DEFINITIVE GUIDE TO ARM® CORTEX®-M23 AND CORTEX-M33 PROCESSORS

About the image on the book cover—Musca-S1 IoT demonstrator

The image on the book cover is a photograph of the Musca-S1, a test chip board with two Arm Cortex-M33 processors, the Arm Corstone-200 foundation IP package and security IP components from the Arm CryptoCell-300 family. The Musca test chip and development board were developed for ecosystem enablement activities and for use as a reference platform to demonstrate the handling of Platform Security Architecture (PSA) level 1 certification and PSA Functional API certification.

The Musca-S1 test chip is the industry's first MRAM-enabled IoT SoC demonstrator.

Further information about the Musca-S1 can be found on the Arm's developer website:

https://developer.arm.com/tools-and-software/development-boards/iot-test-chips-and-boards/musca-s1-test-chip-board

DEFINITIVE GUIDE TO ARM® CORTEX®-M23 AND CORTEX-M33 PROCESSORS

JOSEPH YIU

Distinguished Engineer, Automotive and IoT Line of Business, Arm, Cambridge, UK

ELSEVIER

Newnes
An imprint of Elsevier

Newnes is an imprint of Elsevier
The Boulevard, Langford Lane, Kidlington, Oxford OX5 1GB, United Kingdom
50 Hampshire Street, 5th Floor, Cambridge, MA 02139, United States

Library of Congress Cataloging-in-Publication Data
A catalog record for this book is available from the Library of Congress

British Library Cataloguing-in-Publication Data
A catalogue record for this book is available from the British Library

ISBN: 978-0-12-820735-2

For information on all Newnes publications
visit our website at https://www.elsevier.com/books-and-journals

Publisher: Mara Conner
Acquisitions Editor: Tim Pitts
Editorial Project Manager: Mariana C. Henriques
Production Project Manager: Nirmala Arumugam
Cover Designer: Greg Harris

Typeset by SPi Global, India

Dedication

This book is dedicated to my family,
and,
all the cats and dogs in the neighborhood that kept me entertained ☺
(but no more dead rats under my chair please!!)

Contents

Preface xi
Contributing author: Paul Beckmann xiii
Acknowledgments xv

1. Introduction

1.1 Microcontrollers and processors 1
1.2 Classification of processors 3
1.3 The Cortex-M23 and Cortex-M33
   processors and the Armv8-M
   architecture 3
1.4 Characteristics of the Cortex-M23 and
   Cortex-M33 processors 5
1.5 Why have two different processors? 6
1.6 Applications of the Cortex-M23 and
   Cortex-M33 7
1.7 Technical features 8
1.8 Comparison with previous generations of
   Cortex-M processors 8
1.9 Advantages of the Cortex-M23 and Cortex-M33
   processors 11
1.10 Understanding microcontroller
   programming 14
1.11 Further reading 15
References 16

2. Getting started with Cortex-M programming

2.1 Overview 19
2.2 Some basic concepts 22
2.3 Introduction to Arm Cortex-M
   programming 29
2.4 Software development flow 41
2.5 Cortex Microcontroller Software Interface
   Standard (CMSIS) 44
2.6 Additional information on software
   development 50
Reference 51

3. Technical overview of the Cortex-M23 and Cortex-M33 processors

3.1 Design objectives of Cortex-M23 and
   Cortex-M33 processors 53
3.2 Block diagrams 54
3.3 Processor 57
3.4 Instruction set 58
3.5 Memory map 58
3.6 Bus interfaces 61
3.7 Memory protection 61
3.8 Interrupt and exception handling 62
3.9 Low power features 63
3.10 OS support features 64
3.11 Floating-point unit 64
3.12 Coprocessor interface and Arm Custom
   Instructions 65
3.13 Debug and trace support 65
3.14 Multicore system design support 66
3.15 Key feature enhancements in Cortex-M23 and
   Cortex-M33 processors 66
3.16 Compatibility with other Cortex-M
   processors 70
3.17 Processor configuration options 71
3.18 Introduction to TrustZone 71
3.19 Why TrustZone enables better security? 80
3.20 Firmware asset protection with
   eXecute-Only-Memory (XOM) 83
Reference 84

4. Architecture

4.1 Introduction to the Armv8-M architecture 85
4.2 Programmer's model 87
4.3 Memory system 112
4.4 Exceptions and Interrupts 124
4.5 Debug 131
4.6 Reset and reset sequence 133
4.7 Other related architecture information 136
References 137

5. Instruction set

5.1 Background 139
5.2 Instruction set features in various Cortex-M processors 141
5.3 Understanding the assembly language syntax 143
5.4 Use of a suffix in an instruction 147
5.5 Unified Assembly Language (UAL) 150
5.6 Instruction set—Moving data within the processors 151
5.7 Instruction set—Memory access 158
5.8 Instruction set—Arithmetic operations 182
5.9 Instruction set—Logic operations 185
5.10 Instruction set—Shift and rotate operations 185
5.11 Instruction set—Data conversions (extend and reverse ordering) 191
5.12 Instruction set—Bit field processing 193
5.13 Instruction set—Saturation operations 195
5.14 Instruction set—Program flow control 198
5.15 Instruction set—DSP extension 208
5.16 Instruction set—Floating point support instructions 219
5.17 Instruction set—Exception-related instructions 225
5.18 Instruction set—Sleep mode-related instructions 227
5.19 Instruction set—Memory barrier instructions 228
5.20 Instruction set—TrustZone support instructions 231
5.21 Instruction set—Coprocessor and Arm custom instructions support 232
5.22 Instruction set—Other functions 236
5.23 Accessing special registers with the CMSIS-CORE 240
References 243

6. Memory system

6.1 Overview of the memory system 245
6.2 Memory map 247
6.3 Memory types and memory attributes 251
6.4 Access permission management 254
6.5 Memory endianness 259
6.6 Data alignment and unaligned data access support 262
6.7 Exclusive access support 263
6.8 Memory ordering and memory barrier instructions 267
6.9 Bus wait state and error support 269
6.10 Single-cycle I/O port—Cortex-M23 only 270
6.11 Memory systems in microcontrollers 272
6.12 Software considerations 278
References 279

7. TrustZone support in the memory system

7.1 Overview 281
7.2 SAU and IDAU 283
7.3 Banked and nonbanked registers 285
7.4 Test Target (TT) instructions and region ID numbers 287
7.5 Memory protection controller and peripheral protection controller 292
7.6 Security aware peripherals 296
References 297

8. Exceptions and interrupts—Architecture overview

8.1 Overview of exceptions and interrupts 299
8.2 Exception types 303
8.3 Overview of interrupts and exceptions management 303
8.4 Exception sequence introduction 307
8.5 Definitions of exception priority levels 310
8.6 Vector table and vector table offset register (VTOR) 315
8.7 Interrupt input and pending behaviors 318
8.8 Target states of exceptions and interrupts in TrustZone systems 322
8.9 Stack frames 325
8.10 EXC_RETURN 335
8.11 Classification of synchronous and asynchronous exceptions 340
References 340

9. Management of exceptions and interrupts

9.1 Overview of exception and interrupt management 341
9.2 Details of the NVIC registers for interrupt management 346

9.3 Details of SCB registers for system exception management 354
9.4 Details of special registers for exception or interrupt masking 362
9.5 Vector table definition in programming 369
9.6 Interrupt latency and exception handling optimizations 373
9.7 Tips and hints 378
References 380

10. Low power and system control features

10.1 The quest for low power 381
10.2 Low power features in the Cortex-M23 and Cortex-M33 processors 383
10.3 More on WFI, WFE, and SEV instructions 395
10.4 Developing low power applications 401
10.5 System Control Block (SCB) and system control features 404
10.6 Auxiliary Control Register 413
10.7 Other registers in the System Control Block 415

11. OS support features

11.1 Overview of the OS support features 417
11.2 SysTick timer 418
11.3 Banked stack pointers 427
11.4 Stack limit checking 432
11.5 SVCall and PendSV exceptions 436
11.6 Unprivileged execution level and the Memory Protection Unit (MPU) 444
11.7 Exclusive access 446
11.8 How should an RTOS run in a TrustZone environment? 448
11.9 Concepts of RTOS operations in Cortex-M processors 450
References 462

12. Memory Protection Unit (MPU)

12.1 Overview of the MPU 463
12.2 MPU registers 466
12.3 Configuration of the MPU 474
12.4 TrustZone and MPU 482

12.5 Key differences between the MPU in Armv8-M architecture and the architecture of the previous generations 484
References 485

13. Fault exceptions and fault handling

13.1 Overview 487
13.2 Cause of faults 489
13.3 Enabling fault exceptions 496
13.4 Fault handler designs considerations 497
13.5 Fault status and other information 499
13.6 Lockup 507
13.7 Analysis of fault events 509
13.8 Stack trace 512
13.9 Fault handler to extract stack frame and display fault status 514
Reference 517

14. The Floating-Point Unit (FPU) in the Cortex-M33 processor

14.1 Floating-point data 519
14.2 Cortex-M33 Floating-point Unit (FPU) 524
14.3 Key differences between the FPUs of the Cortex-M33 FPU and the Cortex-M4 539
14.4 Lazy stacking in details 540
14.5 Using the FPU 547
14.6 Floating-point exceptions 553
14.7 Hints and tips 556
References 557

15. Coprocessor interface and Arm Custom Instructions

15.1 Overview 559
15.2 Overview of the architecture 565
15.3 Accessing coprocessor instructions via intrinsic functions in C 566
15.4 Accessing Arm Custom Instructions via the intrinsic functions in C 568
15.5 Software steps to take when enabling the coprocessor and the Arm Custom Instructions 570
15.6 Coprocessor power control 571
15.7 Hints and tips 572
References 573

16. Introduction to the debug and trace features

16.1 Introduction 575
16.2 Debug architecture details 580
16.3 An introduction to debug components 596
16.4 Starting a debug session 633
16.5 Flash memory programming support 634
16.6 Software design considerations 635
References 635

17. Software development

17.1 Introduction 637
17.2 Getting started with the Keil Microcontroller Development Kit (MDK) 639
17.3 Procedure Call Standard for the Arm Architecture 679
17.4 Software scenarios 681
References 683

18. Secure software development

18.1 Overview of Secure software development 685
18.2 TrustZone technical details 688
18.3 Secure software development 701
18.4 Creating a Secure project in Keil MDK 720
18.5 CMSE support in other toolchains 731
18.6 Secure software design considerations 733
References 750

19. Digital signal processing on the cortex-M33 processor

19.1 DSP on a microcontroller? 751
19.2 Why use a Cortex-M processor for a DSP application? 752
19.3 Dot product example 754
19.4 Getting more performance by utilizing the SIMD instructions 757
19.5 Dealing with overflows 759
19.6 Introduction to data types for signal processing 761
19.7 Cortex-M33 DSP instructions 765
19.8 Writing optimized DSP code for the Cortex-M33 processor 779
References 798

20. Using the Arm CMSIS-DSP library

20.1 Overview of the library 799
20.2 Function naming convention 801
20.3 Getting help 802
20.4 Example 1—DTMF demodulation 802
20.5 Example 2—Least squares motion tracking 813
20.6 Example 3—Real-time filter design 818
20.7 How to determine the implemented instruction set features in a Cortex-M33 based system 845
References 847

21. Advanced topics

21.1 Further information on stack memory protection 849
21.2 Semaphores, load-acquire and store-release instructions 851
21.3 Unprivileged interrupt handler 854
21.4 Re-entrant interrupt handler 859
21.5 Software optimization topics 865
Reference 876

22. Introduction to IoT security and the PSA Certified™ framework

22.1 From processor architecture to IoT security 877
22.2 Introduction of PSA Certified 878
22.3 The Trusted Firmware-M (TF-M) project 889
22.4 Additional information 895
References 896

Index 897

The Appendix section of this book, covering information about debug and trace connector layouts and the graphical representations of DSP instructions, is available on the companion website for this book at https://www.elsevier.com/books-and-journals/book-companion/9780128207352.

Preface

It has been a while since the last Definitive Guide to Arm® Cortex®-M Processor book was released. Now, Cortex-M23- and Cortex-M33-based products are arriving in the market and many of them provide sophisticated security features—the definition of "modern microcontrollers" seems to have taken a big step forward. Although the mechanisms of these security features are tailored for small silicon devices with a low power footprint, many of these security technologies are, in principle, similar to high-end computing systems.

While security is a very broad topic, a key aspect of security in billions of connected devices is the "Root of Trust," such as secret keys and secure boot mechanisms—all of which need to be protected. With Arm TrustZone® technology, which is supported by the Cortex-M23 and Cortex-M33 processors, these security-critical assets can be protected in a secure processing environment (Secure world). At the same time, applications running in the normal processing environment (Non-secure world) can be developed easily and are able to utilize security features provided by the secure firmware. Together with other Arm projects, such as the Platform Security Architecture (PSA) and Trusted Firmware-M, software developers are able to easily create software for secure IoT products.

The interaction between Secure and Non-secure software components brings a new dimension of complexity to the architecture. While Non-secure software development is still very similar to that which was needed on previous Cortex-M processors, Secure software developers creating secure firmware now need to be familiar with a range of new architectural features that have been introduced in the Armv8-M architecture.

Unlike previous editions of the Definitive Guides to Arm Cortex-M Processor, this book is focused on the architecture of the Arm Cortex-M23 and Cortex-M33 processors. To enable software developers to create secure solutions based on the Armv8-M architecture, there is a need, as provided in this book, to provide an in-depth explanation of the architectural features which are currently not available elsewhere. As a result, the amount of coverage given to application-level examples and guidance on using development tools is reduced to keep the size of this book manageable. Since application-level examples and application notes for various tools are available from other parties, those materials should satisfy the demand for those aforementioned areas that this book does not cover.

Hopefully, you will find this book useful and well worth reading.

Joseph Yiu

Contributing author: Paul Beckmann

Paul Beckmann's contribution to Chapters 21 and 22 of the Definitive Guide to Arm Cortex-M3 and Cortex-M4 processor has been used in Chapters 19 and 20 of my latest book. I have added new material to these chapters and this includes examples of a real-time filter based on the CMSIS-DSP library.

Paul Beckmann is the founder of DSP Concepts, an engineering services company that specializes in DSP algorithm development and supporting tools. He has many years of experience developing and implementing numerically intensive algorithms for audio, communications, and video. Paul has taught industry courses on digital signal processing and holds a variety of patents in processing techniques. Prior to founding DSP Concepts, Paul spent 9 years at Bose Corporation and was involved in R&D and product development activities.

Acknowledgments

I would like to thank my friends who have been extremely supportive during this book project, especially Ivan who spent 5 months helping me proofread it. (He did not know how bad my writing was when he agreed to help … Sorry!)

I would like to thank the Arm marketing teams for their support on this project, also Thomas Grocutt in Arm Research for providing technical information for Secure software, Sanjeev Sarpal in Advanced Solutions Nederland B.V. for providing support in the digital filter design topic, and Paul Beckmann from DSP Concepts who contributed to the chapters covering digital signal processing.

And of course, thanks to all the readers who gave me feedback on my previous books, which was a great help and assisted me when preparing to write this new book.

Finally, thanks to the staff at Elsevier whose input had enabled this book to be published.

Regards,
Joseph Yiu

1

Introduction

1.1 Microcontrollers and processors

Processors are used in a majority of electronic products: phones, televisions, remote controls, home appliances, electronic toys, computers and their accessories, transportation, building security and safety systems, bank cards, etc. In many cases, those processors are placed inside chips called microcontrollers, which are designed to serve a wide range of applications. Microcontrollers are programmable, which require software developers to write software that runs on those chips. Quite often we call these products embedded systems, as the chips inside the products are usually well hidden.

In order to allow microcontrollers to interact with external environments, they contain a range of functional blocks called peripherals. For example, an analog to digital converter (ADC) allows external voltage signals from sensors to be measured, and a Serial Peripheral Interface (SPI) allows an external LCD display module to be controlled. Different microcontrollers have different peripherals and microcontrollers from different vendors can have similar peripherals, but with different programmer's model and features.

To collect and process the data from peripherals and to control various interfaces, we need to have processors in microcontrollers and software that runs on those processors. In addition to the processor, there are many other components inside a microcontroller. Fig. 1.1 shows the common components in a microcontroller.

In the diagram there are a lot of acronyms. They are explained in Table 1.1.

Some complex microcontroller products can contain a lot more components. In many instances, there are also Direct Memory Access (DMA) controllers, data cryptography accelerators, and complex interfaces like a USB and an ethernet. Some microcontrollers can also contain more than one processor.

Different microcontroller products can have different processors, memory sizes, peripherals, packages, etc. So, even for two microcontrollers that have the same processor inside, they can have different memory maps and peripheral registers. As a result, to carry out the same application function, the program codes required for different microcontroller products can be completely different.

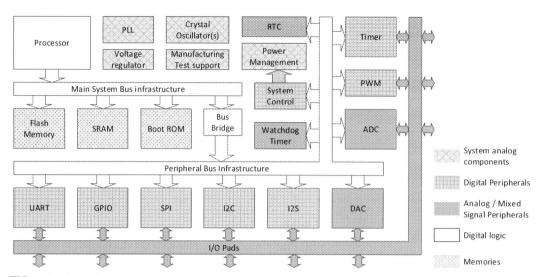

FIG. 1.1   A simple microcontroller.

TABLE 1.1   Typical components in a microcontroller.

Item	Descriptions
ROM	Read-Only Memory: Nonvolatile memory storage for program code.
Flash memory	A special type of ROM that can be reprogrammed many times, typically for storing program code.
SRAM	Static Random Access Memory: for data storage (volatile)
PLL	Phase Lock Loop: a device to generate a programmable clock frequency based on a reference clock.
RTC	Real-Time Clock: a low power timer for counting seconds (typically runs on a low power oscillator) and, in some cases, it also has minutes, hours, and calendar functions.
GPIO	General Purpose Input/Output: a peripheral with a parallel data interface to control external devices and to read back the status of external signals.
UART	Universal Asynchronous Receiver/Transmitter: a peripheral to handle data transfers in a simple serial data protocol.
I2C	Inter-Integrated Circuit: a peripheral to handle data transfers in a serial data protocol. Unlike UART, a clock signal is required which can also provide a higher data rate.
SPI	Serial Peripheral Interface: another serial communication interface for off-chip peripherals.
I2S	Inter-IC Sound: a serial data communication interface specifically for audio information
PWM	Pulse Width Modulator: a peripheral to output waveform with a programmable duty cycle.
ADC	Analog to Digital Converter: a peripheral to convert analog signal level information into digital form.
DAC	Digital to Analog Converter: a peripheral to convert data values to analog signals.
Watchdog timer	A programmable timer device for ensuring the processor is running a program. When enabled, the program running needs to update the watchdog timer within a certain time gap. If the program crashes, the watchdog times out and this can then be used to trigger a reset or a critical interrupt event.

1.2 Classification of processors

There are many different types of processors and many ways of classifying them. A simple classification method is based on the width of the data path (e.g., the data path in an ALU or in a register bank). Using this method, we see 8-bit, 16-bit, 32-bit, and 64-bit processors. Another classification method is based on their applications. For example, Arm® classify their processor products into:

Application processors: These include processors that are used as the main processor in computers, servers, tablets, mobile phones, and smart TVs. Normally those processors support full-feature OS such as Linux, Android™, Windows™, and have a user interface to allow users to operate the device. Typically, these processors run at a high clock frequency and deliver a very high performance.

Real-time processors: Real-time processors are often found in systems that need high performance, but do not require a full-feature OS, and might be well hidden inside the product. In many cases, Real-time Operating Systems (RTOSs) are being used in those processors for task scheduling and intertask messaging. Applications of real-time processors can be found in baseband modems in phones, specialized microcontrollers in automotive systems, and controllers in hard disk drives or solid-state disks (SSDs).

Microcontroller processors: Microcontroller processors are found in most microcontroller products (although some microcontrollers might use application processors or real-time processors instead). The design of these processors is usually focused on low power and fast responsiveness rather than processing power or data processing throughput. In some cases, the design needs to be extremely low power, or low cost, or both at the same time.

To cover these different requirements, Arm developed multiple processor product families:

- Cortex®-A processors for the application processor market
- Cortex-R processors for the real-time processor market
- Cortex-M processors for the microcontroller processor market

In 2018, Arm released a separate product line called Neoverse™, which is a processor product line for servers and infrastructure products.

In some chip designs, it is possible to see a combination of different processors. For example, a chip designed for Network Attached Storage (NAS) devices might contain:

- Cortex-R processors for handling data storage management,
- One or more Cortex-A processor(s) for running network protocol processing and embedded server software to support a web-based administration interface, and
- Cortex-M processors for power management.

1.3 The Cortex-M23 and Cortex-M33 processors and the Armv8-M architecture

The Cortex®-M23 and Cortex-M33 processors are designed by Arm® (https://www.arm.com) and were announced at Arm TechCon in October 2016. Silicon products based on these two processors arrived in the market during 2018.

The Cortex-M23 and Cortex-M33 processors are based on a processor architecture version called Armv8-M, which was announced in 2015. This architecture version is a successor to the previous Armv6-M and Armv7-M architectures, which were used in a number of very successful Cortex-M processor products (Fig. 1.2).

Previously, there were two versions of architecture for the Cortex-M processors:

- Armv6-M architecture: Designed for ultra-low-power applications. Supports a small, compact instruction set and is suitable for general data processing and I/O control tasks.
- Armv7-M architecture: Designed for mid-range and high-performance systems. This architecture supports a richer instruction set (a superset of the instructions in Armv6-M and has an optional floating-point and DSP extensions).

The Armv8-M maintains a similar partitioning by splitting the architecture into two subprofiles:

- Armv8-M Baseline: Architecture designed for ultra-low-power designs. The features and instruction set are a superset of Armv6-M.
- Armv8-M Mainline: Architecture designed for mainstream and high-performance designs. The features and instruction set are a superset of Armv7-M.

From an architectural specification point of view, Armv8-M Mainline is an extension of the Armv8-M Baseline architecture. There are other extensions in the architecture, including:

- DSP instructions (including a range of single instruction multiple data (SIMD) operations), available in Mainline subprofile only.
- A floating-point extension (includes the floating-point unit hardware and instructions), available in Mainline subprofile only.
- A security extension called TrustZone®; available for both Baseline and Mainline subprofiles.
- Helium™ technology, a vector extension also known as M-profile Vector Extension (MVE). This was introduced in Armv8.1-M and is available in the Cortex-M55 processor.

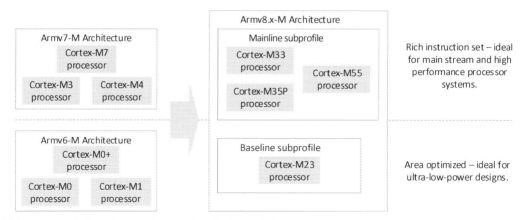

FIG. 1.2   Evolution of architecture versions for Cortex-M processors.

The Cortex-M55 processor was announced in February 2020. (Note: Helium technology is not available in the Cortex-M33 processor).

Those extensions are optional. Additionally, a number of system-level features are also optional in those processors. More detailed explanations are covered in subsequent chapters about each of the system-level features.

The architecture specification document—called Armv8-M Architecture Reference Manual [1]—is a public document that details the programmer's model, instruction set architecture (ISA), exception handling model, and debug architecture. However, this document does not specify how the processors are built. For example, Armv8-M Architecture does not specify how many pipeline stages are needed, what bus interface design should be used, and what the instruction cycle timing looks like.

1.4 Characteristics of the Cortex-M23 and Cortex-M33 processors

Both the Cortex-M23 and Cortex-M33 processors:

- are 32-bit processors, with 32-bit bus interfaces and have a 32-bit arithmetic logic unit (ALU).
- have a 32-bit linear address space, which supports up to 4GB of memories and peripherals.
- use a hardware unit called Nested Vectored Interrupt Controller (NVIC) for interrupt management (includes peripheral interrupts and internal system exceptions).
- include various features for operating system (OS) support such as system tick timer, shadowed stack pointers.
- include sleep mode support and various low-power optimization features.
- support separation of privileged and unprivileged execution levels, which allows the OS (or other privileged software) to restrict unprivileged application tasks from accessing critical system control resources.
- support the optional Memory Protection Unit (MPU), which allows the OS (or other privileged software) to define memory spaces, which are accessible by each unprivileged application tasks.
- can be used in a single processor or in multiprocessor designs.
- support a range of optional debug and trace features to enable software developers to quickly analyze problems and bugs in application codes.
- support an optional TrustZone security extension to allow the software to be further partitioned into different security domains.

There are also a number of differences between the two processors. The Cortex-M23 processor:

- is a two-stage Von-Neumann processor design. The main system bus is based on the Advanced High-performance Bus (AHB) on-chip bus protocol from Advanced Microcontroller Bus Architecture (AMBA®) version 5.
- supports an optional single-cycle I/O interface (which is also available in the Cortex-M0+ processor). This interface allows some of the peripherals to be accessed with just one clock cycle (the normal system bus is based on a pipelined on-chip bus protocol and needs a minimum of two clock cycles per transfer).

- supports a subset of the instructions defined in the Armv8-M architecture (i.e., Baseline subprofile).

The Cortex-M33 processor:

- is a three-stage pipeline design with Harvard bus architecture support. It has two main bus interfaces (based on AMBA 5 AHB) which allow instruction and data accesses to be carried out at the same time. There is also a separate AMBA Advanced Peripheral Bus (APB) interface for extending the debug subsystem.
- supports an optional coprocessor interface. This interface allows chip designers to add hardware accelerators that are tightly coupled to the processor for the acceleration of specialized processing operations.
- supports instructions defined in the Armv8-M Mainline subprofile, including optional DSP instructions and optional single-precision floating-point instructions.

In October 2019, Arm announced that the future release of the Cortex-M33 processor will support Arm Custom Instructions. This new optional feature will enable chip designers to optimize their products for a range of specialized data processing operations.

Traditionally, Arm processors are defined as Reduced Instruction Set Computing (RISC) architecture. However, with the instruction set in Arm processors having evolved over a number of years, the number of instructions supported by the Cortex-M33 processor is quite high compared to classic RISC processors. At the same time, some of the Complex Instruction Set Computing (CISC) processors are designed with pipeline structures similar to RISC processors. As a result, the boundary between RISC and CISC has become blurred and somewhat nonapplicable.

1.5 Why have two different processors?

Both the Cortex-M23 and the Cortex-M33 processors are based on Armv8-M architecture and support the TrustZone security extension. They also share many common features. However, they are also different in the following areas:

Cortex-M23 processor:

- The Cortex-M23 processor is much smaller than the Cortex-M33 (up to 75% smaller in typical configurations).
- The Cortex-M23 processor is 50% more energy efficient than the Cortex-M33 in simple data processing tasks (measured by running Dhrystone benchmark).
- The Cortex-M23 processor supports an optional single-cycle I/O for low latency peripheral access.

Cortex-M33 processor:

- The Cortex-M33 processor is around 50% faster than Cortex-M23 at the same clock frequency (measured by running Dhrystone and CoreMark® benchmarks).
- The Cortex-M33 processor supports an optional DSP extension and an optional single precision floating point unit (These features are not available on the Cortex-M23 processor).

- The Cortex-M33 supports an optional coprocessor interface to enable chip designers to add hardware accelerators, and supports the Arm Custom Instructions feature.

There are also some additional differences in system-level features, such as fault handling exceptions.

The reason for separating the Cortex-M23 (Armv8-M Baseline) and the Cortex-M33 (Armv8-M Mainline) is that there are many different types of embedded systems and they have very different and diverse requirements. In many cases, the processors inside those systems only need to perform simple data processing or control tasks. And, potentially, some of these systems need to be extremely low power. For example, when an energy harvesting method is used to provide the energy for the processor system. In such a case, a simple processor is sufficient and the Cortex-M23 processor would suffice for those applications.

In other cases, where processing requires higher performance, especially where data calculations need to be frequently carried out in a floating-point format, the Cortex-M33 processor would be the one to go for. There are also some applications where the requirement could be met by using the Cortex-M23, the Cortex-M33, as well as other Cortex-M processors. In these instances, the selection decision could be based on the peripherals available on the chip, on other system-level features, and on product pricing, etc.

1.6 Applications of the Cortex-M23 and Cortex-M33

The Cortex-M23 and Cortex-M33 processors are both very versatile and can be used in a wide range of applications.

Microcontrollers: Cortex-M processors are widely used in microcontroller products, particularly designs that are focused on a range of Internet-of-Things (IoT) applications. In some of these products, the TrustZone security extension is utilized to enhance the security of the system. These processors can also be used in other microcontroller applications, including consumer products (e.g., touch sensors, audio control), information technologies (e.g., computer accessories), industrial systems (e.g., motor controls, data acquisitions), fitness/medical devices (e.g., health monitoring). The low gate count nature of the Cortex-M23 processor makes it particularly suitable for a wide range of low-cost consumer products like home appliances and smart lighting.

Automotive: A range of specialized microcontroller products that are built for applications that have very high functional safety requirements, such as those required in the automotive industry. The Cortex-M23 and Cortex-M33 processors are designed to provide real-time responsiveness, which is critical in some of those systems. In addition, the Memory Protection Unit (MPU) in Cortex-M processors enables a high-level of robustness for system-level operations. Furthermore, the Cortex-M23 and Cortex-M33 processors were tested extensively to ensure their functional correctness in various conditions. In recent years, the automotive industry increased its security requirements due to the increased connectivity in cars and to fight against crime (i.e., car theft and hacking). The TrustZone security extension in the Cortex-M23 and Cortex-M33 processors is an important feature that enables automotive system designers to create more dedicated security measures in defense of such attacks.

Data communication: Today's data communication systems can be fairly complex and, at the same time, are battery powered, thus requiring extremely good energy efficiency. Many of these systems have processor(s) embedded inside to handle functions such as communication channel management, encoding, and decoding of communication packets, as well as power management. The energy efficiency and performance of the Cortex-M processors makes them ideal for those applications. Some of the instructions in the Cortex-M33 processor (like bit field operations) make it particularly useful for communication packet processing tasks. Today, many Bluetooth and ZigBee controllers are based on Cortex-M processors. As the security requirements in IoT applications increase, the TrustZone security extension in Cortex-M23 and Cortex-M33 processors have become very attractive because security-sensitive information can be protected without any significant increase in the software overhead.

System-on-Chips (SoC): Although many application SoCs used in mobile phones and tablets use Cortex-A processors (a different range of Arm applications processors which have a much higher level of performance), they also often contain Cortex-M processors for use in various subsystems, e.g., for functions like power management, offloading of peripheral management (e.g., audio), finite state machine (FSM) replacement, and sensor hubs. The Cortex-M processors are designed to support a wide range of multicore design scenarios and, with the introduction of TrustZone for Armv8-M, enables even better integration with the TrustZone support that exists on the Cortex-A processors.

Mixed-signal applications: An emerging range of products like smart sensors, Power Management IC (PMIC), and Microelectromechanical systems (MEMS) now also include processors to provide additional intelligence like calibration, signal conditioning, event detection, and error detection. The low gate count and low power nature of the Cortex-M23 processor make it ideal for most of those applications. In other applications like smart microphones, a level of digital signal processing (DSP) capability is needed and the Cortex-M33 processor is therefore often more suitable.

Today, there are more than 3000 microcontroller parts based on Arm Cortex-M processors. Since the Cortex-M23 and Cortex-M33 processors are new, the number of devices that are presently available based on these two processors is relatively low. However, it is expected that these two processors will in time become much more common.

1.7 Technical features

Table 1.2 is a summary of the key technical features of the Cortex-M23 and Cortex-M33 processors.

1.8 Comparison with previous generations of Cortex-M processors

The Cortex-M processors have been available for quite a long time (over 10 years). The oldest Cortex-M processor is the Cortex-M3, which was announced in 2004. The Cortex-M processors have been tremendously successful; most microcontroller vendors build their microcontroller products using Cortex-M processors and use these processors in a range of multicore System-on-Chips (SoC), Application Specific Integrated Circuits (ASIC), Application Specific Standard Products (ASSP), sensors, etc.

TABLE 1.2   Key features of the Cortex-M23 and Cortex-M33 processors.

	Cortex-M23	Cortex-M33
Architecture	Armv8-M Baseline subprofile	Armv8-M Mainline subprofile
Baseline instructions	Y	Y
Mainline instructions (extension)	–	Y
DSP extension	–	Optional
Floating-point extension	–	Optional (single precision)
Hardware		
Bus architecture	Von Neumann	Harvard
Pipeline	Two stages	Three stages
Main bus interface	1×32-bit AHB5	2×32-bit AHB5
Other bus interface	Single-cycle I/O interface	Private peripheral bus (PPB) for debug components
Coprocessor and Arm Custom Instructions support	–	Support up to eight coprocessors/accelerators
Nested Vectored Interrupt Controller (NVIC)	Yes	Yes
Interrupt support	Up to 240 interrupts	Up to 480 interrupts
Programmable priority levels	2 bits (four levels)	3–8-bits (8–256 levels)
Non-Maskable Interrupt (NMI)	Yes	Yes
Low power support (sleep modes)	Yes	Yes
OS support	Yes	Yes
SysTick (system tick) timer	Optional (up to 2)	Yes (up to 2)
Shadow stack pointers	Y	Y
Memory Protection Unit (MPU)	Optional (4/8/12/16 regions)	Optional (4/8/12/16 regions)
TrustZone security extension	Optional	Optional
Security Attribution Unit (SAU)	0/4/8 regions	0/4/8 regions
Custom attribution unit support	Yes	Yes

Although the previous range of Cortex-M processors fully satisfied the requirement of many applications, there has, in recent years, been a need to enhance the Cortex-M processors to address new challenges in:

- Security
- Flexibility
- Processing capability
- Energy efficiency

As a result, the Cortex-M23 and Cortex-M33 processors were developed. The Cortex-M23 processor contains many enhancements over the previous Cortex-M0 and Cortex-M0+ processors (Fig. 1.3).

The instruction set enhancements from Armv6-M to Armv8-M Baseline include:

- Signed and unsigned integer divide instructions.
- Two compare-and-branch instructions (both 16 bits) and a 32-bit branch instruction (supports a larger branch range).

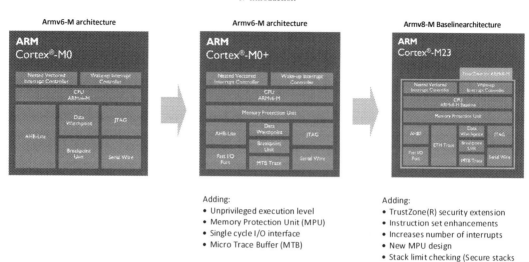

FIG. 1.3   Key enhancements of the Cortex-M23 processor when compared with the Cortex-M0 and Cortex-M0+ processors.

- Additional MOV (move) instructions for immediate data generation.
- Exclusive access instructions for semaphore operations.
- Load acquire, store release instructions for C11 atomic data support.
- Instructions that are required for the TrustZone security extension.

Similarly, the Cortex-M33 also has a number of enhancements when compared to the Cortex-M3 and Cortex-M4 processors (Fig. 1.4).

The instruction set enhancements from the Cortex-M4 (Armv7-M) to Armv8-M Mainline include:

- Floating-point instructions upgraded from FPv4 architecture to FPv5.
- Load acquire, store release instructions for C11 atomic data support.
- Instructions that are required for the TrustZone security extension.

In addition, both the Cortex-M23 and Cortex-M33 processors have a range of other enhancements from a chip-level design point of view. For example:

- Better flexibility in design configuration options.
- Better low power support with new multiple power-domain control interfaces.

Although there are many different enhancements, migration of most applications from the previous Cortex-M processors to the new processors should be straightforward because:

- They are still based on 32-bit architecture and have the same 4GB architecturally defined memory space partitioning. Processor internal components like NVIC and SysTick support the same programming model.
- All instructions in previous processors are supported.

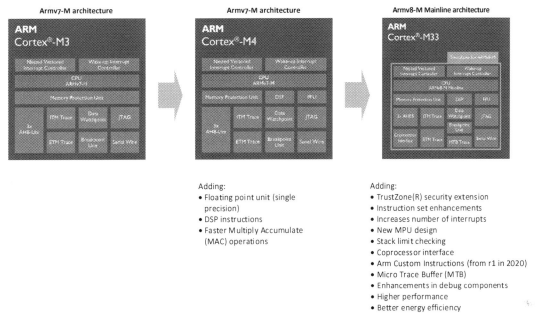

Adding:
- Floating point unit (single precision)
- DSP instructions
- Faster Multiply Accumulate (MAC) operations

Adding:
- TrustZone(R) security extension
- Instruction set enhancements
- Increases number of interrupts
- New MPU design
- Stack limit checking
- Coprocessor interface
- Arm Custom Instructions (from r1 in 2020)
- Micro Trace Buffer (MTB)
- Enhancements in debug components
- Higher performance
- Better energy efficiency

FIG. 1.4 Key enhancements of the Cortex-M33 processor when compared with the Cortex-M3 and Cortex-M4 processors.

While the Armv8-M architecture is designed to be highly compatible with Armv6-M and Armv7-M architectures, software developers will still need to adapt their existing application software when migrating to the new microcontroller devices. For example, there could be software changes needed due to differences in the peripheral programmer's models, memory map, etc. In addition, the development tools and Real Time Operating System (RTOS) will need to be updated to support these new processors.

1.9 Advantages of the Cortex-M23 and Cortex-M33 processors

Similar to the previous Cortex-M processors, the Cortex-M23 and Cortex-M33 processors have a number of advantages compared to most other processors commonly used for microcontrollers, particularly when compared to legacy 8-bit and 16-bit designs.

Small footprint: When comparing the Cortex-M23 and Cortex-M33 processors to most other 32-bit processors, Cortex-M processors are relatively small and, on average, have a very low power requirement. Although they are larger than 8-bit processors and some other 16-bit designs, especially when comparing 8-bit designs like the 8051 to the Cortex-M33 processor, the increase in the processor's size is offset by a higher code density—which enables the same application to be carried out with a smaller program memory space. Since the area and power of the processor are often proportionately small when compared to the area and power of the overall microcontroller system (especially when compared to the area and power of flash memories and analog components), the use of a 32-bit Cortex-M processor in a microcontroller system does not greatly impinge on its cost or increase its power consumption.

Low power: In addition to its small silicon size, the Cortex-M23 and Cortex-M33 processors support a range of low power features. For example, architecturally, the processor supports specialized instructions for entering sleep modes. And there is a range of design optimizations to reduce the power of the processors. For example, by stopping the clock or removing power to sections of the design when those sections are not in use.

Performance: While the Cortex-M23 processor is one of the smallest 32-bit processors on the market, it can still deliver a performance of 0.98DMIPS/MHz (Dhrystone 2.1) and 2.5 CoreMark®/MHz, which is much higher than most 8-bit and 16-bit designs. Additionally, it does not significantly increase the system-level power and silicon area. For applications that need higher performance, the Cortex-M33 processor could be used instead as it offers an impressive performance of 1.5 DMIPS/MHz and 4.02 CoreMark/MHz. With the high throughput of these processors, the systems can complete their processing tasks faster and stay in sleep mode longer to save power. Or run the processor at a slower clock rate to reduce peak power consumption.

Energy efficiency: Combining low power and great performance, the Cortex-M23 and Cortex-M33 are two of the most energy-efficient processors for a wide range of embedded applications. This enables a longer battery life, a smaller battery size, and allows a simpler power supply design at chip and circuit board level. In the past, the low-power capabilities of other Cortex-M processors had already been demonstrated using ULPMark™-CP from EEMBC® (http://www.eembc.org/ulpmark/). It is therefore expected that a number of new microcontroller devices based on the Cortex-M23 and Cortex-M33 processors will achieve similar or better results.

Interrupt handling capabilities: All Cortex-M processors have an integrated Nested Vectored Interrupt Controller (NVIC) for interrupt handling. This unit and the processor core design supports low latency interrupt handling. For example, interrupt latency is only 15 clock cycles in the Cortex-M23 and 12 cycles in the Cortex-M33 processor. In order to reduce the overhead of software executions, the reading of exception vectors (the starting addresses of interrupt service routines), the stacking of essential registers, and the nesting of interrupt services are automatically handled by the hardware. The interrupt management features are also very flexible, e.g., all peripheral interrupts have programmable priority levels. All these characteristics make the Cortex-M processors suitable for many real-time applications.

Security: With the TrustZone security extension, microcontroller vendors and chip designers can build a range of advanced security features for their IoT chip designs. By default, TrustZone technology supports two security domains (Secure and Non-secure), and with additional software, like Trusted Firmware-M, can create more security partitions in the software.

Ease of use: The Cortex-M processors are designed to be easy to use. For example, most applications can be programmed in C language. Since the Cortex-M processors use 32-bit linear addressing they can handle up to 4GB of address range and, by so doing, avoid a range of architectural limitations that are typically found in 8-bit and 16-bit processors (e.g., memory size and stack size restrictions and restrictions on re-entrant code). Typically, application software development environments (except when developing software running on the Secure side in a TrustZone environment) do not require a special C language extension.

Code density: Compared with many other architectures, the instruction set used by Cortex-M processors (called Thumb instructions) offers very high code density. The Thumb instruction set contains both 16-bit and 32-bit instructions (most of the instructions supported by the Cortex-M23 processor are 16-bit), and, when they can, the C/C++ compilers will select the 16-bit version of the instruction to reduce program size while, at the same time generating a very efficient code sequence. The high code density enables applications to be fitted onto a chip with a small program memory, thus reducing cost and, potentially, reducing power, and chip package size.

OS support: Unlike many legacy processors, the Cortex-M processors are designed to support efficient OS operations. The architecture includes features like shadow stack pointers, system tick timers, and dedicated exceptions types for OS operations. Today, there are more than 40 different types of RTOS running on Cortex-M processors.

Scalability: Cortex-M processors are highly scalable in two ways. First, most parts of the programmer's models for these processors are consistent across different designs—from the smallest Cortex-M0 to the highest performance Cortex-M7 processor. This enables software code to be easily ported across different Cortex-M processors. The second aspect is that Cortex-M processors are designed to be very flexible, meaning that they can either be used in a single processor system (e.g., low-power and low-cost microcontrollers), or be part of a complex SoC design where the chips contain many processors working together.

Software portability and reusability: The consistency of the architecture also gives rise to an important benefit of the Cortex-M processors: a high level of software portability and reusability. A range of Arm initiatives such as the Cortex Microcontroller Software Interface Standard (CMSIS) enhances this further by providing a consistent software interface for the various Cortex-M designs. This enables software vendors and developers to safeguard their investment in the long term, as well as enabling them to develop their products much quicker.

Debug features: Cortex-M processors include many debug features that enable software developers to test their codes and easily analyze software problems. In addition to the halting of software execution, breakpoints, watchpoints, and single stepping, which are standard features in modern microcontrollers, the debug features present in Cortex-M processors also include instruction trace, data trace, and profiling supports, which can be linked together in a multicore system to enable the easier debugging of multicore systems. The debug and trace features in the Cortex-M23 and the Cortex-M33 processors have been enhanced to make them more flexible compared to previous designs.

Flexibility: The Cortex-M processor designs are configurable. Chip designers can, therefore, decide which optional features to add to the design during the chip design stage. This enables the design to achieve the best trade-off between functionality, cost, and energy efficiency.

Software ecosystem: Cortex-M processors are supported by a wide range of software development tools, RTOS products, as well as other middleware (e.g., audio codec). In addition to the numerous Cortex-M devices and development boards available, these software solutions enable software developers to create high-quality products in a short time frame.

Quality: Arm processors are thoroughly tested to meet very high-quality levels and most Cortex-M processors, like the Cortex-M23 and Cortex-M33, are designed to be compliant with safety requirements. This enables Cortex-M microcontrollers to be used in a wide range of automotive, industrial, and medical applications. Cortex-M based products are also used in many safety-critical systems, including applications[a] for the space industry.

1.10 Understanding microcontroller programming

If you have been programming on a desktop and learning how to program microcontroller systems, you might be surprised to find that programming microcontrollers are quite different from what you are used to, and what you have learned before. For example:

- Most microcontroller systems do not have a graphic user interface (GUI).
- The microcontroller system might not contain any operating system (typically this is called bare metal). Or, in some instances, a light-weight RTOS is used, which only manages task scheduling and intertask communication. Unlike desktop environments, many of these operating systems do not provide other system Application Programming Interface (API) for data communication and peripheral control.
- In desktop environments, the applications access peripheral functions via APIs or device drivers provided in the OS. Whereas in microcontroller applications, it is not unusual to access the peripheral registers directly. However, most Cortex-M microcontroller vendors also provide device driver libraries to make it easier for software developers to create their applications.
- Memory size and power consumption are constraining factors in many microcontroller systems. In contrast, the amount of memory and processing power in a desktop environment is significantly greater.
- In desktop environments, the use of assembly language is quite rare, and most application developers use a wide range of high-level programming languages, including: Java/ JavaScript, C#, and Python. Today, most microcontroller projects are still based on C and C++. In some instances, a small portion of the software could be written in assembly language.

To learn microcontroller programming on the Cortex-M processor family, you need:

- Some experience in C language programming. Experience in using microcontroller programming tools certainly helps, but this is not always necessary. Compared to using legacy 8-bit and 16-bit microcontrollers, many people find that using microcontrollers based on the Cortex-M processors is far easier.
- A basic understanding of electronics. Knowledge of electronics would be useful to understand some of the examples in this book. For example, understanding what a UART is would help because using a UART to connect to a computer to display a program's operation results is a commonly used technique.
- While not necessary, the experience of using Real-Time Operating Systems (RTOS) would help to understand some of the topics in this book.

Most of the examples in this book are based on the Keil® Microcontroller Development Kit (Keil MDK). However, where relevant, a number of sections have information about the IAR™ Electronic Workbench for Arm (EWARM) and the gcc toolchain.

---

[a] Example: VA10820 from Vorago Technologies (https://www.voragotech.com/products/va10820).

1.11 Further reading

The Arm website is divided into a number of sections which has useful information on various aspects of Arm Cortex-M processor products.

1.11.1 Product pages on developer.arm.com

This is the product information web page where you can find an overview of the products and relevant links to the various parts of the Arm websites.

Web site	
Cortex-M processor page	https://developer.arm.com/products/processors/cortex-m/
Cortex-M23 processor page	https://developer.arm.com/products/processors/cortex-m/cortex-m23
Cortex-M33 processor page	https://developer.arm.com/products/processors/cortex-m/cortex-m33
M-Profile architecture	https://developer.arm.com/products/architecture/m-profile
TrustZone	https://developer.arm.com/ip-products/security-ip/trustzone

1.11.2 Documentation on developer.arm.com

There is a range of documents available on the Arm website that is useful for learning about software development for the Cortex-M23 and Cortex-M33 processors. The main documentation page is called developer.arm.com (https://developer.arm.com/documentation).

The key Cortex-M23/Cortex-M33 document that you find on the website includes:

Reference	Document
[1]	Armv8-M Architecture Reference Manual This is the specification of the architecture on which the Cortex-M23 and Cortex-M33 processors are based. It contains detailed information about the instruction set and about architecture defined behaviors, etc.
[2]	Cortex-M23 Device Generic User Guide This is a user guide written for software developers using the Cortex-M23 processor. It provides information on the programmer's model, details on using core peripherals such as the NVIC and general information about the instruction set.
[3]	Cortex-M23 Technical Reference Manual This is the specification of the Cortex-M23 processor. It gives information on the features that are implemented and details some of the implementation-specific behaviors.
[4]	Cortex-M33 Device Generic User Guide This is a user guide written for software developers using the Cortex-M33 processor. It provides information on the programmer's model, details on using core peripherals such as the NVIC, and general information about the instruction set.

Continued

Reference	Document
[5]	Cortex-M33 Technical Reference Manual This is the specification of the Cortex-M33 processor. It gives information on the features that are implemented and details some of the implementation-specific behaviors.
[6–9]	Arm CoreSight™ MTB-M23/ETM-M23/MTB-M33/ETM-M33 Technical Reference Manual These are the specifications for the instruction trace support components and are intended for debug tool vendors only. Software developers do not need to read these documents.

The developer website also contains various application notes and additional useful documentation. One document I would like to highlight is the Procedure Call Standard for the Arm Architecture (AAPCS), which is referenced in several sections of Chapter 17:

Reference	Document
[10]	Procedure Call Standard for the Arm Architecture This document specifies how software code should work in interfunction calls. This information is often needed for software projects with mixed assembly and C languages.

1.11.3 Community.arm.com

This section of the website allows website users, including Arm experts, to interact and allows individuals (including companies) to post documents or other material relating to Arm technologies. To make it easier for Arm website users to locate information about Cortex-M processors, I have created and continue to maintain several blog pages in the Arm Community website:

Reference	Document
[11]	Armv8-M Architecture Technical Overview This whitepaper summarizes the architecture enhancements of the Armv8-M architecture and gives an overview of how the TrustZone® technology works. I have also included links to various useful documents relating to the Armv8-M architecture.
[12]	Cortex-M resources I maintain a list of useful links to papers, videos, and presentations on various Cortex-M topics.
[13]	Getting started with Arm Microcontroller Resources This is an introductory page for people who want to start using Arm microcontrollers. The blog covers entry-level information for Cortex-A, Cortex-R, and Cortex-M processors.

References

[1] Armv8-M Architecture Reference Manual. https://developer.arm.com/documentation/ddi0553/am (Armv8.0-M only version). https://developer.arm.com/documentation/ddi0553/latest/ (latest version including Armv8.1-M). Note: M-profile architecture reference manuals for Armv6-M, Armv7-M, Armv8-M and Armv8.1-M can be found here: https://developer.arm.com/architectures/cpu-architecture/m-profile/docs.

[2] Arm Cortex-M23 Devices Generic User Guide. https://developer.arm.com/documentation/dui1095/latest/.

[3] Arm Cortex-M23 Processor Technical Reference Manual. https://developer.arm.com/documentation/ddi0550/latest/.

[4] Arm Cortex-M33 Devices Generic User Guide. https://developer.arm.com/documentation/100235/latest/.

[5] Arm Cortex-M33 Processor Technical Reference Manual. https://developer.arm.com/documentation/100230/latest/.

[6] Arm CoreSight MTB-M23 Technical Reference Manual. https://developer.arm.com/documentation/ddi0564/latest/.

[7] Arm CoreSight ETM-M23 Technical Reference Manual. https://developer.arm.com/documentation/ddi0563/latest/.

[8] Arm CoreSight MTB-M33 Technical Reference Manual. https://developer.arm.com/documentation/100231/latest/.

[9] Arm CoreSight ETM-M33 Technical Reference Manual. https://developer.arm.com/documentation/100232/latest/.

[10] Procedure Call Standard for the Arm Architecture (AAPCS). https://developer.arm.com/documentation/ihi0042/latest/.

[11] Armv8-M Architecture Technical Overview. https://community.arm.com/developer/ip-products/processors/b/processors-ip-blog/posts/whitepaper-armv8-m-architecture-technical-overview.

[12] Cortex-M resources. I maintain a list of useful links to papers, videos and presentations on various Cortex-M topics. https://community.arm.com/developer/ip-products/processors/b/processors-ip-blog/posts/cortex-m-resources.

[13] Getting started with Arm Microcontroller Resources. This is an introductory page for people who want to start using arm microcontrollers. The blog covers entry level information for Cortex-A, Cortex-R and Cortex-M processors. https://community.arm.com/developer/ip-products/processors/b/processors-ip-blog/posts/getting-started-with-arm-microcontroller-resources.

Getting started with Cortex-M programming

2.1 Overview

If you have never programmed a microcontroller before, welcome to the exciting world of microcontroller software development. Do not worry, it is not that difficult; Arm® Cortex®-M processors are very easy to use. This book covers many aspects of the processor's architecture. However, you do not need to understand all of those aspects to develop most of the applications.

If you have been using other microcontrollers you will find that programming with Cortex-M based microcontrollers is very straight forward. Almost everything can be programmed in C/C++ because most registers (e.g., peripherals) are memory mapped, and even interrupt handlers can be programmed fully in C/C++. Also, in most normal applications there is no need to use compiler-specific language extensions, which is required in the architecture of some other processors. As long as you have a basic understanding of the C programming language, you will very soon be able to develop and run simple applications on the Cortex-M23 and Cortex-M33 processors.

Usually, the following tools/resources for developing applications on microcontrollers are:

- Development suites (including compilation tools and debug environment software).
- Development board with microcontroller(s).
- Potentially, you might need a debug adaptor. Some development boards provided by MCU vendors have a USB debug adaptor built-in and can be connected directly to the USB port of your computer.
- In some applications, you might need to use an embedded operating system (OS) and firmware packages, like communication software libraries. These are also known as middleware. A range of middleware solutions like Real-Time Operating Systems (RTOSs) is available from the open source community and are free to use.

- Depending on the application, you might need additional electronic hardware (e.g., a motor driver circuit for motor control) and electronic equipment (e.g., multimeter, oscilloscope).

2.1.1 Development suites

A number of development suites are available:

- Commercial development suites such as Keil® Microcontroller Development Kit (Keil MDK, https://www.keil.com), IAR™ Embedded Workbench for Arm (EWARM, https://www.iar.com), Segger Embedded Studio (https://www.segger.com/embedded-studio.html), etc.
- Open source toolchains like gcc (https://developer.arm.com/open-source/gnu-toolchain/gnu-rm) with Eclipse Embedded CDT (https://projects.eclipse.org/projects/iot.embed-cdt).
- Tool chains from microcontroller vendors.
- Web-based development environments such as mbedOS (https://mbed.com).

Some commercial toolchains offer a free trial version, but with limited code size support. Most of the software development examples in this book are based on Keil MDK. You can use toolchains from other vendors. While in most cases the C code should be reusable without modification, a number of projects that illustrate assembly or inline assembly would require modification when using a different toolchain.

2.1.2 Development board

For beginners, it is easier to start by using development/evaluation boards from microcontroller vendors. While it is possible to create your own development boards, it does require a deal of technical knowledge and a range of skills and equipment (e.g., soldering of tiny surface-mounted electronic components require specialized tools).

A range of low-cost development kits are available for Cortex-M processors and typically they come with software packages that contain examples and support files (e.g., C header files and driver libraries for peripheral definitions). Worth noting is that some of the development boards are tied into having to use certain development tools.

Some toolchains also offer instruction set simulator features which allow you to learn programming without real hardware. However, it might be impossible to emulate certain peripheral features in a simulator and, additionally, real hardware development boards do allow you to hook up the application to external devices (e.g., motors, audio, display module).

2.1.3 Debug adaptor

The debug interface of the Cortex-M processors provides access to debug features and flash programming support (for downloading compiled program images to the chip). Most Cortex-M microcontrollers feature a debug interface based on the Serial Wire debug (requires two pins on the chip) or the JTAG (four or five pins) protocols. A debug adaptor is needed to convert a USB/Ethernet interface to one of these debug protocols. A number of low-cost

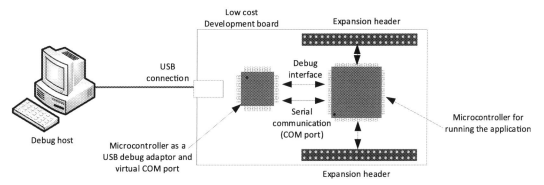

FIG. 2.1 The concept of common low-cost development boards.

development boards come with an extra microcontroller which acts as a debug adaptor, and might also support a virtual COM port feature (Fig. 2.1).

If the board you are using does not have a debug adaptor, you will need to use external debug adaptor hardware. There are a number of products available from Keil, IAR, Segger, and other companies at various price points and with differing feature lists (Fig. 2.2). Many of the development suites support multiple types of debug adaptors.

If you are creating your own microcontroller boards, then you need to ensure the microcontroller can be easily connected to a debug adaptor. Please note that there is a range of standardized connector arrangements and they are covered in Appendix A of this book.

FIG. 2.2 Example of debug adaptors (Keil ULINK™2, Keil ULINKPro, IAR I-Jet, Segger J-Link).

2.1.4 Resources

After obtaining the tools and the development board, remember to view the vendor's website and download some of the reference materials that you might need:

- Software packages, including header files, which provide definitions of peripheral registers and peripheral driver functions.
- Example codes, tutorials.
- Documentation about the microcontroller device and the development board.

Most MCU vendors have online forums to allow you to post questions. If you have questions about Arm products, such as processors and tools, you can post them on the Arm online forum called Arm Community (https://community.arm.com).

2.2 Some basic concepts

If this is the first time you have used a microcontroller, read on. For readers who are already experienced with microcontroller applications, you can skip this part and move to Section 2.3.

In Section 1.1 of Chapter 1, I covered what is inside a microcontroller. I now explain what is needed to get a microcontroller to work.

2.2.1 Reset

A microcontroller needs to be reset to get to a known state before program execution starts. Reset is typically generated by a hardware signal from external sources. For example, you might find a reset button on the development board which generates a reset pulse using a simple circuit (Fig. 2.3) or, in some cases, the reset could be controlled by a more sophisticated

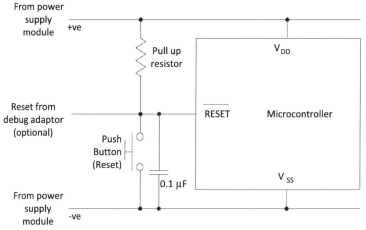

FIG. 2.3   An example of a reset connection on a low-cost microcontroller board (it has been assumed that the reset pin is active low).

power monitoring Integrated Circuit (IC). Most microcontroller devices have an input pin for reset.

On Arm-based microcontrollers, the reset can also be triggered by a debugger connected to microcontroller boards. This allows software developers to reset the microcontroller via the Integrated Development Environment (IDE). Some debugger adaptors can generate a reset using a dedicated pin on their debug connectors. This reset signal can be connected to the microcontroller's reset circuit and thus be controlled by the debugger via the debug connection.

After the reset is released, the internal microcontroller hardware might need a little time (i.e., wait for the internal clock oscillator to become stabilized) before the processor can start executing programs. The delay is usually very short and is not noticeable by users.

2.2.2 Clocks

Almost all processors and digital circuits (including peripherals) need clock signals to operate. Microcontrollers typically support an external crystal for reference clock generation. Some microcontrollers also have internal oscillators (however, the output frequency of some of the implementations like R-C oscillators can be fairly inaccurate).

Many modern microcontrollers allow software to control which clock source is to be used and have programmable Phase Lock Loops (PLLs) and clock dividers to generate the various operation frequencies that are required. As a result, you might have a microcontroller circuit with an external crystal of just 12 MHz, with the processor system running at a much higher clock speed (e.g., well over 100 MHz) and some of the peripherals running at a divided clock speed.

In order to save power, many microcontrollers also allow software to turn on/off individual oscillators and PLLs and to also turn off the clock signal to each of the peripherals. Many microcontrollers also have an additional 32 kHz crystal oscillator (the crystal can be an external component on the board) for the operation of a low-power real-time clock.

2.2.3 Voltage level

All microcontrollers need power to run, so you will find power supply pins on a microcontroller. Most modern microcontrollers need a very low voltage and typically use 3 volts (V). Some of them can even operate with supply voltage of less than 2 V.

If you are going to create your own microcontroller development board, or prototyping circuits, you need to check the datasheet of the microcontroller that you are using and determine the voltage levels of the components that the microcontroller will be connected to. For example, some external interfaces, like a relay switch, might require 5 V signaling, which would not work with a 3 V output signal from a microcontroller. In this case, an additional driver circuit would be needed.

When designing a microcontroller board, one should also make sure that the voltage supply is regulated. Many mains to DC adaptors do not regulate the voltage output, which means the voltage level can constantly fluctuate, and, unless a voltage regulator is added, such an adaptor is not suitable for powering microcontroller circuits.

2.2.4 Inputs and outputs

Unlike personal computers, many embedded systems do not have a display, keyboard, or mouse. The available inputs and outputs can be limited to simple interfaces, like buttons/keypad, LEDs, buzzer, and maybe an LCD display module. This hardware is connected to the microcontroller using electronic interfaces such as digital and analog inputs and outputs (I/Os), UARTs, I2C, SPI, etc. Many microcontrollers also offer USB, Ethernet, CAN, graphic LCD, and SD card interfaces. These interfaces are handled by specialized peripherals.

On Arm-based microcontrollers, peripherals are controlled by memory mapped registers (examples of peripheral accesses are covered in Section 2.3.2 in this chapter). Some of these peripherals are more sophisticated than peripherals available on 8-bit and 16-bit microcontrollers and might have more registers to program during the peripheral setup.

Typically, the initialization process for peripherals often consists of the following:

I. Programming the clock control circuitry to enable the clock signal connected to the peripheral and, if needed, the corresponding I/O pins. In many low-power microcontrollers, the clock signals reaching different parts of the chip can be individually turned on or off for power saving. Typically, by default, most of the clock signals are turned off and need to be enabled before the peripherals are programmed. In some instances, you will also need to enable the clock signal for part of the bus system to access certain peripherals.

II. Programming of I/O configurations. Most microcontrollers multiplex several functions into each of its I/O pins. In order for a peripheral interface to work correctly, the I/O pins assignments (e.g., configuration registers for the multiplexers) might need to be programmed. In addition, some microcontrollers also offer configurable electrical characteristics for the I/O pins. This results in additional I/O configuration steps.

III. Programming of the Peripheral configuration. Since most interface peripherals contain a number of programmable registers to control their operations, a programming sequence is usually needed in order to initialize the peripheral and to get it to work correctly.

IV. Programming of the Interrupt configuration. If a peripheral operation requires interrupt processing, additional configuration steps are required for the interrupt controller (e.g., the NVIC in the Cortex-M processor).

Most microcontroller vendors provide peripheral/device driver libraries to simplify software development. Even though device driver libraries are available, there might still be a fair amount of low-level programming work needed, though this does depend on the applications being used. For example, if a user interface is needed you might need to develop your own interface functions for a user-friendly standalone embedded system. (Note: there is also commercial middleware available for creating Graphic User Interfaces (GUIs).) Nevertheless, the device driver libraries provided by microcontroller vendors should make the development of the embedded applications much easier.

For the development of most deeply embedded systems, it is not necessary to have a rich user interface. However, basic interfaces like LEDs, DIP switches, and push buttons can deliver only a limited amount of information. To assist the debugging of software during development, a simple text input/output console can be very useful. This can be handled by a simple RS-232 connection through a UART interface on the microcontroller to a UART

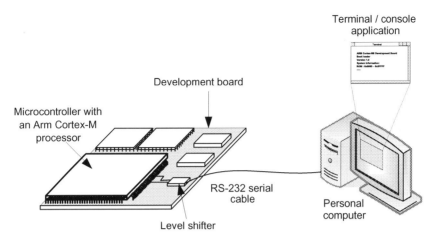

FIG. 2.4   Using a UART interface for user input and output during software development.

interface on a personal computer (or via a USB adaptor). This arrangement allows you to transfer and display text messages from the microcontroller applications and to enter user inputs using a terminal application (see Fig. 2.4). Explanations for creating these message communications are covered in Chapter 17, Section 17.2.7.

An alternative to using UART for message display, some development tools also have features that enable messages to be transferred through the debug connection (an example of this feature is covered in Section 17.2.8).

2.2.5 Introduction to embedded software program flows

There are many different ways to structure the processing flow of an application. Here I will cover a few fundamental concepts. Please note, unlike the programming on a personal computer, most embedded applications do not have an ending of the program flow.

2.2.5.1 Polling method

For simple applications, polling (sometimes also called super loop, see Fig. 2.5) is easy to set up and works fairly well for basic tasks.

When the application is more complex and demands higher processing performance, then polling is not suitable. For example, if process A (in Fig. 2.5) takes a long time to complete, the other peripherals B and C will not get serviced quickly by the processor (i.e., until process A is completed). Another disadvantage of using the polling method is that the processor has to run the polling program all the time, even when no processing is required; thus reducing energy efficiency.

2.2.5.2 Interrupt driven method

In applications that require lower power, processing can be carried out in interrupt service routines so that the processor can enter sleep mode when no processing is required (Fig. 2.6).

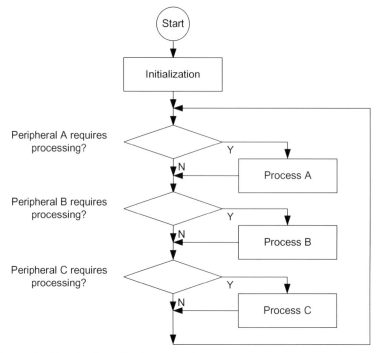

FIG. 2.5   Polling method for simple application processing.

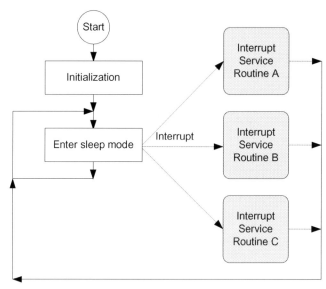

FIG. 2.6   Interrupt driven application.

Interrupts are usually generated by external sources or by on-chip peripherals to wake up the processor.

In interrupt-driven applications, the interrupts from different peripherals can be assigned with different levels of interrupt priority. In this way, a high-priority interrupt request can get serviced even when a lower priority interrupt service is running; in which case the lower priority interrupt service will be temporarily suspended. As a result, the latency (i.e., the delay from the generation of the interrupt request to the servicing of the requesting peripheral) for the higher priority interrupt service is reduced.

2.2.5.3 *Combination of polling and interrupt-driven methods*

In many instances, applications can use a combination of polling and interrupt methods. By using software variables, information can be transferred between interrupt service routines and the application processes (Fig. 2.7).

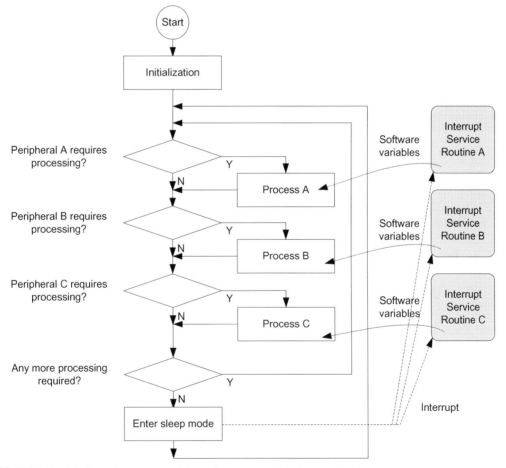

FIG. 2.7 Combination of polling and interrupt-driven methods in an application.

By dividing a peripheral processing task into an interrupt service routine and into a process running in the main program, we can reduce the duration of the interrupt service. By shortening the duration of the various interrupt services, even lower priority interrupt services could be serviced more quickly. At the same time, the system can still enter sleep mode when no processing task is required. In Fig. 2.7, the application is partitioned into processes A, B, and C, but in some instances, it might not be possible to easily partition an application task into individual parts and, thus it would need to be written as a large process. Even then, that does not delay the processing of the peripheral interrupt requests.

2.2.5.4 Handling concurrent processes

In some instances, an application process could take a significant amount of time to complete and therefore it would be undesirable to handle it in a large application loop, as shown in Fig. 2.7. If process A takes too long to complete, processes B and C will not able to respond to peripheral requests fast enough, which might result in a system failure. Common solutions to this are:

1. Breaking down a long processing task to a sequence of states. Each time the process is processed, only one state is executed.
2. Using a Real-Time Operating System (RTOS) to manage multiple tasks.

For method 1 (Fig. 2.8), a process is divided into a number of parts and a software state variable is used to track the state of the process. Each time the process is executed, the state information is updated so that next time the process is executed, the processing sequence is able to correctly resume.

FIG. 2.8 Partitioning a process into multiple parts in an application loop.

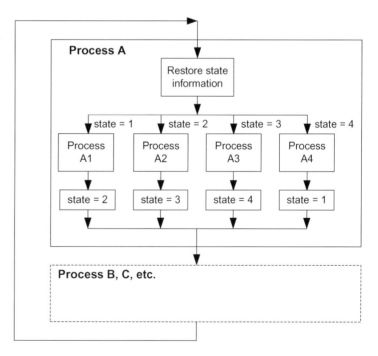

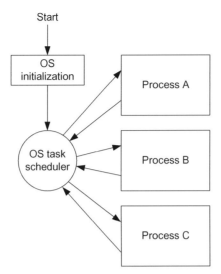

FIG. 2.9 Using an RTOS to handle multiple concurrent application processes.

With this method, since the execution path of the process is shortened, other processes in the main loop can be reached quicker inside the application loop. Although the total time required for the processing remains unchanged (or increased slightly due to the overhead of state being saved and restored), the system does end up being more responsive. However, when the application tasks get ever-more complex, manually partitioning the application task can become impractical.

For more complex applications, a Real Time Operating System (RTOS) can be used (Fig. 2.9). An RTOS allows multiple application processes to be executed concurrently by dividing processor execution time into time slots and then allocating time slots to each task. To use an RTOS, a timer is needed to generate interrupt requests (usually these requests are generated periodically). When each time slot ends, the timer interrupt service triggers the RTOS task scheduler, which then determines whether context switching should be carried out. If context switching is to be carried out, the task scheduler suspends the currently executing task and then switches to the next task that is waiting to be executed.

Using an RTOS improves the responsiveness of a system by ensuring that all tasks will be serviced within a certain amount of time. Examples of using an RTOS are covered in Chapter 17 (Section 17.2.9) and Chapter 20 (Section 20.6.4).

2.3 Introduction to Arm Cortex-M programming

2.3.1 C Programming—Data types

C language supports a number of "standard" data types. However, the implementation of data type is dependent upon processor architecture as well as C compiler features. For Arm Cortex-M processors, the following data types are supported by all C compilers (Table 2.1).

TABLE 2.1 Sizes of data types in Cortex-M processors.

C and C99 (stdint.h) data type	Number of bits	Range (signed)	Range (unsigned)
char, int8_t, uint8_t	8	−128 to 127	0 to 255
short int16_t, uint16_t	16	−32768 to 32767	0 to 65535
int, int32_t, uint32_t	32	−2147483648 to 2147483647	0 to 4294967295
long	32	−2147483648 to 2147483647	0 to 4294967295
long long, int64_t, uint64_t	64	$-(2\char`^63)$ to $(2\char`^63 - 1)$	0 to $(2\char`^64 - 1)$
float	32	$-3.4028234 \times 10^{38}$ to 3.4028234×10^{38}	
double	64	$-1.7976931348623157 \times 10^{308}$ to $1.7976931348623157 \times 10^{308}$	
long double	64	$-1.7976931348623157 \times 10^{308}$ to $1.7976931348623157 \times 10^{308}$	
pointers	32	0x0 to 0xFFFFFFFF	
enum	8/16/32	Smallest possible data type, except when overridden by compiler option	
bool (C++ only), _Bool (C99)	8	True or false	
wchar_t	16	0 to 65535	

When porting applications from other processor architectures to Arm processors, if the data types are of different sizes, it might be necessary to modify the C program code in order to ensure that the program operates correctly.

By default, data variables in Cortex-M programming are aligned, which means the memory address of the variable should be a multiple of the size of the data. However, the Armv8-M Mainline subprofile also allows unaligned data access. Further information on this topic is covered in Chapter 6, Memory System (Section 6.6, Data alignment and unaligned data access support).

In Arm programming, we refer to data sizes as byte, half word, word, and double word (Table 2.2).

These terms are commonly found in Arm documentation, for example, in the instruction set details.

TABLE 2.2 Data size definition in Arm processors.

Term	Size
Byte	8 bits
Half word	16 bits
Word	32 bits
Double word	64 bits

2.3.2 Accessing peripherals in C

In Arm Cortex-M based microcontrollers, peripheral registers are memory mapped and can be accessed by data pointers. In most cases, you can use the device drivers provided by the microcontroller vendors to simplify the software development task and make it easier to port software between different microcontrollers. If it is necessary to access the peripheral registers directly, the following methods can be used.

In a simple scenario of just accessing a few registers, you can define each peripheral register as a pointer using a C macro:

Example registers definition for a UART using pointers and accessing the registers

```c
#define UART_BASE  0x40003000 // Base of Arm Primecell PL011
#define UART_DATA  (*((volatile unsigned long *)(UART_BASE + 0x00)))
#define UART_RSR   (*((volatile unsigned long *)(UART_BASE + 0x04)))
#define UART_FLAG  (*((volatile unsigned long *)(UART_BASE + 0x18)))
#define UART_LPR   (*((volatile unsigned long *)(UART_BASE + 0x20)))
#define UART_IBRD  (*((volatile unsigned long *)(UART_BASE + 0x24)))
#define UART_FBRD  (*((volatile unsigned long *)(UART_BASE + 0x28)))
#define UART_LCR_H (*((volatile unsigned long *)(UART_BASE + 0x2C)))
#define UART_CR    (*((volatile unsigned long *)(UART_BASE + 0x30)))
#define UART_IFLS  (*((volatile unsigned long *)(UART_BASE + 0x34)))
#define UART_MSC   (*((volatile unsigned long *)(UART_BASE + 0x38)))
#define UART_RIS   (*((volatile unsigned long *)(UART_BASE + 0x3C)))
#define UART_MIS   (*((volatile unsigned long *)(UART_BASE + 0x40)))
#define UART_ICR   (*((volatile unsigned long *)(UART_BASE + 0x44)))
#define UART_DMACR (*((volatile unsigned long *)(UART_BASE + 0x48)))
/* ----- UART Initialization ---- */
void uartinit(void) // Simple initialization for Arm Primecell PL011
{
  UART_IBRD  =40;   // ibrd : 25MHz/38400/16 = 40
  UART_FBRD  =11;   // fbrd : 25MHz/38400 - 16*ibrd = 11.04
  UART_LCR_H =0x60;    // Line control : 8N1
  UART_CR    =0x301;  // cr : Enable TX and RX, UART enable
  UART_RSR   =0xA; // Clear buffer overrun if any
}
/* ----- Transmit a character ---- */
int sendchar(int ch)
{
  while (UART_FLAG & 0x20); // Busy, wait
  UART_DATA = ch; // write character
  return ch;
}
/* ----- Receive a character ---- */
int getkey(void)
```

```
{
  while ((UART_FLAG & 0x40)==0); // No data, wait
  return UART_DATA; // read character
}
```

As previously mentioned, this solution (defining each peripheral register as a pointer using a C macro) is fine for simple applications. However, when there are multiple units of the same peripherals available in the system, it will require defining registers for each of those peripherals, which can make code maintenance difficult. In addition, defining each register as an individual pointer could result in a larger program size as each register address is stored as a 32-bit constant in the program flash memory.

To simplify the code and to use program space more efficiently, we can define the peripheral register set as a data structure and then define the peripheral as a memory pointer to this data structure (as shown in the following C program code).

Example of register-definition for a UART using a data structure and a memory pointer based on this structure

```
typedef struct { // Base on Arm Primecell PL011
  volatile unsigned long DATA;        // 0x00
  volatile unsigned long RSR;         // 0x04
          unsigned long RESERVED0[4];// 0x08 - 0x14
  volatile unsigned long FLAG;        // 0x18
          unsigned long RESERVED1;    // 0x1C
  volatile unsigned long LPR;         // 0x20
  volatile unsigned long IBRD;        // 0x24
  volatile unsigned long FBRD;        // 0x28
  volatile unsigned long LCR_H;       // 0x2C
  volatile unsigned long CR;          // 0x30
  volatile unsigned long IFLS;        // 0x34
  volatile unsigned long MSC;         // 0x38
  volatile unsigned long RIS;         // 0x3C
  volatile unsigned long MIS;         // 0x40
  volatile unsigned long ICR;         // 0x44
  volatile unsigned long DMACR;       // 0x48
} UART_TypeDef;
#define Uart0  ((UART_TypeDef *)    0x40003000)
#define Uart1  ((UART_TypeDef *)    0x40004000)
#define Uart2  ((UART_TypeDef *)    0x40005000)

/* ----- UART Initialization ---- */
void uartinit(void) // Simple initialization for Primecell PL011
{
  Uart0->IBRD  =40;  // ibrd : 25MHz/38400/16 = 40
```

```
  Uart0->FBRD  =11;  // fbrd : 25MHz/38400 - 16*ibrd = 11.04
  Uart0->LCR_H =0x60;  // Line control : 8N1
  Uart0->CR    =0x301; // cr : Enable TX and RX, UART enable
  Uart0->RSR   =0xA; // Clear buffer overrun if any
}
/* ----- Transmit a character ---- */
int sendchar(int ch)
{
  while (Uart0->FLAG & 0x20); // Busy, wait
  Uart0->DATA = ch; // write character
  return ch;
}
/* ----- Receive a character ---- */
int getkey(void)
{
  while ((Uart0->FLAG & 0x40)==0); // No data, wait
  return Uart0->DATA; // read character
}
```

In this example, as shown above, the Integer Baud Rate Divider (IBRD) register for UART #0 is accessed by the symbol Uart0->IBRD and the same register for UART #1 is accessed by Uart1->IBRD.

With this arrangement, the same register data structure for the UART peripheral can be shared between multiple UARTs inside the chip, making code maintenance easier. In addition, the compiled code could be smaller due to the reduced requirement of the immediate data storage.

With further modification, a function developed for the peripherals can be shared between multiple units by passing the base pointer to the function:

Example of register-definition for a UART and driver code which support multiple UARTs using passing of the base pointer as a parameter

```
typedef struct { // Base on Arm Primecell PL011
  volatile unsigned long DATA;        // 0x00
  volatile unsigned long RSR;         // 0x04
           unsigned long RESERVED0[4];// 0x08 - 0x14
  volatile unsigned long FLAG;        // 0x18
           unsigned long RESERVED1;   // 0x1C
  volatile unsigned long LPR;         // 0x20
  volatile unsigned long IBRD;        // 0x24
  volatile unsigned long FBRD;        // 0x28
  volatile unsigned long LCR_H;       // 0x2C
  volatile unsigned long CR;          // 0x30
```

```c
    volatile unsigned long IFLS;          // 0x34
    volatile unsigned long MSC;           // 0x38
    volatile unsigned long RIS;           // 0x3C
    volatile unsigned long MIS;           // 0x40
    volatile unsigned long ICR;           // 0x44
    volatile unsigned long DMACR;         // 0x48
} UART_TypeDef;
#define Uart0   (( UART_TypeDef *)      0x40003000)
#define Uart1   (( UART_TypeDef *)      0x40004000)
#define Uart2   (( UART_TypeDef *)      0x40005000)

/* ----- UART Initialization ---- */
void uartinit(UART_Typedef *uartptr) //
{
 uartptr->IBRD  =40;    // ibrd : 25MHz/38400/16 = 40
 uartptr->FBRD  =11;    // fbrd : 25MHz/38400 - 16*ibrd = 11.04
 uartptr->LCR_H =0x60;   // Line control : 8N1
 uartptr->CR    =0x301;    // cr : Enable TX and RX, UART enable
 uartptr->RSR   =0xA;   // Clear buffer overrun if any
}
/* ----- Transmit a character ---- */
int sendchar(UART_Typedef *uartptr, int ch)
{
 while (uartptr->FLAG & 0x20); // Busy, wait
 uartptr->DATA = ch; // write character
 return ch;
}
/* ----- Receive a character ---- */
int getkey(UART_Typedef *uartptr)
{
 while ((uartptr ->FLAG & 0x40)==0); // No data, wait
 return uartptr ->DATA; // read character
}
```

In most instances, peripheral registers are defined as 32-bit words. This is because most peripherals are connected to a peripheral bus (using AMBA® APB protocol, see Section 6.11.2 in Chapter 6) that handles all transfers as 32 bits. Some peripherals might be connected to the processor's system bus (with an AMBA AHB protocol that supports various transfer sizes, also see Section 6.11.2). In such cases, the registers might be accessible in other transfer sizes. Please refer to the user manual of the microcontroller to determine the supported transfer size for each peripheral.

When defining memory pointers for peripheral access, the "`volatile`" keyword should be used in the registers' definitions. This ensures that the compiler correctly generates the access.

2.3.3 What is inside a program image?

After an application is compiled, the toolchain generates a program image. Inside the program image, in addition to the application program code that you have written, there is also a range of other software components. These are:

- A vector table
- A reset handler/startup code
- C startup code
- An application program code
- C runtime library functions
- Other data

In this section, I am going to briefly introduce what these components are.

2.3.3.1 Vector table

In Arm Cortex-M processors, the vector table contains the starting addresses of each exception and interrupt. One of the exceptions is the reset, which means that after reset the processor will fetch the reset vector (the starting address of the reset handler) from the vector table and start the execution from the reset handler. The first word in the vector table defines the starting value of the Main Stack Pointer, which will be introduced in Chapter 4 (Section 4.2 Programmer's Model). If the vector table is not set up correctly in the program image, the device cannot start.

For the Cortex-M23 and Cortex-M33 processors, the initial address of the vector table for boot up is specified by the chip designers. This is different from most of the previous Cortex-M processors (Note: In Cortex-M0/M0+/M3/M4 processors, the vector table initial address is defined as 0x00000000, starting of memory address).

The content of the vector table is device-specific (depending on what exceptions are supported) and is typically merged into the startup code. Further information detailing the vector table will be covered in Sections 8.6 and 9.5.

2.3.3.2 Reset handler/startup code

The reset handler or startup code is the first piece of software to execute after a system reset. Typically, the reset handler is used for setting up configuration data for the C startup code (such as address range for stack and heap memories), which then branches into the C startup code (see Section 2.3.3.3). In some cases, the reset handler also contains a hardware initialization sequence. In projects using CMSIS-CORE (a software framework for Cortex microcontrollers, which will be covered in Section 2.5 of this chapter), the reset handler executes the "`SystemInit()`" function which sets up the configuration for the clocks and the PLLs , before branching to the C startup code.

Depending on the development tools being used, the reset handler can be optional. If the reset handler is omitted, the C startup code is executed directly instead.

The startup code is typically provided by microcontroller vendors and is also often bundled inside toolchains. They can either be in the form of an assembly code or C code.

2.3.3.3 C startup code

If you are programming in C/C++, or are using other high-level languages, the processor will need to execute a piece of program code to set up the program execution environment. This includes (but is not limited to):

- setting up the initial data values in the SRAM, such as global variables.
- zero initializing part of the data memory for variables that are uninitialized at load time.
- initializing the data variables controlling the heap memory (for applications which use C functions, such as "malloc()").

After initialization, the C startup code branches to the start of the "main()" program.

The C startup code is automatically inserted by the toolchain and is toolchain specific, and is not inserted by the toolchain if the program is written in assembly. For Arm compilers, the C startup code is labeled as "__main", while the startup code generated by the GNU C compilers is normally labeled as "_start".

2.3.3.4 Application code

Usually, the application code starts at the beginning of main(). It contains instructions generated from application program code which, when executed, carries out the specified task(s). Apart from the instruction sequence, there are also various types of data inside the program code. These are:

- Initial values of variables. Local variables in functions or subroutines need to be initialized and these initial values are set up during the program execution.
- Constants in program code. Constant data is used in application codes in many ways: data values, addresses of peripheral registers, constant strings, etc. This data is often called literal data and is sometimes grouped together within the program image(s) as a number of data blocks called "literal pools".
- Additional values such as constants in lookup tables and graphic image data, for example, bit map; but only if this data is present in the program code.

This data is merged into the program image(s) during the compilation process.

2.3.3.5 C library code

C library code is inserted into the program image by the linker when certain C/C++ functions are used. In addition, C library code can also be included by way of data processing tasks such as floating-point calculations.

Some development tools offer various versions of C libraries for different purposes. For example, in Keil® MDK or Arm Development Studio (Arm DS) there is an option to use a special version of C library called Microlib. Microlib is targeted for microcontrollers, is very small in memory size, but does not offer all the features or the performance of the standard C library. In embedded applications that do not require a high data processing capability and have a tight program memory requirement, the use of Microlib is a good way to reduce the code size.

Depending on the application, C library code might not be present in simple C applications (if there are no C library function calls) or in pure assembly language projects.

2.3.3.6 *Other data*

The program image might also contain additional data used by other processing hardware, which is not used by the processor itself.

2.3.4 Data in SRAM

The Static Random Access Memory (SRAM) in the processor system is used in a number of ways:

Data: Data usually contains global variables and static variables. (Note: local variables can be placed in the stack memories so that a local variable from a function that is not in use does not take up memory space).

Stack: The role of stack memory includes storage of temporary data when handling function calls (normal stack PUSH and POP operations), storage for local variables, passing of parameters in function calls, saving of registers during exception sequences, etc. The Thumb® instruction set is very efficient in handling data access that uses a Stack Pointer (SP) related addressing mode, i.e., it allows data in the stack memory to be accessed with a very low instruction overhead.

Heap: The use of heap memory is optional and is dependent upon an application's requirements. It is used by C functions that dynamically reserve memory space, like "alloc()", "malloc()" and other function calls that internally uses these functions. In order to allow these functions to correctly allocate memory, the C startup code needs to initialize the heap memory and its control variables.

Depending on the toolchains being used, the size of the stack and the heap spaces could either be defined inside the reset handler or in a project configuration file.

Arm processors also allow program code to be copied into the volatile memory (e.g., SRAM) and to be executed from there. But in most microcontroller applications, the program codes are executed directly from nonvolatile memories, e.g., from flash memories.

There are various approaches in terms of how data is placed in the SRAM. This is often toolchain specific. In simple applications without any OS, the memory layout in the SRAM is typically like the illustration shown in Fig. 2.10. In Arm architecture, the stack pointer is initialized to the top of the stack memory space. The stack pointer decrements as data are placed in the stack by stack PUSH operations and increments as the data are removed from the stack using stack POP operations.

For microcontroller systems with an embedded OS or RTOS (e.g., Keil® RTX), the stacks for each task are separate. Many OS allow software developers to define stack size for each task/thread. Some OS divide the RAM into a number of segments and each segment is then assigned to a task, each containing individual data, stack, and heap regions (Fig. 2.11).

In most systems with an RTOS, the data layout detailed on the left-hand side of Fig. 2.11 would be used and, in this instance, global and static variables and the heap memory would be shared.

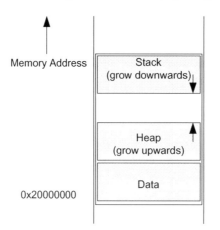

Example RAM usage in systems without OS

FIG. 2.10   Example RAM usage in single-task systems (without OS).

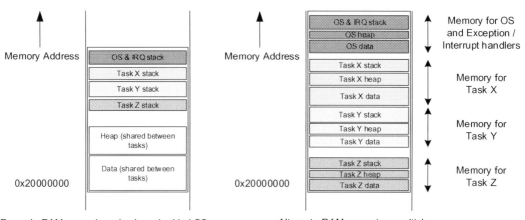

Example RAM usage in a simple embedded OS   Alternate RAM usage in a multiple
                                                      task system with an embedded OS

FIG. 2.11   Example RAM usage in multiple task systems (with an OS).

2.3.5 What happens when a microcontroller starts?

Most modern microcontrollers have on-chip nonvolatile memory (e.g., flash memory) to hold the compiled program. The flash memory holds the program in binary machine code format and thus programs written in C must be compiled before being programmed into the flash memory. Some of those microcontrollers might also have a separate boot ROM, which contains a small boot loader program that is executed when the microcontroller starts before executing the user program in the flash memory. In most cases, only the program code

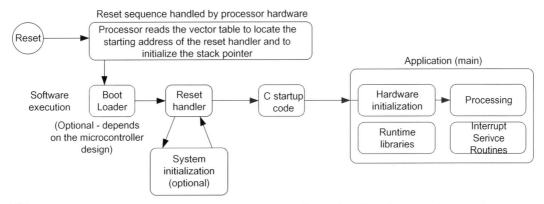

FIG. 2.12   Example boot sequence for Cortex-M microcontrollers without TrustZone security extension.

in the flash memory can be changed, with the program code in the boot loader being fixed by the manufacturer.

In simple Cortex-M microcontrollers without the TrustZone® security extension, the reset and boot sequences are as illustrated in Fig. 2.12. The first phase is a reset sequence which is handled by the hardware for minimal initialization of the stack pointer and the program counter. If the boot loader is present, the initial vector table address should be pointing to the vector table inside the boot loader. The vector table address can be changed by software to point to the vector table in the application program image at the end of the boot loader's execution.

For Cortex-M23 or Cortex-M33 microcontrollers with the TrustZone security extension, the processor inside starts in a Secure state and boots up using the Secure firmware. Once the secure application is up and running, it can then initialize the Non-secure application. This is illustrated in Fig. 2.13.

In such systems, the Secure and Non-secure applications have their own vector tables, stack memories, heap memories, data and program memory spaces. The two application images (Secure and Non-secure worlds), as shown in Fig. 2.13, were separately developed in different projects, but, despite this, there can still be interactions between them using function calls. More of this will be covered in Chapter 18.

2.3.6 Understanding your hardware platform

The designs of Cortex-M processors are very flexible, with many optional features. For example, chip designers can customize:

- Whether the TrustZone security extension is implemented.
- The number of interrupts supported and the number of priority levels implemented (the number of priority levels is configurable in the Cortex-M33 processor design, just like Armv7-M processors).
- In the case of Cortex-M33 based microcontrollers, whether to have a floating-point unit (FPU).

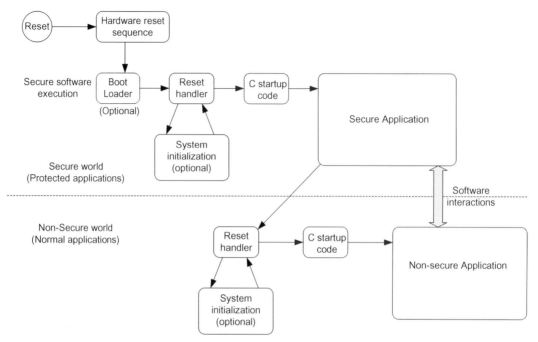

FIG. 2.13   Example boot sequence for Cortex-M microcontrollers with TrustZone security extension.

- Whether the Memory Protection Unit (MPU) should be included and, if it is, the number of MPU regions can be defined. If the TrustZone security extension is implemented, then there could be two optional MPUs in the processor—one for Secure state operations and one for Non-secure state operations. The number of MPU regions in these two MPUs can be configured individually.
- The range of debug and trace features. For example, whether the instruction trace feature is supported and, if it is, whether it is based on the Embedded Trace Macrocell (ETM) or on the Micro Trace Buffer (MTB).

Additional information on the configuration options available is covered in Chapter 3, Section 3.17, Configuration options of the processors.

Understanding the configuration options implemented in the device you are using is important because some of the configuration options directly affect the design of the application software. Also, it can determine the development tool features that can be utilized when the software is developed. Obviously, the memory map of the microcontroller device also affects the software project setup inside the development tools. Additionally, the following processor's configuration options can affect the development of the software:

- If the TrustZone security extension is implemented in the microcontroller, software developers need to know whether they are implementing software for the Secure world (i.e., a protected environment) or for the Non-secure world (i.e., a normal application environment). This is because:

○ Compilation of Secure software requires the use of an additional compiler option (e.g., it can be in the form of a project setting option or a command-line option). Without this, some software features defined in the Arm C Language extension (ACLE) cannot be used.

○ Some of the hardware features in Armv8-M is available only for the Secure world.

○ There are different RTOS design arrangements for TrustZone. So, for the same RTOS, there can be multiple variants and you must use the correct version for your project.

• Some RTOS features might require the availability of an MPU. If your application requires a high level of reliability, the MPU can help by enabling the isolation of memory spaces between the application tasks.

• The system tick timer (SysTick) is optional in the Cortex-M23 processor and is always available in the Cortex-M33 processor. But, for most of microcontroller devices, it is expected that SysTick will usually be available.

• If a floating-point unit (FPU) is present, specific project options might be required to enable the FPU to achieve faster floating-point data processing.

• If the Embedded Trace Macrocell (ETM) is present, you can capture the instruction trace in real-time. To do that, the software developer needs to use a debug probe/adaptor that supports a parallel trace port interface. However, bear in mind that most low-cost development adaptors (including adaptors on some of the development boards based on the open-source CMSIS-DAP) do not support a parallel trace port interface.

Usually, the device data sheet should cover all the information you need.

2.4 Software development flow

There are many development toolchains available for Arm microcontrollers. The majority of them support C/C++ and assembly language. In most cases, the program generation flow is as detailed below in Fig. 2.14.

In most basic applications, the programs can be completely written in the C language. The C compiler compiles the C program code into object files and then generates the executable program image file using the linker. In the case of GNU C compilers, the compile and linking stages are often merged into one single step.

Projects that require assembly programming use the assembler to generate object code from assembly source code. The object files can then be linked together with other object files in the project to produce an executable image.

Aside from the program code, the object files and the executable image may also contain additional data such as debug information to enable the debugger software to provide extra debug features.

Depending on the development tools being used, it is possible to specify the memory layout for the linker using command-line options. However, in projects using GNU C compilers, a linker script is normally required to specify the memory layout. A linker script is also required for other development tools when the memory layout is complicated. With Arm development tools, the linker scripts are often called scatter-loading files. If you are using a Keil® Microcontroller Development Kit (MDK), the scatter-loading file can be generated automatically from the memory layout window. You can, though, use your own scatter-loading file if you prefer.

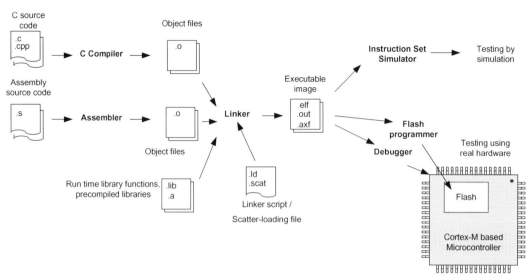

FIG. 2.14 Typical program generation flow.

Apart from the vector table, which must be placed within specific locations in the memory map, there are no other constraints on the placement for the rest of the elements inside a program image. In some cases, if the layout of the items in the program memory is of particular importance, the layout of the program image can be controlled by a linker script. For example, when using the Memory Protection Unit (MPU) for security management, it is common to group program codes and data for the same security partition together to minimize the number of MPU regions needed for defining the access permissions for application tasks.

After the executable image is generated, it can be tested by downloading it to the flash memory or to the internal RAM of the microcontroller. The whole process is quite easy, with most development suites being equipped with a user-friendly Integrated Development Environment (IDE). When working together with a debug probe (sometimes referred to as an In-Circuit Emulator [ICE], or as an in-circuit debugger, or as a USB-JTAG adaptor), you can create a project, build your application and download your embedded application to the microcontroller in just a few steps (Fig. 2.15).

Many microcontroller development boards have a built-in USB debug adaptor. In some instances, the aforementioned adaptor is not provided and a debug probe is needed to connect the debug host (personal computer) to the target board. The Keil® ULINK2/ULINKPro (Fig. 2.2) is one of the products that is available and can be used with the Keil® Microcontroller Development Kit (MDK).

If you are using a Cortex-M23/Cortex-M33 microcontroller with the TrustZone security extension, and if you are creating a software project for Secure firmware, you also need to create a Non-secure project at the same time to test the interactions between the software running in the Secure and Non-secure worlds. Some of the development suites support a feature called multiproject workspace to make this easier—enabling you to simultaneously develop and test multiple software projects.

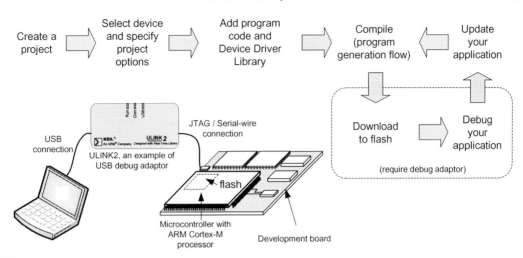

FIG. 2.15 An example of development flow.

The flash programming function can be carried out by the debugger software in the development suite or, in some cases, by utilizing a flash programming utility available from the microcontroller vendor's website. After the program image is programmed into the flash memory in the microcontroller device, the program is then tested. By connecting the debugger software to the microcontroller (via an adaptor), the program execution can then be controlled (stop, single stepping, resume, restart) and its operations can then be observed. All of this can be carried out via the debug interface on the Cortex-M processor (see Fig. 2.16).

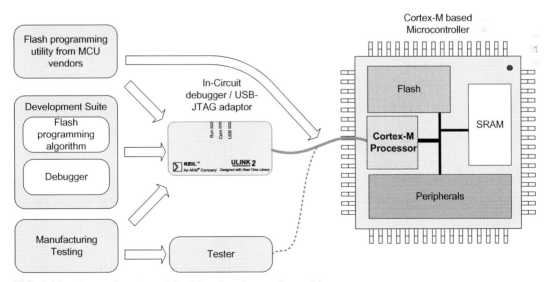

FIG. 2.16 Various functions of the debug interface on Cortex-M processors.

For simple program codes, the program's operations can be tested using a simulator. This allows us to have full visibility of the program's execution sequence and allows testing without using any hardware. However, most simulators only emulate instruction execution and not the behavior of the peripheral hardware. Furthermore, the timing characteristics of the simulated program execution could be inaccurate.

Apart from the fact that the various C Compilers perform differently, the various development suites also provide different C language extension features, as well as different syntax and directives in assembly programming. Chapter 5, Section 5.3 of this book provides assembly syntax information for Arm development tools (including Arm Development Studio 5 and Keil MDK) and for the GNU compiler. In addition, the various development suites provide different debug features and support a range of debug probes. To enable better software portability, the Cortex Microcontroller Software Interface Standard (CMSIS, see Section 2.5) provides a range of consistent software interfaces so that the underlying differences in the toolchain will not affect the application software.

2.5 Cortex Microcontroller Software Interface Standard (CMSIS)

2.5.1 Introduction of CMSIS

As the complexity of embedded systems increases, the compatibility and reusability of software code become ever more important. Having reusable software often helps to reduce development time for subsequent projects and, hence, allows a faster time-to-market. Software compatibility also allows one to use third parties' software components. For example, an embedded system project could consist of the following software components:

- Software developed by in-house software developers.
- Software reused from other projects.
- Device driver libraries from microcontroller vendors.
- Embedded OS/RTOS.
- Other third-party software products, such as a communication protocol stack and a codec (compressor/decompressor).

With so many different software components being used in one project, the compatibility of these components is fast becoming a critical factor in many large-scale software projects. Also, system developers often want, even when those future projects end up using a different processor, to be able to reuse the software they have already developed.

To allow a high level of compatibility between software products and to improve software portability and reusability, Arm has worked with a number of microcontroller and tool vendors, and software solution providers, to develop the CMSIS-CORE—a common software framework covering most of the Cortex-M processors and Cortex-M microcontroller products.

The CMSIS-CORE is implemented as part of the device driver library which is available from microcontroller vendors (Fig. 2.17). It provides a standardized software interface to processor features such as interrupt control and system control functions. Many of these

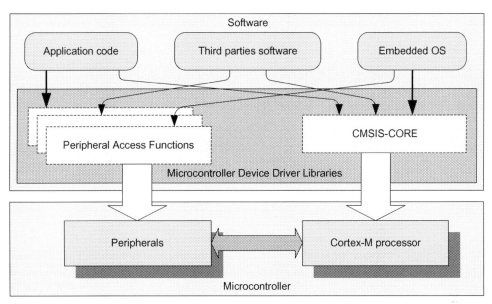

FIG. 2.17   CMSIS-CORE provides standardized access functions for processor features.

processor feature access functions are available across the whole range of Cortex-M processors, allowing easy software porting between the microcontrollers based on those processors.

The CMSIS-CORE is standardized across multiple microcontroller vendors and is also supported by multiple C compiler vendors. For example, it can be used with the Keil® Microcontroller Development Kit (Keil MDK), Arm Development Studio (Arm DS), IAR™ Embedded Workbench, and various GNU-based C compiler suites.

The CMSIS-CORE was the first stage of the CMSIS project and has continued to evolve to encompass additional processors. Over the years, it has integrated various improvements and has added additional toolchain support.

Today, CMSIS has expanded into multiple projects (Table 2.3).

The interactions between various CMSIS projects are shown in Fig. 2.18.

2.5.2 What is standardized in the CMSIS-CORE?

The CMSIS-CORE standardized a range of areas in embedded software. This includes:

- the access functions/Application Programming Interface (API) for accessing the processor's internal peripherals, such as interrupt control and SysTick initialization. These functions will be covered in subsequent chapters of this book.
- the register definitions for the processor's internal peripherals. For the best software portability, we should use standardized access functions. However, in some instances we

TABLE 2.3 List of existing CMSIS projects.

CMSIS project	Description
CMSIS-CORE	A software framework, which includes a set of APIs for processor features and a range of register definitions. It provides a consistent software interface for device driver libraries.
CMSIS-DSP	A free DSP software library available for all Cortex-M processors.
CMSIS-NN	A free Neural Network processing library for machine learning applications.
CMSIS-RTOS	An API specification for interfacing between application codes and RTOS products. This enables middleware to be developed to work with multiple RTOSs.
CMSIS-PACK	A software package mechanism to enable software vendors (including microcontroller vendors that deliver device driver libraries) to deliver software packages, which can then be easily be integrated into development suites.
CMSIS-Driver	A device driver API to enable middleware to access commonly used device driver functions.
CMSIS-SVD	The System View Description (SVD) is a standard for XML based files, which describes the peripheral registers inside a microcontroller device. The CMSIS-SVD files are created by microcontroller vendors. Debuggers supporting CMSIS-SVD can then import these files and visualize the peripheral registers.
CMSIS-DAP	A reference design for a low-cost debug probe with a USB connection. This enables a standard interface for debuggers in development suites to communicate with the USB debug adaptors. With CMSIS-DAP, microcontroller vendors can create low cost debug adaptors that work with multiple toolchains.
CMSIS-ZONE	An initiative to standardize complex system descriptions in XML files to simplify the setup of a project in development tools.

need to directly access those registers, and using the standardized register definitions helps the software to be more portable.
- the functions for accessing special instructions in Cortex-M processors. Some instructions in the Cortex-M processors cannot be generated by using normal C code. If those instructions are needed, they can be generated by utilizing the functions provided. Otherwise, users will have to use intrinsic functions provided by the C compiler or by using embedded/inline assembly language which are toolchain specific and are less portable.
- names for system exceptions handlers. System exceptions are often required by an embedded OS. By having standardized names for the system exception handler means that it is much easier to support different device driver libraries in an embedded OS.
- a name for the system initialization function. The common system initialization function "`void SystemInit(void)`" makes it easier for software developers to set up their system with minimum effort.
- a software variable called "`SystemCoreClock`" to determine the processor clock frequency.

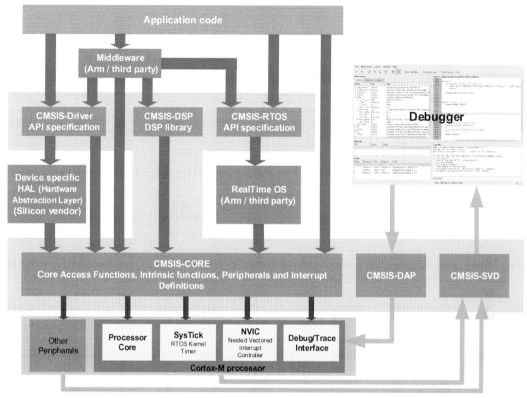

FIG. 2.18   Interactions between different CMSIS projects.

- a common arrangement for device driver libraries, such as a convention for filenames and directory names. This makes it easier for beginners to be familiar with the device driver libraries and also makes it easier for software porting.

The CMSIS-CORE project has been developed to ensure software compatibility for majority of processor operations. Microcontroller vendors can add additional functions to their device driver libraries to enhance their software solutions. As such, CMSIS-CORE does not restrict the functionality and the capability of the vendor's embedded products.

2.5.3 Using CMSIS-CORE

The CMSIS-CORE is an integrated part of the device driver package provided by microcontroller vendors. If you are using the device driver libraries for software development, you are already using the CMSIS-CORE. CMSIS projects are open-source and are and can be accessed freely from the following github website: https://github.com/ARM-software/CMSIS_5 (CMSIS version 5).

For most C program projects, you usually only need to add one header file to your C files. This header file is provided in the device driver library from the microcontroller's vendor.

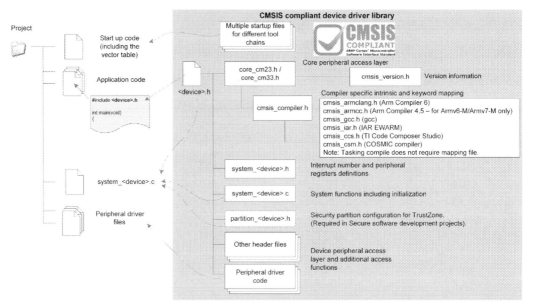

FIG. 2.19   Using a device driver package with CMSIS-CORE in a software project.

Typically, inside this header file, there are device register definitions (additional header files might be needed for other firmware libraries). There are also codes that pull in additional header files for the required features in the CMSIS-CORE. It might also contain header codes that pull in other peripheral functions.

In the project, you will also need to include the CMSIS compliant startup code, which can be in either C or assembly code. CMSIS-CORE provides various templates of startup code for different toolchains.

Fig. 2.19 shows a simple project setup using the CMSIS-CORE package. Some of the filenames are dependent on the name of the actual microcontroller device (indicated as <device> in Fig. 2.19). When you use the header file provided in the device driver library, it automatically includes the other required header files for you (Table 2.4).

Fig. 2.20 shows an example of using a CMSIS compliant driver in a small project.

Typically, information and examples of using a CMSIS compliant device driver library can be found in the libraries package from your microcontroller vendor. Online reference to CMSIS projects can be found at http://www.keil.com/cmsis.

2.5.4 Benefits of CMSIS

For most users, the CMSIS-CORE and other CMSIS offerings provide the following key advantages:

Software Portability and Reusability: Porting of applications from one Cortex-M based microcontroller to another is much easier with the CMSIS-CORE. For example, most of the interrupt control functions are available across the whole range of Cortex-M processors. This

TABLE 2.4   List of CMSIS-CORE files in a typical software project.

File	Description
<device>.h	A file provided by the microcontroller vendor that includes other header files, provides definitions for a number of constants required by the CMSIS-CORE, definitions of device-specific exception types, peripheral register definitions, and peripheral address definitions.
core_cm23.h/core_cm33.h	This file contains the definitions of the registers for processor peripherals such as the NVIC, the System Tick Timer, and the System Control Block (SCB). It also provides the core access functions, i.e., interrupt control and system control.
cmsis_compiler.h	Enables the selection of compiler-specific header files.
cmsis_armclang.h cmsis_armcc.h cmsis_gcc.h cmsis_iar.h cmsis_ccs.h cmsis_csm.h	Provides intrinsic functions and core register access functions. Note: • each compiler/toolchain has their own file • cmsis_armcc.h (Arm compiler 4/5) does not support Cortex-M23 & Cortex-M33. Users of Arm toolchains should use "cmsis_armclang.h"
cmsis_version.h	CMSIS version information
Startup code	Multiple versions of the startup code can be found in the CMSIS-CORE because it is tools specific. The startup code contains a vector table, dummy definitions for a number of system exceptions handlers. In CMSIS-CORE version 1.30 and subsequent, the reset handler in the startup code sequence includes a function call to the system initialization function ("void SystemInit(void)"). This function carries out a range of hardware initialization steps before branching to the C startup code.
system_<device>.h	This is a header file for functions implemented in system_<device>.c
system_<device>.c	This file contains: • the implementation of the system initialization function "void SystemInit(void)" (for clock and PLL setup), • the definition of the variable "SystemCoreClock" (processor clock speed), and • a function called "void SystemCoreClockUpdate(void)" that is used after each change of clock frequency to update the "SystemCoreClock" variable. The "SystemCoreClock" variable and the "SystemCoreClockUpdate" function are available in CMSIS version 1.3 and subsequent.
Other files	There are also additional files for peripheral control code and other helper functions. These files provide access to the device's peripheral functions.

makes it much more straightforward to reuse some of the software components when undertaking a new and different project.

Ease of software development: A number of development tools support CMSIS (CMSIS-CORE, as well as other CMSIS projects) and, by doing so, simplifies the process of setting up new software projects, and hence provides a better out of the box experience for users.

Easy to learn the programming of new devices: Learning to use a new Cortex-M based microcontroller is made easier. Once you have used one Cortex-M based microcontroller you can quickly learn how to use another one because the CMSIS compliant device driver libraries have the same core functions and similar software interfaces.

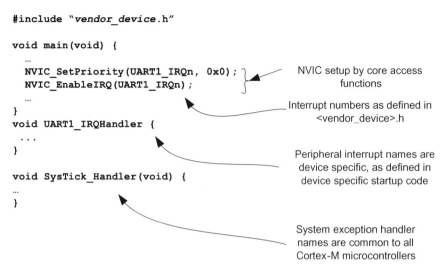

```
#include "vendor_device.h"

void main(void) {
   ...
   NVIC_SetPriority(UART1_IRQn, 0x0);
   NVIC_EnableIRQ(UART1_IRQn);
   ...
}
void UART1_IRQHandler {
  ...
}

void SysTick_Handler(void) {
   ...
}
```

NVIC setup by core access functions

Interrupt numbers as defined in <vendor_device>.h

Peripheral interrupt names are device specific, as defined in device specific startup code

System exception handler names are common to all Cortex-M microcontrollers

FIG. 2.20   Example application based on CMSIS-CORE.

Software component compatibility: Using CMSIS also lowers the risk of incompatibility when integrating third-party software components. Since software components (including RTOS) from different sources are based on the same core level access functions that exist in CMSIS, the risk of having conflicting code is reduced. It also helps to reduce code size as the software components do not have to include their own core level access functions and register definitions.

Future proof: CMSIS helps to ensure that software code is future proof. Future Cortex-M processors and Cortex-M based microcontrollers will have CMSIS support and this means that you can reuse your application codes in future products.

Quality: The CMSIS core access functions have a small memory footprint. The program codes inside CMSIS have been tested by multiple parties and this helps reduce software testing time. CMSIS is Motor Industry Software Reliability Association (MISRA) compliant.

For companies that develop embedded OS or middleware products, the advantage of CMSIS is significant. Since CMSIS supports multiple compiler suites and is supported by multiple microcontroller vendors, the embedded OS or middleware developed for CMSIS can run on multiple microcontroller families and can be compiled with different toolchains. Using CMSIS also means that companies do not have to develop their own portable device drivers, which saves development time and verification efforts.

2.6 Additional information on software development

Cortex-M processors are designed for ease of use and most operations can be coded in standard C/C++ code. However, there are some instances when assembly language might be needed. Most C compilers provide workarounds to allow assembly code to be used within the C programs. For example, many C compilers provide an *Inline Assembler* so that assembly functions can easily be included in the C program code. However, the assembly syntax for using an Inline Assembler is toolchain specific and is not portable.

Some C compilers, including Arm C compilers in the Arm Development Studio (Arm DS) and in Keil MDK, also provide intrinsic functions to allow special instructions to be inserted. This is because those instructions cannot be generated using normal C code. Intrinsic functions are normally toolchain specific. However, toolchain independent intrinsic functions for accessing special instructions in the Cortex-M processors are also available within CMSIS-CORE. This is covered in Chapter 5.

You can mix C, C++, and assembly codes together in a project. This allows most of the program to be written in C/C++ and for the part that cannot be handled in C/C++ to be written in assembly. To handle this, the interface between functions must be handled in a consistent manner to allow input parameters and returned results to be transferred correctly. In Arm software architecture, the interface between functions is specified by a specification document called Arm Architecture Procedure Call Standard (AAPCS) [1]. The AAPCS is part of the Embedded Application Binary Interface (EABI). When writing code in assembly, you should follow the guidelines set by the AAPCS. The AAPCS document and the EABI document can be downloaded from the Arm website.

More information on this is covered in Chapter 17, Section 17.3.

Reference

[1] Procedure Call Standard for the Arm Architecture (AAPCS). https://developer.arm.com/documentation/ihi0042/latest.

Technical overview of the Cortex-M23 and Cortex-M33 processors

3.1 Design objectives of Cortex-M23 and Cortex-M33 processors

The Arm® Cortex®-M processors are widely used in microcontrollers, as well as in a range of low power Application Specific Integrated Circuits (ASICs). In many respects, Cortex-M processor designs are optimized for those applications. This was proven with the previous generations of Cortex-M processors which successfully catered for those particular requirements. With the increasing popularity of Internet-of-Things (IoT) applications, additional requirements have become essential—particularly the security capability of processors.

The design objectives of the Cortex-M23 and Cortex-M33 processors include:

- Low power: Many IoT applications are battery powered, and some could be powered using energy harvesting. The processors also need to support a range of low power features such as sleep modes.
- Small silicon area/low logic gate count: A small processor size is desirable because it helps reduce the cost of the chip. In some applications, for example, mixed-signal designs require a low gate count due to the nature of the transistor geometries.
- Performance: Data processing requirements in microcontrollers have increased over the years. For example, some of them are used for audio processing. Processors used in IoT applications might also need to execute complex communication protocols.
- Real-time capabilities: This includes low interrupt latency and a high level of determinism in software execution behaviors. For example, low interrupt latency is essential in high-speed motor control applications as any delay in responding to an interrupt could reduce the accuracy of the speed/position control, reduce the energy efficiency of the system, increase noise and vibration, and, in the worst-case scenario, could impact safety.
- Ease of use: Microcontrollers are used by many different software developers, including inexperienced users like students and hobbyists. Ease of use can be important for professionals too because in many projects, due to market pressures, they cannot spend a long time studying the architecture of the microcontroller and the processor.

- Security: As many microcontrollers are used in IoT applications security has become a very important requirement. As a result, the TrustZone® security extension has been included in Armv8-M architecture.
- Debug features: As software becomes more complex, the debugging of complex software issues in applications is getting more difficult and thus advanced processor debug features are needed.
- Flexibility: Different chip designs can have very different system design requirements and the processor design must, therefore, be able to cope with each requirement. For example, some of the features can be essential in one application but might need to be removed to enable lower power and a smaller silicon area in another. The Cortex-M23 and Cortex-M33 processors have thus been designed to be highly configurable.
- Ease of system-level integration: The Cortex-M23 and Cortex-M33 processors have been designed with various interface level features and configuration options to enable chip designers to integrate the processors easily into their system-level designs.
- Scalability: Cortex-M processors are used in single core and multicore designs. To meet the scalability requirement, the processor design has a number of features to support multicore system requirements.
- Software reusability: To reduce software development costs, the Cortex-M23 and Cortex-M33 processors are designed to allow most of the software written for previous Cortex-M designs to be reused.
- Quality: The processor designs have been tested extensively using multiple verification methodologies.

As in many engineering projects, there are trade-offs between the many objectives. For example, performance vs energy efficiency, ease-of-use vs security, etc. The Cortex-M23 and Cortex-M33 processors target some of the sweet spots which are optimal for the majority of microcontroller designs.

3.2 Block diagrams

3.2.1 Cortex-M23

The block diagram of the Arm Cortex-M23 processor is illustrated in Fig. 3.1.

The Cortex-M23 processor design contains a number of units, as listed in Table 3.1.

Please note, a number of the aforementioned components are optional (marked with dashed lines in the block diagram).

3.2.2 Cortex-M33

The block diagram of the Arm Cortex-M33 processor is shown in Fig. 3.2.

Compared to the Cortex-M23 processor, the Cortex-M33 processor has one extra AHB5 interface for memory access. In addition, the Cortex-M33 processor has a number of additional units. These are listed in Table 3.2.

Unlike the Cortex-M23 (Armv8-M Baseline), SysTick timers are always present (not optional) in Armv8-M Mainline processors.

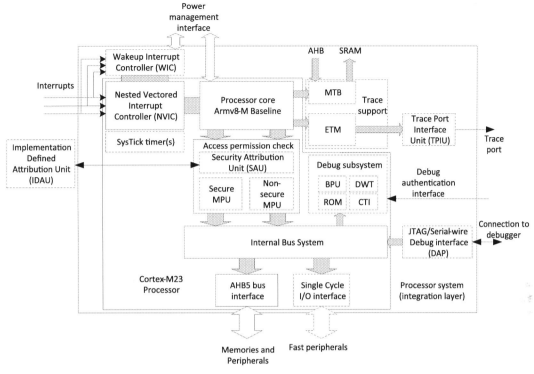

FIG. 3.1 Block diagram of Arm Cortex-M23 processor.

TABLE 3.1 Brief description of processor's internal components

Term	Short description
AHB5	Advanced High-performance Bus (version 5): An on-chip bus protocol with low latency and low hardware cost. Version 5 supports the TrustZone security extension.
SAU	Security Attribution Unit: Defines the partitioning of the memory space between Secure and Non-secure regions.
IDAU	Implementation Defined Attribution Unit: An optional hardware block that works with the SAU to define the partitioning of the memory space.
MPU	Memory Protection Unit: Defines access permission separation between privileged and unprivileged states. If the TrustZone security extension is implemented there can be two MPUs in the processor.
NVIC	Nested Vectored Interrupt Controller: Prioritizes and handles interrupts and internal system exception requests.
WIC	Wakeup Interrupt Controller: Enables the processor to wake up from sleep modes, even if all clocks to the processor are stopped, or if the processor logic is in a low power state with state retention.

Continued

TABLE 3.1   Brief description of processor's internal components—cont'd

Term	Short description
SysTick	System tick timer(s): Basic 24-bit timer for OS periodic interrupt operations, or for other timekeeping purposes. If TrustZone is present there can be up to two SysTick timers.
DAP	Debug Access Port: Allows debug probes to access the processor's memory system and debug features using JTAG or Serial Wire Debug protocol.
BPU	Break Point Unit: Facilitates the handling of breakpoint(s) for debugging
DWT	Data Watchpoint and Trace: Facilitates the handling of data watchpoint(s) and trace operations (data trace support is not included in Armv8-M Baseline).
ROM table	ROM table: A small lookup table to allow debuggers to discover which debug features are implemented in the system.
CTI	Cross Trigger Interface: For debug event communications in multicore systems.
ETM	Embedded Trace Macrocell: A hardware unit to support real-time instruction trace.
TPIU	Trace Port Interface Unit: A hardware block to convert an internal trace bus to trace port protocol.
MTB	Micro Trace Buffer: An alternative instruction trace feature to store instruction trace in on-chip SRAM. This feature allows instruction tracing with low cost debug probes.

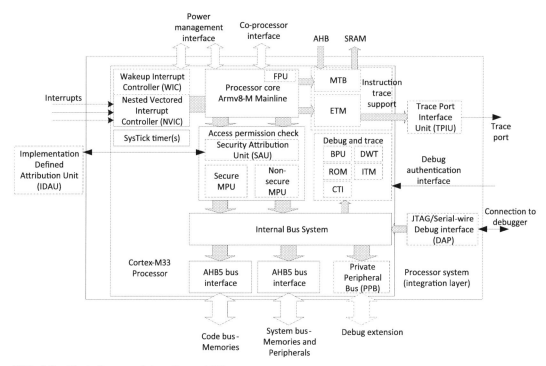

FIG. 3.2   Block diagram of Arm Cortex-M33 processor.

TABLE 3.2 Cortex-M33 additional components

Acronym	Short description
FPU	Floating-Point Unit: Processor hardware for handling floating-point data processing.
ITM	Instrumentation Trace Macrocell: A trace unit to allow software to generate trace stimulus.
PPB	Private Peripheral Bus: A bus interface which allows additional debug components to be easily added.

3.3 Processor

Both the Cortex-M23 and Cortex-M33 are 32-bit processors and are based on Armv8-M architecture.

- Cortex-M23 processor is based on the Baseline subprofile of Armv8-M architecture
- Cortex-M33 processor is based on the Mainline subprofile of Armv8-M architecture

The Cortex-M23 processor has a two-stage pipeline:

- First stage: Instruction fetch and predecoding.
- Second stage: Main instruction decoding and execution.

By using a single two-stage pipeline design, the Cortex-M23 processor is well optimized for applications that need a small silicon area and ultra-low power. To reduce design complexity, the number of instructions supported is relatively few in number. Even so, the processor is well capable of handling general data processing and I/O control tasks.

The Cortex-M33 processor has a three-stage pipeline:

- First stage: Instruction fetch and predecoding.
- Second stage: Decode and simple execution.
- Third stage: Complex execution.

Some of the operations are completed at the second pipeline stage. This arrangement enables low power consumption and also better efficiency. This processor pipeline design also supports the limited dual issue of 16-bit instructions.

The performance of the Cortex-M23 and Cortex-M33 processors is listed in Table 3.3.

The higher performance of Cortex-M33 processor is due to:

- A richer instruction set;
- Use of Harvard bus architecture to allow concurrent data and instruction fetches;
- Limited dual-issue capability.

TABLE 3.3 Integer processing performance of the Cortex-M23 and Cortex-M33 processors

	Cortex-M23	Cortex-M33
Dhrystone version 2.1	0.98 DMIPS/MHz	1.5 DMIPS/MHz
CoreMark® 1.0	2.5 CoreMark/MHz	4.02 CoreMark/MHz

3.4 Instruction set

The instruction set used in Arm Cortex-M processors is called the Thumb® instruction set. This instruction set contains a range of extensions (Table 3.4).

The instruction set of the Cortex-M33 is a superset of the instruction set found in the Cortex-M23 processor. To enable easy project migration, all of the instructions available in previous Cortex-M processors are also available in the Armv8-M architecture (Fig. 3.3).

In general, the instruction set in Cortex-M processors provides an upward compatibility characteristic. For example:

• The instruction set of the Cortex-M23 is a superset of the instruction set found in the Cortex-M0/M0+ processor. A range of instruction set features, such as hardware divide, which is not available in the Cortex-M0/M0+, has been added to the Armv8-M Baseline/Cortex-M23 processor. More information on this can be found in Section 3.15.1.
• The instruction set of the Cortex-M33 is a superset of the instruction set found in the Cortex-M3 and Cortex-M4 processors.
• Except for double-precision floating-point instructions and cache preload instructions, all instruction supported in the Cortex-M7 processors are available in the Cortex-M33. (Note: The Cortex-M33 does not have a double-precision FPU option or a cache memory controller feature.)

This upward compatibility is an important characteristic of the Cortex-M processor family, as it provides software reusability and portability.

Many of the instructions used in the Armv8-M Baseline instruction set are 16-bit in size. This enables high code density. For general data processing and control tasks, the program code can be composed of mostly 16-bit instructions (instead of 32-bit) to reduce the size of program memory.

3.5 Memory map

Both the Cortex-M23 and Cortex-M33 processors have a 4GB unified address space (32-bit address). Unified means that there is only one address space, even though there can be more than one bus interface. For example, the Cortex-M33 processor is based on Harvard bus architecture, which allows simultaneous instruction and data access, but that does not mean that the system has 4GB of memory space for instructions and another 4GB of memory space for data.

TABLE 3.4 Instruction set and extensions

Processor	Instruction set and extensions
Cortex-M23	Armv8-M Baseline instruction set + optional TrustZone security extension
Cortex-M33	Armv8-M Baseline instruction set + Mainline instruction extension + optional DSP extension + optional single precision FPU extension + optional TrustZone security extension

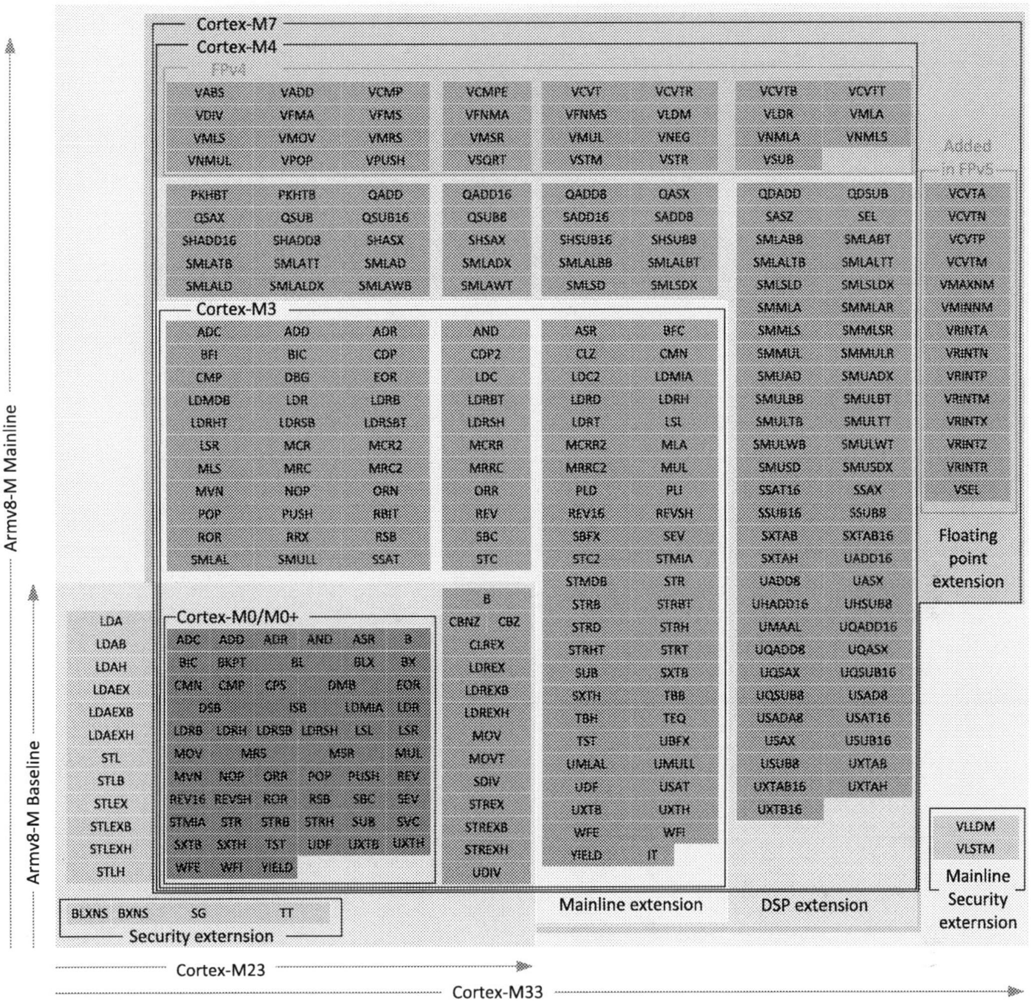

FIG. 3.3 Instruction set compatibility.

This 4GB address space is divided into a number of regions in the architecture's definition (Fig. 3.4).

Some address ranges in the Private Peripheral Bus (PPB) are allocated to internal components, i.e., the Nested Vectored Interrupt Controller (NVIC), Memory Protection Unit (MPU), and a number of debug components.

The rest of the memory regions have predefined memory attributes, making them particularly suitable for storing program (e.g., in the CODE region), data (e.g., in the SRAM region), and for accessing peripherals (e.g., in the Peripheral region). The usage of the memory region is fairly flexible. For example, you can execute programs from the SRAM and RAM regions. If necessary, some of the memory attributes can be overridden with the MPU (Memory Protection Unit).

Memory map

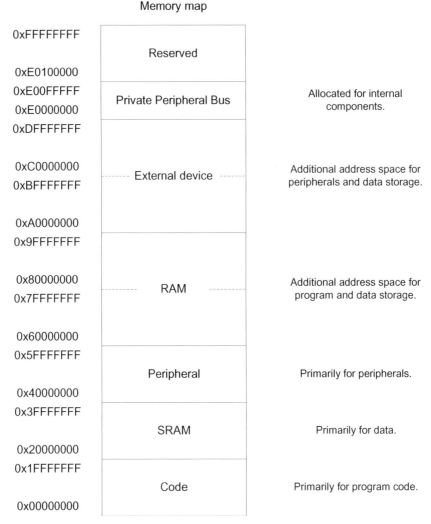

0xFFFFFFFF	Reserved	
0xE0100000		
0xE00FFFFF	Private Peripheral Bus	Allocated for internal components.
0xE0000000		
0xDFFFFFFF		
0xC0000000	External device	Additional address space for peripherals and data storage.
0xBFFFFFFF		
0xA0000000		
0x9FFFFFFF		
0x80000000	RAM	Additional address space for program and data storage.
0x7FFFFFFF		
0x60000000		
0x5FFFFFFF	Peripheral	Primarily for peripherals.
0x40000000		
0x3FFFFFFF	SRAM	Primarily for data.
0x20000000		
0x1FFFFFFF	Code	Primarily for program code.
0x00000000		

FIG. 3.4   Default memory space defined by Armv8-M architecture.

If the Cortex-M23/Cortex-M33 based system supports the TrustZone security extension, then the memory space is divided into Secure and Non-secure address ranges. This partitioning can be programmable using the Security Attribution Unit (SAU) and the Implementation Defined Attribution Unit (IDAU). Both Secure and Non-secure software needs their own program, data, and peripheral address spaces.

The actual memory map of the chip is defined by the chip designers. For the same Cortex-M processor, chip companies can implement different memory sizes and different memory maps. The Cortex-M processors also work with different memory types. For example, most microcontrollers use flash memories for program storage and on-chip SRAM for data storage. But it is also possible to use Mask ROM (a type of Read-Only Memory where the content is fixed in the manufacturing process) for program storage, and use double data rate dynamic random-access memory (DDR-DRAM) for data storage. In theory, it is also possible to use advanced nonvolatile memory (NVM) like Magnetoresistive Random-Access Memory (MRAM) or Ferroelectric RAM (FRAM) for both program and data storage.

3.6 Bus interfaces

Both the Cortex-M23 and Cortex-M33 Processors use Arm® AMBA® 5 AHB protocol (also known as AHB5) for their main system buses. AHB5 (Advanced High-performance Bus) is one of the bus protocols in the Advanced Microcontroller Bus Architecture (AMBA), which is a collection of on-chip bus specifications defined by Arm and is open and widely used in the chip design industry. AHB is a light-weight pipelined bus protocol optimized for low power systems. AHB5 has a number of enhancements when it is compared to the previous AHB specification (AHB-LITE). The highlights of these enhancements are that it supports:

- the TrustZone security extension.
- the official exclusive access sideband signals.
- additional memory attributes.

To simplify system-level integration, the Cortex-M23 processor uses Von Neumann bus architecture (single main bus interface for program, data, and peripherals). The aforementioned processor also has an optional single-cycle I/O interface for low latency hardware/peripheral register access.

The Cortex-M33 processor uses Harvard bus architecture and has two AHB5 master interfaces. One is for access to the CODE region and the other is for access to the rest of the memory space (apart from the Private Peripheral Bus (PPB)). This arrangement allows program fetches to the CODE region and access to data in the RAM or in a peripheral to be carried out at the same time.

The Cortex-M33 processor also has an additional PPB interface for the connection of optional debug components. This interface is based on the Advanced Peripheral Bus (APB) protocol from AMBA 4.

3.7 Memory protection

There are two types of memory access controls in the Cortex-M23 and Cortex-M33 processor systems (Fig. 3.5):

1. A mechanism for defining access permissions based on the separation of Secure and Non-secure memories:

If the TrustZone security extension is implemented, then the memory space is partitioned into Secure and Non-secure address ranges. The Secure software can access both sets of address ranges, but the Non-secure software can only access the Non-secure address range. If a Non-secure software component tries to access a Secure memory address a fault exception is triggered and the access is blocked.

On the system level, further transfer filtering mechanisms can be put in place to block transfers based on the address location and the security attribute of the bus transaction.

The partition of Secure and Non-secure address ranges is handled by the SAU and the IDAU.

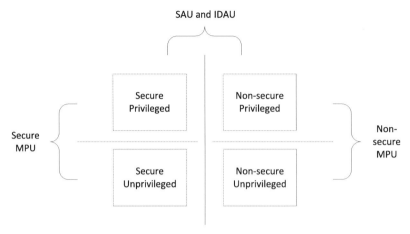

FIG. 3.5   Memory access control mechanisms.

2. A mechanism for defining access permissions based on the separation of Privileged and Unprivileged software:

The concept of privileged and unprivileged execution levels in processors has been around for a number of years. In a system with an Operating Systems (OS), the OS kernel and exception handlers are executed at privileged access level and application threads are (usually) executed using at unprivileged access level. Using a Memory Protection Unit (MPU), the access permission of unprivileged threads/tasks can be restricted.

If the TrustZone security extension is implemented, there can be two MPUs inside the processor (both of them are optional). One would be used for managing access permissions for Secure software and the other would be used for managing access permissions for Non-secure software.

In a TrustZone capable system, the two types of memory protection mechanisms can work together. If the executing software attempts to access a memory location and the access permission check fails one of the protection measures, the transfer is blocked from reaching the memory/peripheral. A fault exception is then raised to handle the issue.

3.8 Interrupt and exception handling

In Arm processors, interrupts (e.g., IRQs generated by peripherals) are a subset of exceptions. Exceptions also include fault event handling and OS supporting exceptions. In Cortex-M processors, exceptions (including interrupts) are handled by the built-in Nested Vectored Interrupt Controller (NVIC). The interrupt controller is designed to make the management and handling of interrupts very easy. The words "Nested" and "Vectored" in NVIC mean:

• Nested interrupt handling: Nesting of interrupt services is automatically handled by the processor without any need for software intervention. For example, during the execution of a low priority interrupt service a high priority interrupt can be serviced as normal.

TABLE 3.5 NVIC specification

	Cortex-M23	Cortex-M33
Number of interrupt inputs	1–240	1–480
Non-Maskable Interrupt (NMI) input	Yes	Yes
Width of priority level registers	2-bit (4 programmable levels)	3-bit (8 programmable levels) to 8-bit (256 programmable levels)
Interrupt masking registers	PRIMASK	PRIMASK, FAULTMASK, and BASEPRI
Interrupt latency in number of clock cycles (assuming a zero wait state memory system is being used)	15	12

• Vectored interrupt handling: The starting program address of interrupt service routines (ISRs) is obtained automatically from a vector table by the processor's hardware. There is no need to use software to determine which interrupt request needs servicing, which reduces the latency of the interrupt service(s).

The NVIC is configurable by chip designers as follows:

• The number of interrupts supported is customizable.
• The number of priority levels supported is configurable in the Cortex-M33 processor, and is fixed to 4 levels in the Cortex-M23 processor.

The NVIC specification in the Cortex-M23 and Cortex-M33 processors is listed in Table 3.5.

If the TrustZone security extension is implemented, each of the interrupt sources can be programmed as Secure or Non-secure. Because there are two vector tables, the Secure and Non-secure vector tables are separated and are respectively placed in Secure and Non-secure memory spaces.

3.9 Low power features

The Cortex-M23 and Cortex-M33 processors support a number of low power features:

• Sleep modes
• Internal low power optimizations
• Wakeup interrupt controller (WIC)
• State Retention Power Gating (SRPG) support

Sleep modes: Architecturally, Cortex-M processors support sleep and deep-sleep modes. How power is reduced during these sleep modes depends on the design of the chip. Chip designers can further expand the number of sleep modes using system-level control hardware.

Internal low power optimization: The Cortex-M23 and M33 processor designs use a range of low power optimization techniques to reduce power consumption, e.g., clock gating and power domain partitioning. The low gate count characteristic also helps reduce the overall power consumption by reducing the amount of leakage current (i.e., the electric current consumption when there is no clocking activity).

Wakeup Interrupt Controller (WIC): This is a small hardware block separated from the NVIC to allow interrupt requests to be detected and will "wake up" the system even when the clock signals to the processor has stopped, or when the processor is placed in a power-down state (e.g., when state-retention power gating is used).

State Retention Power Gating (SRPG) support: The Cortex-M23 and Cortex-M33 processors can be implemented with various advanced low power design technologies. One of these technologies is the SRPG, which, when used with sleep modes, powers down most of the digital logic hardware in the processor. During SRPG sleep, only a small number of transistors are powered to keep the states (0/1) of the processor's registers. In this way, when an interrupt arrives, the processor is able to very quickly resume operations.

3.10 OS support features

Both the Cortex-M23 and Cortex-M33 processors are designed to support a wide range of embedded Operating Systems (OSs) (this includes Real-Time OS (RTOS)). The OS support features include:

- Banked stack pointers to enable easy context switching.
- Stack-limit registers for stack-limit checking.
- The ability to separate between privileged and unprivileged states.
- Memory Protection Unit(s) (MPUs): The OS can use the MPU to restrict access permissions of unprivileged threads.
- Exception types dedicated to OS support: Including SuperVisor Call (SVCall) and Pendable SuperVisor call (PendSV).
- A small 24-bit system tick timer called SysTick for periodic OS interrupt generation. If the TrustZone security extension is implemented there can be two SysTick timers in the processor.

Currently, there are over 40 RTOSs for the Cortex-M processors range. A free reference RTOS design for the Cortex-M23 and Cortex-M33 processors, called RTX, is available from Arm (https://github.com/ARM-software/CMSIS/tree/master/CMSIS/RTOS/RTX).

3.11 Floating-point unit

The Cortex-M33 processor supports an optional Floating-Point Unit (FPU). This FPU supports single precision (i.e., "float" in C/C++) operations and is compliant to the IEEE-754 standard. Although, by using software libraries, a Cortex-M processor (including the Cortex-M23 processor) can handle floating-point calculations without an FPU, the system would be slower and require extra program memory space.

3.12 Coprocessor interface and Arm Custom Instructions

The Cortex-M33 processor supports an optional coprocessor interface to allow chip designers to add hardware accelerators that are directly coupled to the processor. The key features of this interface:

- Includes the support of 32-bit and 64-bit transfers between the processor and the coprocessor's registers in a single clock cycle.
- Include wait state(s) and an error response signal.
- Using a single instruction, a custom-defined operation command can be transferred with data simultaneously.
- Include the ability to support up to eight coprocessors, with each of them able to support a number of coprocessor registers.
- Include support for TrustZone technology. Each coprocessor can be assigned as Secure or Non-secure. At the interface level, there is also a security attribute to allow the fine grain security control of each individual coprocessor register/operation.

The coprocessor interface can be used in many ways. For example, it can be used for connecting accelerators for mathematical operations and for cryptography.

The Arm Custom Instructions (architecturally known as Custom Datapath Extension) is a new feature that was not available in previous Arm processors. Similar to the coprocessor support feature, the Arm Custom Instructions technology was introduced to accelerate processing tasks. This technology was announced in October 2019 at Arm TechCon. An updated release of the Cortex-M33 processor, which was released in mid-2020, is the first Arm processor to support the Arm Custom Instructions feature.

Unlike the coprocessor instructions, which require the hardware accelerators to include their own coprocessor registers, Arm Custom Instructions allows chip designers to create customer accelerator(s) which can then be integrated into the processor's data-path. This arrangement speeds up specialized data processing operations by directly using the processor's registers. This enables lower latency when using hardware accelerator(s).

By architectural definition, the operations in Arm Customer Instructions can support 32-bit, 64-bit, and vector data (including integer, floating-point, and vector operations). Not all of these instructions are included in the Cortex-M33 implementation.

3.13 Debug and trace support

Debug features are necessary for modern microcontroller and embedded processor systems. They help software developers to analyze software problems and assists them in understanding how efficient the code is running (by profiling of the applications). Both the Cortex-M23 and Cortex-M33 processors support a range of standard debug features, for e.g.:

- Program flow control: Halting, single stepping, resume, reset (restarting),
- Access to core registers and memory spaces,
- Program breakpoints and data watchpoints.

In addition, there is also a range of advanced features available, for e.g.:

- Instruction trace (available on both the Cortex-M23 and Cortex-M33 processors)
- Other trace features: Data, event, profiling, and software-generated trace (only available on the Cortex-M33 processor).

The instruction trace feature enables software developers to view the program execution flow inside the hardware so that they can understand how the software problems have occurred. To further aid debugging, other trace features, such as the exception event trace in the Cortex-M33 processor, can complement the instruction trace by adding additional information (e.g., identity and timing of exception events).

Most of the trace features are Noninvasive, which means they allow software developers to collect information about the program's execution without any significant impact on the program's execution behavior (e.g., execution timing).

3.14 Multicore system design support

Cortex-M23 and Cortex-M33 processors can be used as a standalone processor in single core microcontroller devices, as well as being part of a multicore SoC product. With suitable bus interconnect hardware support, the bus interface of multiple processors can be connected to the shared memories and peripherals. The inclusion of exclusive access instructions in the Cortex-M23 processor (compared to the Cortex-M0+ which does not have them) enhances multicore software support. For example, by enabling OS semaphore operations in multicore systems.

The debug architecture also allows multiple processors to be connected to a debugger through a single debug and trace connection. Multicore debugging support in low-end Arm microcontroller development tools has been available since 2011.

3.15 Key feature enhancements in Cortex-M23 and Cortex-M33 processors

3.15.1 Comparison between Cortex-M0+ and Cortex-M23 processors

While the Cortex-M23 processor continues to carry existing Cortex-M0+ features, it has, nonetheless, been considerably enhanced when compared to the Cortex M0+. Fig. 3.6 details those enhancements.

A brief description of the enhancements is as follows:

- TrustZone: An optional security extension.
- Stack limit checking: Detects stack overflow errors in Secure stack pointers and triggers a fault exception to handle the issue.
- Embedded Trace Macrocell (ETM): Optional unit for real-time instruction trace
- MPU (Memory Protection Unit): The programmer's model of the MPU has been updated and is now based on the Protected Memory System Architecture version 8 (PMSAv8). This

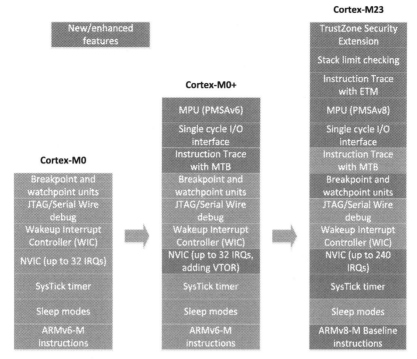

FIG. 3.6   Cortex-M23 processor enhancements when compared to Cortex-M0 and Cortex-M0+ processors.

makes the MPU more flexible and easier to use. The maximum number of MPU regions has also been increased from 8 to 16.

- Single-cycle I/O interface: An optional interface to support single-cycle access to frequently used peripherals. This has been updated to support the TrustZone security extension.
- Micro Trace Buffer (MTB): A low-cost instruction trace solution. This is optional and was first introduced in the Cortex-M0+ processor.
- Breakpoints and watchpoint units: A new programmer's model introduced in Armv8-M architecture to provide greater flexibility. The maximum number of data watchpoint comparators has increased from 2 to 4.
- NVIC (Nested Vectored Interrupt Controller): The NVIC in the Cortex-M0+ added a Vector Table Offset Register (VTOR) for vector table relocation. In the Cortex-M23 processor, the number of interrupts supports increased from 32 to 240.
- SysTick timer: A small 24-bit system tick timer for OS periodic interrupts or for other timing purposes. In Armv8-M, there can be two SysTick timers for Secure and Non-secure operations.
- Instruction set enhancements (see below).

When compared to Armv6-M architecture, there are a number of instructions added to the Armv8-M Baseline architecture. These include several instructions, which were previously only available in the Armv7-M architecture (e.g., Cortex-M3). The instruction set enhancements are summarized in Table 3.6.

TABLE 3.6 Cortex-M23 Instruction set enhancements when compared to Cortex-M0/Cortex-M0+

Feature	Description
Hardware divide	Faster signed and unsigned integer divide operations.
Compare and branch	Combining compare-to-zero and a conditional branch to enable faster control code.
Long branch	32-bit version of the branch instruction to enable longer branch target offset. It also enables some linking stage optimization.
Wide immediate move instructions (MOVW, MOVT)	Generates 16-bit immediate data or 32-bit immediate data (when used in a pair) without needing a literal load. It also enables a firmware protection technique called eXecute-only-memory (XOM, see Section 3.20).
Exclusive access instructions	Load-link/store-conditional support for semaphore usages. This enables common semaphore handling in multicore systems.
Load acquire, store release	Instructions for C11 atomic variables handling (New in Armv8-M).
Secure Gateway, Test Target, and Non-secure branches	Instructions for TrustZone support (New in Armv8-M).

There are also other areas of improvement:

- The Cortex-M23 processor has a small performance increase over the Cortex-M0+ processor due to the enhancement of the instruction set.
- The Cortex-M23 processor allows the initial addresses of the vector tables to be defined by chip designers. This is not configurable in the Cortex-M0 or Cortex-M0+ processors.

3.15.2 Comparison between Cortex-M3/M4 and Cortex-M33 processors

There are many enhancements when one compares the Cortex-M33 processor with the Cortex-M3/M4 range of processors (Fig. 3.7).

A number of the aforementioned enhancements are similar to those that are found in the Cortex-M23 processor:

- TrustZone: An optional security extension.
- MPU (Memory Protection Unit): The programmer's model of the MPU has been updated and is now based on Protected Memory System Architecture version 8 (PMSAv8)—which makes the MPU more flexible and easier to use. Additionally, the maximum number of MPU regions has been increased from 8 to 16.
- MTB (Micro Trace Buffer): A low-cost instruction trace solution. Previously this was not available in the Cortex-M3 and Cortex-M4 processors.
- Breakpoints and watchpoint units: A new programmer's model has been introduced in the Armv8-M architecture to provide better flexibility.
- NVIC (Nested Vectored Interrupt Controller): The maximum number of interrupts supported in the Cortex-M33 has increased to 480 compared to 240 in the Cortex-M3/M4 processor.

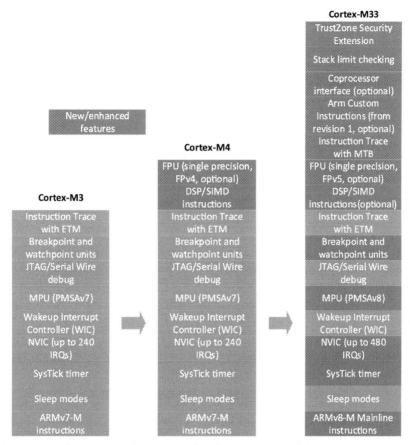

FIG. 3.7   Cortex-M33 enhancements when compared to the Cortex-M3 and Cortex-M4 processors.

- SysTick timer: A small 24-bit system tick timer for OS period interrupts or for other timing purposes. An Armv8-M processor can support up to two SysTick timers—one for Secure operations and the other for Non-secure operations.

  But there are also enhancements that are not available in the Cortex-M23 processor:

- Stack limit checking: Detects stack overflow errors in both Secure and Non-secure stack pointers and triggers a fault exception to handle the issue.
- Floating point unit (FPU): The architecture of the floating-point instructions has been updated from FPv4 to FPv5.
- The DSP/SIMD instruction set is optional, making the processor more configurable than before.
- Coprocessor interface: A new interface allowing chip designers to add hardware accelerators to the chip that are closely coupled to the processor.
- Arm Custom Instructions: This feature allows silicon designers to add custom data processing instructions to a Cortex-M33 processor. This feature is to be added in revision 1 of the Cortex-M33 design during mid-2020.

TABLE 3.7   Cortex-M33 Instruction set enhancements when compared to the Cortex-M4

Feature	Description
Floating-point FPv5	Compared to the FPv4 in the Cortex-M4, FPv5 supports additional instructions for data conversions, finding max/min values, etc.
Load acquire, store release	Instructions for C11 atomic variables handling (New in Armv8-M).
Secure Gateway, Test Target, and Non-secure branches	Instructions for TrustZone support (New in Armv8-M).

There are also a number of instruction-set enhancements (Table 3.7).
And there are also other areas of improvement:

- The Cortex-M33 processor has a performance increase when compared to the Cortex-M3/M4 processor, though the amount of increment is dependent upon the composition of the instruction types used in the applications.
- The Cortex-M33 processor allows the initial addresses of the vector tables to be defined by chip designers. This is not configurable in the Cortex-M3 or Cortex-M4 processors.

3.16 Compatibility with other Cortex-M processors

In many respects, the Cortex-M23 and Cortex-M33 processors are highly compatible with the previous generation of Cortex-M processors:

Instruction set

- All instructions on the Cortex-M0/M0+ processors are available on the Cortex-M23 processor.
- All instructions on the Cortex-M3/M4 processors are available on the Cortex-M33 processor (For Cortex-M4 to Cortex-M33 migration, the compatibility is subject to whether the DSP and floating-point extensions are implemented).

Interrupt handling, SysTick, and sleep modes

- The programmer's model is mostly unchanged and the existing interrupt management code can be reused. If the TrustZone security extension is implemented, additional programming codes have to be added to allow interrupts to be assigned as Secure or Non-secure.
- The SysTick programmer's model is unchanged. If the TrustZone security extension is implemented there can be two SysTick timers.
- Sleep modes and the instructions for entering sleep modes (WFI and WFE) are the same as before. If the TrustZone security extension is implemented, an additional programmable register bit is added to the System Control Register, which defines whether the deep sleep setting is configurable from the Non-secure side.

There are, however, some areas that require software changes:

- Embedded operating systems: The change in the MPU programmer's model and the extension of the EXC_RETURN (exception return) code means that the OS/RTOS (Real-Time Operating System) needs to be updated to support Armv8-M architecture.
- If the TrustZone security extension is implemented, the memory space needs to be partitioned into Secure and Non-secure address ranges. This often means that there is a need to change the memory maps in the microcontroller when one migrates from old to new designs. If the TrustZone is not implemented it is quite straight forward to create new devices with a memory map that is identical with, or compatible to, the previous generation.

For software developers that develop Secure firmware with TrustZone technology, there are new C language extension features that need to be used in order to allow C compilers to generate the new instructions for TrustZone support. These C language extension features, known as Cortex-M Security Extension (CMSE), is part of the Arm C Language Extension (ACLE). ACLE is an open specification and is supported by many compiler vendors.

As in many other project migration scenarios, potentially the execution timing differences between the Cortex-M33 processor and the Cortex-M3/M4 processors could result in having to change code. That said, since the performance/MHz of the Cortex-M33 is higher than the Cortex-M3/M4, and if the memory system characteristics (i.e., wait states) are similar, there should not be a need to do so.

3.17 Processor configuration options

In Section 2.3.6 of Chapter 2, I highlighted the fact that the Cortex-M23 and Cortex-M33 processors are configurable designs and that, as a result, the Cortex-M23/M33 microcontrollers from different vendors could have different features.

Table 3.8 in the next page lists the key configuration options.

Not all of the available options are documented here. For example, there are configuration options that are more relevant to chip designers and are, thus, invisible to software developers (e.g., option to remove unused interrupt lines).

3.18 Introduction to TrustZone

3.18.1 Overview of security requirements

When talking about security, different applications can have very different security requirements. For embedded systems there are typically five common types of security requirements:

Communication protection: Security measures to ensure communications cannot be eavesdropped on or changed by third parties. This typically involves the encrypting and decrypting of communication contents and, potentially, using additional techniques to establish a secure connection link (e.g., key exchanging).

TABLE 3.8 Key feature options of the Cortex-M23 and Cortex-M33 processors

Feature	Description	Cortex-M23	Cortex-M33
Instruction set	DSP (SIMD) instruction extension.	Not available	Optional
	Single precision floating-point instructions.	Not available	Optional
	Instructions for TrustZone support (based on TrustZone configuration)	Optional	Optional
	Multiply implementation	Small/Fast	Fixed
	Divide implementation	Small/Fast	Fixed
	Coprocessor instructions and Arm Custom Instructions	Not available	Optional
Initial vector table	Address of initial vector table for boot sequence.	Configurable	Configurable
Interrupt Controller	Number of interrupts	1–240	1–480
	Number of programmable interrupt priority levels	4	8–256
	Exception vector table relocation (if not implemented, the vector table address is still configurable by chip designers)	Optional	Always available
	Wake up interrupt controller (WIC) for waking up the system in a low power retention state.	Optional	Optional
TrustZone	Security extension that supports Secure and Non-secure states	Optional	Optional
	Number of programmable regions supported by the Security Attribution Unit (SAU)—but only if TrustZone is implemented.	0, 4, 8	0, 4, 8
Memory Protection Unit	MPU for Non-secure world (normal environment), and number of programmable MPU regions.	Optional, 4/8/12/16 regions	Optional, 4/8/12/16 regions
	MPU for Secure world (protected environment), and number of programmable MPU regions (the options are independent of the Non-secure MPU).	Optional, 4/8/12/16 regions	Optional, 4/8/12/16 regions
SysTick timer	Number of timers for periodic system tick interrupt (second SysTick is possible but only if TrustZone is implemented).	0, 1, 2	1, 2
Extra interface	Single-cycle I/O interface	Optional	Not available
	Coprocessor interface	Not available	Optional
Debug	Debug features	Optional	Optional
	Debug interface protocol (JTAG, SWv1 = Serial Wire protocol version 1, SWv2 = Serial Wire protocol version 2)	JTAG or SWv1 or SWv2	JTAG and/or SWv2
	Number of breakpoint comparators	0–4	0/4/8
	Number of data watchpoint comparators	0–4	0/2/4
	Instruction trace using Micro Trace Buffer (MTB) (if implemented, the size of the SRAM connected to the MTB is also configurable).	Optional	Optional
	Instruction trace using Embedded Trace Macrocell (ETM)	Optional	Optional
	Other trace (instrumentation trace, data trace, etc.)	Not available	Optional
	Cross trigger interface (CTI) for multicore debug	Optional	Optional

Data protection: Many devices contain confidential information (e.g., payment account details stored in mobile phones) and security measures are needed to ensure that if the device has been stolen, or if there are other applications running on the device, that third parties cannot access that data.

Firmware protection: Software is a valuable asset to many software developers and to ensure that the software cannot be copied or reverse engineered security measures are needed.

Operation protection: In some embedded systems, certain operations need additional protection to ensure strong robustness in a number of particular features (obviously, up to a certain extent). For example, a microcontroller with certified Bluetooth support might need special arrangements to ensure that the Bluetooth operation is compliant to the Bluetooth specification, even when a user application has crashed. Similar protection requirements can be critical in medical devices and systems with functional safety implications (e.g., automotive and industrial control systems).

Anti-tampering protection: This is needed to make tampering attacks more difficult and to ensure that any that do occur are detected and the appropriate action(s) is taken (e.g., immediately erasing secret data). Typically, this is needed for smartcards and payment related systems.

TrustZone technology can be directly used to provide data protection, firmware protection, and operation protection. It can also indirectly enhance solutions for communication protection (for example, by providing stronger protection for cryptography keys storage). Later in this chapter, I will go into further detail on how TrustZone technology can be deployed.

Since TrustZone technology is focused on software and system architecture, it does not on its own provide any anti-tampering capability. However, since anti-tampering protection measures can be implemented at the product level, circuit board level, chip packaging level, and at chip design level some of the Armv8-M based products (e.g., Cortex-M35P processor) can and do have anti-tampering features.

3.18.2 Evolution of security in embedded systems

Traditionally, many microcontroller systems have either no connectivity or very restricted connectivity features and, thus, the demand for advance security capabilities is relatively low-certainly when compared to application processors (e.g., mobile phone and other computing devices).

Simple microcontroller systems
For simple systems, most microcontrollers come with a read-out protection feature (firmware protection). Once the protection is enabled, the software on the chip cannot be accessed using debug tools and the only way to change the program code is to perform a full chip erase. Some devices though do allow the full chip erase feature to be disabled.

Traditional microcontroller systems with connectivity
In systems with connectivity, security measures are required to protect the communication channels and the storage of cryptography keys. In recent years, many microcontrollers built for connectivity applications have included various types of hardware features, such as crypto engines, a true-random-number-generator (TRNG) and encrypted data storage. These features enable better communication and data protection. A number of these

products also have chip-level anti-tampering features. Therefore, many of the existing Cortex-M devices already have a wide range of security features to cover the common security requirements discussed before.

Before we start looking in depth at TrustZone, it would, I think, be useful to explain the security requirements and security technologies that were present in previous generations (Armv6-M and Armv7-M) of the Cortex-M range of processors.

Security requirements in microcontrollers

As low-cost microcontrollers are increasingly used in ever-more IoT solutions, numbering millions of units or more per product per year, these devices are now becoming of some interest to hackers. While gaining access to a single compromised device is not of any particular benefit to a hacker, being able to gain access to millions of compromised units can be. For example, they can be used as a botnet for launching DDoS attacks. As a result, attacks on IoT devices are getting more sophisticated and frequent.

Since security bugs in software are a fairly regular feature of life, there is, for many products, a need to provide a reliable avenue to enable the update of remote firmware. This means that product designers cannot simply block out the update mechanism (e.g., flash programming feature) when the product is deployed. The firmware update support, thus, must be secure:

- The firmware downloaded via a remote connection must be validated before being used in the update process, and
- The flash programming procedure must not be able to bypass the validation step.

Security features in Armv6-M and Armv7-M architectures

In Armv6-M and Armv7-M architectures, to help create a secure execution environment, most of the Cortex-M processors support the separation of privileged and unprivileged executions. Together with the memory protection unit (MPU), access permission of each application thread is, therefore, defined and enforced. As a result, the failure of a single application thread can be contained as shown in Fig. 3.8.

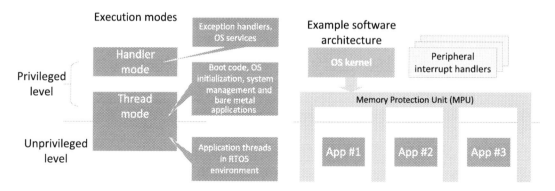

Armv6-M/Armv7-M architecture

FIG. 3.8   Software security in Armv6-M and Armv7-M architectures.

With this arrangement, the MPU is reconfigured by the OS at each context switch and an application running at unprivileged level can only access memories and the peripherals allocated to it. Access to memories or peripherals allocated to other applications or to the OS would result in a fault exception, which the OS can then use to deal with the error (e.g., to terminate or restart the application thread).

With this feature, application developers are able to organize the software structure to run most of the applications, including the communication protocol stacks, at unprivileged level. If one of the threads crashes (for example, if a communication interface is under a packet flood attack, resulting in a stack overflow), the memory corruption will not affect the data used by the OS or other application threads, thus making the system more secure and reliable.

Since application threads have restricted access to the memory space, a compromised application cannot bypass security checks to modify the contents of the flash memory. It also cannot stop other application threads, so this solution provides effective protection of individual operations.

Whilst this security arrangement is suitable for a wide range of applications, there are some instances why this is not sufficient; that is why TrustZone security technology is needed.

- First of all, there are restrictions on the application threads. Since application threads run at unprivileged level, they do not have direct access to interrupt management and, therefore, privileged software must provide interrupt management services to these threads. The system services are typically handled via the SuperVisor Call (SVCall) exception—a process that increases software complexity and overhead in execution timing.
- Unfortunately, in some cases, the peripheral interrupt handlers can have bugs and this could lead to vulnerabilities. Because interrupt handlers execute in a privileged state, if a hacker manages to successfully attack and compromise a peripheral interrupt handler, the hacker would then be able to disable the MPU; and would also be able to access other address spaces that are privileged access only and thus compromise the system.
- Recently, some microcontrollers have been delivered with on-chip software libraries that have included communication protocol software stacks and various software features that enable secure IoT connections. This makes it easier for software developers to create IoT solutions (Fig. 3.9), but does lead to new challenges:
  - Firmware protection features are needed to allow microcontroller vendors to protect their preloaded firmware from being copied or reverse engineered, especially when that software is licensed from a third-party company.
  - Secure storage features are needed to protect data used for establishing secure IoT connections. For example, secret keys or certificates could be stored on the chip. These protection features are needed to prevent device cloning and to prevent the reverse engineering of authentication details.

The trend of delivering IoT solutions on microcontrollers is gaining traction. Since IoT device projects are often cost-sensitive and have tight project schedules, the IoT focused microcontrollers provide an attractive solution because:

- To directly license the middleware from software vendors might have a higher cost,
- Additional work that is needed to integrate middleware can create technical challenges and, thus, lead to slippage in a project's timescale,

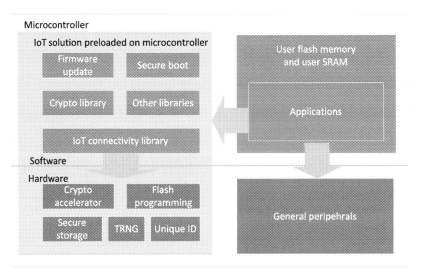

FIG. 3.9   Microcontrollers with preloaded IoT firmware enables a faster time to market.

- Many software engineers do not have the technical knowledge to create secure connections for IoT devices. Using a prepackaged solution is much easier and can reduce the risk of incorrect implementations (which could lead to vulnerabilities).

While system and product designers can easily buy IoT microcontrollers, and can quickly create products based on them, hackers are also able to access those microcontrollers with the aim of reverse-engineering them. Because privileged access to these devices is essential to software developers and therefore has to be allowed, the MPU solution will not be of any use for protecting the firmware assets or the secret keys as previously mentioned. As a result, we need to find a new mechanism for security management, i.e., TrustZone technology.

In Cortex-A processors, TrustZone technology has been available for a long period of time and some concepts of the TrustZone operations can be of benefit for IoT microcontroller applications. As a result, Arm has adopted some of the TrustZone concepts, which have been optimized for Cortex-M based systems. This has become TrustZone for Armv8-M and has been implemented on the Cortex-M23 and Cortex-M33 range of processors.

3.18.3 TrustZone for Armv8-M

TrustZone for Armv8-M is integrated into all aspects of the processor's architecture, including the programmer's model, the interrupt handling mechanism, debug features, bus interfaces, and memory system designs. As previously mentioned, in previous Cortex-M processors there was a separation of privileged and unprivileged execution levels. In Armv8-M, the optional TrustZone security extension provides an additional separation boundary that divides the execution environment into a normal environment (Non-secure world) and into an additional protected environment (Secure world). This is shown in Fig. 3.10.

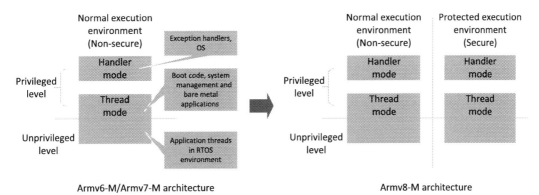

FIG. 3.10 Changing of the processor's execution environment from Armv6-M/Armv7-M to Armv8-M architecture.

Similar to TrustZone available in the Cortex-A processors, software running in the Secure world can access both Secure and Non-secure memories and resources; but the Non-secure world can only access Non-secure memories and resources.

In the Cortex-M23 and Cortex-M33 processors, the TrustZone security extension is optional. If it is not implemented (the decision is made by the chip designer), then only the Non-secure world exists.

The normal execution environment (Non-secure world) is mostly unchanged from previous Cortex-M processors, with many applications written for previous Cortex-M processors being able to run in the Non-secure world without the need for any modification. Where they cannot, minimal modifications are required (e.g., RTOS would need to be updated).

The additional protected environment (Secure world) is also similar to the normal environment. In fact, for most bare metal applications, the same code can run in either world. The Secure world does, however, provide additional control registers for security management. Additionally, there are a number of hardware resources (e.g., SysTick timers, MPUs) available for each of the two worlds.

The separation of Secure and Non-secure world provides a way for security-critical operations and resources to be protected. At the same time, however, because the architecture allows direct function calls to take place between security domain boundaries (Fig. 3.11), with

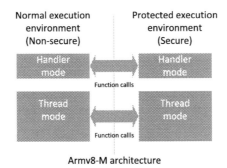

FIG. 3.11 Armv8-M architecture allows direct function calls between Secure and Non-secure worlds.

only a very small amount of software overhead, security features can still be accessed efficiently by normal applications via a range of protected Application Programming Interfaces (APIs).

To make the API call mechanism secure, a function call from a Non-secure to a Secure function is only allowed when the first instruction is an Secure Gateway (SG) instruction and is in a secure memory address marked with a Non-secure Callable (NSC) attribute. This prevents Non-secure code from branching into the middle of a secure API or other secure memory locations. Similarly, switching from a Non-secure to a Secure state when returning from a Non-secure function call is also protected, but by way of a different mechanism: it is called FNC_RETURN (function-return) and is covered in Chapter 18 Section 18.2.5.

The Armv6-M/Armv7-M architecturally defined memory map in the 4GB address space remains unchanged in the Armv8-M architecture. But the security extension divides the memory map further into Secure and Non-secure spaces so that both worlds contain its own program memory, data memory, and peripherals. This partitioning is defined by a new block called the Security Attribution Unit (SAU) and, optionally, an Implementation Defined Attribution Unit (IDAU) (Fig. 3.12). The exact memory partitioning is up to the chip designer and the creators of Secure firmware (who define the memory partitioning configurations in the programming of the SAU).

The security state of the processor is determined by the security attribute of the program address:

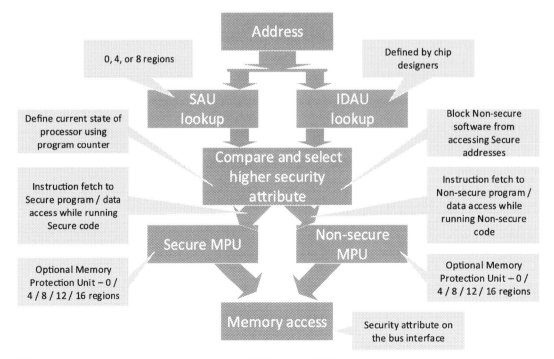

FIG. 3.12 Memory space partitioning using the SAU and the IDAU.

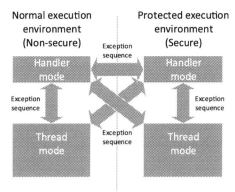

Armv8-M architecture

FIG. 3.13 Security state transition can be caused by exception/interrupt events.

- When executing Secure firmware in the Secure memory the processor is in a Secure state.
- When executing codes in the Non-secure memory the processor is in a Non-secure state.

Switching of the processor state is monitored by hardware to ensure that there are no illegal state transitions.

To ensure the integrity of each world, the stack address spaces and vector tables of the Secure and the Non-secure worlds are separate. As a result, the stack pointers are banked between security states. To facilitate stronger security, a stack limit check feature is used to support Secure stack pointers in both the Cortex-M23 and Cortex-M33 processors, with the Cortex-M33 processor also supporting stack limit checks for Non-secure stack pointers.

Because of the need to have both Secure and Non-secure peripherals, each of the interrupts can be assigned as Secure or Non-secure by the secure software. The security state transitions can be triggered by exception sequences, such as exception preemption and exception return (Fig. 3.13).

Since Secure and Non-secure software use the same physical registers (except stack pointers), Secure register contents are protected automatically by the processor's exception handling sequences to prevent the leaking of Secure information.

To enable Root-of-Trust security, the processor starts up in Secure state. After security management blocks are programmed (e.g., configuration of memory partitioning and interrupt assignments), the Secure software is then able to execute the start-up code in the Non-secure world (Fig. 3.14).

Applications running in the Non-secure world operate in almost the same way as they do in traditional Cortex-M systems. They have full control of:

- its Non-secure (NS) memories,
- its NS peripherals,
- its NS interrupt management registers, and
- the NS Memory Protection Unit (MPU).

In addition, it is also possible to make use of other APIs provided in the secure firmware to access other features (e.g., cryptography functions). Secure firmware can, optionally, also make use of APIs (e.g., I/O driver libraries) that can be placed in the Non-secure memory.

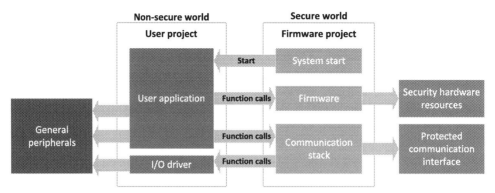

FIG. 3.14   Separation of Secure and Non-secure worlds (Processor starts up in Secure state).

3.19 Why TrustZone enables better security?

Similar to many other security technologies, TrustZone for Armv8-M works by providing a partitioning mechanism to ensure software components can only gain access to resources that are allocated to them. Such an arrangement ensures that an attacker (e.g., a hacker) cannot gain full control of the system or access secret data if one of the software components has been compromised. While previous generations of the Cortex-M processor already provided privileged and unprivileged levels, the aforementioned is inadequate for securing systems in some of the newer scenarios described in Section 3.18.2. For example:

- Software vulnerabilities in privileged codes like peripheral drivers (including interrupt handlers) can potentially allow hackers to gain privileged execution level and hence have full access to the system.
- Microcontrollers with preloaded on-chip firmware might need to be protected against untrusted software developers as hackers could pose as software developers, purchase the chips and then try to reverse engineer them.

In some of the latest IoT microcontroller designs, the chips have a range of preloaded firmware for IoT connectivity. This firmware might include preloaded security certificates or security keys, which allow software developers to create applications that establish secure connections to cloud services by accessing APIs in the preloaded firmware. TrustZone technology is a very good fit in such instances and Fig. 3.15 demonstrates an example of this fit.
In such TrustZone based systems, it is expected that:

- The security keys (including crypto keys) are not accessible from the Non-secure world—all cryptography operations are handled by the preloaded firmware.
- Security resources, such as secure storage, unique ID and True Random Number Generator (TRNG) are also protected. TRNG needs to be protected as it might contain entropy for session keys generation (session keys are used for protecting a secure internet connection).
- The firmware update mechanism is also protected. When the protection feature is enabled, only program images that are validated (e.g., correctly signed using crypto operations) can

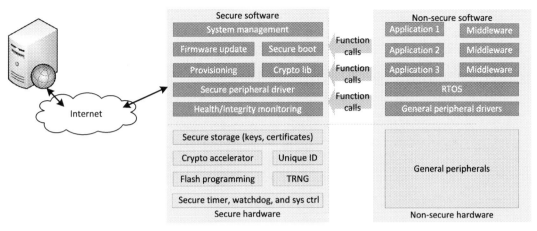

FIG. 3.15 Example concept of an IoT microcontroller—applications establish secure connection to cloud services via Secure APIs.

TABLE 3.9 Examples of Life-Cycle-States in a product

Life Cycle State (LCS)	Flash programming protection status	Debug authentication status
Chip manufactured	Both Secure and Non-secure flash memory pages can be updated.	Both Secure and Non-secure debug allowed.
Secure firmware is preloaded on the chip and is ready for software development	Only Non-secure flash memory pages can be updated. Secure memory is protected (read-out disallowed).	Only Non-secure debug is allowed.
Product is developed and deployed.	Only Non-secure flash memory pages can be updated with verification of signature required. Read-out protection for both Secure and Non-secure memory.	Only Non-secure debug is allowed, with additional debug authentication procedure to enable debug.

be used to update. Such protection is used with the Life Cycle State (LCS) management support of the product and with the debug authentication feature. An example of LCS management can be defined at chip level as (Table 3.9).

- The chip contains Non-volatile memory (NVM) for LCS management. NVM's have a protection mechanism to prevent the reversing of the LCS.
- The Secure software would, optionally, implement system health check services that run in the background when the system is deployed. This can be triggered by a Secure timer interrupt so it is run periodically. The priority level of this timer interrupt can be configured at a higher level than the other Non-secure interrupts so that it cannot be blocked by Non-secure software.

When IoT systems are connected to the internet, they could, potentially, be under attack via connectivity interfaces (e.g., WiFi). As the applications get ever-more complex, there could, inevitably, be bugs in those applications that could result in vulnerabilities and which can then be exploited by hackers. In previous Cortex-M system designs, if a hacker gained privileged level execution, he could gain full control of the system and could potentially then modify the flash program memory to their own version. If that scenario came to fruition, the IoT system would then either need to be replaced or an engineer would have to be on-site to reprogram the device.

In a TrustZone capable IoT microcontroller, the situation is much better. Since the security critical resources are protected, the hacker:

- Cannot reprogram/erase the flash memory
- Cannot steal the secret keys
- Cannot clone the device
- Cannot stop Secure software services (e.g., health checking services)

If a health checking service is implemented, it could potentially detect the attack (or detect abnormal system behavior) and trigger system recovery actions. Since the flash memory would not have been modified, the system would be able to recover by simply restarting.

In general, the capabilities of TrustZone are beneficial to multiple parties because:

- Microcontroller vendors can differentiate their product solution by providing Secure IoT connectivity firmware. And the firmware asset is protected because Non-secure software developers cannot read out the Secure firmware.
- Software developers can make use of the features provided in the Secure IoT connectivity firmware to develop products, resulting in a faster time to market and a lower risk of error (there could, for example, be errors made, when integrating third-party middleware, or when developing in-house secure software solutions).
- The IoT products can be made more secure, thus benefiting the product end users.

Of course, the security level of the system is highly dependent upon the quality of the secure firmware. The preloaded secure firmware should therefore be based on well-established security technologies that have been thoroughly tested and fully reviewed.

In addition to IoT microcontrollers, TrustZone is used for:

- Firmware protection: In some instances, microcontroller vendors need to integrate third-party software components into a device and need to ensure that the firmware assets cannot be reverse engineered. TrustZone technology enables the firmware assets to be protected, while still allowing software developers to make use of the software components.
- Protecting the operations of a certified software stack: Since the operation of critical Secure operations can be protected, some of the certified software like Bluetooth software stacks can use TrustZone to protect its operations. Even if a Non-secure application was programmed incorrectly or crashes, the protected Bluetooth operations remain functional and its certification is not voided.
- Consolidation of multiple processors into one: Previously, in some of the complex SoC designs, there were multiple Cortex-M processor subsystems to isolate Secure and Non-secure data processing. With the TrustZone capability available in the Cortex-M23 and Cortex-M33 processors, it is now possible to merge some of those processor systems.

- Providing a sandboxed software execution environment: In some operating system designs, the security partitioning feature enables the OS to execute software components in a sandboxed environment.

There are, of course, some designs where the processor is just used in a simple system arrangement without the need for IoT security. For example, a smart sensor with an integrated processor might have a serial interface (e.g., I2C/SPI) for connection to a "trusted" host processor. As a result, the need for a TrustZone security extension is optional.

3.20 Firmware asset protection with eXecute-Only-Memory (XOM)

In some cases, a chip designer might, instead of using TrustZone, opt for a simpler firmware asset protection technique called eXecute-Only-Memory (XOM). With the XOM method, the bus system inside the chip is designed so that a portion of the program memory can only be accessed by instruction fetches, but not by data accesses generated by software execution or by the debug host.

The XOM is usually used for protecting functions/APIs so that preloaded functions inside can be called, but the code details cannot be readback by software developers (Fig. 3.16).

The XOM technique helps make the reverse engineering of the software codes inside XOM much harder but is not as Secure as the TrustZone solution. For example, if the execution of an API inside the XOM is frequently interrupted, the effect of each of the executed instructions can be observed by the interrupt handlers, and that might be enough to enable a hacker to guess the instructions being executed.

When using the XOM technique, the program code cannot use literal data reads (see Section 5.7.6) to generate immediate data because that requires a data read operation to read out the immediate data inside the program memory. As a result, the MOVW and MOVT instructions (see Section 5.6.3) are used for immediate data generation when creating codes for XOM. These instructions are supported in all Armv8-M processors. These instructions are

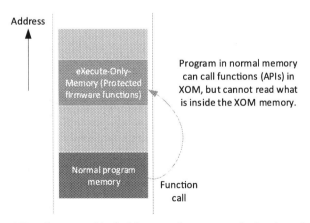

FIG. 3.16 XOM allows APIs to be accessed (called) by normal program codes but the codes inside the APIs cannot be read back.

also supported in the Armv7-M architecture, but are not available in the Armv6-M architecture (e.g., Cortex-M0, Cortex-M0+ processors).

The MOVW and MOVT instructions can also be used in other scenarios that require immediate data generation.

Further information about XOM can be found on the Arm webpage "An introduction to eXecute-only-Memory" [1].

Reference

[1] An introduction to eXecute-only-Memory. https://community.arm.com/developer/ip-products/processors/ b/processors-ip-blog/posts/what-is-execute-only-memory-xom.

4

Architecture

4.1 Introduction to the Armv8-M architecture

4.1.1 Overview

Arm® Cortex®-M23 and Cortex-M33 processors are based on the Armv8-M architecture. The architecture document—Armv8-M architecture reference manual—is a massive document with over 1000 pages [1]. It covers many aspects of the processor including:

- Programmer's model
- Instruction set
- Exception model
- Memory model (e.g., address space, memory ordering)
- Debug

The architecture contains a baseline architecture feature set and a number of optional extensions. Examples of the extensions include:

- Mainline extension—Armv8-M Mainline subprofile is the Armv8-M Baseline plus the Mainline extension.
- DSP extension—a range of instructions for digital signal processing operations, including some instructions with a Single Instruction Multiple Data (SIMD) capability. This optional extension requires the Mainline extension and is available on the Cortex-M33 processor.
- Floating extension—this includes a range of instructions for single precision and double precision processing. This extension requires the Mainline extension. The single precision floating point unit is available on the Cortex-M33 processor as an optional feature.
- MPU extension—Memory Protection Unit (MPU) is optional on both the Cortex-M23 and Cortex-M33 processors.
- Debug extension—debug features are optional.
- Security extension—that is, TrustZone®. It is optional on the Cortex-M23 and Cortex-M33 processors. The TrustZone security extension affects multiple aspects of the processor, including programmer's model, exception handling, debug, etc.

In addition to the architecture's various extensions, a range of optional features in the processor are available. For example, the configuration options described in Chapter 3, Section 3.17 allows a wide range of possible variations to be used in the various Cortex-M23/M33 devices. Please note, the architecture reference manual does not specify the underlying mechanics of how the processor operates. The design of a processor is based on the following concepts of "architecture":

- Architecture—as specified in the Armv8-M architecture reference manual. It defines how the program execution should behave and how the debug tools interact with the processor.
- Micro-architecture—the exact implementation of the processor. For example, how many pipeline stages exist inside; the actual instruction execution timing; the type of bus interface used, etc. Some of the aforementioned are described in more detail in the Technical Reference Manual (TRM) of the processor [2, 3]. This document also specifies what optional features are included in the design.

While the Armv8-M Architecture Reference Manual provides very detailed architectural processor behaviors, like instruction set, it is not easy to read. Fortunately, it is not necessary to have a full understanding of the architecture to use Cortex-M processors. To use a Cortex-M processor-based microcontroller in most applications, you only need to have a basic understanding of

(a) the programmer's model,
(b) how exceptions (including interrupts) are handled,
(c) the memory map,
(d) how to use the peripherals, and
(e) thow to use the driver libraries from the microcontroller vendors.

4.1.2 Background to the Armv8-M architecture

The Armv8-M architecture is evolved from the Armv7-M and Armv6-M architectures, as shown in Fig. 4.1.

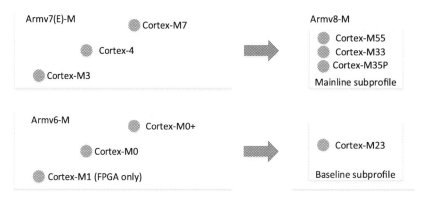

FIG. 4.1   Evolution of architectures for Cortex-M processors.

Note: The letter "E" in "Armv7E-M" refers to the DSP extension in Armv7-M. This is a historical naming convention which began with the Arrm9 processors (architecture v5TE). In Armv8-M, this naming convention is no longer used as there are so many extensions.

When compared to the Armv7-M and Armv6-M, the Armv8-M has many similarities. In fact, most bare metal (i.e., a system without the use of an OS) applications should be able to migrate and run on Cortex-M23/Cortex-M33 based devices with very few changes (e.g., memory map changes). Some examples of the similarities are:

- Armv8-M is still a 32-bit architecture, with an architecturally defined memory map that partitions the 4GB address space into regions.
- It still uses a Nested Vectored Interrupt Controller (NVIC) for interrupt management (All interrupt control registers that are in the Armv6-M/Armv7-M architectures are available in Armv8-M architecture; thus the required software changes are reduced).
- Architectural defined sleep modes (sleep and deep sleep).
- The supported instruction set; All instructions from previous Arvm6-M/Armv7-M architectures are supported in Armv8-M.

There are, however, some areas (listed below) that have been changed and these changes mostly impact the RTOS designs:

- MPU programmer's model
- EXC_RETURN (exception return code) definition
- TrustZone security extension

As explained in Section 3.15, there are also many enhancements when one compares the Cortex-M23 and Cortex-M33 processors to previous generations. To take advantage of the new features, such as the TrustZone security extension, the stack limit checking and the co-processor interface, the software codes will need to be updated.

4.2 Programmer's model

4.2.1 Processor modes and states

As explained in Chapter 3, the operation of the processor can be divided into:

- Privileged and unprivileged states—this state separation is always available,
- Secure and Non-secure states—this state separation is available if the TrustZone security extension is implemented.

When the processor is in unprivileged state, access to some parts of the memory space is restricted. For example, most of the processor's internal peripherals, such as the NVIC, the MPU and its system control registers, are blocked from unprivileged software access. Additional memory access permission rules can be set using the Memory Protection Unit (MPU). For example, an RTOS can use the MPU to further restrict the memory space accessible by an unprivileged application-task. In typical systems, running an RTOS utilizes the privilege level as follows:

- OS software and peripheral interrupt handlers—they execute in privileged state.
- Application threads/tasks—they execute in unprivileged state.

This arrangement allows the software to be more reliable—even if an application thread/task crashes it won't be able to corrupt memories or resources used by the OS or any other application threads/task. Unprivileged state is also sometimes referred to as "User mode" in some documents, a term inherited from legacy Arm processors like Arm7TDMI, which has a User mode for unprivileged operations.

When the processor is in Non-secure privileged state it can then gain access to all resources subject to security access permissions as defined by the Secure software. When the processor is in Secure privileged state it can gain access to all resources.

The concept of Secure and Non-secure states has already been explained in Chapter 3, Section 3.18. In addition to the separation between privileged and unprivileged and the separation between Secure and Non-secure, Cortex-M processors also have the following concepts of processor states and operation modes:

- Thumb® state and Debug state—Thumb state means the processor is executing thumb instructions. Debug state means the processor has halted allowing the debugger to examine its internal registers' states.
- Handler mode and Thread mode—when the processor is executing an exception handler (such as an interrupt service routine) the processor is in Handler mode. Otherwise, it is in Thread mode. The processor's mode is related to the privilege level as follow:

  * Handler mode has privileged access level
  * Thread mode can either be privileged or unprivileged.

When combining all these together, we have the state diagram, as shown in Fig. 4.2.

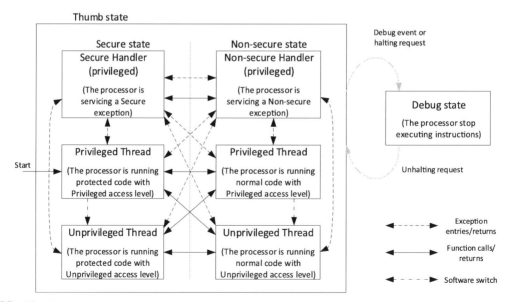

FIG. 4.2   Operation states and modes when TrustZone is implemented.

Please note, software running in privileged thread mode can switch the processor into unprivileged thread mode by programming a special register called "CONTROL"(see nPRIV bit in "CONTROL register" in Section 4.2.2.3).But, once the processor is switched to unprivileged level, the thread mode software cannot switch itself back to privileged thread mode by writing to CONTROL-because the CONTROL register is writable in privileged state only.

Unprivileged code can gain access to privileged system services by triggering one of the system exceptions (e.g., System Service Call, SVC—see Sections 4.4.1 and 11.5). This mechanism is usually used to allow the RTOS to provide OS service Application Programming Interfaces (APIs). Exception handlers can also program the CONTROL register to allow the system to return to a privileged thread operation after an exception return.

Please note, the transition between privileged and unprivileged states can also happen during function calls that switch from one security domain to another. This is because the nPRIV bit in the CONTROL register is banked (Secure and Non-secure states both have their own nPRIV bits). At first glance this might sound strange because typical secure systems do not allow unprivileged code access to privileged level, except via OS's APIs. However, this is not an issue in the Armv8-M processor as explained in the following scenarios:

- Non-secure unprivileged thread software calling Secure privileged APIs (Fig. 4.3): The Secure APIs are created by a Trusted party. The codes in these trusted APIs are designed with security measures in mind to prevent the APIs from being exploited. As a result, allowing a transition from unprivileged to privileged level in the execution of these APIs is not a security issue concern.
- Secure unprivileged thread software calling Non-secure privileged code (Fig. 4.4): As the Secure code is expected to be developed by trusted parties, the security risk in Secure unprivileged code gaining Non-secure privileged is not an issue. Even if the Secure unprivileged software is not fully trusted, allowing it to access Non-secure privileged resources does not pose a security risk. This is because it does not allow the Secure unprivileged software to bypass or disable the security management of the Secure privileged code.

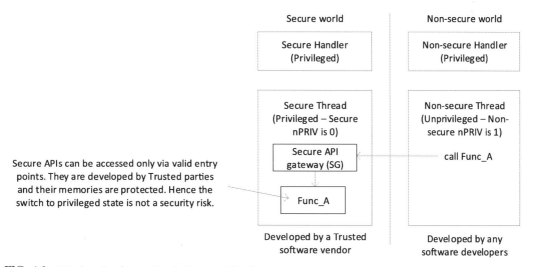

FIG. 4.3 Privilege level transition in Secure API calls.

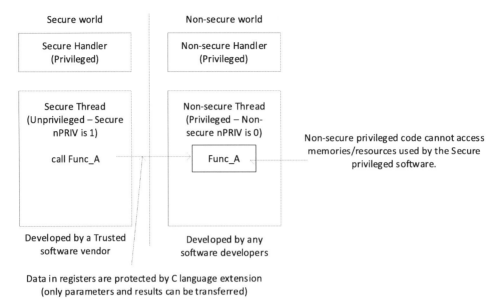

FIG. 4.4   Privilege level transition in Non-secure API calls.

If the TrustZone security extension is not implemented then the state transition diagram can be simplified as follows (Fig. 4.5).

This is identical to the Armv6-M and Armv7-M architectures.

For simple applications, it is possible to leave the unprivileged thread state unused. In this case, only privileged thread (for most of the application code) and Handler mode (e.g., for peripheral's interrupt service routines) are used.

For a system with the TrustZone security extension implemented, it is also possible to leave the Non-secure state unused and to execute the whole application in the Secure state.

The debug state is used during software development. When the halt mode debug features are enabled (this requires a debug connection), the processor can enter the debug state when the software developer halts the processor, or if a debug event like a breakpoint has taken place. This allows the software developer to examine or change the register values of the processor. The memory contents and peripheral registers can be examined or changed via the debugger in either Thumb or debug states. In a deployed system without a debugger connected to it, the processor will not enter the debug state.

4.2.2 Registers

4.2.2.1 *Various types of registers*

There are several types of registers inside Cortex-M processors:

- **Registers in the register bank**—mostly general purpose and used by most of the instructions. A few of them have special usage (e.g., R15 is the Program Counter, see Section 4.2.2.2 for more information).

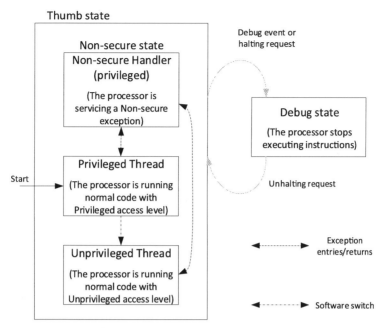

FIG. 4.5   Operation states and modes when the TrustZone security extension is NOT implemented.

- **Special registers**—there are a few special registers with specific purposes (e.g., interrupt masking) that need special instructions (e.g., MRS, MSR) to access them (see Section 4.2.2.3).
- **Memory mapped registers**—the built-in interrupt controller (NVIC) and a number of internal units are managed using memory mapped registers. They are accessible by pointers in C programming. These registers will be covered in various chapters of this book.

At the system level (external to the processor), there are additional registers in the chip:

- Peripheral registers—they are used for managing various peripherals. They are memory mapped and therefore can be easily accessed in C programs using pointers.
- Coprocessor registers—the Cortex-M33 processor has a coprocessor interface that allows chip designers to add coprocessors (hardware for accelerating certain processing tasks). The coprocessor hardware contains coprocessor registers, which can be accessed using coprocessor instructions (see Section 5.21).

In this section, I will cover the registers that are in the register bank and the special registers.

4.2.2.2 Registers in the register bank

Similar to other Arm processors, there are a number of registers in the processor core for data processing and control. To perform an operation on data in the memory, the Arm processor must first load the data in a register, perform the operation in the processor and then, optionally, write back the result to the memory. This is commonly called "load-store architecture". Registers are also used to hold address values to handle data transfers.

By having a sufficient number of registers in the register bank, C compilers can generate code to efficiently handle various operations. The register bank in Cortex-M processors has 16 registers: R0–R15 (see Fig. 4.6). Some of these registers have special usage as detailed below:

- R13—Stack pointer (SP). It is used for accessing the stack memory (e.g., stack PUSH or POP operations). Physically there can be two or four stack pointers—the Secure stack pointers are available only when the TrustZone security extension is implemented. There is more information about the selection of stack pointers in Section 4.3.4.
- R14—Link register (LR). This register is updated automatically to hold the return address when calling a function or subroutine. At the end of the function/subroutine, the value from LR is transferred into the program counter (PC) in order to resume its operation. In the case of nested function calls (i.e., a function call is made within a function which was called by another code), the value in LR must first be saved (e.g., using the stack PUSH operation to save the value into the stack memory) before the second level of function call is

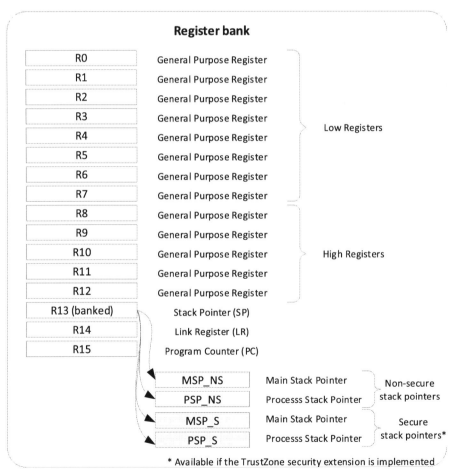

FIG. 4.6 Registers in the register bank.

made. If it is not, the value in LR would be lost and would not be able to return to the original program. LR is also used to hold a special value called EXC_RETURN (Exception Return) during exception/interrupt handling. At the end of the interrupt service routine, the EXC_RETURN value is transferred into the PC to trigger the exception return. Further information on this is covered in Chapter 8, Sections 8.4.5 and 8.10.

- R15—Program Counter (PC). The main advantage of having the PC in the register bank is that it makes accessing constant data in the program code easier (e.g., Obtaining a constant using a data read instruction with the "PC related addressing mode", for accessing a branch offset in a table branch operation). It is also possible to read/write to the PC. When reading this register, the operation returns a value which is the current instruction address (an even number), plus an offset of 4 (this is due to the pipeline nature of the processor and compatibility requirements with legacy processors, e.g., the Arm7TDMI). Writing to this register causes a branch operation. However, it is recommended that normal branch instructions should be used for general branch operations.

The rest of the registers (R0–R12) are general purpose. R0–R7 are also known as **low registers**. Because of the limited space available in a 16-bit instruction, many 16-bit Thumb instructions can only access low registers. The **high registers** (R8–R12) can be used with 32-bit instructions, and a few 16-bit instructions like MOV (move).

The initial values of R0–R12 can be unpredictable at startup. The hardware startup sequence automatically initializes the value of the Secure Main Stack Pointer (MSP_S) if the TrustZone security extension is implemented, or Non-secure Main Stack Pointer (MSP_NS) if it is not. The hardware startup sequence also initializes the program counter (R15/PC).

Further information on these registers is shown in Table 4.1.

TABLE 4.1   Read and write behaviors of registers R0–R15.

Registers	Initial value	Read/Write behaviors
R0–R12	Unknown	32-bit, Read/Write allowed.
R13	MSP_S/MSP_NS is initialized by the hardware startup sequence	32-bit, but the lowest 2 bits are always 0 (stack pointer is always word aligned). Read/Write allowed and write-values to lowest 2 bits are ignored.
R14	Reset to 0xFFFFFFFF for Cortex-M33 (and other processors with the Mainline extension). Unknown for Cortex-M23 (Baseline)	32-bit, Read/Write allowed. The value in R14 is also updated automatically when the processor has called a function or when it starts serving an interrupt/exception service. This allows the software flow to return to the caller or to the interrupted program.
R15	PC is initialized by a hardware startup sequence	Bit 0 is always 0, but when writing to the PC with indirect-branch instructions, bit 0 of the written value has a special meaning. Although it is possible to trigger a branch by writing to the PC (e.g., using a move instruction), it is, nonetheless, recommended to use branch instructions for normal branch operations.

In programming, registers R0–R15 can be accessed using various names in either upper or lower case: R0–R15 or r0–r15. For R13–R15, it can also be accessed as

- R13: SP or sp (current selected **Stack Pointer**)
- R14: LR or lr (**Link Register**)
- R15: PC or pc (**Program Counter**)

As illustrated in Fig. 4.6, the SP is banked between Secure and Non-secure states. When accessing the stack pointer with MSR/MRS instructions, it is possible to specify which stack pointer should be used:

- MSP—Main Stack Pointer of the current security state (could be MSP_S or MSP_NS)
- PSP—Process Stack Pointer of the current security state (could be PSP_S or PSP_NS)
- MSP_NS—This enables Secure software to access the Non-secure Main Stack Pointer
- PSP_NS—This enables Secure software to access the Non-secure Process Stack Pointer

In Arm documentation (e.g., Armv8-M Architecture Reference Manual), the stack pointers are also labeled as SP_main (Main Stack Pointer) and SP_process (Process Stack Pointer).

More information about stack pointer operations is covered in Section 4.3.4.

R0–R15 can also be accessed (read and write) by using debug software (running on a debug host such as a PC) when the processor is in the debug state (i.e., halted).

4.2.2.3 *Special registers*

In addition to the registers in the register bank, there are a number of special registers with special purposes. For example, there are control registers for interrupt masking and condition flags for arithmetic/logic operation results. These registers can be accessed using special register access instructions such as MRS and MSR (see Section 5.6.4, Special register access instructions).

```
MRS <reg>, <special_reg>; Read special register into register
MSR <special_reg>, <reg>; write to special register
```

In programming, the CMSIS-CORE defines a number of C functions for accessing special registers.

Note: Do not confuse special registers as peripheral registers. In some legacy processor architecture, such as the MCS-51/8051 (an 8-bit architecture for basic microcontrollers), special function registers are mostly peripheral registers. In Arm Cortex-M processors, peripheral registers are memory mapped and can be accessed using pointers in C/C++.

Program Status Register (PSR)

The Program Status Register is 32-bit and can be subdivided into:

- Application PSR—contains various "ALU flags" which are required for conditional branches and instruction operations that need special flags (e.g., add with carry flag).
- Execution PSR—contains execution state information.
- Interrupt PSR—contains current interrupt/exception state information.

These three registers can be accessed as one combined register, sometimes referred to as "xPSR" in some documentation (e.g., Armv8-M Architecture Reference Manual), as shown in Fig. 4.7. In programming, the symbol PSR is used when accessing the whole PSR. For example,

```
MRS r0, PSR; Read the combined program status word
MSR PSR, r0; Write combined program state word
```

You can also access each PSR individually. For example:

```
MRS r0, APSR; Read flag states into register r0
MRS r0, IPSR; Read exception/interrupt states into register r0
MSR APSR, r0; Write flag state
```

Table 4.2 shows the register symbols available for accessing xPSR.
Please note, there are some restrictions:

- The EPSR cannot be accessed by software code directly by using the MRS (it is read as zero) or the MSR. But it is visible during exception sequences (when xPSR is saved and restored into the stack), and is visible from debug tools.
- The IPSR is read-only and cannot be changed using a MSR instruction.

Table 4.3 below lists the definitions of the bit fields in the PSRs.

Compared to the Armv6-M architecture, Armv8-M expanded the width of the exception number field in the Program Status Register to 9 bits. This enables the Armv8-M processor to support more interrupts: The Cortex-M23 processor supports up to 240 interrupts compared to 32 interrupts in the Cortex-M0 and Cortex-M0+ processors (the exception number field is 5-bit wide in these processors).

	31	30	29	28	27	26:25	24	23:20	19:16	15:10	9	8	7	6	5	4:0
APSR	N	Z	C	V	Q**				GE*							
IPSR													Exception Number			
EPSR					ICI/IT**		T		ICI/IT**							

The APSR, IPSR, and EPSR registers can be accessed in combination, and is referred as xPSR when accessing all three together.

	31	30	29	28	27	26:25	24	23:20	19:16	15:10	9	8	7	6	5	4:0
xPSR	N	Z	C	V	Q**	ICI/IT**	T		GE*	ICI/IT**			Exception Number			

*GE (Greater than or Equal flags) bits are available in the Cortex-M33 processor when the DSP extension is included. They are also available in the Cortex-M4 and Cortex-M7 processors. They are not available in the Cortex-M23, Cortex-M0, Cortex-M0+, and Cortex-M3 processors.

** Q (Sticky Saturation) bit and ICI/IT (If-Then and Interrupt Continuation) bits are available in the Cortex-M33 processor (Mainline extension), and are also available in Armv7-M processors (Cortex-M3, Cortex-M4, and Cortex-M7 processors). They are not available in the Cortex-M23, Cortex-M0, Cortex-M0+ processors.

FIG. 4.7 Program Status Registers—APSR, IPSR, EPSR, and xPSR.

TABLE 4.2 Valid symbols of xPSR for programming.

Symbol	Description
APSR	Application PSR only
EPSR	Execution PSR only
IPSR	Interrupt PSR only
IAPSR	Combination of APSR and IPSR
EAPSR	Combination of APSR and EPSR
IEPSR	Combination of IPSR and EPSR
PSR	Combination of APSR, IPSR, and EPSR

TABLE 4.3 Bit fields in the Program Status Registers.

Bit	Description
N	Negative flag
Z	Zero flag
C	Carry (or NOT borrow) flag
V	Overflow flag
Q	Sticky saturation flag (Available in Armv8-M Mainline and Arvmv7-M. Not available in Armv8-M Baseline and Armv6-M)
GE[3:0]	Greater-Than or Equal flags for each byte lane (available in Armv8-M Mainline and Arvmv7-M when the DSP extension is implemented). This is updated by a range of instructions in the DSP extension and can be utilized by the SEL (select) instruction.
ICI/IT	Interrupt-Continuable Instruction (ICI) bits and IF-THEN instruction status bit for conditional execution (Available in Armv8-M Mainline and Armv7-M. Not available in Armv8-M Baseline and Armv6-M)
T	Thumb state, always 1 for normal operations. Attempts to clear this bit will cause a fault exception.
Exception Number	Indicates which exception/interrupt service the processor is handling.

Note: *If TrustZone is implemented and if a Secure exception handlers calls a Non-secure function, the value of IPSR is set to 1 during the function call to mask the identity of the Secure exception service.*

The other fields in the xPSR are the same as those in the Armv6-M or Armv7-M architectures. As in the past, some of the bit fields are not available in Armv8-M Baseline (i.e., the Cortex-M23 processor).

Fig. 4.8 shows the PSR bit fields in various Arm architectures. Please note, PSRs in Cortex-M processors are different from classic processors like the Arm7TDMI™. For example, classic Arm processors have Mode (M) bits, and the T bit is in bit 5 rather than bit 24. In addition, the interrupt masking bits (I and F) in classic Arm processors is separated into new interrupt masking registers (e.g., PRIMASK, FAULTMASK).

	31	30	29	28	27	26:25	24	23:20	19:16	15:10	9	8	7	6	5	4:0
Arm general (Cortex-A/R)	N	Z	C	V	Q	IT	J	Reserved	GE[3:0]	IT	E	A	I	F	T	M[4:0]
Arm7TDMI (Armv4)	N	Z	C	V			Reserved						I	F	T	M[4:0]
Armv7-M (Cortex-M3)	N	Z	C	V	Q	ICI/IT	T			ICI/IT		Exception Number				
Armv7E-M (Cortex-M4/M7)	N	Z	C	V	Q	ICI/IT	T		GE[3:0]	ICI/IT		Exception Number				
Armv6-M (Cortex-M0/M0+)	N	Z	C	V			T									Exception Number
Armv8-M baseline (Cortex-M23)	N	Z	C	V			T					Exception Number				
Armv8-M Mainline without DSP ext.	N	Z	C	V	Q	ICI/IT	T			ICI/IT		Exception Number				
Armv8-M Mainline with DSP ext.	N	Z	C	V	Q	ICI/IT	T		GE[3:0]	ICI/IT		Exception Number				

FIG. 4.8 Comparison of Program Status Registers in different Arm architectures.

Detailed behavior of the APSR is covered in Section 4.2.3.

The ICI/IT bits are available in Armv7-M and Armv8-M Mainline and serves two purposes:

- During the execution of an IT (IF-THEN) instruction block, these bits (IT) hold the conditional execution information.
- During the execution of a multiple load/store instruction, these bits (ICI) hold the current progress status of the instruction.

The ICI/IT bit fields overlap as most of the case program codes do not use the two features at the same time. When an exception occurs, the ICI/IT state is saved as part of the automatic stacking operation(see Section 8.4.3—the ICI/IT bits are inside the stacked xPSR). After the interrupt is served, the execution of the interrupted code is resumed using the restored ICI/IT bits.

More information on ICI/IT bits is covered in Section 9.6.2.

Interrupt masking registers

Each of the interrupts can be enabled or disabled at the NVIC. And, in addition, there are several global interrupt/exception masking registers that allow interrupts and exceptions to be blocked based on priority levels. Details as follow:

- PRIMASK—available in all Cortex-M processors. When this is set to 1, all exceptions with programmable priority levels (0 to 0xFF) would be blocked, and only Non-Maskable Interrupt (NMI, level-2) and HardFault (level-1 or -3) are able to invoke. Interrupt masking is disabled when its value is 0, which is the default value.
- FAULTMASK—available in Armv8-M Mainline (Cortex-M33) and Armv7-M (Cortex-M3, Cortex-M4 and Cortex-M7). When this is set to 1, all exceptions with programmable priority levels (0 to 0xFF) and HardFault are blocked (there are some exceptions, see Chapter 9, Table 9.23 in Section 9.4.3). Interrupt masking is disabled when its value is 0, which is the default value.

- BASEPRI—available in Armv8-M Mainline (Cortex-M33) and Armv7-M (Cortex-M3, Cortex-M4 and Cortex-M7). This register allows the blocking of interrupts/exceptions based on their programmable priority levels. It is disabled when the value is 0, which is the default value.

The PRIMARK, FAULTMASK, and BASEPRI registers:

- Can be accessed in privileged state only.
- Are banked between Secure and Non-secure states if the TrustZone security extension is implemented. Secure software can access both the Secure and Non-secure masking registers, but Non-secure software can only access ones that are Non-secure.

PRIMASK and FAULTMASK registers are 1-bit wide and the width of the BASEPRI register ranges from 3 bits to 8 bits (depending on the width of the priority level registers).The most significant bits of the BASEPRI register field is aligned to bit 7, while other bits in this register are unimplemented (Fig. 4.9).

The purpose of the interrupt masking registers is as follows:

- PRIMASK—For general disabling of interrupts and exceptions, e.g., to enable critical regions in program code to be executed without getting interrupted.
- FAULTMASK—Can be used by fault exception handlers to suppress the triggering of further faults (only some types of faults can be suppressed) during fault handling. For example, when it is set it can bypass the MPU and can, optionally, suppress bus error responses. This potentially makes it easier for fault handling code to carry out remedial actions. Unlike PRIMASK, FAULTMASK is cleared automatically at exception exit (except in NMI).
- BASEPRI—for the general disabling of interrupts and exceptions based on priority levels. For some OS operations, there could be a need to block some exceptions for a brief period of time, but, at the same time, still allow high priority interrupts to be serviced. This register is 8-bit wide, but the lowest bits could be unimplemented (see Fig. 4.9). When this register is set to a Nonzero value, it blocks exceptions and interrupts that have the same or a lower priority level than the BASEPRI's level.

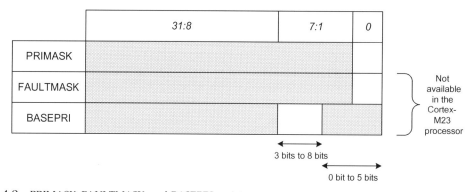

FIG. 4.9   PRIMASK, FAULTMASK, and BASEPRI registers.

These interrupt masking registers can be accessed at privileged level using the MRS and MSR instructions. In C programming, a number of functions for accessing these interrupt masking registers are defined in the CMSIS-CORE header files. For example:

```
x = __get_BASEPRI(); // Read BASEPRI register
x = __get_PRIMARK(); // Read PRIMASK register
x = __get_FAULTMASK(); // Read FAULTMASK register
__set_BASEPRI(x); // Set new value for BASEPRI
__set_PRIMASK(x); // Set new value for PRIMASK
__set_FAULTMASK(x); // Set new value for FAULTMASK
__disable_irq(); // Set PRIMASK, disable IRQ
__enable_irq(); // Clear PRIMASK, enable IRQ
```

The PRIMASK and FAULTMASK registers can also be set or cleared using the CPS (Change Processor State) instructions. For example:

```
CPSIE i ; Enable interrupt (clear PRIMASK)
CPSID i ; Disable interrupt (set PRIMASK)
CPSIE f ; Enable interrupt (clear FAULTMASK)
CPSID f ; Disable interrupt (set FAULTMASK)
```

In programming, access of PRIMASK, FAULTMASK, and BASEPRI using MRS and MSR instructions provide access to the interrupt masking registers of the current security domain. If the TrustZone security extension is implemented and if the processor is in Secure state, Secure privileged software is able to access the Non-secure interrupt masking registers using PRIMASK_NS, FAULTMASK_NS, and BASEPRI_NS symbols.

Further information on interrupt and exception masking is covered in Chapter 9, Section 9.4.

CONTROL register

The CONTROL register contains multiple bit fields for various processor system configuration settings and is available in all Cortex-M processors (Fig. 4.10). This register can be written in privileged state, but can be read by both privileged and unprivileged software.

When the TrustZone security extension is implemented, some of the bit fields are banked between security states. Two of the bit fields in the CONTROL register are only available when the Floating-Point Unit (FPU) is implemented.

The bit fields of the CONTROL register are shown in Table 4.4.

When the processor is reset, the value of the CONTROL register is 0, which means:

- the MSP is the current selected stack pointer (SPSEL bit is 0).
- the program execution starts in privileged thread mode, (nPRIV bit is 0).
- if the FPU is implemented, the FPU does not contain active software context data (indicated by 0 value in the FPCA bit) and does not hold any Secure data (SFPA is 0).

The privileged thread software can, optionally, write to the CONTROL register to:

- Switch the stack pointer selection (the software needs to handle this carefully otherwise the data used by the current software held in the stack will not be accessible if the current selected SP value has changed).

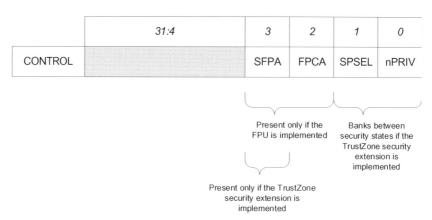

FIG. 4.10   CONTROL register.

TABLE 4.4   Bit fields in the CONTROL Register.

Bit	Bit field	Function
3	SFPA	Secure Floating-Point Active—This bit indicates that the FPU registers contain data belonging to the Secure state software and is used by the context saving mechanism when an exception occurs. This bit is set to 1 when the Secure software has executed a floating-point instruction and clears to 0 when a new context is started (e.g., starting of an ISR). This bit is not accessible from the Non-secure state.
2	FPCA	Floating Point Context Active—This bit is available if the FPU is implemented. This bit is automatically set to 1 when a floating-point instruction is executed and clears to 0 at reset, and when a new context is started (e.g., at the commencement of an ISR). The exception handling mechanism uses this bit to determine whether the registers in the FPU need to be preserved in the stack memory when an exception has occurred.
1	SPSEL	Stack Pointer select—Selects between Main Stack Pointer (MSP) or Processor Stack Pointer (PSP) in Thread mode: - If this bit is 0 (default), the MSP is selected. - If this bit is 1 (default), the PSP is selected. In Handler mode, the MSP is always selected and this bit is 0—writing to this bit is ignored.
0	nPRIV	Not privileged—Defines the privilege level in Thread mode: When this bit is 0 (default) and if the processor is in Thread mode, the processor is at privileged level. Otherwise, the Thread mode is at unprivileged level. In Handler mode, the processor is always at privileged access level. This bit is programmable in Handler mode and this allows an exception handler to change the thread mode privilege access level.

• Switch to unprivileged level—if privileged code changes nPRIV to 1, this switches the processor into unprivileged level. However, the unprivileged thread software cannot switch itself back to privileged by writing 0 to nPRIV (because unprivileged code cannot write to the CONTROL register). It is, however, possible for an exception/interrupt handler to change then PRIV bit (CONTROL bit 0) back to 0.

Unprivileged code is blocked from writing to the CONTROL register. This is essential and ensures a very high level of security—preventing a compromised unprivileged software component from taking over the whole system and, also, preventing an unreliable application thread from crashing the system. Normally an OS can provide various system services, via system exceptions, to enable access to privileged resources (e.g., to enable or disable interrupts). This ensures that it is not a problem for application threads to run in unprivileged state in a system with an OS.

If it is necessary for a thread mode code to regain privileged access, a system exception (e.g., SVC or SuperVisor Call, which is covered in Chapter 11) and the corresponding exception handler is needed. The exception handler can re-program the CONTROL register bit 0 to a value of 0, and, when the exception handler returns to the thread, the processor will be in privileged thread mode (Fig. 4.11).

When an embedded OS is used, it is possible that the OS could program the CONTROL register at each context switch to allow some application threads to run in privileged level and other threads in unprivileged.

For simple applications without an OS, it is perfectly fine to use default settings for CONTROL (there is no need to program the CONTROL register). In some cases, it can be desirable to separate the stack used for the "main()" program and exception/interrupt handlers even if no OS is present. In such instances, privileged code can program the CONTROL register to select PSP for "main()" and MSP for the exceptions and the interrupts handlers (Fig. 4.12).

If an OS is used, the programming of the CONTROL register is normally handled by the OS code.

To access the CONTROL register, in addition to using the MSR and the MRS instructions, you can also use access functions provided in the CMSIS-CORE. Details as follows:

```
x = __get_CONTROL(); // Reads the current value of CONTROL
__set_CONTROL(x); // Sets the CONTROL value to x
```

Secure privileged software can also access the Non-secure CONTROL register using the CONTROL_NS symbol.

There are a couple of specific points you need to be aware of when changing the value of the CONTROL register:

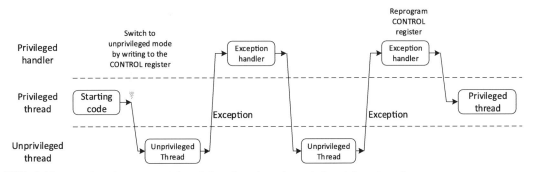

FIG. 4.11   Switching between privileged thread mode and unprivileged thread mode.

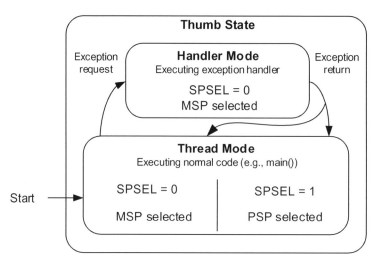

FIG. 4.12 Stack Pointer selection.

- If the FPU is implemented, the FPCA and SFPA bits are automatically set by the processor's hardware when a floating-point instruction is executed. When updating the SPSEL and nPRIV bits in the CONTROL register, care should be taken to preserve the FPCA and SFPA bits. If they are not preserved, the data stored in the FPU registers will not be saved to the stack by the exception handling sequence and could be lost when an exception/interrupt occurs. As a result, generally speaking, software should use a read-modify-write sequence to update the CONTROL register to ensure the FPCA and SFPA are not accidentally cleared.
- After modifying the CONTROL register, as specified by the Armv8-M architecture reference manual, an Instruction Synchronization Barrier (ISB) instruction should be used to ensure the effect of the update applies immediately to any subsequent code. The ISB instruction is accessible using __ISB() function in the CMSIS-CORE.
- Since the SPSEL and then PRIV settings are orthogonal (i.e., they operate independently), there are four possible combinations of settings. However, only three of them are commonly used in real world applications (Table 4.5).

Unlike other special registers, the CONTROL register can be read in unprivileged state. This allows software to determine whether the current execution level is privileged by reading the values of IPSR and the CONTROL registers:

```
int in_privileged(void)
{
  if (__get_IPSR() != 0) return 1; // True when in handler mode
  else // In thread mode
    if ((__get_CONTROL() & 0x1)==0) return 1; // True when nPRIV==0
    else return 0; // False when nPRIV==1
}
```

TABLE 4.5   Different combinations of nPRIV and SPSEL.

nPRIV	SPSEL	Usage scenario
0	0	Simple applications—the whole application is running in privileged access level. Only the main stack is used and the MSP is always selected.
0	1	Applications with an embedded OS with the current executing thread running in **privileged** Thread mode, and with the Process Stack Pointer (PSP) selected for stack operations. In addition, the exception/interrupt handlers (including most of the OS code) are using the main stack.
1	1	Applications with an embedded OS with the current executing thread running in **unprivileged** Thread mode, and with the Process Stack Pointer (PSP) selected for stack operations. In addition, the exception/interrupt handlers (including most of the OS code) are using the main stack.
1	0	Threads/tasks running in unprivileged thread mode and using the MSP as the current stack pointer. Although the exception handlers would be able to see the combination of nPRIV=1 and SPSEL=0 in the CONTROL register (because SPSEL is switched to 0 during handler mode), it is unlikely that the privileged software would use this setup for thread mode operations. This is because with this setup, a stack overflow in an application thread will crash the whole system. Normally in systems with an OS, the stack memory for application threads should be separated from the stack memory used by the privileged codes (including the OS and the exception/interrupt handlers) to ensure a reliable operation.

Stack limit registers

Cortex-M processors use a descending stack operation model. It means the stack pointers are decremented when more data is added to the stack. When too much data is pushed into a stack and the space consumed is more than the allocated stack space, the overflowing stack data can corrupt the OS kernel data and memories used by other application tasks. This can cause various types of errors and, potentially, result in security vulnerabilities.

Stack Limit Registers are used for detecting stack overflow errors. They were introduced in the Armv8-M architecture and were not available in the previous generation of Cortex-M processors. There are four stack limit registers (Table 4.6).

The stack limit registers are 32-bit and can be set to the lowest address of each of the stack address ranges allocated to each stack (Fig. 4.13).Because the lowest 3 bits (bit 2 to bit 0) of these stack limit registers are always zero (writes to these bits are ignored), the stack limits are always aligned to double word boundaries.

By default, the stack limit registers reset to 0 (the lowest address in the memory map) so that the stack limits will not be reached; effectively the stack limit checks are disabled at start-up. The stack limit registers can be programmed when the processor is executing in privileged state. Please note:

- Secure privileged software can access all stack limited registers, and
- Non-secure privileged software can only access Non-secure stack limit registers.

The stack limit is violated if a stack pointer goes lower than the corresponding stack limit register. The violating stack operation (i.e., the memory access to the address below the stack limit) will not take place so as to avoid corrupting memories used by other applications. The stack limit check only happens during stack related operations, such as:

TABLE 4.6　List of stack limit registers.

Symbol	Register	Note
MSPLIM_S	Secure Main Stack Pointer Limit Register	For stack overflow detection of the Secure MSP. Available in the Cortex-M33 and Cortex-M23 processors.
PSPLIM_S	Secure Process Stack Pointer Limit Register	For stack overflow detection of the Secure PSP. Available in the Cortex-M33 and Cortex-M23 processors.
MSPLIM_NS	Non-secure Main Stack Pointer Limit Register	For stack overflow detection of the Non-secure MSP. Available in the Cortex-M33 processor.
PSPLIM_NS	Non-secure Process Stack Pointer Limit Register	For stack overflow detection of the Non-secure PSP. Available in the Cortex-M33 processor.

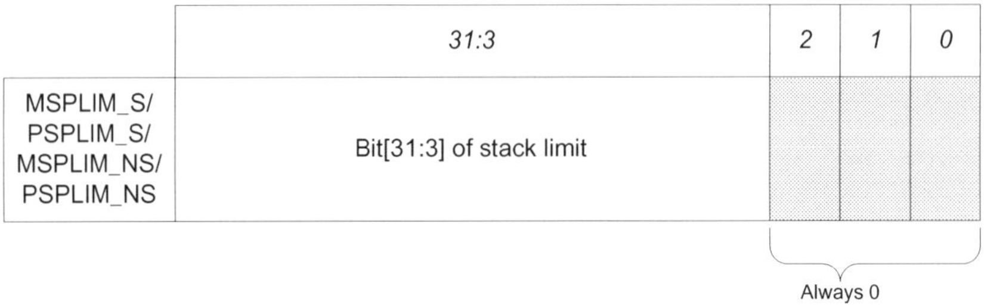

FIG. 4.13　Stack Limit Registers' bit field.

- Stack push, including during exception sequences
- When the stack pointer is updated (e.g., when the stack is allocated for local memory use by a function).

The stack limit check is not performed immediately when the stack limit registers are updated. This simplifies context switching operations in the design of an OS (there is no need to set the stack limit registers to 0 before updating the Process Stack Pointer (PSP)).

If a stack limit violation takes place, a fault exception is triggered (UsageFault/HardFault). With the Cortex-M23 processor, although there are no stack limit registers for the Non-secure stack pointers, it is possible to use the Memory Protection Unit (MPU) to carry out stack limit checks. However, the stack limit registers are easier to use.

4.2.2.4 Floating-point registers in Cortex-M33

The FPU hardware is optional in the Cortex-M33, the Cortex-M4, the Cortex-M7, and other Armv8-M Mainline processors. If the floating-point unit is available, the floating-point unit (FPU) includes an additional register bank containing another 32 registers (S0–S31, each of which are 32-bit), and a Floating-Point Status and Control Register (FPSCR). This is shown in Fig. 4.14.

Each of the 32-bit registers, S0–S31 ("S" for single precision), can be accessed individually using floating point instructions, or accessed as a pair, using the register names D0–D15 ("D" for double-word/double-precision). For example, S1 and S0 are paired together to become D0, and S3 and S2 are paired together to become D1. Although the floating-point unit in

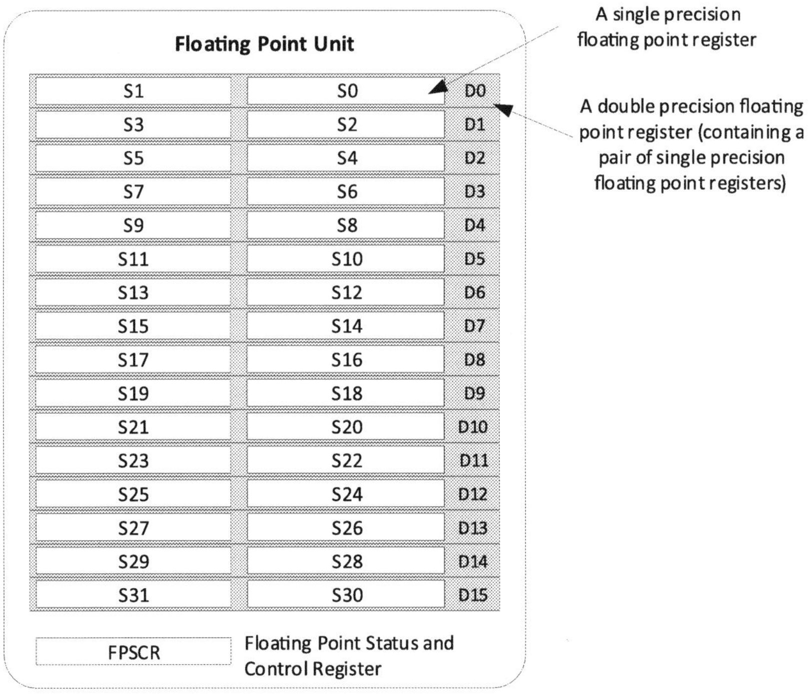

FIG. 4.14   Registers in the Floating-Point Unit (FPU).

	31	30	29	28	27	26	25	24	23:22	21:8	7	6:5	4	3	2	1	0
FPSCR	N	Z	C	V		AHP	DN	FZ	RMode	Reserved	IDC	Reserved	IXC	UFC	OFC	DZC	IOC

Reserved

FIG. 4.15   Bit fields in FPSCR.

the Cortex-M33 processor does not support double precision floating point calculations, you can still use floating point instructions for transferring double precision data.

The FPSCR can only be accessed in privileged state and contains various bit fields (Fig. 4.15). The purposes of these bit fields include:

- defining some of the floating-point operation behaviors
- providing status information about the floating-point operation results

By default, the behavior of the FPU is configured to be compliant with IEEE 754 single precision operations. In normal applications, there is no need to modify the control settings of the FPU. Table 4.7 describes the bit fields in the FPSCR.

Note: The exception bits in the FPSCR can be used by software to detect abnormalities in floating point operations. Bit fields in the FPSCR are covered in Chapter 14.

TABLE 4.7 Bit fields in the FPSCR.

Bit	Description
N	Negative flag (update by floating point comparison operations)
Z	Zero flag (update by floating point comparison operations)
C	Carry/borrow flag (update by floating point comparison operations)
V	Overflow flag (update by floating point comparison operations)
AHP	Alternate half precision control bit: 0—IEEE half precision format (default) 1—Alternative half precision format
DN	Default NaN (Not a Number) mode control bit: 0—NaN operands propagate through to the output of a floating-point operation. (Default) 1—Any operation involving one or more NaN(s) returns the default NaN.
FZ	Flush-to-zero mode control bit: 0—Flush-to-zero mode disabled (default). (IEEE 754 standard compliant.) 1—Flush-to-zero mode enabled.
RMode	Rounding Mode Control field. The specified rounding mode is used by almost all floating-point instructions: 00—Round to Nearest (RN) mode (default). 01—Round toward Plus Infinity (RP) mode. 10—Round toward Minus Infinity (RM) mode. 11—Round toward Zero (RZ) mode.
IDC	Input Denormal cumulative exception bit. Set to 1 when a floating-point exception occurs and is cleared by writing 0 to this bit. (When this bit is 1, it indicates that the result of a floating-point operation is not within the normalized value range, see Section 14.1.2)
IXC	Inexact cumulative exception bit. Set to 1 when a floating-point exception occurs, clear by writing 0 to this bit.
UFC	Underflow cumulative exception bit. Set to 1 when a floating-point exception occurs, clear by writing 0 to this bit.
OFC	Overflow cumulative exception bit. Set to 1 when a floating-point exception occurs, clear by writing 0 to this bit.
DZC	Division by Zero cumulative exception bit. Set to 1 when a floating-point exception occurs, clear by writing 0 to this bit.
IOC	Invalid Operation cumulative exception bit. Set to 1 when a floating-point exception occurs, clear by writing 0 to this bit.

In addition to the registers in the floating-point register bank and the FPSCR, there are a number of additional memory mapped registers that are related to floating-point unit operations. One of the important ones is the Coprocessor Access Control Register (CPACR, Fig. 4.16). By default, the FPU is disabled when the processor is reset to reduce power consumption. Before the FPU can be used, it needs to be enabled first and this is achieved by programming the CPACR.

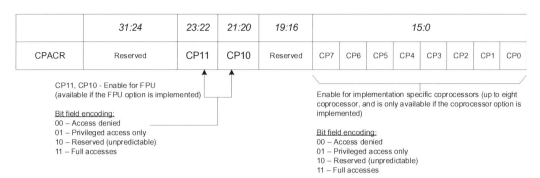

FIG. 4.16 Bit fields in CPACR.

Please note, the CPACR is available in Armv8-M Mainline only:

When programming in C/C++ with CMSIS-CORE compliant drivers, the FPU is enabled in the system's initialization function "SystemInit()" if the C macro "__FPU_USED" is set to 1. This sets up the CPACR value and means that that the CPACR does not need to be programmed within the application codes.

The CPACR is located at address 0xE000ED88, is privileged access only and is cleared to 0 when the processor is reset. If the TrustZone security extension is implemented this register is banked between security states. Secure software can also access the Non-secure version of the CPACR (CPACR_NS) using NS alias address 0xE002ED88. Secure software can also define whether Non-secure software can access each of the coprocessors using a register called the Non-secure Access Control Register (NSACR, see Section 14.2.4). The CPACR and NSACR registers are used for enabling the coprocessor interface and also the Arm Custom Instructions features. For more information on this topic, please refer to Chapter 15.

4.2.3 Behaviors of the APSR (ALU status flags)

The results of arithmetic and logic operations affect a number of status flags in the Application Program Status Register (APSR). These flags include the:

- N-Z-C-V bits: status flags for integer operations
- Q bit: status flag for saturation arithmetic (available in Armv8-M Mainline/Cortex-M33 processor)
- GE bits: status flags for SIMD operations (available in Armv8-M Mainline/Cortex-M33 processor with DSP extension)

4.2.3.1 Integer status flags

Like most other processor architectures, Arm Cortex-M processors have several status flags to indicate the results of integer operations. The flags are updated by data processing instructions and are used:

- For conditional branches
- For certain types of data processing instructions (e.g., carry and borrow flags can be used as input in additions and subtractions. The carry flag is also used in rotate instructions).

TABLE 4.8 ALU flags in the Cortex-M processors.

Flag	Description
N (bit 31)	When it is "1", the result has a negative value (when interpreted as a signed integer), and when it is "0", the result has a positive value or is equal to zero (Effectively this bit has the same value as bit 31 of the processing result).
Z (bit 30)	Set to "1" if the result of the executed instruction is zero. It can also be set to "1" after a compare instruction is executed when the two values are the same.
C (bit 29)	Carry flag of the result. For unsigned additions, this bit is set to "1" if an unsigned overflow occurs. For unsigned subtract operations, this bit is the inverse of the borrow output status. This bit is also updated by shift and rotate operations.
V (bit 28)	Overflow of the result. For signed addition or subtraction, this bit is set to "1" if a signed overflow occurs.

TABLE 4.9 Examples of ALU flags.

Operation	Result, flags
`0x70000000 + 0x70000000`	Result = 0xE0000000, N = 1, Z = 0, C = 0, V = 1
`0x90000000 + 0x90000000`	Result = 0x20000000, N = 0, Z = 0, C = 1, V = 1
`0x80000000 + 0x80000000`	Result = 0x00000000, N = 0, Z = 1, C = 1, V = 1
`0x00001234 - 0x00001000`	Result = 0x00000234, N = 0, Z = 0, C = 1, V = 0
`0x00000004 - 0x00000005`	Result = 0xFFFFFFFF, N = 1, Z = 0, C = 0, V = 0
`0xFFFFFFFF - 0xFFFFFFFC`	Result = 0x00000003, N = 0, Z = 0, C = 1, V = 0
`0x80000005 - 0x80000004`	Result = 0x00000001, N = 0, Z = 0, C = 1, V = 0
`0x70000000 - 0xF0000000`	Result = 0x80000000, N = 1, Z = 0, C = 0, V = 1
`0xA0000000 - 0xA0000000`	Result = 0x00000000, N = 0, Z = 1, C = 1, V = 0

There are four integer flags in the Cortex-M processors (Table 4.8).

A few examples of the ALU flag results are shown in Table 4.9.

In the architecture (Armv6-M, Armv7-M, and Armv8-M) of Cortex-M processors, most of the 16-bit instructions affect some or all of the four ALU flags. In most of the 32-bit instructions the ALU flag update is conditional (one of the bits in the instruction encoding defines whether the APSR flags should be updated or not). Note, some of the data processing instructions do not update the V flag or the C flag. For example, the MULS (multiply) instruction only changes the N flag and the Z flag.

In addition to conditional branch or conditional execution code, the Carry bit of APSR can also be used to extend addition and subtraction operations to over 32 bits. For example, when adding two 64-bit integers together, we can use the carry bit from the lower 32-bit add operation as an extra input for the upper 32-bit add operation:

```
// Calculating Z = X + Y, where X, Y and Z are all 64-bit
Z[31:0] = X[31:0] + Y[31:0]; // Calculate lower word addition using ADD,
                         // carry flag get updated
Z[63:32] = X[63:32] + Y[63:32] + Carry; // Calculate upper
                                      // word addition using ADDC
```

The N-Z-C-V flags are available in all Arm processors.

Please note, the status of floating-point operations is handled by a separate special register in the FPU called FPSCR (Floating Point Status and Control Register). The flags from the FPCSR can be transferred to the APSR and, if needed, be used for conditional branches or data processing.

4.2.3.2 Q status flag

The Q bit in the APSR is available in Armv8-M Mainline and Armv7-M architecture, but is not available in Armv8-M Baseline (Cortex-M23 processor) and all Armv6-M processors. It is used to indicate an occurrence of saturation during saturation arithmetic or saturation adjustment operations. Unlike integer status flags, after this bit is set it remains set until a software write to the APSR clears the Q bit. Saturation arithmetic/adjustment operations do not clear this bit. As a result, you can use this bit to determine whether a saturation has occurred at the end of a sequence of Saturation arithmetic/adjustment operations. There is no need to check the saturation status between each step in the instruction sequence.

Saturation arithmetic is useful for digital signal processing. In some instances, the destination register used to hold calculation results might not have sufficient bit width and, as a result, overflow or underflow could occur. If this happens when a normal data arithmetic instruction is used, the MSB of the result will be lost and this will cause a distortion of output. Instead of just cutting off the MSB, saturation arithmetic forces the result to the maximum value (in the case of overflow) or minimum value (in the case of underflow) to reduce the impact of a signal distortion (Fig. 4.17).

The actual maximum and minimum values which trigger saturation depends on the instructions being used. In most cases, the instructions for saturation arithmetic are mnemonic that starts with the letter "Q", e.g., "QADD16". If saturation occurs, the Q bit is set for the following instructions: QADD, QDADD, QSUB, QDSUB, SSAT, SSAT16, USAT, USAT16; if there is no saturation, the value of the Q bit remains unchanged.

Even without the DSP extension, the Cortex-M33 processor provides a couple of saturation adjustment instructions (USAT and SSAT).If the DSP extension option is implemented, the Cortex-M33 processor provides a full set of saturation arithmetic instructions, as well as saturation adjustment instructions.

4.2.3.3 GE bits

The "Greater-Equal" (GE) is a 4-bit wide field in the APSR and is available in Armv8-M Mainline processors with the DSP extension (i.e., it is available in the Cortex-M33 processor when the DSP option is implemented). It is not available in the Armv8-M Baseline (i.e., Cortex-M23 processor), or in processors where the DSP extension has not been implemented.

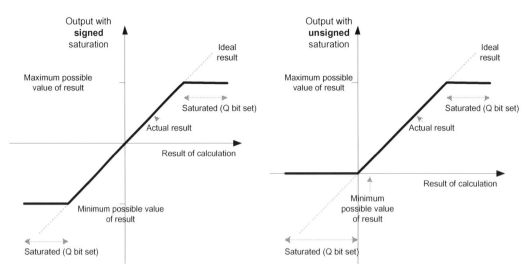

FIG. 4.17   Signed and unsigned saturation.

The GE bits are updated by a number of SIMD instructions where, generally, each bit represents a positive or an overflow of the SIMD operation for each byte (Table 4.10). For SIMD instructions with 16-bit data, bit 0 and bit 1 are controlled by the result of the lower half word, and bit 2 and bit 3 are controlled by the result of the upper half word.

The GE flags are used by the SEL instruction (Fig. 4.18), which multiplexes the byte values from two source registers based on each GE bit. When combining SIMD instructions with the SEL instruction, simple conditional data selection can be created using the SEL instruction for improved performance.

You can also read back the GE bits by reading the APSR into a general-purpose register for additional processing. Further information about the SIMD and the SEL instructions are covered in Chapter 5.

4.2.4 Impact of TrustZone on the programmer's model

Apart from certain special registers, in general there is little difference between the programmer's model for Secure and Non-secure software. It means most runtime libraries and assembly code can be reused in either Secure or Non-secure states when migrating from Armv6-M/Armv7-M to the Armv8-M architecture.

The registers in the programmer's model (excluding memory mapped registers) that are present when the TrustZone security extension is implemented include:

- Secure stack pointers (MPS_S, PSP_S)
- Secure stack limit registers (MSPLIM_S, PSPLIM_S)
- Bit 3 of the CONTROL registers if the FPU is implemented (available in the Cortex-M33 processor)
- A Secure version of the interrupt masking registers (PRIMASK_S, FAULTMASK_S and BASEPRI_S)

TABLE 4.10 GE flags results.

SIMD operation	Results
SADD16, SSUB16, USUB16, SASX, SSAX	If lower half word result >= 0 then GE[1:0]=2′b11 else GE[1:0]=2′b00 If upper half word result >= 0 then GE[3:2]=2′b11 else GE[3:2]=2′b00
UADD16	If lower half word result >= 0x10000 then GE[1:0]=2′b11 else GE[1:0]= 2′b00 If upper half word result >= 0x10000 then GE[3:2]=2′b11 else GE[3:2]= 2′b00
SADD8, SSUB8, USUB8	If byte 0 result >= 0 then GE[0]=1′b1 else GE[0]=1′b0 If byte 1 result >= 0 then GE[1]=1′b1 else GE[1]=1′b0 If byte 2 result >= 0 then GE[6]=1′b1 else GE[6]=1′b0 If byte 3 result >= 0 then GE[8]=1′b1 else GE[8]=1′b0
UADD8	If byte 0 result >= 0x100 then GE[0]=1′b1 else GE[0]=1′b0 If byte 1 result >= 0x100 then GE[1]=1′b1 else GE[1]=1′b0 If byte 2 result >= 0x100 then GE[6]=1′b1 else GE[6]=1′b0 If byte 3 result >=0x100 then GE[8]=1′b1 else GE[8]=1′b0
UASX	If lower half word result >= 0 then GE[1:0]=2′b11 else GE[1:0]=2′b00 If upper half word result >= 0x10000 then GE[3:2]=2′b11 else GE[3:2]= 2′b00
USAX	If lower half word result >= 0x10000 then GE[1:0]=2′b11 else GE[1:0]= 2′b00 If upper half word result >= 0x0 then GE[3:2]=2′b11 else GE[3:2]=2′b00

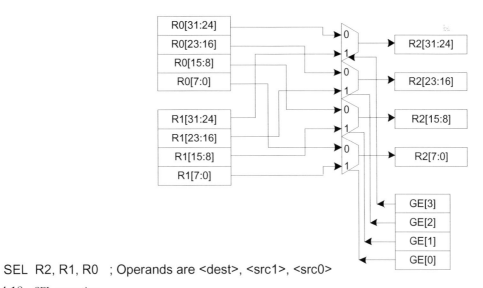

SEL R2, R1, R0   ; Operands are <dest>, <src1>, <src0>

FIG. 4.18 SEL operation.

The other registers are shared between Secure and Non-secure states. If the TrustZone security extension is not implemented, the programmer's model of Armv8-M is very similar to the previous generation of Cortex-M processors; except that the Cortex-M33 processor has additional Non-secure stack limit registers that are not available in the Armv7-M processors.

4.3 Memory system

The Cortex-M23 and Cortex-M33 processors have the following memory system features:

- 4GB linear address space—With 32-bit addressing, the Arm Cortex-M processors can access up to 4GB of memory space. While many embedded systems do not need more than 1MB of memory, the 32-bit addressing capability ensures there are future upgrade and expansion possibilities. The Cortex-M23 and Cortex-M33 processors provide 32-bit buses using a generic bus protocol called AMBA® 5 AHB. The bus interfaces on the Cortex-M processors allows connections to 32/16/8-bit memory devices though the use of suitable memory interface controllers.
- An architecturally defined memory map—the 4GB memory space is divided into a number of regions for various predefined memory and peripheral usage scenarios. This allows the processor design to be optimized for performance and to simplify the initialization process. For example, the Cortex-M33 processor has two bus interfaces to allow simultaneous access to the CODE region (for program code fetches) and to either the SRAM or the Peripheral region (for data operations).
- Support for little endian and big-endian memory systems—The Cortex-M23 and Cortex-M33 processors work with either the little endian or big-endian memory systems. In practice, a microcontroller product is normally designed with just one endian configuration.
- Memory Protection Unit(s) (Optional)—The MPU is a programmable unit to define access permissions for various memory regions. The MPU in the Cortex-M23 and Cortex-M33 processor supports 16 programmable regions and can be used with an embedded OS to provide a robust system.
- Unaligned transfer support—all processors supporting Armv8-M Mainline architecture (including the Cortex-M33 processor) support unaligned data transfers.
- Optional TrustZone® security support—when the system has implemented the TrustZone security extension, the memory system is divided into Secure memory spaces (protected) and Non-secure memory spaces (for normal applications).

The bus interfaces on the Cortex-M processors are designed to be generic and can be connected to different types and sizes of memories via different memory controllers. The memory systems in microcontrollers often contain two or more types of memories. For example, flash memory for program code, static RAM (SRAM) for data and, in some instances, Electrical Erasable Read Only Memory (EEPROM) for configuration data. In most cases, these memories are on-chip and the actual memory interface details are transparent to software developers. As a result, software developers only need to know:

- the address and the size of the program memory,
- the address and the size of the SRAM, and

• how the program memory and SRAM are partitioned in the Secure and Non-secure memory regions (only applies if the TrustZone security extension is implemented).

With two exceptions, the memory features in the Cortex-M3 and the Cortex-M4 processors are available on the Cortex-M33 processor. The two exceptions are:

• Bit band access—The optional bit band feature in the Cortex-M3 and Cortex-M4 processors define two 1MB regions in the memory space to be bit addressable via two-bit band alias regions. The address remapping process of the bit band access can potentially conflict with the TrustZone security arrangements (if the security attributes of the two addresses are setup differently) and cannot therefore be included.
• Write buffer—The Cortex-M3 and Cortex-M4 processors have a single entry write buffer and this is not included in the Cortex-M33 processor. However, potentially a write buffer could be present in a Cortex-M23/M33 based system in bus interconnect components such as bus bridges.

On the other hand, the bus interface of the Cortex-M33 processor overcomes a limitation factor of the Cortex-M3 and Cortex-M4 processors: there is no performance penalty when executing code with the system AHB (address 0x20000000 and above). Whereas, in the Cortex-M3/M4 processors (address 0x20000000 and above) there is a register stage which causes a delay cycle for each instruction fetch.

All of the key memory system features of the Cortex-M0 and Cortex-M0+ processors are available in the Cortex-M23 processor.

4.3.1 Memory map

By default, the 4GB address space of Cortex-M processors is partitioned into a number of memory regions, as shown in Fig. 4.21. The partitioning is based on typical usage so that different areas are primarily designed to be used for:

• Program code access (e.g., the CODE region)
• Data access (e.g., the SRAM region)
• Peripherals (e.g., the Peripheral region)
• The processor's internal control and debug components (e.g., the Interrupt controller). This is located in the Private Peripheral Bus address range, as shown in Fig. 4.19.

The architecture enables a high level of flexibility by allowing most memory regions to be used for other purposes. For example, programs can be executed from the CODE, SRAM, and RAM regions. A microcontroller can also integrate SRAM blocks into most regions, including the CODE region.

Most of the default memory map can be overridden by configuring the Memory Protection Unit (MPU). More information on this is covered in Chapter 12.

Because the Cortex-M33 processor has a Harvard bus architecture, instruction fetches and data access can be carried out simultaneously over two separate bus interfaces. As mentioned in Chapter 3, Section 3.5, it has a unified memory view (i.e., instruction and data access share the same 4GB address space). The CODE bus interface covers the CODE region (address 0x00000000 to 0x1FFFFFFF) and the SYSTEM bus interface covers the rest of the address space

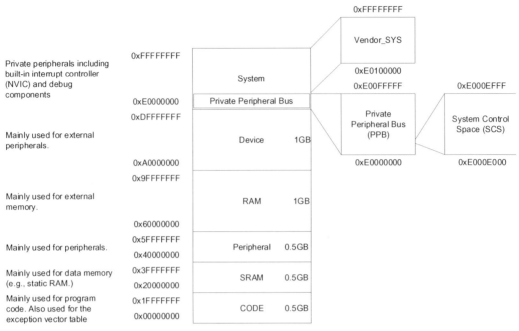

FIG. 4.19 Default memory map of a Cortex-M processor.

(0x20000000 to 0xFFFFFFFF), but not the Private Peripheral Bus (PPB) address range (0xE0000000 to 0xE00FFFFF).

The architecture allocates 512MB of address space for the storage of program codes, 512MB for SRAM and another 512MB for peripherals. In practice, most microcontroller devices only use a small portion of these in each of those regions. Some of the regions can be unused. At the same time, if a Cortex-M processor is being used as a subsystem in a complex SoC with a much larger main memory space, it is also possible to utilize other address regions for accessing the main memory system. Different microcontrollers have different memory sizes and peripheral address locations. This information is usually outlined in user manual or datasheets from microcontroller vendors.

At high level, the memory map arrangements (e.g., the definition of regions, and the addresses of internal blocks on the PPB address range) are identical between all of the Cortex-M processors. The PPB address space hosts the registers for the Nested Vectored Interrupt Controller (NVIC), the processor's configuration registers, as well as the registers for the debug components. It is the same across all Cortex-M devices. This makes it easier to port software from one Cortex-M device to another, allowing better software reusability. It also makes it easier for tool vendors because the debug components have a consistent base address.

4.3.2 Partitioning of address spaces within TrustZone

When a Cortex-M23 or Cortex-M33 processor implements the TrustZone security technology the 4GB is divided into:

- Secure addresses—accessible by Secure software only. Part of the Secure address space can also be defined as Non-Secure Callable (NSC), which allows Non-secure software to call Secure APIs.
- Non-secure addresses—accessible by both Secure and Non-secure software.
- Exempted addresses—These are address regions that are exempted from Security checking. Both Secure and Non-secure software can access Exempted regions. Unlike the Non-secure address(es), the Exempted region(s) setting is enforced even before the processor exits from reset and, typically, is used by debug components.

A comparison of the three address types as detailed above is shown in Table 4.11.

In a TrustZone based microcontroller design, the system contains Secure and Non-secure program spaces, data spaces and peripheral spaces. As a result, the memory regions in the default memory map, as shown in Fig. 4.19, is then further divided into Secure and Non-secure sections. An example of such partitioning is shown in Fig. 4.20.

The memory map shown in Fig. 4.20 is an example which is outlined in a document called "Trusted Based System Architecture for Armv8-M"; a guideline document for chip designers so they can create secure devices. It is possible for chip designers to define the security partitioning differently. The use of address bit 28 for partitioning is commonly used as it gives the largest continuous address space for each Secure and Non-secure region within each region in the default memory map. Another advantage is that the hardware design for the Implementation Defined Attribution Unit (IDAU) for address partitioning is very easy to do.

As mentioned in Chapter 3 Section 3.5, the partitioning of the address space is handled by the Security Attribution Unit (SAU) and the Implementation Defined Attribution Unit (IDAU). The SAU can contain up to 8 programmable regions, and the IDAU (typically a

TABLE 4.11 Address types based on the TrustZone security extension.

Address type	Accessibility	Usage(s)	Bus level security attribute
Secure	Accessible by Secure software only	Secure program, secure data and secure peripherals	Secure
Non-secure Callable (NSC)	Accessible by Secure software only. It also allows Non-secure software to call Secure API entry points in the NSC.	Entry points for Secure API	Secure
Non-secure	Accessible by Secure and Non-secure software.	General program, data and peripherals	Non-secure (even when accessed by Secure software)
Exempted	Accessible by Secure and Non-secure software.	Processor's internal peripherals and debug components.	Based on the current security state of the processor

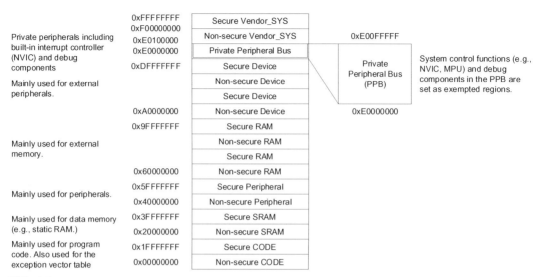

FIG. 4.20 Secure and Non-secure partitioning of the default memory map.

hardware-based address lookup component) can support up to 256 regions. Potentially, the IDAU could contain limited programmability in some devices. The IDAU, typically, is used to define the default security partitioning and the SAU is used by Secure privileged software to, optionally, override some of the IDAU's security region definitions.

Further information about address partitioning, the SAU and the IDAU is covered in Chapters 7 and 18.

4.3.3 System control space (SCS) and system control block (SCB)

As shown in Fig. 4.19, the processor's memory space contains a SCS. This address range contains memory mapped registers for:

- The NVIC
- The MPU
- The SysTick
- A group of system control registers called System Control Block (SCB)

The SCB contains various registers for:

- Controlling processor configurations (e.g., low power modes)
- Providing fault status information (fault status registers)
- Vector table relocation (VTOR)

The SCS address range starts from address 0xE000E000 to 0xE000EFFF. If the TrustZone security extension is implemented, a number of registers (e.g., the MPU and the SysTick) could be banked between security states. In each security state the software accesses its own bank of SCS registers in the SCS address space. Secure software can also access

Non-secure SCS registers using the Non-secure alias of SCS, which is in the range 0xE002E000 to 0xE002EFFF.

Further information about the SCB registers is covered in Chapter 10.

4.3.4 Stack memory

Just like most processor architectures, the Cortex-M processors need a portion of read-write memory, allocated as a stack memory, to operate. Arm Cortex-M processors have dedicated stack pointers (R13) hardware for stack operations. Stack is a kind of memory usage mechanism that allows a portion of memory to be used as a Last-In-First-Out data storage buffer. Arm processors use the main memory address space for stack memory operations and have a PUSH instruction to store data in the stack and a POP instruction to retrieve it. The current selected stack pointer is automatically adjusted for each PUSH and POP operation.

Stack can be used for:

- Temporary storage of original data when a function being executed needs to use registers (in the register bank) for data processing. The values can be restored at the end of the function so the program that called the function will not lose its data.
- Passing information to functions or subroutines.
- Storage of local variables.
- Holding processor status and register values when handling exceptions such as an interrupt.

Cortex-M processors use a stack memory model called "full-descending stack". When the processor is started, the value of the SP (Stack Pointer) is set to the address right after the reserved stack memory space has ended. For each PUSH operation, the processor first decrements the SP, then stores the value to the memory location pointed to by the SP. During operations, the SP points to the memory location where the last stack push data is placed (Fig. 4.21).

In a POP operation:

- The data stored in the memory location pointed to by the SP is read by the processor.
- the value of the SP is then automatically incremented by the processor.

The most common use for PUSH and POP instructions are to save the contents of register banks when a function/subroutine call is made. At the beginning of the function call, the contents of some of the registers can be saved to the stack using a PUSH instruction, and then restored to their original values at the end of the function using a POP instruction. For example, in Fig. 4.22 a simple function/subroutine named "function1" is called from the main program. Since "function1" needs to use and modify R4, R5, and R6 for data processing, and these registers hold values that the main program needs later, they are saved to the stack using PUSH, and then restored using POP at the end of "function1". In this way, the program code that called the function will not lose any data and can continue to execute. Note, for each PUSH (store to memory) operation there must be a corresponding POP (read from memory); and the address of the POP should match that of the PUSH operation.

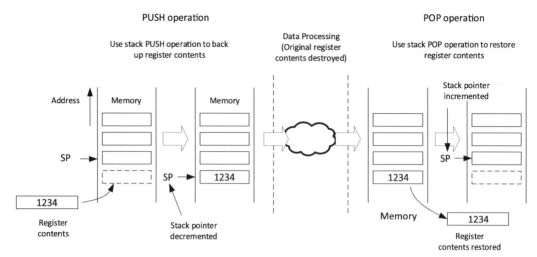

FIG. 4.21   Stack PUSH and POP.

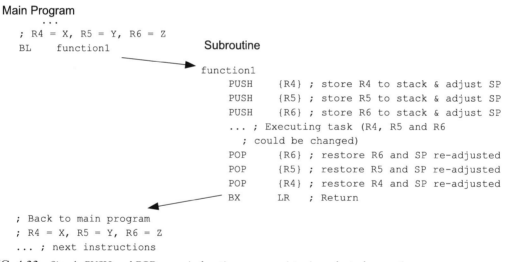

FIG. 4.22   Simple PUSH and POP usage in functions—one register in each stack operation.

Each PUSH and POP instruction can transfer multiple data to/from the stack memory. This is shown in Fig. 4.23. Since the registers in the register bank are 32 bits, each stack PUSH and stack POP operation transfers at least 1 word (4 bytes) of data. The stack addresses are always aligned to 4-byte boundaries and the lowest two bits of the SP are always zero.

You can also combine return with a POP operation. This is achieved by first pushing the value of LR (R14) to the stack memory, and popping it back to PC (R15) at the end of the subroutine/function, as shown in Fig. 4.24.

Main Program

```
        . . .
   ; R4 = X, R5 = Y, R6 = Z        Subroutine
   BL     function1
                                    function1
                                        PUSH     {R4-R6} ; Store R4, R5, R6 to stack
                                        ... ; Executing task (R4, R5 and R6
                                          ; could be changed)
                                        POP      {R4-R6} ; restore R4, R4, R6
                                        BX       LR   ; Return

   ; Back to main program
   ; R4 = X, R5 = Y, R6 = Z
   ... ; next instructions
```

FIG. 4.23   Simple PUSH and POP usage in functions—multiple registers in each stack operation.

Main Program

```
        . . .
   ; R4 = X, R5 = Y, R6 = Z        Subroutine
   BL     function1
                                    function1
                                        PUSH     {R4-R6, LR} ; Save registers
                                                            ; including link register
                                        ... ; Executing task (R4, R5 and R6
                                          ; could be changed)
                                        POP      {R4-R6, PC} ; Restore registers and
                                                            ; return
   ; Back to main program
   ; R4 = X, R5 = Y, R6 = Z
   ... ; next instructions
```

FIG. 4.24   Combining stack POP and a function return.

If the TrustZone security extension is not implemented, then physically there are two stack pointers in the Cortex-M processors. They are the:

- Main Stack Pointer (MSP)—This is the default stack pointer used after reset, and is used for all exception handlers.
- Process Stack Pointer (PSP)—This is an alternative stack pointer that can only be used in Thread mode. It is usually used for application tasks in embedded systems running an embedded operating system (OS).

If the TrustZone security extension is implemented there are four stack pointers. These are:

- Secure MSP (MSP_S)
- Secure PSP (PSP_S)
- Non-secure MSP (MSP_NS)
- Non-secure PSP (PSP_NS)

Secure software uses the Secure stack pointers (MSP_S and PSP_S), and Non-secure software uses the Non-secure stack pointers (MSP_NS and PSP_NS). The stack pointers must be initialized to use the correct address space based on the security partitioning of the memory map.

As mentioned in "CONTROL register" section (Section 4.2.2.3) and Table 4.4, the SPSEL bit (bit 1) of the CONTROL register is used for selecting between MSP and PSP in Thread mode:

- If SPSEL is 0, Thread mode uses the MSP for stack operations.
- If SPSEL is 1, Thread mode uses the PSP for stack operations.

Please note, the SPSEL bit is banked between security states, so Secure and Non-secure software can have different settings for the selection of the stack pointer in thread mode. Also, the values of the SPSEL bits could be automatically updated when returning from exceptions.

As well as saving registers during function calls, the stack memory is also used for saving certain registers during exception events. When an exception (e.g., a peripheral interrupt) takes place some of the processor's registers are automatically saved in the current selected stack (the SP used is the currently selected SP before the exception takes place). Those saved values are restored automatically in exception returns.

For simple systems without TrustZone, a minimal application could use just the MSP for all operations by keeping the SPSEL bit to 0. This is shown in Fig. 4.25. After an interrupt event is triggered, the processor first pushes a number of registers into the stack before entering the Interrupt Service Routine (ISR). This register state saving operation is called "Stacking". At the end of the ISR, these registers are restored to the register bank, an operation is called "Unstacking".

If an operating system is used, the stacks for each of the application threads would normally be separated from each other. The Process Stack Pointer (PSP) is therefore used for the application threads to allow easier context switching without affecting the stacks used by the privileged codes. With this arrangement, privileged codes, such as exception handlers, use the MSP, similar to the previous example (Fig. 4.25). As the thread and handler modes use different stack pointers, the SP selection switches at exception entries and exception exits. This switching is shown in Fig. 4.26. Note, automatic "Stacking" and "Unstacking" operations

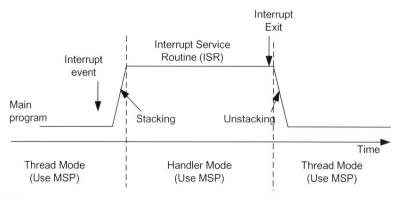

FIG. 4.25   SPSEL set to 0—Both thread and handler modes use the MSP.

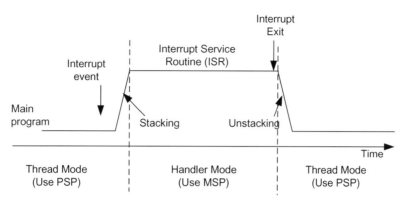

FIG. 4.26 SPSEL set to 1—Thread level codes use the PSP and the handlers use the MSP.

use the PSP because it is the currently selected SP before the exception. The separation of the stacks can prevent a stack corruption or error in an application task from damaging the stack used by the OS. It also simplifies the OS design and hence allows faster context switching.

For systems with the TrustZone security extension implemented, Secure and Non-secure software manage their corresponding SPSEL bits in the CONTROL register, and, thus, in thread mode it is possible for the processor to switch between different SPSEL settings when there are function calls between security states. In handler mode, either MSP_S or MSP_NS would be used, depending on the security domain of the exception/interrupt.

4.3.5 Setting up and accessing of stack pointers and stack limit registers

After the processor powers up:

- If the TrustZone is not implemented, the processor automatically initializes the MSP by reading the vector table.
- If the TrustZone is implemented, the processor automatically initializes the MSP_S by reading the Secure vector table.

More information on the vector table is covered in Section 8.6. Other stack pointers not initialized by the reset sequence have to be initialized by software. This includes the situation where Secure software needs to launch a Non-secure application after finishing its security initialization (The Non-secure MSP (MSP_NS) must be initialized by Secure software before starting the Non-secure application).

Although just one of the SPs is selected at a time (when using SP or R13 to access it), it is possible to specify read/write directly to the MSP and PSP, providing that the processor is in privileged state. If the processor is in Secure privileged state, the software can also access the Non-secure stack pointers. The CMSIS-CORE software framework provides a number of functions for stack pointer access (Table 4.12).

TABLE 4.12 CMSIS-CORE functions for stack pointer access.

CMSIS-CORE function	Usage	Applicable security state
__get_MSP(void)	Gets value of the MSP in the current security state	S/NS
__get_PSP(void)	Gets value of the PSP in the current security state	S/NS
__set_MSP(uint32_t topofstack)	Sets value of the MSP in the current security state	S/NS
__set_PSP(uint32_t topofstack)	Sets value of the PSP in current the security state	S/NS
__TZ_get_MSP_NS (void)	Gets value of the MSP_NS	S
__TZ_get_PSP_NS (void)	Gets value of the PSP_NS	S
__TZ_get_SP_NS(void)	Gets value of the MSP_NS/PSP_NS (dependent upon which one is currently selected in the Non-secure world.)	S
__TZ_set_MSP_NS (uint32_t topofstack)	Sets value of the MSP_NS	S
__TZ_set_PSP_NS (uint32_t topofstack)	Sets value of the PSP_NS	S
__TZ_set_SP_NS (uint32_t topofstack)	Sets value of the MSP_NS/PSP_NS (dependent upon which one is currently selected in the Non-secure world.)	S

Similar to stack pointer access, a number of functions are defined in the CMSIS-CORE for accessing stack limit registers (Table 4.13).

When using assembly language programming, these functions can be carried out using MRS (move from special register to general register) and MSR (move from general register to special register) instructions.

In general, it is not recommended to change the value of a currently selected SP in C functions as part of the stack memory could be used for storing local variables or other data. Most application codes do not need to explicitly access the MSP and PSP. In the case of the passing of parameters in function calls, the compiler automatically handles the stack management and, thus, is totally transparent to application codes.

For software developers working on embedded OS designs, access to the MSP and the PSP is necessary in situations such as:

1. Context switching operations that require the direct manipulation of the PSP.
2. During the execution of an OS's API (MSP is used)—the API might need to read the data pushed into the stack (using a PSP) before the API is called (e.g., the pushed data would contain the registers' states before the execution of an SVC instruction—some of which could be the input parameters for the SVC function).

TABLE 4.13 CMSIS-CORE functions for stack limit registers access.

CMSIS-CORE function	Usage	Applicable security state
__get_MSPLIM(void)	Gets value of the MSPLIM in the current security state	S/NS
__get_PSPLIM(void)	Gets value of the PSPLIM in the current security state	S/NS
__set_MSPLIM(uint32_t limitofstack)	Sets value of the MSPLIM in the current security state	S/NS
__set_PSPLIM(uint32_t limitofstack)	Sets value of the PSPLIM in the current security state	S/NS
__TZ_get_MSPLIM_NS(void)	Gets value of the MSPLIM_NS	S
__TZ_get_PSPLIM_NS(void)	Gets value of the PSPLIM_NS	S
__TZ_set_MSPLIM_NS(uint32_t limitofstack)	Sets value of the MSPLIM_NS	S
__TZ_set_PSPLIM_NS(uint32_t limitofstack)	Sets value of the PSPLIM_NS	S

4.3.6 Memory protection unit (MPU)

The Memory Protection Unit (MPU) is optional in the Cortex-M23 and Cortex-M33 processors. Therefore, not all Cortex-M23 or Cortex-M33 microcontrollers have the MPU feature.

The MPU in the Cortex-M23 and Cortex-M33 processors are different from the ones in the Cortex-M0+, Cortex-M3, Cortex-M4 and Cortex-M7 processors in a number of ways:

- The MPU in the Cortex-M23 and Cortex-M33 processors support 0 (no MPU)/4/8/12 or 16 MPU regions. Whereas, in the Cortex-M0+/M3/M4 processors it supports0 or 8 regions, and in the Cortex-M7 processor it supports 0/8/16 regions.
- The programmer's model of the MPU in Armv8-M is different from that in the Armv6-M and Armv7-M architectures. This change gives better flexibility in the definitions of the MPU regions.
- If the TrustZone security extension is implemented, the Cortex-M23 and Cortex-M33 processors can have up to two MPUs—a Secure MPU and a Non-secure MPU. The number of supported MPU regions in these two MPUs could be different.

The MPU is programmable and the configuration of the MPU regions is managed by a number of memory mapped MPU registers. By default, the MPU(s) are disabled after reset. In simple applications, the MPU is not used and can be ignored. In embedded systems that require high reliability, the MPU can be used to protect memory regions by means of defining access permissions in privileged and unprivileged access states. For example, an embedded OS can define the access permission for each application thread. In other cases, the MPU is configured just to protect a certain memory region, for example, to make a memory range read only.

The MPU also defines memory attributes of the system, e.g., cacheability. If the system contains a system level cache then it might be essential to program the MPU to define the cacheability attribute of certain address spaces.

Further information about the MPU is covered in Chapter 12.

4.4 Exceptions and Interrupts

4.4.1 What are exceptions

Exceptions are events that cause changes to program flow. When it happens, the processor suspends the current executing task and executes a part of the program called the exception handler. After the execution of the exception handler is completed, the processor then resumes to the normal program execution. In Arm architecture, interrupts are one type of exception. Interrupts are usually generated from peripheral or external inputs, and in some cases can be triggered by software. The exception handlers for interrupts are also referred to as Interrupt Service Routines (ISR).

In Cortex-M processors, there are a number of exception sources (Fig. 4.27).

The exceptions are processed by the NVIC. The NVIC can handle a Non-Maskable Interrupt (NMI) request and a number of interrupt requests (IRQs). Usually IRQs are generated by on-chip peripherals or from external interrupt inputs though I/O ports. NMI could be used by a watchdog timer or brown out detector (a voltage monitoring unit that warns the processor when the supply voltage drops below a certain level). Inside the processor there is also a timer called SysTick (potentially two if the TrustZone security extension is implemented) which can be programmed to generate a periodic timer interrupt request. This can be used by an embedded OS for time keeping, or for a simple timing control in applications that do not require an OS.

The processor itself is also a source for exception events. These could be fault events which indicate system error conditions, or exceptions generated by software to support embedded OS operations. The exception types are listed in Table 4.14.

Each exception source has an exception number. Exception numbers 1–15 are classified as system exceptions, and exceptions 16 and above are for interrupts. The design of the NVIC in the Cortex-M23 supports up to 240 interrupt signals and the one in the Cortex-M33 supports up to 480. However, the number of interrupts is defined by chip designers and, in practice, the number of interrupt signals implemented in the design is often far less; and are typically in the

FIG. 4.27 Various exception sources in a Cortex-M processor.

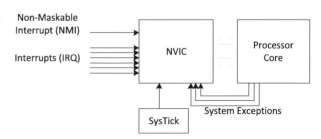

TABLE 4.14 Exception types.

Exception number	CMSIS-CORE interrupt number	Exception type	Priority	Function
1	NA	Reset	−4 (Highest)	Reset
2	−14	NMI	−2	Non-Maskable interrupt
3	−13	HardFault	−3 or −1	All classes of fault:triggered when the corresponding fault handler cannot be activated because it is currently disabled or is masked by exception masking.
4	−12	MemManage (Not available in Armv8-M baseline/Cortex-M23)	Settable	Memory Management fault:caused by MPU violation or an invalid access (such as an instruction fetch from a nonexecutable region)
5	−11	BusFault (Not available in Armv8-M baseline/Cortex-M23)	Settable	Error response received from the bus system:caused by an instruction prefetch abort or data access error
6	−10	UsageFault (Not available in Armv8-M baseline/Cortex-M23)	Settable	Usage Fault: typical causes are invalid instructions or invalid state transition attempts (such as trying to switch to ARM state in the Cortex-M23/M33)
7	−9	SecureFault (Not available in Armv8-M baseline/Cortex-M23)	Settable	Secure Fault: fault event caused by a security violation. Not available in Armv8-M Baseline or when the TrustZone security extension is not implemented.
8–10	−	−	−	Reserved
11	−5	SVC	Settable	Supervisor Call via SVC instruction
12	−4	Debug monitor	Settable	Debug monitor: for software-based debug (often not used) Not available in Armv8-M Baseline
13	−	−	−	Reserved
14	−2	PendSV	Settable	Pendable request for System Service
15	−1	SYSTICK	Settable	System Tick Timer
16–255	0–479 or 0–239	IRQ	Settable	IRQ input #0–479 for Cortex-M33 or IRQ input #0–239 for Cortex-M23

range of 16–100. With this configurability, the silicon size of the design can be reduced, which also reduces power consumption.

The exception number is reflected in various registers, including the IPSR, and is used to determine the exception vector addresses. Exception vectors are stored in a vector table, and the processor reads this table to determine the starting address of an exception handler during the exception entrance sequence. Note, exception number definitions are different from interrupt numbers in the CMSIS-CORE device driver library. In the CMSIS-CORE device driver library, interrupt numbers start from 0, and system exception numbers have negative values.

Unlike classic Arm processors, such as the Arm7^{TM}TDMI, there is no FIQ (Fast Interrupt) in Cortex-M processors. However, the interrupt latency of the Cortex-M23 and Cortex-M33 processors is very low, only 15 and 12 clock cycles, respectively, so the lack of an FIQ feature is not a problem.

Reset is a special kind of exception. When the processor exits from a reset it executes the reset handler in Thread mode (rather than Handler mode as in other exceptions). Also, the exception number in the IPSR is read as zero.

4.4.2 TrustZone and exceptions

If the TrustZone security extension is implemented:

- Each of the interrupts (exception types 16 and above) can be configured as Secure (default) or Non-secure. This is configurable at run time.
- Some of the system exceptions are banked between security states (e.g., SysTick, SVC, PendSV, HardFault (conditionally), MemManage Fault, UsageFault).
- Some of the system exceptions target the Secure state by default, but can be configured to target the Non-secure state by software (NMI, BusFault).
- The target security state of the Debug Monitor exception is defined by the debug authentication setting (see Chapter 16).
- The Secure Fault exception is available on the Armv8-M Mainline (e.g., the Cortex-M33 processor) and targets Secure state only.

4.4.3 Nested Vectored Interrupt Controller (NVIC)

The NVIC is a part of the Cortex$^®$-M processor. It is programmable and its registers are located in the SCS of the memory map (see Fig. 4.19). The NVIC handles the exceptions and interrupt configurations, prioritization and interrupt masking. The NVIC has the following features:

- Flexible exception and interrupt management
- Nested exception/interrupt support
- Vectored exception/interrupt entry
- Interrupt Masking

4.4.3.1 Flexible exception and interrupt management

Each interrupt (apart from the NMI) can be enabled or disabled and can have its pending status set or cleared by software. The NVIC handles various types of interrupt request signals:

- Pulsed interrupt request—the interrupt request is at least one clock cycle long. When the NVIC receives a pulse at its interrupt input the pending status is set and held until the interrupt is serviced.

- Level triggered interrupt request—the interrupt generating source (e.g., peripheral) holds the interrupt request signal at a high (active) level until the interrupt is serviced.

The signal level at the NVIC input is active high (1 = active). However, the actual external interrupt input on the microcontroller could be designed differently (i.e., active low (0 = active)). In this case, on-chip logic is used to convert the signal into active high so that the NVIC can accept the signal.

The interrupt management registers in the NVIC also define the priority levels of exceptions (for exceptions with programmable levels) and also allows, if the TrustZone security extension is implemented, each interrupt to be defined as Secure or Non-secure.

4.4.3.2 Nested exception/interrupt support

Each exception has a priority level. Some exceptions such as interrupts have programmable priority levels and some others (e.g., NMI) have a fixed priority level. When an exception occurs, the NVIC will compare the priority level of this exception to the processor's current level. If the new exception has a higher priority:

- The current running task will be suspended,
- Some of the registers will be stored on the stack memory, and
- The processor will start executing the exception handler of the new exception.

This process is called "preemption". When the higher priority exception handler is completed it is terminated with an exception return operation. The processor then automatically restores the registers from the stack and resumes the task that was previously executing. This mechanism allows nesting of exception services without any software overhead.

In a system with the TrustZone security extension, exception priority levels are shared between Secure and Non-secure exceptions. Therefore,

- If an interrupt is being served in one security state and another interrupt in the other security state with a higher priority level is triggered, the interrupt preemption can take place.
- If an interrupt is being served in one security state it blocks the all interrupts that have a lower or the same priority level, no matter whether those interrupts are configured as Secure or Non-secure.

4.4.3.3 Vectored exception/interrupt entry

When an exception occurs, the processor needs to locate the starting point of the corresponding exception handler. Traditionally, in Arm® processors, such as the Arm7TDMI®, software usually handles this step. The Cortex-M processors automatically locate the starting point of the exception handler from a vector table in the memory. As a result, the delay from the start of the exception to the execution of the exception handler is reduced.

For further information on the vector table topic, please refer to Section 4.4.5.

4.4.3.4 Interrupt masking

The NVIC in the Cortex-M23 and Cortex-M33 processors provide interrupt masking registers, for example, the PRIMASK special register. Setting the PRIMASK register disables all exceptions, excluding HardFault and NMI. This masking is useful for operations that should not be interrupted, such as time critical control tasks or real time multimedia codecs. For a Cortex-M33 based system, you can alternatively use the BASEPRI register to selectively mask exceptions or interrupts which are below a certain priority level.

If the TrustZone security extension is implemented, the interrupt masking registers are banked, and the interrupt masking behavior is based on the combined result of both Secure and Non-secure interrupt masks. Further information on this is covered in Chapter 9.

4.4.4 Interrupt management with CMSIS-CORE

The CMSIS-CORE provides a set of functions which makes it easy to access various interrupt control functions. The flexibility and capability of the NVIC also makes the Cortex-M processors very easy to use and provides a better system response by reducing the software overhead in interrupt processing. By simplifying the interrupt control functions, the memory size needed by the program is reduced.

Further information on this is covered in Chapter 9.

4.4.5 Vector tables

When an exception event takes place and is accepted by the processor core, the corresponding exception handler is executed. To determine the starting address of the exception handler, a vector table mechanism is used. The vector table is an array of 32-bit data inside the system memory, each representing the starting address of one exception type (Fig. 4.28). The vector table is relocatable and the base address of the vector table is controlled by a programmable register in the NVIC called the Vector Table Offset Register (VTOR).

After reset, the VTOR is reset to a value defined by the chip designer; this is different from previous Cortex-M0/M0+/M3/M4 processors where the vector table offset is set to address 0x0 after reset.

The vector address used to determine the starting address is:

Exception type $\times 4$ + VTOR

The bit 0 of the vector read from the vector table is then masked off for use as the ISR starting address.

For example, if the VTOR is reset to 0, then the calculations of the vector address for reset and NMI exceptions are as follow:

(1) When handling a Reset exception, because the reset is exception type 1, the address of the reset vector is therefore 1×4 (each vector is 4 bytes) + VTOR, which equals 0x00000004.
(2) When handling an NMI exception, the NMI vector (type 2) is located in $2 \times 4 +$ VTOR $= 0x00000008$.

The address offset 0x00000000 is used to store the starting value for the MSP.

The LSB of each exception vector indicates whether the exception is to be executed in Thumb state. Since the Cortex-M processors can support only Thumb instructions, the LSB of all the exception vectors should be set to 1.

Exception Type	CMSIS Interrupt Number	Address Offset	Vectors	
18 – 255 or 495	2 – 239 or 479	0x48 – 0x3FC/ 0x7BC	IRQ #2 - #239 or #479	Up to #239 in the Cortex-M23 processor and #479 in the Cortex-M33 processor
17	1	0x44	IRQ #1	
16	0	0x40	IRQ #0	
15	-1	0x3C	SysTick	
14	-2	0x38	PendSV	
NA	NA	0x34	Reserved	
12	-4	0x30	Debug Monitor	
11	-5	0x2C	SVC	
NA	NA	0x28	Reserved	
NA	NA	0x24	Reserved	Not available in the Cortex-M23 processor
NA	NA	0x20	Reserved	
7	-9	0x1C	SecureFault	
6	-10	0x18	Usage fault	
5	-11	0x14	Bus Fault	
4	-12	0x10	MemManage Fault	
3	-13	0x0C	HardFault	
2	-14	0x08	NMI	
1	NA	0x04	Reset	
NA	NA	0x00	Initial value of MSP	

FIG. 4.28 Vector table layout (note: The least significant bit (LSB) of the exception vectors should be set to 1).

In the Cortex-M23 processor, the VTOR is optional to allow chip designers to minimize the silicon area by omitting the VTOR. If the VTOR register is not implemented, it is fixed to a value defined by the chip designer(s) and cannot be changed. The vector table can, therefore, still be nonzero even when the VTOR is not implemented. This is different from the behavior of the Cortex-M0+ processor where the VTOR is fixed to 0 if the VTOR is not implemented.

If the TrustZone security extension is implemented, there two vector tables. The vector table for Secure exceptions should be placed in a Secure address range and the vector table for the Non-secure exceptions in a Non-secure address range. The VTOR register is banked into the VTOR_S (Secure VTOR) and the VTOR_NS (Non-secure).

4.4.6 Fault handling

Several exceptions listed in Table 4.14 are fault handling exceptions. Fault exceptions are triggered when the processor detects an error such as an execution of an undefined instruction, or when the bus system returns an error response to a memory access. The fault exception mechanism (Fig. 4.29) allows errors to be detected quickly and allows the system to respond to an error condition without waiting for a watchdog timer to kick in.

There are some differences between the Armv8-M Baseline and Mainline subprofiles in fault handling features. These are:

• BusFault, UsageFault, MemManage Fault, and SecureFault exceptions are available in Armv8-M Mainline, but not in Armv8-M Baseline (i.e., Cortex-M23 processor).

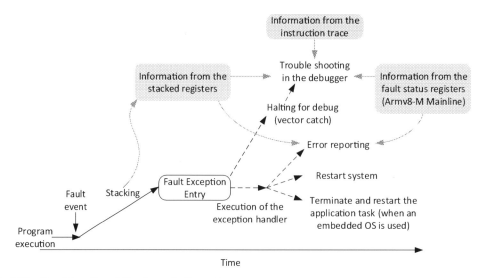

FIG. 4.29   Possible actions following a fault event.

- Armv8-M Baseline does not have fault status registers which allows software to determine the class of the fault.

In Armv8-M Baseline (the Cortex-M23 processor), all fault events trigger the HardFault exception. If the TrustZone security extension is implemented, then the Secure version of the HardFault handler is executed by default (the vector is fetched from the Secure vector table). If the Secure world is not used, the Secure boot code can, optionally, configure the HardFault and the NMI to target the Non-secure state (refer to Section 9.3.4 for more information about the AIRCR.BFHFNMINS register) by default. However, a security violation will, in this situation, trigger a Secure HardFault.

In Armv8-M Mainline architecture (e.g., the Cortex-M33 processor), by default all fault events trigger the HardFault exception. This is because the Bus Fault, Usage Fault, Memory Management Fault and Secure Fault are disabled by default and therefore escalate to HardFault. If these configurable fault exceptions are enabled (these exceptions can, individually, be enabled by software), then they could be triggered by specific classes of fault events. If they are, the corresponding fault handlers can then potentially utilize the fault status registers to determine the exact type of fault, and, if possible, carry out remedial action(s). Similar to Armv8-M Baseline, it is possible to configure the HardFault (as well as the BusFault) to target, except for security violations, the Non-secure state.

In both Armv8-M Mainline and Baseline, HardFault exceptions are always enabled.

Fault exceptions are useful for debugging software issues. When developing software, it is possible to setup the debug tool to configure the processor so that it halts automatically at fault events (this feature is called vector catch, see Section 16.2.5). When such halting takes place, software developers can then use the debugger to analyses the issue (e.g., using the exception stack tracing to locate a faulting code sequence).

It is possible to setup the fault handler in such a way that error information can be reported to the user or to another system. In the case of the Cortex-M33 processor (Armv8-M Mainline), the reporting mechanism could include hints on the error sources by extracting information from the fault status registers. Debug tools could also utilize such information to help with the trouble shooting.

4.5 Debug

As software gets more complex, debug features are becoming more and more important in modern processor architectures. Although quite a compact processor design, the Cortex-M23 and Cortex-M33 processors include a comprehensive list of debugging features: such as program execution controls, including halting and stepping, instruction breakpoints, data watch points, registers and memory accesses, profiling, and traces.

There are two types of interface provided in the Cortex-M processors to help developers to debug and analyze software operations. They are debug and trace.

The debug interface allows a debug adaptor to connect to a Cortex-M based microcontroller to control the debug features and to access the memory space on the chip. The Cortex-M processor supports:

- The traditional JTAG protocol, which uses either four or five pins, or
- A 2-pin protocol called Serial Wire Debug (SWD). The Serial Wire debug protocol was developed by Arm and can handle with just two pins, without any loss of debug performance, the same debug features that are in the JTAG protocol.

In some devices, one debug protocol is implemented, and in others two. If both protocols are implemented, dynamic switching of protocols could be possible through a special signal sequence. There are many debug adaptors, including commercial ones such as the ULINK™ Plus or ULINK Pro products from Keil®, that support both protocols. The two protocols can coexist on the same connector, with the JTAG TCK shared with the Serial Wire clock and with the JTAG TMS shared with the Serial Wire Data. The Serial Wire Data pin is bidirectional when used in SWD protocol mode (Fig. 4.30). Both protocols are widely supported by different debug adaptors from various companies.

The trace interface is used to collect information from the processor during run-time. This can be data values, exception events and profiling information. If the Embedded Trace Macrocell (ETM) is used, it can even provide complete details of the program's execution. Two type of trace interface are supported: a single pin protocol called Serial Wire Output (SWO) and a multi-pin protocol called Trace Port (Fig. 4.31).

The Serial Wire Output (SWO) is a low-cost trace solution which has a lower trace data bandwidth than the parallel trace port. However, the bandwidth is still enough to capture the selective data trace, event trace and basic profiling- which are basic trace features collectively known as the Serial Wire Viewer (SWV). The output signal, which is called SWO, is often shared with the JTAG TDO pin, a fact which means you only need one standard JTAG/SWD connector for both debug and trace. (Obviously the trace data can only be captured when the two pin SWD protocol is used for debugging.)

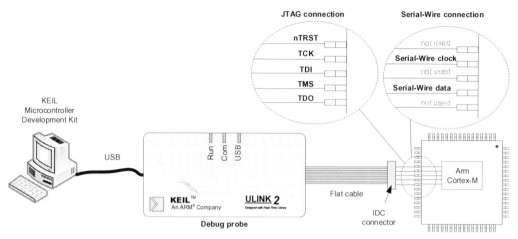

FIG. 4.30   Debug connection.

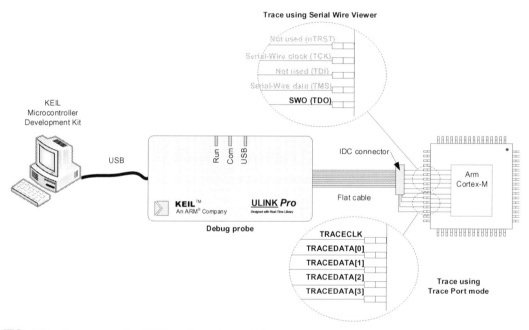

FIG. 4.31   Trace connection (SWO or Trace Port mode).

The Trace Port mode requires one clock pin and multiple data pins. The number of data pins used is configurable, and in most cases the Cortex-M23 and Cortex-M33 microcontrollers support a maximum of four data pins (a total of five pins when one includes the trace clock). The Trace Port mode supports a much higher trace bandwidth than the SWO. You can, if needed, also use the Trace Port mode with fewer pins. For example, when some of the Trace

Data pins are multiplexed with I/O functions and you need to use some of those I/O pins for your application.

The high trace data bandwidth of the Trace Port model allows:

- real-time recording of program execution information (program trace), and
- other trace information you can collect using the SWV.

The real-time program trace requires a companion component called the Embedded Trace Macrocell (ETM) inside the chip. This is an optional component for the Cortex-M23 and Cortex-M33 processors. Some of the Cortex-M23 and Cortex-M33 microcontrollers do not have an ETM and therefore do not provide the real time program/instruction trace feature. An alternative instruction trace solution, called Micro Trace Buffer (MTB), is also available for the Cortex-M23 and the Cortex-M33 processors. This has a limited trace history and only needs a debug connection to retrieve the instruction trace data.

To capture real-time trace data, you can use a low-cost debug adaptor such as the Keil ULINK-Plus or Segger J-Link, which can capture data through the SWO interface. Or, you can use advanced products such as the Keil ULINK Pro or Segger J-Trace to capture trace data in trace port mode.

When compared to the previous generations of Cortex-M processors, the Cortex-M23 and Cortex-M33 processors have a number of debug and trace feature enhancements. For example, both ETM and MTB instruction trace are supported in both of these processors (the previous processors only supported one of those solutions). In addition, the debug architecture has been extended for TrustZone debug authentication support, meaning the chip design can separately control debug accessibility of Secure and Non-secure software.

There are a number of other debug components inside the Cortex-M23 and Cortex-M33 processors. For example, the Instrumentation Trace Macrocell (ITM) in the Cortex-M33 processor allows program code running on the microcontroller to generate data to be output through the trace interface. The data can then be displayed on a debugger window. Further information about debug features is covered in Chapter 16. Appendix A of this book also provides information about standard debug connectors used by various debug adaptors.

4.6 Reset and reset sequence

In most Cortex®-M microcontrollers, there can be several types of reset. From a processor's architectural point of view there are at least two types:

- Power on reset—resets everything in the microcontroller. This includes the processor and its debug support components and peripherals.
- System reset—resets just the processor and peripherals, but not the debug support component of the processor.

In normal operations the processor system receives a power-on reset when the system is first powered up. Potentially, the power-on reset is also applied when the device is turned on after it has been turned off, but it is also possible that the device only receives a system reset in such a scenario. This is dependent upon the design of the chip as well as the design of the circuit board in the product (e.g., one of the factors is whether the chip is actually discon-nected from power when the device is turned "off", or is just in a standby state).

During a system debug or processor reset operation, the debug components in the Cortex-M23 or Cortex-M33 processor are not reset so that the connection between the debug host (i.e., the debugger software running on the computer) and the microcontroller can be maintained. To reset the processor during a debug session, the debug host, in most cases (this might be configurable in the debug tool), makes use of the Application Interrupt and Reset Control Register (AIRCR) in the System Control Block (SCB). This is covered in Section 10.5.3.

The duration of Power-on-reset and System reset depends on the microcontroller design. In some instances, the reset lasts a number of milliseconds as the reset controller needs to wait for a clock source, such as a crystal oscillator, to stabilize.

After a power-on/system reset and before the processor starts executing program, a Cortex-M processor reads the first two words from the vector table (covered in Section 4.4.5) in the memory (Fig. 4.32). The first word of the vector table is the initial value for the Main Stack Pointer (MSP) and the second word is the starting address of the reset han-dler. After these two words are read, the processor starts executing the reset handler.

In a Cortex-M23/Cortex-M33 processor system without the TrustZone security extension, the processor starts in a Non-secure state and the Non-secure vector table (the Secure vector table does not exist in this case) is used for the reset sequence.

In a Cortex-M23/Cortex-M33 processor system with the TrustZone security extension, the processor starts in a Secure state and the Secure vector table is used for the reset sequence. The Non-secure Main Stack Pointer (MSP_NS) is, in this instance, initialized by the Secure software.

The setup of the MSP is necessary because some exceptions, such as the NMI or HardFault handler, could potentially occur shortly after the reset. The stack memory and the MSP will then be needed for the stacking process which is carried out as part of the exception handling.

Note, in most C development environments the C start up code will also update the value of the MSP before entering the main program "main()". The two-step stack initialization method allows a microcontroller device to place the stack in an internal RAM at startup and then update the MSP to place the stack in the external memory later on. For example, if the external memory controller needs an initialization sequence the microcontroller cannot place the stack in the external memory at start up. In this scenario, it must first boot up with the stack placed in an internal SRAM, then initialize the external memory controller in the reset handler and finally execute the C startup code—which then sets up the stack memory to the external memory.

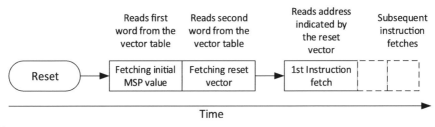

FIG. 4.32   Reset sequence.

The stack pointer initialization behavior is different from that in classic Arm processors, such as the Arm7TDMI®. In those processors, the processor, upon reset, executes instructions from the beginning of the memory (address zero), and the software then initializes the stack pointers. In addition, the vector tables in these processors hold instruction code rather than address values.

Because the stack operations in the Cortex-M23 and Cortex-M33 processors are based on full descending stack (the SP's value decrements before storing the data during a stack PUSH operation), the initial SP value should be set to the first address location after the last allocated address of the stack memory. For example, if you have a stack memory range from 0x20007C00 to 0x20007FFF (1 K bytes), the initial stack value should be set to 0x20008000, as shown in Fig. 4.33.

As explained in Section 4.4.5, the LSB of the exception vectors should be set to 1 to indicate the Thumb state. For that reason, the example in Fig. 4.33 has 0x101 in the reset vector, whereas the boot code starts at address 0x100. After the reset vector is fetched, the Cortex-M processor then starts to execute the program from the reset vector address and begins normal operations.

Normally, the development tool chain automatically sets the LSB of the exception vectors to 1 (the linker should recognize the address is pointing to the Thumb code and will, therefore,

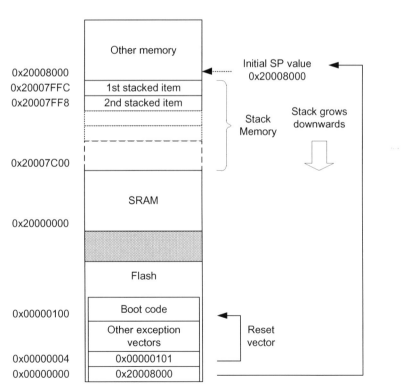

FIG. 4.33   Initial Stack Pointer value and initial Program Counter value example (it is assumed that the vector table is placed in address zero).

set the LSB of the addresses to 1). Various software development tools have different ways of specifying the starting stack pointer value and stack memory allocation. For more information on this topic it is best to look at project examples provided with the development tools.

4.7 Other related architecture information

In addition to the Armv8-M architecture reference manual, there are additional architecture specifications that help define the various aspects of the Cortex-M23 and Cortex-M33 processors. For example, a Cortex-M23 processor system is based on several architectures as shown in Fig. 4.34.

Similarly, the Cortex-M33 processor is based on a range of architecture specifications. The only difference between the Cortex-M23 and the Cortex-M33 processors is:

- the version of the ETM architecture used (the ETM in the Cortex-M33 processor is based on ETMv4.2 and the Cortex-M23 ETM is based on ETMv3.5), and
- the Cortex-M33 processor has the addition of a Private Peripheral Bus (PPB), which is based on the AMBA 4 APB specification.

The documents listed in Figs. 4.34 and 4.35 are mostly targeted at chip designers and development tool vendors. Most software developers using Cortex-M23/M33 based devices will not, therefore, need to read all of those aforementioned documents. For example, the

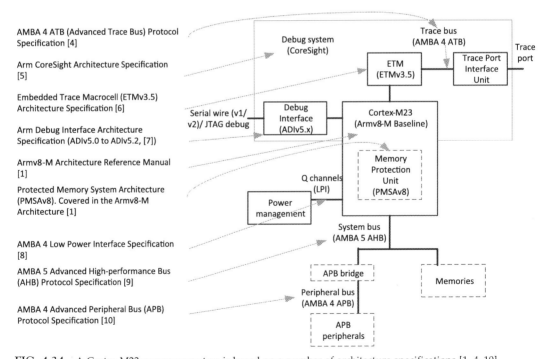

FIG. 4.34 A Cortex-M23 processor system is based on a number of architecture specifications [1, 4–10].

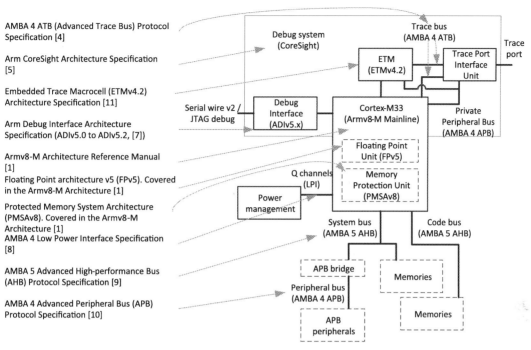

AMBA 4 ATB (Advanced Trace Bus) Protocol
Specification [4]

Arm CoreSight Architecture Specification
[5]

Embedded Trace Macrocell (ETMv4.2)
Architecture Specification [11]

Arm Debug Interface Architecture
Specification (ADIv5.0 to ADIv5.2, [7])

Armv8-M Architecture Reference Manual
[1]
Floating Point architecture v5 (FPv5). Covered
in the Armv8-M Architecture [1]

Protected Memory System Architecture
(PMSAv8). Covered in the Armv8-M
Architecture [1]
AMBA 4 Low Power Interface Specification
[8]

AMBA 5 Advanced High-performance Bus
(AHB) Protocol Specification [9]

AMBA 4 Advanced Peripheral Bus (APB)
Protocol Specification [10]

FIG. 4.35   Architectures related to a Cortex-M33 processor system [1, 4, 5, 7–11].

bus protocol specifications are only useful for chip designers and some of the other architecture specifications (e.g., ETM, ADI, CoreSight®) are only needed by the debug tool vendors. The rest of this book, therefore, will only focus on topics that are relevant to software developers.

References

[1] Armv8-M   Architecture   Reference   Manual.   https://developer.arm.com/documentation/ddi0553/am/ (Armv8.0-M only version). https://developer.arm.com/documentation/ddi0553/latest/ (latest version including Armv8.1-M). Note: M-profile architecture reference manuals for Armv6-M, Armv7-M, Armv8-M and Armv8.1-M can be found here: https://developer.arm.com/architectures/cpu-architecture/m-profile/docs.

[2] Arm   Cortex-M23   Processor   Technical   Reference   Manual.   https://developer.arm.com/documentation/ddi0550/latest/.

[3] Arm Cortex-M33 Processor Technical Reference Manual. https://developer.arm.com/documentation/100230/latest/.

[4] AMBA 4 ATB Protocol Specification. https://developer.arm.com/documentation/ihi0032/latest/.

[5] Arm CoreSight Architecture Specification version 2. https://developer.arm.com/documentation/ihi0029/d/.

[6] Embedded Trace Macrocell (ETMv3.5) architecture specification. https://developer.arm.com/documentation/ihi0014/q.

[7] Arm   Debug   Interface   Architecture   Specification   (ADIv5.0   to   ADIv5.2).   https://developer.arm.com/documentation/ihi0031/e/.

[8] AMBA 4 Low Power Interface Specification. https://developer.arm.com/documentation/ihi0068/c/.

 [9] AMBA 5 Advanced High-performance Bus (AHB) Protocol Specification. https://developer.arm.com/documentation/ihi0033/b-b/.

[10] AMBA 4 Advanced Peripheral Bus (APB) Protocol Specification. https://developer.arm.com/documentation/ihi0024/c/.

[11] Embedded Trace Macrocell (ETMv4.2) architecture specification. https://developer.arm.com/documentation/ihi0064/g/.

Instruction set

5.1 Background

5.1.1 About this chapter

This chapter is an introduction of the instruction set available in the Arm® Cortex®-M23 and Cortex-M33 processors. Full details of the instruction set are covered in the Armv8-M Architecture Reference Manual [1]. In addition, there are also instruction set descriptions in the:

- Cortex-M23 Device Generic User Guide [2]
- Cortex-M33 Device Generic User Guide [3]

For most software developers, the majority of software code is written in C/C++ so, accordingly, it is not essential to have a full understanding of the instruction set in order to use Cortex-M processors. That said, having a general understanding of the instruction set would help in the following cases:

- Debugging (e.g., when single-stepping through assembly code to understand an issue)
- Optimization (e.g., to create an optimized C/C++ code sequence)

There are some instances where assembly coding would be needed. For example:

- In some toolchains, startup codes (e.g., the reset handler) are written in assembly language. Hence, modification of the startup codes (if needed) would require an understanding of assembly language.
- Creating handwritten code for the best optimization (e.g., for DSP processing in Cortex-M33 microcontrollers. Please note, the CMSIS-DSP libraries are already optimized and can therefore be used instead of having to create handwritten codes).
- Assembly coding is required for context switching operations in RTOS designs and where the operation involves the direct manipulation of stack memories. (Usually, the assembly source for context switching is included in the RTOS software and therefore using the RTOS does not require assembly coding.)
- Creating fault exception handlers where the currently selected stack pointer might not point to a valid address range (see Section 13.4.1).

It is possible to add assembly codes into a C/C++ project. Several methods are available. These are:

- Adding an assembly source file to the project, or
- Adding assembly code inside the C/C++ code using an inline assembler.

Further information on this topic is covered in Chapter 17.

5.1.2 Background to the Instruction set in Arm® Cortex®-M processors

The design of the instruction set is one of the most important parts of the processor's architecture. In Arm's terminology, the instruction set design is usually referred to as Instruction Set Architecture (ISA). All Arm Cortex-M processors are based on Thumb-2 technology, which allows a mixture of 16- and 32-bit instructions to be used within one operating state. This is different from classic Arm processors, such as the Arm7™TDMI.

The reason for calling the instruction set "Thumb®" is historical. A brief history of the Thumb instruction set and Cortex-M processors is detailed below:

- Prior to the Arm7TDMI processor, Arm processors supported a 32-bit instruction set called Arm instructions. The architecture evolved over several versions; starting from Arm architecture version 1 to version 4.
- In the Arm7TDMI processor (released around 1994[a]), the processor was designed to support two operating states: The Arm state that utilized the 32-bit Arm instruction set and a Thumb state that used a 16-bit instruction set called the Thumb instruction set. Since the 16-bit version of the instruction size was smaller, the name Thumb was used (as compared to "arm"—a play on words). The Thumb instructions provided a higher code density and were more optimized for 16-bit memory systems. In some instances, the Thumb code provided a 30% code size reduction compared to the equivalent Arm code. As a result, the Arm7TDMI was very attractive to mobile phone designers at that time, especially because memory was a major factor in power consumption and cost. During operations, the processor switched between Arm state for high-performance tasks and exception handling and to Thumb state for the rest of the processing. The architecture version was subsequently updated to version 4T (the T suffix indicates Thumb support).
- Starting from Arm11™56T-2 (an architecture version 6 processor), Thumb-2 technology was released. With Thumb-2 technology, the processor was able to execute 32-bit instructions without switching between Thumb and Arm states. This reduced the switching overhead and made software development easier. Software developers no longer had to manually select which part of the code should run in Arm state and which part in Thumb state. Please note, 32-bit Thumb instructions have different encoding compared to the 32-bit Arm instructions, although some of the instruction's names are the same. Most Arm instructions can be ported to the equivalent Thumb instructions, making application porting fairly easy.
- Thumb-2 was used in subsequent Arm processors. And, in 2006, Arm released the Cortex-M3 processor which only supported a subset of Thumb instructions—not the Arm

[a]Based on information from https://en.wikipedia.org/wiki/ARM7.

instructions. The Cortex-M3 processor was the first release of the Armv7-M architecture. At this stage, processor and architecture development were split into Cortex-A, R, and M families. Cortex-M processors are focused on microcontroller products and embedded systems that require very low power, low response latency and ease of use.

Arm architecture continues to evolve: in 2011, Arm announced the Armv8-A for Cortex-A processors, which included 64-bit support. And Armv8-M architecture was announced in 2015, which added TrustZone and a number of architecture enhancements. Unlike Armv8-A, Armv8-M remains a 32-bit architecture as:

(a) There is not much demand for 64-bit support in small microcontroller systems and
(b) for easier software porting.

5.2 Instruction set features in various Cortex-M processors

All Cortex-M processors support different subsets of the Thumb instructions. This enables some Cortex-M processors to be extremely small and enables others to deliver complex processing with high energy efficiency. An illustration of the instruction set support is shown in Fig. 3.3 in Chapter 3.

Since all of the instructions for a smaller Cortex-M processor are supported by a larger Cortex-M processor, and with consistencies in other aspects of the architecture, software migration from a smaller Cortex-M processor to a larger one is normally straight forward at the processor level. This is called upward compatibility. Of course, at the peripheral level, this can be completely different, especially if the chip is from a different vendor.

The following table (Table 5.1) is a summary of the instruction set features of different Cortex-M processors.

Since a small Cortex-M processor could lack a range of instructions (e.g., floating-point processing instructions), system designers need to consider the instruction set features when selecting the right microcontrollers for their applications. For example:

– Audio processing: the DSP extension is often essential for this type of application. Depending upon the processing algorithms, floating-point support might also be required.
– Communication protocol processing: this might involve a number of bit field operations and, hence, Armv7-M or Armv8-M Mainline processors are likely to be more suitable.
– Complex data processing: when compared to 16-bit Thumb instructions, the 32-bit Thumb instruction set provides
    ○ more choice of data processing instructions,
    ○ more addressing modes in memory access instructions,
    ○ a larger range of immediate data in data processing instructions,
    ○ larger offset ranges in branch instructions,
    ○ access to high registers (r8–r12) in all data processing instructions.
    As a result, for applications dealing with complex operations, Armv7-M and Armv8-M Mainline processors are more suitable.

TABLE 5.1 Instruction set features in Cortex-M processors.

Instruction features	Armv6-M (Cortex-M0, Cortex-M0+, Cortex-M1)	Armv8-M Baseline (Cortex-M23)	Armv7-M (Cortex-M3)	Armv7E-M (Cortex-M4)	Armv7E-M (Cortex-M7)	Armv8-M Mainline (Cortex-M33/ Cortex-M35P/ Cortex-M55)
16-bit Thumb (General data processing and memory accesses)	Y	Y	Y	Y	Y	Y
32-bit Thumb (Additional data processing and memory accesses)			Y	Y	Y	Y
64-bit load/store			Y	Y	Y	Y
32-bit Multiply	Y	Y	Y	Y	Y	Y
64-bit Multiply and MAC			Y	Y	Y	Y
Hardware divide		Y	Y	Y	Y	Y
Bit field processing			Y	Y	Y	Y
Count leading zero			Y	Y	Y	Y
Saturation			Y	Y	Y	Y
16-bit immediate		Y	Y	Y	Y	Y
Compare and branch		Y	Y	Y	Y	Y
Conditional execution (If-Then)			Y	Y	Y	Y
Table branch			Y	Y	Y	Y
Exclusive access (useful for semaphores)		Y	Y	Y	Y	Y
DSP extension				Y	Y	Y (optional)
Single precision floating point				Y (FPv4, optional)	Y (FPv5, optional)	Y (FPv5, optional)
Double precision floating point					Y (FPv5, optional)	
System instructions (sleep, supervisor call, memory barriers)	Y	Y	Y	Y	Y	Y
TrustZone		Y				Y
C11 atomics		Y				Y

– General I/O processing: all Cortex-M processors are well capable of handling this. But for applications that need low power, using the Cortex-M0+ or Cortex-M23 processors has the additional advantage of being small (lower power and a lower silicon area cost). At the same time, these two processors have the single cycle I/O interface which enables fast and efficient I/O access operations.

The number of system-level features also plays a role in terms of selecting a processor/microcontroller device. For example, the availability of a Memory Protection Unit (MPU) might be essential for automotive/industrial applications where the RTOS could utilize the MPU for process isolation to enhance the robustness of the software. A MPU is, except for the Cortex-M0 and Cortex-M1 processors, optional on all Cortex-M processors.

Although the Cortex-M processors support many instructions there is, fortunately, no need to understand them all in detail as C compilers are good enough to generate efficient code. Also, with the availability of the free CMSIS-DSP library and various middle ware (e.g., software libraries), software developers can implement high performance DSP applications without the need to understand the details of each instruction.

Please note, some instructions are available in multiple encoding forms. For example, most of the 16-bit Thumb instructions can also be encoded in a 32-bit equivalent instruction. However, the 32-bit version of the aforementioned instruction has additional bit fields for additional control such as:

- selecting whether flags should be updated,
- wider immediate data/offset, or
- enabling access to the high registers (r8–r12).

These control capabilities are not possible for some of the 16-bit instructions due to the limitation of the instruction encoding space. If an operation can be carried out in either a 16- or 32-bit version of the same instruction, the C compiler can choose:

- a 16-bit version of the instruction for a smaller code size, or
- in some cases, use a 32-bit version of the instruction to align the position of a subsequent 32-bit branch target instruction to align it to a 32-bit boundary (this improves performance as the 32-bit instruction can then be fetched with a single bus transfer).

32-bit Thumb-2 instructions can be half word aligned. For example, you can have a 32-bit instruction located in a half word location (unaligned, Fig. 5.1):

```
0x1000 : LDR r0,[r1] ;a 16-bit instructions (occupy 0x1000-0x1001)
0x1002 : RBIT.W r0   ;a 32-bit Thumb-2 instruction (occupy
                     ;   0x1002-0x1005)
```

5.3 Understanding the assembly language syntax

In most projects, application code is written in C or other high-level languages and therefore it is not necessary for most software developers to have a full knowledge of the assembly language syntax. However, it is still useful to have a general overview of what instructions are

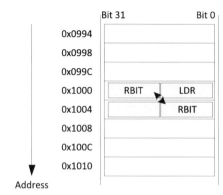

FIG. 5.1   An unaligned 32-bit instruction.

available and to have an understanding of the assembly codes syntax. For example, knowledge in this area can be very useful for debugging. Most of the assembly examples in this book are written for the Arm assembler (armasm), which is used in the Keil® Microcontroller Development Kit (Keil MDK). Assembly tools from different vendors (e.g., the GNU tool chain) have different syntaxes. In most cases, the mnemonics of the assembly instructions are the same, but assembly directives, definitions, labeling and comment syntax can be different.

Knowledge of assembly language syntax is needed when you add assembly codes to C codes. This is commonly known as inline assembly and is available in all major toolchains (the feature that processes inline assembly code is called an inline assembler). However, the exact syntax of an inline assembly is tool chain specific.

With the Arm assembler ("armasm"—applies to Arm DS™, Arm Compiler toolchain and Keil™ Microcontroller Development Kit), the following instruction formatting is used:

```
label
    mnemonic  operand1, operand2, ...      ; Comments
```

The "label" is used as a reference to an address location. It is optional; some instructions might have a label in front of them so that the address of the instruction can be obtained using the label. Labels can also be used to reference data addresses. For example, you can put a label for a lookup table inside the program. After the "label" you can find the "mnemonic", which is the name of the instruction, followed by a number of operands. The information present in an assembly instruction depends on the type of the instruction. For example:

- For data processing instructions written for the Arm assembler, the first operand is the destination of the operation.
- For a single memory read instruction (except multiple load instructions), the first operand is the register in which the data is loaded into.
- For a memory write instruction (except multiple store and exclusive store instructions), the first operand is the register that holds the data to be written to the memory.

Instructions that handle multiple loads and stores have a different syntax compared to single load/store instructions.

The number of operands for each instruction depends on the instruction type. Some instructions do not need any operands and some might need just one.

Note, some mnemonics can be used with different types of operands and this can result in different instruction encodings. For example, the MOV (move) instruction can be used to transfer data between two registers, or can be used to put an immediate constant value into a register.

The number of operands in an instruction depends on what type of instruction it is; and the syntax for the operands can also be different in each case. For example, immediate data is usually prefixed with "#":

```
MOVS  R0, #0x12  ; Set R0 = 0x12 (hexadecimal)
MOVS  R1, #'A'   ; Set R1 = ASCII character A
```

The text after each semicolon ";" is a comment. Comments do not affect the program's operation, but do make the programs easier for humans to understand (… well, usually!).

With the GNU tool chain, the common assembly syntax is:

```
label:
      mnemonic   operand1, operand2,...   /* Comments */
```

The opcode and operands are the same as those used in the Arm assembler syntax, but the syntax for label and comments are different. Using the same instructions as above, the GNU version is:

```
MOVS  R0, #0x12  /* Set R0 = 0x12 (hexadecimal) */
MOVS  R1, #'A'   /* Set R1 = ASCII character A */
```

An alternative way to insert comments in the GNU toolchain is to make use of the inline comment character "@". For example:

```
MOVS R0, #0x12  @  Set R0 = 0x12 (hexadecimal)
MOVS R1, #'A'   @  Set R1 = ASCII character A
```

One of the commonly used features in assembly code is the ability to define constants. By using constant definitions, the program code can be more readable and can thus make code maintenance easier. In Arm assembly, an example of defining a constant is:

```
NVIC_IRQ_SETEN    EQU    0xE000E100
NVIC_IRQ0_ENABLE  EQU    0x1
   ...
   LDR  R0,=NVIC_IRQ_SETEN ; Put 0xE000E100 into R0
          ; LDR here is a pseudo instruction that will be converted
          ; to a PC relativeliteral data load by the assembler
```

```
    MOVS R1, #NVIC_IRQ0_ENABLE ; Put immediate data (0x1) into
                               ; register R1
    STR R1, [R0] ; Store 0x1 to 0xE000E100, this enable external
              ; interrupt IRQ#0
```

In the code above, the address value of a NVIC register is loaded into the R0 register using pseudo instruction LDR. The assembler places the constant value to a location in the program code and inserts a memory read instruction. During the execution of the memory read instruction, the constant value is placed into the R0. The use of a pseudo instruction is needed because the value is too large to be encoded into a single move immediate instruction. When using LDR pseudo instructions to load a value into a register, the value requires an "=" prefix. If a MOV (move) instruction is used for loading an immediate data value into a register, the value is prefixed by "#".

Similar to the previous code example, the same code can be written using the GNU tool chain assembler syntax as shown below:

```
.equ  NVIC_IRQ_SETEN, 0xE000E100
.equ  NVIC_IRQ0_ENABLE, 0x1
...
LDR   R0,=NVIC_IRQ_SETEN /* Put 0xE000E100 into R0
        LDR here is a pseudo instruction that will be
        converted to a PC relative load by the assembler */
MOVS R1, #NVIC_IRQ0_ENABLE /* Put immediate data (0x1) into
                             register R1 */
STR R1, [R0] /* Store 0x1 to 0xE000E100, this enable
               external interrupt IRQ#0 */
```

Another frequently used feature available in assembly tools is one that allows data to be inserted inside a program. For example, this feature allows us to define data in a certain location in the program memory and to access it with memory read instructions. In the Arm assembler, an example of this is:

```
LDR   R3,=MY_NUMBER  ; Get the memory location of MY_NUMBER
LDR   R4, [R3]       ; Read the value 0x12345678 into R4
...
LDR R0,=HELLO_TEXT ; Get the starting address of HELLO_TEXT
BL  PrintText        ; Call a function called PrintText to
                     ; display string
...
ALIGN     4
MY_NUMBER DCD 0x12345678
HELLO_TEXT DCB "Hello\n", 0 ; Null terminated string
```

In the above example, at the bottom of the program code:

- "DCD" is used to insert a word sized data item and
- "DCB" is used to insert byte size data.

When inserting word size data into a program we should use the "ALIGN" directive before the data. The number after the ALIGN directive determines the alignment size. In this case (example above), the value 4 forces the following data to be aligned to a word boundary. By ensuring the data placed at MY_NUMBER is word aligned, the program is able to access the data with just a single bus transfer. By so doing, the code is more portable (unaligned access is not supported in the Cortex-M0/M0+/M1/M23 processors).

The previous example code can also be rewritten in GNU tool chain assembler syntax as follows:

```
    LDR   R3,=MY_NUMBER  /*Get the memory location of MY_NUMBER */
    LDR   R4, [R3]       /* Read the value 0x12345678 into R4 */
    ...
    LDR   R0,=HELLO_TEXT /* Get the starting address of
                            HELLO_TEXT*/
    BL PrintText         /* Call a function called PrintText to
                            display string */
    ...
    .align 4
MY_NUMBER:
    .word 0x12345678
HELLO_TEXT:
    .asciz "Hello\n"      /* Null terminated string */
```

A number of different directives are available in both the Arm and the GNU assemblers, which allows data to be inserted into a program. Listed below are a few commonly used examples (Table 5.2).

In most cases, you can also add a label before the directive so that the address locations of the data can be determined and used in other parts of the program code.

There are a number of other useful directives that are often used in assembly language programming. For example, some of the following Arm assembler directives (Table 5.3) are frequently used and some of these are used in the examples in this book.

Additional information about directives in the Arm assembler can be found in the "Arm Compiler armasm User Guide—version 6.9" [4] (Chapter 21, Directives Reference[b]).

5.4 Use of a suffix in an instruction

When using assembly language for programming Arm processors, some instructions can be followed by suffixes. The suffixes applicable to Cortex-M processors are shown in Table 5.4.

[b]https://developer.arm.com/documentation/100069/0609/directives-reference.

TABLE 5.2 Frequently used directives for inserting data into a program.

Type of data to insert	Arm assembler (e.g., Keil MDK)	GNU assembler
Byte	DCB E.g., `DCB 0x12`	.byte E.g., `.byte 0x012`
Halfword	DCW E.g., `DCW 0x1234`	.hword/.2byte E.g., `.hword 0x01234`
Word	DCD E.g., `DCD 0x01234567`	.word/.4byte E.g., `.word 0x01234567`
Double word	DCQ E.g., `DCQ 0x12345678FF0055AA`	.quad/.octa E.g., .quad 0x12345678FF0055AA
Floating point (single precision)	DCFS E.g., `DCFS 1E3`	.float E.g., .float 1E3
Floating point (double precision)	DCFD E.g., DCFD 3.14159	.double E.g., .double 3f14159
String	DCB E.g., `DCB "Hello\n", 0`	.ascii/.asciz (with NULL termination) E.g., `.ascii "Hello\n` `.byte 0 /* add NULL character */` E.g., `.asciz "Hello\n"`
Instruction	DCI E.g., DCI 0xBE00; Breakpoint (BKPT 0)	.inst/.inst.n/.inst.w E.g., `.inst.n 0xBE00` `/* Breakpoint (BKPT 0) */`

When using a data processing instruction with the Cortex-M33/M3/M4/M7 processors, the instruction can, optionally, update the APSR (flags). Whereas, in the Cortex-M23/M0/M0 + processors, most data processing instructions would always update the APSR (this is not optional for most instructions).

If using the Unified Assembly Language (UAL) syntax, we can specify whether the APSR update should be carried out or not. This might not be supported in some instructions—most data processing instructions in the Cortex-M23 processor always gets updated. For example, when moving data from one register to another, it is possible to use

```
MOVS   R0, R1 ; Move R1 into R0 and update APSR
```

Or

```
MOV    R0, R1 ; Move R1 into R0, and not update APSR
```

The second type of suffix is for:

- Conditional branch instructions. These instructions are supported by all Cortex-M processors.
- Conditional execution of instructions. This is achieved by putting the conditional instructions in an IF-THEN (IT) instruction block and is supported by Cortex-M33/M3/M4/M7 processors.

TABLE 5.3   Frequently used directives.

Directive (GNU assembler equivalent)	Description
THUMB (.thumb)	Specifies assembly code as Thumb instructions in the Unified Assembly Language (UAL) format.
CODE16 (.code 16)	Specifies assembly code as Thumb instructions in legacy pre-UAL syntax.
AREA <section_name>{,<attr>}{,attr}… (.section <section_name>)	Instructs the assembler to assemble a new code or data section. Sections are chunks of code or data that are manipulated by the linker. Each section is: <ul><li>given a name,</li><li>independent of other sections, and</li><li>indivisible by the linker.</li></ul>
SPACE <num of bytes> (.zero <num of bytes>)	Reserves a block of memory and fills it with zeros
FILL <num of bytes>{, <value>{, <value_sizes>}} (.fill <num of bytes>{, <value>{, <value_sizes>}})	Reserves a block of memory and fills it with the specified value. The size of the value is specified by value_sizes (1/2/4) and can be byte (1), half word (2) or word (4).
ALIGN {<expr>{,<offset>{,<pad>{,<padsize>}}}} (.align <alignment>{,<fill>{,<max}}})	Aligns the current location to a specified boundary by padding it with zeros or with NOP instructions. E.g. `ALIGN 8` (It makes sure the next instruction or the data is aligned to an 8-byte boundary)
EXPORT <symbol> (.global <symbol>)	Declares a symbol that is be used by the linker to resolve symbol references in a separate object (e.g., compiled output of a separate C file) or in library files.
IMPORT <symbol>	Declares a symbol reference in a separate object or in a library file that has to be resolved by the linker.
LTORG (.pool)	Instructs the assembler to immediately assemble the current literal pool. A literal pool contains data such as constant values for LDR pseudo instructions.

These suffixes (e.g., EQ, NE, CS) are shown in Table 5.4. By updating the APSR using:

- data operations, or
- a test instruction (TST), or
- compare instructions (e.g., CMP), etc.

the program flow can, based on the result of the instruction operations, be controlled.

TABLE 5.4 Instruction suffixes for Cortex-M processors in assembly programming.

Suffixes	Description
S	Updates the APSR (Application Program Status Register, such as Carry, Overflow, Zero and Negative flags). For example, the following add instruction will update the APSR: `ADDS R0, R1`

EQ, NE, CS, CC, MI, PL, VS, VC, HI, LS, GE, LT, GT, LE	Conditional execution. EQ = Equal, NE = Not Equal, LT = Less Than, GT = Greater Than, etc. With Cortex-M processors these conditions can be applied to conditional branches. For example:
	
	`BEQ label`
	`   ; Branches to label if the previous operation`
	`   ; results in an equal status`
	
	Conditional suffixes can be applied to conditionally executed instructions (see IF-THEN instruction in Section 5.14.6). For example:
	
	`ADDEQ R0, R1, R2`
	`   ; Performs an add operation if the previous`
	`   ; operation results in an equal status`

.N, .W	Specifies the use of 16-bit (N = narrow) instruction or a 32-bit (W = wide) instruction.
.32, .F32	Specifies that the operation is for 32-bit single precision data. In most tool chains, the .32 suffix is optional.
.64, F64	Specifies that the operation is for 64-bit double precision data. In most tool chains, the .64 suffix is optional.

5.5 Unified Assembly Language (UAL)

The assembly language syntax used for Cortex-M assembly programming is called Unified Assembly Language (UAL). Please note, the syntax has slightly stricter rules than that for the legacy Thumb assembly syntax developed for Arm7TDMI, but, at the same time, offers more features (e.g., the .N and .W suffixes).

When the legacy Thumb instruction syntax was developed, the Thumb instruction set that was defined at that time was quite small. Almost all of the data processing instructions in it updated the APSR. As a result, the "S" suffix (see Table 5.4) was not strictly required and by omitting the "S" suffix in an instruction still resulted in an instruction that updated the APSR. With the newer Thumb-2 instruction set, there is more flexibility and data processing instructions can optionally update the APSR. As a result, the use of the ".S" suffix in source code is now needed and needs to explicitly state whether the APSR should be updated.

Another difference between UAL and legacy Thumb syntax is the number of operands needed for some of the instructions. With legacy Thumb syntax, because the 16-bit Thumb instructions used the same bit field for the second operand (register) and the result register, some of the instructions can be written with just two operands. In the 32-bit version of the same Thumb instructions, the result register can be different from the first and second operands. As a result, the assembler tools require the additional operands to be specified to avoid ambiguity.

For example, a pre-UAL ADD instruction for 16-bit Thumb code is

```
ADD  R0, R1 ;   R0 = R0 + R1, update APSR
```

With UAL syntax, this should be written as below, which is more specific on the register usage and APSR update operations:

```
ADDS R0, R0, R1  ;  R0 = R0 + R1, update APSR
```

But, in most cases, depending on the tool chain being used, you can still write the instruction with a pre-UAL coding style (only two operands), but the use of the "S" suffix will have to be explicitly stated. For example:

```
ADDS R0, R1 ; R0 = R0 + R1, updates the APSR (S suffix used)
```

Software developers need to pay attention when they port legacy codes to the Cortex-M development environment. For example, when using Arm tool chains, the legacy Thumb code has the "CODE16" directive. With UAL syntax, the directive use should be "THUMB". In many cases, for the reasons explained above, other additional code changes are required when porting codes from legacy Thumb syntax to the UAL syntax. Optionally, you can specify which instruction you want by adding a suffix to the instruction in the UAL syntax. For example, the codes below show the selection of 16-bit and 32-bit instructions:

```
ADDS R0,    #1 ; Use 16-bit Thumb instruction by default
; for smaller size
ADDS.N R0, #1 ; Use 16-bit Thumb instruction (N=Narrow)
ADDS.W R0, #1 ; Use 32-bit Thumb-2 instruction (W=wide)
```

The .W (wide) suffix specifies a 32-bit instruction. If no suffix is given, the assembler tool can choose either the 32-bit or the 16-bit instruction, but usually defaults to the smaller option to get the best code density. Depending on the tool support, you may also use the .N (narrow) suffix to specify a 16-bit Thumb instruction.

Most of the 16-bit instructions only access registers R0–R7; the 32-bit version of the Thumb instructions does not have this limitation. However, some of the instructions do not allow the use of certain registers, such as PC (R15), LR (R14), and SP (R13). For further information regarding these restrictions, please refer to the Armv8-M Architecture Reference Manual [1] or to the Cortex®-M23/M33 Devices Generic User Guides [2, 3].

5.6 Instruction set—Moving data within the processors

5.6.1 Overview

One of the most basic operations in a processor is to move data around inside the processor. This includes a number of operation types, as shown in Table 5.5.

TABLE 5.5 Instructions for moving data inside a processor.

Operation types	Available in the Cortex-M23	Available in the Cortex-M33
Moves data from one register to another	Y	Y
Moves data between a register and a special register	Y	Y
Moves immediate data (constant) into a register	Y	Y
Moves data between a register in the regular register bank and a register in the floating-point register bank	–	Y (when FPU is present)
Moves data between registers in the floating-point register bank	–	Y (when FPU is present)
Moves data between a register in the regular register bank and a floating-point system register (e.g., FPSCR—Floating Point Status and Control Register)	–	Y (when FPU is present)
Moves immediate data (constant) into a register in the floating-point register bank	–	Y (when FPU is present)
Moves data between a register and a coprocessor register (Please refer to Section 5.21 for coprocessor support instructions)	–	Y (when coprocessor is present)

Please note, memory read operations (load) can be used for creating constant data in the register. This is commonly known as literal (data) load. This is covered in Section 5.7.6.

5.6.2 Moving data between registers

Table 5.6 shows the instructions for moving data between registers.

Table 5.7 details examples of several move instructions.

The MOVS instruction is similar to the MOV instruction apart from the fact that it updates the flags in the APSR, hence the "S" suffix is used.

It is also possible to use an ADD instruction to move data (shown in the instruction below), but this is less common:

TABLE 5.6 Instructions for transferring data within an Armv8-M processor.

Instruction	Description	Restriction in Armv8-M Baseline (Cortex-M23)
MOV Rd, Rm	Moves from register to register	
MOVS Rd, Rm	Moves from register to register, flags update (APSR.Z, APSR.N)	Rm and Rd are both low registers.
MVN Rd, Rm	Moves inverted value to a register	Not supported in Armv8-M Baseline
MVNS Rd, Rm	Moves inverted value to a register, flags update (N, Z)	Rm and Rd are both low registers.

TABLE 5.7 Instructions for transferring data within the processor.

Instruction	Destination	Source	Operations (text in comment)
MOV	R4,	R0	; Copy value from R0 to R4
MOVS	R4,	R0	; Copy value from R0 to R4 with APSR (flags) update
MVN	R3,	R7	; Move bitwise invert value of R7 into R3

ADDS *Rd, Rm*, #0 ; Move Rm into Rd with APSR (Z, N, and C flags) update

For Armv8-M Mainline, the 32-bit encoding of MOV between registers (r0–r13) also allows optional shift/rotate of the data value on-the-fly (i.e., shift/rotate happens at the same time). When using the feature of shift/rotate with MOV, the move instructions are written with a different mnemonic (Table 5.8).

These instructions are not supported in Armv8-M Baseline (e.g., the Cortex-M23 processor).

5.6.3 Immediate data generation

For immediate data generation, there are many instructions to choose from. Table 5.9 shows the move instructions that can be used for the purpose of immediate data generation. The 16-bit version of the MOV instruction can be used if:

- The immediate data is in the range from 0 to 255, and
- The destination register is a low register, and
- An update of the APSR is allowed.

For larger immediate data, the 32-bit version of MOV instructions should be used. There are a number of options:

- If the value is 16 bits or less, the MOVW instruction can be used.

TABLE 5.8 Moves data with rotate/shift.

Instruction	Description	Alternative instruction syntax
ASR{S} *Rd, Rm*, #n	Arithmetic Shift Right	`MOV{S} Rd, Rm, ASR #n`
LSL{S} *Rd, Rm*, #n	Logical Shift Left	`MOV{S} Rd, Rm, LSL #n`
LSR{S} *Rd, Rm*, #n	Logical Shift Right	`MOV{S} Rd, Rm, LSR #n`
ROR{S} *Rd, Rm*, #n	Rotate right	`MOV{S} Rd, Rm, ROR #n`
RRX{S} *Rd, Rm*	Extended rotate right	`MOV{S} Rd, Rm, RRX`

- If the value is 32 bits and can fit into a specific pattern (see example in the last row in Table 5.9), it is possible to encode the immediate data and fit that into a single MOV instruction
- If the two options above do not apply, a pair of MOVW and MOVT instructions can be used together to generate a 32-bit immediate data value.

Table 5.10 details several examples when creating immediate data.

One addition method for placing immediate data into registers is to use a literal load operation (see Section 5.7.6).

5.6.4 Special register access instructions

A number of the registers which are covered in Chapter 4 are special registers (e.g., CONTROL, PRIMASK). To gain access to these registers, MRS and MSR instructions are needed (Table 5.11).

A list of special registers that can be used with MRS and MSR instructions are shown in Table 5.12. Apart from APSR and CONTROL, all other registers can only be updated in privileged state.

Table 5.13 shows some of the examples.

TABLE 5.9 Move instructions for immediate data generation.

Instruction	Description	Restriction in Armv8-M Baseline (Cortex-M23)
MOVS Rd, #immed8	Moves immediate data (0–255) into a register	
MOVW Rd, #immed16	Moves 16-bit immediate data (0–65535)into a register	
MOV Rd, #immed	Moves immediate data into a register where immed is in the format of: 0x000000ab/0x00ab00ab/0xab00ab00/0xabababab/ 0x000000ab<<n (where ab is an 8-bit pattern, n is from 1 to 24)	Not supported in Armv8-M Baseline
MOVT Rd, #immed16	Moves 16-bit immediate data (0–65535) into the top 16-bit of a register. The lower 16-bit remains unchanged.	
MVN Rd, #immed MVNS Rd, #immed	Moves inverted immediate data into a register where #immed is in the format of: 0x000000ab/0x00ab00ab/0xab00ab00/0xabababab/ 0x000000ab<<n (where ab is an 8-bit pattern, n is from 1 to 24) N, Z, and C flags update for the MVNS	Not supported in Armv8-M Baseline

TABLE 5.10 Instructions for immediate data generation.

Instruction	Destination	Source	Operation (text in comment)
MOV	R3,	#0x34	; Set R3 value to 0x34
MOVS	R3,	#0x34	; Set R3 value to 0x34 with the APSR updated
MOVW	R6,	#0x1234	; Set R6 to a 16-bit constant 0x1234
MOVT	R6,	#0x8765	; Set the upper 16-bit of R6 to 0x8765

Instead of using MRS/MSR with the inline assembly feature in C compilers, a number of CMSIS-CORE APIs are available for accessing special registers when programming in C/C++ language. Please see Section 5.23 for further information.

5.6.5 Floating point register access

The Cortex-M33 processor, when it has the Floating-Point Unit (FPU) implemented, supports a number of instructions for accessing registers in the FPU register bank (Table 5.14). Unless specified, the use of the PC (R15) and the SP (R13), with these instructions, are not allowed.

Note: while the Cortex-M33 processor does not have double precision arithmetic operations support, some double precision data move instructions are supported.

For example, the following instructions are available for the Cortex-M33 processor with a floating-point unit (Table 5.15).

5.6.6 Floating point immediate data generation

It is possible to use VMOV for immediate data generation. But the data range is limited. The syntax for this operation is listed in Table 5.16.

By way of an example, the following instruction moves a value of 1.0 into S0, a single precision floating-point register (Table 5.17).

An immediate floating-point value can also be generated using a literal data load (Table 5.18).

Further information about literal data load is covered in Section 5.7.6.

TABLE 5.11 Instructions for special register access.

Instruction	Description	Restriction
MRS *Rd, spec_reg*	Moves from a special register to a register (see Table 5.12)	Rd must not be SP or PC
MSR *spec_reg,Rn*	Moves from a register to a special register (see Table 5.12)	Rn must not be SP or PC

TABLE 5.12   Special registers accessible with MRS and MSR instructions.

Symbol	Description	Restriction
APSR	Application Program Status Register (write is allowed in unprivileged state)	
EPSR	Execution Program Status Register	Read as zero, write ignored
IPSR	Interrupt Program Status Register	Write ignored
IAPSR	APSR + IPSR	See restriction for IPSR
EAPSR	EPSR + APSR	See restriction for EPSR
IEPSR	IPSR + EPSR	See restrictions for IPSR and EPSR
XPSR	APSR + EPSR + IPSR	See restrictions for IPSR and EPSR
MSP	Main Stack Pointer (Current security domain)	
PSP	Process Stack Pointer (Current security domain)	
MSPLIM	MSP Stack Limit (Current security domain)	
PSPLIM	PSP Stack Limit (Current security domain)	
PRIMASK	Interrupt masking register (masks all interrupts with configurable levels)	
BASEPRI	Interrupt masking register (masking by priority level)	Not available in Arvmv8-M Baseline
BASEPRI_MAX	Interrupt masking register (the same register as the BASEPRI, but only updates if the new blocking level is higher than the previous level)	Not available in Arvmv8-M Baseline
FAULTMASK	Interrupt masking register	Not available in Arvmv8-M Baseline
CONTROL	CONTROL register	
MSP_NS	Non-secure MSP	Available in Secure privileged state if the TrustZone is implemented.
PSP_NS	Non-secure PSP	Available in Secure privileged state if the TrustZone is implemented.
MSPLIM_NS	Non-secure MSP Stack Limit	Available in Secure privileged state if the TrustZone is implemented.
PSPLIM_NS	Non-secure PSP Stack Limit	Available in Secure privileged state if the TrustZone is implemented.
PRIMASK_NS	Non-secure PRIMASK	Available in Secure privileged state if the TrustZone is implemented.

TABLE 5.12 Special registers accessible with MRS and MSR instructions—cont'd

Symbol	Description	Restriction
BASEPRI_NS	Non-secure BASEPRI	Available in Secure privileged state if the TrustZone is implemented.
FAULTMASK_NS	Non-secure FAULTMASK	Available in Secure privileged state if the TrustZone is implemented.
CONTROL_NS	Non-secure CONTROL	Available in Secure privileged state if the TrustZone is implemented.
SP_NS	Non-secure current selected stack pointer (this can be used in Secure unprivileged state)	Available in Secure state if the TrustZone is implemented.

TABLE 5.13 Example of MRS and MSR instructions.

Instruction	Destination	Source	Operations
MRS	R7,	PRIMASK	; Copy value of PRIMASK (special register) to R7
MSR	CONTROL,	R2	; Copy value of R2 into CONTROL (special register)

TABLE 5.14 Instructions for transferring data to/from floating point registers.

Instruction	Description	Restriction
VMOV Sn, Rt	Moves a single precision value from Rt to Sn	
VMOV Rt,Sn	Moves a single precision value from Sn to Rt	
VMOV Rt, $Rt2$, Dm	Moves a double precision value from Dm to {$Rt2$, Rt}	
VMOV Dm, Rt, $Rt2$	Moves a double precision value from {$Rt2$, Rt} to Dm	
VMOV Rt, $Rt2$, Sm, $Sm1$	Moves two single precision values from {$Sm1$, Sm} to {$Rt2$, Rt}	"m1" must be "m" + 1.
VMOV Sm, $Sm1$, Rt, $Rt2$	Moves two single precision values from {$Rt2$, Rt} to {$Sm1$, Sm}	"m1" must be "m" + 1.
VMOV Rt, $Dn[0]$	Moves lower half of Dn into Rt	
VMOV Rt, $Dn[1]$	Moves upper half of Dn into Rt	
VMOV.F32 Sd, Sm	Moves a single precision value from Sm to Sd	
VMOV.F64 Dd, Dm	Moves a double precision value from Dm to Dd	
VMRS Rt, FPSCR	Reads FPSCR into Rt	Rt can be R0–R14, or APSR_nzcv (copy FPU flags to APSR)
VMSR FPSCR, Rt	Writes Rt to FPSCR	

TABLE 5.15 Examples of instructions for transferring data between the floating-point unit and registers in the regular register bank.

Instruction	Destination	Source	Operation
VMOV	R0,	S0	; Copy floating point register S0 to general purpose register R0
VMOV	S0,	R0	; Copy general purpose register R0 to floating point register S0
VMOV	S0,	S1	; Copy floating point register S1 to S0 (single precision)
VMRS.F32	R0,	FPSCR	; Copy value in the FPSCR, a floating-point-unit system register, to R0
VMRS	APSR_nzcv,	FPSCR	; Copy flags from the FPSCR to the flags in the APSR
VMSR	FPSCR,	R3	; Copy R3 to the FPSCR, a floating-point-unit system register
VMOV.F32	S0,	#1.0	; Move a single precision value into the floating-point register S0

5.6.7 Moving data between a register and a coprocessor register

This is covered in Section 5.21—coprocessor support instructions.

5.7 Instruction set—Memory access

5.7.1 Overview

In Arm processors, memory access operations are referred to as "Load" and "Store". Armv8-M architecture provides a comprehensive range of memory access instructions. They provide:

– Different data sizes,
– Different address modes, and
– Single and multiple transfers

The base mnemonics of load and store instructions are listed in Table 5.19.

TABLE 5.16 Instructions for generating immediate value in an FPU register.

Instruction	Description	Restriction
VMOV.F32 *Sn, #immed*	Moves a single precision value to *Sn*	The value needs to be encoded in an 8-bit field within the instruction.
VMOV.F64 *Dn, #immed*	Moves a double precision value to *Dn*	The value needs to be encoded in an 8-bit field within the instruction.

TABLE 5.17   Instruction for generating immediate value in an FPU register.

Instruction	Destination	Source	Operation
VMOV.F32	S0,	#1.0	; Moves a single precision value into floating-point register S0

TABLE 5.18   Instructions for generating immediate value in an FPU register.

Instruction	Description	Restriction
VLDR.F32 Sn, [PC, #imm]	Loads a single precision value from memory to Sn	#imm is in range of 0 to +/−1020 and must be a multiple of 4
VLDR.F64 Dn, [PC, #imm]	Loads a double precision value from memory to Dn	#imm is in range of 0 to +/−1020 and must be a multiple of 4

The LDRSB and LDRSH instructions automatically perform a sign-extend operation on-the-fly (i.e., the operation is carried out simultaneously) to convert the read data into a signed 32-bit value. For example, if 0x83 is read in a LDRSB instruction, the value is converted into 0xFFFFFF83 before being placed in the destination register.

If the floating-point unit (FPU) is available and is enabled, the Cortex-M33 processor supports memory access instructions for the FPU. This is covered in Section 5.7.10.

5.7.2 Single memory access

The following single memory load instructions are available in both Armv8-M Baseline and Armv8-M Mainline (Table 5.20) (Note: The imm5 is a 5-bit immediate value for address offset generation. It is optional in assembly programming).

Similar to the load instructions, there is a list of single memory store instructions for both Armv8-M Baseline and Armv8-M Mainline (Table 5.21). As before, the imm5 address offset information is optional.

When using byte and halfword store instructions, the upper 24 bits (for byte) or 16 bits (for half word) of the source registers are not used—the value is truncated to the right size during write operations. There is no need for separate signed and unsigned versions of the store instructions.

When using an Armv8-M Baseline processor, such as the Cortex-M23, data memory access must be aligned. For example, a word size transfer can only be carried out on address locations where the address bit 1 and bit 0 are set to zero. Similarly, a half-word size access can only be carried out on address locations where the address bit 0 is 0. Byte transfers are always aligned. If the software attempts to carry out an unaligned transfer, a HardFault exception would be generated. This behavior is identical to that in Armv6-M architecture, such as the Cortex-M0 and Cortex-M0+ processors. Armv8-M Mainline processors do not have this address alignment restriction for single memory access instructions.

5. Instruction set

TABLE 5.19 Memory access instructions for different data sizes.

Data type	Load (read from memory)	Store (write to memory)
8-bit unsigned	LDRB	STRB
8-bit signed	LDRSB	STRB
16-bit unsigned	LDRH	STRH
16-bit signed	LDRSH	STRH
32-bit	LDR	STR
Multiple 32-bit	LDM	STM
Double word (64-bit) (Not available in Armv8-M Baseline, i.e., the Cortex-M23)	LDRD	STRD
Stack operations (32-bit)	POP	PUSH

TABLE 5.20 Single memory read instructions (Armv8-M Baseline and Mainline).

Instruction	Description	Restriction
LDR *Rt*, [*Rn, Rm*]	Word read. Rt=memory[Rn+Rm]	For Armv8-M Baseline, Rt, Rn, and Rm are low registers. The address must be aligned. Armv8-M Mainline does not have these restrictions.
LDRH *Rt*, [*Rn, Rm*]	Halfword read. Rt=memory[Rn+Rm]	Same as above
LDRSH *Rt*, [*Rn, Rm*]	Halfword read with sign-extend. Rt=memory[Rn+Rm]	Same as above
LDRB *Rt*, [*Rn, Rm*]	Byte read. Rt=memory[Rn+Rm]	Same as above
LDRSB *Rt*, [*Rn, Rm*]	Byte read with sign-extend. Rt=memory[Rn+Rm]	Same as above
LDR *Rt*, [*Rn, #imm5*]	Word read (immediate offset). Rt=memory [Rn+(#imm5<<2)]	Same as above $0 <= \text{Offset} <= 124$
LDRH *Rt*, [*Rn, #imm5*]	Halfword read (immediate offset). Rt=memory[Rn+(#imm5<<1)]	Same as above $0 <= \text{Offset} <= 62$
LDRSH *Rt*, [*Rn, #imm5*]	Halfword read (immediate offset) with sign extend. Rt=memory[Rn +(#imm5<<1)]	Same as above $0 <= \text{Offset} <= 62$
LDRB *Rt*, [*Rn, #imm5*]	Byte read (immediate offset). Rt=memory [Rn+#imm5]	Same as above $0 <= \text{Offset} <= 31$
LDRSB *Rt*, [*Rn, #imm5*]	Byte read (immediate offset) with sign extend. Rt=memory[Rn+#imm5]	Same as above $0 <= \text{Offset} <= 31$

TABLE 5.21 Single memory store (write) instructions (Armv8-M Baseline and Mainline).

Instruction	Description	Restriction
STR *Rt*, [*Rn*, *Rm*]	Word write. memory[Rn+Rm]=Rt	For Armv8-M Baseline, Rt, Rn and Rm are low registers. The address must be aligned. Armv8-M Mainline does not have these restrictions.
STRH *Rt*, [*Rn*, *Rm*]	Halfword write. memory[Rn+Rm]= Rt	Same as above
STRB *Rt*, [*Rn*, *Rm*]	Byte write. memory[Rn+Rm]=Rt	Same as above
STR *Rt*, [*Rn*, #*imm5*]	Word write (immediate offset). memory[Rn+(#imm5<<2)]=Rt	Same as above $0 <= \text{offset} <= 124$
STRH *Rt*, [*Rn*, #*imm5*]	Halfword write (immediate offset). memory[Rn+(#imm5<<1)]=Rt	Same as above $0 <= \text{offset} <= 62$
STRB *Rt*, [*Rn*, #*imm5*]	Byte write (immediate offset). memory[Rn+#imm5]=Rt	Same as above $0 <= \text{offset} <= 31$

Armv8-M Mainline processors (e.g., the Cortex-M33 processor) support additional instructions as follows (Table 5.22).

These memory access instructions provide a wider address offset range compared to the load/store instructions in Armv8-M Baseline.

5.7.3 SP relative load/stores

Another group of load and store instructions use the SP (stack pointer) as a base address with an immediate offset value for the calculation of the address. These instructions are optimized for accessing local variables in C functions. Because there are not enough registers in the register bank for temporary storage of all the variables used by the C functions, these data variables are often stored in stack memory spaces. In this way, if a function is not active, the local variables for the function do not consume any space.

An example of using SP-relative addressing mode is as follows: At the beginning of the function execution, the value of SP can be decremented by a certain amount to reserve space for local variables. The local variables can then be accessed using instructions with SP related addressing. At the end of the function, the value of the SP is incremented back to the original value, which releases the previously allocated stack space. The function then exits and returns to the calling code (Fig. 5.2).

The instructions with SP-relative addressing mode are listed in Table 5.23.

Please note, while architecturally it is possible to have a negative offset for a SP relative access, in general practice the offset being used should be a positive number. This is to ensure that the data being used is within the allocated stack space. If it is not, the data being processed could be changed unexpectedly by an interrupt service.

TABLE 5.22 Additional single memory access instructions in Armv8-M Mainline.

Instruction	Description	Restriction
LDR *Rt*, [*Rn*, #*imm12*]	Word read—immediate offset. Rt=memory[Rn+#imm12]	High registers can be used. Address can be unaligned. −255<=Offset<=4095
LDRH *Rt*, [*Rn*, #*imm12*]	Halfword read—immediate offset. Rt=memory[Rn+#imm12]	Same as above −255<=Offset<=4095
LDRSH *Rt*, [*Rn*, #*imm12*]	Halfword read with sign-extend. Rt=memory[Rn+(imm12)]	Same as above −255<=Offset<=4095
LDRB *Rt*, [*Rn*, #*imm12*]	Byte read—immediate offset. Rt=memory[Rn+#imm12]	Same as above −255<=Offset<=4095
LDRSB *Rt*, [*Rn*, #*imm12*]	Byte read with sign-extend. Rt=memory[Rn+(imm12)]	Same as above −255<=Offset<=4095
LDRD *Rt*, *Rt2*, [Rn, #imm8]	Doubleword Read {Rt2,Rt}=memory[Rn+imm8<<2]	Address must be word aligned. −1020<=Offset<=1020
STR *Rt*, [*Rn*, #*imm12*]	Word write—immediate offset. memory[Rn+#imm12]=Rt	High registers can be used. Address can be unaligned. −255<=Offset<=4095
STRH *Rt*, [*Rn*, #*imm12*]	Halfword write—immediate offset. memory[Rn+#imm12]=Rt	Same as above −255<=Offset<=4095
STRB *Rt*, [*Rn*, #*imm12*]	Byte write—immediate offset. memory[Rn+#imm12]=Rt	Same as above −255<=Offset<=4095
STRD *Rt*, *Rt2*, [Rn, #imm8]	Doubleword Read memory[Rn+imm8<<2]={Rt2,Rt}	Address must be word aligned. −1020<=Offset<=1020

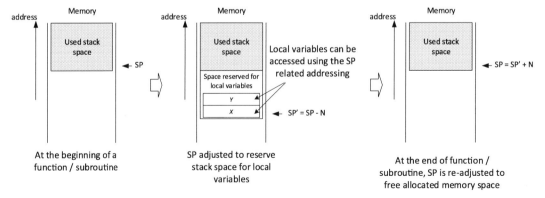

FIG. 5.2   Local variable space allocation and access of those variables in the stack.

TABLE 5.23 Stack Pointer relative memory access instructions.

Instruction	Description	Restriction
LDR *Rt*, [*SP*, #*offset*]	Word read. Rt=memory [SP+(#imm8<<2)]	For Armv8-M Baseline, Rt, is a low register. The address must be word aligned. 0<=offset<=1020
STR *Rt*, [*SP*, #*offset*]	Word write. memory [SP+(#imm8<<2)]=Rt	For Armv8-M Baseline, Rt, is a low register. The address must be word aligned. 0<=offset<=1020
LDR *Rt*, [*SP*, #*offset*]	Word read. Rt=memory[SP+#imm12]	Not available in Armv8-M baseline. −255<=offset<=4095
LDRH *Rt*, [*SP*, #*offset*]	Halfword read. Rt=memory[SP+#imm12]	Not available in Armv8-M baseline. −255<=offset<=4095
LDRSH *Rt*, [*SP*, #*offset*]	Halfword read with signed extend. Rt=memory[SP+#imm12]	Not available in Armv8-M baseline. −255<=offset<=4095
LDRB *Rt*, [*SP*, #*offset*]	Byte read. Rt=memory[SP+(#imm8<<2)]	Not available in Armv8-M baseline. −255<=offset<=4095
LDRSB *Rt*, [*SP*, #*offset*]	Byte read with signed extend. Rt=memory[SP+(#imm8<<2)]	Not available in Armv8-M baseline. −255<=offset<=4095
STR *Rt*, [*SP*, #*offset*]	Word read. memory[SP+#imm12]=Rt	Not available in Armv8-M baseline. −255<=offset<=4095
STRH *Rt*, [*SP*, #*offset*]	Halfword read. memory[SP+#imm12]=Rt	Not available in Armv8-M baseline. −255<=offset<=4095
STRB *Rt*, [*SP*, #*offset*]	Byte read. memory[SP+(#imm8<<2)]=Rt	Not available in Armv8-M baseline. −255<=offset<=4095

The SP relative addressing instructions are 16 bits. The 32-bit version of SP-relative addressing, shown in Table 5.23, is actually the same instruction encoding as the load and store instructions with immediate offset. However, In Armv8-M Baseline, most 16-bit Thumb instructions only use low registers. As a result, there is a pair of dedicated 16-bit versions of the LDR and the STR instructions with SP-relative addressing.

5.7.4 Preindexed and postindex addressing modes

In addition to the addressing mode with an address offset, Armv8-M Mainline processors support postindexed and preindexed addressing modes. The descriptions of these address modes are:

- Preindexed: the address for the transfer is calculated with the offset and the base address register is subsequently updated to the accessed address.
- Postindexed: the address for the transfer does not include the offset, but the base address register is nonetheless subsequently updated with the offset.

Preindexed addressing mode is specified with an exclamation mark (!) after the address. For example:

```
LDR R0, [R1, #0x08]! ; After the access to memory[R1+0x8],
                     ; R1 is also incremented by 0x8.
```

The address for memory access uses the sum of R1+0x8 regardless of whether the exclamation mark (!) is stated. Instructions that have a preindexed addressing mode are listed in Table 5.24.

Postindexed addressing mode is notated by way of having an extra offset value after the address operand. There is no need to add an exclamation mark because, in this form, the base address register is always updated if the data transfer is successfully completed. For example:

```
LDR R0, [R1], #0x08 ; After the access to memory[R1],
                    ; R1 is incremented by 0x8.
```

The postindex address mode is very useful for processing data in an array. As soon as an element in the array is accessed, the address register is automatically adjusted to the next element to save code size and execution time. Instructions that have a postindexed addressing mode are listed in Table 5.25.

TABLE 5.24 Preindexed memory access instructions (Armv8-M Mainline only).

Instruction	Description	Restriction
LDR Rt, [Rn, #{+/-}imm8]!	Word read (preindexed). Rt=memory[Rn+#imm8]	$-255 <=$ Offset $<= 255$
LDRH Rt, [Rn, #{+/-}imm8]!	Halfword read (preindexed). Rt=memory[Rn+(#imm8)]	$-255 <=$ Offset $<= 255$
LDRSH Rt, [Rn, #{+/-}imm8]!	Halfword read (preindexed) with signed extended. Rt=memory[Rn+(#imm8)]	$-255 <=$ Offset $<= 255$
LDRB Rt, [Rn, #{+/-}imm8]!	Byte read (preindexed). Rt=memory[Rn+(#imm8)]	$-255 <=$ Offset $<= 255$
LDRSB Rt, [Rn, #{+/-}imm8]!	Byte read (preindexed) with signed extended. Rt=memory[Rn+(#imm8)]	$-255 <=$ Offset $<= 255$
LDRD Rt, Rt2, [Rn, #{+/-}imm8]!	Doubleword read (preindexed) {Rt2,Rt}=memory[Rn+(#imm8<<2)]	$-1020 <=$ Offset $<= 1020$
STR Rt, [Rn, #{+/-}imm8]!	Word write (preindexed). memory[Rn+#imm8]=Rt	$-255 <=$ Offset $<= 255$
STRH Rt, [Rn, #{+/-}imm8]!	Halfword write (preindexed). memory[Rn+(#imm8)]=Rt	$-255 <=$ Offset $<= 255$
STRB Rt, [Rn, #{+/-}imm8]!	Byte write (preindexed). memory[Rn+(#imm8)]=Rt	$-255 <=$ Offset $<= 255$
STRD Rt, Rt2, [Rn, #{+/-}imm8]!	Doubleword write (preindexed) memory[Rn+(#imm8<<2)]={Rt2,Rt}	$-1020 <=$ Offset $<= 1020$

TABLE 5.25 Postindexed memory access instructions (Armv8-M Mainline only).

Instruction	Description	Restriction
LDRB Rd, [Rn], #offset	Reads byte from memory[Rn] to Rd, then updates Rn to Rn+offset	$-255 <= \text{Offset} <= 255$
LDRSB Rd, [Rn], #offset	Reads and signed extended byte from memory [Rn] to Rd, then updates Rn to Rn+offset	$-255 <= \text{Offset} <= 255$
LDRH Rd, [Rn], #offset	Reads halfword from memory[Rn] to Rd, then updates Rn to Rn+offset	$-255 <= \text{Offset} <= 255$
LDRSH Rd, [Rn], #offset	Reads and signed extended halfword from memory[Rn] to Rd, then updates Rn to Rn+offset	$-255 <= \text{Offset} <= 255$
LDR Rd, [Rn], #offset	Reads word from memory[Rn] to Rd, then updates Rn to Rn+offset	$-255 <= \text{Offset} <= 255$
LDRD Rd1,Rd2,[Rn],#offset	Reads double word from memory[Rn] to Rd1, Rd2, then updates Rn to Rn+offset	$-1020 <= \text{Offset} <= 1020$
STRB Rd, [Rn], #offset	Stores byte to memory[Rn] then updates Rn to Rn +offset	$-255 <= \text{Offset} <= 255$
STRH Rd, [Rn], #offset	Stores halfword to memory[Rn] then updates Rn to Rn+offset	$-255 <= \text{Offset} <= 255$
STR Rd, [Rn], #offset	Stores word to memory[Rn] then updates Rn to Rn +offset	$-255 <= \text{Offset} <= 255$
STRD Rd, [Rn], #offset	Stores doubleword to memory[Rn] then updates Rn to Rn+offset	$-1020 <= \text{Offset} <= 1020$

The postindex memory access instructions are 32 bits. The offset value can be positive or negative. Please note, these single preindexed and postindexed memory access instructions are not supported by Armv8-M Baseline.

5.7.5 Optional shift in register offset (Barrel shifter)

For Armv8-M Mainline, the register offset memory load and store instructions support an optional shift for the second address register operand. For example, the following instruction performs a Logical Shift Left (LSL) to the second address register.

```
LDR R0, [R1, R2, LSL #2]  ;Address used = R1 + (R2<<2)
```

This shift operation is often known as barrel shifter. The general form of the memory access instructions with barrel shift syntax is listed in Table 5.26.

The barrel shift feature in memory access instructions is very useful for handling data arrays where the:

- base address of the array is indicated by Rn (the first address register), and
- array index is indicated by Rm (the second address register), and

TABLE 5.26   Register-relative memory access instructions with optional shift (Armv8-M Mainline only).

Instruction	Description	Restriction
LDR Rt, [Rn, Rm, LSL #n]	Word read. Rt=memory[Rn+Rm<<n]	n is in the range of 0–3 Rn must not be PC Rm must not be PC/SP Rt can be SP for word loads/stores Rt can be PC for word loads.
LDRH Rt, [Rn, Rm, LSL #n]	Halfword read. Rt=memory[Rn+Rm<<n]	Same as above
LDRSH Rt, [Rn, Rm, LSL #n]	Halfword read with sign-extend. Rt=memory[Rn+Rm<<n]	Same as above
LDRB Rt, [Rn, Rm, LSL #n]	Byte read. Rt=memory[Rn+Rm<<n]	Same as above
LDRSB Rt, [Rn, Rm, LSL #n]	Byte read with sign-extend. Rt=memory[Rn+Rm<<n]	Same as above
STR Rt, [Rn, Rm, LSL #n]	Word write. memory[Rn+Rm<<n]=Rt	Same as above
STRH Rt, [Rn, Rm, LSL #n]	Halfword write. memory[Rn+Rm<<n]=Rt	Same as above
STRB Rt, [Rn, Rm, LSL #n]	Byte write. memory[Rn+Rm<<n]=Rt	Same as above

- size of the elements in the array is represented by the barrel shift amount #n (0=byte, 1=half word, 2=word)

The barrel shifter hardware is also be used in data processing instructions (This is covered in Section 5.8).

5.7.6 Literal data read

Program images contain a number of constants and read-only data. Literal data read instructions are for loading that data into registers using the PC (Program Counter) relative addressing mode, i.e., the address of the data is calculated from the current PC value plus an offset.

Due to the pipeline nature of the Cortex-M processors, the effective current PC available is not the same as the address of the literal load instruction. Instead, often a skewed PC value (WordAligned(PC+4)) is used. Literal load instructions are listed in Table 5.27.

If you need to set a register to a 32-bit immediate data value there are several methods:

The most common way to do it is to use a pseudo instruction called "LDR". For example:

```
LDR R0, =0x12345678 ; Set R0 to 0x12345678
```

This is not a real instruction. The assembler converts this instruction into a memory transfer instruction and to a literal data item stored in the program image:

TABLE 5.27 Literal data read (PC relative memory read).

Instruction	Description	Restriction
LDR Rt, [PC, #imm8]	Word read (literal load) Rt=memory[WordAligned (PC+4) + (#imm8<<2)]	Available for Armv8-M Baseline, but the address must be word aligned. *4 < offset < 1020*
LDR Rt, [PC, #{+/-}imm12]	Word read (literal load) Rt=memory[WordAligned (PC+4) + #imm12]	Not available in Armv8-M Baseline. *−4095 < offset < +4095*
LDRH Rt, [PC, #{+/-}imm12]	Halfword read (literal load) Rt=memory[WordAligned (PC+4) + #imm12]	Not available in Armv8-M Baseline. *−4095 < offset < +4095*
LDRB Rt, [PC, #{+/-}imm12]	Byte read (literal load) Rt=memory[WordAligned (PC+4) + #imm12]	Not available in Armv8-M Baseline. *−4095 < offset < +4095*
LDRD Rt, $Rt2$, [PC, #{+/-}imm8]	Doubleword read (literal load) {Rt2,Rt}=memory[Rn +(#imm8<<2)]	Not available in Armv8-M Baseline. *−1020 < offset < +1020*

```
LDR R0, [PC, #offset]
....
DCD 0x12345678
```

In the above example, the LDR instruction reads the memory at [PC+offset] and stores the value into the R0 register. Note, due to the pipeline nature of Cortex-M processors, the value of the PC is not exactly the address of the LDR instruction. However, the assembler will calculate the offset value so you do not have to manually work out the offset value.

Literal pool

Usually the assembler (the tool for converting assembly code to binary) groups various literal data (e.g., DCD 0x12345678 in the above example) into data blocks called literal pools. Since the value of the offset in the LDR instruction is limited, a program will usually need a number of literal pools so that the LDR instruction can access the literal data. We need, therefore, to insert assembler directives, such as "LTORG" (or ".pool"), to tell the assembler where it can insert the literal pools. If this is not undertaken, the assembler will put all the literal data after the end of the program code. The resulting address offsets of the literal data could then be too large to be encoded in the LDR instructions.

5.7.7 Multiple load/store

One of the interesting and very useful features in Arm processors is the multiple load/store instructions. This allows you, using a single instruction, to read or write multiple data that is continuous in the memory. This helps improve code density, and in some cases could also improve performance: For example, by reducing memory bandwidth for instruction fetches. The Load Multiple registers (LDM) and Store Multiple registers (STM) instructions only support 32-bit data.

To use STM/LDM instructions, we need to specify the registers being used to hold read/write data using a register list (shown as `{reg_list}`). It contains at least one register, and:

— Starts with "{" and ends with "}".
— Uses "-" (hypen) to indicate range. For example, R0–R4 means R0, R1, R2, R3, and R4.
— Uses "," (comma) to separate each register.
— Must not contain an SP (Stack Pointer) and, if write back form is used, the base register Rn must not be in the "{reg_list}".

For example, the following instructions read address 0x20000000 to 0x2000000F (four words) into registers R0–R3:

```
LDR   R4,=0x20000000 ; Set R4 to 0x20000000 (address)
LDMIA R4!, {R0-R3}   ; Read 4 words and store them to R0 - R3
```

The register list can be noncontinuous. For example, the register list "{R1, R3, R5–R7, R9, R11–12}" contains registers R1, R3, R5, R6, R7, R9, R11, and R12. However, in Armv8-M Baseline, only low registers (R0–R7) can be used in multiple load/store instructions.

Similar to other load/store instructions, you can use write back (as indicated by "!" in the example below) with STM and LDM. For example,

```
LDR   R8,=0x8000   ; Set R8 to 0x8000 (address)
STMIA R8!, {R0-R3} ; R8 change to 0x8010 after the store
```

In Armv8-M Baseline, the base register is normally updated automatically after the execution of the LDM/STM instruction (Table 5.28)—except for the LDM instruction where the Rn (address register) is one of the registers that will be updated by the read operation (i.e., Rn is included in {reg_list}).

In Armv8-M Mainline, the LDM and STM instructions support two types of preindexing:

TABLE 5.28 Multiple load/store instructions.

Instruction	Description	Restriction
LDMIA Rn!, {reg_list}	Reads multiple registers from the memory address pointed to by Rn (Rn is not in reg_list). Rn is updated to the subsequent address after the last load operation.	For Armv8-M Baseline, registers in reg_list and Rn must be one of the low registers (R0–R7).
STMIA Rn!, {reg_list}	Writes multiple registers to the memory address pointed to by the Rn. Rn is updated to the subsequent address after the last store operation.	Same as above
LDM Rn, {reg_list}	Read multiple registers from the memory address pointed to by Rn (Rn is in the reg_list, and is updated by one of the aforementioned data read operations).	Same as above. This form of LDM instruction is only allowed if Rn is in the reg_list for Armv8-M Baseline. Armv8-M Mainline does not have such a restriction.

– IA: Increment address After each read/write
– DB: Decrement address Before each read/write

The LDM and STM instructions can be used without a base address write back. For example, Armv8-M Mainline supports the instructions listed in Table 5.29.

There are some restrictions for LDM and STM instructions:

- The base register Rn must not be PC
- In any STM instruction, reg_list must not contain PC.
- In any LDM instruction, reg_list must not contain PC and LR at the same time.
- Write-back form (with Rn!) must not be used if Rn is inside reg_list.
- The transfer address must be word aligned.

In general, LDM and STM instructions should be avoided when accessing peripheral registers where the access could have a side effect, e.g., a FIFO register, where a read/write can change the state of the FIFO. This is because Armv8-M Baseline and Armv6-M processors are allowed to abandon and restart an instruction if an interrupt takes place after the instruction has started. When the LDM/STM instruction restarts after the interrupt service routine, the LDM/STM access to some of the registers could be erroneously repeated.

In the architectures of Armv8-M Mainline and Armv7-M, the interrupt continuation bit field in the program status register allows the state of the LDM and STM to be stored and

TABLE 5.29 Additional multiple load/store instructions for Armv8-M Mainline.

Instruction	Description	Restriction
LDMIA Rn,{reg_list}	Reads multiple words and the address is Incremented After (IA) each register is read	See list after this table
LDMDB Rn,{reg_list}	Reads multiple words and the address is Decremented Before (DB) each register is read	See list after this table
STMIA Rn,{reg_list}	Writes multiple words and the address is Incremented After (IA) each register is written	See list after this table
STMDB Rn,{reg_list}	Writes multiple words and the address is Decremented Before (DB) each register is written	See list after this table
LDMIA Rn!,{reg_list}	Reads multiple words and the address is Incremented After (IA) each register is read. Rn is then updated to the subsequent address (write-back).	See list after this table
LDMDB Rn!,{reg_list}	Reads multiple words and the address is Decremented Before (DB) each register is read. Rn is then updated to the subsequent address (write-back).	See list after this table
STMIA Rn!,{reg_list}	Writes multiple words and the address is Incremented After (IA) each register is written. Rn is then updated to the subsequent address (write-back).	See list after this table
STMDB Rn!,{reg_list}	Writes multiple words and the address is Decremented Before (DB) each register is written. Rn is then updated to the subsequent address (write-back).	See list after this table

to resume without having to repeat transfers that have already been carried out. These processors are not, therefore, subject to the same issue highlighted in the previous paragraph.

5.7.8 PUSH/POP

A special form of LDM and STM instructions are the POP and PUSH instructions, which are for stack operations. For clarity, it is recommended that PUSH and POP mnemonics are used for stack operations.

The PUSH and POP instructions use the current selected stack pointer (SP) for address generation, with the SP always being updated for PUSH and POP. The selection of the stack pointer depends on several factors:

- the processor's security state if TrustZone is implemented,
- the current mode of the processor (Thread or Handler mode), and
- the value of bit 1 in the CONTROL register (see "CONTROL register" section in Sections 4.2.2.3 and 4.3.4—Stack Memory).

Instructions for stack push and stack pop operations are shown in the Table 5.30.

The register list (`reg_list`) syntax is the same as that for the LDM and STM instructions. For example,

```
PUSH {R0, R4-R7, R9} ; PUSH R0, R4, R5, R6, R7, R9 into stack
POP  {R2, R3}        ; POP R2 and R3 from stack
```

Usually a PUSH instruction will have a corresponding POP with the same register list but this is not always necessary. For example, a common exception to this rule is when POP is used as a function return:

```
PUSH {R4–R6, LR} ; Save R4 to R6 and LR (Link Register) at the
                 ; beginning of a subroutine. LR contains the
                 ; return address
...              ; processing in the subroutine
POP  {R4-R6, PC} ; POP R4 to R6, and return address from stack.
                 ; the return address is stored directly in the
                 ; PC, this triggers a branch (subroutine return)
```

Instead of popping the return address in the LR, and then writing it to the program counter (PC) as a separate step, we can write the return address directly to the PC in the POP instruction. By so doing, this reduces the instruction and cycle counts.

TABLE 5.30 Stack push and pop instructions for core registers.

Instruction	Description	Restriction
PUSH {*reg_list*}	Store registers in stack	For Armv8-M Baseline, only low registers and LR can be used.
POP {*reg_list*}	Restore registers from stack	For Armv8-M Baseline, only low registers and PC can be used.

The 16-bit versions of PUSH and POP are limited to low registers (R0–R7), LR (for PUSH), and PC (for POP). Therefore, if a high register is modified in a function and the contents of the register need to be saved, you will need to use a pair of 32-bit PUSH and POP instructions.

If the FPU is available, there is also VPUSH and VPOP for saving and restoring FPU registers. This is covered in Section 5.7.10.

5.7.9 Unprivileged access instructions

Usually, APIs provided by an OS execute at privileged level, e.g., when the APIs are accessed via SuperVisor Call (SVC). Since an API might perform memory access on behalf of the unprivileged task that called the API, the API must take care that it is not performing operations on an address space that the unprivileged task is not supposed to have access to. Otherwise, a malicious task could call an OS API to modify an address which is owned by the OS, or by other tasks in the system, resulting in security vulnerabilities.

To solve this problem, traditionally many Arm processors provided memory access instructions that allowed privileged software to access memories at unprivileged level. These instructions are also supported in Armv8-M Mainline (the Cortex-M33 processor). By using these aforementioned instructions, the access permission is restricted by the Memory Protection Unit (MPU). This means that the OS APIs accessing data on behalf of an unprivileged software task have the same permission as the unprivileged software task.

The instructions to allow privileged software to access memory at unprivileged level are listed in Table 5.31. These instructions are not available in Armv8-M Baseline.

TABLE 5.31 Memory access instructions for privileged software to access data with unprivileged access.

Instruction	Description	Restriction
LDRT Rt, [Rn, #$offset$]	Reads 32-bit word at unprivileged level. Rt=memory[Rn+#imm8]	Rn must not be PC. Rt must not be SP/PC. $0 <$ Offset < 255
LDRHT Rt, [Rn, #$offset$]	Reads 16-bit halfword at unprivileged level. Rt=memory[Rn+#imm8]	Same as above
LDRSHT Rt, [Rn, #$offset$]	Reads 16-bit halfword at unprivileged level and then sign extends the data. Rt=memory[Rn+#imm8]	Same as above
LDRBT Rt, [Rn, #$offset$]	Reads 8-bit byte at unprivileged level. Rt=memory[Rn+#imm8]	Same as above
LDRSBT Rt, [Rn, #$offset$]	Reads 8-bit byte at unprivileged level and then sign extends the data. Rt=memory[Rn+#imm8]	Same as above
STRT Rt, [Rn, #$offset$]	Writes 32-bit word at unprivileged level. memory[Rn+#imm8]=Rt	Same as above
STRHT Rt, [Rn, #$offset$]	Writes 16-bit halfword at unprivileged level. memory[Rn+#imm8]=Rt	Same as above
STRBT Rt, [Rn, #$offset$]	Writes 8-bit byte at unprivileged level. memory[Rn+#imm8]=Rt	Same as above

Please note, Armv8-M provides an alternative way for privileged APIs to check whether the pointers from an unprivileged task are permitted to be accessed under the current MPU configuration. The TT (Test Target) instruction, together with the new C intrinsic functions defined in the Arm C Language Extension (ACLE), provides an easier way to handle the pointer check. There is, accordingly, no need to use hand coded assembly APIs to utilize unprivileged memory access instructions.

5.7.10 FPU memory access instructions

For Armv8-M Mainline processors, when the FPU is implemented, there are a number of FPU memory access instructions available to transfer data between the FPU registers and the memory. These instructions are listed in Table 5.32.

For single memory access, the following floating-point memory access instructions are available (Table 5.33).

There are also literal data read instructions for the FPU (Table 5.34).

Load multiple and store multiple operations to the FPU registers are available, including the base register write-back form—which updates the Rn register (write-back is indicated by an exclamation mark "!" after Rn). These instructions are listed in Table 5.35.

Stack memory operations are also available for FPU registers (Table 5.36).

Unlike PUSH and POP, VPUSH and VPOP instructions require that:

- the registers in the register list are consecutive,
- The maximum number of registers stacked/unstacked for each VPUSH or VPOP is 16.

When it is necessary to save more than 16 single precision floating-point registers, you can either use a double precision instruction or use two pairs of VPUSH and VPOP.

5.7.11 Exclusive access

The exclusive access instructions are a special group of memory access instructions for implementing semaphores or Mutual Exclusion (MUTEX) operations. In these operations, atomic read-modify-write behaviors are needed. Exclusive access instructions allow atomic operations to be implemented with a short instruction sequence. Please note, the atomic aspect of the term "atomic read-modify-write" is valid only from a high-level software point of

TABLE 5.32 Memory access instructions for the FPU (Require the FPU extension. Not available in the Cortex-M23 processor).

Data type	Read from memory (Load)	Write to memory (Store)
Single precision data (32-bit)	VLDR.32	VSTR.32
Double precision data (64-bit)	VLDR.64	VSTR.64
Multiple data	VLDM	VSTM
Stack operations	VPOP	VPUSH

TABLE 5.33 Single memory access instructions for the FPU (Require the FPU extension. Not available for the Cortex-M23 processor).

Example Note: the #{+/-} field is optional	Description
VLDR.32 Sd, [Rn, #{+/-}imm8]	Reads single precision data from memory and stores it in the single precision register *Sd* *Offset =+/− (imm8 <<2), i.e., −1020 < offset < +1020*
VLDR.64 Dd, [Rn, #{+/-}imm8]	Reads double precision data from memory and store it in the double precision register *Dd* *Offset =+/− (imm8 <<2), i.e., −1020 < offset < +1020*
VSTR.32 Sd, [Rn, #{+/-}imm8]	Writes single precision data (from the single precision register *Sd*) to memory *Offset =+/− (imm8 <<2), i.e., −1020 < offset < +1020*
VSTR.64 Dd, [Rn, #{+/-}imm8]	Writes double precision data (from the double precision register *Dd*) to memory *Offset =+/− (imm8 <<2), i.e., −1020 < offset < +1020*

view. At an operational level, the read and write operations are handled by separate instructions. As a result, a timing gap can exist between the read and the write operations.

While, at hardware level, there is nothing to prevent the semaphore data being updated by another access carried out by either an interrupt service or by another bus master, such access conflicts are, when that happens, detected by the exclusive access support. When an access conflict is detected, software restarts the whole access sequence in an attempt to carry out the previously unsuccessful semaphore/MUTEX operation.

Semaphores and MUTEX are normally used within an embedded OS where a resource (often hardware, but can be also be software) has to be shared between multiple application tasks or, even, multiple processors.

Exclusive access instructions include exclusive loads and exclusive stores. In Armv8-M architecture, additional variants of exclusive access instructions have been introduced (see Section 5.7.12, Load acquire & store release). Special hardware inside the processor and, optionally, in the bus interconnect are needed to monitor the exclusive access. Inside the

TABLE 5.34 Literal data access instructions for the FPU (Require the FPU extension. Not available for the Cortex-M23 processor).

Example Note: the #{+/-} field is optional	Description
VLDR.32 Sd, [PC, #{+/-}imm8]	Reads single precision data from memory and stores it in the single precision register *Sd* *Offset =+/− (imm8 <<2), i.e., −1020 < offset < +1020*
VLDR.64 Dd, [PC, #{+/-}imm8]	Reads double precision data from memory and stores it in the double precision register *Dd* *Offset =+/− (imm8 <<2), i.e., −1020 < offset < +1020*

TABLE 5.35 Multiple load/store instructions for the FPU (Require the FPU extension. Not available for the Cortex-M23 processor).

Example	Description
VLDMIA.32 Rn, <s_reg list>	Reads multiple single precision data and the address is Incremented After (IA) each register is read.
VLDMDB.32 Rn, <s_reg list>	Reads multiple single precision data and the address is Decremented Before (DB) each register is read.
VLDMIA.64 Rn, <d_reg list>	Reads multiple double precision data and the address is Incremented After (IA) each register is read.
VLDMDB.64 Rn, <d_reg list>	Reads multiple double precision data and the address is Decremented Before (DB) each register is read.
VSTMIA.32 Rn, <s_reg list>	Writes multiple single precision data and the address is incremented after each register is written.
VSTMDB.32 Rn, <s_reg list>	Writes multiple single precision data and the address is decremented before each register is written.
VSTMIA.64 Rn, <d_reg list>	Writes multiple double precision data and the address is incremented after each register is written.
VSTMDB.64 Rn, <d_reg list>	Writes multiple double precision data and the address is decremented before each register is written.
VLDMIA.32 Rn!, <s_reg list>	Reads multiple single precision data and the address is Incremented After (IA) each register is read. *Rn* writes back after the transfer is carried out.
VLDMDB.32 Rn!, <s_reg list>	Reads multiple single precision data and the address is decremented Before (DB) each register is read. *Rn* writes back after the transfer is carried out.
VLDMIA.64 Rn!, <d_reg list>	Reads multiple double precision data and the address is Incremented After (IA) each register is read. *Rn* writes back after the transfer is carried out.
VLDMDB.64 Rn!, <d_reg list>	Reads multiple double precision data and the address is Decremented Before (DB) each register is read. *Rn* writes back after the transfer is carried out.
VSTMIA.32 Rn!, <s_reg list>	Writes multiple single precision data and the address is incremented after each register is written. *Rn* writes back after the transfer is carried out.
VSTMDB.32 Rn!, <s_reg list>	Writes multiple single precision data and the address is decremented before each register is written. *Rn* writes back after the transfer is carried out.
VSTMIA.64 Rn!, <d_reg list>	Writes multiple double precision data and the address is incremented after each register is written. *Rn* writes back after the transfer is carried out.
VSTMDB.64 Rn!, <d_reg list>	Writes multiple double precision data and the address is decremented before each register is written. *Rn* writes back after the transfer is carried out.

TABLE 5.36 Stack push/pop instructions for the FPU registers (Require the FPU extension. Not available for the Cortex-M23 processor).

Example	Description
VPUSH.32 <s_reg list>	Stores single precision register(s) in the stack (i.e., s0–s31)
VPUSH.64 <d_reg list>	Stores double precision register(s) in the stack (i.e., d0–d15)
VPOP.32 <s_reg list>	Restores single precision register(s) from the stack.
VPOP.64 <d_reg list>	Restores double precision register(s) from the stack.

processor, a single bit register is present to record an on-going exclusive access sequence. This is known as a **local exclusive access monitor**. At the system bus level, a **global exclusive access monitor** might also be present to check whether a memory location (or a memory device) used by an exclusive access sequence has been accessed by another processor or another bus master. The processor has an extra signal in the bus interface to indicate whether the transfer is an exclusive access, and another signal for receiving a response from the system bus level exclusive access monitor.

In a semaphore or in a MUTEX operation, a data variable in the RAM is used to represent a token. The variable is used to indicate whether a hardware resource is allocated to an application task. For example,

- if the aforementioned variable is 0, this indicates that the hardware resource is available, and
- if the aforementioned variable is 1, this indicates that the hardware resource has already been allocated to a task.

With this arrangement, an exclusive access sequence for requesting the resource could be as per Fig. 5.3. A number of steps are illustrated in Fig. 5.3 and the description of these is as follows:

1. The variable is accessed with an exclusive load (read): The local exclusive access monitor updates to indicate an active exclusive access transfer and, if a bus level exclusive access monitor is present, it will also update with information about the exclusive load.
2. The variable is checked by the application code to determine whether the hardware resource has already been allocated (i.e., locked): If the value is 1 (already allocated), it can either retry later or return a failure status to the application task that requested the resource. If the value is 0 (resource is free), then it can try to allocate the resource in the next step.
3. The task uses an exclusive store to write a value of 1 to the variable: If the local exclusive access monitor is set and there is no exclusive access conflict reported by the bus level exclusive access monitor, the variable will then be updated and the exclusive store will receive a success return status. If between the execution of the exclusive load and the execution of the exclusive store an event happens that could affect the exclusiveness of the

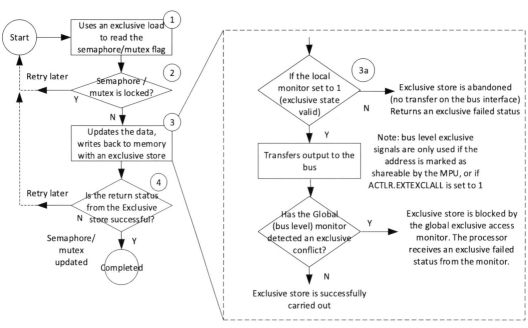

FIG. 5.3 Example exclusive access sequence for requesting a shared resource.

access to the variable, the exclusive store will get a failed return status and the variable will not be updated (the update is either cancelled by the processor or the update is blocked by the bus level exclusive access monitor).

4. Using the return status of the exclusive store, the application task will know whether it has allocated the hardware resource successfully: If it has not, it can retry later or return a failure status to the application task that requested the resource.

The return status of an exclusive store operation is delivered by a register: value of 0 means success and return value of 1 means it failed. The exclusive store fails if:

- The bus level exclusive access monitor returns an exclusive fail response (e.g., the memory location or memory range has been accessed by another processor)
- The local exclusive access monitor is not set. This can be caused by:

  ○ An incorrect exclusive access sequence
  ○ An interrupt entry/exit event between the exclusive load and exclusive store (the memory location or memory range could have been accessed by an interrupt handler or by another application task).
  ○ An execution of a special instruction called CLREX, which clears the local exclusive access monitor.

Exclusive access conflict detection is pessimistic in that an exclusive fail does not always mean that an access conflict has occurred. For example, the bus level exclusive access monitor might not record and compare the few lowest bits of the address value (the address granularity of the exclusive monitor hardware—also known as Exclusives Reservation Granule

(ERG)). Also, if an exception event has taken place, the exception handler might not have accessed the semaphore variable. However, the mechanism does ensure that the access conflict is detected and the only disadvantage of this behavior is, potentially, wasting a small number of clock cycles during the semaphore operations.

The instructions for exclusive access are listed in Table 5.37.

When creating portable semaphore/mutex code, additional memory barrier instructions should be added. This is because high-end processors utilize memory re-ordering techniques for performance reasons, a fact that can cause complications in relation to the operation of semaphores (this topic is covered in Section 5.7.12). Traditionally, DSB or DMB instructions are used (see Section 5.19) to overcome this issue. In Armv8-M, variants of exclusive access instructions with memory barrier semantics have been introduced (i.e., Load-acquire and store release instructions, see Table 5.38).

Further information on memory barriers and load-acquire/store-release instructions are covered in Section 5.7.12.

The behavior of exclusive access in the Cortex-M23 and Cortex-M33 processors are different from the Cortex-M3 and Cortex-M4 processors. In the Cortex-M23 and Cortex-M33 processors, the bus level exclusive signals are only used if:

- The Memory Protection Unit (MPU) marks the address as sharable, or
- The EXTEXCLALL (external exclusive all) bit in the ACTLR (Auxiliary Control Register) is set to 1.

TABLE 5.37 Exclusive access instructions.

Instruction	Description	Restriction
LDREXB Rt, [Rn]	Reads a byte with exclusive read from memory location Rn Rt = memory[Rn]	Rt must not be SP/PC Rn must not be PC
LDREXH Rt, [Rn]	Reads a halfword with exclusive read from memory location Rn Rt = memory[Rn]	Same as above
LDREX Rt, [Rn, #offset]	Reads a word with exclusive read with immediate offset Rt = memory[Rn + (imm8 << 2)]	Same as above 0 < Offset < 1020
STREXB Rd, Rt, [Rn]	Stores a byte with exclusive store in Rt to the memory location Rn. Returns status to Rd.	Same as above
STREXH Rd, Rt, [Rn]	Stores a halfword with exclusive store in Rt to the memory location Rn. Returns status to Rd.	Same as above
STREX Rd, Rt, [Rn, #offset]	Stores a word with exclusive store with immediate offset Memory[Rn + (imm8 << 2)] = Rt. Returns status to Rd.	Same as above 0 < Offset < 1020
CLREX	Forces the local exclusive access monitor to a clear state. This is not a memory access instruction, but is listed here due to its relationship to the exclusive access sequence.	None

TABLE 5.38 Exclusive access instructions with memory barrier semantics.

Instruction	Description	Restriction
DAEXB Rt, [Rn]	Reads byte with an exclusive access from memory location Rn Rt=memory[Rn]	Rt must not be SP/PC Rn must not be PC
LDAEXH Rt, [Rn]	Reads halfword with and exclusive access from memory location Rn Rt=memory[Rn]	Same as above
LDAEX Rt, [Rn]	Reads word with an exclusive access with immediate offset Rt=memory[Rn]	Same as above
STLEXB Rd, Rt, [Rn]	Stores byte in Rt with an exclusive access to memory location Rn. Memory[Rn]=Rt. Returns status in Rd.	Same as above
STLEXH Rd, Rt, [Rn]	Stores halfword in Rt with an exclusive access to memory location Rn. Memory[Rn]=Rt. Returns status in Rd.	Same as above
STLEX Rd, Rt, [Rn]	Stores word in Rt with an exclusive access to memory location Memory[Rn]=Rt. Returns status in Rd.	Same as above

In Cortex-M3 and M4 processors, exclusive side band signals are used for all exclusive access, regardless of the shareability attribute of the address. So, when using the Cortex-M23 and the Cortex-M33 processors, if the semaphore data is to be accessed by multiple processors, you need to either program the MPU to mark the address of the semaphore variable to be shared or set the ACTLR.EXTEXCLALL to 1.

Armv6-M processors (e.g., Cortex-M0, Cortex-M0+ processors) do not support exclusive access.

5.7.12 Load acquire-store release

Load-acquire and store-release instructions are memory access instructions with memory ordering requirements. These instructions are new in the Cortex-M processor family and are designed to help handle data access across multiprocessor systems. This includes the handling of atomic variables, a feature introduced in the C11 standard.

In high performance processors, the processor hardware can re-order memory access to increase performance. This optimization does not cause problems to the software providing that:

(a) the processor keeps track of the access ordering and
(b) ensures that the operation results are not affected.

Memory access re-ordering techniques include the following:

• In the case of reading data, a processor can, optionally, perform the read operation earlier to prevent the subsequent data processing operations that use the data from being stalled.

In a high-performance processor with a long pipeline, the read operation can potentially, as long as the memory location is not a peripheral, speculatively start earlier in the pipeline. The speculative read does not violate security management, such as memory partitioning of the TrustZone security extension.

- In the case of data write, a processor might implement a write buffer with multiple buffer entries. In such a case, a write operation might be delayed and stay in the write buffer for a period of time, resulting in subsequent write operations, potentially, reaching the memory before it.

In single processor systems, such memory access re-ordering is perfectly fine. But, when the system contains two or more processors and there are interactions between the software running on those processors, there could be issues when reordering takes place. By way of an example, I show in Fig. 5.4 an operation sequence where such an issue can occur:

When memory access reordering takes place, processor B will, potentially, take data from memory location X that has not been updated, as shown in Fig. 5.5. Such issue's do not happen in a single core system because the processor's bus interface detects and resolves the potential access conflicts by forwarding the write data in the write buffer to the speculative read access in location X.

In previous Arm processors, there are memory accessing ordering requirements for devices (i.e., peripheral address ranges). But, the memory access ordering behavior for normal memories (e.g., SRAM) is not strictly required and could lead to the problem shown in

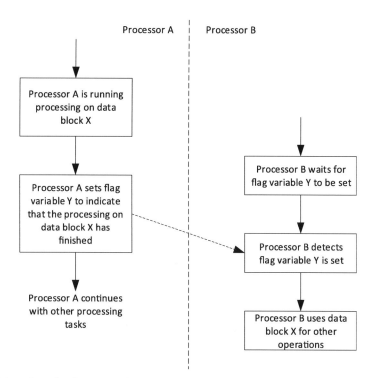

FIG. 5.4   An interaction of software running on two processors.

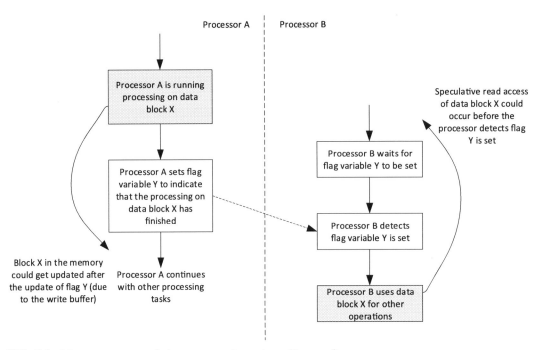

FIG. 5.5   Memory access reordering can cause issues in multicore software.

Fig. 5.5. To solve this issue, memory barrier instructions (see Section 5.19) should be added to ensure the ordering of memory access observed by other bus masters in the system matches the program's intended behaviors (Fig. 5.6). In high performance processors, however, the use of those memory barrier instructions can take many clock cycles, which can impact performance, e.g., all data in the write buffers must be drained and if any of the subsequent reads have started early these must be discarded and re-issued.

To reduce the performance impact, newer Arm processors (from Armv8-M onwards) introduced store release and load acquire instructions (Fig. 5.7).

- Store-release—memory store operations that need to wait until previously issued write operations are complete before they are issued to the bus. In this situation, when other bus masters observe the update of flag variable Y (updated by a store release instruction), the update on data block X must have been completed.
- Load-acquire—memory load operations that prevent subsequent read accesses to be issued in advance until the load acquire operation has been completed. Preceding buffered writes do not have to be drained and thus avoid causing a long delay.

In Armv8-M architecture, the load acquire and store release instructions are available for data sizes of word, halfword, byte (Table 5.39).

Exclusive access variants of load acquire and store release instructions are shown in Table 5.38.

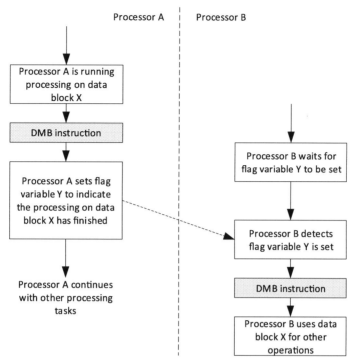

FIG. 5.6   Using Data Memory Barrier (DMB) instructions to avoid access ordering issues.

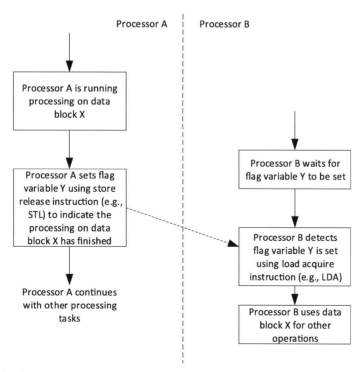

FIG. 5.7   Using load-acquire and store-release instructions to prevent ordering issues.

TABLE 5.39 Load-acquire and store-release instructions.

Instruction	Description	Restriction
LDAB Rt, [Rn]	Reads byte from memory location Rn Rt=memory[Rn]	Rt must not be SP/PC Rn must not be PC
LDAH Rt, [Rn]	Reads halfword from memory location Rn Rt=memory[Rn]	Same as above
LDA Rt, [Rn]	Reads word with immediate offset Rt=memory[Rn]	Same as above
STLB Rt, [Rn]	Stores byte in Rt to memory location Rn.	Same as above
STLH Rt, [Rn]	Stores halfword in Rt to memory location Rn.	Same as above
STL Rt, [Rn]	Stores word in Rt to memory location Rn.	Same as above

In the Cortex-M23 and Cortex-M33 processors, because the pipelines are relatively simple and are without memory access re-ordering, the load-acquire and store-release instructions execute just like normal memory access instructions. The inclusion of these instructions helps to achieve better architecture alignment between the different classes of processors (small and low power Cortex-M as well as the high-performance Cortex-A processors). It is possible to design a Cortex-M processor product to have a superscalar pipeline, similar to that in the Cortex-M7 processor, and the inclusion of these instructions in the architecture enables such designs to be more efficient. This is important for the Cortex-M processor family as this product range has a very long product life cycle.

5.8 Instruction set—Arithmetic operations

Arithmetic operations are key parts of software operations, with all Armv8-M processors supporting a range of arithmetic instructions. For example:

- Addition (including addition with carry)
- Subtractions (including subtraction with borrow)
- Multiplications and multiply-accumulate (MAC). Note: MAC is available in Mainline only.
- Divide

The above arithmetic instructions are available in various forms (different syntaxes and binary encoding). For example:

- Operations between two registers
- Operations between a register and an immediate data

Since the Cortex-M23 processor is designed to be smaller, it only supports a subset of the aforementioned arithmetic instructions, of which most are 16-bit instructions. Most of the arithmetic instructions available on Cortex-M23 processor:

- Are limited to low registers (r0–r7) only.
- Always updates the APSR.
- Supports a smaller range of immediate data values.

Usually 16-bit data processing instructions always updates the APSR and is written with the "S" suffix. However, if one of these instructions is being used in an Armv8-M Mainline processor, like the Cortex-M33, then there is an exception when the APSR is not updated. This is when the instruction is being used in a conditional execution structure "IF-THEN". In such a case, the instruction does not update the APSR and should be written without the "S" suffix.

The following instructions (Table 5.40), which are mostly 16-bit except for the divide instructions, are supported on the Cortex-M23 and Cortex-M33 processors:

TABLE 5.40 Arithmetic instructions which are available for both Armv8-M Baseline and Mainline.

Instruction	Description	Restriction
ADD Rd, Rm	Rd = Rd + Rm	Rd and Rm can be high/low registers
ADD Rd, SP, Rd	Rd = SP + Rd	Rd can be high/low register
ADDS Rd, Rn, Rm	Rd = Rn + Rm, APSR update	Rd, Rn, and Rm are low registers
ADDS Rd, Rn, #imm3	Rd = Rn + Zero_Extend(#imm3), APSR update	Same as above
ADDS Rd, Rd, #imm8	Rd = Rd + Zero_Extend(imm8), APSR update	Same as above
ADD SP, Rm	SP = SP + Rm	Rm can be high/low register
ADD Rd, SP, #imm8	Rd = SP + Zero_Extend (#imm8 << 2)	Rd must be a low register
ADD SP, SP, #imm7	SP = SP + Zero_Extend (#imm7 << 2) (Used for a C function to reserve stack space for local variables)	
ADR Rd, label ADD Rd, PC, #imm8	Rd = (PC[32:2] << 2) + Zero_Extend(imm8 << 2) Used for locating a data address within the program memory (Can be literal data, lookup tables, branch tables). The data address needs to be near the current program counter.	Rd must be a low register. The resulting address must be word aligned.
ADCS Rd, Rm	Add with carry Rd = Rd + Rm + Carry, APSR update	Rd and Rm are low registers
SUBS Rd, Rn, Rm	Rd = Rn − Rm, APSR update	Rd, Rn, and Rm are low registers
SUBS Rd, Rn, #imm3	Rd = Rn − Zero_Extend(#imm3), APSR update	Rd and Rd are low registers
SUBS Rd, #imm8	Rd = Rd − Zero_Extend(#imm8), APSR update	Rd is a low register

Continued

TABLE 5.40   Arithmetic instructions which are available for both Armv8-M Baseline and Mainline—cont'd

Instruction	Description	Restriction
SBCS Rd, Rd, Rm	Subtract with carry (borrow) Rd = Rd − Rm − Borrow, APSR update	Rd and Rm are low registers
RSBS Rd, Rn, #0	Reverse subtract (negative) Rd = 0 − Rn, APSR update	Rd and Rn are low registers
CMP Rn, Rm	Compare: calculate Rn − Rm and update APSR.	Rd and Rm are both low registers, or both high registers.
CMP Rn, #imm8	Compare: calculate Rn − Zero_Extend(#imm8), APSR update	Rn is a low register
CMN Rn, Rm	Compare negative: calculate Rn + Rm and update APSR.	Rd and Rn are low registers
MULS Rd, Rm, Rd	Rd = Rd * Rm (32-bit result), APSR.N and APSR.Z update	Rd and Rm are low registers
UDIV Rd, Rn, Rm	Rd = Rn/Rm (Unsigned divide)	Rd, Rn, and Rm can be high or low registers
SDIV Rd, Rn, Rm	Rd = Rn/Rm (Signed divide)	Rd, Rn, and Rm can be high or low registers

Armv8-M Mainline provides additional range arithmetic instructions with

- larger immediate data ranges
- the ability to utilize high registers
- options for a flexible second operand ("flexible op2")

The flexible second operand feature is partly covered in Section 5.6.3, where op2 can be a constant in the form of (note: X and Y below are hexadecimal digits):

- Any constant that can be produced by shifting an 8-bit value left by any number of bits within a 32-bit word.
- Any constant of the form 0x00XY00XY.
- Any constant of the form 0xXY00XY00.
- Any constant of the form 0xXYXYXYXY.

The second form of flexible second operand is a register with an optional shift/rotate. This is usually indicated by an additional *shift* operand after *Rm*. E.g.

opcode Rd, Rn, Rm, LSL #2; shift operation for Rm is "LSL #2", i.e., logical shift left by 2 bits

Where *Rm* specifies the register holding the data for the second operand and *shift* is an optional specifier of the shift operation to be applied to *Rm*. It can be one of the following (Table 5.41).

The shift operates on-the-fly and does not affect the data held in the Rm register. However, the carry flag could be updated by the shift operations. If the shift specifier is omitted or if the shift expression specifies LSL #0, the instruction will use the value in Rm without changes.

TABLE 5.41 Optional shift operation for second operand (barrel shifter).

Shift expression	Description
ASR #n	Arithmetic shift right n bits, $1 \leq n \leq 32$.
LSL #n	Logical shift left n bits, $1 \leq n \leq 31$.
LSR #n	Logical shift right n bits, $1 \leq n \leq 32$.
ROR #n	Rotate right n bits, $1 \leq n \leq 31$.
RRX	Rotate right one bit, with extend (see RRX description in Section 5.10)

The flexible second operand feature applies to a number of instructions, not just arithmetic operations.

The additional arithmetic instructions provided by the Armv8-M Mainline extension is listed in Table 5.42. This table uses "{S}" (S suffix—APSR update) and "{,shift}" (shift operation specifier) to indicate that these parameters are optional. Both high and low registers can be used with these instructions.

One difference in arithmetic instructions when comparing Armv8-M baseline to Armv6-M is that Armv6-M does not support hardware divide instructions (UDIV and SDIV). These instructions are, however, supported by all Armv8-M processors.

In the Cortex-M33 processor, the behavior of the hardware divide instructions is configurable. By default, if a divide by zero takes place, the result of the UDIV and SDIV instructions will be zero. You can set up the DIVBYZERO bit in the NVIC Configuration Control Register so that when a divide-by-zero situation occurs a fault exception (HardFault/UsageFault) is triggered.

5.9 Instruction set—Logic operations

Another type of data processing instruction are bitwise logical operations. The following instructions (Table 5.43) are supported in the Cortex-M23 and Cortex-M33 processors. Since Rd and Rn must be the same for these 16-bit instructions, the Rd operand is optional.

Armv8-M Mainline processors support a wide range of logic operations, as shown in Table 5.44. Both low and high registers can be used with these instructions.

Note: The C flag could get updated as part of the shift/rotate operation, which is specified by the flexible second operand.

5.10 Instruction set—Shift and rotate operations

The following 16-bit instructions (Table 5.45) are supported on the Cortex-M23 and Cortex-M33 processors.

Please note, when a register is used to specify the length of shift or rotate, the lowest 8 bits are used (the value can be larger than 32). For logical shift operations, the result written to the destination register is 0 if the shift amount is 32 or more.

TABLE 5.42 Arithmetic instructions available for Armv8-M Mainline.

Instruction	Description
`ADD{S} Rd, Rn, Rm {,shift}`	Rd = Rn + shift(Rm), with or without APSR updates
`ADD{S} Rd, Rn, #imm12`	Rd = Rn + #imm12, with or without APSR updates
`ADD{S} Rd, Rn, #imm`	Rd = Rn + #imm (flexible op2 form), with or without APSR updates
`ADD{S} Rd, SP, Rm {,shift}`	Rd = SP + shift (Rm)
`ADDW Rd, SP, #imm12`	Rd = SP + #imm12
`ADD{S} Rd, SP, #imm`	Rd = SP + #imm (flexible op2 form), with or without APSR updates
`ADC{S} Rd, Rn, #imm`	Rd = Rn + imm (flexible op2 form) + carry, with or without APSR updates
`ADC{S} Rd, Rn, Rm {,shift}`	Rd = Rn + shift(Rm) + carry, with or without APSR updates
`ADR Rd, label`	Rd = (WordAlign(PC)+4) +/− #immed12
`SUB{S} Rd, Rn, Rm {,shift}`	Rd = Rn − shift(Rm), with or without APSR updates
`SUB{S} Rd, Rn, #imm12`	Rd = Rn − #imm12, with or without APSR updates
`SUB{S} Rd, Rn, #imm`	Rd = Rn − #imm (flexible op2 form), with or without APSR updates
`SUB{S} Rd, SP, Rm {,shift}`	Rd = SP − shift (Rm)
`SUBW Rd, SP, #imm12`	Rd = SP − #imm12
`SUB{S} Rd, SP, #imm`	Rd = SP − #imm (flexible op2 form), with or without APSR updates
`SBC{S} Rd, Rn, #imm`	Rd = Rn − #imm (flexible op2 form) − borrow, with or without APSR updates
`SBC{S} Rd, Rn, Rm {,shift}`	Rd = Rn − shift(Rm) + borrow, with or without APSR updates
`RSB{S} Rd, Rn, #imm`	Rd = #imm (flexible op2 form) − Rn, with or without APSR updates
`RSB{S} Rd, Rn, Rm`	Rd = shift(Rm) − Rn, with or without APSR updates
`CMP Rn, Rm{,shift}`	Compare: calculate Rn − shift (Rm) and update APSR.
`CMP Rn, #imm`	Compare: calculate Rn − #imm (flexible op2 form) and update APSR.
`CMN Rn, Rm{,shift}`	Compare negative: calculate Rn + shift(Rm) and update APSR.

TABLE 5.42 Arithmetic instructions available for Armv8-M Mainline—cont'd

Instruction	Description
CMN Rn, #imm	Compare negative: calculate Rn + #imm (flexible op2 form) and update APSR.
MUL Rd, Rn, Rm	Rd = Rn * Rm, 32-bit result.
MLA Rd, Rn, Rm, Ra	Rd = Ra + Rn*Rm (32-bit MAC instruction, 32-bit result).
MLS Rd, Rn, Rm, Ra	Rd = Ra − Rn*Rm (32-bit multiply with subtract instruction, 32-bit result)
SMULL RdLo, RdHi, Rn, Rm	32-bit signed multiply with 64-bit result {RdHi, RdLo} = Rn * Rm
SMLAL RdLo, RdHi, Rn, Rm	32-bit signed multiply accumulate with 64-bit result {RdHi, RdLo} += Rn * Rm
UMULL RdLo, RdHi, Rn, Rm	32-bit unsigned multiply with 64-bit result {RdHi, RdLo} = Rn * Rm
UMLAL RdLo, RdHi, Rn, Rm	32-bit unsigned multiply accumulate with 64-bit result {RdHi, RdLo} += Rn * Rm

TABLE 5.43 Logic instructions available for Armv8-M Baseline and Mainline.

Instruction	Description	Restriction
ANDS {Rd,} Rn, Rm	And Rd = Rn AND Rm, APSR(N,Z) update	Rd and Rn must specify the same register. All registers are low registers
ORRS {Rd,} Rn, Rm	Or Rd = Rn OR Rm, APSR(N,Z) update	Same as above
EORS {Rd,} Rn, Rm	Exclusive or Rd = Rn XOR Rm, APSR(N,Z) update	Same as above
BICS {Rd,} Rn, Rm	Bit clear Rd = Rn AND (!Rm), APSR(N,Z) update	Same as above
MVNS Rd, Rm	Bitwise not (also covered in Section 5.6.2) Rd = !Rm, APSR(N,Z) update	Rd and Rm are low registers
TST Rn, Rm	Test (bitwise AND, but without updating the destination register) Calculate Rn AND Rm, only APSR(N,Z) update	Rn and Rm are low registers

TABLE 5.44 Additional logic instructions available for Armv8-M Mainline.

Instruction	Description
AND{S} Rd, Rn, Rm {,shift}	And Rd = Rn AND (shift(Rm)), with or without updating APSR(N,Z,C)
AND{S} Rd, Rn, #imm	And Rd = Rd AND imm (flexible op2 form), with or without updating APSR (N,Z,C)
ORR{S} Rd, Rn, Rm {,shift}	Or Rd = Rn OR Rm, with or without updating APSR(N,Z, C)
ORR{S} Rd, Rn, #imm	Or Rd = Rd OR imm (flexible op2 form), with or without updating APSR(N, Z,C)
ORN{S} Rd, Rn, Rm {,shift}	Or Nor Rd = Rn OR !Rm, with or without updating APSR(N,Z, C)
ORN{S} Rd, Rn, #imm	Or Not Rd = Rd OR !imm (flexible op2 form), with or without updating APSR(N, Z,C)
EOR{S} Rd, Rn, Rm {,shift}	Exclusive or Rd = Rn XOR Rm, with or without updating APSR(N,Z,C)
EOR{S} Rd, Rn, #imm	Exclusive or Rd = Rd XOR imm (flexible op2 form), with or without updating APSR(N, Z,C)
BIC{S} Rd, Rn, Rm {,shift}	Bit clear Rd = Rn AND (!Rm), with or without updating APSR(N,Z,C)
BIC{S} Rd, Rn, #imm	Bit clear Rd = Rd AND (!imm) (flexible op2 form), with or without updating APSR (N,Z,C)
MVN{S} Rd, Rm {,shift}	Bitwise not (also covered in Section 5.6.2) Rd = !Rm, with or without updating APSR(N,Z,C)
TST Rn, Rm {,shift}	Test (bitwise AND, but without updating the destination register) Calculate Rn AND Rm, only APSR(N,Z,C) update
TST Rn, #imm	Test (bitwise AND, but without updating the destination register) Calculate Rn AND imm (flexible op2 form), but only updates APSR(N,Z, C)
TEQ Rn, Rm {,shift}	Test (bitwise XOR, but without update to destination register) Calculate Rn XOR Rm, but only updates APSR(N,Z,C)
TEQ Rn, #imm	Test (bitwise XOR, but without updating the destination register) Calculate Rn XOR imm (flexible op2 form), but only updates APSR(N,Z,C)

TABLE 5.45 Shift and rotate instructions available for Armv8-M Baseline and Mainline.

Instruction	Description	Restriction
ASRS {Rd,} Rm, Rs	Arithmetic Shift Right $Rd = Rn >> Rm$ (shift length 0–255)	Rd and Rm must specify the same register. All registers are low registers
ASRS {Rd,} Rm, #imm	Arithmetic Shift Right $Rd = Rm >> imm$ (shift length 1–32)	Same as above
LSLS {Rd,} Rm, Rs	Logical Shift Left $Rd = Rn << Rm$ (shift length 0–255)	Same as above
LSLS {Rd,} Rm, #imm	Logical Shift Left $Rd = Rm << imm$ (shift length 0–31)	Same as above
LSRS {Rd,} Rm, Rs	Logical Shift Right $Rd = Rn >> Rm$ (shift length 0–255)	Same as above
LSRS {Rd,} Rm, #imm	Logical Shift Right $Rd = Rm >> imm$ (shift length 1–32)	Same as above
RORS {Rd,} Rm, Rs	Rotate Right $Rd = Rm$ rotated by Rs	Same as above

When the ASR is used, the Most Significant Bit (MSB) of the result is unchanged and, at the same time, the Carry flag ("C") is updated using the last bit shifted out (Fig. 5.8).

For logical shift operations, all bits in the register are updated (Figs. 5.9 and 5.10).

The rotate right instruction is illustrated in Fig. 5.11.

The architecture only provides a rotate right instruction. If a rotate left operation is needed, this can be executed using a ROR with a different offset (except that the Carry flag will be different from rotate left):

$$\text{Rotate\_Left}(\text{Data}, \text{offset}) == \text{Rotate\_Right}(\text{Data}, (32 - \text{offset}))$$

The 32-bit version of shift and rotate instructions (Table 5.46) provide additional operation options and the option of updating the APSR.

The RRX operation is illustrated in Fig. 5.12.

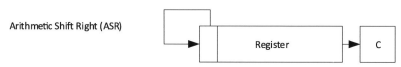

FIG. 5.8 Arithmetic Shift Right.

Logical Shift Left (LSL)

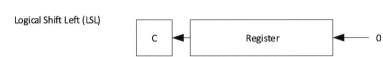

FIG. 5.9   Logical Shift Left.

Logical Shift Right (LSR)

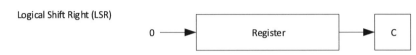

FIG. 5.10   Logical Shift Right.

Rotate Right (ROR)

FIG. 5.11   Rotate Right.

TABLE 5.46   Additional shift and rotate instructions available for Armv8-M Mainline.

Instruction	Description
ASR{S} Rd, Rm, Rs	Arithmetic Shift Right Rd = Rn >> Rm (shift length 0–255)
ASR{S} Rd, Rm, #imm	Arithmetic Shift Right Rd = Rm >> imm (shift length 1–32)
LSL{S} Rd, Rm, Rs	Logical Shift Left Rd = Rn << Rm (shift length 0–255)
LSL{S} Rd, Rm, #imm	Logical Shift Left Rd = Rm << imm (shift length 0–31)
LSR{S} Rd, Rm, Rs	Logical Shift Right Rd = Rn >> Rm (shift length 0–255)
LSR{S} Rd, Rm, #imm	Logical Shift Right Rd = Rm >> imm (shift length 1–32)
ROR{S} Rd, Rm, Rs	Rotate Right Rd = Rm rotated by Rs (rotate range 0–255)
ROR{S} Rd, Rm, #imm	Rotate Right Rd = Rm rotated by imm (1–31)
RRX{S} Rd, Rm	Rotate Right with 1 bit with Extend Rd = Rm rotated right by 1 bit

Rotate Right with Extend (RRX)

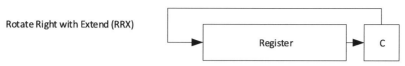

FIG. 5.12   Rotate Right with Extend.

5.11 Instruction set—Data conversions (extend and reverse ordering)

Cortex-M processors support a range of instructions for converting data between different data types. For example, to convert data from 8 bits to 32 bits or from 16 bits to 32 bits. These instructions are available for signed and unsigned data. The 16-bit versions of these instructions are available for all Cortex-M processors and they can only access low registers (r0–r7) (Table 5.47).

SXTB and SXTH instructions sign-extend the input value (Rm) using bit[7] (for SXTB) or bit [15] (for SXTH). With UXTB and UXTH, the input value is zero-extended to a 32-bit result.

For example, if R0 is 0x55AA8765:

```
SXTB R1, R0 ; R1 = 0x00000065
SXTH R1, R0 ; R1 = 0xFFFF8765
UXTB R1, R0 ; R1 = 0x00000065
UXTH R1, R0 ; R1 = 0x00008765
```

32-bit versions of these instructions allow the use of high registers and provide an optional rotate parameter for the input data (Table 5.48).

These instructions are useful for converting data between different data types. Please note, sometimes the sign-extend or unsign-extend operations can also take place on the fly when loading data from memory (e.g., LDRB for unsigned data and LDRSB for signed data).

The DSP extension in Armv8-M Mainline also includes additional extend instructions. This is covered in Section 5.15.

Another type of data conversion instruction is that for converting data between little endian and big endian. These instructions reverse byte order in a register, as shown in Table 5.49.

The operation of these instructions is illustrated in Fig. 5.13.

TABLE 5.47   Signed and unsigned extend instructions for Armv8-M Baseline and Mainline.

Instruction	Description	Restriction
SXTB Rd, Rm	Signed extend byte data into word Rd = signed_extend(Rm[7:0])	Rd and Rm are low registers only
SXTH Rd, Rm	Signed extend byte data into word Rd = signed_extend(Rm[15:0])	Same as above
UXTB Rd, Rm	Unsigned extend byte data into word Rd = unsigned_extend(Rm[7:0])	Same as above
UXTH Rd, Rm	Unsigned extend byte data into word Rd = unsigned_extend(Rm[15:0])	Same as above

TABLE 5.48 Additional sign and unsign extend instructions for Armv8-M Mainline.

Instruction	Description	Restriction
SXTB Rd, Rm {,ROR #n} (n = 0/ 8 / 16/ 24)	Sign extend byte data into word Rd = sign_extend(Rm[7:0]); no rotate Rd = sign_extend(Rm[15:8]); n = 8 Rd = sign_extend(Rm[23:16]); n = 16 Rd = sign_extend(Rm[31:24]); n = 24	
SXTH Rd, Rm {,ROR #n} (n = 0 / 8 / 16/ 24)	Sign extend byte data into word Rd = sign_extend(Rm[15:0]); no rotate Rd = sign_extend(Rm[23:8]); n = 8 Rd = sign_extend(Rm[31:16]); n = 16 Rd = sign_extend(Rm[7:0], Rm[31:24]); n = 24	
UXTB Rd, Rm {,ROR #n} (n = 0 / 8 / 16/ 24)	Unsign extend byte data into word Rd = unsign_extend(Rm[7:0]); no rotate Rd = unsign_extend(Rm[15:8]); n = 8 Rd = unsign_extend(Rm[23:16]); n = 16 Rd = unsign_extend(Rm[31:24]); n = 24	
UXTH Rd, Rm {,ROR #n} (n = 0 / 8 / 16/ 24)	Unsign extend byte data into word Rd = unsign_extend(Rm[7:0]); no rotate Rd = unsign_extend(Rm[15:8]); n = 8 Rd = unsign_extend(Rm[23:16]); n = 16 Rd = unsign_extend(Rm[31:24]); n = 24	

REV reverses the byte order in a data word and REVH reverses the byte order inside a half word. For example, if R0 is 0x12345678, then in executing the following:

```
REV    R1, R0
REV16 R2, R0
```

R1 will become 0x78563412, and R2 will be 0x34127856.

REVSH is similar to REV16 except that it only processes the lower half word and then sign extends the result. For example, if R0 is 0x33448899, then running:

```
REVSH R1, R0
```

R1 will become 0xFFFF9988.

TABLE 5.49 Reverse instructions for Armv8-M Baseline and Mainline.

Instruction	Description	Restriction
REV Rd, Rm	Reverses bytes in word	Armv8-M baseline only supports the 16-bit version, which only supports low registers.
REV16 Rd, Rm	Reverses bytes in each half word	Same as above
REVSH Rd, Rm	Reverses bytes in lower half word and sign-extends the result to 32bits	Same as above

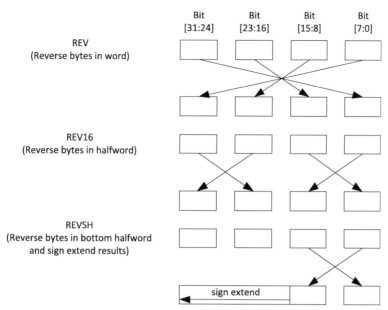

FIG. 5.13   Reverse operations.

The 16-bit form of these instructions (available in both Armv8-M baseline and Mainline) only accesses the low registers (R0–R7). A 32-bit version of these instructions (available in Armv8-M Mainline) can utilize the low and high registers.

5.12   Instruction set—Bit field processing

Bit field processing is common in control applications and for communication protocol processing. Armv8-M Mainline processors support a range of bit field processing instructions as listed in Table 5.50. These instructions are not available in Armv8-M Baseline.

BFC (Bit Field Clear) clears 1–31 adjacent bits in any position of a register. The syntax of the instruction is:

```
BFC  Rd, #lsb, #width
```

For example:

```
LDR  R0,=0x1234FFFF
BFC  R0, #4, #8
```

This will give R0 = 0x1234F00F.

BFI (Bit Field Insert) copies 1–32 bits (#width) from one register to any location (#lsb) in another register. The syntax is:

```
BFI  Rd, Rn, #lsb, #width
```

TABLE 5.50 Bit field processing instructions for Armv8-M Mainline.

Instruction	Description	Restriction
BFC Rd, #lsb, #width	Clears bit field to 0 within a register	lsb: 0–31 width: 1–32 lsb + width <= 32
BFI Rd, Rn, #lsb, #width	Inserts bit field from Rn to Rd at position #lsb	Same as above
SBFX Rd, Rn, #lsb, #width	Copies bit field from register and sign extends	Same as above
UBFX Rd, Rn, #lsb, #width	Copies bit field from register and unsign extends	Same as above
CLZ Rd, Rm	Counts Leading Zeros	
RBIT Rd, Rn	Reverses bit order	

For example:

```
LDR  R0,=0x12345678
LDR  R1,=0x3355AACC
BFI  R1, R0, #8, #16 ; Insert R0[15:0] to R1[23:8]
```

This will give R1 = 0x335678CC.

The CLZ instruction counts the number of leading zeros. If no bits are set the result is 32 and if all bits are set the result is 0. It is commonly used to determine the number of bit shifts required to normalize a value so that the leading bit that is one is shifted to bit 31. It is often used in floating-point calculations.

The RBIT instruction reverses the bit order in a data word. The syntax is:

```
RBIT Rd, Rn
```

This instruction is very useful for processing serial bit streams in data communications. For example, if R0 is 0xB4E10C23 (binary value 1011_0100_1110_0001_0000_1100_0010_0011), then executing the following instruction:

```
RBIT R0, R0
```

R0 will become 0xC430872D (binary value 1100_0100_0011_0000_1000_0111_0010_1101).

UBFX and SBFX are the Unsigned and Signed Bit Field Extract instructions. The syntax of these instructions is:

```
UBFX Rd, Rn, #lsb, #width
SBFX Rd, Rn, #lsb, #width
```

UBFX extracts a bit field from a register starting from any location (specified by the #lsb operand) with any width up to bit 31. The width of the bit field being extracted is specified by the #width operand. After the bit field is extracted, it is then zero-extended and put into the destination register. For example:

```
LDR   R0,=0x5678ABCD
UBFX  R1, R0, #4, #8
```

This will give R1 = 0x000000BC (zero extend of 0xBC).

Similarly, SBFX extracts a bit field but it sign-extends it before putting it in a destination register. For example:

```
LDR   R0,=0x5678ABCD
SBFX  R1, R0, #4, #8
```

This will give R1 = 0xFFFFFFBC (signed extend of 0xBC).

5.13 Instruction set—Saturation operations

Armv8-M Mainline processors support two saturation adjustment instructions called Signed Saturation (SSAT) and Unsigned Saturation (USAT). They are present even if the DSP extension is not included. The DSP extension, when included, provides an additional set of saturating arithmetic instructions. The SSAT and USAT instructions are shown in Table 5.51 and the saturating arithmetic instructions will be covered in Section 5.15.

Saturation is commonly used in signal processing. For example, after certain operations, such as amplification, the amplitude of a signal can exceed the maximum allowed output range. If the value is adjusted by simply cutting off the MSB bits, then the resulting signal waveform could be completely distorted (see Fig. 5.14).

The saturation operation reduces the distortion by forcing the value to the maximum allowed value. The distortion still exists, but if the value does not exceed the maximum range by too much it is less noticeable.

TABLE 5.51 Saturation adjustment instructions for Armv8-M Mainline.

Instruction	Description	Restriction
SSAT Rd,#imm,Rn{,shift}	Saturation for a signed value. The bit position for the saturation is defined by the immediate value (#imm). The Q bit in the APSR (Application Program Status Register) is set to 1 if a saturation occurs.	#imm: 1–32 shift can be ASR #amount(1–31), or LSL #amount(0–31)
USAT Rd,#imm,Rn{,shift}	Saturation for an unsigned value. The bit position for the saturation is defined by the immediate value (#imm). The Q bit in the APSR (Application Program Status Register) is set to 1 if a saturation occurs.	#imm: 0–32 shift can be ASR #amount(1–31), or LSL #amount(0–31)

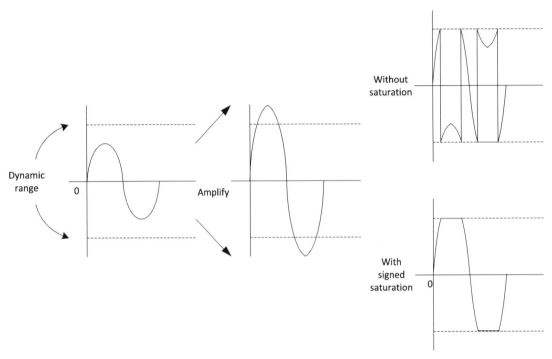

FIG. 5.14   Signed Saturation operation.

The SSAT and USAT instructions store the result of the saturation in the destination register (Rd). In parallel, the Q-flag in the APSR is set to 1 by the SSAT or USAT instruction if saturation takes place during the SSAT/USAT operation. The Q flag is cleared by the software writing 0 to the Q flag of the APSR (see Section 5.6.4). For example, if a 32-bit signed value is to be saturated into a 16-bit signed value, the following instruction can be used:

```
SSAT R1, #16, R0
```

Table 5.52 shows a number of examples of the SSAT operation results.

USAT is slightly different to SSAT in that the result is an unsigned value. This instruction provides a saturation operation, as shown in Fig. 5.15.

To produce the saturation adjustment operation, as shown in Fig. 5.15, you can, for example, convert a 32-bit signed value to a 16-bit unsigned value using the USAT instruction with the following code:

```
USAT R1, #16, R0
```

Table 5.53 shows a number of examples of USAT operation results.

The input value of SSAT and USAT instructions can be shifted before the actual saturation operation. You can add either a "#LSL N" (Logical Shift Left) or a "#ASR N" (Arithmetic Shift Right) parameter to these instructions.

TABLE 5.52 Examples of SSAT results.

Input (R0)	Output (R1)	Q bit
0x00020000	0x00007FFF	Set
0x00008000	0x00007FFF	Set
0x00007FFF	0x00007FFF	Unchanged
0x00000000	0x00000000	Unchanged
0xFFFF8000	0xFFFF8000	Unchanged
0xFFFF7FFF	0xFFFF8000	Set
0xFFFE0000	0xFFFF8000	Set

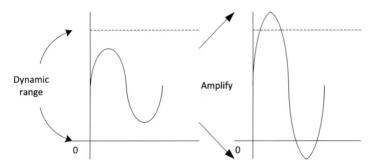
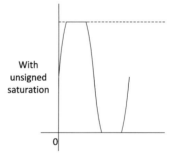

Dynamic range

Amplify

With unsigned saturation

FIG. 5.15 Unsigned Saturation operation.

TABLE 5.53 Examples of USAT results.

Input (R0)	Output (R1)	Q bit
0x00020000	0x0000FFFF	Set
0x00008000	0x00008000	Unchanged
0x00007FFF	0x00007FFF	Unchanged
0x00000000	0x00000000	Unchanged
0xFFFF8000	0x00000000	Set
0xFFFF8001	0x00000000	Set
0xFFFFFFFF	0x00000000	Set

5.14 Instruction set—Program flow control

5.14.1 Overview

There are a number of instruction types for program flow control. These are:

- Branch
- Function call
- Conditional branch
- Combined compare and conditional branch
- Conditional execution (IF-THEN instruction)—Armv8-M Mainline only
- Table branch—Armv8-M Mainline only

The TrustZone security extension has added a few additional branch instructions (e.g., BXNS, BLXNS). These are covered in Section 5.20. Armv8.1-M architecture (e.g., Cortex-M55) added a range of branch instructions, but they are not supported in the Cortex-M23 and Cortex-M33 processors, and, therefore are not covered in this book.

5.14.2 Branch

A number of instructions can cause branch operations. These are:

- Branch instructions (e.g., "B label", "BX Rn")
- A data processing instruction that updates R15 (the Program Counter, PC) (e.g., MOV, ADD)—this method is not used in most cases because branch instructions are usually more optimized.
- A memory read instruction that writes to PC (e.g., LDR, LDM, POP)—a POP instruction with a PC update is often used for function returns.

In general, although it is possible to use any of the above operations to create branches, it is more common to use B (Branch), BX (Branch with Exchange), and POP instructions (commonly used for function return). Sometimes other methods are used in table branches for Armv8-M Baseline and Armv6-M processors. These are not required in Armv8-M Mainline and Armv7-M architecture as those processors have specific instructions for table branches.

Both Armv8-M Baseline and Mainline support the branch instructions listed in Table 5.54.

TABLE 5.54   Unconditional branch instructions (Armv8-M Baseline and Mainline).

Instruction	Description	Restriction
B label	16-bit version of the branch instruction	Branch range of +/−2KB
B.W label	32-bit version of the branch instruction Note: can be written as "B label" if the assembler automatically selects the 32-bit version when offset is >2KB	Branch range of +/−16MB
BX Rm	Branch and exchange. Branches to an address value stored in *Rm*, and sets the execution state of the processor (T-bit) based on bit 0 of *Rm*. (The bit 0 of *Rm* must be 1 because Cortex-M processors only supports Thumb state.)	

TABLE 5.55 Function call instructions (Armv8-M Baseline and Mainline).

Instruction	Description	Restriction
BL label	Branch and link instruction (32-bit). Branches to an address specified by "label", then saves the return address in LR.	Branch range of +/−16MB
BLX Rm	Branch and link with exchange. Branches to an address specified by *Rm*, then saves the return address in LR, and then updates the T-bit in the EPSR with the LSB (Least Significant Bit) of *Rm*.	The LSB of Rm must be 1

Please note, in rare cases, in assembly language programming, it can be necessary to specify a 32-bit version of the branch instruction if the branch target is just near to the +/−2KB range limit.

When one compares Armv8-M Baseline to Armv6-M, the Armv6-M architecture does not support the 32-bit version of the branch instruction ("B.W label"). This is included in Armv8-M Baseline to enable tool chains to provide better optimization mechanisms such as link-time function tail-chaining (which involves branching from the end of a function in one module to the start of another function in a different one).

Please refer to Section 5.20 for information on branch instruction "BXNS" introduced by the TrustZone security extension.

5.14.3 Function call

To call a function, the Branch and Link (BL) instruction or the Branch and Link with eX-change (BLX) instruction can be used (see Table 5.55). When these instructions are executed, the program counter is updated to the targeted address and, at the same time, the return address is saved to the Link Register (LR). The return address is saved in the LR so that the processor can branch back to the original program after the function call has finished.

Since Cortex-M processors only support Thumb instructions, when executing BLX instructions, the LSB of Rm must be set to 1. If it is not set to 1, the execution of the BLX instruction will attempt to switch to the Arm state and this will result in a fault exception.

Please refer to Section 5.20 for information on branch and link instruction "BLXNS" introduced by the TrustZone security extension.

Note: Save the LR if You Need to Call a Subroutine

The BL instruction destroys the current content of the LR register. So, if your program code needs at a later stage the current data held in the LR register, you should save the LR before you use the BL instruction. The usual way to do this is to push the LR to the stack at the beginning of your subroutine. For example:

```
main
    ...
    BL functionA
    ...
functionA
    PUSH {R0, LR} ; Save LR content to stack
    ;(save even number of registers to keep stack pointer aligned
```

```
      ; to double word addresses, a requirement for Arm C interface)
      ...
      BL functionB   ; Note: return address in LR will be changed
      ...
      POP {R0, PC} ; Use stacked LR content to return to main
functionB
      PUSH {R0, LR}
      ...
      POP {R0, PC} ; Use stacked LR content to return to functionA
```

In addition to saving the content in the LR register, if the subroutine called is a C function, you might also need to save the contents in R0–R3 and R12 if these values are also going to be needed at a later stage. According to the *AAPCS* [5], the contents in those registers could be changed by a C function. AAPCS also requires a double word stack alignment at the C function boundaries, thus for the example code above, there is a need to PUSH an even number of registers.

5.14.4 Conditional branch

Conditional branches are executed conditionally based on the current value in the APSR (N, Z, C, and V flags, as shown in Table 5.56).

APSR flags can be affected by:

- Most 16-bit data processing instructions.
- 32-bit (Thumb-2) data processing instructions with the S suffix; for example, ADDS.W.
- Compare (e.g., CMP) and Test (e.g., TST, TEQ) instructions.
- An instruction that writes to APSR/xPSR directly.
- Unstacking operations at the end of an exception/interrupt service.

TABLE 5.56 Flags (status bits) in the APSR which can be used for controlling conditional branches.

Flag	PSR bit	Description
N	31	Negative flag (last operation result is a negative value)
Z	30	Zero (last operation result returned a zero value. For example, the compare of two registers with identical values.)
C	29	Carry flag. – If the last operation is an ADD, and if the Carry flag is SET, this indicates a carry out status. – If the last operation is a SUBTRACT, and if the Carry flag is CLEARED, this indicates a borrow status. – If the last operation is a SHIFT or ROTATE, the Carry flag is the last bit shifted out in the shift or rotate operation.
V	28	Overflow (the last operation resulted in an overflow situation)

TABLE 5.57 Instructions for conditional branch.

Instruction	Description	Restriction
`B<cond> label`	A 16-bit version of the conditional branch. <cond> is one of the condition suffixes in Table 5.58	It has a branch range of −256 bytes to +254 bytes
`B<cond>.W label`	A 32-bit version of the conditional branch Note: this can be written as "B<cond> label" if the assembler automatically selects the 32-bit version when the offset is >2KB. <cond> is one of the condition suffixes in Table 5.58	It has a branch range of +/−1MB. Not supported in Armv8-M Baseline

For Armv8-M Mainline processors, there is another APSR flag bit at bit 27—called the Q flag. It is for saturating arithmetic operations, but is not used for conditional branches.

The condition type of a conditional branch instruction is indicated by a suffix, which is listed in Table 5.58. These suffixes are also used for conditional execution operations (see Section 5.14.6). Conditional branch instructions (Table 5.57, where <cond> is one of the condition suffixes) are available in 16-bit and 32-bit versions. The 16-bit and 32-bit versions have different branch ranges, with the Armv8-M Baseline only supporting the 16-bit version of the conditional branch instructions.

The <cond> is one of the fourteen possible condition suffixes listed in Table 5.58.

An example of using a conditional branch instruction is shown in Fig. 5.16. The operation in the diagram selects a new value for R3 based on the value in R0.

The program flow in Fig. 5.16 can be implemented using conditional branch and regular branch instructions as follows:

```
    CMP   R0, #1  ; compare R0 to 1
    BEQ   p2      ; if Equal, then go to p2
    MOVS R3, #1   ; R3 = 1
    B     p3      ; go to p3
p2                ; label p2
    MOVS R3, #2
p3                ; label p3
    ...           ; other subsequence operations
```

5.14.5 Compare and branches (CBZ, CBNZ)

Armv8-M architecture includes compare and branch instructions, CBZ and CBNZ (Table 5.59). Previously, these two instructions were absent from the Armv6-M processors and were only available on Armv7-M processors. For Armv8-M, CBZ, and CBNZ are available on both Baseline and Mainline subprofiles.

CBZ and CBNZ are very useful in loop structures such as "while" loops. For example:

```
  i = 5;
  while (i != 0 ){
    func1();         // calls a function
    i-;
  }
```

TABLE 5.58 Suffixes for conditional branches and conditional executions.

Suffix	Branch condition	Flags (APSR)
EQ	Equal	Z flag is set
NE	Not equal	Z flag is cleared
CS/ HS	Carry set/unsigned higher or same	C flag is set
CC/ LO	Carry clear/unsigned lower	C flag is cleared
MI	Minus/negative	N flag is set (minus)
PL	Plus/positive or zero	N flag is cleared
VS	Overflow	V flag is set
VC	No overflow	V flag is cleared
HI	Unsigned higher	C flag is set and Z is cleared
LS	Unsigned lower or same	C flag is cleared or Z is set
GE	Signed greater than or equal	N flag is set and V flag is set, or N flag is cleared and V flag is cleared (N==V)
LT	Signed less than	N flag is set and V flag is cleared, or N flag is cleared and V flag is set (N !=V)
GT	Signed greater than	Z flag is cleared, and either both the N flag and V flag are set, or both the N flag and V flag are cleared (Z==0 and N==V)
LE	Signed less than or equal	Z flag is set, or one of the followings: either the N flag is set and the V flag is cleared, or the N flag is cleared and the V flag is set (Z==1 or N !=V)

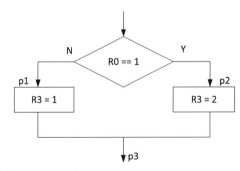

FIG. 5.16 Simple conditional branch example.

TABLE 5.59 Compare and branch instructions (Armv8-M Baseline and Mainline).

Instruction	Description	Restriction
CBZ Rn, label	Compare and branch on zero—branches to label if Rn is zero.	It has a branch range of +4 to +130 bytes
CBNZ Rn, label	Compare and branch on nonzero—branches to label if Rn is not zero.	Same as above

This can be compiled into:

```
      MOV  R0, #5          ; Sets loop counter
loop1 CBZ  R0,loop1exit    ; if loop counter = 0 then it exits the loop
      BL   func1           ; calls a function
      SUBS R0, #1          ; loop counter decrements
      B    loop1           ; next loop
loop1exit
```

The use of CBNZ is very similar to that of CBZ, apart from the fact that the branch is taken if the Z flag is Not set (result is not zero). For example

```
status = strchr(email_address, '@'); // Search '@' in string
if (status == 0){//status is 0 if @ is not in the email_address
      show_error_message(); // A function to display an error msg
      exit(1);
      }
```

This can be compiled into:

```
  ...
  BL   strchr
  CBNZ R0, email_looks_okay ; Branches if result is not zero
  BL   show_error_message
  BL   exit
email_looks_okay
  ...
```

The APSR value is not affected by the CBZ and CBNZ instructions.

5.14.6 Conditional execution (IF-THEN instruction block)

The IT (IF-THEN) instruction is used to support the conditional execution of up to four subsequent instructions. This is supported on Armv8-M Mainline and Armv7-M processors, but is not available on Armv8-M baseline and Armv6-M processors.

An IT instruction block consists of:

- an IT instruction, with conditional execution details, followed by
- one to four conditionally executed instructions. The conditionally execute instructions can be data processing instructions or memory access instructions. The last conditional execution instruction in the IT block can also be a conditional branch instruction.

The IT instruction statement contains the IT instruction opcode with up to three additional optional suffixes of "T" (then) or "E" (else), followed by a condition suffix as shown in Table 5.58(using the same symbols that are used for the condition symbols for conditional branches). Combining the first "T" in the "IT" with up to three additional "T"s or "E"s, the instruction defines one to four conditions for the next one to four instructions. The "T"s specifies an instruction will be executed when the condition is true, and "E"s specifies an instruction will be executed when the condition is false. The first conditional execution in an IT instruction block must use a "T" condition.

An example of using the IT instruction block is as follows. Using the same program flow, as shown in Fig. 5.16, we can write the operation with an IT instruction block as:

```
CMP   R0, #1 ; Compare R0 to 1
ITE   EQ     ; The next instruction executes if Z is set (EQ)&
             ; the one after that executes if Z is cleared (NE)
MOVEQ R3, #2 ; Set R3 to 2 if EQ
MOVNE R3, #1 ; Set R3 to 1 if not EQ (NE)
```

Note, when the "E" suffix is used, the execution condition for the corresponding instruction in the IT block must be the inverse of the condition specified by the IT instruction.

Different combinations of "T" and "E" sequences are possible. They are:

- A sequence with just the one conditional execution instruction: IT
- Sequences with two conditional execution instructions: ITT, ITE
- Sequences with three conditional execution instructions: ITTT, ITTE, ITET, ITEE
- Sequences with four conditional execution instructions: ITTTT, ITTTE, ITTET, ITTEE, ITETT, ITETE, ITEET, ITEEE

Table 5.60 lists various forms of IT instruction block sequences and examples.
With regard to Table 5.60, where:
- $<x>$ specifies the execution condition for the second instruction
- $<y>$ specifies the execution condition for the third instruction
- $<z>$ specifies the execution condition for the fourth instruction
- $<cond>$ specifies the base condition of the instruction block; (the first instruction following IT executes if $<cond>$ is true).

If "AL" is used as $<cond>$, then you cannot use "E" in the condition control as it implies the instruction should not get executed.

In some assembly development environments, the IT instruction can be automatically inserted by the assembler. For example, when using the following assembly code with Arm tool chains, the assembler can, as illustrated in Table 5.61, automatically insert the required IT instruction.

This assembly tool feature assists in the migration of software. Because you do not need to insert the IT instructions manually, assembly application codes for classic Arm processors (e.g., Arm7TDMI®) can be easily ported to the Cortex-M processors (Armv7-M or Armv8-M Mainline).

Data processing instructions inside an IT instruction block should avoid changing the flag values in the APSR for, if it does, then the program could be difficult to debug. Note, when some 16-bit data processing instructions are used inside an IT instruction block the APSR will

TABLE 5.60 IT instruction blocks of various sizes (Armv8-M Mainline/Armv7-M).

	IT block (each of <x>, <y>, and <z> can either be T (true) or E (else))	Example
Only one conditional instruction	`IT    <cond>` `instr1<cond>`	`IT EQ` `ADDEQ R0, R0, R1`

Two conditional instructions	`IT<x><cond>`
	 `instr1<cond>`
	 `instr2<cond or ~(cond)>`
		`ITE GE`
		 `ADDGE R0, R0, R1`
		 `ADDLT R0, R0, R3`

Three conditional instructions	`IT<x><y><cond>`
	 `instr1<cond>`
	 `instr2<cond or ~(cond)>`
	 `instr3<cond or ~(cond)>`
		`ITET GT`
		 `ADDGT R0, R0, R1`
		 `ADDLE R0, R0, R3`
		 `ADDGT R2, R4, #1`

Four conditional instructions	`IT<x><y><z><cond>`
	 `instr1<cond>`
	 `instr2<cond or ~(cond)>`
	 `instr3<cond or ~(cond)>`
	 `instr4<cond or ~(cond)>`
		`ITETT NE`
		 `ADDNE R0, R0, R1`
		 `ADDEQ R0, R0, R3`
		 `ADDNE R2, R4, #1`
		 `MOVNE R5, R3`

TABLE 5.61 The automatic insertion of an IT instruction in the Arm assembler (Armv8-M Mainline/Armv7-M).

Original assembler code	Disassembled assembly code from generated object file
`...`	`...`
`CMP   R1, #2`	`CMP   R1, #2`
`ADDEQ R0, R1, #1`	**`IT    EQ`**`   ; IT added by assembler`
`...`	`ADDEQ R0, R1, #1`
	`...`

not be updated. This is different from the 16-bit instruction's usual behavior, which updates the APSR. This behavioral difference enables the use of 16-bit data processing instructions within IT instruction blocks to reduce the code size.

In many instances, the IT instruction can, because it avoids some of the branch penalties and reduces the number of branch instructions, significantly improve the performance of the program code. For example, a short IF-THEN-ELSE program sequence that normally requires one conditional branch and an unconditional branch can be replaced with a single IT instruction.

In other instances, traditional branch methods can be more effective than an IT instruction because a conditional failed instruction within an IT instruction sequence, which is not executed, will still consume a clock cycle. For example, if you specify ITTTT <cond> and the condition fails due to the APSR value in runtime, this code sequence can take 4 clock cycles. It is, therefore, quicker to use a conditional branch rather than the IT instruction block (which, including the IT instruction itself, is five instructions).

5.14.7 Table branches (TBB and TBH)

Armv8-M Mainline architecture supports two table branch instructions: Table Branch Byte (TBB) and Table Branch Halfword (TBH). These instructions are used with branch tables and are often used to implement switch statements in C code. Since bit 0 of the program counter value is always zero, a branch table using a table branch instruction does not have to store that bit and, thus, the branch offset is multiplied by two in the target address calculation.

The TBB is used when all the entries in a branch table are organized as a byte array (the offset from the base address is less than $2 \times 2^8 = 512$ bytes). The TBH is used when all the entries are organized as a halfword array (the offset from the base address is less than $2 \times 2^{16} = 128K$ bytes). The base address could be the current program counter (PC) value or could be from another register. Due to the pipeline nature of Cortex-M processors, the current PC value is the address of the TBB or the TBH instruction plus 4, and this must be factored in during the generation of the branch table. Both TBB and TBH only support forward branches.

The TBB instruction has the syntax of:

```
TBB    [Rn, Rm]
```

Where *Rn* stores the base address of the branch table and *Rm* is the branch table index. The immediate value for the TBB offset calculation is located in memory[*Rn + Rm*]. If R15/PC is used as Rn, then the operation is as follows (Fig. 5.17).

The operation of the TBH instruction is very similar, except that because each entry in the branch table is two bytes in size, the array indexing is different and the branch offset range is larger. The syntax of TBH is slightly different from that of TBB to reflect the indexing difference. The syntax for the TBH instruction is as follows:

```
TBH    [Rn, Rm, LSL #1]
```

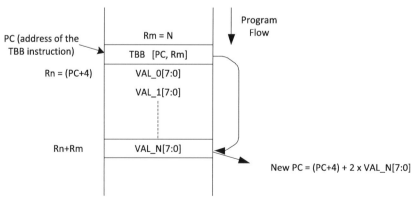

FIG. 5.17   TBB operation.

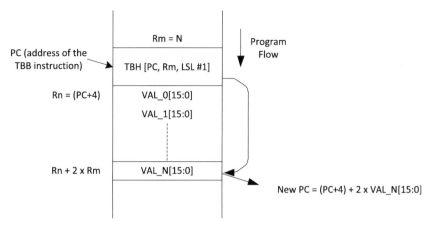

FIG. 5.18 TBH operation.

If R15/PC is used as Rn, then the operation is as follows (Fig. 5.18).

The TBB and TBH instructions are typically used by C compilers in "switch (case)" statements. Using these instructions directly in assembly programming is less straightforward as the values in the branch table are relative to the current program counter value. If the branch target address is not in the same assembly program file, the address offset value cannot be determined at the assembly stage.

In the Arm assembler (armasm in Arm toolchain), including in Keil MDK, the TBB branch table can be created in assembly as follows:

```
            TBB [pc, r0]   ; when executing this instruction, PC is equal
                           ; to the address of the branchtable because
                           ; the size of the TBB instruction is 32-bit
branchtable                ; Label - Start of the branch table
        DCB ((dest0 – branchtable)/2) ; Note that DCB is used
                                   ; because the values are 8-bit
        DCB ((dest1 – branchtable)/2)
        DCB ((dest2 – branchtable)/2)
        DCB ((dest3 – branchtable)/2)
dest0
        ... ; Executes if r0 = 0
dest1
        ... ; Executes if r0 = 1
dest2
        ... ; Executes if r0 = 2
dest3
        ... ; Executes if r0 = 3
```

In the above example, when the TBB instruction is executed the current PC value is the address of the TBB instruction plus 4 (due to the processor's pipeline structure). This address is the same as the starting address of the *branchtable* because the TBB instruction is also 4 bytes in size. (Both TBB and TBH are 32-bit instructions.)

Similar to the TBB example, an example for the TBH instruction can be written as:

```
        TBH [pc, r0, LSL #1]
branchtable ; Label - Start of the branch table
        ; Note that DCI is used
        ; because the values are 16-bit
        DCI ((dest0 - branchtable)/2)
        DCI ((dest1 - branchtable)/2)
        DCI ((dest2 - branchtable)/2)
        DCI ((dest3 - branchtable)/2)
dest0
        ... ; Executes if r0 = 0
dest1
        ... ; Executes if r0 = 1
dest2
        ... ; Executes if r0 = 2
dest3
        ... ; Executes if r0 = 3
```

Please note, the coding syntax needed to create the branch table depends on the development tools being used.

5.15 Instruction set—DSP extension

5.15.1 Overview

The Armv8-M Mainline supports an optional DSP (digital signal processing) extension instruction set. This is available as an optional feature for the Cortex-M33 processor, and is also available on other Armv8-M Mainline processors. Chip designers can decide whether to include this feature in the chip design based on their application requirements. This DSP extension was also available in the Cortex-M4 and Cortex-M7 processors.

The DSP extension contains a range of instructions for integer and fixed-point processing. Examples of these are:

– "Single-Instruction, Multiple-Data" (SIMD) instructions
– Saturating arithmetic instructions
– Multiply and "multiply and accumulate" (MAC) instructions
– Packing and unpacking instructions

Instead of updating the APSR flags (N, C, V, and Z), many of the DSP instructions update the Q bit and the GE (4 bits) in the APSR. The Q bit indicates that a saturation has occurred during the operation and the GE (Greater than or Equal) flags indicate that the result was either greater than or equal to zero (the GE flag is 1 bit per lane in the SIMD operations). Please note, the GE flags are present only when the DSP extension has been implemented.

The DSP extension enables Cortex-M processors to handle real time DSP tasks more efficiently. Please note, some software development tools (e.g., C compilers) are able to utilize some of the instructions in the DSP extension for general data processing. It is, therefore, important to ensure that the correct compilation options are used when compiling the C/C++ codes so that they match the chip's implemented instruction set features.

One of the common methods used to enhance performance is by using Single Instruction Multiple Data (SIMD) technology.

5.15.2 SIMD concept

The data that needs processing in DSP applications is quite often 8 and 16 bits. For example, most audio is sampled using Analog to Digital Converters (ADCs) with a 16-bit resolution or less and image pixels are often represented with multiple channels of 8-bit data (e.g., RGB color space). Since the data path inside the Cortex-M33 processor is 32 bits, we can utilize the data path to handle two pieces of 16-bit data or four pieces of 8-bit data. Because this data can be in a signed or in an unsigned format, the processor's design, will need to take account of this requirement.

The 32-bit registers in the Cortex-M33 processor (and other Armv8-M Mainline processors with the DSP extension) can be used for four types of SIMD data (Fig. 5.19).

In most instances, the data inside a SIMD data set would be the same type (i.e., no mixture of signed and unsigned data and no mixture of 8- and 16-bit data). This arrangement simplifies the SIMD instruction set design.

In order to handle SIMD data, additional instructions are needed and these are covered by the DSP extension in the Armv8-M architecture. The extension in the previous architecture is referred to as the Enhanced DSP extension. In the case of previous Cortex-M processors it is referred to as the Armv7E-M architecture, where "E" indicates the presence of the Enhanced DSP extension.

The DSP extension of Armv8-M is binary compatible to the Enhanced DSP extension in Armv7-M and is source level compatible to the Enhanced DSP extension in the Armv5E architecture. This allows codecs developed for previous Cortex-M processors and Arm9E processors (e.g., the Arm926 and the Arm946) to be easily ported to Cortex-M33 and other Armv8-M Mainline processors. (Note: compatibility with the Armv5E is at source and not at binary level, meaning that the codes need to be recompiled when being reused on Armv7-M/Armv8-M Mainline processors.)

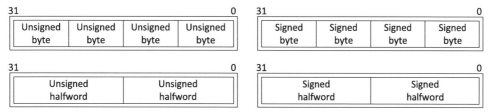

FIG. 5.19 Four possible representations of SIMD data in a 32-bit register.

TABLE 5.62 C99 data types used in the CMSIS-CORE.

Type	Size (bits)	Equivalent C data type
uint8_t	8	unsigned char
uint16_t	16	unsigned short int
uint32_t	32	unsigned int
int8_t	8	signed char
int16_t	16	signed short int
int32_t	32	signed int

Since SIMD data-types are not natively supported in C language, the C compilers cannot usually generate the required DSP instructions by normal C code. In order to make it easier for software developers, intrinsic functions are added to the header files in CMSIS-CORE compliant driver libraries. In this way, the software developers are able to easily access those SIMD instructions. To make it easier to utilize the DSP processing capabilities, Arm provides a DSP library, called CMSIS-DSP, which can be used free of charge by software developers.

Appendix B of this book contains a number of diagrams to illustrate the operation of the DSP instructions. Inside the diagrams in appendix B, C99 data types (see Table 5.62) are used to represent the data.

5.15.3 SIMD and saturating arithmetic instructions

There are quite a large number of SIMD and saturating arithmetic instructions. Some of the saturating arithmetic instructions also support SIMD operations. Many of the SIMD instructions contain similar operations, but with different prefixes to show whether the instruction is intended for signed or unsigned data (Table 5.63).

Base operation descriptions are shows in Table 5.64.

The SIMD instructions also include those listed in Table 5.65.

Some of the saturating instructions (Table 5.66) are not SIMD.

The syntaxes of these instructions are listed in Table 5.67. The Figure numbers in the last column refers to the figures in appendix B. These figures show graphical representations of the operations.

Please note, some of these instructions sets the Q bit in the APSR when saturation has occurred. However, the Q bit is not cleared by those instructions and has to be cleared manually by writing to the APSR. Usually the program code has to examine the value of the Q bit in the APSR to detect if a saturation has taken place in any of the steps during a computation flow. Therefore, the Q bit is not cleared until it is explicitly specified.

5.15.4 Multiply and MAC instructions

The DSP extension includes various multiply and Multiply-and-Accumulate (MAC) instructions. In the earlier section of this chapter, I covered some of the multiply and MAC

TABLE 5.63 SIMD instructions.

Operation (see next table)	Prefix					
	S[a] Signed	Q[b] Signed Saturating	SH[c] Signed Halving	U[a] Unsigned	UQ[b] Unsigned Saturating	UH[c] Unsigned Halving
ADD8	SADD8	QADD8	SHADD8	UADD8	UQADD8	UHADD8
SUB8	SSUB8	QSUB8	SHSUB8	USUB8	UQSUB8	UHSUB8
ADD16	SADD16	QADD16	SHADD16	UADD16	UQADD16	UHADD16
SUB16	SSUB16	QSUB16	SHSUB16	USUB16	UQSUB16	UHSUB16
ASX	SASX	QASX	SHASX	UASX	UQASX	UHASX
SAX	SSAX	QSAX	SHSAX	USAX	UQSAX	UHSAX

[a] "S" and "U"—GE bits (in the APSR register) update.
[b] "Q" and "UQ"—These instructions do not set Q bit when saturation occurs.
[c] "SH" and "UH"—Each value in the SIMD operation result is divided by 2 in Signed Halving (SH) and Unsigned Halving (UH) operations.

TABLE 5.64 Base operations for SIMD instructions.

Operation	Description
ADD8	Adds four pairs of 8-bit data
SUB8	Subtracts four pairs of 8-bit data
ADD16	Adds two pairs of 16-bit data
SUB16	Subtracts two pairs of 16-bit data
ASX	Exchanges halfwords of the second operand register, then adds top halfwords and subtracts the bottom halfword
SAX	Exchanges halfwords of the second operand register, then subtracts top halfwords and adds the bottom halfword

TABLE 5.65 Additional SIMD instructions.

Operation	Description
USAD8	Unsigned Sum of Absolute Difference between four pairs of 8-bit data
USADA8	Unsigned Sum of Absolute Difference between four pairs of 8-bit data and Accumulate
USAT16	Unsigned saturates two signed 16-bit values to a selected unsigned range
SSAT16	Signed saturates two signed 16-bit values to a selected unsigned range
SEL	Selects Byte from first or second operand based on the GE flags

TABLE 5.66 Additional non-SIMD instructions.

Operation	Description
SSAT	Signed saturation (supported without DSP extension)
USAT	Unsigned saturation (supported in without DSP extension)
QADD	Saturating-Adds two signed 32-bit integers
QDADD	Doubles a 32-bit signed integer and adds another 32-bit signed integer. Saturation is possible for both operations.
QSUB	Saturating-Subtract two signed 32-bit integer
QDSUB	Doubles a 32-bit signed integer and subtracts it from another 32-bit signed integer. Saturation is possible for both operations.

TABLE 5.67 Syntax of SIMD and saturation instructions.

Mnemonic	Operands	Brief description	Flag	Figure
SADD8	{Rd,} Rn, Rm	Signed Add 8	GE[3:0]	B.13
SADD16	{Rd,} Rn, Rm	Signed Add 16	GE[3:0]	B.14
SSUB8	{Rd,} Rn, Rm	Signed Subtract 8	GE[3:0]	B.17
SSUB16	{Rd,} Rn, Rm	Signed Subtract 16	GE[3:0]	B.18
SASX	{Rd,} Rn, Rm	Signed Add and Subtract with Exchange	GE[3:0]	B.21
SSAX	{Rd,} Rn, Rm	Signed Subtract and Add with Exchange	GE[3:0]	B.22
QADD8	{Rd,} Rn, Rm	Saturating Add 8		B.5
QADD16	{Rd,} Rn, Rm	Saturating Add 16		B.4
QSUB8	{Rd,} Rn, Rm	Saturating Subtract 8		B.9
QSUB16	{Rd,} Rn, Rm	Saturating Subtract 16		B.8
QASX	{Rd,} Rn, Rm	Saturating Add and Subtract with Exchange		B.10
QSAX	{Rd,} Rn, Rm	Saturating Subtract and Add with Exchange		B.11

TABLE 5.67 Syntax of SIMD and saturation instructions—cont'd

Mnemonic	Operands	Brief description	Flag	Figure
SHADD8	{Rd,} Rn, Rm	Signed Halving Add 8		B.15
SHADD16	{Rd,} Rn, Rm	Signed Halving Add 16		B.16
SHSUB8	{Rd,} Rn, Rm	Signed Halving Subtract 8		B.19
SHSUB16	{Rd,} Rn, Rm	Signed Halving Subtract 16		B.20
SHASX	{Rd,} Rn, Rm	Signed Halving Add and Subtract with Exchange		B.23
SHSAX	{Rd,} Rn, Rm	Signed Halving Subtract and Add with Exchange		B.24
UADD8	{Rd,} Rn, Rm	Unsigned Add 8	GE[3:0]	B.69
UADD16	{Rd,} Rn, Rm	Unsigned Add 16	GE[3:0]	B.70
USUB8	{Rd,} Rn, Rm	Unsigned Subtract 8	GE[3:0]	B.73
USUB16	{Rd,} Rn, Rm	Unsigned Subtract 16	GE[3:0]	B.74
UASX	{Rd,} Rn, Rm	Unsigned Add and Subtract with Exchange	GE[3:0]	B.77
USAX	{Rd,} Rn, Rm	Unsigned Subtract and Add with Exchange	GE[3:0]	B.78
UQADD8	{Rd,} Rn, Rm	Unsigned Saturating Add 8		B.85
UQADD16	{Rd,} Rn, Rm	Unsigned Saturating Add 16		B.84
UQSUB8	{Rd,} Rn, Rm	Unsigned Saturating Subtract 8		B.87
UQSUB16	{Rd,} Rn, Rm	Unsigned Saturating Subtract 16		B.86
UQASX	{Rd,} Rn, Rm	Unsigned Saturating Add and Subtract with Exchange		B.88
UQSAX	{Rd,} Rn, Rm	Unsigned Saturating Subtract and Add with Exchange		B.89
UHADD8	{Rd,} Rn, Rm	Unsigned Halving Add 8		B.71
UHADD16	{Rd,} Rn, Rm	Unsigned Halving Add 16		B.72

Continued

TABLE 5.67 Syntax of SIMD and saturation instructions—cont'd

Mnemonic	Operands	Brief description	Flag	Figure
UHSUB8	{Rd,} Rn, Rm	Unsigned Halving Subtract 8		B.75
UHSUB16	{Rd,} Rn, Rm	Unsigned Halving Subtract 16		B.76
UHASX	{Rd,} Rn, Rm	Unsigned Halving Add and Subtract with Exchange		B.79
UHSAX	{Rd,} Rn, Rm	Unsigned Halving Subtract and Add with Exchange		B.80
USAD8	{Rd,} Rn, Rm	Unsigned Sum of Absolute Differences		B.81
USADA8	{Rd,} Rn, Rm, Ra	Unsigned Sum of Absolute Differences and Accumulate		B.82
USAT16	Rd, #imm, Rn	Unsigned saturate two signed 16-bit values	Q	B.83
SSAT16	Rd, #imm, Rn	Signed saturate two signed 16-bit values	Q	B.62
SEL	{Rd,} Rn, Rm	Select bytes base on GE bits		B.25
USAT	{Rd,} #imm, Rn {, LSL #n} {Rd,} #imm, Rn {, ASR #n}	Unsigned saturate (optionally shifted) value	Q	5.12
SSAT	{Rd,} #imm, Rn {, LSL #n} {Rd,} #imm, Rn {, ASR #n}	Signed saturate (optionally shifted) value	Q	5.11
QADD	{Rd,} Rn, Rm	Saturating Add	Q	B.3
QDADD	{Rd,} Rn, Rm	Saturating double and Add	Q	B.6
QSUB	{Rd,} Rn, Rm	Saturating Subtract	Q	B.7
QDSUB	{Rd,} Rn, Rm	Saturating double and Subtract	Q	B.12

instructions that are always available in the Armv8-M Mainline architecture. These instructions are available even when the DSP extension is not implemented. Those instructions are listed in Table 5.68 (Note: Armv8-M Baseline only supports MULS).

When the DSP extension is included, the processor supports additional multiply and MAC instructions (Table 5.69). And some of these come in multiple forms for selecting lower and upper halfwords from the input operands.

TABLE 5.68 Multiply and MAC instructions which are available in Armv8-M processors without the DSP extension.

Instruction	Description (size)	Flags	Subprofile
MULS	Unsigned multiply (32b × 32b = 32b)	N and Z	All
MUL	Unsigned multiply (32b × 32b = 32b)	None	Mainline
UMULL	Unsigned Multiply (32b × 32b = 64b)	None	Mainline
UMLAL	Unsigned MAC ((32b × 32b) + 64b = 64b)	None	Mainline
SMULL	Signed Multiply (32b × 32b = 64b)	None	Mainline
SMLAL	Signed MAC ((32b × 32b) + 64b = 64b)	None	Mainline

TABLE 5.69 Summary of multiply and MAC instructions in the DSP extension.

Instruction	Description	Flag
UMAAL	Unsigned MAC ((32b × 32b) + 32b + 32b = 64b)	None
SMULxy	Signed multiply (16b × 16b = 32b) **SMULBB**: lower halfword × lower halfword **SMULBT**: lower halfword × upper halfword **SMULTB**: upper halfword × lower halfword **SMULTT**: upper halfword × upper halfword	
SMLAxy	Signed MAC ((16b × 16b) + 32b = 32b) **SMLABB**: (lower halfword × lower halfword) + word **SMLABT**: (lower halfword × upper halfword) + word **SMLATB**: (upper halfword × lower halfword) + word **SMLATT**: (upper halfword × upper halfword) + word	Q
SMULWx	Signed multiply (32b × 16b = 32b, returns upper 32 bits of result, lowest 16 bits ignored) **SMULWB**: word × lower half word **SMULWT**: word × upper half word	
SMLAWx	Signed MAC ((32b × 16b) + 32b <<16 = 32b, returns upper 32 bits of result, lowest 16 bits ignored) **SMLAWB**: (word × lower half word) + (word <<16) **SMLAWT**: (word × upper half word) + (word <<16)	Q
SMMUL	Signed multiply (32b × 32b = 32b, returns upper 32-bit, lowest 32-bit ignored)	
SMMULR	Signed multiply with round (32b × 32b = 32b, round then return upper 32-bit, lowest 32-bit ignored)	
SMMLA	Signed MAC ((32b × 32b) + 32b <<32) = 32b, returns upper 32 bits, lowest 32 bits ignored)	
SMMLAR	Signed MAC with round ((32b × 32b) + 32b <<32 = 32b, rounds and returns upper 32 bits, lowest 32 bits ignored)	
SMMLS	Signed multiply and subtract (32b <<32 − (32b × 32b) = 32b, returns upper 32 bits, lowest 32 bits ignored)	

Continued

TABLE 5.69 Summary of multiply and MAC instructions in the DSP extension—cont'd

Instruction	Description	Flag
SMMLSR	Signed multiply and subtract with round ($32b <<32 - (32b \times 32b) = 32b$, rounds then returns upper 32 bits, lowest 32 bits ignored)	
SMLALxy	Signed MAC $((16b \times 16b) + 64b = 64b)$ **SMLALBB**: (lower halfword × lower halfword) + double word **SMLALBT**: (lower halfword × upper halfword) + double word **SMLALTB**: (upper halfword × lower halfword) + double word **SMLALTT**: (upper halfword × upper halfword) + double word	
SMUAD	Signed dual multiply then add $((16b \times 16b) + (16b \times 16b) = 32b)$	Q
SMUADX	Signed dual multiply with exchange then add $((16b \times 16b) + (16b \times 16b) = 32b)$	Q
SMUSD	Signed dual multiply then subtract $((16b \times 16b) - (16b \times 16b) = 32b)$	
SMUSDX	Signed dual multiply with exchange then subtract $((16b \times 16b) - (16b \times 16b) = 32b)$	
SMLAD	Signed dual multiply then add and accumulate $((16b \times 16b) + (16b \times 16b) + 32b = 32b)$	Q
SMLADX	Signed dual multiply with exchange then add and accumulate $((16b \times 16b) + (16b \times 16b) + 32b = 32b)$	Q
SMLSD	Signed dual multiply then subtract and accumulate $((16b \times 16b) - (16b \times 16b) + 32b = 32b)$	Q
SMLSDX	Signed dual multiply with exchange then subtract and accumulate $((16b \times 16b) - (16b \times 16b) + 32b = 32b)$	Q
SMLALD	Signed dual multiply then add and accumulate $((16b \times 16b) + (16b \times 16b) + 64b = 64b)$	
SMLALDX	Signed dual multiply with exchange then add and accumulate $((16b \times 16b) + (16b \times 16b) + 64b = 64b)$	
SMLSLD	Signed dual multiply then subtract and accumulate $((16b \times 16b) - (16b \times 16b) + 64b = 64b)$	
SMLSLDX	Signed dual multiply with exchange then subtract and accumulate $((16b \times 16b) - (16b \times 16b) + 64b = 64b)$	

Please note, some of these instructions sets the Q bit in the APSR when saturation has occurred. However, the Q bit is not cleared by those instructions and has to be cleared manually by writing to the APSR. Usually the program code has to examine the value of the Q bit in the APSR to detect if a saturation has taken place in any of the steps during a computation flow. Therefore, the Q bit is not cleared until it is explicitly specified.

The syntaxes of those instructions are listed in Table 5.70. The figure numbers in the last column refers to the figures in Appendix B. These figures show graphical representations of the operations.

5.15.5 Packing and unpacking instructions

A number of instructions are available to allow the easy packing and unpacking of SIMD data (Table 5.71). Some of these instructions support an additional operation (barrel shift or rotate) on the second operand. The additional operation on the second operand is optional

TABLE 5.70 Syntax of multiply and MAC instructions in the DSP extension.

Mnemonic	Operands	Brief description	Flags	Figure
MUL{S}	{Rd,} Rn, Rm	Unsigned Multiply, 32-bit result	N, Z	
SMULL	RdLo, RdHi, Rn, Rm	Signed Multiply, 64-bit result		B.26
SMLAL	RdLo, RdHi, Rn, Rm	Signed Multiply and Accumulate, 64-bit result		B.27
UMULL	RdLo, RdHi, Rn, Rm	Unsigned Multiply, 64-bit result		B.90
UMLAL	RdLo, RdHi, Rn, Rm	Unsigned Multiply and Accumulate, 64-bit result		B.91
UMAAL	RdLo, RdHi, Rn, Rm	Unsigned Multiply Accumulate Accumulate Long		B.92
SMULBB	{Rd,} Rn, Rm	Signed Multiply (halfwords)		B.28
SMULBT	{Rd,} Rn, Rm	Signed Multiply (halfwords)		B.29
SMULTB	{Rd,} Rn, Rm	Signed Multiply (halfwords)		B.30
SMULTT	{Rd,} Rn, Rm	Signed Multiply (halfwords)		B.31
SMLABB	Rd, Rn, Rm, Ra	Signed Multiply Accumulate (halfwords)	Q	B.36
SMLABT	Rd, Rn, Rm, Ra	Signed Multiply Accumulate (halfwords)	Q	B.37
SMLATB	Rd, Rn, Rm, Ra	Signed Multiply Accumulate (halfwords)	Q	B.38
SMLATT	Rd, Rn, Rm, Ra	Signed Multiply Accumulate (halfwords)	Q	B.39
SMULWB	Rd, Rn, Rm, Ra	Signed Multiply (word by halfword)		B.40
SMULWT	Rd, Rn, Rm, Ra	Signed Multiply (word by halfword)		B.41
SMLAWB	Rd, Rn, Rm, Ra	Signed Multiply Accumulate (word by halfword)	Q	B.42
SMLAWT	Rd, Rn, Rm, Ra	Signed Multiply Accumulate (word by halfword)	Q	B.43
SMMUL	{Rd,} Rn, Rm	Signed Most significant word Multiply		B.32
SMMULR	{Rd,} Rn, Rm	Signed Most significant word Multiply with rounded result		B.33
SMMLA	Rd, Rn, Rm, Ra	Signed Most significant word Multiply Accumulate		B.34
SMMLAR	Rd, Rn, Rm, Ra	Signed Most significant word Multiply Accumulate with rounded result		B.35
SMMLS	Rd, Rn, Rm, Ra	Signed Most significant word Multiply Subtract		B.44
SMMLSR	Rd, Rn, Rm, Ra	Signed Most significant word Multiply Subtract with rounded result		B.45
SMLALBB	RdLo, RdHi, Rn, Rm	Signed Multiply Accumulate Long (halfwords)		B.46
SMLALBT	RdLo, RdHi, Rn, Rm	Signed Multiply Accumulate Long (halfwords)		B.47
SMLALTB	RdLo, RdHi, Rn, Rm	Signed Multiply Accumulate Long (halfwords)		B.48
SMLALTT	RdLo, RdHi, Rn, Rm	Signed Multiply Accumulate Long (halfwords)		B.49

Continued

TABLE 5.70   Syntax of multiply and MAC instructions in the DSP extension—cont'd

Mnemonic	Operands	Brief description	Flags	Figure
SMUAD	{Rd,} Rn, Rm	Signed Dual Multiply Add	Q	B.50
SMUADX	{Rd,} Rn, Rm	Signed Dual Multiply Add with eXchange	Q	B.51
SMUSD	{Rd,} Rn, Rm	Signed Dual Multiply Subtract		B.56
SMUSDX	{Rd,} Rn, Rm	Signed Dual Multiply Subtract with eXchange		B.57
SMLAD	Rd, Rn, Rm, Ra	Signed Multiply Accumulate Dual	Q	B.52
SMLADX	Rd, Rn, Rm, Ra	Signed Multiply Accumulate Dual with eXchange	Q	B.53
SMLSD	Rd, Rn, Rm, Ra	Signed Multiply Subtract Dual	Q	B.58
SMLSDX	Rd, Rn, Rm, Ra	Signed Multiply Subtract Dual with eXchange	Q	B.59
SMLALD	RdLo, RdHi, Rn, Rm	Signed Multiply Accumulate Long Dual		B.54
SMLALDX	RdLo, RdHi, Rn, Rm	Signed Multiply Accumulate Long Dual with eXchange		B.55
SMLSLD	RdLo, RdHi, Rn, Rm	Signed Multiply Subtract Long Dual		B.60
SMLSLDX	RdLo, RdHi, Rn, Rm	Signed Multiply Subtract Long Dual with eXchange		B.61

TABLE 5.71   Syntax of packing and unpacking instructions in the DSP extension.

Instruction	Operands	Description	Figure
PKHBT	{Rd,} Rn, Rm {,LSL #imm}	Pack Halfword with lower half from first operand and upper half from shifted second operand	B.1
PKHTB	{Rd,} Rn, Rm {,ASR #imm}	Pack Halfword with upper half from first operand and lower half from shifted second operand	B.2
SXTB	Rd,Rm {,ROR #n}	Signed eXtend Byte	B.63
SXTH	Rd,Rm {,ROR #n}	Signed eXtend Halfword	B.67
UXTB	Rd,Rm {,ROR #n}	Unsigned eXtend Byte	B.93
UXTH	Rd,Rm {,ROR #n}	Unsigned eXtend Halfword	B.97
SXTB16	Rd,Rm {,ROR #n}	Signed eXtend two bytes to two halfwords	B.64
UXTB16	Rd,Rm {,ROR #n}	Unsigned eXtend two bytes to two halfwords	B.94
SXTAB	{Rd,} Rn, Rm{,ROR #n}	Signed eXtend and Add byte	B.65
SXTAH	{Rd,} Rn, Rm{,ROR #n}	Signed eXtend and Add halfword	B.68
SXTAB16	{Rd,} Rn, Rm{,ROR #n}	Signed extend two bytes to halfwords and dual add	B.66
UXTAB	{Rd,} Rn, Rm{,ROR #n}	Unsigned eXtend and Add byte	B.95
UXTAH	{Rd,} Rn, Rm{,ROR #n}	Unsigned eXtend and Add halfword	B.98
UXTAB16	{Rd,} Rn, Rm{,ROR #n}	Unsigned extend two bytes to halfwords and dual add	B.96

and, as shown in the table below, the value of "n" for rotate (ROR) can be 8, 16, or 24. The shift operation in PKHBT and PKHTB instructions can support a shift of any number of bits.

5.16 Instruction set—Floating point support instructions

5.16.1 Overview of floating-point support in Armv8-M processors

Armv8-MMainline architecture supports an optional floating-point extension. When the floating-point hardware is included, the processor's implementation could:

(1) Include a single precision (32-bit) floating point unit (FPU) to support single precision floating-point calculations
(2) Include a floating-point unit (FPU) that support both single precision and double precision (64-bit) floating-point calculations

For Cortex-M33 and other Armv8-M Mainline processors, the floating-point unit is optional and, when implemented, the Cortex-M33 processor supports option 1—a single precision FPU. If the FPU is not available, it is still possible to handle single precision floating-point calculations by using software emulation. However, when doing this the performance level would be lower than when using a hardware-based approach. Even when the floating-point unit is implemented, the software emulation approach is required in the Cortex-M33 processor if the application code contains double precision floating-point data processing.

The Cortex-M23 processor does not support the floating-point extension. While it is possible to use software emulation in the Cortex-M23 processor to handle floating-point calculations the performance would, however, be even lower than using a Cortex-M33 without an FPU.

5.16.2 Enabling the FPU

Before using any floating-point instruction, you must first enable the floating-point unit by setting the CP11 and CP10 bit fields in the Coprocessor Access Control Register (SCB-> CPACR at address 0xE000ED88). For software developers using CMSIS-CORE compliant device drivers, this activity is usually undertaken within the *SystemInit(void)* function in the device initialization code provided by microcontroller vendors. In the CMSIS-CORE header file of Cortex-M microcontrollers with an FPU, the "__FPU_PRESENT" directive is set to 1. The CPACR register can only be accessed in privileged state. Accordingly, if unprivileged software attempts to access this register a fault exception would be generated.

In systems where the TrustZone security extension has been implemented, the Secure software needs to consider whether it should allow Non-secure software to access the floating-point unit feature. This is controlled by the Non-secure Access Control Register (SCB-> NSCAR at address 0xE000ED8C), a register which is accessible from Secure privileged state only. To enable Non-secure software to access the FPU, the CP11 (bit 11) and CP10 (bit10) fields of this register must be set to 1. Additionally, if the TrustZone security extension has been implemented, the Coprocessor Access Control Register (CPACR) is banked between security states. And, the access permissions are as follows:

- The Secure version of the CPACR can only be accessed by Secure software using SCB->CPACR (at address 0xE000ED88).
- The Non-secure version of the CPACR can be accessed by both Secure and Non-secure software. Secure software can access this register using the Non-secure alias address (SCB_NS->CPACR at address 0xE002ED880) and Non-secure software can access the same register using SCB->CPACR at address 0xE000ED88.

Secure software will also need to program the Coprocessor Power Control Register (CPPWR) to decide whether Non-secure software can access the FPU's power control bit fields. Further information on this topic can be found in Section 15.16.

5.16.3 Floating point instructions

The floating-point instructions include instructions for floating point data processing as well as floating point data transfers (Table 5.72). All floating-point instructions start with the letter V. The floating-point instruction set in the Cortex-M33 processor is based on the FPv5 (Arm floating point architecture version 5). This is a superset of the floating-point instruction set in the Cortex-M4, which is based on the FPv4. The additional floating-point instruction provides some floating-point processing performance enhancements. The FPv5 is supported in the Cortex-M33, Cortex-M55, and Cortex-M7 processors.

TABLE 5.72 Floating point instructions.

Instruction	Operand	Operation
VABS.F32	Sd, Sm	Floating point Absolute value
VADD.F32	{Sd,} Sn, Sm	Floating point Add
VCMP{E}.F32	Sd, Sm	Compares two floating point registers VCMP: Raises an Invalid Operation exception if either operand is a signaling NaN VCMPE: Raises an Invalid Operation exception if either operand is any types of NaN
VCMP{E}.F32	Sd, #0.0	Compares a floating-point register to zero (#0.0)
VCVT.S32.F32	Sd, Sm	Converts from a floating point to a signed 32-bit integer (round toward zero rounding mode)
VCVTR.S32.F32	Sd, Sm	Converts from a floating point to a signed 32-bit integer (uses a rounding mode specified by the FPCSR)
VCVT.U32.F32	Sd, Sm	Converts from a floating point to an unsigned 32-bit integer (round toward zero rounding mode)
VCVTR.U32.F32	Sd, Sm	Converts from a floating point to an unsigned 32-bit integer (uses rounding mode specified by the FPCSR)
VCVT.F32.S32	Sd, Sm	Converts from a 32-bit signed integer to a floating point

TABLE 5.72 Floating point instructions—cont'd

Instruction	Operand	Operation
VCVT.F32.U32	Sd, Sm	Converts from a 32-bit unsigned integer to a floating point
VCVT.S16.F32	Sd, Sd, #fbit	Converts from a floating point to a signed 16-bit fixed point value. #fbit range from 1 to 16 (fraction bits)
VCVT.U16.F32	Sd, Sd, #fbit	Converts from a floating point to an unsigned 16-bit fixed point value. #fbit range from 1 to 16 (fraction bits)
VCVT.S32.F32	Sd, Sd, #fbit	Converts from a floating point to a signed 32-bit fixed point value. #fbit range from 1 to 32 (fraction bits)
VCVT.U32.F32	Sd, Sd, #fbit	Converts from a floating point to an unsigned 32-bit fixed point value. #fbit range from 1 to 32 (fraction bits)
VCVT.F32.S16	Sd, Sd, #fbit	Converts from a signed 16-bit fixed point value to a floating point. #fbit range from 1 to 16 (fraction bits)
VCVT.F32.U16	Sd, Sd, #fbit	Converts from an unsigned 16-bit fixed point value to a floating point. #fbit range from 1 to 16 (fraction bits)
VCVT.F32.S32	Sd, Sd, #fbit	Converts from a signed 32-bit fixed point value to a floating point. #fbit range from 1 to 32 (fraction bits)
VCVT.F32.U32	Sd, Sd, #fbit	Converts from an unsigned 32-bit fixed point value to a floating point. #fbit range from 1 to 32 (fraction bits)
VCVTB.F32.F16	Sd, Sm	Converts from Half Precision (uses the bottom 16 bits, upper 16 bits is not affected) to Single precision
VCVTT.F32.F16	Sd, Sm	Converts from Half Precision (uses the upper 16 bits, bottom 16 bits is not affected) to Single precision
VCVTB.F16.F32	Sd, Sm	Converts from a Single precision to Half Precision (uses the bottom 16 bits)
VCVTT.F16.F32	Sd, Sm	Converts from a Single precision to Half Precision (uses upper 16 bits)
VCVTA.S32.F32	Sd, Sm	Converts from a floating point to a Signed integer (rounds to nearest with ties to away). Introduced in the FPv5 and is not available on the Cortex-M4.
VCVTA.U32.F32	Sd, Sm	Converts from a floating point to an Unsigned integer (rounds to nearest with ties to away). Introduced in the FPv5 and is not available on the Cortex-M4.
VCVTN.S32.F32	Sd, Sm	Converts from a floating point to a Signed integer (rounds to nearest). Introduced in the FPv5 and is not available on the Cortex-M4.
VCVTN.U32.F32	Sd, Sm	Converts from a floating point to an Unsigned integer (rounds to nearest). Introduced in the FPv5 and is not available on the Cortex-M4.
VCVTP.S32.F32	Sd, Sm	Converts from a floating point to a Signed integer (rounds toward +Infinity). Introduced in the FPv5 and is not available on the Cortex-M4.
VCVTP.U32.F32	Sd, Sm	Converts from a floating point to an Unsigned integer (rounds toward +Infinity). Introduced in the FPv5 and is not available on the Cortex-M4.

Continued

TABLE 5.72   Floating point instructions—cont'd

Instruction	Operand	Operation
VCVTM.S32.F32	Sd, Sm	Converts from a floating point to a Signed integer (rounds toward minus (−) Infinity). Introduced in the FPv5 and is not available on the Cortex-M4.
VCVTM.U32.F32	Sd, Sm	Converts from a floating point to an Unsigned integer (rounds toward minus (−) Infinity). Introduced in the FPv5 and is not available on the Cortex-M4.
VDIV.F32	{Sd,} Sn, Sm	Floating point Divide
VFMA.F32	Sd, Sn, Sm	Floating point Fused Multiply Accumulate Sd = Sd + (Sn*Sm)
VFMS.F32	Sd, Sn, Sm	Floating point Fused Multiply Subtract Sd = Sd − (Sn*Sm)
VFNMA.F32	Sd, Sn, Sm	Floating point Fused Negate Multiply Accumulate Sd = (Sd) + (Sn*Sm)
VFNMS.F32	Sd, Sn, Sm	Floating point Fused Negate Multiply Subtract Sd = (−Sd) − (Sn*Sm)
VLDMIA.32	Rn{!}, {S_regs}	Floating point Multiple Load Increment After (1–16 consecutive 32-bit FPU registers)
VLDMDB.32	Rn{!}, {S_regs}	Floating point Multiple Load Decrement Before (1–16 consecutive 32-bit FPU registers)
VLDMIA.64	Rn{!}, {D_regs}	Floating point Multiple Load Increment After(1–16 consecutive 64-bit FPU registers)
VLDMDB.64	Rn{!}, {D_regs}	Floating point Multiple Load Decrement Before (1–16 consecutive 64-bit FPU registers)
VLDR.32	Sd,[Rn{, #imm}]	Loads single precision data from memory (register + offset). #Imm range from −1020 to +1020 and must be a multiple of 4.
VLDR.32	Sd, label	Loads single precision data from memory (literal data)
VLDR.32	Sd, [PC, #imm]	Loads single precision data from memory (literal data). #Imm range from −1020 to +1020 and must be a multiple of 4.
VLDR.64	Dd,[Rn{, #imm}]	Loads double precision data from memory (register + offset). #Imm range from −1020 to +1020 and must be a multiple of 4.
VLDR.64	Dd, label	Loads double precision data from memory (literal data)
VLDR.64	Dd, [PC, #imm]	Loads double precision data from memory (literal data). #Imm range from −1020 to +1020 and must be a multiple of 4.
VMAXNM.F32	Sd, Sn, Sm	Maximum Number. Compares Sn and Sm and loads Sd with the larger value. Introduced in the FPv5 and is not available on the Cortex-M4.
VMINNM.F32	Sd, Sn, Sm	Minimum Number. Compares Sn and Sm and loads Sd with the smaller value. Introduced in the FPv5 and is not available on the Cortex-M4.
VMLA.F32	Sd, Sn, Sm	Floating point Multiply Accumulate Sd = Sd + (Sn*Sm)
VMLS.F32	Sd, Sn, Sm	Floating point Multiply Subtract Sd = Sd − (Sn*Sm)
VMOV	Rt, Sm	Copy a floating point (scalar) to an Arm core register

TABLE 5.72   Floating point instructions—cont'd

Instruction	Operand	Operation
VMOV{.32}	Rt,Dm[0/1]	Copy the upper[1]/lower[0] half of a double precision register to an Arm core register
VMOV{.32}	Dm[0/1], Rt	Copy an Arm core register to the upper[1]/lower[0] half of a double precision register
VMOV	Sn, Rt	Copy an Arm core register to a floating-point (scalar)
VMOV{.F32}	Sd, Sm	Copy floating-point register Sm to Sd (single precision)
VMOV	Dm, Rt, Rt2	Copy two Arm core registers to a double precision register
VMOV	Rt, Rt2, Dm	Copy a double precision register to two Arm core registers
VMOV	Sm, Sm1, Rt, Rt2	Copy two Arm core registers to two consecutive single precision registers (Alternative syntax: VMOV Dm, Rt, Rt2)
VMOV	Rt, Rt2, Sm, Sm1	Copy two consecutive single precision registers to two Arm core registers (Alternative syntax: VMOV Rt, Rt2, Dm)
VMRS	Rt, FPCSR	Copy value in the FPSCR(a FPU system register) to Rt
VMRS	APSR_nzcv, FPCSR	Copy flags from the FPSCR to the flags in the APSR
VMSR	FPSCR, Rt	Copy Rt to FPSCR (a FPU system register)
VMOV.F32	Sd, #imm	Move a single precision value into a floating-point register
VMUL.F32	{Sd,} Sn, Sm	Floating point Multiply
VNEG.F32	Sd, Sm	Floating point Negate
VNMUL	{Sd,} Sn, Sm	Floating point Multiply with negation $Sd = -(Sn * Sm)$
VNMLA	Sd, Sn, Sm	Floating point Multiply Accumulate with negation $Sd = -(Sd + (Sn * Sm))$
VNMLS	Sd, Sn, Sm	Floating point Multiply Accumulate with negation $Sd = -(Sd - (Sn * Sm))$
VPUSH.32	{S_regs}	Floating point single precision register(s) push
VPUSH.64	{D_regs}	Floating point double precision register(s) push
VPOP.32	{S_regs}	Floating point single precision register(s) pop
VPOP.64	{D_regs}	Floating point double precision register(s) pop
VRINTA.F32.F32	Sd, Sm	Floating point Round to Nearest Integer with Ties to Away. Introduced in the FPv5 and is not available on the Cortex-M4.
VRINTM.F32.F32	Sd, Sm	Floating point Round to Nearest Integer, rounds toward minus ($-$) infinity. Introduced in the FPv5 and is not available on the Cortex-M4.
VRINTN.F32.F32	Sd, Sm	Floating point Round to Nearest Integer. Introduced in the FPv5 and is not available on the Cortex-M4.

Continued

TABLE 5.72 Floating point instructions—cont'd

Instruction	Operand	Operation
VRINTP.F32.F32	Sd, Sm	Floating point Round to Nearest Integer, rounds toward plus (+) infinity. Introduced in the FPv5 and is not available on the Cortex-M4.
VRINTR.F32.F32	Sd, Sm	Floating point Round to Nearest Integer using the rounding mode specified in the FPSCR. Introduced in the FPv5 and is not available on the Cortex-M4.
VRINTX.F32.F32	Sd, Sm	Floating point Round to Nearest Integer using the rounding mode specified in the FPSCR and raises an Inexact exception when the result value is not numerically equal to the input value. Introduced in the FPv5 and is not available on the Cortex-M4.
VRINTZ.F32.F32	Sd, Sm	Floating point Round to Nearest Integer, rounds toward zero. Introduced in the FPv5 and is not available on the Cortex-M4.
VSEL<cond>.F32	Sd, Sn, Sm	Floating point conditional select. If the condition holds then Sd=Sn, else Sd=Sm. Introduced in the FPv5 and is not available on the Cortex-M4. <cond> can be EQ (equal), GE (greater or equal), GT (greater than) or VS (overflow). Other conditions can be met by exchanging the source operands.
VSQRT.F32	Sd, Sm	Floating point Square Root
VSTMIA.32	Rn{!}, <S_regs>	Floating point Multiple Store Increment After
VSTMDB.32	Rn{!}, <S_regs>	Floating point Multiple Store Decrement Before
VSTMIA.64	Rn{!}, <D_regs>	Floating point Multiple Store Increment After
VSTMDB.64	Rn{!}, <D_regs>	Floating point Multiple Store Decrement Before
VSTR.32	Sd,[Rn{, #imm}]	Store a single precision data to memory (register+offset)
VSTR.64	Dd,[Rn{, #imm}]	Store a double precision data to memory (register+offset)
VSUB.F32	{Sd,} Sn, Sm	Floating point Subtract

There are two other FPU related instructions that are specifically for TrustZone security management: VLLDM and VLSTM. They are covered in Section 5.20.

Please note, floating point processing can generate "exceptions". For example, a 32-bit data pattern does not always convert into a valid floating-point number and would, therefore, not be processed by the FPU as normal data—a situation called NaN (Not a Number: further information on this topic can be found in Chapter 14). Although FPU exception signals are exported to the processor's outputs, such an arrangement may not trigger any exceptions in the NVIC. Whether it does or not is dependent upon the chip's system level design. Instead of relying on the occurrence of FPU exceptions via the NVIC exception handling mechanism, software can detect abnormalities (such as NaN) by examining the FPU exception status after the cessation of the floating-point operation(s). Further information on this topic can be found in Section 14.6 of Chapter 14.

TABLE 5.73 Instructions related to exception operations.

Instruction	Description	Restriction
SVC #imm8	SuperVisor Call—generates the SVC exception.	The immediate value range is from 0 to 255. SVC priority setting must be higher than current level.
CPSIE I	Clears PRIMASK (enables interrupts)	Must be in privileged state
CPSID I	Sets PRIMASK (masks interrupts and exceptions with configurable priority levels)	Same as above
CPSIE F	Clears FAULT (enables interrupts)	Not available in Armv8-M Baseline and Armv6-M. The processor must be in privileged state.
CPSID F	Sets FAULTMASK (masks interrupts and exceptions except NMI)	Same as above

5.17 Instruction set—Exception-related instructions

Some instructions are used for exception related operations. These are listed in Table 5.73.

The SuperVisor Call (SVC) instruction is used to generate the SVC exception (exception type 11). Typically, the SVC allows an embedded OS/RealTime OS (RTOS) to provide services (which execute in privileged state) to unprivileged application tasks. The SVC exception provides the transition mechanism from unprivileged to privileged.

The SVC mechanism is optimized for the purpose of being an OS service gateway. This is because application tasks accessing an OS service only need to know the SVC service number and the input parameters: there is no need for the application task to know the actual program memory address of the service.

The SVC instruction requires that the priority level of the SVC exception must be higher than the current priority level and that the exception is not masked by masking registers, e.g., by the PRIMASK register. If it is not higher, the execution of an SVC instruction would instead trigger a fault exception. As a consequence, you cannot use the SVC instruction in a NMI or HardFault handler. This is because the priority levels of those handlers are always higher than the SVC exception.

The SVC instruction has the following syntax:

```
SVC #<immed>
```

The immediate value (#<immed >) is 8 bits. The value itself does not affect the behavior of the SVC exception, but the SVC handler can extract this value by way of software and use it as an input parameter. For example, to determine what service is requested by the application task that executed the SVC instruction.

In traditional Arm® assembly syntax, the immediate value in the SVC instruction does not need the "#" sign. Thus, you can write the instruction as:

```
SVC <immed>
```

You can still use this syntax with most assembler tools, but for new software the use of the "#" sign is recommended.

In a C programming environment, the most common way to insert an SVC instruction is by using an inline assembler and writing the code in the form of inline assembly. For example,

```
__asm volatile ("SVC #3"); // execute SVC instruction with immediate value 3
```

The keyword "volatile" is needed to ensure that the C compiler does not reorder the instruction with another code. If additional parameters need to be passed to the SVC, via registers R0–R3, the SVC function can be written as:

```
__attribute__((always_inline)) void svc_3_service(parameter1,
parameter2,      parameter3, parameter4)
{
    register unsigned r0 asm("r0") = parameter1;
    register unsigned r1 asm("r1") = parameter2;
    register unsigned r2 asm("r2") = parameter3;
    register unsigned r3 asm("r3") = parameter4;
    __asm volatile(
        "SVC #3"
        :
        : "r" (r0), "r" (r1), "r" (r2), "r" (r3)
    );
}
void foo(void)
{
    svc_3_service (0x1, 0x2, 0x3, 0x4);
}
```

For software developers using Arm tool chains, including the Keil Microcontroller Development Kit, it is worth noting that the "__svc" function qualifier for Arm Compiler 5 is not available in Arm Compiler 6 (ARMCLANG) (Reference: http://www.keil.com/support/docs/4022.htm).

Another instruction that is related to exceptions is the Change Processor State (CPS) instruction. With the Cortex-M processors, you can use this instruction to set or clear interrupt masking registers such as PRIMASK and FAULTMASK (available in Armv8-M Mainline only). These registers can also be accessed using the MSR and the MRS instructions.

The CPS instruction can only be used with one of the following suffixes: IE (interrupt enable) or ID (interrupt disable). Because Armv8-M Mainline processors (Cortex-M33 and all other Armv8-M Mainline processors) have several interrupt mask registers, you must also specify which masking register to set/clear. Table 5.74 lists the various forms of the CPS instruction available for the Cortex-M23, Cortex-M33, and other Armv8-M Mainline processors.

The switching of PRIMASK or FAULTMASK to disable and enable interrupts is commonly used to ensure timing critical code can quickly finish without getting interrupted. Another interrupt masking register, BASEPRI, which is available in Armv8-M Mainline and Armv7-M, can be accessed by MSR and MRS instructions only.

In Armv8-M processors with the TrustZone security extension, the interrupt masking registers are banked. The CPS instructions (Table 5.74) can only be used to access the interrupt

TABLE 5.74 Setting and clearing interrupt masking registers in a C programming environment.

Instruction	C programming
CPSIE I	__enable_irq(); // Enables interrupts (clears PRIMASK).

CPSID I	__disable_irq(); // Disables interrupts (sets PRIMASK).
	　　　// Note: NMI and HardFault are not affected.

CPSIE F	__enable_fault_irq(); // Enables interrupt (clears FAULTMASK).
	　　　// Note: Not available in Cortex-M23/M0/M0+/M1

CPSID F	__disable_fault_irq(); // Disables fault interrupt (sets FAULTMASK).
	　　　// Note: NMI is not affected. Not available in Cortex-M23/M0/M0+/M1

masking registers in the current security domain. If Secure privileged software needs to access Non-secure interrupt masking registers, then the MSR and MRS instructions should be used.

5.18 Instruction set—Sleep mode-related instructions

There are two instructions for entering sleep modes. That said, there is another way to enter sleep mode called Sleep-on-Exit, which allows the processor to enter sleep upon exception exit (Section 10.2.5).

One of the two aforementioned instructions is Wait-For-Interrupt. In assembly language programming you can access this instruction as follows:

```
WFI ; Wait for Interrupt (enters sleep)
```

In C programming with a CMSIS-CORE compliant device driver, you can use:

```
__WFI(); // Wait for Interrupt (enters sleep)
```

The WFI (Wait for Interrupt) instruction results in the processor immediately entering sleep mode. The processor can then be woken up from sleep mode by interrupts, by a reset or by a debug operation.

Note: There is a special case where the execution of a WFI instruction does not trigger sleep mode. This is when PRIMASK is set and when an interrupt is pending (Section 10.3.4).

Another instruction called WFE (Wait for Event) causes the processor to conditionally enter sleep mode. In assembly language programming you can access this instruction as follows:

```
WFE ; Wait for Event (conditionally enters sleep)
```

Or in C programming with a CMSIS-CORE compliant device driver, you can use:

```
__WFE(); // Wait for Event (conditionally enters sleep)
```

Inside Cortex-M processors, there is a single bit internal register to record events. If this register is set, the WFE instruction will not enter sleep. Instead, it clears the event register, and then continues to the next instruction. If this register is cleared, the processor enters sleep and wakes up when an event occurs. The event can be one of the following:

- an interrupt,
- a debug operation (following a halting request from the debugger),
- a reset,
- the arrival of a pulse signal at the external-event-interface (via a processor's input pin, Section 10.2.9).

The event input of a processor can be generated from event outputs from other processors in a multiprocessor system. With this arrangement, a processor in WFE sleep (e.g., waiting for a spin lock) can be woken up by other processor(s), which can be useful in semaphore operations in multiprocessor systems. In other cases, the event signal can be triggered by using an I/O port pin of a Cortex-M microcontroller. In other designs, the event input is tied low and not used.

In addition to event input, the event interface signals of Cortex-M processors include an event output. The event output can be triggered using the SEV (Send Event) instruction. In assembly language programming you can access this instruction as follows:

```
SEV ; Send Event
```

In C programming with a CMSIS-CORE compliant device driver, you can use:

```
__SEV(); // Send Event
```

When a SEV is executed, a single cycle pulse is generated at the event output interface. The SEV instruction also sets the event register of the processor that is executing the SEV instruction. In some Cortex-M microcontrollers, the event output is not connected to anything and is, therefore, unused.

Further information on WFI, WFE and SEV instructions, and the event register, is covered in Chapter 10.

5.19 Instruction set—Memory barrier instructions

The Cortex-M23, Cortex-M33, and other Armv8-M processors are all optimized for small embedded systems and, because they have a relatively short pipeline, do not reorder memory access. However, Arm architectures (including Armv6-M, Armv7-M, and Arm8-M) allow the design of processors to reorder memory transfers, that is, memory access could take place, or complete in an order different from the program code, providing that it does not affect the result of the data processing operations.

Memory access re-ordering often happens in high-end processors, such as those designs with caches, superscalar pipeline or out-of-order-execution capabilities. However, by re-ordering memory access, and if the data is shared between multiple processors, then the data sequence observed by another processor can be different from the programmed sequence. This can cause errors or glitches in a range of applications. Examples of the causes of these failures (refer to Fig. 5.4) is covered in Section 5.7.12, Load-acquire and store release instructions.

The memory barrier instructions can be used to:

- enforce ordering between memory accesses,
- enforce ordering between a memory access and another processor's operation,
- ensure the effect of a system configuration change takes place before subsequent operations.

Cortex®-M processors support the following memory barrier instructions (Table 5.75).

In C programming with CMSIS (i.e., using a CMSIS-CORE compliant device driver), these instructions can be accessed using the following functions:

```
void __DMB(void); // Data Memory Barrier
void __DSB(void); // Data Synchronization Barrier
void __ISB(void); // Instruction Synchronization Barrier
```

Since the Cortex-M23 and Cortex-M33 processors have relatively simple pipelines, and because the AMBA® 5 AHB bus protocol used in these processors does not allow the reordering of transfers in the memory system, most applications work without any memory barrier instructions. However, there are several cases (Table 5.76) where the aforementioned barrier instructions should be used.

From an architectural point of view, there can be additional situations (listed in Table 5.77) where memory barrier should be used between two operations. Although, that said, omitting the memory barrier in the current Cortex-M23 and Cortex-M33 processors will not cause any issues.

Some of the memory barriers are essential for high-end processors, like the Cortex-M7, where the bus interface contains write buffers and needs a DSB instruction to ensure that the buffered writes are drained.

An application note on the use of memory barrier instructions for the Cortex®-M processor is available from Arm® and is called "Arm Cortex-M Programming Guide to Memory Barrier instructions" [6] (ArmDAI0321A).

TABLE 5.75 Memory barrier instructions.

Instruction	Description
DMB	Data Memory Barrier; ensures that all memory accesses are completed before new memory access is committed
DSB	Data Synchronization Barrier; ensures that all memory accesses are completed before the next instruction is executed
ISB	Instruction Synchronization Barrier; flushes the pipeline and ensures that all previous instructions are completed before executing a new instruction.

TABLE 5.76 Examples of when memory barrier instruction(s) are needed.

Scenario (Required in the majority of Cortex-M processor implementations)	Barrier instruction(s) needed
After updating the CONTROL register with an MSR instruction, the ISB instruction should be used to ensure the updated configuration is used for subsequent operations.	ISB
If the SLEEPONEXIT bit in the System Control Register is changed inside an exception handler, a DSB should be used before the exception return.	DSB
When an exception which was pending is being enabled, and when you want to ensure the pended exception takes place before a subsequent operation.	DSB, followed by an ISB
When disabling an interrupt using the NVIC clear enable register and when you want to make sure that the effect of the interrupt disabling takes place immediately before starting the next operation.	DSB, followed by an ISB
When a Self-modifying code modifies a portion of program memory (subsequent instructions would already have been fetched and would need to be flushed).	DSB, followed by an ISB
When the program memory map is changed by a control register in a peripheral and when the new program memory map has to be immediately used. (This assumes that the memory map is immediately updated after the write has been completed.)	DSB, followed by and ISB
When the data memory map is changed by a control register in a peripheral and when the new data memory map has to be immediately used. (This assumes that the memory map is immediately updated after the write has been completed.)	DSB
When the configuration in the Memory Protection Unit (MPU) has been updated and when the subsequent program code has immediately fetched and executed an instruction in a memory region which has been affected by the MPU configuration change.	DSB, followed by an ISB

TABLE 5.77 Examples of when memory barrier instruction(s) are recommended by architecture definitions.

Scenario (recommendation based on architecture)	Barrier instruction(s) needed
The software updates the Memory Protection Unit (MPU) configuration and then accesses a data in the memory region affected by the MPU configuration change. (The MPU region affected by the change is for data access only, i.e., there is no instruction fetch.)	DSB
Before entering sleep (WFI or WFE)	DSB
Semaphore operations	DMB or DSB
Changing the priority level of an exception (e.g., SVC) and then triggering it.	DSB
Relocating the vector table to a new location using the Vector Table Offset Register (VTOR) and then triggering an exception with a new vector	DSB
Changing a vector entry in the vector table (if it is relocated to SRAM) and then immediately triggering the same exception.	DSB
Just before a self-reset (there can still be an active ongoing data transfer).	DSB

5.20 Instruction set—TrustZone support instructions

A number of instructions were introduced for Armv8-M to enable the TrustZone security extension to work. The following instructions are available in both Armv8-M Baseline and Mainline processors (Table 5.78).

Information on the handling of Secure and Non-secure software transitions, and the use of TT{A}{T} instructions, are covered in Chapter 7, Section 7.4.2 and in Chapter 18.

VLLDM and VLSTM are two instructions that were added to Armv8-M Mainline processors for context saving and for the restoration of register contents in the floating-point unit (FPU). If Secure software needs to call certain Non-secure functions/subroutines frequently it can, if these two instructions are not available, be very inefficient.

TABLE 5.78 TrustZone support instructions.

Instruction	Description	Restriction
SG	Secure Gateway. SG provides a secure method to allow Non-secure software to call Secure functions with very low latency. If Non-secure code calls a Secure function, the first instruction of the called function must be an SG and must be in an address location defined with a Non-secure Callable (NSC) attribute.	Available in secure world only, and must be placed in a Non-secure Callable region to be a valid entry point.
BXNS Rm	Branch with exchange (Non-secure). Branches to an address stored in a register. If bit 0 of address is 0, and the 32-bit value is not EXC_RETURN or FNC_RETURN, it switches the processor into the Non-secure state.	Available in Secure world only.
BLXNS Rm	Branch with link and exchange (Non-secure). Branches to an address store in a register. If bit 0 of address is 0, and the 32-bit value is not EXC_RETURN or FNC_RETURN, it switches the processor into the Non-secure state. The Link register is saved in the Secure stack and the LR is updated to FNC_RETURN	Available in Secure world only.
TT Rd, Rn TTT Rd, Rn TTA Rd, Rn TTAT Rd, Rn	Test target—queries the Security state and access permissions of a memory location. Rn = memory address location for testing Rd = security and permission results TT and TTT carry the test within the current security domain (TTT carries the test with an unprivileged access level) TTA and TTAT execute from the Secure state and carries out the test with Non-secure security and permission settings. The TTAT instruction differs from the TTA instruction because TTAT specifies Non-secure unprivileged level.	TTA and TTAT are available in Secure world only.

Without the VLLDM and the VLSTM instructions, for each Non-secure function call,

- The data in the FPU would need to be saved to the Secure stack, then
- the FPU registers would need to be erased (to prevent leakage), and then
- the Non-secure function would need to be called.

After the completion of the Non-secure function call, we would then need to restore the registers. This is inefficient because many of the Non-secure functions/subroutines being called might not have used the FPU. The VLSTM and VLLDM instructions were, therefore, introduced to make the process more efficient.

The VLSTM and the VLLDM instructions (Table 5.79) improved the process by saving and restoring the FPU registers only if the Non-secure function used the FPU. Instead of storing all of the FPU register bank data in the Secure stack before calling a Non-secure subroutine, Secure software allocates space in the Secure stack (pointed to by Rn) and uses the VLSTM to enable lazy stacking. This means the actual stacking and clearing of the Secure FPU registers only happens when the Non-secure subroutine uses the FPU. After the Non-secure function/subroutine completes and returns to the Secure world, Secure software uses the VLLDM to restore the saved data from the Secure stack—but only if the Secure FPU data has been pushed to the Secure stack. If the called Non-secure function/subroutine did not use the FPU, then the actual saving and restoring of the FPU registers does not take place and, hence, the number of clock cycles needed is reduced.

If the FPU is not implemented or is disabled, the VLSTM and VLLDM instructions execute as NOPs (no operation).

5.21 Instruction set—Coprocessor and Arm custom instructions support

The coprocessor instructions and Arm custom instructions allow chip designers to extend the processing capability of the processor's system.

The coprocessor instructions were introduced when the Cortex-M33 processor was first released and the Arm Custom Instructions was introduced in the middle of 2020 when the Cortex-M33 revision 1 was released.

The aforementioned instructions are not available on the Cortex-M23 processor.

TABLE 5.79 VLSTM and VLLDM instructions for TrustZone support for Armv8-M Mainline.

Instruction	Description	Restriction
VLSTM Rn	Floating-point Lazy Store Multiple. Enables the lazy stacking of the FPU's Secure data. Rn is the address of the stack space reserved by Secure software to hold, if needed, the Secure FPU data.	Available in Armv8-M Mainline and in Secure state only.
VLLDM Rn	Floating-point Lazy Load Multiple. Restores FPU data from the Secure stack memory (pointed to by Rn) if the FPU data has been pushed to the Secure stack during a Non-secure subroutine/function.	Available in Armv8-M Mainline and in Secure state only.

The coprocessor interface support enables chip designers to add closely coupled hardware accelerators to the Cortex-M33 processor. The functions of the accelerators are defined by chip designers and/or by microcontroller vendors. These hardware accelerators are typically used for mathematical calculations (e.g., trigonometric functions) and crypto acceleration, etc.

The Cortex-M33 processor supports up to eight custom defined coprocessors (#0–#7), with each of them potentially being implemented as:

- A coprocessor hardware unit external to the processor and connected via the coprocessor interface
- A custom data path unit within the processor (This feature is available from the middle of 2020 in the Cortex-M33 revision 1)

A coprocessor hardware unit, which is outside the processor, can have up to 16 coprocessor registers. Although the interface (Fig. 5.20) between the processor and the coprocessor supports 32-bit and 64-bit data transfers between the register bank and the coprocessor's registers, the exact size of the coprocessor registers is defined by chip designers.

The coprocessor instructions are divided into three types:

- Transferring data from the processor's register bank to one or two coprocessor registers, with opcodes for defining operation(s).
- Transferring data from one or two coprocessor registers to the processor's register bank, with opcodes for defining operation(s).
- Coprocessor operations (opcodes + coprocessor register specifiers).

When compared to the memory mapped peripheral approach, a coprocessor interface provides a faster way to access hardware accelerators. This is because:

- The coprocessor interface can transfer up to 64 bits of data at a time, whereas the bus interfaces on the Cortex-M33 processor can only transfer a maximum of 32 bits per cycle.
- Coprocessor transfers are not affected by system level bus traffic (e.g., it is not delayed by another bus transfer which could have multiple clock cycles of wait states).

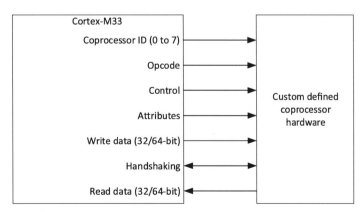

FIG. 5.20 Coprocessor interface.

TABLE 5.80 Coprocessor instructions.

Instruction	Operation
MCR coproc, opc1, Rt, CRn, CRm{, opc2} MCR2 coproc, opc1, Rt, CRn, CRm{, opc2} (e.g. MCR p0, 1, R1, c1, c2, 0)	Transfers 32 bits to coprocessor register (opcode 1 is 4 bits, opcode 2 is 3 bits and is optional)
MRC coproc, opc1, Rt, CRn, CRm{, opc2} MRC2 coproc, opc1, Rt, CRn, CRm{, opc2} (e.g. MRC p0, 1, R1, c1, c2, 0)	Transfers 32 bits from coprocessor register (opcode 1 is 4 bits, opcode 2 is 3 bits and is optional)
MCRR coproc, opc1, Rt, Rt2, CRm MCRR2 coproc, opc1, Rt, Rt2, CRm	Transfers 64 bits from coprocessor register (opcode 1 is 4 bits)
MRRC coproc, opc1, Rt, Rt2, CRm MRRC2 coproc, opc1, Rt, Rt2, CRm	Transfers 64 bits from coprocessor register (opcode 1 is 4 bits)
CPD coproc, opc1, CRd, CRn, CRm {, opc2} CPD2 coproc, opc1, CRd, CRn, CRm {, opc2}	Coprocessor data processing (opcode 1 is 4 bits, opcode 2 is 3 bits and is optional)

- The software does not have to first setup the address in a register before starting the transfer. This is because the coprocessor ID and coprocessor register specifiers are part of the coprocessor instruction's encoding.
- The software does not have to use a separate transfer to define the coprocessor's operation. This is because the coprocessor opcode is part of the coprocessor instruction's encoding.

In some instances, a chip designer can, due to its single cycle access capability, utilize the coprocessor interface to gain faster access to certain peripheral registers.

The coprocessor instructions that are supported on the Cortex-M33 processor are summarized in Table 5.80.

The MRC and MRC2 instructions support the transfer of the APSR.NZVC flags when the processor register field (Rt) is set to PC (0xF).

For historical reasons, multiple instruction encodings are available (e.g., MCR, MCR2). Coprocessor instructions were available in early Arm processors and from Arm architecture v5, more coprocessor instructions (MCR2, MRC2, MCRR2, MRRC2, and CDP2) were introduced into the Arm instruction set (but not the Thumb instruction set). The new additions provide more space for opcode bits, but do not have a conditional execution capability.

Please note, Armv8-M architecture has defined additional coprocessor instructions for memory access. However, these instructions (Table 5.81) are not supported by the Cortex-M33 processor. Any attempt to execute these instructions would result in a fault exception (UsageFault with Undefined Instruction error).

The Arm custom instructions allow chip designers to define custom data processing instructions inside the Cortex-M33 processor. The architecture of the Arm custom instruction instructions supports five data types:

- 32-bit integer,
- 64-bit integer (D—dual variant),

TABLE 5.81 Unsupported coprocessor instructions.

Unsupported coprocessor instruction	Operation
`LDC    coproc, CRd, [Rn {,#imm}]` `LDC2   coproc, CRd, [Rn {,#imm}]`	32-bit Memory read with coprocessor register as data destination
`LDC    coproc, CRd, [Rn ,#imm]!` `LDC2   coproc, CRd, [Rn ,#imm]!`	32-bit Memory read with coprocessor register as data destination with preindex
`LDC    coproc, CRd, [Rn],#imm` `LDC2   coproc, CRd, [Rn],#imm`	32-bit Memory read with coprocessor register as data destination with postindex
`LDC    coproc, CRd, [PC {,#imm}]` `LDC2   coproc, CRd, [PC {,#imm}]`	32-bit Literal memory read with coprocessor register as data destination
`LDCL   coproc, CRd, [Rn {,#imm}]` `LDC2L  coproc, CRd, [Rn {,#imm}]`	64-bit Memory read with coprocessor register as data destination
`LDCL   coproc, CRd, [Rn ,#imm]!` `LDC2L  coproc, CRd, [Rn ,#imm]!`	64-bit Memory read with coprocessor register as data destination with preindex
`LDCL   coproc, CRd, [Rn],#imm` `LDC2L  coproc, CRd, [Rn],#imm`	64-bit Memory read with coprocessor register as data destination with postindex
`LDCL   coproc, CRd, [PC {,#imm}]` `LDC2L  coproc, CRd, [PC {,#imm}]`	64-bit Literal memory read with coprocessor register as data destination
`STC    oproc, CRd, [Rn {,#imm}]` `STC2   coproc, CRd, [Rn {,#imm}]`	32-bit Memory store with coprocessor register as data source
`STC    coproc, CRd, [Rn ,#imm]!` `STC2   coproc, CRd, [Rn ,#imm]!`	32-bit Memory store with coprocessor register as data source with preindex
`STC    coproc, CRd, [Rn],#imm` `STC2   coproc, CRd, [Rn],#imm`	32-bit Memory store with coprocessor register as data source with postindex
`STCL   coproc, CRd, [Rn {,#imm}]` `STC2L  coproc, CRd, [Rn {,#imm}]`	64-bit Memory store with coprocessor register as data source
`STCL   coproc, CRd, [Rn ,#imm]!` `STC2L  coproc, CRd, [Rn ,#imm]!`	64-bit Memory store with coprocessor register as data source with preindex
`STCL   coproc, CRd, [Rn],#imm` `STC2L  coproc, CRd, [Rn],#imm`	64-bit Memory store with coprocessor register as data source with postindex

- single precision float (32-bit, fp32)—supported by the Cortex-M33 r1, if the FPU is included,
- double precision (64-bit, fp64, not supported by the Cortex-M33 r1), and
- MVE vector in Armv8.1-M (128-bit, not supported by the Cortex-M33 r1).

For each data type in the Arm custom instructions, there are three subtypes, which results in a total of 15 classes (Table 5.82). These subtypes support zero to three input operands and an additional immediate data value which enables multiple instructions to be defined.

For each class, there is a normal and an accumulative variant. The Accumulative variant of these instructions (indicated by the {A} suffix), allows the destination register to be used for source data and also as the destination. Only the accumulative variant of integer-type Arm Custom Instructions can be used in IT instruction blocks for conditional execution. Please note, Arm Custom Instructions for floating-point and vector data types, and nonaccumulative variants, cannot be used in IT instruction blocks.

Similar to the coprocessor interface instructions, CX1{A}, CX2{A}, and CX3{A} instructions support the transfer of N,Z, C, V flags when the processor register field (Rd/Rn) is set to APSR_nzcv, which is encoded as 0xF. For the CX1D{A}, CX2D{A}, and CX3D{A} instructions, APSR_nzcv can be used as an input and is encoded as 0xE.

When using double word Arm custom instructions (CX1D{A},CX2D{A},CX3D{A}), the destination is placed in Rd and R(d+1)—where d must be an even number and less than 12.

For information on using these coprocessor instructions in C using intrinsic functions, please refer to Chapter 15, Section 15.4.

Before using coprocessor instructions or Arm custom instructions, the corresponding coprocessor must be enabled by software as, by default, they are disabled. In addition, Secure software should also setup the access permissions of the coprocessors during security initialization. Further information on the setup requirements of access permissions is covered in Chapter 15, Section 15.5.

5.22 Instruction set—Other functions

There are some other miscellaneous instructions.

The Cortex-M processors support a NOP instruction. This instruction can be used to produce instruction alignment or to introduce a delay. When programming in assembly language, the NOP instruction is written as:

```
NOP ; Do nothing
```

Or, when programming in C language with a CMSIS-CORE compliant device driver, it is written as:

```
__NOP(); // Do nothing
```

Please note, in general the delay created by the NOP instruction is not guaranteed and can vary between different systems (e.g., memory wait states, processor types). Therefore, it is not suitable for producing accurate timing delays if the software needs to be used in different systems. If the timing delay needs to be accurate, a hardware timer should be used.

TABLE 5.82 Arm custom instructions (a total of 15 classes).

Class	Instruction	Input data type	Result data type	Width of <imm>
CX1{A}	CX1 <coproc>, <Rd>, #<imm> CX1A <coproc>, <Rd>, #<imm>	32-bit int or APSR_nzcv	32-bit int or APSR_nzcv	13
CX2{A}	CX2 <coproc>, <Rd>, <Rn>, #<imm> CX2A <coproc>, <Rd>, <Rn>, #<imm>	32-bit int or APSR_nzcv	32-bit int or APSR_nzcv	9
CX3{A}	CX3 <coproc>, <Rd>, <Rn>, <Rm>, #<imm> CX3A <coproc>, <Rd>, <Rn>, <Rm>, #<imm>	32-bit int or APSR_nzcv	32-bit int or APSR_nzcv	6
CX1D{A}	CX1D <coproc>, <Rd>,<Rd+1>, #<imm> CX1DA <coproc>, <Rd>, <Rd+1>, #<imm>	Rd: 64-bit int or APSR_nzcv	64-bit int	13
CX2D{A}	CX2D <coproc>, <Rd>, <Rn>, #<imm> CX2DA <coproc>, <Rd>, <Rd+1>, <Rn>, #<imm>	Rd: 64-bit int or APSR_nzcv Rn:32-bit int or APSR_nzcv	64-bit int	9
CX3D{A}	CX3D <coproc>, <Rd>, <Rn>, <Rm>, #<imm> CX3DA <coproc>, <Rd>, <Rd+1>, <Rn>, <Rm>, #<imm>	Rd: 64-bit int or APSR_nzcv Rn, Rm :32-bit int or APSR_nzcv	64-bit int	6
VCX1{A}.S	VCX1 <coproc>, <Sd>, #<imm> VCX1A <coproc>, <Sd>, #<imm>	Float (fp32)	Float (fp32)	11
VCX2{A}.S	VCX2 <coproc>, <Sd>, <Sm>, #<imm> VCX2A <coproc>, <Sd>, <Sm>, #<imm>	float (fp32)	float (fp32)	6
VCX3{A}.S	VCX3 <coproc>, <Sd>, <Sn>, <Sm>, #<imm> VCX3A <coproc>, <Sd>, <Sn>, <Sm>, #<imm>	float (fp32)	float (fp32)	3
VCX1{A}.D	VCX1 <coproc>, <Dd>, #<imm> VCX1A <coproc>, <Dd>, #<imm>	Double (fp64)	Double (fp64)	11
VCX2{A}.D	VCX2 <coproc>, <Dd>, <Dm>, #<imm> VCX2A <coproc>, <Dd>, <Dm>, #<imm>	Double (fp64)	Double (fp64)	6
VCX3{A}.D	VCX3 <coproc>, <Dd>, <Dn>, <Dm>, #<imm> VCX3A <coproc>, <Dd>, <Dn>, <Dm>, #<imm>	Double (fp64)	Double (fp64)	3

Continued

TABLE 5.82   Arm custom instructions (a total of 15 classes)—cont'd

Class	Instruction	Input data type	Result data type	Width of <imm>
VCX1{A}.Q	VCX1 <coproc>, <Qd>, #<imm> VCX1A <coproc>, <Qd>, #<imm>	Vector	Vector	12
VCX2{A}.Q	VCX2 <coproc>, <Qd>, <Qm>, #<imm> VCX2A <coproc>, <Qd>, <Qm>, #<imm>	Vector	Vector	7
VCX3{A}.Q	VCX3 <coproc>, <Qd>, <Qn>, <Qm>, #<imm> VCX3A <coproc>, <Qd>, <Qn>, <Qm>, #<imm>	Vector	Vector	4

Another special instruction which is useful during the development of software is Breakpoint (BKPT). It is used for creating software breakpoints in an application during software development/debugging. If a program being debugged is executed from SRAM, usually the debugger inserts breakpoints to the program by replacing the original instruction (where the breakpoint is) with a BKPT. When the breakpoint is hit, the processor is then halted and the debugger restores the original instruction. The user can then carry out the debug tasks through the debugger. The BKPT instruction can also be used to generate a debug monitor exception. The BKPT instruction has an 8-bit immediate value. The debugger or debug monitor exception handler can extract this data and decide what action to carry out based on the extracted information. By way of an example, one of the uses of the immediate value is that it can be used for indicating a semihosting request using certain special values (this is tool chain dependent).

The syntax of the BKPT instruction in assembly programming language is:

```
BKPT #<immed> ; Breakpoint
```

Similar to the SVC, you can also omit the "#" sign when using most assembler tools:

```
BKPT <immed> ; Breakpoint
```

Or in C programming with a CMSIS-CORE compliant device driver, the BKPT instruction is written as:

```
__BKPT(immed);
```

In addition to the support of the BKPT instruction, the Cortex-M23 and Cortex-M33 processors also support a breakpoint unit which provides up to four (for the Cortex-M23) or eight (for the Cortex-M33) hardware breakpoint comparators. When using a hardware breakpoint unit there is no need to replace the original instructions in the program memory as there is in software breakpoint operations.

TABLE 5.83 Miscellaneous unsupported hint instructions.

Unsupported Instruction	Function
DBG	A hint instruction to the processor's hardware for debug and trace. The exact effect is dependent upon the processor's design. In existing Cortex-M processors this instruction is not used.
PLD	Preload data. This is a hint instruction typically used by the cache memory controller to accelerate data access. However, since there is no data cache inside the Cortex-M23 and Cortex-M33 processors this instruction behaves as a NOP (i.e., no operation).
PLI	Preload instruction. This is a hint instruction typically used for a cache memory controller to accelerate instruction access by indicating where a certain memory region in the program code is to be used. However, since there is no instruction cache inside the Cortex-M23 and Cortex-M33 processors, this instruction behaves as a NOP (i.e., no operation).
YIELD	A hint instruction to allow an application task in a multithreading system to indicate that it is executing a task that can be swapped out (e.g., stalled or waiting for something to happen). This hint information can be used by processors with hardware multithreading support to improve a system's overall performance. Since the Cortex-M23, and Cortex-M33 processors do not have any hardware multithreading support, this hint instruction is executed as a NOP.

There are a number of Hint instructions defined in the Thumb instruction set (Table 5.83). These instructions are executed as NOP on the Cortex-M23 and the Cortex-M33 processors.

All other undefined instructions, when executed, will cause a fault exception to take place, either a HardFault or a UsageFault.

Since the release of the Armv8-M architecture, Armv8-M architecture has been updated to include a number of new instructions. For example, since the discovery of Spectre and Meltdown (security vulnerabilities), Arm has introduced additional instructions to address potential security issues, caused by speculative execution optimization in some processor implementations. Speculative execution is a commonly used optimization technique used in high-end processors with a long pipeline and complex memory systems.

Because the Cortex-M23 and Cortex-M33 processors do not have speculative execution and advanced processor cache systems, they are not subject to vulnerabilities like Spectre and Meltdown. However, to create consistent software architecture, the following instructions (Table 5.84) are supported in the Armv8-M architecture within the Mainline extension (i.e., Mainline subprofile processors such as the Cortex-M33 processor).

These instructions (SSBB, PSSBB, and CSDB) must not be used inside an IT instruction block.

In depth information for these instructions are covered by a whitepaper "Cache Speculation Side-channels", which can be downloaded from https://developer.arm.com/support/arm-security-updates/speculative-processor-vulnerability.

Since Cortex-M processors are not affected by the Spectre and Meltdown vulnerabilities, I have not covered these instructions in this book.

TABLE 5.84 Instructions added to the Armv8-M Mainline Architecture to address spectra and meltdown vulnerabilities.

Instruction	Function
SSBB	Speculative Store Bypass Barrier This instruction prevents speculative loads from: -. Returning data older than the most recent store to the same **virtual** address appearing in the program order before the load -. Returning data from stores using the same **virtual** address appearing in the program order after the load. This instruction executes as DSB in the Cortex-M33 processor.
PSSBB	Physical Speculative Store Bypass Barrier This instruction prevents speculative loads from -. Returning data older than the most recent store to the same **physical** address appearing in the program order before the load -. Returning data from stores using the same **physical** address appearing in the program order after the load. This instruction executes as DSB in the Cortex-M33 processor.
CSDB	Consumption of Speculative Data Barrier This is a memory barrier that, after it has executed, prevents the speculative execution of certain types of subsequent instructions. The prevention lasts until the unresolved condition state has been resolved (no longer speculative). The instructions that are prevented from being speculative execute after a CSDB include: • Nonbranch instructions • Instructions that are the result of data value predictions • Instructions that are the result of ALU flag prediction from instructions other than conditional branch instructions Non-speculative instructions and speculative branch instructions can still be executed. This instruction executes as NOP in the Cortex-M33 processor.

5.23 Accessing special registers with the CMSIS-CORE

In Section 5.6.4 I covered the MRS and MSR instructions that are used for accessing special registers. To make programming easier, the CMSIS-CORE introduced a number of functions for the access of special registers (Table 5.85).

In the Table 5.85:

• The functions with the "__TZ" prefix in their function names can only be used by software running in the Secure state.
• Unless specified, these functions use either the MRS or the MSR instructions.
• Apart from functions that access the APSR and the CONTROL, all other functions need to execute at privileged level.

TABLE 5.85 CMSIS-CORE functions for special register access.

Register	Function	Available on Cortex-M23?
The CONTROL of the current security domain	uint32_t __get_CONTROL(void)	Y
The CONTROL of the current security domain	void __set_CONTROL(uint32_t control)	Y
The Non-secure version of CONTROL	uint32_t __TZ_get_CONTROL_NS (void)	Y
The Non-secure version of CONTROL	void __TZ_set_CONTROL_NS (uint32_t control)	Y
The PRIMASK of the current security domain	uint32_t __get_PRIMASK(void)	Y
The PRIMASK of the current security domain	void __set_PRIMASK(uint32_t priMask)	Y
Clears PRIMASK of the current security domain using the CPS instruction	__enable_irq(void)	Y
Sets PRIMASK of the current security domain using the CPS instruction	__disable_irq(void)	Y
The Non-secure version of the PRIMASK	uint32_t __TZ_get_PRIMASK_NS (void)	Y
The Non-secure version of the PRIMASK	void __TZ_set_PRIMASK_NS (uint32_t priMask)	Y
The BASEPRI of the current security domain	uint32_t __get_BASEPRI(void)	N
The BASEPRI of the current security domain	void __set_BASEPRI(uint32_t basePRI)	N
The Non-secure version of the BASEPRI	uint32_t __TZ_get_BASEPRI_NS (void)	N
The Non-secure version of the BASEPRI	void __TZ_set_BASEPRI_NS(uint32_t basePRI)	N
The FAULTMASK of the current security domain	uint32_t __get_FAULTMASK(void)	N
The FAULTMASK of the current security domain	void __set_FAULTMASK(uint32_t faultMask)	N
Clears FAULTMASK of the current security domain using the CPS instruction	__enable_fault_irq(void)	N
Sets FAULTMASK of the current security domain using the CPS instruction	__disable_fault_irq(void)	N
The Non-secure version of the FAULTMASK	uint32_t __TZ_get_FAULTMASK_NS (void)	N
The Non-secure version of the FAULTMASK	void __TZ_set_FAULTMASK_NS (uint32_t faultMask)	N

Continued

TABLE 5.85 CMSIS-CORE functions for special register access—cont'd

Register	Function	Available on Cortex-M23?
IPSR	uint32_t __get_IPSR(void)	Y
APSR	uint32_t __get_APSR(void)	Y
xPSR	uint32_t __get_xPSR(void)	Y
The MSP of the current security domain	uint32_t __get_MSP(void)	Y
The MSP of the current security domain	void __set_MSP(uint32_t topOfMainStack)	Y
The Non-secure version of the MSP	uint32_t __TZ_get_MSP_NS(void)	Y
The Non-secure version of the MSP	void __TZ_set_MSP_NS(uint32_t topOfMainStack)	Y
The PSP of the current security domain	uint32_t __get_PSP(void)	Y
The PSP of the current security domain	void __set_PSP(uint32_t topOfProcStack)	Y
The Non-secure version of the PSP	uint32_t __TZ_get_PSP_NS(void)	Y
The Non-secure version of the PSP	void __TZ_set_PSP_NS(uint32_t topOfProcStack)	Y
The MSPLIM of the current security domain	uint32_t __get_MSPLIM(void)	Y
The MSPLIM of the current security domain	void __set_MSPLIM(uint32_t MainStackPtrLimit)	Y
The Non-secure version of the MSPLIM	uint32_t __TZ_get_MSPLIM_NS(void)	N
The Non-secure version of the MSPLIM	void __TZ_set_MSPLIM_NS(uint32_t MainStackPtrLimit)	N
The PSPLIM of the current security domain	uint32_t __get_PSPLIM(void)	Y
The PSPLIM of the current security domain	void __set_PSPLIM(uint32_t ProcStackPtrLimit)	Y
The Non-secure version of PSPLIM	uint32_t __TZ_get_PSPLIM_NS(void)	N
The Non-secure version of PSPLIM	void __TZ_set_PSPLIM_NS(uint32_t ProcStackPtrLimit)	N
The Non-secure version of the current SP	uint32_t __TZ_get_SP_NS(void)	Y
The Non-secure version of the current SP	void __TZ_set_SP_NS(uint32_t topOfStack)	Y
The FPSCR (available in the Cortex-M33 with an FPU)	uint32_t __get_FPSCR(void)	N
The FPSCR (available in the Cortex-M33 with an FPU)	void __set_FPSCR(uint32_t fpscr)	N

References

[1] Armv8-M Architecture Reference Manual. https://developer.arm.com/documentation/ddi0553/am/ (Armv8.0-M only version). https://developer.arm.com/documentation/ddi0553/latest/ (latest version including Armv8.1-M). Note: M-profile architecture reference manuals for Armv6-M, Armv7-M, Armv8-M and Armv8.1-M can be found here: https://developer.arm.com/architectures/cpu-architecture/m-profile/docs.

[2] Arm Cortex-M23 Devices Generic User Guide. https://developer.arm.com/documentation/dui1095/latest.

[3] Arm Cortex-M33 Devices Generic User Guide. https://developer.arm.com/documentation/100235/latest.

[4] Arm Compiler armasm user guide—version 6.9. https://developer.arm.com/documentation/100069/0609. Latest version of Arm Compiler armasm user guide is available at https://developer.arm.com/documentation/100069/latest/.

[5] Procedure Call Standard for the Arm Architecture (AAPCS). https://developer.arm.com/documentation/ihi0042/latest.

[6] A Programmer Guide to the Memory Barrier instruction for Arm Cortex-M Family Processor. https://developer.arm.com/documentation/dai0321/latest/.

Memory system

6.1 Overview of the memory system

6.1.1 What is in the memory system?

Arm® Cortex®-M processors provide generic bus interfaces to allow memory blocks (e.g., SRAM, ROM, embedded flash) and peripherals to be connected to the processor. These components are essential for the microcontroller's operation and are present in all Cortex-M-based systems. In addition to the processor, there are, in many microcontrollers, additional bus masters (units that initiate bus transfers) that access memories and peripherals. An example of this is the Direct Memory Access (DMA) controllers which transfer data from one address to another without the processor's intervention (which can help increase throughput or lower the system power level). In this chapter, I will focus on the processor's memory system support. Other blocks, like DMA controllers, can be different between the offerings from different vendors and will not, therefore, be covered in this book.

Although Armv8-M architecture [1] is 32-bit (the same as for the Armv7-M and Armv6-M architectures), there is no restriction on the width of the bus system. The key thing required is that the memory needs to be byte-addressable (the smallest unit of memory that can be accessed by a transfer is a byte). In the Cortex-M23 and Cortex-M33 processors, the bus interfaces are 32-bit. It is possible to connect memory blocks of another data width to these processors, providing that there is a suitable bus infrastructure in place to handle the data transfer width conversions.

The Cortex-M processors support a 4GB address space (32-bit addressing). The exact size and type of the memories in chip design are flexible and, thus, you can find microcontroller products with different memory specifications. Peripherals are memory-mapped, which means that the peripheral registers have their allocated address locations which can be accessed by memory load/store instructions. To simplify the design of the bus systems, the peripheral registers on Arm processors are normally 32-bit aligned (i.e., the address values are a multiple of 4). A portion of the address space is allocated to the registers inside the processors. For example, the NVIC, the MPU, the SysTick timer, and debug components all have memory-mapped registers.

The Cortex-M33 processor is based on Harvard bus architecture, i.e., multiple bus interfaces are used to enable both fetching of instructions and data access to be carried out at the same time. It is worth noting that the memory space in a Cortex-M processor is unified, and therefore, instructions and data share the same address space.

6.1.2 Memory system features

To support a wide range of applications, the memory systems of the Cortex-M23 and the Cortex-M33 processors provide a range of features. These include:

- Bus interface designs based on the AMBA® (Advanced Microcontroller Bus Architecture) 5 AHB™ (Advanced High-performance Bus) protocol [2]. This bus protocol enables pipelined operations in the system bus to access memories and peripherals. The processors also use the Advanced Peripheral Bus (APB) protocol[3] for accessing debug components. AMBA is a collection of bus interface protocol specifications and is a de-facto on-chip bus standard for embedded SoC designs.
- For the Cortex-M23 only, an optional single-cycle I/O interface for low latency peripheral register access.
- For the Cortex-M33 only, a Harvard bus architecture.
- For the Cortex-M33 only, the ability to handle unaligned data.
- Exclusive access (this is commonly used for semaphore operations in systems with an embedded OS or RTOS).
- Optionally, the support for TrustZone® security at the system level.
- A configuration option for little-endian and big-endian memory systems.
- Memory attributes and access permissions for different memory regions.
- Support for the optional Memory Protection Unit (MPU). The Memory attributes and access permissions configurations can, if the MPU is available, be programmed at runtime.

Similar to that in the Armv7-M and Armv6-M architectures, the 4GB address space in the Armv8-M architecture is, as mentioned in Chapter 3, Fig. 3.4, architecturally divided into predefined regions. If the TrustZone security extension is implemented, the address space is further partitioned into Secure and Non-secure address ranges.

6.1.3 Key changes for the Cortex-M23/M33 when compared to the previous Cortex-M processors

Software developers using Cortex-M23 and Cortex-M33 processor-based products will notice several differences in the memory system compared to previous Cortex-M based products. The list in the following section details the changes that are visible to software and excludes chip-level design changes.

Memory system differences between the Cortex-M0/M0+ and the Cortex-M23 include:

- The initial boot vector table is no longer limited to address 0x0. And, if the TrustZone security extension is implemented, the system has separate Secure and Non-secure initial vector table addresses.
- A new programmer's model for the MPU.

- The addition of the TrustZone security extension (This is optional. Some microcontrollers based on the Cortex-M23 processor do not have TrustZone).
- The addition of exclusive access support.

Similarly, memory system differences between the Cortex-M3/M4 and the Cortex-M33 include:

- The initial boot vector table is no longer limited to address 0x0. And, if the TrustZone security extension is implemented, the system has separate Secure and Non-secure initial vector table addresses.
- A new programmer's model for the MPU.
- The addition of the TrustZone security extension (This is optional. Some microcontrollers based on the Cortex-M33 processor do not have TrustZone).
- The removal of the bit band feature that was in the Cortex-M3/M4 processor: this has been removed in Armv8-M because the address remapping nature of the bit band feature sometimes conflicted with the TrustZone security.

There are some architectural definition changes between Armv6-M/Armv7-M and Armv8-M. However, these changes rarely affect the program codes. These changes cover:

- Memory types—Strongly Ordered (SO) memory type becomes a subset of Device type, with new attributes for Device types now defined.
- The Shareability attribute—One of the memory types—Device—is now always shareable in the Armv8-M architecture. In previous architecture, it could be shareable or nonshareable.

The memory maps of microcontroller devices are likely to change when they are migrated from the previous generations of Cortex-M based devices to those on Armv8-M. This is especially true when the TrustZone security is included in the system to separate memory address ranges for Secure and Non-secure resources (e.g., memories and peripherals). This type of change is easily handled by updating the device header files and project settings. The changes required by the application codes are usually straightforward, except when the peripherals are not compatible.

6.2 Memory map

Within the 4GB addressable memory space, some parts of the address ranges are allocated to internal peripherals within the processor, such as the NVIC and debug components. The memory locations of those internal components are fixed. Besides, the memory space is architecturally divided into several memory regions, as shown in Fig. 6.1. This arrangement allows:

- Processors to support different types of memories and devices out of the box. This simplifies the startup process of the software as there is no need to configure the memory attributes for different address ranges before running the application codes.
- An optimized arrangement for higher performance.

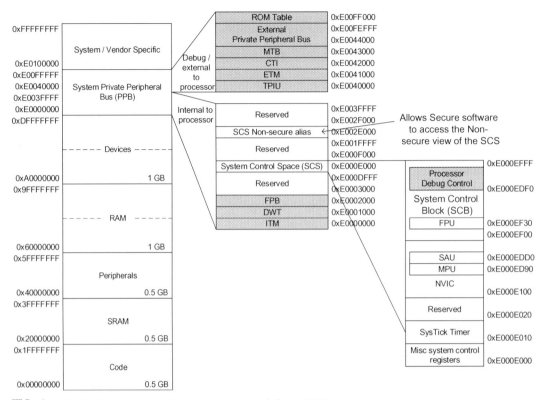

FIG. 6.1   Default memory map of the Cortex-M23 and Cortex-M33 processors.

The architecturally defined memory map is called the default memory map, as shown in Fig. 6.1. Apart from:

- the space allocated for internal components of the processor, and
- the System/Vendor specific address range,

the memory attributes of the rest of the address range can be reconfigured by software using the MPU. In Fig. 6.1, the shaded areas are for debug components.

Although the default memory map is fixed, the architecture allows high flexibility to enable silicon designers to design their products with different memories and peripherals—thus enabling product differentiation.

To begin with, let us look at the memory region definitions shown on the left-hand side of Fig. 6.1. The descriptions of the memory region definitions are listed in Table 6.1.

Program execution from Peripherals, Devices, and System memory regions is not allowed. Architecturally, these regions are preset with the eXecute-Never (XN) attribute which prohibits program execution in these spaces. However, like other memory attributes, the XN attribute of memory regions (like CODE, SRAM, Peripheral, RAM, and Device) can be overridden by software using the MPU.

TABLE 6.1   Memory regions.

Region	Address range
Code	0x00000000 to 0x1FFFFFFF

A 512MB memory space primarily used for program code, which includes the default vector table which is a part of the program memory. This region also allows data access.

SRAM	0x20000000 to 0x3FFFFFFF

The SRAM region is located in the next 512MB of memory space. It is primarily used for connecting SRAM, mostly on-chip SRAM, but there is no limitation of the exact memory type. You can also execute program code from this region.

Peripherals	0x40000000 to 0x5FFFFFFF

The Peripheral memory region is also 512MB in size and is mostly used for on-chip peripherals.

RAM	0x60000000 to 0x9FFFFFFF

The RAM region contains two slots of 512MB memory space (total 1GB) for other RAM, such as off-chip memories. The RAM region can be used for program code as well as data. The two slots of space have different default cache attributes (see Table 6.3).

Devices	0xA0000000 to 0xDFFFFFFF

The Device region contains two slots of 512MB memory space (total 1GB) for other peripherals, such as off-chip peripherals.

System	0xE0000000 to 0xFFFFFFFF

The System region contains several parts:
Internal System Private Peripheral Bus (PPB), 0xE0000000 to 0xE003FFFF

The internal Private Peripheral Bus (PPB) is used to access system components such as the NVIC, SysTick, and the MPU, as well as debug components inside Cortex-M processors. In most cases, this memory space is only accessible by program code running in a privileged state. Some of the registers (e.g., the SAU) are only accessible from the Secure state

External Private Peripheral Bus (PPB), 0xE0040000 to 0xE00FFFFF

An additional PPB region is available for the adding of optional debug components. If a PPB bus is available in the processor's implementation (i.e., on the Cortex-M33), it allows silicon vendors to add their own debug or vendor-specific components. This memory space is only accessible by program code running in a privileged state. Note, the base address of the debug components on this bus can, potentially, be changed by silicon designers.

Vendor Specific area, 0xE0100000 to 0xFFFFFFFF

The remaining memory space is reserved for vendor-specific components and in most instances, it is not used.

The memory space for the NVIC, the MPU, the SCB, and various system peripherals is called the System Control Space (SCS). Further information about these components can be found in various chapters of this book (chapter numbers and descriptions are listed in Table 6.2). The address locations of these built-in components were covered in Fig. 6.1.

TABLE 6.2 Various built-in components in the Cortex-M23 and Cortex-M33 processors.

Component	Description
NVIC	Nested Vectored Interrupt Controller (see Chapter 9) A built-in interrupt controller for exceptions (including interrupts) handling.
MPU	Memory Protection Unit (Chapter 12) An optional programmable unit to setup memory access permissions and memory access attributes (characteristics or behaviors) for various memory regions. Some Cortex-M microcontrollers do not have an MPU.
SAU	Security Attribution Unit (Chapter 18) An optional programmable unit that defines Secure and Non-secure address partitioning when the TrustZone security extension is used.
SysTick	System Tick timer(s) (Chapter 11) A 24-bit timer designed mainly for generating regular OS interrupts. It can also be used by application code if the OS is not in use. If TrustZone is implemented there can be up to two SysTick timers: one for Secure software and one for Non-secure software.
SCB	System Control Block (Chapter 10) A set of registers that can be used to control the behavior of the processor and provides status information.
FPU	Floating-Point Unit (Chapter 14) Several registers are placed here for controlling the behavior of the floating-point unit and to provide status information. These registers are omitted if the FPU has not been implemented.
FPB	Flash Patch and BreakPoint unit (Chapter 16) For debugging operations. It contains up to eight comparators and each can be configured to generate a hardware breakpoint event, e.g., when an instruction at a breakpoint address is executed.
DWT	Data Watchpoint and Trace unit (Chapter 16) For debugging and trace operations. It contains up to four comparators and each can be configured to generate data watchpoint events, e.g., when a certain memory address range is accessed by software. It can also be used to generate data-trace packets to allow a debugger to observe access to monitored memory locations.
ITM	Instrumentation Trace Macrocell—not available on the Cortex-M23 (Chapter 16) A component for debugging and trace. It allows the software to generate a data-trace stimulus that can be captured either by a trace interface or by a trace buffer. It also provides time stamp package generation in the trace system.
ETM	Embedded Trace Macrocell (Chapter 16) A component for generating instruction trace for software debugging.
TPIU	Trace Point Interface Unit (Chapter 16) A component for converting trace packets from trace sources to a trace interface protocol. By using the trace interface protocol, trace data can be easily captured with a minimal set of pins.
ROM table	ROM Table (Chapter 16) A simple lookup table that enables debug tools to extract the addresses of debug and trace components. Using the ROM table(s), debug tools can identify the debug components available in the system. It also provides ID registers which are used for system identification.

6.3 Memory types and memory attributes

6.3.1 Memory type classifications

The key difference between different memory regions in the default memory map is their memory attributes. The last section briefly mentioned the XN (eXecute Never) attribute, but there are others. Different combinations of memory attributes result in different memory types (Fig. 6.2).

6.3.2 Memory attributes overview

The memory map defines the memory attributes of memory access. The memory attributes available in Cortex®-M processors include the following:

Bufferable: A write to the memory can be carried out by a write buffer while the processor continues to execute the next instruction.

Cacheable: Data obtained from memory read can be copied to a memory cache so that the next time it is accessed the value can be obtained from the cache to speed up the program's execution.

Executable: The processor is allowed to fetch and execute program code from this memory region. If a memory region (e.g., the peripheral region) does not allow the execution of program codes, it is marked with an XN (eXecute Never) attribute.

Sharable: Data in this memory region could be shared by multiple bus masters. If a memory region is configured with a shareable attribute, then the memory system needs to ensure the coherency of data between the different bus masters.

Transient: When a memory region is marked with this attribute it suggests that the data in this memory region might not be needed to be accessed shortly.

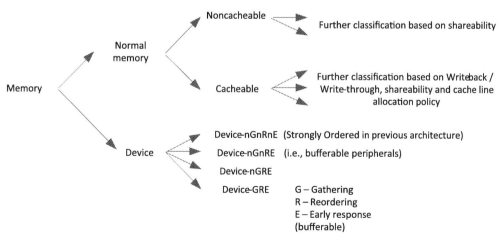

FIG. 6.2 Classification of memory types.

FIG. 6.3   A buffered write operation.

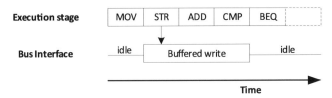

The bufferable attribute can be applied to "Normal memory" and "Device". For example, a cache memory controller can use this attribute to select between Write-Back and Write-Through cache policies. If a write is bufferable, and if the cache controller supports the Write-Back cache policy, then the writes are held in the cache unit as dirty data.

The bufferable attribute is used to improve performance when the memory system contains wait states. For example, if a write buffer is present, a data write to a bufferable memory region can be carried out in a single clock cycle and, even if the actual transfer needs several clock cycles to be completed on the bus interface (Fig. 6.3), it can still immediately execute the next instruction.

Unlike the previous Cortex-M3/M4 processors, there is no internal write buffer in the Cortex-M33 processor. However, write buffers might still be present in system-level components, such as a bus bridge and an external memory interface.

The cacheability attributes for Normal memory can be further divided into:

- inner cache attributes, and
- outer cache attributes

These cacheability attributes are configurable if the MPU has been implemented. The separation of inner and outer attributes allows a processor to use the inner attributes for built-in cache and the outer attributes for system/L2 cache. However, since there are no cache supports in the Cortex-M23 and Cortex-M33 processors, these attributes are only exported to the bus interface. Chip designers can, therefore, utilize the exported cacheability information if they then decide to include cache components in their design.

Another new memory attribute feature in the Armv8-M architecture is that Normal memory has a new Transient attribute. If an address region is marked as Transient it means the data within is unlikely to be frequently used. A cache design could, therefore, utilize this information to prioritize transient data for cacheline evictions. A cacheline eviction operation is needed when the processor needs to store a new piece of data into the cache but all of the cache-ways of the corresponding cache index have already been used by older valid data. In the case of the Cortex-M23 and Cortex-M33 processors, this attribute is not used as (a) there is no data cache support, and (b) the AHB interface does not have any signal for transient indication. Please note, even when an Armv8-M processor has a data cache transient support, is an optional feature. This is because this feature increases the SRAM area needed for cache tags and might, therefore, not be desirable for some designs.

The rest of the attribute information is exported to the processor's top-level boundary and could be used by bus infrastructure components to decide how transfers are handled. In most existing Cortex-M microcontrollers, only the Executable and Bufferable attributes affect the working of the applications. The Cacheable and Sharable attributes are usually used by

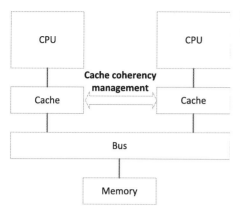

FIG. 6.4 The Shareable attribute is used by Cache coherency management in multiprocessor systems.

the cache controllers and, and although many Cortex-M microcontroller designs do not include a cache controller, small cache units might still be present at the system level, e.g., in an external memory interface such as an external DDR memory controller or a QSPI flash interface.

The Sharable memory attribute is required in systems with multiple processors and multiple cache units with cache coherency control support (Fig. 6.4). When data access is indicated as Sharable, the cache controller needs to ensure that the value is coherent with the other cache units. This is necessary because the value could have been cached and modified by another processor.

Peripherals should be defined as a "Device" memory type. The Device attributes for Armv8-M have been changed when compared with that in the previous architecture. The Device type now has several subcategories which are defined using the following three characteristics:

- Gathering—the bus infrastructure is allowed to merge multiple transfers
- Reordering—the bus infrastructure is allowed to reorder between different transfers
- Early response—the bus infrastructure is allowed to buffer up write transfers and feedback speculative bus responses to the processor (i.e., bufferable)

Although there are three characteristics, there are only four valid combinations (Table 6.3).

For general peripherals, types Device-nGnRE or Device-nGnRnE should be used. Device-nGRE and Device-GRE types could be used for memory-like devices, such as a display buffer, where access order does not matter. However, Device-GRE should not be used if the data transfer size must be retained.

6.3.3 Memory attributes of the default memory map

The default memory access attributes for each memory region are shown in Table 6.4.

By default, all Normal memory regions are defined as Nonshareable, but this can be changed by using an MPU. In single-processor systems, there is no need to change the

TABLE 6.3 Device type subcategories.

Device type	Description
Device-nGnRnE	For a bus transfer targeting a Device-nGnRnE region, the bus interconnect hardware handling the bus transfer must retain the data size and access order. Additionally, the processor must wait for the response from the device before continuing. (Note: Strongly Ordered (SO) memory types from the Armv6-M and Armv7-M processors effectively become the Device-nGnRnE subcategory in Armv8-M.)
Device-nGnRE	For a bus transfer targeting a Device-nGnRE region, the bus interconnect hardware or the processor is allowed to continue operations, before a write operation has finished, by providing an early response to that write operation.
Device-nGRE	For a bus transfer targeting a Device-nGRE region, the bus interconnect hardware or the processor is allowed to • reorder the transfer, and • continue operations, before a write operation has finished, by providing an early response to that write operation.
Device-GRE	For a bus transfer targeting a Device-GRE region, the bus interconnect hardware or the processor is allowed to • reorder the transfer, and • continue operations, before a write operation has finished, by providing an early response to that write operation. Additionally, the data transfer size can be changed as a result of merging transfers, e.g., a write sequence of four successive bytes could be merged into a single word write to achieve higher performance.

memory attribute to shareable, but in multicore processor systems with caches, as shown in Fig. 6.4, then there is a need for the shareability attribute.

6.4 Access permission management

6.4.1 Overview of access permission management

For many years, security management has been available in most Cortex-M processors in the form of Memory Protection and Privilege levels. In Armv8-M, the key enhancement is the TrustZone security extension. Because security is ever more important in embedded systems, many microcontroller vendors are also adding additional security management features at the system level.

A major part of security management is access permission control. This objective is achieved by access permission features inside the processor, at the system level, or both. When software attempts to access a memory location the transfer needs to go through several security checking processes, as shown in Fig. 6.5.

TABLE 6.4 Default memory attributes.

Region	Memory/Device type	XN	Cache, shareability	Note
CODE memory region (0x00000000–0x1FFFFFFF)	Normal	–	WT-RA	Write Through (WT), Read Allocated (RA)
SRAM memory region (0x20000000–0x3FFFFFFF)	Normal	–	WB-WA, RA	Write Back (WB), Write Allocate (WA), Read Allocate
Peripheral region (0x40000000–0x5FFFFFFF)	Device-nGnRE	Y	Shareable	Bufferable, Noncacheable
RAM region (0x60000000–0x7FFFFFFF)	Normal	–	WB-WA, RA	Write Back, Write Allocate, Read Allocate
RAM region (0x80000000–0x9FFFFFFF)	Normal	–	WT, RA	Write Through, Read Allocate
Devices (0xA0000000–0xBFFFFFFF)	Device-nGnRE	Y	Shareable	Bufferable, Noncacheable
Devices (0xC0000000–0xDFFFFFFF)	Devices	Y	Shareable	Bufferable, Noncacheable
System—PPB (0xE0000000-0xE00FFFFF)	Device-nGnRnE (Strongly Ordered)	Y	Shareable	Nonbufferable, Noncacheable
System—Vendor Specific (0xE0100000–0xFFFFFFFF)	Device-nGnRE	Y	Shareable	Bufferable, Noncacheable

6.4.2 Access control mechanisms

As shown in Fig. 6.5, many security checking mechanisms could be involved when checking each memory access. Inside an Armv8-M processor, the following security mechanisms are present:

- The optional TrustZone security extension to prevent Non-secure software from accessing the Secure memory address ranges. The definition of the address partitioning is defined by the:
  - Security Attribution Unit (SAU)—this is programmable and is controlled by Secure firmware
  - Implementation Defined Attribution Unit (IDAU)—this is defined by chip designers, and may or may not be programmable.
- The optional Memory Protection Unit(s) (MPU). This hardware:
  - prevents unprivileged software from accessing privileged only memory
  - prevents software from accessing address ranges not defined by any valid MPU regions
  - prevents writing to address regions defined as read-only by the MPU
- Privilege level management. This is used to prevent unprivileged software from accessing critical processor resources (e.g., the interrupt control). This feature is always present, even without an MPU or when TrustZone is not implemented.

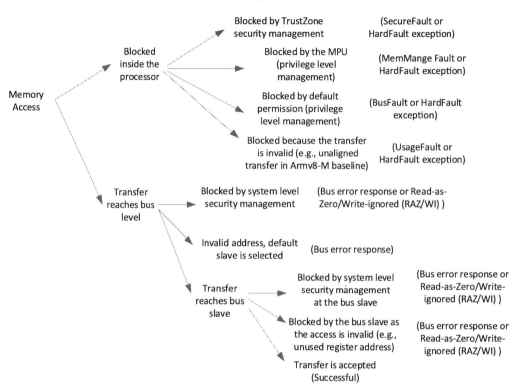

FIG. 6.5 Overview of security checks in a memory access operation.

- Mechanisms to detect illegal software operations. This is not exactly a security feature but could be used for detecting abnormal behaviors (which could be the result of a security incident).

The privilege level and TrustZone attributes of transfers are exported to the processor's bus interfaces so that when the transfer reaches the bus level, system-level security management can permit/deny system-level access permissions. At the system level, security management blocks can include the following features (all of which are device-specific):

- TrustZone bus filters that define whether certain address ranges can be accessed by Non-secure transfers. These can include:
  ○ TrustZone Memory Protection Controller(s)—this unit partitions a memory device into Secure and Non-secure address ranges, either using memory pages or by using a watermark level mechanism.
  ○ TrustZone Peripheral Protection Controller(s)—this unit defines a group of peripherals into Secure and Non-secure peripherals.
- System-level Memory Protection Unit(s). This provides privilege access management for peripherals and could be combined with the TrustZone Peripheral Protection Controller.

Although it is achievable, it is unlikely that a system-level MPU would be used for access permission control for normal memories (e.g., RAM, ROM). This is because the processor in modern microcontrollers is likely to have an architecturally defined MPU. However, because the MPU inside the processor has a limited number of MPU regions, and because a chip can have a large number of peripherals, the processor's MPU would not be sufficient for peripheral access management. To overcome this issue, some microcontroller vendors add system-level MPU(s) to their products.

6.4.3 Differences between the SAU/IDAU and the MPU

Although the SAU and MPU are both used for access permission control, and both have a similar programmer's model that defines regions using starting and ending addresses, they have different purposes. This is illustrated in Fig. 6.6.

The separation of the SAU/IDAU and the MPU is an important characteristic of TrustZone. It allows the RTOS to be decoupled from the security management firmware, which has the following advantages:

- Microcontroller users can either use their own choice of RTOS or use the device as bare metal (no RTOS). In either scenario, applications running on the device are still able to take advantage of the security features provided in the Secure firmware.
- If bugs are present inside the RTOS or in other Non-secure privileged codes, this would not impact the security integrity of the Secure software.
- The OS can be updated using a standard firmware update mechanism for the regular update of the Non-secure program image. This makes product maintenance easier.

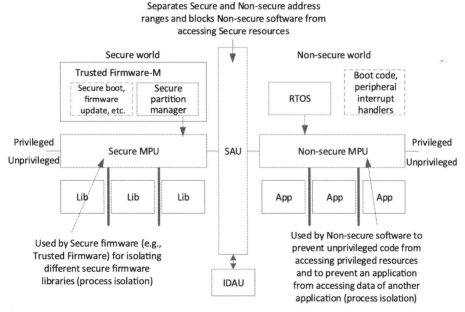

FIG. 6.6 Comparison of the SAU/IDAU and the MPU.

Fig. 6.6 references Trusted Firmware-M (TF-M). This is an open-source project and, as such, the software can be accessed from https://www.trustedfirmware.org/. The TF-M is a part of an initiative called the Platform Security Architecture (PSA), which Arm announced in 2017. It aims to improve security in IoT products and embedded systems.

TABLE 6.5 Default memory access permissions.

Memory region	Address	Access in unprivileged (user) program
Vendor specific	0xE0100000–0xFFFFFFFF	Full access
ROM table	0xE00FF000–0xE00FFFFF	Unprivileged access is blocked and results in a bus fault
PPB, including ETM, TPIU, CTI, MTB	0xE0040000–0xE00FEFFF	Unprivileged access is blocked and results in a bus fault
Internal PPB	0xE000F000–0xE003FFFF	Unprivileged access is blocked and results in a bus fault
NVIC, SCS, core's debug registers, etc.	0xE000E000–0xE000EFFF	Unprivileged access is blocked and results in a bus fault; except if the access is to the Software Trigger Interrupt Register (available in Armv8-M Mainline only) and the configuration is setup to allow unprivileged access In Armv8-M Baseline (i.e., the Cortex-M23), software running on the processor does not have access to the core's debug registers.
FPB/BPU	0xE0002000–0xE0003FFF	Unprivileged access is blocked and results in a bus fault. In Armv8-M Baseline (i.e., the Cortex-M23), software running on the processor does not have access to the Breakpoint Unit (BPU).
DWT	0xE0001000–0xE0001FFF	Unprivileged access is blocked and results in a bus fault. In Armv8-M Baseline (i.e., the Cortex-M23), software running on the processor does not have access to the Data watchpoint Unit (DWT).
ITM (not available in Cortex-M23)	0xE0000000–0xE0000FFF	Unprivileged read is allowed and Unprivileged write is ignored, except for the stimulus port registers which can be setup to allow unprivileged access (runtime configurable)
External Device	0xA0000000–0xDFFFFFFF	Full access
External RAM	0x60000000–0x9FFFFFFF	Full access
Peripheral	0x40000000–0x5FFFFFFF	Full access
SRAM	0x20000000–0x3FFFFFFF	Full access
Code	0x00000000–0x1FFFFFFF	Full access

Further information on:

- PSA and TF-M can be found in Chapter 22.
- TrustZone security management can be found in Chapters 7 and 18.
- the Memory Protection Unit (MPU) can be found in Chapter 12.

6.4.4 Default access permission

The Cortex-M memory map has a default configuration for memory access permissions. This prevents unprivileged (user) applications from accessing system control memory spaces such as the NVIC. The default memory access permission is used when no MPU is present or if the MPU has been disabled.

The default memory access permissions are shown in Table 6.5.

If the MPU is present and enabled, additional access permission rules defined by the MPU setup will also determine whether unprivileged access is allowed for other memory regions.

When unprivileged access is blocked, the fault exception takes place immediately. The fault exception can either be a HardFault or a BusFault exception (not available in Armv8-M Baseline). The fault exception type depends on whether the BusFault exception is enabled and whether its priority level is enough for triggering an exception.

6.5 Memory endianness

Cortex-M processors are used in either Little-Endian or Big-Endian memory systems. With Little Endian memory systems, the first byte of word size data is stored in the least significant byte of the 32-bit memory location (Table 6.6).

In Big Endian memory systems, the first byte of word size data is stored in the most significant byte of the 32-bit address memory location (Table 6.7).

In most Cortex-M microcontrollers, hardware designs are based on a Little-Endian arrangement only. It is important to use the correct endian compilation setting with C compilers, otherwise, the software will fail to work. Please refer to the datasheet and/or reference materials from microcontroller vendors to confirm the endianness of the microcontroller product. The endianness of Cortex-M microcontroller systems is configured as follows:

TABLE 6.6 Little-endian memory representation.

Address	Bits 31–24	Bits 23–16	Bits 15–8	Bits 7–0
0x0003–0x0000	Byte–0x3	Byte–0x2	Byte–0x1	Byte–0x0
...				
0x1003–0x1000	Byte––0x1003	Byte–0x1002	Byte–0x1001	Byte–0x1000
0x1007–0x1004	Byte–0x1007	Byte–0x1006	Byte–0x1005	Byte–0x1004
...				
...	Byte–4xN+3	Byte–4xN+2	Byte–4xN+1	Byte–4xN

TABLE 6.7 Big-endian memory representation.

Address	Bits 31–24	Bits 23–16	Bits 15–8	Bits 7–0
0x0003–0x0000	Byte–0x0	Byte–0x1	Byte–0x2	Byte–0x3
...				
0x1003–0x1000	Byte–0x1000	Byte–0x1001	Byte–0x1002	Byte–0x1003
0x1007–0x1004	Byte–0x1004	Byte–0x1005	Byte–0x1006	Byte–0x1007
...				
...	Byte–4xN	Byte–4xN+1	Byte–4xN+2	Byte–4xN+3

- Armv8-M Baseline (the Cortex-M23 processor) and Armv6-M processors—the endian configuration is set by chip designers and cannot be configured by software.
- Armv8-M Mainline (the Cortex-M33 processor) and Armv7-M processors—the processors determine the endianness of the memory system at a system reset by way of a configuration signal. Once it is started, the endianness of the memory system cannot be changed until the next system reset. However, the system's hardware would likely be designed for one configuration only and thus cannot be changed.

In some instances, some peripheral registers can contain data of different endianness. In those situations, the application codes accessing those peripheral registers would need to convert the data to the correct endianness by using software (e.g., using REV, REV16, and REVSH instructions).

Please note, for the Cortex-M processors:

- Instruction fetches are always in little-endian
- Access to 0xE0000000 to 0xE00FFFFF, including the System Control Space (SCS), the debug components, and the Private Peripheral Bus (PPB), are always little-endian.

If needed, the software can detect the endianness of the system by reading bit 15 (ENDIANNESS) of the Application Interrupt and Reset Control Register (AIRCR) at address 0xE000ED0C. When this bit is 0, it is little-endian, when it is not, it is big-endian. This bit is read-only and can only be accessed in a privileged state or by a debugger.

In Cortex-M processors, the Big-Endian arrangement is called *Byte-Invariant Big-Endian*; but it can also be referred to as BE-8. The Byte-Invariant Big-Endian arrangement is supported on Arm® architectures Armv6, Armv6-M, Armv7, and Armv7-M. The designs of BE-8 systems are different from that of the Big-Endian system built on traditional Arm processors such as the Arm7™TDMI. In classic Arm processors, the Big-Endian arrangement is called *Word-Invariant Big-Endian*, or BE-32. The memory view of both arrangements is the same, but the byte lane usage on the bus interface during data transfers is different. Table 6.8 details the AMBA® AHB byte lane usage for BE-8 and Table 6.9 details the AHB byte lane usage for BE-32.

With Little-Endian systems, the bus lane usage of Cortex-M and classic Arm processors is identical (Table 6.10).

For silicon designers migrating peripherals from legacy Arm processors to Cortex-M processors, the bus interface of these peripherals needs to be modified if the peripherals were

TABLE 6.8 Byte lane usage of a Byte-Invariant Big-Endian (BE-8) system in a 32-bit AHB bus during transfers.

Address, size	Bits 31–24	Bits 23–16	Bits 15–8	Bits 7–0
0x1000, word	Data bit[7:0]	Data bit [15:8]	Data bit [23:16]	Data bit [31:24]
0x1000, half word	–	–	Data bit [7:0]	Data bit [15:8]
0x1002, half word	Data bit [7:0]	Data bit [15:8]	–	–
0x1000, byte	–	–	–	Data bit [7:0]
0x1001, byte	–	–	Data bit [7:0]	–
0x1002, byte	–	Data bit [7:0]	–	–
0x1003, byte	Data bit [7:0]	–	–	–

TABLE 6.9 Byte lane usage of a Word-Invariant Big-Endian (BE-32) system in a 32-bit AHB bus during transfers.

Address, size	Bits 31–24	Bits 23–16	Bits 15–8	Bits 7–0
0x1000, word	Data bit [31:24]	Data bit [23:16]	Data bit [15:8]	Data bit [7:0]
0x1000, half word	Data bit [15:8]	Data bit [7:0]	–	–
0x1002, half word	–	–	Data bit [15:8]	Data bit [7:0]
0x1000, byte	Data bit [7:0]	–	–	–
0x1001, byte	–	Data bit [7:0]	–	–
0x1002, byte	–	–	Data bit [7:0]	–
0x1003, byte	–	–	–	Data bit [7:0]

TABLE 6.10 Byte lane usage of a Little-Endian system in a 32-bit AHB bus during transfers.

Address, size	Bits 31–24	Bits 23–16	Bits 15–8	Bits 7–0
0x1000, word	Data bit [31:24]	Data bit [23:16]	Data bit [15:8]	Data bit [7:0]
0x1000, half word	–	–	Data bit [15:8]	Data bit [7:0]
0x1002, half word	Data bit [15:8]	Data bit [7:0]	–	–
0x1000, byte	–	–	–	Data bit [7:0]
0x1001, byte	–	–	Data bit [7:0]	–
0x1002, byte	–	Data bit [7:0]	–	–
0x1003, byte	Data bit [7:0]	–	–	–

designed for BE-32. A little-endian peripheral designed for previous Arm processors can be reused in an Armv8-M system without modification.

6.6 Data alignment and unaligned data access support

From a programmer's model point of view, the memory system of a Cortex-M processor is 32 bits. In a 32-bit memory system, a 32-bit (4 bytes, or word) data access or a 16-bit (2 bytes, or halfword) data access can either be aligned or unaligned. An aligned transfer means the address value is a multiple of the transfer size (in number of bytes). For example, a word size aligned transfer can be carried out to address 0x00000000, 0x00000004 … 0x00001000, 0x00001004, …, and so on. Similarly, a halfword size aligned transfer can be carried out to 0x00000000, 0x00000002 … 0x00001000, 0x00001002, …, and so on.

Examples of aligned and unaligned data transfers are shown in Fig. 6.7.

Traditionally, most classic Arm® processors (such as the Arm7™/Arm9™) only allowed aligned transfers. This meant that to access memory, a word transfer would have to have both bit[1] and bit[0] of the address equal to 0. Similarly, a half word transfer would have to have an address bit[0] equal to 0. For example, word data can be located at 0x1000 or 0x1004, but it cannot be located in 0x1001, 0x1002, or 0x1003. For half word data, the address can be 0x1000 or 0x1002, but it cannot be 0x1001. All byte size transfers are aligned.

Armv8-M Mainline processors (e.g., the Cortex-M33) and Armv7-M processors (the Cortex-M3, the Cortex-M4 and the Cortex-M7 processors) support unaligned data transfers to memory locations where the memory type is "normal memory" when using single load-store instructions (e.g., LDR, LDRH, STR, STRH).

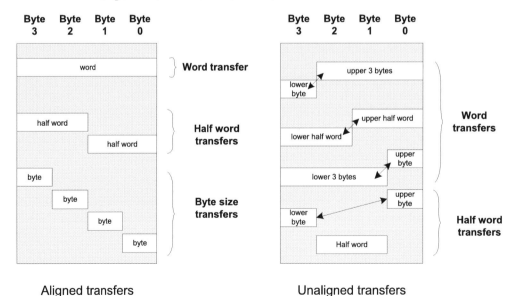

FIG. 6.7   Examples of aligned and unaligned data transfers in a 32-bit Little Endian memory system.

There are several limitations to the unaligned transfer support and these are:

- Unaligned transfers are not supported in Load/Store multiple instructions.
- Unaligned transfers cannot be used on the Private Peripheral Bus (PPB) address range.
- Stack operations (PUSH/POP) must be aligned.
- Exclusive access (such as LDREX or STREX) must be aligned; otherwise, a fault exception (UsageFault) will be triggered.
- Unaligned transfers are not supported on most peripherals. Because most peripherals are not designed to support unaligned transfers, unaligned access to peripherals should generally be avoided.

For the Cortex-M33 processor, unaligned transfers are converted into multiple aligned transfers by the processor's bus interface unit. Because this conversion is carried out by hardware, application programmers do not have to manually divide the access into multiple software steps. However, the conversion of an unaligned transfer to multiple aligned transfers takes multiple clock cycles. As a result, unaligned data access will take longer than aligned access and might not be good for situations in which high performance is required. To guarantee the best performance, therefore, it is worth ensuring that data is properly aligned.

The Armv8-M Baseline processor (the Cortex-M23) and Armv6-M processors (Cortex-M0, Cortex-M0+, and Cortex-M1 processors) do not support unaligned access.

In most instances, C compilers do not generate unaligned data access. It can only happen in:

- Situations where the C/C++ code directly manipulates the pointer values
- Accessing data structures with "__packed" attributes which contain unaligned data
- Inline assembly code

It is possible to set up an Armv8-M Mainline or Armv7-M processor so that an exception is triggered when an unaligned transfer takes place. This is achieved by setting the UNALIGN_TRP (Unaligned Trap) bit in the Configuration Control Register (CCR, address 0xE000ED14) in the System Control Block (SCB). By doing this, the Cortex-M processor generates UsageFault exceptions when unaligned transfers take place. This is useful when developing software as a means to test whether an application produces unaligned transfers. Since Armv8-M Baseline and Armv6-M processors do not support unaligned transfers, such testing is useful to check whether the code can be used on Armv8-M Baseline or Armv6-M processors.

6.7 Exclusive access support

Exclusive access is commonly used for semaphore operations in systems with an OS, which enables resources to be shared by multiple software tasks/applications. Semaphore operations are necessary because many shared resources can only deal with one request at a time. For example:

- Message output handling (e.g., via printf)
- DMA operations (a DMA controller can have very few DMA channels)
- Low-level file system access

When a shared resource can only service one task or one application thread, it is often called Mutual Exclusion (MUTEX). In such a case, when a resource is being used by one process, it is locked to that process and cannot serve another process until the lock is released. To enable a resource to be shared, a memory location is allocated to a piece of the semaphore data (sometimes called a lock flag: if it is set, it indicates that the resource has been locked). Conceptually, semaphore operations when sharing a resource could include:

- The initialization of the semaphore data to indicate that the resource is free/reserved at the beginning of the program (in most cases the resource is free when the system starts).
- Read-modify-write operations on the semaphore data: If an application needs to access the resource, it will first need to read the semaphore data. If the semaphore data indicates the resource is reserved/used by another application, it must then wait. If the resource is available, it can then set the semaphore data to allocate the resource to itself.

On the surface, this simple arrangement should work, but, when looking at the detail, this arrangement could fail if the read-modify-write operation is carried out using normal memory access instructions. This rare situation could occur where both application A and B wishes to access a shared resource at the same time (Fig. 6.8).
The activities in Fig. 6.8 are:

(1) Application A reads the semaphore data first and determines that the shared resource is free.
(2) A context switch is triggered before application A write's back to the semaphore data to allocate the resource.
(3) Application B then reads the semaphore data and also gets the result that the resource is free. It then writes back to the data to allocate the resource.
(4) Application B starts using the resource.
(5) Later on, additional context switching takes place and sometime later, application A is resumed and writes back to the semaphore data to allocate the shared resource.
(6) Application A starts using the shared resource when it was still being used by Application B.

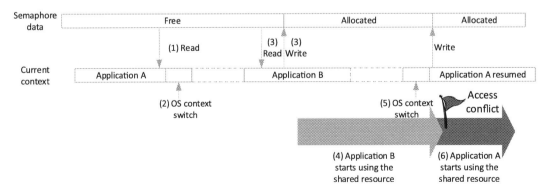

FIG. 6.8 Why a "simple" read-modify-write sequence cannot be used for semaphores.

This sequence of events results in an access conflict, resulting in application A destroying the data from application B.

There are several solutions to avoid this issue:

- Legacy Arm processors, like the Arm7TDMI, provide swap (SWP and SWPB) instructions which provide atomic read-modify-write sequences for semaphore data updates. But this solution is only suitable for simple bus system designs and processors with a short pipeline.
- Semaphores can be handled as an OS service via an SVCall exception. Since only one SVCall exception can take place at any one time, only one application can gain the semaphore. But, the SVCall exception causes additional execution cycles (e.g., latency in exception entry and return) and does not solve the problem for multicore systems where tasks from multiple processors might try to gain the semaphore at the same time.
- By using a device-specific hardware-based semaphore solution. Some chips are designed with semaphore hardware, but the design from each vendor is different and thus making the software less portable.
- By using exclusive access support. The software is portable and works across multiple processors. Exclusive access is supported in most modern Arm-based systems. (Note: Semaphore operations in multicore systems require a bus level exclusive access monitor.)

Exclusive access operations need specific exclusive access instructions, as described in Chapter 5, Section 5.7.11. Exclusive access was first supported in architecture Armv6, e.g., in the Arm1136™.

The concept of exclusive access operations is quite simple but is different from the operations of the swap instructions. Instead of using a locked bus transfer (which the swap instructions use) to block other bus masters or other tasks from accessing the semaphore data during the read-modify-write, it allows and detects the access conflict. When using exclusive access for read-modify-write, if the semaphore has been accessed by another bus master or another process running on the same processor, the complete read-modify-write sequence would need to be repeated (Fig. 6.9).

To support exclusive access, the following hardware features are required:

- Local exclusive access monitor—this is inside the processor and contains a single exclusive status bit that is moved to an exclusive state by an exclusive load. This status bit is moved to an open state by an exclusive store and can also be moved to an open state by either an interrupt/exception enter/exit or by the execution of a CLREX instruction.
- Global exclusive access monitor—this is either in the interconnect or the memory controller and monitors access from different bus masters to detect whether any of the exclusive access sequences conflict with other accesses. If an access conflict is detected, the exclusive store is blocked by the global exclusive access monitor. Through the bus interconnect, the exclusive access monitor also returns the exclusive fail status to the processor. Such an action will cause the return status of the exclusive write to be 1 (i.e., it has failed).

The exclusive write (e.g., STREX) returns a failure status if one of the following conditions takes place:

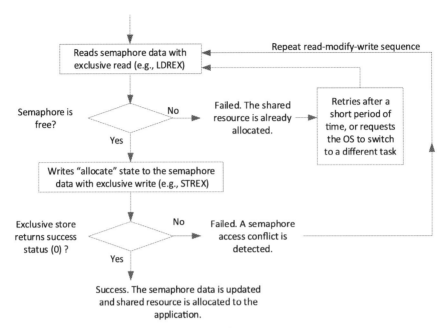

FIG. 6.9   Using exclusive access instruction for a semaphore operation.

- The local exclusive access monitor was in an open state because of the execution of a CLREX instruction.
- The local exclusive access monitor was in an open state because of the occurrence of a context switch or an interrupt/exception event.
- The local exclusive access monitor was in an open state because an LDREX instruction was not executed before the exclusive store instruction.
- External hardware (e.g., A global exclusive access monitor) detected an access conflict and returns an exclusive fail status to the processor via the bus interface.

If the exclusive store receives a failed status the actual write will not take place in the memory. It is either blocked by the processor or by the global exclusive access monitor.

Exclusive access instructions are introduced in Chapter 5 (Section 5.7.11 Exclusive accesses).

Further information about exclusive access can be found in Chapter 11 and example codes for exclusive access can be found in Section 21.2. You can access exclusive access instructions in C using intrinsic functions (Table 6.11) provided in the Cortex Microcontroller Software Interface Standard (CMSIS) compliant device driver libraries:

Please note, there are some differences in exclusive access between the architectures for Cortex-A processors and Cortex-M processors. These differences are:

- In Armv7-A, because the exclusive state in the local monitor is not automatically moved to an open state by an interrupt event, context switching codes need to execute the CLREX instruction (or can use a dummy STREX) to ensure that the local monitor is switched to an

TABLE 6.11　Intrinsic functions for using exclusive accesses in C/C++ programming.

Intrinsic	Instruction	Compatibility
uint8_t __LDREXB (volatile uint8_t *addr)	LDREXB	Not available in Armv6-M
uint16_t __LDREXH(volatile uint16_t *addr)	LDREXH	Same as above.
uint32_t __LDREXW(volatile uint32_t *addr)	LDREX	Same as above.
uint32_t __STREXB(uint8_t, volatile uint8_t *addr)	STREXB	Same as above.
uint32_t __STREXH(uint16_t, volatile uint16_t *addr)	STREXH	Same as above.
uint32_t __STREXW(uint32_t, volatile uint32_t *addr)	STREX	Same as above.
void __CLREX(void)	CLREX	Same as above.
uint8_t __LDAEXB (volatile uint8_t *addr)	LDAEXB	Not available in Armv6-M and Armv7-M.
uint16_t __LDAEXH(volatile uint16_t *addr)	LDAEXH	Same as above.
uint32_t __LDAEX(volatile uint32_t *addr)	LDAEX	Same as above.
uint32_t __STLEXB(uint8_t, volatile uint8_t *addr)	STLEXB	Same as above.
uint32_t __STLEXH(uint16_t, volatile uint16_t *addr)	STLEXH	Same as above.
uint32_t __STLEX(uint32_t, volatile uint32_t *addr)	STLEX	Same as above.

Open Access state. This was changed in the Armv8-A processor family, where interrupt events in those processors automatically clear the exclusive state.
- In Cortex-A processors (both Armv7-A and Armv8-A), exclusive load with an exclusive fail response from a global exclusive access monitor can generate a fault exception. This behavior does not exist in Cortex-M processors.

6.8 Memory ordering and memory barrier instructions

At the beginning of Chapter 4, the differences between architecture and micro-architecture were highlighted. While the Cortex-M23 and Cortex-M33 are small processors that do not have out-of-order[a] execution support and do not reorder memory access on the bus interface, it is possible to implement a high-end Armv8-M processor that does. When developing portable software that can run on a wide range of processors, software developers would find it useful to:

- have a good understanding of memory ordering concepts, and
- know how to use memory barriers to solve memory ordering issues in high-end processors.

[a]The pipeline in a processor that supports an out-of-order execution can start executing some of the later instructions and even complete them while an earlier instruction is still in progress. For example, a memory load operation can take over 100 clock cycles to complete in a high-end processor. This is because it is running at over 1 GHz and because DDR memory has a high latency. An out-of-order processor can start executing subsequent instructions if the data processing is not dependent on the result from the load. The opposite of out-of-order is in-order execution.

Architecturally, memory ordering, based on memory types, which are explained in Section 6.3, has the following requirements (Table 6.12).

In Chapter 5, I covered the use of memory barrier instructions (ISB, DSB, DMB) and load acquire and store release instructions. These instructions help guarantee that memory access from different steps of a software procedure are in the correct order when reaching the memories and the peripherals inside the chip. This is particularly important for multiprocessor systems where the memory access of one processor is observable by another and the ordering between them could be crucial for the interactions.

In Cortex-M processors, memory barrier instructions are also used in the following scenarios, as defined by the requirements of the architecture:

- DSB is used to enforce the ordering between memory access and another processor operation (it does not have to be another memory access).
- DSB and ISB are used to ensure that the effect of a system configuration change takes place before subsequent operations.

The scenarios of where these barrier instructions should be used are covered in Chapter 5, Section 5.19, and Tables 5.76 and 5.77.

Even if the memory barrier instructions are omitted, most applications running on the Cortex®-M23 and the Cortex-M33-based microcontrollers do not suffer from memory ordering issues. This is because:

- These processors do not reorder any memory transfers (this can happen in many high-performance processors).
- These processors do not reorder the execution of instructions (this can happen in many high-performance processors).
- The simple nature of the AHB and APB protocols does not allow a transfer to begin before the previous transfer has finished.
- There is no write buffer in these processors (write buffering is explained in Fig. 6.3).

TABLE 6.12 Memory ordering requirements.

Memory type	Memory ordering requirements
Normal memory	Generally, access to normal memories can be reordered around other memory access, except when: • Data access is separated by a context synchronization event, such as a DSB, a DMB, or load-acquire, and store release instructions. • Instruction fetches are separated by a context synchronization event, such as an ISB.
Device memory without a reordering attribute (Device-nGnRE/nGnRnE)	Bus transactions to a device must match the order of access in the program. Bus transactions to separate devices can have a different access order compared to the program, except when the access is separated by a context synchronization event.
Device with a reordering attribute (Device-GRE/nGRE)	Access can be reordered, except when it is separated by a context synchronization event.

However, for best practice, these memory barrier instructions should, for software portability reasons, be used. Please note, the use of memory barrier instructions might not be sufficient to prevent some of the system level race conditions. For example, after enabling the clock for a peripheral, the software might need to wait for a few clock cycles before accessing the peripheral. This is because the clock control circuit in the microcontroller might need a few clock cycles to enable the peripheral's clock.

6.9 Bus wait state and error support

At the beginning of this chapter, I mentioned that Cortex-M23 and Cortex-M33 processors use AMBA® bus protocols for their bus interfaces. These protocols include:

- AMBA 5 AHB (Advanced High-performance Bus, also known as AHB5) provides a memory system interface(s).
- AMBA 4 APB (Advanced Peripheral Bus, also known as APBv2) provides bus connections for debug component and peripheral interfaces via the "AHB to APB" bridge(s). In some systems, an earlier version of the APB protocol could be used for peripheral connections.
- AMBA 4 ATB (Advanced Trace Bus) for trace packet transfers (this is for debug operations and is not for use by the application).

These interfaces provide support for:

- Bus wait states and OKAY/ERROR response types for AHB (all versions) and APB (this is available following the release of AMBA version 3).
- An exclusive OKAY/FAIL response for AHB5 (see Section 6.7, Exclusive access support)

Wait states are needed when the memories or peripherals are slower than the processors and when latency cycles are added to the bus interconnect infrastructure. Some of the memory access might take several clock cycles to complete. For example, the flash memory used in a low power microcontroller might have a maximum access speed of around 20 MHz, even though the microcontroller can run at over 40 MHz or even 100 MHz. In this situation, the flash memory interface needs to insert wait states to the bus system so that the processor waits for the transfer to complete.
The wait states affect the system in several ways:

- They reduce the performance of the system.
- They can reduce the energy efficiency of the system because of the reduction in performance.
- They increase the interrupt latency of the system.
- They can make the system's behavior less deterministic in terms of the program's execution timing.

Many modern microcontrollers include various types of cache memories to reduce average memory access latency. While the Cortex-M23 and the Cortex-M33 processors do not have internal cache support, many microcontrollers with embedded flash memories do have a cache unit closely integrated with the flash memory controller to:

- Enable the processor to run at a high clock speed with slower embedded flash memory.
- Enable better energy efficiency by reducing memory access in the embedded flash memory (This is because flash memories are usually power-hungry).

Instead of using cache-based designs, some microcontrollers use flash prefetch units that allow sequential fetches with a zero-wait state. Prefetch units are smaller than a cache unit but do not have the same level of advantages as a cache controller because:

(1) They do not prevent wait states if the access is nonsequential.
(2) They do not reduce the number of accesses to the flash memory. Thus, there is no power saving benefit.

Error responses are essential, allowing the hardware to inform the software that something has gone wrong, and ensuring, in the process, that remedial actions can be taken in the form of a fault exception handler. Error responses can be generated by:

- Bus infrastructure components. This can be caused by:
  - Security or privileged level violations (see Section 6.4.1)
  - Access to an invalid address
- Bus slaves. This can be caused by:
  - Security or privileged level violations
  - An operation not being supported by the peripheral

When the processor receives a bus error response, a BusFault exception or a HardFault exception is triggered. The triggered exception is a Bus fault exception if all of the following conditions are met:

- The processor is an Armv8-M Mainline processor, and
- The BusFault exception is enabled (by setting BUSFAULTENA, bit-17 of System Handler Control and State Register, SHCSR at address 0xE000ED24).
- The priority level of the BusFault exception is higher than the processor's current level.

Otherwise, the HardFault exception is triggered.

Further information about fault exception handling is covered in Chapter 13.

6.10 Single-cycle I/O port—Cortex-M23 only

The Cortex-M23 processor has an optional feature called the Single-cycle I/O port. This is a 32-bit bus interface that operates with a single clock cycle (the wait state is not supported on this interface). This feature was first supported on the Cortex-M0+ processor and allows chip designers to assign one or more of the address ranges to this interface to achieve lower access latency.

Microcontroller products based on the Cortex-M0+ and Cortex-M23 processors could be designed to run at a relatively low clock frequency. If a peripheral like a General Purpose Input Output (GPIO) unit is connected to the processor via the system bus, each access takes a minimum of two clock cycles if the bus transfer is carried out using the system AHB. If the peripheral is connected using the APB protocol, the access could have an even longer latency (more than two clock cycles). The latency can also increase further if the AHB to APB bridge introduces additional latencies. Combined with a slow clock rate, the I/O access latency can become undesirable for some of the control applications because it increases the system's response time. To overcome this problem, the single-cycle I/O port feature has been introduced to allow the I/O port registers to be accessed without latency cycles (Fig. 6.10). Multiple access can also be carried out back-to-back, enabling high I/O operation performance.

The single-cycle I/O port is a generic bus interface with features that include:

- 8, 16, and 32-bit transfers
- Privilege and security attribute sideband signals to allow security management on this interface (please note, there is no error response on this interface, so if a transfer needs to be blocked the interface handles the transaction as Read-As-Zero/Write-Ignored).

For software developers, since the registers connected to this interface are just part of the memory map, the registers can be accessed, just like standard peripherals, using pointers in C. As a result, this feature does not affect the software.

In addition to peripherals like the GPIO, for which access latency is often important, the single-cycle I/O port could also be used for connecting registers in hardware accelerators. The single-cycle I/O port is unlikely to be connected to general peripherals like the UART, the I2C, and the SPI. This is because the operations of these peripherals take many clock cycles, so saving a few clock cycles does not bring any significant benefit. Because adding too many registers to the single I/O port interface can cause problems to the timing of the bus interface timing, it is usual, therefore, to just connect a few peripherals to this interface.

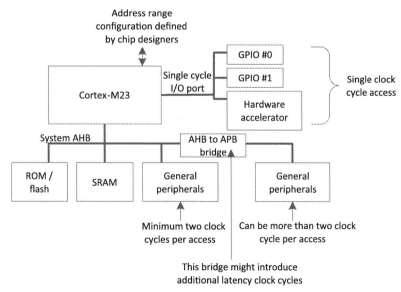

FIG. 6.10   Single cycle I/O port feature.

6.11 Memory systems in microcontrollers

6.11.1 Memory requirements

The bus interfaces on Cortex-M processors are based on generic bus protocols and work with different types of memories, but this is providing that suitable memory interface circuits are implemented. These circuits are not part of the processor design and are often designed by microcontroller vendors or by third-party design houses. Memory interface controllers from different chip vendors can have different characteristics and programmer's models (if programmable).

For the majority of microcontrollers and many standalone Cortex-M based SoC designs, Nonvolatile Memory (NVM) is needed for program storage, such as embedded flash memories or masked ROM. Additionally, read-write memory such as SRAM (static random-access memory) is also essential. SRAM is typically used for data variables and stack memories, as well as for the allocation of heap memory (e.g., for alloc() in C runtime functions).

Cortex-M processors do not have specific restrictions on memory size requirements providing that the program space is large enough to hold one or two program images (two when the TrustZone security is implemented). Each program image contains:

- A vector table,
- C libraries,
- Application code.

Cortex-M microcontrollers designed for the simplest of applications might have memory footprints as small as 8KB of Nonvolatile memory (NVM, e.g., flash) and 1KB of SRAM (e.g., microcontroller MKL02Z8VFG4, one of the Kinetis KL02 series device from NXP, is based on the Cortex-M0 processor). However, modern embedded applications are becoming much more complex, and many microcontrollers designed for IoT applications might provide more than 256KB of flash and 128KB of SRAM. Sometimes, even those memory capacities are not enough, e.g., when an application needs to deal with large amounts of audio or image data. For these applications, microcontrollers with external (off-chip) memories are needed.

Some microcontrollers might support external serial flash for program storage (e.g., using external flash chips based on the Quad SPI interface) and external read/write memories such as DRAM (Dynamic RAM). However, not many Cortex-M microcontrollers support DRAM because DRAM requires lots of connections, a fact which equates to a higher cost. For example, when DRAM support is included, the chip package is more expensive and the circuit board designs would be more complicated. Also, since DRAM controllers have to be initialized before DRAM can be used, an SRAM in the chip is still needed to allow the initialization code to be executed. However, if an application requires more memory, an on-chip SRAM might not be sufficient and, to overcome this, external memory support would be needed. Please note that:

(a) many microcontroller products do not support off-chip memory systems, and
(b) access to external (off-chip) memories are often much slower than access to the on-chip SRAM.

Many microcontrollers have a boot ROM/memory which contains a small program called boot loader, which is provided by MCU vendors. The boot loader executes before the user application, which is stored in the flash memory, starts. The boot loader provides various boot options and might include a flash programming utility. Besides, the boot loader program might also be used for setting configuration data, including:

- factory calibration data for internal clock sources, and
- calibration data for internal voltage references.

With security becoming an important requirement in embedded systems, the boot loader program may also provide:

- Secure boot feature (The ability to validate program images before starting the application)
- Secure firmware updates
- Trusted Firmware-M (TF-M) for security management

Note: Some microcontroller designs do not allow the boot loader to be modified or erased by software developers.

Traditionally, microcontrollers require a separation between Nonvolatile memory (NVM) and SRAM. The NVM in most microcontrollers is based on embedded flash technologies, which, to update, requires a complex programming sequence. As a result, flash memory cannot be used for storing data that needs to be frequently updated (e.g., data variables, stack memories).

Recently, some microcontroller products have started to use Ferroelectric RAM (FRAM) or Magneto-resistive RAM (MRAM). These technologies enable a single memory block to be used for both program code and data storage, with the advantage being that the memory system can be powered down completely and can then resume operations without losing the RAM data. This has the advantage over SRAM because when SRAM is put into state retention mode, the power for the SRAM must still be turned on and, thus, the SRAM still uses a small amount of power. In theory, Cortex-M processors can work with the aforementioned types of memory technologies, but to do so a suitable memory interface circuit is needed to connect those memories to the processor systems. Prototypes of such devices (based on MRAM/ FRAM) already exist and productization of such technologies is likely to happen soon.

6.11.2 Bus system designs

The design of memory and bus systems for Cortex-M processors range from the very simple to the very complex. There are many factors to consider:

- Whether the design has a single bus master (just the processor) or multiple bus masters (e.g., a DMA controller or peripherals that also, like USB controllers, act as bus masters).
- Whether security management is required in the design (e.g., a simple fixed-function smart sensor might not need any security features).
- The type of performance or data bandwidth that is needed for some of the peripherals.
- The low power features required for the applications. Power-saving features affect the design of the bus system. For example, some microcontrollers might have multiple peripheral buses which can be configured to run at different clock speeds. This avoids running all the peripheral bus interfaces at the highest speed when that may only be required for one or more of the peripherals.

A Cortex-M23-based microcontroller without TrustZone could be as simple as the one shown in Fig. 6.11.

The design shown in Fig. 6.11 consists of:

- An AHB system bus for memories and AHB peripherals
- An APB peripheral bus for APB peripherals
- A Single-cycle I/O port bus for low latency peripherals

The default slave component on the AHB is used to provide a bus error response to the processor when a transfer is targeting an invalid address.

Microcontrollers often use APB buses for a range of general peripherals. APB interface designs are simpler than those for AHB. Since the system bus uses the AHB protocol, a bus bridge is needed to convert transactions from AHB to APB. Besides, a bus bridge can provide clock domain separation so that:

- The APB can operate at a different clock speed to that of the processor's system clock.
- The chip designer can avoid having too many bus slaves on the system bus, which can affect the maximum achievable clock frequency of the system.

Similar to the system design for the Cortex-M23 shown in Fig. 6.11, it is possible to have a simple system design for the Cortex-M33 processor. This shown in Fig. 6.12.

Unlike the Cortex-M23 system design in Fig. 6.11, the Cortex-M33 system design has two AHB bus segments to allow instruction fetches and data access to take place in parallel (It uses Harvard bus architecture). Each of the bus segment has its default slave to detect and respond to accesses made to invalid addresses.

While a typical Cortex-M33 system design places NVM memory in the CODE region and SRAM in the SRAM region, it is possible to run code from the SRAM and RAM regions, and put data SRAM in the CODE region. Unlike the Cortex-M3 and Cortex-M4 processors, there is no performance penalty in running a program on the system bus.

There is, on the Cortex-M33 processor's interface, an additional APB-based Private Peripheral Bus (PPB). This is for connecting debug components to the processor and is not to be used for general peripherals. This is because:

FIG. 6.11 Simple system design for a Cortex-M23 processor.

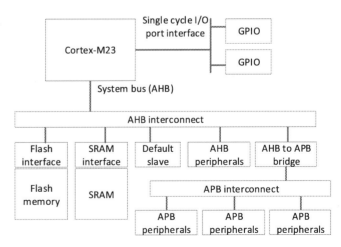

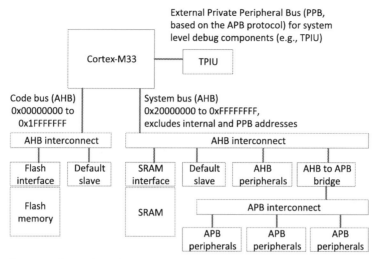

FIG. 6.12 Simple system design for a Cortex-M33 processor.

- The PPB is privileged access only
- Only 32-bit access is supported

Please note, the PPB is little-endian only and cannot be accessed by other bus masters in the system (only software running on the processor and the debugger connected to the processor can access this bus).

In systems with multiple bus masters that have, for example, DMA and USB controllers, the chip designer must ensure that the bus design can cope with the data bandwidth requirements of the applications. To enable a higher bus bandwidth, several techniques are commonly used and these are:

• Having a multilayer AHB design (also known as bus matrix)
• Having multiple banks of SRAM to allow concurrent SRAM access

For example, a Cortex-M33 processor system that contains DMA and USB controllers, both of which could be running concurrently, a system design like the one in Fig. 6.13 could be used to provide sufficient data bandwidth.

This arrangement uses several bus arbiters to allow multiple bus masters to access different bus slaves at the same time. Combined with multiple banks of SRAM, the processor, DMA controller, and USB controller can all access different SRAM at the same time and, by so doing, provide high data throughputs.

6.11.3 Security management

When the TrustZone security feature is implemented, memories for both program storage and data and memories for the Secure and the Non-secure worlds are needed. If separate memory blocks for Secure and Non-secure memory are used, there is likely to be an increase

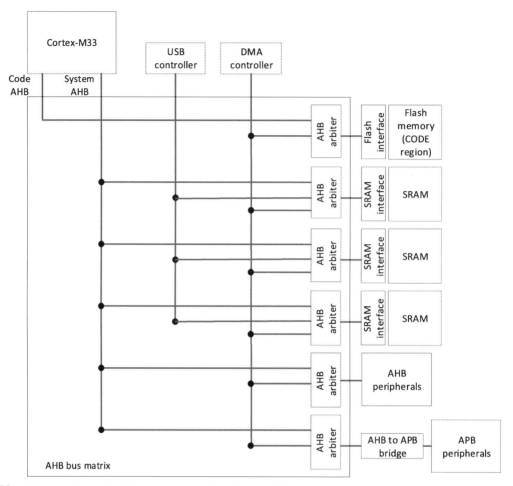

FIG. 6.13   A high bandwidth system design for a Cortex-M33 processor.

in cost and power consumption. Because many microcontrollers are designed to be low cost, it is preferable to use a single memory block and partition that into Secure and Non-secure address ranges. The hardware units that deal with the memory address partitioning are referred to as memory protection controllers (MPC).

In the same way, peripherals need to be partitioned too. Many TrustZone system designs implement peripheral protection controllers (PPC)—a controller that helps Secure software assign some of the peripherals to a Secure or Non-secure state. In theory, if the security domain assignment for peripherals is known in advance, PPCs are not needed because access permissions can be hardwired into the interconnect. However, for many projects, using a fixed security domain assignment for peripherals is unacceptable. For example, with many projects, the design of the software starts after the chips are produced. As a result, the peripheral's security domain requirement is often unknown when the chip is designed. Therefore, the use of PPCs is needed to provide flexibility. Besides, many chip designs are targeted at multiple applications and, therefore, have very diverse requirements. As a result, PPCs are needed as they provide the required flexibility.

Many microcontrollers have integrated legacy bus master components which are designed for non-TrustZone systems. Chip designers might, therefore, need to place additional components, called Master Security Controllers (MSC), in the system to allow legacy bus master components to connect the bus master units to a TrustZone-based system.

When we add MPCs, PPCs, and MSCs to the system design that was shown in Fig. 6.13, this creates the system design as shown in Fig. 6.14.

Information on MPC and PPC operations is covered in Chapter 7, Section 7.5.

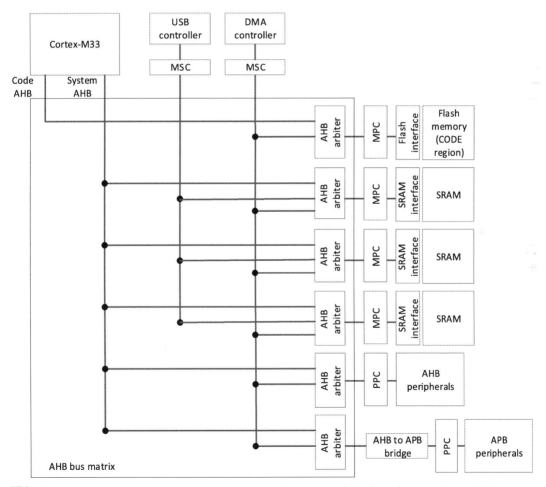

FIG. 6.14   TrustZone security components added to the bus system of a high-performance Cortex-M33 system.

6.12 Software considerations

6.12.1 Bus level power management

When working with modern microcontrollers, because of the nature of multiple buses and their power management control features, there are some areas that software developers need to take into account.

Due to the separation of the main system and peripheral buses, and, in some cases, the separation of the clock frequency controls, an application might need to initialize some clock control hardware in the microcontroller before it can access some of the peripherals. In some instances, there can also be multiple peripheral bus segments running at different clock frequencies, all of which will need to be configured. Apart from allowing part of the system to run at slower clock speed, the separation of bus segments might also allow power to be further reduced by allowing the clock signals of a peripheral system to be stopped completely.

6.12.2 TrustZone security

When the TrustZone security extension is implemented and used, security firmware developers will need to include several initialization steps in the Secure firmware (e.g., setting up various units to define memory and peripheral partitioning). These initialization steps should include the programming of the SAU (potentially the IDAU too, if that is designed to be programmable) and system-level security management hardware such as memory protection and peripheral protection controllers.

In addition to memory partitioning, there are other configurations require setting up by the Secure firmware. This includes interrupt's target states and stack limit checking. Further information on this topic is covered in Chapter 18.

6.12.3 Use of multiple load and store instructions

The multiple load and store instructions in Cortex-M processors can greatly increase the system's performance when they are correctly used. For example, they can be used to speed up a data transfer process or can be used as a means to automatically adjust a register for the memory pointer.

However, when handling peripheral accesses, the use of LDM or STM instructions should, generally, be avoided. The reason for this is that part of the data access in an LDM/STM instruction could be repeated due to an interrupt event. Let us take the following scenario as an example:

On a Cortex-M23 processor (which also applies to Armv6-M processors), if an interrupt request is received during the execution of an LDM or STM instruction, the LDM or STM instruction is abandoned and the interrupt service starts. At the end of the interrupt service, the program execution returns to the interrupted LDM or STM instruction and restarts again from the *first* transfer of the interrupted LDM or STM.

As a result of this restart behavior, some of the transfers in the interrupted LDM or STM instruction could be carried out twice. Though this is not a problem for normal memories, it could be for peripherals if the access is carried out on peripheral register(s) where the repeating of the transfer could cause errors. For example, if the LDM instruction is used for reading data in a First-In-First-Out (FIFO) buffer, then some of the data in the FIFO could be lost as the read operation is repeated.

As a precaution, unless we are sure that the restart behavior does not cause incorrect operation, we should avoid using LDM and STM instructions when accessing peripherals.

Another consideration when using LDM and STM instructions is that we need to ensure that the address is aligned. If it is not aligned, a HardFault (Section 13.2.5) or a UsageFault exception (Section 13.2.3) will occur.

References

[1] Armv8-M Architecture Reference Manual. https://developer.arm.com/documentation/ddi0553/am (Armv8.0-M only version). https://developer.arm.com/documentation/ddi0553/latest/ (latest version including Armv8.1-M). Note: M-profile architecture reference manuals for Armv6-M, Armv7-M, Armv8-M and Armv8.1-M can be found here: https://developer.arm.com/architectures/cpu-architecture/m-profile/docs.

[2] AMBA 5 Advanced High-performance Bus (AHB) Protocol Specification. https://developer.arm.com/documentation/ihi0033/latest/

[3] AMBA 4 Advanced Peripheral Bus (APB) Protocol Specification. https://developer.arm.com/documentation/ihi0024/latest/.

TrustZone support in the memory system

7.1 Overview

7.1.1 About this chapter

The last chapter covered the memory architecture of the Arm®v8-M processors as well as, briefly, detailing aspects of the TrustZone® security extension. In this chapter, I go into further technical detail and describe how the memory systems of Cortex®-M23 and Cortex-M33 processors support the TrustZone security technology. Because some microcontroller devices based on Armv8-M processors do not support TrustZone, and since many software developers might only create software that runs in the Non-secure environment, it may not be necessary for some developers to understand the technical details covered in this chapter. Nevertheless, I hope all developers will find the information in this chapter useful and interesting.

7.1.2 Memory security attributes

The optional TrustZone security extension introduces additional ways to classify memory types. I have already mentioned Secure and Non-secure memories, but there are a further two types. Table 7.1 lists these memory types.

The Secure NSC region and the SG instruction provides a mechanism to prevent Non-secure software from bypassing security checks by branching into the middle of Secure APIs or into other Secure codes. If the Non-secure software does branch into a Secure executable region where either:

- The first instruction is not an SG instruction, or
- The address does not have a Secure NSC attribute

then a security violation fault exception is triggered and the result would be either a SecureFault (Armv8-M Mainline only) or a HardFault.

TABLE 7.1 Memory classification by security attributes.

Memory type	Description	Restriction
Non-secure	Memory regions which are accessible by both Non-secure and Secure software. When executing software in Non-secure memories, the processor is in a Non-secure state. Bus transfers to Non-secure regions are marked as Non-secure, even if they are generated by Secure software.	
Secure	Memory regions which are accessible by Secure software. When executing software in Secure memories, the processor is in a Secure state. Bus transfers to Secure regions are marked as Secure.	Non-secure software cannot gain access to the Secure memory
Secure Non-secure Callable (NSC)	Secure memory with a Non-secure Callable attribute is a type of Secure memory that provides entry points for Secure APIs that can be called from a Non-secure space. Technically, it is possible to put Secure APIs in a Secure NSC. Best practice, however, is to only use Secure NSC region(s) for branch veneers (SG and branch instructions) and to place the APIs in Secure memories. Generally, the memory type of a Secure NSC region should be "Normal memory". Bus transfers to Secure NSC regions are marked as Secure.	Non-secure software cannot read/write to a Secure NSC memory, but can branch into it if the branch target is a SG instruction.
Exempted regions	Also referred to as unchecked regions. These regions can be accessed by both Secure and Non-secure software. When a device (e.g., a peripheral) in an Exempted region receives a bus transfer, it can use the security attribute of the transfer to determine whether the processor accessing it is in a Secure state or not. Using this information, the device is able to handle Secure and Non-secure transfers with different behaviors. Exempted regions are used by system and debug components (e.g., the NVIC, the MPU). It is also possible to use them for peripherals. However, chip designers must not use exempted regions for Normal memories that are executable as this can increase the security risk. Bus transfers to exempted regions are marked as Secure if the processor is in a Secure state and as Non-secure if the processor is in a Non-secure state.	

TABLE 7.2 Relationship between memory security attributes and memory types.

	Normal memory	Device memory
Secure	Valid combination	Valid combination
Secure NSC	Valid combination	Generally invalid (entry points must be in executable regions to be useful and, as a consequence, "Device memory" cannot be used for entry points since they are nonexecutable)
Non-secure	Valid combination	Valid combination
Exempted	Generally invalid (exempted regions must not be executable), unless additional security measures are in place to prevent the code from being executed.	Valid combination

Memory security attributes operate independently to the memory types (as described in Chapter 6), resulting in many different possible combinations (Table 7.2). There are, however, some exceptions, that is, some combinations of security attributes and memory types are invalid.

To avoid security issues, chip designers need, therefore, to design the memory map's security partitioning with these considerations in mind (Table 7.2).

7.2 SAU and IDAU

The security attributes of memory ranges are defined by the Security Attribution Unit (SAU). The SAU can work with additional single or multiple custom-defined address lookup hardware units called Implementation Defined Attribution Units (IDAUs). For each memory access (including data read/write, instruction fetches, and debug access), the address is simultaneously looked up in the SAU and the IDAU(s), and the results are then combined.

The SAU and the IDAU divide the 4GB address space into regions as described below:

- SAU—The SAU is a part of the Armv8-M processor when the TrustZone security extension is implemented and is programmable by Secure privileged software. In the Cortex-M23 and Cortex-M33 processors, the SAU supports 0, 4, or 8 SAU regions. Each region is defined using a pair of address comparators that compare bus transaction addresses against the starting and ending addresses of an SAU region. If the TrustZone security extension is implemented without an SAU region (i.e., the number of SAU regions is zero), the SAU is still present but with only a control register and an IDAU interface(s) to support the address lookup.
- IDAU—IDAU(s) are designed by chip vendors and vary between different devices. Similar to the SAU, they provide address lookups and generate security attributes of the address being accessed. If they are not designed as programmable, they can be less complex than an SAU. IDAU interfaces on the Cortex-M23 and the Cortex-M33 processors support up to 256 regions. A typical IDAU can be a fixed address lookup table, but can, in some designs also

be programmable. If the processor is designed to handle multiple concurrent transfers (as in the Harvard bus architecture), it must have multiple IDAUs and these IDAUs must have consistent security attribute mapping.

After the SAU and the IDAU lookup an address, the results are then combined as shown in Fig. 7.1.

Please note:

- An SAU can only define a region as Non-secure or as Secure NSC. If an address is not covered by an SAU region, it is Secure.
- An IDAU can define a region as Secure, Non-secure, Secure NSC, or Exempted.
- Apart from the exempted region type, the merging of Security levels from the SAU and the IDAU will always result in the higher security level being selected. This prevents Secure software from overriding an IDAU setting and exposing critical security information to the Non-secure world.
- Because the SAU is disabled after reset, all address ranges, apart from the exempted regions defined by the IDAU, are, by default, Secure.
- An exempt region setting is always effective: this enables Non-secure debuggers to access debug components and establish a debug connection to the processor before the SAU is setup.

When the TrustZone security extension is implemented and when the SAU is configured without an SAU region, a minimal level of SAU hardware, including the SAU Control Register, is still present in the processor. For highly constrained systems, the design of the architecture allows a TrustZone system to be built with a minimal additional hardware cost using:

- An SAU with no SAU region
- A basic IDAU(s) for address lookup.

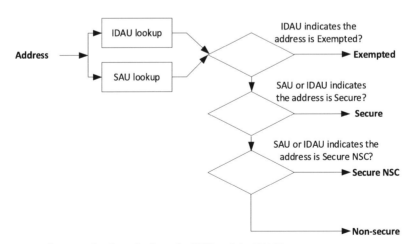

FIG. 7.1   Merging of security level results from the SAU and the IDAU.

In Chapter 6, I made reference to a number of TrustZone system management components (Fig. 6.14), for example, the MPC (Memory Protection Controller) and the PPC (Peripheral Protection Controller). These units are needed if the system requires the flexibility to allow the software to assign security attributes. For chip designs with fixed address partitioning, some of these components can be removed.

Once the security attribute of the address is defined, and if the bus transaction is permitted by the current security settings, the bus transaction can then be carried out with a bus security attribute (e.g., HNONSEC in AMBA® AHB5) [1] as defined by the security attribute of the address.

7.3 Banked and nonbanked registers

7.3.1 Overview

If the TrustZone security extension is implemented, a number of hardware units, including some of the system components inside the processor, such as the NVIC, will contain both Secure and Non-secure information. To help separate the information, banking of registers is sometimes used. There are a number of arrangements for handling security in registers in the System Control Space. They are as follows:

(1) The register is banked (e.g., Vector Table Offset Register, VTOR, Fig. 7.2)

Physically, there are two versions of the same register, for example, VTOR_S and VTOR_NS. When in Secure state, Secure software accessing SCB->VTOR (SCB is the System Control Block, a data structure defined in the CMSIS-CORE header file) sees the Secure VTOR (VTOR_S). When in Non-secure state, Non-secure software accessing SCB->VTOR sees the Non-secure VTOR (VTOR_NS).

(2) The register is not banked (e.g., Software Trigger Interrupt Register, STIR, Fig. 7.3)

Physically, there is only one version of the register and the register does not have any banked contents. However, the behavior of the register can either be identical or different between the Secure and Non-secure states. For SCB->STIR, only Secure software can use this register to trigger Secure interrupts (IRQs).

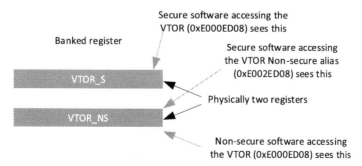

FIG. 7.2   A banked register, for example, the VTOR.

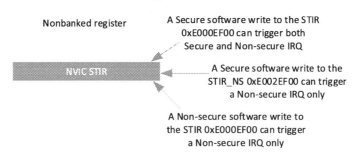

FIG. 7.3   A nonbanked register, for example, the STIR.

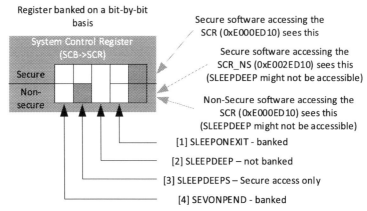

FIG. 7.4   A partially banked register, for example, the SCR.

(3) Some bit fields of the register are banked (e.g., System Control Register, SCR, Fig. 7.4)

Some bit fields of the registers are banked but some bit fields are not. Secure software sees the Secure version of the banked bit fields and Non-secure software sees the Non-secure version.

7.3.2 System Control Space (SCS) NS alias

In Chapter 6, the memory map diagram (Fig. 6.1) showed a System Control Space (SCS) at address 0xE000E000 and a SCS Non-secure alias at address 0xE002E000. The SCS Non-secure alias allows Secure software to access the SCS using the behavior of Non-secure software:

- It is able to access the Non-secure version of banked registers or banked bit fields in the register, and
- It is able to mimic the action of Non-secure software

As a result of this feature, the CMSIS-CORE header files for the Cortex-M23 and the Cortex-M33 processors support additional data structures to allow Secure software to access the registers in the SCS Non-secure alias address range. These data structures are listed in Table 7.3.

TABLE 7.3 CMSIS support for accessing registers in the SCS Non-secure alias.

Data structure for SCS address	Data structure for SCS Non-secure alias address	Description
NVIC	NVIC_NS	Nested Vectored Interrupt Controller
SCB	SCB_NS	System Control Block
SysTick	SysTick_NS	SysTick timer
MPU	MPU_NS	Memory Protection Unit
CoreDebug	CoreDebug_NS	Core debug registers
SCnSCB	SCnSCB_NS	System control registers not in SCB
FPU	FPU_NS	Floating Point Unit

7.4 Test Target (TT) instructions and region ID numbers

7.4.1 Why are the TT instructions needed?

In Chapter 5 (Section 5.20) I detailed the number of instructions that exist for TrustZone support. One of the instructions is TT (Test Target), which has four variants. Here, in this section, I will explain why these instructions are needed.

One of the key functions of TrustZone for Armv8-M is to allow Secure software to provide APIs that can service Non-secure software (an example of this is shown in Fig. 7.5). Since the Secure APIs can process and transfer data on behalf of Non-secure applications, and can themselves access the Secure memory, these Secure APIs have to verify the pointers to ensure that the pointers they have received from the Non-secure applications are indeed pointing to the Non-secure addresses. If that was not the case, it would be essential to stop Non-secure software from erroneously using those APIs to access or modify Secure data.

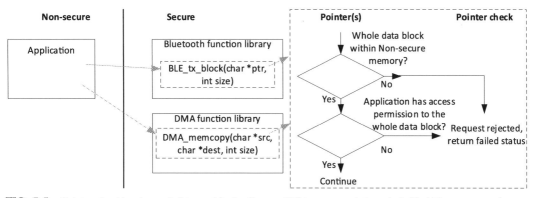

FIG. 7.5 Pointer checking is needed to enable the Secure API to process data on behalf of Non-secure software.

The pointer check functions for the Secure APIs must:

(1) Ensure that the whole data structure/array to be accessed on behalf of Non-secure software is in a Non-secure space—just checking the starting address is not enough.
(2) Ensure that the Non-secure software does have access permission for the data. For example, Non-secure software calling the API can be unprivileged and should not, therefore, be allowed to access memory ranges that are privileged access only. Accordingly, the security check must look up the MPU permissions to prevent the Non-secure unprivileged software using these APIs to attack the Non-secure privileged software.

Traditionally, Arm architecture offers memory access instructions which are unprivileged. Using these instructions (Table 7.4), privileged software, such as the APIs inside an OS, can access memory as unprivileged.

However, there are some limitations with this solution:

- These instructions are not available for Armv8-M baseline and Armv6-M architectures.
- These instructions only cover unprivileged access, but there is no TrustZone variant (there are no instructions for Non-secure access).
- There is no standardized C language feature to force the C compilers to use these instructions instead of the normal load/store instructions.
- It cannot be used in the application scenario where the actual memory access is not carried out by the processor (e.g., where the API is a DMA memory copy service and where the transfers are handled by the DMA controller).
- If an access violation takes place, the APIs need to deal with the fault exceptions, which can be complicated.

In Armv8-M, the TT instructions provide a new mechanism to handle the pointer check by allowing software to determine the security attribute and access permission of a memory location (i.e., the pointer that is passed to a Secure API). This allows security checking to be checked at the beginning of the API service (instead of during the operation when the data is being accessed), thus enabling the APIs to use other hardware resources (e.g., DMA controllers) to access the memory. By moving the pointer checking to the beginning of the API service makes for easier error handling.

To make programming easier, the Arm C Language Extension (ACLE) [2] defines a number of C intrinsic functions to provide pointer checks. After the pointer checks are completed, the data processing is then handled in standard C/C++ code.

TABLE 7.4 Instructions to allow privileged software to access memory as unprivileged.

	Load (read from memory)	Store (write to memory)
8-bit (byte)	LDRBT (unsigned), LDRSBT (signed)	STRBT
16-bit (half word)	LDRHT (unsigned), LDRSHT (signed)	STRHT
32-bit (word)	LDRT (unsigned and signed)	STRT

7.4.2 The TT instructions

A TT instruction has one input and one output (Fig. 7.6):

- 32-bit input—an address
- 32-bit output—a 32-bit value which contains multiple bit fields

TT and TTT instructions are available in both Secure and Non-secure states. If these two instructions are executed in the Non-secure state, only MREGION, MRVALID, R and RW fields are available (Fig. 7.7).

7.4.3 Region ID numbers

The TT instructions return MPU, SAU, and IDAU region numbers. These bit fields enable us to quickly determine whether a whole data structure or a data array is within the Non-secure address range. Since the granularity of address partitioning is 32 bytes, in theory, a simple way to determine whether a data structure/array is entirely within the Non-secure address range is to use a TT instruction to test the address at every 32 bytes interval. This method works, but could be a lengthy process as the data structure pointed to by the pointer can be quite large.

To overcome this and achieve a faster address checking method, the architecture defines the region ID numbering feature for the SAU, the IDAU, and the MPU.

- For each region in the SAU region definition, the SAU region comparator number is used as the SAU region ID.

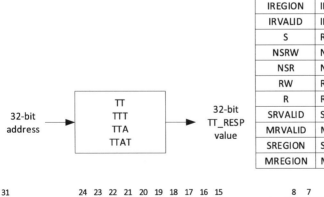

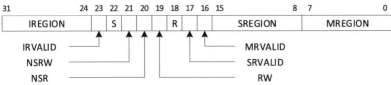

FIG. 7.6   Input and output of TT instructions.

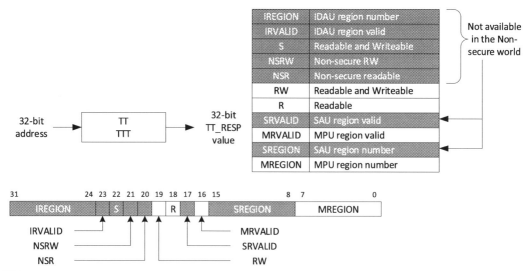

FIG. 7.7   In Non-secure state, TT instructions (TT and TTT) return only RW, R, MRVALID, and MREGION.

- For each Non-secure region/Secure NSC region in the IDAU region definition, the design of the IDAU must assign a unique region number, which is provided to the processor using the IDAU interface.

The region numbers are 8 bit in size, but there is an additional bit to indicate whether the region number is valid or not (e.g., in the SAU, an SAU region might be disabled and thus the region number would be invalid).

To check whether a data structure/array is entirely in a Non-secure region, we only need to use the TT instruction to lookup the starting and ending addresses (both of which are inclusive). The data structure/array is in the Non-secure range if:

- Both the starting and the ending addresses are Non-secure
- The IDAU region numbers of the starting and the ending addresses are identical and are both valid
- The SAU region numbers of the starting and the ending addresses are identical and are both valid

An illustration of how the region numbers in the SAU and the IDAU work is shown in Fig. 7.8.

To get this mechanism to work correctly, chip designers need to make sure that for each Non-secure region defined in the IDAU, each of them has a unique valid region number.

Using the same technique, software can also use the MPU region number to detect whether the data structure/array is in a continuous MPU region. If that is the case, the data structure/array has the same access permission from the starting to the ending addresses. This technique can be used to prevent unprivileged software from using an API to access privileged information.

To make programming easier, a range of C intrinsic functions are defined in the Arm C Language extensions and are supported by multiple C compilers. Additional information on this topic is covered in Chapter 18.

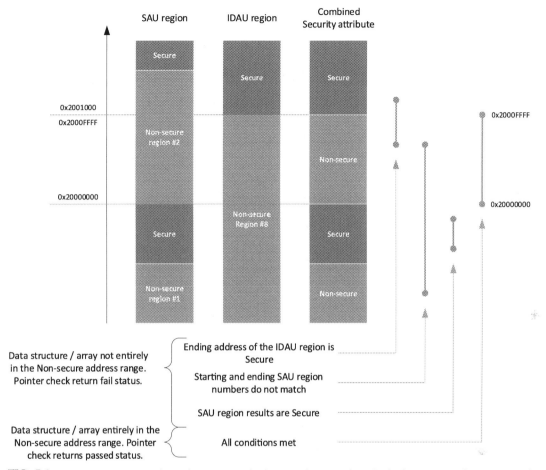

FIG. 7.8 Using region ID numbers, data pointer checking can be carried out by looking up just the starting and ending addresses.

Please note, this technique will not work if the data structure/array being checked goes across two adjacent Non-secure regions (Fig. 7.9).

To avoid the problem shown in Fig. 7.9, chip designers and Secure firmware developers should avoid having adjacent Non-secure regions for continuous memories such as SRAM and ROM. On the other hand, having adjacent Non-secure regions for multiple Non-secure peripherals is not a problem because a data structure or array is unlikely to go across peripheral address boundaries.

Please note, the pointer check feature is used to test whether a data structure/array is entirely in the Non-secure address range but cannot be used to determine whether a data structure/array is entirely in the Secure address range. Since the SAU can only setup Non-secure and Secure NSC regions, Secure address ranges do not have region numbers in the SAU. Fortunately, in normal application scenarios, because Secure APIs only need to determine whether a data structure/array is Non-secure so that it can process the information on behalf

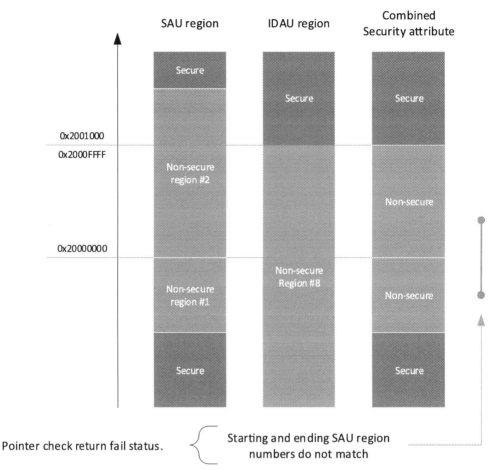

FIG. 7.9 A data structure/array going across two adjacent Non-secure regions gets an incorrect result in the pointer check.

of a Non-secure application, it does not need to determine whether the data is entirely in a Secure address range.

7.5 Memory protection controller and peripheral protection controller

You might wonder whether there is enough region ID space for complex designs. Well, since the SAU is limited to 8 regions (certainly in the current Armv8-M processors) and the IDAU to 256, and because the two pieces of hardware work together in an overlapping region arrangement, it is certainly true that there is a limit on the number of regions that can be created. Although presently most microcontrollers have less than 50 peripherals, it should, in theory in the future, be possible to create microcontroller devices which have hundreds of peripherals.

The limit of the region ID ranges is a big problem for advanced memory partitioning. For example, an embedded flash with several MBs could be divided into thousands of flash pages (a flash page ranges from 256 bytes to 1KB). If part of the flash memory is being used as a file system, it is quite possible that we would need to handle the flash memory partitioning on a page by page basis. In such an example, the IDAU region numbers could easily run out.

Fortunately, there is another way to handle address partitioning without having to utilize a large number of region ID values. This method is based on a memory alias technique and uses a protection controller to divide the memory device—or a group of peripherals—into sections and provides a hardware control to define the accessibility of each section in the Secure and Non-secure alias.

By way of an example, consider a microcontroller with 256KB of embedded flash memory which is connected via a Memory Protection Controller (MPC, Fig. 7.10), with a page size of 512 bytes (256KB/512 bytes = 512 pages). The embedded flash is accessible via a Non-secure alias (0x00000000) and a Secure alias (0x10000000). The MPC is then used to decide which flash pages are visible in the Secure address range and which other pages are visible in the Non-secure address range.

The MPC contains a lookup table that defines the security attribute of each flash memory page and uses this attribute for each access to decide whether a transfer is to be allowed or is to be blocked. In the following diagram (Fig. 7.11), the MPC partitions the embedded flash memory into four parts.

Using this method, we only need one region ID value for the Non-secure address range in the embedded flash, despite the address range containing multiple holes (i.e., flash pages that are blocked). It also prevents a race-condition problem from occurring in multicore systems where:

- One processor changes a memory page from Non-secure to Secure, while
- Another processor running a Secure API treats that memory page as Non-secure (A pointer check would have been carried out when the page was Non-secure).

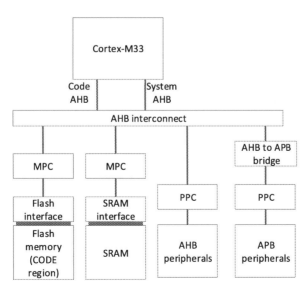

FIG. 7.10 An embedded flash memory which is connected to a processor via a memory protection controller.

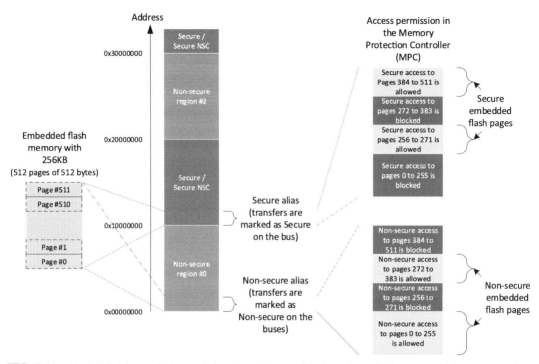

FIG. 7.11 The MPC defines whether each flash page is accessible from either the Secure or the Non-secure alias.

MPC operations are often based on one of the following partitioning methods:

- Partitioning on a page-by-page basis, which needs one configuration bit per page. Or
- If there is only a need to partition the memory device into one Secure and one Non-secure range (i.e., only one boundary), an MPC can be designed to use a watermark level scheme that defines the page number of the boundary. Such a design would require fewer configuration bits in the hardware.

Using the same technique as that used for the MPC operations, a Peripheral Protection Controller (PPC, Fig. 7.12) can be designed to assign a large number of peripherals into the Secure and the Non-secure domains. This is achieved by not having to use a large number of SAU and IDAU region ID values.

In addition to the access control feature based on the security attribute of the transfers, the PPC can also be designed to determine access permissions based on the privileged level. In this way, privileged software is able to control whether a peripheral is accessible by an unprivileged software component.

In short,

- the SAU and the IDAU define the security attributes of the address regions, whereas
- the MPC and the PPC define the effective address for each memory page or for each peripheral. The operation of the MPC and the PPC is handled by masking the memory page or peripheral from one of the Secure or Non-secure alias addresses.

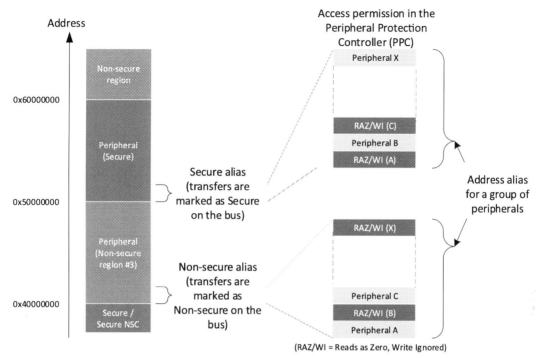

FIG. 7.12 The PPC defines whether each of the peripherals is accessible from either the Secure or the Non-secure alias.

Please note, when using this method, the base address of a peripheral when it is being used as Secure and when it is being used as Non-secure is different. Normally, a peripheral's security state is set up at the bootup of the device and is, as a result, unlikely to be dynamically changed. Thus, it is unlikely to cause an issue with the peripheral control codes. However, in the situation where a peripheral's security state can be changed dynamically, the peripheral control codes might need to detect the security state of the peripheral before accessing it.

When software access to a peripheral is blocked by the PPC, there are two possible responses:

- Bus error (this will trigger a fault exception)
- Read as Zero/write ignored (RAZ/WI)

Both are valid arrangements for Armv8-M systems. Some might argue that the bus error response is more secure as it gives the Secure software a chance to intercept the fault exception and detect whether the Non-secure software that is running is trying to attack the security of the system. But, in many microcontroller device families, which have a range of chip products, with each having a different set of peripherals, it is common practice to allow the software to detect the availability of the peripherals (e.g., by reading the peripheral's ID registers in those peripheral address ranges). In this way, the software is able to ascertain whether a certain peripheral is available.

7.6 Security aware peripherals

Security aware peripherals are accessible by both Secure and Non-secure software. With such peripherals, the device is able to handle Secure and Non-secure transfers with different behaviors. For example, a security-aware peripheral can restrict some of its functional features to Secure software only.

There are a couple of ways that chip designers can create security-aware peripherals. The first solution is to use a memory alias arrangement so that the peripheral is visible in a Secure as well as a Non-secure address (Fig. 7.13). With this solution, the security attribute of the bus transaction depends on which address alias is used. The security attribute of the bus transfer is then used by the peripheral's design to define the peripheral's behavior.

The second way to create a security-aware peripheral is to define the address range of that peripheral as an "exempted" region using the IDAU. By doing so, both the Secure and Non-secure software are able to access the peripheral using the same address range. With this arrangement, the security attribute of the transfer will be based on the security state of the processor.

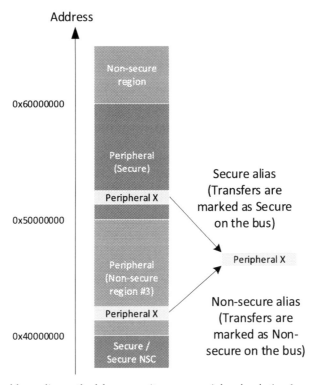

FIG. 7.13　Using an address alias method for a security-aware peripheral, solution 1.

The disadvantage of using an exempted region for peripherals is that you cannot use the intrinsic functions, provided in the Arm C Language Extensions (ACLE), for pointer checks on an exempted address (The pointer check will return a fail status). But an advantage is that both the Secure and Non-secure software are able to use the same base address for the peripheral.

References

[1] AMBA 5 Advanced High-performance Bus (AHB) Protocol Specification. https://developer.arm.com/documentation/ihi0033/b-b/.

[2] Arm C Language Extension (ACLE) home page. https://developer.arm.com/architectures/system-architectures/software-standards/acle.

Exceptions and interrupts— Architecture overview

8.1 Overview of exceptions and interrupts

8.1.1 The need for exceptions and interrupts

Interrupts and exceptions are common features available on all modern processor systems, from simple microcontrollers to high-end computers. For microcontroller systems, interrupts are important for peripheral operations: instead of constantly polling peripheral status, the processor is able to utilize its processing time on other computing tasks and switch over to service the peripheral(s) as and when needed.

In Arm® terminology, interrupts are a type of exception. Exceptions are commonly referred to the processors' mechanism to allow certain events (including hardware generated events such as interrupt requests) to change the program flow and to execute the corresponding exception handlers. Exception handlers are pieces of software that provide services for exception events. Normally, when exception handlers have completed the service the original interrupted program sequence is resumed.

Sources of exceptions include:

- Peripheral interrupt requests (also referred to as IRQs) or other hardware event signals (e.g., architecturally a reset is a kind of exception)
- Error conditions (e.g., bus error in the memory system)
- Software generated events (e.g., execution of an SVC instruction)

In addition to peripheral events handling, exceptions are needed for OS support, fault handling, and security (e.g., a violation of TrustZone® or a memory protection violation can be handled by fault exception handlers). In the case of OS support, exceptions are needed for:

- Context switching between different tasks/threads, and
- Providing OS services to application codes

As a result, exceptions and interrupt handling features are important parts of the processor's architecture [1].

In this chapter, I will introduce architectural topics relating to exceptions and interrupts. Software development topics, such as the registers for interrupt and exception management are covered in Chapter 9.

8.1.2 Basic concepts of peripheral interrupt operations

In a basic scenario, where an interrupt is used for a peripheral control operation, the software must contain:

- Code sequence to initialize the peripheral and to set up the interrupt controller in the processor system.
- A piece of code called the Interrupt Service Routine (ISR) that executes when the peripheral event takes place. This is also known as an interrupt or an exception handler.
- A correct entry in the vector table that contains the starting address of the ISR.

All these are a part of the compiled program image.

Before the peripheral is put into operation, the interrupt controller needs to be set up to enable the interrupt event to be handled. In the case of Cortex®-M processors, software can optionally define a priority level for IRQs so that arbitration hardware can, when multiple IRQs arrive at the same time, elect to serve the higher priority peripheral first. And, of course, a setup sequence is also needed for the peripheral.

When a peripheral or a piece of hardware needs servicing, the following sequence typically occurs:

1. The peripheral asserts an IRQ signal to the processor,
2. The processor suspends the current executing task,
3. The processor executes an ISR to service the peripheral and the ISR optionally clears, if it is needed, the IRQ signal,
4. The processor resumes the previously suspended task.

To resume the interrupted program, the exception sequence needs some method of storing the status of the interrupted program so that the status can be restored after the exception handler has completed its task. In general, this can either be achieved by a hardware mechanism or by way of a mixture of hardware and software operations. In Cortex-M processors, some of the registers are automatically saved to the stack when an exception is accepted and are automatically restored during the exception return sequence. This mechanism allows the exception handlers to be written as normal C functions without having to add any additional software steps for register saving and restoring.

All Cortex-M processors provide a Nested Vectored Interrupt Controller (NVIC) for interrupt and exception handling. The NVIC in Armv8-M processors is similar to that in earlier versions of the Cortex-M processors. There are, obviously, some feature enhancements, but the programmer's models are consistent to allow the easy migration of software.

8.1.3 Introduction to the NVIC

The Nested Vectored Interrupt Controller (NVIC) is an integrated part of the Cortex-M processor. The integration of the NVIC enables lower interrupt latency and allows system exceptions to be handled by the same hardware unit as the one that handles peripheral interrupt events.

In a typical Cortex-M microcontroller, the NVIC receives interrupt requests and exception events from various sources, as shown in Fig. 8.1.

Most IRQs (Interrupt Requests) are generated from peripherals such as timers, I/O ports, and communication interfaces (e.g., UART, I2C). Some of the interrupt requests can be generated by off-chip hardware via an I/O interface port (generally known as a General-Purpose Input/Output, or, in short, a GPIO). For example, a GPIO with interrupt support can be used to enable a push button to generate an interrupt event.

The NMI (Non-Maskable Interrupt) is usually generated from peripherals such as a watchdog timer or a Brown-Out Detector (BOD). The remaining exception sources are generated from the processor core. Interrupts can also be generated using software.

The SysTick timer(s) inside the processor is another source of system exception and, from an exception handling point of view, works just like a timer peripheral. It is an optional feature in the Cortex-M23 processor, but is always available in the Cortex-M33 and other Armv8-M Mainline processors. A range of configuration options for the SysTick timer is shown in Table 8.1.

Information on the SysTick timer is covered in Chapter 11.

The number of interrupt requests supported in the Cortex-M23 and Cortex-M33 processors has increased when one compares the NVIC to the ones present in previous generations of Cortex-M processors. Details as follows (Table 8.2).

In addition, the NVIC in the Cortex-M23 processor has the following enhancements when compared to the Cortex-M0/Cortex-M0+ processors:

- It has optional TrustZone security support

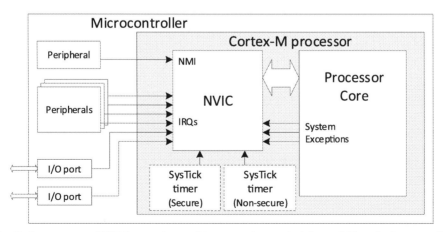

FIG. 8.1   Various sources of NVIC exceptions and interrupts in a typical Cortex-M based microcontroller.

TABLE 8.1 SysTick options.

	Cortex-M23 processor	Cortex-M33/other Armv8-M Mainline processors
TrustZone is not implemented	Options of: • No SysTick timer • One SysTick timer	Always one SysTick timer.
TrustZone is implemented	Options of: • No SysTick timer • One SysTick timer—programmable to be Secure or Non-secure • Two SysTick timers (Secure and Non-secure SysTick).	Always two SysTick timers (Secure and Non-secure SysTick).

TABLE 8.2 Comparison of maximum IRQs in different Cortex-M processors.

	Cortex-M0/M0+	Cortex-M3/M4	Cortex-M23	Cortex-M33
Maximum number of IRQs	32	Up to 240	Up to 240	Up to 480
NMI	Yes	Yes	Yes	Yes
Programmable priority levels	4	8–256	4	8–256

• It has Interrupt Active Status Registers
• It supports sporadic interrupt logic removal (supported in the Cortex-M0+ but not in the Cortex-M0).

The NVIC in the Cortex-M33 processor has the following enhancements when compared to the Cortex-M3/Cortex-M4 processors:

• It has optional TrustZone security support
• It supports sporadic interrupt logic removal
• It has a new SecureFault exception (but only if the TrustZone security extension has been implemented)

The NVIC contains a range of programmable registers that are memory mapped and has a few interrupt masking registers that can be accessed using MRS and MSR instructions. When writing software for Cortex-M processors, the NVIC features can be accessed via a range of APIs provided in the CMSIS-CORE header files. Using those APIs/functions:

- Interrupts can be enabled/disabled,
- The priority levels of interrupts and exceptions can be configured,
- Interrupt masking registers can be accessed.

Further information on interrupt management can be found in Section 8.3 and in Chapter 9.

8.2 Exception types

Cortex-M processors provide a feature-packed exception handling architecture that supports a number of exceptions, including system exceptions and external interrupt requests (IRQs). Exceptions are numbered: numbers 1–15 are reserved for system exceptions and those 16 and above are for IRQs. Most of the exceptions, including all interrupts, have programmable priority, and a few system exceptions have fixed priority.

Cortex-M based microcontrollers from different vendors can have different numbers of interrupt sources and priority levels. This is because chip designers have the ability to configure a Cortex-M processor to match the various application requirements of the chip.

Exception types 1–15 are system exceptions (there is no exception type 0), as outlined in Table 8.3.

Exceptions type 16 and above are external interrupt inputs (see Table 8.4).

The interrupt number in the above table (e.g., Interrupt #0) refers to the numbering of interrupt inputs to the NVIC on the Cortex-M processor. In actual microcontroller products or on system-on-chips (SoCs), the external interrupt input pin number might not match the interrupt input number on the NVIC. For example, the first few interrupt inputs might be assigned to internal peripherals and external interrupt pins could be assigned to the next couple of interrupt inputs. Therefore, when developing an application using interrupts, it is important that you check the chip manufacturer's datasheets to determine the numbering of the interrupts.

The exception number is used as identification for each exception and is used in various ways in the architecture of Armv6-M/Armv7-M/Armv8-M. For example, the value of the current running exception is indicated by the special register Interrupt Program Status register (IPSR, see "Program Status Register (PSR)" in Section 4.2.2.3), as well as by one of the registers in the NVIC called the Interrupt Control State register (the VECTACTIVE field, Section 9.3.2).

When creating applications which use device drivers that are CMSIS-CORE compliant, the interrupt identification is handled by an interrupt enumeration in a header file—starting with the value 0 for Interrupt #0. The system exceptions use negative values in the enumeration, as shown in Table 8.5. The CMSIS-CORE also defines the names of the system exception handlers.

The reason there is a different numbering system in the CMSIS-CORE access functions is to improve the efficiency of some of those access functions (e.g., when setting up priority levels). The interrupt number and enumeration definitions of interrupts are device specific, and are defined in header files provided by microcontroller vendors—in a "typedef" section called "IRQn". The enumeration definitions are used by various NVIC access functions in the CMSIS-CORE.

8.3 Overview of interrupts and exceptions management

Cortex-M processors have a number of programmable registers for the management of interrupts and exceptions (Table 8.6).

The NVIC and SCB data structures are located inside the System Control Space (SCS) address range, which starts from 0xE000E000, and has a size of 4KB. If the TrustZone security extension is implemented and if the processor is in the Secure state, the Non-secure view of the SCS is accessible via a Non-secure SCS alias at 0xE002Exxx. The SCS also contains registers

TABLE 8.3 List of system exceptions 1–15.

Exception number	Exception type	Priority	Description
1	Reset	−4 (Highest)	Reset
2	NMI	−2	Non-Maskable Interrupt (NMI), can be generated from on-chip peripherals or from external sources
3	Hard Fault	−1/−3	All fault conditions—if the corresponding fault handler is not enabled
4	MemManage Fault	Programmable	Memory management fault; caused by an MPU violation or by a program execution from address locations with an XN (eXecute Never) memory attribute. Not available in Armv8-M baseline (i.e., the Cortex-M23 processor).
5	Bus Fault	Programmable	Bus error; usually occurs when the AMBA® AHB™ [2] interface receives an error response from a bus slave (also called *prefetch abort* if it is an instruction fetch or *data abort* if it is a data access). A BusFault can also be caused by an illegal access. Not available in Armv8-M baseline (i.e., the Cortex-M23 processor).
6	Usage Fault	Programmable	Exceptions due to program error. Not available in Armv8-M baseline (i.e., the Cortex-M23 processor).
7	SecureFault	Programmable	Exceptions caused by TrustZone security violations. Not available in Armv8-M baseline (i.e., the Cortex-M23 processor) or when the TrustZone is not implemented.
8–10	Reserved	NA	—
11	SVC	Programmable	SuperVisor Call; usually used in an OS environment to allow application tasks to access system services.
12	Debug Monitor	Programmable	Debug monitor; an exception for debug events, such as breakpoints and watchpoints, when a software-based debug solution is used. Not available in Armv8-M baseline (i.e., the Cortex-M23 processor).
13	Reserved	NA	—
14	PendSV	Programmable	Pendable service call; An exception usually used by an OS in processes such as context switching.
15	SYSTICK	Programmable	System Tick Timer; An exception generated by a timer peripheral which is integrated into the processor. This can be used by an OS, or can be used as a simple timer peripheral.

TABLE 8.4 List of Interrupts.

Exception number	Exception type	Priority	Description
16	Interrupt #0	Programmable	They can be generated from on chip peripherals or from external sources.
17	Interrupt #1	Programmable	Note: The Cortex-M23 supports up to 240 interrupts (exceptions #16–#255).
…	…	…	
495	Interrupt #479	Programmable	

for the SysTick timer, Memory Protection Unit (MPU), debug registers, etc. Additional data structures are defined in the CMSIS-CORE for those registers.

Almost all of the registers in the SCS address range can only be accessed by code running at a privileged access level. The only exception to this is a register called the Software Trigger Interrupt Register (STIR), which is available in Armv8-M Mainline, that can be set up so that it can be accessible in unprivileged mode.

To make it easier to manage interrupts and exceptions, the CMSIS-CORE header files provide a number of access functions to enable a portable software interface. For general

TABLE 8.5 CMSIS-CORE exception definitions.

Exception number	Exception type	CMSIS-CORE enumeration (IRQn)	CMSIS-CORE enumeration value	Exception handler name
1	Reset	–	–	Reset_Handler
2	NMI	NonMaskableInt_IRQn	−14	NMI_Handler
3	Hard Fault	HardFault_IRQn	−13	HardFault_Handler
4	MemManage Fault	MemoryManagement_IRQn	−12	MemManage_Handler
5	Bus Fault	BusFault_IRQn	−11	BusFault_Handler
6	Usage Fault	UsageFault_IRQn	−10	UsageFault_Handler
7	SecureFault	SecureFault_IRQn	−9	SecureFault_Handler
11	SVC	SVCall_IRQn	−5	SVC_Handler
12	Debug Monitor	DebugMonitor_IRQn	−4	DebugMon_Handler
14	PendSV	PendSV_IRQn	−2	PendSV_Handler
15	SYSTICK	SysTick_IRQn	−1	SysTick_Handler
16	Interrupt #0	(device specific)	0	(device specific)
17–495	Interrupt #1–#479	(device specific)	1–479	(device specific)

TABLE 8.6   Various types of registers for interrupt and exception management.

Management function	Register type
To enable and disable interrupts	NVIC Interrupt Set/Clear Enable Registers (memory mapped)
To define the interrupt's priority level	NVIC Interrupt Priority Registers (memory mapped)
To access the interrupt's status	NVIC Set/Clear Pending Registers and NVIC Active Bit Registers (memory mapped)
To define the interrupt's target security state (for TrustZone systems only)	NVIC Interrupt Target Non-secure Registers (memory mapped)
To enable and disable system exceptions (except NMI and HardFault—which cannot be disabled)	SCB (System Control Block) System Handler Control and State Register (memory mapped)
To define the priority levels of system exceptions (except NMI and HardFault—which have fixed priority levels)	SCB (System Control Block) System Handler Priority Registers (memory mapped)
To access the interrupt masking registers (PRIMASK, FAULTMASK and BASEPRI)	Special registers accessible using MRS and MSR instructions, see Section 5.6.4
To access the current exception status	IPSR (Interrupt Program Status Register, a special register, see "Program Status Register (PSR)" in Section 4.2.2.3) and ICSR (Interrupt Control and State Register, a memory mapped register in the SCB)

application programming, best practice is to use the CMSIS-CORE access functions for interrupt management. By way of an example, the most commonly used interrupt control functions are shown in Table 8.7. These functions were also available in previous Cortex-M processors to enable easy software migration.

A few operations do require direct access to the SCB/NVIC registers. For example, if you need to relocate the vector table to a different memory location, the program code needs to update the Vector Table Offset Register (VTOR) directly in the SCB.

TABLE 8.7   Commonly used CMSIS-CORE functions for basic interrupt control.

Function	Usage
void NVIC_EnableIRQ (IRQn_Type IRQn)	Enables an external interrupt
void NVIC_DisableIRQ (IRQn_Type IRQn)	Disables an external interrupt
void NVIC_SetPriority (IRQn_Type IRQn, uint32_t priority)	Sets the priority of an interrupt
void __enable_irq(void)	Clears PRIMASK to enable interrupts
void __disable_irq(void)	Sets PRIMASK to disable all interrupts
void NVIC_SetPriorityGrouping(uint32_t PriorityGroup)	Sets priority grouping configuration. Not available on Cortex-M23 processor (Armv8-M Baseline)

After reset, all interrupts are disabled and are given a priority level value of 0. If the TrustZone security extension is implemented, all interrupts are defined as Secure by default. Before using any interrupts,

- If the TrustZone security extension is implemented, the Secure firmware needs to define for each interrupt whether the interrupt should be targeting the Secure (for Secure peripherals) or the Non-secure state (for Non-secure peripherals). Potentially, a microcontroller system might have most of its interrupts assigned to the Secure domain when the device boots up. To allow the Non-secure application software to use an interrupt, the Non-secure software would, in this scenario, need to call a Secure API in the Secure firmware to request the interrupt to be assigned to the Non-secure domain. This is system dependent.

After the target security states of the interrupts are set up, the application's software would need to carry out the following steps to enable the interrupt feature:

- Setup the priority level of the required interrupt (this step is optional: the default interrupt priority level is 0. If the application needs the interrupt to be set up at a different priority level, then it would be necessary to reprogram the priority level),
- enable the interrupt generation control in the peripheral that triggers the interrupt,
- enable the interrupt in the NVIC.

The application code must also:

- provide a suitable interrupt service routine (ISR) to service the interrupt, and
- ensure the name of the ISR matches the name of the interrupt handler as defined in the vector table (you can usually find this in the startup code provided by the microcontroller vendor). This is required to enable the linker to place the starting address of the ISR in the vector table.

In most typical applications that is all you need to do.

When the interrupt triggers, the corresponding interrupt service routine (ISR) will execute (you might, though, need to clear the interrupt request from the peripheral within the handler).

8.4 Exception sequence introduction

8.4.1 Overview

When an exception or interrupt event occurs a number of steps take place to handle the exception or to service the interrupt. A simplified view of an exception handling is shown in Fig. 8.2.

Sections 8.4.2–8.4.5 describe the operations for each of the steps shown in Fig. 8.2.

8.4.2 Acceptance of exception request

The processor accepts an exception request if the following conditions are met:

- An interrupt or exception event takes place, causing its pending state register to be set to 1
- The processor is running (not halted or in reset state)

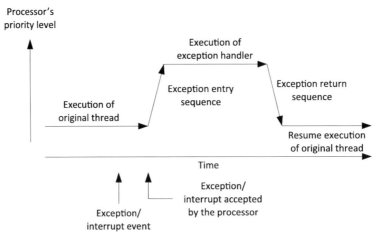

FIG. 8.2   Various steps of an exception handling.

- The exception is enabled (Note: NMI and HardFault exceptions are always enabled)
- The exception has a higher priority than the current priority level
- The exception is not blocked by an exception masking register (e.g., PRIMASK)

Note: For an SVC exception, if the SVC instruction is accidentally used in an exception handler that has the same or a higher priority than the SVC exception itself, the result will be a HardFault exception.

8.4.3 Exception entry sequence

An exception entry sequence contains a number of operations:

- It pushes the contents of a number of registers into the current selected stack—the register values include the return address. This is known as "stacking" and enables an exception handler to be written as a normal C function. If the processor was in Thread mode and was using the Process Stack Pointer (PSP), the stack area pointed to by the PSP will be used for this stacking. Otherwise, the stack area pointed to by the Main Stack Pointer (MSP) will be used.
- It fetches the exception vector (starting address of the exception handler/ISR). For processors with Harvard bus architecture, like the Cortex-M33 processor, this can, to reduce latency, happen in parallel to the stacking operation.
- It fetches instructions for the exception handler to execute. After the starting address of the exception handler is determined by reading the vector table, the instructions are then fetched.
- It updates various NVIC and core registers. This includes the pending status and active status of the exception and registers in the processor core, including the Program Status Register (PSR), Link Register (LR), Program Counter (PC), and Stack Pointer (SP).
- It erases Secure information in the register bank before the ISR starts if the processor was running Secure software and is taking a Non-secure exception. This is to prevent Secure information from leaking to the Non-secure world.

Depending on which stack was used for stacking, either the MSP or PSP value would be adjusted just before the exception handler started. The PC would also be updated to the stating address of the exception handler and the LR would be updated with a special value, called EXC_RETURN (see Section 8.10). This "special" value is 32 bits, with its upper 25 bits set to 1. Some of its lower 7 bits are used to hold status information about the exception sequence (e.g., which stack was used for stacking). This value will be used in the exception return.

8.4.4 Exception handler execution

Within the exception handler, the peripheral that triggered the interrupt request is serviced by software operations. The processor is in Handler mode when executing an exception handler. In Handler mode:

- the Main Stack Pointer (MSP) is used for stack operations,
- the processor executes at privileged access level.

If a higher priority exception arrives at this stage, the new interrupt will be accepted and the current executing handler will be suspended and preempted by the higher priority handler. This situation is called nested exception.

If another exception with the same or with a lower priority arrives during this stage, the newly arrived exception will stay in pending state and will only be serviced when the current exception handler has finished.

When the exception handler is finished, the program code executes a return which causes the EXC_RETURN value to be loaded into the Program Counter (PC). This triggers the exception return mechanism.

8.4.5 Exception return sequence

In some processor architecture, a special instruction is used for an exception return. However, when this is the case it means the exception handlers cannot be written and compiled as normal C code. In Arm Cortex-M processors, the exception return mechanism is triggered using a value called EXC_RETURN. This value is generated at the exception entry sequence and is stored in the Link Register (LR). When this value is written to the PC with one of the allowed exception return instructions, it triggers the exception return sequence.

The exception return can be generated by the instructions shown in Table 8.8.

During an exception return, the register values of the previously interrupted program that were saved to the stack during the exception entrance are automatically restored by the processor. This operation is called unstacking. In addition, when this occurs, a number of NVIC registers (e.g., the active status of interrupts) and registers in the processor core (e.g., PSR, SP, CONTROL) will be updated.

In parallel to the unstacking operation, for processors with the Harvard bus architecture, such as the Cortex-M33, the processor will start fetching the instructions of the previously interrupted program to allow the program to quickly resume its operations.

The use of the EXC_RETURN value for triggering exception returns allows exception handlers (including Interrupt Service Routines) to be written as a normal C function/subroutine.

TABLE 8.8 Instructions that can be used for triggering exception returns.

Return instruction	Description
BX <reg>, or BXNS <reg>	If the EXC_RETURN value is still in the LR when the exception handler ends, we can use the "*BX LR*" instruction to perform the exception return. The BXNS instruction could be used for a Secure exception handler, but this only happens if the handler is also served as a Secure API—a function that is called by Non-secure software. (Note: the BXNS instruction is only available when TrustZone is implemented.)
POP {PC}, or POP {....., PC}	Very often the value of LR is pushed to the stack after entering the exception handler. We can use the "POP {PC}" instruction, or a "POP {..., PC}" operation with multiple registers. With these instructions, the EXC_RETURN value is moved to the Program Counter (PC) and results in the processor performing the exception return.
Load (LDR) or Load multiple (LDM)	With Armv8-M Mainline processors, it is possible to produce an exception return using the LDR or LDM instructions with the PC as the destination register.

In code generation, the C compiler handles the EXC_RETURN value in LR as a normal return address. Because of the values used by the EXC_RETURN mechanism, it is not possible to have a normal function return to address 0xF0000000 to 0xFFFFFFFF. However, since the architecture specifies that this address range cannot be used for program code (because it has a Execute Never (XN) memory attribute) it does not cause any software problems.

8.5 Definitions of exception priority levels

8.5.1 Overview of exception and interrupt priority levels

Each of the interrupts and exceptions in Arm Cortex-M processors has an exception priority level. When a higher priority level interrupt/exception occurs during a lower priority interrupt/exception service, it preempts the lower priority service. This is known as nested interrupt/exception handling. In Cortex-M processors:

- A higher value in the priority level register means a lower priority level (see Fig. 8.3).
- A priority level with a value of zero is the highest level for a programmable interrupt/exception.
- Some system exceptions (NMI, HardFault, and reset) have fixed/non-programmable priority levels of negative values—hence a higher priority than interrupts/exceptions with programmable priority levels.

Architecturally, the programmable priority levels are defined as 8-bit values and range from 0 to 255. However, to reduce hardware cost and timing delays, only the most significant bits of the values are implemented (Fig. 8.4).

In the Cortex-M23 processor (an Armv8-M baseline processor) and in Armv6-M processors:

- Only bit 7 and bit 6 of the priority level registers are implemented, thus providing four programmable priority levels. The unimplemented bits are read as zero, and the write to these bits is ignored.

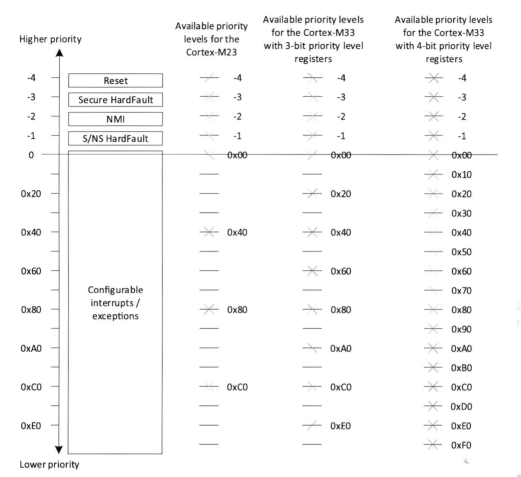

FIG. 8.3 Available priority levels for the Cortex-M23 and Cortex-M33 processors with 3- and 4-bit priority level registers.

In Armv8-M processors with a Main extension (e.g., the Cortex-M33 processor) and in Armv7-M processors:

- The implemented width of the priority level registers is configurable by chip designers. The minimum width is 3 bits (8 levels) and the maximum is 8 bits (256 levels, with a maximum of 128 levels of preemption).

When less than 8 bits are implemented in the priority level registers, the reduction in the number of priority level registers is achieved by cutting out the Least Significant Bit (LSB) portion of the priority configuration registers. In this way, when a software binary image moves to a device which has fewer priority levels, this will not cause, an inversion of the priority levels—which can occur if the MSB (Most Significant Bits) is lost.

Usually, microcontrollers based on the Cortex-M33 or on other Armv7-M/Armv8-M Mainline processors have 8–32 interrupt/exception priority levels. Most real-world applications,

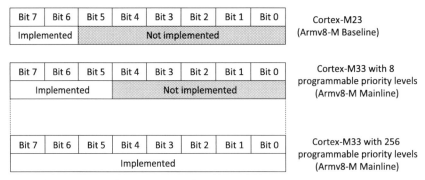

FIG. 8.4   Priority level registers of Cortex-M23 and Cortex-M33 processors.

however, only require a small number of programmable priority levels. A high number of priority levels increases the complexity of the NVIC, which not only increases the silicon area and power consumption but could also reduce the maximum clock speed. As a consequence, 8 and 16 priority levels are the most common choice of implementation on the majority of Cortex-M microcontrollers with Armv7-M/Armv8-M Mainline architectures.

The interrupt/exception priority level decides whether an incoming interrupt/exception is accepted by the processor:

- If the incoming interrupt/exception event has a higher priority level than the processor's current priority level, then the interrupt/exception request will be accepted and the exception entry sequence will start.
- If the incoming interrupt/exception event has the same or a lower priority level than the processor's current priority level, then the incoming interrupt/exception request is blocked and held in a pending status register (to be served later). This is caused when any of the following conditions occurs:
  - The processor is already serving another interrupt/exception of the same/higher priority level, or
  - An interrupt/exception mask register is set which changes the processor's current effective priority level to the same/higher priority level as the incoming interrupt/exception

There are a few exceptions: For example, if an SVC or a synchronous fault exception is triggered and the priority level is insufficient to execute the corresponding fault handler, then the exception event will be escalated to a HardFault exception. Several system exceptions have fixed priority levels of negative values (Table 8.9).

If the TrustZone security extension is not implemented, the Secure HardFault is not present.

AIRCR.BFHFNMIS is a programmable bit and is only accessible by Secure privileged software. If TrustZone is being used then AIRCR.BFHFNMIS should be set to 0. Further information on the AIRCR.BFHFNMIS is covered in Sections 8.8 and 9.3.4.

The priority level of exceptions and interrupts are controlled by priority level registers. These registers are memory mapped and can be accessed in privileged state only. By default, all priority level registers have a value of 0 when the processor starts from reset.

TABLE 8.9   Priority levels of system exceptions.

Exception number	Exception	Priority level
1	Reset	−4 (Note: It is −3 in Armv6-M and Armv7-M and is changed to −4 in Armv8-M)
3	Secure HardFault when AIRCR. BFHFNMIS is 1	−3 (Note: Secure HardFault with priority level −3 is new in Armv8-M)
2	NMI	−2
3	Secure HardFault when AIRCR. BFHFNMIS is 0	−1
3	Non-secure HardFault	−1
4 or above	Other system exceptions and interrupts	Configurable (0–255)

8.5.2 Priority grouping in Armv8-M Mainline

When a chip designer is designing a system with a Cortex-M33 or other Armv8-M Mainline processors, the chip designer can, in theory, define the hardware configuration so that all 8 bits are implemented in the priority level registers. However, instead of having a maximum of 256 (2 to the power of 8 is 256) preemption levels, the maximum number of preemption levels is limited to 128 by the Armv8-M architecture. The reason for this is that the 8-bit priority level registers are further divided into two halves:

- The upper half (left bits) is the group priority for the preemption control
- The Lower half (right bits) is the subpriority

The exact division of group priority and subpriority is controlled by a bit field in the AIRCR called PRIGROUP (priority grouping, Table 8.10). This register is only available for Armv8-M

TABLE 8.10   The definition of Group Priority Field and Subpriority Field in a Priority Level register with various priority group settings.

Priority group	Group Priority Field	Subpriority Field	Maximum number of nested IRQs
0 (default)	Bit [7:1]	Bit [0]	128
1	Bit [7:2]	Bit [1:0]	64
2	Bit [7:3]	Bit [2:0]	32
3	Bit [7:4]	Bit [3:0]	16
4	Bit [7:5]	Bit [4:0]	8
5	Bit [7:6]	Bit [5:0]	4
6	Bit [7]	Bit [6:0]	2
7	None	Bit [7:0]	1 (Only one IRQ at a time, no nesting)

processors with the Main extension (i.e., Mainline subprofile) and is banked between security states. Using the PRIGROUP bit field, the maximum level of interrupt/exception nesting can be controlled.

The *group priority level* defines whether an interrupt can take place when the processor is already running another interrupt handler. The *subpriority level* value is only used when two exceptions with the same group priority level have occurred at the same time. In such a case, the exception with the higher *subpriority* (lower value) will be handled first.

8.5.3 Prioritization of Secure exceptions and interrupts

In some applications, it is essential to arrange for some of the Secure interrupts or Secure system exceptions to have a higher priority than the Non-secure interrupts/exceptions. This is to ensure the background Secure software services operates correctly. For example, a device could have a certified Bluetooth software service running in the background and its operation must not be affected by a failure of applications running on the Non-secure side. To meet this requirement, TrustZone for Armv8-M allows Secure software to prioritize, if needed, Secure exceptions and interrupts.

The Secure exceptions/interrupt prioritization is controlled by a programmable bit in the AIRCR called PRIS (Prioritize Secure exception). By default, this bit is set to 0 out of reset, which means Secure and Non-secure exceptions/interrupts share the same configurable programmable priority level space for level 0 to 0xFF (Fig. 8.5).

When the AIRCR.PRIS is set to 1, although Non-secure software will still see it has exception/interrupt priority levels 0 to 0xFF, the effective level value will be shifted by 1 bit and placed in the lower half of the Secure exception/interrupt priority level space (Fig. 8.6).

While AIRCR.PRIS can, to some extent, protect background Secure exception/interrupt services, the services can still be stopped if the halting debug is enabled (subject to debug authentication configuration). The system can also be stopped by a reset or the powerdown of the device.

The Secure interrupt/exception prioritization feature is available in all Armv8-M processors when the TrustZone security extension is implemented.

8.5.4 Banking of interrupt mask registers

In Armv8-M processors with TrustZone, the interrupt masking registers (PRIMASK, FAULTMASK, and BASEPRI) are banked between security states. Since the priority level space is shared between the Secure and the Non-secure world, setting an interrupt mask register on one side can block some, or all, of the exceptions on the other side.

AIRCR.PRIS also affects the operations of the interrupt masking registers. For example, if the AIRCR.PRIS is set to 1, and the Non-secure software sets the Non-secure PRIMASK (PRIMASK_NS) to 1, then, on the Secure side, although Secure exceptions with priority level 0x80 to 0xFF are blocked, on the Non-secure side all Non-secure exceptions with configurable priority levels (0x0 to 0xFF) are blocked.

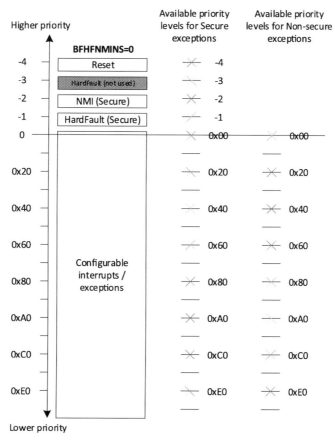

FIG. 8.5 Available priority levels for the Cortex-M33 processor with 3-bit priority level registers and when the AIRCR.PRIS is set to 0.

8.6 Vector table and vector table offset register (VTOR)

One important step of the exception entry sequence is to determine the starting address of the exception handler. In Cortex-M processors, this is automatically handled in the processor hardware by means of reading it from a Vector table—which contains exception vectors (the starting addresses of each handler) arranged in the order of the exception number (Fig. 8.7). When an exception is accepted by the processor, the starting address of the handler is read from a vector table and the address being read is calculated as:

```
Vector address = exception_number  4 + Vector_Table_Offset
```

In a typical software project, the vector table(s) is usually be found in a device specific file for start-up code. Please note, the LSB of the vectors should be set to 1 to indicate Thumb state. The setting of LSB in the vectors is automatically handled by the development toolchain.

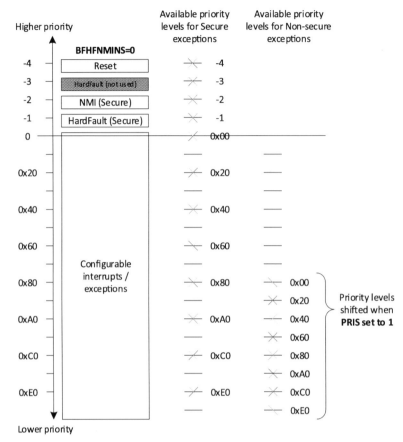

FIG. 8.6 Available priority levels for the Cortex-M33 processor with 3-bit priority level registers and when the AIRCR.PRIS is set to 1.

The first word in the vector table stores the initial value for the Main Stack Pointer (MSP). This value is copied into the MSP register during the reset sequence. This is needed because some exceptions, such as NMI, could occur just as the processor comes out of reset and before any other initialization steps have been carried out.

The vector table offset is defined by a Vector Table Offset Register (VTOR). In Armv8-M processors which have TrustZone support, there are two vector tables:

- The Secure vector table is for Secure exceptions and is placed in the Secure memory. The address of the Secure vector table is defined by VTOR_S (Secure VTOR).
- The Non-secure vector table is for Non-secure exceptions and is placed in the Non-secure memory. The address of the Non-secure vector table is defined by VTOR_NS (Non-secure VTOR).

When TrustZone is not implemented, then only the Non-secure VTOR is present.

In the Cortex-M33 processor, the lowest 7 bits of the VTOR registers are tied to 0, which means the vector table starting address must be multiples of 128 bytes. Similarly, in the

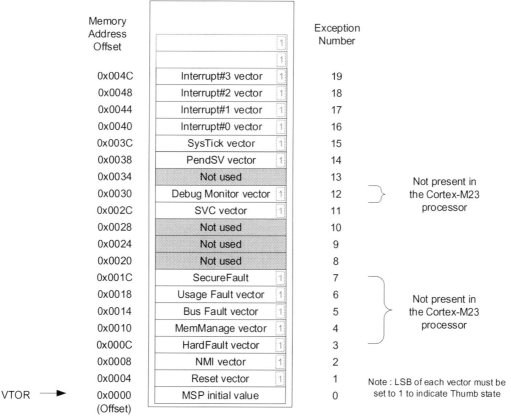

FIG. 8.7   Contents of a vector table.

Cortex-M23 processor, the lowest 8 bits of the VTOR registers are tied to 0, which means the vector table starting address must be multiples of 256 bytes (Fig. 8.8). There are some differences between the VTOR registers in the Cortex-M23 and the Cortex-M33 processors and these are:

- In the Cortex-M23 processor, VTOR(s) are optional. If implemented, bit 31 down to bit 8 of the VTOR is present. If not implemented, the value(s) of the VTOR is defined by chip designers.
- In the Cortex-M33 processor, VTOR(s) are implemented as 25 bits wide (bit 31 down to 7 are implemented).

The VTOR registers are programmable in the privileged state only. The address of the VTOR for a current security state is 0xE000ED08. Secure privileged software can access the Non-secure VTOR (VTOR_NS) using the Non-secure SCB alias 0xE002ED08 (this alias address is not available to a debugger or to Non-secure software).

In some applications, there is a need to relocate the vector table(s) to other addresses. For example, an application might relocate the vector table(s) from Non-volatile memory to SRAM to allow exception vectors to be configurable during the run time. This is achieved by:

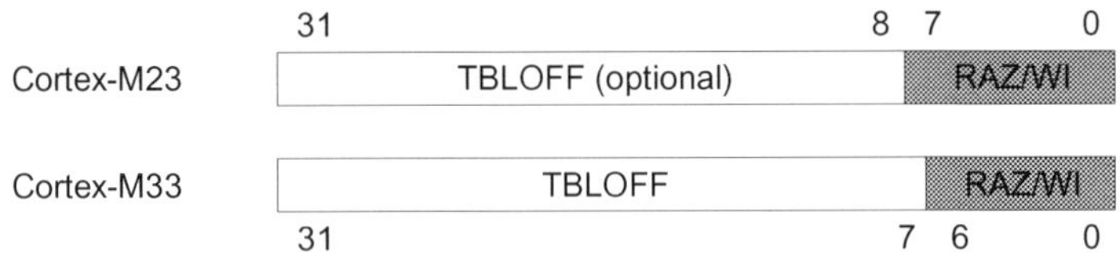

FIG. 8.8   Vector Table Offset Register (VTOR).

Cortex-M23

31	8	7	0
TBLOFF (optional)		RAZ/WI	

Cortex-M33

31	7	6	0
TBLOFF		RAZ/WI	

(1) Copying the original vector table to the new allocated location in SRAM,

(2) Modifying, if needed, some of the exception vectors, then

(3) Programing the VTOR to select the new vector table, and

(4) Executing a DSB (Data Synchronization Barrier) instruction to ensure the change immediately takes place.

An example of the program code for this operation can be found in Chapter 9, Section 9.5.2.

Unlike previous Cortex-M processors (Cortex-M0/M0+/M1/M3/M4), the initial addresses of the vector tables in the Cortex-M23 and the Cortex-M33 processors are defined by silicon designers, whereas in the older Cortex-M processors the initial vector table address was fixed to address 0.

Another difference between the vector table of Armv8-M Mainline and Armv7-M is the addition of a SecureFault vector. This exception was not available in the Armv7-M architecture.

8.7 Interrupt input and pending behaviors

The NVIC design supports a number of interrupt inputs, as mentioned in Section 8.1.3. It is designed to support peripherals that generate pulsed interrupt requests as well as peripherals which continuously hold its interrupt request signal at a high level until the request is serviced. The NVIC does not need configuring to work with either of these interrupt types. Further information on pulsed and level triggered interrupts is as follows:

• For a pulsed interrupt request, the pulse must be at least one clock cycle long.

• For level triggered interrupts, the peripheral requesting the service asserts the request signal until it is cleared by an operation inside the ISR (e.g., writing to a register to clear the interrupt request).

Although the request signals received by the NVIC are active high, the peripherals or external interrupt request at the I/O pin level could be active low (in such cases, chip designers will need to insert some glue logic to convert the signals to active high).

For each of the interrupt inputs, there are several applicable status attributes:

• Each interrupt can either be disabled (default) or enabled.

• Each interrupt can either be pending (a request is waiting to be served) or not pending.

• Each interrupt can either be in an active (being served) or in an inactive state.

To support this, the NVIC contains programmable registers for the interrupt enable control, registers for accessing the pending status, and registers for accessing the active status (the active status registers are read-only). When an interrupt input of the NVIC is asserted, it

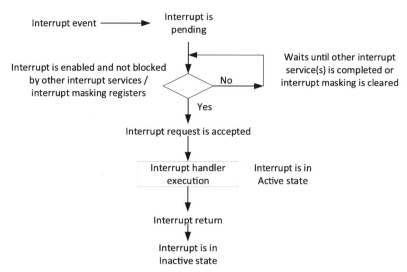

FIG. 8.9 Simplified flow: From interrupt input event, to pending, to interrupt being serviced.

causes the pending status of the interrupt to be asserted (Fig. 8.9). The pending status means that the request is recorded and is waiting for the processor to serve the interrupt. It remains set even when the IRQ signal is de-asserted. In this way, the NVIC can work with pulsed IRQs. When the interrupt is serviced, the pending status is cleared and the active status is set—all of which is automatically carried out by the NVIC hardware.

In most cases, the processor serves the request almost as soon as the interrupt becomes pending. However, if the processor is already serving another interrupt of a higher or of the same priority, or if the interrupt is masked due to one of the interrupt masking registers, the request will remain in pending state until either the other interrupt handler has finished or when the interrupt masking is cleared.

Different combinations of these status attributes are possible. For example, when you are serving an interrupt, which means it is in an active state, you can optionally disable it by software. At the same time, it is also possible for a new request for the same interrupt to arrive again before the interrupt handler exits. In this case, we have a status attribute combination in which the interrupt is disabled while being active and at the same time is also pending.

A simple scenario (Fig. 8.10) of the handling of an interrupt request where:

- interrupt X is enabled,
- the processor is not serving another interrupt, and
- the interrupt request is not blocked by any interrupt masking register.

When the interrupt is being served it is in an active state. Please note, during the interrupt entry sequence a number of registers are automatically pushed into the stack. This is called stacking. In parallel to the stacking operation, the Cortex-M33 processor (and other Armv8-M processors with Harvard bus architecture) fetches the ISR's starting address from the vector table. For the Cortex-M23 processor, which is based on the Von Neumann bus architecture,

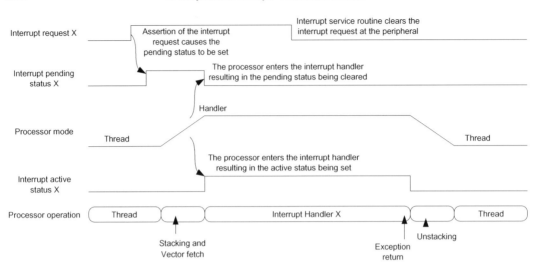

FIG. 8.10   A simple case of interrupt pending and activation behavior.

the fetching of the ISR's starting address occurs after the stacking operation has been completed.

In many microcontroller designs, the peripherals are operating with level triggered interrupts and the ISR will, therefore, have to manually clear the interrupt request by, for example, writing to a register in the peripheral. After the interrupt service has completed, the processor carries out an Exception Return (covered in Section 8.4.5). The registers which were automatically stacked are restored and the interrupted program is resumed. The active status of the interrupt is also cleared automatically.

When an interrupt is active you cannot accept the same interrupt request again, unless and until it is completed and terminated with an exception return (also called an exception exit).

Since the pending status of an interrupt is accessible by software via a number of memory mapped registers, it is possible to manually set or clear the pending status of an interrupt. If an interrupt request arrives when the processor is serving another higher priority interrupt, and the pending status is cleared before the processor starts responding to the pending request, the request is cancelled and will not be served (Fig. 8.11).

FIG. 8.11   The pending status of an interrupt clears before it was serviced.

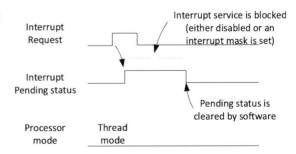

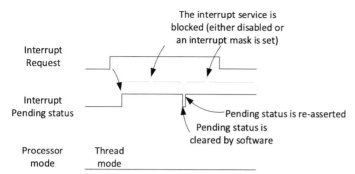

FIG. 8.12 The interrupt pending status clears then re-asserts because of a further interrupt request.

If the peripheral continues to assert the interrupt request, and the software attempts to clear the pending status, the pending status will be set again (Fig. 8.12).

If the interrupt request is not blocked (i.e., it is accepted and serviced by the processor), and if the interrupt source continues to assert its interrupt request at the end of the interrupt service routine, the interrupt will again enter pending state and will again be serviced the by the processor. This situation occurs unless the interrupt is blocked (e.g., by another interrupt service). This is shown in Fig 8.13.

For pulsed interrupt requests, if an interrupt request signal is pulsed several times before the processor starts processing, the request will be treated as one single interrupt request. This is illustrated in Fig. 8.14.

The pending status of an interrupt can be set again when it is being served. For example, in Fig. 8.15, a new interrupt request arrives when the previous request is still being served. This results in a new pending status and causes the processor to serve the interrupt again after the first ISR has been completed.

Please note, the pending status of an interrupt can be set even when the interrupt is disabled. In this case, when the interrupt is enabled later, it can be triggered and then served. In some circumstances, this might not be a desirable outcome and, when it is not, you would need to manually clear the pending status before enabling the interrupt in the NVIC.

In general, the NMI request behavior is the same as that for interrupts. Unless an NMI or a Secure HardFault handler is already running, or the processor has been halted or is in a

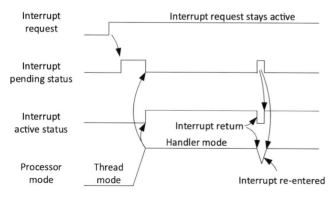

FIG. 8.13 The interrupt pending status is set again if the request remains high after the exception's exit.

FIG. 8.14 Multiple pulsed Interrupt requests merged as a single interrupt pending request.

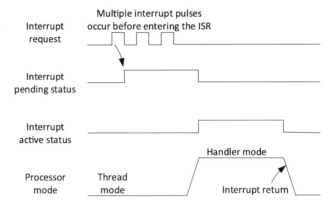

locked-up state, a NMI request will, because it has the second highest priority (the Secure HardFault has the highest) and cannot be disabled, be executed almost immediately.

8.8 Target states of exceptions and interrupts in TrustZone systems

Because peripherals can be allocated to the Secure and the Non-secure worlds, their interrupts must be directed to the interrupt handlers in the correct security domains. In addition, there are a number of system exceptions that need to be handled by either the Secure or the Non-secure handlers. If the TrustZone security extension is implemented:

- All of the interrupts can be configured to be either Secure or Non-secure (e.g., for a peripheral, the interrupt's targeted state should be configured based on the security domain of that peripheral).
- Some of system exceptions are banked, which means that there can be both Secure and Non-secure versions of these exceptions. Both can be triggered and executed independently and have different priority level settings.

FIG. 8.15 Interrupt pending occurs again during the execution of an interrupt service routine.

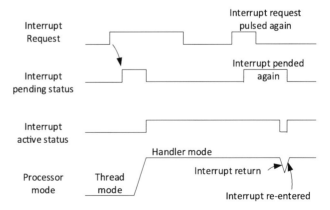

- Some of the system exceptions (NMI, HardFault, BusFault) can be configured to target either the Secure state or the Non-secure state (using AIRCR.BFHFNMINS bit).
- Some of the system exceptions only target the Secure state (e.g., reset, SecureFault).

If the TrustZone security extension is NOT implemented, exceptions and interrupts target the Non-secure state. The SecureFault is not available in this situation.

If an exception is Secure:

- The starting address of the exception is obtained from the Secure vector table in the Secure memory, and
- During the execution of the handler, the Secure Main Stack Pointer (MSP_S) is, by default, used.

Software developers need to ensure that the program codes of Secure exception handlers are placed in the Secure memory. This ensures that these handlers execute in Secure state.

If an exception is Non-secure:

- The starting address of the exception is obtained from the Non-secure vector table in the Non-secure memory, and
- During the execution of the handler, the Non-secure Main Stack Pointer (MSP_NS) is, by default, used.

The program codes for the Non-secure exception handlers are placed in the Non-secure memory and execute in the Non-secure state.

If the exception is setup incorrectly, for example, an interrupt is setup to target the Non-secure state but the vector is pointing to a Secure address, then a SecureFault or HardFault exception would be triggered. However, the architecture allows the use of a Secure API as a Non-secure handler. In such a situation, the vector in the Non-secure vector table points to a valid Secure entry point (the first executing instruction is a Secure Gateway (SG) and this is placed in a Secure NSC memory), which is a Secure address. This situation does not trigger either a SecureFault or HardFault exception.

The types of exceptions and interrupts and their default target states are shown in Table 8.11.

As shown in Table 8.11, a number of exceptions can be configured to target either the Secure or the Non-secure state. The targeted state is defined by programmable registers, or by other mechanisms (Table 8.12), that are only accessible in Secure privileged state (or from a debug connection with Secure debug access).

The bit BFHFNMINS ("Bus Fault, HardFault and NMI Non-secure enable") is a programmable bit in the AIRCR (Application Interrupt and Reset Control Register). This bit is only accessible in Secure privileged state.

When BFHFNMINS is set to 1, BusFault, HardFault and the NMI event will, with the exception of faults that target the Secure state and that are escalated to HardFault, be handled using the Non-secure system exception handlers. If a security error occurs when BFHFNMINS is 1, the exception triggered will still be a Secure HardFault and will target the Secure state.

Worth noting is that the BFHFNMINS feature should only be enabled if the Secure software is to be unused and you want to seal off access to all Secure software features. It is recommended that:

TABLE 8.11   Configurability and default target states for interrupts and exceptions.

Exception number	Exception type	Type	Default target state
1	Reset	Secure only	Secure
2	NMI	Configurable	Secure
3	Hard Fault	Configurable	Secure
4	MemManage Fault	Banked	Banked
5	Bus Fault	Configurable	Secure
6	Usage Fault	Banked	Banked
7	SecureFault	Always Secure	Secure
11	SVC	Banked	Banked
12	Debug Monitor	Configurable	Secure
14	PendSV	Banked	Banked
15	SysTick	Banked or configurable	Banked if two SysTick timers are available. If there is only one SysTick timer, by default the SysTick exception targets the Secure state.
16–495	Interrupt #0– #479	Configurable	Secure

TABLE 8.12   Configuration registers that define the target security states of exceptions and interrupts.

Exception number	Exception type	Configuration method	Note
2	NMI	BFHFNMINS (bit 13) in the Application Interrupt and Reset Control Register (AIRCR)	BFHFNMINS should not be set to 1 if the Secure state execution is required.
3	HardFault	BFHFNMINS bit in the AIRCR	See above
5	BusFault	BFHFNMINS bit in the AIRCR	See above
12	Debug Monitor	If the Secure debug is enabled in the debug authentication interface, it will target the Secure state. Otherwise, the Debug monitor will target the Non-secure state.	
15	SysTick	STTNS bit (bit 24) in Interrupt Control and State Register (ICSR)	Configurable only for Cortex-M23 and only if it is configured to have one SysTick timer
16–495	Interrupt #0–#479	NVIC Interrupt Target State Register (ITNS)	

- Once BFHFNMINS has been set to 1, that the calling of secure functions should be blocked. In addition, the triggering of a secure exception that may return should also be blocked.
- If a Secure fault event is triggered in this setup (i.e., BFHFNMINS is set to 1), that Non-secure codes should not, unless through a reset sequence, be allowed to execute again.

In a Cortex-M23 processor with the TrustZone implemented, it is possible to have just one SysTick timer implemented. In such a case, the Secure privileged software can program the STTNS (bit 24) in the "Interrupt Control and State Register (ICSR)" to decide whether the SysTick should be allocated to the Secure (when STTNS=0) or the Non-secure worlds (STTNS=1).

8.9 Stack frames

8.9.1 Stacking and unstacking overview

In order to allow an interrupted program to resume after the exception/interrupt handler has ended, the Cortex-M processor automatically pushes a number of registers into the stack memory. It then restores those registers from the stack when returning to the interrupted program code. In this way, the interrupted code can resume correctly and is unaffected by the fact that there has been a change of context.

The concept of stacking (the pushing of register contents to stack during an exception entry sequence) and unstacking (the restoration of registers upon the return of exceptions) was briefly covered in Section 8.4. The automatic stacking and unstacking operations use the current selected stack pointer of the interrupted task. For example, if the processor is in the Non-secure state and is running an application task with the Non-secure Process Stack Pointer (PSP_NS) selected as the current SP, then PSP_NS will be used for the stacking and unstacking operations. This is independent from the stack operations within the exception handlers, which use the Main Stack Pointer (either as Secure or Non-secure, which is dependent upon the target state of the exception).

For easier development of Cortex-M software, stacking and unstacking works in a way that enables most exception and interrupt handlers to be programmed as ordinary C functions—without the need to use tool chain specific keywords to specify that they are exception/interrupt handlers.

To understand how this is achieved, we need to understand how the interface of C functions works. This is defined by a specification from Arm called AAPCS (Procedure Call Standard for the Arm Architecture: see Ref. [3]).

8.9.2 Interface of C functions

Based on the AAPCS specification [3], a C function can modify registers R0–R3, R12, LR(R14), and the PSR within C function boundaries. If the floating-point unit is present and enabled, the registers in S0–S15 and the FPSCR (Floating Point Status and Control Register) can also be modified by the C function. The contents on the other registers can also be modified within the C functions, but the contents of these other registers will need to be saved to the stack before being modified. And, before leaving the C function these registers must be restored to their original values.

Because of the aforementioned C function requirements, registers in the register bank and in the floating-point unit register bank are divided into:

- Caller saved registers—R0–R3, R12, LR (also S0–S15 and FPSCR if the FPU is present). If the data in these registers needs to be used after a C function call, the caller needs to save it before calling a C function.
- Callee saved registers—R4-R11 (also S16-S31 if the FPU is present). If the C function needs to modify any of these registers, the C function must first push the affected registers to the stack and then restore them before returning to caller code.

In addition to caller and callee saved register arrangement, the AAPCS specification also specifies how parameters and results can be passed between caller and callee. In a simple scenario, registers R0–R3 can be used as input parameters for C functions. Additionally, register R0 and, optionally, register R1 can be used for returning the results of a function (register R1 is needed when the return value is 64-bit). Fig. 8.16 shows the grouping of callee-saved registers and the usage of several caller saved registers for parameters and result passing.

Another requirement of the AAPCS is that the value of the stack pointer must be aligned to double word boundaries at a function interface. The processor's exception handling hardware handles this automatically.

8.9.3 Exception handler in C

When developing Cortex-M software creating an interrupt handler is very easy. For example, you can declare a Timer handler as:

```
void Timer0_Handler(void)
{
  ... // processing needed
  ... // Clear timer interrupt request at the timer peripheral
  return;
}
```

The function name (Timer0_Handler in the above example) would need to match the handler name declared in the vector table used in the device specific startup code. Additionally, you would need to:

- enable interrupt generation when initializing the peripheral and,
- enable the interrupt at the NVIC (a subject covered in Chapter 9).

To allow a C function to be used as an exception handler, the exception mechanism needs to automatically save the "caller-saved registers" at exception entrances and restore them at exception exits. These operations are under the control of the processor's hardware. In this way, when returned to the interrupted program the registers retain the same value they had before the interrupt took place (this excludes special cases like SVC services, where some of the registers could be used for its return values).

C function

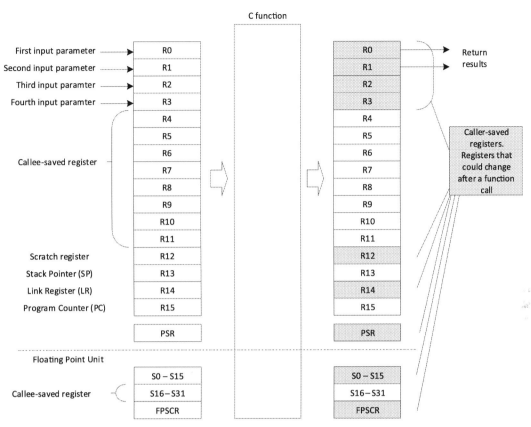

FIG. 8.16 Usage of registers for function inputs and outputs based on the AAPCS's specification.

When TrustZone is implemented and when a Non-secure interrupt takes place during the execution of Secure code, then the "callee-saved registers" must also be saved by the stacking process. This is required because we need to erase the register bank before the Non-secure handler executes. By so doing, this prevents secure information leaking out. However, this behavior (i.e., the saving of the callee-saved registers and the erasing of data in the register bank) does not require the exception handlers, which use a standard C function interface, to be modified.

The exception stacking operations place the caller-saved-registers in a data block in the stack memory. This data block is called exception "stack frame" (Section 8.9.4) and the layout of data inside is defined by the Armv8-M architecture.

8.9.4 Stack frame formats

For the most part, it is not necessary for application software developers to know what data is stored inside stack frames. For interrupt handling, the automatic stack and unstacking is handled by the processor and is transparent to software. There are, however, some instances where an understanding of the stack frame is needed and can be useful. These instances are:

- When OS software developers need to create context switching codes or OS services via SVC exceptions (parameters and results for the OS services can be passed via the stack frame).
- For the analysis of software failures when the processor enters a fault exception (in order to locate the faulting address via the stacked return address in the stack frame). Please note, several commercial development tools have debug features that can extract this information.

Most software developers, do not, however, need this level of detail so can skip the following paragraphs.

There are several formats of stack frame, with each dependent upon several factors:

- Whether it was running Secure code and will be servicing a Non-secure interrupt. If it was, both the caller-saved and callee-saved registers need to be pushed into the stack. If it was not, only the caller-saved registers need to be pushed to the stack during the stacking process.
- Whether the FPU was enabled and used in current context (indicated by CONTROL.FPCA being equal to 1). If it was, the caller-saved registers in the FPU register bank will need to be pushed into the stack.
- Whether the FPU is used by Secure software for Secure processing (determined by the TS bit in the FPCCR). If this bit is set to 1, then the Callee-saved registers in the floating-point register bank must also be saved on the stack when the Secure code execution is interrupted by a Non-secure exception.

At a minimum, an exception stack frame must contain at least 8 data words—Fig. 8.17. The eight words of data contain the "caller-saved registers" in the regular register bank and information to enable the interrupted software to be resumed later. Since exception handlers can be implemented as a normal C function, the contents of R0–R3, R12, LR, and xPSR must be saved. Unlike function calls, the return address for exception handling is not stored in the LR. At the entrance of the exception handler, the value of LR is replaced by a special value called EXC_RETURN (Exception Return), which is used to trigger unstacking at the end of the exception handler. Further information about EXC_RETURN is covered in Section 8.10.

The 8-word stack frame format is used when:

- The FPU is not available, is disabled or is inactive in the current context, and
- The transition is not from a Secure background task to a Non-secure handler

This situation is identical to the stack frame in the Armv6-M and Armv7-M processors, but without an active floating-point context (i.e., CONTROL.FPCA $=0$).

Since AAPCS requires that the value of the stack pointer must be double word aligned at the function boundary, the stacking process automatically inserts a padding word to make sure that, if needed, the stack frame is double word aligned. If such a padding operation is carried out, bit 9 of the stack xPSR is set to 1 to indicate the presence of the padding word. Based on this information, the SP pointer can then re-adjust to the original value during an exception return.

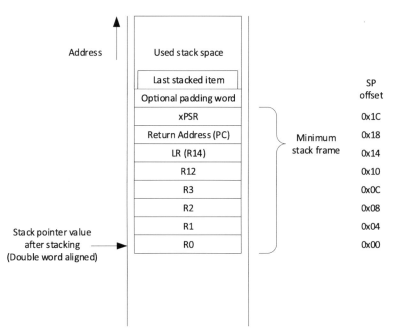

FIG. 8.17 Exception stack frame without an FPU and which is not interrupted from the Secure background code by a Non-secure handler.

If the exception happens when executing Secure code and the interrupt/exception target is in a Non-secure state, then additional registers (callee-saved registers) need to be pushed to the stack, see Fig. 8.18. The extended stack frame also includes an integrity signature (0xFEFA125A or 0xFEFA125B, where a value of 0 in the LSB indicates that the stack frame contains FPU register contents), which is used to prevent the faking of an exception return from the Non-secure to the Secure world. This stack frame layout is new in Armv8-M and is only available if TrustZone is implemented.

Please note, since the additional state context is underneath the previous eight-word stack frame, the stacking of the additional states can, after the previous eight-word state frame has been pushed, be pushed with just an extra stacking step. In fact, stacking of the additional state context can, in certain combinations of an exception event sequence, take place as a completely separate operation. For example, if the processor is running Secure code and receives two interrupts, the first one being Secure and the second Non-secure, the exception stacking operations, as shown in Fig. 8.19, could occur.

The stack frame can get more complex when the FPU is available and is enabled. Assuming that the Secure software did not setup the FPU as Secure (FPCCR.TS==0), and the exception event is not switching the processor from a Secure background task to a Non-secure handler, then the stack frame, as shown in Fig. 8.20, is generated. This situation is identical to the stack frame in Armv7-M processors with a floating-point context (FPU is enabled and is used).

If the processor was executing Secure code (without setting up the FPU as Secure, that is, FPCCR.TS==0) and a Non-secure exception takes place, then the additional state context is

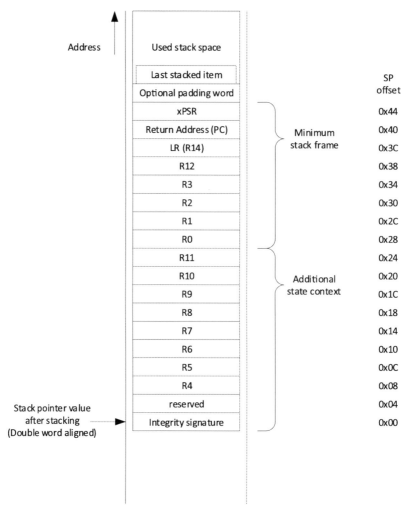

FIG. 8.18   Exception stack frame without an FPU and which is interrupted from Secure background code to the Non-secure handler.

added to the stack frame, as shown in Fig. 8.21. This stack frame layout is new in Armv8-M and is only available if TrustZone is implemented.

And, finally, if the Secure software does need to use the FPU for secure data processing it would need to set FPCCR.TS to 1. On the basis that:

- The processor was executing Secure software and the exception is targeting the Non-secure state,
- The FPU is enabled and is used in the current context (i.e., CONTROL_S.FPCA is 1),

then the maximum size stack frame is used. The stack frame in this scenario would include the additional floating-point context, as shown in Fig. 8.22.

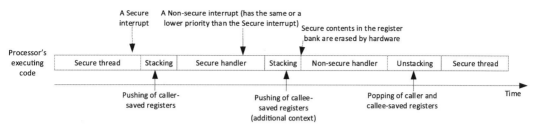

FIG. 8.19 Multistage stacking scenarios.

When the FPCCR.TS is set to 1 and if the processor was executing Secure code and the incoming exception target is in Secure state, the processor will still allocate the stack space for the additional FP (floating-point) context (S16–S31). This is because it is possible for a Non-secure interrupt to take place while the Secure handler is running.

As you can see, the processor might, depending on configuration, need to push a fairly high number of registers to the stack when servicing exceptions/interrupts. The more registers that

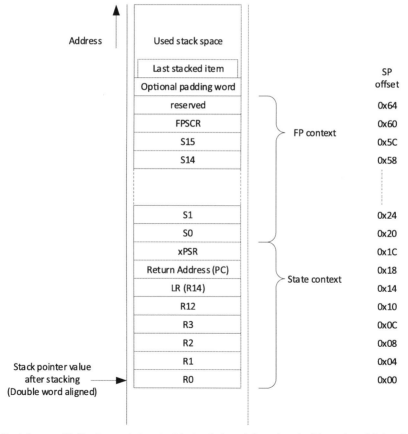

FIG. 8.20 Stack frame with floating-point context (extended stack frame) and without the additional state context.

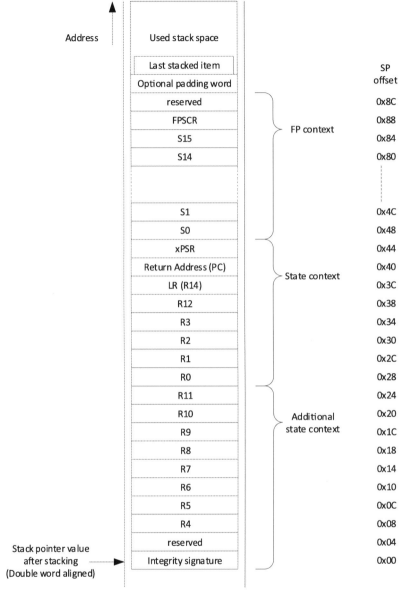

FIG. 8.21 Stack frame with floating-point context (extended stack frame) and with additional state context.

need to be pushed to the stack, the longer the stacking sequence will take. To avoid causing unnecessary delays in interrupt handling, Cortex-M processors with a floating-point unit support a feature called lazy stacking. By default, this feature is enabled. With this feature, although the processor will still allocate stack spaces for the floating-point registers it will not actually take time to push the data into the stack. If the exception/interrupt handler executes a floating-point

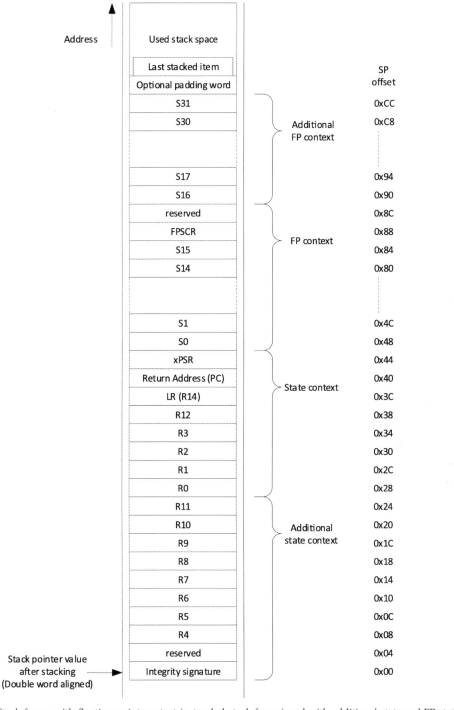

FIG. 8.22 Stack frame with floating-point context (extended stack frame) and with additional state and FP state context.

TABLE 8.13   Stack pointer selection in various situations.

	Processor is in the Secure state		Processor is in the Non-secure state, or TrustZone is not implemented	
	CONTROL_S.SPSEL = 0 (default)	CONTROL_S. SPSEL = 1	CONTROL_NS. SPSEL = 0 (default)	CONTROL_NS. SPSEL = 1
Handler mode	MSP_S	MSP_S	MSP_NS	MSP_NS
Thread mode	MSP_S	PSP_S	MSP_NS	PSP_NS

instruction, this will trigger the lazy stacking which then stalls the pipeline and pushes the floating-point registers into the allocated stack space. If the handler did not use the FPU, the processor will, during the unstacking stage, skip the unstacking of FPU registers. By utilizing the lazy stacking feature, most interrupt/exceptions (i.e., those that do not use the FPU) are, by omitting the saving and restoring of the FPU registers, serviced more quickly.

Further information on lazy stacking can be found in Chapter 14, Section 14.4.

8.9.5 Which stack pointer is used for stacking and unstacking?

The stack pointer used by the interrupted background thread/process is used for stacking and unstacking. This is dependent on the processor's security state, the processor's mode (i.e., whether it is already executing an exception/interrupt handler) and the setting in the CONTROL.SPSEL (this is covered in "CONTROL register" section). The way that the stack pointer is selected is shown in Table 8.13.

Fig. 8.23 shows the selection of the stack pointer for stacking and unstacking in a nested interrupt scenario.

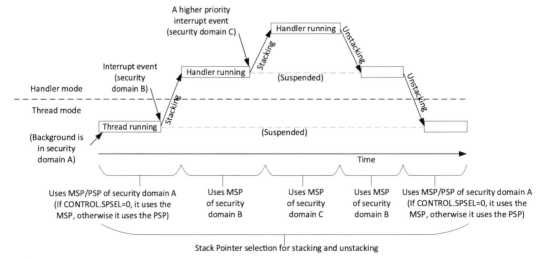

FIG. 8.23   The selection of the stack pointer for stacking and unstacking.

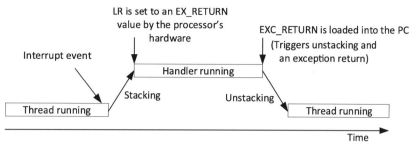

FIG. 8.24 Use of EXC_RETURN to trigger an exception return.

8.10 EXC_RETURN

I mentioned earlier that Cortex-M processors allow interrupt handlers to be written as C functions. In C functions, the function return is normally carried out by loading a return address (which is loaded into the LR when the function call is made) into the PC (Program Counter), for example, by executing a "BX LR" instruction. So, when an interrupt handler executes a return how does the processor know that it is an exception return (which triggers unstacking, rather than a normal function return)? The answer is that Cortex-M processors use a special value called EXC_RETURN (Fig. 8.24) to indicate an exception return when it is loaded into the PC. This is achieved by the use of instructions that updates the PC as shown in Table 8.8.

When the interrupt handler starts, the EXC_RETURN value is generated by hardware and is loaded automatically into the LR. The last step of the interrupt handler loads the EXC_RETURN into the PC, just like a normal return address, which triggers the exception return sequence.

The bit fields inside the EXC_RETURN value is shown in Fig. 8.25.

The bit fields in EXC_RETURN are shown in Table 8.14:

There are many combinations of bit fields and these are shown in Fig. 8.26.

Although Fig. 8.26 does looks a bit complicated it is actually not that hard to follow. The yellow boxes (light gray in print version) are the processor states and the white boxes list the possible values of EXC_RETURN based on one or two conditions. For example, if we assume

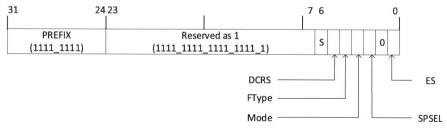

FIG. 8.25 Bit fields in EXC_RETURN.

TABLE 8.14 Bit fields in EXC_RETURN.

Bit	Bit field	Description
6	S	Secure or Non-secure stack (this also indicates the security state of the interrupted program): 0 = use Non-secure stack frame 1 = use Secure stack frame (Always 0 if TrustZone is not implemented)
5	DCRS	Default callee register stacking—indicates whether the default stacking rules apply or whether the callee-saved registers are already on the stack. 0 = Stacking of callee saved registers skipped 1 = Default rules for stacking the callee registers followed (Always 1 if TrustZone is not implemented)
4	FType	Stack Frame type—indicates whether the stack frame is a standard integer only stack frame (i.e., does not contain a floating-point context) or is an extended stack frame (with a floating-point context). 0 = Extended stack frame 1 = Standard (Integer only) stack frame (Always 1 in the Cortex-M23 or processors without an FPU)
3	Mode	Mode—indicates the processor Mode before the preemption 0 = Handler mode 1 = Thread mode
2	SPSEL	Stack pointer selection—The saved copy of SPSEL which was previously in the CONTROL register of the same security domain (i.e., If the exception handler is in Secure state it will hold the previous CONTROL_S.SPSEL.) 0 = Main Stack Pointer 1 = Process Stack Pointer
1	–	Reserved—Always 0
0	ES	Exception Secure—the security domain the exception is taken to 0 = Non-secure 1 = Secure (Always 0 if TrustZone is not implemented)

that the processor is in Non-secure thread mode and running a "bare metal" application (i.e., a software system with no RTOS), the value of the EXC_RETURN in various exception/interrupt events is shown in Fig. 8.27.

If the application deploys an RTOS running in the Non-secure world, then it is very likely that the Non-secure world will be using PSP_NS for its thread. Fig. 8.28 shows a Non-secure thread using PSP_NS being interrupted.

The left hand-side of Fig. 8.26 details several exception transitions where EXC_RETURN. DCRS = 0, which can be caused by one of the following scenarios:

- Scenario 1: The back ground program is Secure, it is interrupted by a Non-secure interrupt and the additional state context information (i.e., callee-save registers) has been pushed to the stack. And then, just before the Non-secure ISR has started, a higher priority Secure

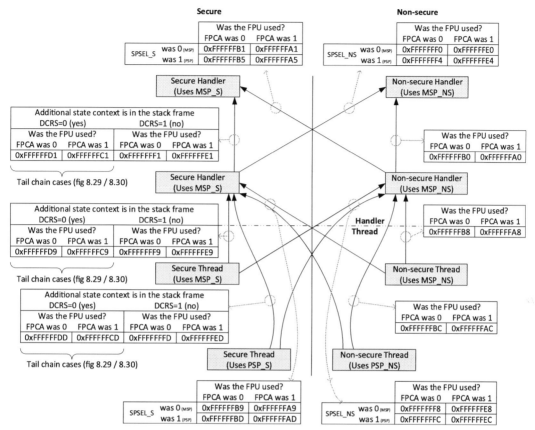

FIG. 8.26 EXC_RETURN value in various exception handling scenarios.

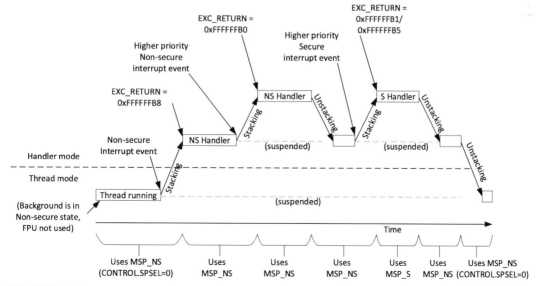

FIG. 8.27 EXC_RETURN example 1—The Non-secure world is using the MSP_NS in thread but is not using the FPU.

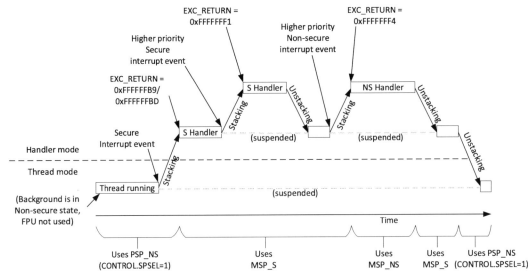

FIG. 8.28   EXC_RETURN example 2—Non-secure world is using the PSP_NS in thread but is not using the FPU.

interrupt takes place and the processor switches to execute the Secure handler first, that is, before the Non-secure interrupt is serviced (see Fig. 8.29).

- Scenario 2: The back ground program is Secure, it is interrupted by a Non-secure interrupt and the additional state context information (i.e., callee-save registers) has been pushed to the stack. And then, during the execution of the Non-secure ISR, a Secure interrupt occurs, which has the same or a lower priority than the priority level of the executing Non-secure interrupt. After the execution of the Non-secure interrupt handler is completed, the processor switches over to execute the pending Secure interrupt handler (see Fig. 8.30).

In the aforementioned scenarios, although both Background and ISR are Secure the stack frame still contains the additional context, which is usually needed when dealing with Non-secure exceptions. Secure handlers can use EXC_RETURN.DCRS to determine whether the additional context is in the stack frame.

Please note, bit fields of EXC_RETURN have been extended when compared to that available in Armv7-M and Armv6-M. In some instances, therefore, source codes will need to be

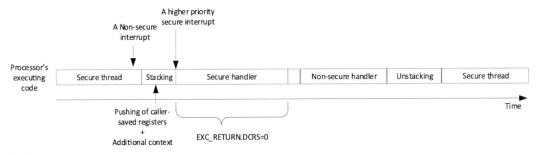

FIG. 8.29   EXC_RETURN.DCRS=0, case #1.

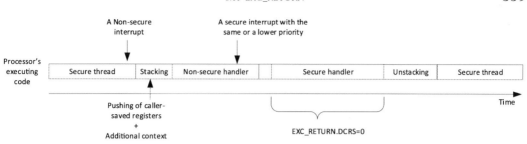

FIG. 8.30 EXC_RETURN.DCRS=0, case #2.

updated to enable them to be used in Armv8-M processors. The areas that source code might contain EXC_RETURN values include:

- RTOS—for example, for starting a task/thread
- Handler redirection code that switches exception handlers to an unprivileged state

In the case of the RTOS, the direct manipulation of the stack frame is often, as shown in Fig. 8.31, used to start a new thread.

As a result of the EXC_RETURN bit field extensions, the RTOS created for Armv7-M/Armv6-M needs to be updated to support Armv8-M processors. This is the case even if the RTOS is being used on a new Armv8-M based microcontroller without the implementation of TrustZone. In addition to the changes for EXC_RETURN update, the RTOS update might also need to include support for stack limit checking (see Chapter 11) and support for the new MPU programmer's model (see Chapter 12).

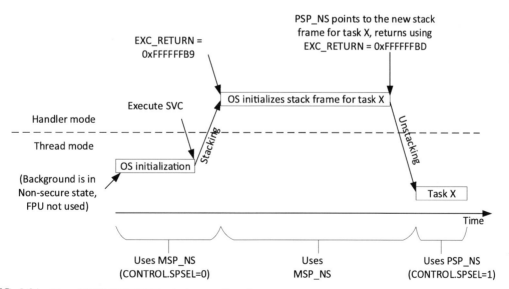

FIG. 8.31 Use of EXC_RETURN to start a new thread.

8.11 Classification of synchronous and asynchronous exceptions

Another way to classify exceptions is basing it on the nature of the timing relationship between the exception response and the code execution that is being interrupted.

- Synchronous exceptions—these are exceptions that must immediately respond to the executed code stream without further code execution in the current thread. Examples of this type of exceptions are:
  - SVCall—The SVC handler must be executed before executing the instructions after the SVC instruction.
  - SecureFault, UsageFault, MemManage fault and synchronous BusFault—An error has occurred in the current thread and should not continue until the fault handling exception has taken place.
- Asynchronous exceptions—This is where the processor is allowed, for a short period of time, to continue current code stream execution before the exception handler starts executing. (The shorter the delay the better for providing a faster interrupt response time.) Examples of this type of exceptions are:
  - Interrupts including the Non-Maskable Interrupt (NMI)
  - SysTick interrupt
  - PendSV exception
  - Asynchronous BusFault—In some processor implementations that contain write buffer(s) in the bus interface, a write operation might be buffered and not take place immediately. At the same time, the processor continues its execution of the subsequent instructions. The delayed write operation might then result in a bus error response which would then be handled as an asynchronous BusFault. (Note: Cortex-M23 and Cortex-M33 processors do not have internal write buffers so asynchronous BusFaults are not applicable to these processors.)

For synchronous exceptions, the exception handler execution usually immediately follows the exception event. However, if another higher priority exception arrives at the same time, one that could preempt the current exception entrance sequence, the processor will service the other higher priority exception first. The deferred synchronous exception is then executed after the higher priority exception handler has completed its task.

In older Arm Cortex-M documentation, an asynchronous BusFault was known as an imprecise BusFault, and a synchronous BusFault was known as a precise BusFault. These classification names were then changed to become synchronous and asynchronous in order to align with the architecture of other Arm Cortex processors.

References

[1] Armv8-M Architecture Reference Manual. https://developer.arm.com/documentation/ddi0553/am/ (Armv8.0-M only version). https://developer.arm.com/documentation/ddi0553/latest/ (latest version including Armv8.1-M). Note: M-profile architecture reference manuals for Armv6-M, Armv7-M, Armv8-M and Armv8.1-M can be found here: https://developer.arm.com/architectures/cpu-architecture/m-profile/docs.

[2] AMBA 5 Advanced High-performance Bus (AHB) Protocol Specification. https://developer.arm.com/documentation/ihi0033/b-b/.

[3] Procedure Call Standard for the Arm Architecture (AAPCS). https://developer.arm.com/documentation/ihi0042/latest/.

Management of exceptions and interrupts

9.1 Overview of exception and interrupt management

9.1.1 Access to exception management functions

Arm® Cortex®-M processors use a combination of memory-mapped registers and special registers for the management of interrupts and system exceptions. These registers reside in various parts of the processor:

- Most management registers for interrupts are in the NVIC.
- System exceptions are managed by registers in the System Control Block (SCB).
- Interrupt masking registers (PRIMASK, FAULTMASK, and BASEPRI) are special registers, and can be accessed by using the MSR and the MRS instructions. (Note: The Cortex-M23 processor does not have FAULTMASK and BASEPRI)

Both the NVIC and SCB registers are in the System Control Space (SCS) address range (0xE000E000 to 0xE000EFFF). If the TrustZone® security extension is implemented, Secure software can also access a Non-secure view of SCS using a SCS Non-secure alias (address range 0xE002E000 to 0xE002EFFF).

To make it easier for software developers to access various interrupt and exception management features, the CMSIS-CORE project provides a range of access functions for Cortex-M processors via the CMSIS-CORE header files. Because these header files are integrated into the device driver libraries by microcontroller vendors, the aforementioned access functions are easily accessible when using these device drivers. Due to the fact that the CMSIS-CORE is supported by all major microcontroller vendors, these access functions can be used with a wide range of Cortex-M based devices.

9.1.2 Basic interrupt management in the CMSIS-CORE

For general application programming, the best practice is to use the CMSIS-CORE access functions for interrupt management. This enables easy migration between a wide range of microcontrollers based on the Arm Cortex-M processors. The most commonly used interrupt control functions are shown in Table 9.1. *Unless specified, all the interrupt management functions that are in the CMSIS-CORE can only be used in a privileged state.*

For the functions in Table 9.1:

- IRQn_Type is an enumeration defined in a device-specific CMSIS header file to identify an individual interrupt/exception. Value of 0 is Interrupt #0 (exception number 16). System exceptions have negative values, as detailed in Table 9.3.
- uint32_t priority is an unsigned integer representing the priority level. The NVIC_SetPriority function automatically shifts the value to the implemented bits in the priority level register (the implemented bits are aligned to the MSB). The Cortex-M23, which has four programmable priority levels, has a valid priority range of 0–3. The Cortex-M33 has a minimum of eight priority levels, thus the minimum valid range is 0–7.
- uint32_t PriorityGroup. This is an unsigned integer with a range of 0 (default) to 7, which is used to separate the bit fields in priority level registers into Group Priority and Subpriority. The definition of PriorityGroup is shown in Table 8.10.
- Please note, the NVIC_EnableIRQ() and NVIC_DisableIRQ() functions are only used to enable or disable interrupts and cannot be used to enable or disable system exceptions.

If priority grouping is used, additional APIs (Table 9.2) are available for encoding and decoding priority level fields (Note: the priority grouping feature is not available for the Cortex-M23 processor or Armv8-M Baseline architecture).

The CMSIS-CORE standardizes handler names for system exceptions and for IRQn_Type enumeration. As shown in Table 9.3, the IRQn_Type uses negative values for system exceptions and positive values for interrupts. This numbering scheme enables interrupts and system exceptions to be easily separated and thus handled efficiently.

A CMSIS-CORE compliant device-specific header file also has a C preprocessing macro called "__NVIC_PRIO_BITS". This macro indicates the number of implemented bits in the priority level registers.

TABLE 9.1 Commonly used CMSIS-CORE functions for basic interrupt control

Function	Usage
void NVIC_EnableIRQ (IRQn_Type IRQn)	Enables an external interrupt
void NVIC_DisableIRQ (IRQn_Type IRQn)	Disables an external interrupt
void NVIC_SetPriority (IRQn_Type IRQn, uint32_t priority)	Sets the priority of an interrupt or a configurable system exception
void __enable_irq(void)	Clears PRIMASK to enable interrupts
void __disable_irq(void)	Sets PRIMASK to disable all interrupts
void NVIC_SetPriorityGrouping(uint32_t PriorityGroup)	Sets priority grouping configuration (unavailable in Armv8-M Baseline)

TABLE 9.2 CMSIS-CORE functions for calculating priority level values when using priority grouping

Function	Usage
uint32_t NVIC_EncodePriority (uint32_t PriorityGroup, uint32_t PreemptPriority, uint32_t SubPriority)	Returns a priority value which is based on the PriorityGroup setting and the values of both the Group Priority and the Sub-Priority.
void NVIC_DecodePriority (uint32_t Priority, uint32_t PriorityGroup, uint32_t* const pPreemptPriority, uint32_t* const pSubPriority)	Decodes a priority level value into both the Group Priority and the SubPriority and is based on the PriorityGroup setting.

TABLE 9.3 CMSIS-CORE exception definition

Exception number	Exception type	CMSIS-CORE enumeration (IRQn)	CMSIS-CORE enumeration value	Exception handler name
1	Reset	–	–	Reset_Handler
2	NMI	NonMaskableInt_IRQn	−14	NMI_Handler
3	HardFault	HardFault_IRQn	−13	HardFault_Handler
4[a]	MemManage Fault[a]	MemoryManagement_IRQn	−12	MemManage_Handler
5[a]	BusFault[a]	BusFault_IRQn	−11	BusFault_Handler
6[a]	Usage Fault[a]	UsageFault_IRQn	−10	UsageFault_Handler
7[a]	SecureFault[a]	SecureFault_IRQn	−9	SecureFault_Handler
11	SVC	SVCall_IRQn	−5	SVC_Handler
12[a]	Debug Monitor[a]	DebugMonitor_IRQn	−4	DebugMon_Handler
14	PendSV	PendSV_IRQn	−2	PendSV_Handler
15	SYSTICK	SysTick_IRQn	−1	SysTick_Handler
16	Interrupt #0	(device specific)	0	(device specific)
17 …	Interrupt #1–#239/479	(device specific)	1–239/479	(device specific)

[a] Not available in Cortex-M23/Armv8-M Baseline.

To set up a peripheral interrupt, the following steps should be taken:

1. Declare an interrupt handler in your program code. The name of the interrupt handler needs to match the handler's name defined in the vector table (you can normally find this in the device-specific startup code).
2. Ensure that the interrupt handler clears the interrupt request at the peripheral. This operation is not required if the peripheral generates an interrupt request in the form of a pulse.

3. Ensure that the software includes the following initialization steps:

* Setting up the interrupt's priority level (default is 0, the highest level for peripheral interrupts). If the peripheral's interrupt priority level needs to be 0, then there is no need to change the priority level.
* Enable the interrupt at the NVIC (e.g., use the NVIC_EnableIRQ function)
* Initialize the peripheral's function
* Enable the interrupt generation at the peripheral (this is device specific)

For the majority of microcontroller applications, these steps are all that is required to enable a peripheral's interrupt. As part of the interrupt's configuration, the priority level of the interrupt might need to be configured—this is supported by the NVIC_SetPriority function. For example, if we assume that the device being used is a Cortex-M33 processor with 16 priority levels (the priority level registers are 4-bit wide), and that we would like to use priority level 0xC0 for the timer0 interrupt, a simple example to set the interrupt up would be:

```
// Set Timer0_IRQn priority level to 0xC0 (4 bit priority)

NVIC_SetPriority(Timer0_IRQn, 0xC); //Shift to 0xC0 by CMSIS function

// Enable Timer 0 interrupt at NVIC

NVIC_EnableIRQ(Timer0_IRQn);

Timer0_initialize(); // Device specific code to initialize timer 0

...

void Timer0_Handler(void)

{

... // timer 0 interrupt processing

... // Clear timer 0 IRQ request (needed for level triggered IRQs)

return;

}
```

To ensure applications work reliably, software developers should make sure that there is enough stack memory for exception handling, otherwise the system could crash if there was a stack overflow. A portion of the stack memory is needed for exception handling; and its size can increase substantially if the application allows multiple levels of nested interrupts and exceptions.

Because exception handlers always use the main stack (i.e., the Main Stack Pointer (MSP) is selected when the processor is in Handler mode), the main stack memory should always contain enough stack space to cater for the worst-case scenario, i.e., the maximum level of nested interrupt/exceptions, with each active handler taking a portion of the main stack memory space. When calculating the stack space, the calculation should include the stack space for use by the handlers plus the space to be used by each level of the stack frame. In most software projects, the main stack size is either part of the project setting or is a parameter in the startup code.

TABLE 9.4 Additional CMSIS-CORE functions for interrupt management (excluding TrustZone related functions)

Function	Usage
uint32_t NVIC_GetEnableIRQ(IRQn_Type IRQn)	Reads back an Interrupt's enable/disable status
uint32_t NVIC_GetPriority(IRQn_Type IRQn)	Reads back the priority level of an interrupt/configurable system exception[a]
void NVIC_SetPendingIRQ(IRQn_Type IRQn)	Sets the pending state of an interrupt
void NVIC_ClearPendingIRQ(IRQn_Type IRQn)	Clears the pending state of an interrupt
uint32_t NVIC_GetPendingIRQ(IRQn_Type IRQn)	Reads back the pending status of an interrupt (returns 0 or 1)
uint32_t NVIC_GetActive(IRQn_Type IRQn)	Reads back the active state of an interrupt (returns 0 or 1)
uint32_t NVIC_GetPriorityGrouping(void)	Reads back the PriorityGrouping value

[a] *Note on the NVIC_GetPriority: this function automatically shifts out the unimplemented bits in the priority level register to make the value aligned to bit 0.*

TABLE 9.5 CMSIS-CORE functions for setting up interrupts as Secure or Non-secure

Function	Usage
uint32_t NVIC_SetTargetState (IRQn_Type IRQn)	Configures the interrupt target state to **Non-secure** and returns the interrupt's target state for checking (0 = Secure, 1 = Non-secure)
uint32_t NVIC_ClearTargetState (IRQn_Type IRQn)	Configures the interrupt target state to **Secure** and returns the interrupt's target state for checking (0 = Secure, 1 = Non-secure)
uint32_t NVIC_GetTargetState (IRQn_Type IRQn)	Reads back the target security state of an interrupt (0 = Secure, 1 = Non-secure)

9.1.3 Additional interrupt management functions in CMSIS-CORE

There are many additional interrupt management functions available in the CMSIS-CORE. They are listed in Table 9.4, and, as previously mentioned, they can only be used in a privileged state.

If the TrustZone security extension is implemented, the Secure privileged software is able to configure and read back the target security domain of each interrupt using the functions listed in Table 9.5.

In addition to accessing the security state of interrupts, Secure software is also able to access the Non-secure view of the NVIC via the interrupt management functions. These are detailed in Table 9.6.

9.1.4 System exception management

In most cases, the management of system exceptions is handled by direct access to registers in the SCB(System Control Block). Information on these registers is covered in Section 9.3.

TABLE 9.6 CMSIS-CORE functions to enable Secure privileged software to access the Non-secure view of the NVIC

Function	Usage
void TZ_NVIC_EnableIRQ_NS (IRQn_Type IRQn)	Enables an external interrupt
void TZ_NVIC_DisableIRQ_NS (IRQn_Type IRQn)	Disables an external interrupt
uint32_t TZ_NVIC_GetEnableIRQ_NS (IRQn_Type IRQn)	Reads back an Interrupt's enable/disable status
void TZ_NVIC_SetPendingIRQ_NS(IRQn_Type IRQn)	Sets the pending state of an interrupt
void TZ_NVIC_ClearPendingIRQ_NS (IRQn_Type IRQn)	Clears the pending state of an interrupt
uint32_t TZ_NVIC_GetPendingIRQ_NS (IRQn_Type IRQn)	Reads back the pending status of an interrupt (returns 0 or 1)
uint32_t TZ_NVIC_GetActive_NS(IRQn_Type IRQn)	Reads back the active state of an interrupt (returns 0 or 1)
void TZ_NVIC_SetPriority_NS (IRQn_Type IRQn, uint32_t priority)	Sets the priority of an interrupt or a configurable system exception
uint32_t TZ_NVIC_GetPriority_NS(IRQn_Type IRQn)	Reads back the priority level of an interrupt/configurable system exception[a]
void TZ_NVIC_SetPriorityGrouping_NS (uint32_t PriorityGroup)	Sets the Non-secure priority grouping configuration (unavailable in Armv8-M Baseline)
uint32_t TZ_NVIC_GetPriorityGrouping_NS (void)	Reads back the Non-secure PriorityGrouping value

[a] *Note on the TZ_NVIC_GetPriority_NS: as for the NVIC_GetPriority, the function automatically shifts out the unimplemented bits in the priority level register to make the value aligned to bit 0.*

9.2 Details of the NVIC registers for interrupt management

9.2.1 Summary

There are a number of registers in the NVIC for interrupt control (exception types 16–495). These registers are located in the address range of the System Control Space (SCS). These registers are listed in Table 9.7.

All these registers, with the exception of the Software Trigger Interrupt Register (STIR), are only accessible at privileged level. The STIR is accessible at privileged level only by default, but can be configured to be accessible at unprivileged level by setting the USERSETMPEND bit in the Configuration and Control Register (Section 10.5.5).

After a system reset, the initial status of the interrupts are as follows:

- All interrupts are disabled (enable bits = 0)
- All interrupts have a priority level of 0 (the highest programmable level)

TABLE 9.7   Summary of the registers in the NVIC for interrupt control

Address	Register	CMSIS-CORE symbol	Function
0xE000E100 to 0xE000E13C	Interrupt Set Enable Registers	NVIC->ISER[0] to NVIC->ISER[15]	Write 1 to set enable
0xE000E180 to 0xE000E1BC	Interrupt Clear Enable Registers	NVIC->ICER[0] to NVIC->ICER[15]	Write 1 to clear enable
0xE000E200 to 0xE000E23C	Interrupt Set Pending Registers	NVIC->ISPR[0] to NVIC->ISPR[15]	Write 1 to set pending status
0xE000E280 to 0xE000E2BC	Interrupt Clear Pending Registers	NVIC->ICPR[0] to NVIC->ICPR[15]	Write 1 to clear pending status
0xE000E300 to 0xE000E33C	Interrupt Active Bit Registers	NVIC->IABR[0] to NVIC->IABR[15]	Active status bits. Read only.
0xE000E380 to 0xE000E3BC	Interrupt Target Non-secure State Registers	NVIC->ITNS[0] to NVIC->ITNS[15]	Write 1 to set an interrupt to Non-secure, clear to 0 to set an interrupt as Secure
0xE000E400 to 0xE000E5EF	Interrupt Priority Registers	NVIC->IPR[0] to NVIC->IPR[495 or 123]	Interrupt Priority Level for each interrupt In Armv8-M Mainline, each IPR register is 8 bits. In Armv8-M Baseline, each IPR register is 32-bit (contains priority levels for four interrupts).
0xE000EF00	Software Trigger Interrupt Register	NVIC->STIR	Writes an interrupt number to set the interrupt's pending status (Armv8-M Mainline only)

- All interrupts pending status are cleared
- All interrupts target the Secure state if the TrustZone security extension is implemented

If an interrupt targets the Secure state, then, from a Non-secure software point of view, all NVIC registers associated with that interrupt are read-as-zero and write is ignored.

Secure software can access the Non-secure view of the NVIC by using the NVIC Non-secure alias address range 0xE002Exxx. The NVIC Non-secure alias is not available to Non-secure software or to the debugger.

9.2.2 Interrupt Enable Registers

The Interrupt Enable register is programmed through two addresses. To set the enable bit, you need to write to the NVIC->ISER[n] register address and, to clear the enable bit, you need to write to the NVIC->ICER[n] register address. By doing this, the enabling or disabling of an interrupt will not affect the enable states of other interrupts. The ISER/ICER registers are 32-bit wide, with each bit representing one interrupt input.

As there are often more than 32 external interrupts in the Cortex-M23 and Cortex-M33 processors, it is likely that each processor will contain more than one ISER and ICER register.

For example, NVIC->ISER[0], NVIC->ISER[1], and so on (Table 9.8). If you only have 32 or fewer interrupt inputs, you will only have one ISER and one ICER. Only the enable bits for interrupts that exist are implemented, e.g., if there are 33 interrupts, only the bit 0 of NVIC-> ISER[1] is implemented.

CMSIS-CORE provides the following functions for accessing Interrupt Enable registers:

void NVIC_EnableIRQ (IRQn_Type IRQn); // Enables an interrupt
void NVIC_DisableIRQ (IRQn_Type IRQn); // Disables an interrupt

9.2.3 Interrupt Set Pending and Clear Pending Registers

If an interrupt takes place but cannot be executed immediately (e.g., because another higher-priority interrupt handler is running), it will be pended. The interrupt-pending status

TABLE 9.8 Interrupt Set Enable Registers (ISER) and Interrupt Clear Enable Registers (ICER)

Address	Name	Type	Reset value	Description
0xE000E100	NVIC->ISER[0]	R/W	0	Enables external interrupts #0–#31. i.e. bit[0] for interrupt #0 (exception #16) bit[1] for interrupt #1 (exception #17) … and so on until bit[31] for interrupt #31 (exception #47) Write 1 to set bit to 1; write 0 has no effect The read value indicates the current status
0xE000E104	NVIC->ISER[1]	R/W	0	Enables external interrupts #32–63 Write 1 to set bit to 1; write 0 has no effect The read value indicates the current status
0xE000E108	NVIC->ISER[2]	R/W	0	Enables external interrupts #64–95 Write 1 to set bit to 1; write 0 has no effect The read value indicates the current status
…	…	…	…	…
0xE000E180	NVIC->ICER[0]	R/W	0	Clears enable for external interrupts #0–#31 bit[0] for interrupt #0 bit[1] for interrupt #1 … and so on until bit[31] for interrupt #31 Write 1 to clear bit to 0; write 0 has no effect The read value indicates the current enable status
0xE000E184	NVIC->ICER[1]	R/W	0	Clears enable for external interrupts #32–#63 Write 1 to clear bit to 0; write 0 has no effect The read value indicates the current enable status
0xE000E188	NVIC->ICER[2]	R/W	0	Clears enable for external interrupts #64–#95 Write 1 to clear bit to 0; write 0 has no effect The read value indicates the current enable status
…	…	…	…	…

is accessible via the Interrupt Set Pending (NVIC->ISPR[*n*]) and Interrupt Clear Pending (NVIC->ICPR[*n*]) registers. Similar to the interrupt-enable registers, the pending status controls, if there are more than 32 external interrupt inputs, will contain more than one register.

Because the values of the pending status registers (Table 9.9) can be changed by software, you can, when necessary, by using software either:

- cancel a current pended exception by writing to the NVIC->ICPR[*n*] register or
- generate a software interrupt by writing to the NVIC->ISPR[*n*] register.

CMSIS-CORE provides the following functions for accessing Interrupt Pending registers:

void NVIC_SetPendingIRQ(IRQn_Type IRQn); // Sets the pending status of an interrupt
void NVIC_ClearPendingIRQ(IRQn_Type IRQn); // Clears the pending status of an interrupt
uint32_t NVIC_GetPendingIRQ(IRQn_Type IRQn); // Reads the pending status of an interrupt

TABLE 9.9 Interrupt Set Pending Registers (ISPR) and Interrupt Clear Pending Registers (ICPR)

Address	Name	Type	Reset value	Description
0xE000E200	NVIC->ISPR[0]	R/W	0	Pending for external interrupts #0–#31 bit[0] for interrupt #0 (exception #16) bit[1] for interrupt #1 (exception #17) … and so on until bit[31] for interrupt #31 (exception #47) Write 1 to set bit to 1; write 0 has no effect The read value indicates the current status
0xE000E204	NVIC->ISPR[1]	R/W	0	Pending for external interrupts #32–#63 Write 1 to set bit to 1; write 0 has no effect The read value indicates the current status
0xE000E208	NVIC->ISPR[2]	R/W	0	Pending for external interrupts #64–#95 Write 1 to set bit to 1; write 0 has no effect The read value indicates the current status
…	…	…	…	…
0xE000E280	NVIC->ICPR[0]	R/W	0	Clears pending for external interrupts #0–#31 bit[0] for interrupt #0 (exception #16) bit[1] for interrupt #1 (exception #17) … and so on until bit[31] for interrupt #31 (exception #47) Write 1 to clear bit to 0; write 0 has no effect The read value indicates the current pending status
0xE000E284	NVIC->ICPR[1]	R/W	0	Clears pending for external interrupts #32–#63 Write 1 to clear bit to 0; write 0 has no effect The read value indicates the current pending status
0xE000E288	NVIC->ICPR[2]	R/W	0	Clears pending for external interrupts #64–#95 Write 1 to clear bit to 0; write 0 has no effect The read value indicates the current pending status
…	…	…	…	…

9.2.4 Active status

Each external interrupt has an active status bit. When the processor executes the interrupt handler, the corresponding active status bit is set to 1 and is cleared when the interrupt return is executed. However, during an Interrupt Service Routine (ISR) execution, another higher-priority interrupt might occur and cause preemption. This results in a nested exception/interrupt scenario, and in such a scenario, the previous servicing interrupt would still be defined as active.

During nested exception/interrupt handling, the IPSR (Interrupt Program Status Register, see "Program Status Register (PSR)" section in Section 4.2.2.3) shows the current executing exception service (i.e., the exception number of the higher-priority interrupt). Although the IPSR cannot be used to identify whether an interrupt is active, the Interrupt Active Status Register addresses this issue by allowing software and debug tools to detect whether an interrupt/exception is active. This information is valid even if it has been preempted by another higher priority exception.

Each Interrupt Active Status Register contains the active status of 32 interrupts. If there are more than 32 external interrupts, there will be more than one active register. The active status registers for external interrupts are read-only (Table 9.10).

CMSIS-CORE provides the following function for accessing the Interrupt Active status registers:

uint32_t NVIC_GetActive(IRQn_Type IRQn); // Reads the active status of an interrupt

9.2.5 Interrupt Target Non-secure Register(s)

When the TrustZone security extension is implemented, Interrupt Target Non-secure Register(s) (NVIC->ITNS[n], Table 9.11) are also implemented to allow Secure privileged software to assign each interrupt as Secure or Non-secure. Similar to other interrupt management registers, the ITNS register will, if there are more than 32 external interrupt inputs, contain more than one register. For each bit, 0 means the targeted security domain is Secure (which is the default), and 1 is Non-secure.

CMSIS-CORE provides the following functions for accessing the Interrupt Active status registers:

TABLE 9.10   Interrupt Active Status Registers

Address	Name	Type	Reset value	Description
0xE000E300	NVIC->IABR[0]	R	0	Active status for external interrupts #0–#31 bit[0] for interrupt #0 bit[1] for interrupt #1 … and so on until bit[31] for interrupt #31
0xE000E304	NVIC->IABR[1]	R	0	Active status for external interrupts #32–#63
…	—	—	—	—

TABLE 9.11 Interrupt Target Non-secure Registers (ITNS)

Address	Name	Type	Reset value	Description
0xE000E380	NVIC->ITNS[0]	R/W	0	Defines the target security domain for external interrupts #0–#31 bit[0] for interrupt #0 bit[1] for interrupt #1 … and so on until bit[31] for interrupt #31
0xE000E384	NVIC->ITNS[1]	R/W	0	Defines the target security domain for external interrupts #32–#63
…	—	—	—	—

```
uint32_t NVIC_SetTargetState(IRQn_Type IRQn); // Sets interrupt as Non-secure
uint32_t NVIC_ClearTargetState(IRQn_Type IRQn); // Sets interrupt as Secure
uint32_t NVIC_GetTargetState(IRQn_Type IRQn); // Reads the target security state
```

The ITNS registers are only accessible in Secure privileged state; there is no NVIC Non-secure alias address for the ITNS registers. If the TrustZone security extension is not implemented, then the ITNS registers are not implemented.

9.2.6 Priority level

Each interrupt has an associated priority-level register, which is 2-bit wide in the Cortex-M23 processor and from 3- to 8-bit wide in the Cortex-M33 processor. As described in Section 8.5.2, for Armv8-M Mainline (e.g., the Cortex-M33 processor) each priority register can be further divided: into group priority level and into a subpriority level, which is based on the priority group settings. In Armv8-M Mainline, the priority-level registers are accessible using byte, half word, or word size transfers. In Armv8-M Baseline, the priority-level registers are accessible using word size transfers only. The number of priority-level registers depends on the number of external interrupts that the chip contains (Table 9.12).

CMSIS-CORE provides the following functions for accessing Interrupt Priority Level registers:

```
void NVIC_SetPriority(IRQn_Type IRQn, uint32_t priority); // Sets the priority level of an
IRQ/ exception
uint32_t NVIC_GetPriority(IRQn_Type IRQn); // Obtains the priority level of an interrupt
or exception
```

When you need to determine the implemented width of the interrupt priority level registers, or the number of priority levels available in the NVIC, you can use the "__NVIC_PRIO_BITS" C preprocessing macro in the CMSIS-CORE header file provided by your microcontroller vendor. Alternatively, you can write 0xFF to one of the Interrupt Priority Level Registers and read back to check how many bits are set. If you are using a device that has eight levels of interrupt priority levels (3 bits), then the read back value is 0xE0.

TABLE 9.12   Interrupt Priority Level Registers

Address	Name	Type	Reset value	Description
0xE000E400	NVIC->IPR[0]	R/W	0 (8 bits in the Cortex-M33, 32 bits in the Cortex-M23)	Cortex-M33: Priority-level external interrupt #0 Cortex-M23: Priority-level external interrupt #3(bits [31:24]), #2, #1 and #0(bits [7:0])
0xE000E401(Cortex-M33) or 0xE000E404 (Cortex-M23)	NVIC->IPR[1]	R/W	0 (8 bits in the Cortex-M33, 32 bits in the Cortex-M23)	Cortex-M33: Priority-level external interrupt #1 Cortex-M23: Priority-level external interrupt #7(bits [31:24]), #6, #5 and #4(bits [7:0])
...	–	–	–	–
0xE000E41F (Cortex-M33) or 0xE000E47C (Cortex-M23)	NVIC->IPR[31]	R/W	0 (8 bits in the Cortex-M33, 32 bits in the Cortex-M23)	Cortex-M33: Priority-level external interrupt #31 Cortex-M23: Priority-level external interrupt #127(bits [31:24]), #126, #125 and #124(bits [7:0])
...	–	–	–	–

9.2.7 Software Trigger Interrupt Register (Armv8-M mainline only)

As well as using the NVIC->ISPR[*n*] registers, you can, if you are using an Armv8-M Mainline processor such as the Cortex-M33, program the Software Trigger Interrupt Register (NVIC->STIR, Table 9.13) to trigger an interrupt. The Cortex-M23 processor does not support this register.

For example, you can generate interrupt #3 by writing the following code in C:

```
NVIC->STIR = 3; // Triggers IRQ #3
```

Triggering an interrupt using NVIC->STIR has the same effect as using the following CMSIS-CORE function call (which uses NVIC->ISPR[*n*]) in C:

```
NVIC_SetPendingIRQ(Timer0_IRQn); // Triggers IRQ #3
// Assume Timer0_IRQn equals 3
// Timer0_IRQn is an enumeration defined in device specific header
```

Unlike the NVIC->ISPR[*n*], which is only accessible with a privileged access level, you can enable unprivileged program code to trigger a software interrupt using NVIC->STIR. To do this, privileged software needs to set bit 1 (USERSETMPEND) of the Configuration Control

TABLE 9.13   Software Trigger Interrupt Register (0xE000EF00)

Address	Name	Type	Reset value	Description
0xE000EF00	NVIC->STIR	W	–	Writing the interrupt number sets the pending bit of the interrupt. Only bits 8 to 0 are valid.

Register (address 0xE000ED14, Section 10.5.5). By default, the USERSETMPEND bit is 0, which means only privileged code can use NVIC->STIR when the system starts.

Similar to NVIC->ISPR[*n*], NVIC->STIR cannot be used to trigger system exceptions such as NMI, SysTick, etc. The Interrupt Control and State Register (ICSR) in the System Control Block (SCB) is, however, available for such system exception management features (Section 9.3.2).

9.2.8 Interrupt Controller Type Register

The NVIC also has an Interrupt Controller Type Register in address 0xE000E004. This read-only register gives the number of interrupt inputs supported by the NVIC in granularities of 32 (Table 9.14).

In a CMSIS-CORE compliant device driver library, the Interrupt Controller Type register is accessible using SCnSCB->ICTR. (SCnSCB refers to "System Control Registers not in the SCB".) While the Interrupt Controller Type register provides an approximate range of the available interrupts, it does not furnish you with the exact number of interrupts that have been implemented. If such information is needed, you can use the following steps to determine how many interrupts have been implemented:

(1) Set the PRIMASK register (to prevent interrupts from being triggered when undertaking this test)
(2) Calculate $N = (((INTLINESNUM + 1) \times 32) - 1)$
(3) Starting with interrupt number N, set the interrupt enable register bit of this interrupt
(4) Read back the interrupt enable register to determine whether the enable bit has been set
(5) If the enable bit is not set, decrement N (i.e., $N = N - 1$) and then retry steps 3 and 4. If the enable bit is set, then the current interrupt number N is the highest available interrupt number.

It is also possible to apply the same techniques with other interrupt management registers (e.g., the pending status or priority level registers) to determine whether a certain interrupt has been implemented.

9.2.9 NVIC feature enhancements

When comparing the NVIC in the Cortex-M23 and the Cortex-M33 processors with the ones in previous Cortex-M processors there are a few noticeable differences:

- The maximum number of interrupt support has increased.
- TrustZone support has been added, including ITNS (Interrupt Target Non-secure Register) and the NVIC Non-secure alias address range.

TABLE 9.14 Interrupt Controller Type Register (SCnSCB->ICTR, 0xE000E004)

Bits	Name	Type	Reset value	Description
4:0	INTLINESNUM	R (read-only)	–	Number of interrupt inputs in increments of 32 0 = 1 to 32 1 = 33 to 64 …

- All Armv8-M processors, including the Cortex-M23 processor, support the Interrupt Active Status registers and the Interrupt Controller Type Register. These registers are not available in the Armv6-M processors. Because the Interrupt Active Status registers are available on Armv8-M processors, privileged software running on these processors is allowed to dynamically change the priority levels of interrupts (this is not allowed in Armv6-M processors such as the Cortex-M0 and the Cortex-M0+ processors).

9.3 Details of SCB registers for system exception management

9.3.1 Summary

The System Control Block (SCB) contains a collection of registers for:

- System management (including system exceptions).
- Fault handling (further information on this is available in Chapter 13).
- Access management for the Coprocessor and the Arm Custom Instructions feature (further information on this is available in Chapter 15).
- Software to determine the processor's available features using a number of ID registers (this is essential in some applications because of the configurability of the processors).

To make software development easier, the CMSIS-CORE provides a standardized software interface for a range of processor features using a SCB data structure definition. A number of SCB register definitions, those that are related to system exception management, are listed in Table 9.15.

TABLE 9.15   Summary of the SCB registers for system exception management

Address	Register	CMSIS-CORE symbol	Function
0xE000ED04	Interrupt Control and State Register	SCB->ICSR	The control and status of system exceptions
0xE000ED08	Vector Table Offset Register	SCB->VTOR	To enable the vector table to be relocated to other address locations
0xE000ED0C	Application Interrupt/Reset Control Register	SCB->AIRCR	For configuration of priority grouping and for self-reset control
0xE000ED18 to 0xE000ED23	System Handler Priority Registers	SCB->SHP[0] to SCB->SHP[1] or SCB->SHP[11]	For the exception priority setting of system exceptions. In Armv8-M Mainline, each SHP register is 8 bits and there are 12 of them. In Armv8-M Baseline, there are two 32-bit SHP registers (each contains priority levels for four exceptions).
0xE000ED24	System Handle Control and State Register	SCB->SHCSR	For controlling fault exceptions (e.g., enable/disable) and for the status of system exceptions

Software can use "NVIC_SetPriority()" and "NVIC_GetPriority()" to configure/access the priority levels of system exceptions. In addition, the CMSIS-CORE provides a SysTick initialization function for configuring the SysTick timer so that it can generate periodic interrupts.

Because the CMSIS-CORE does not define the APIs for system exception management, in order to manage other system exceptions, software needs to directly access the SCB registers. For example:

- To trigger PendSV/NMI/SysTick exception, software needs to access the ICSR.
- To manage (e.g., to enable) configurable fault exceptions (i.e., BusFault, UsageFault, MemManage Fault, and SecureFault) for the Cortex-M33 processor, software needs to access the SHCSR (Note: These fault exceptions are not available on the Cortex-M23 processor).

Further information on the SCB data structure and on other SCB registers is covered in Section 10.5.

9.3.2 Interrupt Control and State Register (SCB->ICSR)

The ICSR register is used by application code to:

- Set and clear the pending status of system exceptions, including SysTick, PendSV, and NMI.
- Determine the current executing exception/interrupt number by reading VECTACTIVE.
- Configure the security state of the SysTick timer in a Cortex-M23 device—but only when TrustZone has been implemented and when the device has just the one SystTick timer.

The ICSR, in addition to being used for software purposes, is also be used by the debugger to determine the processor's interrupt/exception status. The VECTACTIVE field in the SCB->ICSR is equivalent to the IPSR and is easily accessed by a debugger. The bit fields of the ICSR are listed in Table 9.16.

In this register, a fair number of the bit fields are for use by the debugger to determine the system's exception status. In many applications, only the system exception's pending bits and STTNS are used by the software.

Please note, due to the addition of the STTNS bit field in Armv8-M, when migrating Secure software from Armv6-M and Armv7-M Cortex-M processors to the Cortex-M23 processor, additional care needs to be taken to prevent the accidental changing of the STTNS bit field.

9.3.3 System Handler Priority Registers (SCB->SHP[n])

Some of the priority levels of system exceptions are programmable. The programmable level registers for system exceptions have the same width as the interrupt priority level registers. Since the System Handler Priority Registers are byte addressable in Armv8-M Mainline, and are restricted to word size access in Armv8-M Baseline, the CMSIS-CORE header files for the Cortex-M23 and Cortex-M33 processors define these registers in different ways. And this is as follows:

TABLE 9.16   Interrupt Control and State Register (SCB->ICSR, 0xE000ED04)

Bit	Name	Type	Reset value	Description
31	NMIPENDSET	R/W	0	Write 1 to pend the NMI. The read value indicates the NMI's pending status. If AIRCR.BFHFNMINS==0, this bit is read-as-zero and write is ignored from the Non-secure world
30	NMIPENDCLR	W	0	Write 1 to clear the NMI's pending status. Read as zero. If AIRCR.BFHFNMINS==0, this bit is read-as-zero, and write is ignored from the Non-secure world
29	Reserved	–	0	reserved
28	PENDSVSET	R/W	0	Write 1 to pend system call (PendSV). The read value indicates the pending status. This bit is banked between security states.
27	PENDSVCLR	W	0	Write 1 to clear the PendSV's pending status. This bit is banked between security states.
26	PENDSTSET	R/W	0	Write 1 to pend the SYSTICK exception The read value indicates the pending status. If two SysTick's are implemented, this bit is banked between security states.
25	PENDSTCLR	W	0	Write 1 to clear the SYSTICK pending status If two SysTick's are implemented, this bit is banked between security states.
24	STTNS	R/W	0	SysTick targets Non-secure. Available on the Cortex-M23 processor if only one SysTick has been implemented. Secure access only. If set to 1, the SysTick is allocated to the Non-secure world.
23	ISRPREEMPT	R	0	Indicates that a pending interrupt is going to be active in the next step (for single-stepping during debugging) Not available in Armv8-M Baseline.
22	ISRPENDING	R	0	External interrupt pending (excludes system exceptions, such as NMI and fault exceptions) Not available in Armv8-M Baseline.
21	Reserved	–	0	Reserved
20:12	VECTPENDING	R	0	Pending ISR number
11	RETTOBASE	R	0	Sets to 1 when the following conditions are met: • the processor is running an exception handler, and • there are no other pending exceptions. If this bit is 1 and when there is an interrupt return, the processor will return to Thread level. This bit is not available in Armv8-M Baseline
10:0	Reserved	–	0	Reserved
8:0	VECTACTIVE	R	0	The exception type of the current running interrupt service routine

For Armv8-M Baseline (the Cortex-M23 processor):

- Only the priority levels for SVC, PendSV, and SysTick exceptions are programmable.
- The SCB data structure defined SHPR (Fig. 9.1) is an array with two 32-bit unsigned integers. Some of the bytes in those words are not used and are tied to 0.
- The priority level bit fields are 8-bit wide, but only the two most significant bits are implemented. The remaining bits are always 0.

For Armv8-M Mainline (e.g., the Cortex-M33 processor):

- Priority levels for SVC, PendSV, and SysTick, fault exceptions and the Debug Monitor exception are programmable.
- The SCB data structure defined SHPR (Fig. 9.2) is an array with twelve 8-bit unsigned integers. Some of the bytes are not used and are tied to 0.
- The priority level bit fields are 8-bit wide, with configurable number of implemented bits (ranging from 3 to 8). The unimplemented bits are always 0.

In both Armv8-M Baseline and Mainline, some system exception priority levels are banked between Secure and Non-secure state when the TrustZone security extension is implemented (Table 9.17).

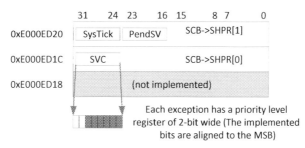

FIG. 9.1   SHPR (System Handler Priority Registers) in the CMSIS-CORE for system exception priority level control in the Cortex-M23 processor.

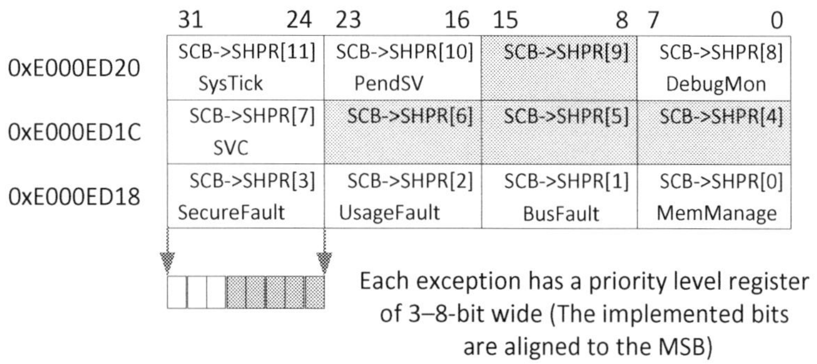

FIG. 9.2   SHPR (System Handler Priority Registers) in the CMSIS-CORE for system exception priority level control in the Cortex-M33 processor.

TABLE 9.17   Banking of priority level registers for system exceptions

Exception number	System exception	Is the priority level register banked?
15	SysTick	Priority level for the SysTick is banked between security states if two SysTick timers are implemented.
14	PendSV	Priority level for the PendSV is banked between security states
12	Debug Monitor	Priority level for the Debug Monitor is not banked between security states
11	SVC	Priority level for the SVC is banked between security states
7	SecureFault	Priority level for the SecureFault is not banked because it is only available in the Secure state.
6	UsageFault	Priority level for the UsageFault is banked between security states.
5	BusFault	Priority level for the BusFault is not banked between security states
4	MemManage Fault	Priority level for the MemManage Fault is banked between security states

Due to differences in the way the system exception priority registers are defined in the CMSIS-CORE between Armv8-M Mainline and Baseline, care must be taken when migrating software between these architecture subprofiles. If the software directly accesses SCB->SHPR [n], it must be modified when ported to another Armv8-M architecture subprofile to ensure it works correctly. To avoid having to modify the software, it is recommended that the portable "NVIC_SetPriority" and "NVIC_GetPriority" functions from the CMSIS-CORE are used for adjusting or accessing the priority level of the system exceptions.

9.3.4 Application Interrupt and Reset Control Register (SCB->AIRCR)

The AIRCR register (Table 9.18) is used for:

- Controlling priority grouping in exception/interrupt priority management.
- Providing information about the Endianness of the system (can be used by software as well as the debugger).
- Providing a self-reset feature.

The priority grouping feature is covered in Section 8.5.2. In most cases, the PRIGROUP field can be accessed by using CMSIS-CORE functions "NVIC_SetPriorityGrouping" and "NVIC_GetPriorityGrouping".

SYSRESETREQ (and SYSRESETREQS) is used for software-generated reset and is used by the debugger to reset a hardware target that is under development. Further information on this topic is covered in Chapter 10, Section 10.5.3.

Please note, there are some differences between the AIRCR in Armv8-M and the same registers in the architectures of Armv6-M and Armv7-M. For example:

TABLE 9.18 Application Interrupt and Reset Control Register (SCB->AIRCR, 0xE000ED0C)

Bits	Name	Type	Reset value	Description
31:16	VECTKEY	R/W	–	Vector key: Value 0x05FA must be written to this bit field when writing to the AIRCR register, otherwise the write will be ignored. The read-back value of this bit field is 0xFA05.
15	ENDIANNESS	R	–	Indicates endianness for data: 1 for big endian (BE8) and 0 for little endian. This can only be changed at reset.
14	PRIS	R/W	0	Prioritize Secure exceptions. Set this bit to 1 to deprioritize Non-secure exceptions. See Section 8.5.3 for further information. This bit is only available when the TrustZone security extension is implemented. It cannot be accessed by Non-secure software.
13	BFHFNMINS	R/W	0	BusFault, HardFault, and NMI Non-secure enable. When this bit is set to 1, these exceptions target the Non-secure state. Do not set to 1 if the Secure code is used. See Section 8.8 for further information. This bit is only available only when the TrustZone security extension is implemented. It cannot be accessed by Non-secure software.
12:11	Reserved	–	0	Reserved
10:8	PRIGROUP	R/W	0	Priority grouping (For further information, refer to Section 8.5.2). Not available on Cortex-M23 (Armv8-M Baseline).
7:4	Reserved	–	0	Reserved
3	SYSRESETREQS	R/W	0	System reset request Secure only. When this bit is set to 1, Non-secure software cannot trigger a system reset using SYSRESETREQ. This bit only affects software generated resets and does not affect a debugger's access to the SYSRESETREQ feature.
2	SYSRESETREQ	W	–	System Reset Request. Requests the chip's control logic to generate a reset.
1	VECTCLRACTIVE	W	–	Clears all active state information for exceptions; typically used when debugging to allow the system to recover from a system error (Note: Reset is a safer option)
0	Reserved	–	0	Reserved

- If TrustZone is implemented, there are new bit fields that are available to the Secure software. These new bit fields include SYSRESETREQS (for managing the accessibility of the self-reset feature), PRIS (for prioritizing Secure exceptions), and BFHFNMINS (for defining the target security states for BusFault, HardFault, and the NMI exceptions).
- The VECTRESET bit in the AIRCR of Armv7-M which generates the processor only reset has been removed. This bit was available in the Cortex-M3 and Cortex-M4 processors. Since this bit was reserved for debugger use, the removal of this bit does not require changes to the software (Note: software should be using SYSRESETREQ for reset generation rather than using VECTRESET. This is because the reset of just the processor without resetting the peripherals could, in some applications, cause a problem).

9.3.5 System Handler Control and State Register (SCB->SHCSR)

With Armv8-M Mainline, configurable fault exceptions (including UsageFault, Memory management (MemManage) faults, BusFault, and SecureFault exceptions) can be enabled by writing to the enable bits in the System Handler Control and State Register (SHCSR, 0xE000ED24). The pending status of faults and the active status of most of the system exceptions are also available in this register (Table 9.19).

TABLE 9.19 System Handler Control and State Register (SCB->SHCSR, 0xE000ED24)

Bit	Name	Type	Reset value	Description
21	HARDFAULTPENDED	R/W	0	HardFault exception pended: HardFault exception was triggered but was preempted by a higher-priority exception (e.g., NMI) This bit is banked between security states. If AIRCR.BFHFNMINS is 0, this bit is not accessible in the Non-secure world.
20	SECUREFAULTPENDED	R/W	0	SecureFault pended: SecureFault exception was triggered but was preempted by a higher-priority exception This bit is not accessible in the Non-secure world. This bit is not available in the Cortex-M23.
19	SECUREFAULTENA	R/W	0	SecureFault exception enable This bit is not available if TrustZone has not been implemented and is not available in the Cortex-M23.
18	USGFAULTENA	R/W	0	UsageFault exception enable This bit is banked between security states. This bit is not available in the Cortex-M23.
17	BUSFAULTENA	R/W	0	BusFault exception enable If AIRCR.BFHFNMINS is 0, this bit is not accessible in the Non-secure world. This bit is not available in the Cortex-M23.
16	MEMFAULTENA	R/W	0	Memory management exception enable. This bit is banked between security states. This bit is not available in the Cortex-M23.
15	SVCALLPENDED	R/W	0	SVC pended: The SVCall was triggered but was preempted by a higher-priority exception This bit is banked between security states.
14	BUSFAULTPENDED	R/W	0	BusFault pended: The BusFault exception was triggered but was preempted by a higher-priority exception This bit is not available in the Cortex-M23.
13	MEMFAULTPENDED	R/W	0	Memory management fault pended: The memory management fault was triggered but was preempted by a higher-priority exception. This bit is banked between security states. This bit is not available in the Cortex-M23.

TABLE 9.19 System Handler Control and State Register (SCB->SHCSR, 0xE000ED24)—cont'd

Bit	Name	Type	Reset value	Description
12	USGFAULTPENDED	R/W	0	Usage fault pended: The UsageFault was triggered but was preempted by a higher-priority exception. This bit is banked between security states. This bit is not available in the Cortex-M23.
11	SYSTICKACT	R/W	0	Reads as 1 if the SYSTICK exception is active. If two SysTick timers are implemented, this bit is banked between security states.
10	PENDSVACT	R/W	0	Reads as 1 if the PendSV exception is active This bit is banked between security states.
9	Reserved	–	0	Reserved
8	MONITORACT	R/W	0	Reads as 1 if the Debug monitor exception is active. This bit is not available in the Cortex-M23.
7	SVCALLACT	R/W	0	Reads as 1 if the SVCall exception is active. This bit is banked between security states.
6	Reserved	–	0	Reserved
5	NMIACT	R/W	0	Reads as 1 if the NMI exception is active. If AIRCR.BFHFNMINS is 0, this bit is not accessible in the Non-secure world. Please refer to the Armv8-M architecture reference manual [1] for additional "write" restrictions.
4	SECUREFAULTACT	R/W	0	Reads as 1 if the SecureFault exception is active. This bit is not available in the Cortex-M23 and is not accessible from the Non-secure world
3	USGFAULTACT	R/W	0	Reads as 1 if the UsageFault exception is active. This bit is not available in the Cortex-M23.
2	HARDFAULTACT	R/W	0	Reads as 1 if the HardFault exception is active. This bit is banked between security states. Please refer to the Armv8-M architecture reference manual [1] for additional "write" restrictions
1	BUSFAULTACT	R/W	0	Reads as 1 if the BusFault exception is active. If AIRCR.BFHFNMINS is 0, this bit is not accessible in the Non-secure world. This bit is not available in the Cortex-M23.
0	MEMFAULTACT	R/W	0	Reads as 1 if the memory management fault is Active. This bit is banked between security states. This bit is not available in the Cortex-M23.

Because the Armv8-M Baseline processor, does not have these configurable fault exceptions, many bit fields in this register are not, therefore, available in the Cortex-M23 processor.

In most instances, this register is used by application code for enabling configurable fault handlers (i.e., MemManage Fault, BusFault, UsageFault, and SecureFault).

Important: Be careful when writing to this register; make sure that the active status bits of the system exceptions (bits 0–11) are not accidentally changed. For example, when enabling the BusFault exception, you could use the following read-modify-write operation:

```
SCB->SHCSR |= 1<<17; // Enable Bus Fault exception
```

Otherwise, if a single write operation is used (i.e., not a read-modify-write), the active state of a system exception could accidentally be cleared. This would result in a fault exception being generated when the active system exception handler executed an exception exit.

9.4 Details of special registers for exception or interrupt masking

9.4.1 Overview of interrupt masking registers

An overview of interrupt masking registers can be found in Chapter 4, "Interrupt Masking Registers" section (see Section 4.2.2.3). Interrupt masking registers can be used as follows:

- **PRIMASK**—For general disabling of interrupts and exceptions, e.g., to enable critical regions in the code to be executed without getting interrupted.
- **FAULTMASK**—Can be used by fault exception handlers to suppress the triggering of further faults during fault handling (Note: only some types of faults can be suppressed). This is not available in the Cortex-M23 processor/Armv8-M Baseline.
- **BASEPRI**—For general disabling of interrupts and exceptions based on priority levels. For some OS operations, it is desirable to block some exceptions for a brief period of time while, at the same time, still allowing certain high priority interrupts to be serviced. This is not available in the Cortex-M23 processor/Armv8-M Baseline.

When TrustZone is implemented, these interrupt masking registers are banked between security states. As you would expect, the Secure interrupt masking registers cannot be accessed from the Non-secure world. The effect of each of the interrupt masking registers on the processor's effective priority level means that these registers can mask both Secure and Non-secure interrupts/exceptions.

Please note, the masked priority levels of the Non-secure PRIMARK_NS, FAULTMASK_NS, and BASEPRI_NS (is) are affected by the PRIS (Prioritize Secure Exceptions) control bit in the Application Handler Control and State Register (AIRCR.PRIS). For example, when PRIMASK_NS is set, the effective masked priority level is 0x80, meaning that Secure interrupts/exceptions with a priority range of 0 to 0x7F can still take place.

The masking registers are accessible in privileged level only. To access these registers, MRS, MSR, and CPS (Change Processor State) instructions should be used. Instead of using assembly instructions, when writing software in C/C++ you can instead use core register access functions provided in the CMSIS-CORE header files. These functions provide access to the interrupt masking registers (Table 9.20).

TABLE 9.20   Interrupt masking registers access functions in the CMSIS-CORE

Function	Usage
void __set_PRIMASK(uint32_t priMask)	Sets the PRIMASK register
uint32_t __get_PRIMASK(void)	Reads the PRIMASK register
void __set_FAULTMASK(uint32_t priMask)	Sets the FAULTMASK register
uint32_t __get_FAULTMASK(void)	Reads the FAULTMASK register
void __set_BASEPRI(uint32_t priMask)	Sets the BASEPRI register
uint32_t __get_BASEPRI(void)	Reads the BASEPRI register
void __set_BASEPRI_MAX(uint32_t priMask)	Sets the BASEPRI register using the BASEPRI_MAX symbol

TABLE 9.21   Access functions in the CMSIS-CORE for Secure software to access Non-secure Interrupt masking registers

Function	Usage
void __TZ_set_PRIMASK_NS(uint32_t priMask)	Sets the PRIMASK_NS register
uint32_t __TZ_get_PRIMASK_NS(void)	Reads the PRIMASK_NS register
void __TZ_set_FAULTMASK_NS(uint32_t priMask)	Sets the FAULTMASK_NS register
uint32_t __TZ_get_FAULTMASK_NS(void)	Reads the FAULTMASK_NS register
void __TZ_set_BASEPRI_NS(uint32_t priMask)	Sets the BASEPRI_NS register
uint32_t __TZ_get_BASEPRI_NS(void)	Reads the BASEPRI_NS register

If TrustZone is implemented, additional access functions (Table 9.21) are available to allow Secure privileged software to access Non-secure interrupt masking registers:

When using interrupt masking registers when writing software, instead of just setting an interrupt masking register before entering the critical code and clearing the register afterward, it is often necessary to use a read-modify-write sequence. When this is the case, it would be necessary to read the current status of the interrupt masking register before setting it. The critical code would then need to be executed and, after the critical code has been executed, the original value of the interrupt masking register would then need to be restored. For example:

```
void foo(void)

{

    ...

    uint32_t prev_PRIMASK;
    ...

    prev_PRIMASK = __get_PRIMASK(); // Saves PRIMASK before changing it

    __set_PRIMASK(1); // Sets PRIMASK to disable interrupts
```

```
... // critical code

__set_PRIMASK(prev_PRIMASK);//Restores PRIMASK to its original value

...

}
```

In the above code example, the arrangement of saving an interrupt masking register and then restoring it prevents the accidental clearance of the interrupt masking register (i.e., if the interrupt masking register was already set when the function "foo" in the above code was called).

9.4.2 PRIMASK

For many applications, you might need to temporarily disable all of the peripheral interrupts in order to carry out a timing-critical task. You can use the PRIMASK register (Table 9.22) for this purpose. The PRIMASK register is only accessible in privileged state.

The PRIMASK register is used to disable all exceptions except the NMI and HardFault (it sets the effective priority level to 0x0). If the AIRCR.PRIS is to 1, the Non-secure PRIMASK is be used to block

- all Non-secure interrupts with priority levels 0x00 to 0xFF (an effective level of 0x80 to 0xFF when viewing from the Secure world), and
- Secure interrupts with priority levels 0x80 to 0xFF.

In C programming, the following functions provided in the CMSIS-CORE to set and clear PRIMASK are:

```
void __enable_irq(); // Clears PRIMASK
void __disable_irq(); // Sets PRIMASK
void __set_PRIMASK(uint32_t priMask); // Sets PRIMASK to value
uint32_t __get_PRIMASK(void); // Reads the PRIMASK value
```

TABLE 9.22   PRIMASK registers

Interrupt masking register	Width (bits)	Description
PRIMASK_S (Secure PRIMASK)	1	When set to 1, it sets the current priority level to 0. i.e., All configurable exceptions (level 0 to 0xFF) are masked. NMI and HardFault can still be invoked.
PRIMASK_NS (Non-secure PRIMASK)	1	When set to 1 and the AIRCR.PRIS is 0, it sets the current priority level to 0, i.e., all configurable exceptions (level 0 to 0xFF) are masked. NMI and HardFault can still be invoked. When set to 1 and the AIRCR.PRIS is 1, it sets the current priority level to 0x80, i.e., all configurable exceptions in the Non-secure world are masked. NMI, HardFault, and Secure exceptions with a priority level of 0x0 to 0x7F can still be invoked.

In assembly language programming, the value of the PRIMASK register is changed by using the following CPS (Change Processor State) instructions:

```
CPSIE I ; Clears PRIMASK (Enables interrupts)
CPSID I ; Sets PRIMASK (Disables interrupts)
```

The PRIMASK register is also accessed using the MRS and MSR instructions. For example:

```
MOVS R0, #1

MSR PRIMASK, R0 ; Write 1 to PRIMASK to disable all

                ; interrupts
```

and:

```
MOVS R0, #0

MSR PRIMASK, R0 ; Write 0 to PRIMASK to allow interrupts
```

When PRIMASK is set, fault events for configurable fault exceptions (i.e., MemManage, Bus Fault, Usage Fault) could be blocked and, if this is the case, it will trigger an escalation, and lead to a HardFault exception.

9.4.3 FAULTMASK

In terms of behavior, FAULTMASK is very similar to PRIMASK, except that it could also block the HardFault handler. The behavior of FAULTMASK is detailed in Table 9.23. It is not available in the Cortex-M23 (Armv8-M Baseline).

FAULTMASK is often used by Configurable Fault Handlers (i.e., MemManage, Bus Fault, Usage Fault) to raise the processor's current priority level. By so doing, this means the aforementioned handlers can:

- Bypass the MPU (Further information on this can be found in Table 12.3, in the description of the HFNMIENA bit in the MPU Control Register)

TABLE 9.23 FAULTMASK registers (not available in the Cortex-M23 processor)

Register	Width (bits)	Description
FAULTMASK_S (Secure FAULTMASK)	1	When set to 1 and if AIRCR.BFHFNMINS is 0, the processor's current priority level is set to −1. When set to 1 and if AIRCR.BFHFNMINS is 1, the processor's current priority level is set to −3.
FAULTMASK_NS (Non-secure FAULTMASK)	1	When set to 1: If AIRCR.BFHFNMINS is 0 and AIRCR.PRIS is 0, the processor's current priority level is set to 0. If AIRCR.BFHFNMINS is 0 and AIRCR.PRIS is 1, the processor's current priority level is set to 0x80. If AIRCR.BFHFNMINS is 1, the processor's current priority level is set to −1.

- Ignore the data Bus Fault for device/memory probing (Further information on this can be found in Section 13.4.5, in the description of the BFHFMIGN bit in the Configuration Control Register)

By using FAULTMASK to raise the current priority level, Configurable Fault Handlers are then able to stop other exceptions or interrupt handlers from being served while an issue is being addressed. Further information about fault handling can be found in Chapter 13.

The FAULTMASK register is only accessible in privileged state. When programming with a CMSIS-CORE compliant driver library, you can use the following CMSIS-CORE functions to set and clear a FAULTMASK:

```
void __enable_fault_irq(void); // Clears FAULTMASK

void __disable_fault_irq(void); // Sets FAULTMASK to disable interrupts

void __set_FAULTMASK(uint32_t faultMask); // Sets FAULTMASK

uint32_t __get_FAULTMASK(void); // Reads FAULTMASK
```

For assembly language users, the current status of the FAULTMASK is changed by using the following CPS instructions:

```
CPSIE F ; Clears FAULTMASK
CPSID F ; Sets FAULTMASK
```

You can also access the FAULTMASK registers by using the MRS and the MSR instructions. The following examples detail the setting and clearing of the FAULTMASK of the current security domain when using the MSR instruction:

```
MOVS R0, #1

MSR FAULTMASK, R0 ; Write 1 to FAULTMASK to disable all interrupts
```

and:

```
MOVS R0, #0

MSR FAULTMASK, R0 ; Write 0 to FAULTMASK to allow interrupts
```

The FAULTMASK register(s) is cleared automatically at an exception return, subject to the following conditions:

- If TrustZone is not implemented, then FAULTMASK_NS is cleared automatically at an exception return, except when the exception is an NMI exception.
- If TrustZone is implemented, then the FAULTMASK of the current exception state (which is indicated by EXC_RETURN.ES) is, except for NMI and HardFault exceptions, cleared to 0.

The characteristic of FAULTMASK being automatically cleared at an exception return provides an interesting application for it: when we want an exception handler to trigger a higher priority handler (except for the NMI), but want this higher priority handler to start AFTER the current handler has completed, we can take the following steps:

1. Set the FAULTMASK to disable all interrupts and exceptions (apart from the NMI exception)
2. Set the pending status of the higher priority interrupt or exception
3. Exit the current handler

Because the pending higher priority exception handler cannot start while FAULTMASK is set, the higher priority exception stays in a pending state until FAULTMASK has cleared; which happens when the lower priority handler finishes. As a result, you can force the higher priority handler to start after the lower priority handler has finished.

9.4.4 BASEPRI

In some instances, you might want to disable interrupts with a priority lower than a certain level. In this case, you could use the BASEPRI register. To do this, simply write the required masking priority level to the BASEPRI register, as detailed in Table 9.24.

The BASEPRI register is not available in the Cortex-M23 processor (Armv8-M Baseline).

For example, if you want to block all exceptions with a priority level equal to or lower than 0x60, you can write the following value to BASEPRI:

```
__set_BASEPRI(0x60); // Disables interrupts with priority

                     // 0x60-0xFF using the CMSIS-CORE function
```

For users of assembly language, the same operation should be written as:

```
MOVS R0, #0x60
MSR BASEPRI, R0 ; Disables interrupts with priority
                ; 0x60-0xFF
```

You can also read back the value of BASEPRI by using the following CMSIS-CORE function:

```
x = __get_BASEPRI(void); // Reads value of BASEPRI
```

or in assembly language:

```
MRS R0, BASEPRI
```

To cancel the masking, just write 0 to the BASEPRI register as follows:

```
__set_BASEPRI(0x0); // Turns off the BASEPRI masking
```

Or in assembly language:

```
MOVS R0, #0x0

MSR  BASEPRI, R0 ; Turns off the BASEPRI masking
```

The BASEPRI register can be accessed by using the BASEPRI_MAX register name. It is actually the same register, but, when you use it with this name, it will give you a conditional write operation. As far as hardware is concerned, BASEPRI and BASEPRI_MAX are the same register, but in the assembler code they use different register name coding. When you use BASEPRI_MAX as a register, the processor hardware automatically compares the current

TABLE 9.24   BASEPRI registers (not available in the Cortex-M23 processor)

Register	Width (bits)	Description
BASEPRI_S (Secure BASEPRI)	3–8 (same width as priority level registers)	When set to 0, BASEPRI_S is disabled. When set to a Nonzero value, • configurable Secure exceptions with the same or with a lower priority levels are blocked. • Non-secure interrupts with an effective priority level that is the same or is lower than BASEPRI_S are blocked. If AIRCR.PRIS is 0, then the effective priority levels of Non-secure interrupts when viewing from the Secure world is the same as the configured priority levels. If AIRCR.PRIS is 1, then the effective priority levels of Non-secure interrupts when viewing from the Secure world is mapped to the lower half of the priority level space—as detailed in Fig. 8.6 in Section 8.5.3.
BASEPRI_NS (Non-secure BASEPRI)	3–8 (same width as priority level registers)	When set to 0, BASEPRI_NS is disabled. When set to a Nonzero value and AIRCR.PRIS is 0, then BASEPRI_NS masks configurable exceptions with the same or with a lower priority level. When set to a Nonzero value and AIRCR.PRIS is 1, then: • Non-secure interrupts with a priority level that is the same or is lower than BASEPRI_NS are blocked (Non-secure interrupts have the same view of priority levels as BASEPRI_NS). • Secure interrupts with priority levels 0 to 0x80 are not blocked. • Secure interrupts with priority levels 0x81 to 0xFF are blocked if the effective priority levels of BASEPRI_NS is the same or is higher than the interrupt's. The mapping of the priority levels is shown in Fig. 8.6 in Section 8.5.3.

value and the new value and only allows the update if it is to be changed to a higher priority level (i.e., a lower value); it cannot be changed to lower priority levels. For example, consider the following instruction sequence:

```
MOVS R0, #0x60

MSR  BASEPRI_MAX, R0 ; Disables interrupts with priority

     ; 0x60, 0x61,..., etc.

MOVS R0, #0xF0

MSR BASEPRI_MAX, R0 ; This write will be ignored because

     ; it has as lower level than 0x60

MOVS R0, #0x40

MSR BASEPRI_MAX, R0 ; This write is allowed and changes the

     ; masking level to 0x40
```

This behavior (conditional write) is very useful when using BASEPRI to protect critical code. Earlier, I mentioned that, when developing software, we would need to consider whether the interrupt masking register might already have been set. With this concept in mind, I have rewritten the example code detailed in Section 9.4.1 to demonstrate the updating of BASEPRI using the BASEPRI_MAX feature. This is shown below:

```
void foo(void)

{

    ...

    uint32_t prev_BASEPRI;

    ...

    prev_BASEPRI = __get_BASEPRI();

    __set_BASEPRI_MAX(0x40); // Conditionally sets BASEPRI to
                             // a higher level

    ... // critical code

    __set_BASEMASK(prev_BASEPRI); // restores BASEPRI to its original value

    ...

}
```

In this example, I have used BASEPRI_MAX to increase the interrupt masking priority level and have used BASEPRI to either lower or remove the interrupt masking level. The BASEPRI/BASEPRI_MAX register cannot be accessed by unprivileged software.

As with other priority-level registers, the formatting of the BASEPRI register is affected by the number of implemented priority register widths. For example, if 3 bits are implemented for priority-level registers, BASEPRI can only be programmed as 0x00, 0x20, 0x40 … 0xC0, and 0xE0.

9.5 Vector table definition in programming

9.5.1 Vector table in startup code

The vector table and the Vector Table Offset Register(s) were introduced in Section 8.6. In a microcontroller software project, the vector table is defined in device-specific startup code. Note: Startup code is often in an assembly format, which is toolchain dependent. Therefore, the software packages from microcontroller vendors often include multiple startup files for different toolchains.

A portion of the vector table that can be found in the startup code of a Cortex-M33 based system using Arm tools (e.g., the Keil Microcontroller Development Kit) is listed below. In this particular example, the code is based on an FPGA prototype of the Cortex-M33 processor:

Fragment of the vector table definition for a Cortex-M33 based system in an example startup file

```
                PRESERVE8
                THUMB

; Vector Table Mapped to Address 0 at Reset

                AREA RESET, DATA, READONLY
                EXPORT __Vectors
                EXPORT __Vectors_End
                EXPORT __Vectors_Size

__Vectors       DCD __initial_sp            ; Top of Stack
                DCD Reset_Handler           ; Reset Handler
                DCD NMI_Handler             ; NMI Handler
                DCD HardFault_Handler       ; Hard Fault Handler
                DCD MemManage_Handler       ; MPU Fault Handler
                DCD BusFault_Handler        ; Bus Fault Handler
                DCD UsageFault_Handler      ; Usage Fault Handler
                DCD SecureFault_Handler     ; Secure Fault Handler
                DCD 0                       ; Reserved
                DCD 0                       ; Reserved
                DCD 0                       ; Reserved
                DCD SVC_Handler             ; SVCall Handler
                DCD DebugMon_Handler        ; Debug Monitor Handler
                DCD 0                       ; Reserved
                DCD PendSV_Handler          ; PendSV Handler
                DCD SysTick_Handler         ; SysTick Handler

                ; Core Interrupts
                DCD NONSEC_WATCHDOG_RESET_Handler ; - 0 NS Watchdog rst hdler
                DCD NONSEC_WATCHDOG_Handler      ; - 1 NS Watchdog Handler
                DCD S32K_TIMER_Handler           ; - 2 S32K Timer Handler
                DCD TIMER0_Handler               ; - 3 TIMER 0 Handler
                DCD TIMER1_Handler               ; - 4 TIMER 1 Handler
                DCD DUALTIMER_Handler            ; - 5 Dual Timer Handler
                ...
```

In the code fragment shown, the vector table is defined with a named region called RESET. Using this name, the linker script can specify where the vector table is placed. A linker script (scatter-loading file) example for the Arm toolchain using the RESET named region is shown below:

Example scatter-loading file

```
LR_IROM1 0x10000000 0x00200000 { ; load : region, size_of_region

ER_IROM1 0x10000000 0x001F0000 { ; Note: load address = execution address

 *.o (RESET, +First)

 *(InRoot$$Sections)

 .ANY (+RO)

 .ANY (+XO)

 }

EXEC_NSCR 0x101F0000 0x10000 {

 *(Veneer$$CMSE)                ; checks with partition.h

 }

RW_IRAM1 0x38000000 0x00200000 { ; Read Write data

 .ANY (+RW +ZI)

 }

 }
```

The third line (i.e., the bolded text) of the example scatter-loading file specifies that the RESET named region is placed as the first item in the internal ROM, starting from address 0x10000000. This address value should match the initial VTOR of the hardware platform being used. If it does not, the startup sequence will fail as the processor will not be able to read the vector table, i.e., the initial value of the MSP (Main Stack Pointer) and the starting address of the reset handler.

Different from previous generations of Cortex-M processors, such as the Cortex-M0/M0+/M3/M4 processors, the initial vector table address on the Cortex-M23 and the Cortex-M33 processors are not fixed to address 0. Because the exact address used is defined by chip designers, you need to either check the documentation supplied, or the project examples provide by the microcontroller vendors, to determine the correct address for the placing of the initial vector table.

9.5.2 Vector table relocation

In some applications, the vector table would need to be relocated to a different address. For example:

- Relocating the vector table from flash to SRAM allows for a faster access speed (this can potentially help reduce interrupt latency).
- Relocating the vector table from flash to SRAM allows for some of the exception vectors to be dynamically changed during the execution of a program.

- When a program image (which has its own vector table) is loaded from an external source to RAM.

To relocate the vector table from flash to SRAM, the following example code can be used:

```
// Macro for word access

#define HW32_REG(ADDRESS) (*((volatile unsigned long *)(ADDRESS)))

#define VTOR_OLD_ADDR     0x00000000

#define VTOR_NEW_ADDR     0x20000000

#define NUM_OF_VECTORS    64

  int i; // loop counter

  ...

  // Copy original vector table to SRAM before programming the VTOR

  for (i=0;i< NUM_OF_VECTORS;i++) {

    // Copy each vector table entry from flash to SRAM

    HW32_REG((VTOR_NEW_ADDR + (i<<2))) = HW32_REG(VTOR_OLD_ADDR + (i<<2));

    }

  __DMB(); // Data Memory Barrier

          // to ensure write to memory is completed

  SCB->VTOR = VTOR_NEW_ADDR; // Sets VTOR to the new vector table location

  __DSB(); // Data Synchronization Barrier

  __ISB(); // Instruction Synchronization Barrier

          // DSB+ISB ensures all subsequence instructions use the new vector table
```

After the vector table is relocated to the SRAM, each of the exception vectors can be easily modified. For example:

```
// Macros for word access

#define HW32_REG(ADDRESS) (*((volatile unsigned long *)(ADDRESS)))

void new_timer0_handler(void); // New Timer 0 Interrupt Handler

unsigned int vect_addr; // address of vector

// Calculates the address of the exception vector

// Assumes that the exception vector to be replaced has an exception number
```

```
// indicated by "Timer0_IRQn"

vect_addr = SCB->VTOR + ((((int) Timer0_IRQn) + 16) << 2);

// Update vector to the address of new_timer0_handler()

HW32_REG(vect_addr) = (unsigned int) new_timer0_handler;

__DSB();    // Executes a Data Synchronization Barrier to ensure the write is

            // completed before subsequent operations
```

When updating exception vectors in the vector table, the bit 0 of the vector must be set to 1 (see Section 8.6). Taking this into account and referring to the above example, because the label of the "`new_timer0_handler`" is recognized as a function address by the compiler, the bit 0 of its vector address value is automatically set to 1. But, if you need to change an exception vector with an address that is not generated by means of a function address, additional address manipulation might be need to force the bit 0 of the address to 1.

The following points need to be considered when relocating the vector table:

- The starting address of the vector table must be a multiple of 128 for the Cortex-M33 and a multiple of 256 for the Cortex-M23. This multiplication requirement is because the starting address of the vector table is indicated by the Vector Table Offset Register (VTOR). And in the VTOR register, some of the lowest bits are not implemented, resulting in the aforementioned 128 bytes/256 bytes alignment requirement. The implemented and unimplemented bits in the VTOR are as follows:
  * In the Cortex-M23 processor, the implemented bits are from bit 8 to bit 31, and the unimplemented bits (i.e., tied to 0) are bits 0–7.
  * In the Cortex-M33 processor, the implemented bits are from bit 7 to bit 31, and the unimplemented bits (i.e., tied to 0) are bits 0–6.

  As a result, the starting address of the vector table must match the alignment characteristic of the address value in the VTOR.
- A data memory barrier would need to be executed after the vector table was updated to ensure that all subsequent operations used the new vector table (Even when an SVC instruction is executed immediately after the vector table was updated, the new vector configurations would still be used).
- A vector table would need to be placed in the address range for the corresponding security domain, i.e., the Secure vector table must be placed in a Secure address and the Non-secure vector table in a Non-secure address.

9.6 Interrupt latency and exception handling optimizations

9.6.1 What is interrupt latency

The term *interrupt latency* refers to the delay that occurs from the start of the interrupt request to the start of the interrupt handler's execution. In Cortex-M23 and Cortex-M33 processors, if the memory system has zero latency, and in the case of the Cortex-M33, provided that the bus system design allows vector fetch and stacking to happen at the same time, the typical interrupt latency is:

- 15 cycles for the Cortex-M23 (the same as the Cortex-M0+), which increases to 24 cycles if the processor is running Secure code and if the interrupt that occurred targeted the Non-secure state.
- 12 cycles for the Cortex-M33 (the same as the Cortex-M3 and the Cortex-M4), which increases to 21 cycles if the processor is running Secure code and if the interrupt that occurred targeted the Non-secure state.

This cycle count includes stacking the registers, vector fetch, and fetching instructions for the interrupt handler.

However, in many cases the latency can be higher due to wait states in the memory system. If the processor is carrying out a memory transfer, the outstanding transfer has, due to the nature of the AMBA® AHB bus protocol (the AHB can deal with just one transaction at a time) [2], to be completed before the exception sequence starts. The duration of the execution sequence also depends on the access speed of the memory.

As well as memory/peripheral wait states, there can be other factors that increase the interrupt latency. For example:

- If the processor was serving another exception of the same or of a higher priority.
- If the processor was running a Secure program and the interrupt targets Non-secure state. In this case, additional context will need to be pushed into the stack frame.
- The debugger accesses the memory system.
- If the processor was carrying out an unaligned transfer (not applicable to the Cortex-M23 or Armv8-M Baseline). From the processor's point of view, this might be a single access, but at the bus level it would be seen as multiple transfers. This is because the processor bus interface converts an unaligned transfer into multiple aligned transfers in order to handle the transfer though the AHB interface.
- In the case of a fault exception, the latency can be different from interrupts because they are handled differently from external interrupt signals.

The Cortex-M23 and Cortex-M33 processors reduce the latency of servicing interrupts in a number of ways. For example, most operations, such as nested interrupt handling, are automatically handled by the processor's hardware, thus reducing latency. This is because there is no need to use software to manage the nesting of the interrupts. Similarly, because of the vectored interrupt support, there is no need to use software to determine which interrupt to service and, additionally, there is no need to look-up the starting address of the Interrupt Service Routines (ISR).

9.6.2 Interrupts during multiple-cycle instructions

Some instructions take multiple clock cycles to execute. If an interrupt request arrives when the processor is executing a multiple cycle instruction (e.g., an integer divide), the instruction could be abandoned and then restarted after the interrupt handler has finished. In the Cortex-M33 and other Armv8-M Mainline processors, this behavior would also apply to load double-word (LDRD) and store double-word (STRD) instructions.

In addition, the Cortex-M33 processor allows exceptions to be taken in the middle of Multiple Load and Store instructions (i.e., LDM, STM, PUSH and POP). If one of these instructions is executing when the interrupt request arrives, the processor will complete the current memory access, and then save the instruction state (i.e., the next register number) in the stacked xPSR (by way of the Interrupt-Continuable Instruction [ICI] bits). After the exception handler completes, using the information from the stacked ICI bits, the multiple load/store/push/pop instruction will be resumed from the point at which the transfer was stopped. The same approach also applies to floating-point memory access instructions (i.e., VLDM, VSTM, VPUSH, and VPOP) for the Cortex-M33 processor with a floating-point unit. There is an exception to this behavior: If the multiple load/store/push/pop instruction being interrupted is part of an IF-THEN (IT) instruction block, then the instruction would be canceled and would only restart upon the completion of the interrupt handler. This is because the ICI bits and IT execution status bits share the same space in the Execution Program Status Register (EPSR).

With the Cortex-M23 processor, if an interrupt takes place in the middle of a Multiple Load and Store instruction (i.e., LDM, STM, PUSH and POP), the instruction would be canceled and would only restart upon the completion of the interrupt handler. (Note: there are no ICI/IT bits in the PSR in Armv8-M Baseline).

If the floating-point unit is implemented in the Cortex-M33 processor, and if an interrupt request arrives when the processor is executing VSQRT (floating-point square root) or VDIV (floating-point divide), the floating-point instruction execution continues in parallel with the stacking operation.

The Cortex-M33 processor has a feature to disable interrupts in the middle of multicycle instructions. This is controlled by setting DISMCYCINT, which is in bit 0 of the Auxiliary Control Register.

9.6.3 Tail chaining

When an exception takes place and the processor is handling another exception of the same or of a higher priority, the exception enters pending state. When the processor finishes executing the current exception handler, it then proceeds to process the pended exception/interrupt request. Instead of restoring the register's data back from the stack (i.e., unstacking) and then pushing that data back to the stack (i.e., stacking), the processor skips some of the unstacking and stacking steps and, as soon as possible, enters the exception handler of the pended exception (Fig. 9.3). With this arrangement, the timing gap between the two exception handlers is considerably reduced.

Tail-chaining optimization makes the processor system more energy efficient because the number of stack memory accesses is reduced and because each memory access consumes energy.

Unlike the Cortex-M3 or Cortex-M4 processors, the tail chain operation does not completely eliminate memory access between the exception handlers. This is because TrustZone brought additional security check requirements to the exception return. For example, the processor might need to check the integrity signature in the Secure stack frame to ensure that the exception return is valid before handling the next exception. If the security checks fail, the processor would first need to trigger a fault exception. The processor might

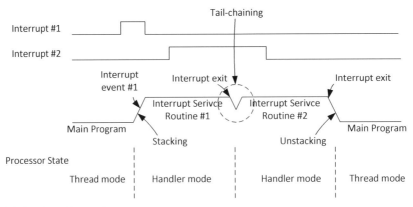

FIG. 9.3   Tail-chaining of exceptions.

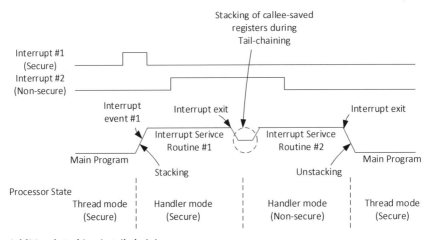

FIG. 9.4   Additional stacking in tail-chaining.

also need to carry out additional stacking operations if the interrupted software and the first ISR were both Secure and the tail-chaining interrupt was Non-secure (Fig. 9.4).

9.6.4 Late arrival

When an exception takes place, the processor accepts the exception request and starts the stacking operation. If during the stacking operation another exception of a higher priority takes place, the higher priority late arrival exception will be serviced first.

For example, if Exception #1 (a lower priority) takes place a few cycles before Exception #2 (a higher priority), the processor will, service Interrupt #2 as soon as the stacking completes, as shown in Fig. 9.5.

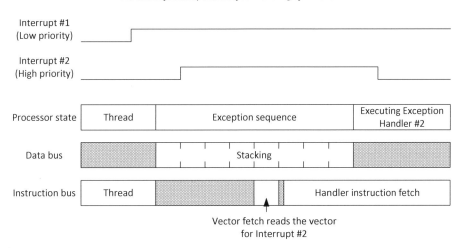

FIG. 9.5 Late arrival exception behavior.

The late arrival of a higher priority interrupt could result in having to stack additional callee-saved registers. This would occur when the interrupted code and the first interrupt event are Secure and when the second interrupt (higher priority) is Non-secure.

9.6.5 Pop preemption

If an exception request arrives during the unstacking process for an exception handler that has just finished, the processor could abandon the unstacking operation and start the vector fetch and instruction fetch for the next exception. This optimization is called pop preemption (Fig. 9.6).

As is the case for tail-chaining, it is possible that the new interrupt event could result in the stacking of additional callee-saved registers.

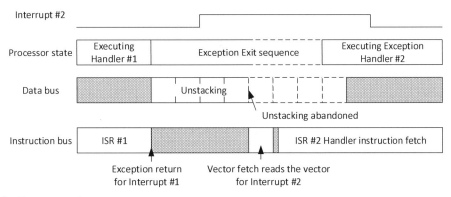

FIG. 9.6 Pop preemption.

9.6.6 Lazy stacking

Lazy stacking is a feature related to the stacking of the registers in the floating-point unit (FPU). It is, therefore, only relevant to Cortex-M based devices with an FPU. It is supported in the Cortex-M33/M35P/M55/M4/M7 processors.

Further information on lazy stacking can be found in Chapter 14, Section 14.4. The following paragraphs are a brief overview of lazy stacking.

If the FPU is available, has been enabled and the FPU has been used when an interrupt arrives, the registers in the FPU's register bank will contain data that will need to be saved. Without lazy stacking, the FPU registers would be pushed to the stack during exception stacking, and would, at the end of the interrupt service, need to be restored to the FPU.

The saving and restoring of these registers could take a number of clock cycles. If the interrupt handler does not contain any floating-point instruction, the saving and restoring of the FPU registers would be a waste of time and would increase interrupt latency. To make Cortex-M processors more efficient, the lazy stacking optimization was introduced.

When an interrupt occurs when the lazy stacking feature is enabled (i.e., default), the processor does not push the FPU registers into the stack, but only reserves the space for them. In addition, a lazy stacking pending register bit is set. If the interrupt handler does not use a floating-point instruction, the restoring of the FPU registers during unstacking does not take place.

If the interrupt handler uses the FPU, the processor's pipeline is stalled when the first floating-point instruction in the interrupt handler is detected. The processor would then carry out the deferred stacking operation (i.e., pushing the FPU registers into the reserved space in the stack frame), clear the lazy stacking pending register, and would then resume its operation. At the end of the interrupt handler, the FPU registers would, during the unstacking process, be restored from the stack frame.

Because of the lazy stacking feature, the interrupt latency of the Cortex-M33 processor with an FPU remains relatively low (e.g., 12, or 21 clock cycles if additional contexts need to be saved).

9.7 Tips and hints

If you are developing an application that is going to be used on a variety of Cortex-M processors there are a number of areas that you need to be aware of:

- The System Control Space (SCS) registers, including NVIC and SCB, are word access only on Armv6-M and Armv8-M Baseline. Whereas, in Armv7-M and Armv8-M Mainline, some of these registers can be accessed as word, halfword, or bytes. As a result, the definitions of the Interrupt Priority Registers NVIC->IPR are different between the two architectures. To ensure software portability, the use of the CMSIS-CORE functions is recommended when handling interrupt configurations. The use of these functions improves the portability of the software code.

TABLE 9.25 Summary of NVIC feature differences for various Cortex-M processors

	Cortex-M0	Cortex-M0+	Cortex-M1	Cortex-M23	Cortex-M3, Cortex-M4, Cortex-M7	Cortex-M33, Cortex-M55
Number of Interrupts	1–32	1–32	1, 8, 16, 32	1–240	1–240	1–480
NMI	Y	Y	Y	Y	Y	Y
Width of priority registers	2	2	2	2	3–8	3–8
Access to interrupt priority level registers	Word	Word	Word	Word	Word, Halfword, Byte	Word, Halfword, Byte
PRIMASK	Y	Y	Y	Y	Y	Y
FAULTMASK	N	N	N	N	Y	Y
BASEPRI	N	N	N	N	Y	Y
Vector Table Offset Register	N	Y (optional)	N	Y (optional)	Y	Y
Software trigger interrupt register	N	N	N	N	Y	Y
Dynamic priority change	N	N	N	Y	Y	Y
Interrupt Active Status	N	N	N	Y	Y	Y
Fault Handling	HardFault	HardFault	HardFault	HardFault	HardFault + three other fault exception	HardFault + four other fault exception
Debug monitor exception	N	N	N	N	Y	Y

- There is no Software Trigger Interrupt Register (NVIC->STIR) in either Armv6-M or Armv8-M Baseline. To set, therefore, the pending status of an interrupt, you need to use the "NVIC_SetPendingIRQ()" function or the Interrupt Set Pending Register (NVIC->ISPR).
- There is no vector table relocation feature in the Cortex-M0. This feature is, however, available on the Cortex-M33, the Cortex-M55, the Cortex-M3, the Cortex-M4, and the Cortex-M7—and is optional on the Cortex-M23 and the Cortex-M0+ processors.
- There are no Interrupt Active Status Registers in Armv6-M. Thus, the NVIC->IABR register and the associated CMSIS-Core function "NVIC_GetActive" are not available for the Cortex-M0 and Cortex-M0+ processors.
- There is no priority grouping in either Armv6-M or Armv8-M Baseline. Accordingly, CMSIS-CORE functions "NVIC_EncodePriority" and "NVIC_DecodePriority" are not available in the Cortex-M23, the Cortex-M0, and in the Cortex-M0+ processors.

- In Armv7-M and Armv8-M, the priority of an interrupt can be changed dynamically at run time. In Armv6-M, the priority of an interrupt should only be changed when it is disabled.
- The FAULTMASK and BASEPRI features are not available on either the Armv8-M Baseline or on the Armv6-M architectures.

A comparison of the NVIC features available in the various Cortex-M processors is shown in Table 9.25.

References

[1] Armv8-M Architecture Reference Manual. https://developer.arm.com/documentation/ddi0553/am (Armv8.0-M only version). https://developer.arm.com/documentation/ddi0553/latest (latest version including Armv8.1-M). Note: M-profile architecture reference manuals for Armv6-M, Armv7-M, Armv8-M and Armv8.1-M can be found here: https://developer.arm.com/architectures/cpu-architecture/m-profile/docs.
[2] AMBA 5 Advanced High-performance Bus (AHB) Protocol Specification. https://developer.arm.com/documentation/ihi0033/b-b/.

Low power and system control features

10.1 The quest for low power

10.1.1 Why low power is important?

Many embedded systems require low power microcontrollers, especially for portable products that run on batteries. Besides, low power characteristics can benefit product designs:

- Smaller battery size can result in a smaller sized, lower-cost product
- It enables products to have a longer battery life
- It lowers electromagnetic interference (EMI) and improves the quality of wireless communication
- It simplifies the power supply design, avoiding heat dissipation issues
- In some instances, a low power embedded system will allow the system to be powered using alternate energy sources (e.g., solar panel, energy harvested from the environment)

Among all those benefits, the most significant benefit for most products is the one that enables a longer battery life. This is particularly important in market segments for wearable products, sensors, and medical implants. For example, many smoke detectors can function for quite long periods without having to change the battery. For many years, microcontroller vendors have utilized the low power capabilities of Arm® Cortex®-M based chip processors, and by adding their low power technologies to the mix, have produced products that have significantly low power capabilities.

10.1.2 What does low power mean? And how to measure it?

Traditionally, microcontroller datasheets quote "active current" and "sleep mode current" of microcontrollers in various states and conditions. In some instances, some of the datasheets also quote the product's energy efficiency. This data can be categorized as shown in Table 10.1.

Depending on the nature of the applications, some of these requirements can be more important than others. For example, if the device is likely to be sleeping for a long period (i.e., hours between each wake-up event), then a low-Sleep Mode Current characteristic would be the most

TABLE 10.1   Typical low power requirements of microcontrollers and related design considerations.

Requirement	Typical measurement and design considerations
Active current	This is usually measured in μA/MHz. Active current is mostly composed of dynamic power that is consumed by memories, peripherals, and the processor. To simplify the calculation, we can assume that the power consumption of the microcontroller is directly proportional to the clock frequency, but this is not strictly true (with this assumption, there is a small margin of error). The active current value might not, in some cases, be accurate because the actual active current value can be dependent upon the nature of the program code. For example, an application which has a lot of data memory access can result in higher power consumption, especially if its memories have a high-power consumption.
Sleep mode current	This is usually measured in μA. In most instances, clock signals are stopped when the microcontroller is in low power sleep mode. The sleep mode current is generally composed of leakage current in the transistors and the current that is consumed by some of the analog circuits and the I/O pads. Typically, most peripherals are turned off when measuring the sleep mode current. However, in the real world, some peripherals will likely, due to the requirements of an application, remain active (e.g., real-time clock, brownout detector, etc.).
Energy efficiency	This measurement is typically based on popular benchmarks such as Dhrystone (DMIPS/μW) or CoreMark® (CoreMark/μW). However, the processor's activities when running these benchmarks can be very different from the data processing activities of a real-world application. It is possible to tune the system (e.g., a microcontroller) to achieve the best DMIPS/μW or CoreMark/μW readings by selecting different combinations for the clocking configuration and specific options for the compiler.
Wake up latency	Wake up latency is often specified as the time it takes to wake up the processor in certain sleep mode(s). This is usually measured in either the number of clock cycles or in μs. Typically, this measurement is measured from the time that a hardware request occurs (e.g., a peripheral interrupt) to the time it takes for the processor to resume the execution of the program. If measured in μs, the clock frequency will directly affect the result. Application developers often need to consider the trade-off between wake-up latency and sleep mode current. To reduce power during sleep mode to a minimum, it is necessary to turn off the majority of the circuit components inside the chip. But some of these components need a long time to power up and to get ready, and, as a result, a lower power sleep mode needs a longer time to wake up. For example, clock circuitry like the PLL could be turned off but, if it is, it will then take longer to resume its normal clock output. Product designers need, therefore, to decide when making their decisions in which sleep modes are best for their application.

important factor when choosing a microcontroller. On the other hand, if the device is designed to run most of the time, then the Energy Efficiency of the microcontroller during its operation would be more important.

To assist system designers in understanding and deciding on the best device to use, EEMBC (Embedded Microcontroller Benchmark Consortium, https://www.eembc.org) has, during the last few years, created several benchmarks to address those needs. Additionally, several chip vendors, using these benchmarks, have created software projects and have made available the results of these projects to product designers. These can be used as a reference to how the claimed low power capabilities can be achieved. Details are as follows:

- ULPMark™-CP (Ultra Low Power Mark—Core Profile): The workload contains simple data processing and sleep operations and is suitable for a wide range of low power microcontrollers including 8-, 16-, and 32-bit processor-based systems.

- ULPMark-PP (Peripheral Profile): The workload contains a range of peripheral operations.
- ULPMark-CoreMark: This standardizes the way energy efficiency is reported and is based on the CoreMark workload operating under consistent test conditions. The result covers fixed voltage, best voltage, and performance-optimized scenarios.
- IoTMark™-BLE: A benchmark to measure the power efficiency of an IoT device (in this case, one based on connectivity using Bluetooth-LE).
- SecureMark™-TLS: A benchmark to measure the power efficiency of a processor system when it is running a Transport Layer Security protocol.

While these benchmarks can be useful in indicating how a device performs, you will often find that though the information supplied is useful, that it is still essential to run real-world applications and measure the results. This is because the test environment of the benchmark is unlikely to fully match the environment of real-world applications.

10.2 Low power features in the Cortex-M23 and Cortex-M33 processors

10.2.1 Low power characteristics

Arm® Cortex®-M processors are designed with low power requirements in mind. To enable these processors to be used in various low power applications, the processors have a range of low power characteristics:

- A small area—Many Cortex-M processors are designed to be very small in terms of silicon area, which helps reduce both static and dynamic current. For example, the Cortex-M23 processor was designed for a range of ultra-low-power applications and made it possible to include advanced security features by supporting the TrustZone® security extension.
- Low power optimization—Within the processor, various low power optimization techniques are used, such as clock gating and multiple power domain support.
- Low power system-level support features—Several low power features, like sleep mode and WIC, are available to enable chip designers to reduce power consumption at the system level.
- High performance—To enable products to deliver the best in class energy efficiency, Cortex-M processors are designed to deliver outstanding performance. For example, the Cortex-M33 processor achieves a performance level of over 4 CoreMark/MHz.
- High code density—Enables applications to fit into a device with a small program space, which also helps reduce the power consumption of the whole system.
- Configurability—Cortex-M processors are highly configurable, which means that chip designers can, to reduce power consumption, omit features that are not required.

Owing to these characteristics, Cortex-M processors are widely used by microcontroller vendors in a range of low power microcontroller and SoC products.

10.2.2 Sleep modes

Sleep modes are commonly used in microcontroller applications to reduce power consumption. Architecturally, the Cortex-M processors support two sleep modes: sleep and deep sleep. System designers can further extend the sleep modes using additional power control methods and system-level low power arrangements. For example, at the processor system level, several power levels can be created, as shown in Fig. 10.1.

At the system level, additional sleep modes can be arranged based on the power management features of other components. For example:

- Some memories (e.g., Flash memory) can be powered down.
- SRAM can be put into various low power states.
- Some of the peripherals can be turned off.
- The voltage level can be reduced when the processor is not running or when the operating frequency is reduced.

Since the Cortex-M processors are designed to cover a wide range of applications, and can be implemented with different semiconductor process nodes, the processor designs do not specify what exactly happens during the various sleep modes. This is not an issue though because the processors' interface supports a range of signals for sleep mode support. This means, therefore, that chip designers can decide what power reduction techniques to use based on their application's requirements.

For simple designs, the internal clock gating of the processor already provides during sleep a good power reduction. In more complex designs, chip designers have the option of either powering down the whole processor or using the state retention power gating arrangement to cut down, when the processor is inactive, its power consumption.

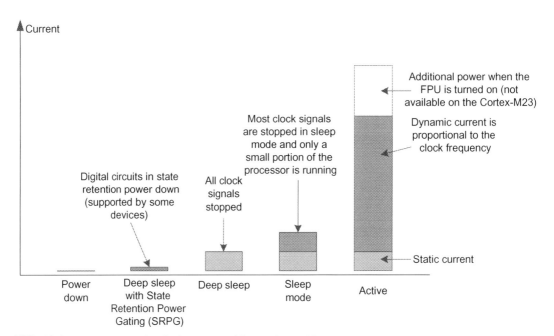

FIG. 10.1 Various power levels that are possible in a Cortex-M processor system.

TABLE 10.2 System Control Register (SCB->SCR, 0xE000ED10).

Bits	Name	Type	Reset value	Description
4	SEVONPEND	R/W	0	Send Event on Pending: When this is set to 1, the processor wakes up from WFE if a new interrupt has pended, regardless of whether the interrupt has a priority higher than the current level and whether it was enabled
3	SLEEPDEEPS	R/W	0	Sleep Deep Secure: If this bit is set to 1, the SLEEPDEEP bit (bit 2) is inaccessible from the Non-secure world. Otherwise (i.e., bit is 0), SLEEPDEEP is accessible by Non-secure privileged software. The SLEEPDEEPS bit is accessible in Secure privileged state and is not implemented if TrustZone is not present.
2	SLEEPDEEP	R/W	0	Sleep Deep: When setting to 1, the Deep Sleep mode is selected. Otherwise (i.e., bit is 0) Sleep mode is selected. If SLEEPDEEPS is set to 1 this bit become read-as-zero and write is ignored from the Non-secure world.
1	SLEEPONEXIT	R/W	0	Sleep on Exit: When this bit is set to 1, it enables the Sleep-On-Exit feature, which causes the processor to automatically enter sleep mode when it is exiting an exception handler and is returning to Thread mode.
0	Reserved	–	–	–

10.2.3 System Control Register (SCB->SCR)

To decide whether sleep or deep sleep mode should be used when entering sleep, one of the bit-fields called SLEEPDEEP would need to be programmed by software. SLEEPDEEP is bit 2 in the System Control Register (SCR). The SCR is a memory-mapped register located in address 0xE000ED10 (For projects using the CMSIS-CORE header file, it can be accessed via the SCB->SCR symbol).

Information on the SCR bit fields is listed in Table 10.2. Just like most other registers in the System Control Block (SCB), the SCR can only be accessed in a privileged state.

The SLEEPDEEP bit (bit 2) can be set to enable the Deep Sleep mode. When TrustZone is implemented, the access of this bit can be controlled by Secure privileged software using SLEEPDEEPS bit (bit 3; this is a new bit field introduced in Armv8-M).

When TrustZone is implemented, Secure privileged software is also able to access the Non-secure privileged view of this register using SCB_NS->SCB (address 0xE002ED10).

The System Control Register is also used to control other lower power features such as Sleep-On-Exit and SEV-On-Pend. I will cover these features in Section 10.2.5 for the Sleep-on-Exit feature and Section 10.2.6 for SEVONPEND.

10.2.4 Entering sleep mode

Cortex-M processors provide two instructions for entering sleep modes (Table 10.3). A third way to enter sleep mode, which is not an instruction, is by using the Sleep-On-Exit feature which is covered in Section 10.2.5.

TABLE 10.3   Instructions for entering sleep mode.

Instruction	CMSIS-CORE intrinsic	Description
WFI	void __WFI (void);	Wait for Interrupt Enter sleep mode. The processor can be woken up by interrupt requests, a debug request, or by a reset.
WFE	void __WFE (void);	Wait for Event Enters sleep mode conditionally. If the internal event register is already cleared, the processor enters sleep mode. If it is not, the internal event register is cleared to 0 and the processor continues without entering sleep mode. The processor can be woken up by interrupt requests, by events, a debug request, or by a reset.

Both WFI sleep and WFE sleep can be woken up by interrupt requests. This depends on the priority of the interrupt, the current priority level, and the interrupt mask settings (Section 10.3.4).

WFE sleep can be woken up by events. Event sources include:

- An exception entrance and exit.
- A SEVONPEND event: When the SEV-On-Pend feature is enabled (bit 4 of the System Control Register), then the event register is set when an interrupt pending status is changed from 0 to 1.
- The assertion of an external event signal (an RXEV input on the processor). This indicates an event from on-chip hardware has occurred. The event signal can be a single cycle pulse and the connection of this signal is device-specific.
- The execution of a SEV (Send Event) instruction.
- A debug event (e.g., a halting request).

The processor can be woken up from WFE sleep by either a current or past event. If the internal event register has been set, this indicates an event has been received since the last WFE execution or sleep. When this happens, the execution of WFE does not enter sleep (it may, potentially, only momentarily cause the processor to enter sleep mode and, if it does, will then immediately wake up). Inside the processor, there is a single bit event register which indicates whether an event has previously occurred. This event register is set by the aforementioned event sources and is cleared by the execution of a WFE instruction.

Similar to WFE sleep, during WFI sleep the processor can be woken up by an interrupt request if the interrupt has a higher priority than the processor's current priority level. The processor's current priority level is based on one of the following:

- the priority level of the running exception service, or
- the priority level of whichever active interrupt masking register (such as BASEPRI) has been set.

These two priority levels are compared by the processor's hardware and the one with the higher priority level is used as the processor's current priority level. The chosen level is then compared against the priority level of a new incoming interrupt and will wake the processor up if the interrupt request has a higher priority.

Alternatively, if the new incoming interrupt has the same or a lower priority than the processor's current priority level, and if the SEV-on-pend feature is enabled, this is treated as an event and will wake the processor up from WFE sleep.

10.2.5 Sleep-on-Exit feature

The Sleep-on-Exit feature is very useful for interrupt-driven applications where all operations (apart from the initialization) are carried out using interrupt handlers. This is a programmable feature and can be enabled or disabled using bit 1 of the System Control Register (SCR—see Section 10.2.3). When enabled, the Cortex®-M processor automatically enters sleep mode (with WFI behavior) when exiting from an exception handler and when returning to Thread mode (i.e., when no other exception request is waiting to be processed).

For example, a program utilizing the Sleep-on-Exit feature might have a program flow as shown in Fig. 10.2.

The activities of the program running in the system shown in Fig. 10.2 are shown in Fig. 10.3. Unlike normal interrupt handling sequences, the stacking and unstacking processes during Sleep-on-Exit are reduced to save power in the processor and its memories. However, the first occurrence of the interrupt, as shown in Fig. 10.3, would still require a full stacking operation.

Please note, the "loop" in Fig. 10.2 is required because the processor could still be woken up by debug requests when a debugger is attached.

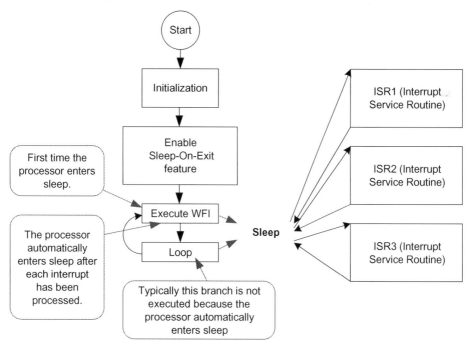

FIG. 10.2 Sleep-on-exit program flow.

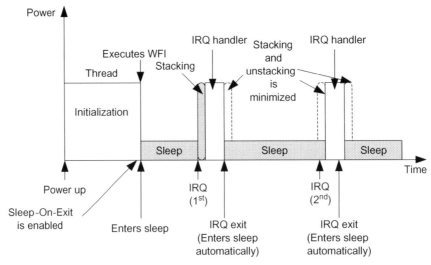

FIG. 10.3   Sleep-on-exit operations.

Important: The Sleep-On-Exit feature should not be enabled until the end of the initialization stage. Otherwise, if an interrupt event happens during the initialization stage, and if the Sleep-on-Exit feature was already enabled, the processor will enter sleep mode even though the initialization stage had not finished.

10.2.6 Send Event On Pend (SEVONPEND)

One of the programmable control bits in the System Control Register (SCR) is the SEVONPEND. This feature is used with the WFE sleep operation. When this bit is set to 1, any new incoming interrupt that sets the interrupt pending status is treated as a wakeup event, and wakes up the processor from WFE sleep mode, regardless of:

- Whether or not the interrupt is enabled in the NVIC
- Whether the priority of the new interrupt has a higher priority than the current priority level

If the pending status of the interrupt was already set to 1 before entering sleep, a new interrupt request will not trigger a SEV-on-pend event and will not wake up the processor.

10.2.7 Sleep extension/wakeup delay

Normally, if a Cortex-M processor is in sleep mode and an interrupt event is triggered, the servicing of the interrupt service routine starts as soon as the processor's clock signals are resumed. In some microcontrollers, the wakeup process could take some time because certain sleep modes might aggressively reduce power consumption by, for example, reducing the voltage supply to the SRAM and by turning off the power to the flash memory. When this happens, starting the interrupt service as soon as possible won't work because the memories are not ready.

To solve this problem, most Cortex-M processors (except the Cortex-M1) support a set of handshaking signals which allows, while the clock is running, the interrupt service to be delayed. This delay allows the rest of the system to get ready. This feature is only visible to silicon designers and is completely transparent to software. However, microcontroller users might observe a longer interrupt latency when this feature is used.

10.2.8 Wakeup Interrupt Controller (WIC)

During certain sleep modes, chip designers might want to stop all the clock signals to the processor or, even, put the processor into a form of power downstate. When this is the case, the NVIC inside the processor is no longer able to either detect incoming interrupts or wake the processor up from sleep. To solve this problem, the Wakeup Interrupt Controller (WIC) was introduced.

The WIC is a small, optional interrupt detection circuit outside the Cortex-M processor, which is coupled to the NVIC in the Cortex-M processor via a dedicated interface. The WIC is typically placed in an always-on power domain so, even when the processor is powered down, the WIC is still operational.

The WIC does not contain any programmable registers, thus requiring the hardware interface to automatically, if the WIC is enabled, transfer interrupts masking information, from the NVIC to the WIC. This transfer occurs just before the processor enters sleep mode. After the processor wakes up, the interrupt masking information is automatically cleared by the WIC's interface. Since the WIC operations are automatically controlled by hardware, the presence of the WIC is, once it is enabled, transparent to software. The WIC is available:

- In Armv8-M Mainline processors and the Armv7-M processor, but only when deep sleep is selected.
- In the Cortex-M23 (Armv8-M Baseline), the Cortex-M0 and the Cortex-M0+ processors (Armv6-M), when either sleep and deep sleep modes are used.

The WIC outputs a WAKEUP signal to the system's power management controller to wake up the system when an interrupt is detected (Fig. 10.4). In addition to handling interrupt signals, the WIC can also handle the detection of a receive event (RXEV) signal (which wakes the processor up from WFE sleep) and, in the case of the Cortex-M33 processor, an external debug request signal called EDBGRQ (Section 16.2.5). The EDBGRQ signal can be used for triggering a debug monitor exception and is, therefore, handled by the WIC like an interrupt signal. The debug monitor exception is not available in the Cortex-M23 processor and its WIC does not, therefore, support the EDBGRQ signal.

During sleep mode, the power used by the processor can be greatly reduced by using a technique called state retention (Fig. 10.5). At the same time, the detection of interrupts is handled by the WIC. When an interrupt request arrives, the WIC detects the request and tells the system's power management controller to restore the clock so that the processor can wake up, can resume operations, and can service the interrupt request.

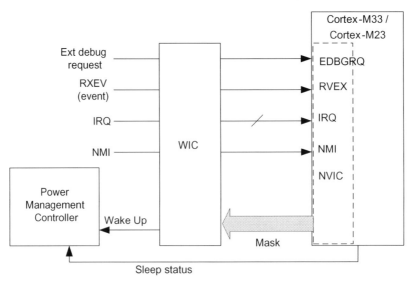

FIG. 10.4 The WIC detects interrupts when the processor is powered down or when all the processor's clocks are stopped.

The interrupt detection logic of the WIC can be customized by silicon designers to, for example, support if needed, a clockless operation.

With the availability of the WIC feature, advanced power-saving techniques, such as State Retention Power Gating (SRPG), can be used to reduce, by a wide margin, the leakage current of a chip. In SRPG designs, the registers (often called flip-flops in IC design terminology) have inside them state retention circuits that have a separate power supply (Fig. 10.6). When the system is powered down, the normal power supply can be turned off, leaving only the power

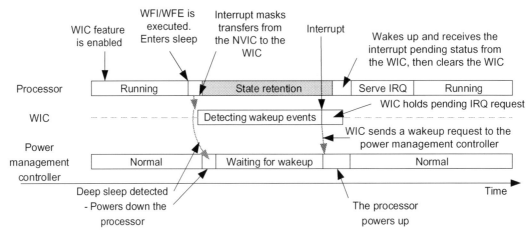

FIG. 10.5 By combining the WIC and state retention techniques, the processor's power consumption during sleep is reduced.

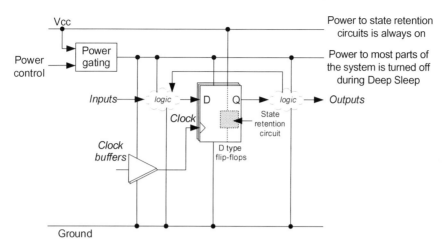

FIG. 10.6   SRPG technology allows most parts of a digital system to be powered down without losing the register's state information.

to the state retention circuits active. The electrical current leakage of the design is greatly reduced because the combinatorial logic, clock buffers, and most of the register's parts are powered down.

When a system with SRPG technology wakes up, because the various states of the processor are retained, the processor can resume operations from the point where the program was suspended. It is, therefore, able to service an interrupt request almost immediately—just like in normal sleep mode. In practice, the power-up sequence does take time to complete and, therefore, can increase the interrupt latency. The exact latency depends on the semiconductor technology used, the memories used, the clocking arrangements, and the design of the power system (e.g., the behavior of the power management controller, i.e., how long it takes for the voltage to be stabilized), and so on.

Please note:

- Not all microcontroller devices based on Cortex-M processors implement the WIC feature.
- In certain sleep modes, when all the clock signals to the processor are stopped, the SysTick timer(s) inside the processor would also stop and would not, therefore, be able to generate SysTick exceptions. Applications or operating systems that need to wake up using a timer will need, therefore, to utilize other peripheral timers in the chip that are not affected by those sleep modes.
- Depending on the chip system-level design, you might need to program some registers to enable the WIC before using some of the sleep modes.
- When a debugger is attached to the processor system, it might disable some of its low power capabilities. For example, the microcontroller could be designed in such a way that when a debugger is connected to the processor system, the processor's SRPG and clock gating features would be disabled (i.e., the processor's clock(s) would continue to run during Deep Sleep mode). With this arrangement, the debugger can examine the system's status even though the application code would be attempting to put the processor into Deep Sleep mode.

10.2.9 Event communication interface

Earlier in this chapter, I mentioned that the WFE instruction can be woken up by a signal, called RXEV (Receive Event), which is an input on the Cortex-M processor. The processor also has an output signal called TXEV (Transmit Event). The TXEV outputs a single-cycle pulse when executing the SEV (Send Event) instruction. These signals are called the event communication interface (Fig. 10.7).

The event communication interface allows the processor to be woken up from WFE sleep by external events, such as another processor or by peripheral hardware.

One of the key uses of this interface is to reduce power when handling semaphores across multiple processors. In Chapter 6, the topic of exclusive access support in Armv8-M processors was discussed and a scenario was highlighted where a semaphore operation needed to poll semaphore data where the semaphore was locked by another processor (Fig. 6.9). If, in the aforementioned scenario, the other processor took a long time to release the semaphore, the processor that was polling the semaphore data (a process known as a spin lock) would have wasted a significant amount of energy during the spinlock.

To solve this problem, WFE instructions can be added to the polling loop to reduce power. By doing so, if the semaphore is already locked up by another processor, the processor enters sleep mode. To wake the processor up when the semaphore is released, an event crossover connection and a SEV instruction are needed: the processor that releases the semaphore would need to execute the SEV instruction, with the event crossover connection delivering the event to the processor which is in WFE sleep (i.e., waiting for the semaphore). For a dual-core system, the event crossover connection required is shown in Fig. 10.8.

Using an event communication connection, the semaphore operation shown in fig. 6.9 can be modified to include a WFE, which will, when applied, result in a reduction in the amount of energy that is wasted. This modified semaphore operation is shown in Fig. 10.9.

The processor waiting for the semaphore could be woken up by other events. This is not an issue because the semaphore data is read and checked again. If the semaphore is still locked by another processor then the processor will again enter sleep mode.

FIG. 10.7 Event communication interface on Cortex-M processors.

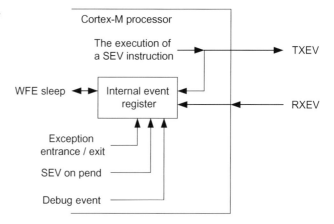

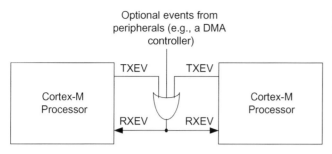

FIG. 10.8 Event communication connection in a dual-core system.

Program examples of using exclusive access for semaphores are covered in Chapter 21, Section 21.2. Please note, RTOS semaphore operations in real-world applications would look different from the diagram shown in Fig. 10.9. When a semaphore has already been locked by another processor, instead of immediately executing a WFE, the RTOS will likely check whether other tasks/threads are waiting to be executed. And, if there are, will then execute those other tasks/threads first. If no tasks/threads are waiting to be processed, then the RTOS will execute a WFE to enter sleep.

Using the same event crossover connection, as shown in Fig. 10.8, it is possible, to avoid wasting energy when using a polling loop, to synchronize operations between two processors (Fig. 10.10). Please note this event passing mechanism does not guarantee precise timing.

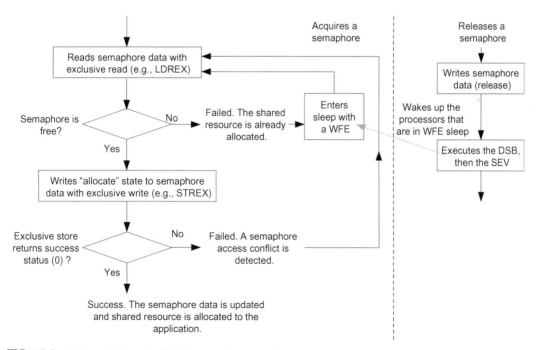

FIG. 10.9 Using a WFE and a SEV in semaphore operations.

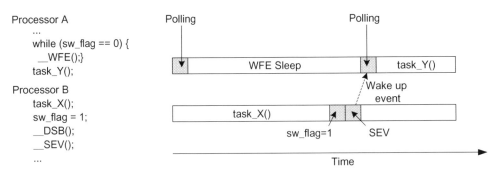

FIG. 10.10 Using a WFE in task synchronization—task Y in processor A needs to execute only after task X in processor B is completed.

Another use of the event communication interface is to allow the processor to enter sleep for a short period while waiting for a hardware event to occur. For example, it can be used in a Direct Memory Access (DMA) operation if the DMA controller has a pulsed output signal (e.g., shown as DMA_DONE in Fig. 10.11) that triggers when a DMA operation has finished. In such an arrangement, after the processor has programmed the DMA controller to start memory copying operations, instead of polling the DMA completion status, the processor executes a WFE instruction in the loop to enter sleep mode. The processor's operation then resumes after an event has been received from the DMA controller.

Because the processor could be woken up by other events, the program code, as detailed in Fig. 10.11, would again need to check the DMA completion status after waking up from WFE sleep. This is to ensure that the DMA controller has completed its operation.

Instead of generating an event (i.e., the DMA_Done signal shown in the example in Fig. 10.11), DMA controllers can also generate interrupts. When comparing the use of an interrupt to the use of the event communication signal (RXEV input) for the scenario shown in Fig. 10.11, the event communication method has the advantage of avoiding the clock cycles which are needed when entering and exiting the interrupt handler. The use of the event

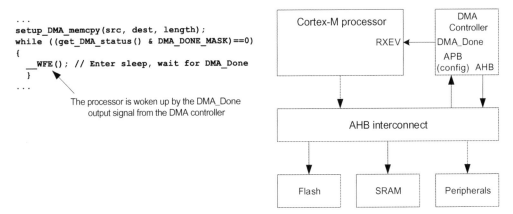

FIG. 10.11 Using a WFE instruction and the RXEV event input to handle small delays.

communication interface when waiting for a hardware event is appropriate when the waiting time is relatively short. However, if the waiting time is longer, instead of waiting for the hardware event, it is more efficient for the processor to handle other processing tasks and, when the DMA operation is finished, to then switch back to handle the completion of the DMA operation using an interrupt mechanism.

10.2.10 Effect of TrustZone on sleep mode support

In Cortex-M23 and Cortex-M33 processors with TrustZone implemented, the Non-secure software can, as in previous generations of Cortex-M processors, enter sleep or deep sleep modes using WFI, WFE or Sleep-on-Exit. However, Secure software can, optionally, prohibit Non-secure software from altering the sleep setting (i.e., SLEEPDEEP, bit 2 in SCB->SCR) by setting SLEEPDEEPS, bit 3 in SCB->SCR. Although SLEEPDEEP cannot be changed by the Non-secure software when the SLEEPDEEPS bit is set, SLEEPDEEP can be changed by way of a Secure API provided by the Secure firmware. This mechanism allows the Non-secure software to access the power management features and, hence change SLEEPDEEP.

The use of Secure APIs for accessing power management features is essential in some TrustZone enabled microcontroller systems. These systems would likely have additional device-specific power management control registers, but setting these registers incorrectly could affect the integrity of the system's security. Because of this, access to those registers must be protected by the system's security permission control. By providing power management APIs in the Secure firmware, application software running in the Non-secure world can utilize the system's low power features and can still protect the security of the device.

10.3 More on WFI, WFE, and SEV instructions

10.3.1 Using WFI, WFE, and SEV instructions in programming

In Chapter 5, I mentioned that WFE, WFI, and SEV instructions can be accessed in a C/C++ programming environment with the following intrinsic functions which are defined in the CMSIS-CORE header files (Table 10.4).

In the case of microcontroller applications, using these instructions alone is unlikely to help you fully utilize the low power features/optimizations of a device. It is important, therefore, to study the documentation supplied and to assess examples of the product(s) from the microcontroller vendors to see what software is needed to take advantage of the low power features. Many microcontroller vendors also provide device driver libraries to support low

TABLE 10.4 CMSIS-CORE Intrinsic functions used to access the WFE, the WFI, and the SEV instructions.

Instruction	Intrinsic function defined in the CMSIS-CORE
WFE	__WFE();
WFI	__WFI();
SEV	__SEV();

power features as a way of making the decision-making process easier for software developers. That said, it is still important to have an understanding of the differences between WFI and WFE instructions so that these instructions are used correctly.

10.3.2 When to use WFI

The WFI instruction unconditionally triggers sleep mode. This is typically used in interrupt-driven applications. For example, an interrupt-driven application is likely to have a program flow as shown as follows:

```
int main(void)
{
  // Initializations
  setup_IO();
  setup_peripherals();
  setup_NVIC();
  ...
  SCB->SCR |= 1<< 1; // Optional: Enables Sleep-on-exit feature
  while(1) {
    __WFI(); // Keeps in sleep mode when not serving the interrupt
  }
}
```

WFI sleep can be used with the sleep-on-exit feature. Normally, the processor enters sleep when the WFI is executed. However, there is a special situation when the execution of a WFI does not result in the processor entering sleep. This occurs when PRIMASK is set, and when there is a pending interrupt that is blocked by PRIMASK (i.e., where the priority level of the pending interrupt has a higher priority level than the processor's current priority level, but, because PRIMASK is set, the interrupt is not taken).

In some application scenarios, the choice of whether a WFI or a WFE instruction should be used depends on the expected timing of the interrupt event: which is used to wake the processor up. For example, the following code programs a timer to trigger an interrupt after N clock cycles, with N equaling 1000. After the timer has been initialized, the processor then enters sleep by executing a WFI instruction and wakes up when the timer reaches the programmed value:

```
NVIC_EnableIRQ(Timer0_IRQn); // Enables Timer0 interrupt

setup_timer0_trigger(N);// Sets up a timer to trigger an

                        // interrupt after N=1000 cycles

__WFI(); // Enters sleep and waits for the Timer0 IRQ event

...      // Resumes operation and starts processing
```

Using the previously mentioned code where N equals 1000, the control function works as expected. However, when using the same code, but shortening the timer delay to just 1 (i.e., "N" equals 1), then the Timer0 interrupt is likely to be triggered before the WFI has executed. And, when the WFI instruction has finally executed, the system will, because there is no timer interrupt to wake the system up, stay in sleep mode.

Even if N is 1000, a similar issue can occur if other interrupt events occur shortly after Timer0 has been setup. In such a situation, during the execution of the other interrupt service routines, the Timer0 IRQ would be triggered and then serviced. By the time the WFI had been executed, the processor would, because the Timer0 interrupt had already been triggered and serviced, be stuck in sleep mode.

Some people might try to fix the aforementioned problem by changing the previously mentioned code so that WFI is executed conditionally. The modified code to do this is:

```
volatile int timer0_flag = 0;

// the timer0_flag is set to a Non-zero in the Timer0 ISR

...

NVIC_EnableIRQ(Timer0_IRQn); // Enables Timer0 interrupt

setup_timer0_trigger(N);// Sets up a timer to trigger an

                        // interrupt after N cycles

if (timer0_flag==0) { // if timer 0 ISR has not been executed

__WFI();} // Enters sleep and waits for the Timer0 IRQ event

...        // Resumes operation and starts processing
```

Unfortunately, this modified code does not completely solve the problem. If the timer delay N is set to a value which results in the Timer0 interrupt being triggered just after the timer0_flag's value has been checked by software, then the WFI instruction will still execute after the Timer0 interrupt event. And, as a consequence, the processor will still be stuck in sleep mode.

To resolve this problem, the WFE instruction should be used (Section 10.3.3).

10.3.3 When to use WFE

The Wait for Event (WFE) instruction is commonly used in idle loops, including the timer delay example, I detailed in the last section. This instruction is also used in the "idle task" which are in RTOS designs. When the WFE is executed:

- If the internal event register is 0, the processor enters sleep.
- If the internal event register is 1, the processor clears the internal event register and continues to the next instruction without entering sleep.

Please note, the WFE instruction needs to be used in a loop. As a result, you cannot simply modify a piece of code by replacing WFI with WFE. Based on the last example that entered sleep and then woke up using a timer interrupt, we can modify the code to get the desired behavior by using a WFE instruction and by replacing the "if" to a "while" loop as follows:

```
volatile int timer0_flag=0;

...

NVIC_EnableIRQ(Timer0_IRQn); // Enables Timer0 interrupt

timer0_flag = 0; // Clears flag

setup_timer0_trigger(N);// Sets up a timer to trigger an

                        // interrupt after N cycles

while (timer0_flag==0) {

    __WFE(); // Enters sleep and waits for the timer #0 interrupt

    };

...              // Resumes operation and starts processing
```

In the earlier code example, I changed the sleep operation (i.e., the WFE instruction) so that it is now inside a loop. The loop operations are as follows:

- If the internal event register was set (e.g., due to a previous interrupt event) when the WFE instruction was first executed, the processor's internal event register would clear and would then continue without entering sleep. Because the WFE instruction is placed in a loop, the WFE would then execute again and, if no other interrupt events are happening, the processor would then enter sleep.
- If the processor enters sleep, the Timer0 interrupt would then wake up the processor, which would then execute the Timer 0 interrupt handler. The software flag (timer0_flag) would then be set to a nonzero value by the Timer 0 interrupt handler. When the handler code had completed its task, the processor would then return to the interrupted code. The checking of the software flag (timer0_flag) in the interrupted code would then detect that a Timer 0 interrupt had occurred and would then exit the loop.
- If the Timer 0 interrupt is triggered after entering the Idle loop and after the software flag (timer0_flag) was checked, the internal event register would be set by the Timer 0 interrupt event. As a result, the processor would not enter sleep when the WFE instruction was executed. Because the processor had not entered sleep, the idle loop would then execute again and, because the software flag (timer0_flag) was set, the loop would end.
- If the Timer 0 interrupt is triggered before entering the Idle loop, the software flag (timer0_flag) would be set, the loop would be skipped and the WFE instruction would not execute (i.e., the processor does not enter sleep).

As you can see, the behavior of the WFE instruction ensures that the aforementioned event sequences operate reliably, i.e., the processor can enter sleep and the software can resume operations after the timer 0 interrupts.

Please note, the status of the internal event register cannot be read directly by software code. However, you can set the internal event register to 1 by executing a SEV instruction. If you need to clear the event register, you can do so by executing a SEV and then a WFE:

```
__SEV(); // Sets the internal event register
__WFE(); // Because the event register was set,
         // this WFE does not trigger sleep and
         // only clears the event register.
```

If an interrupt event takes place just after the execution of the WFE instruction, the event register is set again.

Because a single WFE instruction may not result in the processor entering sleep, to make the processor enter sleep using WFE, the following sequence of WFE instructions can be used:

```
__SEV(); // Sets the internal event register
__WFE(); // Clears the event register
__WFE(); // Enters sleep
```

However, this code sequence only works if there are no other interrupt events taking place. If an interrupt occurs just after the first WFE instruction is executed, the second WFE will not enter sleep because the event register would have been set by the interrupt event.

A WFE instruction should also be used if the SEVONPEND feature is required.

10.3.4 Wake up conditions

In most instances, interrupts (including NMI and SysTick timer interrupts) can be used to wake up Cortex-M based microcontrollers from sleep modes. However, some of the sleep modes might turn off clock signals to the NVIC or peripherals, and, as a result, prevent some of those interrupts from waking up the processor. Therefore, before starting a project, you need to check the microcontroller's reference manual to understand which sleep mode(s) are suitable for your project's needs.

If sleep mode is entered using WFI or Sleep-On-Exit, for the wake-up to occur, the interrupt request would need to be enabled and would need to have a higher priority level than the current level (Table 10.5). For example, if the processor enters sleep mode whilst running an exception handler, or if the BASEPRI register was set before entering sleep mode, then the priority of the incoming interrupt will need to be higher than the current interrupt priority level to wake the processor up.

TABLE 10.5 Wake up conditions for WFI or Sleep-on-Exit.

IRQ priority condition	PRIMASK	Wake up	IRQ execution
Incoming IRQ higher than the current priority level: (IRQ priority > Current priority) AND (IRQ priority > BASEPRI)	0	Y	Y
Incoming IRQ the same or lower than the current priority level: ((IRQ priority =< Current priority) OR (IRQ priority =< BASEPRI))	0	N	N
Incoming IRQ higher than the current priority level: (IRQ priority > Current priority) AND (IRQ priority > BASEPRI)	1	Y	N
Incoming IRQ the same or lower than the current priority level: (IRQ priority =< Current priority) OR (IRQ priority =< BASEPRI)	1	N	N

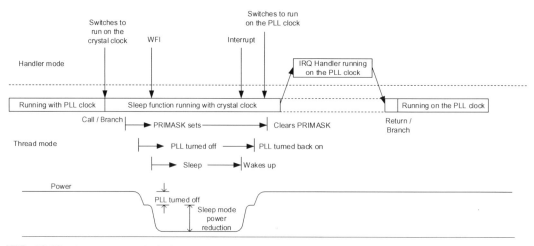

FIG. 10.12   Setting PRIMASK before executing the WFI allows the processor to wake up and resume execution without executing the ISR.

The PRIMASK wake up condition is a special feature that enables, immediately after the processor has woken up, a piece of software to be executed so that, before the execution of the Interrupt Service Routines (ISRs), certain system resources can be restored. For example, a microcontroller could allow its Phase Locked Loop (the PLL is used for internal clock generation) to be turned off during sleep mode to reduce power. The PLL's operation would then need to be restored before the execution of the ISR(s). The operation to achieve this is shown in Fig. 10.12 and the steps required are as follows:

(i)   Before entering sleep mode, PRIMASK should be set, the clock source should be switched to crystal clock and the PLL should then be turned off.
(ii) With the PLL turned off to save power, the microcontroller then enters sleep mode.
(iii) The interrupt request arrives, wakes up the microcontroller, and resumes the program's execution from the point right after the WFI instruction.
(iv) The software code then re-enables the PLL, switches back to using the PLL clock, and then clears the PRIMASK before servicing the interrupt request.

If an interrupt arrives before the WFI is executed, the processor does not enter sleep and instead turns the PLL clock on and clears PRIMASK. When this stage is reached, the ISR is executed.

If sleep mode is entered using the WFE instruction, the wake-up conditions are slightly different (Table 10.6). In addition to interrupts, a WFE can be woken up by other events (this is covered in Section 10.2.4). One of the wake-up events is a feature called SEVONPEND (Section 10.2.6). When this feature is enabled, and when an interrupt request arrives, the pending status is set and a wake-up event is generated. This applies even when the interrupt is disabled or when the interrupt has the same or a lower priority level than the processor's current level.

Please note, the SEVONPEND feature generates the wake-up event only when a pending status switches from 0 to 1. If the pending status of the incoming interrupt was already set, it will not generate the wake-up event.

TABLE 10.6 Wake up conditions for WFE.

IRQ priority condition	PRIMASK	SEVONPEND	Wake up	IRQ execution
Incoming IRQ higher than the current priority level: (IRQ priority > Current priority) AND (IRQ priority > BASEPRI)	0	0	Y	Y
Incoming IRQ same or lower than the current priority level: (IRQ priority =< Current priority) OR (IRQ priority =< BASEPRI)	0	0	N	N
Incoming IRQ higher than the current priority level: (IRQ priority > Current priority) AND (IRQ priority > BASEPRI)	1	0	N	N
Incoming IRQ the same or lower than the current priority level: (IRQ priority =< Current priority) OR (IRQ priority =< BASEPRI)	1	0	N	N
Incoming IRQ higher than the current priority level: (IRQ priority > Current priority) AND (IRQ priority > BASEPRI)	0	1	Y	Y
Incoming IRQ the same or lower than the current priority level: (IRQ priority =< Current priority) OR (IRQ priority =< BASEPRI)	0	1	Y	N
Incoming IRQ higher than the current priority level: (IRQ priority > Current priority) AND (IRQ priority > BASEPRI)	1	1	Y	N
Incoming IRQ the same or lower than the current priority level: (IRQ priority =< Current priority) OR (IRQ priority =< BASEPRI)	1	1	Y	N

10.4 Developing low power applications

10.4.1 Getting started

Most Cortex-M microcontrollers come with various low power features to help product designers reduce the power consumption of products. Because every microcontroller product is different, designers must spend time understanding the low power features of the microcontrollers they are using. Various sources of information are available from microcontroller vendors and these include:

- Examples or tutorials
- Application notes/technical articles

Because it is impossible to cover all the low power design methods for the many different types of microcontrollers, I will, therefore, only cover the basics considerations one needs to take into account when designing low power embedded systems.

10.4.2 Reducing the active power

10.4.2.1 Choose the right microcontroller device

The choice of the microcontroller device plays a significant role in achieving low power consumption. In addition to considering a device's electrical characteristics, you should also consider the size of the memory required for your project(s). You could, for example, waste power if the microcontroller you intend using has a much larger flash or SRAM than needed.

10.4.2.2 Running at the right clock frequency

Most applications do not need a high clock frequency; thus, you could potentially reduce the power consumption of the system by reducing the clock frequency. However, pushing the clock frequency too low might run the risk of reducing the system's responsiveness, or even failing the timing requirements of the application.

In most instances, the microcontroller should be run at a decent clock speed to ensure that the system is responsive and to ensure that the system goes into sleep mode when there are no outstanding processing tasks. Sometimes, benchmarking might be needed so that a decision can be made as to whether the system should run faster and then enter sleep, or run slower to keep the active current down.

10.4.2.3 Select the right clock source

Some microcontrollers provide multiple clock sources with different capabilities in terms of frequency and accuracy. Depending on your application, you could be better off using an internal clock source to save power. This is because the combined power consumption of an oscillator and an external crystal could be much higher than that used by the internal clock source. Alternatively, you could switch between different clock sources basing that selection on the requirements of the workload.

10.4.2.4 Turn off unused clock signals

Many modern microcontrollers allow you to turn off the clock signals for peripherals not being used, or to turn the clock signals on before the peripherals are used. In addition, some devices also allow you to power down some of these unused peripherals to save power.

10.4.2.5 Utilized clock system features

Some microcontrollers provide various clock dividers for different parts of the system. You can use them to reduce the speed of peripherals, peripheral buses, and so on.

10.4.2.6 Power supply design

A good power supply design is another key factor in achieving high energy efficiency. For example, if you use a voltage source with a higher voltage than required you will need to reduce the voltage and, by so doing, often waste power.

10.4.2.7 Modify the idle thread of RTOS

In an application that has an RTOS, it is often beneficial to customize the idle thread to utilize sleep mode features to reduce power consumption. The idle thread/task is a part of the RTOS that executes when there are no other threads/tasks to process. By default, the idle thread might use a WFE instruction to put the processor to sleep. You can customize the idle thread codes by using examples that are available from microcontroller vendors. By doing so, when the system is idle (i.e., the idle thread is executing), it is possible to further reduce the power consumption of the system.

10.4.2.8 Modify the clock control of RTOS

Many RTOS designed for Cortex-M processors use a SysTick timer for timekeeping. Because SysTick is available in most Cortex-M based systems, it allows the RTOS to work straight "out of the box". However, it is possible to achieve lower power by switching the RTOS's clock control code so that it uses a system-level timer peripheral. Some of these system-level timers have a lower power requirement than the SysTick and can still run, even when the clocks to the processor have stopped (e.g., when the processor is in sleep mode with state retention).

10.4.2.9 Running program from SRAM

If the program code is small enough, you can consider running the application code entirely from SRAM and, to save power, turn off the power to the internal flash memory. To achieve this, the microcontroller would need to start up with the program code in flash memory, the reset handler would need to copy the program image to SRAM and execute from there and then, to save power, turn off the flash memory.

Because many microcontrollers only have a limited amount of SRAM, it is often impossible to copy the whole program to it. It is still possible, however, to reduce the system's power by copying the frequently used parts of the program to the SRAM. Once this is undertaken, these program parts are then executed from the SRAM and the flash memory is only turned on as and when the remaining parts of the program are needed.

10.4.2.10 Choosing the right I/O port configuration

Some microcontrollers have programmable I/O port options to control the drive strength (i.e., the electrical current supported by the I/O pins on the chip) and the skew rate. Depending on the devices connected to the I/O pins, the power consumption of the I/O interface logic can be reduced by having a lower drive strength or a slower skew rate configuration.

10.4.3 Reduction of active cycles

10.4.3.1 Utilizing the sleep modes

One of the ways to reduce power consumption is, as often as possible, to utilize the sleep mode features of the microcontroller. Even if each idle period only lasts for a short period, utilizing sleep mode for those idle periods could still make a difference. In addition, features like sleep-on-exit can also assist in reducing the active cycles.

10.4.3.2 *Reducing the run time*

When a C compiler is configured to compile a project with the speed optimization option, the program size usually increases due to the optimization method used (e.g., loop unrolling). If you have spare memory space in the flash memory, you can select speed optimization in the project's compilation options (at least for the codes that frequently run). By so doing, the tasks are completed quicker and the system can stay in sleep mode longer.

10.4.4 Sleep mode current reduction

10.4.4.1 *Using the right sleep mode*

Some microcontrollers provide various sleep modes and some peripherals can operate in some of those sleep modes without waking up the processor. By using the right sleep mode for your application, you can significantly reduce the power consumption of the microcontroller. However, since some sleep modes have a much longer wake up latency, the sleep mode configuration needs to be carefully chosen. For applications that need a fast response, those sleep modes with a long wake up latency would be undesirable.

10.4.4.2 *Utilizing the power control features*

Some microcontrollers allow you the option to fine-tune the power profile settings in different modes, i.e., active and sleep. For example, for each mode, the microcontroller can automatically turn off the PLL and a selection of peripherals. However, this can, in some cases, affect the wake-up latency of the system.

In some microcontroller systems, the flash memory can automatically be switched off in certain sleep modes. By so doing, a significant reduction in the sleep mode current can be achieved.

10.5 System Control Block (SCB) and system control features

10.5.1 Registers in the System Control Block (SCB)

The System Control Block (SCB) is a group of hardware registers inside the Cortex-M processor which handles the processor's control functions. They are accessible by the privileged software and by the debugger.

The SCB registers for exception and interrupt management were covered in Chapter 9 and are also detailed in Table 10.7.

If the TrustZone security extension is implemented, some of these registers are banked between security states:

- When in Secure state, privileged software access to the SCB data structure sees the Secure view of the SCB registers.
- When in a Non-secure state, privileged software access to the SCB data structure sees the Non-secure view of the SCB registers.
- When in Secure state, privileged software can see the Non-secure view of the SCB registers using Non-secure alias (SCB_NS) address 0xE002EDxx (Fig. 10.13).

TABLE 10.7 SCB registers for management of exceptions and interrupts (covered in Chapter 9).

Address	Register	Covered in section	CMSIS-CORE symbol	Non-secure alias
0xE000ED04	Interrupt Control and State Register	9.3.2	SCB->ICSR	SCB_NS->ICSR (0xE002ED04)
0xE000ED08	Vector Table Offset Register	9.5	SCB->VTOR	SCB_NS->VTOR
0xE000ED0C	Application Interrupt/Reset Control Register	9.3.4	SCB->AIRCR	SCB_NS->AIRCR (0xE002ED0C)
0xE000ED18 to 0xE000ED23	System Handler Priority Registers	9.3.3	SCB->SHP[n]	SCB_NS->SHP[n] (0xE002ED18 to 0xE002ED23)
0xE000ED24	System Handle Control and State Register	9.3.5	SCB->SHCSR	SCB_NS->SHCSR (0xE002ED24)

A debugger with permission to debug the Secure world software can access both the Secure and the Non-secure SCB data structures. However, the alias method used by Secure software, which allows the registers to be accessed with the SCB and the SCB_NS views, is not suitable for the aforementioned debugger. Because the SCB data view at address 0xE000EDxx is dependent on the processor's security state, the SCB view is, as a result, frequently changed (Note: When the processor is running, it can frequently switch between Secure and Non-secure states). Instead of using the same alias method that is used by software, the debug tool uses the SBRSEL (Secure Bank Register Select) and the SBRSELEN control bits in the DSCSR (Debug Security Control and Status Register) to decide which SCB view to use. With this arrangement, even though the processor often switches between the Secure and Non-secure states, the processor's state does not affect the debugger's access to the SCB. This ensures that the debugger is always able to access the desired SCB register.

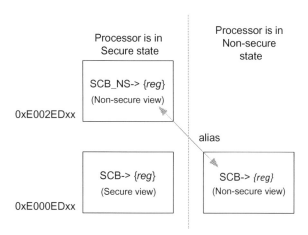

FIG. 10.13 SCB registers, the Secure and the Non-secure view.

If the TrustZone security extension is not implemented, there is only a Non-secure view of the SCB and, as a consequence, SCB_NS alias does not exist.

There are many other registers in the SCB. The full list of SCB registers is shown in Table 10.8.

Please note, the CMSIS-CORE header file includes several Media and VFP Feature registers and additional registers for cache maintenance support and. Architecturally, these are not part of the SCB but, for convenience, they are included in the SCB data structure.

10.5.2 CPU ID base register

Inside the System Control Block (SCB) there is a register called CPU ID Base Register (Table 10.9). It is a read-only register containing the processor's ID value and revision number. The address of this register is 0xE000ED00 (it is privileged access only). In C language programming this register can be accessed using the "SCB->CPUID" symbol.

Software and debug tools read this register to detect which Cortex-M processor is in the device. For reference, the CPU ID values of previous Cortex-M processors are as per Table 10.10.

If TrustZone is implemented and if the processor is in Secure privileged state, software running on the processor can read the Non-secure alias of the CPU ID base register at 0xE002ED00 (using symbol SCB_NS->CPUID). By reading SCB_NS->CPUID, privileged software can detect whether it is running in a Secure or a Non-secure state: if it is in the Secure state, the read value is nonzero. If it is in the Non-secure state, the read value is zero because Non-secure software does not see the SCB's Non-secure alias addresses.

10.5.3 AIRCR—Self-reset generation (SYSRESETREQ)

One of the key usages of the Application Interrupt/Reset Control Register (SCB->AIRCR, see Section 9.3.4) is to allow software or the debugger to trigger a system reset. This is needed:

- When an error is detected in the system (e.g., a fault handler is triggered) and the software decides to recover it using a self-reset.
- When during a debug session, the system reset is either requested by the software developer via the debugger interface or by the debug tools generating a system reset when establishing a debug connection.

The SYSRESETREQ bit (bit 2 of SCB->AIRCR) is used for generating a system reset request. For the request to be accepted, several conditions must be met:

- That bit 2 of the write data (SYSRESETREQ) is 1.
- That the upper 16 bits of the write data is a key-value (i.e., 0x05FA. If the upper 16 bits is not this key value, the write is ignored).
- That one of the following permission conditions exist:

  * That write is triggered from a debug connection, or
  * That write is generated by Secure privileged software, or

TABLE 10.8 SCB registers for Armv8.0-M.

Address	Register	CMSIS-CORE symbol	Comment
0xE000ED00	CPUID Base register	SCB->CPUID	See Section 10.5.2
0xE000ED04	Interrupt Control and State Register	SCB->ICSR	See Section 9.3.2
0xE000ED08	Vector Table Offset Register	SCB->VTOR	See Section 9.5
0xE000ED0C	Application Interrupt/Reset Control Register	SCB->AIRCR	See Sections 9.3.4 and 10.5.3
0xE000ED10	System Control Register	SCB->SCR	See Section 10.2.3
0xE000ED14	Configuration and Control Register	SCB->CCR	See Section 10.5.5
0xE000ED18 to 0xE000ED23	System Handler Priority Registers	SCB->SHP[n]	See Section 9.3.3
0xE000ED24	System Handle Control and State Register	SCB->SHCSR	See Section 9.3.5
0xE000ED28	Configurable Fault Status Register	SCB->CFSR	See Section 13.5
0xE000ED2C	HardFault Status Register	SCB->HFSR	See Section 13.5.6
0xE000ED30	Debug Fault Status Register	SCB->DFSR	See Section 13.5.7
0xE000ED34	MemManage Fault Address Register	SCB->MMFAR	See Section 13.5.9
0xE000ED38	BusFault Address Register	SCB->BFAR	See Section 13.5.9
0xE000ED3C	Auxiliary Fault Status Register	SCB->AFSR	See Section 13.5.8
0xE000ED40 to 0xE000ED44	Processor Feature Register 0,1	SCB->ID_PFR[n]	Not covered in this book.
0xE000ED48	Debug Feature Register	SCB->ID_DFR	Not covered in this book.
0xE000ED4C	Auxiliary Feature Register	SCB->ID_ADR	Not covered in this book.

Continued

TABLE 10.8   SCB registers for Armv8.0-M—cont'd

Address	Register	CMSIS-CORE symbol	Comment
0xE000ED50 to 0xE000ED5C	Memory Model Feature Register 0 to 3	SCB->ID_MMFR[n]	Not covered in this book.
0xE000ED60 to 0xE000ED74	Instruction Set Attribute Register 0 to 5	SCB->ID_ISAR[n]	See Section 20.7
0xE000ED78	Cache Level ID Register	SCB->CLIDR	Not available in the Cortex-M23 or Cortex-M33 processor (because there is no internal cache support for these two processors).
0xE000ED7C	Cache Type Register	SCB->CTR	
0xE000ED80	Current Cache Size ID Register	SCB->CCSIDR	
0xE000ED84	Cache Size Selection Register	SCB->CSSELR	
0xE000ED88	Coprocessor Access Control Register	SCB->CPACR	Available in the Cortex-M33 if the FPU, a coprocessor, or the Arm Custom Instructions feature is implemented. Refer to Chapter 14 for information on the FPU and Chapter 15 for information on the coprocessor and the Arm Custom Instructions support.
0xE000ED8C	Non-secure Access Control Register	SCB->NSACR	

∗ That write is generated by Non-secure privilege software and SYSRESETREQS (bit 4 of SCB->AIRCR) is not set to 1 by the Secure software. If the Cortex-M23/M33 device does not have TrustZone implemented, privileged software is always able to generate a system reset request.

To access the AIRCR register (including accessing the SYSRESETREQ feature), the program must be running in a privileged state. The easiest way to access the SYSRESETREQ feature is to use a function that is provided in the CMSIS-CORE header file called "`NVIC_SystemReset (void)`".

TABLE 10.9   CPU ID base register (SCB->CPUID, 0xE000ED00).

Processor and revision	Implementer bit [31:24]	Variant bit [23:20]	Constant bit [19:16]	PartNo bit [15:4]	Revision bit [3:0]
Cortex-M23—r0p0	0x41	0x0	0xC	0xD20	0x0
Cortex-M23—r1p0	0x41	0x1	0xC	0xD20	0x0
Cortex-M33—r0p0–r0p4	0x41	0x0	0xC	0xD21	0x0–0x4

TABLE 10.10 CPU ID base registers in Arm Cortex-M processors (SCB->CPUID, 0xE000ED00).

Processor and revision	Implementer bit [31:24]	Variant bit [23:20]	Constant bit [19:16]	PartNo bit [15:4]	Revision bit [3:0]
Cortex-M0—r0p0	0x41	0x0	0xC	0xC20	0x0
Cortex-M0+—r0p0/r0p1	0x41	0x0	0xC	0xC60	0x0/0x1
Cortex-M1—r0p0/r0p1	0x41	0x0	0xC	0xC21	0x0/0x1
Cortex-M1—r1p0	0x41	0x1	0xC	0xC21	0x0
Cortex-M3—r0p0	0x41	0x0	0xF	0xC23	0x0
Cortex-M3—r1p0/r1p1	0x41	0x0/0x1	0xF	0xC23	0x1
Cortex-M3—r2p0/r2p1	0x41	0x2	0xF	0xC23	0x0/0x1
Cortex-M4—r0p0/r0p1	0x41	0x0	0xF	0xC24	0x0/0x1
Cortex-M7—r0p2	0x41	0x0	0xF	0xC27	0x2
Cortex-M7—r1p0–r1p2	0x41	0x1	0xF	0xC27	0x0–0x2

Instead of using the CMSIS-CORE, you can also directly access the AIRCR register by way of the following code:

```
// Use a DMB (Data Memory Barrier) instruction so that the
// processor waits until all outstanding memory access has
// finished
__DMB();
// Read back PRIGROUP and merge with SYSRESETREQ
SCB->AIRCR = 0x05FA0004 | (SCB->AIRCR & 0x700);
while(1); // Wait until reset happens
```

The Data Memory Barrier (DMB) instruction is needed so that previous data memory accesses are completed before the reset happens. When writing to the AIRCR, the upper 16 bits of the write value should be set to 0x05FA: this key-value was introduced in the architecture to prevent a self-reset request from accidentally being generated.

The SCB->AIRCR register has other bit fields and, to prevent problems, it is recommended that a read-modify-write sequence is used to request the reset.

Depending on the design of the reset circuitry in the microcontroller, after writing 1 to SYSRESETREQ, the processor could continue to execute several instructions before the reset takes place. To overcome this problem it is advisable, therefore, to add an endless loop after the system reset request.

The self-reset logic in Armv8-M has several differences when compared to Armv7-M. These are:

- The VECTRESET bit available in Armv7-M processors (e.g., Cortex-M3/Cortex-M4) has been removed.
- The addition of the SYSRESETREQS bit, which allows Secure privileged software to stop Non-secure software from generating a self-reset by setting SYSRESETREQS to 1.

In some instances, you might want to set PRIMASK so it disables interrupt processing before starting the self-reset operation. This is to ensure that if the system reset takes some time to trigger, that an interrupt occurring during the delay does not result in the execution of an interrupt handler. Otherwise, the system reset could happen in the middle of an interrupt handler which might be undesirable for some applications.

10.5.4 AIRCR—Clearing all interrupt states (VECTCLRACTIVE)

During halt mode debugging, when the processor is halted within an exception handler (e.g., a Fault exception), a software developer might want to force the processor to jump directly into a piece of code outside the handler. Although changing the PC (program counter) and resuming the program's execution is quite straight forward, a problem could arise if the processor continues while still in exception Handler mode. If the code was written for Thread mode, the code might not work when the processor is in Handler mode (e.g., executing an SVC might not be possible when the processor is in Handler mode with a high interrupt priority level).

Fortunately, the VECTCLRACTIVE bit in the Application Interrupt/Reset Control Register (SCB->AIRCR, Section 9.3.4) allows the interrupt state in the processor to be cleared for the aforementioned debugging scenario. When using the VECTCLRACTIVE feature, the upper 16 bits of the write data must be set to 0x05FA when writing to the AIRCR (i.e., the same requirement when using the SYSRESETREQ bit in the AIRCR).

Since the VECTCLRACTIVE feature does not reset the rest of the system, generating a full system reset via SYSRESETREQ is, generally speaking, a much better option. This feature is for use with debug tools and should not be used by application software.

10.5.5 CCR—Configuration and Control Register (SCB->CCR, 0xE000ED14)

10.5.5.1 CCR overview

The CCR is a register in the SCB for controlling several processor configurations (Table 10.11). This register is privileged access only.

10.5.5.2 CCR—STKOFHFNMIGN bit

STKOFHFNMIGN (Stack Over-Flow HardFault NMI Ignore) allows HardFault and NMI handlers to bypass stack limit checks. This bit, when using the stack limit check feature, is useful when you want to reserve some memory space at the end of the main stack for the HardFault and NMI handlers.

TABLE 10.11 Configuration and Control Register (SCB->CCR, 0xE000ED14).

Bits	Name	Type	Reset value	Description
31:19	Reserved	–	0	Reserved
18	Reserved—BP	–	0	Enables branch prediction (Not available in the Cortex-M23 and Cortex-M33 processors)
17	Reserved—IC	–	0	Enables the L1 (level 1) instruction cache (Not available in the Cortex-M23 and Cortex-M33 processors)
16	Reserved—DC	–	0	Enables the L1 (level 1) data cache (Not available in the Cortex-M23 and Cortex-M33 processors)
15:11	Reserved	–	0	Reserved
10	STKOFHFNMIGN	R/W	0	Controls the action of a stack limit violation while executing a HardFault or an NMI handler (i.e., all exceptions with an interrupt priority of less than 0). When 0—stack limit fault not ignored. When 1—stack limit fault ignored. This bit is not available in the Cortex-M23 (Armv8-M Baseline)
9	Reserved	–	1	Reserved—always 1 Note: in the Cortex-M3/Cortex-M4, this is STKALIGN. It forces exception stacking to start in a double word-aligned address. In Armv8-M processors, the exception stack frames are always double word-aligned.
8	BFHFNMIGN	R/W	0	Ignores data bus fault during the execution of the HardFault handler and the execution of the NMI handler. This bit is not available in the Cortex-M23 (Armv8-M Baseline)
7:5	Reserved	–	–	Reserved
4	DIV_0_TRP	R/W	0	Trap on divide by 0 This bit is not available in the Cortex-M23 (Armv8-M Baseline)
3	UNALIGN_TRP	R/W	0 for Cortex-M33, always 1 for Cortex-M23	Trap on unaligned accesses. This bit is not writeable in the Cortex-M23 (Armv8-M Baseline)
2	Reserved	–	–	Reserved
1	USERSETMPEND	R/W	0	If set to 1, it allows unprivileged code to write to the Software Trigger Interrupt Register. This bit is not available in the Cortex-M23 (Armv8-M Baseline)
0	Reserved	–	1	Reserved It was used as NONBASETHRDENA (Nonbase thread enabled) in the Armv7-M processors. If set to 1, it allows the exception handler to return to the thread state at any level by controlling the EXC_RETURN value.

10.5.5.3 CCR—BFHFNMIGN bit

When this bit is set, handlers with a priority of −1 (e.g., HardFault) or −2 (e.g., NMI) will ignore data bus faults caused by load and store instructions. This can also be used when configurable fault exception handlers (i.e., BusFault, Usage Fault, or MemMenage fault) are executing with the FAULTMASK bit set to 1.

If this bit is not set, a data bus fault in the NMI or the HardFault handler will result in the system entering into a lock upstate (see Section 13.6).

The bit is typically used in fault handlers that need to probe various memory locations to detect the presence of issues relating to system buses and memory controller(s).

10.5.5.4 CCR—DIV_0_TRP bit

When this bit is set, a Usage Fault exception is triggered when a divide by zero occurs in the SDIV (signed divide) or the UDIV (unsigned divide) instructions. When it is not set, the operation will complete with a quotient of 0.

If the Usage Fault handler is not enabled, the HardFault exception would be triggered (see Sections 13.2.3 and 13.2.5).

10.5.5.5 CCR—UNALIGN_TRP bit

The Cortex-M33 processor supports unaligned data transfers (see Section 6.6). However, unaligned data access can be less efficient than aligned data access. This is because multiple clock cycles are required for each unaligned transfer. Also, in some instances, the occurrence of unaligned transfers might indicate the use of incorrect program code (e.g., the use of an incorrect data type). To allow software developers to detect and remove unnecessary unaligned transfers, a trap exception mechanism is, therefore, implemented in the processor to detect the presence of unaligned transfers.

If the UNALIGN_TRP bit is set to 1, the Usage Fault exception is triggered when an unaligned transfer occurs. If it is not (i.e., the UNALIGN_TRP is set to 0—the default value), unaligned transfers are allowed but only for the following single load and store instructions: LDR, LDRT, LDRH, LDRSH, LDRHT, LDRSHT, LDA, LDAH STR, STRH, STRT, STRHT, STA, STAH.

Multiple transfer instructions such as LDM, STM, LDRD, and STRD always trigger faults if the address is unaligned, regardless of the UNALIGN_TRP value.

Bytes size transfers are always aligned.

10.5.5.6 CCR—USERSETMPEND bit

By default, the Software Trigger Interrupt Register (NVIC->STIR) can only be accessed in a privileged state. If the USERSETMPEND is set to 1, unprivileged access is allowed on this register.

Please note: setting USERSETMPEND does not allow unprivileged access to other NVIC and SCB registers.

Setting USERSETMPEND can result in the following scenario. After it is set, unprivileged tasks can trigger, apart from system exceptions, any software interrupt. As a result, if USERSETMPEND is used and the system contains untrusted user tasks, the interrupt handlers need to check whether, because it could have been triggered from untrusted programs, there is an actual need for the exception handling to be carried out.

10.6 Auxiliary Control Register

10.6.1 Overview of the Auxiliary Control Register

Some Cortex-M processors provide an Auxiliary Control Register for controlling processor-specific behaviors. Many of the control bits in this register (apart from EXTEXCLALL, bit 29) are for debug purposes only and are unlikely to be used in normal application programming.

The address of the Auxiliary Control Register is 0xE000E008. Programming with a CMSIS-CORE compliant driver, the Auxiliary Control Register can be accessed using the "SCnSCB->ACTLR" symbol when the processor is in a privileged state. For Cortex-M processors with TrustZone implemented, Secure software can access the Non-secure view of the Auxiliary Control Register using the "SCnSCB_NS->ACTLR" symbol (address 0xE002E008).

10.6.2 Auxiliary Control Register for the Cortex-M23 processor

The Cortex-M23 processor has only one bit in its Auxiliary Control Register (Table 10.12).

The EXTEXCLALL bit enables the use of the system level global exclusive access monitor without the need to use an MPU to mark the memory address range as sharable. By default, most of the memory regions are nonsharable. Although privileged software can use the MPU to mark certain address ranges as sharable, the processor system must have an MPU implemented to do so. In some ultra-low power designs, an MPU might not be available due to its power consumption and the silicon area cost. Accordingly, the EXTEXCLALL bit provides an alternative way of being able to use the system level global exclusive access monitor.

EXTEXCLALL bit should be set to 1 if:

- There is more than one bus master in the system, and
- The multiple bus masters are likely to try and access the same data used for the exclusive access sequence (e.g., semaphore), and

TABLE 10.12 Auxiliary Control Register (SCnSCB->ACTLR, 0xE000ED08) for the Cortex-M23 processor.

Bits	Name	Type	Reset value	Description
31:30	Reserved	–	0	Reserved
29	EXTEXCLALL	R/W	0	When this bit is 0 (default), only the exclusive access to the sharable memory utilizes the exclusive access sideband signals (this enables the use of a global exclusive access monitor, see Section 6.7). When this bit is 1 (default), all exclusive access utilizes the exclusive access sideband signals.
28:0	Reserved	–	0	Reserved

- The software is unable to use the MPU to set up the memory region for the exclusive access data (e.g., when the MPU is not available).

10.6.3 Auxiliary Control Register for the Cortex-M33 processor

As well as having the EXTEXCLALL bit, the Auxiliary Control Register in the Cortex-M33 processor also has the following additional control bits (Table 10.13).

TABLE 10.13   Auxiliary Control Register (SCnSCB->ACTLR, 0xE000ED08) for the Cortex-M33 processor.

Bits	Name	Type	Reset value	Description
31:30	Reserved	–	0	Reserved
29	EXTEXCLALL	R/W	0	When this bit is 0 (default), only the exclusive access to the sharable memory can utilize the exclusive access sideband signals (this enables the use of a global exclusive access monitor, see Section 6.7). When this bit is 1 (default), all exclusive access utilizes the exclusive access sideband signals.
38:13	Reserved	–	0	Reserved
12	DISITMATBFLUSH	R/W	0	When set to 1, it disables the ATB flush in the ITM and the DWT debug components. When the ATB flush is disabled, the flush request signal (AFVALID) is ignored and the flush acknowledgment signal (AFREADY) is held high. This allows the trace interface to have the same behavior as in the previous Cortex-M3/Cortex-M4 processors, which do not support the ATB flush. This feature is only required when the debug tools have an issue with the ATB flush support.
11	Reserved	–	0	Reserved
10	FPEXCODIS	R/W	0	When set to 1, it disables the FPU exception outputs (see Section 14.6). This bit is only available when the FPU is implemented.
9	DISOOFP	R/W	0	When set to 1, the interleaved floating-point and nonfloating-point instructions are completed in the same order as defined in the instruction sequence (out-of-order completion is disabled). Only available when the FPU is implemented.
8:3	Reserved	–	0	Reserved
2	DISFOLD	R/W	0	When set to 1, it disables the dual issue capability (by doing so, the performance of the processor will be reduced)
1	Reserved	–	0	Reserved
0	DISMCYCINT	R/W	0	Disables the interruption of multiple cycle instructions, such as LDM, STM, 64-bit multiply, and the divide instructions. Because an LDM or STM instruction must complete before the processor can stack the current state and enter the interrupt handler, setting this bit will increase the interrupt latency of the processor.

Other than EXTEXCLALL, the control bit fields detailed in Table 10.13 are only used for debugging.

10.7 Other registers in the System Control Block

There are several other registers in the System Control Block. These are:

- The fault status registers—this is covered in Chapter 13, Section 13.5.
- The coprocessor access control (CPACR and NSACR)—this is covered in Sections 14.2.3 and 14.2.4.
- The cache management registers—not available in the Cortex-M23 and Cortex-M33 processors.
- A range of read-only registers that allow software and debug tools to identify the processor's available features.l

OS support features

11.1 Overview of the OS support features

Arm® Cortex®-M processors are designed to support embedded Operating Systems (OS) and provide a range of features to enable the efficient and secure execution of the OS and its applications. Many embedded OS's which are designed for Cortex-M processors are referred to as Real-Time Operating Systems (RTOS). They provide task scheduling capabilities that deliver deterministic responses, that is, a critical task that can be executed within a predefined timing window after the occurrence of a certain hardware event.

Cortex-M processors are designed with features that support OS operations. If TrustZone® is not implemented, the following features are available in the majority of Cortex-M processors, including the Cortex-M23 and Cortex-M33:

- SysTick timer: A simple timer inside the processor for generating periodic interrupt events for OS operations (i.e., System Ticks). It enables the OS to support Cortex-M processors out-of-the-box. Software developers can also use the SysTick timer for other timing purposes if the SysTick is not being used by an OS, that is, either the system does not have an OS, or the OS uses another device specific timer peripheral for the system tick interrupt.
- Banked stack pointer: The stack pointer is banked between the Main Stack Pointer (MSP) and the Process Stack Pointer (PSP)
  - The MSP is used for booting up, system initialization, and for exception handlers (including the OS Kernel).
  - The PSP is used by application tasks.
- Stack limit checking: This detects stack overflow errors and is a new feature in Armv8-M. (Note: This feature is not available in the Cortex-M23 processor without TrustZone and, when TrustZone is included, only the Secure stack pointers support the stack limit checking feature.)
- SVC and PendSV exceptions: The SVC instruction trigger's the SVCall exception event, which allows application tasks (which usually execute as unprivileged thread) to access OS services (which execute with privileged access permission). The PendSV exception is

triggered by the Interrupt Control and State Register in the System Control Block (SCB-> ICSR: see Section 9.3.2). It can be used for context switching operations (Section 11.9).

- Unprivileged execution level and Memory Protection Unit (MPU): This allows a basic security model which restricts the access rights of unprivileged application tasks. The separation of privileged and unprivileged software can also be used in conjunction with the Memory Protection Unit (MPU), thus further enhancing the robustness of the embedded systems.
- Exclusive access: The exclusive load and store instructions are useful for semaphore and mutual exclusive (MUTEX) operations in the OS.

When TrustZone is implemented, a range of the aforementioned OS features are banked between the Secure and the Non-secure states. The following are additional features which are available when TrustZone is implemented:

- Banked stack pointer—a total of four stack pointers are available: MSP_S (Secure MSP), PSP_S (Secure PSP), MSP_NS (Non-secure MSP), and PSP_NS (Non-secure PSP).
- Stack limit checking for Secure stack pointers for all Armv8-M processors.
- Banked MPU (Both Secure and Non-secure).
- Banked SVCall and PendSV exception.
- Secure SysTick Timer (optional on Armv8-M Baseline/Cortex-M23 processor).

In addition to the above, a number of features in the processor also indirectly benefit OS deployment in the Cortex-M processors. For example, the Instrumentation Trace Macrocell (ITM) in the Cortex-M33 processor (as well as all Armv7-M processors) can be used to enable OS aware debugging. The low interrupt latency characteristic of the Cortex-M processor also improves the performance of context switching.

11.2 SysTick timer

11.2.1 Purpose of the SysTick timer

When using an embedded OS, the OS relies on a timer peripheral to schedule OS exceptions for context switching between multiple application tasks. In simple OS designs, the OS uses a timer peripheral to generate periodic interrupts (sometimes referred to as system ticks). In the timer's interrupt handler, the software reevaluates the tasks' priorities and can, if required, context switch to another task. The SysTick timer is designed to fit this need: since the SysTick timer is available in most Cortex-M devices, an embedded OS can rely on the presence of this timer and run it straight out-of-the-box without the need to make any custom changes.

If the application does not contain an RTOS, or if the RTOS is configured to use another peripheral timer, the SysTick timer can then be used for other timing purposes, that is:

- For a periodic interrupt for control purposes
- For timing measurement
- For producing a delay

The SysTick timer is optional on the Armv8-M Baseline (i.e., the Cortex-M23 processor). SoC designers creating a Cortex-M23 based design can, therefore, omit the SysTick timer to reduce the total silicon area. But, in most microcontroller devices, it is likely that the SysTick timer would be available and, thus, will enable software developers to quickly get the OS code up and running.

The SysTick timer is always present in Armv8-M Mainline processors, such as the Cortex-M33 processor.

When TrustZone is implemented, there can be up to two SysTick timers in the processor. The possible configurations are listed in Table 11.1.

Further information about the banked SysTick operations in a TrustZone enabled system can be found in Section 11.2.4.

11.2.2 SysTick timer operations

The SysTick timer is a simple 24-bit timer and contains 4 registers (Fig. 11.1).

The timer operates as a down counter and triggers the SysTick exception when it reaches 0 (Fig. 11.2). After reaching zero, at the next transition it automatically reloads using the value in the reload value register. It can run at the processor's clock frequency but can also be set up to decrement using, if available, a reference clock. Normally such a reference clock would be an on-chip clock source with a fixed clock speed. Please note, if the processor's clock has stopped, which occurs during certain sleep modes, the SysTick timer would also stop.

For easier access to the SysTick registers, a data structure called SysTick is defined in the CMSIS-CORE header file to allow these registers to be accessed (Table 11.2).

Some points:

- The SysTick registers are accessible in privileged state only.
- Unprivileged access to SysTick triggers an error response.
- Access to the registers should be carried out using 32-bit aligned transfers.

TABLE 11.1 SysTick implementation options.

	Cortex-M23	**Cortex-M33**
TrustZone not implemented	Options of: - no SysTick timer, or - One SysTick timer	One SysTick timer
TrustZone implemented	Options of: - no SysTick timer, or - one SysTick timer (programmable as Secure or Non-secure), or - two SysTick timers (1 Secure, 1 Non-secure)	Two SysTick timers (1 Secure, 1 Non-secure)

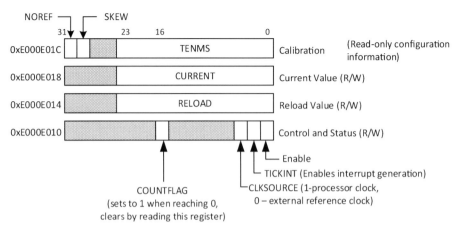

FIG. 11.1 SysTick registers.

When SysTick is enabled (i.e., bit 0 of the SysTick->CTRL is set to 1), the down counter register (SysTick->VAL) decrements at either the processor's clock speed (applies if bit 2 of the SysTick->CTRL is 1), or at the rising edge (i.e., 0 to 1 transitions) of a reference clock (applies if bit 2 of the SysTick->CTRL is 0). The reference clock, if available, must be one half slower than the processor clock speed for it to correctly synchronize. In some devices there is no reference clock available; in which case the NOREF bit (bit 31 of the SysTick->CALIB)

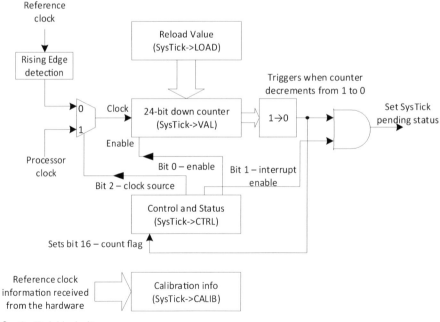

FIG. 11.2 SysTick block diagram.

TABLE 11.2   Summary of the SysTick registers.

Address	CMSIS-CORE symbol	Register
0xE000E010	SysTick->CTRL	SysTick Control and Status Register
0xE000E014	SysTick->LOAD	SysTick Reload Value Register
0xE000E018	SysTick->VAL	SysTick Current Value Register
0xE000E01C	SysTick->CALIB	SysTick Calibration Register

should be 1 and, when it is, the CLKSOURCE bit (which determines when the SysTick decrements) is forced to 1.

When the down counter (SysTick->VAL) counts down to 0, the COUNTFLAG (bit 16 of the SysTick->CTRL) is automatically set to 1 by the hardware. If the TICKINT bit is set, the SysTick exception pending status will be triggered and the processor will execute, when possible, the SysTick exception handler (exception type 15). The Reload value (SysTick->LOAD) is then loaded into the SysTick's current counter (SysTick->VAL) at the SysTick's next decrement. The COUNTFLAG, in this scenario, will not clear until there is either a register read or until the current counter value has been cleared.

An additional register, called the SysTick Calibration Register, is available to allow the on-chip hardware to provide calibration information for the software. In the CMSIS-CORE, the use of the SysTick Calibration Register is normally not needed because the CMSIS-CORE provides a software variable called "SystemCoreClock". This variable is set up in the system initialization function "SystemInit()" and is also updated each time the system clock configuration is changed. This software approach is better than using the SysTick Calibration Register as it is more flexible (e.g., the "SystemCoreClock" variable is easily updated).

The programmer's models for the SysTick registers are shown in Tables 11.3–11.6.

The SysTick Calibration Value Register (SysTick->CALIB) is read only and was designed to provide timing calibration information. If this information is available, the lowest 24 bits of

TABLE 11.3   SysTick Control and Status Register (0xE000E010).

Bit	Name	Type	Reset value	Description
16	COUNTFLAG	R	0	Returns 1 if the timer counted to 0 since the last read of this register; clears to 0 automatically when read or when current counter value is cleared
2	CLKSOURCE	R/W	0	0 = Uses External reference clock (STCLK) 1 = Uses processor clock
1	TICKINT	R/W	0	1 = Enables SYSTICK interrupt generation when SYSTICK timer reaches 0 0 = Does not generate interrupt
0	ENABLE	R/W	0	SYSTICK timer enable (1 = enabled, 0 = disabled)

TABLE 11.4 SysTick Reload Value Register (0xE000E014).

Bits	Name	Type	Reset value	Description
23:0	RELOAD	R/W	–	Reloads value when timer reaches 0

the SysTick->CALIB register provide the reload value required to achieve a SysTick interval of 10 ms. However, because many microcontrollers do not have this information, the TENMS bit field would normally read as zero. You can also use bit 31 of the SysTick Calibration register to determine whether a reference clock is available.

Instead of relying on SysTick->CALIB, the CMSIS-CORE's approach of providing a software variable (i.e., the **SystemCoreClock**) for clock frequency information is more flexible and is supported by most microcontroller vendors.

In software projects with a CMSIS-CORE header file, the SysTick exception handler is called "SysTick_Handler(void)".

11.2.3 Using the SysTick timer

11.2.3.1 *Using the SysTick timer for RTOS*

Many RTOS's already have built-in support for a SysTick timer straight out of the box so do not, unless you want to change the use of a device-specific peripheral timer for OS operations, require software changes to be made. For further information on this, please refer to the relevant RTOS documentation.

11.2.3.2 *Using the SysTick timer with CMSIS-CORE*

The CMSIS-CORE header file provides a function for periodic SysTick interrupt generation using the processor's clock as the clock source:

```
uint32_t SysTick_Config(uint32_t ticks);
```

This function sets the SysTick interrupt interval to "ticks"; enables the counter using the processor clock; and enables the SysTick exception with the lowest exception priority.

For example, if you have a clock frequency of 30 MHz and you want to trigger a SysTick exception of 1 kHz, you can use the following function call:

```
SysTick_Config(SystemCoreClock / 1000);
```

TABLE 11.5 SysTick Current Value Register (0xE000E018).

Bits	Name	Type	Reset value	Description
23:0	CURRENT	R/ Wc	–	Reads the current value of the timer. A write to clear counter to 0. Clearing of current value also clears COUNTFLAG in SYSTICK Control and Status Register

TABLE 11.6 SysTick Calibration Value Register (0xE000E01C).

Bits	Name	Type	Reset value	Description
31	NOREF	R	–	1 = No external reference clock 0 = External reference clock available
30	SKEW	R	–	1 = Calibration value is not exactly 10 ms 0 = Calibration value is accurate
23:0	TENMS	R	–	Calibration value for 10 ms: A chip designer could provide this value via a hardware input signal on the processor. If this value is read as 0, the calibration value is not available

This example assumes the variable "SystemCoreClock" holds the correct clock frequency value of 30×10^6. If it does not, you can just use:

```
SysTick_Config(30000); // 30MHz / 1000 = 30000
```

The SysTick_Handler() will then trigger at a rate of 1 kHz.

If the input parameter of the SysTick_Config function cannot fit into the 24-bit reload value register (i.e., it is larger than 0xFFFFFF), the SysTick_Config function returns 1 to indicate that the operation has failed. If the operation is successful, it returns 0.

11.2.3.3 Using SysTick timer without using SysTick_Config()

If you:

- would like to use the SysTick timer with a reference clock, or
- would like to use the SysTick timer without generating a SysTick exception

then you will have to manually create the SysTick timer setup code. To do so, the following sequence is recommended:

(1) Disable the SysTick timer by writing 0 to SysTick->CTRL. This step is optional. It is recommended for reusable code because the SysTick could have been previously enabled.

(2) Write the new reload value to SysTick->LOAD. The reload value should be the interval value——1.

(3) Write to the SysTick Current Value register SysTick->VAL with any value to clear the current value to 0.

(4) Write to the SysTick Control and Status register SysTick->CTRL to start the SysTick timer.

Because the SysTick timer counts down to 0, the reload value should be programmed to the interval value minus 1. For example, if you want to set the SysTick interval to 1000, you should set the reload value (SysTick->LOAD) to 999.

If you want to use the SysTick timer in polling mode, you can use the count flag in the SysTick Control and Status Register (SysTick->CTRL) to determine when the timer reaches zero. For example, you can create a timed delay by setting the SysTick timer to a certain value and wait for it to reach zero:

```
SysTick->CTRL = 0;      // Disables SysTick
SysTick->LOAD = 0xFF;  // Counts from 255 to 0 (256 cycles)
SysTick->VAL  = 0;      // Clears current value as well as count flag
SysTick->CTRL = 5;      // Enables SysTick timer with processor clock
while ((SysTick->CTRL & 0x00010000)==0);// Waits until count flag is set
SysTick->CTRL = 0;      // Disables SysTick
```

If you want to schedule the SysTick interrupt for a "one-shot" operation which triggers in a certain time, you can reduce the reload value by 12 cycles to compensate for the interrupt latency. For example, if we want to have the SysTick handler to execute in a 300-clock cycle time:

```
volatile int SysTickFired; // A global software flag to
                           // indicate the SysTickAlarm has executed
...
SysTick->CTRL = 0;         // Disables SysTick
SysTick->LOAD = (300-12); // Sets Reload value
                           // Minus 12 because of exception latency
SysTick->VAL  = 0;      // Clears current value to 0
SysTickFired  = 0;      // Sets up software flag to zero
SysTick->CTRL = 0x7;   // Enables SysTick, enables SysTick
                       // exception and uses the processor clock
while (SysTickFired == 0); // Waits until the software flag is set by
                           // SYSTICK handler
```

Inside the "one-shot" SysTick Handler, we need to disable the SysTick so that the SysTick exception only triggers once. We might also need to clear the SysTick pending status in case the pending status had been set again due to the required processing task taking some time. The example of the "one-shot" SysTick Handler is as follow:

```
void SysTick_Handler(void)   // SYSTICK exception handler
{
SysTick->CTRL = 0x0;         // Disables SysTick
...;                         // Executes the required processing task
SCB->ICSR |= 1<<25;          // Clears the SYSTICK pend bit
                             // in case it has been pended again
SysTickFired++;              // Updates the software flag so that the
                             // main program knows that the SysTick alarm
                             // task has been carried out
return;
}
```

Please note, if another exception happens at the same time, the SysTick exception is likely to be delayed.

11.2.3.4 Using the SysTick timer for timing measurement

The SysTick timer can be used for timing measurements. For example, you can measure the duration of a short function using the following code:

```
unsigned int start_time, stop_time, cycle_count;
SysTick->CTRL = 0;              // Disables SysTick
SysTick->LOAD = 0xFFFFFFFF;     // Sets the Reload value to maximum
SysTick->VAL  = 0;              // Clears the current value to 0
SysTick->CTRL = 0x5;            // Enables the SysTick, uses the processor clock
while(SysTick->VAL != 0);       // Waits until the SysTick is reloaded
start_time = SysTick->VAL;      // Obtains the start time
function();                     // Executes the function to be measured
stop_time  = SysTick->VAL;      // Obtains the stop time
cycle_count = start_time - stop_time; // Calculates the time taken
```

Since the SysTick is a decrement counter, the value of the "start_time" is greater than that for the "stop_time". If the execution time of the function being measured is too long (i.e., over 2^24 clock cycles), then the timer would underflow. With this in mind, there might be a need to include a check for the count_flag at the end of the timing measurement. If the count_flag is set, the duration being measured would be more than 0xFFFFFF clock cycles. If that is the case, the SysTick exception will have to be enabled and the SysTick Handler used to count how many times the SysTick counter underflowed. The total number of clock cycles measured would then also include the SysTick exceptions.

11.2.4 TrustZone and SysTick timer

As detailed in Table 11.1 in Section 11.2.1, an Armv8-M processor with TrustZone implemented can have up to two SysTick timers, that is, a Secure SysTick and a Non-secure SysTick. Non-secure software can only see the Non-secure SysTick, but the Secure software can see both the Secure SysTick and the Non-secure SysTick (via the Non-secure SysTick alias address). This is shown in Fig. 11.3.

The SysTick exception is banked between the Secure and the Non-secure worlds. The SysTick exceptions are linked to the SysTick timer of the same security domain as described below:

- The Secure SysTick timer triggers the Secure SysTick exception and the exception entry uses the SysTick vector in the Secure vector table. The base address of the Secure vector table is pointed to by the VTOR_S.
- The Non-secure SysTick timer triggers the Non-secure SysTick exception and the exception entry uses the SysTick vector in the Non-secure vector table. The base address of the Non-secure vector table is pointed to by the VTOR_NS.

SysTick exceptions can also be triggered by software using SCB->ICSR (Interrupt Control and State Register: see Section 9.3.2). The behavior of triggering a SysTick exception using SCB->ICSR is shown in Table 11.7.

SysTick is optional in the Armv8-M Baseline processor. If the chip designer decides to implement just one SysTick timer, Secure privileged software can program the STTNS bit (SysTick Targets Non-secure, bit 24 in the SCB->ICSR) to decide whether the implemented SysTick timer is to be selected as:

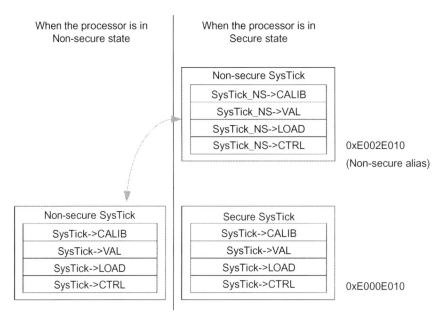

FIG. 11.3 SysTick in address space.

- the Secure SysTick (when STTNS in SCB->ICSR is 0, the default value), or
- the Non-secure SysTick (when STTNS in SCB->ICSR is 1)

The STTNS control bit is not available if:

- SysTick is not implemented, or
- Two SysTick timers have been implemented, or
- TrustZone is not implemented

    The STTNS bit is only accessible from Secure privileged state.

11.2.5 Other considerations

A number of considerations need to be made when using the SysTick timer:

1. The registers in the SysTick timer are only be accessed when in privileged state and can only be accessed using a 32-bit aligned access.

TABLE 11.7 Banked SysTick pending status behavior.

If the processor is in Secure state:	If the processor is in Non-secure state:
Setting PENDSTSET in the SCB->ICSR sets the pending status of the Secure SysTick Setting PENDSTSET in the SCB_NS->ICSR sets the pending status of the Non-secure SysTick	Setting PENDSTSET in the SCB->ICSR sets the pending status of the Non-secure SysTick

2. The reference clock might not be available in some microcontroller designs.
3. When you are using an embedded OS in your application, the SysTick timer might be used by the OS and should therefore not be used by application tasks.
4. The SysTick Timer stops counting when the processor is halted during debugging.
5. Depending on the design of the microcontroller, the SysTick timer may stop in certain sleep modes.

11.3 Banked stack pointers

11.3.1 Benefits of banked stack pointers

The stack pointer registers and stack operations are covered in Chapter 4 (Section 4.2.2 Registers and Section 4.3.4 Stack Memory). Armv8-M processors can either have two stack pointers (when TrustZone is not implemented) or four stack pointers (when TrustZone is implemented). The fundamental reasons for having multiple stack pointers are:

- **For security and system robustness:** Multiple stack pointers are needed to allow the stack memories for unprivileged application threads to be separated from stack spaces for privileged codes (including the OS kernel). If TrustZone is implemented, the stack spaces for Secure and Non-secure software components would need to be separated.
- **For ease and efficiency of context switching during RTOS operations**: When an RTOS is used in a Cortex-M processor, the Process Stack Pointer (PSP) is used by multiple application threads and needs to be reprogrammed during each context switching operation. For each context switching, the PSP updates and points to the stack space of each thread that is due to be executed. When the processor is running the OS kernel functions (e.g., task scheduling, context switching), the codes inside the OS operate using their own stack memory. Hence a separate stack pointer (i.e., the Main Stack Pointer (MSP)) is needed so that the stacked data used by the OS is not be affected by the reprogramming of the PSP. By having a separate MSP and PSP, the OS design is simpler and is more efficient.
- **Improved memory usage:** With application threads using PSP and exception handlers using MSP, software developers only need, therefore, to consider the first level of the exception stack frame when allocating stack space for application threads. This is because only the Main Stack allocation needs to support the total stack space required for multiple levels of nested exceptions/interrupts. Because there is no need to preserve stack space for nested exceptions in each of the application thread's stack, memory usage is more efficient.

11.3.2 Operations of banked stack pointers

As shown in Fig. 4.6, there can be up to four stack pointers in an Armv8-M processor. These are:

- Secure Main Stack Pointer (MSP_S)
- Secure Processor Stack Pointer (PSP_S)

- Non-secure Main Stack Pointer (MSP_NS)
- Non-secure Process Stack Pointer (PSP_NS)

The selection of stack pointers being used is determined by the processor's security states (either Secure or Non-secure), the processor's mode (Thread or Handler), and the SPSEL setting in the CONTROL register. This is covered in Sections 4.2.2.3 and 4.3.4. If TrustZone is not implemented, only the Non-secure stack pointers are available.

For programming purposes, normally:

- The MSP and the PSP symbols refer to the stack pointer in the current selected state:
  - If the processor is in a Secure state, MSP means MSP_S and PSP means PSP_S
  - If the processor is in a Non-secure state, MSP means MSP_NS and PSP means PSP_NS
- Secure software can access the MSP_NS and PSP_NS using MSR and MRS instructions

By default, a Cortex-M processor uses the Main Stack Pointer (MSP) to boot up:

- if TrustZone is implemented, the processor boots up in Secure privileged state and, by default, selects MSP_S (the Secure MSP). The default value of CONTROL_S.SPSEL (bit 1 in the CONTROL_S register) is 0, which indicates that the MSP has been selected.
- if TrustZone is not implemented, the processor boots up in (Non-secure) privileged state and, by default, selects MSP. The default value of CONTROL.SPSEL (bit 1 in the CONTROL register) is 0, which indicates that the MSP has been selected.

In most applications without an embedded OS or RTOS, the MSP can be used for all operations and the PSP can be ignored.

For most RTOS based systems without TrustZone, the PSP is used by application threads for stack operations. The MSP is used for booting up, for initialization and for exception handlers (including OS kernel codes). For each of these software components, stack operation instructions (such as PUSH, POP, VPUSH, and VPOP) and most instructions that use SP (e.g., using SP/R13 as a base address for data access), will use the currently selected stack pointer.

Each application task/thread has its own stack space (Fig. 11.4: Note that the placement of the stack space in this diagram is just an example) with the context switching code in the OS updating the PSP each time the context is switched.

Within the context switching operations, the OS code accesses the PSP directly using the MRS and MSR instructions. The access of PSP include:

- saving the PSP value of the task to be switched out
- setting the PSP to the previous PSP value of the task to be switched into

By separating the stack spaces, the OS can use either the MPU (Memory Protection Unit) or the stack limit check feature to restrict the maximum amount of stack space each task/thread uses. In addition to restricting the stack memory that is consumed, the OS can also utilize the MPU to restrict which memory address ranges an application task/thread is able to access. More information on this topic is covered in Chapter 12.

Cortex-M processor systems with TrustZone have four stack pointers. In a typical system which has security software solutions such as Trusted Firmware-M [1] and secure libraries, the way the four stack pointers could be used is as per Fig. 11.5.

Using the software architecture as shown in Fig. 11.5:

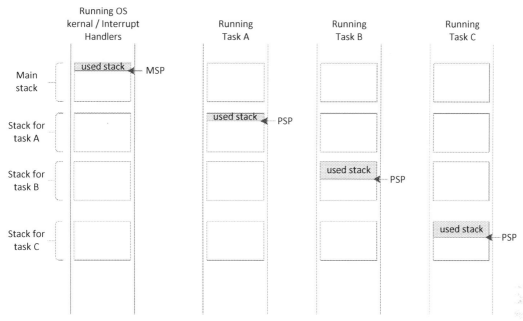

FIG. 11.4 The stack memory allocated for each task/thread is separated from other stacks.

- the security management software (such as the Secure Partition Manager in Trusted Firmware-M) [1] executes in Secure privileged state, and
- the secure libraries (such as IoT cloud connectors/clients) execute in Secure unprivileged state.

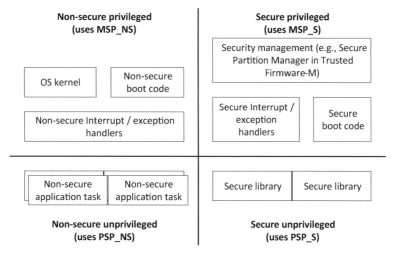

FIG. 11.5 Stack pointer usage in a TrustZone system.

By so doing, the security management software can configure the Secure MPU to isolate the various Secure libraries and, thus, prevent those libraries from accessing/corrupting critical data being used by the security management software. The use of PSP_S (Secure Process Stack Pointer) allows us to separate the stacks of these libraries.

Similar to the execution of multiple tasks on the Non-secure side in an RTOS environment, these Secure unprivileged libraries might need to be accessed at different times and, to do so, will need security management software to handle the context switching of these libraries. This will involve reprogramming the PSP_S and the reconfiguration of the Secure MPU at each context switch.

11.3.3 Banked stack pointers in bare metal systems

While the use of banked stack pointers is mostly for embedded OS/RTOS systems, it is possible to utilize banked stack pointers for bare metal (i.e., the OS not being used) applications. Such an arrangement could be interesting because:

- Even when an application running in thread mode (which is using the PSP) has crashed due to a stack corruption, the fault exception handler (e.g., the HardFault_Handler) can still execute.
- In devices where there are multiple RAM regions that are not continuous you can configure the thread stack (using MSP) to one RAM region and the Handler stack to another.

A simple way to achieve this arrangement is as follows (Fig. 11.6):

(1) At the start of the program, define the initial stack using the MSP (this is the normal practice for Cortex-M projects).
(2) Reserve a separate stack space for the handlers.

FIG. 11.6 Using banked stack pointers in a bare metal system.

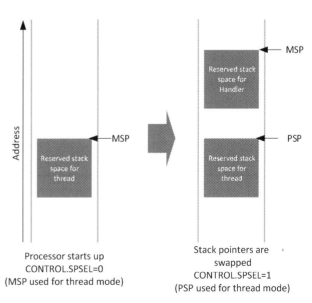

(3) At thread execution level, copy the value of the MSP into the PSP.

(4) With interrupts disabled (e.g., by setting PRIMASK to 1), switch the stack pointer selection to use the PSP in thread mode and sets the MSP to the address at the top of the handler's stack.

(5) Clear PRIMASK to enable interrupts.

When using assembly startup code, the aforementioned stack setup steps 1–5 can be carried out inside the reset handler. Alternatively, the same steps can be carried out in a C programming environment as follows:

A simple way to initialize and use the PSP (suitable for a bare-metal system only; not suitable for an RTOS environment)

```
        uint64_t MainStack[1024]; // Space for the new Main Stack
        ...
    int main(void)
    {
        ...
        // Sets initial Main Stack value to the address at the top of the new
        // Main Stack
        uint32_t new_msp_val = ((unsigned int) MainStack) + (sizeof (MainStack));
        ...

        __set_PSP(__get_MSP());
        __disable_irq(); // Disables interrupts by setting PRIMASK
        __set_CONTROL(__get_CONTROL()|0x2); // Sets SPSEL
        __ISB(); // ISB after update CONTROL is an architectural recommendation
        __set_MSP(new_msp_val); // Points MSP to top of MainStack[]
        __enable_irq(); // Enables interrupts by clearing PRIMASK
        ...
```

It is essential that the interrupts are disabled for a short period of time when executing this code sequence. If the interrupts are not disabled and an interrupt arrives just after setting the SPSEL bit in the CONTROL register, the following events can occur:

- The exception stacking pushes a number of registers into the stack using the PSP.
- During the execution of the ISR (using the MSP, which is pointing to the old PSP before stacking), the stack operations in the ISR can end up corrupting the existing stacked contents.
- After the ISR has finished and when the "main()" program has resumed, a software failure could occur because the data in the stack used by the "main()" program was corrupted by the ISR.

The aforementioned software steps (1–5) are applicable only for bare metal systems. For RTOS based systems, the handling of multiple stacks is usually integrated into the RTOS and is hidden away from software developers. Please refer to the RTOS documentation, and to code examples supplied by RTOS vendors, for stack configuration information when using an RTOS in software projects.

11.4 Stack limit checking

11.4.1 Overview

Stack overflow is a common software error and is where an application, or an application task within a multitasking system, consumes more stack space than it is allocated. Such an occurrence might end up corrupting other data and, in turn, might cause an application to fail (e.g., getting incorrect results or making it crash). It could also negatively impact on the security of IoT applications.

Prior to Armv8-M architecture, software was able to use the MPU to define the memory space allocation for stacks to detect stack overflow. Some RTOS products support stack overflow detection in application threads using software steps during context switching. In Armv8-M architecture, a dedicated stack limit checking feature has been added. By having stack limit registers (Fig. 11.7), privileged software is able to define the maximum stack sizes allocated to both the main and the process stacks.

The lowest 3 bits of the Stack Limit Registers are tied to 0, which means that stack limits are always double word aligned.

If the value of a stack pointer goes below the stack limit, and if a stack-related operation occurs when using the stack pointer, the stack operation violation would be detected and will trigger a fault exception as follows:

- For Armv8-M Baseline, the HardFault exception is triggered (i.e., the Secure HardFault—this is because the stack limit check feature is available in Secure state only).
- For Armv8-M Mainline, the UsageFault exception is triggered and the STKOF fault status bit in the UsageFault Status Register is set to 1 to reflect this fault condition. The UsageFault exception can be either Secure or Non-secure, depending on whether the stack overflow violation is related to the Secure or to the Non-secure stack. If the UsageFault was not enabled, or if the priority level of the UsageFault was insufficient for it to be triggered, the fault event would be escalated to HardFault.

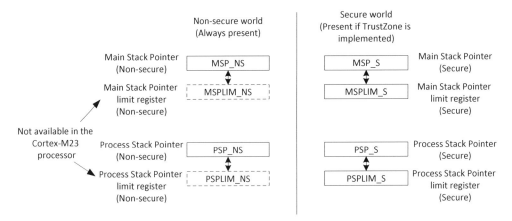

FIG. 11.7   Stack limit registers.

A stack overflow fault exception is synchronous, which means, as soon as the fault is detected, the processor is unable to execute any further instructions in the current context. The only instance where the processor would continue to execute is when a higher priority interrupt (e.g., an NMI) arrives at the same time; in which cause the fault exception will stay in a pending state and will only execute when the ISR of the higher priority interrupt has been completed.

Stack-related operations that can trigger a stack overflow fault include:

- Stack push/pop
- Memory access instructions that update the stack pointers (e.g., load/store instructions that update a stack pointer because of a base register update)
- Add/sub/move instructions that update the stack pointer
- Exception sequences (e.g., exception entry, tail-chaining from a Secure to a Non-secure ISR)
- Secure code calling a Non-secure function (e.g., some secure states being pushed into the current selected Secure stack)

Please note:

- Changing the stack limit registers using the MSR instruction, or
- Changing the Secure stack pointer using the MSR instruction

will not immediately trigger a fault exception for violating the stack overflow. By not triggering a fault exception until a stack-related operation is taking place, it is easier to design the OS context switching software. For example:

- The RTOS running in the Non-secure world only needs to update the PSPLIM_NS and then the PSP_NS in a context switch, even though the new PSPLIM_NS value could be higher than the previous PSP_NS, that is, there is no need to set PSPLIM_NS to zero to disable the stack limit check during the PSP update.
- Secure privileged software can update the MSP_S/PSP_S and its MSPLIM_S/PSPLIM_S registers in any order.

11.4.2 Access to the stack limit registers

To access the stack limit registers, MSR and MRS instructions are used. The register symbols for the access are shown in Table 11.8.

To make it easier to access these registers when writing software, CMSIS-CORE has implemented the following functions for accessing the stack limit registers (Table 11.9).

Because the Cortex-M23 processor does not have MSPLIM_NS and PSPLIM_NS, an attempt to read these stack limit registers (e.g., using the CMSIS-CORE function mentioned in Table 11.9) on the Cortex-M23 processor would return zero, and the write to these registers would be ignored.

11.4.3 Protection of the Main Stack Pointer(s)

The benefit of applying a stack limit checking feature on the Process Stack Pointers (PSPs) (e.g., using the PSPLIM_NS for stack overflow protection in the RTOS and the PSPLIM_S for

TABLE 11.8 Register symbols for accessing stack limit registers when using the MSR and MRS instructions.

Operation to be carried out	Stack limit register symbol to use when the processor is in Non-secure state	Stack limit register symbol to use when the processor is in Secure state
Access MSPLIM_NS (Non-secure Main Stack Pointer Limit Register)	MSPLIM	MSPLIM_NS
Access PSPLIM_NS (Non-secure Process Stack Pointer Limit Register)	PSPLIM	PSPLIM_NS
Access MSPLIM_S (Secure Main Stack Pointer Limit Register)	– (Not allowed)	MSPLIM
Access PSPLIM_S (Secure Processor Stack Pointer Limit Register)	– (Not allowed)	PSPLIM

TABLE 11.9 Stack limit register access functions.

Function	Description
void __set_MSPLIM(uint32_t ProcStackPtrLimit)	Sets the PSPLIM of the current security domain
uint32_t __get_MSPLIM(void)	Returns the MSPLIM of the current security domain
void __set_PSPLIM(uint32_t ProcStackPtrLimit)	Sets the PSPLIM of the current security domain
uint32_t __get_PSPLIM(void)	Returns the PSPLIM of the current security domain
void __TZ_set_MSPLIM(uint32_t ProcStackPtrLimit)	Sets the PSPLIM_NS (available to Secure software only)
uint32_t __TZ_get_MSPLIM(void)	Returns the MSPLIM_NS (available to Secure software only)
void __TZ_set_PSPLIM(uint32_t ProcStackPtrLimit)	Sets the PSPLIM_NS of the current security domain (available to Secure software only)
uint32_t __TZ_get_PSPLIM(void)	Returns the PSPLIM_NS (available to Secure software only)

stack protection for Secure libraries) is easily understood. This security measure is easily implemented and is deployed in multiple RTOS products and in other security software (e.g., Trusted Firmware-M). The stack limit check feature is also used for protecting the Main Stack Pointer(s) (MSP) from stack overflow. This is needed because a stack overflow can occur because of either a software error or because the number of nested exception levels is higher than expected.

When using the stack limit checking on the Main Stack Pointer(s), there is a need to ensure that the fault handler can execute (Note: the fault handlers also uses the MSP). There are several ways to handle this:

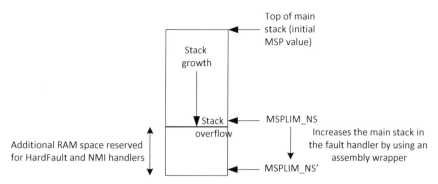

FIG. 11.8 MSP overflow handling with an assembly wrapper adjusting the stack limit at runtime.

1. By adding assembly wrappers to the HardFault and UsageFault handlers to update the MSPLIM before starting the C/C++ portion of the fault handler

When setting the stack limit, you need to make sure that extra RAM space is available after the stack limit and then reserve that for the UsageFault/HardFault handlers. The UsageFault/HardFault handlers require an assembly wrapper to update the MSPLIM in order that the C/C++ portion of the fault handler can execute (Fig. 11.8).

This method can be used in all Armv8-M processors.

2. By using the Secure HardFault handler to handle the stack overflow in the MSP_NS (Non-secure MSP)

For Cortex-M systems with TrustZone, by default the HardFault targets the Secure side—which uses the MSP_S during the execution of the fault handler (Fig. 11.9). So, even when the Non-secure main stack has been corrupted, or the MSP_NS points to an invalid memory, the fault handler can still execute.

This method can be used in Armv8-M Mainline processors. It is not suitable for an Armv8-M Baseline processor, like the Cortex-M23, because the Non-secure MSP does not have a stack limit register.

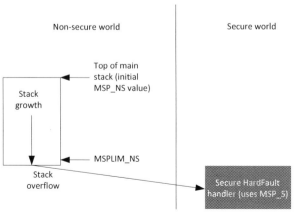

FIG. 11.9 MSP_NS overflow handling with a handler using the MSP_S.

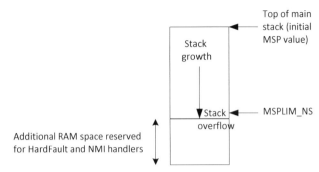

FIG. 11.10   MSP overflow handling.

3. By reserving stack space for the fault handler and the NMI and by setting the STKOFHFNMIGN bit in SCB->CCR

When STKOFHFNMIGN (bit 10 of SCB->CCR, see Section 10.5.5) is set to 1, the stack limit check is ignored when executing either the HardFault or the NMI handler(s). By so doing, it allows software developers to reserve additional stack space for the HardFault handler that deals with the stack overflow (Fig. 11.10).

The STKOFHFNMIGN bit is reset to 0 and banks between security states. It is only available in Armv8-M Mainline only.

11.5 SVCall and PendSV exceptions

11.5.1 Overview of SVCall and PendSV

The SVCall (Supervisor Call) and PendSV (Pendable Service Call) exceptions are important processor features that are designed to assist OS operations. SVCall is exception type 11 and PendSV is exception type 14. Both have a programmable exception priority level.

A summary of the key aspects of these two exceptions is shown in Table 11.10.

11.5.2 SVCall

In order to make embedded systems more secure and robust, application threads/tasks are usually executed at unprivileged level. When using privilege level separation and utilizing the Memory Protection Unit (MPU) for controlling access permission, unprivileged threads can only access the memory and resources they are supposed to have access to. However, since application threads/tasks might, from time to time, need to access privileged features, many OS's provide a range of OS services for this purpose. The SVC instruction and the SVCall exception provide a gateway for those unprivileged threads to access the privileged level OS services (Fig. 11.11).

TABLE 11.10 Key aspects of SVCall and PendSV exceptions.

Characteristic	SVCall (exception type 11)	PendSV (exception type 14)
How it is used in an OS environment	Allows unprivileged threads (application tasks) access to privileged OS services.	Handles context switching.
Triggering mechanism	Execution of an SVC instruction	Sets its pending status by writing to SCB->ICSR (Interrupt Control and State Register, Section 9.3.2).
Priority level	Programmable	Programmable. In an OS environment, it is usually set to the lowest priority level so that context switching can be executed when no other exception handler is running.
Targets security state in a TrustZone system	Banked: The SVCall exception has the same security state as the software that executed the SVC instruction.	Banked: The PendSV pending status control bits in the SCB->ICSR is banked between security states. The security state of the PendSV exception depends on which one was set.
The name of the exception handler in the CMSIS-CORE	void **SVC_Handler**(void)	void **PendSV_Handler**(void)
Exception nature	Synchronous: after the execution of the SVC subsequent instructions in the current context are not allowed to execute until the SVC Handler has been taken.	Asynchronous: after setting the PendSV status bit, the processor is able to execute additional instructions in the current context before the PendSV handler executes.

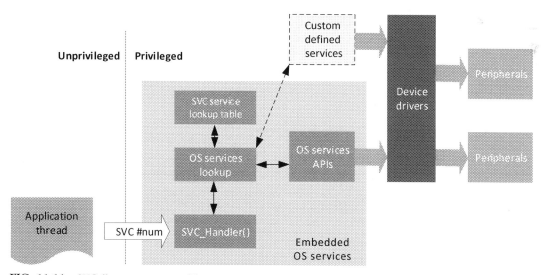

FIG. 11.11 SVCall as a gateway to OS services.

Inside an SVC handler, the SVC service in privileged state extracts the parameters passed from the application and then looks up which application has made the service request (e.g., by checking a current OS task ID from the OS kernel). It then decides whether the requested service should be allowed.

The SVC instruction has an 8-bit integer parameter. This value does not affect the exception entry sequence of the SVCall exception. However, during the execution of the SVCall handler, software can extract this data from the program memory and use this value to decide which SVC service is being requested by the unprivileged application. Because of this, an OS can provide a range of OS services to the unprivileged application. In many OS designs, the SVC service look up can be extended to provide custom defined privileged services.

To insert an SVC instruction in an assembly program, the following example code can be used:

```
SVC #0x3 ; Call SVC function 3
```

The immediate value ranges from 0 to 255.

In C programming, you can use inline assembly to generate an SVC instruction. To carry out the same operation as the above SVC assembly instruction, we can use:

```
__asm("SVC #0x3"); // Call SVC function 3
```

If we need to enable the SVC service to take input parameters using registers r0–r3 and return a result using r0, the following inline assembly code can be used:

```
// This function uses named register variables to create a call.
// The four arguments to the system call are held in r0-r3,
// the SVC service number is 3, and
// the result is placed in r0.
int foo(register int d1, unsigned d2, int d3, unsigned d4) {
        register int       r0 __asm("r0") = d1;
        register unsigned r1 __asm("r1") = d2;
        register int       r2 __asm("r2") = d3;
        register unsigned r3 __asm("r3") = d4;
        __asm("svc #3"
                : "+r" (r0)
                : "r"  (r1), "r"  (r2), "r"  (r3));
        return r0;
}
```

Note: The above example is based on the Arm Compiler 6. For additional information on using register variables in inline assembly code, please see Arm Compiler armclang Reference Guide [2]: https://developer.arm.com/documentation/100067/0612/armclang-Inline-Assembler/Forcing-inline-assembly-operands-into-specific-registers.

After triggering the SVC instruction, we then need an SVC handler to deal with the SVC request. In a typical SVC handler:

- We need to extract the SVC service number from the program memory. To do that, we need to extract the stacked PC in the stack frame and then use this value to read the SVC number

FIG. 11.12 Interaction between the SVC assembly wrapper and the SVC Handler in C.

- Depending on the SVC service being accessed, we might need to extract arguments—that is, parameters—from the stack frame
- And, depending on the SVC service being accessed, we might need to return the result(s) via the stack frame

To allow the SVC service to directly manipulate the stack memory, the SVC handler needs an assembler wrapper. This assembly wrapper collects two pieces of information which are then passed to the SVC Handler as function arguments (Fig. 11.12). The two pieces of information are:

- The value of EXC_RETURN
- The value of the MSP when it enters the SVC Handler—this is needed because the prologue of an SVC Handler in C can update the MSP. Whereas, the PSP value can be accessed using the CMSIS-CORE function __get_PSP().

The assembly wrapper code of the SVC Handler could be as simple as:

```
void __attribute__((naked)) SVC_Handler(void)
{
    __asm volatile ("mov r0, lr\n\t"
            "mov r1, sp\n\t"
            "B SVC_Handler_C\n\t"
        );
}
```

The example SVC Handler code detailed below is written in C. To allow it to be used for OS services, the handler code needs to:

1. Extract the right stack pointer (Either the MSP or the PSP with the same security domain as the SVC)
2. Calculate the stack frame address. For the Secure SVC, the handler code needs to determine whether the stack frame contains Additional State Context (r4–r11 and integrity signature) (Figs. 8.18, 8.21, 8.22) from the DCRS bit in the EXC_RETURN, and to then adjust the stack frame address calculation accordingly.
3. Extract the SVC number from the program memory and the function arguments in the stack frame.

The aforementioned C handler code is as follows:

```
void SVC_Handler_C(uint32_t exc_return_code, uint32_t msp_val)
{
    uint32_t    stack_frame_addr;
```

```
unsigned int *svc_args;
uint8_t     svc_number;
uint32_t    stacked_r0, stacked_r1, stacked_r2, stacked_r3;
// Determines which stack pointer was used
if (exc_return_code & 0x4) stack_frame_addr = __get_PSP();
else stack_frame_addr = msp_val;
// Determines whether additional state context is present
if (exc_return_code & 0x20) {
   svc_args = (unsigned *) stack_frame_addr;}
else {// additional state context present (only for Secure SVC)
   svc_args = (unsigned *) (stack_frame_addr+40);}
// extracts SVC number
svc_number = ((char *) svc_args[6])[-2];//Memory[(stacked_pc)-2]
stacked_r0 = svc_args[0];
stacked_r1 = svc_args[1];
stacked_r2 = svc_args[2];
stacked_r3 = svc_args[3];
...
// Returns result (e.g. sum of the first two arguments)
svc_args[0] = stgacked_r0 + stacked_r1;
return;
}
```

Unlike triggering an exception using the NVIC's Interrupt Pending Set Registers, the SVCall exception is synchronous, which means after an SVC instruction is executed, the processor is unable to execute any further instructions in the current context. This is different for software triggered IRQ services using NVIC->ICSR, where the processor could execute additional instructions before the ISR itself is executed. Please note, because of the way exceptions are handled, if an interrupt with a priority level that is higher than the one for the SVCall exception arrives at the same time, the interrupt's ISR would get executed first, and then tail-chained into the SVC handler.

Due to the nature and mechanics of exception handling, software designs need to consider the following aspects when using the SVC:

- The SVC instruction should not be used in an exception/interrupt service routine that has the same or a higher priority than the SVCall exception, or when an interrupt masking register is set that blocks the SVCall exception. If the SVCall exception cannot be executed, a HardFault exception would be triggered.
- When passing parameters to an SVC service via registers r0–r3, the SVC service needs to extract these parameters from the exception stack frame rather than take the current values in the register bank. This is because if another interrupt service executes just before the SVC handler and is tail-chained into the SVC service, the values in r0–r3, and r12 might have been changed by the previous ISR.
- If an SVC service needs to return a value back to the calling task/thread, the return value should be written to the exception stack frame in order that it can be read back into r0–r3 during the unstacking of the exception.

One interesting aspect of using the SVC service is that application code only needs to know the SVC number and the parameters/return results (i.e., the function prototype). It does not need to know the address of the SVC services. Accordingly, it is possible to separately link the application code and the OS (i.e., They can be created as separate projects).

11.5.3 PendSV

The PendSV feature allows software to trigger an exception service. Similar to IRQs, PendSV is asynchronous (i.e., it can be deferred). But, instead of using an IRQ, for deferring processing tasks in an embedded OS/RTOS, OS's can use the PendSV exception for this purpose. Unlike IRQs, where the exception number assignments are device specific, because the exception number and control register bits of PendSV are identical, the same PendSV control code can be used by all Arm Cortex-M processors. Therefore, PendSV enables, without customization, an embedded OS/RTOS to run out of the box on all Cortex-M based systems.

In an RTOS environment, PendSV is usually configured to have the lowest interrupt priority level. The OS kernel code, which executes in Handler mode at a high priority level, is able to schedule, for carrying out at a later time, some OS operations using PendSV. By using PendSV, those deferred OS operations can be carried out at the lowest exception priority level when no other exception handler is running. One of those deferred OS operations is OS context switches, which is an essential part of a multitasking system.

To understand this better, let's first look at some basic concepts of context switching. In a simple OS design, the execution time is divided into a number of time slots. For a system with two tasks, an OS might execute those tasks alternately, as shown in Fig. 11.13.

In the above example (Fig. 11.13), the SysTick timer is used to generate a periodic exception to trigger context switching. Please note, in a realistic OS environment the context switching might not happen at every OS tick. In addition to the SysTick exception, the OS kernel code running in exception state could, potentially, be triggered by an SVC through in an OS service call. For

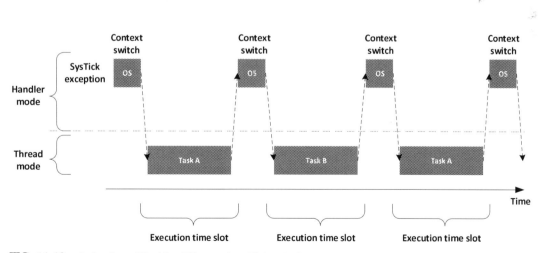

FIG. 11.13 A simple multitasking OS scenario with two tasks.

example, when an execution thread is waiting for an event and cannot proceed further, it can call an OS "yield" service so that the processor can, earlier than envisaged, swap into a different task.

If a peripheral interrupt request has a lower priority than the SysTick that took place just before the SysTick exception, this results in a nested exception scenario (Fig. 11.14). In such a case, it would not be a good time for a context switch because by doing so would delay the peripheral's ISR. As a result, in a very simple OS design, if an OS tick interrupt is triggered while an ISR is still running, the context switching operation would be delayed to the next tick.

Now, imagine that the peripheral is a timer and that the interrupt rate is getting close to the SysTick interrupt rate, or close to an integer multiple of the SysTick interrupt rate. In this scenario we would have a problem as the timer IRQ could stop the OS from context switching for a long period of time.

Potentially, this problem could be avoided by setting the priority level of the SysTick timer to the lowest level. But, if there are a number of interrupt events happening at the same time, it is possible that because the other ISRs would have filled up the current execution time slot, that the SysTick exception would not execute in that time slot. When this occurs, the scheduled tasks could end up being delayed.

Fortunately, for Cortex-M processors, this is not a problem because OS designers are able to separate the context switching operation from the SysTick handler by placing the operation into a separate PendSV exception handler. By having separate exceptions:

- The SysTick handler, which handles the task scheduling evaluation, can still run at a high priority level and, if there is no other interrupt service running, carry out context switching.
- The PendSV exception, which is triggered by the OS scheduling code, can run at the lowest priority level and carry out the deferred context switching when needed. This is needed when the OS code in the SysTick handler needs to carry out a context switch but has detected that the processor is servicing another interrupt.

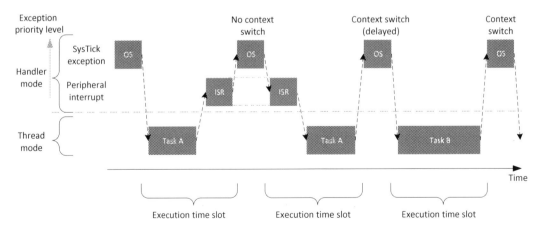

FIG. 11.14 OS software code delays a context switch because the OS detected an interrupt handler was still running.

The concept of using PendSV to handle a deferred context switching operation is shown in Fig. 11.15.

The deferral of the context switch is illustrated in Fig. 11.15 and follows the following path:

(1) A peripheral interrupt is triggered and enters the peripheral's ISR.

(2) During the execution of the peripheral ISR, a SysTick exception is triggered and the OS kernel starts task-scheduling evaluation and, by so doing, decides that it is time to context switch into task B.

(3) However, because the OS kernel detects that the processor was servicing an interrupt and will not directly return to the thread (either by checking the EXC_RETURN code generated when entering SysTick or by checking RETTOBASE bit (bit 11 of the SCB-> ICSR, which is available in Armv8-M Mainline only)), the OS defers the context switch and sets the pending status of the PendSV exception.

(4) When the SysTick handler finishes, the processor resumes the execution of the peripheral ISR.

(5) When the peripheral ISR finishes its task, the processor tail-chains into the PendSV handler, which then handles the context switch. When the PendSV handler ends by triggering an exception return, the processor returns to Task B in the Thread mode.

If the SysTick did not preempt another interrupt, then the OS can either execute the context switch inside the SysTick exception handler, or set the PendSV pending status to trigger the context switch after the SysTick handler has finished.

Another use for PendSV is that it allows part of a processing sequence associated with an interrupt service to be carried out at a lower interrupt priority level. This is useful when there is a need to divide an interrupt service into two parts:

- The first part of the interrupt service is usually a timing-critical procedure of short duration that needs to be handled by an ISR with a high priority level.

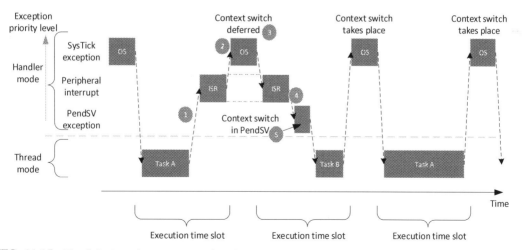

FIG. 11.15 The deferring of a context switch to the PendSV handler when an ISR is already running.

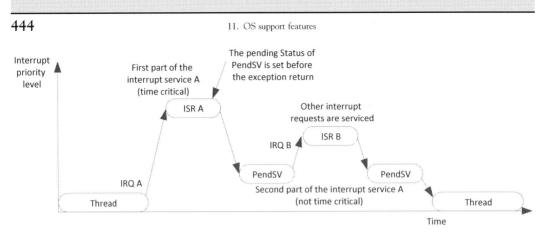

FIG. 11.16 Using PendSV to partition an interrupt service into two sections.

- The second part of the interrupt service is a longer processing task, but does not have a strict timing requirement and can be handled by an ISR with a low priority level.

In this scenario, PendSV is set to a low interrupt priority level and is then used for the second part of the processing (Fig. 11.16). This allows other interrupt requests to be serviced during the ongoing second part of the interrupt service.

If the TrustZone security extension is implemented in the device, the PendSV exception is banked between security states. The access permission for setting the PendSV pending status is as follows and as per Table 11.11:

- Secure privileged software can access the pending status of both the Secure and the Non-secure PendSV.
- Non-secure privileged software is only able to access the pending status of the Non-secure PendSV.

11.6 Unprivileged execution level and the Memory Protection Unit (MPU)

The separation of privileged and unprivileged execution levels is a common feature in modern embedded processors, and has been part of the architecture of Arm Cortex-M processors right from the start (i.e., when the Cortex-M3 was developed). A robust OS can be created to utilize the separation of privileged and unprivileged execution levels in

TABLE 11.11 Banked PendSV pending status behavior.

If the processor is in Secure state:	If the processor is in Non-secure state:
Setting PENDSVSET in SCB->ICSR sets the pending status of Secure PendSV	Setting PENDSVSET in SCB->ICSR sets the pending status of Non-secure PendSV
Setting PENDSVSET in SCB_NS->ICSR sets the pending status of Non-secure PendSV	

conjunction with the MPU feature. By so doing, a rogue application thread/task running in unprivileged state:

- Cannot access/modify memory locations which are used by the OS or by other application tasks/threads.
- Cannot affect critical operations (i.e., interrupt handling settings and system configurations cannot be changed).

With this arrangement, even when an application task crashes, or has been attacked by a hacker and has been compromised, the OS and other application tasks would still be able to execute. Although other application tasks could still be affected, the system is able to implement fail-safe mechanisms, such as generating a self-reset (see Section 10.5.3), to recover the system.

This arrangement not only benefits security (e.g., from the aspect of IoT applications), but also helps functional safety (e.g., in automotive and industrial applications where the robustness of the system is critical).

To satisfy the requirements of security and functional safety, Cortex-M processors have been designed to have the following characteristics:

- Restrictions to system resource management functions—these functions (e.g., most special registers and the registers in key hardware units such as the NVIC, the SCB, the MPU and in SysTick), are not accessible by unprivileged software.
- Memory protection—Privileged software, such as the OS, can configure the MPU to restrict the access permission of unprivileged threads. In an OS environment, the MPU configuration is changed at each context switch of the unprivileged threads (Note: because there are separate MPU's for the Secure and the Non-secure worlds, switching between a Secure and Non-secure context does not always require the MPU to reconfigure).
- Restrictions to system instructions—Some instructions that change a processor's settings (e.g., CPS instructions can be used to disable interrupts) cannot be used in unprivileged state.
- Supports a system-wide security arrangement—Chip designers can utilize the processor's security information on the bus interface to implement system level security management control functions to prevent security breaches. The security information on the bus interface includes the privilege level and also the security attribute of the bus transactions.

The Memory Protection Unit (MPU) is essential for protecting the memory used by privileged software and critical software components. The Cortex-M23 and Cortex-M33 processors both support optional MPUs, with the MPUs in those processors having a number of enhancements when compared to the MPUs in the previous generations of Cortex-M processors. These enhancements are:

- Up to 16 MPU regions compared to a maximum of 8 regions in previous designs.
- A new programmer's model enabling a more flexible approach when programming memory region settings in the MPU.

The MPU components in Cortex-M processors are optional. Because the privilege level is exported to the bus interface, it is possible:

- to implement system level MPUs for managing access permissions for peripherals.
- to implement bus level security management control hardware using a customized bus interconnect instead of using the MPU. This is usually only found in specialized ultra-low power SoC products. Although this is not as flexible as an MPU it can have a smaller silicon area and a lower power consumption.

Further details on the MPU can be found in Chapter 12.

11.7 Exclusive access

Exclusive access instructions, including new load-acquire/store-release variants are covered in Sections 5.7.11, 5.7.12, and 6.7. Compared to previous generations of Cortex-M processors, the Cortex-M23 and the Cortex-M33 processors have the following enhancements:

- Exclusive access instructions—these were not available in the Armv6-M architecture.
- Load-acquire/store-release—this enables OS semaphores to be handled without the need for explicit memory barrier instructions. This enhancement shortens the code and, potentially, achieves a better performance.
- The use of AMBA® 5 AHB—this provides a standardized system level of exclusive access signaling and improves the reusability of the design.

Exclusive access is mostly used for semaphores. In a multitasking system, it is usual for a number of tasks to share a limited number of resources. For example, there might be one console display output available which needs to be used by a number of different tasks. As a result, almost all OS's have a built-in mechanism that allows a task to "lock" a resource and to then "free" it when the task no longer needs it. The locking mechanism is usually based on software variables. If a lock variable is set, other tasks see that it is "locked" and have to wait. This feature is usually called a semaphore. When only one resource is available, it is called a Mutual Exclusive (MUTEX).

More detailed information on MUTEX can be found in Section 6.7.

A semaphore can also support multiple tokens. For example, a communication stack might support up to four channels, which means up to four application tasks can use the communication stack at the same time. To limit the number of application tasks (i.e., 4) that can access the communication stack, a semaphore operation of four tokens is needed. To achieve this, a semaphore software variable can be implemented, with a starting value of 4, as a "token counter" (Fig. 11.17). When a task needs to access a channel, it decrements the counter using the exclusive access instructions. When the counter reaches zero, it indicates that all the available channels are used and that any task needing a communication channel will have to wait. When one of the tasks that gained access finishes using a channel and releases the token by incrementing the counter, if there are any task's that are still waiting, it can then acquire a channel using the exclusive access instructions.

If exclusive access instructions are not available and if the semaphore is implemented using normal memory access instructions (i.e., read, modify, and then write back), then the semaphore access is not atomic and, unless other protection mechanisms are implemented, could lead to the following failure. For example, if an OS context switch

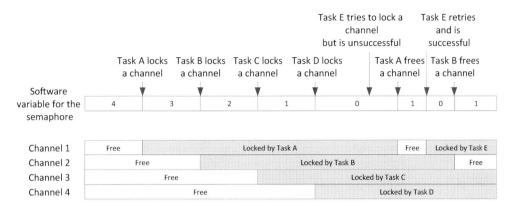

FIG. 11.17 Semaphore examples with multiple tokens.

happens in the middle of a read-modify-write sequence with normal memory access, another task could gain the same semaphore at the same time and cause a conflict (Fig. 11.18).

Potentially the problem can be avoided by either:

- Disabling interrupts during semaphore read-modify-write (this will affect interrupt latency)
- Using an OS service (e.g., via an SVC exception) to handle the semaphore (but this method has a much longer execution time than that for exclusive access).

Please note, these solutions only work for single processor systems.

Although a hardware semaphore (using dedicated memory mapped semaphore registers) could solve the access conflict problem, the software for it is not, because different devices could have different hardware semaphore registers, so portable.

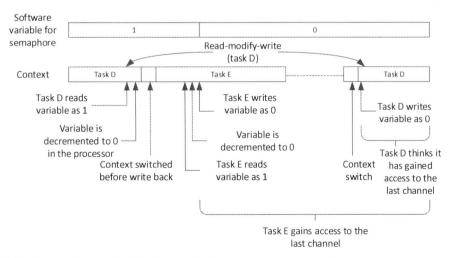

FIG. 11.18 A semaphore could fail without exclusive access or other protection.

By using exclusive load and exclusive store instructions to implement the semaphore read-modify-write sequence, the aforementioned access conflict problem can be avoided. The exclusive access sequence has the following major characteristics:

- Semaphore data is not updated if the exclusive store fails
- Software can read back the success/fail status of an exclusive store

As shown in the flow chart in Chapter 6, Fig. 6.9, the application thread should, if it sees an exclusive fail status, restart the read-modify-write sequence in a further attempt to access the semaphore. It is worth noting, however, that an exclusive fail status does not necessarily mean that the semaphore has been claimed by another thread. In Cortex-M processors an exclusive fail can be caused by:

- A CLREX instruction that has been executed and has switched the local monitor to an Open Access state.
- The occurrence of a context switch (e.g., an interrupt).
- An exclusive load (e.g., LDREX) that was not executed before the exclusive store instruction.
- External hardware returning an exclusive fail status to the processor via the bus interface.

When a semaphore access gets an exclusive fail response, it is likely that the exclusive fail was caused by a peripheral interrupt or a context switch. If an exclusive fail response occurs, the code retries the read-modify-write sequence in an attempt to gain the semaphore.

11.8 How should an RTOS run in a TrustZone environment?

When looking at the various OS support features that are available in Armv8-M architecture, many experienced software developers might notice that a number of OS support features are banked between security states, and that, as a result, there are multiple ways to run an RTOS on an Armv8-M processor with the TrustZone security extension. For example:

- An RTOS running in Secure state—application threads/tasks can either be Secure or Non-secure
- An RTOS running in Non-secure state—application threads/tasks can only be Non-secure

To enable better IoT security across the ecosystem, Arm has started an initiative called Platform Security Architecture (PSA) [3]. Through the PSA project, Arm liaises with various parties in the industry to define the specifications for secure IoT platforms. In addition, the initiative also provides recommendations, as well as delivering reference security firmware (e.g., Trusted Firmware-M for Cortex-M processors). During this initiative, Arm researched the requirements of a range of applications and, by so doing, was able to provide guidelines for designing security software for, for example, the RTOS. Based on the PSA's recommendations, it was decided that the RTOS in Armv8-M processors should run in a Non-secure state.

By running the RTOS in the Non-secure state:

- Software developers can select their choice of RTOS for their projects and customize them, even when the Secure firmware has been locked down.

- The RTOS can be easily updated during the product's life cycle by way of a standard firmware update.
- The IoT device would not, even when there are vulnerabilities in the RTOS codes, be completely compromised. This aligns with the "least privilege" approach which is strongly recommended by the IoT security industry.

When an RTOS and its application tasks/threads are running in the Non-secure world, there is a deal of complexity when dealing with the access of secure APIs. Consider a simple case where there are two application threads in the Non-secure world and each of them call a Secure API. In this scenario, context switching in both the Non-secure and the Secure worlds would be needed at the same time (Fig. 11.19).

As shown in Fig. 11.19, the switching from application #1 to application #2 also requires the switching of the PSP_S and, potentially, the Secure MPU configurations (if used by the Secure

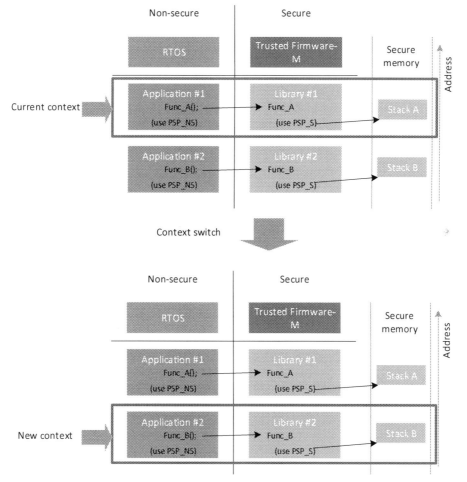

FIG. 11.19 Context switching in Non-secure RTOS threads requires context switching in the Secure world.

Partition Manager inside the Trusted Firmware-M). In order to support this coordinated switching, Trusted Firmware-M include OS helper APIs which interact with the Non-secure RTOS to facilitate the context switching operations. The OS helper APIs, as well as the Trusted Firmware-M source code, are all open-sourced.

Further information on this topic is covered in a paper published in Embedded World "How should an RTOS work in a TrustZone for Armv8-M environment" [4] (https://pages.arm.com/rtos-trustzone-armv8m). For more information about Trusted Firmware-M, including how to get access to Trusted Firmware-M source code, please visit https://www.trustedfirmware.org/ [1].

11.9 Concepts of RTOS operations in Cortex-M processors

11.9.1 Starting a simple OS

In this section, I look at some of the building blocks that are required for a simple OS and begin with how an OS starts. To simplify the examples, I have assumed that TrustZone is not implemented or is not used (i.e., everything operates in the Non-secure state). Consider:

- the system boots up in privileged state (Non-secure) and uses MSP (MSP_NS)
- The first application thread executes in unprivileged state and uses PSP

An RTOS initialization can be undertaken by:

1. Initializing the stack frames for all the threads that will be used.
2. Initializing the SysTick for the periodic OS tick interrupt.
3. Writing to the CONTROL register to set bits 0 and 1 in order to switch the thread execution state to unprivileged and to select the PSP as the current stack pointer.
4. Branching to the starting point of the first application thread.

However, if we need to enable the MPU for memory protection, this method will not work due to the following conflicting requirements:

- Firstly, for security reason, the MPU needs to be enabled and the processor needs to be switched to unprivileged level before it can enter an application thread.
- Secondly, the OS code that is used to start the first application thread cannot be executed at the unprivileged level. This is because as soon as the MPU is enabled and the processor is switched to unprivileged state, the OS code, which is in a memory region that is privileged access only, would be blocked by the MPU.

The following example program sequence demonstrates this issue. The sequence used is:

Enable MPU -> Set CONTROL register -> Branch to thread

Using this sequence, an MPU violation would occur as soon as the CONTROL register was updated to a value of 0x3. To overcome this violation problem, most OS's uses an exception return to start the first thread instead of using a branch operation. With this arrangement, the OS initialization code switches itself to Handler mode by using an SVC instruction, and then configures the MPU and the CONTROL register. Since the processor is in Handler mode, the

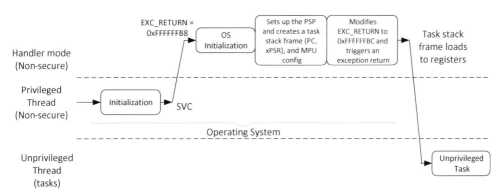

FIG. 11.20 Entering first thread in a simple OS (running in Non-secure state).

OS code is not blocked by the MPU. When the OS is ready to switch to the first thread, it uses an exception return operation, which allows the privileged level and the program address to be changed at the same time (Fig. 11.20).

11.9.2 Context switching

A simple RTOS can use a timer peripheral to generate a periodic Tick interrupt for:

- Executing a task scheduler to evaluate the task priority and to then decide if a context switch is needed. If it is,
- Executing the context switching code. This involves:

  ○ Saving the data of the current executing thread, that is, the registers in the register bank, the PSP value, the FPU active status (if the FPU is present).
    Note: To obtain the FPU active status, software can either extract the CONTROL. FPCA state of the task from the EXC_RETURN value or just save the whole EXC_RETURN value and reuse it when switching back into this thread.
  ○ Reconfiguring the MPU to define the memory access permission for the next thread
  ○ Restoring the data of the next running thread
  ○ Selecting the right EXC_RETURN value to trigger an exception return—which switches the processor to thread and then executes the next thread

The context switching code can get executed inside the timer tick exception handler if there are no other active ISRs running (i.e., not a nested exception). If there are other active ISRs running, the PendSV exception is used to handle the context switch, as described in Section 11.5.3 (Fig. 11.21).

Note: It is possible for an OS to only use the PendSV to handle the context switching.

Please note, for context switching support, the exception priority of the PendSV exception is normally programmed to the lowest priority level. This is to prevent context switching from occurring during the middle of an interrupt handler. This is explained in detail in Section 11.5.3.

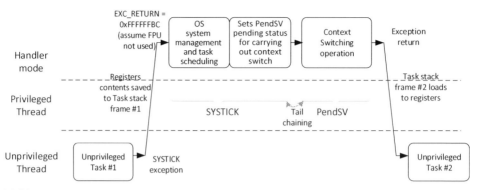

FIG. 11.21 Example of a context switch.

11.9.3 Context switching in action

To demonstrate the context switching operation in a real example, I have created a simple task scheduler that switches between two tasks in a round robin arrangement. This is covered in a later part of this section. For this example, I have made the following assumptions:

1. That the RTOS is running in the Non-secure side—Note: this has an additional advantage in that we do not need to worry about the additional state context in the stack frames.
2. That the processor is a Cortex-M33 (with the optional FPU support).
3. That context switching is handled in the PendSV handler and that this handler is not used for other purposes.

During context switching in Handler mode, the stack frame created by the exception entry contains the caller saved registers, r0–r3, r12, LR, and, if the FPU is present and enabled, registers s0–s15 and register FPSCR. In addition to the caller saved registers, the context switching code will also need to save additional callee save registers and any other data that assists in context switching. To simplify the example, my context switching code example pushes these additional callee save registers to the process stack, as shown in Fig. 11.22.

Once the data layout in the stack frame has been defined, we can then define the code for handling the context switches. The followings codes are needed for handling the data layout in the stack:

- OS kernel code that defines the Task Control Block (TCB)
- PendSV_Handler code which executes the context switching

For this OS example, which has only two tasks, the following data variables would need to be defined for task identification and for the Task Control Block (TCB):

```
// Data use by OS
uint32_t curr_task=0;    // Current task
uint32_t next_task=0;    // Next task

struct task_control_block_elements {
  uint32_t psp_val;
  uint32_t psp_limit;
};
struct task_control_block_elements tcb_array[2]; // Only two tasks
```

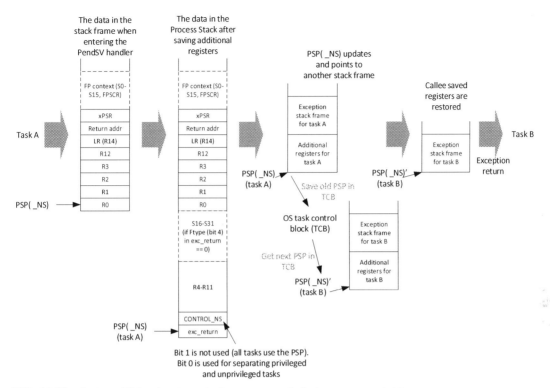

FIG. 11.22 Saving additional registers in the process stack during context switching.

The PendSV handler code (context switching) is written as:

```
// -----------------------------------
// Context switching code
void __attribute__((naked)) PendSV_Handler(void)
{ // Context switching code
  __asm(
  "mrs    r0, psp\n\t"   // Obtains current PSP value
  "tst    lr, #0x10\n\t" // Tests bit 4 of EXC_RETURN. If 0, needs to save regs s16-s31
  "it     eq\n\t"
  "vstmdbeq r0!,{s16-s31}\n\t" // Saves FPU callee-saved registers
  "mov    r2, lr\n\t"          // copies EXC_RETURN
  "mrs    r3, CONTROL\n\t"     // Copies CONTROL
  "stmdb  r0!,{r2-r11}\n\t"    // Saves EXC_RETURN, CONTROL and R4-R11
  "bl     PSP_update\n\t"      // Saves the PSP in the TCB, and gets the PSP for
                               // the next task in the return value
  "ldmia  r0!,{r2-r11}\n\t"    // Loads EXC_RETURN, CONTROL and R4-R11 from the task stack
  "mov    lr, r2\n\t"          // Sets EXC_RETURN
```

```
  "msr    CONTROL, r3\n\t"      // Sets CONTROL
  "isb    \n\t"                 // Executes an ISB after CONTROL updates
                                // (architecture recommendation)
  "tst    lr, #0x10\n\t"        // Tests bit 4, If zero, unstacks FPU s16-s31
  "it     eq\n\t"
  "vldmiaeq r0!,{s16-s31}\n\t"  // Loads the FPU callee-saved registers
  "msr    psp, r0\n\t"          // Sets the PSP for the next task
  "bx     lr\n\t"               // Exception return
  );
}

// Switches the PSP value to a new task - used by the PendSV_Handler
uint32_t PSP_update(uint32_t Old_PSP)
{
  tcb_array[curr_task].psp_val = Old_PSP; // Saves the PSP of the old task to the TCB
  curr_task = next_task; // Updates task ID
  __set_PSPLIM(tcb_array[curr_task].psp_limit); // Sets stack limit for task
  return (tcb_array[curr_task].psp_val); // Returns the PSP of the new task to the PendSV
}
```

Because there are multiple tasks in an RTOS environment, a function is created to make the creation of the stack frame and the various tasks easier. This function (as shown below) initializes the data in the Task Control Block (TCB), as well as the essential data in the stack frame for context switching operations.

```
/* Macros for word access */
#define HW32_REG(ADDRESS) (*((volatile unsigned long *)(ADDRESS)))

// Creates stack frame for new task
void create_task(uint32_t task_id, uint32_t stack_base, uint32_t stack_size, uint32_t
privilege, uint32_t task_addr)
{
  uint32_t stack_val; // Starting address of new stack frame

  // Initial stack structure with stack frame (8 words) +
  // additional registers (10 words)
  stack_val = (stack_base + stack_size - (18*4));
  tcb_array[task_id].psp_val = stack_val;
  // Stack limit - since we use the task's process stack to store extra registers
  // We need to reserve 26 words (26x4 bytes)
  // (or 10 words in the Cortex-M23/M33 without an FPU)
  // for holding this data.
  tcb_array[task_id].psp_limit = stack_base + (26*4);
  HW32_REG(stack_val ) = 0xFFFFFFBCUL;   // Exception return value: Handler(NS) to
                                         // Thread(NS) transition, uses PSP, FPCA=0
```

```
HW32_REG(stack_val+ 4) = privilege;    // Sets to 0 if task is privileged or
                                        // Sets to 1 if task is unprivileged
HW32_REG(stack_val+64) = task_addr;    // Return address
HW32_REG(stack_val+68) = 0x01000000UL; // xPSR
return;
}
```

In order to start the first thread, a separate piece of code is needed because we cannot use PendSV (i.e., the context switching code). This is because there is no current running thread to swap out from. As mentioned in Section 9.1, we can though use an SVC service to handle the start of the first thread. To do that, we need to point the PSP to the bottom of the exception stack frame (excluding the additional stack data) so that the exception return of the SVC handler can be handled correctly (Fig. 11.23).

As well as using the SVC service to start the OS, we also need to create the following codes:

- a SysTick handler for the task scheduling (a round robin scheme that swaps between the two tasks in the example)
- the two example application tasks

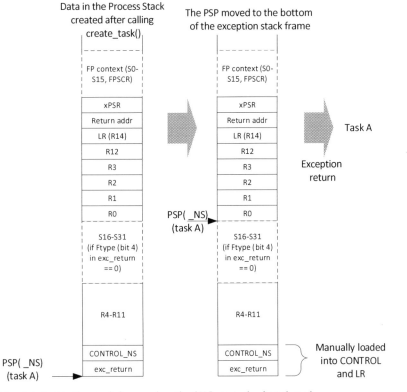

FIG. 11.23   The data inside the stack frame when the SVC starts the first thread.

Once the aforementioned codes have been created, we can then put a simple context switching operation into action using the following code:

```c
#include "stdio.h"
#include "IOTKit_CM33_FP.h"

/* Macros for word, half word and byte access */
#define HW32_REG(ADDRESS)  (*((volatile unsigned long *)(ADDRESS)))
#define TASK_UNPRIVILEGED  0x1
#define TASK_PRIVILEGED    0x0

// Function prototypes
extern void UART_Config(void);

// System handlers
void                      SysTick_Handler(void);
void __attribute__((naked)) PendSV_Handler(void);
void __attribute__((naked)) SVC_Handler(void);
uint32_t SVC_Handler_C(uint32_t exc_return_code, uint32_t msp_val);

void    os_start(void); // SVC #0
void    create_task(uint32_t task_id, uint32_t stack_base, uint32_t stack_size,
uint32_t privilege, uint32_t task_addr);
uint32_t PSP_update(uint32_t Old_PSP); // Saves the old PSP into the TCB, and
                                       // loads the new PSP from the TCB

// Threads
void task0(void);       // Toggles LED0
void task1(void);       // Toggles LED1

// Stack for each task (8Kbytes each - 1024 x 8 bytes)
uint64_t task0_stack[1024], task1_stack[1024];

// Data use by OS
uint32_t  curr_task=0;     // Current task
uint32_t  next_task=0;     // Next task

struct task_control_block_elements {
  uint32_t  psp_val;
  uint32_t  psp_limit;
};
struct task_control_block_elements tcb_array[2]; // Only two tasks

// LED I/O functions
extern int32_t LED_On (uint32_t num);
extern int32_t LED_Off (uint32_t num);
```

```c
void error_handler(void);


// ----------------------------------------------------------------
void __attribute__((noreturn)) task0(void) // Toggles LED #0
{
   int32_t loop_count=0;
   while (1) {
     LED_On(0);
     for (loop_count=0;loop_count<50000; loop_count++) {
       __ISB();}
     LED_Off(0);
     for (loop_count=0;loop_count<50000; loop_count++) {
       __ISB();}
   }
}
// ----------------------------------------------------------------
void __attribute__((noreturn)) task1(void) // Toggles LED #1
{
   int32_t loop_count=0;
     while (1) {
       LED_On(1);
       for (loop_count=0;loop_count<110000; loop_count++) {
         __ISB();}
       LED_Off(1);
       for (loop_count=0;loop_count<110000; loop_count++) {
         __ISB();}
   }
}
// ----------------------------------------------------------------
int main(void)
{
  UART_Config();
  printf("Non-secure Hello world\n");
  // Create two tasks
  create_task(0, // task ID
     (((unsigned) &task0_stack[0])), // stack base
          (sizeof task0_stack), // stack size
     TASK_PRIVILEGED ,   // privileged/unprivileged level
     ((uint32_t) task0));   // starting address of thread
  create_task(1, // task ID
     (((unsigned) &task1_stack[0])), // stack base
          (sizeof task1_stack), // stack size
     TASK_PRIVILEGED ,      // privileged/unprivileged level
     ((uint32_t) task1));  // starting address of thread

  os_start(); // Start OS
```

```
  while(1){
    error_handler(); // Program flow should not reach here
  }
}
void error_handler(void)
{ // Program flow should not reach here
   __BKPT(0); // halt by breakpoint.
}
// ------------------------------------------------------------
void os_start(void) {
   __asm("svc #0");
   return;
}
// Assembly wrapper
void __attribute__((naked)) SVC_Handler(void)
{
   __asm volatile (
   "mov r0, lr\n\t" // 1st argument, EXC_RETURN
   "mov r1, sp\n\t" // 2nd argument, MSP value
   "BL SVC_Handler_C\n\t"
   "bx r0\n\t" // Uses return value as EXC_RETURN
   );
}
// SVC handler - C portion
uint32_t SVC_Handler_C(uint32_t exc_return_code, uint32_t msp_val)
{
   uint32_t     stack_frame_addr;
   volatile unsigned int *svc_args;
   uint8_t      svc_number;                // The Extracted SVC number
   uint32_t     new_exc_return;

// Determines which stack pointer was used
if (exc_return_code & 0x4) stack_frame_addr = __get_PSP();
else stack_frame_addr = msp_val;
// Determines if additional state context is present
if (exc_return_code & 0x20) {
   svc_args = (unsigned *) stack_frame_addr;}
else {
   svc_args = (unsigned *) (stack_frame_addr+40);}
// extracts SVC number from program image
svc_number = ((char *) svc_args[6])[-2]; // Memory[(stacked_pc)-2]
// Returns with the same exc_return by default
new_exc_return = exc_return_code;
```

```
// SVC services
switch (svc_number) {
  case 0: // OS initialization
    // Note: needs to update the PSPLIM_NS before updating the PSP_NS
    __set_PSPLIM(tcb_array[0].psp_limit); // Stack limit for task
    __set_PSP(tcb_array[0].psp_val + 40); // 40 for R4-R11, CONTROL_NS and
    EXC_RETURN
    new_exc_return = HW32_REG(tcb_array[0].psp_val); // Get exc_return for the
    task, and
                                               // Return to thread with the PSP
    // Sets to unprivileged if needed
    __set_CONTROL(__get_CONTROL() | (HW32_REG((tcb_array[0].psp_val+4)) & 0x1));
    __ISB(); // Executes the ISB after CONTROL has been updated
             // (architectural recommendation)
    NVIC_SetPriority(PendSV_IRQn, 0xFF); // Sets PendSV to the lowest priority level
    if (SysTick_Config(SystemCoreClock/1000) != 0){ // Enables the SysTick timer
      error_handler();
    }
    break;
  default:
    break;
  }
  return new_exc_return;
}
// ---------------------------------------------------------------
// Create stack frame for new task
void create_task(uint32_t task_id, uint32_t stack_base, uint32_t stack_size,
uint32_t privilege, uint32_t task_addr)
{
  uint32_t stack_val; // Starting address of the new stack frame

  // Initial stack structure with stack frame (8 words) +
  // additional registers (10 words)
  stack_val = (stack_base + stack_size - (18*4));
  tcb_array[task_id].psp_val = stack_val;
  // Stack limit - since we use the task's process stack to store extra registers
  // We need to reserve 26 words (or 10 words in Cortex-M23/M33 without FPU)
  // to hold this data.
  tcb_array[task_id].psp_limit = stack_base + (26*4);
  HW32_REG(stack_val )   = 0xFFFFFFBCUL;   // Exception return - Handler(NS) to
                                           // Thread(NS) transition, uses PSP, FPCA=0
  HW32_REG(stack_val+ 4) = privilege;     // Sets to 0 if task is privileged or
                                           // Sets to 1 if task is unprivileged
  HW32_REG(stack_val+64) = task_addr;     // Return address
  HW32_REG(stack_val+68) = 0x01000000UL; // xPSR
```

```
    return;
}
// ------------------------------------------------------------
// Context switching code
void __attribute__((naked)) PendSV_Handler(void)
{ // Context switching code
   __asm(
   "mrs   r0, psp\n\t"   // Obtains current PSP value
   "tst   lr, #0x10\n\t" // Tests bit 4 of EXC_RETURN. If 0, needs to save regs s16-s31
   "it    eq\n\t"
   "vstmdbeq r0!,{s16-s31}\n\t" // Saves FPU callee-saved registers
   "mov   r2, lr\n\t"            // copies EXC_RETURN
   "mrs r3, CONTROL\n\t"         // copies CONTROL
   "stmdb r0!,{r2-r11}\n\t"      // Saves EXC_RETURN, CONTROL, R4-R11
   "bl PSP_update\n\t"           // Saves the PSP in the TCB, and gets the PSP for
                                 // the next task in the return value
   "ldmia r0!,{r2-r11}\n\t"      // Loads EXC_RETURN, CONTROL and R4-R11 from the task
   stack
   "mov lr, r2\n\t"              // Sets EXC_RETURN
   "msr CONTROL, r3\n\t"         // Sets CONTROL
   "isb \n\t"                    // Executes an ISB after CONTROL updates
                                 // (architecture recommendation)
   "tst lr, #0x10\n\t"           // Tests bit 4, If zero, unstacks FPU s16-s31
   "it eq\n\t"
   "vldmiaeq r0!,{s16-s31}\n\t"  // Loads the FPU callee-saved registers
   "msr psp, r0\n\t"             // Sets PSP for the next task
   "bx  lr\n\t"                  // Exception return
   );
}
// Switches the PSP value to a new task - used by PendSV_Handler
uint32_t PSP_update(uint32_t Old_PSP)
{
   tcb_array[curr_task].psp_val = Old_PSP; // Saves the PSP of the old task to the TCB
   curr_task = next_task; // Update task ID
   __set_PSPLIM(tcb_array[curr_task].psp_limit); // Sets stack limit for task
   return (tcb_array[curr_task].psp_val); // Returns the PSP of the new task to the PendSV
}
// ------------------------------------------------------------
// SysTick Handler
void SysTick_Handler(void)
{
   // A simple task scheduler (round robin)
   switch(curr_task) {
     case(0): next_task=1; break;
     case(1): next_task=0; break;
```

```
        default: next_task=0;
        printf("ERROR:curr_task = %x\n", curr_task);
        error_handler();
        break; // // Program flow should not reach here
        }
    if (curr_task!=next_task){ // Context switching needed
        SCB->ICSR |= SCB_ICSR_PENDSVSET_Msk; // Sets PendSV to pending
        }
    return;
}
```

When porting the same example to the Cortex-M23 processor, the following changes would need to be made:

• Removal of stack limit checking if the software is to be used in the Non-secure world. This is because there is no stack limit checking on the Non-secure side in the Cortex-M23 processor.
• Simplification of the context switching code: Because there is no FPU in the Cortex-M23 processor, the context switch code in the PendSV_Handler is able to skip the context saving and restoring of the FPU registers.
• Modification of the PendSV handler: Because the load-store multiple instructions (LDMDB and STMIA) in Armv8-M Baseline do not support the high registers (r8–r12), the PendSV handler would need to be modified to save and restore these registers by copying the content via the low registers.

If this simple OS example is to be run on the Secure side, the hard-coded initial EXC_RETURN value in create_task() will need to be changed from 0xFFFFFFBC to 0xFFFFFFFD. For OS code previously prepared for Armv7-M, it is likely value 0xFFFFFFFD would be used. Accordingly, the create_task() (or equivalent) would needed to be updated before being used on an Armv8-M processor.

Please note, this example does not illustrate the functionalities found in a typical RTOS. A typical RTOS:

• has more task scheduling capability features, for example, it can put a thread into an inactive state and can prioritize tasks based on a task's priority levels.
• would have additional SVC services, for example, to activate/disable tasks and for configuring task priorities.
• would have additional interprocess communications, for example, event handling, message queue, and semaphores.

Since the aforementioned example is not a full OS implementation, it does not show integration with the OS helper APIs in the Trusted Firmware-M. Further information on this can be found in the Embedded World paper mentioned in section 8 [4], and detailed examples can be found on the Trusted Firmware website (https://www.trustedfirmware.org/) [1].

This simple example makes no mention of MPU support. This is because the various parts of the codes used in this example, including the application tasks, are merged into a single file. Because of this arrangement, it is difficult to define separate memory regions for the OS and for application code/data. If an MPU was used, each of the application tasks would normally be in a separate code file. With this arrangement, the memory allocation of each task would accordingly be separately handled during the linking stage.

References

[1] Trusted Firmware-M. https://www.trustedfirmware.org/.
[2] Arm Compiler armclang Reference Guide—inline assembly example. https://developer.arm.com/documentation/100067/0612/armclang-Inline-Assembler/Forcing-inline-assembly-operands-into-specific-registers.
[3] Platform Security Architecture. https://developer.arm.com/architectures/security-architectures/platform-security-architecture
[4] How should an RTOS work in a TrustZone for Armv8-M environment. https://pages.arm.com/rtos-trustzone-armv8m.

Memory Protection Unit (MPU)

12.1 Overview of the MPU

12.1.1 Introduction

The Memory Protection Unit (MPU) is an optional feature in the Arm® Cortex®-M processor. It has two main purposes:

- To define the access permission of an application or process
  - In an OS environment, the MPU can be used for process isolation—which means application tasks running in unprivileged state can only access memory spaces that are assigned to them. Therefore, if an application task crashes, or has been compromised by a hacker, it cannot corrupt or access memories used by the OS or by other application tasks. Hence, it improves the security and robustness of the system.
  - The MPU can be used to force some of the address ranges to be read-only. For example, after loading a program image into RAM, you can, to prevent it from accidentally changing the program image inside, use the MPU to force the program location in RAM to be read-only.
  - The MPU can be used to mark certain data address ranges (e.g., stack, heap) as non-executable. This is a useful countermeasure to prevent hackers from attacking a system using code injection techniques. Using the MPU to mark a portion of the SRAM as non-executable prevents the code injected into the stack and heap from being executed.
- To define the memory attributes of the address ranges
  - For systems with caches (either built-in as a part of the processor or integrated at the system level), the MPU can be used for defining whether certain address ranges should be cacheable. If they are cacheable, the MPU can then be used to define the type of caching scheme (e.g., write-back, write-through) and the shareability attributes of the memory regions.
  - While possible, although in general not recommended, the MPU can be used to override the memory/device type definition of the default memory map (see Chapter 6, Section 6.3 for Memory Types and Memory Attributes, and Table 6.4 regarding the

Memory Attributes in the default memory map). Note: In normal applications, however, software developers should avoid switching an address from "Normal" to "Device" (or vice-versa) because a debugger would not know that the default memory/device type in the memory map had been overridden. A consequence of the aforementioned action is that the debugging of the system could become more difficult. This is because the bus transfers generated by the debugger would have mismatching memory attributes, resulting in inconsistencies between the application and the debug views.

In some RTOS's designed for Armv6-M and Armv7-M based Cortex-M processors, the MPU is used for stack overflow detection in application threads. However, in Armv8-M processors, stack overflow detection can be handled by the stack limit check registers. Specifically, in the:

- Cortex-M33: the stack limit check registers (see Section 11.4) can be used for both Secure and Non-secure software.
- Cortex-M23: the stack limit check registers are only available in the Secure world. An RTOS running in the Non-secure world might, therefore, still use an MPU for stack overflow detection.

When an MPU violation is detected, the transfer is blocked and a fault exception is generated:

- If the MemManage Fault (exception type 4) is available (it is not available in the Cortex-M23 processor), is enabled and has a higher priority than that of the current level, then the MemManage Fault would be instantly triggered.
- If that is not the case (either MemManage Fault is not available, is disabled or its priority level is same or lower than the current priority level), then HardFault (exception type 3) would be triggered.

The exception handler can then decide how best to deal with the error, i.e., whether the system should reset or, in the case of an OS environment, whether the OS should either terminate the offending task or restart the whole system.

The MemManage Fault is banked between security states:

- If a Secure MPU violation takes place, a Secure MemManage Fault is triggered
- If a Non-secure MPU violation takes place, a Non-secure MemManage Fault is triggered

When a MemManage Fault event is escalated to HardFault, the target security state depends on whether TrustZone® is implemented on the device and on the configuration of the AIRCR.BFHFNMINS bit (Table 9.18).

Unlike the Memory Management Unit (MMU) in application processors (e.g., Cortex-A processors), the MPU does not offer address translation (i.e., it has no virtual memory support). The reason for Cortex-M processors not supporting the MMU feature is to ensure that the processor system can deal with real-time requirements: When an MMU is used for virtual memory support and when there is a Translation Lookup Buffer (TLB) miss (i.e., a logical address needs to be translated to a physical address but the address translation details are not available in the local buffer), the MMU needs to carry out a page table walk. The page table walk operation is needed to obtain the address translation information. However, because during the page table walk operation the processor might not be able to deal with interrupt requests, the use of an MMU is not ideal for real-time systems.

12.1.2 MPU operation concepts

The MPU is a programmable unit and is controlled by privileged software. By default, the MPU is disabled, which means that:

- The memory access permission in the system's memory map is based on the default memory access permission (see Section 6.4.4)
- The memory attribute in the system's memory map is based on the default memory map (see Section 6.3.3)

The use of default memory access permission and default memory attribute also applies when the MPU has not been implemented.

The MPU operates by defining MPU regions. In Armv8-M, each MPU region has a starting and an ending address, with a 32-byte granularity. Before enabling the MPU, privileged software needs to program the MPU to define the MPU regions for both the privileged and the unprivileged software. The settings for each region include:

- The starting and ending addresses of the MPU region,
- The access permissions of the MPU region (i.e., whether the region is privileged access only or is full access), and
- The attributes of the MPU region (i.e., the memory/device type, cache attributes, etc.).

After programming the MPU regions, the MPU can then be enabled.

In an OS environment, the MPU region settings are likely to be reconfigured at each context switch so that each unprivileged application/thread has their own accessible address ranges. Each application/thread uses several MPU regions for code (including regions for shared libraries), data (such as stack), and peripherals. OS code also provides MPU regions for privileged code (e.g., interrupt handlers).

To simplify the MPU setup, the MPU for Cortex-M processors also provides a programmable background region feature. When this is enabled, privileged software is, unless the settings are overridden by an enabled MPU region, able to see the access permissions and memory attributes of the default memory map. By using the background region feature, OS code only needs to program the MPU regions required for the unprivileged code.

12.1.3 MPU support in Arm Cortex-M23 and Cortex-M33 processors

In the Cortex-M23 and Cortex-M33 processors, the MPU feature is optional. When implemented, the MPU could have 4/8/12 or 16 MPU regions. If the TrustZone security extension is implemented, there can be up to two MPUs, one for the Secure and one for the Non-secure world. The number of MPU regions for the Secure and the Non-secure MPU can be different.

Although the Cortex-M23 and Cortex-M33 processors do not have an internal level 1 cache, the cache attributes produced by the MPU settings are exported to the processor's top level so, if a system level cache is available, it can utilize the attribute information.

12.1.4 Architectural requirements when using the MPU

The design of the MPU is based on the Protected Memory System Architecture (PMSA). PMSAv8 is part of the Armv8-M Architecture [1]. When configurating the MPU:

- Before changing the MPU configuration, a DMB instruction should be executed to ensure that the previous memory accesses (if some of those are still outstanding) are not affected.
- If a system level cache is present, and if the configuration of the MPU is going to change the caching scheme, you will need to clean the cache before updating the MPU configuration.
- After the MPU has configured, you should execute a DSB and then an ISB instruction to ensure that the subsequent program operations are using the new MPU settings.

12.2 MPU registers

12.2.1 Summary of the MPU registers

The MPU registers (Table 12.1) are memory mapped and are placed in the System Control Space (SCS). In Armv8-M architecture, the access to the MPU registers should always be 32-bit in size.

Please note, the programmer's model of the MPU in the Armv8-M architecture is, apart from the MPU_TYPE, the MPU_CTRL, and the MPU_RNR registers, different from the MPU in the Armv6-M and Armv7-M architectures.

TABLE 12.1 Summary of the registers in the MPU (Alias registers are not available in the Cortex-M23 processor).

Address	Register	CMSIS-CORE symbol	Function
0xE000ED90	MPU_TYPE	MPU->TYPE	MPU Type Register
0xE000ED94	MPU_CTRL	MPU->CTRL	MPU Control Register
0xE000ED98	MPU_RNR	MPU->RNR	MPU Region Number Register
0xE000ED9C	MPU_RBAR	MPU->RBAR	MPU Region Base Address Register
0xE000EDA0	MPU_RLAR	MPU->RLAR	MPU Region Limit Address Register
0xE000EDA4	MPU_RBAR_A1	MPU->RBAR_A1	MPU Region Base Address Register Alias 1
0xE000EDA8	MPU_RLAR_A1	MPU->RLAR_A1	MPU Region Limit Address Register Alias 1
0xE000EDAC	MPU_RBAR_A2	MPU->RBAR_A2	MPU Region Base Address Register Alias 2
0xE000EDB0	MPU_RLAR_A2	MPU->RLAR_A2	MPU Region Limit Address Register Alias 2
0xE000EDB4	MPU_RBAR_A3	MPU->RBAR_A3	MPU Region Base Address Register Alias 3
0xE000EDB8	MPU_RLAR_A3	MPU->RLAR_A3	MPU Region Limit Address Register Alias 3
0xE000EDC0	MPU_MAIR0	MPU->MAIR0	MPU Memory Attribute Indirection Register 0
0xE000EDC4	MPU_MAIR1	MPU->MAIR1	MPU Memory Attribute Indirection Register 1

When TrustZone is implemented:

- If the processor is running Non-secure privileged software, software can access the Non-secure MPU registers via address 0xE000ED90 to 0xE000EDC4.
- If the processor is running Secure privileged software, software can access the Secure MPU registers via address 0xE000ED90 to 0xE000EDC4.
- If the processor is running Secure privileged software, software can access the Non-secure MPU registers via address 0xE002ED90 to 0xE002EDC4 (i.e., Non-secure MPU alias address).

When using the CMSIS-CORE header file, Secure privileged software uses the MPU_NS data structure instead of the MPU data structure to access the Non-secure MPU registers.

12.2.2 MPU Type register

The MPU Type register (Fig. 12.1 and Table 12.2) details the number of MPU regions implemented in the MPU for the selected security state. If the DREGION bit field is 0, the MPU is not implemented for the selected security state. This MPU Type register is read-only.

12.2.3 MPU Control register

The MPU Control register (Fig. 12.2 and Table 12.3) defines the feature enable control for the MPU.

The PRIVDEFENA bit in the MPU Control Register is used to enable the background region. By using PRIVDEFENA, and if no other regions are set up, privileged programs can

FIG. 12.1 MPU TYPE register.

TABLE 12.2 MPU Type Register (MPU->TYPE, 0xE000ED90).

Bits	Name	Type	Reset Value	Description
31:16	Reserved	RO	0	Reserved
15:8	DREGION	RO	Implementation defined	Number of MPU regions that are supported by the MPU in the selected security state.
7:1	Reserved	RO	0	Reserved
0	SEPARATE	RO	0	Indicates the support for separate instruction and data regions. Because Armv8-M only supports unified MPU regions, this bit is always 0.

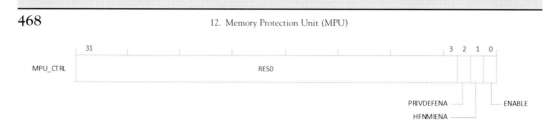

FIG. 12.2 MPU CTRL register.

TABLE 12.3 MPU Control Register (MPU->CTRL, 0xE000ED94).

Bits	Name	Type	Reset Value	Description
31:3	Reserved	RO	0	Reserved
2	PRIVDEFENA	R/W	0	Privileged default memory map enables. When set to 1 and if the MPU is enabled, the default memory map is used for privileged access that is not mapped into any MPU region (i.e., it provides a background region for privileged code). If this bit is not set, the background region is disabled and any access not covered by an enabled MPU region will cause a fault.
1	HFNMIENA	R/W	0	If set to 1, the MPU is used when the HardFault handler and NMI handler are being executed; If set to 0, the MPU is bypassed during the execution of the HardFault handler and the NMI, and the MPU is also bypassed when the FAULTMASK is set to 1.
0	ENABLE	R/W	0	Enables the MPU if set to 1.

access all memory locations. Memory access generated from unprivileged programs will, however, be blocked. However, if other MPU regions are programmed and enabled, they can override the background region. For example, Fig. 12.3 shows two systems with similar region setups, but only the one on the right-hand side has the PRIVDEFENA bit set to 1, which means this system allows privileged access to the background regions.

The HFNMIENA bit is used to define the behavior of the MPU during the execution of the NMI and the HardFault handlers, or when the FAULTMASK is set. By default (i.e., when the HFNMIENA bit is 0), the MPU is bypassed (disabled) when one or more of these conditions is met. This allows the HardFault handler and the NMI Handler to execute even when the MPU has been incorrectly set up.

Setting the enable bit in the MPU Control register is usually the last step in the MPU setup code. If it was not, the MPU might accidentally generate faults before the region configuration was completed. In many cases, especially one with an embedded OS with dynamic MPU configurations, the MPU should be disabled at the start of the MPU configuration routine to ensure that the MemManage fault is not accidentally triggered during the configuration of the MPU regions.

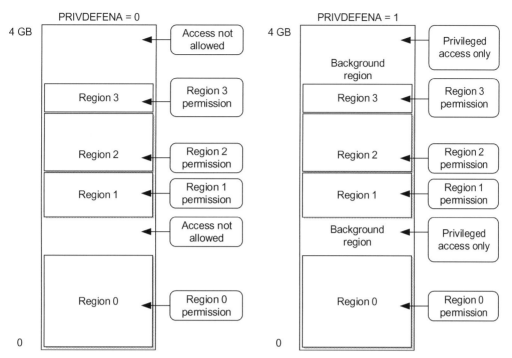

FIG. 12.3   The effect of the PRIVDEFENA bit (Background region enabled).

12.2.4 MPU Region Number Register

In theory, an Armv8-M processor can support more than 16 MPU regions. Instead of allocating individual addresses for all of the MPU's region registers, the MPU register access is indexed and controlled by the MPU's Region Number Register. Because of this, you only need a small number of register addresses in order to access all of the MPU's region configuration registers.

The MPU Region Number Register (Fig. 12.4 and Table 12.4) is 8 bit, so, in theory, could allow 256 MPU regions to be configured. But, because having 256 MPU regions significantly increases the cost of the silicon area and the power usage, the Cortex-M23 and Cortex-M33 processors only support up to 16 MPU regions. Before setting up an MPU region, software needs to write to this register to select the region to be programmed.

Note: In Armv7-M it was possible to skip the programming of the MPU_RNR by merging the region number into the write value for the MPU Region Base Address Register. This mechanism is not, however, supported in Armv8-M.

FIG. 12.4   MPU Region Number Register.

TABLE 12.4 MPU Region Number Register (MPU->RNR, 0xE000ED98).

Bits	Name	Type	Reset Value	Description
31:8	Reserved	RO	0	Reserved
7:0	REGION	R/W	–	Selects the region for programming.

12.2.5 MPU Region Base Address Register

The MPU Region Base Address Register (Fig. 12.5 and Table 12.5) defines the starting address of an MPU region and the access permission of that region.

Although the Cortex-M23 and Cortex-M33 processors do not have built-in caches, the designs do support external caches, including level 1 (i.e., it uses the inner cache attribute) and level 2 (i.e., it uses the outer cache attribute). The cacheability and shareability attributes from the MPU region lookup is propagated alongside the bus system transfers in order that the

FIG. 12.5 MPU Region Base Address Register.

TABLE 12.5 MPU Region Base Address Register (MPU->RBAR, 0xE000ED9C).

Bits	Name	Type	Reset Value	Description
31:5	BASE	R/W	–	Base address of the MPU region—contains bit 31 to bit 5 of the lower inclusive address limit of the MPU region. The lowest 5 bits of the address value (bit 4 to 0) are padded with zeros for MPU region checking purposes.
4:3	SH	R/W	–	Shareability—defines the shareability attribute of this region for Normal memory. If this region is configured as Device, it is always treated as shared. 00—Non-shareable 11—Inner Shareable 10—Outer Shareable
2:1	AP [2:1]	R/W	–	Access permission 00—Read/Write by privileged code only 01—Full access (read/write for any privilege level) 10—Read-only for privileged code only 11—Read-only for both privileged and unprivileged code
0	XN	R/W	–	Execute Never—when set to 1, the execution of code from this MPU region is not allowed.

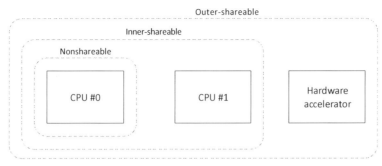

FIG. 12.6 A simplified view of shareability grouping.

cache units can, based on the memory attributes defined in the MPU, correctly handle the transfer.

In systems with multiple bus masters, the bus masters are partitioned into shareability groups (Fig. 12.6), with the shareability attribute from the bus transaction being used to decide whether a cache unit needs to handle the coherency management for the transfer.

The coherency management schemes shown in Fig. 12.6 are explained below:

- Non-shareable: An update of data in a Non-shareable region by CPU #1 is not always observable by any other bus masters in the system. This has the benefit of achieving a higher performance, but if, at some stage, the data needs to be accessed by other bus master(s), a software operation, such as cache clean, will be needed.
- Inner shareable: An update of data in an inner-shareable region by CPU #1 is only observable by other bus masters in the same inner shareability group. Other bus masters that are not in the same group, may not, however, be able to see the updated data. For example, some Arm Cortex-A processors support cluster configurations and cache coherency between multiple processor cores. This makes sharing data between processors easier. However, to handle coherency, a snoop control unit (SCU) inside the cache hardware is likely to introduce small delays in some bus transactions.
- Outer shareable: Some systems contain other bus masters and could have a shared level 2 cache to allow the processors and other bus master(s) to have a coherent view in some memory regions. With this arrangement, the aforementioned processors and bus masters are easily able to use these regions to share data. When a memory region is defined as outer shareable it is also inner shareable.

12.2.6 MPU Region Limit Address Register

The MPU Region Limit Address Register (Fig. 12.7 and Table 12.6) defines the ending address of an MPU region and the memory attributes of that region. It also contains the enable control bit of the MPU region. Unused MPU regions should have its region enable bit set to 0 before the MPU is enabled. The MPU enable is controlled by the control bit MPU_CTRL.ENABLE (Table 12.3).

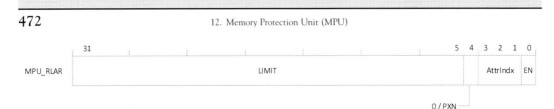

FIG. 12.7   MPU Region Limit Address Register.

TABLE 12.6   MPU Region Limit Address Register (MPU->RLAR, 0xE000EDA0).

Bits	Name	Type	Reset Value	Description
31:5	LIMIT	R/W	–	Upper limit address of the MPU region—contains bit 31 to bit 5 of the upper inclusive address limit of the MPU region. The lowest 5 bits of the address value (bit 4 to 0) are padded with "1"s for MPU region checking purposes.
4	Reserved/ PXN	– R/W	–	Reserved in Armv8.0-M The Privileged eXecute Never (PXN) attribute is available in Armv8.1-M (e.g., Cortex-M55) and is not available in the Cortex-M23 and Cortex-M33 processors.
3:1	AttrIndx	R/W	–	Attribute Index—for selecting memory attributes from MAIR0 and MAIR1
0	EN	R/W	0	Region Enable

The MPU region limit address is generated by taking the LIMIT bit field and padding it with 5 bits of one's. For example, if the MPU_RLAR is set to 0x2000FFE7, then the settings are interpreted as follows:

- The LIMIT provides bit 31 down to bit 5 of the limit address. Before bit 4 down to bit 0 of the address is replaced with "1"s, the address is 0x2000FFE0. After replacing the lowest 5 bits of the LIMIT address to "1", the actual limit address value obtained is 0x2000FFFF.
- Bit 4 (Reserved/PXN bit) is 0—this is not used in the Cortex-M23 and Cortex-M33 processors.
- The lowest 4 bits has a binary value of 0111 (i.e., 7) and this maps to the value of the Attribute Index (i.e., AttrIndx), which is 3, and to the value of the enable control bit (i.e., EN) for the MPU region, which is 1 (i.e., the MPU region is enabled).

The "AttrIndx" is an index value for obtaining the correct memory attribute settings from the MAIR0 and MAIR1 registers. By using an indexing method, the total number of memory attribute bits for the MPU regions can be reduced.

The PXN attribute bit was introduced in the Armv8.1-M architecture (e.g., the Cortex-M55 processor) and is not available in Armv8.0-M. This allows an MPU region containing unprivileged application or library codes to be marked as unprivileged-execution-only to prevent privileged escalation attacks.

12.2.7 MPU RBAR and RLAR alias registers

The MPU RBAR and RLAR alias registers are only available in Armv8-M Mainline and are not supported by the Cortex-M23 processor. The purpose of those aforementioned registers is to speed up the programming of the MPU. This is achieved by avoiding the need to program the MPU Region Number Register (MPU_RNR) each time a region is programmed. To use the alias registers, you program the MPU_RNR to a value of N, where N is multiple of 4, and then access MPU regions N+1, N+2, and N+3 using the MPU RBAR and RLAR alias registers. The aliasing of the MPU region registers is shown in Table 12.7.

The bit fields inside the MPU RBAR and RLAR alias registers (i.e., MPU_RBAR_A1/2/3 and MPU_RLAR_A1/2/3) are exactly the same as the bit fields inside the MPU_RBAR and MPU_RLAR registers. The only difference is the region number of the MPU region being accessed.

If the MPU_RNR is not set to multiples of 4, bits 1 and 0 of the MPU_RNR are ignored when accessing the MPU RBAR and MPU RLAR alias registers, i.e., the region number used is (MPU_RNR[7:2]) $<<2+$ alias_number.

12.2.8 MPU Attribute Indirection Register 0 and 1

Memory system behaviors in modern computing systems can be quite complex. For the memory access behaviors to be controlled, many bits are needed in the MPU's memory attributes to cover the required control needs. However, an embedded system is likely to only have a few types of memory. So, instead of having a number of control bits for the memory attributes in each of the MPU regions, the MPU Attribute Indirection Registers (Fig. 12.8) provide a lookup table of up to eight memory attribute types. Each MPU region selects the memory attribute from those eight memory attribute types using the AttrIndx bit field in the MPU_RLAR register.

For more information on Memory and Device types, please refer to Section 6.3.

The MPU in Armv8-M introduces a new memory attribute called "transient". Its purpose is to provide a hint to the cache units that the data in the MPU region might only need to be in the cache for a short period of time. This hint can be useful during cache line replacement. In

TABLE 12.7 MPU regions being accessed when using the MPU RBAR and the MPU RLAR alias registers.

	When MPU_RNR = 0	When MPU_RNR = 4	When MPU_RNR = 8	When MPU_RNR = 12
MPU_RBAR	MPU_RBAR[0]	MPU_RBAR[4]	MPU_RBAR[8]	MPU_RBAR[12]
MPU_RLAR	MPU_RLAR[0]	MPU_RLAR[4]	MPU_RLAR[8]	MPU_RBAR[12]
MPU_RBAR_A1	MPU_RBAR[1]	MPU_RBAR[5]	MPU_RBAR[9]	MPU_RBAR[13]
MPU_RLAR_A1	MPU_RLAR[1]	MPU_RLAR[5]	MPU_RLAR[9]	MPU_RBAR[13]
MPU_RBAR_A2	MPU_RBAR[2]	MPU_RBAR[6]	MPU_RBAR[10]	MPU_RBAR[14]
MPU_RLAR_A2	MPU_RLAR[2]	MPU_RLAR[6]	MPU_RLAR[10]	MPU_RBAR[14]
MPU_RBAR_A3	MPU_RBAR[3]	MPU_RBAR[7]	MPU_RBAR[11]	MPU_RBAR[15]
MPU_RLAR_A3	MPU_RLAR[3]	MPU_RLAR[7]	MPU_RLAR[11]	MPU_RBAR[15]

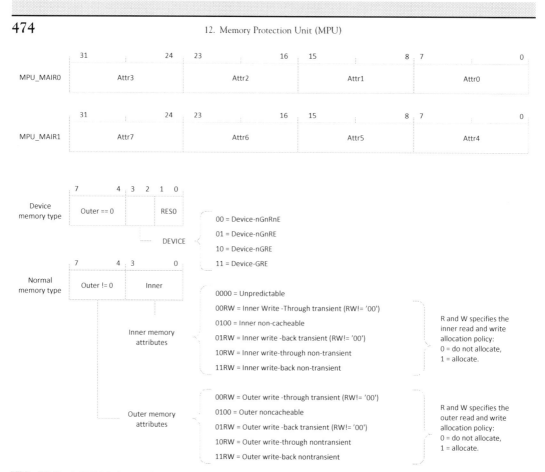

FIG. 12.8   MPU_MAIR0 and MPU_MAIR1 registers.

systems based on the Cortex-M23 and Cortex-M33 processors, transient information is not used because these processors do not have internal caches and the AMBA® 5 AHB bus protocol [2] does not provide signals for the transfer of transient attributes.

12.3 Configuration of the MPU

12.3.1 Overview of the MPU's configuration steps

A typical MPU setup sequence is illustrated in Fig. 12.9.

If using an Armv8-M Mainline processor, the number of iterations in the MPU configuration loop can be reduced by making use of the MPU RBAR and RLAR alias registers.

Some things to consider when setting up the MPU:

- It is not necessary to setup MPU regions for the processor's internal memory mapped components such as the hardware registers in the System Control Space (SCS) and the Private Peripheral Bus (PPB, address 0xE0000000 to 0xE00FFFFF).

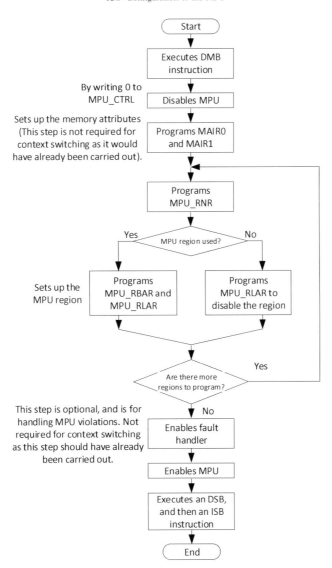

FIG. 12.9 A simple MPU setup sequence.

- Exception vector fetches always use the default memory map and there is, therefore, no need to setup an MPU region for the vector table.
- Using the background region (i.e., set PRIVDEFENA to 1) reduces the number of MPU regions needed—because the MPU region configuration only needs to cover the requirements of the unprivileged software.
- When setting HFNMIENA to 1, you need to make sure that the MPU region settings cover the memory space needed for the execution of both the HardFault and the Non-Maskable Interrupt (NMI) handler. Alternatively, you can enable the background region by setting

PRIVDEFENA to 1 and, by so doing, allow the HardFault and the NMI handler to execute using the default memory map. If HFNMIENA is 1 and if you do not set PRIVDEFENA to 1, the MPU will be used when these handlers execute (i.e., all accesses would be subjected to MPU permission checking). This will, if a memory is accessed by one of those handlers and is blocked by the MPU, result in the processor entering LOCKUP (Section 13.6).

- Avoid overriding Normal memories to Device and vice versa. If software does override the memory type, a debugger might not be able generate a debug access with matching memory attributes. And, if a system cache is present, the debugger could end up, due to mismatching memory attributes, with a different data view from that seen in the software.
- For microcontroller applications, the MPU region setup can often be simplified by using a single MPU region to cover all of the program flash (or other forms of Nonvolatile memory). In many microcontroller applications, even when an RTOS is used, it is often unnecessary and impractical to define separate MPU regions for application threads. This is because these application threads often use shared C functions (e.g., C runtime libraries and OS-specific APIs), making it difficult to separate the program memories for each of the unprivileged software threads into separate MPU regions. In addition, because application software developers usually have full visibility of the program memory, allowing those unprivileged software threads to read the whole program is unlikely to cause security concerns.

12.3.2 Defining the memory attributes for MAIR0 and MAIR1

One of the first things to think about when defining the MPU configuration is what memory types will need to be supported. This information is required for the configuration of MAIR0 and MAIR1. In an embedded system based on a microcontroller, there are usually only a few memory types. Several examples of common memory types for microcontrollers are listed in Table 12.8.

The inner and outer attributes can be used by either system level caches or by memory interface controllers (Fig. 12.10).

Once the required attributes are defined, the rest of the MPU's programming sequence can reference the memory attributes by specifying AttrIndx (Attribute Index) in the MPU_RLAR (Region Limit Address Register). During context switching in the OS, memory attributes in MAIR0 and MAIR1 do not need to be updated (Fig. 12.11).

12.3.3 MPU programming

12.3.3.1 Overview

A range of low-level MPU configuration functions has been defined in the CMSIS-CORE (in a header file "include/mpu_v8.h"). In addition, another CMSIS project called the CMSIS-Zone provides a utility that is able to generate MPU configuration codes from project settings (in the form of an XML file format).

The low-level MPU control functions as defined in the CMSIS-CORE are as follows.

TABLE 12.8   Examples of memory attribute.

Memory/device type	Description	Example of memory attribute value (binary)
Program memory such as embedded flash (cacheable)	Inner and outer write back, nontransient. Read and write allocate (although write is unlikely to take place).	(8-bit)11111111
On-chip fast SRAM	Fast SRAM that is closely coupled to the processor. This can be configured as Noncacheable so that access to the fast SRAM will not replace other cached information.	(8-bit)01000100
Slow RAM with shared level 2 cache	Memory devices with long access latency. E.g., DRAM. Cacheable on both inner and outer cache	(8-bit)11111111
Peripherals (Bufferable)	General peripherals	(8-bit)00000001
Peripherals (Non-bufferable)	Usually for specialized hardware blocks. E.g., Hardware registers for system control. Marked as non-bufferable so that the effect on the register update is almost immediately visible to the subsequent code.	(8-bit)00000000

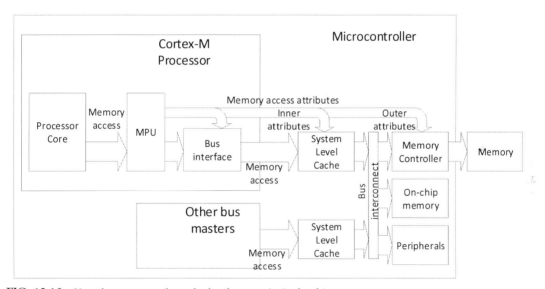

FIG. 12.10   Use of memory attributes by hardware units in the chip.

12.3.3.2 Disable MPU

To disable the MPU (this might be needed when updating the MPU's configuration), the following function is used.

```
void ARM_MPU_Disable(void);
```

If TrustZone is implemented, the following function allows the Secure software to disable the Non-secure MPU:

```
void ARM_MPU_Disable_NS(void);
```

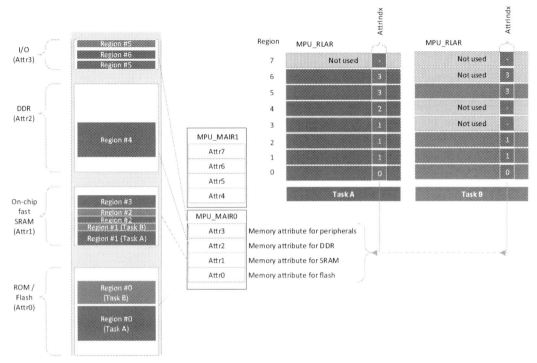

FIG. 12.11 During context switching, only MPU_RBAR and MPU_RLAR are updated, with the settings in the MAIRx remaining unchanged.

12.3.3.3 Program MAIR0 and MAIR1

One of the key steps for initializing the MPU (Fig. 12.9) is to program the MPU attribute redirection registers (MAIR0 and MAIR1). The header files in the CMSIS-CORE provide the following functions:

```
// for the current selected MPU
void ARM_MPU_SetMemAttr(uint8_t idx, int8_t attr);
```

When TrustZone is implemented, the following function allows Secure software to setup attribute redirection registers to one of the explicitly selected MPUs:

```
// for explicit MPU selection (Use "MPU" for the current selected MPU,
// or "MPU_NS" for the Non-secure MPU)

void ARM_MPU_SetMemAttrEx(MPU_Type* mpu, uint8_t idx, int8_t attr);
```

Another function to use when setting up the attribute redirection registers of the Non-secure MPU is:

```
// for MPU_NS

void ARM_MPU_SetMemAttr_NS(uint8_t idx, int8_t attr);
```

Where the function parameters are:

- "mpu" is either `MPU` or `MPU_NS`,
- "idx" is index value 0–7, and
- "attr" is the 8-bit memory attribute.

When using these functions, there are a number of defined C macros which makes the code more readable. To enable the use of these functions, a number of constants have been defined (Table 12.9).

To create the appropriate memory attribute values from these C macros, the following C macro codes can be used (Table 12.10).

12.3.3.4 Region Base Address and Limit Address registers

When MAIR0 and MAIR1 are programmed, the MPU Base Address and the Limit Address Registers (RBAR and RLAR) can then be programmed. The header files in the CMSIS-CORE provides the following functions:

```
// for current selected MPU

void ARM_MPU_SetRegion(uint32_t rnr, uint32_t rbar, uint32_t rlar);
```

When TrustZone is implemented, the following function allows Secure software to setup the RBAR and the RLAR registers to one of the explicitly selected MPUs:

```
// for explicit MPU selection (Use "MPU" for the current selected MPU,
// or "MPU_NS" for the Non-secure MPU)

void ARM_MPU_SetRegionEx(MPU_type* mpu, uint32_t rnr, uint32_t rbar,
uint32_t rlar);
```

TABLE 12.9 C macros to support the creation of memory attributes.

Feature	Macro	Value	Description
DEVICE	ARM_MPU_ATTR_DEVICE	0	Upper 4 bit of attr for Devices
Device type bit 3 to bit 2	ARM_MPU_ATTR_DEVICE_nGnRnE	0	Non-bufferable device
	ARM_MPU_ATTR_DEVICE_nGnRE	1	Bufferable device
	ARM_MPU_ATTR_DEVICE_nGRE	2	Device allowing read/write reordering
	ARM_MPU_ATTR_DEVICE_GRE	3	Device allowing read/write re-ordering and gathering (e.g., resizing)
Memory Type	ARM_MPU_ATTR(O, I)	–	Combining Outer (O) and Inner (I) attributes.
	ARM_MPU_ATTR_NON_CACHEABLE	4	Noncacheable Normal Memory
	ARM_MPU_ATTR_MEMORY_(NT, WB, RA, WA)	–	4-bit cacheable memory attribute for inner and outer cache policy

TABLE 12.10 Example of generating memory attributes using the C macros.

Example of device and memory types	C macro example
DEVICE-nGnRnE	(ARM_MPU_ATTR_DEVICE << 4) | (ARM_MPU_ATTR_DEVICE_nGnRnE <<2)
DEVICE-nGnRE	(ARM_MPU_ATTR_DEVICE << 4) | (ARM_MPU_ATTR_DEVICE_nGnRE <<2)
DEVICE-nGRE	(ARM_MPU_ATTR_DEVICE << 4) | (ARM_MPU_ATTR_DEVICE_nGRE <<2)
DEVICE-GRE	(ARM_MPU_ATTR_DEVICE << 4) | (ARM_MPU_ATTR_DEVICE_GRE <<2)
Inner and outer Noncacheable normal memory	ARM_MPU_ATTR(ARM_MPU_ATTR_NON_CACHEABLE, ARM_MPU_ATTR_NON_CACHEABLE)
Inner noncacheable, outer cacheable normal memory	ARM_MPU_ATTR(ARM_MPU_ATTR_MEMORY_(NT,WB,RA,WA), ARM_MPU_ATTR_NON_CACHEABLE) *where NT (Nontransient), WB (Write-back), RA (Read-allocate) and WA (Write-allocate) has values or 0 or 1.*
Inner cacheable, outer cacheable normal memory	ARM_MPU_ATTR(ARM_MPU_ATTR_MEMORY_(NT,WB,RA,WA), ARM_MPU_ATTR_MEMORY_(NT,WB,RA,WA)) *where NT (Nontransient), WB (Write-back), RA (Read-allocate) and WA (Write-allocate) has values or 0 or 1.*

Another function to use when setting up the RBAR and RLAR registers of the Non-secure MPU is:

```
// for MPU_NS

void ARM_MPU_SetRegion_NS(uint32_t rnr, uint32_t rbar, uint32_t rlar);
```

When using these functions, there are a number of defined C macros for creating RBAR and RLAR values, which makes the code more readable (Table 12.11).

If an MPU region is not used, the following function can be used to clear the MPU regions:

```
// for current selected MPU

void ARM_MPU_ClrRegion(uint32_t rnr);
```

When TrustZone is implemented, the following function allows Secure software to clear an MPU region in one of the explicitly selected MPUs:

```
// for explicit MPU selection (Use "MPU" for the current selected MPU,
// or "MPU_NS" for the Non-secure MPU)

void ARM_MPU_ClrRegionEx(MPU_Type* mpu, uint32_t rnr);
```

Another function to use when clearing a region of the Non-secure MPU is:

```
// for MPU_NS

void ARM_MPU_ClrRegion_NS(uint32_t rnr);
```

TABLE 12.11 C macros to support the creation of RBAR and RLAR values.

Feature	Macro	Value	Description
RBAR	ARM_MPU_RBAR(BASE, SH, RO, NP, XN)	–	Region Base Address Register value
			- BASE: Base address - SH: Shareability - RO: Read-only (0 or 1-true) - NP: Nonprivileged allowed (0 or 1-true) - XN: eXecute Never (0 or 1-true)
RLAR	ARM_MPU_RBAR(LIMIT, IDX) Or ARM_MPU_RBAR_PXN(LIMIT, IDX, PXN) - for Armv8.1-M only, not suitable for Cortex-M23/Cortex-M33	–	Region Limit Address Register value
			- LIMIT: Region upper limit address - IDX: index to attr in MAIR0, MAIR1 - PXN: Privileged eXecute Never (0 or 1-true, for Armv8.1-M only)
Shareability (SH in MPU_RBAR)	ARM_MPU_SH_NON	0	The MPU region is not shared
	ARM_MPU_SH_OUTER	2	The MPU region is outer sharable (implicitly inner sharable)
	ARM_MPU_SH_INNER	3	The MPU region is inner sharable

12.3.3.5 Enable the MPU

After all the MPU regions are configured and all the unused regions are disabled, we can then enable the MPU. The header files in the CMSIS-CORE provide the following function:

```
// for current selected MPU

void ARM_MPU_Enable(uint32_t MPU_Control);
```

In this function, the bit 0 of the MPU_Control value is set to 1 before it is written into the MPU_CTRL. When TrustZone is implemented, there is another function which allows Secure software to enable the Non-secure MPU:

```
// for MPU_NS

void ARM_MPU_Enable_NS(uint32_t MPU_Control);
```

These two functions include the execution of the required memory barrier instructions (DSB and ISB). You should ensure that all configurations relating to fault exception handling (e.g., the enabling of MemManage Fault and the setting up of its priority level) is completed before enabling the MPU.

12.4 TrustZone and MPU

If TrustZone is not implemented in an Armv8-M processor, there can be only one MPU in the processor. If TrustZone is implemented, then the processor can have up to two MPUs. These are:

- The Secure MPU (MPU_S), which monitors the operations of the Secure software (including access to the Non-secure memories).
- The Non-secure MPU (MPU_NS), which monitors the operations of the Non-secure software.

Each of the MPU's can have a different number of MPU regions and can operate independently of each other. One could, for example, be enabled and the other not. In a typical TrustZone enabled environment:

- The Non-secure MPU can be used to handle process isolation for unprivileged applications.
- The Secure MPU can be used to handle process isolation for unprivileged Secure libraries.

A concept of how the MPUs could be used is shown in Fig. 12.12.

In such an environment, if a Secure MPU is used, the Secure MPU configuration would be based on which Secure APIs are being called from the Non-secure world. When there is a context switch in the Non-secure world, the Secure MPU configuration will also need to be switched. This requirement is supported by the OS helper APIs as described in Section 11.8.

Two approaches can be used to ensure that the Secure MPU is configured to the right secure library context:

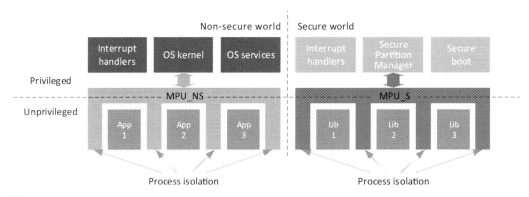

FIG. 12.12   Use of both Secure and Non-secure MPU's in a TrustZone enabled system.

- Before an application in the Non-secure world starts to call a library function in the Secure world, it calls a function in the secure firmware to request access to the library so that the Secure Partition Manager can setup the Secure MPU for this context. If the Non-secure software needs to call another function in another Secure library, it needs to call a Secure function to request the context switch of the Secure MPU.
- For Armv8-M Mainline, instead of calling a Secure function in the Secure world to request access to a Secure library, it is possible to call the library directly. The Secure MemManage fault handler detects the need to context switch the Secure MPU and deals with that accordingly. The call to the Secure APIs can then resume. This method is not suitable for Armv8-M Baseline (i.e., the Cortex-M23 processor) due to the lack of the Secure MemManage fault and the lack of fault status registers in the Baseline subprofile.

The Secure Partition Manager keeps track of which Secure library is being used in each Non-secure thread so that the Secure MPU is updated accordingly in each context switch.

When using the MPU setup shown in Fig. 12.12, the MPU regions for the Secure and Non-secure MPU are different. In order to allow a Secure API to provide services to a Non-secure application, the Secure software needs to setup the Secure MPU so that it can access Non-secure application data and carry out operations on behalf of the Non-secure application. For example, when an application calls a Secure API to process its data, it needs to pass a pointer to the Secure API, as shown in Fig. 12.13.

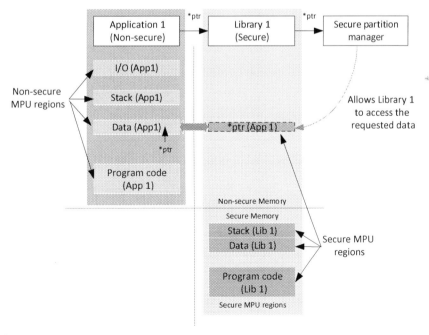

FIG. 12.13   Secure library accessing Non-secure application data.

If in the example shown in Fig. 12.13 the Secure library is executing in an unprivileged state, then it is unable to update the Secure MPU settings by itself. Instead, the Secure library passes the pointer to and requests the Secure Partition Manager for permission to access the data. Since the Secure Partition Manager is aware that library 1 is called from application 1, it can decide if the requested access permission should be granted by checking the access permission of application 1. This permission check is carried out by checking the Non-secure MPU configuration (using the TT instruction) as follows:

- If application 1 has access permission to the address pointed to by the pointer, then the Secure Partition Manager grants Secure Library 1 access to the data referenced to by that pointer.
- If application 1 does not have access permission to the address pointed to by the pointer, the request is rejected and the Secure API returns an error status to application 1.

With this setup, a Non-secure application cannot use Secure APIs to bypass the security measures in the Non-secure OS (i.e., the process isolation) to attack the privileged software.

12.5 Key differences between the MPU in Armv8-M architecture and the architecture of the previous generations

Although the concepts for MPU operations are similar to that in Armv6-M and Armv7-M, the MPU in Armv8-M architecture has a different programmer's model. There is a range of other differences and these are as follows:

- In Armv8-M architecture, the size of an MPU region can be any size in the granularity of 32 bytes. The previous restriction where region size must be 2^N (i.e., 2 to the power of N) has been removed.
- The starting address of an MPU region can now also be in any address which is a multiple of 32 bytes. This allows more flexibility for the MPU region placement.
- In the new programmer's model for Armv8-M, the subregion disable feature has been removed. Because the size of an MPU region is no longer restricted to 2^N, it can, therefore, be difficult to equally divide a region into eight subregions.
- The new design does not allow MPU regions to be overlapped. With the new programmer's model, the MPU region definition is already much more flexible so the need to overlap an MPU region is no longer necessary (apart from overlapping with the background region).
- In Armv7-M and Armv6-M MPUs, you can declare an MPU region as having no access. This is not required in Armv8-M. By not mapping an address to an MPU region, the address is automatically nonaccessible (except when the address maps to an internal memory mapped component like the NVIC, the SysTick, etc.). Access to an unmapped address location, when the MPU is enabled, triggers the MemManage fault (except where the background region is enabled and when the software is executing in privileged state).
- There are new attribute definitions of device memories.
- Attribute Indirection for memory attribute generation is now used in Armv8-M: using an index value which is then looked up in memory attribute registers.

The addition of TrustZone technology also impacts the MPU program code. When the optional Security Extension (i.e., TrustZone) is implemented, the processor can have:

- one set of MPU configuration registers for the Secure state and another set of MPU configuration registers for the Non-Secure state, or
- an MPU feature available in just one of the security states or
- no MPU at all.

When TrustZone and the Non-secure MPU is implemented, Secure software can access the Non-Secure MPU by using an alias address (address 0xE002ED90).

References

[1] Armv8-M Architecture Reference Manual. https://developer.arm.com/documentation/ddi0553/am/ (Armv8.0-M only version). https://developer.arm.com/documentation/ddi0553/latest/ (latest version including Armv8.1-M). Note: M-profile architecture reference manuals for Armv6-M, Armv7-M, Armv8-M and Armv8.1-M can be found here: https://developer.arm.com/architectures/cpu–architecture/m–profile/docs.
[2] AMBA 5 Advanced High-performance Bus (AHB) Protocol Specification, https://developer.arm.com/documentation/ihi0033/latest/.

Fault exceptions and fault handling

13.1 Overview

Fault exceptions are exception types dedicated to error handling and are a part of the system exceptions in the Arm®v8-M architecture [1]. For example, in the last chapter I mentioned that an MPU violation could trigger either a MemManage Fault or a HardFault. In addition to those faults, Arm® Cortex®-M processors provide several other fault exceptions and hardware resources for:

* Managing fault events
* Analyzing fault exception (Fault Status Registers are available in Armv8-M Mainline only)

A summary of the fault exceptions available in Arm Cortex-M23 and Cortex-M33 processors are listed in Table 13.1.

MemManage Fault, BusFault, UsageFault, and SecureFault are often referred to as configurable faults because they can be enabled/disabled by software, and because their exception priority levels are programmable.

In Chapter 4, the available fault exceptions were briefly introduced (Table 4.14). When a fault event is detected, the corresponding fault exception handler is executed. In Armv8-M Baseline (i.e., the Cortex-M23 processor), because there is only one fault exception available, all fault events trigger the HardFault handler. In Armv8-M Mainline processors (e.g., the Cortex-M33 processor), several fault exceptions are available and can, optionally, be enabled by software to deal with different types of faults.

Fault events can be triggered by many different reasons:

* Hardware failure—potentially caused by transient factors such as power instability, various forms of interference, issues with the environment that the system is operating in (e.g., the temperature range), and possibly, if there is a bug in the hardware.
* Software issues—these can be caused by software bugs, or by the system operating under undesirable conditions (e.g., the system crashing under a heavy processing load) or because of software vulnerabilities.
* User error—e.g., incorrect data input.

TABLE 13.1 Fault exceptions availability in Armv8-M processors.

Exception number	Exception name	Available in Cortex-M33	Available in Cortex-M23	Description
3	HardFault	Yes	Yes	For vector fetch fault and escalated faults
4	MemManage fault	Yes	No—escalates to HardFault	For faults related to the MPU and for faults related to the violation of access permissions in the default memory map
5	BusFault	Yes	No—escalates to HardFault	For faults related to bus level error responses and for faults caused by the access of registers in the private peripheral bus while in unprivileged state.
6	UsageFault	Yes	No—escalates to HardFault	Faults related to instruction operations/executions
7	SecureFault	Yes	No—escalates to HardFault	For faults related to TrustZone® security (this is new in Armv8-M)

Traditionally, many microcontrollers integrated watchdog timers to detect operational timeout. The watchdog is a hardware peripheral that contains a counter, which once enabled, cannot be disabled or stopped. However, software can regularly reset the counter value to prevent the counter from reaching a timeout value. If the counter reaches the timeout value (i.e., if the software does not reset the watchdog counter before it times out), the watchdog timer automatically resets the system.

Although the watchdog timer can restart a system when the processor has crashed, there can, however, be a delay from the time the system stops functioning to the time the watchdog reset takes place. This is, potentially, undesirable because the system will not respond to hardware events, and additional data corruptions could take place during the delay.

The fault exceptions in Cortex-M processors allow remedial action to take place as quickly as possible after an issue has been detected. Once the fault exception handler executes, there are several ways the software can deal with the error. For example, it can:

- Safely stop the system.
- Inform users or other systems that it has encountered a problem and request the user to intervene.
- Carry out a self-reset.
- In the case of multitasking systems, terminate the offending tasks and then restart them.
- Carry out other remedial action to try and fix the problem, e.g., executing a floating-point instruction with the floating-point unit (FPU) turned off can cause an error, but this issue is easily solved by turning the FPU back on.

Depending on the type of fault detected, a system could carry out several operations from the list above in order to resolve the matter.

To detect the error type that was triggered in the fault handler, the Cortex-M33 processor has several Fault Status Registers (FSRs). The status bits inside these FSRs indicate the fault type that has been detected. Although it might not pin-point exactly when or where things had gone wrong, locating the source of the problem is made easier when these additional pieces of information are available. Additionally, in some instances, the faulting address is also captured by Fault Address Registers (FARs). Further information on FSRs and FARs are covered in Section 13.5.

When software is being developed, programming errors can lead to fault exceptions. To fix those errors, the information provided by the FSRs and the FARs can be used by software developers to identify these software issues. To make the analysis of the software issues easier, software developers can utilize a feature called instruction tracing. This feature can either be enabled by using the Embedded Trace Macrocell (ETM) or the Micro Trace Buffer (MTB) in the processor (Chapter 16, Sections 16.3.6 and 16.3.7). With instruction tracing support, software developers can extract the program flow before the fault exception occurred.

The fault exception mechanism also allows applications to be debugged safely. For example, when developing a motor control system, you can turn off the motor in the fault handlers before stopping the processor for debugging, instead of halting immediately and leaving the motor running.

Due to the requirement of keeping the processor very small (in terms of silicon area) and as low power as possible, the Cortex-M23 processor does not have the same level of fault diagnostic features as the Cortex-M33 processor. For example, features such as fault status registers and multiple fault exception handlers are not available in the Cortex-M23 processor, but instruction trace is supported, which greatly assists fault debugging.

Following on from my last paragraph, fault events in the Cortex-M23 processor are considered unrecoverable as there are no fault status registers to help the software determine the cause of the fault exception. Moreover, since there is no multiple fault handler, all fault events are handled by the HardFault handler. The only way, therefore, to handle the error is to stop the system, and optionally, report the error (e.g., via a user interface) and/or carry out a self-reset.

13.2 Cause of faults

13.2.1 Memory management (MemManage) fault causes

MemManage faults can be caused by a violation of access rules, which are defined by the MPU's configuration. For example:

- Unprivileged tasks trying to access a memory region, which is privileged access only.
- Access to a memory location which is not defined by any defined MPU region (except the Private Peripheral Bus (PPB), which is always accessible by privileged code).
- Writing to a memory location which is defined as Read-Only by the MPU.
- A program execution in a memory region that is marked as eXecute Never (XN).

The accesses that trigger the fault exception could be data accesses during a program execution, program fetches, or stack operations during exception handling sequences.

When the TrustZone security extension is implemented, there can be two MPUs in the processor: one Secure and one Non-secure.

- For data access during a program execution:
  - The selection of the MPU is based on the security state of the processor—i.e., whether the processor is in Secure or Non-secure states.
- For instruction fetches:
  - The selection of the MPU is based on the security attribute of the program address. This allows the program to fetch instructions from the other security state (this is needed when calling functions/subroutines that are in the other security domain).
  - For instruction fetches that trigger a MemManage fault, the fault triggers only when the failed program location enters the execution stage.
- For a MemManage fault triggered by stack operations during an exception handling sequence:

  - The MPU selected is based on the security state of the interrupted background code.
  - If the MemManage fault occurred during stack pushing in the exception entrance sequence, it is called a stacking error.
  - If the MemManage fault occurred during stack popping in the exception exit sequence, it is called an unstacking error.

The MemManage fault can also be triggered when attempting to execute program code in the eXecute Never (XN) regions, e.g., the PERIPHERAL region, the DEVICE region or the SYSTEM region (Table 6.4). This fault occurs even when the Cortex-M23 and Cortex-M33 processors do not have the optional MPU implemented.

13.2.2 Bus faults

Bus faults can be triggered by error responses received from the processor bus interface during a memory access. For example:

- An instruction fetch (read)—also called prefetch abort in traditional Arm processors.
- A data read or data write—also called data abort in traditional Arm processors.

In addition to the aforementioned memory access, the bus fault can also occur during the stacking and unstacking of an exception handling sequence. If the bus error is caused by:

- stack pushing during the exception entry sequence, it is called a stacking error.
- stack popping during the exception exit sequence, it is called an unstacking error.

If the bus error happens during an instruction fetch, the bus fault only triggers when the failed program location enters the execution stage. Therefore, even though a branch shadow access would result in a bus error response, the bus fault exception would not be triggered because the instruction would not enter the execution stage. (Note: A branch shadow contains instructions that are fetched by the processor but which are not executed because of a previous branch operation.)

Please note, if a bus error is returned at a vector fetch, the HardFault exception is activated even when the Bus Fault exception is enabled.

There are several reasons why a memory system might return an error response. These are:

- When the processor attempts to access an invalid memory location: When this happens, the transfer is sent to a default slave module in the bus system. The default slave returns an error response and triggers the processor's bus fault exception.
- When the device is not ready to accept a transfer: For example, when it tries to access DRAM without initializing the DRAM controller it might trigger a bus error. This behavior is device specific.
- When the bus slave receiving the transfer request returns an error response: This could happen if the transfer type/size is not supported by the bus slave or if the peripheral determines that the operation is not allowed.
- When unprivileged software accesses a privileged-access only register on the Private Peripheral Bus (PPB). This violates the default memory access permission (see Section 6.4.4).
- When a system level TrustZone access permission control component (e.g., a memory protection controller, a peripheral protection controller, or other types of TrustZone access filter components. Section 7.5 refers) detects a disallowed transfer, these components, optionally, generate a bus error response when blocking the disallowed transfer.

Bus faults can be classified into:

- Synchronous bus faults—fault exceptions that happen as soon as the memory access instruction is executed. When this happens, the processor is not allowed to complete the faulting instruction and cannot continue. During the entry to the fault exception, the return address in the exception stack frame points to the faulting instruction (Note: In early versions of the Arm Cortex-M document a synchronous bus fault was referred to as a precise bus fault).
- Asynchronous bus faults—fault exceptions that happen sometime after the memory access instruction has been executed. This happens if the bus error response is not immediately received by the processor. (Note: In early versions of the Arm Cortex-M document an asynchronous bus fault was referred to as an imprecise bus fault.)

The reason a bus fault becomes asynchronous (imprecise) is due to the presence of write buffers or caches in the processor's bus interface. For example, when the processor writes data to a Device-E address (i.e., a device address location, which allows an instruction to be completed while the actual transfer is still ongoing, see Table 6.3 and Fig. 6.3), the processor can complete the write instruction and execute the next instruction(s). At the same time, the write operation is handled by the write buffer at the bus interface. If the bus slave responds with a bus error, by the time the processor receives the bus error, the processor could have executed several other instructions after the write, and as a result, the bus fault is asynchronous (i.e., the fault event timing is decoupled from the processor's pipeline). Similarly, the presence of a data cache can also delay a write transfer and thus result in an asynchronous bus fault.

Write buffer and data caches allow the processor system to achieve a high performance but the downside to this is that it can make debugging more difficult. This is because when an asynchronous bus fault exception has been triggered the processor could have executed several instructions. If one of those instructions is a branch instruction, and if the branch target is accessible via several execution paths, it could be hard to tell, unless you have access to instruction trace information (Sections 16.3.6 and 16.3.7), where the faulting memory access took place.

In the Cortex-M23 and Cortex-M33 processors, there are no internal caches and internal write buffers. Therefore, bus errors received by way of the execution of data access instructions are always synchronous. If a system level cache is present, the cache unit usually forwards asynchronous bus errors back to the processor in the form of an interrupt signal(s).

13.2.3 Usage Faults

There are a wide range of reasons for a Usage Fault exception. This could be:

- The execution of an undefined instruction (including the execution of floating-point instructions when the floating-point unit is disabled or is not present).
- The execution of coprocessor instructions or Arm Custom Instructions—Although, the Cortex-M33 processor supports coprocessor instructions and Arm Custom Instructions, for the instruction to execute successfully, the coprocessor or hardware accelerator specified by the instruction needs to be present, enabled, and must not return an error response to the processor. Otherwise, a Usage Fault is triggered. The Cortex-M23 does not support coprocessor and Arm Custom Instructions.
- Trying to switch to Arm state—Classic Arm processors, such as the Arm7TDMI®, support both the Arm and Thumb instruction sets, while the Cortex-M processors only support Thumb ISA. Software ported from classic Arm processors could contain code that switches the processor to Arm state and which then needs to be updated in order to run on the Cortex-M processor.
- An invalid EXC_RETURN code occurring during an exception-return sequence (see Section 8.10 for information on the EXC_RETURN code). An example of this would be trying to return to Thread level, but when the stacked IPSR in the stack frame is nonzero (i.e., there are still other exception(s) active).
- An unaligned memory access on the Cortex-M23 processor, or when using an unaligned address with the Armv8-M Mainline processor (e.g., the Cortex-M33 processor) for multiple load or multiple store instructions (including load double and store double, see Section 6.6).
- An exception return with Interrupt-Continuable Instruction (ICI) bits in the unstacked xPSR, but where the instruction being executed after the exception return is not a multiple-load/store instruction.
- A violation of stack limit checking (see Section 11.4). This is new in Armv8-M and is not available in either the Armv6-M or the Armv7-M.

It is also possible, by setting up the Configuration Control Register (CCR, see Sections 10.5.5.4 and 10.5.5.5), to generate usage faults for the following instances:

- Divide by zero
- All unaligned memory accesses

Please note, to enable the floating-point unit or to use the coprocessor instructions (e.g., MCR, MRC, see Section 5.21) software needs to write to:

- The Coprocessor Access Control Register (CPACR, see Section 14.2.3), and

- If TrustZone is implemented, the Non-secure Access Control Register (NSACR, see Section 14.2.4).

If these steps are not carried out, a UsageFault is generated when attempts are made to access the FPU or the coprocessor(s).

13.2.4 SecureFault

The Secure fault exception is triggered by violations of security rules as outlined in the TrustZone. The Secure fault exception is not available when TrustZone has not been implemented and is not available in the architectures of either Armv6-M or Armv7-M. There are a range of security violations that trigger the Secure fault and some of these are:

- Memory accesses that violate security permission. These can be:
  - Data read/write
  - Exception stacking, unstacking
- An illegal transition between security domains. For example:
  - A branch from the Non-secure to Secure world without going through a valid entry point (Note: a valid entry point requires an SG instruction in a region marked as Non-secure Callable).
  - A branch from the Secure to the Non-secure world without using a correct instruction (e.g., BXNS, BLXNS)
- When a security integrity check fails during an exception sequence. Examples of this are:
  - An invalid EXC_RETURN code
  - An invalid integrity signature in an exception stack frame. The integrity signature is inserted in a Secure exception stack frame when a Non-secure interrupt is triggered when executing a piece of Secure code. When the processor returns from a Non-secure interrupt handler and switches back into the Secure software, and the integrity signature is invalid or missing, a Secure fault would be triggered.

Please note, at the system level, bus access could be filtered by TrustZone security compo-nents (the Memory Protection Controller, the Peripheral Protection Controller, etc.). These components can, instead of triggering a SecureFault, trigger a BusFault using the bus error response.

13.2.5 HardFault

The HardFault exception can be triggered by:

- A bus error response received for the vector fetch.
- A security or MPU violation for the vector fetch.
- An SVC instruction execution when the priority level of the SVCall exception is the same or is lower than the current level.
- The execution of a breakpoint (BKPT) instruction where the debug has been disabled (i.e., there is no debug connection and the debug monitor exception has been disabled, or has a lower priority than the current level).

The HardFault can also be triggered by the escalation of the MemManage Fault, the BusFault, the UsageFault and the SecureFault when these fault exceptions are:

- Not available (e.g., in the Cortex-M23 processor and in Armv8-M Baseline, all fault events escalate to HardFault), or
- Not enabled (The aforementioned configurable fault exception handlers need to be enabled by software before they can be used), or
- Of the same or of a lower priority than the current exception priority level. When this occurs, the priority level of the aforementioned configurable fault exception is insufficient, which means that the configurable fault exception cannot be carried out and, is instead, escalated to the HardFault exception. The exception to this is an asynchronous BusFault, which can be pended and then handled when the other higher priority interrupt handler(s) has finished.

13.2.6 Faults triggered by exception handling

The MemManage Fault, the Bus Fault, the UsageFault (but only when triggered by a stack limit violation) and the SecureFault can all be triggered by memory access during an exception entry and an exception return sequence. For example,

- Stacking/unstacking. If normal stack operations are functioning correctly, the stacking error could be caused by a stack overflow. If stacking is working correctly but failed during an unstacking operation, the cause could be:
  ○ Unexpected changes in the MPU configurations
  ○ An incorrect change in the EXC_RETURN (e.g., the incorrect stack pointer was used for the unstacking)
  ○ An incorrect change in the stack pointer value.
- Lazy stacking—but only if the FPU is available and is enabled. Further information on lazy stacking can be found in Chapter 14, Section 14.4. In normal applications, it is likely that if the lazy stacking of an exception results in a fault then the same fault would, unless the MPU configuration was changed in between, have occurred at the stacking stage. Another possible cause of a fault during lazy stacking could be that the contents of the Floating-point Context Address Register (FPCAR) had been unexpectedly modified or corrupted.
- Vector fetches—this always triggers a HardFault and could be caused by the:
  ○ Incorrect configuration of the Vector Table Offset Register (VTOR), or
  ○ Incorrect configuration of the SAU/IDAU—resulting in the security attribute of the vector table address being incorrect.
- EXC_RETURN failing integrity checking—The corruption of the EXC_RETURN during exception handling routines is another likely cause for the occurrence of fault exceptions during exception returns. The Cortex-M processor contains several integrity checks in its exception handling sequencing and the failing of any integrity check can result in a fault exception.

If a stacking or unstacking error occurs during an exception sequence, the current priority level for error handling is based on the priority level of the interrupted process/task (level X), as shown in Fig. 13.1.

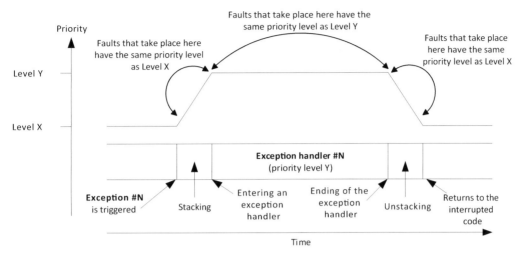

FIG. 13.1   Priority levels of fault exception at stacking and unstacking sequences for the handling of exception #N.

Based on the diagram shown in Fig. 13.1, if a fault event takes place during the exception handler sequence, the following scenarios could happen:

- A fault occurs during stacking/unstacking #1—If the fault exception (i.e., the BusFault, the MemManage Fault, the UsageFault, or the SecureFault) is disabled, or has the same or a lower priority level than the current priority level, it is immediately escalated to the HardFault exception.
- A fault occurs during stacking/unstacking #2—If the fault exception is enabled and has a higher priority level than both the current level and the priority level of the exception to be serviced, the fault exception is executed first and exception #N is pended.
- A fault occurs during stacking/unstacking #3—If the fault exception is enabled and has a priority level between the background level and the level of the to be serviced exception #N, the handler for exception #N would be executed first and the triggered fault handler would be executed afterwards.
- A fault occurs during Lazy stacking—If the FPU has been implemented and has been enabled, if the lazy stacking feature is also enabled (i.e., the default setting), and if the exception handler #N also use the FPU, then the stacking of the FPU registers happens later during the execution of exception handler #N. The lazy stacking feature, which is covered in Chapter 14, Section 14.8, helps reduce interrupt latency.

For the aforementioned lazy stacking scenario, if the memory access for lazy stacking triggers a fault event, it is handled as though the fault had occurred during stacking. For example:

- If the configurable fault exception is disabled, or has the same or a lower priority level than priority level X then it will escalate to HardFault.
- If the configurable fault exception is enabled and has a higher priority level than level Y (i.e., the level that the exception handler #N currently executing has), then the configurable fault exception executes immediately.

- If the configurable fault exception is enabled and has the same or a lower priority level than level Y (i.e., the level that the exception handler #N currently executing has), then the pending status of the configurable fault exception is set and will execute when exception handler #N has finished.

13.3 Enabling fault exceptions

When using the Cortex-M23 processor (Armv8-M Baseline), there is no need to enable the fault exception because the only fault exception available is the HardFault, which is always enabled. When programming with the CMSIS-CORE compliant driver, the HardFault handler is defined in the vector table/startup code as:

```
void HardFault_Handler(void)
```

When using the Cortex-M33 processor (or other Armv8-M Mainline processors), the MemManage Fault, the BusFault, the UsageFault and the SecureFault can, optionally, be enabled; but SecureFault is only available when writing software running in the Secure world. Before enabling these handlers, the exception priority levels should be set up based on the application's requirements. One way to do this is by using the following functions:

```
NVIC_SetPriority(MemoryManagement_IRQn, <priority>);
NVIC_SetPriority(BusFault_IRQn, <priority>);
NVIC_SetPriority(UsageFault_IRQn, <priority>);
NVIC_SetPriority(SecureFault_IRQn, <priority>);
```

The enable control bits of these fault handlers are in the System Handler Control and State Registers (SCB->SHCSR). The fault exception can be enabled by setting the corresponding enable bit to 1 as per the following examples:

```
SCB->SHCSR |= SCB_SHCSR_MEMFAULTENA_Msk; //Set bit 16 to 1
SCB->SHCSR |= SCB_SHCSR_BUSFAULTENA_Msk; //Set bit 17 to 1
SCB->SHCSR |= SCB_SHCSR_USGFAULTENA_Msk; //Set bit 18 to 1
SCB->SHCSR |= SCB_SHCSR_SECUREFAULTENA_Msk; //Set bit 19 to 1
```

When programming with the CMSIS-CORE compliant driver, these fault handlers are declared in the vector table/startup code as:

```
void MemManage_Handler(void)
void BusFault_Handler(void)
void UsageFault_Handler(void)
void SecureFault_Handler(void)
```

A dummy version of these handlers (i.e., an empty function) might be defined in the startup code file. These dummy handlers are normally defined with a "weak" C attribute and are overridden when your own fault handler definitions are added.

13.4 Fault handler designs considerations

13.4.1 Stack pointer validation check

In many instances, starting the fault handler in C might not be ideal as the fault could be caused by a stack issue (i.e., the stack pointer pointing to an invalid address space). If the HardFault handler is written in C and the Main Stack Pointer (MSP) being used is pointing to an invalid address when the HardFault is triggered, the execution of the HardFault could result in a LOCKUP situation (see Section 13.6).

The LOCKUP occurs because the HardFault handler also uses memory space in the main stack. For example, when the HardFault handler is programmed as a standard C function, the C compiler could insert a PUSH operation at the beginning of the HardFault handler's code (as a part of the C function's prologue). This is illustrated by the following example code:

```
HardFault_Handler
      PUSH  {R4-R7,LR}  ; <= This causes a LOCKUP if the MSP is invalid
      ...
```

As a result, for some applications, it is desirable to add an assembly wrapper to check that the value of the MSP is still in a valid range before calling the fault handler in C. In Armv8-M, the assembly wrapper might also be required because of the stack limit check feature (as described in Section 11.4.3). If the MSP is in an invalid range, the MSP should be moved to a valid range before branching into the C code (Fig. 13.2). Please note that the software operations would not be recoverable in this situation and would need to be reset in order to resume its operation. The use of the assembly wrapper to allow the HardFault handler to run correctly is particularly important for systems with functional safety requirements.

13.4.2 Making sure the SVC is not accidentally used in the HardFault and NMI handlers

Another consideration when creating a fault handler is to avoid the accidental use of SVC functions inside the HardFault and NMI handlers. In some software designs, high level message output functions (e.g., for error reporting) could be redirected to OS functions—such as

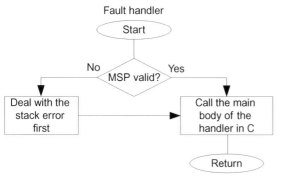

FIG. 13.2   Adding a SP value check before entering the fault handler in C.

semaphore calls, which manage shared hardware resources. Using those OS functions in the HardFault handler will result in a LOCKUP situation because the SVC exception is always of a lower priority level than the HardFault handler. Similarly, using OS functions in other fault exception handlers can have similar issues because the SVC exception may have the same or a lower priority level than the other fault exception handlers. As a result, care must be taken to ensure that the SVC is not being used in fault handlers, which have the same or a higher priority level than the SVC.

13.4.3 Triggering self-reset or halting

In many applications, triggering a self-reset in fault handler(s) is a good way to recover the system. However, during application development, triggering a self-reset can make it more difficult to debug the system as the system's state is immediately lost. Therefore, while writing and debugging software, the best way forward is to halt the system when a fault exception occurs.

There are several ways of halting the system at the beginning of a fault exception handler. These are:

- By setting a breakpoint via the debugger/IDE
- By placing a breakpoint instruction (BKPT) at the beginning of the fault handler
- By using the vector catch feature (a debug feature, supported by some of the commercial IDEs). When this feature is enabled, the processor automatically halts when entering a fault handler. Further information on the vector catch feature is covered in Chapter 16, Section 16.2.5.

13.4.4 Partitioning of fault handler

If you are using the Cortex-M33 or other Armv8-M Mainline processors, the system might be able to recover and continue to run after a fault event has occurred. This is dependent upon the nature of the fault. In this situation, the fault handling process could be partitioned into two parts:

- The first part of the fault handling process, which is handled by the fault handler that was triggered by the fault event, takes the immediate remedial action to address the fault event, and attempts to recover the system.
- The remaining part of the fault handling process, such as error reporting, is carried out in a separate handler running at a low exception priority level (e.g., using the PendSV exception).

By partitioning the fault handling process, the application shortens the time it takes to execute a high priority exception. If the application uses a high priority fault exception to handle the whole process, this will affect the responsiveness of the system.

13.4.5 Using the Fault Mask in a configurable fault handler

When using the Cortex-M33 or other Armv8-M Mainline processors, the configurable fault handlers (i.e., the BusFault, the MemManage Fault, the Usage Fault and the SecureFault handler), are able to utilize the FAULTMASK feature (see "Interrupt Masking Registers" section in Section 4.2.2.3) to:

- Bypass the MPU (using the HFNMIENA bit in the MPU Control register, Chapter 12, Section 12.2.3)
- Suppress stack limit checking (using the STKOFHFNMIGN bit in the Configuration and Control Register, Chapter 10, Section 10.5.5.2)
- Suppress bus faults (using the BFHFNMIGN bit in the Configuration and Control Register, Chapter 10, Section 10.5.5.3)

Setting FAULTMASK also disables all interrupts (this is essential because we do not want to allow other interrupt handlers to bypass the security checking mechanism), with the exception of the Nonmaskable interrupt (NMI).

Potentially, FAULTMASK can also be used outside of fault handlers. For example, if you need to use a piece of software to detect the memory size in a processor system, you can set the FAULTMASK and the BFHFNMIGN bit in the Configuration and Control Register to suppress the BusFault. A memory read-write-test can then be carried out to detect the memory size without triggering the BusFault exception.

13.5 Fault status and other information

13.5.1 Overview of fault status registers and fault address registers

One of the features of Armv8-M Mainline processors is its fault status registers, which assist in the diagnosis of fault events. These registers can be used by the debugger to assist in fault diagnosis when a fault exception takes place. Fault exception handlers could also use these registers for fault handling (e.g., in some instances, simple remedial actions can be taken to enable the application to resume its operations) and for the reporting of errors.

Due to the requirement of keeping the Cortex-M23 processor very small (in terms of silicon area) and as low power as possible, most of the fault status registers are omitted from it and the only fault status register that it has is the Debug Fault Status Register (DFSR, address 0xE000ED30). This is not for general fault handling but is there to enable the debugger to determine the reason(s) for any halting.

Table 13.2 is a summary of the fault status and fault address registers. These registers are only accessible in privileged state.

If the processor is in Secure state, Secure privileged software is able to access the Non-secure view of these registers (except SFSR and SFAR) using the Non-secure alias 0xE002EDxx.

The Configurable Fault Status Register (CFSR) is further divided into three parts (Table 13.3 and Fig. 13.3).

The CFSR register can be accessed as a whole using a 32-bit data transfer, or each part within the CFSR can be accessed using byte and half word transfers. However, when programming with a CMSIS-CORE compliant software driver, the only available software symbol is 32 bits (either SCB->CFSR or SCB_NS->CFSR). There is no individual CMSIS-CORE symbol for the divided MMSR (8 bits), BFSR (8 bits), and UFSR (16 bits).

TABLE 13.2   Fault Status Registers and Fault Address Registers.

Address	Register	CMSIS-Core symbol	Function
0xE000ED28	Configurable Fault Status Register	SCB->CFSR	Status information for Configurable Faults
0xE000ED2C	HardFault Status Register	SCB->HFSR	Status for the HardFault
0xE000ED30	Debug Fault Status Register	SCB->DFSR	Status for Debug Events
0xE000ED34	MemManage Fault Address Register	SCB-> MMFAR	If available, shows the accessed address that triggered the MemManage fault
0xE000ED38	BusFault Address Register	SCB->BFAR	If available, shows the accessed address that triggered the bus fault
0xE000ED3C	Auxiliary Fault Status Register	SCB->AFSR	Device specific fault status—optional in the architecture but not implemented in the current Cortex-M23 and Cortex-M33 processors.
0xE000EDE4	Secure Fault Status Register	SAU->SFSR	Status for SecureFault (available if TrustZone is implemented)
0xE000EDE8	Secure Fault Address Register	SAU->SFAR	If available, shows the accessed address that triggered the SecureFault

TABLE 13.3   Dividing Configurable Fault Status Register (SCB->CFSR) into three parts.

Address	Register	Size	Function
0xE000ED28	MemManage Fault Status Register (MMFSR)	Byte	Status information for the MemManage Fault
0xE000ED29	Bus Fault Status Register (BFSR)	Byte	Status for the BusFault
0xE000ED2A	Usage Fault Status Register (UFSR)	Halfword	Status for the UsageFault

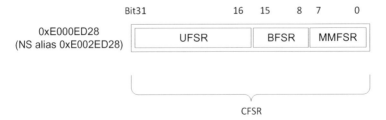

FIG. 13.3   Partitioning of the Configurable Fault Status Register (CFSR).

13.5.2 MemManage Fault Status Register (MMFSR)

The programmer's model for the MemManage Fault Status Register is shown in Table 13.4. When the TrustZone security extension is implemented, this register is banked between security states, and the following views of MMFSR are available:

- The Secure view of MMFSR shows the cause of the MemManage Fault for the Secure MPU
- The Non-secure view of MMFSR shows the cause of the MemManage Fault for the Non-secure MPU (Secure privileged software can access the Non-secure view of the MMFSR using the Non-secure SCB alias).

Each fault indication status bit (but not including MMARVALID) is set when the fault occurs, and stays high until a value of 1 is written to the register. The MemManage fault is triggered:

- When an MPU violation occurs during the execution of a data access instruction and is indicated by the fault status bit DACCVIOL.
- When an instruction fetch triggers an MPU violation, including executing code from a memory region marked as XN, and the faulting instruction reaches the execution stage—in this fault condition, the fault status bit IACCVIOL is set to 1.
- When an MPU violation occurs during stacking, unstacking, and lazy stacking (see Section 13.2.6) and is indicated by the fault status bits MSTKERR, MUNSTKERR, and MLSPERR, respectively.

Bit 7 of the MMFSR, i.e., the MMARVALID bit, is not a fault status indicator. When the MMARVALID bit is set, it is possible to determine the accessed memory location that caused the fault using the MemManage Fault Address Register (SCB->MMFAR).

When the MMFSR indicates that the fault is a data access violation (indicated by DACCVIOL being set to 1), or an instruction access violation (indicated by IACCVIOL being

TABLE 13.4 MemManage Fault Status Register (MMFSR) (the lowest 8 bits in the SCB->CFSR register).

Bit	Name	Type	Reset value	Description
7	MMARVALID	Read only	0	Indicates that MMFAR is valid
6	–	–	– (read as 0)	Reserved
5	MLSPERR	R/Wc (Read, Write to clear)	0	Floating-Point lazy stacking error (only available on the Cortex®-M33 when it has a floating-point unit)
4	MSTKERR	R/Wc	0	Stacking error
3	MUNSTKERR	R/Wc	0	Unstacking error
2	–	–	– (read as 0)	Reserved
1	DACCVIOL	R/Wc	0	Data access violation
0	IACCVIOL	R/Wc	0	Instruction access violation

set to 1), the faulting code address is usually indicated by the stacked program counter in the stack frame (i.e., if the stack frame is still valid).

13.5.3 BusFault Status Register (BFSR)

The programmer's model for the Bus Fault Status Register is shown in Table 13.5. When the TrustZone security extension is implemented and if AIRCR.BFHFNMINS is zero (i.e., default), this register is not accessible from the Non-secure world (i.e., read as zero, write ignored).

Each fault indication status bit (not including BFARVALID) is set when the fault occurs, and stays high until a value of 1 is written to the register. The BusFault is triggered:

- By a bus error during an instruction fetch and when the faulting instruction enters the execution stage of the pipeline. This fault condition is indicated by the IBUSERR bit.
- When an MPU violation occurs during the execution of a data access instruction, and is indicated by either the PRECISERR or the IMPRECISERR status bit. PRECISERR indicates a synchronous (i.e., precise) bus error (see Section 13.2.2). When PRECISERR is set, the faulting instruction address is available from the stacked program counter value in the stack frame. Although the address of the data access that triggered the fault is also written to the Bus Fault Address Register (SCB->BFAR), the fault handler still needs to check if BFARVALID is still 1 after reading the BFAR. When the IMPRECISERR is set (i.e., the bus fault is asynchronous or imprecise), the stacked program counter does not reflect the faulting instruction address. For an asynchronous bus fault, the address of the faulting transfer will not show in the BFAR, with, therefore, the BFARVALID bit being 0.
- When a bus error occurs during stacking, unstacking, and lazy stacking (see Section 13.2.6) and is indicated by the fault status bits STKERR, UNSTKERR, and LSPERR, respectively.

TABLE 13.5 BusFault Status Register (BFSR) (second byte in the SCB->CFSR register).

CFSR bit	Name	Type	Reset value	Description
15	BFARVALID	–	0	Indicates that BFAR is valid
14	–	–	– (read as zero)	Reserved
13	LSPERR	R/Wc (Read, Write to clear)	0	Floating-Point lazy stacking error (only available on the Cortex®-M33 when it has a floating-point unit)
12	STKERR	R/Wc	0	Stacking error
11	UNSTKERR	R/Wc	0	Unstacking error
10	IMPRECISERR	R/Wc	0	Imprecise data access error
9	PRECISERR	R/Wc	0	Precise data access error
8	IBUSERR	R/Wc	0	Instruction access error

When the BFARVALID bit is set, it is possible to determine the accessed memory location that caused the fault using the Bus Fault Address Register (SCB->BFAR).

When the BFSR indicates that the fault is a synchronous bus error (indicated by PRECISERR being set to 1), or an instruction access bus error (indicated by IBUSERR being set to 1), the faulting code address is usually indicated by the stacked program counter in the stack frame (i.e., if the stack frame is still valid).

13.5.4 Usage Fault Status Register (UFSR)

The programmer's model for the Usage Fault Status Register is shown in Table 13.6. When the TrustZone security extension is implemented, this register is banked between security states. Secure privileged software can access the Non-secure view of the UFSR using the Non-secure SCB alias.

Each fault indication status bit is set when the fault occurs and stays high until a value of 1 is written to the register.

13.5.5 Secure Fault Status Register (SFSR)

The programmer's model for the SecureFault Status Register is shown in Table 13.7. The SFSR and the Secure Fault Address Register (SFAR) registers are only available when the TrustZone security extension has been implemented. When the SecureFault is triggered,

TABLE 13.6 UsageFault Status Register UFSR (Upper half word in the SCB->CFSR register).

CFSR bits	Name	Type	Reset value	Description
25	DIVBYZERO	R/Wc	0	Indicates a divide by zero has taken place (can only be set if the DIV_0_TRP is set)
24	UNALIGNED	R/Wc	0	Indicates that an unaligned access fault has taken place
23:21	–	–	– (read as zero)	Reserved
20	STKOF	R/Wc	0	Stack Overflow flag (a violation of stack limit checking)
19	NOCP	R/Wc	0	An attempt to execute a coprocessor instruction or Arm Custom Instruction when the coprocessor/Arm Customer Instruction is not present/disabled/not accessible.
18	INVPC	R/Wc	0	An attempt to carry out an exception return with a bad value in the EXC_RETURN number
17	INVSTATE	R/Wc	0	An attempt to switch to an invalid state (e.g., EPSR.T is cleared, which indicates that the Arm state or the EPSR.IT value does not match the instruction type)
16	UNDEFINSTR	R/Wc	0	An attempt to execute an undefined instruction

TABLE 13.7   SecureFault Status Register (SFSR) (SAU->SFSR).

SFSR bit	Name	Type	Reset value	Description
7	LSERR	R/Wc	0	Lazy state error flag—This flag is set to 1 during an exception entry and return and when the security integrity checks have failed. This checking mechanism detects the following combinations that should not happen under normal circumstances: Exception entry -. If CONTROL.FPCA is set (it indicates the FPU has been used) but the lazy stacking pending status is still active. Exception return -. If CONTROL.FPCA is set but the secure view of the lazy stacking pending status is still active. -. If EXC_RETURN.Ftype is 0, but is returning from a Secure exception and CONTROL.FPCA is set
6	SFARVALID	Read only	0	Indicates the SFAR is valid.
5	LSPERR	R/Wc	–	Lazy state preservation error—A SAU/IDAU violation during a lazy stacking operation for floating-point registers.
4	INVTRAN	R/Wc	0	Invalid transition error flag—indicates a branch from Secure to Non-secure without using BXNS/BLXNS; or the target state of the destination (LSB) in the instruction's operand was not marked as Non-secure.
3	AUVIOL	R/Wc	0	Attribution unit violation—indicates a software generated memory Non-secure access (not including lazy stacking, which is indicated by LSPERR or by vector fetch) attempt to access a Secure address.
2	INVER	R/Wc	0	Invalid exception return flag. This can be caused by EXC_RETURN. DCRS being set to 0 when returning from an exception in the Non-secure state; or by EXC_RETURN.ES being set to 1 when returning from an exception in the Non-secure state.
1	INVIS	R/Wc	0	Invalid integrity signature—when an exception return switches the processor from Non-secure to Secure state and the Secure stack being used for the unstacking does not have a valid integrity signature.
0	INVEP	R/Wc	0	Invalid entry point—Non-secure code trying to branch into a Secure address where the first instruction is not an SG instruction; or the address is not marked as Non-secure Callable by the SAU/IDAU.

one of the fault status bits (not including the SFARVALID bit) in the SFSR is set to 1 to indicate the cause of the error.

Each fault indication status bit is set when the fault occurs and stays high until a value of 1 is written to the register.

TABLE 13.8   HardFault Status Register (HFSR) (SCB->HFSR).

HFSR bits	Name	Type	Reset value	Description
31	DEBUGEVT	R/Wc	0	Indicates that a hard fault has been triggered by a debug event
30	FORCED	R/Wc	0	Indicates that a hard fault has been triggered because of a bus fault, a memory management fault or a usage fault
29:2	–	–	– (read as zero)	Reserved
1	VECTBL	R/Wc	0	Indicates that a hard fault has been triggered by a failed vector fetch
0	–	–	– (read as zero)	Reserved

13.5.6 HardFault Status Register (HFSR)

The programmer's model for the Hard Fault Status Register is shown in Table 13.8. When the TrustZone security extension is implemented and if AIRCR.BFHFNMINS is zero (i.e., default), this register is not accessible from the Non-secure world (i.e., read as zero, write ignored).

A HardFault handler uses this register to determine whether a HardFault was caused by any of the Configurable Faults. If the FORCED bit is set, it indicates that the fault has been escalated from one of the Configurable Faults and that the fault handler should check the value of the CFSR to see what the cause of the fault was.

Similar to other Fault Status Registers, each status bit in the HardFault Status Register is set when the fault occurs and stays high until a value of 1 is written to the register.

13.5.7 Debug Fault Status Register (DFSR)

Unlike other Fault Status Registers, the DFSR is designed to be used by debug tools such as debugger software running on a debug host (e.g., a Personal Computer) or by debug agent software running on the microcontroller. The status bits in this register indicate which debug event has occurred.

The programmer's model for the Debug Fault Status Register is shown in Table 13.9. This register is not banked between security states.

Similar to other Fault Status Registers, each fault indication status bit is set when the fault occurs and stays high until a value of 1 is written to the register.

13.5.8 Auxiliary Fault Status Register (AFSR)

Architecturally, an Armv8-M processor is able to support an Auxiliary Fault Status Register to provide processor-specific or device fault status information. This register is not available in either the Cortex-M23 or the Cortex-M33 processor.

The programmer's model for the AFSR is shown in Table 13.10.

TABLE 13.9 Debug Fault Status Register (DFSR) (SCB->DFSR).

Bits	Name	Type	Reset value	Description
31:5	–	–	–	Reserved
4	EXTERNAL	R/Wc	0	Indicates the debug event is caused by an external debug event signal called EDBGRQ (Chapter 16, Section 16.2.5). The EDBGRQ signal is an input on the processor and is typically used in multiprocessor designs for synchronizing debug activities.
3	VCATCH	R/Wc	0	Indicates the debug event is caused by a vector catch, a programmable feature that allows the processor to automatically halt when coming out of a reset and when entering certain types of system exceptions.
2	DWTTRAP	R/Wc	0	Indicates the debug event is caused by a watchpoint
1	BKPT	R/Wc	0	Indicates the debug event is caused by a breakpoint
0	HALTED	R/Wc	0	Indicates the processor has been halted by a debugger request (including single step)

TABLE 13.10 Auxiliary Fault Status Register (AFSR) (SCB->AFSR).

Bits	Name	Type	Reset value	Description
31:0	Implementation Defined	R/W	0	Implementation defined fault status—not available in the Cortex-M23 or the Cortex-M33 processors.

Similar to other Fault Status Registers, if implemented, each fault indication status bit is set when the fault occurs and stays high until a value of 1 is written to the register.

13.5.9 Fault address registers (BFAR, MMFAR, and SFAR)

In addition to fault status registers, Armv8-M Mainline processors also provide fault address registers (Table 13.11). These registers allow fault handlers to determine the address values of the transfers that trigger the fault. Because this information is not always available, the values of these address registers need to be quantified by a valid bit in the corresponding fault status register.

The reset values of these registers are unpredictable.

Armv8-M architecture permits these fault address registers to share physical register resources, and because of this, a valid fault address could be replaced by another fault address of a higher priority fault. This happens when a lower priority fault handler is running and when a higher priority fault occurs in the middle of the lower priority fault handler (i.e., a nested fault situation). The processor design takes account of this situation by ensuring:

(a) that the valid status bits of the shared fault address register are either one-hot or zero, and
(b) that it does not leak information between security states.

TABLE 13.11 Fault Status and Fault Address Registers.

Address	Register	CMSIS-CORE symbol	Valid status	Note
0xE000ED34	MemManage Fault Address Register	SCB->MMFAR	MMARVALID (bit 7 of SCB->CFSR)	When TrustZone is implemented, this register is banked between security states.
0xE000ED38	BusFault Address Register	SCB->BFAR	BFARVALID (bit 15 of SCB->CFSR)	When TrustZone is implemented and if AIRCR.BFHFNMINS is 0, this is not accessible from Non-secure software.
0xE000EDE8	Secure Fault Address Register	SAU->SFAR	SFARVALID (bit 6 of SAU->SFSR)	Only available when TrustZone is implemented. Secure privileged access only.

Due to the possibility of the nested fault situation occurring, software must take this into account when reading the fault address register by handling the read as follows:

(1) Software reads the fault address register (either MMFAR, BFAR, or SFAR, with the read depending on which fault exception handler is running), then
(2) Software reads the corresponding valid status bit; if the valid bit is 0, then the value of the fault address register must be discarded.

If the memory access that triggered the fault is unaligned the following could occur: the memory access could be divided into multiple transactions at the bus interface level, and, if a fault has taken place, the address value placed into the fault address register could be the generated bus transaction address instead of the original address (i.e., different from the address value used in the program code).

13.6 Lockup

13.6.1 What is Lockup?

When an error condition occurs, one of the fault handlers will be triggered. If another fault happens inside a Configurable Fault handler, then either:

• Another Configurable Fault handler is triggered and executed (if the fault is different from the one already triggered and if it has a higher priority than the current level fault), or
• The HardFault handler is triggered and executed.

However, what happens if another fault event occurs during the execution of the HardFault handler? (it is a very unlikely situation, but can happen). In this case, a lockup situation will take place.

Lockups can occur if:

– A fault occurs during the execution of the HardFault or the Non-Maskable Interrupt (NMI) exception handler

- A bus error occurs during the vector fetch for the HardFault or NMI exceptions
- The SVC instruction is accidentally included in the HardFault or in the NMI exception handler
- The Vector fetches during the startup sequence

During lockup, the processor stops executing the program and asserts an output signal called LOCKUP. How this signal is used inside the chip depends on the system level design of the chip. In some cases, it can be used to automatically generate a system reset.

If the lockup is caused by a fault event inside the HardFault handler (a double fault condition) at priority level −1, it is still possible for the processor to respond to an NMI (priority level −2) and execute the NMI handler. But, after the NMI handler finishes, it will return to the lockup state and the priority level will return to −1. If, however, the system is in the Secure HardFault when the AIRCR.BFHFNMIS is set to 1 (i.e., the priority level of the Secure HardFault is −3), or if the processor has entered LOCKUP state from within an NMI handler (priority level −2), the processor will not be able to respond to the NMI event.

There are various ways to exit the lockup state:

- By way of a system reset or power on reset
- If the lockup happens during a debug session, the debugger can halt the processor and clear the error state(s) (e.g., by using reset or by clearing the current exception handling status, and by updating the program counter value to a new starting point, etc.).

Usually, a system reset or power-on reset are the best methods for exiting the lockup state as they ensure that the peripherals, and all the interrupt handling logic, return to the reset state.

Now, you may be wondering why we do not automatically reset the processor when a lockup takes place. Well, doing that may be good for a live system. But when writing and debugging software, it is important that we should find out the cause of any problems that occur and resolve the issue. If we reset the system automatically, it will be impossible to analyze what went wrong because the hardware status would have changed.

Cortex-M processors are designed to export the lockup status to their interface, thus enabling chip designers to implement a programmable auto reset feature so that when the auto reset feature is enabled the system can automatically reset itself.

Note: When entering a HardFault or NMI Handler, a fault (e.g., a bus error or an MPU access violation) that occurs during stacking or unstacking (except one that involves a vector fetch), does not cause the system to enter into a lockup state (Fig. 13.4). If a bus error is triggered during stacking, the BusFault exception would end up pended and will only execute after the HardFault handler has finished.

13.6.2 Avoiding Lockup

In some applications, it is important to avoid lockup and, thus, extra care is needed when developing the HardFault and NMI Handlers. As explained in Section 13.4.1, stack pointer checks should be in place at the beginning of the HardFault and NMI Handlers to ensure that the main stack pointer is within a valid memory range.

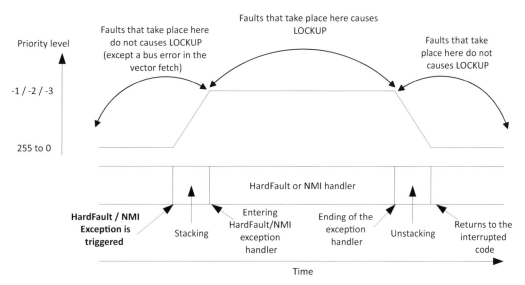

FIG. 13.4   Bus errors occurring during the stacking or the unstacking of the HardFault or the NMI does not cause LOCKUP.

One approach for developing HardFault and NMI handlers is to partition the exception handling tasks so that the HardFault and NMI handlers only carry out essential tasks. The other tasks, such as error reporting for the HardFault exception, can then be carried out using a separate exception—such as PendSV (this chapter, Section 13.4.4 and Chapter 11, Fig. 11.16 in Section 11.5.3). The partitioning helps ensure that the HardFault handler and/or the NMI are kept small (i.e., it is easier to check and improve the quality of the code) and are robust.

Furthermore, we need to ensure that the NMI and HardFault handler code does not call functions that accidentally utilize the SVC. Further information on this is in Section 13.4.2.

13.7 Analysis of fault events

13.7.1 Overview

Fault exceptions are not uncommon during the development of software. Fortunately, there are several ways to obtain the required information to determine the cause of the issue(s). These are as follows:

- Instruction trace: If the device you are using supports Embedded Trace Macrocell (ETM) or Micro Trace Buffer (MTB), the ETM and MTB can be utilized to understand how the fault occurred, i.e., to view the instructions that were executed just before the fault exception. This information can then be used to identify the processor operations that led to the failure. It is also possible to set up the debug environment to automatically halt the processor when the fault handler has started (see Section 13.4.3). The Cortex-M23 and Cortex-M33 processors support both the ETM and the MTB, but please note, the devices based on these processors might not always include these features. When using ETM trace, a debug probe with the Trace Port capture function is required. Although instruction trace using the MTB does not require a Trace Port capture function, it provides less information than the ETM as it only captures a limited history. Further information on the ETM and the MTB can be found in Chapter 16.

- Event trace: Sometimes fault exceptions can be related to exception handling (e.g., the system configuration was unexpectedly changed by an exception handler). If you are using the Cortex-M33 or other Armv8-M Mainline processors, the event trace capability in the Data Watchpoint and Trace unit (For more information on the DWT, see Chapter 16, Section 16.3.4) can help you to not only determine what exception has taken place but might also help you to determine the cause of the issue. An event trace can either be captured with a low-cost debug probe with Single Wire Output (SWO) support or with a debug probe with Trace Port support.
- Stack trace: Even with a low-cost debugger without a trace capture capability, you should be able to extract the stack frame when entering a fault exception if the stack pointer configuration was still valid at the point of the fault event. Assuming that you stopped the processor at the beginning of the fault handler (see the vector catch feature description in Section 13.4.3), you would then be in a position to examine the processor status and the contents of the memory. The stack frame created when the processor enters the fault exception provides useful information for debugging, e.g., the stacked Program Counter (PC) indicates where the program was executed to when the fault exception was triggered. Using the information gleaned from the stack frame and the values in the Fault Status Registers, a determination can then be made of the source of the issue.
- Fault status and fault address registers: If you are using the Cortex-M33 or other Armv8-M Mainline processors, the information in the fault status and fault address registers could provide important clues as to what has gone wrong. Some debug tools have a built-in capability to analyze errors based on the information obtained from those registers. To assist further, you can use a communication interface to output the contents of those registers to a console to further assist the debugging process. An example of a fault handler that can report the stacked PC and fault status registers can be found in Section 13.9.

In some debug tools, the debugger software contains features to allow you to easily access the fault status information. For example, in Keil® MDK, you can access the Fault Status Registers using the "Fault Report" window, as shown in Fig. 13.5. This can be accessed from the pull-down menu "Peripherals" -> "Core Peripherals" -> "Fault Reports".

13.7.2 Key differences between the fault handling in Armv8-M architecture and the architecture of previous generations

There are several key changes in fault handling when comparing Armv8-M processors to the previous generations of the Cortex-M processors:

When comparing Armv6-M processors to the Cortex-M23 processor (Armv8-M Baseline), the changes are:

- The HardFault is now handled by the Secure state when TrustZone is enabled and when AIRCR.BFHFNMINS is 0 (i.e., default). This means that if a device has TrustZone

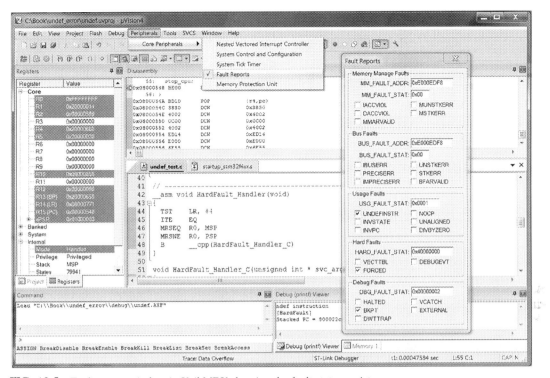

FIG. 13.5 Fault report window in Keil MDK showing the fault status registers.

implemented and the Secure world is used, a fault event occurrence will always execute the HardFault handler in the Secure world first. When this occurs, the Secure HardFault handler is then able to carry out the required security checks (in case the fault is related to a security attack) and once it does, is then able to, optionally, (a) utilize a communication interface to inform users of a fault, (b) enter halting, or (c) trigger a self-reset.

- If the Secure world has been locked down and the software developer does not have Secure debug permission, the processor cannot enter halting state while in the Secure world's HardFault exception. If the Secure HardFault handler does not utilize a communication interface to report the fault, a Non-secure software developer would have no easy way of debugging the system. It is, therefore, useful if Non-secure software enables the Non-secure UsageFault and Non-secure MemManage Fault so that these fault events can be debugged by Non-secure software developers. Additional information about handling faults in the Secure world is covered in Chapter 18.
- The addition of stack limit checking for the Secure stack pointers.
- An extension of the EXC_RETURN code: Because of the extension of the EXC_RETURN code and because there are additional stack pointers, the fault exception handlers for reporting errors might need to be updated. Further information on this can be found in Section 13.9.

When comparing Armv7-M processors to the Cortex-M33 processor (Armv8-M Mainline), the changes include those mentioned above (from Armv6-M to Armv8-M Baseline), and additionally:

- The addition of stack limit checking for Non-secure stack pointers (i.e., both the Secure and the Non-secure stack pointer has stack limit checking).
- The addition, when TrustZone is implemented, of the SecureFault exception.

13.8 Stack trace

When the processor enters a fault exception, several registers are pushed into the stack (i.e., the stack frame). If the stack pointer is still pointing to a valid RAM location, the information in the stack frame can be used for debugging. The analysis of the stack frame is often called stack tracing and can be carried out either inside the debug tools or inside the fault handlers.

The first step of stack trace is to determine which stack pointer was used for the stacking operation (Fig. 13.6). In Cortex-M processors, this is identified using the EXC_RETURN value and the CONTROL_S and CONTROL_NS registers. Please note, if TrustZone is implemented and if there is no Secure debug access permission, Secure fault events (e.g., SecureFault, Secure MemManage Fault, etc.) and faults that were triggered during the execution of the Secure software cannot be analyzed.

The second step is to determine whether the stack frame contains additional state context (Fig. 13.7). This information is needed if we want to extract the stacked return address. If TrustZone is implemented and if there is no Secure debug access permission, only the Non-secure stack frames, which do not have the additional state context, can be examined.

Note: If the Secure code is interrupted by a Non-secure IRQ and is halted inside the Non-secure ISR, the additional state context in the Secure stack frame is visible—even when EXC_RETURN.DCRS is 1—to a debugger which has Secure debug permission.

Once the stack frame contents have been identified, the stacked registers, such as the stacked return address and the stacked xPSR, are then easily located. These stacked values are useful for debugging in the following ways:

- Stacked return address: In many instances, the stacked return address provides the most important help when debugging faults. By generating a disassembled code listing of the program image in the tool chain, the code fragment where the fault occurred is easily pin-pointed. With the additional information provided from the current stacked register values, and the Fault Status Registers, it should be easy to understand why the fault exception occurred.
- Stacked xPSR: This can be used for identifying whether the processor was, when the fault occurred, in Handler mode and whether there had been an attempt to switch the processor into Arm state (if the T-bit in the EPSR is cleared, then one can safely assume that there has been an attempt to switch the processor into Arm state).
- EXC_RETURN value in the Link Register (LR): The EXC_RETURN value in the LR when entering the fault handler might also provide information about the cause of the fault. If the fault event is caused by an invalid EXC_RETURN value during an exception return, the fault event would cause a tail chaining of the fault exception. In this situation, the EXC_RETURN value of the fault handler will show the partial value of the invalid

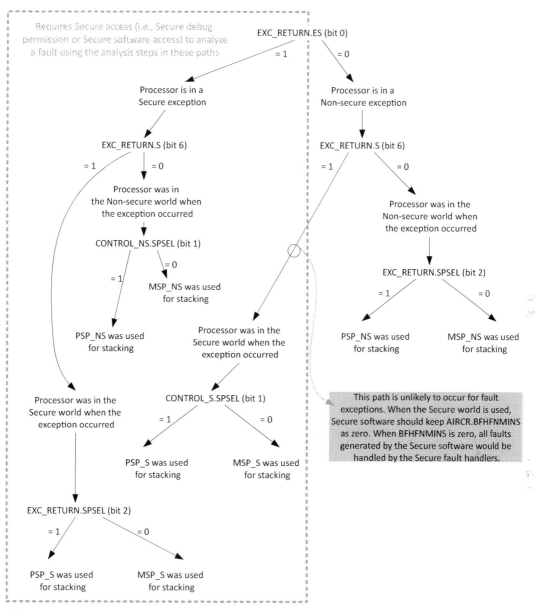

FIG. 13.6 Checking of the EXC_RETURN and the SPSEL bit in the CONTROL register to determine which stack pointer was used.

EXC_RETURN (some of the bits in the EXC_RETURN could be different because the fault handler could be in a different security state than the previous faulting exception handler). The fault handler can, optionally, report the EXC_RETURN value in the LR and could be used by software programmers to determine whether the fault was caused by a corruption of the EXC_RETURN value in the exception handler.

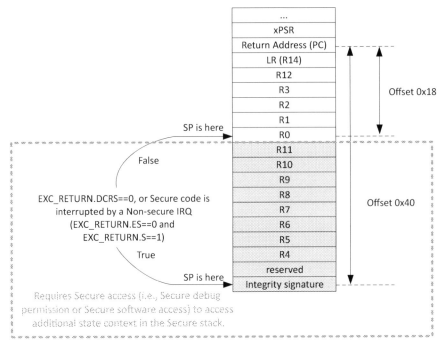

FIG. 13.7   Identifying the stack frame format for the stack trace.

13.9 Fault handler to extract stack frame and display fault status

After establishing the method to extract information from the stack frame, we can then create a fault handler to extract and display that information in a console (assuming "printf" redirection or semihosting is in place). To do this, we need to have an assembly wrapper:

– To extract the stack pointer value (because the C compiler inserts stack operations in a prologue of C function, which would change the current selected SP value)
– To extract the value of the EXC_RETURN

Based on the SVC example in Section 11.5.2, a simple assembly wrapper could take the form:

```
void __attribute__((naked)) HardFault_Handler(void)
{
    __asm volatile ("mov r0, lr\n\t"
          "mov r1, sp\n\t"
          "B HardFault_Handler_C\n\t"
    );
}
```

In the C handler, we then need to:

- Extract the right stack pointer, and
- Extract various pieces of useful information (e.g., stacked register values)

If the fault handler is written for the Non-secure world, the fault handler code is similar to the SVC example:

```
void HardFault_Handler_C(uint32_t exc_return_code, uint32_t msp_val)
{
  uint32_t stack_frame_r0_addr;
  unsigned int *stack_frame;
  uint32_t stacked_r0, stacked_r1, stacked_r2, stacked_r3;
  uint32_t stacked_r12, stacked_lr, stacked_pc, stacked_xPSR;
  // Check source of fault
  if (exc_return_code & 0x40) { // EXC_RETURN.S is 1 - error
    printf ("ERROR: fault is from Secure world.\n");
    while(1); } // dead-loop

  // Determine which stack pointer was used
  if (exc_return_code & 0x4) stack_frame_r0_addr = __get_PSP();
  else stack_frame_r0_addr = msp_val;

  // Extract stack frame
  stack_frame = (unsigned *) stack_frame_r0_addr;

  // Extract stacked registers in the stack frame
  stacked_r0 = stack_frame[0];
  stacked_r1 = stack_frame[1];
  stacked_r2 = stack_frame[2];
  stacked_r3 = stack_frame[3];
  stacked_r12 = stack_frame[4];
  stacked_rlr = stack_frame[5];
  stacked_pc = stack_frame[6];
  stacked_xPSR = stack_frame[7];
  ...
  return;
}
```

If the fault handler is written for the Secure world, additional steps are needed. For example, it is possible for a Secure configurable fault handler to view the additional state context (it contains the integrity signature and stacked values of r4–r11) in the stack frame if it is configured to be of a lower priority level than that of a Non-secure IRQ. If a Secure configurable fault is triggered and stacking commences, a higher priority Non-secure IRQ arriving at that time could be served first, causing the additional state context to be pushed to the Secure stack. This additional state information would remain on the stack frame when the configurable fault handler executed: the calculation of stack frame address would need to take this into account (The following handler code refers):

```c
void HardFault_Handler_C(uint32_t exc_return_code, uint32_t msp_val)
{
  uint32_t stack_frame_r0_addr; // address of r0
  uint32_t stack_frame_extra_addr;// address of additional state
  unsigned int *stack_frame_r0;
  unsigned int *stack_frame_extra;
  uint32_t sp_value;

  uint32_t stacked_r0, stacked_r1, stacked_r2, stacked_r3;
  uint32_t stacked_r12, stacked_lr, stacked_pc, stacked_xPSR;
  uint32_t stacked_r4, stacked_r5, stacked_r6, stacked_r7;
  uint32_t stacked_r8, stacked_r9, stacked_r10, stacked_r11;

  // Check source of fault
  if (exc_return_code & 0x40) { // EXC_RETURN.S is 1 - Secure
    // Determine which stack pointer was used
    if (exc_return_code & 0x4) sp_value = __get_PSP();
    else                       sp_value = msp_val;
    }
  else { // Non-secure
    // Determine which stack pointer was used
    if (__TZ_get_CONTROL_NS() & 0x2) sp_value = __TZ_get_PSP_NS();
    else                             sp_value = __TZ_get_MSP_NS();
    }

  if ((exc_return_code & 0x20)!=0) { // EXC_RETURN.DCRS
    // No additional state context
    stack_frame_r0_addr    = sp_value;
    stack_frame_extra_addr = 0; // assume 0 means not available
  }
  else {
    // Additional state context present
    stack_frame_r0_addr = sp_value+40;
    stack_frame_extra_addr = sp_value;
    // Extract additional state context in stack frame
    stack_frame_extra = (unsigned *) sp_value;
  }
  // Extract stack frame
  stack_frame_r0 = (unsigned *) stack_frame_r0_addr;

  // extract stack frame
  stacked_r0 = stack_frame_r0[0];
  stacked_r1 = stack_frame_r0[1];
```

```
stacked_r2 = stack_frame_r0[2];
stacked_r3 = stack_frame_r0[3];
stacked_r12 = stack_frame_r0[4];
stacked_rlr = stack_frame_r0[5];
stacked_pc = stack_frame_r0[6];
stacked_xPSR = stack_frame_r0[7];
if (stack_frame_extra_addr!=0){
  stacked_r4 = stack_frame_extra[2];
  stacked_r5 = stack_frame_extra[3];
  ...
  }
...
return;
}
```

Because there are more stack pointers to choose from, the operation of this handler is somewhat more complex than the SVC example detailed in Chapter 11.

After the stack frame is extracted, the information can be displayed using the "printf" statements. If available, the handler can also display the fault status registers, which contain fault event information.

Please note, this handler will not work correctly if the stack pointer is pointing to an invalid memory region (e.g., because of stack overflow). This affects all C code as most C functions need stack memory.

To help debug the issue, a disassembled code list file can be generated so that the instruction, which triggered the fault can be located using the report stacked program counter value.

Reference

[1] Armv8-M Architecture Reference Manual. https://developer.arm.com/documentation/ddi0553/am (Armv8.0-M only version). https://developer.arm.com/documentation/ddi0553/latest (latest version including Armv8.1-M). Note: M-profile architecture reference manuals for Armv6-M, Armv7-M, Armv8-M and Armv8.1-M can be found here: https://developer.arm.com/architectures/cpu-architecture/m-profile/docs.

The Floating-Point Unit (FPU) in the Cortex-M33 processor

14.1 Floating-point data

14.1.1 Introduction

In C programming, numerical values can be defined as floating-point data. For example, the value of π can be declared as a single precision float:

```
float   pi = 3.141592F;
```

or double precision:

```
double pi = 3.14159265358979323846426433832795;
```

The floating-point data allows the processor to handle a much wider data range (compared to integers or fixed-point data), as well as very small values. There is also a half precision floating-point data format, which is 16 bits. The half precision floating-point format is not supported by some C compilers. In the gcc and in the Arm® C compiler, a half precision floating-point value is declared using __fp16 data type (Note: additional command option needed, Table 14.14).

14.1.2 Single precision floating-point numbers

The single precision data format is shown in Fig. 14.1.

In most cases, the exponent is in the value range of 1–254, with the single precision value being represented by the equation shown in Fig. 14.2.

To convert a value to a single precision floating-point, we need to normalize it between the range of 1.0 and 2.0. Examples are shown in Table 14.1.

When the exponent value is 0, then there are several possible scenarios:

(1) When the Fraction is equal to 0 and the Sign bit is also 0, then it is a zero (+0) value.

FIG. 14.1   Single precision floating-point format.

$$\text{Value} = (-1)^{\text{Sign}} \times 2^{(\text{exponent} - 127)} \times (1 + (\tfrac{1}{2} * \text{Fracion}[22]) + (\tfrac{1}{4} * \text{Fraction}[21]) + (1/8 * \text{Fraction}[20]) \dots (1/(2^{23}) * \text{Fraction}[0]))$$

FIG. 14.2   A normalized number in single precision format.

TABLE 14.1   Examples of floating-point values.

Floating-point value	Sign	Exponent	Fraction in binary form	Hex value
1.0	0	127 (0x7F)	000_0000_0000_0000_0000_0000	0x3F800000
1.5	0	127 (0x7F)	100_0000_0000_0000_0000_0000	0x3FC00000
1.75	0	127 (0x7F)	110_0000_0000_0000_0000_0000	0x3FE00000
0.04 → 1.28 * 2^(−5)	0	127 − 5 = 122 (0x7A)	010_0011_1101_0111_0000_1010	0x3D23D70A
−4.75 → −1.1875 *2^2	1	127 + 2 = 129 (0x81)	001_1000_0000_0000_0000_0000	0xC0980000

(2) When the Fraction is equal to 0 and the Sign bit is 1, then it is a zero (−0) value. Usually the +0 and −0 show the same behavior during an operation. In a few instances though there would be differences. For example, when a divide-by-zero occurs, the sign of the infinity result will be dependent on whether the divider is +0 or −0.

(3) When the Fraction is not 0, it is a denormalized value, i.e., a very small value between $-(2^{(-126)})$ and $(2^{(-126)})$.

A single precision denormalized value is represented by the equation shown in Fig. 14.3. When the exponent value is 0xFF, there are also several scenarios:

(1) When the Fraction is equal to 0 and the Sign bit is also 0, then it is an infinity ($+\infty$) value.

(2) When the Fraction is equal to 0 and the Sign bit is 1, then it is a minus infinity ($-\infty$) value.

(3) When the Fraction is not 0, then the floating-point data indicates that the floating-point value is invalid. It is more commonly known as Not a Number (NaN).

There are two types of NaN:

– When bit 22 of the Fraction is 0, it is a signaling NaN. The rest of the bit in the Fraction can be any value apart from zero.

– When bit 22 of the Fraction is 1, it is a quiet NaN. The rest of the bit in the Fraction can be any value.

$$\text{Value} = (-1)^{\text{Sign}} \times 2^{(-126)} \times ((\tfrac{1}{2} * \text{Fracion}[22]) + (\tfrac{1}{4} * \text{Fraction}[21]) + (1/8 * \text{Fraction}[20]) \dots (1/(2^{23}) * \text{Fraction}[0]))$$

FIG. 14.3   A denormalized number in a single precision format.

The two types of NaN can result in different floating-point exception behaviors in several floating-point instructions, e.g., VCMP and VCMPE.

In some floating-point operations, if the result is invalid it will return a "Default NaN" value. This has the value of 0x7FC00000 (Sign=0, Exponent=0xFF, bit 22 of Fraction is 1 and the rest of the Fraction bits are 0).

14.1.3 Half precision floating-point numbers

In many ways, the half precision floating-point format is similar to single precision, but differs by using fewer bits in the Exponent and Fraction fields (Fig. 14.4).

When 0 < Exponent < 0x1F, the value is a normalized value, with the value of the half precision value being represented by the equation in Fig. 14.5.

When the exponent value is 0 there are several scenarios:

(1) When the Fraction is equal to 0 and the Sign bit is also 0, then it is a zero (+0) value.
(2) When the Fraction is equal to 0 and the Sign bit is 1, then it is a zero (−0) value. Usually the +0 and −0 show the same behavior during an operation. In a few instances though, there would be differences. For example, when a divide-by-zero occurs, the sign of the infinity result will depend on whether the divider is +0 or −0.
(3) When the Fraction is not 0, then it is a denormalized value, i.e., it is a very small value between −(2^(−14)) and (2^(−14)).

A half precision denormalized value is represented by the equation in Fig. 14.6.

When the exponent value is 0x1F, the situation is a bit more complex. The floating-point feature in Armv8-M architecture [1] (Note: this is the same as in Armv7-M [2]) supports two operation modes for half precision data:

– IEEE Half precision
– Alternative Half precision. This does not support Infinity or NaN, but does have a large number range, and, in some cases, achieves a higher performance. However, if the application needs to be IEEE 754 [3] compliant, this operation mode cannot be used.

FIG. 14.4   Half precision floating-point format.

$$\text{Value} = (-1)^{\text{Sign}} \times 2^{(\text{exponent}-15)} \times (1 + (\tfrac{1}{2} * \text{Fracion}[9]) + (\tfrac{1}{4} * \text{Fraction}[8]) + (1/8 * \text{Fraction}[7]) \ldots (1/(2^{10}) * \text{Fraction}[0]))$$

FIG. 14.5   A normalized number in half precision format.

$$\text{Value} = (-1)^{\text{Sign}} \times 2^{(-14)} \times ((\tfrac{1}{2} * \text{Fracion}[9]) + (\tfrac{1}{4} * \text{Fraction}[8]) + (1/8 * \text{Fraction}[7]) \ldots (1/(2^{10}) * \text{Fraction}[0]))$$

FIG. 14.6   A denormalized number in half precision format.

In IEEE Half precision mode, with an exponent value that equals 0x1F, there are several scenarios:

(1) When the Fraction is equal to 0 and the Sign bit is also 0, then it is an infinity ($+\infty$) value.
(2) When the Fraction is equal to 0 and the Sign bit is 1, then it is a minus infinity ($-\infty$) value.
(3) When the Fraction is not 0, then the floating-point data indicates that the floating-point value is invalid. It is more commonly known as Not a Number (NaN).

Similar to single precision, a NaN can be signaling or quiet:

- When bit 9 of the Fraction is 0, it is a signaling NaN. The rest of the bit in the Fraction can be any value apart from Zero.
- When bit 9 of the Fraction is 1, it is a quiet NaN. The rest of the bit in the Fraction can be any value.

In some floating-point operations, if the result is invalid it will return a "Default NaN" value. This has the value of 0x7E00 (Sign=0, Exponent=0x1F, bit 9 of the Fraction is 1 and the rest of the Fraction bits are 0).

In Alternative Half precision mode, with an exponent value that equals 0x1F, the value is a normalized number and is represented by the equation shown in Fig. 14.7.

14.1.4 Double precision floating-point numbers

Although the floating-point unit in the Arm® Cortex®-M33 processor does not support double precision floating-point operations, you can still have double precision data in your applications. When this is needed, the C compiler and linker will insert the appropriate run time library functions to handle the required calculations.

The double precision data format is shown in Fig. 14.8.

In a little-endian memory system, the least significant word is stored in the lower address of a 64-bit address location and the most significant word is stored in the upper address. In big-endian memory systems it is the other way around.

$$\text{Value} = (-1)^{\text{Sign}} \times 2^{16} \times (1 + (\tfrac{1}{2} * \text{Fracion[9]}) + (\tfrac{1}{4} * \text{Fraction[8]}) + (1/8 * \text{Fraction[7]}) \dots (1/(2^{10}) * \text{Fraction[0]}))$$

FIG. 14.7   Alternate normalized number in half precision format.

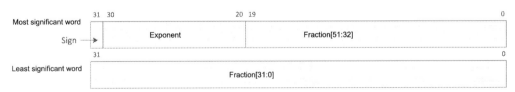

FIG. 14.8   Double precision floating-point format.

Value = (-1)^{Sign} x 2$^{(exponent-1023)}$x (1 + (½ * Fracion[51]) + (¼ * Fraction[50]) + (1/8 * Fraction[49]) ... (1/(2^{52}) * Fraction[0]))

FIG. 14.9 A normalized number in double precision format.

When $0 <$ Exponent $< 0x7FF$, the value is a normalized value, with the value of the double precision value being represented by the equation in Fig. 14.9.
When the exponent value is 0, there are several scenarios:

(1) When the Fraction is equal to 0 and the Sign bit is also 0, then it is a zero (+0) value.
(2) When the Fraction is equal to 0 and the Sign bit is 1, then it is a zero (−0) value. Usually the +0 and −0 show the same behavior during an operation. In a few instances though there would be differences. For example, when a divide-by-zero occurs, the sign of the infinity result would be dependent on whether the divider is +0 or −0.
(3) When the Fraction is not 0, then it is a denormalized value, i.e., it is a very small value between $-(2\char94(-1022))$ and $(2\char94(-1022))$.

A double precision denormalized value is represented by the equation in Fig. 14.10.
When the exponent value is 0x7FF, there are also several scenarios:

(1) When the Fraction is equal to 0 and the Sign bit is also 0, then it is an infinity (+∞) value.
(2) When the Fraction is equal to 0 and the Sign bit is 1, then it is a minus infinity (−∞) value.
(3) When the Fraction is not 0, then it is a Not a Number (NaN).

There are two types of NaN number values:

– When bit 51 of the Fraction is 0, it is a signaling NaN. The rest of the bit in the Fraction can be any value apart from zero.
– When bit 51 of the Fraction is 1, it is a quiet NaN. The rest of the bit in the Fraction can be of any value.

14.1.5 Floating-point support in Arm Cortex-M processors

The floating-point unit is optional in several Cortex-M processors (Table 14.2).
The Cortex®-M33 processor has the option of including a single-precision floating-point unit. If the floating-point unit is available, you can use the floating-point unit to accelerate single precision floating-point operations. However, double precision calculations still need to be handled by the C runtime library functions.
Even when the floating-point unit is available and the operation is single precision, you might still need the run-time library functions. For example, when dealing with functions like sinf(), cosf(), etc. These functions require a sequence of calculations, which cannot be performed by a single or a few instructions.

Value = (-1)^{Sign} x 2$^{(-1022)}$ x ((½ * Fracion[51]) + (¼ * Fraction[50]) + (1/8 * Fraction[49]) ... (1/(2^{52}) * Fraction[0]))

FIG. 14.10 A denormalized number in double precision format.

TABLE 14.2   Cortex-M processors with optional floating-point units.

Processor	FPU options
Cortex-M4	Optional single-precision FPU (FPv4)
Cortex-M7	Optional single-precision FPU (FPv5), or Optional single-precision and double precision FPU (FPv5)
Cortex-M33, Cortex-M35P	Optional single-precision FPU (FPv5)
Cortex-M55	Optional half-precision, single-precision and double precision FPU (FPv5), optional vector half-precision and single-precision when Helium® is implemented.

Some Cortex-M processors do not support a floating-point unit. This includes:

— The Cortex-M0, the Cortex-M0+, the Cortex-M1 (for FPGA), the Cortex-M3, and the Cortex-M23 processor

With these processors, all floating-point calculations must be carried out using runtime library functions.

Even when you are using a microcontroller with a floating-point unit, with well-established tool chains you can compile an application and decide not to enable the floating-point unit support. By doing so, the compiled code can be used on another Cortex-M microcontroller product which does not have a floating-point unit. This does mean, however, that the floating-point data processing will be carried out as a software runtime function and will execute slower.

For some applications, a software developer can use fixed point data. Fundamentally, fixed-point operations are just like integer operations, but add to the mix additional shift adjustment operations. While fixed-point processing is quicker than using the floating-point run time library functions, it can only handle a limited data range because the exponent is fixed. Arm® has an application note (Application note 33) [4] on how to create fixed point arithmetic operations in Arm architecture.

14.2 Cortex-M33 Floating-point Unit (FPU)

14.2.1 FPU overview

In Armv8-M architecture, the floating-point data and operations are based on IEEE Std 754-2008, which is the IEEE Standard for Binary Floating-Point Arithmetic. The Floating-Point Unit (FPU) in the Cortex-M33 processor is designed to enable floating-point data to be efficiently processed. This feature is not available in the Cortex-M23 processor.

The FPU support in the Cortex-M33 processor is optional; supports single precision floating-point calculations, as well as some conversion and memory access functions. The

FPU design is compliant to the IEEE 754 standard, but is not a complete implementation. For example, the following operations are not implemented by hardware:

- Double precision data calculations,
- Floating-point remainder (e.g., z = fmod(x, y)),
- Binary-to-decimal and decimal-to-binary conversions,
- Direct comparison of single precision and double precision values (the two values being compared must be of the same data type).

The operations that are not implemented would need to be handled by software.

The FPU in the Cortex-M33 processor is based on an extension of the Armv8-M architecture called FPv5-SP-D16M (Floating-point version 5—Single Precision). This is a subset of the FPv5 extension for Armv8-M architecture, where the full FPv5 also supports double precision floating-point processing. The FPU architecture extension came from the Cortex-A architecture and supports Vectored Floating-point operations. As many floating-point instructions are common to both the Cortex-A and Cortex-M architectures, floating-point instruction mnemonics begin—as they were first introduced in the Vectored Floating-point (VFP) extensions—with the letter "V".

The floating-point unit design supports:

- A floating-point register bank, which contains thirty-two 32-bit registers. These can be used as 32 single precision data registers or used in pairs as 16 double-precision registers.
- Single-precision floating-point calculations.
- Conversion instructions for:
  - "integer ↔ single precision floating-point",
  - "fixed point ↔ single precision floating-point",
  - "half precision ↔ single precision floating-point".
- Data transfers of single-precision and double word data between the floating-point register bank and the memory.
- Data transfers of single-precision between the floating-point register bank and the integer register bank.
- Lazy-stacking operations.

In the past, Arm processors treated the FPU as a coprocessor. To be consistent with other Arm architectures, the floating-point units in Armv8-M processors are defined as Coprocessor #10 and #11 in the CPACR, NSACR, and CPPWR programmer's models (see Sections 14.2.3, 14.2.4, and 15.6). However, in terms of floating-point operations, a set of floating-point instructions are used instead of using the coprocessor access instructions.

An FPU feature available in the Cortex-M33 is lazy stacking, a feature for reducing interrupt latency. Because the FPU has its own register bank, the exception handling mechanism needs to save and restore additional registers in the FPU during an exception sequence if the FPU is:

(a) enabled and
(b) used by both the interrupted software and the exception handler.

However, if the exception handler does not need to use the floating-point unit, the lazy stack feature avoids the timing overhead of the saving and restoring of the FPU context. Further information on lazy stacking can be found in Section 14.4.

TABLE 14.3   Additional FPU memory map registers for FPU control.

Address	Register	CMSIS-CORE symbol	Function
0xE000EF34	Floating-Point Context Control Register	FPU->FPCCR	FPU control data
0xE000EF38	Floating-Point Context Address Register	FPU->FPCAR	Holds the address of the unpopulated floating-point register space in the stack frame
0xE000EF3C	Floating-Point Default Status Control Register	FPU-> FPDSCR	Default values for the floating-point status control data (FPSCR).
0xE000EF40	Media and FP Feature Register 0	FPU->MVFR0	Read-only: Details information about the implemented VFP instruction features.
0xE000EF44	Media and FP Feature Register 1	FPU->MVFR1	Read-only: Details information about the implemented VFP instruction features
0xE000EF48	Media and FP Feature Register 2	FPU->MVFR2	Read-only: Details information about the implemented VFP instruction features

14.2.2 Floating-point registers overview

The FPU adds several registers to the processor:

- The Coprocessor Access Control Register (CPACR) in the System Control Block (SCB)
- The Non-secure Access Control Register (NSACR) in the SCB
- Registers in the Floating-point register bank (s0–s31, or d0–d15)
- The Floating-point Status and Control Register (FPSCR) is a special register
- The Coprocessor Power Control Register (CPPWR, Section 15.6)
- Additional registers in the FPU for floating-point operations and control (as shown in Table 14.3).

When the TrustZone® security extension is implemented, Secure software has access to the Non-secure view of those registers, listed in Fig. 14.3, via the Non-secure address alias 0xE002Exxx.

14.2.3 CPACR register

The CPACR register is a part of the SCB. It allows you to enable or disable:

- the FPU,
- coprocessors (if implemented), and
- Arm Custom Instructions (An optional feature available in revision 1 of the Cortex-M33).

The CPACR is located in address 0xE000ED88 and is accessed as "SCB->CPACR" in the CMSIS-CORE. Bits 0–15 are reserved for the coprocessor and for Arm Custom Instructions. Bits 16–19 and bits 24–31 are not implemented and are reserved (see Fig. 14.11).

The programmer's model of this register provides the bit fields, which enable/disable up to 16 coprocessors. In the Cortex-M33 processor, the FPU is defined as coprocessors

SCB->CPACR, 0xE000ED88

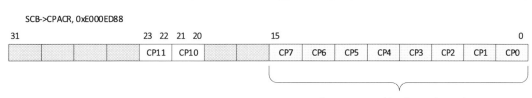

For coprocessor / Arm Custom Instructions

FIG. 14.11   Coprocessor Access Control Register (SCB->CPACR, 0xE000ED88).

TABLE 14.4   The setting bit field for CP0–CP11 in the CPACR.

Bits	Settings for CP0–CP11 in the CPACR
00	Access denied. Any attempted access generates a Usage Fault (type NOCP—No Coprocessor)
01	Privileged Access only. Unprivileged access generates a Usage Fault
10	Reserved—result unpredictable
11	Full access

10 (CP10) and 11 (CP11). When programing this register, the settings for CP10 and CP11 must be identical. The settings bit field for each of the coprocessors in the CPACR register is shown in Table 14.4.

By default, the settings for CP10 and CP11 in the CPACR are zero after reset. This setting disables the FPU and should provide for lower power consumption. Before using the FPU, you first need to program the CPACR to enable the FPU. For example:

```
SCB->CPACR|= 0x00F00000; // Enables the floating-point unit for full access
```

This step is typically carried out inside the SystemInit() function provided in the device specific software package file. SystemInit() is executed by the reset handler.

When the TrustZone security extension is implemented, this register is banked between security states so that the FPU can be enabled in one security domain and not in another.

14.2.4 NSACR register

When the TrustZone security extension is implemented, the Non-secure Access Control Register (NSACR) in the SCB allows you to define whether, for each coprocessor; it can be accessed from the Non-secure state. This register is accessible from Secure privileged state only. If TrustZone is not implemented, then this register is read-only and all available coprocessors are available for Non-secure use.

NSACR is located in address 0xE000ED8C and is accessed as "SCB->NSACR" in the CMSIS-CORE. Bits 0–7 are reserved for the coprocessor and for Arm Custom Instructions. Bits 8–9 and bits 12–31 are not implemented and are reserved (see Fig. 14.12).

This register can only be accessed from the Secure privileged state. By default, the access control bits for CP10 and CP11 are zero after reset, which means the FPU is then Secure access only. To enable the FPU to be used by Non-secure software, Secure software needs to set both the CP10 and the CP11 to 1. For example:

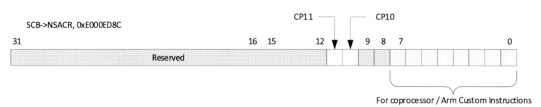

FIG. 14.12   Coprocessor Access Control Register (SCB->NSACR, 0xE000ED8C).

```
SCB->NSACR|= 0x00000C00; // Enables the floating-point unit for Non-secure use
```
The value written to the CP10 and CP11 bits must be identical, for if it is not then the result is architecturally unpredictable.

14.2.5 Floating-point register bank

The floating-point register bank contains thirty-two 32-bit registers, which can be viewed as sixteen 64-bit double word registers for double precision floating-point processing (Fig. 14.13).

64-bit →			
	S1	S0	D0
32-bit →	S3	S2	D1
	S5	S4	D2
	S7	S6	D3
	S9	S8	D4
	S11	S10	D6
	S13	S12	D6
	S15	S14	D7
	S17	S16	D8
	S19	S18	D9
	S21	S20	D10
	S23	S22	D11
	S25	S24	D12
	S27	S26	D13
	S29	S28	D14
	S31	S30	D15

caller saved registers (D0–D7)

callee-saved registers (D8–D15)

FIG. 14.13   Floating-point register bank.

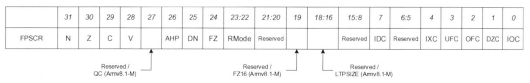

	31	30	29	28	27	26	25	24	23:22	21:20	19	18:16	15:8	7	6:5	4	3	2	1	0
FPSCR	N	Z	C	V		AHP	DN	FZ	RMode	Reserved			Reserved	IDC	Reserved	IXC	UFC	OFC	DZC	IOC

Reserved / QC (Armv8.1-M)

Reserved / FZ16 (Armv8.1-M)

Reserved / LTPSIZE (Armv8.1-M)

FIG. 14.14 Bit fields in the FPSCR.

S0–S15 are caller-saved registers: If a function A calls a function B, function A must save the contents of these registers (e.g., on the stack) before calling function B because these registers can be changed by the function call (e.g., returning a result).

S16–S31 are callee-saved registers: If a function A calls a function B and function B needs to use more than 16 registers for its calculations, it must, first, save the contents of these registers (e.g., on the stack) and then restore these registers from the stack before returning to function A.

The initial values of these registers are undefined.

14.2.6 Floating-point Status and Control Register (FPSCR)

The FPSCR is a special register and holds the result flags and sticky status flags for arithmetical operations, as well as bit fields to control the behavior of the floating-point unit (Fig. 14.14 and Table 14.5).

The N, Z, C, and V flags are updated by floating-point comparison operations (Table 14.6).

TABLE 14.5 Bit fields in the FPSCR.

Bit	Description
N	Negative flag (updates by floating-point comparison operations)
Z	Zero flag (updates by floating-point comparison operations)
C	Carry/borrow flag (updates by floating-point comparison operations)
V	Overflow flag (updates by floating-point comparison operations)
Reserved/QC	Reserved/Cumulative saturation bit for vector saturation (available in Armv8.1-M/Cortex-M55 only). Not available in the Cortex-M33 processor.
AHP	Alternative half precision control bit: 0—IEEE half precision format (default) 1—Alternative half precision format, see Section 14.1.3
DN	Default Not a Number (NaN) mode control bit: 0—NaN operands propagate through to the output of a floating-point operation. (Default) 1—Any operation involving one or more NaN(s) returns the default NaN.
FZ	Flush-to-zero mode control bit for single precision (and architecturally applicable to double precision, although double precision support is not implemented in the Cortex-M33 FPU): 0—Flush-to-zero mode disabled (default). (IEEE 754 standard compliant.)

Continued

TABLE 14.5 Bit fields in the FPSCR—cont'd

Bit	Description
	1—Flush-to-zero mode enabled. Denormalized values (tiny values with an exponent equal to 0) are flushed to 0.
RMode	Rounding Mode Control field. The specified rounding mode is used by almost all floating-point instructions: 00—Round to Nearest (RN) mode (default). 01—Round toward Plus Infinity (RP) mode. 10—Round toward Minus Infinity (RM) mode. 11—Round toward Zero (RZ) mode.
Reserved/FZ16	Reserved/Flush-to-zero mode for half precision data processing. (Available in Armv8.1-M/Cortex-M55 only.) Not available in the Cortex-M33 processor. 0—Flush-to-zero mode disabled (default). (IEEE 754 standard compliant.) 1—Flush-to-zero mode enabled.
Reserved/LTPSIZE	Reserved/Vector element size when applying a low-overhead-loop tail predication to vector instructions. (Available in Armv8.1-M with Helium/MVE.) Not available in the Cortex-M33 processor.
IDC	Input Denormal cumulative exception bit. Sets to 1 when a floating-point exception has occurred, clears by writing 0 to this bit.
IXC	Inexact cumulative exception bit. Sets to 1 when a floating-point exception has occurred, clears by writing 0 to this bit.
UFC	Underflow cumulative exception bit. Sets to 1 when a floating-point exception has occurred, clears by writing 0 to this bit.
OFC	Overflow cumulative exception bit. Sets to 1 when a floating-point exception has occurred, clears by writing 0 to this bit.
DZC	Division by Zero cumulative exception bit. Sets to 1 when a floating-point exception has occurred, clears by writing 0 to this bit.
IOC	Invalid Operation cumulative exception bit. Sets to 1 when a floating-point exception has occurred, clears by writing 0 to this bit.

TABLE 14.6 Operation of the N, Z, C, and V flags in the FPSCR.

Comparison result	N	Z	C	V
Equal	0	1	1	0
Less Than	1	0	0	0
Greater than	0	0	1	0
Unordered	0	0	1	1

The results of the floating-point compare can be used for conditional branch/conditional execution by first copying, as follows, the flags to the APSR:

```
VMRS    APSR_nzcv, FPSCR ; Copy flags from the FPSCR to the flags in the APSR
```

The bit fields AHP, DN, and FZ are control register bits for special operation modes. By default, all these bits default to 0, with the behavior compliant with the IEEE 754 single-precision standard. In most applications, there is no need to modify the settings of the floating-point operation control. It is important though, that these bits are not changed if your application requires IEEE 754 compliance.

The RMode bit field controls the rounding mode for calculation results. The IEEE 754 standard defines several rounding modes. These are listed in Table 14.7:

The bits IDC, IXC, UFC, OFC, DZC, IOC are sticky status flags that show any abnormities (floating-point exceptions) during floating-point operations. Software, optionally, checks these flags after the floating-point operations have occurred and then clears them by writing zero to those flags. Further information on floating-point exceptions can be found in Section 14.6.

Please note, Armv8.1-M architecture added a number of new bit fields (QC, FZ16, LTPSIZE) to the FPSCR register. They are not implemented in the Cortex-M33 processor's FPU, and therefore, are not covered here.

Even when TrustZone is implemented, the FPSCR register is not banked between security states. This is because the switching of the FPSCR value is automatically handled during exception sequences as follows:

• During stacking (a part of exception handling), the FPSCR is saved as part of the extended stack frame for floating-point registers; and then

TABLE 14.7   Rounding modes available in the FPUs for Cortex-M processors.

Rounding mode	Description
Round to nearest	Rounds to the nearest value. This is the default configuration. IEEE 754 subdivides this mode to:
	— Round to nearest, ties to even: rounds to the nearest value with an even (zero) Least Significant Bit (LSB). This is the default setting for a binary floating-point and is the recommended default setting for the decimal floating-point.
	— Round to nearest, ties away from zero: rounds to the nearest value above (for positive numbers) or below (for negative numbers). This is intended as an option for the decimal floating-point.
	Since the floating-point unit uses the binary floating-point only, the "Round to nearest, ties away from zero" mode is not available.
Round toward $+\infty$	Also known as rounding up or ceiling.
Round toward $-\infty$	Also known as rounding down or flooring.
Round toward 0	Also known as truncation.

- When entering an exception handler (i.e., the start of a new context), the configurations in the FPSCR are copied from the Floating-point Default Status Control Register (see Section 14.2.9); and then
- During unstacking, the FPSCR is restored from the extended stack frame.

When there is a function call across security domains, the update of the FPSCR is handled by software and the required code is automatically generated by the C compilers.

14.2.7 Floating-Point Context Control Register (FPU->FPCCR)

The Floating-Point Context Control Register (FPCCR, Fig. 14.15 and Table 14.8) allows the exception handling behavior to be controlled. The behavior and features controlled by this register include "lazy stacking" and, if TrustZone is implemented, the security settings for handling the floating-point context. In addition, this register allows access to some of the control information.

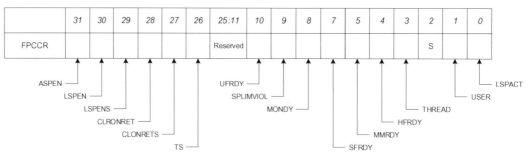

FIG. 14.15   Bit fields in the FPCCR.

TABLE 14.8   Floating-point Context Control Register (FPU->FPCCR, 0xE000EF34).

Bits	Name	Type	Reset value	Description
31	ASPEN	R/W	1	Automatic state preservation enable. Enables/disables the automatic setting of the FPCA (bit 2 of the CONTROL register). When this bit is set to 1 (i.e., default), it enables the automatic state preservation and restoration of the caller saved registers (S0–S15 and the FPSCR) on exception entry and exception exit. When this bit is cleared to 0, the automatic saving of the FPU registers is disabled. Software using the FPU will in this scenario need to manually manage the context saving. This bit is banked between Security states.
30	LSPEN	R/W	1	Lazy state preservation enable. Enables/disables lazy stacking (state preservation) for S0–S15 and the FPSCR. When this is set to 1 (i.e., default), the exception sequence uses the lazy stacking feature to ensure low interrupt latency.

TABLE 14.8 Floating-point Context Control Register (FPU->FPCCR, 0xE000EF34)—cont'd

Bits	Name	Type	Reset value	Description
29	LSPENS	R/W	0	Lazy state preservation enable Secure. This bit determines whether the Non-secure software can write to LSPEN (bit 30) – if 0 (default), the Secure and Non-secure worlds can read and write to LSPEN. – If 1, LSPEN can be written to in the Secure world and is read-only in the Non-secure world. This bit is not available if TrustZone is not implemented. This bit is not accessible from the Non-secure software/Non-secure debugging.
28	CLRONRET	R/W	0	Clear on return. When set to 1 it clears the floating-point caller save registers (s0–s15, FPSCR and VPR for Armv8.1-M) on the exception return.
27	CLRONRETS	R/W	0	Clear on return, Secure only. If CLRONRETS is 0 (i.e., default), Non-secure privileged code can write to CLRONRET. If CLRONRETS is 1, then CLRONRET is read-only from the Non-secure world. This bit is not available if TrustZone is not implemented. This bit is not accessible from the Non-secure software/Non-secure debugging.
26	TS	R/W	0	Treat as Secure. Treats Floating-point registers as Secure enable – When 0 (i.e., default), the data in the FPU is treated as Non-secure even when Secure software is using the FPU – When 1, all data in the FPU in the current context is treated as Secure when Secure software is used in the FPU. Setting this bit to 1 has the side effect of increasing interrupt latency when pushing the FPU context to the stack. (Additional FP context is included in the stack frame, Fig. 8.22) This bit is not available if TrustZone is not implemented. This bit is not accessible from the Non-secure software/Non-secure debugging.
25:11	–	–	–	Reserved.
10	UFRDY	R	–	UsageFault enable. Indicates that if a fault occurs during lazy stacking, whether the fault event is allowed to trigger the UsageFault exception. 0 = When the floating-point stack frame was allocated, the UsageFault was either disabled or the UsageFault priority level did not permit the UsageFault handler to enter pending state. 1 = When the floating-point stack frame was allocated, the UsageFault was enabled and the UsageFault priority level permitted the UsageFault handler to enter pending state. This bit is banked between Security states.

Continued

TABLE 14.8   Floating-point Context Control Register (FPU->FPCCR, 0xE000EF34)—cont'd

Bits	Name	Type	Reset value	Description
9	SPLIMVIOL	R	–	Stack pointer limit violation. Sets to 1 if the lazy stacking triggers a stack pointer limit violation. Note: if a stack limit violation occurs when serving a Non-secure interrupt and when the FPU has Secure data, the data in the FPU registers would still be zero to zero to prevent data leakage during the Non-secure ISR execution. In this situation, the Secure FPU data is lost. This bit is banked between Security states.
8	MONRDY	R	–	DebugMonitor ready. Indicates that if a debug event occurs during lazy stacking, whether the debug event is allowed to trigger the DebugMonitor exception. 0 = When the floating-point stack frame was allocated, the DebugMonitor was either disabled or the DebugMonitor priority level did not permit the setting of the MON_PEND bit (the pending status of the DebugMonitor). 1 = When the floating-point stack frame was allocated, the DebugMonitor was enabled and the DebugMonitor priority level permitted the setting of the MON_PEND bit. When TrustZone is implemented and the Debug Monitor is enabled for the Secure debug, this bit is inaccessible from the Non-secure state.
7	SFRDY	R	–	SecureFault ready. Indicates that if a fault occurs during lazy stacking, whether the fault event is allowed to trigger the SecureFault exception. 0 = When the floating-point stack frame was allocated, the SecureFault was either disabled or the SecureFault priority level did not permit the SecureFault handler to enter pending state. 1 = When the floating-point stack frame was allocated, the SecureFault was enabled and the SecureFault priority level permitted the SecureFault handler to enter pending state. This bit is banked between Security states. This bit is not available if TrustZone is not implemented. This bit is not accessible from the Non-secure software/Non-secure debugging.
6	BFRDY	R	–	BusFault ready. Indicates that if a fault occurs during lazy stacking, whether the fault event is allowed to trigger the BusFault exception. 0 = When the floating-point stack frame was allocated, the BusFault was either disabled or the BusFault priority level did not permit the BusFault handler to enter pending state. 1 = When the floating-point stack frame was allocated, the BusFault was enabled and the BusFault priority level permitted the BusFault handler to enter pending state.
5	MMRDY	R	–	MemManage ready. Indicates that if a fault occurs during lazy stacking, whether the fault event is allowed to trigger the MemManage exception. 0 = When the floating-point stack frame was allocated, the MemManage was either disabled or the MemManage priority level did not permit the

TABLE 14.8 Floating-point Context Control Register (FPU->FPCCR, 0xE000EF34)—cont'd

Bits	Name	Type	Reset value	Description
				MemMange handler to enter pending state.
				1 = When the floating-point stack frame was allocated, the MemManage was enabled and the MemManage priority level permitted the MemManage handler to enter pending state.
				When TrustZone is implemented, this bit is banked between Security states.
4	HFRDY	R	–	HardFault ready.
				Indicates that if a fault occurs during lazy stacking, whether the fault event is allowed to trigger the pending status of the HardFault exception.
				0 = When the floating-point stack frame was allocated, the processor's priority level did not permit the HardFault handler to enter pending state.
				1 = When the floating-point stack frame was allocated, the processor's priority level permitted the HardFault handler to enter pending state.
3	THREAD	R	0	Thread mode.
				Indicates the processor mode when it allocates the floating-point stack frame.
				0 = Processor was in Handler Mode when the floating-point stack frame was allocated.
				1 = Processor was in Thread Mode when the floating-point stack frame was allocated.
				When TrustZone is implemented, this bit is banked between Security states.
2	S	–	–	Security.
				The security state of the data in the FPU (Floating-point context).
				0 = the data belongs to the Non-secure state software
				1 = the data belongs to the Secure state software
				This bit is not available when TrustZone is not implemented.
				This bit is not accessible from the Non-secure software / Non-secure debugging.
1	USER	R	00	User privilege.
				0 = Mode was in Handler Mode when the floating-point stack frame was allocated.
				1 = Mode was in Thread Mode when the floating-point stack frame was allocated.
				This bit is banked between Security states.
0	LSPACT	R	0	Lazy state preservation active.
				0 = Lazy state preservation is not active.
				1 = Lazy state preservation is active. The floating-point stack frame would have been allocated but the state had not, as yet, been saved to the stack (i.e., it was deferred).
				This bit is banked between Security states.

In most applications:

- Secure software needs to configure the FPU's security settings in the FPCCR.
- Non-secure software does not need to change the settings in the FPCCR.

The usual FPU security settings that need to be configured by the Secure privileged software include those listed in Table 14.9.

The other use of this register is to configure the lazy stacking mechanism. By default, the "automatic FPU context saving and restoration" (controlled by the ASPEN bit in the FPCCR) and the "lazy stacking" (controlled by the LSPEN bit in the FPCCR) are enabled to reduce interrupt latency. ASPEN and LSPEN can be set in the following configurations (Table 14.10).

TABLE 14.9 Examples of security configurations for the FPCCR.

Typical usage	Typical configuration
If Secure software does not use the FPU	Secure privileged software, optionally, enables the Non-secure software to access the FPU by setting the CP11 and the CP10 bits in the SCB->NSACR
If both Secure and Non-secure software uses the FPU	Secure privileged software sets FPCCR.TS, FPCCR.CLRORET and FPCCR.CLRORETS bits to 1 and enables the Non-secure software to access the FPU by setting the CP11 and the CP10 bits in the SCB->NSACR. It also configures the CPPWR (Section 15.6) to prevent the Non-secure world from modifying the FPU's power control setting.
If the FPU is for Secure use only	Secure privileged software sets FPCCR.TS to 1 and configures the CPPWR (Section 15.6) to prevent the Non-secure world from modifying the FPU's power control setting.

TABLE 14.10 Available context saving configurations.

ASPEN	LSPEN	Configuration
1	1	Automatic state saving enabled, Lazy stacking enabled (default) CONTROL.FPCA is automatically set to 1 when the floating-point unit is used. If CONTROL.FPCA is 1 at the exception entry, the processor reserves space in the stack frame and sets LSPACT to 1. But the actual stacking does not happen until the interrupt handler uses the FPU.
1	0	Lazy stacking disabled, automatic state saving enabled. CONTROL.FPCA is automatically set to 1 when the FPU is used. At the exception entry, the floating-point registers S0–S15 and the FPSCR are, if CONTROL.FPCA is 1, pushed to the stack.
0	0	No automatic state preservation. This setting can be used: 1. In applications without an embedded OS or without a multitask scheduler and if none of the interrupt or exception handlers use the FPU. 2. In application code where only one exception handler uses the FPU and where it is not used by Thread. If multiple interrupt handlers use the FPU, they must not be allowed to nest. This can be achieved by giving all the handlers the same priority level. 3. In applications where the saving/restoration of the FPU context is manually handled by software to avoid conflicts (e.g., All exception handlers that use the FPU would need to manually save and restore the used FPU registers).
0	1	Invalid configuration

14.2.8 Floating-Point Context Address Register (FPU->FPCAR)

Earlier in this chapter and in Chapter 8 (Section 8.9.4), I briefly covered the Lazy Stacking feature. When an exception takes place, and if the current context has an active floating-point context (i.e., the FPU has been used), then the exception stack frame will contain registers from the integer register bank (R0–R3, R12, LR, the Return Address, and the xPSR) and from the FPU (S0–S15, the FPSCR, and, if TrustZone is implemented and if the Secure software also uses the FPU, registers S16–S31). To reduce interrupt latency, lazy stacking is, by default, enabled to ensure that the stacking mechanism reserves the stack space for the FPU registers but does not, in the process, push these registers to the stack until there is a need to do so.

The FPCAR register is part of the Lazy stacking mechanism (Fig. 14.16). It holds the address of the allocated space for the FPU registers in the stack frame so that the lazy stacking mechanism knows where to push the FPU registers to when required to do so. Bits 2 to 0 are not used because the stack frame is double word aligned.

When the TrustZone security extension is implemented, the FPCAR register is banked between security states.

When an exception occurs during lazy stacking, the FPCAR is updated to the address of the FPU S0 register space in the stack frame, as shown in Fig. 14.17.

FIG. 14.16 Bit assignments in the Floating-point context address register (FPU->FPCAR, address 0xE000EF38).

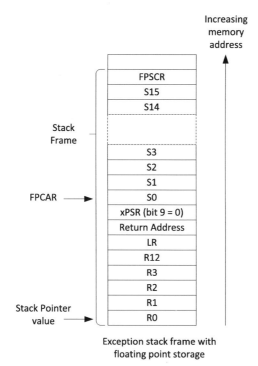

FIG. 14.17 FPCAR points to the reserved FPU register memory space in the stack frame.

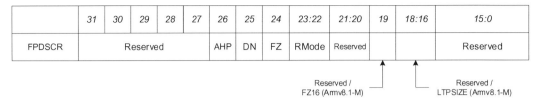

FPDSCR	31	30	29	28	27	26	25	24	23:22	21:20	19	18:16	15:0
	Reserved					AHP	DN	FZ	RMode	Reserved			Reserved

Reserved / FZ16 (Armv8.1-M)   Reserved / LTPSIZE (Armv8.1-M)

FIG. 14.18   Bit assignment in the Floating-point default status control register (FPU->FPDSCR).

14.2.9 Floating-Point Default Status Control Register (FPU->FPDSCR)

The FPDSCR register holds default configuration information (i.e., operation modes) for the floating-point status control data. The values are copied to the FPSCR at exception entries (Fig. 14.18).

At system reset, AHP, DN, FZ, and RMode are reset to 0. When the TrustZone security extension is implemented, this register is banked between Security states.

In a complex system there can be different types of applications running in parallel, with each having a different FPU configuration (e.g., rounding mode). In order to cope with this, the FPU configuration needs to automatically switch between exception entry and exception return. The FPDSCR defines the FPU configuration when the exception handlers start. Because most parts of the OS execute in Handler mode, the default FPU configuration used by the OS kernel are defined by the settings in the FPDSCR.

When using an RTOS, if each of the application tasks requires different FPU settings, there would be a need for each task to set the FPSCR up when they start. Once a task has set the FPSCR up, its configuration is saved and restored with the FPSCR during each context switching.

14.2.10 Media and FP Feature Registers (FPU->MVFR0 to FPU->MVFR2)

The FPU in the Cortex-M33 processor has three read-only registers to allow software to determine what instruction features are supported. The values of MVFR0, MVFR1, and MVFR2 are hard coded (Table 14.11). Software uses these registers to determine what floating-point features are available (Fig. 14.19).

TABLE 14.11   Media and FP feature registers.

Address	Name	CMSIS-CORE symbol	Value in the Cortex-M33 processor when the FPU is implemented
0xE000EF40	Media and FP Feature Register 0	FPU->MVFR0	0x10110021
0xE000EF44	Media and FP Feature Register 1	FPU->MVFR1	0x11000011
0xE000EF48	Media and FP Feature Register 2	FPU->MVFR2	0x00000040

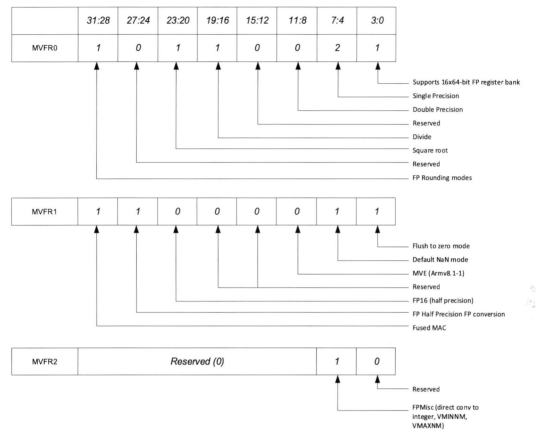

FIG. 14.19   Media and Floating-point feature registers.

When the bit fields are 0, the features in Fig. 14.19 are not available. When the bit fields are 1 or 2 the features are supported. The Single Precision field is set to 2 to indicate that, apart from normal single precision calculations, it can also handle floating divide and square root functions.

14.3 Key differences between the FPUs of the Cortex-M33 FPU and the Cortex-M4

There are some changes in the floating-point unit of the Cortex-M33 when compared to the one in the Cortex-M4. These are:

Instruction set: The FPU in the Cortex-M4 is based on FPv4, whereas the one in the Cortex-M33 is based on the FPv5 architecture, which supports additional data conversions and max and min comparison instructions. This enables a marginally higher floating-point performance. (For reference, the FPU in the Cortex-M7 processor is also based on the FPv5.)

TrustZone support: TrustZone support in Armv8-M means that Secure software needs to configure the FPU to decide whether security measures are needed in dealing with the FPU context. During initialization, Secure software sets up the configuration settings for the FPU. A range of new configuration bits have been added to the FPU registers (e.g., FPU->FPCCR, FPSCR) to support the TrustZone security extension. Some of these configuration registers are banked between Security states.

Stack limit checking: In Armv8-M, the lazy stacking mechanism is subject to stack limit checking, with new bit fields being added to the FPCCR to deal with UsageFault and stack limit violations.

14.4 Lazy stacking in details

14.4.1 Key elements of the Lazy Stacking feature

Lazy stacking is an important feature of the Cortex-M33 processor. Without this feature, the time required for every exception would, if the FPU was available and was used, be increased. This is because instead of pushing only the registers in the regular register bank to the stack it would also need to push the registers in the floating-point register bank.

As we have seen in the stack frame diagrams at Figs. 8.20–8.22, when we need to stack the required floating-point registers for each exception, additional memory pushes for the FPU registers would be required each time an exception occurred. Depending on the number of FPU registers that need to be pushed to the stack, interrupt latency would accordingly be increased.

In order to reduce the interrupt latency, Cortex-M processors with a floating-point unit have a feature called *lazy stacking*. When an exception arrives with the floating-point unit enabled and used, which is indicated by bit 2 of the CONTROL register (called floating-point context active (FPCA)), the longer stack frame format is used. However, the values of these floating-point registers are not actually written into the stack frame. Accordingly, the Lazy stacking mechanism only reserves the stack space for the FPU registers and only stacks R0–R3, R12, LR, the Return Address, and the xPSR, and, if needed, the optional additional context.

When lazy stacking happens, an internal register called Lazy Stacking Preservation Active (LSPACT) is set and another 32-bit register, called the Floating-Point Context Address Register (FPCAR), stores the address of the reserved stack space for the floating-point register.

If the exception handler does not require a floating-point operation, the floating-point registers remain unchanged throughout the exception service and are not restored at the exception's exit. If the exception handler does need a floating-point operation, the processor detects the conflict, stalls the processor, pushes the floating-point registers into the reserved stack space and clears the Lazy stacking pending state. After those actions have been carried out, the exception handler resumes. Because of this, the floating-point registers are only stacked as and when necessary.

If the current executing context (either Thread or Handler) does not use the floating-point unit when an interrupt arrives, as indicated by a zero value in the FPCA (bit 2 of the CONTROL register), the shorter stack frame formats would be used.

Because of the Lazy Stacking feature, for a zero-wait state memory system and assuming that there is no need to push additional state context, the exception latency stays at just 12 clock cycles—the same number of clock cycles as previous Armv7-M Cortex-M processors.

By default, the Lazy Stacking feature is enabled (the control bits FPCCR.LSPEN and FPCCR.ASPEN are both reset to 1, Section 14.2.7), and therefore, there is no need for software developers to configure registers to take full advantage of this particular feature. Moreover, there is no need to setup any registers during exception handling as all the required operations are automatically managed by the hardware.

There are several key elements in the Lazy Stacking mechanism:

The FPCA bit in the CONTROL register: CONTROL.FPCA indicates whether the current context (e.g., the task) has a floating-point operation. It is:

- set to 1 when the processor executes a floating-point instruction,
- cleared to zero at the beginning of an exception handler,
- set to the inverse of bit 4 in EXC_RETURN at exception return,
- cleared to zero after a reset.

The EXC_RETURN: Bit 4 of the EXC_RETURN is set to 0 at exception entry if the interrupted task has a floating-point context (i.e., the FPCA was 1). When bit 4 of the EXC_RETURN is 0, it indicates that the longer stack frame (contains R0–R3, R12, LR, the Return Address, the xPSR, S0–S15, the FPSCR and, if the FPCCR.TS was set to 1, registers S16–S31) was used for stacking. If this bit is set to 1 at exception entry, it indicates that the stack frame was the shorter version (contains R0–R3, R12, LR, Return Address, xPSR).

LSPACT bit in FPCCR: Lazy stack pending active—When the processor enters an exception handler, when Lazy Stacking is enabled and when the interrupted task has a floating-point context (i.e., FPCA is 1), the longer stack frame is used in stacking and the LSPACT is set to 1. This indicates that the stacking of the floating-point registers has been deferred and that space has been, as indicated by the FPCAR, allocated in the stack frame. If the processor executes a floating-point instruction when LSPACT is 1, the processor will stall the pipeline, start the stacking of the floating-point registers, and when completed, resume operations. At this stage the LSPACT will also be cleared to 0—to indicate that there is no outstanding deferred floating-point register stacking required. This bit is also cleared to 0 in an exception return if bit 4 of EXC_RETURN value was 0.

FPCAR register: The FPCAR register holds the address for use when floating-point registers S0–S15 and the FPSCR are being pushed to the stack. This register automatically updates at exception entry.

14.4.2 Scenario #1: no floating-point context in an interrupted task

When there is no floating-point context before an interrupt, the CONTROL.FPCA is zero and the short version of the stack frame is used (Fig. 14.20). This situation applies to all Cortex-M processors where the FPU is either disabled or is not implemented. If the exception handler or an ISR uses the FPU, the FPCA bit is set to 1 and is cleared at the end of the ISR during the exception return.

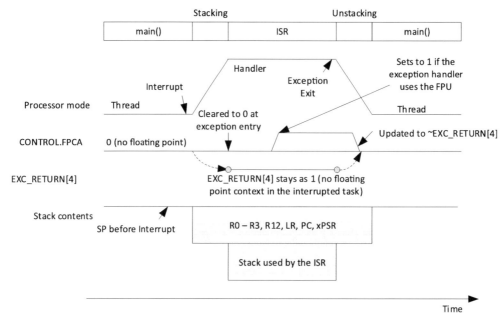

FIG. 14.20   Exception handling with no floating-point context in the interrupted task.

14.4.3 Scenario #2: floating-point context in an interrupted task but not in the ISR

If the FPU is used before an interrupt arrives, the interrupted task has a floating-point context. In this scenario, CONTROL.FPCA is set to 1 to indicate the presence of the floating-point context, with the long version of the stack frame being used during stacking (Figs. 8.20–8.22). Unlike normal stacking, which pushes all the registers to the stack, the stack frame contains space for S0–S15, the FPSCR, and potentially, S16–S31. However, the values of these registers are not pushed to the stack. Instead, LSPACT is set to 1 to indicate the deferment of the stacking of the floating-point registers (Fig. 14.21).

In Fig. 14.21, at the exception return, the processor sees that although EXC_RETURN[4] is 0 (i.e., the long stack frame), the LSPACT is 1, which indicates that the floating-point registers were not pushed to the stack. This would mean that the unstacking of S0–S15, the FPSCR, and potentially, S16–S31 would not be carried out and would remain unchanged.

14.4.4 Scenario #3: floating-point context in an interrupted task and in the ISR

If the interrupt code has a floating-point context and there is a floating-point operation inside the ISR, the deferred lazy stack process has to be carried out. When the first floating-point instruction in the ISR reaches the decode stage, the processor detects the presence of the floating-point operation, stalls the processor and then pushes the floating-point registers S0–S15, the FPSCR and, potentially, S16–S31 to the reserved space in the stack. This process

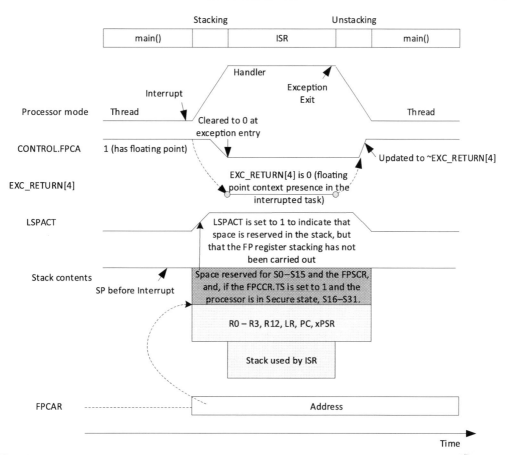

FIG. 14.21 Exception handling with floating-point context in the interrupted task and where there are no FPU operations in the ISR.

is shown in Fig. 14.22. Once the stacking is finished, the ISR then resumes and is able to execute the floating-point instruction.

In Fig. 14.22, a floating-point instruction is executed during the ISR execution and triggers the deferred stacking. During this operation, the address of the reserved stack space, which was stored in the FPCAR, is used for the stacking of the FPU registers during lazy stacking.

In Fig. 14.22, at the exception return, when the processor sees that EXC_RETURN[4] is 0 (i.e., the long stack frame) and that the LSPACT is also 0, it proceeds to unstack the floating-point registers from the stack frame.

14.4.5 Scenario #4: Nested Interrupt with FP context in the second handler

The Lazy Stacking feature also works across multiple levels of nested interrupts. For example, if

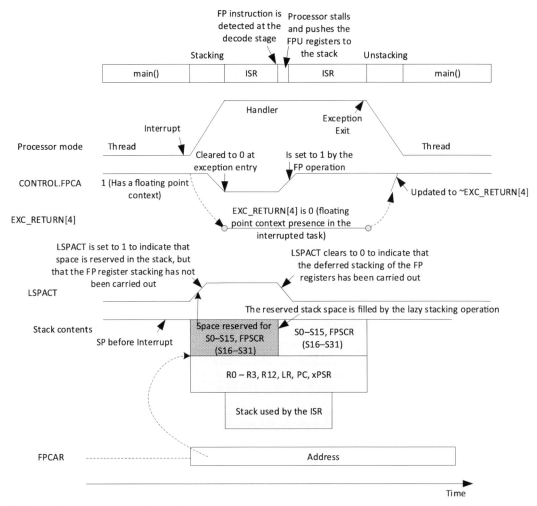

FIG. 14.22   Exception handling with a floating-point context in the interrupted task and in the ISR.

(a) The thread has a floating-point context; and
(b) The low priority ISR does not; and
(c) The higher priority ISR does,

the deterred Lazy Stacking will push the floating-point registers to the first level of the stack frame pointed to by the FPCAR (Fig. 14.23).

14.4.6 Scenario #5: Nested interrupt with FP context in the both handlers

The Lazy Stacking mechanism also works for nested ISRs with an FP context in both low and high priority ISRs. In this scenario, the processor reserves stack space for the floating-point registers' multiple times (Fig. 14.24).

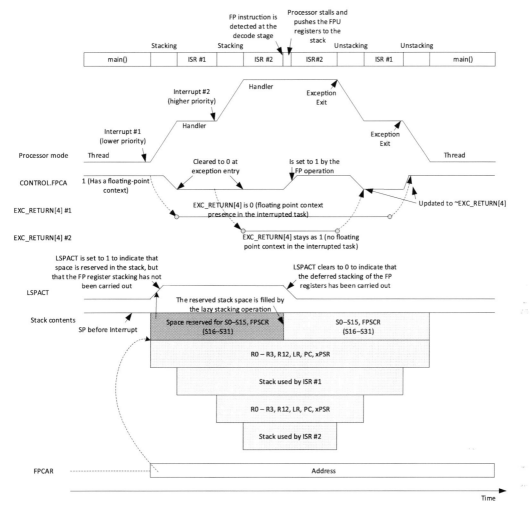

FIG. 14.23 Nested exception handling with a floating-point context in the interrupted task and in the higher priority ISR.

In Fig. 14.24, at each of the exception returns, when the processor sees that EXC_RETURN [4] is 0 (i.e., the long stack frame) and that the LSPACT is also 0, it proceeds, in both instances, to unstack the floating-point registers from the stack frame.

14.4.7 Interrupt during a lazy stacking operation

A deferred lazy stacking operation may be interrupted during its operation. When this happens, the lazy stacking operation is suspended to allow the higher priority interrupt to be serviced without further delay (Note: the normal stacking process would still be needed).

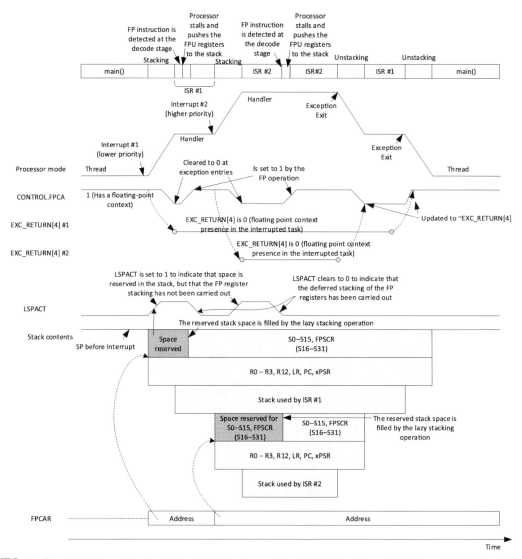

FIG. 14.24 Nested exception handling with a floating-point context in the interrupted task and in both levels of ISRs.

Because the floating-point instruction that triggered the lazy stacking would still be in the decode stage and would not have been executed, the return PC in the stack frame would point to the address of this floating-point instruction. If the higher priority interrupt does not use a floating-point operation, the floating-point instruction that triggered the lazy stacking the first time will, after the higher priority interrupt is returned, enter the processor pipeline again and trigger the lazy stacking for the second time.

14.4.8 Interrupt of floating-point instructions

Many floating-point instructions take multiple clock cycles.

If an interrupt takes place during the VPUSH, the VPOP, the VLDM, and the VSTM instructions (i.e., multiple memory transfers), the processor will suspend the current instruction and use the ICI bits in the EPSR (further information on EPSR can be found in Chapter 4, "Program Status Register (PSR)" section) to store the status of those instructions. It will then execute the exception handler and will, based on the restored ICI bits, resume the instruction from where it was suspended.

If the interrupt takes place during a VSQRT (a floating-point square root instruction) or a VDIV (a floating-point divide instruction), the processor will continue the calculation and handle the stacking operation in parallel.

14.5 Using the FPU

14.5.1 Floating-point support in the CMSIS-CORE

To use the floating-point unit, it first needs to be enabled. The enabling of the FPU (using the SCB->CPACR register) is usually handled inside the `SystemInit()` function. The FPU enabling code is enabled by C macros—there are three preprocessing directives/macros in the CMSIS-CORE relating to FPU configurations (Table 14.12).

The data structure for the FPU is only available if the __FPU_PRESENT macro is set to 1. If __FPU_USED is set to 1, then the `SystemInit()` function enables the FPU by writing to the CPACR when the reset handler is executed.

14.5.2 Floating-point programming in C language

For most applications, the accuracy of the single precision floating-point computation is sufficient. In some applications though, there is a need to use double precision floating point calculations to obtain high accuracy. Although it is possible to use double-precision calculations in the Cortex-M33 processor, to do so would increase code size and the calculations would take longer to complete. This is because the FPU in the Cortex-M33 processor only

TABLE 14.12 Preprocessing macros in the CMSIS-CORE related to the FPU.

Preprocessing directive	Description
__FPU_PRESENT	Indicates whether the Cortex®-M processor in the microcontroller has an FPU. If it does, this macro is set to 1 by the device specific header.
__FPU_USED	Indicates whether an FPU is being used. Must be set to 0 if __FPU_PRESENT is 0. It can either be 0 or 1 if __FPU_PRESENT is 1. This is set by the compilation tools (it could be controlled by the project settings).
__FPU_DP	Indicates whether the FPU supports double precision operations (This macro is not used in the Cortex-M33).

supports single precision calculations and, as a result, double precision operations have to be undertaken by software (using the run time library functions inserted by the development tool chains).

Most software developers endeavor to limit the floating-point calculations in the code to single precision. However, it is not uncommon for software developers to accidentally use double precision floating-point operations in their codes. To illustrate this, the following lines of code from the Whetstone benchmark can be used as an example (it was designed for computers which have double precision floating-point support). Using the following codes, even if we attempt to restrict the operations to single precision only by defining variables X, Y, T, and T2 as "float" (single precision), a C compiler will still generate compiled code with double precision operations:

```
X=T*atan(T2*sin(X)*cos(X)/(cos(X+Y)+cos(X-Y)-1.0));
Y=T*atan(T2*sin(Y)*cos(Y)/(cos(X+Y)+cos(X-Y)-1.0));
```

This is because the mathematical functions used are double precision by default and, in addition, the constant 1.0 is also treated as double precision. To generate a single precision calculation version of the above code, the code would need to be modified as follows:

```
X=T*atanf(T2*sinf(X)*cosf(X)/(cosf(X+Y)+cosf(X-Y)-1.0F));
Y=T*atanf(T2*sinf(Y)*cosf(Y)/(cosf(X+Y)+cosf(X-Y)-1.0F));
```

To confirm that the compiled code does not accidentally use double precision calculations, compilation report files can be used to check whether double precision runtime functions are inserted in the compiled code. Some development tools are able to report when double precision operations are used, with some of these also allowing floating-point operations to be forced to single precision.

14.5.3 Compiler command line options

In most tool chains, by selecting the FPU option in in the project Integrated Development Environment (IDE), the command line options are setup by the IDE to enable you to easily use the FPU. For example, to enable the use of the FPU feature in the µVision IDE of Keil® MDK, this is achieved by simply selecting the "Single precision" in the project option (Fig. 14.25).

By selecting the FPU to be used in the project settings, the toolchain automatically sets the compiler options to include the following FPU support options:

```
"-mcpu=cortex-m33 -mfpu=fpv5-sp-d16 -mfloat-abi=hard"
```

For users of Arm Compiler 6 (which comes with Arm DS or DS-5), the following command line options can be used to enable the FPU feature during compilation with the hard abi (I will cover the hard/soft abi topic in Section 14.5.4):

```
"armclang --target=arm-arm-none-eabi -mcpu=cortex-m33 -mfpu=fpv5-sp-d16 -
mfloat-abi=hard", or
```

```
"armclang --target=arm-arm-none-eabi -marmv8-m.main -mfpu=fpv5-sp-d16 -
mfloat-abi=hard"
```

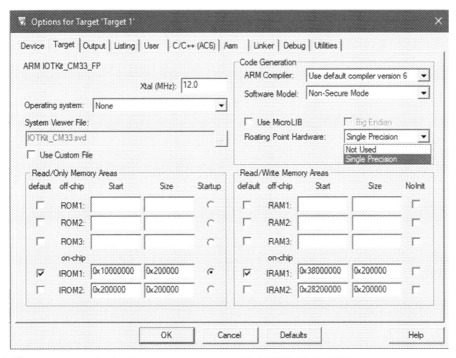

FIG. 14.25 FPU options for the Cortex-M33 processor in Keil MDK μVision IDE.

For GNU C Compiler (gcc) users, the following command line options can be used to use the FPU:

```
"arm-none-eabi-gcc -mthumb -mcpu=cortex-m33 -mfpu=fpv5-sp-d16 -mfloat-abi=hard",
or
```

```
"arm-none-eabi-gcc -mthumb -march=armv8-m.main -mfpu=fpv5-sp-d16 -
mfloat-abi=hard"
```

14.5.4 ABI options: Hard-vfp and soft-vfp

In most C compilers you can specify how the parameters and the results of the floating-point calculations are transferred across function boundaries using different Application Binary Interface (ABI) arrangements. For example, even if you have an FPU in the processor, you still need to use a number of C runtime library functions because many of the math functions require a sequence of calculations.

The ABI options affect:

− Whether the floating-point unit is used;
− How parameters and results are passed between caller and callee functions

With most development tool chains [5], there are three different ABI options (Table 14.13). The operational differences of the options listed in Table 14.13 are detailed in Fig. 14.26.

TABLE 14.13 Command line options for various floating-point ABI arrangements.

Arm® C compiler 6 and gcc floating-point ABI options	Description
`-mfloat-abi=soft`	Soft ABI without FPU hardware: All floating-point operations are handled by the runtime library functions. Values are passed via the integer register bank.
`-mfloat-abi=softfp`	Soft ABI with FPU hardware: This allows the compiled code to generate codes that directly access the FPU. But, if a calculation needs to use a runtime library function, a soft-float calling convention is used (i.e., by using the integer register bank).
`-mfloat-abi=hard`	Hard ABI: This allows the compiled code to generate codes that directly access the FPU and use FPU-specific calling conventions when calling runtime library functions.

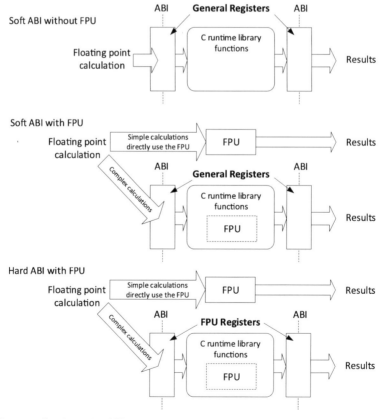

FIG. 14.26 Common floating-point ABI options.

When a software library is compiled for multiple Cortex-M33-based products, which include devices with and without an FPU, the soft ABI option should be used. During the linking stage of an application, if the target processor supports the FPU, a version of the runtime library functions that use the FPU can be inserted by the linker. Although, using soft ABI when compiling a program does not generate floating-point instructions, the application can, because of the library inserted by the linker, still take advantage of the FPU feature when running the runtime library function.

For an enhance performance over the soft ABI, the hard ABI should, if all the floating-point calculations are single precision only, be used. However, for applications which mostly require double precision calculations, the performance of the hard ABI could be lower than one achieved by the soft ABI. This is because when using the hard ABI, the values to be processed are usually transferred using the floating-point register bank. Because the FPU in the Cortex-M33 processor does not support double precision floating-point calculations, the values have to be copied back to the integer register bank to be processed by the software. Since this creates additional overhead, you would, as a result, be better off using the soft ABI with the FPU hardware.

That said, for most applications, where the required access to the floating-point runtime function is far and few between, the performance is about the same whether you are using the hard or the soft ABI.

14.5.5 Special FPU modes

By default, the FPU in the Cortex-M33 processor is already IEEE 754 compliant. Therefore, in most cases there is no need to change the FPU mode settings, which will be detailed below. Please note, if you need to use any of the special FPU modes in your application, you will, typically, need to program the FPSCR and the FPDSCR. If you do not, because the exception handlers use the default IEEE 754 behavior and the rest of the applications use other special FPU modes, there could be inconsistencies, which could subsequently result in floating-point calculation issues.

The special FPU modes are:

Flush-to-Zero mode

Flush-to-Zero mode allows some floating-point calculations to be faster by avoiding the need to calculate results in the denormalized value range (i.e., exponent $=0$). When the value is too small to be represented by the normalized value range (i.e., $0 < $ exponent $ < 0xFF$), the value is replaced with a zero. Flush-to-Zero mode is enabled by setting the FZ bit in the FPSCR and the FPDSCR.

Default NaN mode

In default Not a Number (NaN) mode, if any of the inputs of a calculation is a NaN, of if the operation results in an invalid result, the calculation returns the default NaN (i.e., a non-signaling NaN, which is also known as a quiet NaN). This is slightly different from the default configuration. By default, the default NaN mode is disabled and has the following IEEE 754 standard behaviors:

• An operation that produces an Invalid Operation floating-point exception generates a quiet NaN.

- An operation involving a quiet NaN operand, but is not a signaling NaN operand, returns an input NaN.

The default NaN mode is enabled by setting the DN bit in the FPSCR and in the FPDSCR. In some instances, using the default NaN mode enables the quicker checking of NaN values when calculations are being undertaken.

Alternative Half Precision mode

This mode only affects applications with half precision data __fp16 (see Section 14.1.3). By default, the FPU follows the IEEE 754 standard. If the exponent of the half precision floating-point data is 0x1F, the value is infinity or NaN. In the alternative half precision mode, the value is a normalized value. The alternative half precision mode allows a wider value range, but does not support infinity or NaN.

The Alternative half precision mode is enabled by setting the AHP bit in the FPSCR and in the FPDSCR. To use half precision data, you need to set up your compiler command line options as per Table 14.14.

Rounding modes

The FPU supports four rounding modes as defined in the IEEE 754 standard. You can change the rounding mode in runtime. In C99 (a C language standard), fenv.h defines the four available modes as listed in Table 14.15.

These definitions can be used with the C99 functions defined in fenv.h:

`int fegetround (void)`—returns the currently selected rounding mode and is represented by one of the values of the defined rounding mode macros

`int fesetround(int round)`—changes the currently selected rounding mode. fesetround() and returns zero if the change is successful and non-zero if it is not.

The C library functions should be used when adjusting the rounding mode to ensure that the C runtime library functions are adjusted in the same way as they are in the FPU.

TABLE 14.14 Command line options for using half precision data (__fp16).

	Command line option
Arm Compiler 6 IEEE Half precision	`-mcpu=cortex-m33+fp16` `-march=armv8-m.main+fp16`
gcc IEEE Half precision	`-mfp16-format=ieee`
gcc alternate Half Precision	`-mfp16-format=alternative`

TABLE 14.15 C99 definitions for floating-point rounding modes.

fenv.h macros	Description
FE_TONEAREST	Round to Nearest (RN) mode (default)
FE_UPWARD	Round toward Plus Infinity (RP) mode.
FE_DOWNWARD	Round toward Minus Infinity (RM) mode.
FE_TOWARDZERO	Round toward Zero (RZ) mode.

14.5.6 Power down the FPU

The design of the Cortex-M33 processor allows the FPU to have a power domain that is separated from the processor's core logic. With this optional arrangement, it is possible to power down the FPU when it is not used. And, if the design supports the state retention feature, the FPU can automatically enter state retention mode when the processor is sleeping—or when the FPU is disabled.

If a Cortex-M33 based device has a separate FPU power domain, and if the state retention feature is not available, software can power down the FPU by taking the following steps:

(1) Disabling the FPU by clearing the CP10 and CP11 bit fields in the CPACR, then
(2) Setting both the SU10 and the SU11 bit fields in the CPPWR (Section 15.6).

When the FPU is powered down using the previous steps, the data inside the FPU's registers are lost. Therefore, if the data contents in the FPU are required for a later operation, the FPU should not be powered down. Instead, power can be reduced by simply disabling the FPU by clearing the CP10 and CP11 bit fields.

If the TrustZone security extension is implemented, the Secure software might need to prevent the Non-secure software from accessing the SU10 and the SU11 bit fields in the CPPWR, which, if it did, could result in the Secure data in the FPU being lost. This can be prevented by setting the SUS10 and SUS11 bit fields in the CPPWR, which, when they are, prevents the Non-secure software from accessing the SU10 and the SU11 bit fields.

If a Cortex-M33 based device implements a separate power domain for the FPU, and if the state retention feature is available, then the FPU can automatically switch to state retention mode when the processor is sleeping, or when the FPU is disabled, by clearing the CP10 and CP11 bit fields in the CPACR.

If the SU10 and SU11 bits in the CPPWR is set, the execution of an FPU instruction always results in a UsageFault exception, regardless of whether the FPU has its own power domain.

14.6 Floating-point exceptions

In Section 14.2.6 (which described the FPSCR) I highlighted several floating-point exception status bits. In this section the term exception is not the same as the term exceptions or interrupts, which are present in the NVIC. The floating-point exceptions refer to issues encountered during floating-point processing. Table 14.16 lists the exceptions that are defined in the IEEE 754 standard [3].

In addition to the FPU exceptions listed in Table 14.16, the FPU in the Cortex-M33 also supports an additional exception for "Input Denormal". This is shown in Table 14.17.

The FPSCR provides six sticky bits so that software code can check the sticky bit values to determine whether the calculations carried out were successful. In most cases these flags (i.e., the sticky bits) are ignored by the software (compiler generated code does not check these values).

If you are designing software with high safety requirements, you could add the checking of the FPSCR in your code. However, in some instances not all floating-point calculations are

TABLE 14.16 Floating-point exceptions defined in the IEEE 754 standard.

Exception	FPSCR bit	Example
Invalid operation	IOC	Square root of a negative number (returns a quiet NaN by default)
Division by zero	DZC	Divide by zero or log(0) (returns $+/- \infty$ by default)
Overflow	OFC	A result that is too large to be correctly represented (returns $+/- \infty$ by default)
Underflow	UFC	A result that is very small (returns a denormalized value by default)
Inexact	IXC	The result has been rounded (returns a rounded result by default)

TABLE 14.17 Additional floating-point exception provided in the FPU of the Cortex-M33 processor.

Exception	FPSCR bit	Example
Input Denormal	IDC	A denormalized input value is replaced with a zero in the calculation due to the Flush-to-Zero mode.

carried out by the FPU. Some could be carried out by the C runtime library function. C99 has defined the following functions for checking and clearing the floating-point exception status:

```
#include <fenv.h>

// check floating-point exception flags
int fegetexceptflag(fexcept_t *flagp, int excepts);

// clear floating-point exception flags
int feclearexcept(int excepts);
```

In addition, you can examine and change the configuration of the floating-point runtime library using:

```
int fegetenv(envp);
int fesetenv(envp);
```

For detailed information on these functions, please refer to the C99 documentation and to the manuals supplied by the tool chain vendors.

An alternative to the C language features in C99; some development suites also provide additional functions for accessing the FPU control. For example, in the Arm Compiler (including Keil™ MDK) the __ieee_status() function allows you to easily configure the FPSCR. The function prototype is as follows:

```
// Modify the FPSCR (the older version of the __ieee_status() was __fp_status())
unsigned int __ieee_status(unsigned int mask, unsigned int flags);
```

When using __ieee_status(), the "mask" parameter defines the bits that you want to modify and the "flags" parameter specifies the parameters of the new values of the bit covered by the mask. To make these functions easier to use, fenv.h defines the following macros:

```
#define FE_IEEE_FLUSHZERO              (0x01000000)
#define FE_IEEE_ROUND_TONEAREST        (0x00000000)
#define FE_IEEE_ROUND_UPWARD           (0x00400000)
#define FE_IEEE_ROUND_DOWNWARD         (0x00800000)
#define FE_IEEE_ROUND_TOWARDZERO       (0x00C00000)
#define FE_IEEE_ROUND_MASK             (0x00C00000)
#define FE_IEEE_MASK_INVALID           (0x00000100)
#define FE_IEEE_MASK_DIVBYZERO         (0x00000200)
#define FE_IEEE_MASK_OVERFLOW          (0x00000400)
#define FE_IEEE_MASK_UNDERFLOW         (0x00000800)
#define FE_IEEE_MASK_INEXACT           (0x00001000)
#define FE_IEEE_MASK_ALL_EXCEPT        (0x00001F00)
#define FE_IEEE_INVALID                (0x00000001)
#define FE_IEEE_DIVBYZERO              (0x00000002)
#define FE_IEEE_OVERFLOW               (0x00000004)
#define FE_IEEE_UNDERFLOW              (0x00000008)
#define FE_IEEE_INEXACT                (0x00000010)
#define FE_IEEE_ALL_EXCEPT             (0x0000001F)
```

For example, to clear the Underflow sticky flag, you can use:

```
__ieee_status(FE_IEEE_UNDERFLOW, 0);
```

In the Cortex-M33 processor, the FPU exception status bits are exported to the top level of the processor. Potentially, these exception status bits can be used to trigger an exception at the NVIC. Fig. 14.27 shows a possible hardware signal connection arrangement to enable the FPU exception status bits to be used as an interrupt.

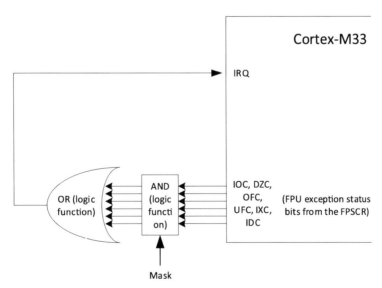

FIG. 14.27   Use of floating-point exception status bit for hardware exception generation.

By connecting the FPU exception status bit to the NVIC, as shown in Fig. 14.27, a system can trigger an interrupt almost immediately when an error condition such as "divide by zero" or "overflow" occurs.

Please note, since interrupt events are imprecise, the generated exception shown in Fig. 14.27 could be delayed by a few cycles. This delay occurs even when the exception is not blocked by other exceptions. As a result, you cannot determine which floating-point instruction triggered the exception. If the processor was executing a higher priority interrupt handler, the interrupt handler for the floating-point exception would not be able start until the other interrupt handler task had finished.

When the FPU exception status is used to trigger exceptions in the NVIC, before the end of the interrupt service routine (i.e., the exception-return), the exception handler needs to clear the following:

- The exception status bits in the FPSCR, and
- The stacked FPSCR in the exception stack frame

If it is not cleared, the exception could be triggered again.

14.7 Hints and tips

14.7.1 Runtime libraries for microcontrollers

Some development suites provide special run time libraries that are optimized for microcontrollers with small memory footprints. For example, with Keil MDK, Arm® DS or DS-5 you can select the MicroLIB for a mathematic function library that is optimized for microcontroller applications (see Fig. 14.25, just above the FPU option). In most cases, these libraries provide the same floating-point functionality as the standard C libraries. However, there can be limitations that impact on IEEE 754 support.

The MicroLIB has the following limitations in terms of IEEE 754 floating-point support:

- Operations involving NaNs, infinities or input denormals that produce indeterminate results. For example, operations that produce a result that is very close to zero, return zero as the result. In IEEE 754, this would normally be represented by a de-normalize value.
- IEEE exceptions cannot be flagged by MicroLIB, and there are no __ieee_status()/ __fp_status() register functions in the MicroLIB.
- The sign of zero is not treated as significant by MicroLIB, and zeroes that are output from the MicroLIB floating-point arithmetic have an unknown sign bit.
- Only the default rounding mode is supported.

Notwithstanding the aforementioned limitations, it is worth pointing out that:

(a) For the majority of embedded applications such limitations do not cause any problem, and
(b) MicroLIB allows applications to be compiled to a smaller size by reducing the size of the library.

14.7.2 Debug operation

Lazy stacking adds some complexity when debugging. When the processor has halted in an exception handler, the stack frame might not contain the contents of the floating-point registers. If the lazy stacking is pended, while you are debugging your code by single stepping, the deferred stacking will take place when the processor executes a floating-point instruction.

References

[1] Armv8-M Architecture Reference Manual. https://developer.arm.com/documentation/ddi0553/am/ (Armv8.0-M only version). https://developer.arm.com/documentation/ddi0553/latest/ (latest version including Armv8.1-M). Note: M-profile architecture reference manuals for Armv6-M, Armv7-M, Armv8-M and Armv8.1-M can be found here: https://developer.arm.com/architectures/cpu-architecture/m-profile/docs.

[2] Armv7-M Architecture Reference Manual. https://developer.arm.com/documentation/ddi0403/latest.

[3] IEEE 754 specifications, IEEE 754-1985: https://ieeexplore.ieee.org/document/30711. IEEE 754-2008: https://ieeexplore.ieee.org/document/4610935.

[4] AN33-Fixed-pointarithmetic on the Arm. https://developer.arm.com/documentation/dai0033/a/.

[5] Arm Compiler 6 ABI options. https://developer.arm.com/documentation/100748/0614/Using-Common-Compiler-Options/Selecting-floating-point-options. GCC ABI options. https://gcc.gnu.org/onlinedocs/gcc/ARM-Options.html.

15

Coprocessor interface and Arm Custom Instructions

15.1 Overview

15.1.1 Introduction

The coprocessor interface and the Arm® Custom Instructions are both optional features on the Arm Cortex®-M33 processor to enable silicon designers to add custom hardware accelerators.

Conceptually, the key difference between these two features is whether the hardware accelerator sits inside or outside of the processor. The coprocessor design concept is shown in Fig. 15.1.

The coprocessor interface has the following characteristics:

- The coprocessor hardware is external to the processor.
- The coprocessor hardware has its own registers, and, optionally, can have its own interface to other hardware. For example, it can have its own bus master interface to access the memory system.

The Arm Custom Instructions concept is shown in Fig. 15.2.
For Arm custom instructions:

- The custom data path for custom-defined data processing is internal to the processor.
- The Arm custom instructions use registers in the existing processor's register banks and does not have its own interface to external hardware.

For both the coprocessor and the Arm Custom Instructions, the instruction encodings are defined in the Armv8-M architecture [1]. Since the Arm Custom Instructions are very new, when this book was written the full details of these instructions were not merged into the Armv8-M Architecture Reference Manual. However, they are now available in a supplementary document for the Armv8-M architecture [2]. The Armv8-M architecture document refers to the Arm Custom Instructions as the Custom Datapath Extension (CDE). They are

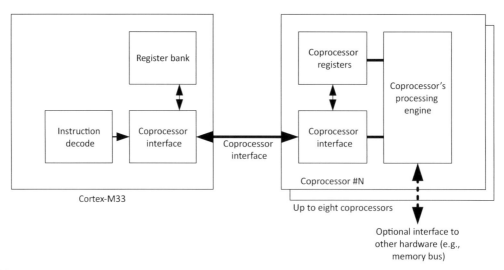

FIG. 15.1　Concept of coprocessor interface.

effectively the same feature. The "Arm Custom Instructions" name is reserved only for Arm products, whereas Custom Datapath Extension (CDE) is a general technical term.

To make it easier for software developers to access the coprocessor and Arm Custom Instructions features in C/C++ programming environments, C intrinsic functions for these instructions have been defined in the Arm C Language Extension (ACLE) [3]. To make use of these new features, software developers only need to upgrade their development tools to the version that supports the new intrinsic functions. Although the design of the coprocessor and Arm Custom Instructions hardware from chip vendors are different, there is no need for chip

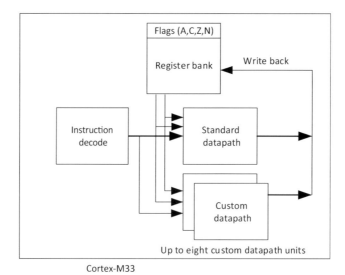

FIG. 15.2　Concept of Arm Custom Instructions.

vendors to customize their compilation tool chains because the instruction encodings and intrinsic functions are predefined in the architecture and tools.

Please note, Arm custom instruction support on the Cortex-M33 processor is available from revision 1, which was released around the mid- 2020. Cortex-M33 based products released prior to revision 1 do not support the Arm Custom Instructions.

Some of the Cortex-M33 based products may not include these features because both the coprocessor interface and the Arm Custom Instructions features are optional.

15.1.2 The purpose of coprocessors and Arm custom instructions

In general, coprocessors and Arm custom instructions enable chip vendors to optimize the design for some of the specialized processing workloads, and, potentially, enable better product differentiation. The coprocessor interface has already been used in several Cortex-M33 based microcontroller products. For example, it has been used for:

- Acceleration of mathematical functions (e.g., trigonometric functions such as sine and cosine)
- Acceleration of DSP functions
- Acceleration of cryptography functions

Because the coprocessor hardware is external to the processor and has its own registers, it can, after a coprocessor operation has started and while the processor executes other instructions, continue to operate in parallel with the Cortex-M33 processor.

Because the coprocessor registers can be accessed with a single clock cycle using coprocessor instructions, a chip design can, in some instances, utilize the coprocessor's interface to enable the quicker access of certain peripheral registers.

Arm custom instructions are designed for the acceleration of specialized data operations and are suitable for operations that are either single cycle or just take a few cycles. Some operations that could benefit from Arm custom instructions include:

- Cyclic redundancy check (CRC) computations
- Specialized data format conversions (e.g., RGBA color data)

Because the execution of Arm Custom Instructions requires direct access to the processor's register banks, the processor cannot, in parallel, execute other instructions. Therefore, if a custom processing operation is expected to take some time (more than a few clock cycles), it is best to implement the hardware accelerator as a coprocessor instead of using the Arm Custom Instructions. By doing so, the processor is able to execute other instructions when the hardware accelerator is running.

15.1.3 Coprocessor interface and Arm Custom Instructions features

The coprocessor interface on the Cortex-M33 supports:

- Up to eight coprocessors.
- For each coprocessor, up to 16 registers. Each of them can be up to 64-bit wide.

- A 64-bit data interface to allow the single-cycle transfer of 64-bit and 32-bit data between the registers of the coprocessor and the processor.
- A handshaking interface, which supports wait states and error response.
- Up to two operation opcodes (op1 and op2)
  - Op1 can be up to 4 bits wide, but some instructions only support a 3-bit op1 field.
  - Op2 is 3 bits wide. This is supported by the MCR, MCR2, MRC, MRC2, CDP, and CDP2 instructions.
- An additional op field bit to indicate instruction variants (i.e., MCR2, MRC2, MCRR2, MRRC2, CDP2).
- The TrustZone® security extension
  - Each coprocessor can be defined as Secure or Non-secure using the SCB->NSACR register.
  - The coprocessor interface supports a security attribute sideband signal to allow the coprocessor to determine the security permission at the finer grained level (i.e., it is possible to define permission per operation—based on the coprocessor register(s) that is used and/or on the type of operation based on the op1 and the op2 signals).
- Power management

  - The Cortex-M33 processor provides a power management interface to allow each coprocessor to be separately powered up or down.
  - The status of the Coprocessor Power Control Register (CPPWR, Section 15.6) in the Cortex-M33 processor is exported from the processor to the coprocessors—this signal connection controls whether each of the coprocessors is allowed to enter a non-retentive low power state (Note: When the coprocessor is in a nonretentive low power state the data inside the coprocessor would be lost). If the TrustZone security extension is implemented, the CPPWR supports TrustZone security.

  Similarly, the Arm custom instruction supports a range of features:

- It supports up to eight custom datapath units.
- It supports the TrustZone security extension by allowing each of the custom datapath units to be defined as Secure or Non-secure using the SCB->NSACR register.
- By architectural definition, Arm Custom Instructions supports up to 15 classes of data processing instructions (Note: some of these instructions are not supported in the Cortex-M33 processor). These instructions have the following characteristics:
  - A wide choice of 32-bit and 64-bit operations, including integer, floating-point and vector (vector support is for the M-profile vector extension in the Armv8.1-M architecture).
  - For each supported data type class, there are a range of instructions for operations with zero, one, two and three operands.
  - For Arm Custom Instructions that operates integer data, there is a choice of updating either the destination register(s) or the APSR flags.
  - For each class of Arm Custom Instructions, there is a normal and an accumulative variant—accumulative variant means the destination register is also one of the input operands.

* For each class of Arm Custom Instructions, there is an immediate data value, which ranges from 3 to 13 bits. This allows multiple Arm custom instructions to be defined and individually identified.
* Arm Custom Instructions support single and multiple cycle operations.
* Arm Custom Instructions support error handling. The custom datapath returns an error status if the instruction/operation specified is not supported. This triggers the UsageFault (i.e., the Undefined Instruction (Undef) and No Coprocessor (NoCP) Table 13.6).

15.1.4 Comparing the coprocessor and the Arm Custom Instructions with memory mapped hardware accelerators

Before the Cortex-M33 processor was available, chip designers had already integrated hardware accelerators into many of their projects using memory mapped hardware (Fig. 15.3).

In many ways, this is similar to the coprocessor interface solution; however, the coprocessor interface method has a number of advantages:

* The coprocessor's interface between the processor and the coprocessor hardware is 64-bit wide and can handle 64-bit and 32-bit transfers. Whereas, the AMBA® AHB bus interface on the Cortex-M33 processor is 32 bits, and therefore, the coprocessor interface provides a higher bandwidth.
* When using a memory mapped register to transfer data, we first need an instruction to place the address value (or base address value of the accelerator) into one of the processor's register. Then another instruction is needed to carry out the actual data transfer. In contrast to the memory map register method, a coprocessor instruction contains the coprocessor number and its register number(s), thus there is no need to use a separate instruction to set up the address.
* A coprocessor instruction can transfer data between the processor and the coprocessor register, as well as pass control information (i.e., custom-defined opcode) at the same time.

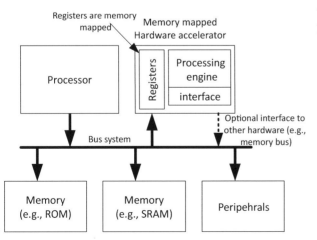

FIG. 15.3 Concept of memory mapped hardware accelerators.

Whereas for memory mapped hardware accelerators you will need to transfer the control information with an additional memory access.

- The data transfers between the processor and the coprocessor hardware is not affected by other activities on the bus systems. For example, it is not delayed by another bus transfer, which could have multiple clock cycles of wait states.

All these advantages also apply to the Arm custom instructions.

15.1.5 Why these are called coprocessors?

Historically, Arm processors, such as the Arm9™ processors, used a separate hardware unit to handle floating-point computations. These hardware units were called coprocessors because they had their own pipeline structure and were coupled to the main processor pipeline with a complex interface. This interface was needed because the coprocessor hardware needed a "pipeline follower" to monitor the flow of instructions. Those coprocessors had their own instruction decoders to decode the floating-point instructions (Fig. 15.4).

As the use of floating-point data became more common, it made sense that the later Arm processors merged the FPU into the main processor. Moreover, as the processor's pipeline got ever more complex, having a complex pipeline follower interface (which differs from processor to processor) was becoming increasingly infeasible. Therefore, the coprocessor interface was removed from subsequent Arm processors (e.g., the Arm11™ processor). However, the concept of having coprocessors remained, and thus, are still being used in many Arm processors as internal units. For example, several coprocessor numbers are reserved inside Arm processors:

- CP15 is used for various system control functions (used by Cortex-A and Cortex-R processors, not used by Cortex-M processors)
- CP14 is reserved for debug functions (used by Cortex-A and Cortex-R processors, not used by Cortex-M processors)
- CP10 and CP11 are reserved for the floating-point unit (used by all Cortex processors)

FIG. 15.4 Concept of coprocessors in the older generation of Arm processors, e.g., Arm9.

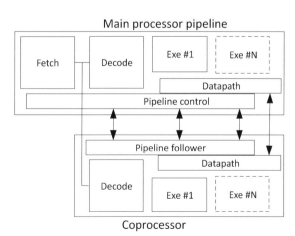

Main processor pipeline

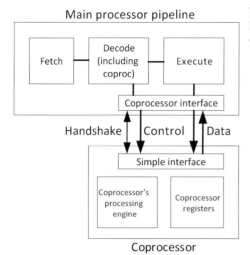

FIG. 15.5 Concept of a coprocessor interface in the Cortex-M33 processor which greatly simplifies the design of coprocessors.

When the product concept for the Cortex-M33 processor was being defined, it was clear that there was an increasing demand in the marketplace to enable chip vendors to differentiate their products from their competitors. To satisfy this demand, Arm re-introduced the coprocessor feature. However, instead of requiring customers to build coprocessor hardware that required a complex interface to couple with the main processor pipeline, a new design concept was used, which provides a much simpler interface. In the new design, the initial decode of the coprocessor instructions is handled by the instruction decoder in the main processor, with the transfer of control information and data between the processor and the coprocessors controlled by using simple handshaking signals (Fig. 15.5).

In addition to the Cortex-M33 processor, the coprocessor interface feature is now also available in the Cortex-M35P and Cortex-M55 processors.

15.2 Overview of the architecture

The coprocessor interface and the Arm Custom Instructions features, both use the concept of a coprocessor ID value. The instruction set architecture uses a bitfield (4-bit) to define which coprocessor is accessed, meaning, in theory, that there could be up to 16 coprocessors attached to a processor. However, only coprocessors ID #0–#7 are allocated for custom-defined solution(s), with these eight units being either:

- coprocessors connected via the coprocessor interface, or
- custom data path units inside the processor.

Other coprocessor numbers are reserved for internal use by the Arm processor (e.g., CP10 and CP11 are used by the FPU and by the Helium processing unit for the Cortex-M55 processor).

Please note, software cannot change how each coprocessor ID is used.

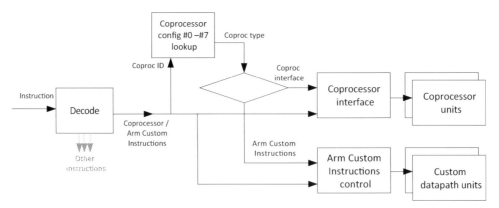

FIG. 15.6 An instruction can be decoded as a coprocessor interface or as Arm Custom Instructions based on the hardware's configuration.

The coprocessor ID #0–#7 are shared between the coprocessor interface and Arm custom instructions. For each coprocessor ID, chip designers need to decide, which way the instruction should be handled, that is, as a coprocessor or as a custom data path unit. This is a decision that needs to be made during the chip design stage.

The instruction encoding of the coprocessor interface operation and Arm Custom Instructions overlaps, and, as such, the instruction decode logic inside the processor needs to take account of the coprocessor hardware configuration that was setup by the chip designer (Fig. 15.6).

Since the instruction encoding overlaps, you may need to provide the Cortex-M33's hardware configuration information to the development tool(s) so that the tool(s) can correctly disassemble the instructions during debugging.

15.3 Accessing coprocessor instructions via intrinsic functions in C

To utilize the coprocessor instructions in the C programming environment, the Arm C language extension (ACLE) [3] defines a range of intrinsic functions to access the coprocessor instructions. These are shown in Table 15.1.

To use these intrinsic functions, you must include the Arm ACLE header file:

```
#include <arm_acle.h>
```

The header file is available when the "__ARM_FEATURE_COPROC" feature macro is defined.

An example of reading a coprocessor register is as follow:

```
unsigned int val;
// CP[x],op1,CRn,CRm,op2
val = __arm_mrc(1, 0, 0, 0, 0);
// coprocessor #1, Opc1=0, CRn=c0, CRm=c0, Opc2=0
```

TABLE 15.1   ACLE defined intrinsic functions for coprocessor access.

Instruction	ACLE defined intrinsic function for coprocessor access
MCR	`void __arm_mcr(coproc, opc1, uint32_t value, CRn, CRm, opc2)`
MCR2	`void __arm_mcr2(coproc, opc1, uint32_t value, CRn, CRm, opc2)`
MRC	`uint32_t __arm_mrc(coproc, opc1, CRn, CRm, opc2)`
MRC2	`uint32_t __arm_mrc2(coproc, opc1, CRn, CRm, opc2)`
MCRR	`void __arm_mcrr(coproc, opc1, uint64_t value, CRm)`
MCRR2	`void __arm_mcrr2(coproc, opc1, uint64_t value, CRm)`
MRRC	`uint64_t __arm_mrrc(coproc, opc1, CRm)`
MRRC2	`uint64_t __arm_mrrc2(coproc, opc1, CRm)`
CDP	`void __arm_cdp(coproc, opc1, CRd, CRn, CRm, opc2)`
CDP2	`void __arm_cdp2(coproc, opc1, CRd, CRn, CRm, opc2)`

and when writing a coprocessor register:

```
unsigned int val;
// CP[x],op1, value,CRn,CRm,op2
__arm_mcr(1, 0, val, 0, 4, 0);
// coprocessor #1, Opc1=0, CRn=c0, CRm=c0, Opc2=0
```

There are also additional intrinsic functions which can be used to support other data types (Table 15.2).

When using the intrinsic functions listed in Table 15.2, the constant character string (that is, "`*special_register`") is based on the following format:

```
cp<coprocessor>:<opc1>:c<CRn>:c<CRm>:<op2>
```

There is an equivalent alternative syntax that can be used and this is:

```
p<coprocessor>:<opc1>:c<CRn>:c<CRm>:<op2>
```

The following code shows how a coprocessor register can be read using one of the intrinsic functions listed in Table 15.2:

```
unsigned int val;
val = __arm_rsr("cp1:0:c0:c0:0"); // coproc #1, op1=0, op2=0
```

To write to a coprocessor register, the following code can be used:

```
unsigned int val;
__arm_wsr("cp1:0:c0:c0:0", val); // coproc #1, op1=0, op2=0
```

Using various programming techniques, for example, C macros, it is straightforward to create easy-to-use software wrappers that layer on top of those intrinsic functions. The use of the software wrappers can make the software much more readable.

TABLE 15.2   Additional ACLE defined intrinsic functions for coprocessor access.

Data types	ACLE defined intrinsic functions for coprocessor access (RSR = Read System Register, WSR = Write System Register)
32-bit	uint32_t __arm_rsr(const char *special_register)
64-bit	uint64_t __arm_rsr64(const char *special_register)
float	float __arm_rsrf(const char *special_register)
double	float __arm_rsrd(const char *special_register)
pointer	void* __arm_rsrp(const char *special_register)
32-bit	void __arm_wsr(const char *special_register, uint32_t value)
64-bit	void __arm_wsr64(const char *special_register, uint64_t value)
float	void __arm_wsrf(const char *special_register, float value)
double	void __arm_wsrf64(const char *special_register, double value)
pointer	void __arm_wsrp(const char *special_register, const void *value)

Please note, because the opcodes (opc1 and opc2) and the "value" parameter (Table 15.1) are encoded within the instructions, the coprocessor number, register identifier and opcode values must be constants. If you attempt to pass a variable into a register or opcode field in an intrinsic function call, you will get an error message during compilation. For example, the symbol "i" in the example below is a variable, leading to the compiler reporting an error:

```
test.c:234:12: error: argument to '__builtin_arm_mrc' must be a constant integer
   data = __arm_mrc(1, 0, i, 1, 0); // Read result
              ^                    ~

.../linux-x86_64/bin/../include/arm_acle.h:639:49: note: expanded from macro
'__arm_mrc'
#define __arm_mrc(coproc, opc1, CRn, CRm, opc2) __builtin_arm_mrc(coproc, opc1,
CRn, CRm, opc2)
                                                        ^         ~~~

1 error generated.
```

The ACLE specification [4] can be found on the Arm website at: https://developer.arm.com/architectures/system-architectures/software-standards/acle.

15.4 Accessing Arm Custom Instructions via the intrinsic functions in C

Revision 1 of the Cortex-M33 processor, which was released mid-2020, supports Arm Custom Instructions. So that software developers have access to the Arm Custom Instructions, Intrinsic functions have been defined for them. However, at the time of writing this book, the specification [3] for this is in beta state and there is, therefore, a remote possibility that some changes could occur after this book has been published.

To use the intrinsic functions for the Arm Custom Instructions, you must include the Arm ACLE header file:

```
#include <arm_cde.h>
```

The header file is available when the "__ARM_FEATURE_CDE" feature macro is defined.

For Arm Custom Instructions that return a result of either a 32-bit integer value or a 64-bit integer value, the following intrinsic functions can be used (Table 15.3).

Similar to the coprocessor intrinsic functions, the coprocessor ID number (that is, "coproc") and the immediate data value (i.e. "imm") that is used when using these functions must be compile-time constant.

When the FPU and the Arm Custom Instructions support are implemented, the following intrinsic functions are available for handling the 32-bit floating point registers (Table 15.4).

Additional intrinsic functions are architecturally defined but are not available in the Cortex-M33 processor. The functions that are not available for the Cortex-M33 processor are the intrinsic functions that deal with double FPU data type and intrinsic functions that deal with vectors in the M-profile vector extension (i.e., Helium).

When using Arm Custom Instructions with Arm Compiler 6 and with the GCC, additional command line options are needed. Instead of using the name "Arm Custom Instructions", these options use the technical term "Custom Datapath Extension" (CDE). For Arm Compiler 6,

TABLE 15.3 ACLE defined intrinsic functions for Arm Custom Instructions for 32-bit and 64-bit scalar data types.

Instruction	ACLE defined intrinsic function for Arm Custom Instructions access
CX1	`uint32_t __arm_cx1(int coproc, uint32_t imm);`
CX1A	`uint32_t __arm_cx1a(int coproc, uint32_t acc, uint32_t imm);`
CX2	`uint32_t __arm_cx2(int coproc, uint32_t n, uint32_t imm);`
CX2A	`uint32_t __arm_cx2a(int coproc, uint32_t acc, uint32_t n, uint32_t imm);`
CX3	`uint32_t __arm_cx3(int coproc, uint32_t n, uint32_t m, uint32_t imm);`
CX3A	`uint32_t __arm_cx3a(int coproc, uint32_t acc, uint32_t n, uint32_t m, uint32_t imm);`
CX1D	`uint64_t __arm_cx1d(int coproc, uint32_t imm);`
CX1DA	`uint64_t __arm_cx1da(int coproc, uint64_t acc, uint32_t imm);`
CX2D	`uint64_t __arm_cx2d(int coproc, uint32_t n, uint32_t imm);`
CX2DA	`uint64_t __arm_cx2da(int coproc, uint64_t acc, uint32_t n, uint32_t imm);`
CX3D	`uint64_t __arm_cx3d(int coproc, uint32_t n, uint32_t m, uint32_t imm);`
CX3DA	`uint64_t __arm_cx3da(int coproc, uint64_t acc, uint32_t n, uint32_t m, uint32_t imm);`

TABLE 15.4   ACLE defined intrinsic functions for Arm Custom Instructions for 32-bit single precision register access.

Instruction	ACLE defined intrinsic function for Arm Custom Instructions access
VCX1	`uint32_t __arm_vcx1_u32(int coproc, uint32_t imm);`
VCX1A	`uint32_t __arm_vcx1a_u32(int coproc, uint32_t acc, uint32_t imm);`
VCX2	`uint32_t __arm_vcx2_u32(int coproc, uint32_t n, uint32_t imm);`
VCX2A	`uint32_t __arm_vcx2a_u32(int coproc, uint32_t acc, uint32_t n, uint32_t imm);`
VCX3	`uint32_t __arm_vcx3_u32(int coproc, uint32_t n, uint32_t m, uint32_t imm);`
VCX3A	`uint32_t __arm_vcx3a_u32(int coproc, uint32_t acc, uint32_t n, uint32_t m, uint32_t imm);`

you can specify which coprocessor number is assigned to the CDE when compiling a program by using the following option:

- `"armclang __target=arm-arm-none-eabi -march=armv8-m.main+cdecpN"`

The above command is for an Armv8-M processor with the Main Extension, where N is in the range 0–7.

The command line for the "fromelf" utility in the Arm Compiler 6 toolchain also needs to be updated when using the CDE Instructions. To specify which coprocessor, number is used for the CDE, the "__coprocN=*value*" command line option should be added: where N is the coprocessor ID in the range of 0–7, and where "*value*" is either "cde" or "CDE". If a coprocessor ID is not used for the CDE, the "*value*" should be "generic". Please note, you must use the "__cpu" option when using "__coprocN=value".

For the GCC tool chain, the CDE instructions are supported from version 10 (i.e., GCC10) and the following command line options are used to define which coprocessor ID ("N" in the following commands) is used for integer, floating-point and vector CDE instructions:

- `"-march=armv8-m.main+cdecpN -mthumb"`
- `"-march=armv8-m.main+fp+cdecpN -mthumb"`
- `"-march=armv8.1-m.main+mve+cdecpN -mthumb"`

15.5 Software steps to take when enabling the coprocessor and the Arm Custom Instructions

By default, all coprocessors are disabled at reset and, thus, to proceed software needs to undertake the following steps to enable the coprocessor or the Arm Custom Instructions:

(1) Configure the security attribute of each coprocessor ID: Because each of the coprocessors can be defined as either Secure or Non-secure, that is, by using a register called NSACR (Non-secure Access Control Register, Section 14.2.4), Secure firmware needs to program the NSACR register to define, which coprocessor(s) should be accessible from the Non-secure world. The NSACR register is Secure privileged access only. The coprocessor interface also contains a security attribute signal, so, even if a coprocessor is defined as Non-secure, a chip designer can design coprocessor hardware, which filters the operations based on the security attribute. This means that some of the operations/features would only be available to Secure software. Because the coprocessor power control is TrustZone aware, Secure firmware must also set up the CPPWR (Section 15.6) if the TrustZone security extension is being used.

(2) Enable the coprocessor: After reset, coprocessors are, by default, disabled/powered-down to save power. Before using the coprocessor instructions and/or the Arm Custom Instructions, the corresponding coprocessor (#0–#7) would need to be enabled by programming the SCB->CPACR (Section 14.2.3).

If the coprocessor specified in the coprocessor instruction(s) is not implemented, or is disabled, a UsageFault would be triggered. If the UsageFault is disabled or masked, the HardFault would execute instead.

15.6 Coprocessor power control

If a coprocessor unit is disabled, it can be powered down to save power. Inside the Cortex-M33 processor, there is a programmable register called Coprocessor Power Control Register (CPPWR). This register is used for power management purposes (Fig. 15.7).

This register is only be accessible in privileged state and is not banked between security states. In the CPPWR, there are two bits for each of the coprocessor ID (#0–#7), and they are described as follows (the coprocessor ID is, for reference purposes, noted as <n> below):

- The State Unknown (SU<n>)bit, if set to 1, allows the coprocessor to be completely powered down (that is, the state becomes unknown) when it is disabled by the SCB->CPACR register. If the SU<n> bit is set to 0 (that is, default), then the coprocessor is not allowed to completely power down. If the coprocessor <n> is enabled, it does not get powered down (except in the case of a system power loss).

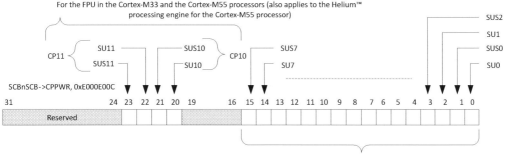

FIG. 15.7   Coprocessor Power Control Register (SCBnSCB->CPPWR, 0xE000E00C).

- The State Unknown Secure (SUS) bit indicates whether the corresponding SU<n> bit is Secure access only (when the SUS is set to 1) or whether it is accessible from both the Secure and Non-secure worlds (when the SUS is set to 0, i.e., default).

If the TrustZone security extension is not implemented, then the SUS bits are not implemented.

When the TrustZone security extension is implemented, Secure privileged software can access the Non-secure view of the CPPWR register via the Non-secure alias address 0xE002E00C (SCBnSCB_NS->CPPWR).

The SUS11, SU11, SUS10, and SU10 bits in the CPPWR register are allocated to the FPU (and the Helium processing unit in the Cortex-M55 processor). The setting for CP10 and CP11 must be identical—that is, SUS11==SUS10, and SU11==SU10.

When a coprocessor <n> is disabled and if the corresponding SU is set to 1, the power management in the chip could power down the coprocessor and, as a result, the previous state of the logic hardware could be lost. However, depending on the power management design of the chip, a power down feature might not be available or, potentially, a state retention feature could be implemented. In these cases, the state of the coprocessor unit might be retained even though the software control had allowed the coprocessor to be powered down.

Although the custom datapath units for Arm Custom Instructions do not have internal state storage (i.e., the operational states are stored in the processor's register bank), software must still ensure that the SU bit in the CPPWR is 0 before using Arm Custom Instructions.

15.7 Hints and tips

Software developers creating application codes are unlikely to require the direct use of the intrinsic functions described in Sections 15.3 and 15.4. This is because microcontroller vendors can make the chips easier to use by:

- Creating software libraries—software developers creating applications only need to access APIs in the libraries.
- Adding C macros that map into intrinsic function calls—By doing so, software developers can access the intrinsic functions indirectly via the aforementioned C macros. This has the same look and feel as calling C APIs.

When using coprocessor units connected via the coprocessor interface, and if multiple application tasks are trying to access the same coprocessor unit, then software will need to deal with the management of the resource conflict by adding semaphores or something of a similar nature. In this aspect, this is no different to what occurs when using a memory mapped hardware accelerator. The resource conflict problem is not applicable when using Arm Custom Instructions because all software states are held in the processor's registers and the context switching of these registers is handled by the embedded OS.

Please note, the debugger does not have a direct view of the coprocessor registers because they are external to the processor. As a result, many chip designers add a bus interface to make those registers visible in the memory map. Using this method, the debugger is able to examine those coprocessor registers as peripheral registers.

References

[1] Armv8-M Architecture Reference Manual. https://developer.arm.com/documentation/ddi0553/am" (Armv8.0-M only version). https://developer.arm.com/documentation/ddi0553/latest (latest version including Armv8.1-M). Note: M-profile architecture reference manuals for Armv6-M, Armv7-M, Armv8-M and Armv8.1-M can be found here: https://developer.arm.com/architectures/cpu-architecture/m-profile/docs.

[2] Arm Architecture Reference Manual Supplement, Custom Datapath Extension for Armv8-M Documentation. https://developer.arm.com/documentation/ddi0607/latest.

[3] ACLE Version Q2 2020—Custom Datapath Extension. https://developer.arm.com/documentation/101028/0011/Custom-Datapath-Extension.

[4] ACLE Specification. https://developer.arm.com/architectures/system-architectures/software-standards/acle.

Introduction to the debug and trace features

16.1 Introduction

16.1.1 Overview

A processor is not going to be of any use unless you can program it. And to program a processor-based system like a microcontroller you need a range of features to help you develop and test the codes. This is where debug and trace features come to the fore. What makes these features even more important is that many embedded systems have no display or keyboard (unlike a personal computer). As such, the debug and trace connection(s) are the key communication channels which enable software developers to not only gain visibility of the software operations, but the internal state of the processor system as well.

As illustrated in Figs. 2.1 and 2.2 in Chapter 2, debug connections are present on many development boards and some of these come with a built-in USB debug adaptor (or debug probe). If the board is not so equipped, you will need to use an external one. Whether internal or external, the essential debug connection helps you to:

- Download the compiled program image to the board: this might involve the programming of the embedded flash memories.
- Handle debug operations (e.g., halting, resuming, reset, single stepping, etc.).
- Access the memories in the device, including trace buffer (if implemented on the device); which helps provide crucial information when troubleshooting.

In microcontroller devices, there are two types of commonly used debug communication protocols. They might coexist on the same device and, when they do, they share connection pins, but only one of them can be used at a time. These protocols are:

- Serial Wire Debug (SWD)—this only requires two signals (SWDCLK and SWDIO) and is very popular in Arm® based microcontrollers.

- JTAG—this uses either four signals (TCK, TMS, TDI, TDO) or five signals (with the additional nTRST for test reset).

In order to reduce debug pin usage, some microcontrollers omit the Joint Test Action Group (JTAG) debug protocol capability and only support the Serial Wire Debug protocol. Some Cortex®-M microcontrollers support both the SWD and JTAG debug protocols and also supports dynamic switching between the two protocols with a special bit sequence on the TMS/SWDIO pin. Because these two protocols can share pins (Fig. 16.1), you can have a single debug connection that supports both protocols and, by adjusting the debug setting of the project in the debug environment, can select which debug protocol to use.

Some of the debug adaptors also provide real-time trace connections. At protocol level, debug and trace connections are separated, but they can still coexist on the same debug connector and debug adaptor. With real-time trace, you can collect information about the execution of the software when the processor system is still running. This provides the following:

- Instruction execution information (But only when the Embedded Trace Macrocell (ETM) is implemented and a parallel trace connection is supported in the setup),
- Profiling information,
- Selective data trace,
- Software generated trace information (e.g., the printf message can be redirected to the trace connection).

On many Cortex-M devices there are two types of trace protocol:

- A single pin trace output called SWO—this has limited trace data bandwidth but is supported by many low-cost debug adaptors. This signal can be shared with the TDO and is enabled when using the Serial Wire Debug protocol.
- A parallel trace port mode—this typically has five signals (4 bits of trace data and a trace clock) and has higher trace bandwidth (this is essential when using ETM trace).

There are several standardized debug and trace connector arrangements, and these are detailed in appendix A. With these debug connector layouts, a single connect can offer JTAG/ Serial Wire Debug and, optionally, a trace connection (Fig. 16.2).

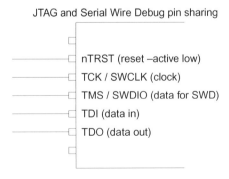

JTAG and Serial Wire Debug pin sharing

nTRST (reset –active low)
TCK / SWCLK (clock)
TMS / SWDIO (data for SWD)
TDI (data in)
TDO (data out)

FIG. 16.1 Pin sharing between JTAG and Serial Wire debug protocol.

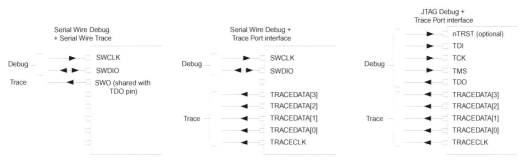

FIG. 16.2   Common debug and trace connection arrangements.

The left-hand side of Fig. 16.2 shows a setup which is commonly used for low cost debug adaptors. With just three pins of connection, as well as being able to carry out debug operations you also get access to basic trace features. Although this is unable to support real-time instruction trace using the ETM (which needs a higher trace bandwidth), it does support many other trace features.

The trace connection is not available in a number of Cortex-M based microcontrollers. However, not all trace features require a dedicated trace connection. For example, if the microcontroller device supports the Micro Trace Buffer (MTB) for instruction tracing, a portion of the SRAM can be allocated for the trace buffer and the trace data can then, after the processor has stopped, be collected via a debug connection.

16.1.2 CoreSight architecture

The debug and trace support in the Cortex processors are based on the CoreSight™ architecture. This architecture covers a wide spectrum, including the debug interface protocols, on chip bus for debug access, control of debug components, security features, trace data interface, etc.

It is not necessary to have in-depth knowledge of CoreSight technology to develop software. For readers who would like more information on the CoreSight technology, I recommend, for an overview of the architecture, the CoreSight Technology System Design Guide [1]. For those wanting even more information on the CoreSight Debug Architecture and on the Cortex-M specific debug system designs, the following documents should be viewed:

- CoreSight Architecture Specification (version 2.0 ARM IHI 0029) [2].
- ARM® Debug Interface v5.0/5.1 (e.g., ARM IHI 0031) [3]—this contains programmer's model details for the debug connection components (I will cover Debug Port and Access Port later in this chapter) and covers Serial Wire and JTAG communication.
- Embedded Trace Macrocell™ Architecture Specification (ARM IHI 0014 and ARM IHI 0064)—details the ETM trace packet format and the programmer's model [4, 5].
- Armv8-M Architecture Reference Manual [6]: this covers the debug support that is available on the Cortex-M23 and Cortex-M33 processors.

This CoreSight debug architecture is very scalable and:

- Supports single as well as multiple processor systems- and even other design blocks that are not processors (e.g., Mali GPU).
- Allows multiple options for debug and trace interface protocols.

One characteristic of the CoreSight debug system is that the debug interface (Serial Wire Debug/JTAG) and the trace interface (e.g., Trace Port Interface Unit) modules are separated from the debug components inside the processor (Fig. 16.3). This arrangement enables a single debug and trace connection to be shared between multiple processors using a scalable debug bus and trace bus network; and allows processors to be used in both single processor and multiple-processor systems with the same generic debug and trace bus interfaces.

In addition to supporting single and multiple processors, CoreSight architecture also:

- Supports TrustZone debug authentication.
- Allows debug tools to detect the available debug and trace components via a look-up-table based mechanism.

The debug and trace interface components (e.g., trace port interface unit) used in many Cortex-M based microcontrollers are designed to be compatible with CoreSight. However, these components are different from those that are used on high-end System-on-Chip designs because they are designed specifically for the smaller silicon area and low power Cortex-M processor systems.

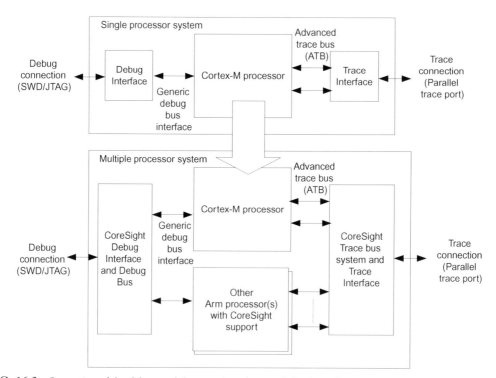

FIG. 16.3   Separation of the debug and the trace interface modules from the processor.

16.1.3 Classification of debug and trace features

CoreSight debug and trace features are classified as per Fig. 16.4.
Invasive debugging: this includes the following features

- Core debug—Program halting, single stepping, reset, resume
- Breakpoints
- Data watchpoints
- Direct access to the processor's internal register via the debug connection (either read or write: this can only be carried out when the processor is halted)

Note: When the Debug Monitor exception handler is used for debugging, it changes the program execution flow and therefore is classified as invasive.
Non-invasive debugging: this includes the following features

- On-the-fly memory/peripheral access
- Instruction trace (through the ETM or the MTB)
- Data trace (available on Armv8-M Mainline processors. It uses the same comparators that are used for data watchpoint, but in this instance they are configured for data trace)
- Software generated trace, which is also known as Instrumentation Trace. To use this feature, software code would need to be added and would have to be executed during runtime. However, the overall application timing is unlikely to be affected by adding this additional software.
- Profiling (using profiling counters or PC sampling features)

Note: These features have very little or no effect on the program flow and therefore are classified as non-invasive.

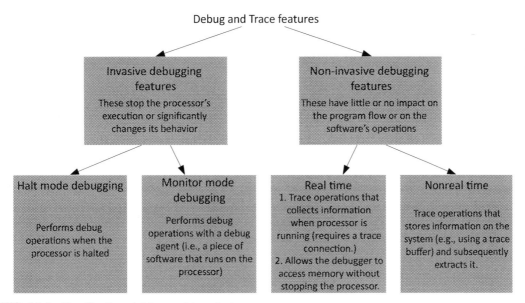

FIG. 16.4 Classification of debug and trace features.

In CoreSight architecture, the separation of Invasive and Non-invasive debug and trace operations is closely related to debug authentication support in the TrustZone security extension. The debug authentication settings of the Cortex-M processor are defined using an interface which controls, with separate signals, invasive, and non-invasive debug/trace permissions. Further information on this can be found in Section 16.2.7.

16.1.4 Debug and trace features summary

A summary of the available debug and trace features are listed in Table 16.1. Please note, these features are optional, and therefore may not be used by the chip designers. Some of the options, like the number of hardware comparators for breakpoint and watchpoint, can be configured by chip designers.

Many of these debug features are configurable by chip designers. For example, an ultra-low power sensor device based on a Cortex-M processor can have a reduced number of breakpoint and watchpoint comparators for lowering the power consumption. Also, because some of the components, such as the MTB and the ETM are optional, some Cortex-M23 and Cortex-M33 microcontrollers might not have instruction trace support.

The trace features offered by the DWT and the ITM are often referred to as the Serial Wire Viewer (SWV), which are a collection of trace capabilities that are available on the Cortex-M33 and Armv7-M processors. With a single pin serial protocol, a wide range of information, such as data trace, exception event trace, profiling trace, and instrumentation trace (i.e., software generated trace), can be transmitted to the debug host in real-time. By so doing, the visibility of the system's operations is enhanced.

16.2 Debug architecture details

16.2.1 Debug connection

Inside an Arm processor system, the Serial Wire/JTAG signals are connected to the debug system via a number of stages, as shown in Fig. 16.5. The hardware module that handles the SWD or JTAG interface protocol is called the Debug Access Port (DAP).

The DAP provides a generic AMBA® AHB bus interface—the same bus protocol that is used by the processor to access the memory system [7]. For the majority of Cortex-M based devices, an area optimized DAP is used which supports just one processor connection. For devices with multiple processors, a configurable DAP from CoreSight SoC-400/SoC-600, which can be configured to include multiple Access Port submodules to support multiple processor systems, is normally used.

The first stage of the debug connection is handled by the DP (Debug Port) submodule, which translates the SWD or JTAG protocol to a generic read/write bus access using the AMBA® APB protocol [8]. By using a generic bus protocol to handle the debug transfers in the DAP module, the structure of the DAP can be expanded to support multiple processors. In theory, you can have hundreds of Cortex-M processors connected to the internal debug bus inside the DAP, each via an Access Port (AP) submodule. The DP submodule also provides a power management handshaking interface so that the debug subsystem in a system-on-chip

TABLE 16.1 Debug and trace features in the Cortex-M23 and Cortex-M33 processors.

Feature	Cortex-M23	Cortex-M33	Notes
JTAG or Serial Wire debug protocol	Typically, just one of the debug protocols is implemented to reduce area/power	Typically supports both, and allows dynamic switching	The debug interface is external to the processor and can be swapped to a different CoreSight debug access port module
Core debug—halting, single stepping, resume, reset, register accesses	Yes	Yes	—
Debug Monitor exception	No	Yes	This is only available in Armv8-M Mainline processors
On-the-fly memory and peripheral access	Yes	Yes	Yes
Hardware breakpoint comparators	Up to four	Up to eight	—
Software breakpoints (Breakpoint instruction)	Unlimited	Unlimited	See Section 5.22
Hardware watchpoint comparators	Up to four	Up to four	—
Instruction Trace with ETM	Yes (ETMv3.5)	Yes (ETMv4.2)	Requires a trace connection
Instruction Trace with MTB	Yes	Yes	—
Selective data trace using DWT	No	Yes	Requires a trace connection
Software trace (Instrumentation Trace)	No	Yes	Requires a trace connection
Profiling counters	No	Yes	Requires a trace connection
PC Sampling	Via a debugger read access only	Via a debugger read access or via a trace connection	With the Cortex-M33, periodic PC samples can be exported to the trace output
Debug authentication	Yes	Yes	Four control signals if TrustZone is implemented, otherwise only two signals
CoreSight architecture compliant	Yes	Yes	Allows the easy integration of the debug system for larger multicore SoC designs

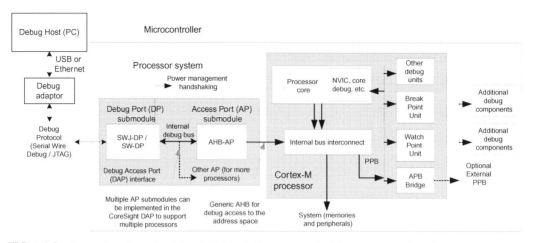

FIG. 16.5 Connections from the debug interface to the processor's debug components and memory system.

design can be powered down when the debug system is not being used. When a debugger is connected, the debug host requests the debug subsystem of the chip to be powered up using the handshaking interface. After doing so, debug operations can then be carried out.

The AP (Access Port) submodule provides the second stage of converting the debug transfer. Although each AP submodule only takes up a small address space on the internal debug bus, the conversion of the debug transfers handled by the AP submodule allows "read/write" access to the 4GB address range of the Cortex-M processor. The AHB-AP submodule provides an AMBA® AHB interface, which is connected to the internal interconnect of the processor, and has access to the memories, peripherals as well as the debug components inside the processor(s). In CoreSight SoC-400/SoC-600, there are other types of Access Port which provide other forms of bus interfaces, e.g., APB and AXI.

In a TrustZone based system, the DAP can be programmed to mark a debug access as Secure or Non-secure. Additional debug authentication control features (see Section 16.2.7 for further information) are provided in Armv8-M processors to handle the permission checks. If a debug access is disallowed by the TrustZone authentication setting, an error response is returned to the DAP.

Because the DAP is decoupled from the processor and is connected to the processor via a generic bus interface, the DAP can be exchanged with a different version/variant of the DAP. The DAP modules that come with the Cortex-M23 and Cortex-M33 processors are optimized for a small silicon area, and are based on the Arm Debug Interface (ADI), specification v5.0–v5.2 [3]. However, if a chip designer is designing a debug system with Arm CoreSight SoC-600 for the Cortex-M23/Cortex-M33 processor, the DAP interface would be based on Arm ADIv6 [9]. Although there are differences between ADIv5.x and ADIv6 from the debug tool perspective, the differences are handled by the debug tools, and should not, therefore, affect the application software being developed. Software developers are thus unlikely to notice any difference when using a device with a different release of the DAP module.

Please note, software running on the Cortex-M33 processor is able to access its debug components and debug registers. However, for the Cortex-M23 processor, only the debug host connected to the processor can gain access to the debug components, but the software running on the processor cannot. Because Armv8-M Baseline does not support the Debug Monitor feature, software does not need to be enabled to access the debug components. This means that the processor's internal bus system can be simplified, which, in turn, reduces the silicon area and the power consumption of the processor.

16.2.2 Trace connection—Real time trace

Trace connection provides a method of outputting real time information on the processor's operations. There are various types of trace sources inside a Cortex-M processor. These are:

- Embedded Trace Macrocell (ETM)—This provide instruction trace.
- The Data Watchpoint and Trace (DWT) unit—The DWT in Armv8-M Mainline processors can be used to generate selective data trace, profiling trace and event (i.e., exception) trace.
- Instrumentation Trace Macrocell—This unit allows software to generate debug messages (e.g., printf, RTOS aware debugging support).

Note: Unlike the ETM, instruction tracing using the Micro Trace Buffer (MTB) does not require a trace connection.

The trace data from the aforementioned trace sources are transferred via an internal trace bus network using the AMBA® ATB (Advanced Trace Bus) protocol [10]. The information transfer is based on a packetized protocol, each packet containing a number of bytes of information. Each trace source has their own packet encoding, with the debug host needing to decode the packets once it has received the information.

Trace data from various trace sources are merged into a single ATB bus using the CoreSight Trace Funnel component, as shown in Fig. 16.6. Each trace source is assigned an ID value, with the ID being propagated with the trace packets in the ATB trace bus system. When the trace data reaches the Trace Port Interface Unit (TPIU), the trace ID values are encapsulated inside the trace port data formatting so that the debug host can again separate the trace streams.

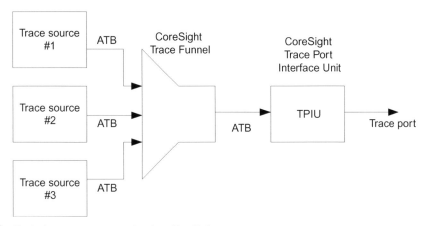

FIG. 16.6   Typical trace stream merging in a CoreSight system.

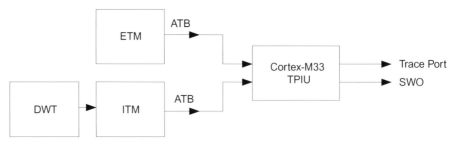

FIG. 16.7   Trace sources and trace connections in a single Cortex-M processor system.

After being enabled by a debugger, the trace sources operate independently. In order to enable correlation between the different trace streams, a timestamp mechanism is provided. In the Cortex-M23 and Cortex-M33 processors, the trace source components (e.g., an ETM) support a 64-bit timestamp input value which is shared between multiple trace sources.

In the Cortex-M33 (Armv8-M Mainline) and Armv7-M processors, the DWT and ITM share the same trace data FIFO and ATB interface (i.e., they are considered as a single trace source in the ATB bus). In order to reduce the silicon area, the TPIU for Cortex-M is designed to combine the functions of both the Trace Point Interface Unit (TPIU) and the trace funnel (Fig. 16.7). Additionally, the TPIU also supports the single pin SWO output, which itself supports a low bandwidth trace connection with a single pin—something which is very popular with microcontroller software developers.

The trace packet protocols for the DWT and the ITM are documented in the Armv8-M Architecture Reference Manual [6]. For Armv7-M processors, please refer to Armv7-M Architecture Reference Manual [11]. For ETM trace packet format details, please refer to the ETM Architecture Specification Documentation (Ref. [4] for the Cortex-M23 ETM and Ref. [5] for the Cortex-M33 ETM).

16.2.3 Trace buffer

Instead of using the TPIU to output trace data, it is possible to direct the trace information into a trace buffer for it to be then collected by the debugger using a debug connection. In Cortex-M processors systems there are two types of trace buffer solutions:

- Micro Trace Buffer (MTB)—this uses a small portion of the system's SRAM for instruction trace. It contains the trace generation unit, SRAM interface and bus interface. When MTB trace is not in use, this unit works as a normal AHB to SRAM bridging device. Further information on the MTB is covered in Section 16.3.7 [12].
- CoreSight Embedded Trace Buffer (ETB) [13]—this uses a dedicated SRAM to hold trace data which has been generated by various trace sources and which has been transferred by the trace bus (AMBA® ATB) [10].

When a Cortex-M based device only has a small number of interface pins and the application has used all the pins, the use of trace port for trace capturing is not possible. When this occurs, the CoreSight ETB can be used for trace data collection. To make the design more flexible, the trace bus system in the chip can include a trace replicator component which

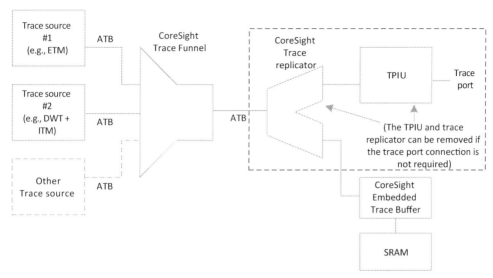

FIG. 16.8   Using a CoreSight Embedded Trace Buffer (ETB) with a Cortex-M processor.

selectively directs trace data to either the ETB for storage in the SRAM or, when the application does not need all the pins, to a trace connection (Fig. 16.8). To allow a debugger to collect the trace data from the trace buffer using normal memory access, the ETB module is accessed via either the Private Peripheral Bus or via the system bus.

Potentially, the TPIU and replicator can be removed, with the trace output from the trace funnel being directly collected by the ETB.

The ETB and TPIU each have their own particular advantages (Table 16.2).

For most Cortex-M microcontrollers, the TPIU solution is used as it does not require a dedicated SRAM, which means a lower silicon cost.

16.2.4 Debug modes

When writing software, there is often a need to analyze software operations to

- understand how the system operates
- determine the reason for a particular failure
- see if there are better ways to optimize the software.

TABLE 16.2   Comparison of the ETB and TPIU trace capture solutions.

Advantages of the ETB trace solution	Advantages of the TPIU trace solution
It does not require a trace connection and uses the same JTAG or Serial Wire debug connection to extract trace information.	Trace history could be unlimited as trace data is streamed to the debug host in real-time.
The ETB can operate at a high clock speed and provides a very high trace bandwidth. In contrast, the trace bandwidth available by using the TPIU is restricted by the trace pin's toggling speed.	Does not require a dedicated SRAM.

To achieve these aims, it is often essential to stop the application, to examine and, optionally, modify the system's states. There are two ways to do this:

1. Halt mode debugging: When the software developer requests the suspension of the software, or when a debug event has occurred, the processor enters halt mode, which stops the processor from executing any further instructions. Once the processor is halted, the debugger is able to examine and modify the internal states of the processor (e.g., the registers in the register banks) and decide whether to resume the operation, whether to single step, or, if needed, whether to reset the system.

2. Monitor mode debugging: A piece of software called a debug agent can either be integrated into the software or can be integrated into preloaded firmware to support the debug operations. The debug agent communicates with the debugger through a communication channel so that debug operations can, via software, be carried out (Fig. 16.9). When a debug event occurs, the processor executes the Debug Monitor exception (Type 12) in the debug agent so that the "application" which was running is suspended. Instead of triggering the debug agent by way of a debug event, the debug agent can, instead, be triggered by a "stop/suspend" request from the software developer via the communication channel. When the debug agent is running, the state(s) of the suspended application (which is saved in the memory) can be examined and can then be resumed or single stepped. But, at the same time, the higher priority interrupts can, while the debugging operations are being carried out, still be executed.

Inside the Cortex-M processor System Control Space (SCS), there are a number of debug control registers for controlling debug operations. These include registers for enabling/disabling halt mode or monitor mode debugging. Although halt mode debugging is the most popular debug method by far, it is worth pointing out that monitor mode debugging is also supported by the Arm eco-system (e.g., Segger—https://www.segger.com/products/debug-probes/j-link/technology/monitor-mode-debugging/).

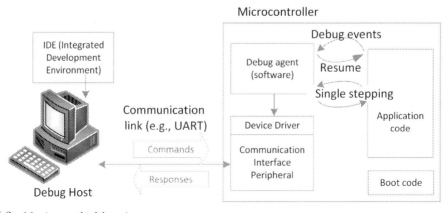

FIG. 16.9   Monitor mode debugging concept.

TABLE 16.3 Comparison of Halt mode and Monitor mode debugging.

Halt mode debugging	Monitor mode debugging
Is supported on all Arm Cortex-M processors	Supported on Armv7-M and Armv8-M Mainline processors. Not available on Armv8-M Baseline (e.g., Cortex-M23) or Armv6-M processors.
Does not require memory for debug agent	Requires some program and RAM memory spaces. Some RAM locations can be changed by the debug agent software as the debug agent needs program and RAM space.
Debugs over Serial-Wire Debug or JTAG interface	Debugs over communication channel (e.g., UART).
Can debug any code, including NMI and HardFault handlers	Can debug codes that have a lower exception priority level than the debug monitor, but cannot debug the NMI, HardFault or other exception handlers with the same or a higher priority level. Debugging is also prohibited when the Debug Monitor is blocked by interrupt mask registers.
Suitable for silicon bring-up (when there is no software preloaded on the chip)	It is possible to allow some software to continue to execute while other software components are being debugged.
Debug operations can be carried out even if the main stack is in an invalid state (e.g., the MSP pointing to an invalid address)	Requires the main stack and communication interface driver (for the debug agent) to be in an operational state.
The SysTick timer is stopped in Halt mode	The SysTick timer continues to run during debugging.
Interrupts can be pended, invoked or masked during single stepping.	A newly arrived interrupt can be pended and served if it has higher priority level than the debug monitor.

Table 16.3 compares halt mode debugging with monitor mode debugging.

In most microcontroller development projects, halt mode debugging is much more popular because it is powerful and because of its ease of use. However, there are instances where monitor mode debugging is more suitable. For example, if the microcontroller is used to control an engine or a motor, stopping the microcontroller for halt mode debugging might mean that we lose control of the engine or the motor, which, obviously, can be undesirable or even dangerous. In some cases, the sudden termination of a motor control circuit could cause physical damage to the system being tested. In such a case monitor mode debugging should be used.

In a system that uses a debug agent for debugging, the debug agent starts and enables the communication interface (which communicates with the debugger running on the debug host) after booting up. To stop the application, the debug host issues a command to stop and, by so doing, the execution stays inside the debug agent. The software developer can then examine the system states via the software control process inside the debug agent. Similarly, if a debug event is triggered during the execution of the application code, the debug agent takes over and the debug host receives a notification that the application code has stopped, enabling the software developer to debug the application.

16.2.5 Debug events

During debugging, the processor enters halt mode or debug monitor when:

- A stop (halt) request is raised by the software developer, or
- After the execution of an instruction during single stepping, or
- When a debug event has occurred

On a Cortex-M processor, a debug event can be caused:

- By the execution of a breakpoint instruction (BKPT)
- When a program execution hits a breakpoint indicated by the breakpoint unit
- By an event emanating from the Data Watchpoint and Trace (DWT) unit: the event could be triggered by a data watchpoint, a program counter match or a cycle counter match.
- By an external debug request: at the processor's boundary, there is an input signal called EDBGRQ. The connection of this signal is device specific. It could be tied low, connected to a vendor specific debug component or could be used for multicore synchronized debug support.
- By a vector catch event: this is a programmable feature that, when enabled, either halts the processor right after a system reset or when certain fault exceptions have occurred. It is controlled by a register called the Debug Exception and Monitor Control Register (DEMCR, at address 0xE000EDFC). Further information on the DEMCR can be found in Table 16.11. The vector catch mechanism is commonly used by debuggers to halt the processor at the beginning of a debug session (after the flash image has updated), or after the processor has reset.

When a debug event occurs, the processor might enter halt mode, it might enter the debug monitor exception or it might ignore the request based on a range of conditions (Fig. 16.10).

The handling of a monitor mode debug is a different from halt mode because the Debug Monitor exception is just another type of exception and can be affected by the current priority level of the processor.

After debug operations:

- If the halt mode debugging is used, the debugger resumes operations by writing to one of the debug control registers in the processor to clear the halting request.
- If the monitor debug is used, the debug agent resumes operations by carrying out an exception return.

Similar to exceptions, debug events are either synchronous or asynchronous. For example:

- The execution of a breakpoint instruction, a "vector catch" or when a program execution hits a breakpoint set in the breakpoint unit, are all synchronous. When the breakpoint event is accepted, the processor stops the execution of the instruction and either enters halt mode or the debug monitor. The program counter visible to the debugger, or the stacked return address in the case of monitor mode debugging, is the same address as the breakpoint location, or is the first instruction of the exception handler for vector catch events.

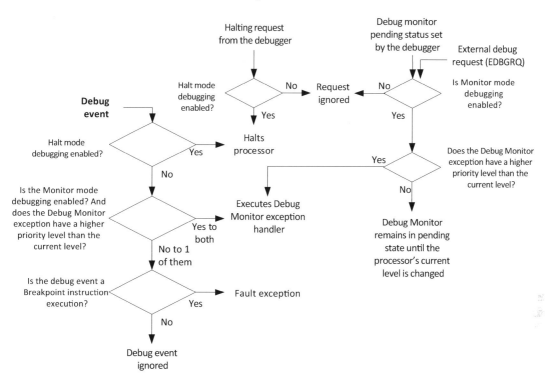

FIG. 16.10 Debug event handling (a simplified view without considering the TrustZone debug permission).

- Data watchpoint events (including PC match and cycle counter match) and external debug request are asynchronous. This means that the processor might, before stopping, continue to execute additional instructions that are already in the pipeline.

Debuggers must take account of these situations when handling debug operations. For example, to resume an operation after a breakpoint for halt mode debugging, the debugger needs to:

(1) Disable the breakpoint, then
(2) Use the single stepping feature to move the program counter to the next instruction, then
(3) Re-enable the breakpoint so that the processor can halt again if it subsequently executes to the same location, then
(4) Clear the halting request to resume the operation

If the above steps are not carried out, when the software developer attempts to resume the program execution after the program is halted by a breakpoint, the processor would immediately hit the same breakpoint because the program counter would, as the instruction pointed to by the breakpoint had not been executed, still set to the breakpoint location (not the address after the breakpoint).

16.2.6 Using the breakpoint instruction

When writing software, the breakpoint instruction can be inserted to stop the program execution at points of interest. Unlike hardware breakpoint comparators, you can insert as many software breakpoints as you like (subject, obviously, to the available memory size). The breakpoint instruction (BKPT #immed8) is a 16-bit Thumb® instruction and uses the encoding 0xBExx—only the upper 8 bits of 0xBE is decoded by the processor. The lower 8 bits of the instruction depend on the immediate data that is given following the instruction. If the debug tool supports semihosting, the immediate data can be used for requesting semihosting services. In this scenario, the debugger would have to extract the immediate data value from the program memory, or from the compiled program image if this was available and if the contents in the program memory was guaranteed to be identical to the current program image in the chip. For Arm development tools, the semihosting service usually uses the value 0xAB, the lower 8 bits in the BKPT instruction.

In a C programming environment using the CMSIS-CORE driver, a breakpoint instruction can be inserted using the CMSIS-CORE defined function:

```
void __BKPT(uint8_t value);
```

For example, a breakpoint can be inserted using

```
__BKPT(0x00);
```

Most C compilers have their own intrinsic functions for generating breakpoint instructions. When using semihosting features (e.g., redirecting "printf" messages to a semihosting communication channel), the breakpoint instructions and associate semihosting support codes are automatically inserted by the development toolchain. Please note, when using semihosting with halt mode debugging, the processor could frequently stop. This would, obviously, significantly reduce the performance of the processor and in general is not suitable for real-time applications.

When finalizing the software for production, it is very important that the breakpoint instructions in the codes that were inserted for debugging are removed. If the breakpoint instruction is not removed and is executed without the debug being enabled (e.g., no debugger connection), the processor would enter the HardFault exception. The cause of this HardFault would be indicated by the fault status bit "DEBUGEVT" in the Hard Fault Status register (HFSR) and the "BKPT" bit in the Debug Fault Status register (DFSR).

16.2.7 Debug authentication and TrustZone

The debug authentication mechanism allows the system to define the permission levels of the debug and trace features. Although basic debug authentication features were available in the Armv6-M and Armv7-M architectures, these have, for the Armv8-M architecture been enhanced and now support TrustZone.

To support debug authentication features, there are a number of input signals at the processor's top level (i.e., the boundary of the processor's design) and these are shown in Table 16.4.

TABLE 16.4 Debug authentication control signals.

Signal	Name	Description
DBGEN	Invasive debug enable	If the signal is 1, the invasive debug features for the normal (i.e., the Non-secure) world are enabled.
NIDEN	Non-invasive debug enable	If the signal is 1, the non-invasive debug features (e.g., trace) for the normal (i.e., the Non-secure) world are enabled.
SPIDEN	Secure privilege invasive debug enable	If the signal is 1, the invasive debug features for the Secure world are enabled. Only available when TrustZone is implemented.
SPNIDEN	Secure privilege non-invasive debug enable	If the signal is 1, the non-invasive debug features (e.g., trace) for the Secure world are enabled. Only available when TrustZone is implemented.

Not all combinations of these signals are allowed. For example:

- If SPIDEN is high (i.e., logic level 1) then DBGEN must also be high
- Similarly, if SPNIDEN is high then NIDEN must also be high
- If an invasive debug is allowed in a security domain, it is expected that non-invasive debugs are also allowed.

The commonly used combinations are listed in Table 16.5.

These debug authentication signals are controlled by debug authentication control software, either running on the processor (Fig. 16.11) or on another system management processor, e.g., a Secure enclave.

The debug authentication process, as illustrated in the gray rectangle in Fig. 16.11, uses a cryptography function(s) to validate the information in the software developer's credentials and then compares that against the secret information held in the chip's secure storage. This ensures that only authorized software developers can gain debug access. Since the debug authentication configuration is dependent upon the life cycle of the chip, a nonvolatile memory

TABLE 16.5 Combinations for the debug authentication control signals.

DBGEN	NIDEN	SPIDEN	SPNIDEN	Description
0	0	0	0	All debug and trace features disabled.
0	1	0	0	Only allows a Non-invasive debug (e.g., trace) in the Non-secure world.
1	1	0	0	Only allows debug and trace features in the Non-secure world.
0	1	0	1	Only allows a Non-invasive debug (e.g., trace) in both worlds.
1	1	0	1	Only allows a Non-invasive debug (e.g., trace) in the Secure world. Allows both invasive and non-invasive debugs in the Non-secure world.
1	1	1	1	Allows all debug and trace features for both the Secure and the Non-secure world.

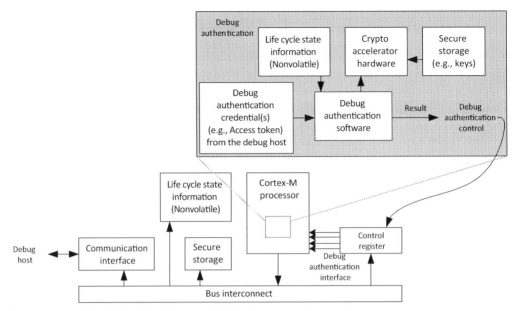

FIG. 16.11   Example of debug authentication system.

is needed to hold the life cycle states. The typical device life cycle states are after the device has been manufactured; after the Secure firmware has been loaded; after the Non-secure firmware has been loaded; once the product is in deployment and once the product is retired, etc.

Secure privileged software can override the value of SPIDEN and SPNIDEN by programming the Debug Authentication Control Register (DAUTHCTRL, address 0xE000EE04). This feature works as follows:

- When the DAUTHCTRL.SPNIDENSEL (bit 2) is set to 1, the value of DAUTHCTRL. INTSPNIDEN (bit 3) overrides the value of SPNIDEN.
- When the DAUTHCTRL.SPIDENSEL (bit 0) is set to 1, the value of DAUTHCTRL. INTSPIDEN (bit 1) overrides the value of SPIDEN.

When all debug features are disabled, it is still possible to access certain memory locations, e.g., the ID registers and the ROM tables. This is required so that the debugger can detect the available debug resource and processor type. In some instances, a SoC product designer might want to disable all debug accesses. To achieve this, an additional debug permission control signal is available on the DAP module to allow all debug accesses to be disabled.

With Armv8-M architecture, it is possible to allow a debug in the Non-secure world while, at the same time, disabling access for a Secure debug. When this is the case:

- Secure memories are not accessible by software developers. Although the DAP (see Section 16.2.1) can be programmed by a debugger to generate Secure or Non-secure transfers, when the Secure debug is disallowed all debug access is handled as Non-secure and is blocked from accessing Secure addresses.

- The processor can neither halt at the middle of a Secure API nor single step into it.
- A reset vector catch debug event would be pended so that the processor halts as soon as it branches into a Non-secure program. Other vector-catch events that are caused by Secure exceptions would be ignored.
- Trace sources (e.g., ETM, DWT) would stop generating instruction/data trace packets when the processor is in the Secure state.
- Trace sources (e.g., ETM, DWT) would still allow other trace packages to be generated when the processor is in the Secure state, providing that it did not lead to a leakage of Secure information.
- If the debugger attempted to change the program counter to a Secure program address when the processor was halted at a Non-secure address, the processor would enter SecureFault or Secure HardFault when attempts were made to single step or to resume.

If a halting request, from either the debugger or from the external debug request signal EDBGRQ, is received during the execution of a Secure API, the halting request would be pended and only accepted when the processor returned to the Non-secure state (Fig. 16.12).

During the single stepping of a Non-secure application, if the Non-secure code calls a Secure API the processor halts at the first instruction of the Secure API (i.e., the SG instruction). But, at the next step of single stepping, the processor would not stop until it was returned to the Non-secure world (Fig. 16.13). Although the processor halts at a Secure address location (i.e., the address of the SG instruction), this behavior does not result in a leakage of Secure information because:

- The Secure API codes and Secure data in the Secure memory would not be visible to the software developers, and
- The Secure API has not carried out any processing at that point.

Please note, the halting address (i.e., the entry point of the Secure API) is not considered as Secure information. The Non-secure software developers would already know the addresses of the entry points because this information is needed by them so they can call the Secure APIs in their program codes.

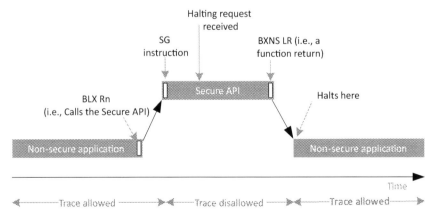

FIG. 16.12   Debug authentication scenario—halting request received when running a Secure API.

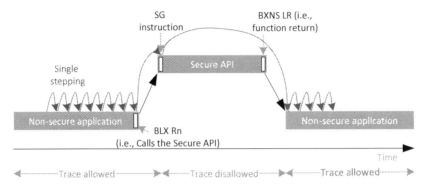

FIG. 16.13 Debug authentication scenario—single stepping over a Secure API.

The debug authentication setting defines whether the Debug Monitor exception target is either in the Secure or in the Non-secure state. If the Secure debug is allowed, the Debug Monitor exception (type 12) targets the Secure state and, if it is not, it targets the Non-secure state.

16.2.8 CoreSight discovery: The identification of debug components

CoreSight Debug Architecture is very scalable and can be used in complex System-on-Chip designs with a large number of debug components. In order to support a wide range of system configurations, CoreSight Debug Architecture provides a mechanism to allow debuggers to automatically identify debug components in the system. This involves the use of ID registers inside each debug component and one or more lookup ROM table(s).

When a debugger connects to a CoreSight based debug system, a range of steps are taken and these are detailed below:

1. The debugger detects what type of Debug Port component (see left-hand side of Fig. 16.5) it is connected to using the detected ID value—via JTAG or the Serial Wire debug protocol.
2. Using the debug connection, the debugger issues a power-up request to the debug system and, if needed, the system logic. This wakeup request is handled by a hardware interface on the Debug Port module. A handshaking mechanism is used so that the debugger can tell when it is ready to issue the next command.
3. After the handshaking of the power-up request is completed, the debugger scans through the DAP's internal debug bus to see how many Access Port components are connected to it. Based on CoreSight architecture version 2.0, there can be up to 256 AP modules in the internal debug bus. However, for the majority of Cortex-M devices, only one processor would be shown and this would only have one AP module connected to the DP module.
4. The debugger is now able to detect the type of AP module connected by reading its ID registers. For a single-core Cortex-M based device, this is shown as an AHB-AP module (on the right of the Debug Port module in Fig. 16.5).
5. After confirming the AP module is an AHB-AP, the debugger identifies the base address of the primary ROM table by reading one of the registers inside the AHB-AP. This register contains the base address, which is a read-only value. The ROM table is used for detecting debug components as described in steps 6–8.

6. Using the ROM table base address obtained in step 5, the debugger reads the ID registers of the primary ROM table and confirms that it is a ROM table.

7. The debugger reads though the entries in the ROM table to collect the base addresses of the debug components and, if it is available, an additional ROM table. The ROM table contains one or more debug components entries. Each entry has:
   ○ An address offset value that indicates the address offset (from the base address of the ROM table) of the component. Because bus slaves are normally aligned to 4KB address boundaries, not all bits of the 32-bit entry are used for the address.
   ○ One bit (one of the lowest bits of an entry) and this is used to indicate whether a component has been implemented at the address pointed to by that entry, and
   ○ One bit (one of the lowest bits of an entry) and this is used to indicate whether that entry is the last one in the current ROM table.

8. The debugger then uses this information to build a tree-like database of all the available devices.

If the debugger detects an additional ROM table(s) during the scanning, the debugger would also scan the entries in the additional ROM table(s)

Fig. 16.14 illustrates the aforementioned steps 1–8.

The debug component identification process continues until all of the entries in all of the ROM tables are detected. The debug components have a number of ID registers located at the

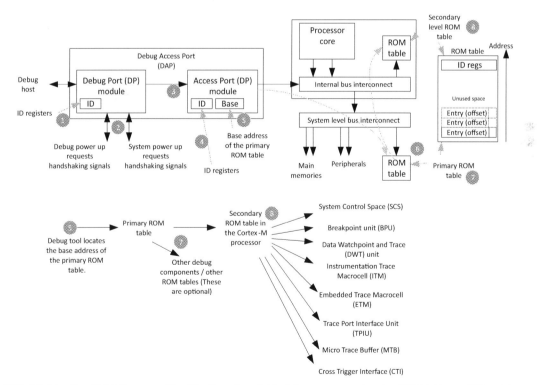

FIG. 16.14 CoreSight discovery: identification of available debug components using ROM tables and ID registers.

end of their address range—values that are available to debug tool vendors so that debug tools can be designed to identify what components are present in the system.

Most modern Cortex-M based microcontrollers have two levels of ROM tables: system level (primary) and processor level (secondary). When this is the case, one of the entries in the primary ROM table points to the secondary ROM table inside the Cortex-M processor and the secondary ROM table then provides entries to the processor's debug components (e.g., the breakpoint unit, the Data Watchpoint and Trace unit, etc.). All of the debug components and the secondary ROM table have a range of ID values which allows the debugger to determine which components are available. In some instances, more than two levels of ROM tables are present. When this is the case, the ROM table inside a Cortex-M processor could be located at a deeper level (e.g., The third level) of the ROM table lookup.

16.3 An introduction to debug components

16.3.1 Overview

There are a number of debug components inside a Cortex-M processor. The Cortex-M23 and Cortex-M33 processors have the following debug components:

- A debug control block inside the processor core
- A Breakpoint unit (BPU—but, for historical reasons, also called the Flash Patch and Breakpoint unit "FPB")
- A Data Watchpoint and Trace (DWT) unit (Note: on the Cortex-M23 the DWT does not have trace functions)
- An Instrumentation Trace Macrocell (ITM) for software generation of trace stimulus— available in Armv8-M Mainline processors only
- An Embedded Trace Macrocell (ETM) for real-time instruction trace
- A Micro Trace Buffer (MTB) for instruction trace with buffer
- A Cross Trigger Interface (CTI) for debug synchronization in multicore systems
- A Trace Port Interface Unit (TPIU) for outputting trace data

Generally, application developers do not need a detailed understanding of debug components. But, that said, it could be useful to understand how they work at a high level. For example, this can be helpful in troubleshooting when certain debug features are not working as expected. If you are a chip designer, knowledge of how the debug system works could be important because it could help you implement the debug support for the chip.

In most cases, debug components, such as the BPU, the DWT and the ETM, are managed by debug tools and are not accessed by software. In the Cortex-M23 processor, debug registers are accessible by the debugger only and software executing on the processor cannot access the debug components. In the Cortex-M33 processor, software executing on the processor is allowed to access the debug registers. This is needed to support the debug agents, which use the Debug Monitor feature.

However, there are likely to be a few instances where software developers would like to directly access certain debug features in their software. These could be:

- When adding a software breakpoint to code during debugging.
- So Secure privileged software can override the Secure debug authentication setting when using the DAUTHCTRL register in the debug control block.
- When using ITM to generate a trace stimulus in software (available in Armv8-M Mainline processors, but not available in Armv8-M Baseline)
- When integrating a debug agent for monitor mode debugging (available in Armv8-M Mainline processors, but not available in Armv8-M Baseline)

Unless specifically specified, the registers for debug components in Armv8.0-M are only accessed in privileged state and are only accessed using 32-bit transfers. In Armv8.1-M architecture it is possible to allow unprivileged access to debug components. However, this is beyond the scope of this book and is not covered.

16.3.2 Debug support registers in the processor core

At the processor's core there are several registers for debug control functions. These include:

- A control register (DHCSR) for halt mode debugging. This register handles halting and single stepping.
- A control register (DEMCR) for monitor mode debugging. This register handles management of the Debug Monitor exception and single stepping using a Debug Monitor.
- A pair of registers(DCRSR and DCRDR) for accessing various registers inside the processor (e.g., registers in the register banks, special registers).
- A control register (DEMCR) for Vector Catch debug event handling.
- A control register (DAUTHCTRL) for management of debug authentication. This register is new in Armv8-M.

The debug registers are not banked between security states, but some of the bit fields in these debug registers are only accessible in Secure state. In the processor's debug control block, there are six registers (Table 16.6).

In addition, there are other registers in the Debug Identification Block and System Control Space that are needed for debug functions. There are detailed in Table 16.7.

In most scenarios, application software does not need to access these registers (unless a debug agent for monitor mode debugging is being created). If, in some cases, software modified these registers, it would cause a problem for the debug tools. For example, the DHCSR is used by the debugger that is connected to the device and if this register is read by software, the read operation can change some of its status bits. Accordingly, application code should avoid accessing the DHCSR because it could cause problems for debugger tools. Information on the DHCSR is shown in Table 16.8.

Note: For the DHCSR, bits 5, 2, and 0 are reset by power on reset only. Bit 1 can be reset by the power-on-reset (cold reset) and the system reset. Additional bitfields are added to this register in the Armv8.1-M architecture, they are not covered here.

TABLE 16.6 Debug control block registers.

Address (NS alias)	Name	Type	Reset value
0xE000EDF0 (0xE002EDF0)	Debug Halting Control Status Register (DHCSR)	R/W	0x00000000
0xE000EDF4 (0xE002EDF4)	Debug Core Register Selector Register (DCRSR)	W	–
0xE000EDF8 (0xE002EDF8)	Debug Core Register Data Register (DCRDR)	R/W	–
0xE000EDFC (0xE002EDFC)	Debug Exception and Monitor Control Register (DEMCR)	R/W	0x00000000
0xE000EE04 (0xE002EE04)	Debug Authentication Control Register (DAUTHCTRL). This is only accessible from Secure privileged software and is not accessible by the debugger.	R/W	0x0
0xE000EE08 (0xE002EE08)	Debug Security Control and Status Register (DSCSR)	R/W	0x00020000

TABLE 16.7 Other debug related registers in the processor's core.

Address (NS alias)	Name	Type	Reset value
0xE000EFB8 (0xE002EFB8)	Debug Authentication Status Register (DAUTHSTATUS). This allows the debugger/software to determine the debug authentication status. (This is new in Armv8-M.)	RO	Implementation defined
0xE000ED30 (0xE002ED30)	Debug Fault Status Register (DFSR). This allows the debugger/software to determine which event triggered halting or the Debug Monitor exception (Section 13.5.7).	RW	0x00

To enter halt mode, the C_DEBUGEN bit in the Debug Halting Control and Status register (DHCSR) must be set. Because this bit can only be programmed through the debugger connection, via the Debug Access Port (DAP), you cannot halt the Cortex-M processor without a debugger. After C_DEBUGEN is set, the core can be halted by setting the C_HALT bit in the DHCSR. The C_HALT bit can be set by either the debugger or, if it is in an Armv8-M Mainline processor, by the software running on the processor. The C_DEBUGEN bit can only be accessed by the debugger.

The bit field definition of the DHCSR differs between read and write operations. For write operations, a debug key value must be used for bits 31 to 16. For read operations, there is no debug key and the return value of the upper half word contains the status bits.

When the processor is halted (indicated by S_HALT), a debugger can access the processor's register bank and special registers using DCRSR (Table 16.9) and DCRDR (Table 16.10).

To use these registers to read register contents, the following procedure must be followed:

- Make sure the processor is halted.
- Write to the DCRSR with bit 16 set to 0: this indicates that it is a read operation.
- Poll until the S_REGRDY bit in DHCSR (0xE000EDF0) is 1.
- Read the DCRDR to obtain the register content.

TABLE 16.8 Debug Halting Control and Status Register in the Armv8.0-M architecture (CoreDebug-> DHCSR, 0xE000EDF0).

Bits	Name	Type	Reset Value	Description
31:16	KEY	W	–	Debug key; value of 0xA05F must be written to this field so it can write to this register, otherwise the write would be ignored.
26	S_RESTART_ST	R	–	Indicates the processor execution has been restarted (unhalted); this bit is cleared when read.
25	S_RESET_ST	R	–	Core has been reset or is being reset; this bit is cleared when read.
24	S_RETIRE_ST	R	–	Instruction has completed since the last read; this bit is cleared when read.
20	S_SDE	R	–	Secure debug enabled (If 1, the Secure invasive debug is allowed). If TrustZone is not implemented this bit is always 0.
19	S_LOCKUP	R	–	When this bit is 1, the core is in a locked-up state.
18	S_SLEEP	R	–	When this bit is 1, the core is in sleep mode.
17	S_HALT	R	–	When this bit is 1, the core is halted.
16	S_REGRDY	R	–	Register read/write operation has completed.
15:6	Reserved	–	–	Reserved
5	C_SNAPSTALL	R/W	0^a	Used to break a stalled memory access (for Armv8-M Mainline only and not available in the Cortex-M23). If the processor is stuck due to a stalled transfer, it might not be able to enter halt mode even when a halting request is received. C_SNAPSTALL allows the transfer to be abandoned and helps to force the processor into a debug state.
4	Reserved	–	–	Reserved
3	C_MASKINTS	R/W	–	Masks interrupts while stepping; can only be modified when the processor is halted.
2	C_STEP	R/W	0^a	Single steps the processor; valid only if C_DEBUGEN is set.
1	C_HALT	R/W	0	Halts the processor core; valid only if C_DEBUGEN is set.
0	C_DEBUGEN	R/W	0^a	Enables halt mode debug.

[a] Reset by power-on-reset.

Similar operations are needed for writing to a register:

- Make sure the processor is halted.
- Write data value to the DCRDR.
- Write to the DCRSR with bit 16 set to 1: this indicates that it is a write operation.
- Poll until the S_REGRDY bit in DHCSR (0xE000EDF0) is 1.

The DCRSR and the DCRDR registers can only transfer register values during a halt mode debug. For debugging using a debug monitor handler, the contents of some of the registers can be accessed from the stack memory; the others can be accessed directly within the monitor exception handler.

TABLE 16.9 Debug Core Register Selector Register in the Armv8.0-M architecture (CoreDebug->DCRSR, 0xE000EDF4).

Bits	Name	Type	Reset value	Description
16	REGWnR	W	–	Direction of data transfer: Write = 1, Read = 0
15:7	Reserved	–	–	–
6:0	REGSEL	W	–	Register to be accessed: 0000000 = R0 0000001 = R1 … 0001111 = R15 (Debug return address) 0010000 = xPSR/flags 0010001 = MSP (Current Main Stack Pointer) 0010010 = PSP (Current Process Stack Pointer) 0010100 = Special registers: [31:24] Control [23:16] FAULTMASK (read as zero for Armv8-M Baseline) [15:8] BASEPRI (read as zero for Armv8-M Baseline) [7:0] PRIMASK 0011000 = MSP_NS (Available when TrustZone is implemented) 0011001 = PSP_NS (Available when TrustZone is implemented) 0011010 = MSP_S (Available when TrustZone is implemented) 0011011 = PSP_S (Available when TrustZone is implemented) 0011100 = MSPLIM_S (Available when TrustZone is implemented) 0011101 = PSPLIM_S (Available when TrustZone is implemented) 0011110 = MSPLIM_NS (Available for Armv8-M Mainline) 0011111 = PSPLIM_NS (Available for Armv8-M Mainline) 0100001 = Floating Point Status and Control Register (FPSCR) 0100010 = Secure special registers: [31:24] CONTROL_S [23:16] FAULTMASK_S (reads as zero for Armv8-M Baseline) [15:8] BASEPRI_S (reads as zero for Armv8-M Baseline) [7:0] PRIMASK_S 0100011 = Non-secure special registers: [31:24] CONTROL_NS [23:16] FAULTMASK_NS (reads as zero for Armv8-M Baseline) [15:8] BASEPRI_NS (reads as zero for Armv8-M Baseline) [7:0] PRIMASK_NS 1000000 = Floating point register S0 … 1011111 = Floating point register S31 Other values are reserved

TABLE 16.10 Debug Core Register Data Register (CoreDebug->DCRDR, 0xE000EDF8).

Bits	Name	Type	Reset value	Description
31:0	Data	R/W	–	Data register to hold the result of a register read or for writing data into a selected register.

The DCRDR can also be used for semihosting if suitable function libraries and debugger support are available. For example, when an application executes a printf statement, the text output could be generated by a number of putc (put character) function calls. The putc function calls can be implemented as functions that first store the output character and status to the DCRDR and then, second, trigger the debug mode. When the processor is halted, the debugger then detects that the processor is halted and collects the output character for display. This operation, however, requires the processor to halt, whereas the printf solution using ITM (Section 16.3.5) does not have this requirement.

When debugging is carried out in monitor mode, the debug agent software needs to use the features provided in the DEMCR (Debug Exception and Monitor Control Register). Information on the DEMCR is shown in Table 16.11.

Please note, for the DEMCR:

- Bits 16–19 are reset by system reset as well as power on reset. Other bits are reset by power on reset only.
- Bits 4–9 and bit 11 are not available in Armv8-M Baseline
- Additional bitfields are added in the Armv8.1-M architecture and they are not covered here.

The DEMCR register is used to control the Vector Catch feature and the Debug Monitor Exception and enables the trace subsystem. Before being able to use any trace features (e.g., instruction trace, data trace), or being able to access any trace component (e.g., DWT, ITM, ETM, and TPIU), the TRCENA bit must be set to 1.

In Armv8-M, the addition of TrustZone support adds, for security, additional debug management. The Debug Authentication Control Register (CoreDebug->DAUTHCTRL) enables Secure privileged software to override the settings of SPIDEN and SPNIDEN input signals (Table 16.12).

The DAUTHCTRL register is accessible from Secure privileged software only. Additional bitfields are added to this register in the Armv8.1-M architecture and they are not covered here.

The debugger and software can determine the debug authentication status using the Debug Authentication Status Register (DAUTHSTATUS) (Table 16.13). Note: Additional bitfields are added to this register in the Armv8.1-M architecture and they are not covered here.

Many resources are banked between security states when TrustZone is implemented. When handling an access that targets the System Control Space (SCS) address range, the way that the transfer is handled is different between the access that is generated by a debugger and the access generated by software. For software generated access, the same address could be directed to either Secure or Non-secure resources, dependent upon the security state of the processor at the time. For debug access, this method cannot be used because the processor could be running and could, while the debug is being carried out, be in either a Secure or a Non-secure state. To solve this problem, the Debug Security Control and Status Register (DSCSR) has been implemented to allow the debug access view to be controlled, no matter what the security state of the processor is, by the debugger (Table 16.14).

TABLE 16.11 Debug Exception and Monitor Control Register in the Armv8.0-M architecture (CoreDebug-> DEMCR, 0xE000EDFC).

Bits	Name	Type	Reset value	Description
24	TRCENA	R/W	0^a	Trace system enable; to use the DWT, the ETM, the ITM and the TPIU this bit must be set to 1.
23:20	Reserved	–	–	Reserved
20	SDME	RO	–	Secure Debug Monitor enable. The status of this bit depends on the debug authentication setting. It determines whether the Debug Monitor exception should target the Secure (1) or the Non-secure state (0).
19	MON_REQ	R/W	0	An indication that the debug monitor is caused by a manual pending request rather than by hardware debug events.
18	MON_STEP	R/W	0	Single steps the processor. This is only valid when MON_EN is set.
17	MON_PEND	R/W	0	Pends the monitor exception request; the core will enter the monitor exception when priority allows.
16	MON_EN	R/W	0	Enables the debug monitor exception.
15:12	Reserved	–	–	Reserved
11	VC_SFERR	R/W	0^a	Debug trap on a SecureFault.
10	VC_HARDERR	R/W	0^a	Debug trap on a HardFault.
9	VC_INTERR	R/W	0^a	Debug trap on interrupt/exception service errors.
8	VC_BUSERR	R/W	0^a	Debug trap on a BusFault.
7	VC_STATERR	R/W	0^a	Debug trap on UsageFault state errors.
6	VC_CHKERR	R/W	0^a	Debug trap on UsageFault checking errors. This enables the debug trap on a UsageFault caused by unaligned checking or by divide by zero checking.
5	VC_NOCPERR	R/W	0^a	Debug trap on a UsageFault caused by access to invalid coprocessor (i.e., a NOCP error).
4	VC_MMERR	R/W	0^a	Debug trap on a memory management fault.
3:1	Reserved	–	–	Reserved
0	VC_CORERESET	R/W	0^a	Debug trap on a core reset.

[a] Reset by power-on-reset.

TABLE 16.12 Debug Authentication Control Register in the Armv8.0-M architecture (CoreDebug-> DAUTHCTRL, 0xE000EE04).

Bits	Name	Type	Reset value	Description
31:4	Reserved	–	–	Reserved
3	INTSPNIDEN	R/W	0	When SPNIDENSEL is set to 1, INTSPNIDEN overrides the SPNIDEN setting.
2	SPNIDENSEL	R/W	0	
1	INTSPIDEN	R/W	0	When SPIDENSEL is set to 1, INTSPNIDEN overrides the SPIDEN setting.
0	SPIDENSEL	R/W	0	

TABLE 16.13 Debug Authentication Status Register in the Armv8.0-M architecture (DAUTHSTATUS, 0xE000EFB8).

Bits	Name	Type	Description
31:8	Reserved	–	Reserved
7:6	SNID	RO	Secure non-invasive debug 00—TrustZone security extension not implemented 01—Reserved 10—Secure non-invasive debug disabled (TrustZone implemented) 11—Secure non-invasive debug allowed (TrustZone implemented)
5:4	SID	RO	Secure invasive debug 00—TrustZone security extension not implemented 01—Reserved 10—Secure invasive debug disabled (TrustZone implemented) 11—Secure invasive debug allowed (TrustZone implemented)
3:2	NSNID	RO	Non-secure non-invasive debug 0×—Reserved 10—Non-invasive debug disabled 11—Non-invasive debug allowed
1:0	NSID	RO	Non-secure invasive debug 0×—Reserved 10—Invasive debug disabled 11—Invasive debug allowed

TABLE 16.14 Debug Security Control and Status Register (DSCSR, 0xE000EE08).

Bits	Name	Type	Description
31:18	Reserved	–	Reserved
17	CDSKEY	W/read as 1	Current domain secure (CDS) write-enable key: This bit should be 0 when updating the CDS bit (i.e., bit 16). When writing to the DSCSR, write to CDS is ignored if CDSKEY is 1. This prevents the CDS bit being accidentally changed when the processor is running and when the bit is writing to the DSCSR.
16	CDS	R/W	Current domain secure—allows the debugger to check/change the current security state of the processor. 0—Non-secure, 1—Secure. When writing to the CDS, the write to CDS is ignored if CDSKEY is 1.
15:2	Reserved	–	Reserved
1	SBRSEL	R/W	Secure banked register select (This bit is used only when the DSCSR.SBRSELEN is set to 1). -. 0—Non-secure view -. 1—Secure view
0	SBRSELEN	R/W	Secure banked register select enable. If the DSCSR.SBRSELEN bit is 1, SBRSEL determines whether debug access should target the Secure or the Non-secure registers. If it is not 1, the current security state of the processor determines whether the debug access should see the Secure or the Non-secure view.

The DSCSR also allows the debugger to change the security state of the processor. This must be carefully executed as a fault exception would be triggered if the security state and the security attribute of the program address did not match after the change.

The DSCSR register is not available if the TrustZone security extension is not implemented.

In addition to these debug registers, the processor core has a few more debug features for multicore debug support:

- External debug request signal EDBGRQ (see Section 16.2.5): The processor provides an external debug request signal that allows the Cortex-M processor to enter debug mode through an external event, such as the debug status of other processors in a multiprocessor system. This feature is very useful for debugging a multiprocessor system. In simple microcontrollers, this signal is likely to be tied low.
- Debug restart interface: The processor provides a hardware handshaking signal interface to allow the processor to be unhalted using other hardware on the chip. This feature is commonly used for synchronized debug restart in a multiprocessor system. In a single processor system, the handshaking interface is normally not used.

These features are available in both the Cortex-M23 and the Cortex-M33 processors.

16.3.3 Breakpoint unit

The breakpoint unit in the Cortex-M23 and Cortex-M33 processors allows breakpoints to be set to a specific program address without manually adding breakpoint instructions inside the program code. By doing this, the program code does not have to be modified. However, there is a limit on how many hardware breakpoints can be set:

- The Cortex-M23 processor supports up to four hardware breakpoint comparators
- TheCortex-M33 processor supports up to eight hardware breakpoint comparators

The breakpoint function is fairly easy to understand. During debugging, you can set one or multiple breakpoints to the program addresses. If the program code at the breakpoint addresses is executed, this triggers a breakpoint debug event and causes the program execution to either halt (for the halt mode debug) or to trigger the debug monitor exception (if the debug monitor is used). Once this occurs, the register's contents, memories and peripherals status can then be examined, and debug operations (e.g., using single stepping) can be carried out.

For historical reasons, the breakpoint unit is called the Flash Patch and Breakpoint (FPB) unit. In the Cortex-M3 and Cortex-M4 processors, the breakpoint comparators can also be used for remapping transfers to patch the ROM image. This feature is not supported in Armv8-M due to complications with TrustZone relating to the remap process.

The key registers in the breakpoint units are listed in Table 16.15.

By default, the breakpoint unit is disabled. To enable the breakpoint unit, the debug tool needs to set the ENABLE bit in the Flash Patch Control Register (FP_CTRL) (Table 16.16).

The breakpoint comparator registers start from address 0xE0002008 (FP_COMP0) and continue in subsequent addresses, i.e., 0xE000200C (FP_COMP1), 0xE0002010 (FP_COMP2), etc. To configure a hardware breakpoint, the debug tool would need to program one of these breakpoint comparator registers (Table 16.17).

Unlike the breakpoint unit in the Cortex-M0/M0+/M1/M3/M4 processors, the use of FPB revision 1 architecture allows the breakpoint to be set in any executable region. Whereas in

TABLE 16.15   Breakpoint unit registers.

Address (NS alias)	Name	Type	Reset value
0xE0002000 (0xE0022000)	Flash Patch Control Register (FP_CTRL).	R/W	0x00000000
0xE0002004 (0xE0022004)	Reserved—FP_REMAP register in an earlier version of the FPB programmer's model. Not used in Armv8-M.	–	–
0xE0002008+n*4 (0xE0022008+n*4)	Flash Patch Comparator Register (FP_COMPn).	R/W	–
0xE0002FBC (0xE0022FBC)	FPB Device Architecture Register (FP_DEVARCH). For supporting auto discovery in CoreSight debug components.	RO	0x47701A03 (Cortex-M33)/0x0 (Cortex-M23)
0xE0002FCC (0xE0022FCC)	FPB Device Type Register (FP_DEVTYPE).	RO	0x00000000
0xE0002FD0—0xE0002FFC (0xE0022FD0—0xE0022FFC)	Flash Patch peripheral and component ID registers. For supporting auto discovery CoreSight debug components.	RO	

TABLE 16.16   FP_CTRL register.

Bits	Name	Type	Reset value	Description
31:28	REV	RO	0001	FPB architecture revision—always 1 in the Cortex-M23 and Cortex-M33 processors.
27:15	Reserved	–	–	Reserved
14:12	NUM_CODE [6:4]	RO	–	NUM_CODE is the number of implemented code comparators in the breakpoint unit. This bit field (bits 14 to 12—3 bits wide) only provides bits 6 to 4 of the NUM_CODE. Because both the Cortex-M23 and Cortex-M33 have less than 16 code comparators, this is always 0.
11:8	NUM_LIT	RO	0	Number of implemented literal comparators—this is always 0 in the current Armv8-M processors.
7:4	NUM_CODE [3:0]	RO		Number of implemented code comparators. It is -. 0–4 in the Cortex-M23 processor -. 0, 4, or 8 in the Cortex-M33 processor It is 0 when the debug feature is not implemented.
3:2	Reserved	–	–	Reserved
1	Key	WO	–	Write-enable key. To write to the FP_CTRL register, this bit must be set to 1, otherwise the write is ignored.
0	ENABLE	R/W	0	Enable. When set to 1 the breakpoint unit is enabled.

TABLE 16.17   FP_COMPn register(s).

Bits	Name	Type	Reset value	Description
31:1	BPADDR	R/W	–	Breakpoint address[31:1].
0	BE	R/W	0	Breakpoint enable. When set to 1, the breakpoint comparator is enabled.

previous designs the breakpoint comparators only worked in the CODE region (in the first 512MB of memory).

16.3.4 Data Watchpoint and Trace Unit (DWT)

The DWT contains a range of functions:

- The DWT comparators. They can be used for:
  - Data watchpoint event generation (for halting or Debug Monitor exception)
  - An ETM Trigger (if the ETM is implemented)
  - Data trace generation (for Armv8-M Mainline only, not available in the Cortex-M23 processor)
- Profiling counters (available in Armv8-M Mainline only). They can be used for:
  - Profiling trace
- A 32-bit cycle counter (available in Armv8-M Mainline only). It can be used for:
  - Program execution time measurement
  - Generating a periodic control for trace synchronization and for program counter sampling trace
- A PC sample register. It is used for coarse grained profiling of executed code. When this feature is used, the debugger periodically samples the PC value via a debug connection. (Note: in Armv8-M Mainline processors PC sampling can also be carried out via trace.)

The number of DWT comparators is configurable, with both the Cortex-M23 and the Cortex-M33 processors each supporting up to four hardware DWT comparators.

Before accessing the DWT registers, the TRCENA bit in the DEMCR (Table 16.11) must be set to 1 to enable the DWT. And if the trace features in the DWT are used,

- The TXENA bit (bit 3) in the ITM Trace Control Register (ITM_TCR) must be set to 1; and
- The TPIU needs to be initialized to enable trace output.

The DWT contains the following key registers (Table 16.18).
The DWT Control Register contains many functions:

- Bit fields to allow software/the debugger to determine the availability of hardware resources
- Various enable control bit fields

The bit fields of the DWT Control Register are detailed in Table 16.19.
The DWT Cycle Count Register (DWT_CYCCNT) is available in Armv8-M Mainline only and is used for:

- The measurement of the processor's execution cycle
- The control of the periodic PC sampling trace packet (this feature is dependent on the settings of DWT_CTRL.PCSAMPLENA and DWT_CTRL.CYCTAP)

TABLE 16.18 Data Watchpoint and Trace unit registers.

Address (NS alias)	Name	Type
0xE0001000 (0xE0021000)	DWT Control Register (DWT_CTRL).	R/W
0xE0001004 (0xE0021004)	DWT Cycle Count Register (DWT_CYCCNT) (Not available in the Cortex-M23).	R/W
0xE0001008 (0xE0021008)	DWT CPI Count Register (DWT_CPICNT) (For profiling trace—Not available in the Cortex-M23).	R/W
0xE000100C (0xE002100C)	DWT Exception Overhead Count Register (DWT_EXCCNT) (For profiling trace—Not available in the Cortex-M23).	R/W
0xE0001010 (0xE0021010)	DWT Sleep Count Register (DWT_SLEEPCNT) (For profiling trace—Not available in the Cortex-M23).	R/W
0xE0001018 (0xE0021018)	DWT Folded Instruction Count Register (DWT_FOLDCNT) (For profiling trace—Not available in the Cortex-M23).	R/W
0xE000101C (0xE002101C)	DWT Program Counter Sample Register.	R/W
0xE0001020+16*n (0xE0021020+16*n)	DWT Comparator Register n (DWT_COMP[n]).	R/W
0xE0001028+16*n (0xE0021028+16*n)	DWT Comparator Function Register n (DWT_FUNCTION[n]).	R/W
0xE0001FBC (0xE0021FBC)	DWT Device Architecture Register (FP_DEVARCH). For supporting CoreSight debug component identification.	RO
0xE0001FCC (0xE0021FCC)	DWT Device Type Register (FP_DEVTYPE).	RO
0xE0001FD0–0xE0001FFC (0xE0021FD0–0xE0021FFC)	DWT peripheral and component ID registers. For supporting CoreSight debug component identification.	RO

- The control periodic trace synchronization packet (this feature is dependent on the settings of DWT_CTRL.SYNCTAP)
- The control periodic cycle count trace packet (this feature is controlled by the DWT_CTRL. CYCEVTENA bit)

The DWT Cycle Count Register (Table 16.20) is 32-bit wide.

When TrustZone is implemented, setting DWT_CTRL.CYCDISS to 1 prevents CYCCNT from incrementing during the Secure state. The DWT_CTRL.CYCDISS is not accessible from the Non-secure world.

In Armv8-M Mainline, the DWT contains a number of profiling counters for counting the number of cycles used for different types of activities (e.g., Sleep, memory access and interrupt processing overhead). These counters are listed in Tables 16.21–16.25.

These profiling counters are 8-bit and during operations easily overflow. Because of this, they should be used with a trace connection so that each time any of the counters overflow, a corresponding trace packet is generated and recorded by the debug host. By doing so, the debug host is able, when the profiling operation stops, to calculate the total counts by adding the "number of trace packets $\times 256$" to the values in these counters. (Note: each overflow

TABLE 16.19 DWT Control Register (DWT_CTRL, 0xE0001000).

Bits	Name	Type	Reset value	Description
31:28	NUMCOMP	RO	–	Number of DWT comparators that are implemented.
27	NOTRCPKT	RO	–	No trace packets—always 1 in the Cortex-M23 to indicate that trace is not supported.
26	NOEXTTRIG	RO	–	No External Triggers. Reserved (read as zero).
25	NOCYCCNT	RO	–	No cycle count register—always 1 in the Cortex-M23 to indicate that the Cycle Count register is not implemented.
24	NOPRFCNT	RO	–	No profile counters—always 1 in the Cortex-M23 to indicate that the profile counters are not implemented.
23	CYCDISS	R/W	0	Cycle count disable secure—if set to 1, it prevents the cycle counter from incrementing in Secure state. In the Cortex-M23 processor, this bit is always zero as the cycle counter is not implemented.
22	CYCEVTENA	R/W	0	Cycle event enable—if set to 1, it enables the Event Counter packet generation on the POSTCNT underflow. POSTCNT is a 4-bit counter that decrements if the tapped bit of the CYCCNT counter overflows (the tapped bit is controlled by the CYCTAP, bit 9 of DWT_CTRL) In the Cortex-M23 processor, this bit is always zero as the cycle counter is not implemented.
21	FOLDEVTENA	R/W	0	Enables the DWT_FOLDCNT counter when this bit is set to 1. In the Cortex-M23 processor, this bit is always zero as FOLDCNT is not implemented.
20	LSUEVTENDA	R/W	0	Enables the DWT_LSUCNT counter when this bit is set to 1. (LSU = Load Store unit. When enabled, LSUCNT increments for every pipeline stall cycle caused by memory access.) In the Cortex-M23 processor, this bit is always zero as LSUCNT is not implemented.
19	SLEEPEVTENA	R/W	0	Enables the DWT_SLEEPCNT counter when this bit is set to 1. (When enabled, SLEEPCNT increments for every sleep cycle.) In the Cortex-M23 processor, this bit is always zero as SLEEPCNT is not implemented.
18	EXCEVTENA	R/W	0	Enables the DWT_EXCCNT counter when this bit is set to 1. (When enabled, the EXCCNT increments for every cycle of the interrupt entry/exit overhead.) In the Cortex-M23 processor, this bit is always zero as EXCCNT is not implemented.
17	CPIEVTENA	R/W	0	Enables the DWT_CPICNT counter when this bit is set to 1. (When enabled, the CPICNT increments additional cycles (the first cycle is not counted) that are required to execute instructions—except those recorded by DWT_LSUCNT.) In the Cortex-M23 processor, this bit is always zero as CPICNT is not implemented.

TABLE 16.19   DWT Control Register (DWT_CTRL, 0xE0001000)—cont'd

Bits	Name	Type	Reset value	Description
16	EXCTRCENA	R/W	0	Enables the exception event trace. In the Cortex-M23 processor, this bit is always zero as profiling trace is not implemented.
15:13	Reserved	–	–	Reserved.
12	PCSAMPLENA	R/W	0	Enables PC sampling trace. When set to 1, the PC value is sampled and is outputted to trace when the selected tapped bit (by POSTCNT) changes value. In the Cortex-M23 processor, this bit is always zero as FOLDCNT is not implemented.
11:10	SYNCTAP	R/W	0	Synchronization tap—defines the rate of the synchronization packets 00—The synchronization packet is disabled. 01—The synchronization packet taps at bit 24 of CYCCNT 10—The synchronization packet taps at bit 26 of CYCCNT 11—The synchronization packet taps at bit 28 of CYCCNT In the Cortex-M23 processor this bit is always zero as CYCCNT is not implemented.
9	CYCTAP	R/W	0	The cycle count tap for the POSTCNT counter. 0—POSTCNT taps at bit 6 of CYCCNT 1—POSTCNT taps at bit 10 of CYCCNT POSTCNT is a decrement counter and decrements when the tapped bit (selected by CYCTAP) changes value. In the Cortex-M23 processor, this bit is always zero as CYCCNT is not implemented.
8:5	POSTINIT	R/W	–	The initial value for the POSTCNT counter. In the Cortex-M23 processor, this bit is always zero as POSTCNT is not implemented.
4:1	POSTPRESET	R/W	–	POSTCNT PRESET—A reload value for the POSTCNT counter. In the Cortex-M23 processor, this bit is always zero as POSTCNT is not implemented.
0	CYCCNTENA	R/W	0	CYCCNT enable—when set to 1, it enables the increment of CYCCNT.

TABLE 16.20   DWT Cycle Count Register (DWT_CYCCNT, 0xE0001004).

Bits	Name	Type	Reset value	Description
31:0	CYCCNT	RW	–	Cycle counter—increments when DWT_CTRL.CYCCNTENA is 1 and DEMCR.TRCENA is 1. When it overflows, it wraps to zero.

TABLE 16.21   DWT CPI Count Register (DWT_CPICNT, 0xE0001008).

Bits	Name	Type	Reset value	Description
31:8	Reserved	–	–	Reserved
7:0	CPICNT	R/W	–	Counts the additional cycles required to execute multicycle instructions and stall cycles in instruction fetches. The first cycle of the instruction cycle and the delay cycle, which are recorded by LSUCNT, are not included. Initializes to zero when the counter is disabled and when DWT_CTRL.CPIEVTENA is written with 1.

TABLE 16.22   DWT Exception Overhead Count Register (DWT_EXCCNT, 0xE000100C).

Bits	Name	Type	Reset value	Description
31:8	Reserved	–	–	Reserved
7:0	EXCCNT	R/W	–	Counts the total cycles spent in exception processing. Initializes to zero when the counter is disabled and when DWT_CTRL.EXCEVTENA is written with 1.

TABLE 16.23   DWT Sleep Count Register (DWT_SLEEPCNT, 0xE0001010).

Bits	Name	Type	Reset value	Description
31:8	Reserved	–	–	Reserved
7:0	SLEEPCNT	R/W	–	Counts the processor's total sleep cycles. Initializes to zero when the counter is disabled and when DWT_CTRL.SLEEPEVTENA is written with 1.

TABLE 16.24   DWT LSU Count Register (DWT_LSUCNT, 0xE0001014).

Bits	Name	Type	Reset value	Description
31:8	Reserved	–	–	Reserved
7:0	LSUCNT	R/W	–	Counts the additional cycles that are required to execute the load or store instructions (the first clock cycle of the load and store execution is not counted). Initializes to zero when the counter is disabled and when DWT_CTRL.LSUEVTENA is written with 1.

TABLE 16.25 DWT Folded Instruction Count Register (DWT_FOLDCNT, 0xE0001018).

Bits	Name	Type	Reset value	Description
31:8	Reserved	–	–	Reserved
7:0	FOLDCNT	R/W	–	Counts the additional instructions that are executed (e.g., dual-issued). Initializes to zero when the counter is disabled and when DWT_CTRL.FOLDEVTENA is written with 1.

packet represents 256 cycles because the counters are 8-bit wide.) By way of an example, if during a debug session the debug host receives 6 Sleep-event-counter packets and, if at the end of the session, the SLEEPCNT counter value is 9, then the processor would, during that session, enter sleep mode for 1545 clock cycles (i.e., $6 \times 256 + 9 = 1545$).

By combining the total cycle count (either by reading DWT_CYCCNT, or by trace—enabled via DWT_CTRL.CYCEVTENA), the total number of instructions that have been executed over a period of time can be measured as follows:

$$\text{Total instruction executed} = \text{Total cycle count} - \text{CPICNT} - \text{EXCCNT} - \text{SLEEPCNT} - \text{LSUCNT} + \text{FOLDCNT}$$

By correlating the program trace information (by either using the ETM instruction trace or the PC sampling trace), it is possible to identify some of the performance issues. For example, Fig. 16.15 show a possible profiling scenario in which a DWT trace shows some interesting aspects during the code's execution.

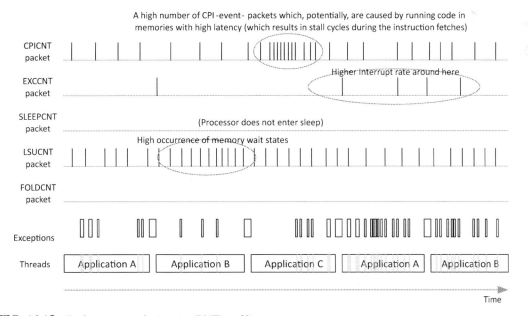

FIG. 16.15 Performance analysis using DWT profiling counters.

TABLE 16.26   DWT Program Counter Sample Register (DWT_PCSR, 0xE000101C).

Bits	Name	Type	Reset value	Description
31:0	EIASAMPLE	RO	–	Execution instruction address sample value.

Although the EXCCNT packets provide exception overhead information, they do not provide information detailing which exceptions have taken place. To obtain this information, you can enable exception tracing by setting DWT_CTRL.EXCTRCENA. This details which exception has occurred and, if timestamp is enabled for tracing, it can also show the time the exception handler was started and when it ended.

When TrustZone is implemented and if Secure trace (Non-invasive debug) is disabled, the profiling counters will not increment during Secure software activities. In addition, the profiling counters will also stop when the processor is halted.

Some basic profiling can also be carried out by PC sampling through a debug connection. To achieve this, the PC value can be read periodically via the DWT Program Counter Sample Register (Table 16.26) without the need for a trace connection. This is supported in both the Cortex-M23 and Cortex-M33 processors.

When the read value of the DWT PC Sample Register is 0xFFFFFFFF, it means that one of the follow conditions is true:

- That the processor has halted.
- That TrustZone is implemented, that the processor is running in Secure state and that the debug authentication setting does not allow a Secure debug.
- That the debug authentication setting does not allow debugging.
- That DWT is disabled (The DEMCR.TRCENA is set to 0).
- That the address of a recently executed instruction is not available (e.g., immediately after reset).

Because of debug connection speed limitations, the sampling rate of PC sampling via a debug connection is usually quite low. As a result, PC sampling via trace is, if available, a better option or, better still, ETM instruction trace—which provides more profiling information.

The data watchpoint feature of the DWT is handled by the DWT_COMP[n] and DWT_FUNCTION[n] registers, where the value of "n" is 0–3 in the Cortex-M23 and Cortex-M33 processors (Note: There are up to four DWT comparators in both processors; though architecturally there can be more than four).

The definition of value in DWT_COMP[n] depends on the functions defined in the DWT_FUNCTION[n] (Table 16.27).

The bit fields of the DWT_FUNCTION[n] are listed in Table 16.28.

The match types (i.e., the lowest 4 bits of the DWT_FUNCTION[n] registers) that are available are listed in Table 16.29.

Some of the functions described in Table 16.29 require two DWT comparators to be used as a pair. Usually, if more than one comparator has been implemented, at least one of the comparators supports linking. Usually, the linking feature is supported by odd-numbered comparators (e.g., COMP1, COMP3, etc.), and because there is no comparator #-1, comparator #0 does not support linking.

TABLE 16.27   DWT Comparator Register[n] (DWT_COMP[n], 0xE0001020 + 16*n).

Bits	Name	Type	Reset value	Description
31:0	DWT_COMP[n]	R/W	–	The value depends on the function of the DWT comparator: • CYCVALUE—When DWT_FUNCTIONn.MATCH==0001 (Cycle Match) • PCVALUE—When DWT_FUNCTIONn.MATCH==001x (PC match: only bits 31 to 1 are used, bit0 should be 0) • DVALUE—when DWT_FUNCTIONn.MATCH==10xx (Data value match, not supported in Armv8-M Baseline/Cortex-M23 processor) • DADDR—when DWT_FUNCTIONn.MATCH==x1xx (Data address match)

TABLE 16.28   DWT Comparator Function Register[n] (DWT_FUNCTION[n], 0xE0001028 + 16*n).

Bits	Name	Type	Reset value	Description
31:27	ID	RO	–	Identifies the capabilities of MATCH for comparator "n", see Table 16.30.
26:25	Reserved	–	–	Reserved
24	MATCHED	RO	–	Comparator matched status (clears to 0 when read).
23:12	Reserved	–	–	Reserved
11:10	DATAVSIZE	R/W	–	Data value size—the size of data being watched by the Data Value and Data Address comparators: 00=byte, 01=half word, 10=word. Please note: • DATAVSIZE must be set to 10 (0x2) when being used as an instruction address or an instruction address limit comparator. • If this DWT comparator is being used to pair with another DWT comparator for data address range checking, the DATAVSIZE should be set to 00.
9:6	Reserved	–	–	Reserved
5:4	ACTION	R/W	–	Action on match: • 00=Trigger only (for trigger packet generation/ETM triggering). • 01=Generates a debug event (for halting or for the Debug monitor). • 10=Generates a Data Trace Match packet or a Data Trace Data Value packet. • 11=Generates a Data Trace Data Address Packet, or a Data Trace PC Value Packet, or both a Data Trace PC Value Packet and a Data Trace Data Value Packet.
3:0	MATCH	R/W	–	Match type, see Table 16.29.

TABLE 16.29   DWT_FUNCTION[n].MATCH description.

MATCH [3:0]	Description
0000	Disable
0001	Cycle counter matching: The value of DWT_COMP[n] is compared against the value of DWT_CYCCNT(Not available in Armv8-M Baseline).
0010	Instruction address: The value of DWT_COMP[n] is compared against the instruction address.
0011	Instruction address limit: A match event is triggered when the program execution address is between the lower instruction address limit (This is indicated by comparator [n-1]) and the upper instruction address limit (This is indicated by comparator [n]). Both addresses are inclusive. A pair of DWT comparators are needed for this feature. For two comparators to be used as a pair, the MATCH bit field of Comparator[n] should be set to 0011 and the MATCH bit field of Comparator[n-1] should be set to either 0010 (Instruction address) or 0000 (Disabled).
0100	Data address: The value of DWT_COMP[n] is compared against the data address when it is not linked to by a Data Address limit comparator. Used for normal data watchpoints: DATAVSIZE should be set to the size of the watched data.
0101	Data address, similar to 0100, but for monitoring write access only.
0110	Data address, similar to 0100, but for monitoring read access only.
0111	Data address limit: A match event is triggered when the data access address is between the lower data address limits (This is indicated by comparator [n-1]) and the upper data address limits (This is indicated by comparator [n]). Both addresses are inclusive. A pair of DWT comparators are needed for this feature. For two comparators to be used as a pair, the MATCH bit field of Comparator[n] should be set to 0111 and the MATCH bit field of Comparator [n-1] should be set to 0100/0101/0110 (Data address), or 1100/1101/1110 (Data Address with Data Value) or 0000 (Disable).
1000	Data value: The value of DWT_COMP[n] is compared against the data value. (Only available in Armv8-M Mainline.)
1001	Data value, similar to 1000, but for monitoring write access only.
1010	Data value, similar to 1000, but for monitoring read access only.
1011	Linked data value. A match event is triggered when the data address matches the value in comparator [n-1] and the data value matches the value in comparator [n]. Comparator [n-1] must be set to 0100/0101/0110 (Data address), or 1100/1101/1110 (Data Address with Data Value) or 0000 (Disable). Comparator [n-1] and [n] are used as a pair to allow both the address and the data value conditions to be defined for a match.
1100	Data Address with Value. Similar to Data address (0100), except that the data value is traced. (Available for the first 4 comparators only.)
1101	Data Address with Value for write only. Similar to Data address for write (0101), except that the data value is traced. (Available for the first four comparators only.)
1110	Data Address with Value for read only. Similar to Data address for read (0110), except that the data value is traced. (Available for the first four comparators only.)

TABLE 16.30 DWT_FUNCTION[n].ID description.

Features available	The values of DWT_FUNCTION[n].ID in binary form							
	01000	01001	01010	01011	11000	11010	11100	11110
Data address	Y	Y	Y	Y	Y	Y	Y	Y
Data address with value (Not available in the Cortex-M23 processor)	Y	Y	Y	Y	Y	Y	Y	Y
Data address limit					Y	Y	Y	Y
Data value							Y	Y
Linked Data value							Y	Y
Instruction address			Y	Y		Y		Y
Instruction address limit						Y		Y
Cycle counter (Not available in the Cortex-M23 processor)		Y		Y				

Debug tools can determine the DWT comparator features that are available by reading the ID bit field of DWT_FUNCTION[n]. The mapping of DWT_FUNCTION[n]. ID to the features that are available can be found in Table 16.30 (Note: the value of 00000 is reserved).

When the Cycle Counter (DWT_CYCCNT) is implemented, the DWT comparator #0 must support the Cycle counter compare function.

Using DWT comparators, a selection of data variables can be traced when the processor is running. This is achieved by setting the DWT_FUNCTION.MATCH to 1100/1101/1110 (Data Address with Value). For example, when using the Logic Analyzer feature with Keil® MDK, the selective data trace feature allows data value changes to be visualized (Fig. 16.16).

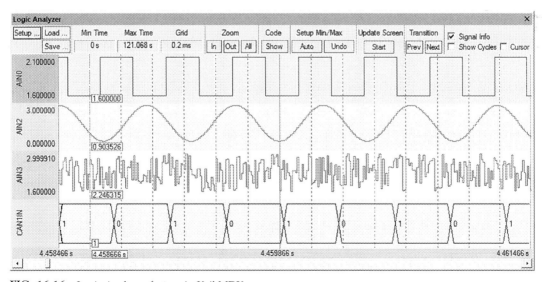

FIG. 16.16 Logic Analyzer feature in Keil MDK.

16.3.5 Instrumentation Trace Macrocell (ITM)

16.3.5.1 *Overview*

The ITM is available in the Cortex-M33 processor but is not in the Cortex-M23 processor. It has multiple functionality. It has:

- Software generated trace—Software is able to directly write messages to the ITM stimulus port registers to generate trace data. By doing so, the ITM can then encapsulate the data in trace packets and output them through the trace interface.
- Timestamp packet generation—The ITM can be programmed to generate time stamp packets that are inserted into the trace stream to assist the debugger in reconstructing the timing of events.
- Trace packet merging—The ITM works as a trace packet merging device inside the processor to merge trace packets from the DWT, to merge software generated trace packets from the stimulus port registers and to merge timestamp packets from the timestamp packet generator (Fig. 16.17).
- FIFO—There is a small First-In-First-Out (FIFO) buffer in the ITM to reduce the chance of trace overflow.

To use the ITM for debugging, the microcontroller or SoC device must have a trace port interface. If the device does not have a trace interface, or if the debug adaptor does not support trace capture, console text messages can, by using other peripheral interfaces (e.g., a UART or an LCD module), still be output. However, other features such as DWT profiling will not work. Some debuggers also support printf (and other semihosting features) by using the core debug registers (e.g., CoreDebug->DCRDR) as a communication channel.

Before accessing any ITM registers or using any ITM features, the TRCENA bit (Trace Enable) in CoreDebug->DEMCR (see Table 16.11) must be set to 1.

In a CoreSight trace system, each trace source must be assigned with a trace source ID value. This is a programmable value and is one of the bit fields (TraceBusID) in the ITM Trace

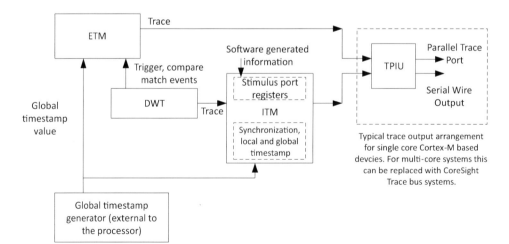

FIG. 16.17   Merging of Trace Packets in the ITM.

Control Register. Normally, this trace ID value is automatically setup by a debugger. So that the debug host receiving the trace packet can separate the ITM's trace packets from other trace packets, this ID value must be totally different from the IDs for the other trace sources.

16.3.5.2 Programmer's model

The ITM contains the following key registers (Table 16.31).

Before using the ITM features we first need to write to the ITM Trace Control Register (ITM_TCR) to set the master enable bit. The bit fields of ITM_TCR are listed in Table 16.32.

The ITM Stimulus Port Registers are used by software to generate messages for the debug host. Multiple message channels are available via the use of the multiple stimulus ports registers. When data is written to one of the stimulus ports registers, the stimulus port number is encapsulated in the trace packet so that the debug host can identify which message channel the data belongs to. In the Cortex-M33 and in existing Armv7-M processors, the ITM supports 32 stimulus ports. The most common use of the stimulus port (usually Stimulus port #0) is for handling "printf" messages so that the message can be displayed on the console program which is running on the debug host.

In Keil MDK and when using the RTX RTOS, stimulus port #31 is used for OS aware debug support. The OS outputs information about its status so that the debugger can tell when context switching has taken place and, additionally, which task the processor is running.

Before using an ITM stimulus port:

- The ITM needs to be enabled (DEMCR.TRCENA must be set, then ITM_TCR.ITMENA must be set).
- The ITM Trace Enable Register (ITM_TER) must be configured to enable the stimulus port to be used.
- The TraceBusID in ITM_TCR must be configured.

For a read operation, the ITM_STIM[n] has the following return value (Table 16.33).

TABLE 16.31 ITM registers.

Address (NS alias)	Name	Type
0xE0000000+n*4 (0xE0020000+n*4)	ITM Stimulus Port Register n (ITM_STIM[n]).	R/W
0xE0000E00+n*4 (0xE0020E00+n*4)	ITM Trace Enable Register n (ITM_TER[n]).	R/W
0xE0000E40 (0xE0020E40)	ITM Trace Privilege Register (ITM_TPR).	R/W
0xE0000E80 (0xE0000E80)	ITM Trace Control Register (ITM_TCR).	R/W
0xE0000FBC (0xE0020FBC)	ITM Device Architecture Register (FP_DEVARCH). For supporting the identification of the CoreSight debug component.	RO
0xE0000FCC (0xE0020FCC)	ITM Device Type Register (FP_DEVTYPE).	RO
0xE0000FD0—0xE0000FFC (0xE0020FD0—0xE0020FFC)	ITM peripheral and component ID registers. For supporting the identification of the CoreSight debug component.	RO

TABLE 16.32 ITM Trace Control Register (ITM_TCR, 0xE0000E80).

Bits	Name	Type	Reset value	Description
31:24	Reserved	–	–	Reserved
23	BUSY	RO	–	When 1, it indicates that the ITM is currently generating a trace packet (either by software, the ITM itself or by handling a packet from the DWT).
22:16	TraceBusID	R/W	–	Bus ID on the ATB (Advanced Trace Bus). Set to 0x01 to 0x6F for normal use.
15:12	Reserved	–	–	Reserved
11:10	GTSFREQ	R/W	00	Global Timestamp Frequency. 00—Global timestamp disabled. 01—Generates a global timestamp approximately every 128 cycles. 10—Generates a global timestamp approximately every 8192 cycles. 11—Generates a global timestamp after every packet when the FIFO in the trace output stage is empty.
9:8	TSPrescale	R/W	00	Prescaler for local timestamp. This controls the prescaler of the timestamp generator. This setting applies to timestamps of trace packets transmitted via the ITM. 00—No prescaling (Timescale generator running at the same speed as the processor) 01—Divide by 4 (Timescale generator running at ¼ of the processor's speed) 10—Divide by 16 (Timescale generator running at 1/16 of the processor's speed) 11—Divide by 64 (Timescale generator running at 1/64 of the processor's speed)
7:6	Reserved	–	–	Reserved
5	STALLENA	R/W	–	Stall enable—When set to 1, the processor is stalled when the ITM FIFO is full so that the trace system can catch up and the data trace packets can be delivered. When set to 0, DWT data trace packets are dropped when the FIFO is full and an Overflow packet is used to indicate that the packet has been lost. Architecturally, this feature is optional. It is included in the Cortex-M33 from release version r0p1.
4	SWOENA	R/W	–	SWO enable—enables asynchronous clocking of the local time stamp counter.
3	TXENA	R/W	0	Transmit enable—When set to 1, it enables the forwarding of DWT packets.
2	SYNCENA	R/W	0	Synchronization enable—enables synchronization packet generation.
1	TSENA	R/W	0	Local timestamp enable—enables local timestamp packet generation.
0	ITMENA	R/W	0	Master enable for the ITM.

TABLE 16.33 ITM_STIM[n] Register read value (ITM_STIM[n], 0xE0000000 + 4*n).

Bits	Name	Type	Reset value	Description
31:2	Reserved	–	–	Reserved
1	DISABLED	R	–	If the value is 1, the stimulus port is disabled.
0	FIFOREADY	R	–	If the value is 1, the stimulus port is ready to accept one piece of data.

TABLE 16.34 ITM_STIM[n] Register write value (ITM_STIM [n], 0xE0000000 + 4*n).

Bits	Name	Type	Reset value	Description
31:0	STIMULUS	W	–	Stimulus data

If the stimulus port is not disabled (i.e., ITM_STIM[n].DISABLE is 0) and if the FIFO status is ready (i.e., ITM_STIM[n].FIFOREADY is 1), software can output data to the ITM stimulus port by writing to it (Table 16.34).

The write to the ITM Stimulus Port Registers can be byte, half word or word size. The write transfer size defines the size of the data to be output to trace. The ITM encapsulate the data size in the trace packet protocol so that a sequence of character writes for "printf" can be correctly displayed on the debug host (i.e., the host is able to tell what the correct size of the data is).

For example, the µVision IDE in the Keil MDK development tool can collect and display the printf text output in the ITM viewer shown in Fig. 16.18.

Unlike UART-based text output, using the ITM to output does not delay the application too much. Although a FIFO buffer is used inside the ITM and thus, writing output messages are buffered, it is still necessary to check whether the FIFO is full before you write to it.

The output messages can either be collected at the trace port interface or the Serial Wire Output interface (SWO) on the TPIU. It is not essential to remove the code that generated the debug messages from the final code because, when there is no debugger connected, the trace system is disabled (the TRCENA control bit is low) and the writes to the ITM are simply ignored. If the text message generation function is available in the final code, the output message can be switched on in a "live" system as and when needed. In this scenario, the ITM stimulus ports can be selectively enabled by controlling the Trace Enable register so that only some of the messages in the specific stimulus ports are outputted.

To assist software development, the CMSIS-CORE provides a function, as detailed below, for handling text messages using the ITM stimulus port:

```
unit32_t ITM_SendChar (uint32_t ch)
```

This function uses stimulus port #0 and returns the value of the "ch" input. Normally the debugger sets up the trace port and ITM for you, meaning that you only need to call this function to output each of the characters you want to display. To use this function, you must setup the debugger to enable trace capture. For example, if the SWO signal is used, the debugger

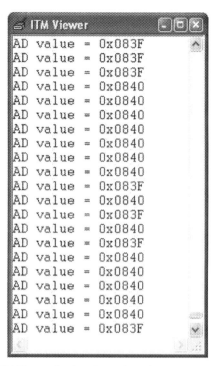

FIG. 16.18 In Keil MDK, the ITM Viewer display shows the software generated text output.

must capture the trace using the correct transmission speed. Usually the debugger's Graphic User Interface (GUI) allows you to configure the TPIU frequency and the speed of the Serial Wire Output (This is handled by adjusting the clock divide ratio in the SWO part of the TPIU). In addition, if the SWO output is shared with the TDO pin, the Serial Wire Debug communication protocol must be selected.

Although the ITM only allows data output, the CMSIS-CORE header file also includes a function to allow the debugger to output a character to the application running on the microcontroller. This function is:

```
int32_t ITM_ReceiveChar (void)
```

Although this function has the "ITM_" prefix in its name, the transferring of a character from the debug host to the software running on the Cortex-M processor is actually handled by the debug interface (i.e., the Serial Wire Debug or the JTAG connection). To use this feature, a variable called ITM_RxBuffer needs to be declared, allowing the debug tool to update this variable by directly accessing the memory where the variable is stored. If there is no data to receive, the ITM_ReceiveChar() function returns −1. If data is available, then it returns the character received. Another function available for checking whether a character has been received is:

```
int32_t ITM_CheckChar (void)
```

The ITM_CheckChar() returns 1 if a character is available. Otherwise it returns 0.

TABLE 16.35 ITM Trace Enable Register n (ITM_TER[n], 0xE0000E00 +4*n).

Bits	Name	Type	Reset value	Description
31:0	STIMENA	R/W	0	Stimulus port enable (when set to 1, the stimulus port is enabled) For ITM_TER0: Bit[0]—Stimulus port #0 Bit[1]—Stimulus port #1 … Bit[31]—Stimulus port #31

A stimulus port needs to be enabled before it can be used. This is controlled by the ITM Trace Enable Register (ITM_TER[n]) (Table 16.35). Architecturally, there can be more than one ITM_TER if there are more than 32 ITM Stimulus Port Registers. However, because the Cortex-M33 processor only has 32 ITM Stimulus Port Registers implemented, just one ITM_TER register is available, with each bit in it representing the enable control for one stimulus port.

It is also possible to setup an ITM Stimulus Port so that unprivileged applications can use it. This is controlled by the ITM Trace Privileged Register (ITM_TPR[n]) (Table 16.36). Similar to the ITM Trace Enable Register (ITM_TER[n]), architecturally there can be more than one ITM_TPR[n] if there are more than 32 ITM Stimulus Port Registers. In the Cortex-M33 processor, however, there is only one ITM Trace Privileged Register, with each bit of this register representing the privileged level control for one stimulus port.

16.3.5.3 Hardware trace with ITM and DWT

The ITM handles the merging of packets from the DWT. To enable DWT trace, the TXENA bit in the ITM Trace Control Register would need to be set and, additionally, the DWT trace settings would need to be configured. Usually the trace features (e.g., data trace, event trace) are configured via the GUI of a debugger and, when they are, the trace settings are then automatically set up by the debugger.

TABLE 16.36 ITM Trace Privilege Register n (ITM_TPR[n], 0xE0000E40 +4*n).

Bits	Name	Type	Reset value	Description
31:0	STIMENA	R/W	0	Stimulus port privilege control—when set to 1, the stimulus port is privileged access only. When it is not, unprivileged code can access this stimulus port. For ITM_TER0: Bit[0]—Stimulus port #0 Bit[1]—Stimulus port #1 … Bit[31]—Stimulus port #31

16.3.5.4 ITM *timestamp*

The ITM has a timestamp feature that allows trace capture tools to determine timing information. This is achieved by inserting timestamp packets into the traces every time a new trace packet enters the FIFO inside the ITM. The timestamp packet is also generated when the timestamp counter overflows.

In the Cortex-M33 processor, there is

- A local timestamp mechanism for reconstructing timing relationships between the ITM/DWT packets.
- A global timestamp mechanism for reconstructing timing relationships between ITM/DWT trace and other trace sources (e.g., the ETM).

A local timestamp packet provides the time difference (delta) between a current trace packet and a previously transmitted packet. Using the delta timestamp packets, the trace capture tools establish the timing of each generated packet and, thus, can reconstruct the timing of the various debug events.

The global timestamp mechanism allows the correlation of trace information between different trace sources (e.g., between the ITM and the ETM, or even between multiple processors).

Combining the trace functionality of the DWT and ITM enables software developers to collect a great deal of useful information. For example, the exception trace windows in the Keil MDK development tool (Fig. 16.19) are able to display the exceptions that have been carried out and the amount of time that was spent on the exceptions.

16.3.6 Embedded Trace Macrocell (ETM)

The ETM is used for providing instruction traces. Information collected can be useful for:

- Analyzing the reasons for program failure
- Checking code coverage
- Obtaining detailed profiling of the application

Num	Name	Count	Total Time	Min Time In	Max Time In	Min Time Out	Max Time Out	First Time [s]	Last Time [s]
2	NMI	0	0 s						
3	HardFault	0	0 s						
4	MemManage	0	0 s						
5	BusFault	0	0 s						
6	UsageFault	0	0 s						
11	SVCall	475	158.236 us	77.500 us	80.736 us	135.861 us	14.549 s	0.00021660	25.44279225
12	DbgMon	0	0 s						
14	PendSV	0	0 s						
15	SysTick	2576	4.309 ms	1.417 us	93.694 us	765.222 us	10.066 ms	0.00087276	25.47015878
16	ExtIRQ 0	0	0 s						
17	ExtIRQ 1	0	0 s						
18	ExtIRQ 2	0	0 s						
19	ExtIRQ 3	0	0 s						
20	ExtIRQ 4	0	0 s						
21	ExtIRQ 5	0	0 s						
22	ExtIRQ 6	0	0 s						
23	ExtIRQ 7	0	0 s						

FIG. 16.19   Exception trace in the Keil MDK debugger.

The ETM is optional and might not be available on some Cortex-M23 and Cortex-M33 based products. When enabled, the program flow information (i.e., instruction trace) is generated in real-time and is collected by a debug host via the parallel trace port on the TPIU (Trace Port Interface Unit). Because the debug host is likely to have a copy of the program image, it is able to reconstruct the program execution's history. Fig. 16.20 shows an instruction trace display in Keil MDK.

The ETM trace protocol is designed to minimize the bandwidth needed to transfer trace data. To reduce the amount of data generated, the ETM does not generate a trace packet for every instruction it executes. Instead, it only outputs information about program flow and only outputs full addresses as and when needed (e.g., if an indirect branch has taken place). That said, the ETM does generate quite a lot of data, especially if branches frequently occur. To enable the data trace to be captured, a FIFO buffer is provided in the ETM to allow sufficient time for the Trace Port Interface Unit (TPIU) to process and reformat the trace data.

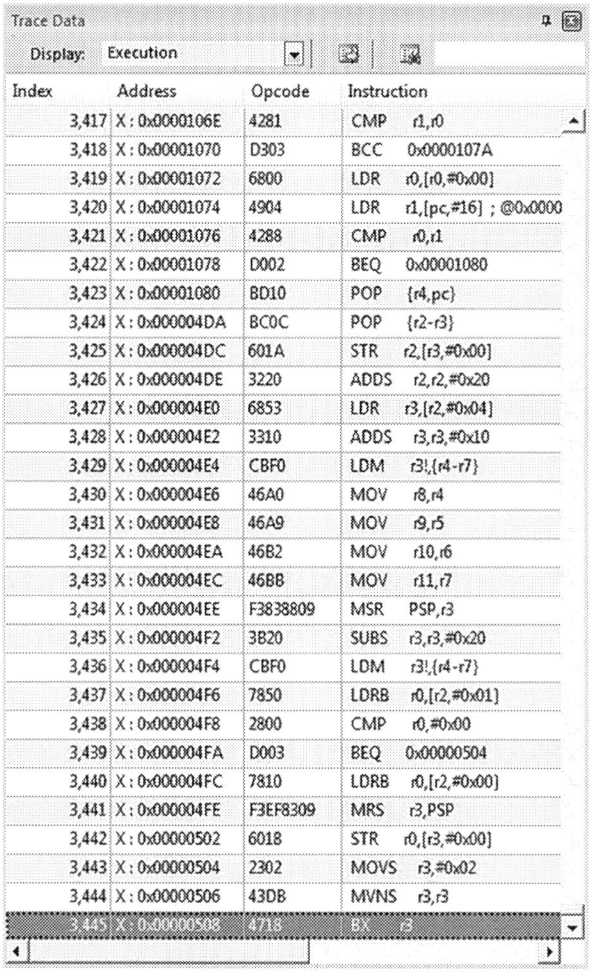

Index	Address	Opcode	Instruction	
3,417	X : 0x0000106E	4281	CMP	r1,r0
3,418	X : 0x00001070	D303	BCC	0x0000107A
3,419	X : 0x00001072	6800	LDR	r0,[r0,#0x00]
3,420	X : 0x00001074	4904	LDR	r1,[pc,#16] ; @0x0000
3,421	X : 0x00001076	4288	CMP	r0,r1
3,422	X : 0x00001078	D002	BEQ	0x00001080
3,423	X : 0x00001080	BD10	POP	{r4,pc}
3,424	X : 0x000004DA	BC0C	POP	{r2-r3}
3,425	X : 0x000004DC	601A	STR	r2,[r3,#0x00]
3,426	X : 0x000004DE	3220	ADDS	r2,r2,#0x20
3,427	X : 0x000004E0	6853	LDR	r3,[r2,#0x04]
3,428	X : 0x000004E2	3310	ADDS	r3,r3,#0x10
3,429	X : 0x000004E4	CBF0	LDM	r3!,{r4-r7}
3,430	X : 0x000004E6	46A0	MOV	r8,r4
3,431	X : 0x000004E8	46A9	MOV	r9,r5
3,432	X : 0x000004EA	46B2	MOV	r10,r6
3,433	X : 0x000004EC	46BB	MOV	r11,r7
3,434	X : 0x000004EE	F3838809	MSR	PSP,r3
3,435	X : 0x000004F2	3B20	SUBS	r3,r3,#0x20
3,436	X : 0x000004F4	CBF0	LDM	r3!,{r4-r7}
3,437	X : 0x000004F6	7850	LDRB	r0,[r2,#0x01]
3,438	X : 0x000004F8	2800	CMP	r0,#0x00
3,439	X : 0x000004FA	D003	BEQ	0x00000504
3,440	X : 0x000004FC	7810	LDRB	r0,[r2,#0x00]
3,441	X : 0x000004FE	F3EF8309	MRS	r3,PSP
3,442	X : 0x00000502	6018	STR	r0,[r3,#0x00]
3,443	X : 0x00000504	2302	MOVS	r3,#0x02
3,444	X : 0x00000506	43DB	MVNS	r3,r3
3,445	X : 0x00000508	4718	BX	r3

FIG. 16.20 Instruction trace window in the Keil MDK debugger.

Owing to the trace bandwidth required, the single pin SWO trace output mode is not suitable for ETM trace.

Although the ETM protocol allows data to be traced, the ETM for the Cortex-M23 and Cortex-M33 processors does not support data trace. Instead, the selective data trace feature in the DWT is available for use when capturing data.

When compared to the MTB, which I will introduce next, ETM instruction trace has many advantages:

- It has unlimited trace history.
- It provides timing information via timestamp packets.
- It operates in real-time—information is collected by the debug tools while the processor is still running.
- It does not take any room in the system's SRAM.

The ETM also interacts with other debugging components, such as the DWT. The comparators in the DWT can be used to generate trigger events or the trace start/stop control function in the ETM. Because of the interactions between the DWT and the ETM, the ETM does not need dedicated trace start/stop control hardware.

16.3.7 Micro Trace Buffer (MTB)

Similar to the ETM, the MTB is also used to provide instruction trace. However, instead of outputting the instruction trace data through the TPIU in real time, the MTB solution uses a portion of on-chip SRAM to hold the instruction trace data. The MTB is an optional component in the Cortex-M0+, the Cortex-M23 and the Cortex-M33 processors.

During program execution, program flow change information is captured and stored in the SRAM. When the processor is halted, the program flow information in the trace buffer is then retrieved via the debug connection and made available for reconstruction.

Although the MTB does not provide instruction trace in real time and its trace history is limited (It is restricted by the size of the SRAM region allocated for instruction tracing), the MTB instruction trace solution does have several advantages:

- Software developers can use a low-cost debug probe to collect the MTB trace result. For the ETM trace, however, a debug probe that supports parallel trace port capturing is needed and is usually more expensive.
- With the MTB, there is no need to use extra pins for parallel trace output. This is an important consideration for some devices with low pin counts.
- The overall silicon area of the MTB is smaller than the area of an ETM plus the TPIU (meaning a lower chip manufacturing cost). Since the MTB can use part of the system's SRAM as a trace buffer, there is no need for a dedicated SRAM buffer.

The MTB is a small component that is placed between the SRAM and the system bus (Fig. 16.21). In normal operations, the MTB acts as an interface module to connect the on-chip SRAM to the AMBA® AHB.

During debug operations, the debugger configures the MTB so that it allocates a small portion of the SRAM as a trace buffer for storing trace information. Of course, care must be taken

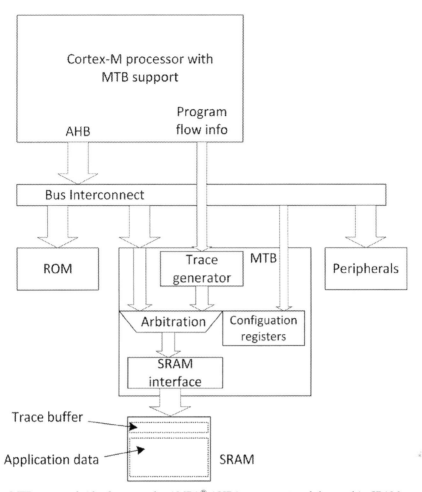

FIG. 16.21 MTB acts as a bridge between the AMBA® AHB interconnect and the on-chip SRAM.

to ensure that the application does not use the same SRAM space that has been allocated for trace operations.

When a program branch occurs, or when the program flow has changed due to interrupts, the MTB stores the source program counter and the destination program counters in the SRAM. A total of 8 bytes of trace data per branch is needed for storing each program flow change. For example, if just 512 bytes of the SRAM is allocated for instruction trace, we can store up to 64 of the most recent program flow changes. This is a great help when debugging software for, for example, determining what program code sequence led to a HardFault.

The MTB supports two operation modes:

Circular buffer mode—the MTB uses the allocated SRAM in circular buffer mode. The MTB trace operates continuously, with the old trace data being constantly overwritten by the new trace data. If the MTB is used for software failure analysis (e.g., HardFault), the debugger sets up the processor, using the Vector Catch feature (see Section 16.2.5), so that it enters halt automatically when a HardFault occurs. When the processor enters HardFault, the debugger extracts the information in the trace buffer and recreates the trace history. The circular buffer mode is the most commonly used operation mode for the MTB.

One shot mode—the MTB starts writing trace from the start of the allocated trace buffer and automatically stops tracing when the trace write pointer reaches a specific watermark level. The MTB can, optionally, stop the processor's execution by asserting a debug request signal.

The impact of MTB operations on an application is negligible because when the processor executes a branch it does not generate any data access to the SRAM. There is the chance, however, that another bus master like a DMA controller, might attempt to access the SRAM at the same time. To manage this, the MTB has an internal bus arbitrator to handle access conflicts.

The MTB solution was first introduced in the Arm Cortex-M0+ processor; and was subsequently made available in the Cortex-M23 and Cortex-M33 processors. In the Cortex-M33 processor, the MTB solution is able to coexist with the ETM. In the Cortex-M23 processor, to reduce the silicon area, chip designers can only implement one of the trace solutions, i.e., either the ETM or the MTB.

16.3.8 Trace Port Interface Unit (TPIU)

The TPIU module is used to output trace packets to the external world in order that trace data can be captured by trace capturing devices, e.g., like Keil ULINKPro. The TPIU module used in Cortex-M devices is usually a version of the TPIU that is area-optimized for microcontrollers. It supports two output modes:

• Parallel trace port mode (clocked mode): provides up to 4-bit parallel data output and a trace clock output.
• Serial Wire Output (SWO) mode: it uses a single-bit serial output. There can be two different output modes with the SWO. These are:
  ◦ Manchester coding
  ◦ Non-Return to Zero (NRZ)

The NRZ is used in most debug probes that support the SWO.

In clocked mode, the actual number of trace data bits used on the trace interface can be programmed to accommodate different sizes (i.e., trace data can be 1/2/4 bit, plus the trace clock). For devices with small pin counts, using 5 bits for the trace output might not be feasible, especially if the application is already using a lot of I/O pins. Therefore, the ability to use a fewer number of pins is highly desirable. Chip designers can restrict the maximum port size using a configuration input port, making the setting visible from the hardware registers and meaning that debug tools can then determine the maximum allowed width of the trace port.

In SWO mode, a 1-bit serial protocol is used and this not only reduces the number of output signals to 1, but also reduces the maximum bandwidth for the trace output. In addition to the aforementioned, the speed of the trace data output can be programmed using a prescaler. When combining the SWO with the Serial-Wire debug protocol, the Test Data Output (TDO) pin normally used for the JTAG protocol can be shared with the SWO (Fig. 16.22).

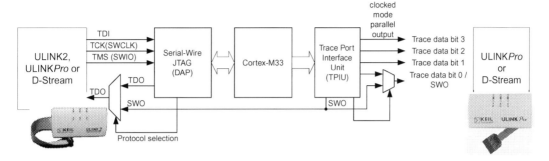

FIG. 16.22   Trace connection and pin sharing on the Serial Wire Output.

For example, the trace output in SWO mode can be collected using a standard debug connector for the JTAG using a Keil ULINK2 debug probe.

An alternative to sharing the SWO with the TDO, the SWO output can also share a pin with the parallel trace output pin. The trace data (either in clocked mode or in SWO mode) can then be collected by an external trace port analyzer, e.g., like the Arm D-Stream or the Keil ULINKPro.

Please note, the restriction of the trace data bandwidth in SWO mode means it is not suitable for use with the ETM instruction trace. However, the SWO is sufficient for "printf" message output and for basic event/profiling trace. Potentially, the trace port's clock can run at a higher frequency to provide more bandwidth, but only up to a point, as the maximum speed of the I/O pins are also limited.

Inside the TPIU, the trace bus interface (AMBA® ATB), which connects to the trace bus from the processor, operates asynchronously to the trace port interface's clock (Fig. 16.23). This allows the trace port to operate at a higher clock frequency than the processor and

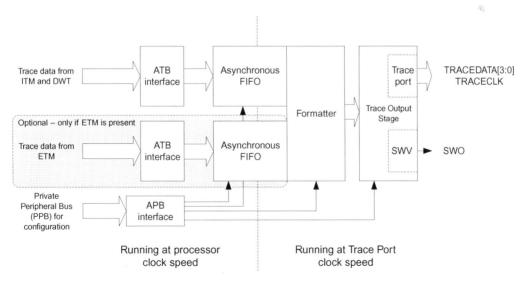

FIG. 16.23   Cortex-M TPIU block diagram.

provides a higher trace bandwidth. This is fine for parallel trace port mode as the trace clock is also outputted to the trace capturing unit. But for the SWO trace there is no reference clock. As a result, you would need to configure the project settings in the debug tool you are using so that the SWO trace is captured at the right speed.

Potentially, a debug initialization script might be needed to configure the trace clock at the beginning of the debug session (i.e., if the trace interface clock setting is controlled by hardware registers).

Because there can be multiple trace sources connected to the TPIU, the TPIU includes a formatter which encapsulates the trace bus ID value into the trace data output. This allows trace streams to be merged and to be separated by the debug host. When using SWO mode for trace without an ETM, there is only one active trace bus; and in this case the formatter can be switched off (i.e., bypass mode) to enable a higher data throughput. When in bypass mode, trace bus ID values are not encapsulated in the trace data.

To use the Cortex-M TPIU:

- The TRCENA bit in the DEMCR must be set to 1.
- The clock signal for the TPIU's trace interface port needs to be enabled (This is device specific). In many instances, the TRCENA bit in the DEMCR is also used for the enabling of the clock signal for the TPIU's trace interface port.
- The protocol (mode) selection register and trace port size control registers need to be programmed by the trace capture software.

Because the TPIU is not within the System Control Space, the TPIU registers do not have a Non-secure alias address. The TPIU contains the following key registers and these are listed in Table 16.37.

The TPIU Supported Parallel Port Size Register (TPIU_SPPSR) allows debug tools to determine the maximum width of the trace port (Table 16.38).

The TPIU Current Parallel Port Size Register (TPIU_CSPSR) allows debug tools to set the width of the trace port (Table 16.39).

TABLE 16.37 Key registers in the Cortex-M TPIU.

Address	Name	Type
0xE0040000	TPIU Supported Parallel Port Size Register (TPIU_SPPSR)	RO
0xE0040004	TPIU Current Parallel Port Size Register (TPIU_CSPSR)	R/W
0xE0040010	TPIU Asynchronous Clock Prescaler Register (TPIU_ACPR)	R/W
0xE00400F0	TPIU Selected Pin Protocol Register (TPIU SPPR)	R/W
0xE0040300	Formatter and Flush Status Register (TPIU_FFSR)	RO
0xE0040304	Formatter and Flush Control Register (TPIU_FFCR)	R/W
0xE0040308	Periodic Synchronization Control Register(TPIU_PSCR)	R/W
0xE0040FA0	Claim tag set	R/W
0xE0040FA4	Claim tag clear	R/W

TABLE 16.38 Supported Parallel Port Size Register (TPIU_SPPSR, 0xE0040000).

Bits	Name	Type	Reset value	Description
31:0	SWIDTH	RO	–	Maximum width of trace port 0x00000001—1-bit width 0x00000003—2-bit width 0x00000007—3-bit width 0x0000000F—4-bit width …

TABLE 16.39 Current Parallel Port Size Register (TPIU_CSPSR, 0xE0040004).

Bits	Name	Type	Reset value	Description
31:0	CWIDTH	RO	–	Current width of trace port 0x00000001—1-bit width 0x00000002—2-bit width 0x00000004—3-bit width 0x00000008—4-bit width …

The Asynchronous Clock Prescaler Register (TPIU_ACPR) allows debug tools to define clock prescaling for the asynchronous SWO output (Table 16.40).

The TPIU Selected Pin Protocol Register (TPIU SPPR) selects the output mode (Table 16.41).

The Formatter and Flush Status Register (TPIU_FFSR) shows the status of the formatter and flushing logic (Table 16.42). CoreSight debug architecture supports an optional trace

TABLE 16.40 Asynchronous Clock Prescaler Register (TPIU_ACPR, 0xE0040010).

Bits	Name	Type	Reset value	Description
31:12	Reserved	–	–	Reserved
11:0	PRESCALER	RW	0	Divisor for trace clock input is PRESCALER+1 Note: architecture supports a prescaler ratio of up to 16 bits, but in the existing Cortex-M TPIU only 12 bits are implemented.

TABLE 16.41 Selected Pin Protocol Register (TPIU_SPPR, 0xE00400F0).

Bits	Name	Type	Reset value	Description
31:2	Reserved	–	–	Reserved
1:0	TXMODE	RW	1	Transmit mode 00—parallel trace port mode 01—asynchronous SWO using Manchester encoding 10—asynchronous SWO using NRZ encoding

TABLE 16.42   Formatter and Flush Status Register (TPIU_FFSR, 0xE0040300).

Bits	Name	Type	Reset value	Description
31:4	Reserved	–	–	Reserved
3	FtNonStop	RO	1	Formatter cannot be stopped.
2	TCPresent	RO	0	This bit is always 0.
1	FtStopped	RO	0	This bit is always 0.
0	FlInProg	RO	0	Flush in progress: 0—Flush completed or no flushing in progress. 1—A flush is initiated.

bus flush feature that forces trace components to flush out remaining data in the internal trace buffer(s). After a debug session, the debugger can, optionally, issue a trace flush command to the TPIU and, when it does, the flush command is then propagated to various trace sources using signals on the trace bus. After receiving the flush request, the trace sources then flush out the remaining trace data in the internal FIFO buffer, which enables the data to be collected by the debug host.

The Formatter and Flush Control Register (TPIU_FFSR) allows debug tools to initiate a flush of trace data on the trace bus (Table 16.43).

The TPIU Periodic Synchronization Control Register (TPIU_PSCR) determines how frequently the TPIU synchronization packets are generated (Table 16.44).

The TPIU Claim Tag Set/Clear Registers (TPIU_CLAIMSET, TPIU_CLAIMCLR) allows debug agent software components to decide which software component takes control of the TPIU; this is similar to a hardware semaphore (Tables 16.45 and 16.46). Architecturally,

TABLE 16.43   Formatter and Flush Control Register (TPIU_FFCR, 0xE0040304).

Bits	Name	Type	Reset value	Description
31:9	Reserved	–	–	Reserved
8	TrigIn	RO	1	This bit reads as one and indicates that triggers are inserted to trace interface signaling when a trigger event has been detected. The trigger event could be generated by either the DWT or the ETM.
7	Reserved	–	–	Reserved
6	FOnMan	RW	0	Flush on manual. A write to 1 generates a trace bus flush. This clears to 0 when either the flush is completed or when the TPIU has been reset.
5:2	Reserved	–	–	Reserved
1	EnFCont	RW	1	Enable continuous formatting. 0—Continuous formatting disabled (bypass mode) 1—Continuous formatting enabled
0	Reserved	–	–	Reserved

TABLE 16.44 TPIU Periodic Synchronization Control Register (TPIU_PSCR, 0xE0040308).

Bits	Name	Type	Reset value	Description
31:5	Reserved	–	–	Reserved
4:0	PSCount	RW	0	Periodic Synchronization Count. When set to a nonzero value, it determines the approximate number of bytes of TPIU trace data output between synchronization. 00000—synchronization disabled 00111—synchronization packet after every 128 bytes 01000—synchronization packet after every 256 bytes … 11111—synchronization packet after every 2 31 bytes

TABLE 16.45 TPIU Claim Tag Set Register (TPIU_CLAIMSET, 0xE0040FA0).

Bits	Name	Type	Reset value	Description
31:4	Reserved	–	–	Reserved
3:0	CLAIMSET	RW	0xF	Read -. If 0, indicates that the claim tag bit is not implemented -. If 1, indicates the claim tag bit is implemented Write -. Writing a 0 has no effect -. Writing a 1 sets the claim tag bit

TABLE 16.46 TPIU Claim Tag Clear Register (TPIU_CLAIMCLR, 0xE0040FA4).

Bits	Name	Type	Reset value	Description
31:4	Reserved	–	–	Reserved
3:0	CLAIMCLR	RW	0	Read -. Current claim tag value Write -. Writing a 0 has no effect -. Writing a 1 clears the claim tag bit

this register is not required and is rarely used in modern debug tools. But it is included to maintain upward compatibility for the TPIU's of the previous Cortex-M processors.

In system-on-chips with multiple processors, the TPIU being used will be different from that used in a single processor microcontroller. In a multiprocessor system, the TPIU will likely be a CoreSight TPIU, which supports a wider trace data port width (up to 32 bits). In such a system, additional trace bus components would be needed to merge the trace data received from multiple trace sources. Because the SWO output is unlikely to provide enough trace data bandwidth for multiple trace sources, the CoreSight TPIU does not have a SWO output. However, it does have a similar programmer's model to that in the Cortex-M's TPIU.

16.3.9 Cross Trigger Interface (CTI)

The Cross-Trigger Interface is an optional component to assist multiprocessor debug handling. In multiprocessor systems, each processor has a CTI block linked to it, with multiple CTIs being linked together using a debug event propagation network consisting of Cross Trigger Matrix (CTM) components (Fig. 16.24).

With CTI and CTM components, debug activities between different processors can be linked. For example:

- When one processor enters halt state due to a debug event, it can halt other processors in the system at the same time.

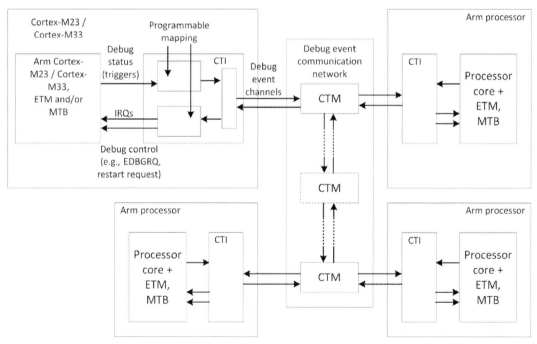

FIG. 16.24 ACTI in a multiprocessor system.

- When multiple processors are halted, you can restart all of them at the same time.
- A trace trigger event can be sent to multiple trace sources so that trace trigger packets can be generated from multiple trace components at almost the same time-allowing you to easily correlate the activities of multiple processors around a trigger event.
- A debug event from one processor can trigger an interrupt on another, e.g., in a system that controls a high-power motor, when one processor enters halt state, it can trigger an interrupt on another processor and request it manage the potentially still rotating motor.
- A debug event from one processor can be used to trigger debug/trace operations on another processor. For example, a DWT/ETM event on a processor can be used to trigger the trace start/stop of an ETM on another processor.

The mapping between debug triggering events and debug channels is programmable. Usually this is managed by debug tools. In single processor systems, the CTI component is unlikely to be present. In the previous generation of Arm processors, the CTI components were outside of the processor, but are now integrated as optional components to make the design of the system easier.

16.4 Starting a debug session

When the debugger connects to a debug target, a number of steps are carried out by the debug host:

1. It first attempts to detect the ID register value in the JTAG or Serial Wire Debug interface (Debug Port module).
2. It issues a debug power up request in the debug port and waits for the handshaking to be completed. This ensures that the system is ready for the debug connection.
3. It, optionally, scans through the internal debug bus of the Debug Access Port (DAP) to check what type of Access Port (AP) is available. In the case of a Cortex-M system, the ID register values will indicate that it is an AHB-AP module.
4. The debugger than checks that it can access the memory map.
5. It, optionally, obtains the address of the primary ROM table from the AHB-AP module and detects the debug components in the system via the ROM table (as explained in Section 16.2.8).
6. It, optionally, downloads a program image to the device based on the settings of the project.
7. It, optionally, enables the reset Vector Catch feature and resets the system using SCB-> AIRCR (SYSRESETREQ). The reset vector-catch feature halts the processor before any code is executed.

If step 7 is carried out, the processor is halted at the beginning of the execution of the program and is ready for the user to issue a run command to execute the software.

It is possible to connect to a running system without stopping and resetting the application by skipping steps 6 and 7.

If the system does not have a valid program image, the processor is likely to enter HardFault shortly after coming out of reset. If it does enter HardFault, it is still possible to connect to the processor, reset it and make sure it halts before doing anything by using the reset vector-catch feature. From that position, the software developer can download the program image to the memory and execute it.

16.5 Flash memory programming support

Although flash memory programming is not classified as a debug feature, flash programming operations often rely on the debug features that are present on the Cortex-M processors. Flash programming support is often an integrated part of the toolchain and can, optionally, be carried out at the start of a debug session.

Flash memories are usually partitioned into a number of pages (e.g., this can range from 512 bytes to a few Kbytes). Because of this, flash programming operations are usually designed to handle the flash updates page by page.

The flash programming of a Cortex-M microcontroller could be undertaken by a debugger using the following steps:

1. By using the debug connection and carrying out steps 1–5 as detailed in Section 16.4.
2. By enabling the reset Vector-Catch feature and resetting the system using SCB->AIRCR (SYSRESETREQ).
   Note: This action halts the processor.
3. By using the debugger to download a small piece of flash programming code and downloading the first page of program data to the SRAM.
   Note: To enable the flash programming to stop and halt the processor, a breakpoint instruction is inserted at the end of the code.
4. By changing the program counter to the starting point of the flash programming code in the SRAM and by unhalting the processor.
   Note: This starts the execution of the flash programming code.
5. By detecting the completion of the flash page programming, the debugger updates SRAM with the next block of data to be programmed and restarts the flash programming process.
   Note: At the end of the downloaded flash programming code, a breakpoint instruction is used which places the processor in halt state after the flash programming code is executed. When the debugger detects the halting, it checks to see if there has been any error, downloads the next page of the program image to the SRAM, sets the PC back to the beginning of the flash programming code and reruns it.
6. By repeating the programming steps until all the flash pages have been updated.
   Note: At this stage, the debugger can, optionally, run another piece of code to verify that the programmed flash pages have the correct contents by using a checksum algorithm.
7. By issuing another system reset, using SCB->AIRCR (SYSRESETREQ), the processor is halted and ready to execute the new program image.
   Note 1: The flash program code might start with an initialization of hardware resources, such as clock and power management, in order that the flash programming is carried out at the right speed and conditions (e.g., voltage settings).

Note 2: The flash programming procedure inside the downloaded flash programming code depends on the nature of the microcontroller system as follows:

a. When TrustZone security is implemented and if the Secure firmware is preloaded, the downloaded flash programming code calls the Secure firmware update functions in the Secure firmware to update the flash memory.

b. If TrustZone security is not implemented, or if the Secure firmware update function has not been preloaded, the downloaded flash programming code will need to include the flash programming algorithm and carry out the flash programming control steps.

16.6 Software design considerations

Cortex-M processors provide a wide range of debug features. However, to make the most of the debug feature, software developers should be aware of the following:

- Depending on the chip's design, some of the low power optimizations might be disabled in order to allow the debugger to continue accessing the processor's states and its memories. This could lead to the application consuming slightly higher power during debugging.
- Some of the low power modes in certain Cortex-M devices could result in the debug connection being lost. For example, when the processor is powered down the debugger will not be able to access the processor's states.
- During halting, the SysTick timers stop. However, the peripheral on the system level (outside of the processor) could still be running.
- Generally, application code should avoid modifying debug registers as this can interfere with debug operations.
- To use DWT data-trace, the data being traced should be declared as global or static so that it has a fixed address location. This is because local variables are dynamically allocated in the stack memories and, thus, with no fixed address and cannot be traced.
- Many devices have I/O pins that combine debug signals with functional I/O features. Although those I/O pins are, right after reset, normally assigned for debug purposes, it is possible to lockout a device from further debugging activities by switching the functions of the debug pins. This arrangement, however, is not a secure way to prevent debug connections or to stop access to the debug feature. It is usual, therefore, for silicon vendors to provide other read-out protection features to enable product designers to stop their software assets from being read-out by third parties.
- Some development tools provide a range of profiling features to allow software developers to optimize their applications.

References

[1] CoreSight Technology System Design Guide. https://developer.arm.com/documentation/dgi0012/latest/.

[2] CoreSight Architecture Specification v2.0. https://static.docs.arm.com/ihi0029/d/IHI0029D_coresight_architecture_spec_v2_0.pdf.

[3] Arm Debug Interface Architecture Specification (ADIv5.0 to ADIv5.2). https://developer.arm.com/documentation/ihi0031/d.

[4] ETM Architecture Specification v1.0 to v3.5, Applicable to Arm Cortex-M23 Processor. https://developer.arm.com/documentation/ihi0014/latest/.

[5] ETM Architecture Specification v4.0 to v4.5, Applicable to Arm Cortex-M33 Processor. https://developer.arm.com/documentation/ihi0064/latest/.

[6] Armv8-M Architecture Reference Manual. https://developer.arm.com/documentation/ddi0553/am (Armv8.0-M only version). https://developer.arm.com/documentation/ddi0553/latest/ (latest version including Armv8.1-M). Note: M-profile architecture reference manuals for Armv6-M, Armv7-M, Armv8-M and Armv8.1-M can be found here: https://developer.arm.com/architectures/cpu-architecture/m-profile/docs.

[7] AMBA 5 Advanced High-performance Bus (AHB) Protocol Specification. https://developer.arm.com/documentation/ihi0033/latest/.

[8] AMBA 4 Advanced Peripheral Bus (APB) Protocol Specification. https://developer.arm.com/documentation/ihi0024/latest/.

[9] Arm Debug Interface Architecture Specification (ADIv6.0). https://developer.arm.com/documentation/ihi0074/latest/.

[10] AMBA 4 ATB Protocol Specification. https://developer.arm.com/documentation/ihi0032/latest/.

[11] Armv7-M Architecture Reference Manual. https://developer.arm.com/documentation/ddi0403/ed/.

[12] Arm CoreSight MTB-M33 Technical Reference Manual. https://developer.arm.com/documentation/100231/latest/.

[13] Embedded Trace Buffer in CoreSight SoC-400. https://developer.arm.com/documentation/100536/0302/embedded-trace-buffer.

CHAPTER

17

Software development

17.1 Introduction

17.1.1 Software development overview

An overview of software development has already been covered in Chapter 2, Section 2.4. When using Arm®v8-M architecture [1], there can be various software development scenarios. For example, a device might or might not have TrustZone® implemented and, even if does, the application software developer creating software for it might not need, as explained in Chapter 3, Section 3.18, to know anything about it.

For information purposes, I have illustrated in Fig. 17.1, various software development scenarios.

In this chapter, I will focus on the scenarios where only a single project is created and used (i.e., scenarios #1, #2, and #5 in Fig. 17.1) and will detail the basic concepts of a typical software project setup. Information covering Secure software projects is covered in Chapter 18, and that is where scenarios #3 and #4 are covered. For these two scenarios, interactions between Secure and Non-secure projects are involved.

17.1.2 Inside a typical Cortex-M software project

As mentioned in Section 2.5.3, a basic software project based on the CMSIS-CORE compliant software driver usually includes several software files (Fig. 17.2).

Behind the scenes, the device-specific header file pulls in additional CMSIS-CORE header files, which also include some generic Arm® CMSIS-CORE files (as shown in Chapter 2, Fig. 2.19). By so doing, it enables access to a range of CMSIS functions; such as interrupt management, the SysTick timer configuration, and the special registers access function.

When using a typical microcontroller device, you would likely find example software packages from the microcontroller vendor. These example projects usually contain:

- The CMSIS-CORE header files for the Cortex®-M processor(s).
- A device-specific header file based on the CMSIS-CORE.

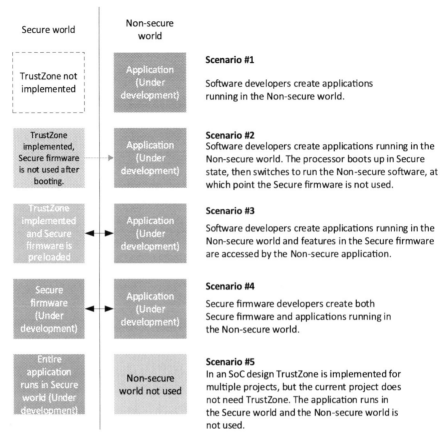

FIG. 17.1   Software development scenarios in Armv8-M processors.

- Device-specific startup code(s) (this can be in assembly language or in C language). There can be multiple versions for different toolchains.
- Device driver program files.
- Example applications.
- Project configuration files. There can be multiple versions for different toolchains.

To help the distribution and integration of these essential files, some of the device-specific files are packaged into software packs based on the CMSIS-Pack standard. Inside these software specific packages, an XML file is used to specify and detail the software components that are available. This enables the software developers to:

- Download and integrate essential and optional files
- Ensure software dependency requirements are met

The CMSIS-Pack support utility is often integrated as part of the microcontroller toolchain, and in the Keil® Microcontroller Development Kit (MDK) it is called the "Pack Installer".

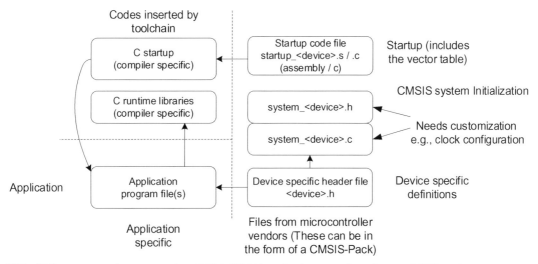

FIG. 17.2   An example project with a CMSIS-CORE-based software package from an MCU vendor.

Arm also provides CMSIS-Pack Eclipse Plug-ins (https://github.com/ARM-software/cmsis-pack-eclipse/releases) to enable third party software development tools to take advantages of the CMSIS-Pack. The advantage of using the CMSIS-PACK is that it makes the creation of a Cortex-M application quite straight forward.

It is still possible to create projects without using the CMSIS-Pack by manually adding various files into the software project. But, to do so, will require a deal more effort as one will need to make sure that everything is in place. Instead of creating a software project from scratch, you can, alternatively, start out with an example project from the microcontroller vendor and modify the project from there.

17.2 Getting started with the Keil Microcontroller Development Kit (MDK)

17.2.1 Overview of Keil MDK features

When developing software on an Armv8-M-based device you need a software development toolchain that supports the Armv8-M processors. To demonstrate the software development process, most of the examples in this book have been created using the Keil Microcontroller Development Kit (MDK). However, there are many other toolchains, including those provided by microcontroller vendors that also support Armv8-M architecture.

Keil MDK contains the following components:

- µVision Integrated Development Environment (IDE)
- Arm Compilation Tools including
  - A C/C++ Compiler
  - An Assembler
  - A Linker and its utilities

- A Debugger—which includes support for multiple types of debug probes: e.g., Keil debug probes (ULINK™ 2, ULINK Pro, ULINK Plus), CMSIS-DAP-based probes, and several third-party products such as the ST-LINK (from ST Microelectronics, multiple versions), the UDA Debugger from Silicon Labs, and the NULink Debugger.
- A Simulator
- An RTX Real-Time OS Kernel
- Support for the CMSIS-PACK—which enables software developers to access reference software packages for over 6000 microcontrollers; these software packages include device-specific header files, program examples, flash programming algorithms, etc.
- Optionally, in some editions of Keil MDK, middleware such as the USB stack, the TCP/IP stack.

Various versions of Keil MDK are available from Keil (www.keil.com). There are also free-to-use editions of Keil MDK available for microcontroller devices from specific microcontroller vendors. To get started, you do not, therefore, need to spend too much money; you only need to factor in the cost of the board as many development boards have a low-cost debug probe built-in.

17.2.2 Typical program compilation flow

Typically, the program compilation flow of a project using Keil MDK would be as per Fig. 17.3. Once the project has been created, the compilation flow is handled by the Integrated Development Environment (IDE), which means that, after taking a few simple steps, you can program your microcontroller and test the application.

Please note, Keil MDK contains two types of C compilers. These are the:

- Arm Compiler 6—this is the latest version and supports the Armv8-M architecture.
- Arm Compiler 5—this is the previous generation C compiler and does not support Armv8-M architecture.

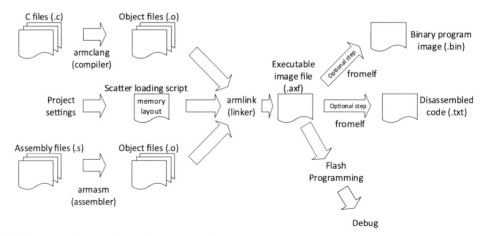

FIG. 17.3 Example compilation flow using Keil MDK.

As a result of switching over from Arm Compiler 5 to Arm Compiler 6, which is based on a different compiler technology, some of the compiler-specific features have been changed. As a result, in some cases the C codes created for Arm Compiler 5 might need to be updated (e.g., function attributes, the use of the embedded assembler). Full information about the software migration is covered in the following Keil application note: http://www.keil.com/appnotes/files/apnt_298.pdf [2].

17.2.3 Creating a new project from scratch

The easiest path to take when developing new software is to reuse an existing project example from the MCU vendor (the project files have the ".uvproj" extension in their filenames). However, to demonstrate how the MDK development tool works, the following paragraphs detail the steps to take when creating from scratch a new Keil MDK-based project. The target hardware used for the purpose of this exercise is an Arm FPGA board called MPS2+.[a] It is configured with a processor system design called IoTKit, which contains a Cortex-M33 processor. Although the example software package for the board (in the form of a CMSIS-Pack) would be different if a standard microcontroller device was being used, the concept is, nonetheless, the same.

The name of the Integrated Development Environment (IDE) in Keil MDK is called μVision®. After starting the μVision IDE, a screen similar to the one shown in Fig. 17.4 is displayed. But, if the Keil MDK is run for the first time after its installation, the Pack Installer will start automatically, and the screen will be as per Fig. 17.6.

If the IDE opens showing a previous project's details, the old project can be closed by using the pull-down menu: select Project → Close project.

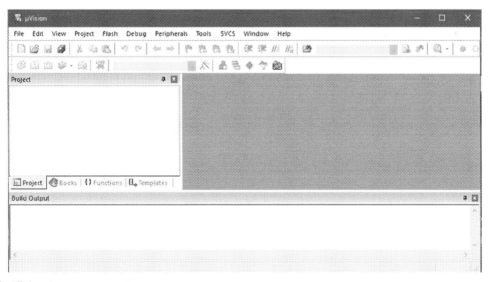

FIG. 17.4 Blank project window in μVision IDE.

[a] https://developer.arm.com/tools-and-software/development-boards/fpga-prototyping-boards/mps2.

FIG. 17.5   Access to the Pack Installer in Keil μVision IDE.

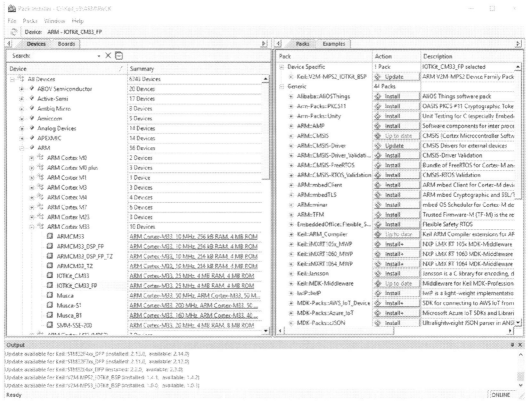

FIG. 17.6   Pack Installer.

Before creating a new project, it is recommended that the Pack Installer is used to install the right software packages to the Keil MDK and to update software packs that might be out of date. The pack installer can be accessed via the toolbar shown in Fig. 17.5.

An example screen of the Pack Installer is shown in Fig. 17.6.

A freshly installed Pack Installer might take several minutes to execute as it will need to download the latest CMSIS-Pack index, and will need to check whether any previously installed software packs are out of date. Using the Pack Installer (Fig. 17.6), the "IOTKit_CM33_FP" hardware platform (or a hardware platform of your choice), which is listed on the left-hand side, along with other available hardware platforms, should be selected. Once done, the "Install" button, which is on the right-hand side, and where the available software packs are listed, should be clicked to install the required software packs.

If the button next to a software component displays "Update", as it does in the Keil::V2M-MPS2_IOTKit_BSP and ARM::CMSIS-Driver in Fig. 17.6, it should be clicked so that the software pack can be updated.

After the required software packs have been installed, the process of creating a software project can begin. To begin the new project, the "new project" item in the pull-down menu should be clicked (Fig. 17.7).

The IDE will then ask for the location and name of the project, as shown in Fig. 17.8

Once the project name and location has been entered, the microcontroller device to be used in the project would need to be selected. For this example, the "IOTKit_CM33_FP" hardware platform, which is based on the Cortex-M33 processor with an FPU, is selected. This can be found in the device list: Arm → Arm Cortex-M33 → IOTKit_CM33_FP, as shown in Fig. 17.9. Because the devices that are listed in the "Select Device" dialog are based on the CMSIS-Packs that have been installed, if the device you would like to use is not available in this list, it means that the CMSIS-Pack of the device you want to use has either not been installed, or there is no CMSIS-Pack for this device.

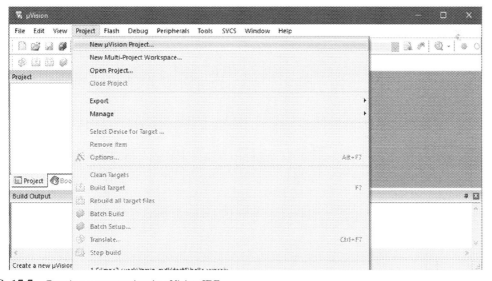

FIG. 17.7   Creating a new project in µVision IDE.

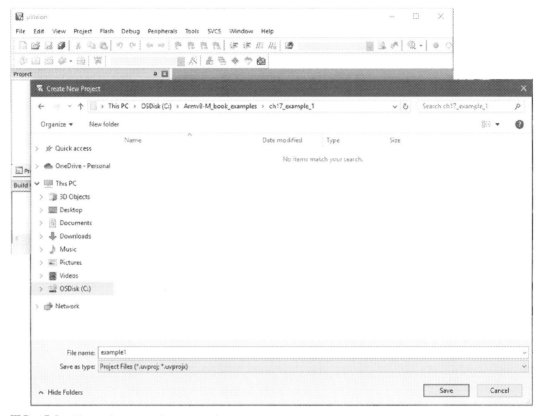

FIG. 17.8 Choose the project directory and project name.

Once the required microcontroller device has been selected, the Manage Run-Time Environment window (Fig. 17.10) is shown. This window allows a range of software components to be selected.

By default, Keil MDK imports the specified software components in groups, as shown in Fig. 17.11.

Once the required software components have been selected and the project has been created, the next step is adding the application code (i.e., a C program). To do so, right-clicking on the Source Group 1 and selecting "Add New Item to Group …", as shown in Fig. 17.12, should be carried out.

Once done, the file type would then need to be selected and the filename entered, as shown in Fig. 17.13.

Following on from this, a piece of program code to toggle an LED (i.e., LED blinky) should be added to example_1.c (Note: this is the filename entered in Fig. 17.13). The program code is as follows:

example_1.c

```c
// Device specific header
#include "IOTKit_CM33_FP.h"  /* Device header */
#include "Board_LED.h"        /* ::Board Support:LED */
int main(void)
{
  int i;
  LED_Initialize();
  while (1) {
    LED_On(0);
    for (i=0;i<100000;i++){
      __NOP();
    }
    LED_Off(0);
    for (i=0;i<100000;i++){
      __NOP();
    }
  }
}
```

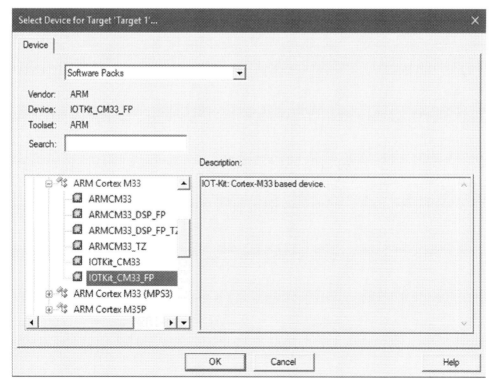

FIG. 17.9   Device selection when creating a project.

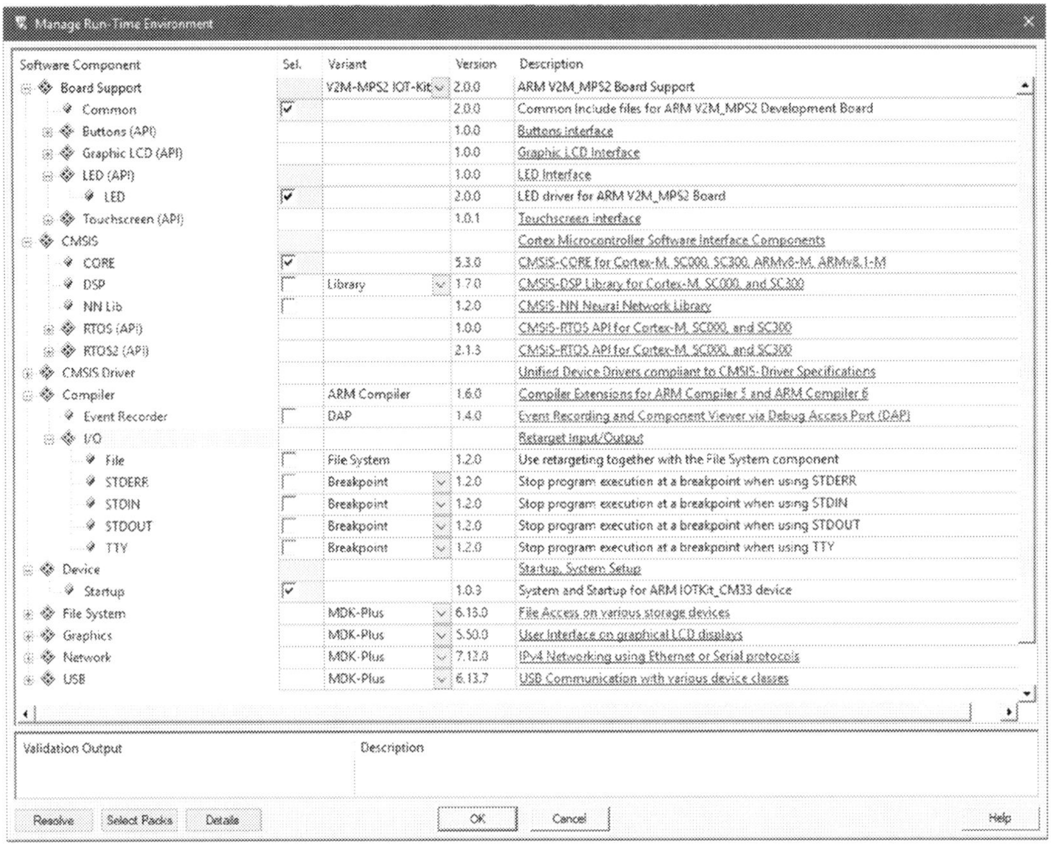

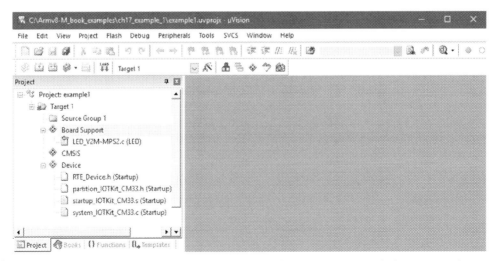

Software Component	Sel.	Variant	Version	Description
⊟ ◇ Board Support		V2M-MPS2 IOT-Kit ✓	2.0.0	ARM V2M_MPS2 Board Support
◆ Common	✓		2.0.0	Common Include files for ARM V2M_MPS2 Development Board
⊞ ◇ Buttons (API)			1.0.0	Buttons interface
⊞ ◇ Graphic LCD (API)			1.0.0	Graphic LCD Interface
⊟ ◇ LED (API)			1.0.0	LED Interface
◆ LED	✓		2.0.0	LED driver for ARM V2M_MPS2 Board
⊞ ◇ Touchscreen (API)			1.0.1	Touchscreen interface
⊟ ◇ CMSIS				Cortex Microcontroller Software Interface Components
◆ CORE	✓		5.3.0	CMSIS-CORE for Cortex-M, SC000, SC300, ARMv8-M, ARMv8.1-M
◆ DSP	☐	Library ✓	1.7.0	CMSIS-DSP Library for Cortex-M, SC000, and SC300
◆ NN Lib	☐		1.2.0	CMSIS-NN Neural Network Library
⊞ ◇ RTOS (API)			1.0.0	CMSIS-RTOS API for Cortex-M, SC000, and SC300
⊞ ◇ RTOS2 (API)			2.1.3	CMSIS-RTOS API for Cortex-M, SC000, and SC300
⊞ ◇ CMSIS Driver				Unified Device Drivers compliant to CMSIS-Driver Specifications
⊟ ◇ Compiler		ARM Compiler	1.6.0	Compiler Extensions for ARM Compiler 5 and ARM Compiler 6
◆ Event Recorder	☐	DAP	1.4.0	Event Recording and Component Viewer via Debug Access Port (DAP)
⊟ ◇ I/O				Retarget Input/Output
◆ File	☐	File System	1.2.0	Use retargeting together with the File System component
◆ STDERR	☐	Breakpoint ✓	1.2.0	Stop program execution at a breakpoint when using STDERR
◆ STDIN	☐	Breakpoint ✓	1.2.0	Stop program execution at a breakpoint when using STDIN
◆ STDOUT	☐	Breakpoint ✓	1.2.0	Stop program execution at a breakpoint when using STDOUT
◆ TTY	☐	Breakpoint ✓	1.2.0	Stop program execution at a breakpoint when using TTY
⊟ ◇ Device				Startup, System Setup
◆ Startup	✓		1.0.3	System and Startup for ARM IOTKit_CM33 device
⊞ ◇ File System		MDK-Plus ✓	6.13.0	File Access on various storage devices
⊞ ◇ Graphics		MDK-Plus ✓	5.50.0	User Interface on graphical LCD displays
⊞ ◇ Network		MDK-Plus ✓	7.12.0	IPv4 Networking using Ethernet or Serial protocols
⊞ ◇ USB		MDK-Plus ✓	6.13.7	USB Communication with various device classes

FIG. 17.10 Selecting software components for inclusion in the project.

FIG. 17.11 Example of a project created after selecting the software components; which are arranged in groups.

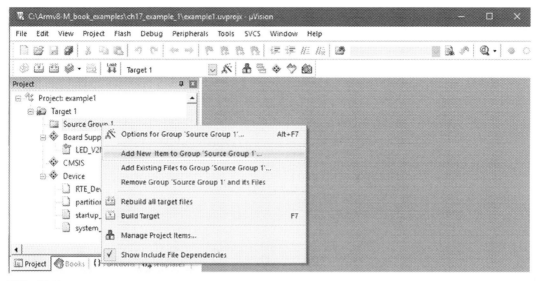

FIG. 17.12   Adding new program code file to the project.

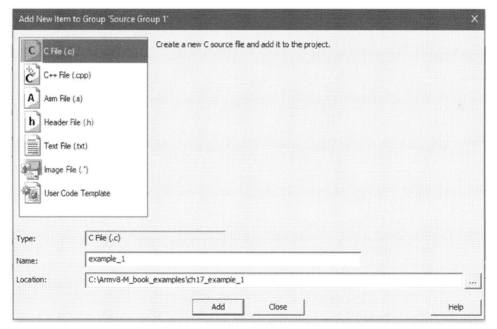

FIG. 17.13   Specifying new C program file ("example_1.c").

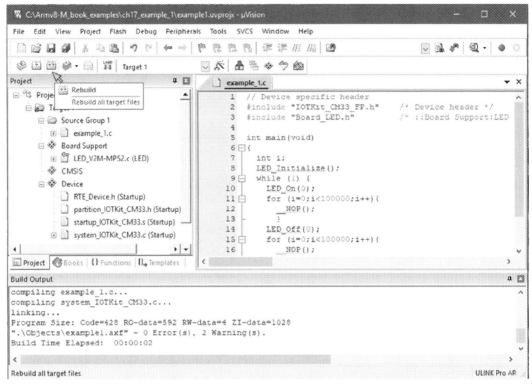

FIG. 17.14 Compilation output message.

Once all the source files are ready, the project can then be compiled. This is achieved by:

- Clicking on the Build Target icon on the tool bar, or
- Selecting "Project → Build Target" from the pull-down menu, or
- Right clicking on Target 1 in the project browser and selecting "Build Target", or
- Using the "F7" hotkey.

After the project's compilation, the compilation output is as per Fig. 17.14.

The program compilation process generates an executable image called "example1.axf". After the program image is generated, several more steps need to be carried out before the program can be downloaded to the board and tested. These steps are:

- Checking whether the Device driver for the debug probe needs to be installed. If it does, the required device driver should be installed.
- Updating the debug settings, so that the correct debug probe is selected, and the required settings are configured.

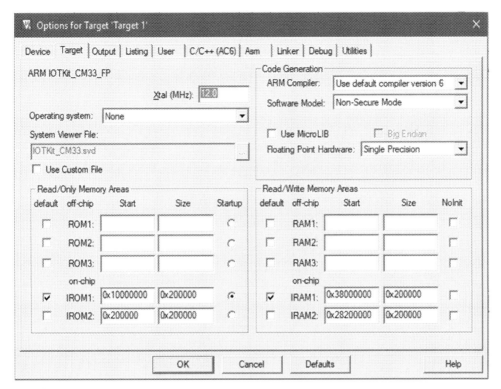

FIG. 17.15   Project option default window.

The debug settings are accessible from the project options menu. There are several ways to access it:

- Right-clicking on the "Target 1" on the project browser and selecting "Options for target 'Target 1'", or
- From the pull-down menu, selecting "Project→ Options for target 'Target 1'", or
- Using the hot-key Alt-F7, or
- Clicking on the target option button 🔧 on the tool bar

When the project option is opened, a project option window as shown in Fig. 17.15 should appear:

The top of the project options dialog window contains a number of tabs. Please note:

- The memory map settings, the C preprocessing macros, and the flash programming options should already be correctly configured based on the information provided in the CMSIS-Pack.
- Some project options (e.g., whether the FPU should be used for the project and the clock speed settings) need to be configured by software developers. The definition of these options depends on the needs of the application.

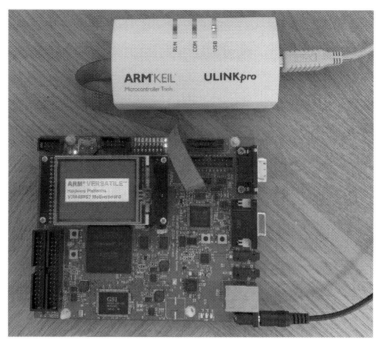

FIG. 17.16   A ULINKPro debug probe connected to the MPS2+ FPGA board.

- The debug probe options (under the debug tab) need to be configured by the software developer based on the debug probe being used.

For the example project being demonstrated here, the debug probe setting would need to be modified to allow the compiled project to be tested. In this scenario, a ULINKPro (Fig. 17.16) from Keil is being used (Further information about the ULINKPro can be found on this web page: www.keil.com/mdk5/ulink/ulinkpro/).

In order that the project can be tested, the right debug probe needs to be selected in the debug option (Fig. 17.17).

Once the correct debug probe is selected, the "Settings" button next to the debug probe selection need to be clicked so that the debug settings (Fig. 17.18) for the following areas can be defined:

- The JTAG or Serial Wire Debug connection protocols and connection speed
- The program "download" and reset options
- The trace option (under the Trace tab)
- The flash programming option (under the Flash Download tab)
- The debug setup sequence (under the "Pack" tab. This is optional and can be used, for example, to setup the debug authentication control sequence)

Because an FPGA board (it has no flash memory) is being used in this example, the flash programming options have been removed, leaving only the "Do not erase" option available

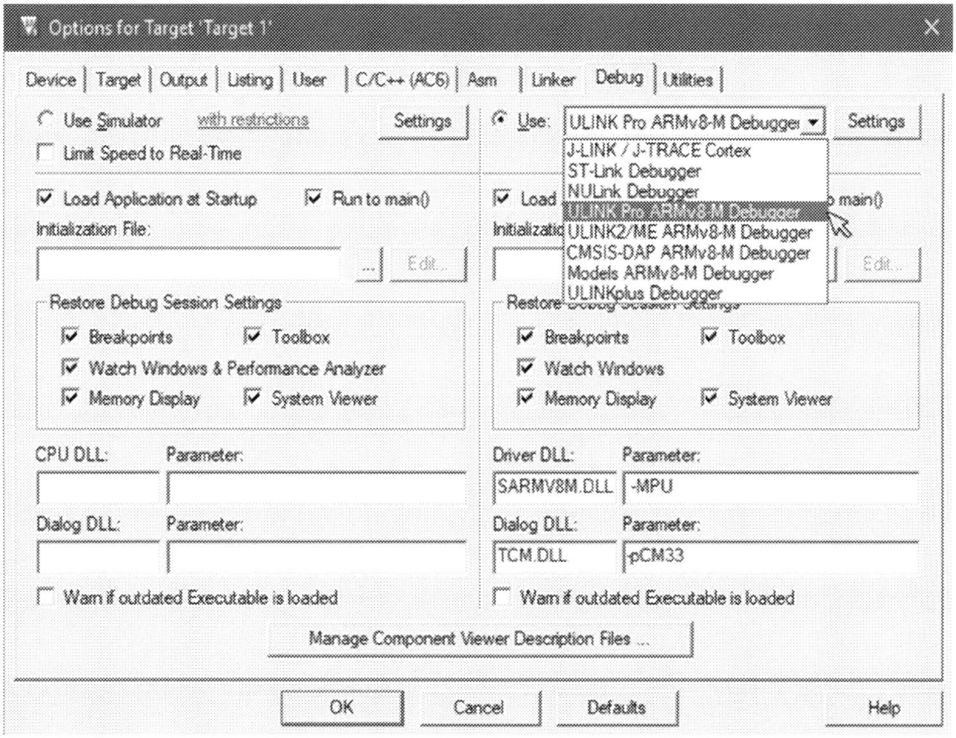

FIG. 17.17   Selecting the right debug probe in debug options.

for selection. Usually though, when using standard microcontrollers there will be a flash programming algorithm that will need to be defined.

Once the debug settings have been correctly set, and once the development board is connected and powered up, the debugger tool will be in a position to detect, via the Debug Settings window (Fig. 17.18), whether the JTAG or Serial Wire Debug interface has connected. If it has, an IDCODE would be displayed.

At this stage, the project option window can be closed and the debug session can be started by one of the following options. By:

- Using the pull-down menu "Debug → Start/Stop Debug Session", or
- Using the Ctrl-F5 hot key, or
- Clicking on the button on the tool bar

The debugger window (Fig. 17.19) should now appear.
The program execution can be started by:

- Clicking on the "Debug → Run" item in the pull-down menu, or
- Using the F5 hot key, or
- Clicking on the Run button on the tool bar,

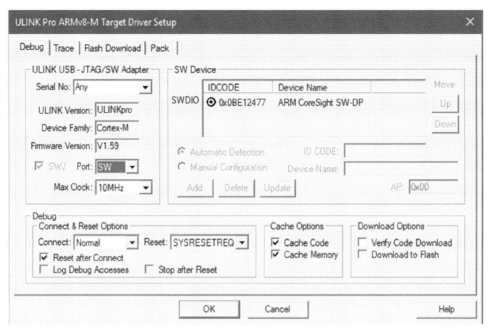

FIG. 17.18   Debug settings.

If everything is setup correctly, the LEDs on the board should start flashing and, if they do, this indicates that the Cortex®-M project is functioning correctly.

Once the example is up and running, the debug session can then be stopped by:

- Using pull down menu "Debug → Start/Stop Debug Session", or
- Using the Ctrl-F5 hot key, or
- Clicking on the ⓠ button

Note: These steps are almost the same as that used for starting the debug session.

17.2.4 Understanding the project options

17.2.4.1 Overview

As Fig. 17.15 showed, there is a range of project options under the various tabs of the project setting window, and these are now shown in more detail in Fig. 17.20.

It is possible to define multiple sets of project options in a project, and switch between sets of options when compiling the project. This is useful for software projects because you can then have:

- One (or more) set of project options when debugging software. For debugging purposes, the project options can be set at a lower optimization level (which makes debugging easier) and the output of debug symbols in the compilation outputs can be enabled.

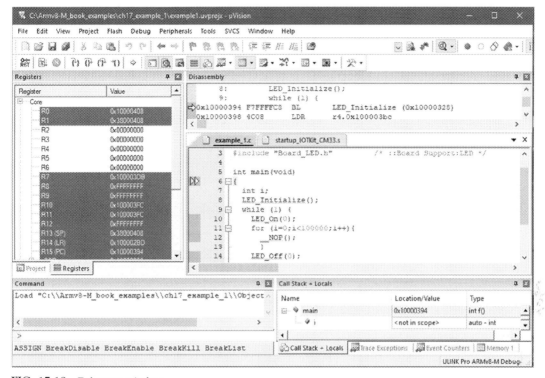

FIG. 17.19   Debugger window.

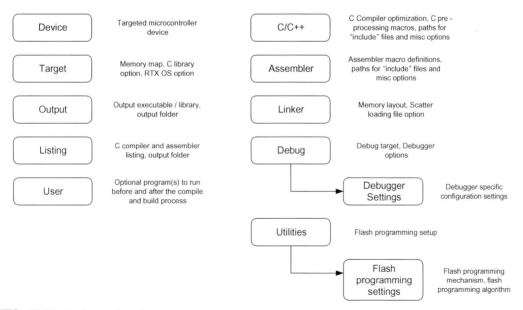

FIG. 17.20   Project option tabs.

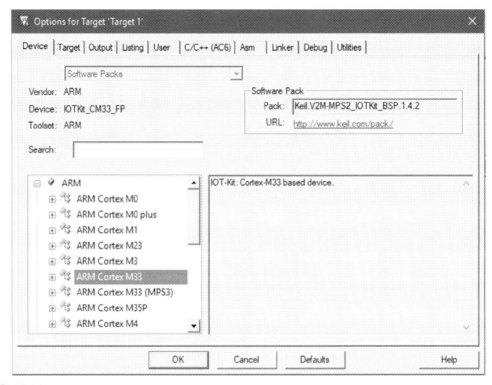

FIG. 17.21   Device options.

- Another set of project options for release, which uses a higher optimization level and which do not have the debug symbols.

When using Keil MDK, each set of options is called a target. In the example project shown in Fig. 17.11, the project window has a "Target 1". The name of a target can be customized (e.g., using names such as "Development" or "Release" can be an intuitive way to define the target's purpose). To add a target, right-click on the target name, select "Manage Components" and then click on the button for the "New (Insert)" target. When there are multiple targets in a project, you can switch between targets using the target selection box on the tool bar.

17.2.4.2 Device options

This tab defines the hardware device/platform that is being used for the project. After the device-specific software pack (i.e., the CMSIS-Pack) is installed, the device of your choice can be selected from this option tab. When selecting a device from this dialog (Fig. 17.21), compiler flags, memory maps, and flash algorithm settings are preconfigured for that device. If the device that you are using is not listed, you can still select the Cortex-M23 or Cortex-M33 processors under the Arm section and then manually set the configuration options.

17.2.4.3 *Target options*

The target option tab (already shown in Fig. 17.15) allows you to define:

- The memory map of the device (please note, you can also define the memory map of the project using a scatter file and pass this file to the linker using an option in the linker tab).
- The version of the compiler you want to use (for Armv8-M devices, Arm compiler 6 should be selected and for Armv6-M or Armv7-M devices you have a choice of either selecting Arm Compiler 5 or Arm Compiler 6).
- Whether the FPU feature is used. Even when the hardware platform does have an FPU, if the application does not require floating-point data processing the FPU can be left unused and disabled to save power.
- Whether the project is compiled for Non-secure or Secure software. If the Secure software model is selected, a range of TrustZone features (e.g., intrinsic functions for pointer security checks) are available. These features are needed when creating Secure firmware or Secure libraries. For software development scenarios #1, #2, and #3 in Fig. 17.1, the Non-secure software model should be used.
- The type of C runtime library that is used—This can be either the standard C runtime library, which is fully featured and is optimized for speed or the MicroLib, which is a memory size optimized C runtime library.
- Whether the built-in RTX operating system is used.
- The crystal frequency—this setting is used by the instruction set simulator and, potentially, by the flash programming algorithm. This should be set to the frequency of the main crystal oscillator, which is usually external to the device.

The options in the target option tab are automatically updated when a different microcontroller device is selected.

17.2.4.4 *Output options*

The output option tab (Fig. 17.22) allows you to select whether the project should generate an executable image or generate a library. It also allows you to specify the directory where the generated files will be created. For example, you can create a subdirectory in your project directory and then set the output directory to this location using the "Select Folder for Objects" dialog. This is very useful as it helps you keep your main project directory clean and tidy. During a project compilation, a large number of files (e.g., C object files) are likely to be generated, and if the output directory is not separated from the main project directory, it could clutter the project directory and make project file maintenances (e.g., backup) difficult.

The output option tab also allows you to generate a batch file (a script file for Windows/DOS command prompt), which after the first compilation, can be repeatedly used for batch mode regression testing. This compilation can be carried out without using the Keil μVision IDE.

17.2.4.5 *Listing options*

The listing option tab (Fig. 17.23) allows you to enable/disable assembly listing files. By default, the C Compiler listing file is turned off. When debugging software issues, it can be useful to turn on the option to generate the C compiler listing so that you can see exactly

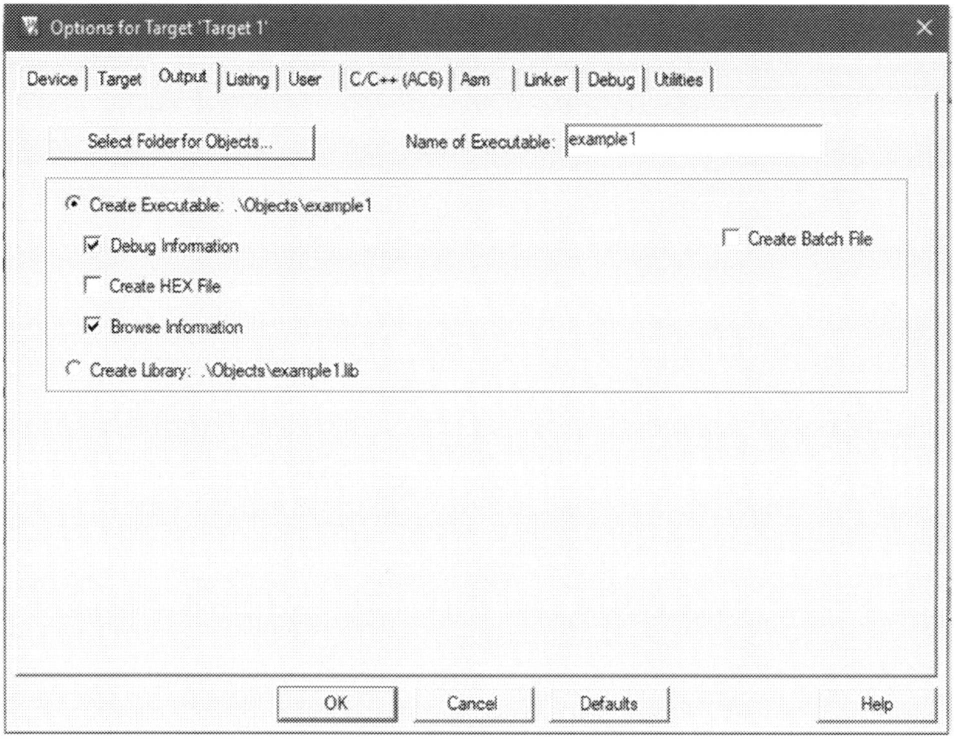

FIG. 17.22 Output options.

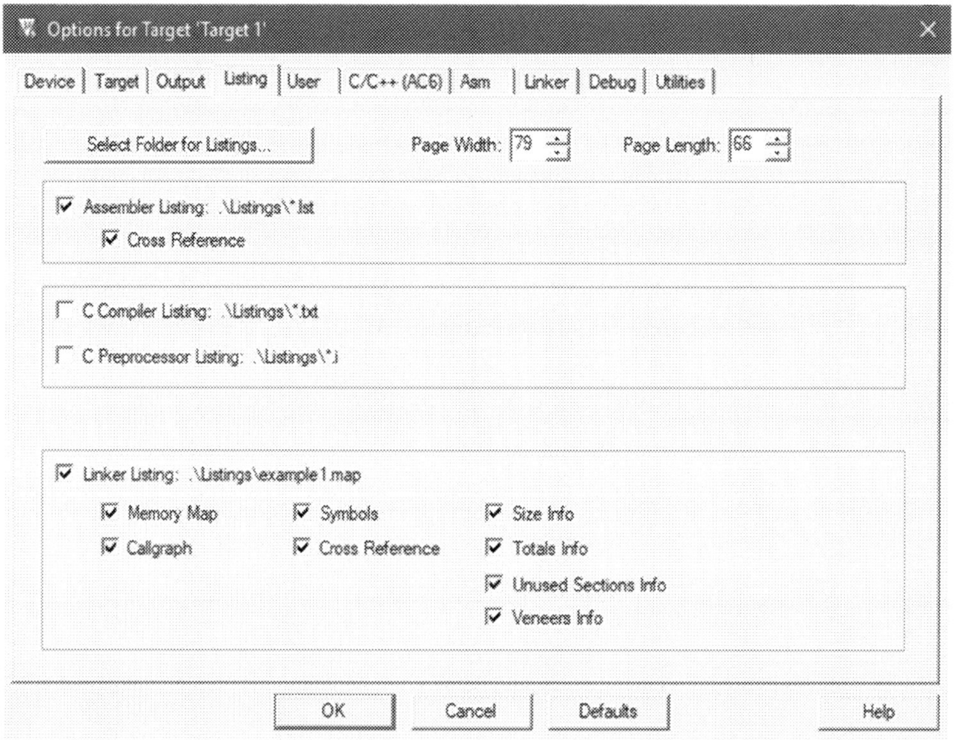

FIG. 17.23 Listing options.

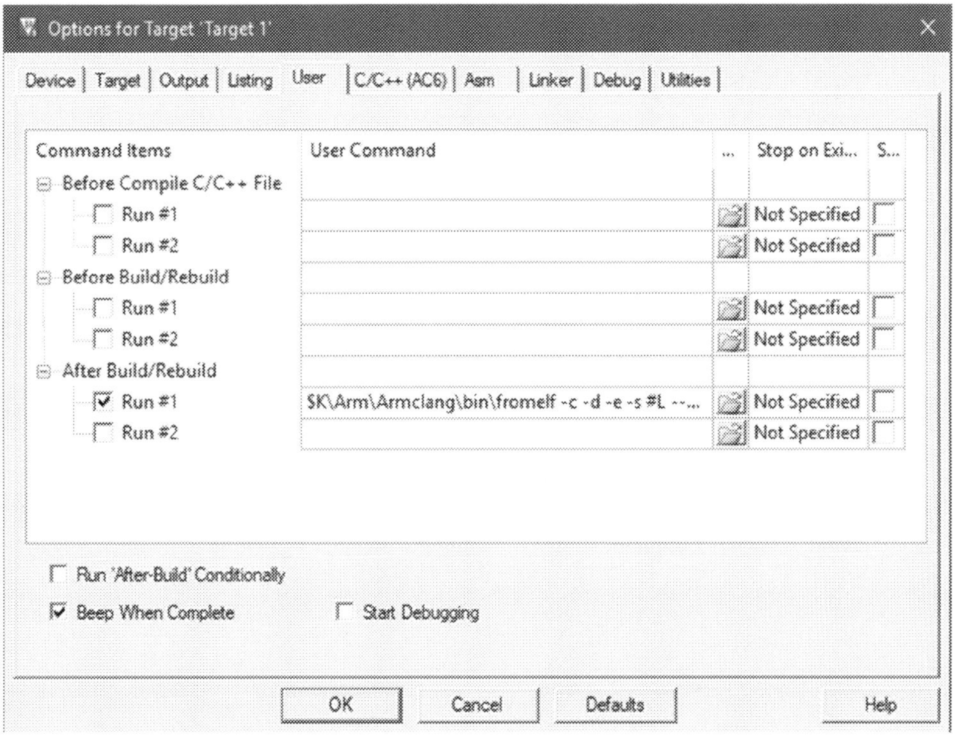

FIG. 17.24 User options.

what assembly instruction sequence has been generated. Similar to the "Output" options, you can click on the "Select Folder for Listings" to define where the output listing files should be stored. Another method to generate a disassembly listing is to add a user command that executes after the linking stage—this is described in the User options in Section 17.2.4.6.

17.2.4.6 User options

The User option tab allows you to specify additional commands that need to be executed at each stage of the software's compilation. For example, in Fig. 17.24, a command line to generate the disassembled listing of the complete program image has been added and will execute after the compilation stage has concluded.

The full command added in the user option in Fig. 17.24 is

```
$K\Arm\Armclang\bin\fromelf -c -d -e -s #L --output list.txt –cpu=cortex-m33
```

This command generates a file called list.txt, which is the full disassembly of the program image generated. In the command example shown above, "$K" is the root folder of the Keil development tool, and "#L" is the linker output file. These special keywords are called key sequences and can be used to pass arguments to external user programs. A list of key sequence code can be found in this link on the Keil web site: http://www.keil.com/support/man/docs/uv4/uv4_ut_keysequence.htm.

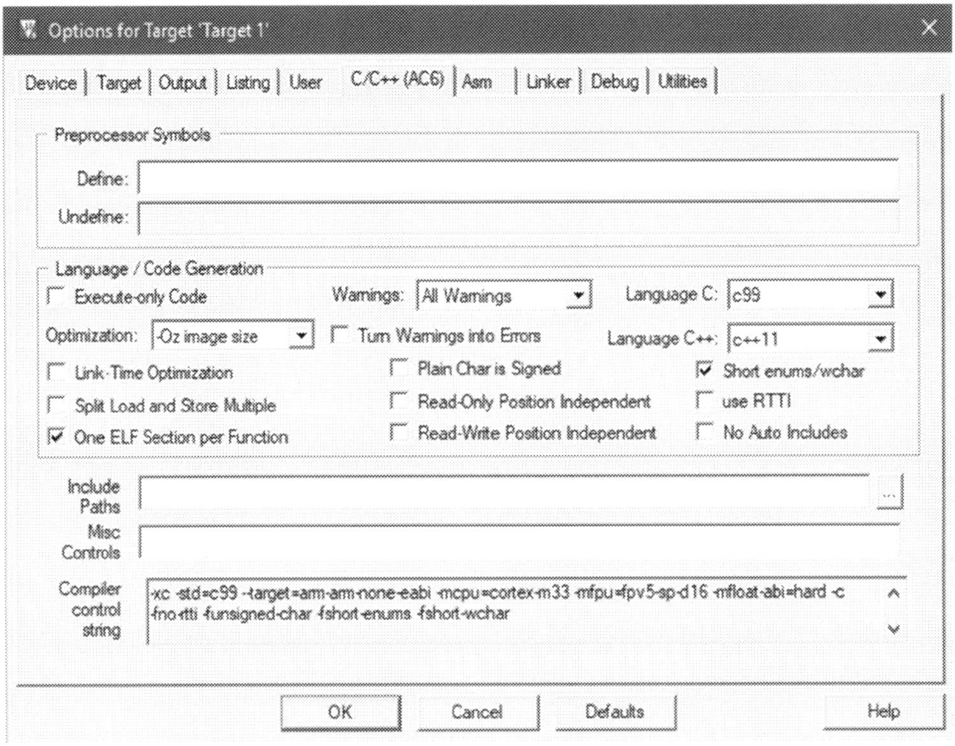

FIG. 17.25   C/C++ options.

17.2.4.7 C/C++ options

The C/C++ option tab (Fig. 17.25) allows you to define the optimization options, the C preprocessing directives (defines) and the search path for the "include-files", and the miscellaneous compile switches. Please note, by default a number of include-file directories are automatically included in the file search path of a Keil MDK project (You can determine which directories are included in these search paths from the Compile control string listed at the bottom of the C/C++ option tab). For example, the CMSIS-CORE include-files, and sometimes the device-specific header files, are often automatically included. If you want to use a specific version of a CMSIS-CORE file, you will need to disable this automatic include path feature by clicking on the "No Auto Includes" box in the option tab.

For an in-depth overview of the optimization level options, please refer to Keil application note AN298: http://www.keil.com/appnotes/files/apnt_298.pdf.

17.2.4.8 Assembler options

The assembler option tab allows you to define preprocessing directives, the "include-paths" and, if required, the additional assembler command switches.

Assembler options are shown in Fig. 17.26.

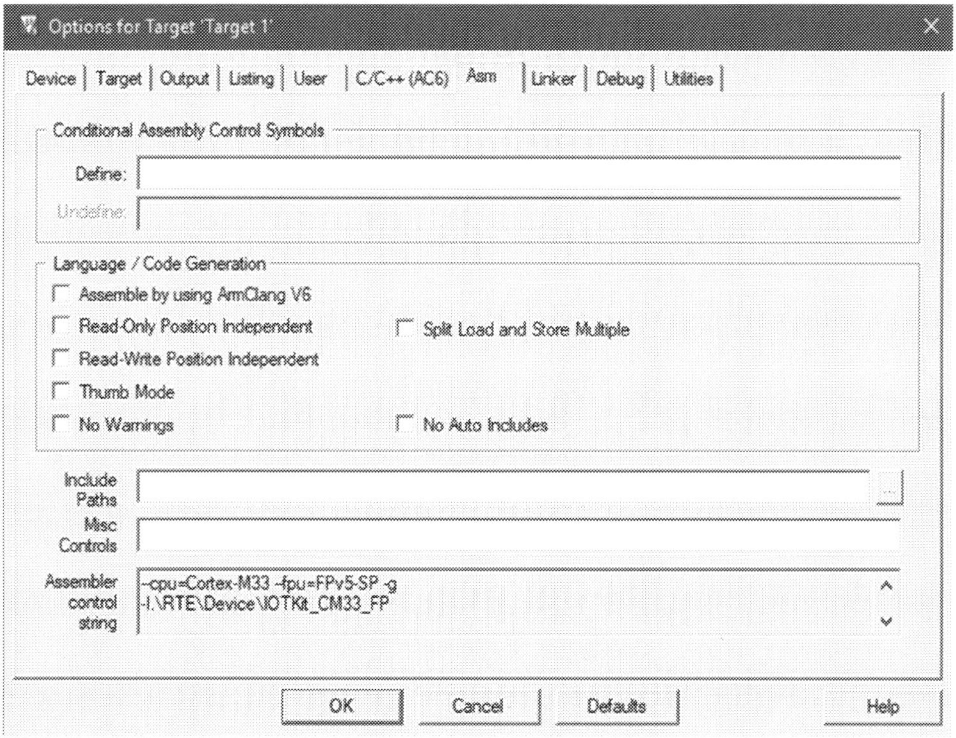

FIG. 17.26 Assembler options.

17.2.4.9 Linker options

The linker option tab allows you to define the memory map of a software project by selecting one of two options:

1. By generating the memory layout from the settings in the Target option (see Fig. 17.15 and Section 17.2.4.3). By so doing, the build process automatically generates a configuration file (also known as a scatter file) based on the memory layout details. This file is then passed to the linker.
2. By specifying a scatter file. The scatter file can either be created by the software developer (i.e., custom defined) or can be provided by the microcontroller vendor. To use this method, the "Use Memory Layout from the Target Dialog" option needs to be unchecked, and the location of the scatter file needs to be added to the "Scatter File" option box.

If a device with a relatively new CMSIS-Pack is being used, it is very likely that the start-up code will be written using C language. In this scenario, the CMSIS-Pack will most likely come with a scatter file, which will help define the memory layout of the vector table, the stack, and the heap memories. If this is the case, the scatter file that comes with the CMSIS-Pack should

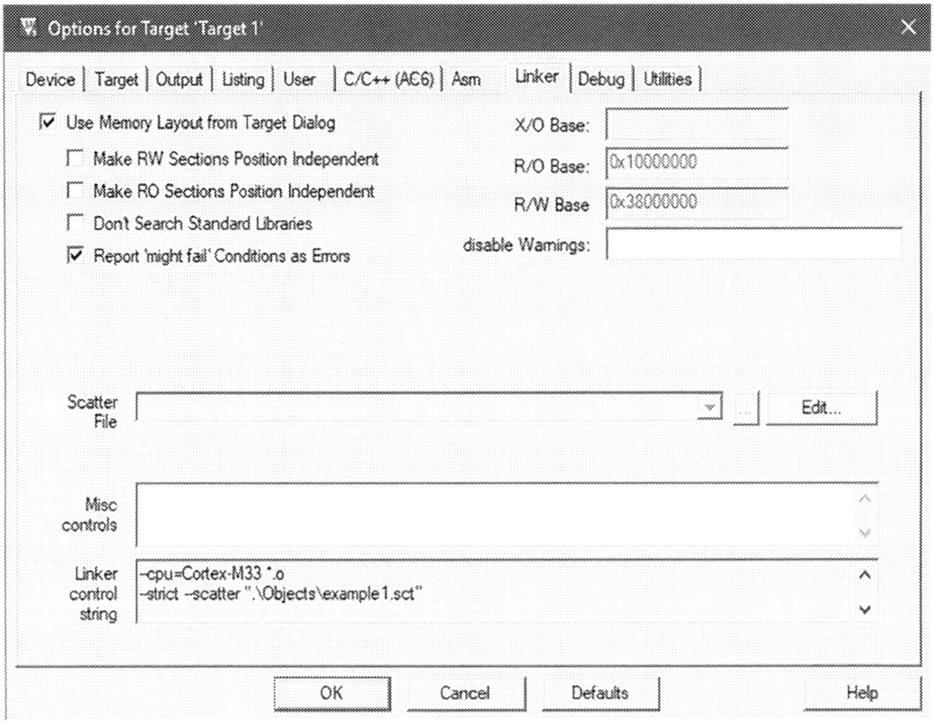

FIG. 17.27 Linker options.

be specified in the linker option and the "Use Memory Layout from the Target Dialog" option should be unchecked.

Linker options are shown in Fig. 17.27.

17.2.4.10 Debug options

Some of the debug options in the debug option tab have already been covered in Section 17.2.3. In addition, the debug option tab also allows you the option to either select running the code in the instruction set simulator (left-hand side of Fig. 17.28) or to use actual hardware with a debug adaptor (right-hand side of Fig. 17.28). The debug options tab also allows you to select the type of debug adaptor (Fig. 17.17) and allows you to access debug adaptor specific options from the submenu.

An additional script file (i.e., An "Initialization file"), which executes before each debug session starts, can be defined in the debug option tab.

Inside the sub menu for the debug adaptor, there are several different tabs:

1. Debug (see Fig. 17.18)
2. Trace (see Fig. 17.29)
3. Flash download

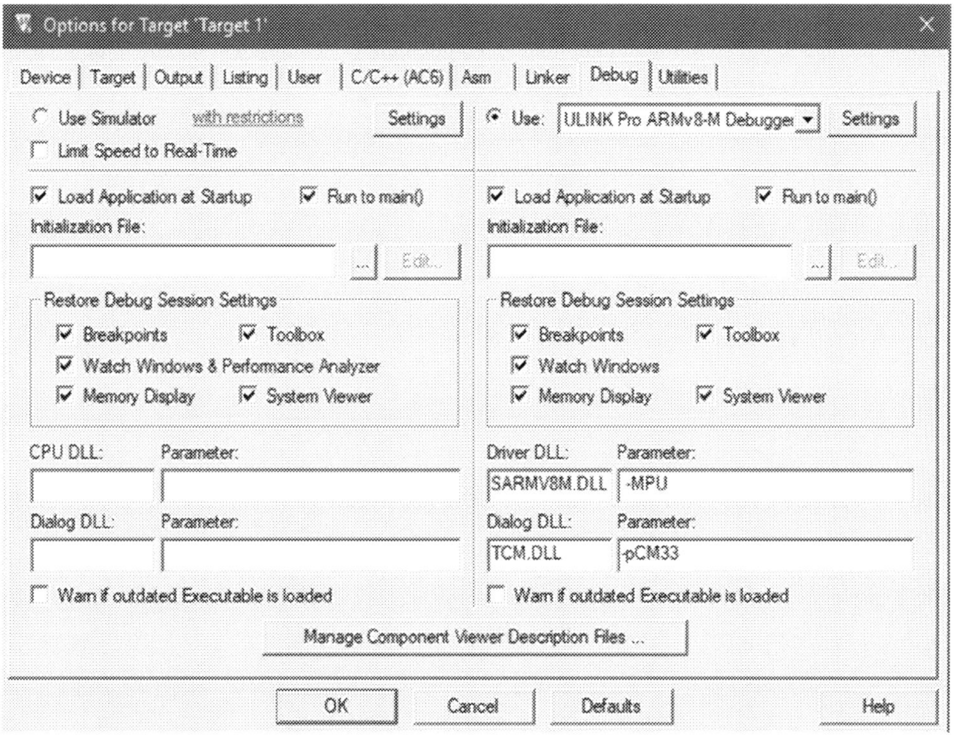

FIG. 17.28 Debug options.

If you are planning to use the trace feature (e.g., using the Serial Wire Viewer for a printf message display, which is covered in Section 17.2.8), you will need to setup the configurations, such as the clock frequencies, in the trace options tab as shown in Fig. 17.29.

In addition to the clock frequency and trace port protocol settings, you can, optionally, enable "Trace Events" for obtaining additional profiling information.

17.2.4.11 Utilities options

The Utilities options tab (Fig. 17.30) allows you to define, which debug adaptor is used for flash programming. For some devices, a hardware initialization sequence would need to be executed before the flash programming can be carried out. This is achieved by adding a hardware initialization script to the "Init File" option in the Utilities option tab.

17.2.5 Defining stack and heap sizes in a Keil MDK project

17.2.5.1 Determining the required stack and heap sizes

One of the important tasks when undertaking an embedded software project is to ensure that there are sufficient memories allocated to the main stack and heap. Heap memory is needed when using memory allocation functions, such as "malloc()". Heap memory could be also be used when, for some toolchains, functions like "printf" are used.

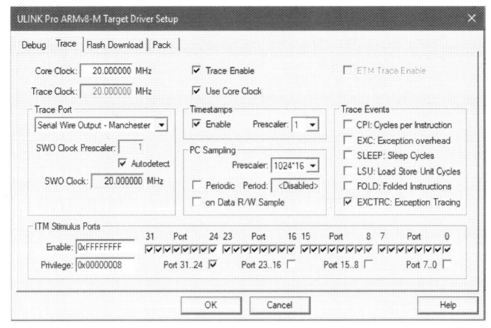

FIG. 17.29   Trace options.

If you are using Keil MDK, when the software compilation has ended you should see an HTML file in the "Objects" directory. This shows a function call tree and details the maximum stack size for each function and for the call tree itself. There is a need to consider when defining the allocation of memory space the amount of additional memory space required for exception stack frame(s), and for the stack space required by exception handlers. To demonstrate this, let us assume that we have a Cortex-M33-based system running a bare-metal project in the Non-secure state which:

• Has the main thread using up to 1000 bytes of stack memory space, which utilizes the FPU for processing
• Utilizes two levels of interrupt priority levels:
  ○ The first level using 200 bytes of stack space, which utilizes the FPU for processing
  ○ The second level using 300 bytes of stack space (the FPU is not used)
• Has a HardFault exception handler that could use up to 100 bytes of stack space

Assuming, for this example, that the Non-Maskable Interrupt (NMI) is not used for the application, the maximum stack memory size that would be required is as per the calculation in Fig. 17.31.

At each execution level of the software, space needs to be provided, unless it has the highest priority level, for an exception stack frame. The space required for the stack frames is dependent upon whether an FPU is used in the code. Assuming that both the background code and the handler code are both Non-secure then:

• When the FPU is not used, the stack frame is 8 words in size
• When the FPU is used, the stack frame is 26 words in size

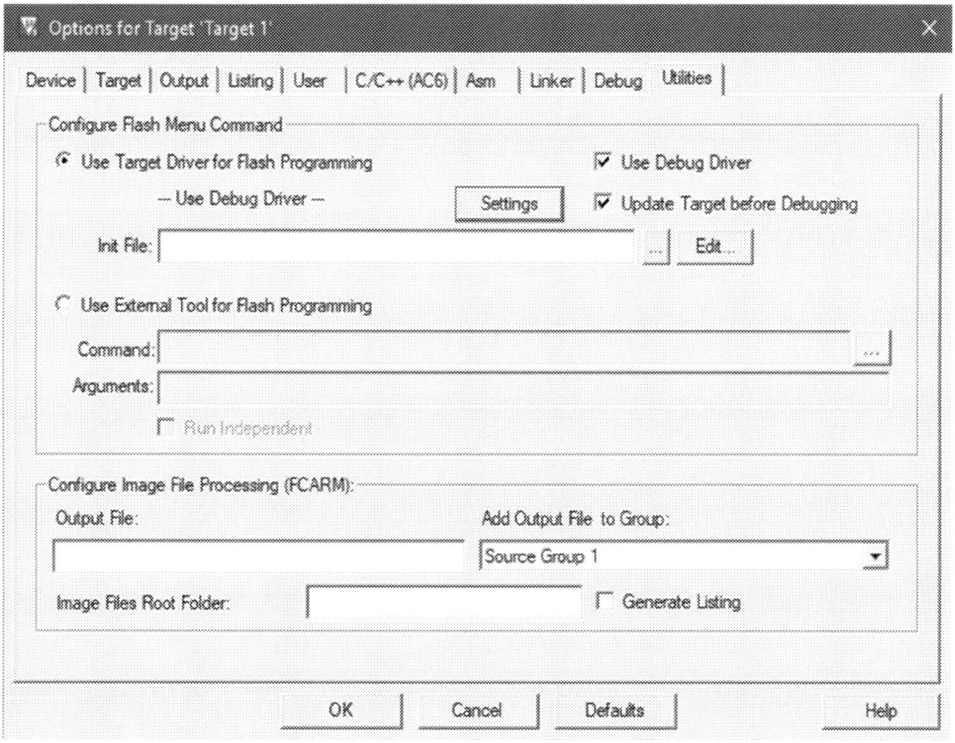

FIG. 17.30 Utilities options.

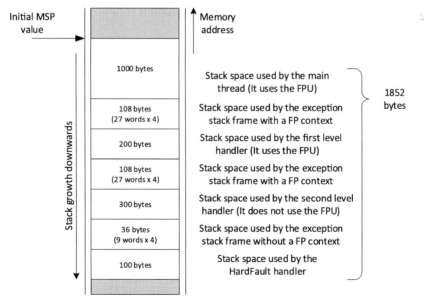

FIG. 17.31 A calculation detailing the maximum amount of the main stack required.

In the calculation shown in Fig. 17.31, I included a 4-byte padding space for each level of the exception stack frame. The padding space is needed because exception stack frames need to be aligned to double word address boundaries; and a padding word is needed if the SP value is not double word aligned when the exception took place. Further information on stack frames is covered in Chapter 8, Section 8.9.

When using an RTOS in the application, the stack usage for each thread is:

- The maximum stack size used by the thread's codes in the call-tree, plus
- The maximum stack frame size.

There could also be a need to include additional space in the calculation of the required stack space if the RTOS uses the thread's stack for "other data" storage.

Determining the heap memory size requirement would be easier if the application code always allocated the same amount of heap space. Unfortunately, because this is not always possible, a trial-and-error approach is sometimes needed. To detect whether the allocation of memory has been successful, there is a need to check the return status information of the memory allocation functions. When using memory allocation functions provided by an OS, you might need to customize the error detection handler of the OS to help you to detect whether an OS thread has used up too much memory.

17.2.5.2 Projects with assembly startup codes

In the example project that I detailed earlier in this chapter, the initial stack and heap sizes were defined in the assembly startup file as shown in Fig. 17.32.

The startup code includes several blocks of metadata. Using that metadata, the startup code can be configured using the "Configuration Wizard". By clicking on the "Configuration Wizard" tab underneath the code, the configurable settings can then be easily edited in the user interface (Fig. 17.33).

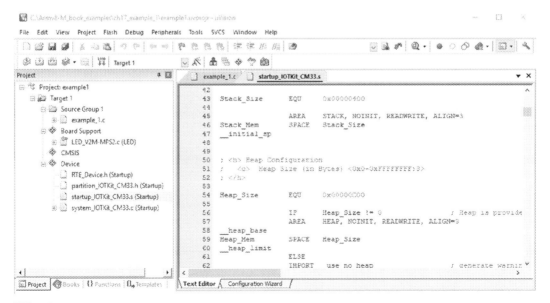

FIG. 17.32   Heap and stack memory size definition in the startup code.

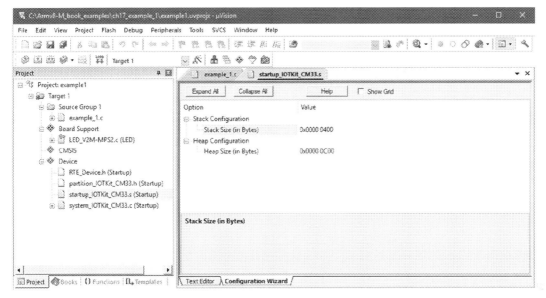

FIG. 17.33   Configuring the heap and stack memory sizes using the Configuration Wizard.

Clicking on the "Text Editor" tab at the bottom of the user interface returns the user interface to the code editor view.

17.2.5.3 *Projects with C startup codes*

When using a project with C startup code, it is likely that a scatter file will be available that enables you to define the initial heap and stack sizes. This will contain the following text:

```
...
/*.................. Stack / Heap Configuration ....................*/
#define __STACK_SIZE    0x00000400
#define __HEAP_SIZE     0x00000C00
...
```

These values can be edited to define the stack and heap sizes based on the project's requirements.

17.2.6 Using the IDE and the debugger

The Keil μVision Integrated Development Environment (IDE) provides a number of features that are easily accessible via the toolbar. Fig. 17.34 shows the various toolbar icons in the IDE that can be used during code editing.

When the debugger starts, the IDE display changes (as shown in Fig. 17.19) and presents information and controls that are useful during the debugging process. From the display, you can see and change the core registers (left-hand side) and can also see the source and disassembly windows. The icons on the tool bar also change during this period (Fig. 17.35).

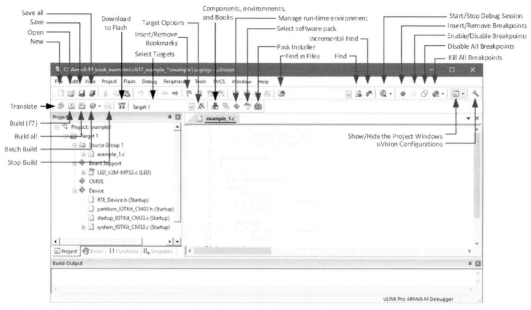

FIG. 17.34   Tool bar icons in the µVision IDE.

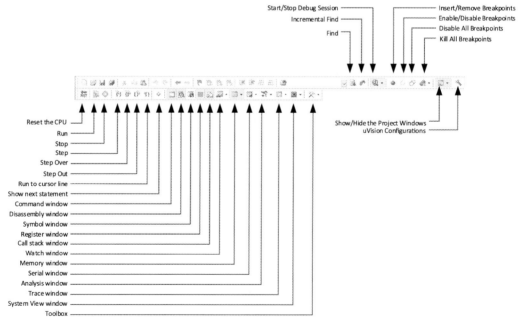

FIG. 17.35   Icons in the tool bar during a debug session.

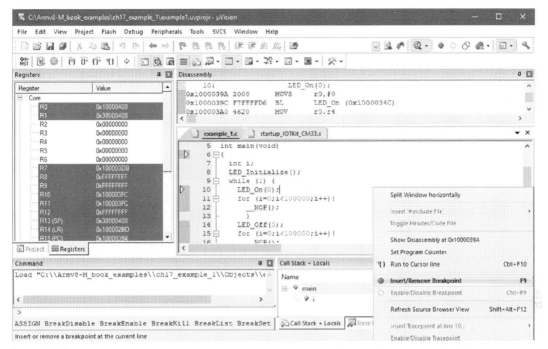

FIG. 17.36 A breakpoint can be inserted by right clicking on the code and selecting insert breakpoint.

Debug operations can either be carried out at instruction or source level. If the source window is highlighted, the debug operation process (e.g., single stepping, breakpoints) is carried out by taking account of each line of the C or assembly code. If the disassembly window is highlighted, the debug operation is based on instruction-level code—meaning that each assembly instruction can be single stepped even if it is compiled from C code.

When using source or disassembly windows, a breakpoint can be inserted or removed using icons in the toolbar, near the top right-hand corner of the IDE Window. This can also be achieved by right-clicking on the source/instruction line and selecting the "insert breakpoint" (Fig. 17.36).

When a program execution halts at a breakpoint, this is highlighted and enables you to start your debug operation (Fig. 17.37). For example, you can use "single-stepping" to execute your program code and can then examine the results using the register window.

The "Run to main()" debug option (see Fig. 17.28) sets a breakpoint at the beginning of "main()". When this option is set, and when the debugger is started, the processor begins execution from the reset vector and halts once "main()" is reached.

There are many features available in the debugger, but it is not possible to cover them all here. Further information for using Keil debugger features with various Cortex-M development boards can be found at http://www.keil.com/appnotes/list/arm.htm.

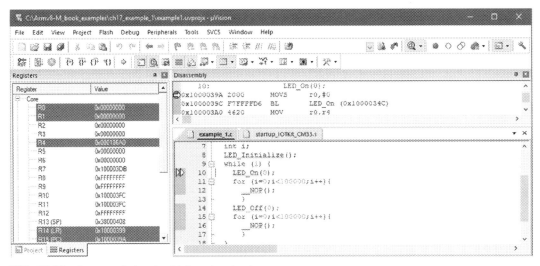

FIG. 17.37   Processor halts after hitting a breakpoint.

17.2.7 Printf with UART

When developing software, it is often useful to be able to display debug messages using the printf function in C/C++. A common technique is to direct the printf messages to a UART interface and to display them on a debug host. To do this, you would need to install terminal software (e.g., Tera Term or Putty) on the debug host (e.g., a PC).

In Keil MDK, the Manage Run-Time Environment dialog allows you to install a piece of program code to redirect printf message. This is achieved as follows: Compiler → I/O → STDOUT (Fig. 17.38). Please note, the type of STDOUT support selected can be one of the following:

- User—For directing printf messages to a peripheral interface.
- Breakpoint—For use with a debug tool with semihosting support, e.g., the Arm Development Studio.
- EVR (Event Recorder)—A software approach, which allows the debugger to access event information via a debug connection.
- ITM—Instrumentation Trace Macrocell (available on Armv8-M Mainline and Armv7-M processors only; not available for the Cortex-M23 processor). This allows printf messages to be directed to the trace interface (Section 17.2.8).

After adding the STDOUT software component, an additional file called "`retarget_io.c`" becomes available, as shown in Fig. 17.39.

Once the STDOUT option, with user defined output support, is added to the project, the program codes for the "user defined" output would need to be added. In the following example, a few lines of code (in bold text) are added to the main program:

```
// Device specific header
#include "IOTKit_CM33_FP.h" /* Device header */
#include "Board_LED.h"       /* ::Board Support:LED */
#include <stdio.h>
extern void UART_Config(void);
extern int UART_SendChar(int txchar);
// Retargeting support
int stdout_putchar (int ch);


int main(void)
{
  int i;
  LED_Initialize();
UART_Config();
printf ("Hello world\n");

  while (1) {
    LED_On(0);
    for (i=0;i<100000;i++){
      __NOP();
    }
    LED_Off(0);
    for (i=0;i<100000;i++){
      __NOP();
    }
  }
}
// Function used by retarget_io.c
int stdout_putchar (int ch)
{
    return UART_SendChar(ch);
}
```

The retarget_io.c file requires that the "stdout_putchar(int ch)" function is defined. This function, in the above example, calls a UART output function ("UART_SendChar()"), which transmits a character. A function for the initialization of the UART interface also needs to be added and this, in the example, is listed as "UART_Config()". The "UART_Config()" and "UART_SendChar()" functions are, in the example, implemented as a separate program file called "uart_funcs.c". The coding details of UART_Config() and UART_SendChar() are device specific and are not covered in this book.

To collect the UART display message on the debug host, a UART to USB adaptor is needed. Some development boards have this feature built-in. Assuming this has been setup, and once the program code has been compiled and executed, the terminal software connected to the board will display the "Hello world" message.

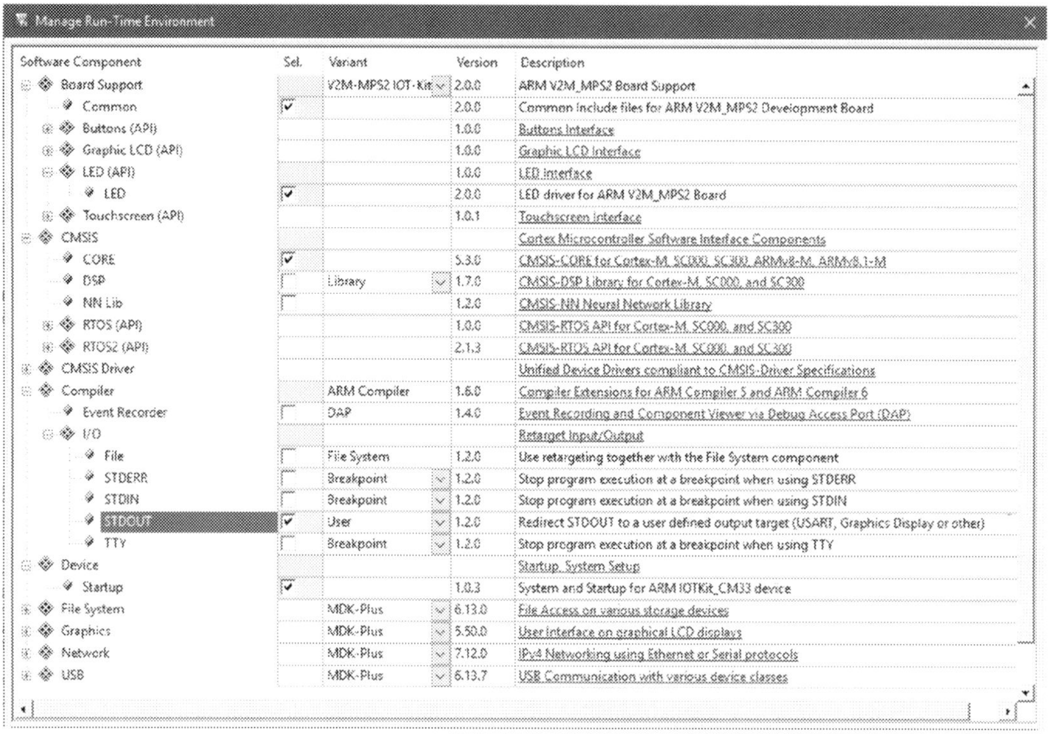

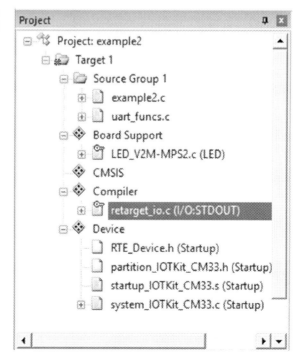

FIG. 17.38   Adding standard output (STDOUT) support in a Keil MDK project.

FIG. 17.39 Keil MDK automatically includes retarget_io.c in a project when the standard output (STDOUT) support is selected.

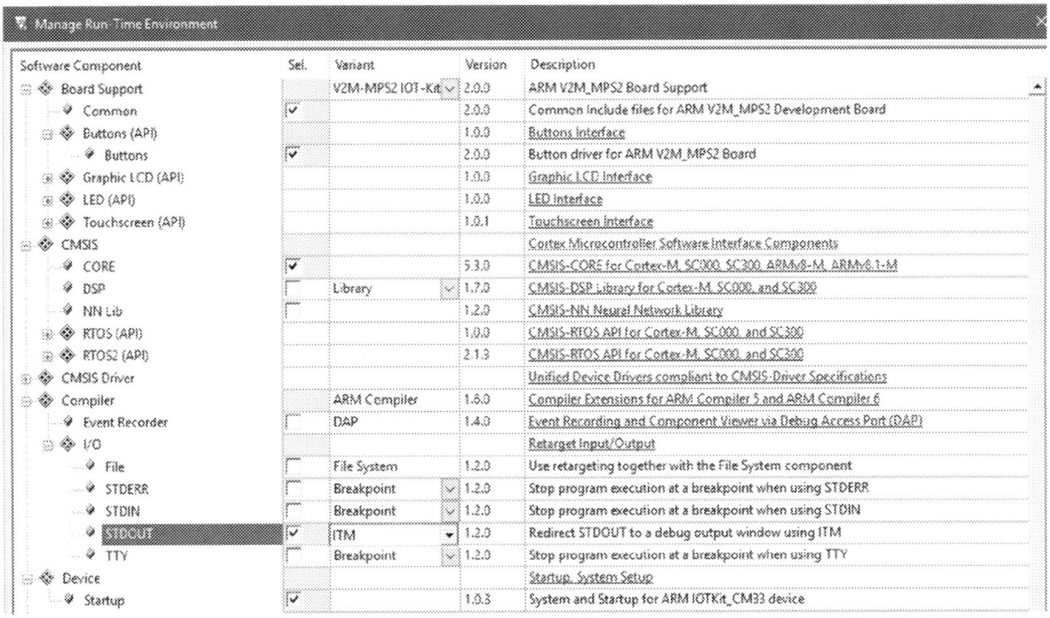

FIG. 17.40　Adding a standard output (STDOUT) via ITM in a Keil MDK project.

17.2.8 Printf with ITM

Armv8-M Mainline processors (e.g., the Cortex-M33 processor) and Armv7-M processors support an Instrumentation Trace Macrocell (ITM) feature to allow debug tools to collect debug messages using a trace connection. To enable debug messages to be outputted via the ITM, the STDOUT option should be enabled and the ITM output type should be selected, as shown in Fig. 17.40.

Adding the ITM standard output (STDOUT) support in a project is easier than adding support for UART STDOUT. All that is required is to add the printf code and the "stdio.h" C header, as detailed below:

```
// Device specific header
#include "IOTKit_CM33_FP.h" /* Device header */
#include "Board_LED.h"       /* ::Board Support:LED */
#include <stdio.h>

int main(void)
{
  int i;
  LED_Initialize();
  printf ("Hello world\n");

  while (1) {
    LED_On(0);
    for (i=0;i<100000;i++){
      __NOP();
    }
```

```
      LED_Off(0);
      for (i=0;i<100000;i++){
        __NOP();
      }
    }
  }
}
```

Although it is very easy to enable printf with ITM in the program code, additional debug configurations are needed to get this up and running. Assuming we want to use a low-cost debug adaptor that collects trace via the SWO pin (see Section 16.1.1 and the left-hand side of Fig. 16.2), then we need to make sure that we are using the Serial Wire Debug (SWD) protocol in the debug setting (Fig. 17.41). JTAG protocol is not suitable because the TDO pin of this protocol and the SWO pin are shared and cannot be used at the same time.

Note: If the parallel Trace port mode is used, it is safe to use the JTAG protocol as there would be no pin assignment conflict.

As part of the process of configuring debug settings to enable tracing with the SWO pin, we also need to enable trace in the debug setting (Fig. 17.42) and, when we do, we must make sure that:

- The setting of the trace clock speed matches that of the hardware platform being used.
- The Non-Return to Zero (NRZ) output mode is used (for most debug adaptors).
- The stimulus port #0 is enabled.

After the trace configuration is setup, the software can be compiled and the debug session can start. Though, before executing the software, the Debug (printf) viewer needs to be enabled from the pull-down menu, as shown in Fig. 17.43.

After the Debug (printf) Viewer is enabled and after the application has started, the "Hello world" printf message will be displayed (Fig. 17.44).

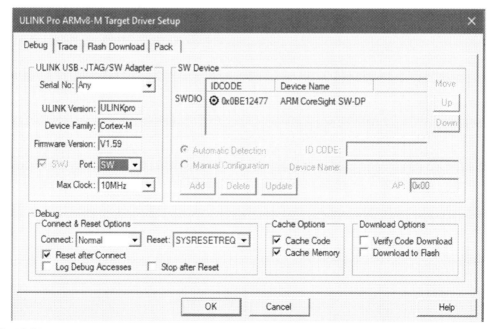

FIG. 17.41 Selecting SWD protocol for a debug connection when using ITM printf with SWO.

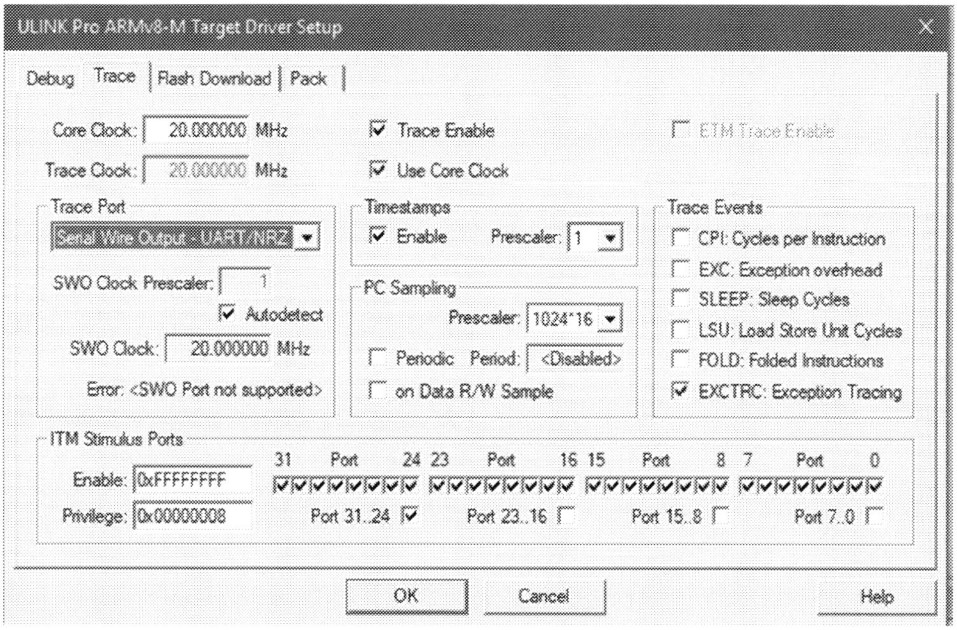

FIG. 17.42 Trace setting for ITM trace via SWO.

17.2.9 Using a Real-Time OS—RTX

A particular feature of Keil MDK is how easy it is to integrate an RTX RTOS into a software project. An RTOS is, typically, needed where there is a need for processing to be partitioned and placed into a number of concurrent tasks. In these applications, the RTOS is used for:

- Task scheduling—in most RTOS designs the task scheduling supports task prioritization capabilities.
- Intertask events and message communications (e.g., mailbox).
- Semaphores (including MUTEX).
- Handling process isolation. This is optional and requires MPU support. The OS can also utilize stack limit checking for detecting stack overflow errors.

Some RTOSs available in the market could include features such as communication stacks and file systems. The aforementioned features are available in MDK Professional and MDK Plus but will have to be added as separate software components. Unlike full feature OSs, such as Linux, most RTOSs, such as RTX, do not require virtual memory support features, e.g., a Memory Management Unit (MMU). Because these RTOSs have a very small memory footprint, they can fit into small microcontroller devices.

Keil RTX is one of the royalty-free RTOSs that was designed for microcontroller systems. It is:

- Open source and is released on Github under the permissive Apache 2.0 license (Further information can be found at https://github.com/ARM-software/CMSIS_5/tree/develop/CMSIS/RTOS2/RTX).

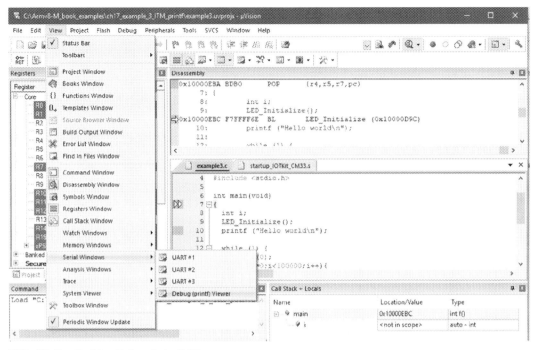

FIG. 17.43   Enabling Debug (printf) Viewer.

- Of commercial quality, is fully configurable and offers a fast response time.
- Based on the design of the open CMSIS-RTOS 2 APIs (Further information can be found at www.keil.com/pack/doc/CMSIS/RTOS2/html/index.html).
- Compatible with multiple toolchains (e.g., Arm/Keil, IAR EW-ARM, and GCC).

Please note, the CMSIS-RTOS APIs have been enhanced, and version 2 is now available. Software being developed for the Armv8-M processor will need to use the RTX codes for CMSIS-RTOS 2. RTX code with CMSIS-RTOS version 1 is not supported on Armv8-M architecture.

The steps for creating an RTX-based application with only one application thread that toggles an LED are as follows.

Step 1: Adding the RTX OS to a Keil MDK project

To add the RTX OS kernel in a Keil MDK project, the RTX software in the "Manage Run-Time Environment" window, as shown in Fig. 17.45, would have to be selected. Please note, there are a number of options for the RTX in the "Manage Run-Time Environment" window and it is important that the right type of RTX component is selected. The options are as follows:

- Whether the RTX integrated is in source code or in library form, and
- Whether the RTOS operates in the Secure or the Non-secure world (Note: Because of differences in the EXC_RETURN code values between Secure and Non-secure exceptions, this would need to match the situation that exists in your project).

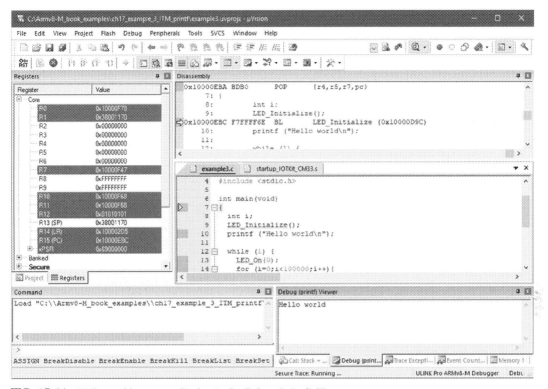

FIG. 17.44 Hello world message display in the Debug (printf) Viewer.

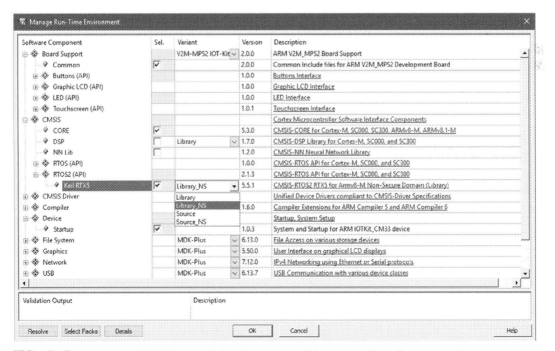

FIG. 17.45 Adding an RTX RTOS to a Keil MDK project in "Manage Run-Time Environment".

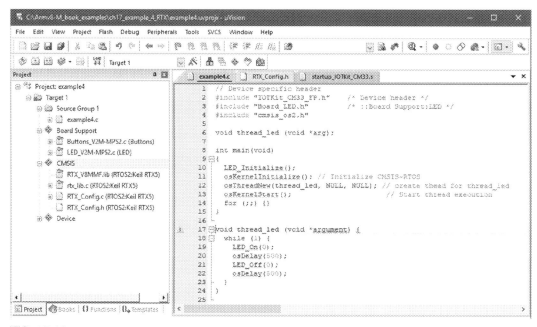

FIG. 17.46   An RTX project example.

By this stage, the RTX files would have been added, and this is reflected in the project window as shown in Fig. 17.46.

Step 2: Adding an application thread in the program code

The application code needs to:

- Include a header file called "cmsis_os2.h" in order to allow the program code to access the OS functions.
- Add OS function calls for OS initialization (osKernelInitialize), OS thread creation (osThreadNew), and OS starting (osKernelStart).
- Include the thread code that toggles an LED (thread_led).

These codes are shown in Fig. 17.46.

Step 3: Customization of RTX configurations

A range of OS configurations can be customized in the file "RTX_Config.h". To make the configuration easier, this file includes metadata to allow the "Configuration Wizard" to be used when editing the configuration of the OS (Fig. 17.47).

By default, the RTX RTOS uses the SysTick timer for generating a periodic OS tick interrupt. Using the "SystemCoreClock" variable defined in the CMSIS-CORE file "system_<device>.c", and the "OS_TICK_FREQ" (Kernel Tick Frequency) defined in "RTX_Config.h", the RTX code calculates the required clock divide ratio.

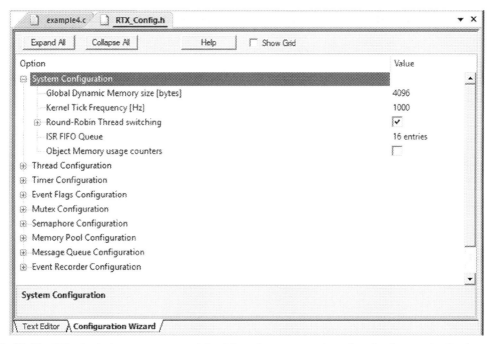

FIG. 17.47   RTX_Config.h contains most of the OS configurations and can be edited using the Configuration Wizard.

Once the project is compiled, it can then be downloaded to the development board for testing.

The RTX RTOS contains many features and it is, therefore, impossible to cover all of its aspects in this book. For further information, please refer to the CMSIS-RTOS2 documentation for details and examples. This can be found at: https://arm-software.github.io/CMSIS_5/RTOS2/html/index.html.

17.2.10 Inline assembly

Inline assembly enables assembly code sequences to be added in C code. When writing programs for Cortex-M processors, inline assembly is needed for creating an OS's context switching routine, an OS's SVCall handler, and, in some cases, fault handlers (e.g., for extracting stacked registers from the stack frame).

To use inline assembly, the assembly codes need to be written in a code syntax that is specific to a toolchain. As a result of changes in the underlying compiler technology, there are changes to the inline assembly features when migrating from Arm Compiler 5 to Arm Compiler 6 (which is based on the LLVM compiler technology). Fortunately, the inline assembly support in the LLVM is highly compatible with the widely adopted GCC compiler. As a result, in many instances, the inline assembly for GCC can be reused on Arm Compiler 6.

For the GCC and for Arm Compiler 6, the general syntax for an inline assembly code fragment, with parameter support is as follows:

```
__asm ("    inst1  op1, op2, ... \n"
       "    inst2  op1, op2, ... \n"

       ...

       "    instN  op1, op2, ... \n"
      : output_operands      /* optional */
      : input_operands       /* optional */
      : clobbered_operands   /* optional */

      );
```

When the assembly instruction does not require parameters, the syntax can be as simple as:

```
void Sleep(void)
{ // Enter sleep using WFI instruction
  __asm (" WFI\n");
  return;
}
```

If the assembly code requires input and output parameters, or if other registers need to be modified by the inline assembly operation, then the input and output operands and the clobbered register lists would need to be defined. For example, an inline assembly code for multiplying a value by 10 would be written as follows:

```
int my_mul_10(int DataIn)
{
  int DataOut;
    __asm(" movs r3, #10\n"
          " mul r2, %[input], r3\n"
          " movs %[output], r2\n"
         :[output] "=r" (DataOut)
         :[input] "r" (DataIn)
         : "cc", "r2", "r3");
  return DataOut;
}
```

The "__asm" in the above code indicates the start of the inline assembly code text and, within the code, register symbolic names ("input" and "output") are used. Following the release of GCC version 3.1, as well as recent releases of the LLVM compilers, symbolic name features are now available to help software developers create intuitive codes.

In the above inline assembly code example, there are a few lines of operands after the inline assembly code text. The operand order is:

- output_operands,
- input_operands, and
- clobbered_operands.

Because the assembly code modifies the values in registers R2 and R3, and the condition flags ("cc"), these registers need to be added to the clobbered operand list.

It is possible to create an assembly function within a C file. An example of how to create an assembly function in C code is shown in Section 13.9. The "naked" C function attribute is used when declaring an inline assembly function to prevent the C compiler from generating C function prologue and epilogue (i.e., additional instruction sequences before and after the function body). For example, the inline assembly example above can be rewritten as:

```
/* r0 is used as input parameter as well as return result */
int __attribute__((naked)) my_mul_10(int DataIn)
{
    __asm(" movs r3, #10\n\t"
          " mul  r0, r0, r3\n\t"
          " bx   lr\n\t"
          );
}
```

For this type of inline assembly function, it is not necessary to provide operands (input operands, output_operands, and clobbered operands). However, when creating this type of function, it is essential that the interaction between functions and the standard practice regarding the transfer of a function's parameters, and its results are fully understood and followed. For Arm architecture, this information can be found in a document called "Procedure Call Standard for the Arm Architecture" [3]. This document is also known as the AAPCS, as mentioned in Section 17.3.

17.3 Procedure Call Standard for the Arm Architecture

When a function is written using assembly language and needs to interact with other C codes, there is a range of requirements that need to be followed/met to allow the interface between the software functions to work. These requirements are documented in a document called "Procedure Call Standard for the Arm Architecture" AAPCS [3]. This document describes how multiple software functions interact with each other when running on Arm processors.

By following the programming conventions set out in the AAPCS document:

- Various software components (including compiled program images generated by different toolchains) can seamlessly interact with each other.
- Software code can be reused in multiple projects.
- Problems when integrating assembly code with program code generated by compilers or program code from third parties can be avoided.

Even if you are creating an application that only contains assembly code (this is very unlikely in a modern programming environment), it would still be useful to follow the AAPCS guidelines because debug tools might make assumptions about the operation of assembly functions based on the practices as defined in the AAPCS document.

The main areas covered by the AAPCS document are as follows:

- Register usage in function calls—The document details which registers are caller saved and which are callee saved. For example, a function or a subroutine should retain the values in R4–R11. If these registers are changed during the function or the subroutine, the values should be saved in the stack and be restored before returning to the calling code.
- Passing of parameters to functions—For simple cases, input parameters can be passed on to a function using R0 (first parameter), R1 (second parameter), R2 (third parameter), and R3 (fourth parameter). If a 64-bit value is to be used as an input parameter, a pair of 32-bit registers (e.g., R0–R1) would be used. If the four registers (R0–R3) are not enough for the passing of all the parameters (e.g., more than four parameters have to be passed on to a function), the stack would be used (details can be found in the AAPCS). If floating-point data processing is involved and the compilation flow specifies the Hard-ABI (see Section 14.5.4), the registers in the floating-point register bank could also be used.
- Passing of return results to the caller—Usually, the return value of a function is stored in the R0. If the return result is 64 bits, both R1 and R0 would be used. Similar to parameter passing, if floating-point data processing is involved and the compilation flow specifies the Hard-ABI (see Section 14.5.4), the registers in the floating-point register bank could also be used.
- Stack alignment—If an assembly function needs to call a C function, it should ensure that the current selected stack pointer points to a double word-aligned address location (e.g., 0x20002000, 0x20002008, 0x20002010, etc.). This is a requirement for the Embedded-ABI (EABI) standard [4]: this requirement allows the EABI compliant C compiler to assume that the stack pointer is pointing to a double word aligned location when generating program codes. If the assembly code does not call any C function, either directly or indirectly, then the assembly code does not need to keep the stack pointer aligned to a double word address at function boundaries.

Based on these requirements, for simple function calls (assuming they do not use floating-point registers for data passing, and that fewer than four registers are needed), the data transfers between a caller and the callee functions would be as per Table 17.1

In addition to the parameter and result usages,

- The code inside a function must ensure that the values of "callee saved registers" when leaving the function are the same as when the function was entered.
- The code that calls a function must ensure that if data in "caller saved registers" needs to be accessed again later on, that this data is saved to the memory (e.g., stack) before calling a C function. This is necessary because C functions are allowed to remove data in caller saved registers.

The aforementioned requirements are summarized in Table 17.2.

Please note, there is a need to be careful with the doubleword stack alignment requirement. When using the Arm assembler (armasm) in the Arm toolchain, the assembler provides:

- The REQUIRE8 directive to indicate whether the function requires doubleword stack alignment, and
- The PRESERVE8 directive to indicate whether a function has preserved the doubleword alignment.

TABLE 17.1 Simple parameter passing and returning results in a function call.

Register	Input parameter	Return value
R0	First input parameter	Function return value
R1	Second input parameter	–, or return value (64-bit result)
R2	Third input parameter	–
R3	Fourth input parameter	–

TABLE 17.2 Requirements of caller saved and callee saved registers at function boundaries.

Registers	Function call behavior
R0–R3, R12, S0–S15	Caller Saved Register—The contents of these registers can be changed by a function. Assembly code calling a function might need to save the values in these registers if they are required for operations at a later stage.
R4–R11, S16–S31	Callee Saved Register—Contents in these registers must be retained by a function. If a function needs to use these registers for processing, they need to be saved to the stack and restored before the function returns.
R14 (LR)	The value in the Link Register needs to be saved to the stack if the function contains a "BL" or "BLX" instruction (i.e., calling another function). This is because the value in LR will be overwritten when "BL" or "BLX" is executed.
R13 (SP), R15 (PC)	Should not be used for normal processing

These directives help the assembler to analyze the assembly code and generate a warning if a function that requires a doubleword aligned stack frame has been called by another function that does not guarantee doubleword stack alignment. Depending on the application, these directives might, especially for projects built entirely with assembly code, not be required.

17.4 Software scenarios

17.4.1 A recap of the software development scenarios

At the beginning of this chapter, I detailed five different software development scenarios. So far, the software development examples I have covered were mostly focused on scenario #1 in Fig. 17.1; where the software is running in only one security domain (i.e., the Non-secure world). The same software development steps for scenario #1 can also be applied to scenarios #2, #3, and #5. In this section, I will look at the differences that exist between scenarios #1, #2, #3, and #5. Scenario #4 will be covered in Chapter 18.

17.4.2 Scenario #1—The Armv8-M system does not implement TrustZone

The software development process is almost the same as that that exists in the traditional Armv6-M and Armv7-M Cortex-M processors. There is no separation of Secure and Non-secure states, and with a debug connection, software developers have full visibility of the system.

There are, however, changes to software codes that need to be taken into account when one is migrating Armv6-M/Armv7-M projects to Armv8-M-based systems. These are as follows:

- MPU configuration code changes—Due to changes in the programmer's model of the Memory Protection Unit (MPU), the code that utilizes the MPU will need to be updated.
- hOS code changes—The OS would need to be changed due to changes in the definition of EXC_RETURN code values (see Section 8.10). A software developer should select an OS version that can run in the Non-secure state (see Fig. 17.45). And, if the processor being used is a Cortex-M33 processor (or another Armv8-M Mainline processor), the OS can take advantage of the stack limit checking feature to make the system more robust.
- Removal of the bit-band feature—The bit band feature, an optional feature on Cortex-M3 and Cortex-M4 processors, is not available in Armv8-M processors.
- Vector table address—Unlike Cortex-M0, Cortex-M0+, Cortex-M3, and Cortex-M4 processors, the initial vector table address on Armv8-M processors can be Non-zero.

For most application codes, minimal software code changes are needed. Due to the various changes made to the debug components (e.g., Breakpoint unit, the data watchpoint unit, the ETM), development tools will need to be updated to a version that supports Armv8-M architecture.

17.4.3 Scenario #2—Development of Non-secure software where the Secure world is not used

In this scenario, software developers will need to update the software for the same areas as in scenario #1. And, in addition, software developers might notice the following differences:

- Optional API for disabling Secure firmware—At the beginning of the initialization of the Non-secure software, the Non-secure software might need to call a Secure API to tell the Secure software that the Secure world software is not going to be used. This allows the Secure world to release more hardware resources (e.g., SRAM and peripherals) to the Non-secure software. In addition, this Secure API configures the NMI, HardFault, and the BusFault exception to target the Non-secure state by setting the BFHFNMINS bit in the Application Interrupt and Reset Control Register (AIRCR, see Section 9.3.4). Note: This is optional because this Secure API might not be available.
- Memory map—Memory ranges containing Secure program and Secure resources are not accessible.

Other than that, the software development on such a system is very similar to that when using Armv6-M and Armv7-M processors.

17.4.4 Scenario #3—Development of Non-secure software when the Secure world is used

In this scenario, the software developer will need to update the software in the same areas as in Scenario #1. And, in addition, software developers would notice the following changes:

- The application can make use of various features via the available Secure APIs.
- A need to use an RTOS with Trusted Firmware-M support—If the software uses an RTOS, the RTOS being used needs to support Trusted Firmware-M integration— or support other Secure firmware if the Secure world of the chip uses another Secure software solution. This topic is covered in Section 11.8.
- Fault handling and fault analysis—Because the NMI, HardFault, and the BusFault exception targets Secure state, Non-secure software does not have direct access to these features. To allow Non-secure software developers to be aware of software issue(s), some of the Secure firmware offers mechanisms to report an error if a HardFault or BusFault exception takes place. When the ETM/MTB instruction trace is available, the Non-secure operations that are carried out before a HardFault/BusFault is observable in the instruction trace. As a result, software developers are able to analyze the fault event using the ETM/MTB instruction trace. Software developers are also able to enable MemManage Fault and UsageFault in the Non-secure world so that the error conditions that triggered those fault exceptions can be diagnosed in the Non-secure debug environment. If the Non-secure MemManage Fault and UsageFault are not enabled, those fault events would be escalated to a Secure HardFault.

17.4.5 Scenario #5—Development of Secure software where the Non-secure world is not used

In this scenario, software developers will need to update the software for the same areas as in scenario #1. The only difference is that if they are using an RTOS, the RTOS variant being selected (Fig. 17.45) needs to support the Secure world instead of the Non-secure world.

References

[1] Armv8-M Architecture Reference Manual. https://developer.arm.com/docs/ddi0553/am (Armv8.0-M only version). https://developer.arm.com/documentation/ddi0553/latest/ (latest version including Armv8.1-M). Note: M-profile architecture reference manuals for Armv6-M, Armv7-M, Armv8-M and Armv8.1-M can be found here: https://developer.arm.com/architectures/cpu-architecture/m-profile/docs.
[2] Keil application note 298—Migrate Arm Compiler 5 to Arm Compiler 6. http://www.keil.com/appnotes/files/apnt_298.pdf.
[3] Procedure Call Standard for the Arm Architecture (AAPCS). https://developer.arm.com/documentation/ihi0042/latest.
[4] Arm Application Binary Interface. https://developer.arm.com/architectures/system-architectures/software-standards/abi.

CHAPTER

18

Secure software development

18.1 Overview of Secure software development

18.1.1 Introduction

In Chapter 3, Section 3.18, I covered the benefits of using the Arm® TrustZone® security extension and gave a high-level overview of how TrustZone is used in IoT microcontroller products. The majority of software developers using these IoT microcontrollers are likely to create applications in the Non-secure world only. By accessing the various security features via Application Programming Interfaces (APIs) provided by Secure firmware, they can enable robust security in their projects without having to have an in-depth understanding of TrustZone's.

That said, since many software developers work on Secure software projects, there is a need for them to understand the whys and wherefores of programming with TrustZone. This chapter is for those developers, and will cover how to develop Secure software and, via a range of guidelines, how to make it secure.

18.1.2 The separation of Secure and Non-secure in software projects

When TrustZone technology is being used, Secure and the Non-secure software projects are separately compiled and linked. Each of them has their own boot codes and C libraries. This is illustrated in Fig. 18.1.

Because it is expected that Secure software developers will need to create a Non-secure project so that they can test the interactions between the two sides, many toolchains support a feature called multiproject workspace—allowing the simultaneous development and debugging of multiple projects. An example of this is shown in Section 18.4.

When a Secure project has been created, the Secure software developer will need to provide the following files to the Non-secure software developer(s) so that Non-secure projects can access the Secure APIs:

- The function prototype of the Secure APIs (i.e., header file(s)).
- An export library that only provides information about the addresses of the APIs (i.e., address symbols, which are needed by the linker tools when linking Non-secure projects).

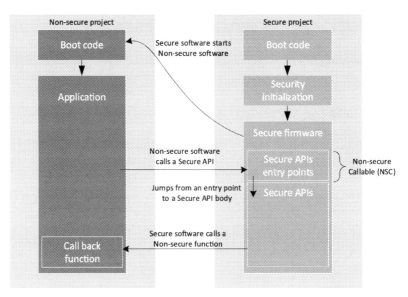

FIG. 18.1   Separation of Secure and Non-secure worlds in software projects.

Please note, the internal details of the APIs, such as instruction codes, are omitted from this library.

Using the information in these files, a Non-secure software project that contains function calls to the Secure APIs can then be compiled and linked. The Non-secure software project can then either be created by the same person who created the Secure project or by a third party developer who only creates Non-secure applications.

Please note:

- Secure and Non-secure projects can be created using different tool chains. This is achievable because the method of parameters and result passing is standardized in the Procedure Call Standard for the Arm Architecture [1].
- The Secure project must be generated before the Non-secure project is compiled and linked. This is so the export library that is generated from the linking stage of the Secure project is available during the linking stage of the Non-secure project.

Where a Secure code has to call a Non-secure function, the Non-secure code, first of all, needs to transfer the pointer of the Non-secure function to the Secure world via a Secure API. When it does, the Secure API validates the fact that the function pointer is pointing to a Non-secure address and then later executes the function pointer when it is needed.

18.1.3 Cortex®-M Security Extension (CMSE)

To assist the development of Secure software, Arm has introduced a range of C compiler support features called the Cortex-M Security Extension (CMSE). This is documented in

"Armv8-M Security Extension: Requirements on Development Tools" [2] and is a part of the Arm C language Extension (ACLE[a]) [3].

The CMSE features are supported in multiple toolchains, including Arm Compiler 6, gcc, IAR™ Embedded Workbench® for ARM, etc. As a result, Secure software codes are portable across the range of different toolchains.

18.1.4 Trusted Firmware-M

To help the electronic industry address security challenges, Arm announced, in 2017, the Platform Security Architecture (PSA) initiative. As part of this initiative, Arm started the Trusted Firmware-M (TF-M) project, which provides reference security firmware to silicon vendors who use Cortex®-M processors in their devices. The TF-M project has many different security features and these will be covered in Chapter 22.

18.1.5 Development platform considerations

Notably, some Cortex-M23 and Cortex-M33 devices do not implement the TrustZone security extension. For devices that support TrustZone, the Secure world on those devices could potentially be locked down (i.e., The Secure world cannot be modified and the debug features are limited to the Non-secure world only). If this is the case, although software developers can create applications that can access the Secure APIs to utilize the security features, they will not be able to create software to run on the Secure world.

As a result, a software developer who wants to create their Secure software solution will need to ensure that the hardware platform they are using supports the development of Secure software. Additionally, there would probably be a need to ensure that the hardware platform offers suitable debug authentication features. This would ensure that if the development boards were subsequently transferred to a 3rd party for Non-secure software development, the Secure software developed would be protected.

Last but not least, the TrustZone feature is only one part of the security features that are available on a hardware platform. With this in mind, security in IoT applications can be further enhanced if the microcontroller or SoC provides a range of hardware security features e.g., secure storage, a True Random Number Generator (TRNG), a cryptography engine, and so on.

It is important to note that TrustZone itself does not protect a system against various forms of physical attack. For example, if a hacker has physical access to the device, they can launch physical attacks, such as voltage glitching, clock glitching, or fault injection, or for them to extract secrets from the device using side-channel attacks. Some TrustZone enabled devices might have a reasonable level of physical protection, but to be sure that the devices support physical protection features, a software developer should always check the device's security capabilities with the device's manufacturer.

---

[a]https://developer.arm.com/architectures/system-architectures/software-standards/acle.

18.2 TrustZone technical details

18.2.1 Processor state

When TrustZone is implemented, the processor can either be in a Secure or a Non-secure state (Fig. 18.2).

Similar to previous Armv6-M and Armv7-M architectures, an Armv8-M processor is in a privileged state when executing an exception handler (Handler mode). When the processor is executing in thread mode (i.e., not in Handler mode), the processor can either be in a privileged or an unprivileged state, depending on the value of the nPRIV bit in the CONTROL register (see "CONTROL register" section in Section 4.2.2.3).

Put simply,

- The processor is in the Secure state when it is executing code from the Secure memory
- The processor is in the Non-secure state when it is executing code from the Non-secure memory.

At the detailed level, there is an exception to this simplified description. This occurs during the transition from the Non-secure state to the Secure state when a Non-secure code calls a Secure API. This exception is covered in Section 18.2.4.

When the processor starts up from reset, the processor executes in Secure privileged thread mode. After the system has started up, security state transitions happen when:

- Secure code branches into the Non-secure application code to start up the Non-secure world.
- A Non-secure application calls a Secure API and returns to the Non-secure world when the API has executed its task.
- A Secure function calls a Non-secure function and returns to the Secure world when the function has executed its task.
- A Secure interrupt/exception event occurs during the execution of the Non-secure code. The state transition will occur for both the exception entry and the return.

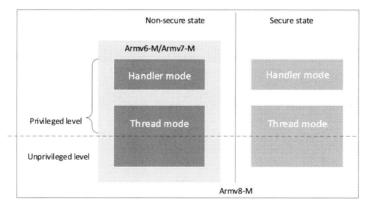

FIG. 18.2   Processor states in Armv8-M processors.

- A Non-secure interrupt/exception event occurs during the execution of Secure code. The state transition will occur for both the exception entry and the return.
- There is tail chaining between the Secure and Non-secure exception handlers (see Figs. 8.29 and 8.30 in Section 8.10).
- A reset occurs during the execution of a Non-secure code.

Theoretically, during a debug session, a debugger can change the security state of a processor when the processor has been halted. However, to stop a security violation occurring when the processor resumes its instruction execution, or when the debugger single steps into the next instruction, the program counter would also need to change so that the security attribute of the software execution address matches the processor's state.

18.2.2 Memory separation

The partitioning of the memory space into Secure and Non-secure ranges is handled by the Security Attribution Unit (SAU) and by Implementation Defined Attribution Units (IDAU)—both are covered in Chapter 7, Section 7.2. The SAU is an integrated part of the Armv8-M processor. The IDAU's are device-specific hardware units that are designed by chip/SoC designers and are closely coupled to the processor.

The SAU and the IDAU work together: for each address lookup, the results from the SAU and the IDAU are compared and the higher security level is then selected; except when the IDAU lookup result indicates that the address is exempted from a security check (Fig. 7.1). Exempted address ranges are typically used by debug components that are security-aware (i.e., they ensure that Secure data and Secure operations are protected from Non-secure access), or are used where Non-secure access does not pose any security risk (e.g., CoreSight™ ROM tables).

The SAU in the Cortex-M23 and Cortex-M33 processors can be configured to support 0, 4, or 8 programmable SAU regions, while the IDAU can support up to 256 regions. As part of the security initialization process, the security initialization procedure (see the right-hand side of Fig. 18.1) includes programming the SAU and, potentially, if the device vendor made the configuration of the IDAU programmable, the IDAUs.

The usual reason for making IDAUs programmable is that although it allows the processor to contain few, or none, SAU regions, it still allows the NSC (Non-secure Callable) attribute of a Secure region to be setup by software. By way of an example, as shown in Fig. 18.3, if a device does not have an SAU region, and if the security partition memory map is entirely handled by the IDAU, then the IDAU would need to be programmable to allow the software to control the location and the size of the NSC region.

Another aspect of configuring memory partitioning in a TrustZone based system is setting up system-level security management hardware such as the Memory Protection Controllers (MPCs) and the Peripheral Protection Controllers (PPCs). Although these units are also for resource partitioning, they operate differently when compared to the SAU and IDAUs. The difference is:

- The SAU and IDAU define how the 4GB address-space is partitioned into Secure and Non-secure regions

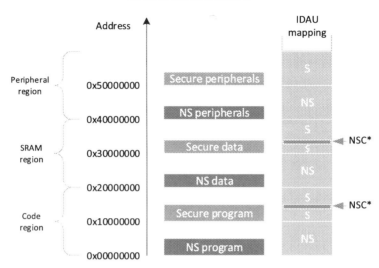

FIG. 18.3   An example of an IDAU memory map.

- The MPCs and PPCs define, for each memory page or each peripheral, whether they are accessible from a Secure or a Non-secure address alias.

The address aliasing concept for MPCs and PPCs is covered in Section 7.5 (Fig. 7.11). Using the MPC and PPC method, it is possible to manage the targeted security domain for a large number of memory pages or peripheral resources, even though the processor is limited to 8 SAU and 256 IDAU regions. This avoids dynamically changing address partitioning during run time (i.e., reprogramming the SAU and the IDAU), which can result in software complexity and can be prone to error, e.g., a pointer passed from Non-secure software to Secure software could, unexpectedly, be switched from Non-secure to Secure when the address partitioning changed.

To ensure that the system is Secure, secure software developers must make sure that resources used by Secure software are placed in the Secure address ranges. This includes:

- Secure firmware codes,
- Secure data memories (including stacks and heap memories),
- The Secure vector table, and
- Secure peripherals.

By so doing, Non-secure software is unable to gain direct access to those Secure resources. Additionally, to make the system secure, software developers must take great care when creating Secure APIs which provide services to Non-secure software. A range of design considerations for creating Secure software is covered in Section 18.6.

18.2.3 SAU programmer's model

18.2.3.1 *Summary of SAU registers and concepts*

The Security Attribution Unit (SAU) contains several programmable registers. These registers are placed in the System Control Space (SCS) and are only accessible from the Secure privileged state. Access to the SAU registers is always 32-bit in size. A summary of SAU registers is detailed in Table 18.1.

The SAU sets up work in a similar way to the MPU by defining memory regions using a base (starting) address and a limit (ending) address, with a granularity of 32 bytes. The SAU in the Cortex-M23 and Cortex-M33 processors can have 0, 4, or 8 SAU regions. In an Armv8-M processor with TrustZone support, even when the SAU has been configured with zero SAU regions, the SAU would still be available. In this instance, the memory partitioning would be entirely handled by the IDAUs. The exact memory partitioning would be defined by the chip designers that designed the IDAU.

The SAU address lookup function is summarized in Fig. 18.4.

The SAU address lookup behavior, as shown in Fig. 18.4, is explained in detail as follows:

- If the SAU is enabled, and if an address matches an SAU region, the result will be based on the setting on the address comparator, be either Non-secure or Secure Non-secure Callable (NSC).
- If the SAU is enabled, and if the address does not match any SAU region, the result is Secure.
- If the SAU is disabled, and if the ALLNS (All Non-secure) bit in the SAU Control register is set, the result is Non-secure (i.e., the memory map is entirely decided on by the IDAU).
- If the SAU is disabled, and if the ALLNS (All Non-secure) bit in the SAU Control register is zero, the result is Secure. This is the default setting after a reset.

During the execution of a TT (Test Target) instruction, when an SAU region matches the address of the TT checking input, the region number of the matching SAU region is reported as a part of the result for the TT execution (Section 7.4.2 and Fig. 7.6).

TABLE 18.1 SAU register summary.

Address	Register	CMSIS-CORE symbol	Full name
0xE000EDD0	SAU_CTRL	SAU->CTRL	SAU Control Register
0xE000EDD4	SAU_TYPE	SAU->TYPE	SAU Type Register
0xE000EDD8	SAU_RNR	SAU->RNR	SAU Region Number Register
0xE000EDDC	SAU_RBAR	SAU->RBAR	SAU Region Base Address Register
0xE000EDE0	SAU_RLAR	SAU->RLAR	SAU Region Limit Address Register
0xE000EDE4	SAU_SFSR	SAU->SFSR	SAU Secure Fault Status Register
0xE000EDE8	SAU_SFAR	SAU->SFAR	SAU Secure Fault Address Register

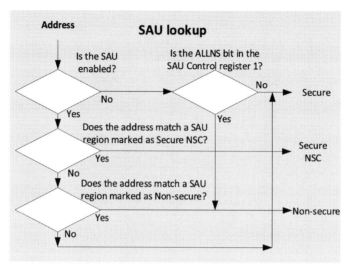

FIG. 18.4 SAU address lookup summary.

At the same time as an address is being looked up using the SAU, the IDAUs are also, in parallel, undertaking the address lookup. The results from the SAU and IDAU lookup are then combined, as shown in Fig. 18.5.

Chips that are designed for ultra-low power applications and which have a tiny silicon area can use the IDAUs for address partitioning and can have an SAU with no region comparators.

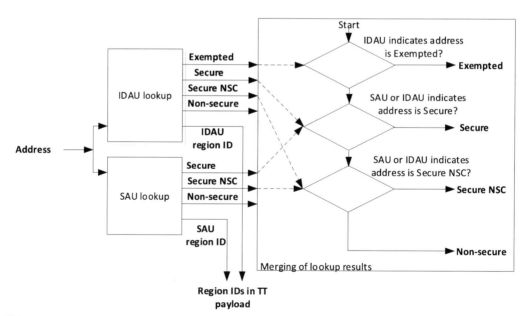

FIG. 18.5 Combined SAU and IDAU address lookups.

TABLE 18.2 SAU Control Register (SAU->CTRL, 0xE000EDD0).

Bits	Name	Type	Reset value	Description
31:2	Reserved	–	0	Reserved
1	ALLNS	R/W	0	All Non-secure. When set to 1, the SAU lookup result is always Non-secure. Otherwise, the result is Secure.
0	ENABLE	R/W	0	When set to 1, it enables the SAU. If the SAU has a zero region, this bit is tied to 0.

In this scenario, the Secure software that handles the TrustZone initialization only needs to set the ALLNS bit in the SAU Control register to 1 so that the security partitioning is only handled by the IDAUs.

18.2.3.2 SAU Control Register

The SAU Control Register (Table 18.2) provides the global enable control bit for the SAU. Even if the SAU is configured to have a zero SAU region, the SAU Control Register is still present. By default, the SAU is disabled and the ALLNS bit is cleared, which means the whole memory map is, by default, Secure.

Please note, before setting the ENABLE bit in the SAU Control Register, the software initializing the SAU must clear the region's "enable" bit of the unused SAU region(s). This is required because the individual enable bit of each SAU region is undefined after a reset.

18.2.3.3 SAU Type Register

The SAU Type Register (Table 18.3) details the number of regions implemented in the SAU.

18.2.3.4 SAU Region Number Register

The SAU Region Number Register (Table 18.4) selects the SAU region to be configured.

TABLE 18.3 SAU Type Register (SAU->TYPE, 0xE000EDD4).

Bits	Name	Type	Reset value	Description
31:8	Reserved	–	0	Reserved
7:0	SREGION	RO	0	The number of implemented SAU regions (0, 4, or 8).

TABLE 18.4 SAU Region Number Register (SAU->RNR, 0xE000EDD8).

Bits	Name	Type	Reset value	Description
31:8	Reserved	–	0	Reserved
7:0	REGION	R/W	0	Selects the region currently accessed by the SAU_RBAR and the SAU_RLAR registers

TABLE 18.5 SAU Region Base Address Register (SAU->RBAR, 0xE000EDDC).

Bits	Name	Type	Reset value	Description
31:5	BADDR	R/W	–	Region base (starting) address
4:0	Reserved	–	0	Reserved. Reads as zero, write is ignored.

18.2.3.5 SAU Region Base Address Register

The SAU Region Base Address Register (Table 18.5) details the starting address of the SAU region currently selected by the SAU Region Number Register.

18.2.3.6 SAU Region Limit Address Register

The SAU Region Limit Address Register (Table 18.6) details the limit address of the SAU region currently selected by the SAU Region Number Register. The ending address of the SAU region is inclusive of the limit address set in this register, with the lowest 5 bits of the SAU region ending address automatically padded with value 0x1F. Because of this, even the last byte of the 32-byte granularity is included in the SAU region.

18.2.3.7 Secure Fault Status Register (SFSR) and Secure Fault Address Register (SFAR)

The SFSR and SFAR registers are available in Armv8-M Mainline processors (e.g., the Cortex-M33) but are not available on the Armv8-M Baseline processor (i.e., the Cortex-M23). These registers are covered in Chapter 13 as follows:

- Information on the SFSR is covered in Chapter 13, Section 13.5.5
- Information on the SFAR is covered in Chapter 13, Section 13.5.9

These registers allow a SecureFault exception handler to report information about the fault exception and, potentially, allows the fault exception handler to deal with the issue. The obtained information can also be used during a debug session to help software developers understand any issues that have arisen during the software operations.

TABLE 18.6 SAU Region Limit Address Register (SAU->RLAR, 0xE000EDE0).

Bits	Name	Type	Reset value	Description
31:5	LADDR	R/W	–	Region limit (ending) address
4:2	Reserved	–	0	Reserved. Reads as zero, write is ignored.
1	NSC	R/W	–	Non-secure callable. If this bit is set to 1, an SAU region match will return a Secure Non-secure Callable (NSC) memory type. If not set to 1, the SAU region match will return a Non-secure memory type.
0	ENABLE	R/W	–	If set to 1, it enables the SAU region. If not set to 1, the region is disabled.

18.2.4 Non-secure software calling a Secure API

One of the key features of "TrustZone for Armv8-M" is its ability to allow direct function calls between Secure and Non-secure software. This allows Secure firmware to provide a range of services, e.g., APIs for cryptography operations, secure storage, and APIs for establishing a secure IoT connection to cloud services.

To make the design secure, a range of hardware features have been introduced to prevent illegal state transitions. In the case of Non-secure software calling a Secure API/function, this function call can only take place if both of the following conditions are met (Fig. 18.6):

(1) The first instruction in the Secure API is an SG (Secure Gateway) instruction, and
(2) The SG instruction is in a memory region marked as Non-secure Callable.

If neither of these conditions is met, a security violation is detected and either a SecureFault or HardFault exception is triggered to deal with the error. Because of this, it is impossible to branch into the middle of a Secure function and bypass the security checks.

When a Non-secure code is calling a Secure API, the Secure address location where the Non-secure code branches into the Secure API is called an entry point. There is no limit on how many entry points can exist in the Secure firmware: each NSC region can have multiple entry points, and there can be multiple NSC regions in the memory map. Please note, because an ordinary branch and link instruction (i.e., either a BL or BLX instruction) is used when Non-secure software calls a Secure API, the Non-secure software project does not require any special compilation support from the toolchain to enable it to work with Secure software.

Please also note, at the execution of an SG instruction, the processor is still in Non-secure state. Only after the SG instruction has successfully executed is the processor then in Secure state. If a software developer has only Non-secure debug access, they will still, during a debug session, see the execution of the branch to the entry point. Although the address of the Secure entry point is visible to the Non-secure software developer, it is not a problem because memory contents in the Secure memory are not accessible unless Secure debug permission is granted. The only Secure firmware information that would be seen by the Non-secure software developer is the address of the entry points, which are available inside the export library provided by the developers of the Secure software.

The reason why the Non-secure callable (NSC) memory attribute is needed is to prevent binary data within the Secure software, which contains a pattern that matches the opcode of

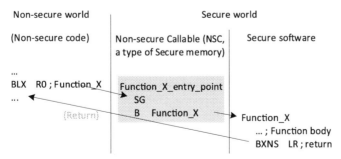

FIG. 18.6 Non-secure code calling a Secure API.

the SG instruction, being abused by a hacker who branches into it. By making sure that only the entry points are placed in memories marked as NSC, the risk of having inadvertent entry points is eliminated.

Another part of the protection mechanism is the function return at the end of a Secure API. Instead of using the usual "BX LR" instruction to return to the calling code, the "BXNS LR" instruction should be used. Armv8-M introduced "BXNS <reg>" and "BLXNS <reg>" instructions so that the processor can switch from the Secure to the Non-secure state when bit 0 of the address register (specified by <reg>) is zero. When the SG instruction is executed, the processor automatically:

- Clears bit 0 of the Link Register (LR) to zero if the processor was, before the SG instruction is executed, in Non-secure state.
- Sets bit 0 of the LR to 1 if the processor was, before the SG instruction is executed, in Secure state.

When the function-return takes place at the end of the Secure API, with bit 0 of the LR being zero (it would have been cleared by SG at the function entry), the processor knows it must return to the Non-secure world. In this scenario, a fault exception would be triggered if the processor returned to a Secure address. This mechanism detects and prevents a hacker from calling a Secure API with a fake return address pointing to a Secure program location.

If the same Secure API is called by another Secure function, the execution of the SG instruction at the function entry will set bit 0 of the LR to 1. At the end of the Secure API, the LR value, which has a bit 0 value of 1, is used for the function-return. Using bit 0 of the LR, the processor knows that it will be returning to a Secure program location. This arrangement allows a Secure API to be used by either Non-secure or Secure code.

To help software developers create Secure APIs in C/C++, the Cortex-M Security Extension (CMSE) defines a C function attribute called "cmse_nonsecure_entry". An example of how "cmse_nonsecure_entry" is used can be found in Section 18.3.4.

18.2.5 Secure code calling a Non-secure function

TrustZone for Armv8-M allows Secure software to call a Non-secure function. This is useful when:

- A middleware software component in the Secure world needs to access a peripheral driver in the Non-secure world to access a certain peripheral function.
- Secure firmware needs to access an error handling function (i.e., a call-back function) in the Non-secure world. The call-back mechanism allows Secure software to notify Non-secure software when an error has occurred. For example, a Secure API, which handles a background memory copying service on behalf of a Non-secure software component, could carry out the operation using a Secure DMA controller. Secure software is then able to use the call-back mechanism to notify the Non-secure software when a DMA operation error occurs.

When Secure software needs to call a Non-secure function, the BLXNS instruction should be used (Fig. 18.7). Similar to using the BXNS instruction, bit 0 of the register holding the branch target address is used to indicate the security state of the function being called. If that

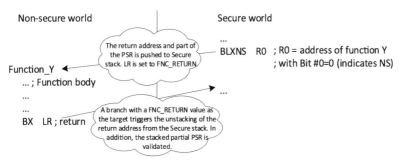

FIG. 18.7 Secure code calling a Non-secure function.

bit is 0, the processor must switch to the Non-secure state at this branch. If the bit is 1, the branch targets a Secure function.

When branching to a Non-secure function, the BLXNS instruction saves the return address and the partial xPSR to the Secure stack and updates the LR to a special value, which is called FNC_RETURN (i.e., Function Return). Partial information in the PSR (Program Status Register) is also saved in the Secure stack and is used later when returning to Secure state.

The value of the FNC_RETURN (Table 18.7) is either 0xFEFFFFFF or 0xFEFFFFFE.

At the end of the Non-secure function, the return operation (e.g., "BX LR") loads the FNC_RETURN value into the Program Counter (PC), triggering the unstacking of the real return address from the Secure stack. An integrity check is also carried out using the partial PSR, which was previously pushed to the Secure stack.

The use of FNC_RETURN hides the Secure program address from the Non-secure world to avoid the leakage of any secret information. It also stops Non-secure software from modifying the Secure return address which is stored in the Secure stack.

If the processor is in Secure handler mode when calling a Non-secure API, part of the Program Status Register (the value of IPSR) is saved in the Secure Main Stack and the value in the IPSR is switched to 1 to mask the identity of the calling Secure handler. When the Non-secure API finishes and returns to the Secure world, an integrity check is carried out to ensure that the processor's mode has not been changed. The IPSR, which was changed to 1 when calling the Non-secure API, is then returned to the previous value.

TABLE 18.7 FNC_RETURN code.

Bits	Description
31:24	PREFIX—must be 0xFE
23:1	Reserved—These bits must be "one"
0	S (Secure)—Indicates the security state of the caller code. 0—the function was called from the Non-secure state 1—the function was called from the Secure state This bit is normally 1 because the FNC_RETURN mechanism is used when the Secure code calls a function in the Non-secure world. However, in some function chaining situations, this bit might be cleared by an SG instruction. To overcome this, the function return mechanism ignores bit 0 when processing a branch to the FNC_RETURN.

TABLE 18.8   Behavior of BXNS and BLXNS instructions.

Execution state (instruction)	Condition	Result
Secure state (BX, BLX)	LSB of Address is 1	Branches to an address in the Secure state
Secure state (BX, BLX)	LSB of Address is 0	Causes a HardFault/UsageFault
Secure state (BXNS, BLXNS)	LSB of Address is 1	Branches to an address in the Secure state
Secure state (BXNS, BLXNS)	LSB of Address is 0	Branches to an address in the Non-Secure state
Non-Secure state (BX, BLX)	LSB of Address is 1	Branches to an either a Secure or a Non-secure address
Non-Secure state (BX, BLX)	LSB of Address is 0	Causes a HardFault/UsageFault
Non-Secure state (BXNS, BLXNS)	BXNS, BLXNS not supported	Causes a HardFault/UsageFault

18.2.6 Additional information for the BXNS and BLXNS instructions

The BXNS and BLXNS instructions are available on Armv8-M processors when TrustZone is implemented and can only be used by Secure software. When the processor is in the Non-secure state, any attempt to execute these instructions would be handled as an error of an undefined instruction and would trigger either a HardFault or a UsageFault exception (Table 18.8).

In C/C++ programming, when using CMSE features to create Secure APIs, or for calling Non-secure functions, there is no need to use an inline assembler to manually insert these instructions. This is because the BXNS and BLXNS instructions are generated by the C compiler.

18.2.7 Security state transition—Privileged level change

Security state transitions that are caused by function calls or function returns can result in the processor's privileged level being changed. This is because the nPRIV bit in the processor's CONTROL register is banked between Security states (Fig. 18.8).

A privilege level change caused by function calls or function returns only occurs when the processor is in thread mode.

If the processor is in handler mode, the processor is kept at a privileged level at the cross-domain function call/return. This is because:

(1) The Interrupt Program Status Register (IPSR)—see "Program Status Register (PSR)" section in Section 4.2.2.3—is shared between the Secure and the Non-secure world, and

(2) The architecture definition specifies that the processor has to be in a privileged state while in Handler mode.

Because of the way the Armv8-M architecture is defined, a Secure API in a Secure software library is executed at a privileged access level when it is being called by a Non-secure exception handler. If there is a need to restrict the access permission of a Secure API to an unprivileged level, the Secure API's entry point must:

(1) First, redirect the function call to the Secure firmware codes that check the privileged level, then

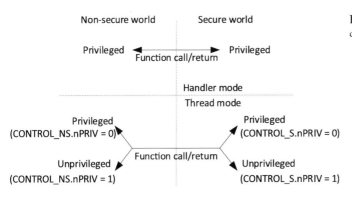

FIG. 18.8 Security state transition can change the processor's privileged level.

(2) If required, switch the processor to unprivileged state, then
(3) Execute the function body of the Secure API.

By running the Secure API in an unprivileged state, the operation of the API can be restricted to a selection of memory regions using the Secure Memory Protection Unit (MPU).

18.2.8 Security state transitions and their relationship with exception priority levels

Some of the system exceptions are banked between security states, e.g., exceptions like SysTick, SVC, and PendSV. Because of this, there are, for those exceptions, Secure and Non-secure exception priority level registers. When one of the aforementioned system exception handlers calls a function from the opposite security domain, the exception priority level of the first triggered exception is used. In the example in Fig. 18.9, the Non-secure SVC calls a Secure API, and, even though the processor is in Secure state and its IPSR (Interrupt Program Status Register) is indicating that it is running an SVC handler, the exception priority level of the Non-secure SVC is used.

Please note, there are special cases where the exception priority level changes in cross-domain function calls/returns.

When Secure exceptions are prioritized by setting the PRIS (Prioritize Secure) bit in the AIRCR (Application Interrupt and Reset Control Register), the switching of one security state

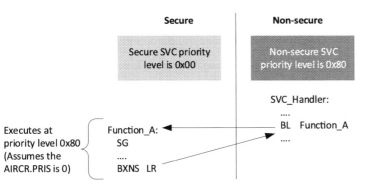

FIG. 18.9 Exception priority level of banked system exceptions at cross-domain function calls.

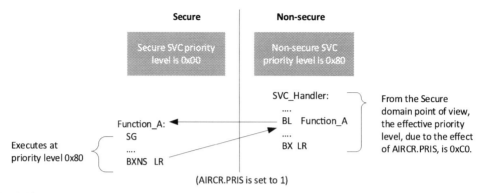

FIG. 18.10   Security state transition can change the processor's exception priority level.

to another via a function call/return can affect the processor's current exception priority level. For example, when the same code example detailed in Fig. 18.9 is executed, and if the AIRCR. PRIS is set to 1, the effective exception priority level during the execution of the Non-secure SVC handler would be 0xC0. However, the effective priority level would change to 0x80 during the execution of the Secure function (i.e., function A) (Fig. 18.10).

18.2.9 Other TrustZone instructions

To support the various TrustZone operations, Armv8-M introduced several instructions. These are listed in Table 18.9.

Information on these instructions can be found in Chapter 5, Section 5.20.

The TT instructions are accessed via intrinsic functions and are covered in Section 18.3.6. The VLSTM and VLLDM instructions are generated by the C/C++ compiler as follows:

- Before the Non-secure function call is made, the Secure software reserves a small portion of memory space on the stack for the FPU registers and then executes the VLSTM instruction. This marks the data in the FPU and tells it that it needs to be protected from the Non-secure state software, but this action does not push the FPU registers into the allocated stack space.
- The Non-secure C function is called and executed. This means that:

TABLE 18.9   Other TrustZone support instructions.

Instruction	Purpose
Test Target (TT, TTA, TTT, TTAT)	These instructions are used for pointer checking (see Sections 5.20 and 18.3.6).
VLSTM, VLLDM Note: These are available in Armv8-M Mainline (e.g., the Cortex-M33 processor) but not in Armv8-M Baseline (e.g., the Cortex-M23 processor)	When Secure code needs to call a Non-secure function, these instructions save and restore Secure data in the FPU. By reusing the lazy-stacking support hardware, the latency of calling Non-secure functions can, if the Non-secure code does not utilize the FPU, be reduced.

    ○ When the Non-secure C function executes an FPU instruction, the stacking of the FPU registers takes place and saves the Secure data in the FPU to the Secure stack. The FPU registers are then cleared to prevent leakage of the Secure information. Once the stacking and clearing of the registers is completed, the Non-secure function is resumed and operations continue.

- After returning from the Non-secure API, the processor executes the VLLDM instruction. When this instruction is executed:
  - ○ If the executed Non-secure function did not use the FPU, the FPU registers would not be touched and the VLLDM instruction would only clear the pending FPU stacking request.
  - ○ If the executed Non-secure function did use the FPU, the previous Secure FPU data would be in the Secure stack and the VLLDM instruction would restore the Secure FPU context.

When the FPU is not implemented or is disabled, the VLSTM and VLLDM instructions execute as NOPs (No operation).

18.3 Secure software development

18.3.1 Overview of Secure software development

To build a Secure project, we need to

(1) Tell the C/C++ compiler that we are building a Secure project. This is required so that codes generated by the compiler satisfy the requirements defined in the document "Armv8-M Security Extension: Requirements on Development Tools" [2]. For Arm Compiler 6 and the GCC, the "-mcmse" option is available for this purpose. For the IAR compiler, the equivalent command-line option is "--cmse".

(2) Include a header file in the C/C++ code using the following line of code:

```
#include <arm_cmse.h>
```

If you are using the Keil® Microcontroller Development Kit (MDK), you can specify the Secure project option in the target option menu, as per Fig. 18.11.

When compiling Secure software, the C compiler generates a built-in preprocessing macro called __ARM_FEATURE_CMSE (Table 18.10), which is set to a value of 3.

The __ARM_FEATURE_CMSE built-in preprocessing macro enables software to adapt to the Secure and the Non-secure environments. For example, the following C codes executes "function_1" if compiled for the Secure state:

```
    . . .
#if defined (__ARM_FEATURE_CMSE) && (__ARM_FEATURE_CMSE == 3U)
    function_1();
#endif
    . . .
```

The use of this feature is often found in Armv8-M software projects. For example, you often find the __ARM_FEATURE_CMSE preprocessing macro being used in the CMSIS-CORE header files and device driver libraries.

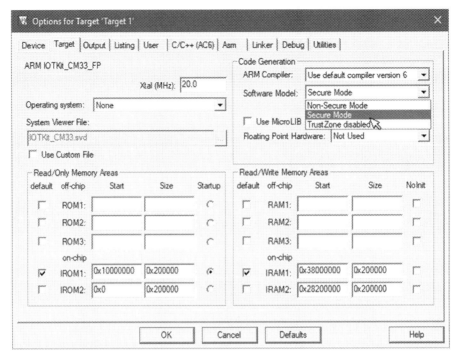

FIG. 18.11   For Keil MDK, select the Secure Mode in the target option to compile the Secure software.

TABLE 18.10   Values and the definitions of the __ARM_FEATURE_CMSE macro.

__ARM_FEATURE_CMSE value	Definition
0 or undefined	The TT instruction is not available
1	TT instruction support is available. However, the software is not compiled for Secure mode and, therefore, TrustZone variants of TT (TTA, TTAT) are not available.
3	Compilation target for Secure state. TT support for TrustZone is available.

18.3.2 Security setup

The security configuration of a device usually needs to be setup when initializing the Secure software. The areas to be considered when setting up the security configuration of a Cortex-M23/Cortex-M33 based system are as follows:

- Configuring the Memory map. This includes the programming of:
   ○ The SAU to define the Non-secure and the NSC regions
   ○ The IDAU (but only when the IDAU is programmable). Note: Potentially, a system can contain programmable register(s) that control the IDAU's configurations.
   ○ The system-level Memory Protection Controllers (MPCs)

- The system-level Peripheral Protection Controllers (PPCs)
- Configuring the security domains of exceptions and other exception related settings. For example:
  - For each interrupt, whether it should target the Secure or the Non-secure state. This is defined using the Interrupt Target Non-secure Register (NVIC->ITNS, see Section 9.2.5).
  - For the Cortex-M33 processor, optionally enabling the SecureFault exception and, potentially, other system exceptions.
  - Setting up the Application Interrupt and Reset Control Register (AIRCR, see Section 9.3.4). The bit fields in this register that are related to TrustZone include:
    - AIRCR.BFHFNMIHF: Typically, this bit is kept at 0 (NMI, HardFault, and BusFault exceptions remain in Secure state) when TrustZone is used.
    - AIRCR.PRIS: Optionally, this bit is set to prioritize Secure exceptions.
    - AIRCR.SYSRESETREQS: Optionally, this bit is set to decide whether Non-secure software can trigger a self-reset.
- Defining the features available to Non-secure software: For the Cortex-M33 processor, the Non-secure Access Control Register (SCB->NSACR) should be programmed to define whether the FPU, the coprocessor, and the Arm Custom Instructions features are accessible from the Non-secure state (see Sections 14.2.4 and 15.5). In addition, the CPPWR (Section 15.6) might also need configuring to prevent the Non-secure software from accessing the power control of the FPU and custom accelerators.
- Configuring the FPU settings (only applicable to Armv8-M processors with an FPU): If the Secure software is expected to use the FPU (or the Helium feature in an Armv8.1-M processor) for sensitive data, the Secure software should, at boot time, set the TS, CLRONRET, and CLRONRETS control bits to 1 in the FPU Floating-point Context Control Register (FPU->FPCCR, see Section 14.2.7). These bits should not be changed and should always remain high. If the Secure software does not use the FPU/Helium registers for sensitive data, the Secure software can leave the TS and CLRONRETS control bits as zero; Non-secure privileged software can then set the CLRONRET control bit to 1 to prevent privileged data in the FPU from being visible to unprivileged software.
- Deciding whether the Non-secure software can control, by programming the SLEEPDEEPS bit in the System Control Register (SCB->SCR), the SLEEPDEEP feature.
- Configuring the system level/Device-specific security management features—each chip design could have additional security features that might need to be configured or enabled before being used.
- Configuring the debug security settings: When required, Secure software can override the Secure debug authentication setting (Section 16.2.7).

For Armv8-M devices with a CMSIS-CORE compliant driver, most of these configurations are carried out in a function called "TZ_SAU_Setup()". This function and its parameters are placed inside a file called partition_<device>.h (Note: The exact name is device-specific i.e., "<device>" is replaced by the name of the device being used). The "TZ_SAU_Setup()" function is accessed from the "SystemInit()" function and is executed during the execution of the reset handler.

When using Keil MDK for a Secure software project, the parameters inside partition_<device>.h are easily edited using the Configuration Wizard (Fig. 18.12).

FIG. 18.12   Partition_<device>.h is configured using the Configuration Wizard.

Please note:

- The debug authentication override is not part of the "TZ_SAU_Setup()".
- In addition to the security configurations for the processor and the memory map, there could be other system-level security configurations that need to be setup. For example, the power management and clock control system could contain security management control register(s) that would also need to be programmed.

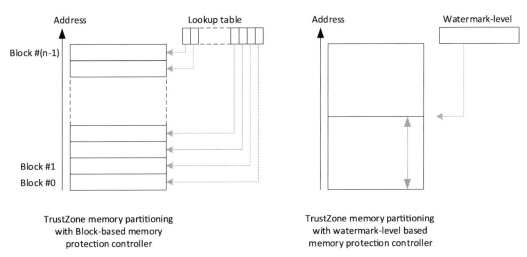

FIG. 18.13 Memory partitioning approach in a block-based and a watermark-level based MPC.

The configuration code for setting up the Memory Protection Controller (MPC) and the Peripheral Protection Controller (PPC) can usually be found in the CMSIS-CORE file "partition_<device>.h" or in the CMSIS-CORE file "system_<device>.c". The programmer's model for the MPC and the PPC are device-specific. There are two types of MPC based on the following partitioning methods (Fig. 18.13):

- Memory-block based design—The memory block connected to the MPC is divided into several memory pages, with the target security state of each memory page defined by a small programmable look-up table (LUT) inside the MPC hardware. Each bit of the LUT represents the target security state of a page.
- Watermark-level based design—The memory block connected to the MPC is divided into two sections, with the boundary location controlled by a programmable register.

Whereas the memory-block based design is highly flexible, the watermark-level based MPC design can be smaller and is thus ideal for a range of ultra-low-power systems. The programmer's model for the MPC is vendor/device-specific. For microcontrollers based on the Arm Corstone™-200 foundation IPs, the MPC design is memory-block based. The programmer's model for this component can be found using the following link [4]: https://developer.arm.com/documentation/ddi0571/e/programmers-model/ahb5-trustzone-memory-protection-controller.

In the Arm Corstone-200 MPC design:

- The lookup table is accessible by the BLK_LUT[n] register. Each bit in this register represents the security state of a memory block. Because there can be more than 32 memory blocks, there can, consequently, be more than one BLK_LUT register.
- A read/write register called BLK_IDX (i.e., the block index register) defines the value of the index "n". This is used for selecting which BLK_LUT[n] register should be accessed. Before accessing the lookup table, the index "n" of BLK_LUT[n] needs to be set via BLK_IDX.

- Additional read-only registers are available to allow the software to determine the block size, via the BLK_CFG register, and the maximum number of blocks available, via the BLK_MAX register.
- The MPC can, optionally, send an interrupt to the processor if a security abnormality is detected. For example, when a Non-secure program attempts to access a memory block that has been allocated to the Secure world via a Non-secure alias address. To assist the management of interrupt generation and interrupt handling, the MPC has interrupt control and status registers.

Similar to the MPC, the PPC is also vendor/device-specific. Typically, a simple programmable register is used to provide a lookup table, with each bit representing whether a peripheral is Secure or Non-secure. Some PPC designs, including those for the Arm Corstone™-200 foundation IP, also allow the peripherals to be accessed either at the privileged level or at both the privileged and unprivileged level. The programmer's models for the PPCs in Arm Corstone-200 can be found using the following links:

- AMBA® AHB5 PPC: https://developer.arm.com/documentation/ddi0571/e/functional-description/ahb5-trustzone-peripheral-protection-controller/functional-description [5]
- AMBA APB4 PPC: https://developer.arm.com/documentation/ddi0571/e/functional-description/apb4-trustzone-peripheral-protection-controller/functional-description [6]

The control registers for the AHB5 PPC and APB4 PPC in Arm Corstone-200 are not included in the PPC components and are, therefore, vendor/device-specific.

When undertaking Secure and Non-secure software projects, the settings for the TrustZone memory partitioning must match the project's memory usage settings. The TrustZone memory partitioning settings include:

- Configuring the SAU, and, optionally, the IDAU if it is programmable, and
- Configuring the MPC and the PPC.

A software project's memory usage is usually defined by the project's linker settings, either linker scripts or command-line options. With this in mind, a Secure software developer would need to configure:

- The memory map of the Secure project, including where the NSC region(s) should be placed, and, optionally,
- The memory map of the Non-secure project.

If there are inconsistencies between the TrustZone partitioning and the software project settings, the security of the device could be compromised. To reduce the risk of this occurring, the CMSIS-Zone project has been created which delivers a tool that automatically generates various setup codes and linker scripts using a single source of data. Using XML based files and a CMSIS-Zone utility (a software tool):

- Setup codes—for the SAU, the IDAU, the MPC, and the PPC,
- The linker scripts, and
- Optionally, the MPU setup codes for process isolation, which can be used by Trusted Firmware-M and the RTOS,

can be generated. This approach makes the development process much easier and less prone to error.

18.3.3 Initial switching to the Non-secure world

When the security initialization process has been carried out and before starting the application(s) in the Non-secure world, the following actions might be needed:

- Depending on an application's requirements, the initialization of the Secure peripherals (e.g., Secure watchdog timers).
- The initialization of the Secure firmware framework.
- Setting up the stack limits for the Secure stack pointers.

Once completed, we should then be in a position to branch into the Non-secure application. The starting point for the Non-secure software (i.e., the starting address of the Non-secure reset handler) is in the Non-secure vector table. Secure firmware starts the Non-secure world by reading the starting address and then branches to it. To ensure that Non-secure software, such as an RTOS, correctly operates, the processor must be in privileged Thread mode when starting the Non-secure software.

An example code that can be used to branch into the Non-secure world is listed in the following section. In this example, a function attribute from the Cortex-M Security Extension (CMSE) is used to define a Non-secure function pointer. This action enables the C compiler to generate the correct BLXNS instruction to branch to the reset handler in the Non-secure world.

```
// Non-secure int function typedef with cmse_nonsecure_call attribute
typedef int __attribute__((cmse_nonsecure_call)) nsfunc(void);
...
int nonsecure_init(void) {
  // Example modified from Arm website
  // https://community.arm.com/developer/ip-products/processors/trustzone-for-
armv8-m/b/blog/posts/a-few-intricacies-of-writing-armv8-m-secure-code

  // If needed, setup the Non-secure VTOR.
  // In the Cortex-M33 based FPGA platform used for creating this example
  // (i.e. a system called IoT Kit, which runs on the MPS2 FPGA board), the
  // Non-secure code image starting address is 0x00200000
  SCB_NS->VTOR=0x00200000UL; // Optional for most hardware platforms.
  // But it is needed in the FPGA platform used here
  // The following line creates a pointer to the Non-secure vector table
  uint32_t *vt_ns = (uint32_t *) SCB_NS->VTOR;

  // Setup the Non-secure Main Stack Pointer (MSP_NS)
  __TZ_set_MSP_NS(vt_ns[0]);
  // Setup the function pointer to the NS reset vector
  nsfunc *ns_reset = (nsfunc*)(vt_ns[1]);
```

```
  // Branch into the Non-secure reset handler
  ns_reset(); // Branches to the Non-secure world
#ifdef VERBOSE
  // Displays error for debug
  printf("ERROR: should not be here\n");
#endif
  while(1);
}
```

18.3.4 Creating a simple Secure API

When developing Secure software, it is easy to create a simple Secure API. In the following code example, a simple Secure function to return the value of x^2 has been created.

```
// Non-secure int function prototype
int __attribute__((cmse_nonsecure_entry)) entry1(int x);
...
int __attribute__((cmse_nonsecure_entry)) entry1(int x)
{
  return (x * x);
}
```

Because the SG instructions (i.e., the entry points) are produced by the linker, the "simple" code detailed above is all that is required for creating a Secure API. To prevent Secure information from being leaked, the C compiler generates a code sequence which ensures that Secure data inside the register banks, except the return result, is erased before it is returned to the Non-secure world.

During the linking stage (Fig. 18.14), the linker identifies all the Secure APIs that are in the Secure project and generates an entry point table, which is placed in a location specified in the linker setting configuration (e.g., a linker script).

At the same time, the linker generates an export library. This file contains the symbols and addresses of the entry points and can be used by Non-secure software developers to handle the linking of Non-secure projects. Note: Because Non-secure projects can contain function calls to the Secure APIs, the linker needs the information in the export file to carry out the linking process.

In some cases, a Secure program image might be a new revision of an existing one, and additional Secure functions might have to be added. To avoid the need to recompile existing Non-secure projects (which could mean that Non-secure programs in released products would need to be updated), the address of the entry points that exist in the previous version of the Secure program image would need to remain unchanged after the update. To ensure this occurs, the linker has to import the old version of the export library so that it knows the addresses of the old entry points and does not change them.

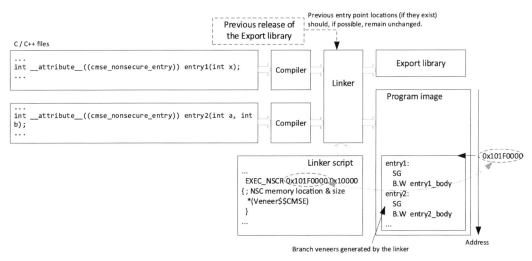

FIG. 18.14 Creation of entry points during the linking stage.

18.3.5 Calling a Non-secure function

Secure software is allowed to call Non-secure functions. However, the process is not as straight forward as a normal function call because the address locations of the Non-secure functions to be called are, when the software is compiled, often unavailable (this is because the compilation of Non-secure software takes place after the compilation of the Secure software). The most common solution used to solve this problem is to use Secure API(s) for passing function pointers from the Non-secure software to the Secure world. In this scenario, once the Secure software receives the Non-secure function pointer, the Non-secure functions can then subsequently be called by the Secure software.

The following example demonstrates the process of a Non-secure function pointer being passed to the Secure world and then calling the Non-secure function from the Secure world. To begin the process, a Secure API needs to be created so that a function pointer from the Non-secure world can be passed to the Secure world. The Non-secure function for the call has an integer input and an integer return value.

```
typedef int __attribute__((cmse_nonsecure_call)) tdef_nsfunc_o_int_i_int(int x);
int __attribute__((cmse_nonsecure_entry))
pass_nsfunc_ptr_o_int_i_int(tdef_nsfunc_o_int_i_int *callback);

void default_callback(void);

// Declare function pointer *fp
// fp can point to either a secure or a non-secure function
// Initialized to a default callback
tdef_nsfunc_o_int_i_int *fp = (tdef_nsfunc_o_int_i_int *) default_callback;

// This is a Secure API with a function pointer as an input parameter
```

```
int __attribute__((cmse_nonsecure_entry))
pass_nsfunc_ptr_o_int_i_int(tdef_nsfunc_o_int_i_int *callback) {
  // Result for the function pointer
  cmse_address_info_t tt_payload;
    tt_payload = cmse_TTA_fptr(callback);
    if (tt_payload.flags.nonsecure_read_ok) {
      fp = cmse_nsfptr_create(callback); // Non-secure function pointer
      return (0);
    } else {
      printf ("[pass_nsfunc_ptr_o_int_i_int] Error: input pointer is not NS\n");
      return (1); // Function pointer is not accessible from the Non-secure side
    }
}

void default_callback(void) {
  __BKPT(0);
  while(1);
}
```

This Secure API (i.e., `pass_nsfunc_ptr_o_int_i_int`) uses two of the following CMSE defined intrinsic functions:

(1) `cmse_TTA_fptr`—This intrinsic function checks the function pointer using the TT instruction. It makes sure that (a) the function pointer is accessible from the Non-secure world and (b) the function code is readable. This intrinsic function returns a 32-bit result using the cmse_address_info_t data structure (Chapter 7, Section 7.4.2), which is defined in the CMSE support.

(2) `cmse_nsfptr_create`—This intrinsic function converts a normal function pointer to a Non-secure function pointer (i.e., it clears bit 0 to zero) so that the BLXNS instruction can handle it as a Non-secure function call.

Within the aforementioned example code, a default call-back function is defined (i.e., `default_callback(void)`). This is needed in case the Secure software attempts to call the Non-secure function before the Secure API (i.e., pass_nsfunc_ptr_o_int_i_int) is used to setup the Non-secure function pointer.

When the Secure API (i.e., pass_nsfunc_ptr_o_int_i_int) for receiving a function pointer is in place, the Non-secure software is then in a position to use this Secure API to pass a function pointer to the Secure world. This is shown in the following code:

```
extern int __attribute__((cmse_nonsecure_entry)) pass_nsfunc_ptr_o_int_i_int(void
*callback);

  ...
  int status;
  ...

// Pass a Non-secure function pointer to the Secure world
status = pass_nsfunc_ptr_o_int_i_int(&my_func);
```

```
if (status==0) {
    // Call a secure function
    printf ("Result = %d\n", entry1(10)); // Note: this Secure API calls my_func
    } else {
    printf ("ERROR: pass_nsfunc_ptr_o_int_i_int() = %d\n", status);
}

int my_func(int data_in)
{
printf("[my_func]\n");
return (data_in * data_in);
}
```

Once the Non-secure function pointer is received from the Non-secure world, Secure software can then call the Non-secure function using the following code:

```
int call_callback(int data_in) {
    if (cmse_is_nsfptr(fp)){
        return fp(data_in);        // Non-secure function call
    } else {
        ((void (*)(void)) fp)(); // normal function call to the default call-back
        return (0);
    }
}
```

The aforementioned code uses a CMSE intrinsic function (i.e., `cmse_is_nsfptr`) to detect whether the function pointer is, by checking the value of bit 0, Non-secure. If it is, the Non-secure function can then be called. If it is not, meaning that the Non-secure function pointer has not been transferred, the default call-back function would, in this example, be executed instead.

The Secure code generated by the C/C++ compiler ensures that, apart from the function parameter, no Secure data remains in the register bank when the Non-secure function is called. Because of this, the contents of a number of registers need to be saved to the Secure stack before the BLXNS instruction is executed. After returning from the Non-secure call, the previously saved Secure contents in the register bank are then restored from the Secure stack.

18.3.6 Pointer checking

Because Secure APIs often have to carry out operations on behalf of Non-secure software, there is a need for Non-secure software to pass data pointers to the Secure software to indicate where the data sources are and where to put the operation results.

When a Secure API processes data on behalf of Non-secure software the security risks are:

- The pointer passed to the Secure API could point to Secure data which the Non-secure software is, ordinarily, not supposed to access. If the pointer points to a Secure address

location and a pointer check is not carried out, the Secure API could, as a result, readout or modify the Secure data. This is a serious security problem and must be avoided.
• Non-secure unprivileged software passes to a Secure API a pointer that points to an address that is privileged access only. In this example, if the Secure API does not carry out a pointer check, the Non-secure software could use the Secure API to bypass the security mechanism (e.g., the Non-secure MPU) in the Non-secure world.

These two security risks are shown in Fig. 18.15.

To complicate things, when a Secure API is executed, the processor can service Non-secure interrupts, and, when it does, the Non-secure data pointed to by the pointer could be accessed and modified by the Non-secure interrupt handler. As a result, the design of a Secure API must consider the instances where the Non-secure data being processed could be unexpectedly changed. Further information on this topic can be found in Section 18.6.4.

The TT (Test Target) instructions (see Sections 5.20 and 7.4) are designed to allow pointer checking to be carried out. To make these operations easier in a C/C++ programming environment, the Arm C Language Extension (ACLE) has defined a range of intrinsic functions for dealing with pointer checks. The example in Section 18.3.5 showed the use of the `cmse_TTA_fptr` function for checking whether a function pointer is pointing to a Non-secure address.

The following intrinsic functions (Table 18.11) are available for both Non-secure and Secure software, and can be used even if TrustZone is not implemented.

The intrinsic functions detailed in Table 18.11 return a 32-bit result (payload) called `cmse_address_info_t` (see Fig. 7.6 for the result returned for Secure state software and Fig. 7.7 for the result returned for Non-secure state software). In C/C++ programming, when using the features of the Cortex-M Security Extension (CMSE), the `cmse_address_info_t` is declared in the CMSE support header. For Non-secure software, the "typedef" details are as follows:

```
typedef union {
  struct cmse_address_info {
    unsigned mpu_region:8;
    unsigned :8;
```

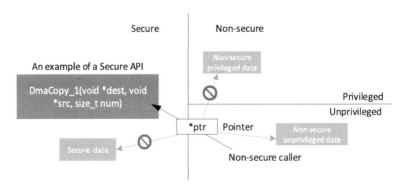

FIG. 18.15   Secure APIs need to check data pointers from the Non-secure world.

TABLE 18.11 Intrinsic functions for checking a single pointer.

Intrinsic function	Semantic
cmse_address_info_t cmse_TT(void *p)	Generates a TT instruction.
cmse_address_info_t cmse_TT_fptr(p)	Generates a TT instruction. Argument p can be any function pointer type.
cmse_address_info_t cmse_TTT(void *p)	Generates a TT instruction with the T flag.
cmse_address_info_t cmse_TTT_fptr(p)	Generates a TT instruction with the T flag. The argument p can be any function pointer type.

```
      unsigned mpu_region_valid:1;
      unsigned :1;
      unsigned read_ok:1;
      unsigned readwrite_ok:1;
      unsigned :12;
    } flags;
    unsigned value;
} cmse_address_info_t;
```

For Secure software, the "typedef" details are as follows:

```
typedef union {
  struct cmse_address_info {
    unsigned mpu_region:8;
    unsigned sau_region:8;
    unsigned mpu_region_valid:1;
    unsigned sau_region_valid:1;
    unsigned read_ok:1;
    unsigned readwrite_ok:1;
    unsigned nonsecure_read_ok:1;
    unsigned nonsecure_readwrite_ok:1;
    unsigned secure:1;
    unsigned idau_region_valid:1;
    unsigned idau_region:8;
  } flags;
  unsigned value;
} cmse_address_info_t;
```

The `cmse_address_info_t` definition for the Secure software provides additional bit fields detailing access permissions for the Non-secure world and the attributes of the security regions.

TABLE 18.12 Secure intrinsic function for checking a single pointer.

Intrinsic function	Semantic
`cmse_address_info_t` `cmse_TTA(void *p)`	Generates a TT instruction with the A flag.
`cmse_address_info_t` `cmse_TTA_fptr(p)`	Generates a TT instruction with the A flag. The argument p can be any function pointer type.
`cmse_address_info_t` `cmse_TTAT(void *p)`	Generates a TT instruction with the T and A flags.
`cmse_address_info_t` `cmse_TTAT_fptr(p)`	Generates a TT instruction with the T and A flags. The argument p can be any function pointer type.

So that Secure software can handle pointer checks on Non-secure software, TTT and TTAT instructions are available. Additional intrinsic functions (Table 18.12) are also available so that Secure software can access these instructions.

As explained in Section 7.4.3, the region's ID is one of the bit-fields returned by the TT instructions, a value that is used for detecting whether a data structure/data array is placed entirely in a Non-secure region (Fig. 7.8). Instead of using the intrinsic functions in Table 18.12 to manually check the security attribute of the aforementioned data structure/ data array, CMSE has defined additional intrinsic functions (Table 18.13) for checking data objects and address ranges.

When using these intrinsic functions, the access permission condition needs to be specified by using the flags parameter. The flag values are defined in CMSE using C macros (Table 18.14).

These flags can be combined to help the Secure APIs specify the type of access permissions that are required when pointer checks are carried out. The commonly used combinations are listed in Table 18.15.

TABLE 18.13 Secure intrinsic functions for checking the address range and the data object.

Intrinsic function	Semantic
`void *cmse_check_pointed_object` `(void *p, int flags)`	Checks that the specified object meets the access permissions outlined by the flags. Returns NULL on a failed check and *p on a successful check.
void *cmse_check_address_range(void *p, size_t size, int flags)	Checks that the specified address range meets the access permissions outlined by the flags. Returns NULL on a failed check and *p on a successful check.

TABLE 18.14 C macros defined in CMSE to assist the checking of the address range and the data object.

Macro	Value	Description
(Flag not used)	0	A TT instruction without any flag is used to retrieve the permission of an address. The result is returned in a cmse_address_info_t structure.
CMSE_MPU_UNPRIV	4	This macro sets the T flag on the TT instruction used to retrieve the permission of an address. Retrieves the unprivileged mode access permission.
CMSE_MPU_READWRITE	1	Checks if the readwrite_ok field is set in the permission.
CMSE_MPU_READ	8	Checks if the read_ok field is set in the permission.
CMSE_AU_NONSECURE	2	Checks if the secure field is *unset* in the permission.
CMSE_MPU_NONSECURE	16	Sets the A flag on the TT instruction used to retrieve the permission of an address.
CMSE_NONSECURE	18	The combined semantics of CMSE_AU_NONSECURE and CMSE_MPU_NONSECURE.

TABLE 18.15 Combination of flags enable various pointer checks.

#	Combination of C macros for use with CMSE intrinsic functions (Used for pointer checks)	Usage (i.e., The required access permission for the pointer check to pass).
1	CMSE_MPU_NONSECURE | CMSE_MPU_READWRITE	Address range/Object is readable and writeable by the Non-secure world caller
2	CMSE_MPU_NONSECURE | CMSE_MPU_READ	Address range/Object is readable by the Non-secure world caller
3	CMSE_MPU_NONSECURE | CMSE_MPU_READWRITE | CMSE_MPU_UNPRIV	Address range/Object is readable and writeable by the Non-secure unprivileged software.
4	CMSE_MPU_NONSECURE | CMSE_MPU_READ | CMSE_MPU_UNPRIV	Address range/Object is readable by the Non-secure unprivileged software.

When a data pointer is passed from the caller directly to the Secure API, the first two combinations (i.e., #1 and #2), listed in Table 18.15, are usually sufficient for handling the pointer checking. The last two combinations (i.e., #3 and #4) are different from the first two (i.e., #1 and #2) because they include the CMSE_MPU_UNPRIV flag. When this flag is set, the pointer checks that are carried out use the access permission settings of the unprivileged software. This arrangement is needed when a software service request, and the corresponding data pointer, originates from a Non-secure unprivileged caller, and when the software service

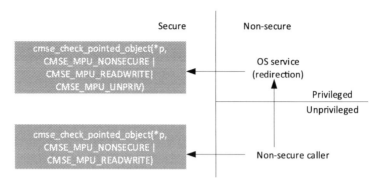

FIG. 18.16   Example showing flag combinations for object check functions and address range checks.

is redirected to the Secure API via Non-secure privileged software (e.g., an OS service running on the Non-secure side, as shown in Fig. 18.16). When the CMSE_MPU_UNPRIV flag is set, the pointer check intrinsic function provides a result based on the access permission of the Non-secure unprivileged caller, even though the Secure API was called by Non-secure privileged software.

The address range and object check functions return NULL (0) if the check fails. For example, in the following code an abort function "cmse_abort()" is called if the pointer check fails.

```
int DmaCopy_1(void *dest, void *src, size_t, num){
void *dest_chk, *src_chk;
// Check source pointer. The source for copying only needs a read permission
src_chk = cmse_check_address_range(*src, size, CMSE_MPU_NONSECURE | CMSE_MPU_READ);
if (src_chk==0) {
  cmse_abort();
  }
// Check destination pointer (read/write)
dest_chk = cmse_check_address_range(*dest, size, CMSE_MPU_NONSECURE |
CMSE_MPU_READWRITE);
if (dest_chk==0) {
  cmse_abort();
  }
...
```

The "cmse_abort()" function in the previously mentioned code is part of the C runtime library and is available when CMSE support has been enabled. It has a "weak" declaration so that it can be overridden by a customized application specific abort handling code. By default, the "cmse_abort()" function in the C library calls the "abort()" function, which is a standard C function provided by the toolchain, and then remains in the abort function. In real-world applications, instead of using the default "cmse_abort()" function, application-specific error handling code can be used instead to handle software errors when a pointer check fails.

TABLE 18.16 CMSE functions that are not pointer check intrinsic functions.

Combination	Usage
cmse_nsfptr_create(p)	Returns the value of p with its bit 0 cleared. The argument p can be any function pointer type.
cmse_is_nsfptr(p)	Returns nonzero if bit 0 of p is unset (zero) and returns zero if bit 0 of p is set. The argument p can be any function pointer type.
int cmse_nonsecure_caller (void)	Used in a Secure API—Returns nonzero if the entry function is called from the Non-secure state and zero if it is not.
cmse_abort()	The default CMSE error handling function. By default this function calls abort().

18.3.7 Other CMSE features

In addition to pointer checking intrinsic functions, the CMSE support in C/C++ compilers also provides several other functions (Table 18.16).

Most of the functions listed in Table 18.16 (except for "cmse_nonsecure_caller()") have already been detailed in previous examples and will not be covered again. The cmse_nonsecure_caller() function allows a Secure API to determine whether it was called by Non-secure or Secure software. For example, if the previous DmaCopy function was called by either a Secure or a Non-secure software component, then this function is used to decide whether a pointer check should be carried out. This is illustrated by the following code:

```
int __attribute__((cmse_nonsecure_entry)) DmaCopy_1(void *dest, void *src, size_t,
num){
void *dest_chk, *src_chk;
if (cmse_nonsecure_caller()) {
  // Caller is Non-secure. Pointer check is needed.
  // Check the source pointer. Only read permission is required for the data
  // source for the copying operation.
  src_chk = cmse_check_address_range(*src, size, CMSE_MPU_NONSECURE |
    CMSE_MPU_READ);
  if (src_chk==0) {
  cmse_abort();
   }
  // Check the destination pointer. Read/write permission is required.
  dest_chk = cmse_check_address_range(*dest, size, CMSE_MPU_NONSECURE |
    CMSE_MPU_READWRITE);
  if (dest_chk==0) {
  cmse_abort();
   }
 }
...
```

18.3.8 Passing parameters across security domains

Even when CMSE support is included and enabled in a C/C++ compiler, the passing of parameters using the stack in a cross-security-domain API will not necessarily be supported by the C compiler. This is because the passing of parameters using the stack memory is an optional feature (not mandatory) based on the CMSE specification: "Armv8-M Security Extension: Requirements on Development Tools" [2]. As a result, software developers creating Secure APIs will, if they don't know which C/C++ compiler Non-secure software developers will use, have to make sure that all of the Secure APIs parameters can be passed using just the registers (e.g., r0–r3).

Full details relating to the passing of parameters and the results are documented in an Arm specification document called Procedure Call Standard for Arm Architecture [1]. This document is also known as AAPCS and was briefly covered in Section 17.3.

18.3.9 Software environments when TrustZone is not used

When TrustZone is implemented, the Non-Maskable Interrupt, HardFault, and BusFault exceptions, for security reasons and by default, target the Secure state. If an application runs entirely in the Non-secure state and TrustZone is not used, it is possible to change the target state of those aforementioned exceptions to Non-secure. This is achieved by setting the BFHFNMINS bit in the AIRCR (Application Interrupt and Reset Control Register). However, the AIRCR.BFHFNMINS bit should only be used when the Secure world is not used. In a system that is designed to support both a TrustZone environment and a Non-TrustZone environment, it is possible to:

- Use Secure firmware that disables the TrustZone features after the Secure boot, which sets AIRCR.BFHFNMINS and that then branches into the Non-secure world.
- Boot up the system using Secure firmware and with TrustZone support enabled. The Secure firmware provides a Secure API that disables the Secure world features and also disables further access to all of the Secure APIs. The initialization software in the Non-secure world uses the Secure API to set the AIRCR.BFHFNMINS bit and to disable the Secure world from being used.

In both scenarios, disabling the Secure world features requires that:

- All Non-secure Callable (NSC) regions are removed. This means that the Non-secure world would no longer be able to access Secure APIs.
- If a secure software framework (e.g., Trusted Firmware-M) has been initialized, that the services provided by the secure software framework are disabled.
- Background Secure services (e.g., Secure timer peripherals) are disabled.
- Secure interrupts are disabled.

The security software that disables the Secure world features also, optionally, erases part of the Secure SRAM and releases the erased SRAM space to the Non-secure world. Please note, the Secure HardFault Handler could still take place, and if it does, the Secure HardFault handler should either reset the system or power down the device. If the powering down method is used, then the processor system must reset when it exits the power downstate.

18.3.10 Fault Handler

When the TrustZone security features are used, Secure firmware should be configured so that the HardFault and the BusFault exceptions target the Secure state (i.e., the AIRCR. BFHFNMINS bit is kept at zero). Additionally, it is recommended that the fault exceptions in the Secure firmware are setup so that after a fault exception is triggered in the Secure world, the further execution of Non-secure codes that could trigger operations in the faulting Secure context (e.g., Non-secure to Secure function calls, exception returns, etc.) is prevented. This is needed because, potentially, during a security attack, although a fault exception in the Secure world (e.g., MemManage or HardFault) would be triggered, the Secure stack for the faulting Secure context could be corrupted and, thus, the Secure context needs to be stopped. As a result, there is also a need to prevent the execution of Non-secure codes that could trigger further operations in the faulting Secure context.

If the stack that is corrupted is a Secure process stack (i.e., PSP_S was used) and the Secure context (i.e., a software thread) associated with that stack can be terminated, it is safe to resume normal execution. In this situation, the Secure software can, optionally, include a call back API feature so that the Non-secure software is notified when a fault has occurred. If the stack that is corrupted is a Secure main stack or if the faulting Secure context cannot be terminated, the system should be restarted (Note: If the Secure main stack is corrupted there is no safe way to resume operation).

To reduce the security risk further, Secure software can prevent Non-secure software from launching an attack on the Secure software once a fault event has occurred in the Secure world. This is achieved by setting the priority levels of the fault exceptions in the Secure world to a higher exception priority level than the Non-secure exceptions. There are several ways to achieve this:

(a) Set AIRCR.PRIS to 1 and ensure that the Secure fault exceptions (the BusFault, UsageFault, SecureFault, and MemManage fault) for the Secure world are in the exception priority range 0 to 0x7F.
(b) Alternatively, do not enable BusFault, UsageFault, SecureFault, and MemManage faults in the Secure world so that fault events targeting the Secure state escalate to the Secure HardFault.

Because the HardFault and BusFault exceptions target the Secure state, it can be hard for the Non-secure software developers to work out the cause of software failures during debugging. This is because the fault status information for those fault exceptions is not accessible from the Non-secure world. To enable some of the fault events to be easily debugged, Non-secure software developers using the Cortex-M33 processor should enable the UsageFault and the MemManage fault (see Sections 9.3.5 and 13.3) and set the priority level of those fault exceptions to a higher level than the other interrupts. By so doing, this will allow those fault events to be debugged in the Non-secure environment.

To help Non-secure software developers debug software, Secure software can, optionally, utilize a communication interface to report the occurrence of fault events to software developers. Instead of calling a Non-secure function to process the error messages, it is more secure for the fault handler in the Secure firmware to handle the message output directly (e.g., by using the ITM feature). If a communication interface is not available, a Non-secure RAM buffer can be declared in the project, and the Secure firmware can then output the error messages in the buffer so that Non-secure software developers can extract the messages.

18.4 Creating a Secure project in Keil MDK

18.4.1 Creating a Secure project

To develop a Secure project, you normally need to create a Non-secure project at the same time so that you can test the interface between the Secure and the Non-secure worlds. To assist in this, using a toolchain (e.g., Keil MDK) that supports a multiproject workspace would be helpful. The usual steps when creating a secure project are:

(1) Create a Secure project—using project settings (e.g., compiler command-line options that enable Secure code compilation, see Section 18.3.1) for the Secure software environment
(2) Create a Non-secure project—using project settings for the Non-secure software environment
(3) Create a multiproject workspace and add both Secure and Non-secure projects to it.

When creating this example Secure project, the same FPGA hardware platform (MPS2+ with a Cortex-M33 processor) that was used in the example project detailed in Chapter 17 will be used. By following the steps detailed in Section 17.2.3 (Figs. 17.4–17.13, but calling the project "example_s" rather than "example_1": to indicate that this a Secure project) a Secure project is created. Unlike the example in Chapter 17, the "Secure Mode" in the target option tab should be selected (Fig. 18.17).

When creating a Secure project "Secure mode" must be selected. To simplify this example, it is assumed that the Secure world does not use the FPU.

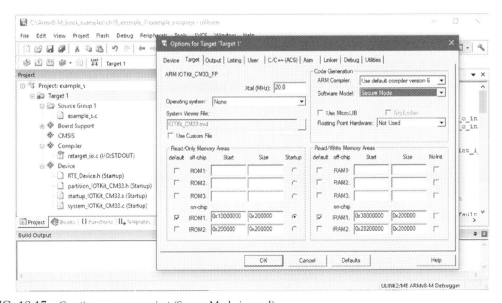

FIG. 18.17   Creating a secure project (Secure Mode is used).

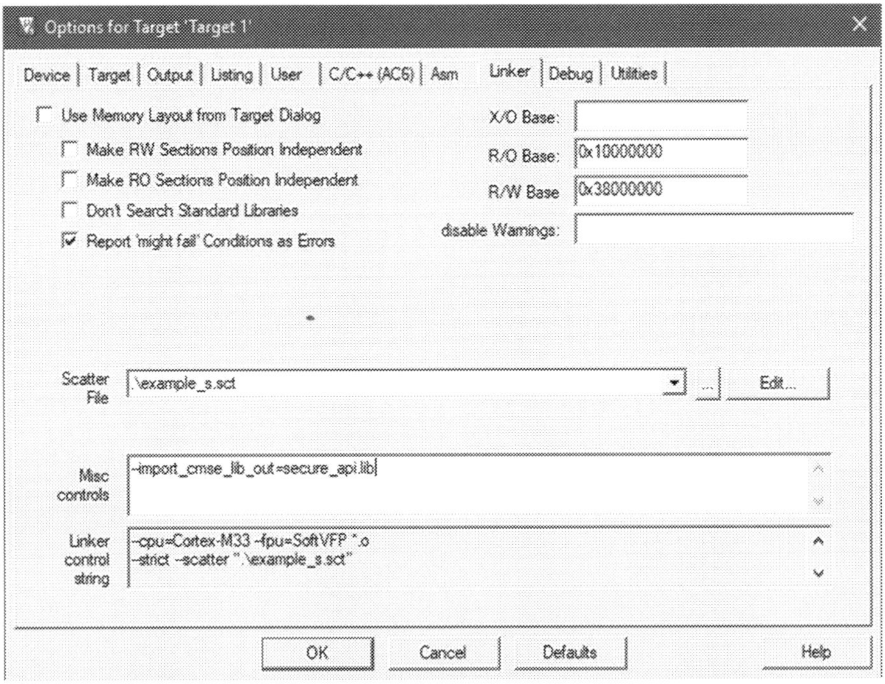

FIG. 18.18   Linker settings for the Secure project example.

The next important step is configuring the linker settings. By default, the project takes the memory map settings from the target dialog (see "Use Memory Layout from Target Dialog" option in Fig. 17.27). For a Secure project, the layout of the NSC region needs to be customized, and as a result, the linker setting (Fig. 18.18) is different from that used by the default setting.

The linker scatter file (example_s.sct) contains the following setup:

```
LR_IROM1 0x10000000 0x00200000 { ; load region (size of region=0x00200000)
  ER_IROM1 0x10000000 0x00200000 { ; load address = execution address
   *.o (RESET, +First)
   *(InRoot$$Sections)
   .ANY (+RO)
   .ANY (+XO)
  }
  EXEC_NSCR 0x101F0000 0x10000 {
   *(Veneer$$CMSE)     ; check with partition.h
  }
  RW_IRAM1 0x38000000 0x00200000 { ; RW data
   .ANY (+RW +ZI)
  }
}
```

The difference between the default scatter file generated by the IDE and the customized version is that the latter version has a different setup for the memory region used by the Secure entry points. This setup is indicated by the section containing "Veneer$$CMSE" in the scatter file. This address range needs to match the Non-secure Callable (NSC) region setup defined in the CMSIS-CORE file "partition_<device>.h". If it does not, the Secure calls either might not work or the mismatch could result in security vulnerabilities.

The final step for setting up the Secure project is to add the following command to instruct the linker to generate the export library. This is inserted in the "Misc controls" of the linker setting dialog.

Command to instruct linker to generate an export library:

```
--import_cmse_lib_out=secure_api.lib
```

So that a range of features that I detailed earlier in this chapter can be demonstrated, the example program code contains the following operations (Fig. 18.19):

- An initial switch into the Non-secure world (Section 18.3.3)
- Non-secure software calling a Secure API (Section 18.3.4)
- The passing of a callback function pointer from the Non-secure world to the Secure world (Section 18.3.5)
- Secure software calling a callback function in the Non-secure world (Section 18.3.5)

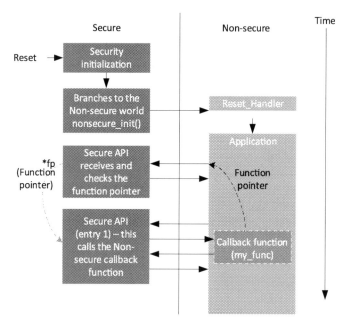

FIG. 18.19   The program flow in the example project.

The following is the actual Secure example code illustrated by Fig. 18.19:

```c
#include <arm_cmse.h>
#include "IOTKit_CM33_FP.h"
#include "stdio.h"

typedef int __attribute__((cmse_nonsecure_call)) tdef_nsfunc_o_int_i_void(void);
typedef int __attribute__((cmse_nonsecure_call)) tdef_nsfunc_o_int_i_int(int x);

int __attribute__((cmse_nonsecure_entry)) entry1(int x);
int __attribute__((cmse_nonsecure_entry)) pass_nsfunc_ptr_o_int_i_int
(tdef_nsfunc_o_int_i_int *callback);

int nonsecure_init(void);
void default_callback(void);
int call_callback(int data_in);

// Declare function pointer *fp
// *fp can point to either a secure function or a non-secure function
// Initializes to a default callback
tdef_nsfunc_o_int_i_int *fp = (tdef_nsfunc_o_int_i_int *) default_callback;

int main(void)
{
  printf("Secure Hello world\n");
  nonsecure_init();
  while(1);
}

int nonsecure_init(void) {
  // Example modified from
  // https://www.community.arm.com/iot/embedded/b/blog/posts/a-few-intricacies-of-
writing-armv8-m-secure-code

  // If needed, setup the Non-secure VTOR.
  // In the Cortex-M33 based FPGA platform used for creating this example
  // (i.e. a system called IoT Kit, which runs on the MPS2 FPGA board), the
  // Non-secure code image starting address is 0x00200000
  SCB_NS->VTOR=0x00200000UL; // Optional for most hardware platforms.
  // But it is needed in the FPGA platform used here.

  // The following line creates a pointer to the Non-secure vector table
  uint32_t *vt_ns = (uint32_t *) SCB_NS->VTOR;
  // Setup Non-secure Main Stack Pointer (MSP_NS)
  __TZ_set_MSP_NS(vt_ns[0]);
  // Setup the function pointer to NS reset vector
  tdef_nsfunc_o_int_i_void *ns_reset = (tdef_nsfunc_o_int_i_void*)(vt_ns[1]);
  // Branch into the Non-secure reset handler
  ns_reset(); // Branch to the Non-secure world
```

```
  // If Reset Handler executes a return, the program execution will reach here
  printf("ERROR: should not be here\n");
  while(1);
}

// This is a Secure API
int __attribute__((cmse_nonsecure_entry)) entry1(int x)
{
  int result;
  result = call_callback(x);
  return (result);
}

// This is a Secure API with a function pointer as the input parameter
int __attribute__((cmse_nonsecure_entry)) pass_nsfunc_ptr_o_int_i_int
(tdef_nsfunc_o_int_i_int *callback) {
  // Result for function pointer
  cmse_address_info_t tt_payload;
  tt_payload = cmse_TTA_fptr(callback);
  if (tt_payload.flags.nonsecure_read_ok) {
    fp = cmse_nsfptr_create(callback); // non-secure function pointer
    return (0);
  } else {
    printf ("[pass_nsfunc_ptr_o_int_i_int] Error: input pointer is not NS\n");
    return (1); // Function pointer is not accessible from the Non-secure side
  }
}
// Call back a Non-secure function
int call_callback(int data_in) {
  if (cmse_is_nsfptr(fp)){
    return fp(data_in);  // Non-secure function call
  } else {
    ((void (*)(void)) fp)(); // Call default callback as normal function call
    return (0);
  }
}
// Default callback function
void default_callback(void) {
  __BKPT(0);
  while(1);
}
```

In addition to creating the example Secure program code, the address partitioning setup (e.g., the SAU, the MPC, and the PPC) would, based on the project's requirements, need to be updated. In this example, the SAU setup detailed in Fig. 18.20 is used, with the setup for the MPC and the PPC located inside the file "system_<device>.c".

After the setup is finished, the Secure project can then be compiled. This generates the export library "`secure_api.lib`", which is needed for the Non-secure project. At this stage, the Secure project can be closed and a new project can be opened for the Non-secure world.

18.4.2 Creating a Non-secure project

The steps for creating a Non-secure project are almost the same as that for the Secure project, except that:

(1) The project is setup in Non-secure mode
(2) The memory map is setup for Non-secure memory
(3) The memory map settings in the project's target dialog can be used to create the linker's settings
(4) The export library generated from the Secure project to the Non-secure project needs to be added

The Non-secure project is called example_ns. It is important that the Non-secure memories are selected and the "Startup" is set to the Non-secure memory program (Fig. 18.21).

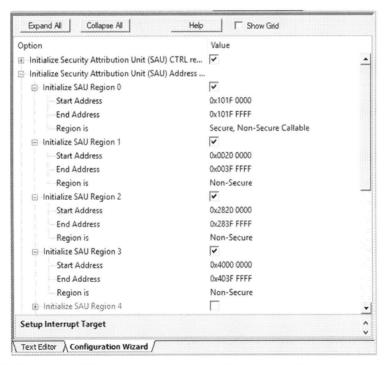

FIG. 18.20 SAU setup (e.g., NSC region) needs to match the linker script setting.

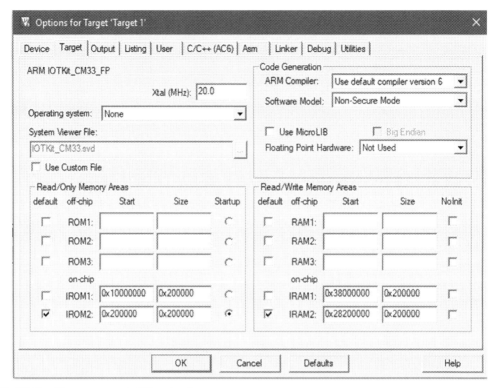

FIG. 18.21   Non-secure project Target options.

The program code for the Non-secure project is as follows:

```
#include "IOTKit_CM33_FP.h"
#include "stdio.h"

extern int entry1(int x);
extern int pass_nsfunc_ptr_o_int_i_int(void *callback);

int my_func(int data_in); // Call back function

int main(void)
{
  int status;
  printf("Non-secure Hello world\n");
  // Pass a Non-secure function pointer to the Secure world
  status = pass_nsfunc_ptr_o_int_i_int(& my_func);
  if (status==0) {
    // Call a Secure function
    printf ("Result = %d\n", entry1(10));
  } else {
    printf ("ERROR: pass_nsfunc_ptr_o_int_i_int() = %d\n", status);
  }
```

```
// Normally, Non-secure software only passes a Non-secure function
// pointer to the Secure world. In this example, because I want to
// illustrate the checking of the function pointer by a Secure API, an
// attempt is made to pass a function pointer with a Secure address.
status = pass_nsfunc_ptr_o_int_i_int((void* )0x100000F1UL);
if (status==0) {
  // Call secure function
  printf ("Result = %d\n", entry1(10));
} else {
  printf ("Expected: pass_nsfunc_ptr_o_int_i_int() = %d\n", status);
}
printf("Test done\n");
while(1);
}
int my_func(int data_in)
{
  printf("[my_func]\n");
  return (data_in * data_in);
}
```

In addition to creating the Non-secure program code, the export library "`secure_api.lib`" would need to be added to the project (Fig. 18.22).

Once this stage is reached the Non-secure project is ready for compilation. The Non-secure project should be closed and a multiproject workspace created. In the example project, a multiproject workspace called "`example`" is created and the "`example_s`" (Secure) and "`example_ns`" (Non-secure) projects have been added to it.

18.4.3 Creating a multiproject workspace

To create a multiproject workspace, the pull-down menu "Project → New multi-project workspace" is used. In the "Create New Multi-Project Workspace" dialog, the "New (Insert)" icon at the top right-hand corner should be clicked on (Fig. 18.23).

After clicking on that icon, the "…" button on the right-hand side of the row should be clicked to add "example_s" and again to add "example_ns" to the project (Fig. 18.24).

After the projects are added, both projects are then listed in the Workspace in the project window (Fig. 18.25).

When working with a multiproject workspace, one of the projects needs to be selected as the "Active Project". This allows us to define which project will be selected for compilation, debug, etc. The Active project selection is achieved by right-clicking on the project name in the project window and then selecting "Set as Active Project" (Fig. 18.26).

The final step to take before running the example programs on the hardware is to setup the debug options. A range of debug settings have already been highlighted in Chapter 17 (Figs. 17.17, 17.18, and 17.29). Additionally, there might also be a need to setup the debug option so, when a debug session starts, it loads both images to the device at the same time. This is optional when using devices with flash memories because the program images can be

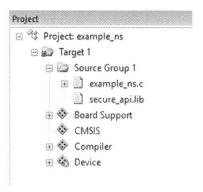

FIG. 18.22 Export library (secure_api.lib) added to the Non-secure project.

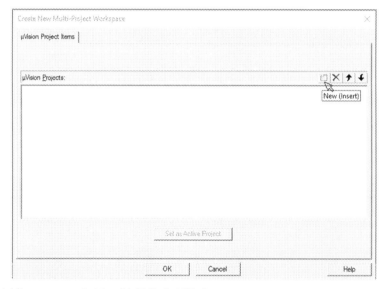

FIG. 18.23 Adding a new project to a Multi-Project Workspace.

individually downloaded after each program image is compiled, and the software can then be tested after both images are programmed to the flash memory. However, without using a debug setup to ensure that both the Secure and the Non-secure program images are programmed to the flash memory, the software testing and debugging process could be prone to error because it is easy to forget to program one of the program images.

By using a debug script (Fig. 18.27), we can make sure that both compiled images are loaded to the device at the start of a debug session. If the active project is Non-secure, the debug script can also be used to configure the debug session so that it starts at the beginning of the Secure startup.

Please note, in Fig. 18.27 the "Run to main()" option has been disabled. This is because if it was not, the program would run until it reached the beginning of the Non-secure "main()"

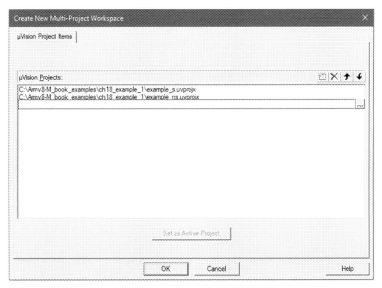

FIG. 18.24 "example_s" and "example_ns" projects added to a Multi-Project Workspace.

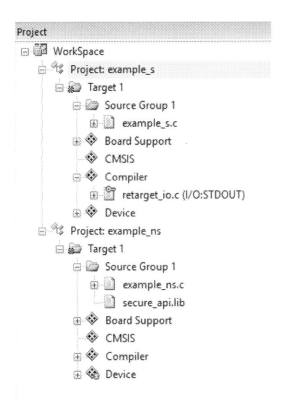

FIG. 18.25 Multi-Project Workspace created with Secure and Non-secure projects.

FIG. 18.26   Selecting a project as "Active".

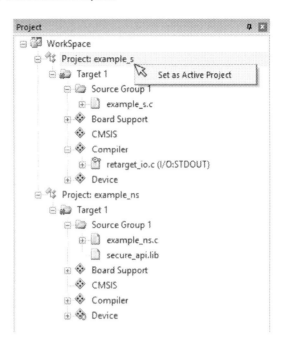

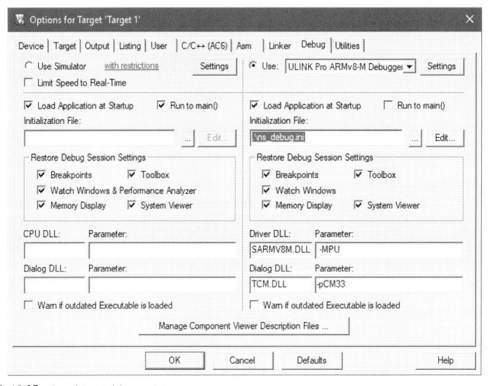

FIG. 18.27   Specifying a debug script.

function, which is not we want to occur when we want to debug the Secure initialization code. An example of a Non-secure debug script "ns_debug.ini" is shown in the following section. In addition to loading the program images, this script sets up the debug control settings that are specific to the hardware platform used and also sets up the SP and PC values to the starting values for the Secure software.

Non-secure debug script "ns_debug.ini"

```
FUNC void Setup (void) {
  _WDWORD(0x50021104, 0x00000010);     // Sets bit 4 of the RESET_MASK register
  // Setup SP and PC to use values for Secure software
  SP = _RDWORD(0x10000000);            // Sets up the Stack Pointer
  PC = _RDWORD(0x10000004);            // Sets up the Program Counter
}

LOAD "Objects\\example_s.axf" incremental
LOAD "Objects\\example_ns.axf" incremental

Setup();

RESET                                  /* Resets the target processor */
```

For a Secure project, a similar debug script is as follows:

Secure debug script "s_debug.ini"

```
FUNC void Setup (void) {
  _WDWORD(0x50021104, 0x00000010);     // Sets bit 4 of the RESET_MASK register
}

LOAD "Objects\\example_s.axf" incremental
LOAD "Objects\\example_ns.axf" incremental

Setup();

RESET                                  /* Resets the target processor */
```

The Secure debug script is simpler than the Non-secure one because, by default, the debug session already sets up the settings for the debugging of a Secure software environment.

18.5 CMSE support in other toolchains

18.5.1 GNU C compiler (GCC)

When using an Arm GCC compiler with an Armv8-M processor, the "-mcmse" command-line option is needed to compile Secure state software.

To specify the location of the Non-secure Callable (NSC) region in the Secure software using the GCC, you can either use the:

- Command-line option: "--section-start=.gnu.sgstubs=<address>" or the
- Linker script: For this, an output section description for ".gnu.sgstubs" with a specified runtime address needs to be created

Two command-line options for handling export libraries would also need to be added. These are:

- "--out-implib=<import library>", and
- "--cmse-implib"

and are used to generate the import library. An example of creating an export library when compiling the Secure project, and importing the export library when compiling the Non-secure project, is shown in Fig. 18.28.

18.5.2 IAR

The IAR™ Embedded Workbench® for Arm (EWARM) has supported Armv8-M architecture since the release of version 7.70. When using an IAR compiler with an Armv8-M processor, the "--cmse" command-line option is needed to enable the compilation of Secure state software. To specify that the compilation is for an Armv8-M processor, you can either:

- Use a processor option: e.g., "--cpu=Cortex-M23" or "--cpu=Cortex-M33", or
- Use an architecture option: e.g., "--cpu=8-M.baseline" or "--cpu=8-M.mainline"

For the linker, a command-line option "--import_cmse_lib_out FILE/DIRECTORY" should be used for specifying the export library and "--import_cmse_lib_in FILE" for specifying the import library.

```
# Secure build command
arm-none-eabi-gcc -march=armv8-m.base -mthumb -mcmse -static --specs=nosys.specs \
-Wl,--section-start,.gnu.sgstubs=0x190000,--out-implib=sg_veneers.lib,--cmse-implib -Wl,\
-Tsecure.ld -I$MDK/CMSIS/Include  main_s.c Board_LED.c -I. \
$DEVICE_SRC $DEVICE_INC $OPTS \
-o secure_blinky_baseline.out

# Non-secure build command
arm-none-eabi-gcc -march=armv8-m.base -mthumb \
-static --specs=nosys.specs -Wl,-Tnonsecure.ld -I$MDK/CMSIS/Include \
main_ns.c Board_LED.c -I. sg_veneers.lib -ffunction-sections \
$DEVICE_SRC $DEVICE_INC $OPTS \
-o nonsecure_blinky_baseline.out
```

FIG. 18.28   GCC compilation command example.

18.6 Secure software design considerations

18.6.1 Initial branching to the Non-secure world

In the example shown in Section 18.3.3, the Non-secure reset handler was declared as a Non-secure function pointer and was then called, using a BLXNS instruction, to start the Non-secure world. It is possible that the reset handler might only contain a return, which if it did would mean that the code execution flow would return to the Secure world. As a result, the Secure code that handles the switching has to be able to deal with this situation, e.g., by having an error reporting code placed after the branch.

Instead of using BLXNS to branch to the Non-secure world, you can use inline assembly code to use a BXNS instruction instead. However, when using this method, the assembly code needs to add additional steps to manually clear the contents of the register bank before the branch (This is needed because the register bank can contain Secure information). Furthermore, two additional data words need to be pushed on to the Secure stack before executing the BXNS instruction (see stack sealing descriptions in Section 18.6.6.4). If this method is used, the Non-secure code cannot return to the Secure code because (a) there is no return address or FNC_RETURN in the Link Register (LR), and (b) the Secure stack does not have a stacked return address.

Before branching into the Non-secure software, the stack pointer limits for the Secure stack pointers need to be setup.

18.6.2 Non-secure callable (NSC)

18.6.2.1 NSC region definition matching

The location and size of the NSC region, as defined by the SAU/IDAU, should only cover the CMSE veneer ("Veneer$$CMSE") in the linker script. If the NSC region definition in the SAU/IDAU is too large, it could cover the other program's binary data, which might contain binary data matching an SG instruction, resulting in an inadvertent entry point. If, on the other hand, the NSC region definition in the SAU/IDAU is too small, some of the valid entry points will not be covered by the NSC region. Ideally, the definition of the NSC, as defined by the SAU/IDAU, should match the definition in the linker script.

Note: When defining the NSC region, because there is often a need to update Secure firmware throughout the life cycle of a product, it can be beneficial to reserve additional space in the NSC region, i.e., more space than is needed by the existing entry points. When the NSC memory space is more than the space needed by the entry points, the CMSE compatible toolchain makes sure that the unused address space in the NSC is filled with predefined data values (e.g., 0 is used in the Arm toolchain) that are not matched to an SG instruction, and which do not result in an unexpected entry point.

18.6.2.2 NSC region in SRAM

Since the contents of SRAM is unknown when it powers up, the NSC attribute to a region in the SRAM should not be setup until that region has been initialized. This security measure prevents inadvertent entry points caused by unknown SRAM data.

18.6.3 Memory partitioning

18.6.3.1 MPC and PPC behavior

Depending on the implementation of the Memory Protection Controller (MPC) and the Peripheral Protection Controller (PPC), it is likely that a Secure transaction targeting a Non-secure memory portion or peripheral will be blocked. For example, if the MPC/PPC defines a memory portion or a peripheral as Non-secure, but the SAU has not been enabled, then the memory portion or the peripheral might not be accessible. This is because when the SAU is disabled (i.e., SAU_CTRL equals 0), the attribute of the memory address is treated as Secure (i.e., a Secure transaction is generated for the access). However, because the MPC or the PPC expects transfers targeting a Non-secure memory portion/peripheral to be Non-secure, the transfer could be blocked.

This MPC and PPC behavior is to ensure that correct configurations are being used. If the Secure software mistakenly configures the MPC/PPC so that a memory portion/peripheral, which is supposed to be Secure, is handled as Non-secure, other Non-secure bus masters might be able to access that memory portion/peripheral. If the Secure software then treats the memory portion/peripheral as Secure, and the processor is allowed to access that memory portion/peripheral via a Secure address alias (using Secure transactions), Secure data could then be leaked and result in a breach of security.

18.6.3.2 Dynamic switching of the security attribute of an SRAM page

During runtime, if there is a need to update the memory partitioning to switch a memory page which has been used by Secure software from Secure to Non-secure, the Secure software must carry out the following steps:

1. Clears Secure information from the SRAM page.
2. If a system level cache is implemented, flush the cached data for that page so that the main memory system is also cleared.
3. Execute a data memory barrier to make sure that the data memory has been updated (This is normally part of the cache maintenance routine).
4. Write to the SAU or the device-specific registers (e.g., MPC) to update the security attribute of the memory page.

If, on the other hand, there is a need to switch a Non-secure memory page in the SRAM to Secure, the following steps would be needed to reduce the risk of a code injection attack.

1. If a system level cache is present, the Non-secure interrupts (e.g., using a combination of BASEPRI_S and AIRCR.PRIS) would need to be disabled to prevent a Non-secure ISR from updating the memory page during switching.
2. The Secure MPU would need to be setup so that the memory region is marked as XN (eXecute Never).
3. If a system level cache is present, the cached data for that page would need to be flushed (if the data in that memory page is to be used) or invalidated (if the data in that memory page is to be discarded).
4. A data memory barrier would need to be executed to ensure that the data memory is updated (This is normally part of the cache maintenance routine).

5. A write to the SAU or device-specific registers (e.g., MPC) would be needed to update the security attribute of the memory page.
6. If the Non-secure interrupts have been disabled for the switching, they should now be re-enabled.
7. If the data in the SRAM page can be discarded, the data should be erased.
8. If the data in the SRAM page is to be used, the data might need to be validated.

18.6.3.3 Dynamic switching of a peripheral's security attribute

When switching a peripheral from one security domain to another, if that peripheral generates interrupts, the NVIC's Interrupt Target Non-secure State Register (NVIC_ITNS[n]) should be updated.

When switching a peripheral from the Secure to the Non-secure world, the following steps should be taken:

1. Ensuring that no Secure data remains in the peripheral when the peripheral is disabled.
2. Updating the memory map configuration (e.g., the control registers in the PPC) to switch the peripheral to the Non-secure state.
3. Updating the peripheral's interrupts' target state.

It is also possible to switch a peripheral that has been used by the Non-secure world to Secure. When switching a peripheral from Non-secure to Secure, the following steps should be taken:

1. Non-secure interrupt generation (e.g., using a combination of BASEPRI_S and AIRCR. PRIS) should be temporarily disabled. This prevents a Non-secure interrupt handler from re-enabling the peripheral in the middle of the switching process.
2. The peripheral should be disabled.
3. The memory map configuration (e.g., the control register(s) in the PPC) should be updated to switch the peripheral to the Secure state.
4. The NVIC_ITNS register should be updated to set the target state of the peripheral interrupt to Secure.
5. Non-secure interrupts should be re-enabled.

Temporarily disabling Non-secure interrupts prevents a Non-secure exception handler re-enabling the peripheral between the 2nd and 3rd steps, which, if it did, would mean that the peripheral had been enabled under Non-secure software control when it was transitioning to the Secure state.

18.6.4 Input data and pointer validations

18.6.4.1 Validation of input data in the Non-secure memory

When input data of a Secure function is passed by a pointer, the data needs to be copied into the Secure memory before its value is validated. If the data is not copied into the Secure memory, the data can be modified by a Non-secure handler which can lead to a security breach. The following Secure API code illustrates this issue:

Bad code example

```
int __attribute__((cmse_nonsecure_entry)) entry2a(int *idx)
{
  const char textstr[] = "Hello world\n";
  if (cmse_check_pointed_object(idx, CMSE_NONSECURE|CMSE_MPU_READ) != NULL) {
    if ((*idx>=0) && (*idx < 12)) {
      return ((int) textstr[*idx]); // Using data in the Non-secure memory
                                    // as an index
    } else {
      return(0);
    }
  } else
    return (-1);
}
```

Although a pointer-check and a value range check have been carried out in the above code, the index value (idx) being used is in the Non-secure memory (Fig. 18.29). If a Non-secure interrupt occurs during the execution of this function, the value of the index (idx) could be changed and, in theory, a hacker could then setup the index value (idx) to read the data in the Secure memory.

To fix this problem, the data needs to be copied into the Secure memory before its value is validated. This process is shown in the following code:

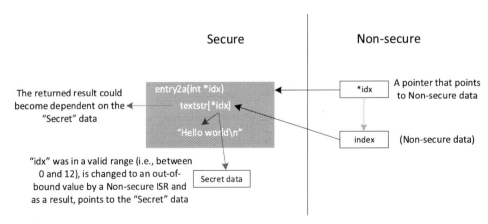

FIG. 18.29 Using Non-secure data as an array index can lead to a security breach.

Good code example

```
int __attribute__((cmse_nonsecure_entry)) entry2(int *idx)
{
  const char textstr[] = "Hello world\n";
  int idx_copy;
  if (cmse_check_pointed_object(idx, CMSE_NONSECURE|CMSE_MPU_READ) != NULL) {
    idx_copy = *idx;
    if ((idx_copy >=0)&&(idx_copy < 12)) { // Validates a Secure copy of the index
      return ((int) textstr[idx_copy]); // Uses the Secure copy of the index
    } else {
      return(0);
    }
  } else
    return (-1);
}
```

Similar challenges apply to any data that is stored in the Non-secure memories, including pointers. For example, when a double pointer (i.e., a pointer of pointer) is used as an input parameter for a Secure API, there is a great risk that the pointer stored in the Non-secure SRAM could, at any time, be changed by a Non-secure exception handler. This is illustrated by the following code:

Bad code example

```
int __attribute__((cmse_nonsecure_entry)) entry3a(int **idx)
{
  const char textstr[] = "Hello world\n";
  int *idx_ptr;
  int idx_copy;
  // Check the pointer of pointer is in the Non-secure world
  if (cmse_check_pointed_object(*idx, CMSE_NONSECURE|CMSE_MPU_READ) != NULL) {
    // Pointer of pointer is Non-secure
    idx_ptr = *idx;
    // Validate that the location of idx is Non-secure
    if (cmse_check_pointed_object(idx_ptr, CMSE_NONSECURE|CMSE_MPU_READ) != NULL)
{
    // ISSUE: the pointer of idx in the Non-secure world could be
    // changed by a Non-secure ISR
      idx_copy = **idx; // Copy value
      if ((idx_copy>=0) && (idx_copy < 12)) { // Value validation
        return ((int) textstr[idx_copy]); // Uses the Secure copy of the index
```

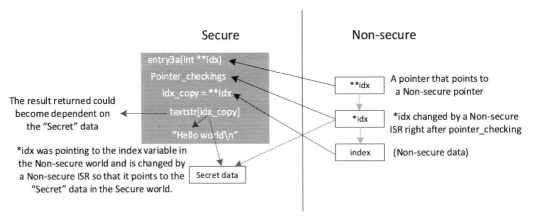

FIG. 18.30 Directly using a pointer in the Non-secure memory can lead to a security breach.

```
    } else {
      return(0);
    }
  } else
    return (-1);
} else {
  return (-1);
}
}
```

In the earlier example code, although we have validated that:

- The pointer of pointer is in the Non-secure address, and
- The pointer of idx (index) is in the Non-secure address, and
- The value of idx (index)

there would still be a security issue. This is because if a Non-secure interrupt takes place just after the pointer-check, the pointer of the index in the Non-secure world could be changed and end up pointing to a Secure address (Fig. 18.30).

To overcome this problem, we need to make sure that the Secure API makes a secure copy of the index pointer and then uses the secure copy for copying the index variable to the Secure memory. The code for this is:

Good code example

```
int __attribute__((cmse_nonsecure_entry)) entry3b(int **idx)
{
  const char textstr[] = "Hello world\n";
  int *idx_ptr;
  int idx_copy;
```

```
  // Check that the pointer of pointer is in the Non-secure world
  if (cmse_check_pointed_object(*idx, CMSE_NONSECURE|CMSE_MPU_READ) != NULL) {
    // Pointer of pointer is Non-secure
    idx_ptr = *idx;
    // Validate that the location of idx is Non-secure
    if (cmse_check_pointed_object(idx_ptr, CMSE_NONSECURE|CMSE_MPU_READ) != NULL) {
      idx_copy = *idx_ptr; // Copy value using a validated pointer
      if ((idx_copy>=0) &&(idx_copy < 12)) { // Value validation
        return ((int) textstr[idx_copy]); // Use the Secure copy of the index
      } else {
        return(0);
      }
    } else
      return (-1);
  } else {
    return (-1);
  }
}
```

Please be aware that double pointers can exist in the form of pointers within data structures in the Non-secure world.

18.6.4.2 *Always check a pointer before using it*

It is important to validate a pointer before accessing the data. Even if the Secure API only reads the data and the pointer check is carried out afterward, a security issue can still arise if the pointer is not validated before it is used. This is illustrated by the following code:

Bad code example

```
int __attribute__((cmse_nonsecure_entry)) entry4a(char * src, char * dest)
{
#define MAX_LENGTH_ALLOWED 128
  int string_length;
  // Pointer is used before being validated
  string_length = strnlen(src, MAX_LENGTH_ALLOWED);
  if ((string_length == MAX_LENGTH_ALLOWED) && (src[string_length] != '\0')) {
    // string is too long
    return (-1); // return error
  } else { // Pointer-check for the source
    if (cmse_check_address_range ((void *)src, (size_t) string_length,
(CMSE_NONSECURE | CMSE_MPU_READ)) == NULL) {
      return (-1); // return error
    }
```

```
    // Pointer-check for the destination
    if (cmse_check_address_range ((void *)dest, (size_t) string_length,
(CMSE_NONSECURE | CMSE_MPU_READWRITE)) == NULL) {
       return (-1); // return error
    }
    memcpy (dest, src, (size_t) string_length); // Memory copy operation
    return (0);
  }
}
```

Although pointer checks are carried out before those of the memory copy (i.e., memcpy), there could still be a security issue because the data pointed to by the Secure API is read by the strnlen function before the pointer is validated. This is a problem when the "src" pointer is pointing to a Secure peripheral and where the reading of certain register(s) can affect the operations of the Secure world. For example, if a FIFO data register is in the peripheral, the data in the FIFO could, as a result, be lost.

To overcome this problem, the responsibility for executing the string length function needs to be moved from the Secure world back to the Non-secure world. This would result in the string length (i.e., the "len" parameter in the code in the following section) becoming an additional parameter of the Secure API function. The code for this is:

Good code example

```
int __attribute__((cmse_nonsecure_entry)) entry4b(char * src, char * dest,
  int32_t len) // Good example – string length is a parameter
{
#define MAX_LENGTH_ALLOWED 128
  if ((len < 0) || (len > MAX_LENGTH_ALLOWED)) return (-1);

  // Pointer-check for the source
  if (cmse_check_address_range ((void *)src, (size_t) len, (CMSE_NONSECURE |
CMSE_MPU_READ)) == NULL) {
     return (-1); // return error
  }
  // Pointer-check for the destination
  if (cmse_check_address_range ((void *)dest, (size_t) len, (CMSE_NONSECURE |
CMSE_MPU_READWRITE)) == NULL) {
     return (-1); // return error
  }
  memcpy (dest, src, (size_t) len);
  return (0);
}
```

18.6.4.3 *The danger of "printf" in a Secure API*

While printf can be a handy function for a Secure software developer to use when debugging their applications, we need to be very careful about using printf to display string messages from the Non-secure world. Firstly, the string message stored in the Non-secure world could be modified by a Non-secure exception handler when the printf function is executing, which might result in the string not terminating inside the Non-secure memory. When this happens, the Secure memory contents that are adjacent to the Non-secure memory could be printed out and result in a leak of Secure information.

Secondly, if the displayed text string contains a "%s" format specifier, the printf function inside the Secure API assumes that a specific memory location in the Secure stack contains the address of the string to be displayed. However, this might not be the case, i.e., If the Non-secure software uses a printf function provided by the Secure world to print a message with the "%s" format specifier, there might not be a valid string pointer in the parameter of the function call. The printf code will then mistakenly use data in the Secure stack as the string pointer, which could be interpreted as a Secure address location—a situation that could end up leaking Secure information.

Another risk associated with the printf function is the use of the special format specifier "%n", which writes the number of character outputs to a data pointer specified in the input parameter. This feature is useful when using "printf" to send messages to peripherals, such as an LCD module, as it allows the software to control the cursor position based on the number of printed characters. An example of how the %n is used in printf is as follows:

Example use of %n in printf

```
int lcd_cursor_x_pos; // LCD cursor x position
int lcd_cursor_y_pos; // LCD cursor y position
...
printf ("Speed: %d %n", currend_speed, &lcd_cursor_x_pos);
// LCD cursor information is updated by printf
if (lcd_cursor_x_pos > 30){ // Move cursor to the next line
  lcd_cursor_x_pos= 0;
  lcd_cursor_y_pos++; // next line
  ...
```

Unfortunately, if a Secure API allows Non-secure software to use a printf function in the Secure world, this feature can result in security issues: If the pointer points to a Secure memory location, a Non-secure function could craft a special string message causing a Secure API to write a value into a Secure memory location. Needless to say, this would result in a serious breach of security.

For the aforementioned reasons, we should avoid providing a "printf" capability in the API which takes text strings from the Non-secure world. If an API is needed for the display of messages, functions like "puts" and "putchar"/"putc" should be directly used, with custom defined Secure APIs added to handle the printing of integers and other values.

When using puts, the string should be copied from a Non-secure to a Secure memory before calling the puts because the puts function itself does not provide a maximum character count. Since the text string in the Non-secure world can be changed by a Non-secure exception handler, the text string needs to be copied to the Secure world before the "puts" are called. Example code for this is:

---

puts example

```
int __attribute__((cmse_nonsecure_entry)) entry5(char * src, int32_t len)
{
  int string_length;
  char ch_buffer[128];
#define MAX_LENGTH_ALLOWED 128
  if ((len < 0) || (len > MAX_LENGTH_ALLOWED)) return (-1);

  if (cmse_check_address_range ((void *)src, (size_t) len, (CMSE_NONSECURE |
CMSE_MPU_READ)) == NULL) {
    return (-1); // return error
    }
  // copy to buffer - please note the text could be changed by the Non-Secure ISR
  memcpy (&ch_buffer[0], src, (size_t) len);
  string_length = strnlen(src, MAX_LENGTH_ALLOWED);
  if ((string_length == MAX_LENGTH_ALLOWED) && (src[string_length] != '\0')) {
    // The string is too long
    return (-1); // return error
  }
  puts (ch_buffer);
  return (0);
}
```

18.6.4.4 *Using the CMSE pointer check functions*

If a Secure API needs to process data on behalf of Non-secure software, the Secure API must use the CMSE defined pointer checking functions to detect the access permission of the data coming from the Non-secure caller. The reason for this was explained in Section 18.3.6.

To prevent Non-secure unprivileged software (e.g., application tasks) from attacking Non-secure privileged software (e.g., the OS kernel), the pointer check takes the MPU permission level into account. As a result, the flag CMSE_AU_NONSECURE, which only checks the security attribute from the SAU and the IDAU, is rarely used. In most cases, the flag CMSE_NONSECURE is used, together with either CMSE_MPU_READ or CMSE_MPU_R-EADWRITE: the actual flag used depends on whether the data needs to be modified by the function.

The execution of a TTA instruction automatically detects the privileged state of the Non-secure software (based on IPSR and CONTROL_NS.nPRIV) and, armed with that information, determines whether access is restricted by the Non-secure MPU settings. Because an OS service running in the Non-secure world could call a Secure API to request a service on behalf of an unprivileged software task (Fig. 18.16), the Secure API, in this scenario, should carry out pointer checking based on the access permission of the unprivileged software. In this scenario, the CMSE_MPU_UNPRIV flag, which forces the pointer check function to use the TTAT instruction, would be used by the pointer checking code. To allow the Secure software to provide a Secure API service to both the Non-secure privileged software and the Non-secure unprivileged software (via a privileged OS redirection mechanism), two variants of the same Secure API service are needed:

1. A Secure API for servicing Non-secure privileged software (e.g., the OS kernel) and Non-secure unprivileged software (the Non-secure unprivileged software directly accesses the Secure API). This variant uses the TTA instruction for pointer checking.
2. A Secure API for servicing Non-secure unprivileged software via the OS redirection mechanism. This variant uses the TTAT instruction for pointer checking (i.e., the CMSE_MPU_UNPRIV flag is used).

Similar to data pointers, function pointers passing from the Non-secure world also need to be checked to ensure that they are safe to use. A function pointer should either be:

(a) Processed by "cmse_nsfptr_create", which clears bit 0 of the address value, to indicate that it is Non-secure, or
(b) Checked by TTA/TTAT, e.g., using "cmse_TTA_fptr" to ensure that the address is Non-secure.

Method (a) is quicker because it only needs to clear the bit 0 of the address value. Although it is a simple operation, it ensures that a security violation exception is triggered if the BXNS/BLXNS instruction is used with a function pointer that is pointing to a Secure address. This is because when bit 0 of the target address is 0, the BXNS/BLXNS instruction checks that the processor is branching to, or is calling, a Non-secure address location.

The advantage of method (b) is that it allows the Secure API used for transferring the pointer to immediately return an error status.

18.6.5 Peripheral driver

18.6.5.1 Definition of peripheral registers

When a Peripheral Protection Controller (PPC) is used, the peripherals connected via the PPC have both Secure and Non-secure alias addresses. (This topic was covered in Section 7.5.) When creating the definition of a peripheral, a data structure to represent the registers in the peripheral should be defined, followed by the definition of separate Secure and Non-secure pointers. For example:

```
/*------------ Universal Asynchronous Receiver Transmitter (UART) -----------*/
typedef struct
```

```
{
  __IOM uint32_t DATA;      /* Offset: 0x000 (R/W) Data Register */
  __IOM uint32_t STATE;     /* Offset: 0x004 (R/W) Status Register */
  __IOM uint32_t CTRL;      /* Offset: 0x008 (R/W) Control Register */
  union {
  __IM uint32_t INTSTATUS;  /* Offset: 0x00C (R/ ) Interrupt Status Register */
  __OM uint32_t INTCLEAR;   /* Offset: 0x00C ( /W) Interrupt Clear Register */
    };
  __IOM uint32_t BAUDDIV;   /* Offset: 0x010 (R/W) Baudrate Divider Register */
} IOTKIT_UART_TypeDef;
  ...
  // Secure base addresses
#define IOTKIT_SECURE_UART0_BASE              (0x50200000UL)
#define IOTKIT_SECURE_UART1_BASE              (0x50201000UL)
  ...
  // Non-secure base addresses
#define IOTKIT_UART0_BASE            (0x40200000UL)
#define IOTKIT_UART1_BASE            (0x40201000UL)
  ...
  // Secure peripheral pointers
#define IOTKIT_UART0            ((IOTKIT_UART_TypeDef *) IOTKIT_UART0_BASE )
#define IOTKIT_UART1            ((IOTKIT_UART_TypeDef *) IOTKIT_UART1_BASE )
  ...
  // Non-secure peripheral pointers
#define IOTKIT_SECURE_UART0  ((IOTKIT_UART_TypeDef *) IOTKIT_SECURE_UART0_BASE )
#define IOTKIT_SECURE_UART1  ((IOTKIT_UART_TypeDef *) IOTKIT_SECURE_UART1_BASE )
  ...
```

18.6.5.2 *Peripheral driver code*

When creating a driver code, it is common to pass the peripheral pointer as an argument (i.e., a parameter) of the driver function so that the same function can be used for multiple instantiations of the peripheral (e.g., When a chip has multiple UARTs, the UART initialization function can be used on all of them because they are of the same design). By so doing, the caller of the driver function can decide whether the Secure or Non-secure version of the peripheral pointer should be used. Example code for this is:

```
// Driver function
int UART_init(IOTKIT_UART_TypeDef * UART_PTR, int baudrate ...) {
  {
  ...
  UART_PTR->CTRL |= IOTKIT_UART_CTRL_TXEN_Msk|IOTKIT_UART_CTRL_RXEN_Msk;
  ...
  }
  // caller
  ...
```

```
UART_init(IOTKIT_UART0, 9600, ...); // UART0 is set as Non-secure
...
UART_init(IOTKIT_SECURE_UART1, 9600, ...); // UART1 is set as secure
...
```

In some cases, a Secure library function might need to access a peripheral and operate on it regardless of whether it is configured as Secure or Non-secure. When this occurs, the code determines which peripheral pointer should be used by reading back the security setting of the peripheral from the Peripheral Protection Controller (PPC). It then defines the peripheral pointer based on this information. Example code for this is:

```
  // Driver function
int UART_putc(int ch ...) {
  {
  IOTKIT_UART_TypeDef * UART_PTR;
  ...
  if (check_uart0_is_Secure()) { // Automatically selects the right pointer
    UART_PTR = IOTKIT_SECURE_UART0;
  } else {
    UART_PTR = IOTKIT_UART0;
  }
  // Waits if the buffer is full
  while (UART_PTR->STATE & IOTKIT_UART_STATE_TXBF_Msk);
  UART_PTR->DATA = (uint32_t) ch;
  ...
  }
```

In addition to selecting the peripheral pointer, the peripheral driver code can, optionally, utilize the CMSE predefined macros to enable the peripheral pointer selection code to be conditionally compiled (i.e., when needed, it uses the preprocessing method to insert the code that detects the security settings). By doing so, the same piece of code is available for use by both Secure and Non-secure software developers. For example, the previous code detailed in the earlier section that detected the security settings can be changed as follows:

```
  // Driver function
int UART_putc(int ch ...) {
  {
  IOTKIT_UART_TypeDef * UART_PTR;
  ...
#if defined (__ARM_FEATURE_CMSE) && (__ARM_FEATURE_CMSE == 3U)
  // Secure software might need to decide whether the peripheral is
  // accessible from the Secure or the Non-secure aliases
  if (check_uart0_is_Secure()) { // Automatically selects the right pointer
    UART_PTR = IOTKIT_SECURE_UART0;
  } else {
    UART_PTR = IOTKIT_UART0;
  }
```

```
#else
   // Non-secure software only uses the Non-secure peripheral pointer
   UART_PTR = IOTKIT_UART0;
#endif
   // Waits if the buffer is full
   while (UART_PTR->STATE & IOTKIT_UART_STATE_TXBF_Msk);
   UART_PTR->DATA = (uint32_t) ch;
   ...
   }
```

18.6.5.3 *Peripheral interrupts*

Normally, a system should not be configured to allow Non-secure software to generate Secure exceptions. This is to avoid security attacks such as a denial of service or the triggering of a Secure interrupt event that the Secure software was not expecting. Accordingly, when a peripheral is to be configured as Non-secure, its interrupt should also be configured as Non-secure (by using the NVIC_ITNS registers). There are a few instances where it is acceptable for Non-secure software to generate Secure interrupts/ exceptions. These are:

- Fault exceptions, e.g., A bus error triggered by a Non-secure operation results, when TrustZone is used, in the HardFault/BusFault exception targeting the Secure state.
- Interprocessor communications (IPC), e.g., In a system that has an IPC mailbox, the Secure software might allow Non-secure software to generate messages for the Secure software. Note: Usually a Secure API should be sufficient for sending messages to Secure software when the Secure and Non-secure software projects are running on the same processor. However, the IPC mechanism enables message passing to work even when the Secure and Non-secure software projects are running on different processors.

18.6.6 Other general recommendations

18.6.6.1 *Parameter passing*

Based on the CMSE specification, it is not mandatory for C compilers to support parameter passing by using the stack for cross security domain function calls. If you are creating a Secure API and do not know whether the toolchain used by the Non-secure software developers supports this feature, you need to ensure that the function's pass parameters only use registers. Using registers for passing parameters potentially achieves better performance because when using the stack for parameter passing, more software steps need to be carried out. If a Secure API's operation requires a lot of parameters, instead of passing the parameters individually, a data structure can be defined to group the parameters, and the pointer of the data structure can then be passed to the Secure API as a single parameter.

18.6.6.2 Defining the stack, the heap, and the data RAM with the XN (eXecute Never) attribute

It is generally good practice to use the MPU to set the XN (eXecute Never) attribute for regions in the Secure SRAM that are used for the stack, heap, and data. This is because the aforementioned regions in the Secure SRAM often contain data which, for various reasons, has originated from the Non-secure world. Some of these reasons are as follows:

- During the execution of Secure APIs, data often needs to be copied from the Non-secure to the Secure world for processing.
- Non-secure data in the registers could be pushed to the Secure stack during Secure API calls and Secure exceptions.

By utilizing the XN attribute in the Secure MPU, the risk of code injection attack is reduced.

18.6.6.3 Stack limit for the main stack

In general, software developers should utilize the stack limit checking feature to reduce the risk of the stack overflowing. However, before setting up the stack limit, software developers need to estimate how much stack space is required, and this is particularly true when dealing with the main stack. Because the main stack is used by system exceptions (including fault handling), if the main stack limit size is too small then some of the fault exceptions will not be able to function.

Software developers should, therefore, avoid using too many exception priority-levels to reduce the chance of having too many levels of nested interrupts, which can result in excessive main stack usage.

18.6.6.4 Preventing a stack underflow attack

In some cases, e.g., when a Secure stack is empty (this happens when a new thread is created), a hacker could, potentially, use a fake EXC_RETURN or FNC_RETURN operation to trigger a stack underflow scenario. Because the contents above the stack memory could be unpredictable, there is a possibility that the 32-bit data value, which is just above the stack region, could match a stack frame integrity signature or match a Secure executable address value. If this occurs, and if a hacker uses a fake EXC_RETURN or FNC_RETURN operation to switch from the Non-secure world to the Secure world, this illegal operation could be undetected.

To ensure that the aforementioned attack is detected and stopped, Secure software developers can reserve two words (8 bytes) of stack memory and place a special value 0xFEF5EDA5 just above the real stack space (Fig. 18.31).

Two words of stack space are needed to keep the stack double word-aligned. Because the aforementioned special value 0xFEF5EDA5 is never going to match the stack frame integrity signature and cannot be used as program address because the address range 0xE0000000 to 0xFFFFFFFF is nonexecutable, a fake EXC_RETURN or FNC_RETURN operation would always result in a fault exception.

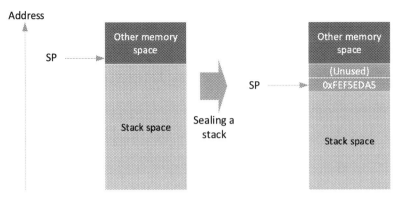

FIG. 18.31   Adding a special value in the stack to detect stack underflow attack.

This technique is referred to as sealing a stack. Secure privileged software should seal the Secure process stack before setting the CONTROL_S.SPSEL bit, and also seal the Secure main stack when switching to thread level (Section 18.6.6.8). By applying this technique, a fake EXC_RETURN or FNC_RETURN operation would always be detected.

18.6.6.5 Check all Secure entry points to prevent unintentional entry points

Because it is common to copy-and-paste codes between projects, a function declared as a Secure entry point in one project might not be a Secure entry point in another. It is, therefore, important to review the function prototype declarations to make sure that the Secure entry attributes are not mistakenly copied across.

18.6.6.6 Restricting a Secure library to unprivileged execution level

If a Secure software library needs to be restricted to unprivileged level, then:

(a) The Secure CONTROL register (CONTROL_S) must be setup so that the Secure thread is unprivileged and so that the processor uses, when in thread mode, the PSP_S as the stack pointer.
(b) The Secure MPU should be setup so that the Secure unprivileged software cannot access the privileged memory.
(c) If the processor being used is based on Armv8.1-M (e.g., Cortex-M55 processor), the Secure MPU region for the library code should be configured with the PXN MPU attribute to ensure that the code in the region can only execute in the unprivileged state. In this scenario, the library code region could have its own Non-secure Callable (NSC) region(s).
Alternatively, a system-level protection measure could be implemented to achieve a similar outcome. If the processor being used, however, is an Armv8.0-M processor and no system-level mechanism is deployed to prevent the execution of the library in a privileged state, the library code memory region must not be configured with the NSC attribute.

18.6.6.7 Reentrancy of Secure functions

Some Secure APIs might not support reentrancy and, if this is the case, additional measures need to be taken to prevent reentrancy occurring in respect of those Secure API functions. Reentrancy of a Secure API happens when the following sequences occur:

(1) A Non-secure software calls a Secure API,
(2) The processor then takes a Non-secure interrupt, and
(3) The Non-secure software then calls the same Secure API.

If a Secure API needs to execute in Handler mode, it should be designed to support reentrancy.

If a Secure API cannot handle reentrancy, it should use Thread mode to execute in an unprivileged state. In this situation, the following arrangement should be used to prevent software issues:

- When using an Armv8.0-M processor, a Secure API should undertake additional software steps to detect whether a previous API call is still in progress before it executes the API function code. One approach for doing this is to implement a simple "API busy" flag in the software, but, when doing so, care must be taken to ensure that the sequence of checking and setting the flag is a thread-safe step. This thread-safe step can be achieved by using the LDREX/STREX instructions.
- When using an Armv8.1-M processor (e.g., Cortex-M55), the CCR_S.TRD bit should be set to 1 so that when reentrancy has occurred it is detected and so when it is, a fault exception is triggered. (Note: the CCR_S.TRD bit is only used for protecting thread mode APIs).

18.6.6.8 The Secure handler must seal the Secure main stack when switching an exception handler to unprivileged execution

Some Secure interrupt handlers might need to be executed at an unprivileged level. If that is the case, the Secure interrupt(s) should first execute a process in the Secure firmware to switch the processor to an unprivileged level and then execute the Secure interrupt handler. The switching process involves the use of an SVC exception, with the SVC's exception return using a fake stack frame to switch the processor to an unprivileged state. In addition to creating the fake stack frame on the process stack, the SVC handler also seals the main stack (Section 18.6.6.4) before executing the exception return that starts the unprivileged handler code. Sealing of the Secure main stack is also required when Secure privileged software creates a new unprivileged process using an exception return.

18.6.6.9 Secure world not used

When AIRCR.BFHFNMINS is set to 1, the following measures must be used to prevent the Non-secure software from re-entering the Secure state:

- All NSC region attributes should be disabled.
- Secure interrupts should be disabled.
- Secure stacks should be sealed (Section 18.6.6.4).

18.6.6.10 PSA certification

In respect of Secure firmware development, as well as reviewing code to ensure code quality, PSA (Platform Security Architecture) certification should also be considered. "PSA certified" is a security evaluation scheme for the IoT era that provides industry-wide trust in security products, and enables a higher quality definition of IoT security. An overview of PSA is covered in Chapter 22. Information on the requirements for PSA certification is outside the scope of this book, but further information on this topic can be found at www.psacertified.org.

References

[1] Procedure Call Standard for the Arm Architecture (AAPCS). https://developer.arm.com/documentation/ihi0042/latest.

[2] Armv8-M Security Extension: Requirements on Development Tools. https://developer.arm.com/documentation/ecm0359818/latest.

[3] ACLE specification. https://developer.arm.com/architectures/system-architectures/software-standards/acle.

[4] Corstone-200/201 foundation IP: Memory Protection Controller. https://developer.arm.com/documentation/ddi0571/e/programmers-model/ahb5-trustzone-memory-protection-controller.

[5] Corstone-200/201 foundation IP: AMBA AHB5 Peripheral Protection Controller. https://developer.arm.com/documentation/ddi0571/e/functional-description/ahb5-trustzone-peripheral-protection-controller/functional-description.

[6] Corstone-200/201 foundation IP: AMBA APB4 Peripheral Protection Controller. https://developer.arm.com/documentation/ddi0571/e/functional-description/apb4-trustzone-peripheral-protection-controller/functional-description.

Digital signal processing on the cortex-M33 processor

19.1 DSP on a microcontroller?

Digital Signal Processing (DSP) includes a wide range of mathematically intensive algorithms. The umbrella term includes applications in audio, video, measurement, and industrial control. Increasingly, digital signal processing has become one of the key requirements in many microcontroller applications. Since the introduction of the Arm® Cortex®-M4 processor in 2010, which included a DSP extension in the Armv7-M architecture, the use of Cortex-M based systems in signal processing applications has increased significantly.

Many of these applications are focused on audio, such as portable audio players, and, in 2019, we saw the Cortex-M4 system being used in the Amazon Alexa Voice Service (AVS).[a] As well as that, we have also seen Arm Cortex-M processors being used in other forms of signal processing and these include:

- Sensor fusion applications for use in mobile phones and wearable devices
- Image processing (e.g., the OpenMV project[b] utilizes a Cortex-M7 microcontroller to handle image processing)
- Detecting and analyzing sound (e.g., ai3™—a sound detection software solution[c] from Audio Analytic that runs on an entry-level Cortex-M0 processor)
- Vibration analysis[d] for predictive maintenance

---

[a] AWS Press release: https://aws.amazon.com/about-aws/whats-new/2019/11/new-alexa-voice-integration-for-aws-iot-core-cost-effectively-brings-alexa-voice-to-any-connected-device/.

[b] The OpenMV project: https://openmv.io/.

[c] Audio Analytic ai3™ running on a Cortex-M0 microcontroller: https://www.audioanalytic.com/the-cortex-m0-challenge-part-one/.

[d] A technical presentation slide on predictive maintenance from ST Microelectronics.

TABLE 19.1   DSP processing features in Cortex-M processors.

	Multiply-accumulate (MAC), saturation adjustments	DSP extension (SIMD, single-cycle MAC, saturation arithmetic instructions)	Helium (M-profile vector extension)
Cortex-M0, Cortex-M0+, Cortex-M23	–	–	–
Cortex-M3	Yes	–	–
Cortex-M4, Cortex-M7	Yes	Yes	–
Cortex-M33	Yes	Optional	–
Cortex-M55	Yes	Yes	Optional

The various members of the Cortex-M processor family have different levels of signal processing capabilities (Table 19.1).

The Cortex-M33 processor supports, as an optional feature, the same DSP instruction set that is in the Cortex-M4 and Cortex-M7 processors. These instructions accelerate numerical algorithms and open the door to performing real-time signal processing operations directly on the Cortex-M processors, without the need for an external digital signal processor. This chapter starts with some motivation behind the DSP extensions, and provides a simple introduction to the feature using, as an example, the dot product calculation.

I continue with a detailed look at the Cortex-M33 instruction set and provide tips and tricks for optimizing the DSP code on this processor. Chapter 20 presents the CMSIS-DSP library—an off-the-shelf optimized DSP library provided by Arm for the Cortex-M processors.

19.2   Why use a Cortex-M processor for a DSP application?

Before the arrival of modern microcontrollers with DSP capabilities, the first choice that comes to mind when looking for a processor to execute Digital Signal Processing applications on is the Digital Signal Processor, which, sharing the same acronym, is also called a DSP. The architecture of a DSP is tuned to perform the mathematical operations found in these algorithms. However, in some sense, they are crippled savants that excel at certain focused operations while struggling with some of the requirements we see in embedded applications.

Microcontrollers, on the other hand, are general purpose and excel at control tasks: interfacing to peripherals, handling user interfaces, and general connectivity. As a result, microcontrollers have a wide range of peripherals, making it easy for them to interface to other sensors and ICs with common interfaces, such as ADC, DAC, SPI, I2C/I3C, USB, and the Ethernet. Microcontrollers also have a long history of being embedded in portable products and a greater focus on minimizing power consumption, as well as delivering excellent code density. Many legacy microcontrollers, however, are not necessarily great at performing intense mathematical algorithms because they lack registers and a proper set of instructions that support these computations.

The recent boom in connected devices creates a need for products with both microcontroller and DSP features. This is evident in devices which handle multimedia content. They require both peripheral connectivity and a capability to handle DSP processing. Traditionally, these connected devices either have:

- Two separate chips—a general-purpose microcontroller and a digital signal processor.
- One chip that contains both a general-purpose processor and a digital signal processor.

Modern Cortex-M based microcontrollers, especially those that support a DSP instruction extension, enable a wide range of applications that demand a certain level of DSP processing capabilities to run on those microcontroller systems. This has many advantages:

- There is no need for a dedicated DSP chip on the circuit board, reducing product and design costs.
- Embedded product developers can use a single development toolchain to develop the whole application.
- Reduces software complexity by running all software tasks on a single processor system.
- IoT security management features on the Cortex-M processors, such as TrustZone, can be useful for a range of signal processing applications (e.g., the handling of biometric data such as fingerprints).
- On a Cortex-M processor you can utilize its RTOS support capabilities to handle multiple signal processing threads with very little context switching overhead. In comparison, many digital signal processors do not have dedicated RTOS support.

Some microcontrollers have multiple Cortex-M processors, which means that one or more of the Cortex-M processors could be dedicated to DSP processing, which is useful when the DSP processing workload is heavy. The other processors in the chip could then be used for other purposes such as running communication stacks, handling user interface processing tasks, etc. Although these devices have multiple processors, software developers, when developing software for these devices, are able to use a single toolchain. With the CoreSight debug architecture, multicore debugging on microcontrollers with multiple Cortex-M processors is easier than debugging a multicore system with a general-purpose processor and a digital signal processor. This is because you are likely to need multiple debug connections to debug such systems.

With the availability of the CMSIS-DSP library, DSP application development on Cortex-M based systems is made much easier. In contrast, it can be very hard to find experienced DSP software developers who are familiar with certain proprietary DSP architectures. Cortex-M based development boards are also widely available, making them ideal starting points for teaching/learning about digital signal processing.

While the Cortex-M33 processor can be a good match for applications that demand some digital signal processing capabilities, it is not designed to deliver the superior signal processing performance that is achieved by many dedicated digital signal processors. In 2020, Arm announced the Cortex-M55 processor, which is designed to offer a signal processing performance which is similar to a modern, mid-range digital signal processor. To achieve this performance level, the Cortex-M55 processor supports Helium technology, an extension that includes over 150 new instructions, including many vector operations. Information about Helium is not detailed here because the Cortex-M55 processor and the Armv8.1-M architecture are beyond the scope of this book. Nevertheless, because the

CMSIS-DSP library is available for all Arm Cortex-M processors, an application developed for the Arm Cortex-M processors using the CMSIS-DSP library can easily migrate to a Cortex-55 based device.

Please note that the DSP extension is optional in the Cortex-M33 processor. This means that silicon chip designers can omit the DSP extension if the target usage for a chip does not involve signal processing and if ultra-low power is a higher priority requirement. If this is the case, when the DSP extension is omitted (i.e., the SIMD or the saturate arithmetic instructions are unavailable), a few variants of the multiply-accumulate instructions and saturation adjustment instructions are still available.

Unlike the Cortex-M33 processor, the Cortex-M23 processor does not have a DSP extension and does not have the same level of processing capabilities. It can, however, still be used for lightweight signal processing tasks, such as voice activity detection and for the analysis of signals that have relatively low sampling rates (e.g., the detection of mechanical vibration).

19.3 Dot product example

This section discusses the salient features of DSPs with an eye toward how they improve overall performance. There are many types of processing algorithms that are useful for signal processing. Examples of low-level algorithms include filtering functions, transformations, matrix, and vector operations. Many of these processing algorithms involve a series of multiplication and add operations (i.e., multiply-accumulate) and here I will start with some of the simple functions that involve multiply-accumulate.

By way of example, I will look at the dot product operation that multiplies two vectors and accumulates the products, element by element (Fig. 19.1).

Assuming that inputs $x[k]$ and $y[k]$ are arrays of 32-bit values and that we want to use a 64-bit representation for z. In C code, the dot product would be implemented as:

---

dot product implemented in C code

```
int64_t dot_product (int32_t *x, int32_t *y, int32_t N) {
        int32_t xx, yy, k;
        int64_t sum = 0;
            for(k = 0; k < N; k++) {
                    xx = *x++;
                    yy = *y++;
                    sum += xx * yy;
            }
        return sum;
        }
```

$$z = \sum_{k=0}^{N-1} x[k]y[k]$$

FIG. 19.1   Dot product mathematical representation.

The dot product consists of a series of multiplications and additions. This "multiply-accumulate" or MAC operation is at the heart of many DSP functions.

Now, consider the execution time of this algorithm on the Cortex-M33 processor. Fetching data from memory and incrementing the pointer takes just 1 clock cycle

```
xx = *x++; // 1 cycle (LDR with post increment addressing mode)
```

Similarly, the next fetch also takes 1 cycle

```
yy = *y++; // 1 cycle
```

Unlike the Cortex-M4 processor, which takes 2 clock cycles for a single load operation, the Cortex-M33 processor can be slightly faster for memory access operations.

The multiply-accumulate operation (multiplication and addition) is of the form $32 \times 32 + 64$ and the Cortex-M33 processor can do this with a single instruction. In an ideal situation, the multiply-accumulate operation is single cycle and operates back-to-back. However, if the input data for the multiplication operations (not including the accumulator value) was loaded into the register bank at the last executed instruction, there can be a 1 cycle load-use penalty.

The loop itself (shown in the aforementioned C code example) introduces an additional overhead. This usually involves decrementing the loop counter and then branching to the beginning of the loop. The standard loop overhead ranges from 2 to 3 cycles on the Cortex-M33 processor. Thus, on the Cortex-M33, the inner loop of the dot product takes 8 cycles with the execution time being data dependent:

```
xx = *x++;        // 1 cycle
yy = *y++;        // 1 cycle
sum += xx * yy;   // 2 cycles (1 cycle pipeline due to load-use penalty)
(loop overhead)   // 4 cycles including loop counter update and compare
```

The whole dot product function can be rewritten in assembly code as follows:

Inline assembly code for simple dot product

```
int64_t __attribute__((naked)) dot_product (int32_t *x, int32_t *y, int32_t N)
{
    __asm(
        "    PUSH {R4-R5}\n\t"          /* 2 cycle */
        "    MOVS R4, #0\n\t"           /* 1 cycle */
        "    MOVS R5, #0\n\t"           /* 1 cycle */
    "loop: \n\t"
        "    LDR R3 , [R0], #4\n\t"     /* 1 cycle */
        "    LDR R12, [R1], #4\n\t"     /* 1 cycle */
        "    SMLAL R4, R5, R3, R12\n\t" /* 2 cycles - pipeline hazard */
        "    SUBS R2, R2, #1\n\t"       /* 1 cycle */
        "    BNE loop\n\t"              /* 3 cycles */
```

```
   "    MOVS R0, R5\n\t"            /* 1 cycle */
   "    MOVS R1, R4\n\t"            /* 1 cycle */
   "    POP {R4-R5}\n\t"           /* 2 cycle2 */
   "    BX LR\n\t");               /* 3 cycle2 */
}
```

With a simple rescheduling of instructions, we can remove the pipeline bubble of SMLAL and reduce the inner loop to 7 cycles:

Inline assembly code for simple dot product

```
int64_t __attribute__((naked)) dot_product (int32_t *x, int32_t *y, int32_t N)
{
    __asm(
    "    PUSH {R4-R5}\n\t"         /* 2 cycle */
    "    MOVS R4, #0\n\t"          /* 1 cycle */
    "    MOVS R5, #0\n\t"          /* 1 cycle */
   "loop: \n\t"
    "    LDR R3 , [R0], #4\n\t"    /* 1 cycle */
    "    LDR R12, [R1], #4\n\t"    /* 1 cycle */
    "    SUBS R2, R2, #1\n\t"      /* 1 cycle - placed between LDR and SMLAL*/
    "    SMLAL R4, R5, R3, R12\n\t" /* 1 cycle */
    "    BNE loop\n\t"             /* 3 cycles */
    "    MOVS R0, R4\n\t"          /* 1 cycle */
    "    MOVS R1, R5\n\t"          /* 1 cycle */
    "    POP {R4-R5}\n\t"          /* 2 cycles */
    "    BX LR\n\t");              /* 3 cycles */
}
```

The loop overhead can be reduced by utilizing loop unrolling. For example, if you know that the length of the vectors is a multiple of four samples, then you can unroll the loop by a factor of 4. Computing four samples would require 15 cycles. In other words, the dot product operation would only require 3.75 cycles on the Cortex-M33, whereas on the Cortex-M4 processor it would require 4.75 cycles per sample; and on the Cortex-M3 processor it would take from 7.75 to 11.75 cycles per sample.

Inline assembly code for simple dot product with loop unrolling

---

```
int64_t __attribute__((naked)) dot_product (int32_t *x, int32_t *y, int32_t N)
{
    __asm(
    "    PUSH {R4-R11}\n\t"        /* 8 cycle */
    "    MOVS R3, #0\n\t"          /* 1 cycle */
    "    MOVS R4, #0\n\t"          /* 1 cycle */
```

```
"loop: \n\t"
    "    LDMIA R0 , {R5-R8}\n\t"        /* 4 cycles */
    "    LDMIA R1 , {R9-R12}\n\t"       /* 4 cycles */
    "    SMLAL R3, R4, R5, R9\n\t"      /* 1 cycle */
    "    SMLAL R3, R4, R6, R10\n\t"     /* 1 cycle */
    "    SMLAL R3, R4, R7, R11\n\t"     /* 1 cycle */
    "    SMLAL R3, R4, R8, R12\n\t"     /* 1 cycle */
    "    SUBS R2, R2, #4\n\t"           /* 1 cycle */
    "    BNE loop\n\t"                  /* 3 cycle */
    "    MOVS R0, R3\n\t"               /* 1 cycle */
    "    MOVS R1, R4\n\t"               /* 1 cycle */
    "    POP {R4-R11}\n\t"              /* 8 cycles */
    "    BX LR\n\t");                   /* 3 cycles */
}
```

Please note:

- The assembly code examples are manually created: C compiler generated code can look quite different from what is illustrated here.
- The number of clock cycles needed for the processing is dependent on the memory wait state and, in some cases, the alignment of the instructions in the memory.

19.4 Getting more performance by utilizing the SIMD instructions

In the dot product example in Section 19.3, the SMLAL instruction (a MAC operation) was used. The SMLAL instruction is available even when the DSP extension is not implemented. When the DSP extension is implemented, the "Single-Instruction, Multiple-Data" (SIMD) instruction feature can be utilized to accelerate the processing of 16-bit dot product operations.

For example, if the dot product operation is based on 16-bit data instead of 32 bits, the SMLALD, a dual MAC instruction, can be used. The operation of SMLALD is illustrated in Fig. 19.2.

With input data arrays x[ ] and y[ ] in the dot product example in Section 19.3 both based on 16-bit data, two samples can be loaded using a single load operation; resulting in the overall dual MAC operation (as shown in Fig. 19.3, excluding the loop handling overhead) taking only 3 clock cycles, or just 1.5 clock cycle per MAC.

Utilizing the loop unrolling technique, as illustrated in Section 19.3, the average loop overhead can be reduced. Please note, the loop counter decrement value changes from 4 to 8 as each dual MAC processes two data samples. The rewritten dot product assembly code which utilizes the SIMD operation is as follows:

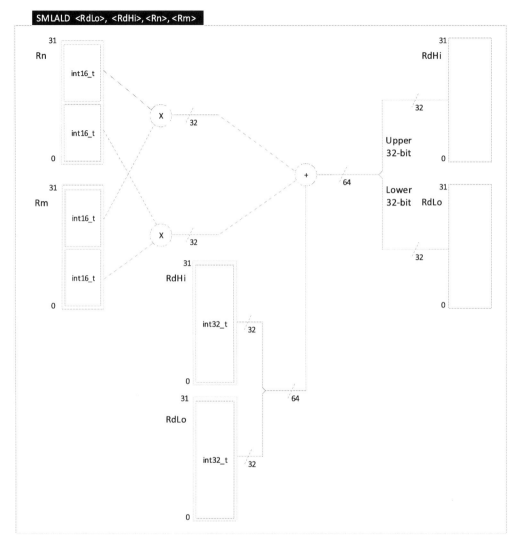

FIG. 19.2   SMLALD instruction.

FIG. 19.3   Reducing the number of instruction cycles using SIMD operations.

Inline assembly code for simple dot product with SIMD and loop unrolling

```
int64_t __attribute__((naked)) dot_product (int16_t *x, int16_t *y, int32_t N)
{
    __asm(
        " PUSH {R4-R11}\n\t"              /* 8 cycle */
        " MOVS R3, #0\n\t"               /* 1 cycle */
        " MOVS R4, #0\n\t"               /* 1 cycle */
    "loop: \n\t"
        " LDMIA R0 , {R5-R8}\n\t"        /* 4 cycles */
        " LDMIA R1 , {R9-R12}\n\t"       /* 4 cycles */
        " SMLALD R3, R4, R5, R9\n\t"     /* 1 cycle */
        " SMLALD R3, R4, R6, R10\n\t"    /* 1 cycle */
        " SMLALD R3, R4, R7, R11\n\t"    /* 1 cycle */
        " SMLALD R3, R4, R8, R12\n\t"    /* 1 cycle */
        " SUBS R2, R2, #8\n\t"           /* 1 cycle */
        " BNE loop\n\t"                  /* 3 cycles */
        " MOVS R0, R3\n\t"               /* 1 cycle */
        " MOVS R1, R4\n\t"               /* 1 cycle */
        " POP {R4-R11}\n\t"              /* 8 cycles */
        " BX LR\n\t");                   /* 3 cycles */
}
```

In addition to undertaking dot product calculations, the SIMD dual MAC can also be deployed to many other DSP processing tasks, e.g., handling the finite impulse response (FIR) filter. For example, each of the dotted rectangles in the FIR filter shown in Fig. 19.4 can be implemented as a dual MAC.

19.5 Dealing with overflows

In the dot product example in Section 19.3, the input data is 32-bit wide and the accumulator is 64-bit wide. If the input values for the MAC operation are often close to the limits of the input value range, and there are a high number of elements in the array, the accumulation operations could easily overflow because the multiplication results are 64 bits.

To solve this problem, many traditional DSPs use a dedicated accumulator register which is wider than the width of the multiplication results. For example, in some traditional DSPs (e.g., the SHARC processor from Analog Devices), a dedicated accumulator register with a width of 80 bits is available so that this problem does not occur.

The Cortex-M33 processor does not, however, have a dedicated accumulator register. To avoid the aforementioned issue, an application developer could, therefore, simply restrict the input data value ranges to reduce the chance of the accumulator overflowing. Thankfully, in most signal processing applications, the input source data values, such as those for audio signals, are only 16–24 bits in size. If the data processing is carried out in a fixed-point format, the input data values can be scaled accordingly to reduce the chance of an overflow.

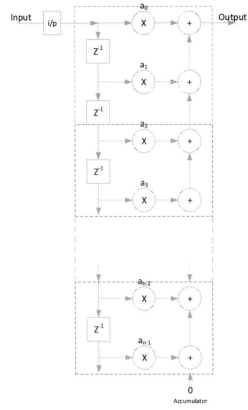

FIG. 19.4   Use of dual MAC in FIR filter.

In some instances, it is impractical to scale input data to prevent an overflow from happening. For example, if we want to utilize the SIMD to maximize processing performance, we cannot do so as the input data values are already restricted to 16 bits (-32768 to $+36767$ for integer data). To help overcome this problem, the DSP extension of the Cortex-M33 processor supports *saturation* arithmetic. Instead of having the calculation results wrapping around at the overflow values, which is standard behavior for two's complement arithmetic, saturation arithmetic operations limit the operation results to the maximum (e.g., $+32767$ for 16-bit value) or minimum (e.g., -32768 for 16-bit value). Consider the waveforms shown in Fig. 19.5. In this example, the wave forms are represented as 16-bit integers and are limited to the range -32768 to $+32767$. The top plot shows the ideal result, which exceeds the allowable range. The middle plot shows how the result wraps when using the standard two's complement addition. The bottom plot shows the result with saturation. The signals are slightly clipped but are still recognizable as sine waves.

Basic saturating arithmetic operations are supported in the DSP extension of Cortex-M33 processors, other Armv8-M Mainline processors, Cortex-M4 and Cortex-M7 processors. The processor provides saturating addition and subtraction instructions but no saturating MAC instructions. To perform a saturating MAC instruction, you have to separately multiply the two values and then perform a saturating addition. This takes one more clock cycle.

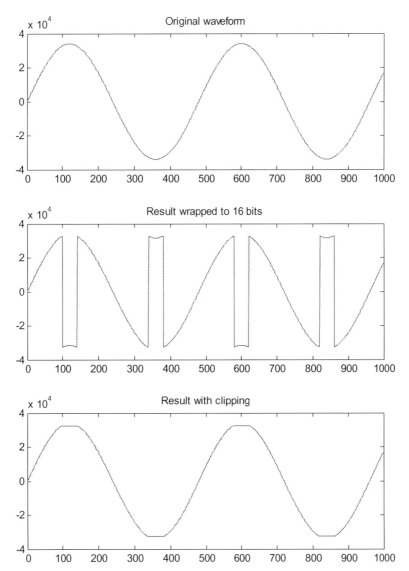

FIG. 19.5 The effects of processing with and without saturation. The top plot shows the ideal result of processing, but it exceeds the allowable 16-bit range. The middle plot is the result wrapped to 16 bits and has severe distortion. The bottom plot is the result saturated to the allowable range and has mild distortion.

19.6 Introduction to data types for signal processing

19.6.1 Why we need the fixed-point data format

Before we start going into the details of signal processing, we need to understand how signal values are represented in embedded processor systems. Various data types can be used for signal processing:

- Integers of various sizes
- Floating-point values (single precision, double precision, etc.)
- Fixed point values of various sizes

In many signal processing applications, because the floating-point data format provides a very wide dynamic range of signal values, the floating-point support enables signal processing algorithms to be easily implemented. However, many traditional embedded processors (including some legacy Digital Signal Processors) do not support Floating-point Unit (FPU) hardware and rely on software emulation to handle floating-point calculations. However, software emulation can be very slow (in the magnitude of up to 10 times slower). At the same time, there is often a need for presenting fractional data values. While using integers with additional scaling ratios can work, it can be error prone when transferring values between different data types.

To solve this problem, the fixed-point format was introduced to enable fractional values to be handled with integer operations. Many signal processing algorithms were developed using fixed-point format(s), which can use integer processing instructions to handle the computation—with a certain level of compromise in the signal value's dynamic range. However, fixed-point computations can, potentially, achieve a higher performance compared to floating-point computations because many embedded processors require multiple clock cycles to execute a floating-point calculation instruction. In comparison, integer processing instructions usually take a single clock cycle.

19.6.2 Fractional arithmetic

Fractional data types are commonly used in signal processing and are unfamiliar to many software programmers. Accordingly, I have spent a bit of time introducing them and detailing their benefits in this section.

Fixed-point data operations use regular integer data types (8-bit, 16-bit, 32-bit, etc.) and divide the bit fields into multiple parts (Fig. 19.6). Typically, these data values are signed, so the MSB (Most Significant Bit) is used for the sign bit in most cases. The rest of the bits in the data is divided into integer and fraction parts. The bit position for the integer and fraction part partitioning is called the radix point.

The choice of radix point is application dependent. It is possible to omit the integer portion and just have the sign bit and fractional part (Table 19.2). This arrangement is quite common for a range of embedded applications.

It is possible to use other arrangements for the partitioning of integer bit and fraction bit fields. For example, with 8-bit signed data, you can have the following fixed-point data types (Table 19.3).

An N-bit signed integer using a standard two's complement representation represents values in the range $[-2^{(N-1)}, 2^{(N-1)} - 1]$. A fractional N-bit integer has an implied division

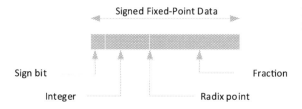

FIG. 19.6 A generalized fixed-point data format representation.

TABLE 19.2 Common fixed-point data types.

Common fixed-point data types	Data type definition in programming	Number of sign bit	Number of integer bits	Number of fraction bits
q0.7 (often refers as q7)	q7_t	1	0	7
q0.15 (often refers as q15)	q15_t	1	0	15
q0.31 (often refers as q31)	q31_t	1	0	31

TABLE 19.3 Various radix point arrangements are possible.

8-bit fixed-point data types	Number of sign bit	Number of integer bits	Number of fraction bits
q0.7	1	0	7
q1.6	1	1	6
q2.5	1	2	5
q3.4	1	3	4
q4.3	1	4	3
q5.5	1	5	2
q6.7	1	6	1
q7.0 (same as signed integer data)	1	7	0

by $2^{(N-1)}$ and represents values in the range $[-1, 1-2^{-(N-1)}]$. If I is the integer value then $F = \frac{I}{2^{(N-1)}}$ is the corresponding fractional value. 8-bit fractional values are in the range

$$\left[\frac{-2^7}{2^7}, \frac{2^7 - 1}{2^7}\right] \text{ or } \left[-1, 1-2^{-7}\right].$$

In binary, some common signed values in two's complement are represented as:

Maximum	=	01111111	$=1-2^{-7}$
Smallest positive	=	00000001	$=2^{-7}$
Zero	=	00000000	$=0$
Smallest negative	=	11111111	$=-2^{-7}$
Minimum	=	10000000	$=-1$

Similarly, 16-bit fractional values are in the range

$$\left[-1, 1-2^{-15}\right]$$

Note that the ranges of values are almost identical for the 8- and 16-bit fractional representations. This simplifies scaling in mathematical algorithms because instead of having to keep in mind a particular integer range, you simply have to remember -1 to about $+1$.

You may be wondering why 8-bit fractional values are named "q7_t" rather than "q8_t". The reason is that there is an implied sign bit in the representation and there are actually only 7 fractional bits. The individual bit values are:

$$\left[S, \frac{1}{2}, \frac{1}{4}, \frac{1}{8}, \frac{1}{16}, \frac{1}{32}, \frac{1}{64}, \frac{1}{128} \right]$$

where S represents the sign bit. We can generalize fractional integers to include both integer and fractional bits. Qm.n refers to a fractional integer with 1 sign bit, m integer bits, and n fractional bits. For example, q0.7 is the familiar 8-bit data type (q7_t) mentioned above with 1 sign bit, no integer bits, and 7 fractional bits. q8.7 is a 16-bit fractional integer with 1 sign bit, 8 integer bits, and 7 fractional bits. The bit values are:

$$\left[S, 128, 64, 32, 16, 8, 4, 2, 1, \frac{1}{2}, \frac{1}{4}, \frac{1}{8}, \frac{1}{16}, \frac{1}{32}, \frac{1}{64}, \frac{1}{128} \right]$$

The integer bits can be used as guard bits in signal processing algorithms.

Fractional values are represented as integers and stored in integer variables or registers. Addition of fractional values is identical to integer addition. Multiplication, however, is fundamentally different. Multiplying two N-bit integers yields a $2N$-bit result. If you need to truncate the result back to N bits you typically take the low N bits.

Since fractional values are in the range $[-1\ +1]$, multiplying two values will yield a result in the same[e] data result range. Let us examine what happens if you multiply two N-bit fractional values:

$$\frac{I_1}{2^{(N-1)}} \times \frac{I_2}{2^{(N-1)}}$$

You end up with a $2N$-bit result

$$\frac{I_1 I_2}{2^{(2N-2)}}$$

where $I_1 I_2$ is standard integer multiplication. Since the result is $2N$ bits long and there is a factor of 2^{2N-2} in the denominator, this represents a q1.$(2N-2)$ number. For example, for two 8-bit q0.7 fixed point data of 0.5 (i.e., binary 01000000), their integer multiplication result is 0x1000 (i.e., binary 0001_0000_0000_0000). As we know, the result should be 0.25 which should have been 0x2000. To turn this into a q0.$(2N-1)$ fractional number it would be left shifted by 1 bit. Alternatively, this can be turned into a q0.$(N-1)$ bit number by either:

1. Left shifting by 1 bit and taking the high N bits, or
2. Right shifting by $N-1$ bits and taking the low N bits.

[e] Well almost. The only place where this falls apart is if you multiply $(-1) \times (-1)$ and obtain $+1$. This value is technically one LSB out of the allowable range and needs to be truncated to the largest allowable positive value.

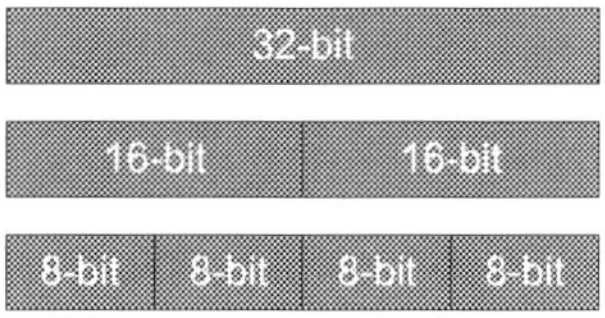

FIG. 19.7 SIMD data.

These operations describe a true fractional multiplication in which the result is back in the range [−1 +1].

The Cortex-M processors uses approach (1) for fractional multiplication, but omits the left shift by 1 bit. Conceptually, the result is scaled down by 1 bit and lies in the range [−1/2 +1/2]. You have to keep this in mind when developing algorithms and, at some point, incorporate the missing bit shift.

19.6.3 SIMD data

When the DSP extension is implemented, the Cortex-M33 processor also provides SIMD instructions that operate on packed 8- or 16-bit integers. A 32-bit register can hold either 1×32-bit value, 2×16-bit values, or 4×8-bit values, as illustrated below (Fig. 19.7).

Instructions which operate on 8- or 16-bit data types are useful for processing data (e.g., video or audio data) which do not require full 32-bit precision. Software developers can utilize SIMD operations with fixed-point data types, and many of the program codes in the CMSIS-DSP library are already optimized in this way.

To use the SIMD instructions in C code, you load values into int32_t variables and then invoke the corresponding SIMD intrinsic instructions.

19.7 Cortex-M33 DSP instructions

The instructions available in the DSP extension for the Cortex-M33 processor is identical to those in the Cortex-M4 and Cortex-M7 processors. These instructions operate on data in the regular register bank: Cortex-M processors have a core register set containing sixteen 32-bit registers. The bottom 13 registers, R0–R12, are general purpose and can hold intermediate variables, pointers, function arguments, and return results. The upper three registers are reserved for special purposes.

```
R0 to R12 - General purpose
R13 - Stack pointer    [reserved]
R14 - Link register    [reserved]
R15 - Program counter [reserved]
```

When optimizing code, you need to keep in mind that the register set can only hold 13 intermediate values. If you exceed this, the compiler will need to store intermediate values on the stack causing the application's performance to slowdown. Consider the dot product C code example from Section 19.3. The registers required are:

```
x - pointer
y - pointer
```

```
xx – 32-bit integer
yy – 32-bit integer
z – 64-bit integer [2 registers required]
k – loop counter
```

In total, this function needs seven registers. The dot product is quite basic and already half of the registers are used.

The optional floating-point unit (FPU) on the Cortex-M33 processor has its own set of registers. This extension register file contains 32 single-precision registers (32 bits each) labeled S0–S31. One obvious advantage of floating-point code is that you have access to these additional 32 registers. R0–R12 are still available to hold integer variables (pointers, counters, etc.), yielding a total of 45 registers that can be used by the C compiler. We will see later on that floating-point operations are typically slower than integer ones, but the extra registers can lead to more efficient code, especially for more complicated functions such as Fast Fourier Transforms (FFTs). Savvy C compilers make use of the floating-point registers when performing integer arithmetic. They store intermediate results to the floating-point register file, rather than to the stack, since register-to-register transfers take 1 cycle as opposed to register-to-memory transfers which may, if the memory access has wait states, take multiple clock cycles.

To use the Cortex-M33 DSP instructions, start by including the main CMSIS file core_cm33.h (this should be pulled in automatically when "including" the device header file). This defines a variety of integer, floating-point, and fractional data types as shown below:

Signed Integers

```
int8_t    8-bit
int16_t  16-bit
int32_t  32-bit
int64_t  64-bit
```

Unsigned Integers

```
uint8_t    8-bit
uint16_t  16-bit
uint32_t  32-bit
uint64_t  64-bit
```

Floating-Point

```
float32_t single precision  32-bit
float64_t double precision  64-bit
```

Fractional

```
q7_t     8-bit
q15_t   16-bit
q31_t   32-bit
q63_t   64-bit
```

19.7.1 Load and store instructions

Loading and storing 32-bit data values can be accomplished with standard C constructs. On the Cortex-M33 processor, each load or store instruction takes 1 cycle to execute. However, the read data is fetched into the processor in the third stage of pipeline. If the subsequent instruction processes the read data immediately in the second stage of the pipeline, the pipeline would have to be stalled for 1 cycle. However, this pipeline stall can be avoided by scheduling other useful instructions in between the data load and the data processing.

Please note, this pipeline characteristic is different from the Cortex-M3 and the Cortex-M4 processors where a single data load instruction takes two cycles and where subsequent loads or stores take 1 cycle. *When working with these processors, whenever possible, group loads and stores together to take advantage of this situation,* i.e., *saving 1 cycle.*

To load or store packed SIMD data, define int32_t variables to hold the data. Then perform the loads and stores using the __SIMD32 macros supplied in the CMSIS library. For example, to load four 8-bit values in one instruction use

```
q7_t *pSrc *pDst;
int32_t x;
x = *__SIMD32(pSrc)++;
```

This also increments pSrc by a full 32-bit word (so that it points to the next group of four 8-bit values). To store the data back to memory, use

```
*_SIMD32(pDst)++ = x;
```

The macro also applies to packed 16-bit data

```
q15_t *pSrc *pDst;
int32_t x;
x = *__SIMD32(pSrc)++;
*__SIMD32(pDst)++ = x;
```

19.7.2 Arithmetic instructions

This section describes the Cortex-M arithmetic operations which are most frequently used in DSP algorithms. The goal is not to cover each and every Cortex-M arithmetic instruction but rather to highlight the ones that are most frequently used in practice. In fact, I only cover a fraction of the available commands. The focus is on:

Signed data	[Ignore unsigned]
Floating-point	
Fractional integers	[Ignore standard integer math]
Sufficient precision	[32-bit or 64-bit accumulators]

I also ignore fractional operations with rounding, add/subtract variants, carry bits, and variants based on top or bottom placement of 16-bit words within a 32-bit register. I have ignored these instructions because they are less frequently used and once the content of this section is understood, it should be easy to apply the other variants.

The instructions vary on how they are invoked by the C compiler. In some cases, the compiler determines the correct instruction to use based on standard C code. For example, fractional addition is performed using:

```
z = x + y;
```

In other cases, you have to use an *idiom*. This is a predefined snippet of C code that the compiler recognizes and maps to the appropriate single instruction. For example, to swap bytes 0 and 1, and 2 and 3 of a 32-bit word, use the idiom

```
(((x&0xff)<<8)|((x&0xff00)>>8)|((x&0xff000000)>>8)|((x&0x00ff0000)<<8));
```

The compiler recognizes this and maps it to a single REV16 instruction.

And finally, in some cases there is no C construct that maps to the underlying instruction and the instruction can only be invoked via an *intrinsic*. For example, to carry out a saturating 32-bit addition use

```
z = __QADD(x, y);
```

In general, it is better to use idioms because they are standard C constructs and provide portability across processors and compilers. The idioms described in this chapter apply to Keil® Microcontroller Development Kit (MDK) and the idioms map to precisely 1 Cortex-M instruction. Some compilers do not provide full support for idioms and may yield several instructions. Check your compiler documentation to see which idioms are supported and how they map to Cortex-M instructions. Alternatively, a range of portable intrinsic functions are available in the CMSIS-CORE. Information appertaining to this is available in the CMSIS reference page: https://arm-software.github.io/CMSIS_5/Core/html/group__intrinsic__SIMD__gr.html.

19.7.2.1 32-bit integer instructions

ADD—32-bit addition

Standard 32-bit addition without saturation—may result in an overflow situation. It supports both int32_t and q31_t data types.

Processor support: All Cortex-M processors [Takes 1 cycle].

C code example

```
q31_t x, y, z;
z = x + y;
```

SUB—32-bit subtraction

Standard 32-bit subtraction without saturation—may result in an overflow situation. It supports both int32_t and q31_t data types.

Processor support: All Cortex-M processors [Takes 1 cycle].

C code example

```
q31_t x, y, z;
z = x - y;
```

SMULL—Long signed multiply

Multiplies two 32-bit integers and returns a 64-bit result. This is useful for computing products of fractional data while maintaining high precision.

Processor support: Cortex-M3 [Takes 3–7 cycles] and Cortex-M4, Cortex-M7, Cortex-M33, Cortex-M55 [Takes 1 cycle].

C code example

```
int32_t x, y;
int64_t z;
z = (int64_t) x * y;
```

SMLAL—Long signed multiply accumulate

Multiplies two 32-bit integers and adds the 64-bit result to a 64-bit accumulator. This is useful for computing MACs of fractional data and maintaining high precision.

Processor support: Cortex-M3 [3–7 cycles] and Cortex-M4, Cortex-M7, Cortex-M33, Cortex-M55 [1 cycle].

C code example

```
int32_t x, y;
int64_t acc;
acc += (int64_t) x * y;
```

SSAT—Signed saturation

Saturates a signed x integer to a specified bit position B. The result is saturated to the range

$$-2^{B-1} \leq x \leq 2^{B-1} - 1$$

where B = 1, 2, …, 32. The instruction is available in C code only via the intrinsic:

```
int32_t __SSAT(int32_t x, uint32_t B)
```

Processor support: All Armv7-M and Armv8-M Mainline processors [Takes 1 cycle].

C code example

```
int32_t x, y;
y = __SSAT(x, 16); // Saturate to 16-bit precision.
```

SMMUL—32-bit multiply returning 32-most-significant-bits

Fractional q31_t multiplication (if the result is left shifted by 1 bit). Multiplies two 32-bit integers, generates a 64-bit result, and then returns the high 32 bits of the result.

Processor support: Cortex-M4, Cortex-M7, and Armv8-M Mainline processors with the DSP extension [Takes 1 cycle].

The instruction is available in C code via the following idiom:

```
(int32_t) (((int64_t) x * y) >> 32)
```

C code example

```
// Performs a true fractional multiplication but loses the LSB of the result
int32_t x, y, z;
```

```
z = (int32_t) (((int64_t) x * y) >> 32);
z <<= 1;
```

A related instruction is SMULLR, which rounds the 64-bit result of multiplication rather than simply truncating. The rounded instruction provides slightly higher precision. SMULLR is accessed via the idiom:

```
(int32_t) (((int64_t) x * y + 0x80000000LL) >> 32)
```

SMMLA—32-bit multiply with 32-most-significant-bit accumulate

Fractional q31_t multiply accumulate. Multiplies two 32-bit integers, generates a 64-bit result, and adds the high bits of the result to a 32-bit accumulator.

Processor support: Cortex-M4, Cortex-M7, and Armv8-M Mainline processors with the DSP extension [Takes 1 cycle].

The instruction is available in C code via the following idiom:

```
(int32_t) (((int64_t) x * y + ((int64_t) acc << 32)) >> 32);
```

C code example

```
// Performs a true fractional MAC
int32_t x, y, acc;

acc = (int32_t) (((int64_t) x * y + ((int64_t) acc << 32)) >> 32);
acc <<= 1;
```

Related instructions are SMMLAR which includes rounding and SMMLS which performs subtraction rather than addition.

QADD—32-bit saturating addition

Adds two signed integers (or fractional integers) and saturates the result. Positive values are saturated to 0x7FFFFFFF and negative values are saturated to 0x80000000; wrap around does not occur.

The instruction is available in C code only via the intrinsic:

```
int32_t __QADD(int32_t x, uint32_t y)
```

Processor support: Cortex-M4, Cortex-M7, and Armv8-M Mainline processors with the DSP extension [Takes 1 cycle]
C code example

```
int32_t x, y, z;
z = __QADD(x, y);
```

Related instruction:
QSUB—32-bit saturating subtraction

SDIV—32-bit division

Divides two 32-bit values and returns a 32-bit result.
Processor support: Armv7-M and Armv8-M processors [Takes 2–12 cycles]

C code example

```
int32_t x, y, z;
z = x / y;
```

19.7.2.2 16-bit integer instructions

SADD16—Dual 16-bit addition

Adds two 16-bit values using SIMD. If overflow occurs then the result wraps around.

Processor support: Cortex-M4, Cortex-M7, and Armv8-M Mainline processors with the DSP extension [Takes 1 cycle]

C code example

```
int32_t x, y, z;
z = __SADD16(x, y);
```

Related instructions
SSUB16—Dual 16-bit subtraction

QADD16—Dual 16-bit saturating addition

Adds two 16-bit values using SIMD. If an overflow occurs then the result is saturated. Positive values are saturated to 0x7FFF and negative values are saturated to 0x8000.

Processor support: Cortex-M4, Cortex-M7, and Armv8-M Mainline processors with the DSP extension [Takes 1 cycle]

C code example

```
int32_t x, y, z;
z = __QADD16(x, y);
```

Related instructions
QSUB16—Dual 16-bit saturating subtraction

SSAT16—Dual 16-bit saturate

Saturates two signed 16-bit values to bit position B. The resulting values are saturated to the range

$$-2^{B-1} \leq x \leq 2^{B-1} - 1$$

where $B = 1, 2, \ldots 16$. The instruction is available in C code only via the intrinsic:

```
int32_t __ssat16(int32_t x, uint32_t B)
```

Processor support: Cortex-M4, Cortex-M7, and Armv8-M Mainline processors with the DSP extension [Takes 1 cycle]

C code example

```
int32_t x, y;
y = __SSAT16(x, 12); // Saturate to bit 12.
```

SMLABB—Q setting 16-bit signed multiply with 32-bit accumulate, bottom by bottom

Multiplies the low 16 bits of two registers and adds the result to a 32-bit accumulator. If an overflow occurs during the addition then the result will wrap.

Processor Support: Cortex-M4, Cortex-M7, and Armv8-M Mainline processors with the DSP extension [Takes 1 cycle]

The instruction is available in C code using standard arithmetic operations:

```
int16_t x, y;
int32_t acc1, acc2;
acc2 = acc1 + (x * y);
```

SMLAD—Q setting dual 16-bit signed multiply with single 32-bit accumulator

Multiplies two signed 16-bit values and adds both results to a 32-bit accumulator. (top * top) + (bottom * bottom). If an overflow occurs during the addition then the result will wrap. This is the SIMD version of SMLABB.

Processor Support: Cortex-M4, Cortex-M7, and Armv8-M Mainline processors with the DSP extension [Takes 1 cycle]
The instruction is available in C code using the intrinsic:

```
sum = __SMLAD(x, y, z)
```

Conceptually, the intrinsic performs the operations:

```
sum = z + ((short)(x>>16) * (short)(y>>16)) + ((short)x * (short)y)
```

Related instructions are.
SMLADX—Dual 16-bit signed multiply add with 32-bit accumulate. (top * bottom) + (bottom * top).

SMLALBB—16-bit signed multiply with 64-bit accumulate, bottom by bottom

Multiplies the low 16 bits of two registers and adds the result to a 64-bit accumulator.
Processor Support: Cortex-M4, Cortex-M7, and Armv8-M Mainline processors with the DSP extension [Takes 1 cycle]

The instruction is available in C code using standard arithmetic operations:

```
int16_t x, y;
int64_t acc1, acc2;
acc2 = acc1 + (x * y);
```

See also SMLALBT, SMLALTB, SMLALTT.

SMLALD—Dual 16-bit signed multiply with single 64-bit accumulator

Performs two 16-bit multiplications and adds both results to a 64-bit accumulator. (top * top) + (bottom * bottom). If an overflow occurs during the accumulation then the result wraps. The instruction is only available in C code via the intrinsic:

```
uint64_t __SMLALD(uint32_t val1, uint32_t val2, uint64_t val3)
```

C code example

```
// Input arguments each containing 2 packed 16-bit values
// x[31:16] x[15:0], y[31:15] y[15:0]
uint32_t x, y;

// 64-bit accumulator
uint64_t acc;

// Computes acc += x[31:15]*y[31:15] + x[15:0]*y[15:0]
acc = __SMLALD(x, y, acc);
```

Related instructions are

SMLSLD—Dual 16-bit signed multiply subtract with 64-bit accumulate

SMLALDX—Dual 16-bit signed multiply add with 64-bit accumulate. (top * bottom) +(bottom * top).

19.7.2.3 8-bit integer instructions

SADD8—Quad 8-bit addition

Adds four 8-bit values using SIMD. If an overflow occurs then the result wraps around.

Processor support: Cortex-M4, Cortex-M7, and Armv8-M Mainline processors with the DSP extension [Takes 1 cycle]

C code example

```
// Input arguments contain 4 8-bit values each:
// x[31:24] x[23:16] x[15:8] x[7:0]
// y[31:24] y[23:16] y[15:8] y[7:0]
int32_t x, y;

// Result also contains 4 8-bit values:
// z[31:24] z[23:16] z[15:8] z[7:0]
int32_t z;

// Computes without saturation:
//    z[31:24] = x[31:24] + y[31:24]
//    z[25:16] = x[25:16] + y[25:16]
//     z[15:8] = x[15:8]  + y[15:8]
//      z[7:0] = x[7:0]   + y[7:0]

z = __SADD8(x, y);
```

Related instructions

SSUB8—Quad 8-bit subtraction

QADD8—Quad 8-bit saturating addition

Adds four 8-bit values using SIMD. If an overflow occurs then the result is saturated. Positive values are saturated to 0x7F and negative values are saturated to 0x80.

Processor support: Cortex-M4, Cortex-M7, and Armv8-M Mainline processors with the DSP extension [Takes 1 cycle]

C code example

```
// Input arguments contain 4 8-bit values each:
// x[31:24] x[23:16] x[15:8] x[7:0]
// y[31:24] y[23:16] y[15:8] y[7:0]
int32_t x, y;

// Result also contains 4 8-bit values:
// z[31:24] z[23:16] z[15:8] z[7:0]
int32_t z;

// Computes with saturation:
//    z[31:24] = x[31:24] + y[31:24]
//    z[25:16] = x[25:16] + y[25:16]
//     z[15:8] = x[15:8]  + y[15:8]
//      z[7:0] = x[7:0]   + y[7:0]

z = __QADD8(x, y);
```

Related instructions
QSUB8—Quad 8-bit saturating subtraction

19.7.2.4 Floating-point instructions

The floating-point instructions on the Cortex-M33 processors are fairly straightforward and most of them are directly accessible via C code. The instructions execute natively if the Cortex-M33 processor includes the floating-point unit (FPU). Most instructions execute in 1 cycle if the result is not used in the next instruction. The floating-point instructions are IEEE 754 standard compliant [1].

If the FPU is not implemented, then the instructions are emulated in software and execute much more slowly. I provide here only a quick overview of the floating-point instructions.

VABS.F32—Floating-point absolute value

Computes the absolute value of a floating-point value.

```
float x, y;
y = fabs(x);
```

VADD.F32—Floating-point addition

Adds two floating-point values.

```
float x, y, z;
z = x + y;
```

VDIV.F32—Floating-point division

Divides two floating-point values (multicycles).

```
float x, y, z;
z = x / y;
```

VMUL.F32—Floating-point multiplication

Multiplies two floating-point values.

```
float x, y, z;
z = x * y;
```

VMLA.F32—Floating-point multiply accumulate

Multiplies two floating-point values and adds the result to a floating-point accumulator.[f]

```
float x, y, z, acc;
acc = z + (x * y);
```

VFMA.F32—Fused floating-point multiply accumulate

Multiplies two floating-point values and adds the result to a floating-point accumulator. This is slightly different from the standard floating-point multiply accumulate (VMLA), which performs two rounding operations; one after the multiplication and then a second one after the addition. The fused multiply accumulate maintains full precision of the multiplication result and performs a single rounding operation after the addition. This yields a slightly more precise result, with roughly half the rounding error. The main use of the fused MAC is in iterative operations such as divisions or square roots.

```
float x, y, acc;
acc = 0;
__fmaf(x, y, acc);
```

VNEG.F32—Floating-point negation

Multiplies a floating-point value by −1.

```
float x, y;
y = -x;
```

VSQRT.F32—Floating-point square root

Computes the square root of a floating-point value (multicycles).

```
float x, y;
y = __sqrtf(x);
```

VSUB.F32—Floating-point subtraction

Subtracts two floating-point values.

```
float x, y, z;
z = x - y;
```

[f] I recommend not using the multiply accumulate instruction but rather separate multiplication and addition instructions because, by doing so, it is possible to achieve a 1 cycle saving. Refer to Section 19.7.3.4 for further information.

19.7.3 General Cortex-M33 optimization strategies

This section builds upon the instruction set introduction from the previous section and describes common optimization strategies that can be applied to DSP algorithms on the Cortex-M33 processor.

19.7.3.1 Scheduling of load and store instructions

Load or store instructions on the Cortex-M33 processor take 1 cycle, but if the next instruction uses the loaded data, the pipeline could stall due to the nature of its design. To maximize performance, try scheduling other instructions between the load and the data processing instruction. For example, in the dot product example shown in Section 19.3, the loop counter update was placed between the load and the MAC (SMLAL instruction) to avoid the waste clock cycle. This optimization applies to both integer and floating-point operations.

19.7.3.2 Examine the intermediate assembly code

The underlying DSP algorithm may appear straightforward and easy to optimize, but compilers can and do get confused when setting it up. The way forward is to double check the intermediate assembly output of the C compiler to make sure that that the proper assembly instructions are being used. Also, check the intermediate code to see whether the registers are being properly used or whether intermediate results are being stored on the stack. If something does not look right, double check the compiler settings or refer to the compiler documentation.

If you are using Keil MDK, you can enable the generation of intermediate assembly output files by adjusting the project settings as follows: go to the "Listings" tab of the target options window and check "Assembly Listing". Then rebuild the project.

19.7.3.3 Enable optimization

This may seem obvious, but it is worth mentioning. The code generated by a compiler varies greatly between debug mode and optimization mode. The code generated in debug mode is made for ease of debugging and not for the speed of execution.

Compilers also provide various levels of optimization. In Arm Compiler 6, which is used in the Keil MDK, the options provided are listed in Table 19.4.

For the best performance, a high optimization level, e.g., -O3 or -Ofast is typically used. However, I have found that when code is carefully written to schedule instructions in a certain way, using the "–O3" or the high optimization levels may result in a reordering of instructions—which is not, obviously, what you want. Accordingly, you may have to experiment with the optimization level options to determine what is the best performance for a specific algorithm.

19.7.3.4 Performance considerations in MAC instructions

Conceptually, the MAC instruction computes a multiplication followed immediately by an addition. Since the addition requires the result of the multiplication, the overall operation of the MAC can take multiple cycles. However, back-to-back integer MAC operations are possible providing that the result of the MAC is not being used as an input for the multiplication

TABLE 19.4 Optimization levels available in Arm Compiler 6.

Level	Description
-O0	Turns off most optimizations. When debugging is enabled, this option generates code that directly maps to the source code and can, therefore, result in a significantly large program image. This optimization level is not, therefore, recommended for general debugging.
-O1	Restricted Optimization. When debugging is enabled, this option selects a good compromise between image size, performance and the quality of the debug view. This is currently the recommended level for source level debugging.
-O2	High optimization for speed. Code size will increase due to loop unrolling and function inlining. Also, the debug view might be less satisfactory because the mapping of object code to source code is not always that clear.
-O3	Very high optimization for speed. At this optimization the debug visibility is generally poorer.
-Ofast	Enables all optimizations from level 3, including those optimizations that are performed with the fast math (-ffp-mode=fast armclang option). This level also performs other aggressive optimizations that might violate strict compliance with language standards.
-Omax	Maximum optimization. Specifically targets performance optimization. Enables all the optimizations from fast level, together with other aggressive optimizations. Link Time Optimization (LTO) is enabled at this level. This level is not, by default, available in the Keil MDK project option as the generated code is not guaranteed to be full standards-compliant. If this level of optimization is needed, you need to manually add this option in the "Misc control" field.
-Os	Performs optimizations to reduce code size—balancing code size against code speed.
-Oz	Performs optimizations to minimize image size.

stage. In other words, the register(s) for holding the accumulator result is solely used by the MAC at the addition stage.

For floating-point MAC operations, the cycle count for the MAC instruction (VMLA.F32/VFMA.F32) is 3 cycles. By splitting the MAC into separate multiplication (VMUL.F32) and addition (VADD.F32) parts, and by properly scheduling the instructions, by, for example, interleaving two sets of MAC operation sequences, it is possible to perform a floating-point MAC in 2 cycles. *When optimizing for speed for the Cortex-M33 processor, it is good practice to avoid the floating-point MAC and to only use separate arithmetic operations.* The penalty is an increase in code size and not being able to take advantage of the slightly better accuracy in the fused MAC; but the increase in code size is usually negligible and, in most cases, has no impact on the results.

19.7.3.5 Loop unrolling

The Cortex-M33 has a 2 or 3 cycle overhead per loop iteration (3 cycles if the branch target is an unaligned 32-bit instruction). Unrolling a loop by a factor of N effectively reduces the loop overhead to $2/N$ or $3/N$ cycles per iteration. This can be a considerable saving, especially if the inner loop consists of only a few instructions.

You can either manually unroll a loop by repeating a set of instructions or by having the compiler do it for you. The Keil MDK compiler supports *pragmas*, which guides the operation of the compiler. For example, to instruct the compiler to unroll a loop use,

```
#pragma unroll
for(i= 0; i < L; i++)
   {
    ...
   }
```

In Arm Compiler 6, this pragma only has an effect when the optimization level is -O2 or higher. By default, Arm Compiler 6 (i.e., armclang) fully unrolls the loop whereas in Arm Compiler 5 (i.e., armcc) the loop is unrolled by a factor of 4. This pragma can be used with "for", "while", and "do-while" loops. Specifying #pragma unroll(N) causes the loop to be unrolled N times.

Be sure to examine the generated code to make sure that the loop unrolling is effective. *When unrolling, the key thing to watch for is register usage.* Unrolling the loop too much may exceed the number of registers available and intermediate results will, thus, be stored on the stack leading to a degradation of performance.

19.7.3.6 Focus on the inner loop

Many DSP algorithms contain multiple nested loops. The processing in the inner loop is executed most frequently and should be the target of the optimization work. Savings in the inner loop are essentially multiplied by the outer loop counts. Only once the inner loop is in good shape should you consider optimizing the outer loops. Many engineers spend time optimizing nontime critical code with little performance benefits to show for it.

19.7.3.7 Inline functions

There is some overhead associated with each function call. If your function is small and executed frequently, consider inserting the code of the function in-line instead to eliminate the function call overhead.

19.7.3.8 Count registers

The C compiler uses registers to hold intermediate results. If the compiler runs out of registers, then the results are placed on the stack. As a result, costly load and store instructions are needed to access the data on the stack. When developing an algorithm, it is good practice to start with pseudo-code to count the number of registers needed. In your count, be sure to include pointers, intermediate numerical values, and loop counters. Often, the best implementation is the one which uses the fewest intermediate registers.

Be especially careful with register usage in fixed-point algorithms. The Cortex-M33 processor only has 13 general-purpose registers available for storing integer variables. The floating-point unit, on the other hand, adds 32 floating-point registers to the 13 general-purpose registers. The large number of floating-point registers makes it easy to apply loop unrolling and grouping of load and store instructions.

19.7.3.9 Use the right amount of precision

The Cortex-M33 processor provides several multiply accumulate instructions which operate on 32-bit numbers. Some provide 64-bit results (e.g., SMLAL) and others provide 32-bit results (e.g., SMMUL). Although they both execute in a single instruction, SMLAL requires two registers to hold the 64-bit result and may execute more slowly. This could be caused by the values being frequently transferred between the processor and the memory or could be because the registers have been used up. In general, 64-bit intermediate results are preferred, but check the generated code to make sure that the implementation is efficient.

19.7.4 Instruction limitations

The set of DSP instructions available for the Cortex-M33 processor is quite comprehensive, but there are a few gaps that make it different from some of the full feature DSP processors. These differences are:

- Saturating fixed-point arithmetic is only available for additions and subtractions, but not for MAC instructions. For performance reasons, you will often use the fixed-point MAC and need to scale down intermediate operations to avoid overflows.
- There is no SIMD MAC support for 8-bit values; use 16-bit SIMD MAC instead.

19.8 Writing optimized DSP code for the Cortex-M33 processor

This section shows how to use the optimization guidelines and DSP instructions to develop optimized code. I look at the Biquad filter, FFT butterfly, and FIR filter. For each, I start with generic C code and then map to the Cortex-M33 DSP instructions while applying the optimization strategies.

19.8.1 Biquad filter

A Biquad filter is a second order recursive or infinite impulse response (IIR) filter. Biquad filters are used throughout audio processing for equalization, tone controls, loudness compensation, graphic equalizers, crossovers, etc. Higher order filters can be constructed using cascades of second-order Biquad sections. In many applications, Biquad filters are the most computationally intensive part of the processing chain. Biquad filters are also similar to PID controllers used in control systems and many of the techniques developed in this section apply directly to PID controllers.

A Biquad filter is a linear time-invariant system. When the input to the filter is a sine wave, the output is a sine wave at the same frequency but with a different magnitude and phase. The relationship between the filter's input and output magnitudes and phases is called *"frequency response"*. A Biquad filter has 5 coefficients and the frequency response is determined by those coefficients. By changing coefficients, it is possible to implement lowpass, highpass, bandpass, shelf, and notch filters. For example, Fig. 19.8 shows how the magnitude response of an audio "peaking filter" varies in response to coefficient changes. Filter coefficients are typically generated by design equations[g] [2] or by using tools such as Matlab.

---

[g]Useful design formulas for computing Biquad coefficients for a wide number of filter types have been provided by Robert Bristow-Johnson. See https://webaudio.github.io/Audio-EQ-Cookbook/audio-eq-cookbook.html.

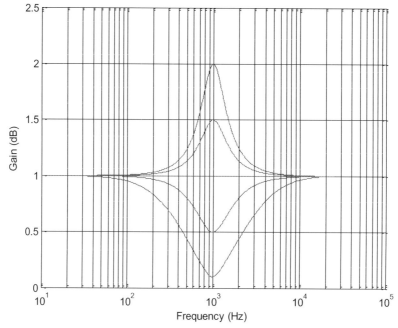

FIG. 19.8 Typical magnitude response of a Biquad filter. This type of filter is called a "peaking filter" and boosts or cuts frequency by around 1 kHz. The plots show several variants with center gains of 0.1, 0.5, 1.0, 1.5, and 2.0.

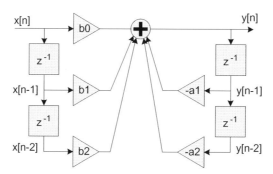

FIG. 19.9 Direct Form I Biquad filter. This implements a second-order filter and is a building block used in higher order filters.

The structure of a Biquad filter implemented in Direct Form I is shown in Fig. 19.9. The input $x[n]$ arrives and feeds a delay line with two sampling stages. The boxes labeled z^{-1} represent a one sample delay. The left-hand side of the figure is the feed-forward processing and the right-hand side is the feedback processing. Because the Biquad filter includes feedback, it is also referred to as a *recursive* filter. A Direct Form I Biquad filter has five coefficients, four state variables, and takes a total of five MACs per output sample.

Since the system shown in Fig. 19.9 is linear and time invariant, we can switch the feedforward and feedback sections as shown in Fig. 19.10. With this change, the delay lines for the feedback and feed-forward sections can both take the same input and can thus be

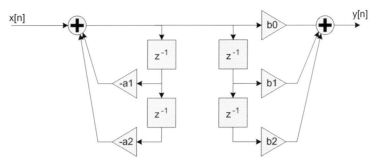

FIG. 19.10   In this figure, the feed-forward and feedback portions of the filter have been exchanged. The two delay chains receive the same input and can be combined as shown in Fig. 19.11.

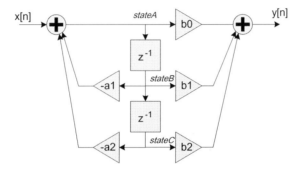

FIG. 19.11   The Direct Form II Biquad structure. This requires five multiplications but only two delay state variables. It is preferred when undertaking floating-point processing.

combined. This leads to the structure shown in Fig. 19.11, which is called Direct Form II. The Direct Form II filter has five coefficients, two state variables, and requires a total of five MACs per output sample. *Direct Form I and Direct Form II filters are mathematically equivalent.*

   The obvious advantage of the Direct Form II filter over Direct Form I is that it requires half the number of state variables. Other benefits of each structure are more subtle. If you study the Direct Form I filter you will notice that the input state variables hold delayed versions of the input. Similarly, the output state variables contain delayed versions of the output. Thus, if the gain of the filter does not exceed 1.0 then the state variables in Direct Form I will never overflow.[h] The state variables in the Direct Form II filter, on the other hand, have no direct relationship to the input or output of the filter. In practice, the Direct Form II state variables have a much higher dynamic range than the inputs and outputs of the filter. Thus, even if the gain of the filter does not exceed 1.0, it is possible for the state variables in Direct Form II to exceed 1.0. Because of this, Direct Form I implementations are preferred for fixed-point implementations (for better numerical behavior) while Direct Form II is preferred for floating-point implementations (because there are fewer state variables).

[h]This is not 100% true; there are cases where you can still have overflows. Nevertheless, this rule of thumb is still useful.

Standard C code for computing a single stage of an implemented Biquad filter using Direct Form II is shown below. The function processes a total of blockSize samples through the filter. The input to the filter is taken from the buffer inPtr[] and the output is written to outPtr[]. Floating-point arithmetic is used.

```
// b0, b1, b2, a1, and a2 are the filter coefficients.
// a1 and a2 are negated.
// stateA, stateB, and stateC represent intermediate state variables.

for (sample = 0; sample < blockSize; sample++)
   {
   stateA = *inPtr++ + a1*stateB + a2*stateC;
   *outPtr++ = b0*stateA + b1*stateB + b2*stateC;
   stateC = stateB;
   stateB = stateA;
   }

// Persist state variables for the next call
state[0] = stateB;
state[1] = stateC;
```

The intermediate state variables stateA, stateB, and stateC are shown in Fig. 19.11.

Next, I will examine the inner loop of the function and see how many cycles are required. I will break down the operation into individual Cortex-M33 instructions:

```
stateA = *inPtr++;      // Data fetch [1 cycle]
stateA += a1*stateB;    // MAC with result used in next inst [3 cycles]
stateA += a2*stateC;    // MAC with result used in next inst [3 cycles]
out = b0*stateA;        // Mult with result used in next inst [2 cycles]
out += b1*stateB;       // MAC with result used in next inst [3 cycles]
out += b2*stateC;       // MAC with result used in next inst [3 cycles]
*outPtr++ = out;        // Data store [1 cycle]
stateC = stateB;        // Register move [1 cycle]
stateB = stateA;        // Register move [1 cycle]
                        // Loop overhead [2 to 3 cycles]
```

Altogether, the inner loop of the generic C code requires a total of 20–21 cycles per sample to execute.

The first step in optimizing the function is to split the MAC instructions into separate multiplications and additions. Then reordering the computation so that the result of a floating-point operation is not required in the next cycle. Some additional variables are used to hold the intermediate results.

```
stateA = *inPtr++       // Data fetch [1 cycle]
prod1 = a1*stateB;      // Mult [1 cycle]
prod2 = a2*stateC;      // Mult [1 cycle]
stateA += prod1;        // Addition [1 cycle]
prod4 = b1*stateB;      // Mult [1 cycle]
```

```
stateA += prod2;        // Add [1 cycle]
out = b2*stateC;        // Mult [1 cycle]
prod3 = b0*stateA       // Mult [1 cycle]
out += prod4;           // Add [1 cycle]
out += prod3;           // Add [1 cycle]
stateC = stateB;        // Register move [1 cycle]
stateB = stateA;        // Register move [1 cycle]
*outPtr++ = out;        // Data store [1 cycle]
                        // Loop overhead [2 to 3 cycles]
```

These changes reduce the inner loop of the Biquad from 20 to 15 cycles. This is a step in the right direction, but there are a number of techniques that can be applied to the Biquad for further improvement:

1. Eliminate the register moves by careful use of intermediate variables. The state variables in the structure from top to bottom are initially:

   stateA, stateB, stateC

   After the first output is computed, the state variables are shifted right. Instead of actually shifting the variables I will reuse them in situ using the ordering:

   stateC, stateA, stateB

   After the next iteration, the state variables are reordered as

   stateB, stateC, stateA

   And finally, after the fourth iteration, the variables are

   stateA, stateB, stateC

   The cycle then repeats and it has a natural period of three samples. That is, if we start with

   stateA, stateB, stateC

   then after three output samples are computed we will be back to:

   stateA, stateB, stateC

2. Unroll the loop by a factor of 3 to reduce loop overhead. The loop overhead of 2–3 cycles will be amortized over three samples.

3. Schedule instructions to avoid stall cycles in the pipeline (applicable to the Cortex-M33 processor). If a result is produced in the third stage of the pipeline for an instruction (e.g., a memory load or a MAC) and the result is immediately used by the next instruction in the second stage of the pipeline, a stall cycle could occur. To avoid the stall, another instruction should be scheduled so that it is executed between the load/MAC instruction and the other instruction that uses the result of the load/MAC instruction.

4. Group load and store instructions (only applicable to the Cortex-M3/M4 processors). In the above code, the load and store instructions are isolated, with each requiring 2 cycles (for the Cortex-M3/M4 processors). By loading and storing several results, the second and subsequent memory accesses only takes 1 cycle.

The resulting code is now quite a bit longer due to loop unrolling:

```
in1 = *inPtr++;        // Data fetch [1 cycle]
in2 = *inPtr++;        // Data fetch [1 cycle]
in3 = *inPtr++;        // Data fetch [1 cycle]

prod1 = a1*stateB;     // Mult [1 cycle]
prod2 = a2*stateC;     // Mult [1 cycle]
stateA = in1+prod1;    // Addition [1 cycle]
prod4 = b1*stateB;     // Mult [1 cycle]
stateA += prod2;       // Add [1 cycle]
out1 = b2*stateC;      // Mult [1 cycle]
prod3 = b0*stateA;     // Mult [1 cycle]
out1 += prod4;         // Add [1 cycle]
out1 += prod3;         // Add [1 cycle]

prod1 = a1*stateA;     // Mult [1 cycle]
prod2 = a2*stateB;     // Mult [1 cycle]
stateC = in2+prod1;    // Addition [1 cycle]
prod4 = b1*stateA;     // Mult [1 cycle]
stateC += prod2;       // Add [1 cycle]
out2 = b2*stateB;      // Mult [1 cycle]
prod3 = b0*stateC;     // Mult [1 cycle]
out2 += prod4;         // Add [1 cycle]
out2 += prod3;         // Add [1 cycle]

prod1 = a1*stateC;     // Mult [1 cycle]
prod2 = a2*stateA;     // Mult [1 cycle]
stateB = in3+prod1;    // Addition [1 cycle]
prod4 = b1*stateC;     // Mult [1 cycle]
stateB += prod2;       // Add [1 cycle]
out3 = b2*stateA;      // Mult [1 cycle]
prod3 = b0*stateB;     // Mult [1 cycle]
out3 += prod4;         // Add [1 cycle]
out3 += prod3;         // Add [1 cycle]

outPtr++ = out1;       // Data store [1 cycle]
outPtr++ = out2;       // Data store [1 cycle]
outPtr++ = out3;       // Data store [1 cycle]
                       // Loop overhead [2 to 3 cycles]
```

Counting cycles, we end up with 35 or 36 cycles to compute three output samples or 12 cycles per sample. The code presented here operates on vectors that are a multiple of three samples in length. Generally, if the total number of samples is not a multiple of 3, the code needs another stage which handles the remaining one or two samples (this is not shown in the above code).

Is it possible to optimize this further? How far can we take loop unrolling? The core arithmetic operations for the Biquad filter consists of five multiplications and four additions. These operations when properly ordered to avoid stalls take 9 cycles on the Cortex-M33 processor. The memory load and store each take at best 1 cycle. Putting this together, the absolute lowest number of cycles for a Biquad is 11 cycles per sample. This assumes that all data loads and stores are 1 cycle and there is no loop overhead. If we unroll the inner loop still further, the following would be found:

Unroll by	Total Cycles	Cycles/sample
3	36	12
6	71	11.833
9	104	11.55
12	137	11.41

At some point, the processor runs out of intermediate registers to hold the input and output variables and no further gains are possible. Unrolling by three or six samples is a reasonable choice. Beyond this the gains are marginal.

19.8.2 Fast Fourier Transform

The Fast Fourier Transform (FFT) is a key signal processing algorithm that is used in frequency-domain processing, compression, and fast filtering algorithms. The FFT is actually a fast algorithm to compute the discrete Fourier transform (DFT). The DFT transforms an N-point time-domain signal $x[n]$ into an N separate frequency component $X[k]$, where each component is a complex value containing both magnitude and phase information. The DFT of a finite-length sequence of length N is defined as:

$$X[k] = \sum_{n=0}^{N-1} x[n] W_N^{kn}, k = 0,1,2,\ldots,N-1$$

where W_N^k is a complex value representing the kth root of unity:

$$W_N^k = e^{-j2\pi k/N} = \cos(2\pi k/N) - j\sin(2\pi k/N).$$

The inverse transform which converts from the frequency domain back to the time domain is nearly identical:

$$x[n] = \frac{1}{N} \sum_{n=0}^{N-1} X[k] W_N^{-kn}, n = 0,1,2,\ldots,N-1$$

Directly implementing the formulas above would require $O(N^2)$ operations to compute all N samples of the forward or inverse transform. With the FFT we will see that this reduces to $O(N\log_2 N)$ operations. The savings can be substantial for large values of N, with the FFT having made possible many new signal processing applications. The FFT was first described by Cooley and Tukey in 1965 [3] and a good general reference for FFT algorithms can be found here [4].

FFTs generally work best when the length N is a composite number that can be represented as a product of small factors:

$$N = N_1 \times N_2 \times N_3 \cdots N_m$$

The easiest to follow algorithms are when N is a power of 2; they are called radix-2 transforms. The FFT follows a "divide and conquer" algorithm and an N point FFT is computed using two separate $N/2$ point transforms, together with a few additional operations. There are two main classes of FFTs: decimation-in-time and decimation-in-frequency. Decimation-in-time algorithms compute an N-point FFT by combining $N/2$-point FFTs of the even and odd time-domain samples. Decimation-in-frequency algorithms are similar and compute the even and odd frequency-domain samples using two $N/2$-point FFTs. Both algorithms have a similar number of mathematical operations. The CMSIS-DSP library uses decimation-in-frequency algorithms and, in this chapter, I focus on these.

The first stage of an eight-point radix-2 decimation-in-frequency FFT is shown in Fig. 19.12. The eight-point transform is computed using two separate four-point transforms.

The multiplicative factor W_N^k defined earlier appears above and the values are referred to as *twiddle factors*. For speed, twiddle factors are precomputed and stored in an array rather than being computed in the FFT function.

The decomposition continues and the four-point FFTs are each decomposed into two 2-point FFTs. Then at the end, four 2-point FFTs are computed. The final structure is shown in Fig. 19.13. Note that there are $\log_2 8 = 3$ stages in the processing.

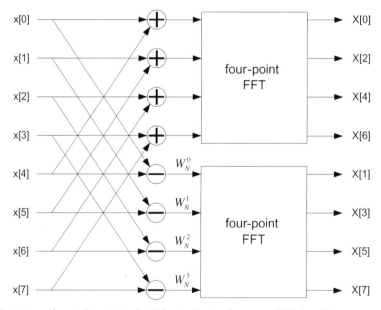

FIG. 19.12   First stage of an eight-point radix-2 decimation-in-frequency FFT algorithm.

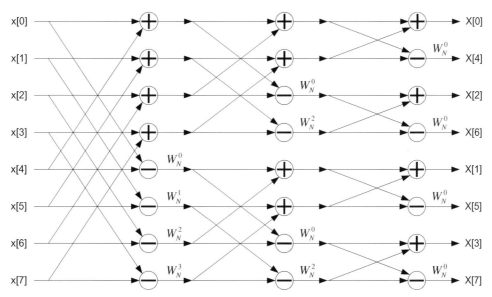

FIG. 19.13   Overall structure of an eight-point FFT. There are three stages and each stage consist of four butterflies.

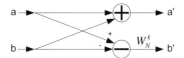

FIG. 19.14   Single butterfly operation.

Each stage consists of four *butterfly* operations and a single butterfly is illustrated in Fig. 19.14.

Each butterfly includes a complex addition, subtraction, and multiplication. A property of the butterfly is that it can be done in place in memory. That is, it can fetch the complex values a and b, perform the operations and then place them back into the memory in the same locations where the array is. In fact, the entire FFT can be done in place with the output being generated in the same buffer that was used for the input.

The input in Fig. 19.13 is in normal order and proceeds sequentially from x[0] to x[7]. The output after processing is scrambled and the ordering is referred to as *bit-reversed order*. To understand the order, write the indexes 0–7 in binary, flip the bits, and convert back to decimal:

$0 \rightarrow 000 \rightarrow 000 \rightarrow 0$
$1 \rightarrow 001 \rightarrow 100 \rightarrow 4$
$2 \rightarrow 010 \rightarrow 010 \rightarrow 2$
$3 \rightarrow 011 \rightarrow 110 \rightarrow 6$
$4 \rightarrow 100 \rightarrow 001 \rightarrow 1$
$5 \rightarrow 101 \rightarrow 101 \rightarrow 5$
$6 \rightarrow 110 \rightarrow 011 \rightarrow 3$
$7 \rightarrow 111 \rightarrow 111 \rightarrow 7$

Bit-reversed ordering is a natural side effect of the in-place processing. Most FFT algorithms (including the ones in the CMSIS-DSP Library) provide the option of reordering the output values back into sequential order.

Butterflies are at the heart of FFT algorithms and I will analyze and optimize the computation for a single butterfly in this section. The eight-point FFT requires $3 * 4 = 12$ butterflies. In general, a radix-2 FFT of length N has $\log_2 N$ stages each with $N/2$ butterflies for a total of $(N/2)\log_2 N$ butterflies. The decomposition into butterflies yields the $O(N\log_2 N)$ operation count for FFTs. In addition to the butterflies themselves, the FFT requires indexing to keep track of which values should be used in each stage of the algorithm. In this analysis, I will ignore this indexing overhead, but it must be accounted for in the final algorithm.

The C code for a floating-point butterfly is shown below. The variables index1 and index2 are the array offsets for the two inputs to the butterfly. The array x[] holds interleaved data (real, imag, real, imag, etc.).

C code implementation of a floating-point butterfly

```
// Fetch two complex samples from memory [4 cycles]
x1r = x[index1];
x1i = x[index1+1];

x2r = x[index2];
x2i = x[index2+1];

// Compute the sum and difference [4 cycles]
sum_r = (x1r + x2r);
sum_i = (x1i + x2i);

diff_r = (x1r - x2r);
diff_i = (x1i - x2i);

// Store sum result to memory [2 cycles]
x[index1] = sum_r;
x[index1+1] = sum_i;

// Fetch complex twiddle factor coefficients [2 cycles]
twiddle_r = *twiddle++;
twiddle_i = *twiddle++;

// Complex multiplication of the difference [6 cycles]
prod_r = diff_r * twiddle_r - diff_i * twiddle_i;
prod_i = diff_r * twiddle_i + diff_i * twiddle_r;

// Store back to memory [2 cycles]
x[index2] = prod_r;
x[index2+1] = prod_i;
```

The code also shows cycle counts for the various operations and it can be seen that a single butterfly takes 20 cycles on a Cortex-M33 processor. Looking more closely at the cycle count, it can also be seen that 10 cycles are due to memory accesses and 10 cycles are due to arithmetic operations. To avoid stall cycles, instructions should be scheduled carefully as explained earlier in this chapter (see Section 19.8.1). Even so, on a Cortex-M33 processor a radix-2 butterfly is dominated by memory accesses and this will be true for the overall FFT algorithm. Little can be done to speed up the radix-2 FFT butterfly code. Instead, to improve performance, we need to consider higher radix algorithms.

In a radix-2 algorithm, two complex values are operated on at a time and there is a total of $\log_2 N$ stages of processing. At each stage we need to load N complex values, operate on them and then store them back into the memory. In a radix-4 algorithm, four complex values are operated on at a time and there is a total of $\log_4 N$ stages. This cuts memory access down by a factor of 2. Higher radixes can be considered as long as we do not run out of intermediate registers. I have found that up to

- Radix-4 butterflies using the fixed-point format, and
- Radix-8 butterflies using the floating-point format

can be efficiently implemented on a Cortex-M33 processor.

A radix-4 algorithm is limited to FFT lengths, which are powers of 4: {4, 16, 64, 256, 1024, etc.}, while a radix-8 algorithm is restricted to lengths which are powers of 8: {8, 64, 512, 4096, etc.} To efficiently implement any length which is a power of 2, a *mixed-radix* algorithm is used. The trick is to use as many radix-8 stages as possible (they are the most efficient) and then use a single radix-2 or radix-4 stage, as needed, to achieve the desired length. Here is how the various FFT lengths break down into butterfly stages:

Length	Butterflies
16	2×8
32	4×8
64	8×8
128	$2 \times 8 \times 8$
256	$4 \times 8 \times 8$

The FFT function in the CMSIS-DSP library uses this mixed radix approach for floating-point data types. For fixed-point, you must select either radix-2 or radix-4. In general, pick the radix-4 fixed-point algorithm if it supports the length you want.

Many applications also require that inverse FFT transforms are computed. Comparing the equations for the forward and inverse DFTs, it will be seen that the inverse transform has a scale factor of (1/N) and that the sign of the exponent of the twiddle factors is inverted. This leads to two different ways of implementing inverse FFTs:

1. Compute the forward FFT as before but use a new twiddle factor table. The new table is created using positive rather than negative exponents. This leads to twiddle factors simply being conjugated. Then divide by N.
2. Keep the same twiddle factor table as before but modify the FFT code to negate the imaginary portion of the twiddle factor table while performing twiddle factor multiplications. Then divide by N.

Both approaches detailed above are somewhat inefficient. Approach (1) saves on code space but doubles the size of the twiddle factor table; Approach (2) reuses the twiddle factor table but requires more code. Another approach is to use the mathematical relationship:

$$\text{IFFT}(X) = \frac{1}{N}\text{conj}\left(\text{FFT}\left(\text{conj}(X)\right)\right)$$

This requires conjugating the data twice. The first (inner) conjugate is carried out at the start and the second conjugate (outer) can be combined with the division by N. The real overhead of this approach compared to approach (2) is that, roughly, only the inner conjugate is required—which does not substantially increase the processing time.

When implementing an FFT in the fixed-point format it is crucial to understand scaling and the growth of values throughout the algorithm. A butterfly performs addition and subtraction operations and it is possible for the values at the output of the butterfly to be double those at the input. In the worst-case scenario, values double at every stage and the output is N times larger than the input. Intuitively, the worst case occurs if all input values equal 1.0. This represents a DC signal and the resulting FFT is all zeros except that bin $k = 0$ contains a value of N. In order to avoid overflow in fixed-point implementations, each butterfly stage must incorporate a scale of 0.5 as part of the addition and subtraction. This is in fact the scaling used by the fixed-point FFT functions in the CMSIS-DSP library, with the net result being that the output of the FFT is scaled down by $1/N$.

The standard FFT operates on complex data and there are variations for handling real-data. Typically, an N-point real FFT is computed using a complex N/2 point FFT, together with some additional steps. An excellent reference can be found in Ref. [5].

19.8.3 FIR filter

The third standard DSP algorithm that I will consider is the Finite Impulse Response (FIR) filter. FIR filters occur in a number of audio, video, control algorithms, and are used for analyzing data problems. FIR filters have several useful properties compared to IIR filters (like the Biquad):

1. FIR Filters are inherently stable. This is true for all possible coefficients.
2. Linear phase can be achieved by making the coefficients symmetric.
3. Simple design formulas.
4. Well-behaved even when implemented using fixed-point.

The operation of an FIR filter can be represented by the following formula: Let $x[n]$ be the input to the filter at time n and let $y[n]$ be the output. The output is computed using the difference equation:

$$y[n] = \sum_{k=0}^{N-1} x[n-k]h[k]$$

where $h[n]$ are the filter coefficients. In the difference equation above, the FIR filter has N coefficients

$$\{h[0], h[1], \cdots, h[N-1]\}$$

and the output is computed using N previous input samples

$$\{x[n], x[n-1], \cdots, x[n-(N-1)]\}$$

The previous input samples are called the *state variables*. Each output of the filter requires N multiplications and $N-1$ additions. A modern DSP can compute an N point FIR filter in roughly N cycles.

The most straightforward way of organizing the state data in the memory is to use a FIFO as shown in Fig. 19.15. When sample $x[n]$ arrives, the previous samples $x[n-1]$ through $x[n-N]$ are shifted down by one position and then $x[n]$ is written to the buffer. Shifting data like this is very wasteful and requires $N-1$ memory reads and $N-1$ memory writes per input sample.

A better way to organize the data is to use a circular buffer as shown in Fig. 19.16. The circular state index points to the oldest sample in the buffer. When sample $x[n]$ arrives, it overwrites the oldest sample in the buffer and then circularly increments. That is, it increments in normal fashion, and if the end of the buffer is reached it wraps around back to the beginning.

The standard C code for the FIR filter is shown below. The function is designed to operate on a block of samples and incorporates circular addressing. The outer loop is over the samples in the block while the inner loop is over the filter taps as shown in the aforementioned difference equation.

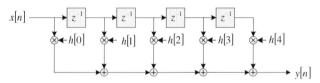

FIG. 19.15   FIR filter implemented using a shift register. In practice this is rarely used since the state variables have to be shifted right whenever a new sample arrives.

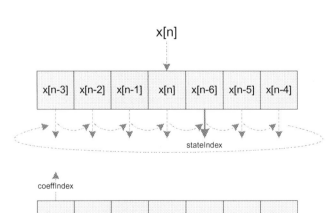

FIG. 19.16   FIR filter implemented using a circular buffer for the state variables (top). The stateIndex pointer advances to the right and then circularly wraps when it reaches the end of the buffer. The coefficients are accessed in linear order.

Standard C code for implementing a FIR filter by utilizing a circular buffer. The code processes a block of samples.

```
// Block-based FIR filter.
// N equals the length of the filter (number of taps)
// blockSize equals the number of samples to process
// state[] is the state variable buffer and contains the previous N
//     samples of the input
// stateIndex points to the oldest sample in the state buffer. It
//     will be overwritten with the most recent input sample.
// coeffs[] holds the N coefficients
// inPtr and outPtr point to the input and output buffers, respectively

for(sample=0;sample<blockSize;sample++)
{
   // Copy the new sample into
   state[stateIndex++] = inPtr[sample]
   if (stateIndex >= N)
     stateIndex = 0;

   sum = 0.0f;
   for(i=0;i<N;i++)
     {
        sum += state[stateIndex++] * coeffs[N-i];
        if (stateIndex >= N)
         stateIndex = 0;
     }
   outPtr[sample] = sum;
}
```

In order to compute each output sample, N state variables $\{x[n], x[n-1], \cdots, x[n-(N-1)]\}$ and N coefficients $\{h[0], h[1], \cdots, h[N-1]\}$ have to be fetched from the memory. DSPs have been optimized to compute FIR filters. The state and coefficients can be fetched in parallel with the MACs and the corresponding memory pointers incremented. DSPs also have hardware support for circular addressing and can perform circular addressing without any overhead. Using these features together, a modern DSP can compute an N-point FIR filter in about N cycles.

The Cortex-M33 processor will have difficulty implementing the FIR code efficiently. The Cortex-M33 processor does not have native support for circular addressing and the bulk of the time will be spent evaluating the "if" statement in the inner loop. A better approach is to use a FIFO for the state buffer and to shift in a block of input data. Instead of shifting the FIFO data every sample, just shift it once every block. This requires increasing the length of the state buffer by blockSize samples. This process is illustrated in Fig. 19.17 for a block size of four samples. Input data is shifted in on the right side of the block. The oldest data then appears on the left-hand side. Coefficients continue to be time flipped as shown in Fig. 19.16.

Four new input samples are
shifted in

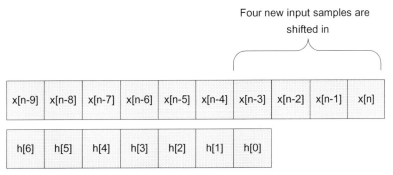

FIG. 19.17 Work around for circular addressing. The size of the state buffer is increased by blockSize-1 samples which in this example equals three samples.

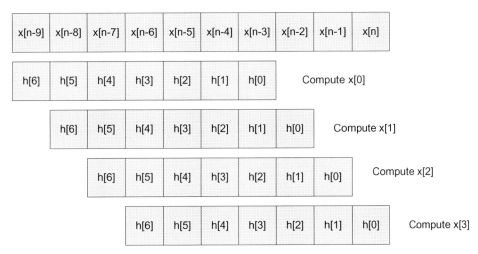

FIG. 19.18 With the work around for circular addressing, each inner loop computation operates on continuous data.

The coefficients in Fig. 19.17 have $h[0]$ aligned with $x[n-3]$. This is the position needed to compute the first output $[n-3]$:

$$y[n-3] = \sum_{k=0}^{6} x[n-3-k]h[k]$$

To compute the next output sample, the coefficients conceptually shift over by one. This then repeats for all output samples (Fig. 19.18). By using this block-based approach with a FIFO state buffer, we are able to eliminate the costly circular addressing from the inner loop.

To optimize the FIR filter further, there is a further need to again focus on memory access. In the standard FIR implementation, N coefficients and N state variables are accessed for each output sample. The approach to take is to simultaneously compute multiple output samples and cache intermediate state variables in the registers. In the following example, four output samples are computed simultaneously.[i] A single coefficient is loaded and then multiplied by four state variables. This has the net effect of reducing memory access by a factor of 4. For the sake of simplicity and brevity, the code shown below only supports block sizes that are a multiple of four samples. The CMSIS-DSP library, on the other hand, is general purpose and imposes no constraints on the length of the filter or block size. Even with these simplifications, the code is still quite involved.

Partially optimized floating-point FIR code. The example shows how the number of memory accesses can be reduced by simultaneously computing multiple results.

```
/*
** Block based FIR filter. Arguments:
** numTaps - Length of the filter. Must be a multiple of 4
** pStateBase - Points to the start of the state variable array
** pCoeffs - Points to the start of the coefficient array
** pSrc - Points to the array of input data
** pDst - Points to where the result should be written
** blockSize - Number of samples to process. Must be a multiple of 4.
*/

void arm_fir_f32(
    unsigned int numTaps,
    float *pStateBase,
    float *pCoeffs,
    float *pSrc,
    float *pDst,
    unsigned int blockSize)
{
    float *pState;
    float *pStateEnd;
    float *px, *pb;
    float acc0, acc1, acc2, acc3;
    float x0, x1, x2, x3, coeff;
    float p0, p1, p2, p3;
    unsigned int tapCnt, blkCnt;

    /* Shift the data in the FIFO down and store the new block of input data
    ** at the end of the buffer. */
```

---

[i] The number of outputs to simultaneously compute depends upon how many registers are available. In the CMSIS-DSP library, Q31 FIR three samples are simultaneously computed. In the floating-point version, eight samples are simultaneously computed.

```
        /* Points to the start of the state buffer */
        pState = pStateBase;

        /* Points ahead blockSize samples */
        pStateEnd = &pStateBase[blockSize];

        /* Unroll by 4 for speed */
        tapCnt = numTaps >> 2u;
        while(tapCnt > 0u)
        {
                *pState++ = *pStateEnd++;
                *pState++ = *pStateEnd++;
                *pState++ = *pStateEnd++;
                *pState++ = *pStateEnd++;

                /* Decrement the loop counter */
                tapCnt-;
        }

        /* pStateEnd points to where the new input data should be written */
        pStateEnd = &pStateBase[(numTaps - 1u)];
        pState = pStateBase;

        /* Apply loop unrolling and compute 4 output values simultaneously.
         * The variables acc0 ... acc3 hold output values that are being computed:
         *
         *    acc0 = b[numTaps-1]*x[n-numTaps-1]+b[numTaps-2]*x[n-numTaps-2] +
         *           b[numTaps-3]*x[n-numTaps-3]+ ... + b[0]*x[0]
         *    acc1 = b[numTaps-1]*x[n-numTaps]+b[numTaps-2]*x[n-numTaps-1] +
         *           b[numTaps-3]*x[n-numTaps-2] +... + b[0]*x[1]
         *    acc2 = b[numTaps-1]*x[n-numTaps+1]+b[numTaps-2]*x[n-numTaps] +
         *           b[numTaps-3]*x[n-numTaps-1] + ... + b[0]*x[2]
         *    acc3 = b[numTaps-1]*x[n-numTaps+2] + b[numTaps-2]*x[n-numTaps+1] +
         *           b[numTaps-3]*x[n-numTaps] + ... + b[0]*x[3]
         */

blkCnt = blockSize >> 2;

/* Processing with loop unrolling. Compute 4 outputs at a time. */
while(blkCnt > 0u)
{
        /* Copy four new input samples into the state buffer */
        *pStateEnd++ = *pSrc++;
        *pStateEnd++ = *pSrc++;
        *pStateEnd++ = *pSrc++;
        *pStateEnd++ = *pSrc++;

        /* Set all accumulators to zero */
```

```
acc0 = 0.0f;
acc1 = 0.0f;
acc2 = 0.0f;
acc3 = 0.0f;

/* Initialize state pointer */
px = pState;

/* Initialize coeff pointer */
pb = pCoeffs;

/* Read the first three samples from the state buffer:
      x[n-numTaps], x[n-numTaps-1], x[n-numTaps-2] */
x0 = *px++;
x1 = *px++;
x2 = *px++;

/* Loop unrolling. Process 4 taps at a time. */
tapCnt = numTaps >> 2u;

/* Loop over the number of taps. Unroll by a factor of 4.
** Repeat until we have computed numTaps-4 coefficients. */
while(tapCnt > 0u)
{
    /* Read the b[numTaps-1] coefficient */
    coeff = *(pb++);

    /* Read x[n-numTaps-3] sample */
    x3 = *(px++);

    /* p =b[numTaps-1] * x[n-numTaps] */
    p0 = x0 * coeff;

    /* p1 =b[numTaps-1] * x[n-numTaps-1] */
    p1 = x1 * coeff;

    /* p2 =b[numTaps-1] * x[n-numTaps-2] */
    p2 = x2 * coeff;

    /* p3 =b[numTaps-1] * x[n-numTaps-3] */
    p3 = x3 * coeff;

    /* Accumulate */
    acc0 += p0;
    acc1 += p1;
    acc2 += p2;
    acc3 += p3;

    /* Read the b[numTaps-2] coefficient */
    coeff = *(pb++);
```

```
/* Read x[n-numTaps-4] sample */
x0 = *(px++);

/* Perform the multiply-accumulate */
p0 = x1 * coeff;
p1 = x2 * coeff;
p2 = x3 * coeff;
p3 = x0 * coeff;
acc0 += p0;
acc1 += p1;
acc2 += p2;
acc3 += p3;

/* Read the b[numTaps-3] coefficient */
coeff = *(pb++);

/* Read x[n-numTaps-5] sample */
x1 = *(px++);

/* Perform the multiply-accumulates */
p0 = x2 * coeff;
p1 = x3 * coeff;
p2 = x0 * coeff;
p3 = x1 * coeff;
acc0 += p0;
acc1 += p1;
acc2 += p2;
acc3 += p3;

/* Read the b[numTaps-4] coefficient */
coeff = *(pb++);

/* Read x[n-numTaps-6] sample */
x2 = *(px++);

/* Perform the multiply-accumulates */
p0 = x3 * coeff;
p1 = x0 * coeff;
p2 = x1 * coeff;
p3 = x2 * coeff;
acc0 += p0;
acc1 += p1;
acc2 += p2;
acc3 += p3;

/* Read the b[numTaps-5] coefficient */
```

```
                coeff = *(pb++);

                /* Read x[n-numTaps-7] sample */
                x3 = *(px++);

                tapCnt-;
        }

        /* Advance the state pointer to process the next
         * group of 4 samples */
        pState = pState + 4;

        /* Store the 4 results in the destination buffer. */
        *pDst++ = acc0;
        *pDst++ = acc1;
        *pDst++ = acc2;
        *pDst++ = acc3;

        blkCnt-;
    }
}
```

Depending on the compilation toolchain and optimization settings of the compiler, the inner loop of the floating-point FIR filter, which performs a total of 16 MACs, might take around 43 cycles. The CMSIS-DSP library takes this a step further and computes eight intermediate sums, leading to a further performance gain in the inner loop.

The q15 FIR filter functions in the CMSIS-DSP library use similar memory optimizations to the floating-point function example that I have just presented. As a further optimization, the q15 functions apply the dual 16-bit SIMD capabilities of the Cortex-M33 processor. Two q15 functions are provided:

arm_fir_q15()—uses 64-bit intermediate accumulators and the SMLALD and SMLALDX instructions.

arm_fir_fast_q15()—uses 32-bit intermediate accumulators and the SMLAD and SMLADX instructions.

References

[1] IEEE 754 specifications: IEEE 754–1985. https://ieeexplore.ieee.org/document/30711. IEEE 754–2008. https://ieeexplore.ieee.org/document/4610935.

[2] Cookbook formulae for audio equalizer biquad filter coefficients. https://www.w3.org/2011/audio/audio-eq-cookbook.html.

[3] J.W. Cooley, J.W. Tukey, An algorithm for the machine calculation of complex Fourier series, Math. Comput. 19 (90) (1965) 297–301.

[4] C.S. Burrus, T.W. Parks, DFT/FFT and Convolution Algorithms, Wiley, 1984.

[5] R. Matusiak, Implementing Fast Fourier Transform Algorithms of Real-Valued Sequences With the TMS320 DSP Platform, Texas Instruments Application Report SPRA291(August 2001).

Using the Arm CMSIS-DSP library

20.1 Overview of the library

The CMSIS-DSP library is a suite of common signal processing and mathematical functions that have been written for the Arm® Cortex®-M and Cortex-A processors. It has been optimized on Cortex-M processors with the DSP extension and on Cortex-A processors with the Neon (Advanced SIMD) extension. The library is freely available as part of the CMSIS release from Arm and includes all source codes. The functions in the library are divided into several categories:

1. Basic math functions
2. Fast math functions
3. Complex math functions
4. Filters
5. Matrix functions
6. Transforms
7. Motor control functions
8. Statistical functions
9. Support functions
10. Interpolation functions

The library has separate functions for operating on 8-bit integers, 16-bit integers, 32-bit integers, and 32-bit floating-point values.

The library has been optimized to take advantage of the DSP extensions found in the Cortex-M processors, including the Armv8.1-M processor with Helium technology. Although the library is available for other Cortex-M processors without a DSP extension, the functions have not been optimized for these cores; the functions operate properly but run more slowly.

If you are using the Keil® Microcontroller Development Kit (Keil MDK), you can easily add the CMSIS-DSP library into your project. By using the Manage Run-Time Environment settings, the prebuilt library file or source codes of the CMSIS-DSP can be added into a project (Fig. 20.1).

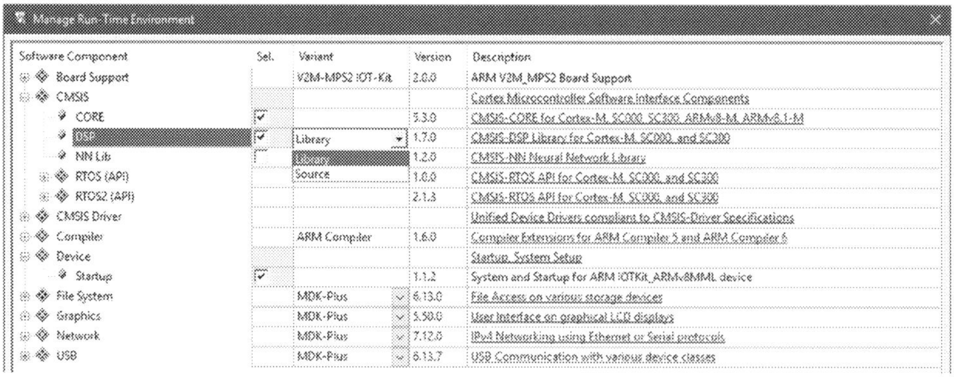

FIG. 20.1   Adding the CMSIS-DSP library into a Keil MDK project.

When integrating the CMSIS-DSP library into the project there is the option of selecting the precompiled library or the source code. Usually, the precompiled library is preferred because the precompiled libraries are optimized for use with Arm toolchains (e.g., Keil MDK) and provide the best performance.

In addition to the prebuild libraries for Arm toolchains, such as Keil MDK, prebuilt libraries for GCC and the IAR Embedded Workbench® for Arm are also available. Multiple library files are also available for various Cortex-M processors in various FPU configurations (e.g., there are multiple versions of the library for the Cortex-M7 processor due to the availability of multiple FPU configurations), and there are also separate library files for little-endian and big-endian memory configurations. The following library files (Table 20.1) are currently available for the CMSIS installation in the Keil MDK toolchain.

TABLE 20.1   Precompiled CMSIS-DSP library files which are available for Arm toolchains.

Library name	Processor	Endianness	Use DSP extension	Uses FPU
arm_ARMv8MMLldfsp_math.lib	Cortex-M33/Cortex-M35P	Little	Yes	Yes
arm_ARMv8MMLld_math.lib		Little	Yes	No
arm_ARMv8MMLlfsp_math.lib		Little	No	Yes
arm_ARMv8MMLl_math.lib		Little	No	No
arm_ARMv8MBLl_math.lib	Cortex-M23	Little	No	No
arm_cortexM7lfdp_math.lib	Cortex-M7	Little	Yes	Yes (single +double precision)
arm_cortexM7bfdp_math.lib		Big	Yes	Yes (single +double precision)
arm_cortexM7lfsp_math.lib		Little	Yes	Yes (single precision)
arm_cortexM7bfsp_math.lib		Big	Yes	Yes (single precision)

TABLE 20.1 Precompiled CMSIS-DSP library files which are available for Arm toolchains—cont'd

Library name	Processor	Endianness	Use DSP extension	Uses FPU
arm_cortexM7l_math.lib		Little	Yes	No
arm_cortexM7b_math.lib		Big	Yes	No
arm_cortexM4lf_math.lib	Cortex-M4	Little	Yes	Yes
arm_cortexM4bf_math.lib		Big	Yes	Yes
arm_cortexM4l_math.lib		Little	Yes	No
arm_cortexM4b_math.lib		Big	Yes	No
arm_cortexM3l_math.lib	Cortex-M3	Little	No	No
arm_cortexM3b_math.lib		Big	No	No
arm_cortexM0l_math.lib	Cortex-M0/Cortex-M0+	Little	No	No
arm_cortexM0b_math.lib		Big	No	No

A similar range of prebuilt libraries are available for the IAR and the GCC, but the filenames are slightly different, and the precompiled libraries for the GCC are available for little endian only. If for any reason, you need to rebuild the libraries, the CMSIS-DSP library HTML documentation should be your first port of call.

20.2 Function naming convention

The functions in the library follow the naming convention:
arm_OP_DATATYPE
where OP is the operation performed and DATATYPE describes the operands

- q7—8-bit fractional integers
- q15—16-bit fractional integers
- q31—32-bit fractional integers
- f32—32-bit floating-point

For example, some of the library function names are:

```
arm_dot_prod_q7 — the dot product of 8-bit fractional integers
arm_mat_add_q15 — the matrix addition of 16-bit fractional integers
arm_fir_q31 — a FIR filter with 32-bit fractional data and coefficients
arm_cfft_f32 — a complex FFT of 32-bit floating-point values
```

20.3 Getting help

The library document is in HTML format and is located in the following folder in the CMSIS-PACK:

`CMSIS\Documentation\DSP\html`

The file `index.html` is the main starting point. The documentation can also be accessed on the github web page for Arm software [1].

20.4 Example 1—DTMF demodulation

A standard touch-tone dial pad with four rows and three columns is shown in Fig. 20.2 below. Each row and column has a corresponding sine wave associated with it. When a button is pressed, the dial pad generates two sine waves; one based on the row index and another based on the column index. For example, if the number 4 is pressed then a 770 Hz sine wave is generated (corresponding to the row) plus a 1209 Hz sine wave (corresponding to the column). This signaling method is referred to as Dual-tone multi-frequency (DTMF) signaling and is the standard signaling method used by analog phone lines.

In this example, we demonstrate three different methods of detecting the tones in the DTMF signal. These are:

- FIR filter [q15]
- FFT [q31]
- Biquad Filter [float]

Although I will focus on decoding one frequency, 697 Hz, the example can easily be extended for decoding all seven tones. Other aspects of DTMF decoding such as setting thresholds and decision making are not covered. All of the code used in this example is shown in Section 20.4.5, Example of DTMF Code.

The goal of the example is to show how to use various CMSIS-DSP functions and how to handle different data types. As it turns out, the Biquad filter is computationally much more

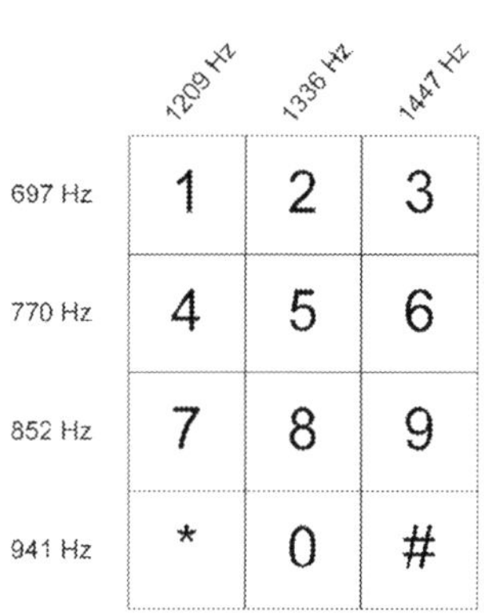

FIG. 20.2   Keypad matrix in a DTMF signaling scheme. Each row and column has a corresponding sine wave, which is generated when a button is pressed.

	1209 Hz	1336 Hz	1447 Hz
697 Hz	1	2	3
770 Hz	4	5	6
852 Hz	7	8	9
941 Hz	*	0	#

efficient than the FIR filter. The reason for this is that a single Biquad stage can be used to detect a sine wave rather than a 202-point FIR filter. The Biquad is roughly 40 times more efficient than the FIR. The FFT might seem like a good choice, especially since, in a full DTMF implementation, seven frequencies will need to be checked. Still, taking all of this into account, the Biquad is still computationally more efficient than the FFT and requires much less memory as well. In practice, most DTMF receivers use the Goetzel algorithm, which is computationally very similar to the Biquad filter used in this example.

20.4.1 Generating the sine wave

In a typical DTMF application, the input data will be taken from an A/D converter. In this example, I generate the input signal using math functions. At the start of the example code, a sine wave at 697 Hz or 770 Hz is generated. The sine wave is first generated using a floating-point and is then converted to Q15 and Q31 representations. All of the processing is performed at an 8 kHz sample rate, which is the standard sample rate used in telephony applications. To test the algorithms, 512 samples of the sine wave were generated with amplitude of 0.5.

20.4.2 Decoding using a FIR filter

The first approach I will use for demodulating the DTMF signal is an FIR filter. The FIR filter will have a passband centered around 697 Hz and must be narrow enough to filter out the next closest frequency of 770 Hz. The following MATLAB® code designs the filter.

```
SR = 8000;    % Sample rate
FC = 697;     % Center frequency of the pass band, in Hz

NPTS = 202;

h = fir1(NPTS-1, [0.98*FC 1.02*FC] / (SR/2), 'DC-0' );
```

Some experimentation was needed in order to determine the correct length of the filter, so that by 770 Hz there was sufficient attenuation. I found that a filter length of 201 points was sufficient. Since the CMSIS library requires an even length filter for the Q15 FIR filter function, the filter length was rounded up to 202 points. The impulse response of the designed filter is shown in Fig. 20.3 and the magnitude response is shown in Fig. 20.4.

The filter was designed to have a gain of 1.0 in the passband. The largest coefficient of the resulting filter has a value of about 0.019. If converted to an 8-bit format (q7), the largest coefficient would only be about 2 LSBs large. The resulting filter would be severely quantized and unusable in 8-bits. At least 16-bits are required, and this example uses Q15 math. MATLAB was also used to convert the filter coefficients to the Q15 format and write them to the console window (the code below refers). The coefficients were then copied into the Cortex-M33 project.

```
hq = round(h * 32768);      // Quantize to Q15

fprintf(1, 'hfir_coeffs_q15 = {\n');
for i=1:length(hq);
        fprintf(1, '%5d', hq(i));
```

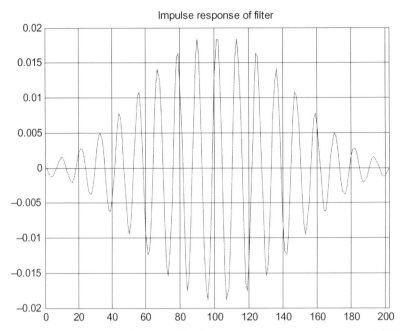

FIG. 20.3 Impulse response of the FIR filter. The filter has a strong sine wave component at 697 Hz, which is the center of the passband.

```
if (i == length(hq))
        fprintf(1, '};\n');
else
        fprintf(1, ', ');
        if (rem(i, 8) == 0)
                fprintf(1, '\n');
        end
    end
end
```

The CMSIS-DSP code to use to apply the FIR filter is straightforward. First, the function arm_fir_init_q15() is called to initialize the FIR filter structure. The function just checks to make sure that the filter length is even and greater than four samples, and then sets a few structural elements. Next, the function processes the signal one block at a time. A macro BLOCKSIZE is defined as 32 and equals the number of samples that will be processed in each call to the arm_fir_q15() function. Each call generates 32 new output samples, and these are written into the output buffer.

The output of the filter was computed for 697 Hz and 770 Hz inputs and the results are shown in Fig. 20.5. The top plot shows the output when the input is 697 Hz. The sine wave falls into the middle of the band and has the expected output amplitude of 0.5 (Remember that the input sine wave has amplitude of 0.5 and the filter has a gain of 1.0 in the center

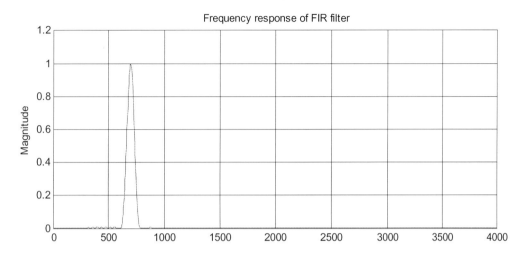

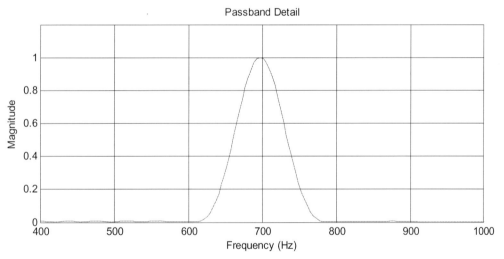

FIG. 20.4 Frequency response of the filter. The top figure shows the magnitude response across the entire frequency band. The bottom figure shows the detail around the passband frequency of 697 Hz.

of the band.). The bottom plot shows the output when the input frequency is increased to 770 Hz. The output is, as expected, greatly attenuated.

20.4.3 Decoding using an FFT

The next approach to decoding the DTMF tones that I will explore is by using an FFT. The advantage of using the FFT is that it provides a complete frequency representation of the signal and can be used to simultaneously decode all seven DTMF sine waves. A Q31 FFT and a

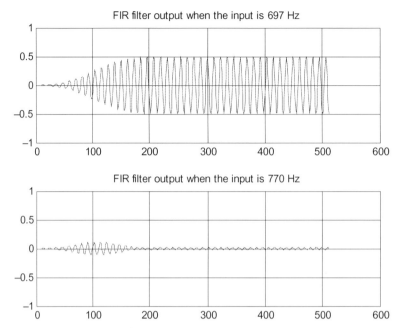

FIG. 20.5 Output of the FIR filter for two different sine wave inputs. The top plot shows the output when the input is a 697 Hz sine wave, which is centered in the middle of the band. The bottom plot shows the output when the input is a 770 Hz sine wave and is properly attenuated.

buffer with a 512 sample length will be used in this example. Since the input data are real, a real transformation (i.e., a real-FFT) will be used.

The FFT operates on an entire buffer of 512 samples. Several steps are involved. First, the data are windowed in order to reduce the transients at the edge of the buffer. There are several different types of window functions (i.e., methods to extract signal samples within a specific period from a longer sequence of samples): Hamming, Hanning, Blackman, etc.—with the choice depending upon the desired frequency resolution and the separation between the neighboring frequencies. In our application, I used a Hanning, or raised cosine, window. The input signal is shown at the top of Fig. 20.6, and the result after windowing is shown at the bottom. You can see that the windowed version decays smoothly to zero at the edges. All data are represented by Q31 values.

The Arm CMSIS-DSP library function arm_rfft_init_q31 is applied to the data. The function produces complex frequency domain data. The function arm_cmplx_mag_q31 then computes the magnitude of each frequency bin. The resulting magnitude is shown in Fig. 20.7. Since the FFT is 512 points long and the sample rate is 8000 Hz, the frequency spacing per FFT bin is

$$\frac{8000}{512} = 15.625\,\text{Hz}$$

The largest magnitude is found at bin 45, which corresponds to a frequency of 703 Hz—the closest bin to 697 Hz.

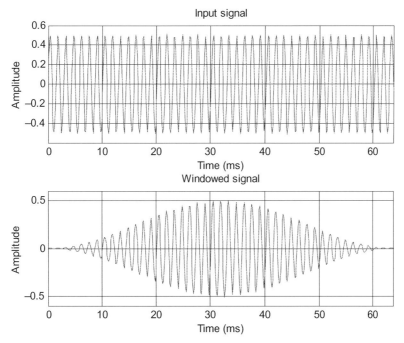

FIG. 20.6 The top figure shows the input sine wave of 697 Hz. Some discontinuities at the signal edges can be seen and these could cause the peak frequency to be misidentified. The bottom figure shows the sine wave after it was windowed by a Hanning window.

If the input frequency is 770 Hz, the FFT produces the magnitude plot shown in Fig. 20.8. The peak occurs at bin 49, which corresponds to 766 Hz.

20.4.4 Decoding using a Biquad filter

The final approach taken was to use a second-order Infinite Impulse Response (IIR) filter to detect the tone. The approach is similar to the Goertzel algorithm that is used in most DSP-based decoders. The Biquad filter is designed to have a pole near the unit circle at the desired frequency of 697 Hz and zeros at DC (i.e., 0 Hz) and Nyquist (i.e., half of the sampling rate). This yields a narrow bandpass shape. The gain of the filter is adjusted so that it has a peak gain of 1.0 in the passband. By moving the pole closer to the unit circle the sharpness of the filter can be adjusted. I settled on placing the pole at a radius of 0.99 and at an angle of

$$\omega = 2\pi \left(\frac{697}{8000} \right)$$

The pole forms part of a complex conjugate pair, and there is a matching pole at the negative frequency. The MATLAB code to generate the filter coefficients is shown below. The scaling by K creates a peak gain of 1.0 in the passband.

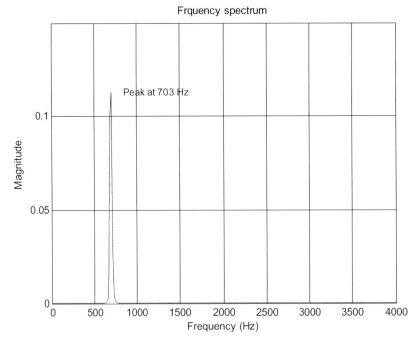

FIG. 20.7 Magnitude of the FFT output. The peak frequency component occurs at 703 Hz, which is the bin closest to the actual frequency of 697 Hz.

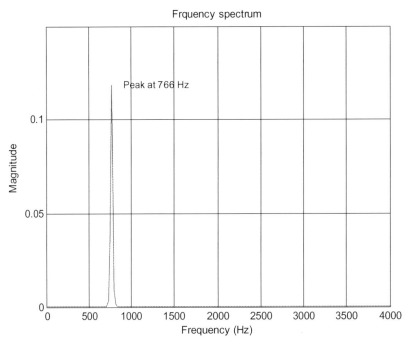

FIG. 20.8 FFT output when the input frequency is 770.

```
r = 0.99;

p1 = r * exp(sqrt(-1)*2*pi*FC/SR);   % Pole location
p2 = conj(p1);                        % Conjugate pole
P = [p1; p2];                         % Make the array of poles

Z = [1; -1];                          % Zeros at DC and Nyquist

K = 1 - r;                            % Gain factor for unity gain
SOS = zp2sos(Z, P, K);                % Convert to biquad coeffs
```

The resulting frequency response of the filter is shown in Fig. 20.9. The filter is sharp and passes frequencies within a very narrow band.

The CMSIS-DSP library provides two versions of the floating-point Biquad filter: Direct Form I and Transposed Direct Form II. For biquad processing using the floating-point format, the best version to use is always the Transposed Direct Form II. This is because it only requires two state variables per Biquad rather than four. With fixed-point, you should always use Direct Form I, but, in this case, the Transposed Direct Form II is the correct version to use.

The code for processing the Biquad filter is straightforward. This example uses a second-order filter, which corresponds to a single Biquad filter stage. The filter has two associated arrays:

Coefficients—five values
State variables—two values

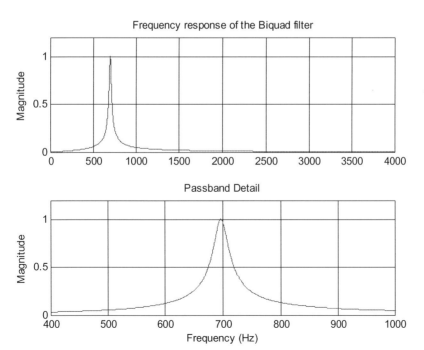

FIG. 20.9 Frequency response of the IIR filter used in DTMF tone detection.

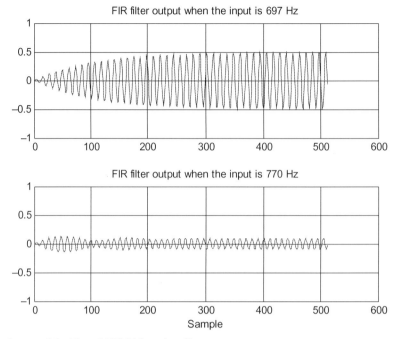

FIG. 20.10   Output of the Biquad DTMF detection filter.

These arrays are defined at the top of the function and the coefficient array is set to the values computed by MATLAB. The only change is that the feedback coefficients are negated compared to the standard MATLAB representation. Next, the function arm_biquad_cascade_df2T_init_f32() is called to initialize the Biquad instance structure. The processing of the filter is handled by the arm_biquad_cascade_df2T_f32() function, which is called to process the input data in blocks in a program loop. Each call processes 32 samples (i.e., BLOCKSIZE) through the filter and stores the result in the output array.

The output of the Biquad filter is shown in Fig. 20.10. The top part of the figure shows the output when the input is at 697 Hz; the bottom part shows the output when the input is 770 Hz. When the input is 697 Hz, the output builds-up to the expected amplitude of 0.5. When the input is a 770 Hz sine wave, there is still a bit of signal in the output, and the rejection is not as great as the FIR result shown in Fig. 20.5. Still, the filter does a reasonable job discerning the various signal components.

20.4.5   Example of DTMF code

The following code demonstrates the three DTMF decoding techniques using the CMSIS-DSP library functions.

Example DTMF program code

```
#include "IOTKit_CM33_FP.h"
#include <stdio.h>

#include "arm_math.h"

#define L 512
#define SR 8000
#define FREQ 697
// #define FREQ 770
#define BLOCKSIZE 8

q15_t inSignalQ15[L];
q31_t inSignalQ31[L];
float inSignalF32[L];

q15_t outSignalQ15[L];
float outSignalF32[L];

q31_t fftSignalQ31[2*L];
q31_t fftMagnitudeQ31[2];

#define NUM_FIR_TAPS 202
q15_t hfir_coeffs_q15[NUM_FIR_TAPS] = {
  -9  , -29,  -40,  -40,  -28,   -7,   17,   38,
  49  ,  47,   29,    1,  -30,  -55,  -66,  -58,
  -31 ,   9,   51,   82,   91,   72,   29,  -28,
  -82 , -117, -119,  -84,  -20,   57,  124,  160,
  149 ,  91,    0,  -99, -176, -206, -175,  -88,
  33  , 153,  235,  252,  193,   72,  -80, -217,
  -297, -293, -199,  -40,  141,  289,  358,  323,
  189 ,  -9, -213, -364, -412, -339, -161,   73,
  294 , 436,  453,  336,  114, -149, -376, -499,
  -477, -312,  -51,  233,  456,  548,  480,  269,
  -27 , -320, -525, -579, -462, -207,  113,  404,
  580 , 587,  422,  131, -201, -477, -614, -572,
  -362, -45,  287,  534,  626,  534,  287,  -45,
  -362, -572, -614, -477, -201,  131,  422,  587,
  580 , 404,  113, -207, -462, -579, -525, -320,
  -27 , 269,  480,  548,  456,  233,  -51, -312,
  -477, -499, -376, -149,  114,  336,  453,  436,
  294 ,  73, -161, -339, -412, -364, -213,   -9,
  189 , 323,  358,  289,  141,  -40, -199, -293,
  -297, -217,  -80,   72,  193,  252,  235,  153,
```

Continued

```
  33 , -88, -175, -206, -176, -99,    0,   91,
 149 , 160,  124,   57,  -20, -84, -119, -117,
 -82 , -28,   29,   72,   91,  82,   51,    9,
 -31 , -58,  -66,  -55,  -30,   1,   29,   47,
  49 ,  38,   17,   -7,  -28, -40,  -40,  -29,
  -9 ,   0};

q31_t hanning_window_q31[L];

q15_t hfir_state_q15[NUM_FIR_TAPS + BLOCKSIZE] = {0};

float biquad_coeffs_f32[5] = {0.01f, 0.0f, -0.01f, 1.690660431255413f, -0.9801f};
float biquad_state_f32[2] = {0};

/*---------------------------------------------------------------
main program
*----------------------------------------------------------------*/

int main (void) {    /* execution starts here     */
   int i, samp;
   arm_fir_instance_q15 DTMF_FIR;
   arm_rfft_instance_q31 DTMF_RFFT;
   arm_biquad_cascade_df2T_instance_f32 DTMF_BIQUAD;

   // Generates the input sine wave
   // The signal will have an amplitude of 0.5 and a frequency of FREQ Hz
   // Creates floating-point, Q31, and Q7 versions.

   for(i=0; i<L; i++) {
      inSignalF32[i] = 0.5f * sinf(2.0f * PI * FREQ * i / SR);
      inSignalQ15[i] = (q15_t) (32768.0f * inSignalF32[i]);
      inSignalQ31[i] = (q31_t) ( 2147483647.0f * inSignalF32[i]);
   }

   /* -----------------------------------------------------------
   ** Process with FIR filter
   ** ----------------------------------------------------------- */

   if (arm_fir_init_q15(&DTMF_FIR, NUM_FIR_TAPS, &hfir_coeffs_q15[0],
                        &hfir_state_q15[0], BLOCKSIZE) != ARM_MATH_SUCCESS) {
      // error condition
      // exit(1);
   }

   for(samp = 0; samp < L; samp += BLOCKSIZE) {
      arm_fir_q15(&DTMF_FIR, inSignalQ15 + samp, outSignalQ15 + samp, BLOCKSIZE);
   }
```

```
/* ————————————————————————————————————————————————————
** Process with a floating-point Biquad filter
** ———————————————————————————————————————————— */

arm_biquad_cascade_df2T_init_f32(&DTMF_BIQUAD, 1, biquad_coeffs_f32,
                                 biquad_state_f32);

for(samp = 0; samp < L; samp += BLOCKSIZE) {

    arm_biquad_cascade_df2T_f32(&DTMF_BIQUAD, inSignalF32 + samp,
                                outSignalF32 + samp, BLOCKSIZE);

}

/* ————————————————————————————————————————————————————
** Process with Q31 FFT
** ———————————————————————————————————————————— */

// Creates the Hanning window. This is usually done once at the
// start of the program.

for(i=0; i<L; i++) {
    hanning_window_q31[i] =
            (q31_t) (0.5f * 2147483647.0f * (1.0f - cosf(2.0f*PI*i / L)));
}

// Applies the window to the input buffer
arm_mult_q31(hanning_window_q31, inSignalQ31, inSignalQ31, L);

arm_rfft_init_q31(&DTMF_RFFT, 512, 0, 1);

// Computes the FFT
arm_rfft_q31(&DTMF_RFFT, inSignalQ31, fftSignalQ31);

arm_cmplx_mag_q31(fftSignalQ31, fftMagnitudeQ31, L);
}
```

20.5 Example 2—Least squares motion tracking

Tracking the motion of an object is a common requirement for many applications. Examples include navigation systems, exercise equipment, video game controllers, and factory automation. Noisy measurements of past positions of the object are available and they need to be combined to estimate future positions. One approach to solve this challenge is to combine multiple noisy measurements in order to estimate the underlying trajectory (position, velocity, and acceleration) and to then project this into the future.

Consider an object under constant acceleration. The motion of the object as a function of time t will be:

$$x(t) = x_0 + v_0 t + a t^2$$

where

x_0 is the initial position
v_0 is the initial velocity
a is the acceleration

In this example, I will assume that the acceleration is constant but the approach used can be extended to time-varying acceleration.

Assume that we have measurements of the past location of the object at times $t_1, t_2, ..., t_N$. Assume also that the position measurements are noisy and that we only know an approximate position. Place the measurements and times into column vectors:

$$x = \begin{bmatrix} x_1 \\ x_2 \\ \vdots \\ x_N \end{bmatrix} \quad t = \begin{bmatrix} t_1 \\ t_2 \\ \vdots \\ t_N \end{bmatrix}$$

The overall equation that relates the measurements to the unknowns x_0, v_0, and a is then

$$\begin{bmatrix} x_1 \\ x_2 \\ \vdots \\ x_N \end{bmatrix} = x_0 + v_0 \begin{bmatrix} t_1 \\ t_2 \\ \vdots \\ t_N \end{bmatrix} + a \begin{bmatrix} t_1^2 \\ t_2^2 \\ \vdots \\ t_N^2 \end{bmatrix}$$

This expression can be computed using a matrix multiplication

$$x = Ac$$

where

$$A = \begin{bmatrix} 1 & t_1 & t_1^2 \\ 1 & t_2 & t_1^2 \\ \vdots & \vdots & \vdots \\ 1 & t_N & t_N^2 \end{bmatrix}$$

and

$$c = \begin{bmatrix} x_0 \\ v_0 \\ a \end{bmatrix}.$$

Since there are three unknowns, at least three measurements are required to compute the result vector c. In most cases, there are many more measurements than unknowns, and the problem is overdetermined. One standard solution to this problem is to carry out the least-squares fit. The solution $\hat{c}$ is the one which minimizes the error between the N estimated positions and the actual N measurement positions. The least-squares solution can be found by solving the matrix equation:

$$\hat{c} = \left(A^T A\right)^{-1} A^T x$$

Equations of this type can be solved using the matrix functions within the CMSIS-DSP library. A matrix in the CMSIS-DSP library is represented using a data structure. For floating-point data, the structure is:

```
typedef struct
{
    uint16_t numRows;  /**< number of rows of the matrix.    */
    uint16_t numCols;  /**< number of columns of the matrix. */
    float32_t *pData;  /**< points to the data of the matrix. */
} arm_matrix_instance_f32;
```

Essentially, the matrix structure keeps track of the size of the matrix (numRows, numCols) and contains a pointer to the data (pData). Element (R, C) of the matrix is stored at location

```
pData[R*numRows + C]
```

in the array. That is, the array contains the first row of data, followed by the second row of data, and so on. You can either manually initialize the matrix instance structure yourself by setting internal fields or you can use the function arm_mat_init_f32(). In practice, it is easier to manually initialize the matrix.

The overall code that computes the least-squares solution is shown in Section 20.5.1. The top of the function allocates memory for all of the pData arrays used by the matrices. Matrices t and x are initialized with actual data while all other matrices are initially set to zero. After this, the individual matrix instance structures are initialized. Note: multiple matrices are defined so that the intermediate results can be stored. The following matrices are defined:

A—matrix A from above
AT—transpose of A
ATA—the product $A^T A$
invATA—the inverse of $A^T A$
B—the product $(A^T A)^{-1} A^T$
c—the final result from above

The start of the main function initializes the values for matrix A. After this, several matrix math functions are called to finally arrive at the result vector c. The result contains three elements and they can be seen by inspecting the cData within the debugger. By so doing, it will be found that:

$$x_0 = c[0] = 8.7104$$

$$v_0 = c[1] = 38.8748$$

$$a = c[2] = -9.7923$$

The original input data and the resulting fit are shown in Fig. 20.11. The thin line is the measured data showing the random noise, and the thick line is the resulting data fit. The figure shows that the underlying least-squares fit is quite accurate, and the fit could be used to extrapolate the measured data into the future.

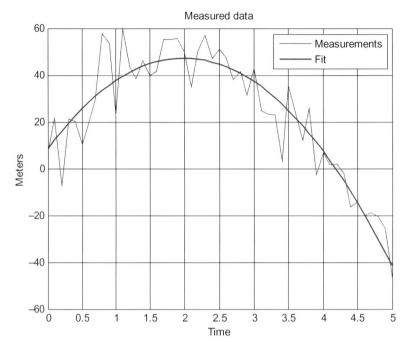

FIG. 20.11   Raw measurements *(thin line)* and resulting least-squares fit *(thick line)*.

20.5.1 Example of least squares code

Example code for least square computation

```
#include "arm_math.h"    /* Main include file for CMSIS-DSP       */

#define NUMSAMPLES 51    /* Number of measurements                */
#define NUMUNKNOWNS 3    /* Number of unknowns in polynomial fit */

// Allocate memory for the matrix arrays. Only t and x have initial data defined.

// Contains the times at which the data was sampled. In this example, the data
// is evenly spaced but this is not required for the least squares fit.
float32_t tData[NUMSAMPLES] =
{
   0.0f, 0.1f, 0.2f, 0.3f, 0.4f, 0.5f, 0.6f, 0.7f,
   0.8f, 0.9f, 1.0f, 1.1f, 1.2f, 1.3f, 1.4f, 1.5f,
   1.6f, 1.7f, 1.8f, 1.9f, 2.0f, 2.1f, 2.2f, 2.3f,
   2.4f, 2.5f, 2.6f, 2.7f, 2.8f, 2.9f, 3.0f, 3.1f,
   3.2f, 3.3f, 3.4f, 3.5f, 3.6f, 3.7f, 3.8f, 3.9f,
   4.0f, 4.1f, 4.2f, 4.3f, 4.4f, 4.5f, 4.6f, 4.7f,
   4.8f, 4.9f, 5.0f
};
```

```
// Contains the noisy position measurements
float32_t xData[NUMSAMPLES] =
{
  7.4213f, 21.7231f, -7.2828f, 21.2254f, 20.2221f, 10.3585f, 20.3033f, 29.2690f,
  57.7152f, 53.6075f, 22.8209f, 59.8714f, 43.1712f, 38.4436f, 46.0499f, 39.8803f,
  41.5188f, 55.2256f, 55.1803f, 55.6495f, 49.8920f, 34.8721f, 50.0859f, 57.0099f,
  47.3032f, 50.8975f, 47.4671f, 38.0605f, 41.4790f, 31.2737f, 42.9272f, 24.6954f,
  23.1770f, 22.9120f, 3.2977f, 35.6270f, 23.7935f, 12.0286f, 25.7104f, -2.4601f,
  6.7021f, 1.6804f, 2.0617f, -2.2891f, -16.2070f, -14.2204f, -20.1870f, -18.9303f,
  -20.4859f, -25.8338f, -47.2892f
};

float32_t AData[NUMSAMPLES * NUMUNKNOWNS];
float32_t ATData[NUMSAMPLES *NUMUNKNOWNS];
float32_t ATAData[NUMUNKNOWNS * NUMUNKNOWNS];
float32_t invATAData[NUMUNKNOWNS * NUMUNKNOWNS];
float32_t BData[NUMUNKNOWNS * NUMSAMPLES];
float32_t cData[NUMUNKNOWNS];

// Array instance structure initialization. For each instance, the form is:
//      MAT = {numRows, numCols, pData};

// Column vector t
arm_matrix_instance_f32 t = {NUMSAMPLES, 1, tData};

// Column vector x
arm_matrix_instance_f32 x = {NUMSAMPLES, 1, xData};

// Matrix A
arm_matrix_instance_f32 A = {NUMSAMPLES, NUMUNKNOWNS, AData};

// Transpose of matrix A
arm_matrix_instance_f32 AT = {NUMUNKNOWNS, NUMSAMPLES, ATData};

// Matrix product AT * A
arm_matrix_instance_f32 ATA = {NUMUNKNOWNS, NUMUNKNOWNS, ATAData};

// Matrix inverse inv(AT*A)
arm_matrix_instance_f32 invATA = {NUMUNKNOWNS, NUMUNKNOWNS, invATAData};

// Intermediate result invATA * AT
arm_matrix_instance_f32 B = {NUMUNKNOWNS, NUMSAMPLES, BData};
```

Continued

```
// Solution
arm_matrix_instance_f32 c = {NUMUNKNOWNS, 1, cData};

/*-----------------------------------------------------------
** main program
**-----------------------------------------------------------*/

int main (void) {
  int i;
  float y;

  y = sqrtf(xData[0]);
  cData[0] = y;

  // Fills in the values for matrix A. Each row contains:
  // [1.0f t t*t]
  for(i=0; i<NUMSAMPLES; i++) {
    AData[i*NUMUNKNOWNS + 0] = 1.0f;
    AData[i*NUMUNKNOWNS + 1] = tData[i];
    AData[i*NUMUNKNOWNS + 2] = tData[i] * tData[i];
  }

  // Transpose
  arm_mat_trans_f32(&A, &AT);

  // Matrix multiplication AT * A
  arm_mat_mult_f32(&AT, &A, &ATA);

  // Matrix inverse inv(ATA)
  arm_mat_inverse_f32(&ATA, &invATA);

  // Matrix multiplication invATA * x;
  arm_mat_mult_f32(&invATA, &AT, &B);

  // Final result.
  arm_mat_mult_f32(&B, &x, &c);

  // Examine cData in the debugger to view the final values
}
```

20.6 Example 3—Real-time filter design

20.6.1 Overview of filter design

Filtering is one of the most commonly used signal processing tasks in real-time embedded systems. In Section 20.4 I showed how to apply filtering to an input signal sequence. However, in many applications the input signals are active all of the time and, thus, continuous filtering is needed. In this section, I am going to look into how to create real-time filters using the CMSIS-DSP library.

The first step of filter design is to define the filter specification. Some of the areas that need to be defined include:

- Filter type
- Data type used by the digital filter
- Sampling frequency
- Frequency response

The frequency response of a filter can be characterized using various aspects. For example, Fig. 20.12 shows some of these characteristics.

There can be a lot of factors to consider when designing filters. In addition to the frequency response (e.g., rejection ratio), phase response can also be important in some applications. In some cases, you might also need to take the delay of the filter response into account when making the design decision. Although filter design techniques are not covered in detail in this book, information about filter design is widely available (e.g., an IIR filter design guide from Advanced Solution Nederland provides a good overview of this topic [2]). There is also a range of filter design tools to make life easier.

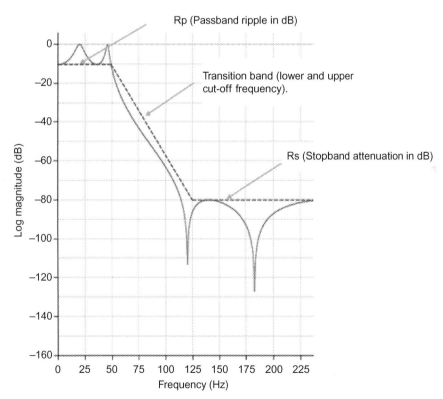

FIG. 20.12   A range of filter characteristics to consider in filter design. *Image courtesy of Advanced Solution Nederland.*

In Section 20.4, the use of MATLAB for filter design was briefly covered. MATLAB is one of the most popular mathematical tools available on the market and includes features that support the design of filters. There are other filter-design software tools available on the market, including some in the form of open-source projects.

A number of commercial filter-design software tools are designed specifically for filter-design tasks and make it easier to analyze a filter's characteristics. For software developers who are not familiar with filter designs, these tools can be a great help. In the following examples, the filters were created using ASN Filter Designer Professional (Version 4.33), which have been developed by Advanced Solution Nederland (http://www.advsolned.com).

The ASN Filter Designer Professional software supports a wide range of filter types. Its design allows filters to be designed via an interactive user interface, where various parameters can be adjusted and the design's output can immediately be viewed. It also supports the simulation of the filter's response so that the simulation outputs can be examined to determine whether the filter meets the requirements of the application. An added bonus, for developers creating software for Cortex-M processors, is that it generates C codes that directly call CMSIS-DSP library functions (the designed filters can also be exported to C/C++, Python, MATLAB, etc.).

When the ASN Filter Designer starts, and assuming that the license key has been installed, a default startup screen, as shown in Fig. 20.13, will appear.

In this example, I am going to design a low pass biquad filter for a system with 48 kHz sampling rate and with single-precision floating-point data types. The first step to take when starting a basic filter design is to define the sampling rate. This is achieved by clicking on the "Fs" icon on the toolbar and entering the sampling rate in the Sampling Frequency dialog (Fig. 20.14).

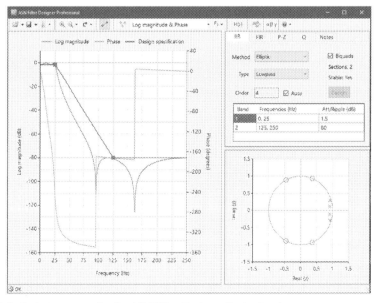

FIG. 20.13   Default startup screen for the ASN Filter Designer Professional.

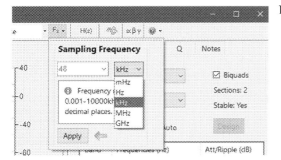

FIG. 20.14 Setting up the sampling rate.

The next step is to define the filter type. By default, the filter type is "Elliptic IIR" filter; this can be changed to a simple Butterworth Biquad filter by selecting the filter "Method" on the top right-hand side of the user interface (Fig. 20.15).

The next step is to then define the data type and structure. These settings can be found by clicking on the "Q" tab on the top right-hand side of the user interface, as shown in Fig. 20.16. For Cortex-M33 processors with an FPU, because the FPU supports a single-precision floating-point unit this is the option I have selected for this example. A fixed-point data format can, if preferred, also be selected. If that is required, a suitable fixed-point data format (Word length and number of bits for the fractional part in the data) should be selected.

At this stage of the process, the filter characteristic (Fig. 20.17) should be defined. To do so, the IIR tab should be clicked again, whereupon the number of biquad sections required, and the filter order will be displayed. The square cursors in the graph on the left-hand side can be adjusted to control the filter's frequency response. After you have adjusted the filter response, you then need to click on the "Design" button in the IIR filter tab (on the right) to update the filter design.

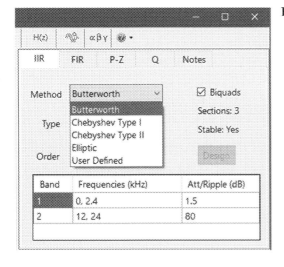

FIG. 20.15 Defining the filter type.

FIG. 20.16 Defining the filter's data type and structure.

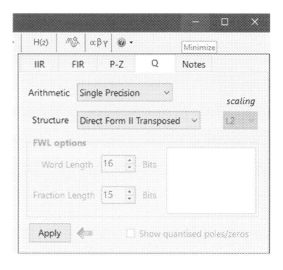

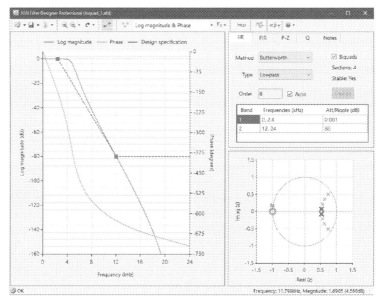

FIG. 20.17 Defining the frequency response of the filter.

Once the filter is defined, the design can then be exported into C code (using the Arm CMSIS-DSP option). The C code contains the generated filter coefficients and the function calls that access the required CMSIS-DSP library functions. The function to export the C code is accessed by clicking on the "H(z)" button on the toolbar (Fig. 20.18).

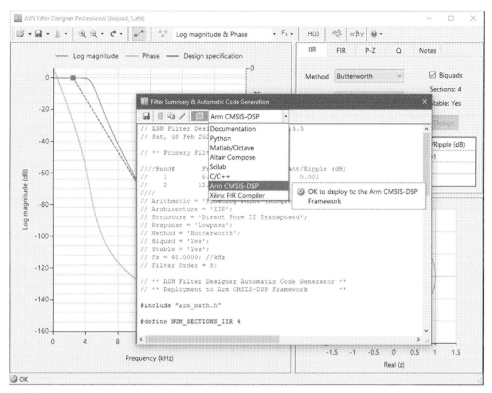

FIG. 20.18 Exporting the filter design to C code using the CMSIS-DSP library.

The generated biquad filter code is as follows:

Generated Biquad filter C code utilizing the CMSIS-DSP library

```
// ASN Filter Designer Professional v4.3.3
// Sat, 08 Feb 2020 11:50:38 GMT

// ** Primary Filter (H1)**

////Band#        Frequencies (kHz)        Att/Ripple (dB)
//    1        0.000,    2.400            0.001
//    2       12.000,   24.000           80.000
////
// Arithmetic = 'Floating Point (Single Precision)';
// Architecture = 'IIR';
// Structure = 'Direct Form II Transposed';
// Response = 'Lowpass';
// Method = 'Butterworth';
// Biquad = 'Yes';
```

Continued

```
// Stable = 'Yes';
// Fs = 48.0000; //kHz
// Filter Order = 8;

// ** ASN Filter Designer Automatic Code Generator **
// ** Deployment to Arm CMSIS-DSP Framework   **

#include "arm_math.h"

#define NUM_SECTIONS_IIR 4

// ** IIR Direct Form II Transposed Biquad Implementation **
// y[n] = b0 * x[n] + w1
// w1 = b1 * x[n] + a1 * y[n] + w2
// w2 = b2 * x[n] + a2 * y[n]

// IIR Coefficients
float32_t iirCoeffsf32[NUM_SECTIONS_IIR*5] =
        {// b0, b1, b2, a1, a2
            0.0582619, 0.1165237, 0.0582619, 1.0463270, -0.2788444,
            0.0615639, 0.1231277, 0.0615639, 1.1071010, -0.3531238,
            0.0688354, 0.1376707, 0.0688354, 1.2402050, -0.5158056,
            0.0815540, 0.1631081, 0.0815540, 1.4713260, -0.7982877
        };

// ************************************************************
// Test loop code (Right mouse button -> Show test loop code)
// ************************************************************

#define ARM_MATH_CM4 // Cortex-M4 (default). Can be omitted if deploying to CMSIS-DSP
v1.7.0 or greater

#define TEST_LENGTH_SAMPLES 128
#define BLOCKSIZE 32
#define NUMBLOCKS (TEST_LENGTH_SAMPLES/BLOCKSIZE)

float32_t iirStatesf32[NUM_SECTIONS_IIR*5];

float32_t OutputValues[TEST_LENGTH_SAMPLES];
float32_t InputValues[TEST_LENGTH_SAMPLES];

float32_t *InputValuesf32_ptr = &InputValues[0]; // declares Input pointer
float32_t *OutputValuesf32_ptr = &OutputValues[0]; // declares Output pointer

arm_biquad_cascade_df2T_instance_f32 S;

int32_t main(void)
{

  uint32_t n,k;
```

```
    // sets up the test sinusoid input
    for (n=0; n<TEST_LENGTH_SAMPLES; n++)
        InputValues[n]= arm_sin_f32(2*PI*4.8*n/48.0);

    // Initialises the Biquads
    arm_biquad_cascade_df2T_init_f32 (&S, NUM_SECTIONS_IIR, &(iirCoeffsf32[0]), &
    (iirStatesf32[0]));

    // Performs the IIR filtering operation
    for (k=0; k < NUMBLOCKS; k++)
        arm_biquad_cascade_df2T_f32 (&S, InputValuesf32_ptr + (k*BLOCKSIZE),
     OutputValuesf32_ptr + (k*BLOCKSIZE), BLOCKSIZE); // performs filtering

    while (1);
  }
```

If the selected filter design is not supported by the CMSIS-DSP library, the filter design can be exported as C/C++ codes instead.

By default, the generated C code assumes that the Cortex-M4 processor is being used. Because the CMSIS-DSP APIs for all Cortex-M processors are identical, the code can be used on the Cortex-M33 processor. By using a set of precalculated input values (which are stored in a data array), the generated code demonstrates the operation of the filter design. The program ends when all the data in the input data array has been processed. To convert the code into a real-time filter, which processes input data continuously, the code would need to be modified.

20.6.2 Creating a real-time filter: A bare metal project example

To make the filter computation more efficient, the filter in the CMSIS-DSP library only executes after a block of samples has been collected. The block size is dependent on the filter design and, in the example biquad I have highlighted, the block size is 32—which means the filter function executes every time 32 samples have been collected. To support this behavior, the input and output buffers need to be defined (Fig. 20.19).

If the filter processing function finishes within 1 sampling period, then the same set of input and output buffers can, after the biquad filter calculation has taken place, be immediately reused for the next block of samples. However, the processing time needed for the filter function to execute often exceeds the timing gap of one sample. As a result, having just one set of input and output buffers is not enough. To solve this problem, two sets of input and output data buffers are, typically, needed. When one pair of input and output buffer's is used for the filter processing, the other pair is used for the input of data samples and the output of the previously executed processing results. This is often called a ping-pong buffer operation (Fig. 20.20).

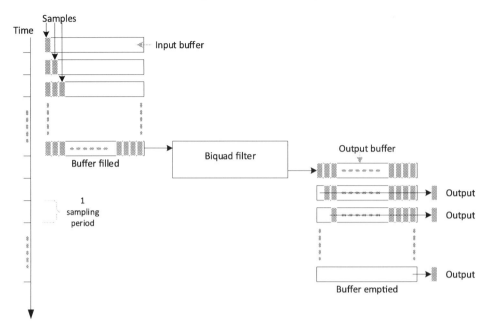

FIG. 20.19 CMSIS-DSP filter functions operate on blocks of samples and therefore require input and output buffers.

For the purpose of demonstrating a real-time filter using a "ping-pong" buffer operation, I have created an example code for an audio filter. In this example, the input and the output are handled by an audio interface interrupt handler. This triggers the sampling rate (i.e., 48 kHz in my setup) and the biquad filter function runs in thread mode (which can be interrupted by the audio interface interrupt). To enable the processing to be kick-started after a buffer is filled, the following data variables are required:

- A data variable for counting the number of samples collected in the input buffer A/B ("Sample_Counter")
- A data variable to indicate ping-pong state ("PingPongState")
- A data variable, which allows the audio interrupt handler to trigger the start of the filter processing once enough samples have been collected ("processing_trigger")
- And of course, two pairs of input/output buffers ("InputValues_A/B", "OutputValues_A/B")

At the start of the program, the buffers and the aforementioned variables, the biquad filter data structure, and the audio interface hardware (including the interrupt configuration of the NVIC) will all need to be initialized. Because the filter code generated by the ASN Filter Designer targets the Cortex-M4 processor by default, the code contains the C macro "ARM_MATH_CM4". This C macro is not used in the recent releases of the CMSIS-DSP library and can be ignored.

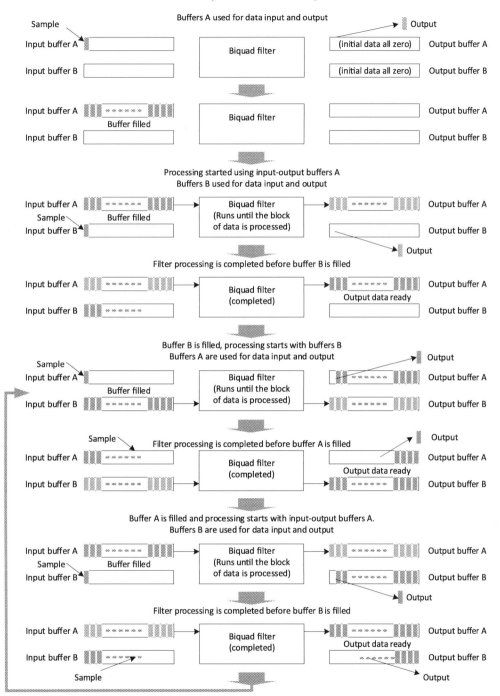

FIG. 20.20 CMSIS-DSP filter with a "ping pong" buffer.

After all the aforementioned modifications have been carried out, the real-time audio filter design can then be tested. The program code for doing this is detailed below:

Real-time filter code

```
// ASN Filter Designer Professional v4.3.3
// Fri, 07 Feb 2020 18:41:12 GMT

// ** Primary Filter (H1)**

////Band#        Frequencies (kHz)        Att/Ripple (dB)
//    1             0.000,    2.400            0.001
//    2            12.000,   24.000           80.000
////
// Arithmetic = 'Floating Point (Single Precision)';
// Architecture = 'IIR';
// Structure = 'Direct Form II Transposed';
// Response = 'Lowpass';
// Method = 'Butterworth';
// Biquad = 'Yes';
// Stable = 'Yes';
// Fs = 48.0000; //kHz
// Filter Order = 8;

// ** ASN Filter Designer Automatic Code Generator **
// ** Deployment to Arm CMSIS-DSP Framework   **

// Included Headers
#include "IOTKit_CM33_FP.h"
#include "arm_math.h" // CMSIS-DSP library header

extern uint8_t audio_init(void); // Initializes audio hardware
extern void read_sample(int16_t *left, int16_t *right);
extern void play_sample(int16_t *left, int16_t *right);
void I2S_Handler(void);

#define BLOCKSIZE 32

#define NUM_SECTIONS_IIR 4

// ** IIR Direct Form II Transposed Biquad Implementation **
// y[n] = b0 * x[n] + w1
// w1 = b1 * x[n] + a1 * y[n] + w2
// w2 = b2 * x[n] + a2 * y[n]

// IIR Coefficients
// IIR Coefficients
float32_t const static iirCoeffsf32[NUM_SECTIONS_IIR*5] =
```

```
          {// b0, b1, b2, a1, a2
              0.0582619f, 0.1165237f, 0.0582619f, 1.0463270f, -0.2788444f,
              0.0615639f, 0.1231277f, 0.0615639f, 1.1071010f, -0.3531238f,
              0.0688354f, 0.1376707f, 0.0688354f, 1.2402050f, -0.5158056f,
              0.0815540f, 0.1631081f, 0.0815540f, 1.4713260f, -0.7982877f
          };

float32_t static iirStatesf32[NUM_SECTIONS_IIR*5];

static arm_biquad_cascade_df2T_instance_f32 S;

// Ping-pong buffer
float32_t static InputValues_A[BLOCKSIZE];
float32_t static OutputValues_A[BLOCKSIZE];
float32_t static InputValues_B[BLOCKSIZE];
float32_t static OutputValues_B[BLOCKSIZE];
volatile int static PingPongState=0; // 0 = processing A, I/O = B
                                     // 1 = processing B, I/O = A
volatile int static Sample_Counter=0; // Counts sample from 0 to BLOCKSIZE-1,
  // then triggers processing and returns to 0
volatile int static processing_trigger=0;
  // When it is set to 1, it starts processing
  // Sets to 2 during processing & returns to 0 when processing is completed

// Samples from both audio channels
int16_t static left_channel_in;
int16_t static right_channel_in;
int16_t static left_channel_out;
int16_t static right_channel_out;

int main(void) {
  int i;

  // Initializes data in ping-pong buffer
  for (i=0;i<BLOCKSIZE;i++) {
    OutputValues_A[i] = 0.0f;
    OutputValues_B[i] = 0.0f;
    }

  // Initializes Biquads
  arm_biquad_cascade_df2T_init_f32 (&S, NUM_SECTIONS_IIR, &(iirCoeffsf32[0]), &
(iirStatesf32[0]));

  audio_init();               // Initializes the audio interface
```

Continued

```
  // Waits for I2S IRQs to occur and then services them.
  // WFE sleep is used to allow power saving
  while(1){
    if (processing_trigger>0) {
    // processing_trigger is set to 1 by I2S_Handler when a BLOCK of data is sampled
      processing_trigger=2; // indicates the biquad is running
      if (PingPongState==0) {
        arm_biquad_cascade_df2T_f32 (&S, &InputValues_A[0], &OutputValues_A[0],
BLOCKSIZE); // performs filtering
      } else {
        arm_biquad_cascade_df2T_f32 (&S, &InputValues_B[0], &OutputValues_B[0],
BLOCKSIZE); // performs filtering
      } // endif-if (PingPongState==0)
      processing_trigger=0; // returns state to 0
    } // end-if (processing_trigger!=0)
    __WFE(); // enters sleep when the processing is finished
  }

}
/**************************************************************************/
/* I2S audio IRQ handler. Triggers at 48KHz.          */
/**************************************************************************/
void I2S_Handler(void) {
  int local_Sample_Counter;

  // Sample_Counter counts from 0 to BLOCKSIZE-1
  local_Sample_Counter = Sample_Counter;

  // Reads sample from the ADC
  read_sample(&left_channel_in, &right_channel_in);

  if (PingPongState==0) {
  InputValues_B[local_Sample_Counter] = (float) left_channel_in;
    left_channel_out=(int16_t) OutputValues_B[local_Sample_Counter];
  } else {
    InputValues_A[local_Sample_Counter] = (float) left_channel_in;
    left_channel_out=(int16_t) OutputValues_A[local_Sample_Counter];
  }
  right_channel_out = right_channel_in; // Only left channel is processed

  // Writes sample to the DAC
  play_sample(&left_channel_out, &right_channel_out);

  local_Sample_Counter++;
  if (local_Sample_Counter>=BLOCKSIZE) {
    // Wraps around and toggles the ping-pong buffer
```

```
    local_Sample_Counter = 0;
    PingPongState = (PingPongState+1) & 0x1; // toggles the ping-pong state
    if (processing_trigger==2) {
      // Biquad is still running - an overrun error has occurred
      __BKPT(1); // Error
    } else {
      processing_trigger = 1; // Starts new biquad
    }
  }
  Sample_Counter = local_Sample_Counter; // saves new Sample_Counter

  return;
}
```

In a real-world application, a device is likely to have a number of interrupt sources. In the unlikely scenario that the processor receives a large number of interrupt requests in a short period of time, the filter function might not be able to complete the processing before the next block of samples is received. To detect when this occurs, a check is carried out inside the I2S handler. If the value of the "`processing_trigger`" is still 2 when a block of samples is received, this is flagged up as an error as it means the filter processing function running in the thread mode is still running.

20.6.3 Filter processing in a low priority handler

To reduce the possibility of the processor not being able to finish the filter processing in time for the next block of data, the filter processing function could be run as another interrupt handler at a low priority level (i.e., a lower priority than the audio interface interrupt). This arrangement also allows us to run some slow processing functions (nonreal-time) at the thread level. By running the filter processing as an interrupt handler, codes for measuring the filter's processing duration and for displaying the result (using a printf statement) can be added to the project in the form of thread-level background operations. This arrangement avoids the filter processing from being delayed.

In the following example, the same filter algorithm that was used in the previous example is used, but the execution of the filter function is carried out inside the PendSV exception handler.

Real-time filter code using the PendSV exception for filter processing. Thread mode is used for displaying the processor's load.

```
// ASN Filter Designer Professional v4.3.3
// Fri, 07 Feb 2020 18:41:12 GMT

// ** Primary Filter (H1)**
```

Continued

```
////Band#   Frequencies (kHz) Att/Ripple (dB)
//    1     0.000,    2.400      0.001
//    2    12.000,   24.000     80.000
////
// Arithmetic = 'Floating Point (Single Precision)';
// Architecture = 'IIR';
// Structure = 'Direct Form II Transposed';
// Response = 'Lowpass';
// Method = 'Butterworth';
// Biquad = 'Yes';
// Stable = 'Yes';
// Fs = 48.0000; //kHz
// Filter Order = 8;

// ** ASN Filter Designer Automatic Code Generator **
// ** Deployment to Arm CMSIS-DSP Framework  **

// Included Headers
#include "IOTKit_CM33_FP.h"
#include "arm_math.h" // CMSIS-DSP library header
#include "stdio.h"

extern uint8_t audio_init(void); // Initializes audio hardware
extern void read_sample(int16_t *left, int16_t *right);
extern void play_sample(int16_t *left, int16_t *right);
void I2S_Handler(void);
void PendSV_Handler(void);

#define BLOCKSIZE 32

#define NUM_SECTIONS_IIR 4

// ** IIR Direct Form II Transposed Biquad Implementation **
// y[n] = b0 * x[n] + w1
// w1 = b1 * x[n] + a1 * y[n] + w2
// w2 = b2 * x[n] + a2 * y[n]

// IIR Coefficients
// IIR Coefficients
float32_t const static iirCoeffsf32[NUM_SECTIONS_IIR*5] =
        {// b0, b1, b2, a1, a2
           0.0582619f, 0.1165237f, 0.0582619f, 1.0463270f, -0.2788444f,
           0.0615639f, 0.1231277f, 0.0615639f, 1.1071010f, -0.3531238f,
           0.0688354f, 0.1376707f, 0.0688354f, 1.2402050f, -0.5158056f,
           0.0815540f, 0.1631081f, 0.0815540f, 1.4713260f, -0.7982877f
        };
```

```
float32_t static iirStatesf32[NUM_SECTIONS_IIR*5];

static arm_biquad_cascade_df2T_instance_f32 S;

// Ping-pong buffer
float32_t static InputValues_A[BLOCKSIZE];
float32_t static OutputValues_A[BLOCKSIZE];
float32_t static InputValues_B[BLOCKSIZE];
float32_t static OutputValues_B[BLOCKSIZE];
volatile int static PingPongState=0; // 0 = processing A, I/O = B
                                     // 1 = processing B, I/O = A
volatile int static Sample_Counter=0; // Counts sample from 0 to BLOCKSIZE-1,
 // then triggers processing and returns to 0
volatile int static processing_trigger=0;
 // When it is set to 1, it starts processing
 // Sets to 2 during processing & returns to 0 when processing is completed

// Samples from both audio channels
int16_t static left_channel_in;
int16_t static right_channel_in;
int16_t static left_channel_out;
int16_t static right_channel_out;

// Number of cycles per block of samples
#define CPUCYCLE_MAX ((20000000/48000)*BLOCKSIZE)
static volatile uint32_t cycle_cntr=0;

int main(void) {
  int i;

// Initializes data in ping-pong buffer
for (i=0;i<BLOCKSIZE;i++) {
   OutputValues_A[i] = 0.0f;
   OutputValues_B[i] = 0.0f;
   }

// Initializes Biquads
arm_biquad_cascade_df2T_init_f32 (&S, NUM_SECTIONS_IIR, &(iirCoeffsf32[0]), &
(iirStatesf32[0]));

NVIC_SetPriority(PendSV_IRQn, 7); // PendSV sets to Low priority

audio_init();    // Initializes the audio interface

// Waits for I2S IRQs to occur and then services them.
```

Continued

```
while(1){
    printf ("cpu load=%d percent\n", (100*cycle_cntr/CPUCYCLE_MAX));
}

}
/********************************************************************/
/* PendSV handler. Triggers at 48KHz/BLOCKSIZE.       */
/********************************************************************/
void PendSV_Handler(void)
{
      processing_trigger=2; // indicates the biquad is running
      SysTick->LOAD=0x00FFFFFFUL;
      SysTick->VAL=0;
      SysTick->CTRL=SysTick_CTRL_CLKSOURCE_Msk|SysTick_CTRL_ENABLE_Msk;

      if (PingPongState==0) {
             arm_biquad_cascade_df2T_f32 (&S, &InputValues_A[0], &OutputValues_A[0],
BLOCKSIZE); // performs filtering
      } else {
             arm_biquad_cascade_df2T_f32 (&S, &InputValues_B[0], &OutputValues_B[0],
BLOCKSIZE); // performs filtering
      } // endif-if (PingPongState==0)
      processing_trigger=0; // returns state to 0
      cycle_cntr = 0x00FFFFFFUL - SysTick->VAL;
      SysTick->CTRL=0;
      return;
}
/********************************************************************/
/* I2S audio IRQ handler. Triggers at 48KHz.                    */
/********************************************************************/
void I2S_Handler(void) {
int local_Sample_Counter;

// Sample_Counter counts from 0 to BLOCKSIZE-1
local_Sample_Counter = Sample_Counter;

// Reads sample from the ADC
read_sample(&left_channel_in, &right_channel_in);

if (PingPongState==0) {
InputValues_B[local_Sample_Counter] = (float) left_channel_in;
    left_channel_out=(int16_t) OutputValues_B[local_Sample_Counter];
} else {
    InputValues_A[local_Sample_Counter] = (float) left_channel_in;
    left_channel_out=(int16_t) OutputValues_A[local_Sample_Counter];
}
```

```
right_channel_out = right_channel_in; // Only left channel is processed

// Writes sample to the DAC
play_sample(&left_channel_out, &right_channel_out);

local_Sample_Counter++;
if (local_Sample_Counter>=BLOCKSIZE) {
    // Wraps around and toggles the ping-pong buffer
    local_Sample_Counter = 0;
  PingPongState = (PingPongState+1) & 0x1; // toggles ping-pong state
  if (processing_trigger==2) {
      // Biquad is still running – an overrun error has occurred
      __BKPT(1); // Error
    } else {
      processing_trigger = 1; // Starts new biquad
      SCB->ICSR |= SCB_ICSR_PENDSVSET_Msk; // Triggers PendSV
    }
  }
Sample_Counter = local_Sample_Counter; // saves new Sample_Counter

return;
}
```

The FPGA platform I am using contains a Cortex-M33 processor running at 20 MHz, and the measured processing loading is around 22%. Please note, the measured utilization ratio for the processor is more than the filter processing time because it also includes the clock cycles that are needed for handling the audio interface interrupt services.

20.6.4 Use of an RTOS for handling filter processing

In many applications, an RTOS is used to manage large numbers of processing tasks. Using the task prioritization capability of a modern RTOS, we can prioritize the filter processing over other less time-critical processing tasks and, by so doing, achieve the same effect as running the filter processing function using a low priority exception handler.

In the following example, an RTX RTOS is used to demonstrate how the filter processing task is executed as one of the application threads in an RTOS environment. To allow the audio interface interrupt to trigger the execution of the filter processing task, an OS event is used. The filter processing task (i.e., "biquad_processing()" in the following code) waits for the OS event and proceeds when the OS event is received from the audio interface interrupt handler (i.e., the "I2S_Handler()").

Real-time filter code using RTX, with filter processing running as a real-time application thread

```
// ASN Filter Designer Professional v4.3.3
// Fri, 07 Feb 2020 18:41:12 GMT

// ** Primary Filter (H1)**

////Band#        Frequencies (kHz)       Att/Ripple (dB)
//   1           0.000,    2.400              0.001
//   2          12.000,   24.000             80.000
////
// Arithmetic = 'Floating Point (Single Precision)';
// Architecture = 'IIR';
// Structure = 'Direct Form II Transposed';
// Response = 'Lowpass';
// Method = 'Butterworth';
// Biquad = 'Yes';
// Stable = 'Yes';
// Fs = 48.0000; //kHz
// Filter Order = 8;

// ** ASN Filter Designer Automatic Code Generator **
// ** Deployment to Arm CMSIS-DSP Framework        **

// Included Headers
//#include "IOTKit_CM33_FP.h"
#include "SMM_MPS2.h"

#include "arm_math.h" // CMSIS-DSP library header
#include "stdio.h"
#include "cmsis_os2.h"

extern uint8_t audio_init(void); // Initializes audio hardware
extern void read_sample(int16_t *left, int16_t *right);
extern void play_sample(int16_t *left, int16_t *right);
void        biquad_processing (void *arg);
void        report_utilization (void *arg);

void I2S_Handler(void);

osEventFlagsId_t evt_id;   // message event id
osThreadId_t     biquad_tread_id;
osThreadId_t     report_tread_id;
#define FLAGS_MSK1 0x00000001ul
```

```
const osThreadAttr_t report_thread1_attr = {
 .stack_size = 1024    // Creates the thread stack with a size of 1024 bytes
};

#define BLOCKSIZE 32

#define NUM_SECTIONS_IIR 4

// ** IIR Direct Form II Transposed Biquad Implementation **
// y[n] = b0 * x[n] + w1
// w1 = b1 * x[n] + a1 * y[n] + w2
// w2 = b2 * x[n] + a2 * y[n]

// IIR Coefficients
// IIR Coefficients
float32_t const static iirCoeffsf32[NUM_SECTIONS_IIR*5] =
        {// b0, b1, b2, a1, a2
            0.0582619f, 0.1165237f, 0.0582619f, 1.0463270f, -0.2788444f,
            0.0615639f, 0.1231277f, 0.0615639f, 1.1071010f, -0.3531238f,
            0.0688354f, 0.1376707f, 0.0688354f, 1.2402050f, -0.5158056f,
            0.0815540f, 0.1631081f, 0.0815540f, 1.4713260f, -0.7982877f
        };

float32_t static iirStatesf32[NUM_SECTIONS_IIR*5];

static arm_biquad_cascade_df2T_instance_f32 S;

// Ping-pong buffer
float32_t static InputValues_A[BLOCKSIZE];
float32_t static OutputValues_A[BLOCKSIZE];
float32_t static InputValues_B[BLOCKSIZE];
float32_t static OutputValues_B[BLOCKSIZE];
volatile int static PingPongState=0; // 0 = processing A, I/O = B
                           // 1 = processing B, I/O = A
volatile int static Sample_Counter=0; // Counts sample from 0 to BLOCKSIZE-1,
  // then triggers processing and returns to 0
volatile int static processing_trigger=0;
  // When it is set to 1, it starts processing
  // Sets to 2 during processing & returns to 0 when processing is completed

// Samples from both audio channels
int16_t static left_channel_in;
int16_t static right_channel_in;
int16_t static left_channel_out;
int16_t static right_channel_out;
```

Continued

```
// Number of cycle per block of samples
#define CPUCYCLE_MAX ((20000000/48000)*BLOCKSIZE)
static volatile uint32_t cycle_cntr=0;

int main(void) {
  int i;
  osStatus_t status;

  // Initializes data in ping-pong buffer
  for (i=0;i<BLOCKSIZE;i++) {
    OutputValues_A[i] = 0.0f;
    OutputValues_B[i] = 0.0f;
    }

  // Initializes Biquads
  arm_biquad_cascade_df2T_init_f32 (&S, NUM_SECTIONS_IIR, &(iirCoeffsf32[0]), &
(iirStatesf32[0]));

  osKernelInitialize(); // Initializes CMSIS-RTOS
  // creates thread for the biquad_processing
  biquad_tread_id=osThreadNew(biquad_processing, NULL, NULL);
  // Sets thread priority
  status = osThreadSetPriority (biquad_tread_id, osPriorityRealtime);
  if (status == osOK) {
    // Thread priority successfully changed
  }
  else {
    // Fails to set the priority
    __BKPT(0);
  }

  // creates a thread for reporting the processor's utilization
  report_tread_id=osThreadNew(report_utilization, NULL, &report_thread1_attr);
  // Sets thread priority
  status = osThreadSetPriority (report_tread_id, osPriorityNormal);
  if (status == osOK) {
    // Thread priority successfully changed
  }
  else {
    // Fails to set the priority
    __BKPT(0);
  }

  evt_id = osEventFlagsNew(NULL); // Creates an event object (Cannot be called until
osKernelInitialize is complete)
```

```
  audio_init();        // Initializes the audio interface

  osKernelStart();     // Starts the thread execution
  while(1);

}
/************************************************************************/
/* Biquad thread. Triggers at 48KHz/BLOCKSIZE.                        */
/************************************************************************/
void biquad_processing (void *arg)
{
  uint32_t flags;
  while (1) {
    flags = osEventFlagsWait (evt_id,FLAGS_MSK1,osFlagsWaitAny, osWaitForever);
    processing_trigger=2; // indicates the biquad is running
    MPS2_SECURE_FPGAIO->COUNTER=0;

    if (PingPongState==0) {
      arm_biquad_cascade_df2T_f32 (&S, &InputValues_A[0], &OutputValues_A[0],
BLOCKSIZE); // performs filtering
    } else {
      arm_biquad_cascade_df2T_f32 (&S, &InputValues_B[0], &OutputValues_B[0],
BLOCKSIZE); // performs filtering
    } // endif-if (PingPongState==0)
    processing_trigger=0; // returns to 0
    cycle_cntr = MPS2_FPGAIO->COUNTER;
  }
  return;
}
/************************************************************************/
/* Processor load reporting thread                                    */
/************************************************************************/
void report_utilization (void *arg)
{
  while (1) {
    osDelay(1000);
    printf ("cpu load=%d percent\n", (100*cycle_cntr/CPUCYCLE_MAX));
  }
}

/************************************************************************/
/* I2S audio IRQ handler. Triggers at 48KHz.                          */
/************************************************************************/
void I2S_Handler(void) {
  int local_Sample_Counter;
```

Continued

```
// Sample_Counter counts from 0 to BLOCKSIZE-1
local_Sample_Counter = Sample_Counter;

// Reads sample from the ADC
read_sample(&left_channel_in, &right_channel_in);

if (PingPongState==0) {
InputValues_B[local_Sample_Counter] = (float) left_channel_in;
  left_channel_out=(int16_t) OutputValues_B[local_Sample_Counter];
} else {
  InputValues_A[local_Sample_Counter] = (float) left_channel_in;
  left_channel_out=(int16_t) OutputValues_A[local_Sample_Counter];
}
right_channel_out = right_channel_in; // Only left channel is processed

// Writes sample to the DAC
play_sample(&left_channel_out, &right_channel_out);

local_Sample_Counter++;
if (local_Sample_Counter>=BLOCKSIZE) {
  // Wraps around and toggles the ping-pong buffer
  local_Sample_Counter = 0;
  PingPongState = (PingPongState+1) & 0x1; // toggle ping-pong state
  if (processing_trigger==2) {
    // Biquad is still running - an overrun error has occurred
    __BKPT(1); // Error
  } else {
    processing_trigger = 1; // Start new biquad
    osEventFlagsSet(evt_id, FLAGS_MSK1);
  }
}
Sample_Counter = local_Sample_Counter; // saves new Sample_Counter

return;
}
```

When running the filter processing task in an RTOS, you might see that the measured processing time needed to complete the filter processing task increases compared to the example that I mentioned in Section 20.6.3. This is because the measured processing time included the time it took to execute:

- The audio interrupt services,
- The processing of the audio filter,
- The OS tick exception handler and, potentially,
- Other real-time threads.

20.6.5 Stereo audio biquad filter

In many audio applications, the filter processing tasks operate on stereo audio data. A simple way to handle this is to run the filter algorithm twice: once for the left channel and once for the right. To make the processing more efficient, the CMSIS-DSP library also provides a biquad filter function for processing stereo data.

When dealing with stereo data, the values for the left and right channels interleave. As a result of combining the left and right channels, the input and output buffers are double the size. Because the same filtering is applied to both channels, the filter coefficients are shared between the two channels. The example stereo filter code is shown below:

Stereo filter example—bare metal environment (i.e., no OS)

```
// ASN Filter Designer Professional v4.3.3
// Fri, 07 Feb 2020 18:41:12 GMT

// ** Primary Filter (H1)**

////Band#  Frequencies (kHz)  Att/Ripple (dB)
//   1      0.000,    2.400    0.001
//   2     12.000,   24.000   80.000
////
// Arithmetic = 'Floating Point (Single Precision)';
// Architecture = 'IIR';
// Structure = 'Direct Form II Transposed';
// Response = 'Lowpass';
// Method = 'Butterworth';
// Biquad = 'Yes';
// Stable = 'Yes';
// Fs = 48.0000; //kHz
// Filter Order = 8;

// ** ASN Filter Designer Automatic Code Generator **
// ** Deployment to Arm CMSIS-DSP Framework        **

// Included Headers
#include "IOTKit_CM33_FP.h"
#include "arm_math.h" // CMSIS-DSP library header

extern uint8_t audio_init(void); // Initializes audio hardware
extern void read_sample(int16_t *left, int16_t *right);
extern void play_sample(int16_t *left, int16_t *right);
void I2S_Handler(void);
```

Continued

```
#define BLOCKSIZE 32

#define NUM_SECTIONS_IIR 4

// ** IIR Direct Form II Transposed Biquad Implementation **
// y[n] = b0 * x[n] + w1
// w1 = b1 * x[n] + a1 * y[n] + w2
// w2 = b2 * x[n] + a2 * y[n]

// IIR Coefficients
// IIR Coefficients
float32_t const static iirCoeffsf32[NUM_SECTIONS_IIR*5] =
        {// b0, b1, b2, a1, a2
            0.0582619f, 0.1165237f, 0.0582619f, 1.0463270f, -0.2788444f,
            0.0615639f, 0.1231277f, 0.0615639f, 1.1071010f, -0.3531238f,
            0.0688354f, 0.1376707f, 0.0688354f, 1.2402050f, -0.5158056f,
            0.0815540f, 0.1631081f, 0.0815540f, 1.4713260f, -0.7982877f
        };

float32_t static iirStatesf32[NUM_SECTIONS_IIR*5];

static arm_biquad_cascade_stereo_df2T_instance_f32 S;

// Ping-pong buffer
float32_t static InputValues_A[BLOCKSIZE*2];
float32_t static OutputValues_A[BLOCKSIZE*2];
float32_t static InputValues_B[BLOCKSIZE*2];
float32_t static OutputValues_B[BLOCKSIZE*2];
volatile int static PingPongState=0; // 0 = processing A, I/O = B
                            // 1 = processing B, I/O = A
volatile int static Sample_Counter=0; // Counts sample from 0 to BLOCKSIZE-1,
  // then triggers processing and returns to 0
volatile int static processing_trigger=0;
  // When it is set to 1, it starts processing
  // Sets to 2 during processing & returns to 0 when processing is completed

// Samples from both audio channels
int16_t static left_channel_in;
int16_t static right_channel_in;
int16_t static left_channel_out;
int16_t static right_channel_out;

int main(void) {
  int i;

  // Initializes data in ping-pong buffer
```

```
  for (i=0;i<BLOCKSIZE*2;i++) {
    OutputValues_A[i] = 0.0f;
    OutputValues_B[i] = 0.0f;
    }

  // Initializes Biquads
  arm_biquad_cascade_stereo_df2T_init_f32 (&S,NUM_SECTIONS_IIR,&(iirCoeffsf32[0]),
&(iirStatesf32[0]));

  audio_init();     // Initializes the audio interface

  // Waits for I2S IRQs to occur and then services them.
  // WFE sleep is used to allow power saving
  while(1){
    if (processing_trigger>0) {
    // processing_trigger is set to 1 by I2S_Handler when a BLOCK of data is sampled
      processing_trigger=2; // indicates biquad is running
      if (PingPongState==0) {
        arm_biquad_cascade_stereo_df2T_f32 (&S,&InputValues_A[0],&OutputValues_A[0],
BLOCKSIZE); //performs filtering
      } else {
        arm_biquad_cascade_stereo_df2T_f32 (&S,&InputValues_B[0],&OutputValues_B[0],
BLOCKSIZE); //performs filtering
      } // endif-if (PingPongState==0)
      processing_trigger=0; // returns state to 0
    } // end-if (processing_trigger!=0)
    __WFE(); // enters sleep when the processing is finished

  }

}
/*********************************************************************/
/* I2S audio IRQ handler. Triggers at 48KHz.      */
/*********************************************************************/
void I2S_Handler(void) {
  int local_Sample_Counter;

  // Sample_Counter counts from 0 to BLOCKSIZE-1
  local_Sample_Counter = Sample_Counter*2;

  // Reads sample from the ADC
  read_sample(&left_channel_in, &right_channel_in);

  if (PingPongState==0) {
```

Continued

```
    InputValues_B[local_Sample_Counter ] = (float) left_channel_in;
    InputValues_B[local_Sample_Counter+1] = (float) right_channel_in;
    left_channel_out =(int16_t) OutputValues_B[local_Sample_Counter];
    right_channel_out=(int16_t) OutputValues_B[local_Sample_Counter+1];
  } else {
    InputValues_A[local_Sample_Counter] = (float) left_channel_in;
    InputValues_A[local_Sample_Counter+1] = (float) right_channel_in;
    left_channel_out =(int16_t) OutputValues_A[local_Sample_Counter];
    right_channel_out=(int16_t) OutputValues_A[local_Sample_Counter+1];
  }

  // Writes sample to the DAC
  play_sample(&left_channel_out, &right_channel_out);

  local_Sample_Counter=local_Sample_Counter+2;
  if (local_Sample_Counter>=(2*BLOCKSIZE)) {
    // Wraps around and toggles the ping-pong buffer
    local_Sample_Counter = 0;
    PingPongState = (PingPongState+1) & 0x1; // toggles the ping-pong state
    if (processing_trigger==2) {
      // Biquad is still running – an overrun error has occurred
      __BKPT(1); // Error
    } else {
      processing_trigger = 1; // Starts new biquad
    }
  }
  Sample_Counter = local_Sample_Counter>>1; // saves new Sample_Counter

  return;
}
```

20.6.6 Alternative buffer arrangement

The real-time filter examples detailed so far have used two pairs of input and output buffers, i.e., a total of four blocks of buffer space. In microcontroller systems with a small amount of SRAM space, it is often desirable to reduce the SRAM usage. To achieve this, an alternative buffer arrangement can be used and an example of this is shown in Fig. 20.21. In this alternative buffer arrangement:

- Three buffers are used.
- Each buffer is used for both input and output.
- The buffer system operates with three states (different from the previous examples that use two Ping-pong states).

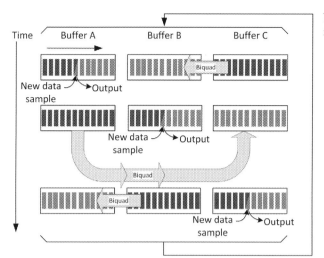

FIG. 20.21 An alternative buffer arrangement for real-time filters.

Although this design can reduce memory usage, the software could be harder to debug because each buffer is used for both inputs and outputs.

20.7 How to determine the implemented instruction set features in a Cortex-M33 based system

Since the FPU and DSP extensions are optional in the Cortex-M33 processor, a Cortex-M33-based device might not have these extensions implemented. Normally, information about the implemented features should be available from the device's specification/datasheet. In some instances, though, you might need to determine what is implemented in the chip via a debug connection or by executing software on the system.

The Cortex-M33 processor includes a number of read-only registers to allow software or a debugger to determine what instruction set features have been implemented (Table 20.2).

In addition to directly reading the registers listed in Table 20.2, the CMSIS-CORE has a function call for determining what type of FPU has been implemented. This function is:

```
uint32_t SCB_GetFPUTyper(void);
```

and returns the following values:

- 0—no FPU is implemented
- 1—Single precision FPU is implemented
- 2—Double + single precision FPU is implemented

TABLE 20.2 Registers that can be used for determining the implemented instruction set in the Cortex-M33 processor.

Register	Address (Non-secure alias)	CMSIS-CORE symbol	Description
ID_ISAR1	0xE000ED64 (0xE002ED64)	SCB-> ID_ISAR[1] SCB_NS-> ID_ISAR[1]	Instruction Set Attribute Register 1 • If the DSP Extension is not implemented, this register reads as 0x02211000. • When the DSP Extension is implemented, this register reads as 0x02212000.
ID_ISAR2	0xE000ED68 (0xE002ED68)	SCB-> ID_ISAR[2] SCB_NS-> ID_ISAR[2]	Instruction Set Attribute Register 2 • With bits [11:8] masked, if the DSP Extension is not implemented, this register reads as 0x20112032. • With bits [11:8] masked, when the DSP Extension is implemented, this register reads as 0x20232032.
ID_ISAR3	0xE000ED6C (0xE002ED6C)	SCB-> ID_ISAR[3] SCB_NS-> ID_ISAR[3]	Instruction Set Attribute Register 3 • If the DSP Extension is not implemented, this register reads as 0x01111110. • When the DSP Extension is implemented, this register reads as 0x01111131.
MVFR0	0xE000EF40 (0xE002EF40)	FPU->MVFR0 FPU_NS-> MVFR0	Media and VFP Feature Register 0 • If the Floating-point Extension is not implemented this register reads as 0x00000000. • Where only a single-precision floating-point unit is supported this register reads as 0x10110021. • Where a single and double-precision floating-point unit are supported this register reads as 0x10110221. (This configuration is not supported in the Cortex-M33 processor)
MVFR1	0xE000EF44 (0xE002EF44)	FPU->MVFR1 FPU_NS-> MVFR1	Media and VFP Feature Register 1 • If the floating-point extension is not implemented this register reads as 0x00000000. • Where only a single-precision floating-point unit is supported this register reads as 0x11000011. • Where single and double-precision floating-point are supported this register reads as 0x12000011. (This configuration is not supported in the Cortex-M33 processor)
MVFR2	0xE000EF48 (0xE002EF48)	FPU->MVFR2 FPU_NS-> MVFR2	Media and VFP Feature Register 2 • If the floating-point extension is not implemented this register reads as 0x00000000. • When the floating-point unit is implemented this register reads as 0x00000040.

References

[1] CMSIS-DSP library documentation. https://arm-software.github.io/CMSIS_5/DSP/html/index.html.

[2] The Advanced Solution Nederland web site has a good article on filter design. Classical IIR filter design: a practical guide. http://www.advsolned.com/iir-filters-a-practical-guide/.

Advanced topics

21.1 Further information on stack memory protection

21.1.1 Determining the stack memory usage

Stack overflow is a common software issue and can lead to software failures, as well as security vulnerabilities. In Arm®v8-M architecture [1], a stack limit check feature was introduced to enhance the security of a range of embedded applications. Information on this feature, and information about the protection of the Main Stack, was covered in Chapter 11, Section 11.4. While the stack checking feature is very useful, it is, still best, however, to reserve sufficient memory space for the stack(s) to avoid potential stack issues. Accordingly, the amount of stack required by the application(s) should be estimated so that the stack memory settings can be correctly configured.

Several methods have been developed for estimating stack size. Traditionally, it is common for a software developer to fill the SRAM with a predefined pattern (e.g., "0xDEADBEEF"[a]), then, after executing the program for a short period of time, stopping the processor and, by examining the stack content, determining how much stack space had been used. This method works to an extent, but is not particularly accurate because the conditions for maximum stack usage may not have been triggered.

In some tool chains, the required stack size can be estimated from report files after the project has been compiled. For example, if you are using:

(1) Keil® Microcontroller Development Kit (MDK): After the compilation, an HTML file in the project directory will provide, as one of the pieces of supplied information, the maximum stack size the functions will use.
(2) IAR Embedded Workbench®: After enabling two project options (the "Generate linker map file" option in the "List" tab for the Linker and the "Enable stack usage analysis" option in the "Advanced" tab for the Linker), you will, after compilation, then be able to

---

[a]This is a well known special debug value used in early IBM systems—https://en.wikipedia.org/wiki/Deadbeef.

view the "Stack Usage" section in the linker report (.map) in the "Debug\List" subdirectory.

Some software analysis tools can also be used to give you a report on stack usage, and additionally, detailed information to help you improve the quality of the program code.

While compilation tools can report the stack usage of the functions, including total stack usage in a function call chain, this analysis does not include the additional stack space required for exception handling. Software developers must do this themselves by:

Step 1: Looking at the maximum level of nested interrupt/exception's based on the exception priority level configurations, and then,
Step 2: By estimating, adding the stack usage of the exception handlers and the sizes of stack frames together, the worst-case stack usage for the exception handling.

However, if there are stack issues, such as a stack leak in the software, the compilation report files and other stack analysis methods will be of no use. As a result, further mechanisms to detect the stack overflow error would, in some applications, still be required.

21.1.2 Detecting stack overflow

Although Armv8-M architecture introduced a stack limit check feature, this feature is not available for the Non-secure world in the Cortex®-M23 processor. Fortunately, there are several other methods to detect stack overflows.

One such method is to use the MPU to detect a stack overflow, i.e., either use the MPU to define an MPU region for stack usage, or use the MPU to define a read only memory region at the end of the stack space, which is reserved for the HardFault exception handler. By setting MPU_CTRL.HFNMIENA (Table 12.3 in Chapter 12) to 0, the HardFault exception bypasses the MPU and, even if a stack overflow occurs, is still able to correctly execute by using the reserved SRAM.

Another method, which is only suitable for bare metal applications, is to separate the thread's stack (which uses the Process Stack Pointer) and the handler's stack (which uses the Main Stack Pointer), and place the thread's stack near the bottom of the SRAM space. When the stack overflows during a stack push operation, the processor will, because the transfer is no longer in a valid memory region, receive a bus error response and execute the fault handler. The fault handler that uses the handler's stack will, in this scenario, still be able to operate correctly. Further information about separating the thread's and handler's stacks is covered in Section 11.3.3.

During software development, it is also possible to detect a stack overflow in the Non-secure world by setting a data watchpoint (a debug feature) at the limit of the stack memory. If a stack push operation reaches the limit, the data watchpoint event will halt the processor so that the software developer is able to analyze the issue. Because the Cortex-M23 processor does not support the Debug Monitor exception, this method can only be used during halt mode debugging. This method is not required for the Secure world or when using the Cortex-M33 processor because the stack limit checking feature is available for these.

For applications with an OS, the OS can check the Process Stack Pointer (PSP) value during each context switch to ensure that the application tasks only use the allocated stack space.

While this is not as reliable as using the MPU, this is still a useful method and is easy to implement in the design of an RTOS.

If you are using the RTX (an RTOS from Arm/Keil), together with the Keil MDK toolchain, you can analyze the stack usage of each thread by enabling the Stack usage watermark feature in the RTX configuration file (i.e., RTX_Config.h). Once this feature is enabled and the project is compiled, the stack usage information can be accessed from the RTX RTOS viewer window in the Keil MDK debugger (via the pull-down menu View→Watch windows→RTX RTOS).

21.2 Semaphores, load-acquire and store-release instructions

In Chapter 5, Section 5.7.12, the load-acquire and store-release instructions were introduced. And then in Chapter 11, Section 11.7, I covered the relationship between exclusive access operations and semaphores. In this section, I cover the use of load-acquire and store release instructions in semaphores/mutexes.

A mutex (mutual exclusive) is a special form of semaphore, which only has one available token, and governs access to a shared resource. When a mutex is used, only one software process can gain access to the shared resource when it is granted the token.

A semaphore/mutex operation is divided into two parts—acquire the semaphore/mutex and release the semaphore/mutex. Using traditional exclusive access instructions, the simplest code for acquiring a mutex is written as:

```
// Function to lock a shared resource with a MUTEX (mutual exclusive)

void acquire_mutex(volatile int * Lock_Variable)

{ // Note: __LDREXW and __STREXW are functions in the CMSIS-CORE
  int status;
  do {
    while ( __LDREXW(Lock_Variable) != 0);
        // Polling: Wait until the lock variable is free

    status = __STREXW(1, Lock_Variable);
        // Tries to set the Lock_Variable to 1 by using the STREX instruction
  } while (status != 0);
        // Retries the read-modify-write operation until the lock is successful
  __DMB(); // Data memory Barrier
  return;

}
```

Once a shared resource is no longer needed, the code for releasing the semaphore can be written as:

```
// Function to release a shared resource with a MUTEX (mutual exclusive)

void release_mutex(volatile int * Lock_Variable)

{

   __DMB();              // Data memory Barrier

  Lock_Variable = 0; // Frees the semaphore by clearing the lock variable

  return;

}
```

For both functions, a Data Memory Barrier (DMB) instruction is needed to prevent the reordering of the memory access from causing errors to the functionality of the application. Memory access reordering, which is allowed in the Armv8-M architecture, is a common optimization technique used in high-end processors to enhance their performance. Although the Cortex-M23 and Cortex-M33 processors do not support memory access reordering, adding the DMB (or Data Synchronization Barrier, i.e., DSB) memory barrier instructions to the aforementioned mutex functions (`acquire_mutex()` and `release_mutex ()`) ensure that the program code can be reused on high-end Arm processors. Essentially, the DMB (or DSB) instruction safeguards the mutex/semaphore operations in the following way:

- In the "`acquire_mutex()`" function—DMB prevents the processor from carrying out a data memory access for the critical section (the code sequence guarded by the mutex) before the mutex is acquired.
- In the "`release_mutex()`" function—DMB ensures that all data memory access in the critical section are completed before the mutex is released.

The barrier behavior that is required in these two mutex functions only has to work in a single direction. The use of the DMB instruction does, however, result in a separation of the memory access before and after the DMB (a barrier, which separates data access in two directions). For high-end processors, this can result in a performance penalty. For example, in the "`acquire_mutex()`" function the DMB instruction execution causes the processor's write buffers (if implemented) to be unnecessarily drained.

To solve the problem, load-acquire and store-release instructions include exclusive access variants, which allow the semaphore code to operate safely, but without using a DMB instruction. With these instructions, the "`acquire_mutex()`" function can be modified to:

```
// Function to lock a shared resource with a MUTEX (mutual exclusive)

void acquire_mutex(volatile int * Lock_Variable)

{ // Note: __LDAEX and __STREXW are functions in the CMSIS-CORE
 int status;

do {

   while ( __LDAEX(Lock_Variable) != 0);

      // Polling: Wait until the lock variable is free
```

```
        // Note: LDAEX has ordering semantic properties
    status = __STREXW(1, Lock_Variable);
        // Tries to set the Lock_Variable to 1 by using the STREX instruction
} while (status != 0);
        // Retries the read-modify-write operation until the lock is successful
return;
}
```

The "release_mutex()" function can be modified to:

```
// Function to release a shared resource with a MUTEX (mutual exclusive)
void release_mutex(volatile int * Lock_Variable)
{
    __STL(0, Lock_Variable);
    // Frees the semaphore by clearing the lock variable
    // Note: STL has ordering semantic properties
    return;
}
```

To further improve the design, the polling loop in the "acquire_mutex()" can be modified to prevent processing bandwidth and energy from being wasted. If the Lock_variable is non-zero, indicating that the mutex has been locked by another software process, the processor could:

- If an RTOS is running, and if other software processes are ready to execute, execute them; or
- Enter sleep mode

To achieve this, the "acquire_mutex()" function can be updated by way of the following example:

```
// Function to lock a shared resource with a MUTEX (mutual exclusive)
void acquire_mutex(volatile int * Lock_Variable)
{ // Note: __LDAEX and __STREXW are functions in CMSIS-CORE
  int status;
  do {
    while ( __LDAEX(Lock_Variable) != 0){//Waits until the lock variable is free
      osThreadYield(); //CMSIS-RTOS2 function: passes control to the next thread
                // that is awaiting execution. If all threads are in a
                // waiting state (i.e. not ready for execution) then the
                // processor enters sleep using a WFE instruction
    }
```

```
   status = __STREXW(1, Lock_Variable);
       // Tries to set the Lock_Variable to 1 by using the STREX instruction
 } while (status != 0);
       // Retries the read-modify-write until the lock is successful
 return;
}
```

For the "`release_mutex()`" function, the code can be modified as follows:

```
// Function to release a shared resource with MUTEX (mutual exclusive)
void release_mutex(volatile int * Lock_Variable)
{
  __STL(0, Lock_Variable);
  // Frees the semaphore by clearing the lock variable
  // Note: STL has ordering semantic properties
  __DSB(); // Ensures write to the Lock_Variable is completed before executing
          // the SEV instruction
  __SEV(); // Sends event
  return;
}
```

A Data Synchronization Barrier (DSB) instruction is needed to prevent the event pulse generated by the SEV instruction reaching another processor before the write to Lock_Variable has finished.

Using this arrangement, the mutex/semaphore works across multiple processors. Fig. 21.1 shows the interaction of two mutex operations running on two separate processors.

21.3 Unprivileged interrupt handler

In Cortex-M processors, exception handlers are, by default, executed at privileged level. This is required so that exception requests can be served with low latency. Without this characteristic, the settings in the Memory Protection Unit (MPU) would have to be reprogrammed before handling an exception request. This would result in an increase in both latency and software overhead.

In some cases, however, it is beneficial to execute, for security reasons, some functions at unprivileged level within exception handlers. For example, the handler might need to execute functions inside an untrusted third party software library. This can be carried out in Armv8-M and Armv7-M processors by using a feature previously known as "Non-base thread enable". In Armv7-M architecture this feature has to be enabled manually by setting the bit 0 of the Configuration and Control Register (SCB->CCR). In Armv8-M processors, this capability is always enabled as a part of the exception handling architecture and the term "Non-base thread enable" is no longer used.

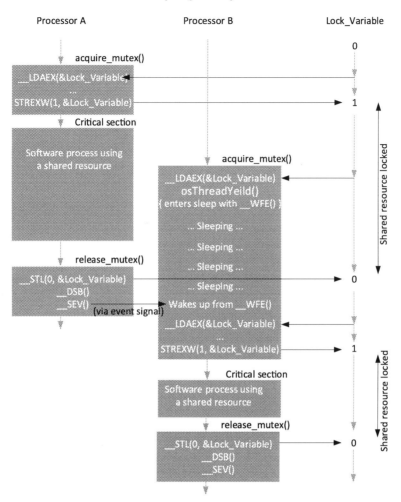

FIG. 21.1 Mutex/semaphore operation between two processors, with the processor releasing the semaphore waking up the other processor from WFE sleep using a SEV instruction.

Use this feature with caution

Because of the need to adjust the stack pointers and to manually manipulate data in the stacked memory, software developers must, when creating such code, carefully test its operation.

To change the execution of the handler to unprivileged and then, before ending the interrupt service routine, restore it back to privileged, an additional exception, usually the SVCall, is required to help with the switching steps (Fig. 21.2).

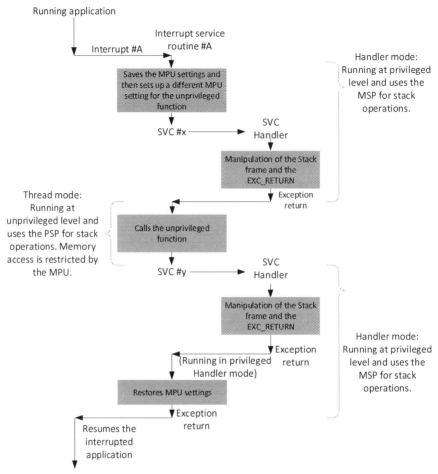

FIG. 21.2 Use of SVC services to switch the handler code execution to unprivileged level and then restore it back to privileged level.

In a TrustZone®-based system, both Secure and Non-secure MPU settings need to be updated when switching the exception handler to unprivileged. When creating the code for handling the MPU settings, a couple of different approaches can be taken. These are:

1. If an unprivileged function is allowed to call a function in an alternative security domain, the MPU settings of the alternative security state must also be updated so that the cross-security domain function call executes at the correct memory permission.
2. If an unprivileged function does not need to call a function in the alternative security domain, the processor's MPU can be set up to block code from executing in the alternative security state. This arrangement can be achieved by:

a. Setting up the alternative domain's MPU to only have a privileged background region. This is achieved by using the MPU_CTRL.PRIVDEFENA control bit in the MPU and by disabling all of the MPU regions.

b. Configuring the alternative domain's thread mode to unprivileged by setting the CONTROL.nPRIV bit of the alternative domain to 1 (i.e., thread mode is unprivileged).

If the second approach is used and if the unprivileged function does call a function in the alternative security state, an MPU violation would occur and the fault handler would carry out a full MPU reconfiguration so that the unprivileged function call can be resumed.

To create a code to demonstrate how an exception handler executes a function call in an unprivileged state, we first need to create the exception handler that contains the SVC calls and the call to the unprivileged code. I have used the SysTick exception handler for this example (refer to the code in the following section). To simplify things, the MPU setup is not included. Please note, because part of this function will be executed in an unprivileged state, that when defining MPU regions for this method in a real application, the program codes for this function (which switch the processor between privileged and unprivileged states) should be placed in an MPU region that is accessible by the unprivileged code.

Example SysTick handler code that calls the SVC services and calls the unprivileged handler

```
void SysTick_Handler(void)
{
  // Note: MPU configuration code is skipped in this example
  __ASM("svc #0\n\t");
  unprivileged_handler(); // Calls the unprivileged function
  __ASM("svc #1\n\t");
  // Note: Restoration of MPU settings is skipped in this example
  return;
}
```

The next step is to create the SVC handler. This handler is based on the SVC example shown in Chapter 11 and is divided into an assembly wrapper, which extracts the EXC_RETURN value and the MSP value when entering the interrupt service routine (ISR), and a handler written in C for the rest of the operation. The C handler returns a value to the assembly wrapper, with the assembly wrapper using this value as the EXC_RETURN value for exiting the exception handler. The assembly wrapper and the C code for the SVC handler is shown in the following section:

```
#define PROCESS_STACK_SIZE 512
#define MEM32(ADDRESS) (*((unsigned long *)(ADDRESS)))
static uint32_t saved_exc_return;
static uint32_t saved_old_psp;
static uint32_t saved_old_psplim;
static uint32_t saved_control;
static uint64_t process_stack[PROCESS_STACK_SIZE/8];
void __attribute__((naked)) SVC_Handler(void)
```

```c
{
  __asm volatile (
    "mov r0, lr\n\t"
    "mov r1, sp\n\t"
    "bl SVC_Handler_C\n\t"
    "bx r0\n\t"
    ); /* the return value of the SVC handler in C is used as EXC_RETURN */
}
uint32_t SVC_Handler_C(uint32_t exc_return_code, uint32_t msp_val)
{
  uint32_t new_exc_return;
  uint32_t stack_frame_addr;
  uint8_t  svc_number;
  unsigned int *svc_args;
  uint32_t temp, i;
  new_exc_return = exc_return_code; // Default return
  // ─────────────────────────────────────────────
  // Extracts SVC number
  // Determines which stack pointer was used
  if (exc_return_code & 0x4) stack_frame_addr = __get_PSP();
  else stack_frame_addr = msp_val;
  // Determines whether additional state context is present
  if (exc_return_code & 0x20) {// Additional state context is not present
    svc_args = (unsigned *) stack_frame_addr;}
  else {// Additional state context is present (Secure SVC only)
    svc_args = (unsigned *) (stack_frame_addr+40);}
  // Extracts SVC number
  svc_number = ((char *) svc_args[6])[-2]; // Memory[(stacked_pc)-2]
  if (svc_number == 0) {
    // ─────────────────────────────────────────────────
    // SVC Service to switch handler from privileged to
    // unprivileged and sets EXC_RETURN to use
    // the PSP on the exception return
    saved_exc_return = exc_return_code; // Saved for later use
    saved_old_psp = __get_PSP(); // Saved for later use
    saved_old_psplim = __get_PSPLIM(); // Saved for later use
    saved_control = __get_CONTROL(); // Saved for later use
    // Sets PSP to top of reserved process stack space - 32 (stack frame size)
    temp = ((uint32_t)(&process_stack[0])) + sizeof(process_stack) - 32;
    __set_PSP(temp);
    __set_PSPLIM(((uint32_t)(&process_stack[0])));
    for (i=0;i<7;i++){ // Copies stack frame to the stack pointed to by the PSP
      MEM32((temp + (i*4))) = svc_args[i];
      }
    // Clears the IPSR and stack alignment bit in the stacked xPSR
```

```
    MEM32((temp+0x1C)) = (svc_args[7]) & (~0x3FFUL);
    // Sets CONTROL[0] so Thread runs in unprivileged state
    __set_CONTROL(__get_CONTROL()|0x1);
    // Updates EXC_RETURN to return to thread with PSP, DCRS=1 & Ftype=1
    new_exc_return = new_exc_return|(1<<5)|(1<<4)|(1<<3)|(1<<2);
  } else if (svc_number == 1) {
    // ─────────────────────────────────────────────
    // SVC Service for switching handler from unprivileged to
    // privileged
    new_exc_return = saved_exc_return;
    __set_PSP(saved_old_psp);
    __set_PSPLIM(saved_old_psplim);
    __set_CONTROL(saved_control);
  } else {
    printf ("ERROR: Unknown SVC service number %d\n", svc_number);
  }
  return (new_exc_return);
}
```

The priority levels of the exceptions involved during the initialization of the hardware would also need to be defined. Because the SVC service is called from within the SysTick handler, the SysTick exception must have a lower priority level than the SVC exception. For example:

```
...
NVIC_SetPriority(SysTick_IRQn , 7); // Low priority
NVIC_SetPriority(SVCall_IRQn , 4);  // Medium priority
...
```

And, of course, we also need to create the custom defined unprivileged function ("`unprivileged_handler()`") that is executed when the processor is in unprivileged state.

The SVC services are used because the Interrupt Program Status register (IPSR) cannot be modified by writing directly to it. The only way you can change the IPSR is via an exception entry or return. Other exceptions, such as software-triggered interrupts, could be used, but they are not recommended because they are imprecise and could be masked; potentially resulting in the stack copying and switching operations not being carried out.

The overall sequence of events, which enables an exception handler to call a function in an unprivileged state, including the required SVC services, is shown in Fig. 21.3.

In Fig. 21.3, the manual adjustments of the PSP inside the SVC services are highlighted by circles, which are made up of dotted lines.

21.4 Re-entrant interrupt handler

One of the differences when comparing the architecture of Cortex-M processors to some other processor architectures is that Cortex-M processors do not have native support for

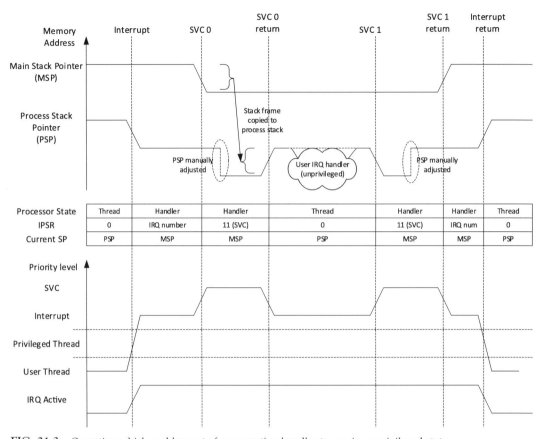

FIG. 21.3   Operation which enables part of an exception handler to run in unprivileged state.

re-entrant exceptions. In Cortex-M processors, the processor's priority level is updated automatically when an exception is accepted and when an exception service ends. During the servicing of the exception (including interrupts), exceptions with the same or a lower priority level are not accepted, if they are triggered. They instead remain in pending state and are serviced later when the on-going handler has completed its task.

The blocking of exceptions with the same or a lower priority level is beneficial to a system's reliability as the possibility of too many levels of re-entrant interrupts/exceptions can lead to stack overflow and deadlocks in software. However, this blocking behavior can be a problem for software developers that need to port legacy software because some of the legacy software relies on re-entrant exception behavior to work.

There is, fortunately, a software workaround for this issue. A wrapper can be created for the interrupt handler so that it switches itself into Thread mode, enabling it to again, if needed, be interrupted by the same interrupt. The wrapper code contains two parts: the first part is the interrupt handler that switches itself back to Thread state and executes the ISR task, and the second part is the SVC exception handler that restores the processor's exception state and resumes the original thread.

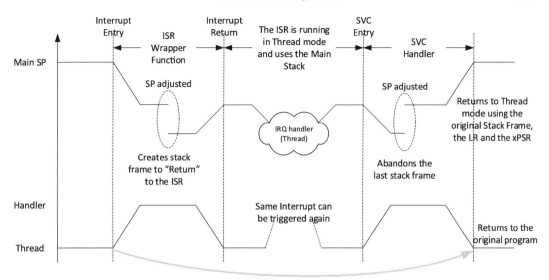

FIG. 21.4 Using a code wrapper to run an ISR in Thread mode to allow a re-entrant interrupt.

Use this workaround with caution

Generally, the use of re-entrant interrupts should be avoided. This method can, potentially, allow a very high number of nested interrupt executions and can, as a result, cause the stack to overflow. The re-entrant interrupt mechanism I have demonstrated here also requires the priority level of the example interrupt to be the lowest exception priority level in the system. If it was not, this workaround would fail if the re-entrant exception had preempted another lower priority exception.

The concept of the re-entrant interrupt code's operation is shown in Fig. 21.4.

An example code to demonstrate the operations showing in Fig. 21.4 is shown in the following code example:

```
#include "IOTKit_CM33_FP.h"
#include "stdio.h"
// Function declarations
void Reentrant_SysTick_Handler(void);
    // The C handler for the demonstration of the exception re-entrant
void __attribute__((naked)) SysTick_Handler(void); // handler wrapper
void __attribute__((naked)) SVC_Handler(void);
                        // SVC #0 is used to restore the stack state
uint32_t Get_SVC_num(uint32_t exc_return_code, uint32_t msp_val);
uint32_t Get_SVC_stackframe_top(uint32_t exc_return_code, uint32_t msp_val);
// Variable declaration
int static SysTick_Nest_Level=0;
```

```c
int main(void)
{
  printf("Reentrant handler demo\n");
  NVIC_SetPriority(SysTick_IRQn , 7); // Sets to a Low priority
  SCB->ICSR |= SCB_ICSR_PENDSTSET_Msk; // Sets SysTick pending status
  __DSB();
  __ISB();
  printf("Test ended\n");
  while(1);
}
void Reentrant_SysTick_Handler(void)
{
  printf ("[SysTick]\n");
  if (SysTick_Nest_Level < 3){
    SysTick_Nest_Level++;
    SCB->ICSR |= SCB_ICSR_PENDSTSET_Msk; //Sets pending status for the SysTick
    __DSB();
    __ISB();
    SysTick_Nest_Level-;
  } else {
    printf ("SysTick_Nest_Level = 3\n");
  }
  printf ("leaving [SysTick]\n");
  return;
}
// Handler wrapper code
void __attribute__((naked)) SysTick_Handler(void)
{
/* Now we are in Handler mode, MSP is selected and should be doubleword aligned */
  __asm volatile (
#if (__CORTEX_M >= 0x04)
#if (__FPU_USED == 1)
    /* The following 3 lines are only for Cortex-M processors with an FPU */
    "tst lr, #0x10\n\t" /* Test bit 4 & if zero, trigger stacking*/
    "it eq\n\t"
    "vmoveq.f32 s0, s0\n\t" /* Triggers lazy stacking */
#endif
#endif
    "mrs r0, CONTROL\n\t"
    "push {r0, lr}\n\t"      /* Saves CONTROL and LR in stack */
    "bics r0, r0, #1\n\t"    /* Sets thread as privileged */
    "msr CONTROL, r0\n\t"    /* Updates CONTROL */
    "sub sp, sp, #0x20\n\t" /* Reserves 8 words for a fake stack-frame for */
                            /* carrying out an exception return */
    "ldr r0,=SysTick_Handler_thread_pt\n\t" /* Obtains the return address */
```

```
    "str r0,[sp, #24]\n\t"     /* Places the return address in the stack frame*/
    "ldr r0,=0x01000000\n\t"  /* Creates default APSR for the fake stack frame */
    "str r0,[sp, #28]\n\t"     /* Places the xPSR in the stack frame */
    "mov r0, lr\n\t"           /* Obtains EXC_RETURN */
    "ubfx r1, r0, #0, #1\n\t"/* Copies EXC_RETURN.ES to EXC_RETURN.S so that*/
    "bfi r0, r1, #6, #1\n\t"  /* it returns to the same security domain */
    "orr r0, r0, #0x38\n\t"   /* Sets DCRS - std, FType - no FP, Mode - thread */
    "bics r0, r0, #0x4\n\t"   /* Uses the MSP for the handler in the thread */
    "mov lr, r0\n\t"
    "bx lr\n\t"    /* Carries out an exception return */
  "SysTick_Handler_thread_pt:\n\t"
    "bl Reentrant_SysTick_Handler\n\t"
    /* Blocks SysTick from being triggered just before SVC */
    "ldr r0,=0xe000ed23\n\t" /* Loads address of SysTick priority level reg*/
    "ldr r0,[r0] \n\t"
    "msr basepri, r0\n\t"     /* Blocks SysTick from being triggered */
    "isb\n\t"                 /* Instruction Synchronization Barrier */
    "mrs r0, CONTROL\n\t"
    "bics r0, r0, #0x4\n\t"   /* Clears CONTROL.FPCA to simplify stack frame*/
    "msr CONTROL, r0\n\t"     /* Updates CONTROL */
    "svc #0\n\t"              /* Uses an SVC to switch back to privileged */
    "b  .\n\t"                /* Program execution should not reach here */
    );
}
void __attribute__((naked)) SVC_Handler(void)
{
    __asm volatile (
    "movs r0, #0\n\t" /* Clears BASEPRI to allow SysTick */
    "msr basepri, r0\n\t"
#if (__CORTEX_M >= 0x04)
#if (__FPU_USED == 1)
    /* The following 3 lines are only for Cortex-M processors with an FPU */
    "tst lr, #0x10\n\t"     /* Test bit 4 & if zero, trigger stacking */
    "it eq\n\t"
    "vmoveq.f32 s0, s0\n\t" /* Triggers lazy stacking */
#endif
#endif
    "mov r0, lr\n\t"
    "mov r1, sp\n\t"
    "push {r0, r3}\n\t" /* r3 is not needed but pushed to keep SP 64b aligned*/
    "bl Get_SVC_num\n\t" /* "Get_SVC_num" function places SVC number in r0 */
    "pop {r2, r3}\n\t"   /* EXC_RETURN is now in r2 */
    "cmp r0, #0\n\t"
    "bne Unknown_SVC_Request\n\t"
    "mov r0, r2\n\t" /* EXC_RETURN is set as the 1st parameter*/
```

```
    "mov r1, sp\n\t"   /* MSP is set as the 2nd parameter */
    "bl Get_SVC_stackframe_top\n\t" /* top of SVC stack frame returns in r0 */
    "mov sp, r0\n\t"
    "pop {r0, lr}\n\t" /* Obtains original CONTROL and EXC_RETURN */
    "msr CONTROL, r0\n\t"
    "bx lr\n\t"             /* Returns to the original interrupted code */
  "Unknown_SVC_Request: \n\t" /* Error condition - Unknown SVC number (not 0) *
    "bkpt 0\n\t"            /* Triggers breakpoint to halt the processor */
    "b .\n\t"              /* Program execution should not reach here */
 );
}
// ————————————————————————————
uint32_t Get_SVC_num(uint32_t exc_return_code, uint32_t msp_val)
{ /* Extract SVC number */
  uint32_t stack_frame_addr;
  uint8_t  svc_number;
  unsigned int *svc_args;
  // ————————————————————————————
  // Determines which stack pointer was used
  if (exc_return_code & 0x4) stack_frame_addr = __get_PSP();
  else stack_frame_addr = msp_val;
  // Determines if the additional state context is present
  if (exc_return_code & 0x20) {
     svc_args = (unsigned *) stack_frame_addr;}
  else {// additional state context is present but only for the Secure SVC
     svc_args = (unsigned *) (stack_frame_addr+40);}
  // extracts SVC number
  svc_number = ((char *) svc_args[6])[-2]; // Memory[(stacked_pc)-2]
  return (svc_number);
}
// ————————————————————————————
uint32_t Get_SVC_stackframe_top(uint32_t exc_return_code, uint32_t msp_val)
{ // Returns the top of the stack frame. Assumptions are:
  // - No FP context in FPU because CONTROL.FPCA is cleared before SVC #0
  // - No need to include padding word in the calculation because SVC #0 is
  // called when stack is double word aligned
  uint32_t stack_frame_addr;
  // ————————————————————————————
  // Determines which stack pointer was used
  if (exc_return_code & 0x4) stack_frame_addr = __get_PSP();
  else stack_frame_addr = msp_val;
  // Determines if the additional state context is present
  if ((exc_return_code & 0x20)==0)
    {// additional state context is present but only for the Secure SVC
    stack_frame_addr = stack_frame_addr+40;
    }
```

```
stack_frame_addr = stack_frame_addr+0x20; // adjusts by 8 words to get to the
                                          // top of the stack frame
return (stack_frame_addr);
}
```

Note:

- The priority level of the re-entrant interrupt handler needs to be set to the lowest when compared to the rest of the interrupts and exceptions.
- The BASEPRI should be set before triggering the SVC. This prevents the re-entrant exception (i.e., the SysTick in this case) from triggering just before the SVC, which results in a tail-chaining transition from the re-entrant interrupt handler to the SVC. If this happens, the SVC handler cannot correctly re-adjust the stack pointer because the SP value is changed by the re-entrant exception.
- The handlers force the deferred lazy stacking to take place to ensure that the FPU contexts are saved in the nested ISR when the FPU operations have been carried out.

21.5 Software optimization topics

21.5.1 Complex decision trees and conditional branches

When creating a program code, there is often a need to create conditional branches that are based on a complex set of conditions. For example, a conditional branch might depend on the value of an integer variable. If the range of the variable is small, e.g., 0–31, there are ways to simplify the program code to make the decision-making process inside the program more efficient.

Assuming we want to detect whether the value of an integer in the range of 0–31 is a prime number, the simplest code to use is:

```
int is_a_prime_number(unsigned int i)
{
  if ((i==2) || (i==3) || (i==5) || (i==7) ||
     (i==11) || (i==13) || (i==17) || (i==19) ||
     (i==23) || (i==29) || (i==31)) {
    return 1;
  } else {
    return 0;
  }
}
```

However, the compilation of this code could potentially generate a very long-branch tree. We can prevent this from happening by encoding the condition into a binary pattern and use this for the following conditional branch operation:

```
int is_a_prime_number(unsigned int i)
{
  /* Bit pattern is
```

```
    31:0 - 1010 0000 1000 1010 0010 1000 1010 1100 = 0xA08A28AC */
  if ((1<<i) & (0xA08A28ACUL)) {
    return (1);
  } else {
    return (0);
  }
}
```

This example greatly simplifies the condition checking code, results in a faster program speed and a smaller code size. Please note, some modern C compilers can handle the code transformation for you.

There are several ways of optimizing this code at the assembly programming level. The first method is as per the following steps and as per Fig. 21.5:

(1) By shifting, that is in this example, using the "LSLS" instruction, the value #1 left by N bits (where N represents the condition input).
(2) Then by performing an "ANDS" operation between the shift result and a condition pattern (i.e., the bit patterns in the bottom part of Fig. 21.5). This results in the Z flag being updated by the "ANDS" operation.
(3) And finally, by using a conditional branch using the Z flag.

The second method, which requires $N > 0$ (where N represents the condition input), is as follows (Fig. 21.6):

(1) By shifting the condition pattern right by N bit ($N > 0$) so that the required condition bit is shifted into the carry flag
(2) By then using a conditional branch with the decision based on the status of the carry flag

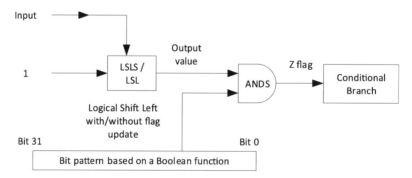

FIG. 21.5 Conditional branch with predefined condition pattern table—method 1.

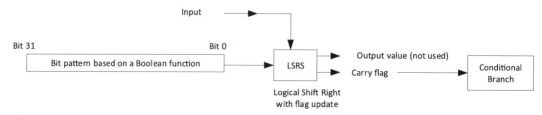

FIG. 21.6 Conditional branch with a predefined condition pattern table—method 2.

Method 2 could be 1 cycle quicker than method 1 if the input value (i.e., the binary representation of the condition input) is always greater than 0. If this requirement is not met, an extra ADD instruction would be needed to adjust the input, resulting in both method 1 and method 2 taking around the same number of clock cycles to execute.

A modified version of this condition lookup method can be used when the decision of a conditional branch is dependent upon several binary inputs. For example, in a software-based Finite State Machine (FSM) design, you might need to determine the next state, based on several binary inputs. The following code merges four binary inputs into an integer and uses it for a conditional branch:

```c
int branch_decision(unsigned int i0, unsigned int i1, unsigned int i2,
unsigned int i3,unsigned int i4,unsigned int i)
{
  unsigned int tmp;
  tmp = i0<<0;
  tmp |= i1<<1;
  tmp |= i2<<2;
  tmp |= i3<<3;
  tmp |= i4<<4;
  if ((1<<tmp) & (0xA08A28AC)) { // Pattern of conditions (i.e. a Lookup table)
    return(1);
  } else {
    return(0);
  }
}
```

If the number of possible conditions is more then 32, then multiple words (each word is 32 bits) of the condition look-up pattern is needed. For example, to determine whether an input number with a value of 0–127 is a prime number, the following code could be used:

```c
int is_a_prime_number(unsigned int i)
{
/* Bit pattern is
  31: 0 - 1010 0000 1000 1010 0010 1000 1010 1100 = 0xA08A28AC
  63:32 - 0010 1000 0010 0000 1000 1010 0010 0000 = 0x28208A20
  95:64 - 0000 0010 0000 1000 1000 0010 1000 1000 = 0x02088288
 127:96 - 1000 0000 0000 0010 0010 1000 1010 0010 = 0x800228A2
  */
  const uint32_t bit_pattern[4] = {0xA08A28AC,
            0x28208A20, 0x02088288, 0x800228A2};
  uint32_t i1, i2;
  i1 = i & 0x1F;          // Bit position
  i2 = (i & 0x60) >> 5;   // Mask index
  if ((1<<i1) & (bit_pattern[i2])) {
    return(1);
  } else {
    return(0);
  }
}
```

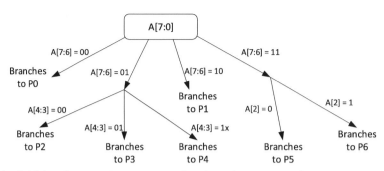

FIG. 21.7   A bit field decoder example—a situation that shows how UBFX and TBB instructions are utilized.

21.5.2 Complex decision tree

In many instances, a decision tree of conditional branches can have many different destination paths (i.e., the result is not binary). Two of the important instructions in the Armv8-M Mainline and Armv7-M processors for handling these branching operations are the table branch instructions TBB and TBH. Information about table branch instructions can be found in Chapter 5, Section 5.14.7. In the same chapter, the bit field extract instructions, UBFX and SBFX, were covered in Section 5.12. In this section, I will explain how complex decision trees can be efficiently handled by combining bit field extract's and table branch instructions.

In many applications, such as communication protocol handling, the decoding of communication packet headers, or other forms of binary information, can take up a significant amount of processing time. In this type of processing, data can be packed into various types of packet formats, with specific bit fields in the data header being used to select the packet format type to use for the decoding of the data. A decoding operation such as this can be represented in the form of a decision tree. For example, a decision tree, which decodes an 8-bit value (Input A) is shown in Fig. 21.7.

The aforementioned decision tree can be broken down into several smaller table branches, as demonstrated by the example assembly code in the following section:

```
DecodeA
    LDR   R0,=A           ; Obtains the value of A from memory
    LDR   R0,[R0]
    UBFX  R1, R0, #6, #2  ; Extracts bit[7:6] into R1
    TBB   [PC, R1]
BrTable1
    DCB   ((P0      -BrTable1)/2) ; Branches to P0      if A[7:6] = 00
    DCB   ((DecodeA1-BrTable1)/2) ; Branches to DecodeA1 if A[7:6] = 01
    DCB   ((P1      -BrTable1)/2) ; Branches to P1      if A[7:6] = 10
    DCB   ((DecodeA2-BrTable1)/2) ; Branches to DecodeA1 if A[7:6] = 11
DecodeA1
    UBFX  R1, R0, #3, #2  ; Extracts bit[4:3] into R1
    TBB   [PC, R1]
```

```
BrTable2
    DCB ((P2 -BrTable2)/2) ; Branches to P2  if A[4:3] = 00
    DCB ((P3 -BrTable2)/2) ; Branches to P3  if A[4:3] = 01
    DCB ((P4 -BrTable2)/2) ; Branches to P4  if A[4:3] = 10
    DCB ((P4 -BrTable2)/2) ; Branches to P4  if A[4:3] = 11
DecodeA2
    TST R0, #4 ; Because only 1 bit is tested there is no need to use the UBFX
    BEQ P5
    B   P6
P0 ... ; Process 0
P1 ... ; Process 1
P2 ... ; Process 2
P3 ... ; Process 3
P4 ... ; Process 4
P5 ... ; Process 5
P6 ... ; Process 6
```

The example code completes the decision tree by way of a short assembler code sequence. If the branch target address offsets are too large for the TBB instruction, some of the table branch operations can be implemented using the TBH instruction instead.

Of course, for many application developers it is rare to use assembly language for modern projects. Fortunately, it is possible to efficiently handle bit fields using the C/C++ programming language—a topic that is covered in Section 21.5.3.

21.5.3 Bit data handling in C/C++

In C or C++, you can define bit fields, and by correctly using this feature, can generate more efficient code in the areas of bit data and bit field handling. For example, when dealing with I/O port control tasks, you can define a data structure of bits and a union in C to make coding easier:

Helper C structure and union definition in bit data handling

```
typedef struct /* structure to define 32-bits */
{
  uint32_t bit0:1;
  uint32_t bit1:1;
  uint32_t bit2:1;
  uint32_t bit3:1;
  uint32_t bit4:1;
  uint32_t bit5:1;
  uint32_t bit6:1;
  uint32_t bit7:1;
  uint32_t bit8:1;
  uint32_t bit9:1;
```

Continued

```
  uint32_t bit10:1;
  uint32_t bit11:1;
  uint32_t bit12:1;
  uint32_t bit13:1;
  uint32_t bit14:1;
  uint32_t bit15:1;
  uint32_t bit16:1;
  uint32_t bit17:1;
  uint32_t bit18:1;
  uint32_t bit19:1;
  uint32_t bit20:1;
  uint32_t bit21:1;
  uint32_t bit22:1;
  uint32_t bit23:1;
  uint32_t bit24:1;
  uint32_t bit25:1;
  uint32_t bit26:1;
  uint32_t bit27:1;
  uint32_t bit28:1;
  uint32_t bit29:1;
  uint32_t bit30:1;
  uint32_t bit31:1;
} ubit32_t;         /*!< Structure used for bit access */
typedef union
{
  ubit32_t ub; /*!< Type used for unsigned bit access */
  uint32_t uw; /*!< Type used for unsigned word access */
} bit32_Type;
```

Using this newly created data type, variables can then be declared and the bit field access made easier. For example:

```
bit32_Type foo;
foo.uw = GPIOD->IDR; // .uw access using word size
if (foo.ub.bit14) { // .ub access using bit size
    GPIOD->BSRRH = (1<<14); // Clears bit 14
  } else {
    GPIOD->BSRRL = (1<<14); // Sets bit 14
  }
```

In the earlier discussed example, the compiler generates a UBFX instruction to extract the required bit value. If the bit fields are defined as signed integers, the SBFX instruction will be used instead.

The bit field typedef can be used in various ways, e.g., it can be used to declare a pointer to the register as follows:

```
volatile bit32_Type * LED;
LED = (bit32_Type *) (&GPIOD->IDR);
if (LED->ub.bit12) { // uses the extracted bit for a conditional branch
   GPIOD->BSRRH = (1<<12); // Clears bit 12
 } else {
   GPIOD->BSRRL = (1<<12); // Sets bit 12
 }
```

Please note, writing to a bit or bit field using this kind of code can result in a software read-modify-write sequence being generated by the C compiler. For I/O control this might be undesirable because if another bit is changed by an interrupt handler, which takes place between the read and write operations, the bit change made by the interrupt handler could be overwritten after the interrupt returns.

A bit field can have multiple bits. For example, the complex decision tree described in Section 21.5.2 can be written in C as follows:

```
typedef struct
{
uint32_t bit1to0:2;
uint32_t bit2 :1;
uint32_t bit4to3:2;
uint32_t bit5 :1;
uint32_t bit7to6:2;
} A_bitfields_t;
typedef union
{
  A_bitfields_t ub; /*!< Type used for bit access */
  uint32_t      uw; /*!< Type used for word access */
} A_Type;
void decision(uint32_t din)
{
  A_Type A;
  A.uw = din;
  switch (A.ub.bit7to6) {
  case 0:
     P0();
     break;
 case 1:
   switch (A.ub.bit4to3) {
      case 0:
        P2();
        break;
```

```
        case 1:
           P3();
           break;
        default:
           P4();
           break;
     };
     break;
   case 2:
     P1();
     break;
   default:
     if (A.ub.bit2) P6();
     else P5();
     break;
   }
   return;
}
```

21.5.4 Other performance considerations

In general, the Cortex-M based microcontrollers and SoC products that are available in the market are already well optimized for performance. During the design stage of the microcontroller or the SoC, the chip designer(s) has usually:

- Ensured that the memory access paths are at least 32-bit wide.
- When using the Cortex-M33 processor, optimized the memory system design to, whenever possible, allow instruction and data access to be carried out at the same time.

For software developers, there are a number of things that are worth considering for maximizing the system's performance and/or efficiency:

(1) Avoid memory wait states by running the Cortex-M device at optimal clock speed: Most microcontroller devices use flash memories for storing programs. If the processor system is set to run at a clock speed faster than the embedded flash, wait states are introduced during program fetches, resulting in stall cycles that reduces the energy efficiency of the system. Therefore, it is possible to achieve better energy efficiency by running the system at a slower clock speed to avoid wait states in the flash memory. For Cortex-M systems with a system level cache, the impact of flash memory wait states could be marginal as the flash memory is only accessed when there is a cache miss—an occurrence that is relatively rare.

(2) Arrange memory layout to enhance the performance of the program: If the processor is based on Harvard bus architecture (e.g., Cortex-M33 processor), memory configurations used in the software project should utilize its nature. For example, the memory map of the project should be arranged so that:(1) the program is executed from the CODE region and, (2) the majority of data accesses (apart from literal data within program codes) are carried out via the system bus. By doing so, data accesses and instruction fetches can be carried out at the same time.

(3) Utilize Harvard bus architecture to reduce interrupt latency: When using a processor with Harvard bus architecture, the memory layout of the project should be arranged so that stacking operations (i.e., RAM accesses), and access to the interrupt vector table and instructions (program accesses), can be carried out in parallel. This arrangement will reduce interrupt latency. This can be achieved by putting the program code, including the vector table, in the CODE region and the stack memories in the SRAM region.

(4) If possible, avoid using unaligned data transfers in the software: Since unaligned data transfers take two or more bus transactions to complete, they can reduce performance. Although compilations of most C programs do not generate unaligned data, unaligned data access can occur in program codes that contain direct pointer manipulations and packed structures (`__pack`). If you plan the data structure layouts carefully, the need for packed structures can usually be avoided. In assembly language programming, you can use the ALIGN directive to ensure that a data location is aligned.

(5) Avoid stack-based parameter passing: If possible, limit your function calls to four or fewer input parameters so that only registers are used for parameter passing. When there are more input parameters, the remaining parameters are transferred via the stack memory and, therefore, take longer to set up and to access. When there is a lot of information to be transferred, it is best to group the data into a data structure, and pass a pointer, which points to the data structure, to reduce the number of parameters needed.

Unlike the Cortex-M3 and Cortex-M4 processors, the performance of the Cortex-M33 processor is not reduced by running the program code from the system bus. Assuming that a Cortex-M33-based system has memories with a zero wait-state, the performance of the following scenarios (a) and (b) will be the same:

(a) Running a program from the CODE region with data in the SRAM region
(b) Running a program from the SRAM region with data in the CODE region

However, in most instances, for devices based on the Cortex-M33 processor, the memory system is optimized for scenario (a) because peripherals are placed on the system bus in the Peripheral region. As a result, arrangement (a) allows the peripheral accesses and instruction accesses to be carried out in parallel.

21.5.5 Optimizations at assembly language level

Most software developers use C/C++ language for embedded programming, but for those who use assembly, you can use a few tricks to speed up parts of the program.

Note: In the following code examples, I used the NVIC priority level configuration to illustrate several optimization techniques. In real-world applications, however, because CMSIS-CORE APIs are more portable, it is more common to use them to configure the NVIC priority levels.

(1) Use memory access instructions with offset addressing: When multiple memory locations in a small region are to be accessed, instead of writing:

```
LDR R0, =0xE000E400 ; Sets interrupt priority #3,#2,#1,#0 address
LDR R1, =0xE0C02000 ; priority levels (#3,#2,#1,#0)
STR R1,[R0]
LDR R0, =0xE000E404 ; Sets interrupt priority #7,#6,#5,#4 address
LDR R1, =0xE0E0E0E0 ; priority levels (#7,#6,#5,#4)
STR R1,[R0]
```

Reduce the program code to the following:

```
LDR R0, =0xE000E400 ; Sets interrupt priority #3,#2,#1,#0 address
LDR R1, =0xE0C02000 ; priority levels (#3,#2,#1,#0)
STR R1,[R0]
LDR R1, =0xE0E0E0E0 ; priority levels (#7,#6,#5,#4)
STR R1,[R0,#4] ;
```

The second store (i.e., the STR instruction) uses an offset from the first address, and hence, reduces the number of instructions.

(2) Combine multiple memory access instructions into a single Load/Store Multiple instruction (LDM/STM): The preceding example can be further reduced by using the STM instruction as follows:

```
LDR R0,=0xE000E400 ; Sets interrupt priority base
LDR R1,=0xE0C02000 ; priority levels #3,#2,#1,#0
LDR R2,=0xE0E0E0E0 ; priority levels #7,#6,#5,#4
STMIA R0, {R1, R2}
```

(3) Utilize memory addressing modes: You can improve performance by making use of the available addressing mode features. For example, when reading a look-up table, instead of calculating the read address with an LSL (shift) and an ADD operation (code in the following section refers):

```
Read_Table
 ; Input R0 = index
 LDR R1,=Look_up_table ; Address of the lookup table
 LDR R1, [R1]           ; Obtains lookup table base address
 LSL R2, R0, #2         ; Index multiplied by 4
                        ; (each item in the table is 4 bytes)
 ADD R2, R1             ; Calculates the actual address(base+offset)
 LDR R0, [R2]           ; Reads table
 BX  LR                 ; Function-return
 ALIGN 4
 Look_up_table
 DCD 0x12345678
 DCD 0x23456789
 . . .
```

You can, in the Cortex-M33 processor, by using the code in the following section, significantly reduce the code by utilizing the shift operation in the register's relative addressing mode:

```
Read_Table
 ; Input R0 = index
 LDR R1,=Look_up_table ; Address of the lookup table
 LDR R1, [R1]   ; Obtains lookup table base address
```

```
LDR R0, [R1, R0, LSL #2] ; Reads table with base + (index << 2)
BX LR    ; Function-return
ALIGN 4
Look_up_table
DCD 0x12345678
DCD 0x23456789
. . .
```

(4) Replace a small branch with the IT (IF-THEN) instruction block: Because the Cortex-M33 is a pipelined processor, a branch penalty happens when a branch operation occurs. Replacing some of the conditional branches with IT instruction blocks avoids the branch penalty issues and may achieve a better performance. This is demonstrated in the following code:

Using a conditional branch	Replacing a conditional branch using an IT instruction block
```CMP R0, R1 ; 1 cycle` `BNE Label1 ; 2 cycles or 1 cycle` `ADDS .... ; 1 cycle` `B Label2 ; 2 cycles` `Label1` `MOVS .... ; 1 cycle` `Label2```	```CMP R0, R1 ; 1 cycle` `ITTTT EQ ; 1 cycle` `ADDEEQ ....; 1 cycle` `MOVNE .... ; 1 cycle```
Note: condition "not equal" takes 4 cycles, condition "equal" takes 5 cycles	Note: Assume IT folding does not take place, both execution paths take 4 cycles. (Saving 1 clock cycle if the condition is "equal").

However, you need to check the clock cycle saving on a case-by-case basis. For example, in the following example code you will not be able to save any clock cycles by using the IT instruction:

Using conditional branch	Using IT
```CMP R0, R1 ; 1 cycle` `BNE Label ; 2 cycles or 1 cycle` `MOVS .... ; 1 cycle` `MOVS .... ; 1 cycle` `MOVS .... ; 1 cycle` `MOVS .... ; 1 cycle` `Label```	```CMP R0, R1 ; 1 cycle` `ITTTT EQ ; 1 cycle` `MOVEQ .... ; 1 cycle` `MOVEQ .... ; 1 cycle` `MOVEQ .... ; 1 cycle` `MOVEQ .... ; 1 cycle```
Note: Condition "not equal" takes 3 cycles and condition "equal" takes 6 cycles.	Note: Assume IT folding does not take place, both paths take 6 cycles. Performance is slower when compared to the conditional branch method

(5) Reduce instruction counts: In the Cortex-M23 and Cortex-M33 processors, if an operation can be carried out by either two Thumb instructions or a single Thumb-2 instruction, the Thumb-2 instruction method should be used. This is because even though the memory size is the same, it might give a shorter execution time.[b]

(6) Place a 32-bit branch target instruction at a 32-bit aligned address: If the target of a branch is a 32-bit instruction and is not aligned to a 32-bit address, the branch takes one extra clock cycle because it takes two bus transfers to fetch the complete instruction. This performance penalty can be avoided by ensuring that the 32-bit branch target instruction is aligned. To enable the alignment, you might need to replace a preceding 16-bit thumb instruction with a 32-bit version.

(7) Optimize instruction sequences based on the processor's pipeline behavior: If you are using the Cortex-M33 processor, a data read instruction, followed by a data processing instruction which process the read data, can result in a stall cycle. The reduction of performance caused by the stall cycle can be avoided by scheduling other instructions in between the read and the data processing instructions.

Reference

[1] Armv8-M Architecture Reference Manual. https://developer.arm.com/documentation/ddi0553/am/ (Armv8.0-M only version). https://developer.arm.com/documentation/ddi0553/latest/ (latest version including Armv8.1-M). Note: M-profile architecture reference manuals for Armv6-M, Armv7-M, Armv8-M and Armv8.1-M can be found here: https://developer.arm.com/architectures/cpu-architecture/m-profile/docs.

[b]Not always the case for the Cortex-M33 processor because it has a limited dual-issue capability.

Introduction to IoT security and the PSA Certified™ framework

22.1 From processor architecture to IoT security

In previous chapters, the contents were focused on low-level processor operations/behaviors and its architecture. Many application developers rarely need to go into low-level detail because the security capabilities of the systems or the software projects they are working on are often defined by product level security features. These features include:

- The cryptography of communication data,
- Authentication,
- Secure boot,
- Secure firmware updates…

Although the Arm® TrustZone® technology security features of Armv8-M processors appear to be very different from the aforementioned application-level security features, the fact of the matter is that TrustZone support provides the essential hardware required to build and safeguard those previously mentioned features.

That said, there is a need to bridge the gap between the application-level requirements and the processor's security capabilities. This is not an easy task as multiple aspects of security needs are involved, even in the most basic of IoT applications. To create secure IoT product solutions, these security aspects need to be addressed by both software and hardware developers who have the required specialized knowledge and experience.

In the past, a range of security software solutions was available from the embedded software ecosystem, but most of these solutions only addressed a few aspects of the IoT's security requirements; additional efforts were, therefore, needed to integrate the multiple security solutions that were available to satisfy all of the requirements. If the integration of those software solutions is not correctly undertaken, or if one of the security aspects is missing from the solution, there is a high likelihood that the integrated solution will still suffer from security vulnerabilities.

Even when the software solution is complete, because of potential shortcomings in the design of a silicon product's security features, security issues could still arise. Accordingly, it was clear that there was a need to define the essential security requirements for hardware system designs.

It was also clear that there was a need for the IoT industry to establish a "gold standard" for affordable and scalable IoT product security. This was a significant undertaking and despite Arm being a leading provider of processors and system component designs, and having heavily invested in various open-source projects, it was apparent that, rather than Arm tacking this challenge on its own, collaboration between companies within the electronic industry was the way forward. To this end, Arm set up working relationships with silicon partners, various ecosystem partners, and other companies that work with and within the IoT industry.

In October 2017, Arm announced[a] the Platform Security Architecture (PSA) [1], a framework that defined the security requirements for IoT devices; which, in 2019, was expanded to become PSA Certified™ [2]. This is an ongoing journey to drive the security standard in connected devices and to make the development of secure IoT products easier.

At launch, PSA Certified was widely endorsed by the technology ecosystem and among those that did so were as follows:

• A wide range of world-leading silicon partners
• RTOS vendors
• Original equipment manufacturers (OEMs)
• Security software solution vendors
• System solution vendors
• Cloud service providers

Increasingly, a number of government regulators are becoming more aware of the security issues surrounding IoT products and are working on legislation to ensure that IoT products have sound IoT security capabilities. There is now, therefore, an even stronger need for product developers to ensure that their designs are secure.

In addition to making products more secure, PSA Certified also aims to make life easier for software developers. The PSA Functional APIs (which are implemented as part of Trusted Firmware-M, also known as TF-M) provide a portable software interface for applications and for firmware development. Further information on this can be found in Section 22.3.3, PSA Functional APIs.

22.2 Introduction of PSA Certified

22.2.1 Overview of the security principles

IoT security covers many aspects. Traditionally, when talking about security, the first thing people might think about is the security of data transfers between IoT devices and cloud services. Often cryptography techniques are involved to ensure that the information is not

---

[a]https://www.arm.com/company/news/2017/10/a-common-industry-framework.

leaked. However, there is a need for security well before we get to the stage of securely transferring the aforementioned data. For example:

- Before a device can connect to an IoT service, some form of authentication is needed. This is often handled by attestation (the process could be hidden inside product activation), with a mechanism inside the chip for establishing the identity of the device.
- Since the software on a device might have bugs, secret information such as crypto keys needs to be stored in secure storage (storage areas, which cannot be accessed during the execution of general software).
- Overtime, software bugs might be found and there might be a need for updating the device's software to allow additional features to be added/updated. To enable this, a secure firmware update mechanism would be needed.
- Because big data (composed of "small" data from potentially millions of IoT devices) could be maliciously manipulated if a person was able to clone or modify the millions of IoT devices that generate the "small" data, there is a need for these devices to support secure boot and unique ID features.

So, how do you define security requirements? It is a challenging question: in many respects, the security requirements are dependent on the applications, which can be subjected to a number of security threats. The identification of threats that are applicable to an application and the definition of countermeasures are typically referred to as "threat model". Once the threat model is defined, we are then in a position to define the method(s) needed to address the threats and work out what solutions are required to address them.

After an in-depth analysis of a number of IoT applications and their threat models, PSA Certified^{TM} identified 10 security goals (Fig. 22.1) [3], which were common to the majority of IoT systems and which would need to be implemented to meet the security requirements.

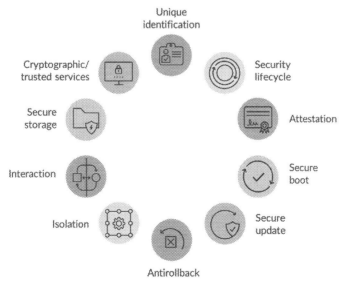

FIG. 22.1 PSA Certified defines 10 security goals to meet security best practices.

FIG. 22.2 The PSA Root of Trust (PSA-RoT) defines the four key requirements for source of integrity and confidentiality.

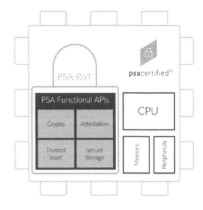

Defining the security goals enables a product's security requirements to be defined, but because each application has specific security needs, further product-specific definitions are required.

For an IoT product to achieve its security goals, it must meet the requirements of one of the key anchor points known as "Root of Trust". Fig. 22.2 shows the PSA Certified key elements, which make up the Root of Trust.

The PSA Root of Trust (PSA-RoT) is a source of confidentiality (it can keep secrets such as crypto keys) and integrity (you can rely on this system being unaltered from its intended state). To help software developers access the Root of Trust features, PSA Certified defines a set of PSA Functional APIs.[b] These simple to use APIs cover secure storage, cryptography, and attestation operations. Because the secure boot (i.e., the Trusted boot shown in Fig. 22.2) is used when a device starts up and is not used once the system is running, there is no need for a secure boot API.

22.2.2 How to get there?

22.2.2.1 The four pillars of PSA Certified

To address security needs, PSA Certified defines four key stages for addressing the security challenges. These are shown in Fig. 22.3.

Note: The documents referred to in the following sections can be downloaded by using the following Arm web page link [4]: https://developer.arm.com/architectures/security-architectures/platform-security-architecture/documentation.

22.2.2.2 Stage 1—Analyze

The first stage when addressing the security requirements of a product is to analyze what the security risks are and then identifying the key security measures that are needed. To help the industry, PSA Certified offers, at no cost, several examples of Threat Model and Security

---

[b]https://www.psacertified.org/functional-api-certification/psa-developer-apis/.

FIG. 22.3 The four stages for addressing security needs with PSA Certified.

Analysis (TMSA) that are applicable for the most common IoT applications. At the time of writing this book, the following TMSA documents were available:

- Asset Tracker TMSA
- Smart Water Meter TMSA
- Network Camera TMSA

These documents have been written with terminologies that are aligned with industrial standards (such as Common Criteria). Using TMSA as a starting point, security objectives and detailed Security Functional Requirements (SFRs) can be defined.

Although the TMSA documents provided do not cover all IoT applications, they are useful as a starting point for system designers who want to create a TMSA for their own IoT projects.

22.2.2.3 Stage 2—Architect

The architect stage defines the architecture required to cover the security requirements identified in stage 1. There is a range of specifications, which covers various topics. These include:

- Security Model (PSA-SM)—details the top-level requirements for secure designs of all products. This document outlines the key goals for designing products with known security properties. In addition, it also provides important terminology and methodology for PSA Certified.
- "PSA Trusted Base System Architecture for Armv6-M, Armv7-M, and Armv8-M" (TBSA-M) [5]—a specification document for microcontrollers and SoC hardware designs based on Arm Cortex®-M processors.
- Trusted Boot and Firmware Update (PSA-TBFU)—a specification covering system and firmware requirements for firmware boot and update.
- PSA Firmware Framework for M (PSA-FF-M)—a specification for a standard programming environment and fundamental Root of Trust (RoT) for secure applications on a Cortex-M based product.
- PSA Firmware Framework for A (PSA-FF-A)—a specification for a standard programming environment and fundamental Root of Trust (RoT) for secure applications on a Cortex-A-based product.

For products aiming to be PSA Functional API Certified, the software framework used needs to follow the requirements as defined in PSA-FF-M/A. Additional information about PSA Functional API Certified is covered in Section 22.2.4.

22.2.2.4 Stage 3—Implement

The third stage of implementing a security system is the implementation itself. Implementing secure software requires a great deal of knowledge. In addition to understanding the processor's security features, software developers also need to understand cryptography and other specialized topics, for example, have knowledge about the various forms of software attacks and how to prevent them from occurring.

Based on the PSA Functional APIs, the secure firmware provides a consistent interface to the underlying Root of Trust hardware and security features. The APIs are divided into three areas:

- PSA Functional APIs for RTOS and software developers,
- PSA Firmware Framework APIs for security specialists, and
- TBSA APIs for silicon manufacturers.

Since the majority of the firmware's framework is common between connected devices, Arm offers an open-source reference implementation of the PSA Firmware framework called Trusted Firmware-M (TF-M). It provides the source code for the PSA Firmware Framework APIs and PSA Functional APIs. (Note: TF-M provides Hardware Abstraction Layer (HAL) APIs, which, although they are not the same as the TBSA APIs, they cover functionalities as required by the TBSA specification.)

The Trusted Firmware-M reference implementation is designed for Arm Cortex-M processors. It can be used with Armv8-M processors with TrustZone for security isolation, or on systems with multiple Cortex-M processors—which use the isolation between processors as a mechanism for providing the security capabilities.

To help Secure software developers test the Trusted Firmware-M software, which has been ported to their designs, the TF-M comes with an API test suite. Overall, the TF-M offering makes security easier for the whole IoT ecosystem and enables a path for security certification. Further information on PSA Certified can be found in Section 22.2.2.5.

22.2.2.5 Stage 4—Certify

The certify stage makes it possible to define a security capability as a tangible measure of a product's capability. The certify stage of PSA Certified is an independent evaluation and certification scheme developed and maintained by seven founders (https://www.psacertified. org/what-is-psa-certified/founding-members/). With the PSA Certified scheme:

- The IoT industry has a common definition they can use to demonstrate the security capabilities of their IoT products. Previously, companies described their product's security capabilities by highlighting individual features, which can be misleading because that does not give an overall picture. The PSA Certified scheme solved this issue by evaluating the security capabilities against a broader range of security goals (Fig. 22.1).
- Consumers buying connected electronic goods have an easy way to identify secure products. Because PSA Certified has been adopted and is supported by many parties in the

electronics industry, PSA Certified could, in the future, become a product requirement for organizations that purchase electronic products.

- It is possible to drive the alignment of regulation and security standards. Today, there are multiple regional guidelines (e.g., ETSI 303645 for Europe, NIST 8259, and SB-327 for the United States). PSA Certified is actively aligning certification to these schemes to reduce fragmentation.

The PSA Certified scheme contains the following key areas:

- PSA Functional API Certified—checks, by way of an API test suite, that software has correctly implemented the PSA software interface.
- PSA Certified consists of three progressive levels of assurance and robustness testing that enables device makers to choose third party solutions and/or the certification level that is appropriate for their applications.

The certification process is handled by independent test labs and the following web page lists those participating test labs: https://www.psacertified.org/getting-certified/evaluation-labs/.

An independent certification body ensures the quality of the test lab-based evaluations.

The following webpage lists the products that are PSA Certified: https://www.psacertified.org/certified-products/.

22.2.3 PSA Certified security evaluation levels

22.2.3.1 Overview

Without a formal evaluation of a device's or a system's security capabilities, there is a chance that some of an application's security needs could get overlooked. There are many documented cases where white-hat hackers and security researchers have, ethically, shown ways of hacking into devices to (a) show what their vulnerabilities are and (b) to encourage security improvements. But there are also numerous cases where hackers have criminally launched attacks on connected products for nefarious reasons.

To reduce the chance of criminal attacks happening, the bar for the security of IoT devices must be raised. This is where PSA Certified comes in: by addressing this issue, by creating security evaluation schemes that are suitable for the IoT market and working with many partners in the industry to ensure that security evaluations are carried out fairly, independently, and meet the needs of the IoT industry.

Different connected products have different security needs. For example, a smart meter connected to the infrastructure of a power grid has completely different security needs to that of a low-cost electronic toy whose chip contains a limited amount of data. To ensure that the security requirements for the myriad of products are addressed, PSA Certified defines three levels of security. The definition of these levels is based on the security capabilities of the system as well as the software architecture that is deployed.

Note: Not all of the PSA Certified security evaluation levels are relevant to each of the IoT solutions. Table 22.1 shows the applicable levels for a range of IoT solutions.

Once the test lab has assessed that a chip, an OS, or a device has passed evaluation, a digital certificate is provided along with a unique digital certificate number (International Article

TABLE 22.1   PSA Certified levels for a range of IoT products.

IoT solution	Applicable levels	What it means
Silicon devices	1, 2, and 3	Chip vendors are able to demonstrate the security level of their device(s) and its capability when matched against the PSA-RoT standard. Having a silicon product with a PSA Certified Level 1–3 assessment means that because the product's security has been independently evaluated, an OEM can rely on the test results and, thus, undertake less testing.
Real-time OS (RTOS)	1	Applicable to RTOSs with integrated PSA Functional APIs. RTOS vendors marketing the aforementioned RTOS complete a PSA Certified Level 1 questionnaire showing that they have adhered to the 10 security goals (Fig. 22.1) and the industry's best practices.
Products/ devices	1	Product makers developing connected products/devices complete a PSA Certified Level 1 "Document and Declare" questionnaire, which is then checked by a test lab to confirm that they have followed the security model goals and the industry's best practice.

Number EAN-13 is used). As recommended by PSA Certified, the EAN-13 reference is used in the chip's attestation token as a "Hardware version claim" to enable third parties (e.g., service providers) to identify the PSA-RoT and to then link the chip or device with the certification level of the PSA-RoT.

At the beginning of 2020, PSA Certified Level 2 arrived in the market, with PSA Certified Level 3 due to arrive later in the year.

22.2.3.2 *PSA Certified level 1*

PSA Certified Level 1 is the minimum level of PSA Certified security certification. In a PSA Certified Level 1 system, the hardware has to support:

- The PSA Root-of-Trust (PSA-RoT, see Fig. 22.2).
- The isolation of secure domain resources to prevent them from being accessed by normal applications. For example, when using a Cortex-M23 or a Cortex-M33 processor, the system design can be based on the recommendations outlined in the "Trusted Base System Architecture for Armv6-M, Armv7-M, and Armv8-M" (TBSA-M) [5]. Those TBSA-M recommendations specify the hardware requirements needed to achieve isolation and other security measures.

The software architecture utilizes the hardware's isolation capability to protect Secure software from normal applications running in the Non-secure world. For example, when a Cortex-M23 or a Cortex-M33 based microcontroller is used, the TrustZone security extension can be used to provide the protection required to safeguard the integrity of the PSA-RoT (Isolation type 1, Fig. 22.4). Optionally, a device can also opt for additional isolations within the Secure world, by, for example, having isolation type 2 or above (Figs. 22.6 and 22.8).

PSA Certified Level 1 provides independent assurance of security best practices for IoT products such as microcontrollers, RTOSs, and IoT products. To obtain a product PSA Certified Level 1, a vendor self-assesses by way of completing a questionnaire containing a set of

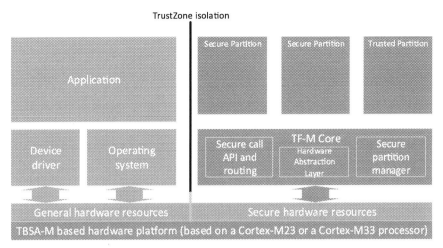

FIG. 22.4 High-level representation of isolation type 1 using an Armv8-M processor and Trusted Firmware-M.

critical security questions. This is followed-up by a laboratory review, with both actions ensuring that the product has been developed with a security-based design.

A product that passes PSA Certified Level 1 gains a quality marker (a logo, Fig. 22.5) showing that it has the essential security capabilities, including PSA-RoT. Product developers can, therefore, rely on these capabilities to build, providing that the product design is properly carried out, connected devices that met common IoT security requirements.

22.2.3.3 PSA Certified level 2

PSA Certified level 2 is targeted at silicon devices, and its aim is to add additional security robustness so that devices are better protected against scalable remote software attacks. Compared to level 1, the additional requirements to achieve PSA Certified Level 2 are as follows:

- Unique cryptographic keys for each device in the PSA-RoT.
- Additional security capabilities within the secure firmware—PSA Root of Trust (PSA-RoT) is protected from being accessed by the Application Root of Trust. For example, with PSA Certified Level 2, Trusted Firmware-M uses the Secure MPU to isolate Secure unprivileged partitions, and stop them from accessing the Secure privileged codes. This is known as isolation type 2 and is shown in Fig. 22.6.

psacertified™
level one

FIG. 22.5 PSA Certified Level 1 quality marker.

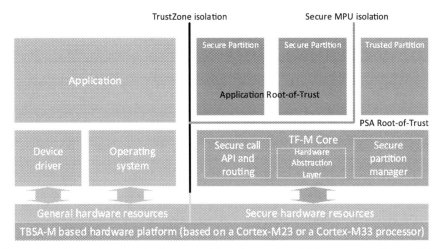

FIG. 22.6   High-level representation of isolation type 2 based on an Armv8-M processor and Trusted Firmware-M.

To gain PSA Certified Level 2 status, the chip has to pass a range of penetration tests carried out by security labs. This takes less than a month. The assessment also covers security function requirements, as outlined in the PSA Certified Level 2 PSA-RoT Protection Profile (This can be downloaded using the link https://www.psacertified.org/development-resources/).

In some instances, hardware platform developers might need to demonstrate the security capability of their solution when using a Field Programmable Gate Array or a test-chip. When this is the case, instead of using the PSA Certified Level 2 scheme, the PSA Certified Level 2 Ready scheme should be used for a precertification assessment. This particular scheme demonstrates the security capability of hardware prototypes and paves the way for a subsequent full PSA Certified evaluation. The quality markers of PSA Certified Level 2 and the PSA Certified Level 2 Ready schemes are shown in Fig. 22.7.

Optionally, a device can also be designed to have additional isolations within the Secure world by, for example, having an isolation type 3 arrangement in the Secure software (Fig. 22.8). Please note, as of May 2020, Trusted Firmware-M support for isolation type 3 is not available.

FIG. 22.7   PSA Certified Level 2 and PSA Certified Level 2 Ready quality markers.

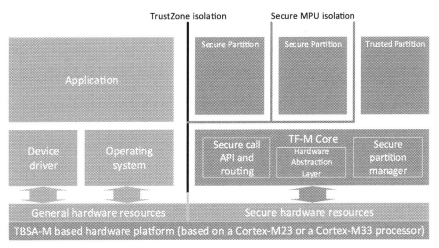

FIG. 22.8   High-level representation of isolation type 3 based on an Armv8-M processor and Trusted Firmware-M.

22.2.3.4 *PSA Certified level 3*

Similar to PSA Certified Level 2, PSA Certified Level 3 is for silicon devices. And, in addition to the security requirements required for PSA Certified Level 2, devices targeting PSA Certified Level 3 need to have a range of protections against physical attacks (i.e., anti-tampering features). When this book was written, PSA Certified Level 3 was still under development and is not, therefore, covered here.

22.2.4 PSA Functional API Certification

Separate from PSA Certified security levels, IoT solution vendors can also certify their product by way of PSA Functional API Certification. The quality marker for the PSA Functional API Certification is shown in Fig. 22.9.

PSA Functional APIs provide software developers with access to security functions, and by obtaining PSA Functional API Certification, demonstrate that their software is compatible with the PSA Functional API specification (Fig. 22.10). To obtain this certification, software solution(s) must pass a set of software tests, which check the correctness of the implemented software. A test suite is available for this test process. For further information about the

FIG. 22.9   PSA Functional API Certification quality marker.

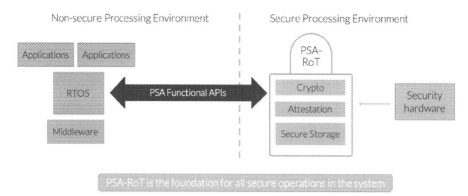

FIG. 22.10   PSA Functional APIs.

test suite, please visit https://www.psacertified.org/getting-certified/functional-api-certification/.

Please note, PSA Functional API Certified does not imply that a system/device has a security capability or is robust. Only PSA Certified Levels 1–3 does this.

22.2.5 Why PSA is important?

PSA defines a common language for security needs, thread models, and security capabilities. PSA is

- A holistic approach to security, with multiple profiles to address the requirements of different applications.
- Processor architecture agnostic—meaning that PSA activities such as PSA Certified and the designs of the PSA Functional APIs are not limited to Arm products.
- Independent—PSA Certified evaluations are carried out by independent security labs.
- Open—the specifications can be downloaded free of charge and the reference implementations (e.g., Trusted Firmware-M) are open source projects. PSA Certified is managed by seven founders and the specifications are created with ecosystem partners with security expertise.
- Flexible—the PSA approach allows system designers to define the Threat Model and Security Analysis (TMSA) document based on their own specific application requirements and can, thus, choose a PSA security level that is suitable for their target market.
- A standard that addresses the challenge of Root of Trust—When a device is connected to a service (e.g., cloud service), the service providers will be able to get "trust evidence" on the devices they are connected to via an Entity Attestation Token (a built-in "report card" which enables the device to make a set of claims that are cryptographically signed).

Due to various PSA activities and the joined-up effort between Arm and its security partners, it is now much easier for the IoT industry to achieve better security in their IoT products and solutions. In addition to the reference firmware and the architecture specifications, PSA resources, like TMSA and the Security Model document, enable product designers to see how best to address the security requirements of IoT devices.

With PSA Certified, the industry now has an independent "security standard" for quantifying IoT security. Although addressing the IoT security challenge is challenging and complex, the PSA project is gaining momentum and is making good progress. Many modern IoT microcontroller products and RTOS's have achieved PSA Certified Level 1, and many silicon partners have achieved PSA Certified Level 2.

Product makers, such as OEMs, can decide which silicon product to use by factoring in the chip's PSA Certification levels. By selecting a silicon product that is PSA Certified, product makers not only reduce the risk of using chips with security vulnerabilities but also demonstrate their commitment to security.

22.3 The Trusted Firmware-M (TF-M) project

22.3.1 About the TF-M project

TF-M is an open-source project, developed by security experts from various parties to cover the Implement stage of the Platform Security Architecture (PSA). It has been designed to address common security needs and to run on Cortex-M based microcontroller devices. The TF-M project codes are developed and tested to a production-quality level; using the codes developed, the IoT industry can quickly adopt the PSA principles and achieve a faster time-to-market.

Trusted Firmware is hosted by an open-source governance community project and contains both Cortex-M and Cortex-A Trusted Firmware. The link for the Trusted Firmware project is https://www.trustedfirmware.org. The technical direction of TF-M is overseen by a Technical Steering Committee. As well as Armv8-M processors, TF-M also works with Armv6-M and Armv7-M processors. But when using these processors, the system must contain multiple processors so that the Secure and Non-secure processing environments are separate.

Anybody can join the Trusted Firmware project and contribute to it. To take part, please visit the Trusted Firmware website and subscribe to the following mailing list: https://lists.trustedfirmware.org/mailman/listinfo/tf-m. The TF-M project source codes are hosted in the Trusted Firmware Git repository. The list to this is: https://git.trustedfirmware.org/trusted-firmware-m.git/.

22.3.2 Software execution environment using TF-M

TF-M is designed for Cortex-M processor systems with a PSA Root of Trust (PSA-RoT) capability. You can use TF-M with either:

- An Armv8-M processor with TrustZone implemented, or
- A multiprocessor Cortex-M system, which uses the separation of processors as a basis for software isolation.

In the rest of this chapter, I will describe how TF-M is deployed on a TrustZone based Armv8-M processor system.

In a TrustZone based system with TF-M, the software execution environment is divided into Secure and Non-secure processing environments (Fig. 22.11).

The Secure boot, the TF-M core, as well as a number of Secure partitions, execute in the Secure world. The applications and the RTOS run in the normal application environment (i.e., the Non-secure world), as explained in Chapter 11, Section 11.8. In the same section, it was also mentioned that interactions between the RTOS and Secure software are required to facilitate context switching. This capability has been integrated into the TF-M and is supported by a number of RTOSs that support Armv8-M architecture.

The TF-M is divided into the TF-M core and into a number of partitions. This arrangement allows the Secure MPU to isolate the Secure partitions (unprivileged) from the TF-M Core (privileged). Because there are multiple Secure partitions, the configurations of the Secure MPU need to be managed and this is undertaken by the Secure Partition Manager (SPM)—which handles the MPU settings (Secure isolation) and the scheduling (i.e., the context switching of the Secure library).

The PSA Functional APIs, which include APIs for cryptography, attestation, etc., are placed in the Trusted partitions. There are also Secure partitions for external facing APIs, such as those for protected storage and, if applicable, other third party APIs. This software partitioning arrangement in the TF-M ensures that critical data and code are protected.

The overall software architecture of the TF-M is illustrated in Fig. 22.12.

TF-M also includes a Hardware Abstraction Layer (HAL) to enable it to be ported to new hardware platforms. However, because this specific HAL is not accessible to Non-secure applications it is not part of the PSA Functional APIs.

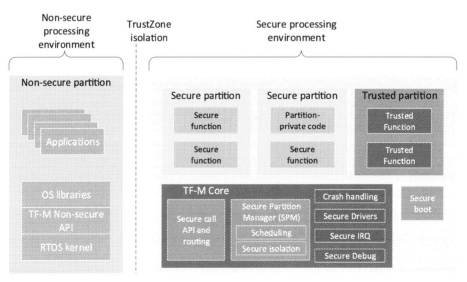

FIG. 22.11 Secure and Non-secure processing environments in a software system with TF-M.

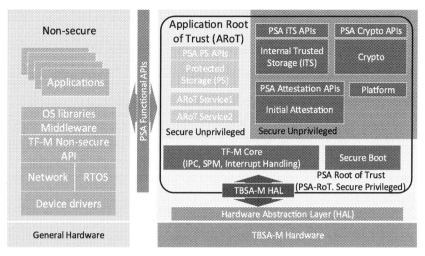

FIG. 22.12 TF-M software architecture—PSA Functional APIs.

To support the requirements of PSA Certified Level 2, the TF-M was designed to support a range of security functions. These functions (Table 22.2) are specified in the "PSA Certified Level 2 Protection Profile" [6], which can be found in the following link: https://www.psacertified.org/app/uploads/2019/12/JSADEN002-PSA_Certified_Level_2_PP-1.1.pdf.

The majority of the functional requirements in the protection profile document are well aligned to established security standards such as the "Common Criteria". This characteristic enables easy adoption of the PSA Certified Level 2 protection profile by organizations that are already using other security standards.

22.3.3 PSA Functional APIs

The TF-M project currently supports a range of PSA Functional APIs. These are:

- PSA Crypto APIs
- PSA Attestation APIs
- PSA Internal Trusted Storage APIs
- PSA Protected Storage APIs

The key aim for these APIs is to simplify application developments in the Non-secure world by providing a set of easy to use APIs. By using these APIs, software developers can, without having to fully understand the underlying complex technical operations, utilize the security features provided by the microcontrollers. Another advantage of having these APIs is that they are standardized across various hardware platforms, meaning that applications can be reused on another hardware platform.

The TF-M codebase is designed to be modular, with Secure software developers able to choose the required isolation level. The full details of the APIs are documented in Table 22.3.

TABLE 22.2   Security requirements documented in the PSA Certified Level 2 protection profile specification.

Security function	What takes place to satisfy the Security function requirement
F.INITIALIZATION	The system starts through a secure initialization process that affirms the authenticity and integrity of the firmware.
F.SOFTWARE_ISOLATION	The system provides isolation between the Non-secure processing environment (NSPE) and the Secure processing environment (SPE); and also, between the PSA Root-of-Trust and other executable codes (such as the Application Root of Trust) in the Secure Processing Environment.
F.SECURE_STORAGE	The system protects the confidentiality and integrity of assets in secure storage. The secure storage is bound to the platform. And only the trusted Secure firmware can retrieve and modify assets from this secure storage.
F.FIRMWARE_UPDATE	The system verifies the integrity and authenticity of the system update prior to performing the update; and also rejects attempts to downgrade the firmware.
F.SECURE_STATE	The system ensures its security functions operate correctly. In particular, the system: • Protects itself against abnormal situations caused by programmer errors or from the violation of good practices from code executed outside of the system, that is, either from the SPE or the NSPE. • Controls access to its services by Applications and checks the validity of parameters of any operation requested from Applications • Enters a secure state upon platform initialization error or software failure detection, without exposing any sensitive data.
F.CRYPTO	The system implements state-of-the-art cryptographic algorithms and key sizes for the protection of the system's secure assets. Recommendations may come from national security agencies (such NIST for the United States, BSI for Germany, CESG for the United Kingdom, ANSSI for France) or from academia. Weak cryptographic algorithms or key sizes may be available for specific usages and with specific guidance, but they should not reduce the security of the provided state-of-the-art cryptography.
F.ATTESTATION	The system provides an attestation service, which reports on the device's identity, its firmware measurements, and its runtime state. The attestation should be verified by remote entities.
F.AUDIT	The system maintains a log of all significant security events and allows access and analysis of those logs to authorized users only (such as the system's Admin).
F.DEBUG	The system restricts access to debug features by deactivation or by way of an access control mechanism, which has the same level of security assurance as other security functions implemented in this system.

The specification documents for these APIs are available at the following Arm Developer website location [4]: https://developer.arm.com/architectures/security-architectures/platform-security-architecture/documentation.

These documents contain a great deal of information appertaining to the aforementioned APIs. For information purposes, the following example details the use of the PSA API for Secure storage. In an IoT application, the application might have a crypto key that needs to be securely stored. Using TF-M, the secure storage is handled by using a range of features

TABLE 22.3 PSA API specifications.

Specification
PSA Firmware Framework for M (PSA-FF-M)
PSA Cryptography API
PSA Storage API (This covers PSA Internal Trusted Storage APIs and PSA Protected Storage APIs)
PSA Attestation API

provided in the PSA Cryptography API and PSA Storage API libraries. Although the underlying operations are fairly complex, the application running on the Non-secure side only needs to call the high-level functions shown in Fig. 22.13.

As shown in Fig. 22.13, an application running in the Non-secure world only has to call two functions to handle the Secure key storage. The application:

- Calls the psa_crypto_init function to initialize the crypto library, and then, when a crypto key needs to be saved,
- Calls the psa_import_key function, which then uses the PSA Internal Trusted Storage API psa_its_set to store the key in the internal trusted storage.

If the operation is successful, the API function returns an updated "key_handle" to the application, which can then be used for further operations. For example:

- psa_cipher_encrypt—for symmetric encryptions
- psa_cipher_decrypt—for symmetric decryptions
- psa_asymmetric_encrypt—for asymmetric encryptions
- psa_asymmetric_decrypt—for symmetric decryptions
- psa_destroy_key—to destroy the key.

By way of another example, an application might need to save data in a data storage device such as an external serial flash. Because this data could be sensitive, it would need to be

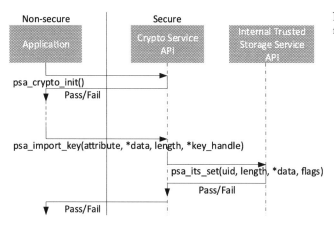

FIG. 22.13 Using PSA Functional APIs for storing a crypto key.

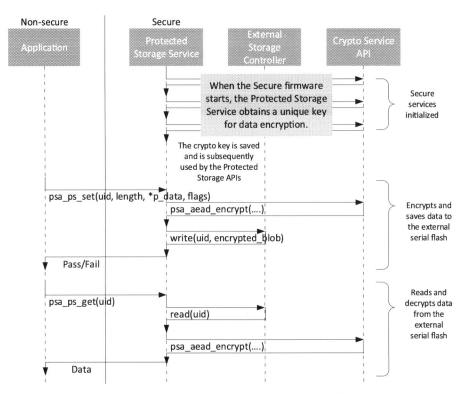

FIG. 22.14 Using PSA Functional APIs for accessing protected data storage with an external encrypted memory.

encrypted to prevent other applications running on the same microcontroller from reading it. In this example, the PSA Protected Storage APIs could be used as follows (Fig. 22.14):

When secure firmware boots up, a range of steps are carried out within the TF-M to generate a unique crypto key for use by the protected storage hardware. The key is then saved for future use by the Protected Storage APIs. When an application needs to securely save data in the external serial flash, it only has to use the Protected Storage API psa_ps_set() to encrypt and save the data and psa_ps_get() to retrieve it.

For the Protected Storage APIs in the aforementioned example to work, software developers creating Secure firmware for this hardware platform would need to develop the device's "Platform" code. This would include the Hardware Abstraction Layer (HAL) code, which is the software's interface between the TF-M and the hardware driver. The "Platform" code for the hardware platform, including the HAL for the external storage controller (i.e., the external serial flash), is device specific.

22.3.4 PSA interprocess communication

In addition to the Cryptography, Storage, and Attestation APIs, TF-M also supports IPC (Inter-Process Communication) APIs that allow Non-secure client libraries to communicate with and between Secure partitions. Fig. 22.15 shows the use of the IPC in the TF-M.

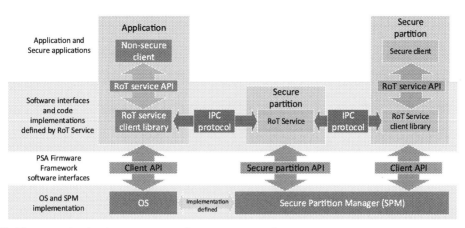

FIG. 22.15   Example of IPC usage in Root-of-Trust services in the TF-M.

The specification of the IPC APIs is detailed in the PSA Firmware Framework.

Application codes utilizing an additional RoT Service(s) are usually expected to use the RoT service client library, which runs in the Non-secure world, instead of connecting directly by way of IPC interface.

For a developer developing a Root of Trust client library, it is essential that the IPC protocol support is used to create an RoT service wrapper.

22.4 Additional information

22.4.1 Getting started

For application developers using microcontrollers with TF-M support, it is best, when starting a project, to study the examples provided by microcontroller vendors. In addition to TF-M support, there are, at the microcontroller product level, a number of other security features, which, if used, will enable product designers to build secure IoT products. Product designers should, therefore, spend time to acquaint themselves with information appertaining to the product they are going to use, understand its features, and then make sure the features are correctly used.

22.4.2 Design considerations

Although the TF-M and the PSA Cryptography APIs support a wide range of crypto methods, silicon vendors are able to decide what crypto functions to support. It is, therefore, necessary that the documentation from microcontroller vendors is fully read and understood to make sure what has, and what has not been implemented.

Please note, PSA Functional API Certification only tests against the compatibility and functional correctness of the APIs and does not provide any indication of the device's security capability. Therefore, when choosing a microcontroller or SoC product for a security application, you should consider both its PSA Certified Level as well as its PSA Functional API Certification.

References

[1] Platform Security Architecture (PSA). https://developer.arm.com/architectures/security-architectures/platform-security-architecture.
[2] PSA Certified. https://www.psacertified.org/.
[3] PSA Certified Security Goals. https://www.psacertified.org/psa-certified-10-security-goals-explained/.
[4] Platform Security Architecture Documentation. https://developer.arm.com/architectures/security-architectures/platform-security-architecture/documentation.
[5] Trusted Base System Architecture for Armv6-M, Armv7-M, and Armv8-M (TBSA-M). https://developer.arm.com/architectures/security-architectures/platform-security-architecture/documentation.
[6] PSA Certified Level 2 Protection Profile. https://www.psacertified.org/app/uploads/2019/12/JSADEN002-PSA_Certified_Level_2_PP-1.1.pdf.

Index

Note: Page numbers followed by *f* indicate figures and *t* indicate tables.

A

AAPCS. *See* Procedure Call Standard for Arm Architecture (AAPCS)
ABI. *See* Application binary interface (ABI)
Access permission management
  access control mechanisms, 255–257
  default, 258*t*, 259
  overview, 254
  security attribution unit/implementation defined attribution unit and memory protection unit, 257–259
ACLE. *See* Arm C language extension (ACLE)
ADCs. *See* Analog to digital converters (ADCs)
AFSR. *See* Auxiliary fault status register (AFSR)
AIRCR. *See* Application interrupt and reset control register (AIRCR)
Amazon Alexa Voice Service (AVS), 751–752
Analog to digital converters (ADCs), 1, 209
Application binary interface (ABI)
  command line options, 550*t*
  floating-point, 550*f*
  hard-vfp and soft-vfp, 549–551
Application interrupt and reset control register (AIRCR), 134, 358–359
Application processors, 3
Application specific integrated circuits (ASICs), 53
Architecture
  Armv8-M, 85–87
  debug, 131–133
  exceptions and interrupts, 124–131
  information, 136–137
  memory system, 112–124
  programmer's model (*see* Programmer's model)
  reset and reset sequence, 133–136
Arithmetic instructions, 182–185, 186–187*t*
  8-bit integer instructions, 773–774
  16-bit integer instructions, 771–773
  32-bit integer instructions
    ADD—32-bit addition, 768
    SDIV—32-bit division, 770–771
    SUB—32-bit subtraction, 768
Arm Architecture Procedure Call Standard (AAPCS), 51

Arm C language extension (ACLE), 41
  Arm custom instructions, 568–570, 569–570*t*
  coprocessor interface, 566, 567–568*t*
Arm CMSIS-DSP library
  categories, 799
  Cortex-M33 based system, 845, 846*t*
  dual-tone multifrequency (DTMF) demodulation, 802–813
  function naming convention, 801
  Keil® Microcontroller Development Kit (Keil MDK), 799, 800*f*
  least squares motion tracking, 813–818
  precompiled, 800, 800–801*t*
  real-time filter design, 818–845
Arm custom instructions, 65, 237–238*t*.
    See also Coprocessor interface
  concept, 559, 560*f*
  custom datapath extension (CDE), 559–560
  features, 562–563
  intrinsic functions in C, 568–570, 569–570*t*
  memory mapped hardware accelerators, 563–564, 563*f*
  purpose, 561
  software steps, 570–571
Armv6-M architecture, 4
Armv7-M architecture, 4
Armv8-M architecture, 4, 484–485, 487
  background, 86–87
  overview, 85–86
ASICs. *See* Application specific integrated circuits (ASICs)
Assembly language syntax, 143–147
Assembly programming, 150*t*
Auxiliary control register
  Cortex-M23 processor, 413–414
  Cortex-M33 processor, 414–415
  overview, 413
Auxiliary fault status register (AFSR), 505–506, 506*t*
AVS. *See* Amazon Alexa Voice Service (AVS)

B

Banked and nonbanked registers, 285–286
Banked stack pointers
  bare metal systems, 430–431, 430*f*, 431*t*

Banked stack pointers (*Continued*)
  benefits, 427
  memory allocated for each task/thread, 428,
    429*f*
  operations, 427–430
  TrustZone system, 428–430, 429*f*
Banking of interrupt mask registers, 314
Barrel shifter, 165–166
BASEPRI register, 367–369
BFSR. *See* BusFault status register (BFSR)
Biquad filter
  digital signal processing (DSP), 779–785, 780–781*f*
  dual-tone multifrequency (DTMF) demodulation,
    807–810, 810*f*
Bit field processing instructions, 193–195
Bit fields
  CONTROL register, 100*t*
  coprocessor access control register (CPACR), 107*f*
  EXC_RETURN, 335*f*, 336*t*
  floating-point status and control register (FPSCR),
    105*f*, 106*t*
  program status registers, 96*t*
Bit-reversed order, 787–788
Boot sequence, Cortex-M microcontrollers, 40*f*
Brown-out detector (BOD), 301
BusFault status register (BFSR), 502–503, 502*t*
Bus interfaces, 61
Bus system designs, 273–275
Bus wait state and error support, 269–270

C

Cacheable and sharable attributes, 252–253
CDE. *See* Custom datapath extension (CDE)
CFSR. *See* Configurable fault status register (CFSR)
C library code, 36–37
Clocks, 23
CMSE. *See* Cortex-M security extension
CMSIS. *See* Cortex Microcontroller Software Interface
    Standard (CMSIS)
Coherency management schemes, 471
Compare and branch instructions, 201–203
Compatibility with Cortex-M processors, 70–71
Complex Instruction Set Computing (CISC) processors, 6
Conditional branches, 200–201
Configurable fault status register (CFSR), 499, 500*f*, 500*t*
CONTROL register, 89, 99–102
Coprocessor access control register (CPACR), 106,
    526–527, 527*t*, 527–528*f*
Coprocessor and Arm custom instructions support,
    232–236
Coprocessor interface, 65
  architecture, 565–566, 566*f*
  characteristics, 559

concept, 559, 560*f*
Cortex-M33 processor, 565, 565*f*
features, 561–562
intrinsic functions in C, 566–568, 567–568*t*
memory mapped hardware accelerators, 563–564, 563*f*
older generation of Arm processors, 564–565, 564*f*
power control, 571–572
purpose, 561
software steps, 570–571
Coprocessor power control register (CPPWR),
    571–572, 571*f*
Coprocessor registers, 91
Cortex-M33 floating-point unit (FPU)
  C language, 547–548
  CMSIS-CORE, 547, 547*t*
  compiler command line options, 548–549
  vs. Cortex-M4, 539–540
  exceptions, 553–556, 554*t*, 555*f*
  floating-point data, 519–524
  lazy stacking, 540–547
  modes, 551–552
  overview, 524–525
  registers
    context saving configurations, 536, 536*t*
    coprocessor access control register (CPACR),
      526–527, 527*t*, 527–528*f*
    floating-point context address register (FPCAR),
      537, 537*f*
    floating-point context control register (FPCCR),
      532–536, 532*f*, 532–536*t*
    floating-point default status control register
      (FPDSCR), 538, 538*f*
    floating-point register bank, 528–529, 528*f*
    floating-point status and control register (FPSCR),
      529–532, 529–530*t*, 529*f*
    media and floating-point (FP) feature, 538–539,
      538*t*, 539*f*
    non-secure access control register (NSACR),
      527–528
    overview, 526, 526*t*
  rounding modes, 531, 531*t*, 552*t*
Cortex Microcontroller Software Interface Standard
    (CMSIS), 13, 266
  benefits, 48–50
  CORE compliant device driver, 228, 236, 238
  CORE standardized, 45–47, 305*t*, 547, 547*t*
  data types, 210*t*
  device driver package with CORE, 47–48
  functions, special register access, 241–242*t*
  introduction, 44–45
  projects, 46*t*
Cortex-M23 processors
  advantages, 11–14

applications, 7–8
architecture version, 4, 4*f*
block diagrams, 54–56
characteristics, 5–6
vs. Cortex-M0 and Cortex-M0+ processors, 10*f*
design objectives, 53–54
enhancements, 66–70
features, 6–7
operating systems (OSs) support features, 64
technical features, 8, 9*t*
Cortex-M33 processors
advantages, 11–14
applications, 7–8
architecture version, 4, 4*f*
block diagrams, 54–56
characteristics, 5–6
vs. Cortex-M3 and Cortex-M4 processors, 11*f*
design objectives, 53–54
enhancements, 66–70
features, 6–7
operating systems (OSs) support features, 64
technical features, 8, 9*t*
Cortex-M55 processor, 4–5
Cortex-M security extension (CMSE), 686–687, 696,
    707–708, 717
CPACR. *See* Coprocessor access control register
    (CPACR)
CPPWR. *See* Coprocessor power control register
    (CPPWR)
Cross trigger interface (CTI), 632–633, 632*f*
C startup code, 36
Custom datapath extension (CDE), 559–560

D
DAP. *See* Debug access port (DAP)
Data alignment, 262–263
Data communication, 8
Data memory barrier (DMB), 181*f*, 852
Data synchronization barrier (DSB), 854
Data type, 29–30
Data watchpoint and trace unit (DWT)
comparator function register[n], 612, 613*t*
comparator register[n], 612, 613*t*
control register, 606, 608–609*t*
CPI count register, 607, 610*t*
cycle count register, 607, 609*t*
DWT_FUNCTION[n].MATCH, 612, 614*t*, 615
exception overhead count register, 607, 610*t*
folded instruction count register, 607, 611*t*
functions, 606
logic analyzer, 615, 615*f*
LSU count register, 607, 610*t*
performance analysis, 611, 611*f*

program counter sample register, 612, 612*t*
registers, 606, 607*t*
sleep count register, 607, 610*t*
DCRDR. *See* Debug core register data register (DCRDR)
DCRSR. *See* Debug core register selector register
    (DCRSR)
Debug, 131–133
Debug access port (DAP), 580
Debug adaptor, 20–21
Debug and trace features
architecture (*see* Debug architecture)
classification, 579–580, 579*f*
communication channels, 575
components (*see* Debug components)
connection arrangements, 577, 577*f*
CoreSight architecture, 577–578
flash memory programming support, 634–635
internal/external connection, 575
protocols, 575–576
session, 633–634
software design considerations, 635
Debug and trace support, 65–66
Debug architecture
authentication, 590–594, 591*t*, 592–594*f*
breakpoint instruction, 590
connection, 580–583, 582*f*
CoreSight discovery, 594–596, 595*f*
events, 588–589, 589*f*
modes, 585–587, 586*f*
trace buffer, 584–585, 585*f*
trace connection, 583–584, 583–584*f*
TrustZone, 590–594
Debug authentication control register, 601, 602*t*
Debug authentication status register, 601, 603*t*
Debug components
breakpoint unit, 604–606, 605*t*
control block registers, 597, 598*t*
core register data register (DCRDR), 598, 600*t*
core register selector register (DCRSR), 598, 600*t*
Cortex-M23 and Cortex-M33 processors, 596
cross trigger interface (CTI), 632–633
data watchpoint and trace unit (DWT), 606–615
embedded trace macrocell (ETM), 622–624
exception trace, 622, 622*f*
FP_COMPn register(s), 604, 606*t*
FP_CTRL register, 604, 605*t*
halting control and status register, 597, 599*t*
instruction trace window, 623, 623*f*
instrumentation trace macrocell (ITM), 616–622
micro trace buffer (MTB), 624–626, 625*f*
support registers in processor core, 597–604, 598*t*
trace port interface unit (TPIU), 626–632
Debug core register data register (DCRDR), 598, 600*t*, 601

Debug core register selector register (DCRSR), 598, 600*t*

Debug exception and monitor control register (DEMCR), 601, 602*t*

Debug fault status register (DFSR), 505, 506*t*, 590

Debug features, 13

Debug interface, functions, 43*f*

Debug operation, 557

Debug security control and status register (DSCSR), 601, 603*t*, 604

Deep sleep, 385, 391

Default memory access permission, 259

Default memory attributes, 255*t*

Default memory map, 248*f*

DEMCR. *See* Debug exception and monitor control register (DEMCR)

Development board, 20, 21*f*

Development suites, 20

DFSR. *See* Debug fault status register (DFSR)

DFT. *See* Discrete Fourier transform (DFT)

Digital signal processing (DSP), 8

arithmetic instructions, 767–775

biquad filter, 779–785, 780–781*f*

Cortex-M33 optimization strategies

amount of precision, 778–779

count registers, 778

enable optimization, 776, 777*t*

inline functions, 778

inner loop, 778

intermediate assembly code, 776

load and store instructions, scheduling of, 776

loop unrolling, 777–778

MAC instructions, performance considerations, 776–777

Cortex-M processors, 752–754, 752*t*

data types

fixed-point data format, 761–762, 762*f*, 763*t*

fractional arithmetic, 762–765

single-instruction, multiple-data (SIMD), 765, 765*f*

dot product, 754–757, 754–757*t*, 754*f*

fast Fourier transform (FFT), 785–790, 786–787*f*

finite impulse response (FIR) filter, 790–798, 791–792*t*, 791*f*, 794–798*t*

floating-point instructions, 774–775

instruction limitations, 779

load and store instructions, 767

microcontroller, 751–752

overflows, 759–760

registers, 765–766

single-instruction, multiple-data (SIMD), 757–759, 757–759*t*, 758*f*

Digital signal processing (DSP) extension instruction set

multiply and MAC instructions, 210–216

overview, 208–209

packing and unpacking instructions, 216–219

saturating arithmetic instructions, 210

single-instruction, multiple-data (SIMD) concept, 209–210

Digital signal processing (DSP) instructions

QADD, 770

QADD8, 773–774

QADD16, 771

SADD8, 773

SADD16, 771

SMLABB, 772

SMLAD, 772

SMLAL, 769

SMLALBB, 772

SMLALD, 757, 758*f*, 772–773

SMMLA, 770

SMMUL, 769–770

SMULL, 769

SSAT16, 771

Directives, 148*t*

Direct memory access (DMA) controllers, 1, 245, 394

Discrete Fourier transform (DFT), 785

DMA. *See* Direct memory access (DMA)

DMB. *See* Data memory barrier (DMB)

DSB. *See* Data synchronization barrier (DSB)

DSP. *See* Digital signal processing (DSP)

Dual-tone multifrequency (DTMF) demodulation

decoding

biquad filter, 807–810, 810*f*

fast Fourier transform (FFT), 805–807, 808*f*

finite impulse response (FIR) filter, 803–805, 804*f*, 806*f*

program code, 810–813, 810–813*t*

decoding one frequency, 802

Goetzel algorithm, 802–803

keypad matrix, 802, 802*f*

sine wave generation, 803

types, detecting tones, 802

DWT. *See* Data watchpoint and trace unit (DWT)

E

Electromagnetic interference (EMI), 381

Embedded Application Binary Interface (EABI), 51

Embedded software program flows

concurrent processes, handling, 28–29

interrupt driven method, 25–28

polling method, 25, 27–28

Embedded trace macrocell (ETM), 40, 66, 131, 133, 489, 622–624

EMI. *See* Electromagnetic interference (EMI)

Entering sleep modes, 385–387

ETM. *See* Embedded trace macrocell (ETM)

Event communication interface, 392–395

Exception handling, 62–63
Exception handling optimizations
    late arrival, 376–377
    lazy stacking, 378
    pop preemption, 377
    tail chaining, 375–376
Exception/interrupt masking
    BASEPRI, 367–369
    FAULTMASK, 365–367
    overview, 362–364
    PRIMASK, 364–365
Exception priority levels
    overview, 310–312
    priority grouping in Armv8-M Mainline, 313–314
Exception-related instructions, 225–227
Exceptions
    CMSIS-CORE, 305t
    definition, 124
    management, 303–307
    overview, 299–302
    sources, 124f
    synchronous and asynchronous, 340
    target states, TrustZone systems, 322–325
    and TrustZone, 126
    types, 125t, 303
Exception sequence
    acceptance of exception request, 307–308
    entry sequence, 308–309
    handler execution, 309
    overview, 307
    return sequence, 309–310
Exclusive access, 446–448, 447f
Exclusive access instructions, 172–178
Exclusive access support, 263–267
EXC_RETURN (exception return)
    bit fields, 335f, 336t
    exception return, 335f
    value in exception handling scenarios, 337f
eXecute-Never (XN) attribute, 248
eXecute-Only-Memory (XOM), 83–84

F
Fast Fourier transforms (FFTs)
    digital signal processing (DSP), 766, 785–790, 786–787f
    dual-tone multifrequency (DTMF) demodulation, 805–807, 808f
Fault address registers (FARs), 489, 499–500, 506–507, 507t
Fault events analysis
    Armv8-M vs. Cortex-M processors, 510–512
    event trace, 510
    fault status and fault address registers, 510
    instruction trace, 509
    stack trace, 510

Fault exceptions
    Armv8-M processors, 487, 488t
    causes
        bus faults, 490–492
        exception handling, 494–496
        hard fault status register (HFSR), 493–494
        memory management, 489–490
        SecureFault, 493
        usage faults, 492–493
    configurable faults, 487
    enabling, 496
    events, 487–488
    software error, 488
    stacking and unstacking sequences, 495, 495f
    watchdog timer, 488
Fault handler designs considerations
    extract stack frame and display fault status, 514–517
    fault mask, configurable, 498–499
    hard fault status register (HFSR) and NMI handlers, 497–498
    partitioning, 498
    stack pointer validation check, 497
    triggering self-reset/halting, 498
Fault handling, 129–131, 747
FAULTMASK register, 365–367
Fault status registers (FSRs)
    auxiliary (AFSR), 505–506, 506t
    BusFault Status Register (BFSR), 502–503, 502t
    Cortex-M33 processor, 489
    debug (DFSR), 505, 506t
    hard fault status register (HFSR), 505, 505t
    MemManage (MMFSR), 501–502, 501t
    overview, 499–500
    secure (SFSR), 503–504, 504t
    usage (UFSR), 503, 503t
Ferroelectric RAM (FRAM), 273
FFT. See Fast Fourier transform (FFT)
Filter design
    ASN Filter Designer Professional, 820, 820f
    buffer arrangement, 844–845, 845f
    C code, 822–825, 823f, 823–825t
    characteristics, 819, 819f
    data type and structure, 821, 822f
    defining the filter type, 821, 821f
    frequency response, 821, 822f
    low priority handler, 831–835
    MATLAB, 820
    real-time, bare metal project, 825–831, 831–835t
    real-time operating systems (RTOS), 835–840, 835–840t
    sampling rate, 820, 821f
    signal processing tasks, 818
    specification, 819
    stereo audio biquad, 841–844, 841–844t

Finite impulse response (FIR)
    digital signal processing (DSP), 790–798, 791–792*t*,
        791*f*, 794–798*t*
    dual-tone multifrequency (DTMF) demodulation,
        803–805, 804*f*, 806*f*
Finite state machine (FSM), 8
Firmware asset protection, 83–84
Flash memory programming support, 634–635
Flash patch and breakpoint (FPB), 604
Floating point
    calculations, 194
    immediate data generation, 155–157
    memory access instructions, 172
    register access, 155
    support instructions
        enabling FPU, 219–220
        floating point instructions, 220–224
        overview, 219
Floating-point context active (FPCA), 540
Floating-point context address register (FPCAR), 537,
        537*f*, 540
Floating-point context control register (FPCCR), 532–536,
        532*f*, 532–536*t*
Floating-point data
    Arm Cortex-M processors, 523–524, 524*t*
    double precision format, 522–523, 522–523*f*
    half precision format, 521–522, 521–522*f*
    single precision format, 519–521, 520*f*
Floating-point default status control register (FPDSCR),
        538, 538*f*
Floating-point instructions, 220–224*t*
    VABS.F32—floating-point absolute value, 774
    VADD.F32—floating-point addition, 774
    VDIV.F32—floating-point division, 774
    VFMA.F32—fused floating-point multiply
        accumulate, 775
    VMLA.F32—floating-point multiply accumulate, 775
    VMUL.F32—floating-point multiplication, 775
    VNEG.F32—floating-point negation, 775
    VSQRT.F32—floating-point square root, 775
    VSUB.F32—floating-point subtraction, 775
Floating-point register bank, 528–529, 528*f*
Floating-point registers, 104–107
Floating-point status and control register (FPSCR), 104,
        529–532, 529–530*t*, 529*f*
Floating-point unit (FPU), 39, 64
    CONTROL register, 99
    literal data access instructions, 173*t*
    multiple load/store instructions, 174*t*
    registers, 105*f*
    stack push/pop instructions, 175*t*
FNC_RETURN code, 697, 697*t*
Formats, stack frame, 327–334

FPB. *See* Flash patch and breakpoint (FPB)
FPCA. *See* Floating-point context active (FPCA)
FPCAR. *See* Floating-point context address register
        (FPCAR)
FPCCR. *See* Floating-point context control register
        (FPCCR)
FPDSCR. *See* Floating-point default status control
        register (FPDSCR)
FPSCR. *See* Floating-point status and control register
        (FPSCR)
FPU. *See* Floating-point unit (FPU)
FRAM. *See* Ferroelectric RAM (FRAM)
Frequency response, 779
FSM. *See* Finite state machine (FSM)
FSRs. *See* Fault status registers (FSRs)
Full-descending stack, 117
Function call instructions, 199*t*

G
General purpose input output (GPIO), 270–271
Global exclusive access monitor, 173–175
GNU C compiler (GCC), 731–732
Goetzel algorithm, 802–803
Graphic user interface (GUI), 14, 24
Greater-equal (GE) bits, 109–110
Group priority level, 314
GUI. *See* Graphic user interface (GUI)

H
Half precision. *See* Floating-point data
Halt mode *vs.* monitor mode debugging, 587, 587*t*
HardFault, 493–494, 497–498
Hard fault status register (HFSR), 505, 505*t*, 590
Hardware platform, 39–41
Harvard bus architecture, 6, 57–58, 61, 113–114, 246, 309,
        872–873

I
ICER. *See* Interrupt clear enable registers (ICER)
ICPR. *See* Interrupt clear pending registers (ICPR)
ICSR. *See* Interrupt control and state register (ICSR)
IDAU. *See* Implementation defined attribution unit
        (IDAU)
IIR. *See* Infinite impulse response (IIR)
Immediate data generation, 153–154
Implementation defined attribution unit (IDAU), 60, 78,
        115–116, 255, 257–259, 283–285, 689, 690*f*
Infinite impulse response (IIR), 779, 807
Inline assembler, 50–51
Inline assembly, 677–679
Instruction set, 58
    arithmetic operations, 182–185
    assembly language syntax, 143–147

background, 139–141
bit field processing, 193–195
coprocessor and Arm custom instructions support, 232–236
data conversions, 191–193
DSP extension (*see* Digital signal processing (DSP) extension instruction set)
exception-related instructions, 225–227
features in Cortex-M processors, 141–143
floating point support instructions, 219–224
functions, 236–239
logic operations, 185
memory access
    exclusive access, 172–178
    floating-point unit (FPU) memory access instructions, 172
    literal data read, 166–167
    load acquire-store release, 178–182
    multiple load/store, 167–170
    optional shift in register offset, 165–166
    overview, 158–159
    preindexed and postindex addressing modes, 163–165
    PUSH/POP, 170–171
    single memory access, 159–161
    stack pointer relative load/stores, 161–163
    unprivileged access instructions, 171–172
memory barrier instructions, 228–230
moving data
    between coprocessor register, 158
    floating point immediate data generation, 155–157
    floating point register access, 155
    immediate data generation, 153–154
    overview, 151–152
    between registers, 152–153
    special register access instructions, 154–155
program flow control (*see* Program flow control)
saturation operations, 195–197
shift and rotate operations, 185–190
sleep mode-related instructions, 227–228
suffix, 147–149
TrustZone support instructions, 231–232
unified assembly language (UAL), 150–151
Instruction Set Architecture (ISA), 140
Instruction suffixes, 150*t*
Instruction synchronization barrier (ISB) instruction, 102
Instruction tracing, 489
Instrumentation trace macrocell (ITM), 133, 671–672, 672–673*f*
    first-in-first-out (FIFO), 616
    hardware trace, 621
    programmer's model, 617–621
    registers, 616, 617*t*

software generated text output, 619, 620*f*
software generated trace, 616
timestamp, 622
timestamp packet generation, 616
trace control register, 617, 618*t*
trace enable register, 621, 621*t*
trace packet merging, 616, 616*f*
Integer Baud Rate Divider (IBRD), 33
Integer processing performance, 57*t*
Integer status flags, 107–109
Integrated circuit (IC), 22–23
Integrated Development Environment (IDE), 23, 42
Internet-of-Things (IoT), 53
Interprocess communication (IPC), 894–895, 895*f*
Interrupt, 62–63
Interrupt active status register, 350
Interrupt clear enable registers (ICER), 348–349
Interrupt clear pending registers (ICPR), 348–349
Interrupt control and state register (ICSR), 355, 356*t*
Interrupt controller type register, 353
Interrupt driven method, 25–27
Interrupt enable register, 347–348
Interrupt latency, 373–374
Interrupt management, 128
    CMSIS-CORE functions, 341–345
    nested vectored interrupt controller (NVIC) registers
        active status, 350
        enhancements, 353–354
        interrupt controller type register, 353
        interrupt enable register, 347–348
        interrupt set pending and clear pending registers, 348–349
        interrupt target non-secure register(s), 350–351
        priority level, 351
        software trigger interrupt register, 352–353
        summary, 346–347
Interrupt masking registers, 97–99
    access functions in the CMSIS-CORE, 363*t*
    BASEPRI, 367–369
    FAULTMASK, 365–367
    overview, 362–364
    PRIMASK, 364–365
Interrupt priority level registers, 351
Interrupt requests (IRQs), 303
Interrupts
    input and pending behaviors, 318–322
    management, 303–307
    during multiple-cycle instructions, 374–375
    overview, 299–302
    target states, TrustZone systems, 322–325
Interrupt service routine (ISR), 120, 300, 307
Interrupt set enable registers (ISER), 348–349
Interrupt set pending registers (ISPR), 348–349

Interrupt target non-secure registers (ITNS), 350–351
Intrinsic functions, 172, 210, 236
Invasive debugging, 579
IoT. *See* Internet-of-Things (IoT)
IoT security, processor architecture, 877–878
IPC. *See* Interprocess communication (IPC)
IRQs. *See* Interrupt requests (IRQs)
ISER. *See* Interrupt set enable registers (ISER)
ISPR. *See* Interrupt set pending registers (ISPR)
ISR. *See* Interrupt service routine (ISR)
ITM. *See* Instrumentation trace macrocell (ITM)
ITNS. *See* Interrupt target non-secure registers (ITNS)

J

Joint test action group (JTAG), 576, 576*f*

K

Keil Microcontroller Development Kit (MDK)
　breakpoint, 667, 667–668*f*
　compilation output message, 648, 648*f*
　components, 639–640
　creating scratch project, 641–652
　debugger window, 651, 653*f*
　debug script, 728, 730*f*, 731*t*
　debug settings, 651, 652*f*
　device selection, 643, 645*f*
　inline assembly, 677–679
　instrumentation trace macrocell (ITM) printf, 671–672,
　　672–675*f*
　integrated development environment (IDE) and
　　debugger, 665–667, 666*f*
　multiproject workspace, 727–731, 728–729*f*
　μVision integrated development environment (IDE),
　　641, 641–643*f*
　non-secure project, 725–727, 725–726*f*, 728*f*
　Pack Installer, 642–643, 642*f*
　program code file, 644, 647*f*
　program compilation flow, 640–641, 640*f*
　project directory and project name, 643, 644*f*
　project option default window, 649, 649*f*
　RTX RTOS, 673–677, 675–677*f*
　secure project, 720–725, 720–721*f*
　software components, 644, 646*f*
　stack and heap sizes, 661–665
　standard output (STDOUT), 668, 670–671*f*
　UART, 668–670
　ULINKPro debug probe, 650, 650*f*
　understanding project options, 652–661

L

Late arrival exception behavior, 377*f*
Lazy stacking, 378
　elements, 540–541

floating-point context in interrupted task and in ISR,
　542–543, 544*f*
floating-point context in interrupted task but not in
　ISR, 542, 543*f*
interrupted during operation, 545–546
interrupt of floating-point instructions, 547
nested interrupt with floating-point context in both
　handlers, 544–545, 546*f*
nested interrupt with floating-point context in second
　handler, 543–544, 545*f*
no floating-point context in interrupted task, 541, 542*f*
Lazy stacking preservation active (LSPACT), 540
LCS. *See* Life cycle state (LCS)
Least squares motion tracking
　floating-point data, 815
　noisy measurements, 813
　program code, 816–818, 816–818*t*
　time-varying acceleration, 814
Life cycle state (LCS), 81*t*
Link register (LR), 308–309
Load-acquire instructions, 178–182, 851–854
Load double-word (LDRD) instructions, 374
Load-store architecture, 91
Load/store instructions, 168–169*t*
Local exclusive access monitor, 173–175
Lockup
　avoiding, 508–509
　bus errors, 508, 509*f*
　definition, 507–508
Logical operations, 185
Logic instructions, 187–188*t*
Low power
　applications developing
　　active cycles, reduction, 403–404
　　active power, reducing, 402–403
　　microcontroller vendors, 401–402
　　sleep mode current reduction, 404
　benefits, 381
　characteristics, 383
　entering sleep mode, 385–387
　event communication interface, 392–395
　requirements of microcontrollers, 382*t*
　send event on pend (SEVONPEND), 388
　sleep extension/wakeup delay, 388–389
　sleep modes, 383–384
　sleep-on-exit feature, 387–388
　system control register, 385
　TrustZone on sleep mode support, 395
　wakeup interrupt controller (WIC), 389–391
Low power features, 63–64
LR. *See* Link register (LR)
LSPACT. *See* Lazy stacking preservation active
　　(LSPACT)

M

Magneto-resistive RAM (MRAM), 273
Main stack pointer (MSP), 119, 308, 316
Master security controllers (MSC), 277
MemManage fault status register (MMFSR), 501–502, 501*t*
Memory access control mechanisms, 62*f*
Memory access, instruction set
  exclusive access, 172–178
  floating-point unit (FPU) memory access instructions, 172
  literal data read, 166–167
  load acquire-store release, 178–182
  multiple load/store, 167–170
  optional shift in register offset, 165–166
  overview, 158–159
  preindexed and postindex addressing modes, 163–165
  PUSH/POP, 170–171
  single memory access, 159–161
  stack pointer relative load/stores, 161–163
  unprivileged access instructions, 171–172
Memory access ordering, 267–269
Memory attributes
  default memory map, 253–254
  overview, 251–253
Memory barrier instructions, 228–230, 267–269
Memory endianness, 259–262
Memory map, 58–61, 113–114
  components, 250*t*
  default, 248*f*
  memory attributes, 251–252
  regions, 249*t*
Memory mapped hardware accelerators, 563–564, 563*f*, 572
Memory mapped registers, 91
Memory partitioning
  block-based and watermark-level, 705, 705*f*
  dynamic switching
    peripheral's security attribute, 735
    static random access memory (SRAM) page, 734–735
  memory protection controller (MPC) and peripheral protection controller (PPC), 734
Memory protection, 61–62
Memory protection controllers (MPCs), 275–276, 292–295, 689–690, 705
Memory protection unit (MPU), 40, 42, 59, 62, 66, 74, 87–88, 123–124, 303–305
  architectural requirements, 466
  Armv8-M architecture, 484–485
  configurations
    MAIR0 and MAIR1, memory attributes for, 476, 477*t*, 477*f*, 479*t*
    setup sequence, 474, 475*f*

  context switching, 478*f*
  Cortex-M23 and Cortex-M33, 465
  fault exception, 464
  operation, 465
  programming
    disable, 477
    enable, 481–482
    MAIR0 and MAIR1, 478–479
    overview, 476
    region base address and limit address registers, 479–480, 481*t*
  purposes, 463–464
  registers (*see* Memory Protection Unit (MPU) registers)
  stack overflow detection, 464
  TrustZone, 482–484, 482*f*
  unprivileged execution level, 444–446
  virtual memory support, 464
Memory protection unit (MPU) registers
  attribute indirection register 0 and 1, 473–474, 474*f*
  control, 467–468, 468*t*, 468*f*
  PRIVDEFENA bit, 467–468, 469*f*
  RBAR and RLAR alias, 473, 473*t*
  region base address, 470–471, 470*t*, 470*f*
  region limit address, 471–472, 472*f*, 472*t*
  region number, 469, 469*f*, 470*t*
  summary, 466–467, 466*t*
  type register, 467, 467*t*, 467*f*
Memory regions, 249*t*
Memory security attributes, 281–283
Memory space partitioning, 78*f*
Memory system
  access permission management, 254–259
  bus wait state and error support, 269–270
  Cortex-M3/M4, 247
  data alignment and unaligned data access support, 262–263
  exclusive access support, 263–267
  features, 246
  memory endianness, 259–262
  memory map, 113–114, 247–250
  memory protection unit (MPU), 123–124
  microcontrollers
    bus system designs, 273–275
    requirements, 272–273
    security management, 275–277
  ordering and barrier instructions, 267–269
  overview, 245–247
  partitioning of address spaces within Trustzone, 115–116
  single-cycle I/O port, 270–271
  software considerations
    bus level power management, 278
    multiple load and store instructions, 278–279
    TrustZone security, 278

Memory system *(Continued)*
  stack memory, 117–121
  stack pointers and stack limit registers, 121–122
  system control block (SCB), 116–117
  system control space (SCS), 116–117
  TrustZone support
    banked and nonbanked registers, 285–286
    implementation defined attribution units (IDAUs), 283–285
    memory protection controller and peripheral protection controller, 292–295
    region ID numbers, 289–292
    security attribution unit (SAU), 283–285
    security aware peripherals, 296–297
    test target (TT) instructions, 287–292
  types and attributes, 251–254
Memory types, 251, 283*t*
MEMS. *See* Microelectromechanical systems (MEMS)
Microcontroller Development Kit (MDK), 41
Microcontrollers, 2*f*, 556, 895
  clocks, 23
  components, 2*t*
  Cortex-M processors, 7
  inputs and outputs, 24–25
  low power requirements, 382*t*
  memory systems, 272–277
  processors, 3
  programming, 14
  reset, 22–23
  tools/resources for developing applications, 19–20
  voltage level, 23
Microelectromechanical systems (MEMS), 8
Micro trace buffer (MTB), 40, 133, 489, 577, 624–626, 625*f*
Mixed-signal applications, 8
MMFSR. *See* MemManage fault status register (MMFSR)
Most significant bit (MSB), 189, 311
MPCs. *See* Memory protection controllers (MPCs)
MPU. *See* Memory protection unit (MPU)
MRAM. *See* Magneto-resistive RAM (MRAM)
MSB. *See* Most significant bit (MSB)
MSC. *See* Master security controllers (MSC)
MSP. *See* Main stack pointer (MSP)
MTB. *See* Micro trace buffer (MTB)
Multicore system design support, 66
Multiply and accumulate (MAC) instructions, 208, 210–216
Mutual exclusive (MUTEX), 264, 446, 851, 855*f*

N
NAS. *See* Network attached storage (NAS)
Neoverse™, 3
Nested interrupt/exception handling, 310

Nested vectored interrupt controller (NVIC), 12, 59, 62–63
  exceptions and interrupts, 301–302
  flexible exception and interrupt management, 126–127
  interrupt management
    active status, 350
    enhancements, 353–354
    interrupt controller type register, 353
    interrupt enable register, 347–348
    interrupt set pending and clear pending registers, 348–349
    interrupt target non-secure register(s), 350–351
    software trigger interrupt register, 352–353
  interrupt masking, 127–128
  nested exception/interrupt support, 127
  SysTick options, 302*t*
  vectored exception/interrupt entry, 127
Network attached storage (NAS), 3
Noninvasive debugging, 579
Non-maskable interrupt (NMI), 301
Non-secure access control register (NSACR), 527–528
Non-secure callable (NSC), 78, 281, 284, 695–696
  definition matching, 733
  static random access memory (SRAM), 733
Nonvolatile memory (NVM), 272
Not a Number (NaN), 224, 520–522
NSACR. *See* Non-secure access control register (NSACR)
NSC. *See* Non-secure callable (NSC)
NVIC. *See* Nested vectored interrupt controller (NVIC)
NVM. *See* Nonvolatile memory (NVM)

O
Operating systems (OS) support features
  banked stack pointers, 427–431
  context switching, 451, 452*f*
  context switching in action, 452–462, 453*f*
  exclusive access, 446–448, 447*f*
  overview, 417–418
  real-time *(see* Real-time operating systems (RTOS))
  stack limit checking, 432–436
  supervisor call (SVCall) and pendable service call (PendSV) exceptions, 436–444
  SysTick timer *(see* SysTick timer)
  unprivileged execution level and memory protection unit (MPU), 444–446
Operation states and modes, 88*f*, 91*f*

P
Packing and unpacking instructions, 216–219
PC. *See* Program counter (PC)
Peaking filter, 779, 780*f*
Pendable service call (PendSV), 437*t*, 441–444, 443–444*f*, 444*t*, 453–454

Peripheral interrupt operations, 300
Peripheral protection controllers (PPCs), 292–295, 689–690, 705
Peripheral registers, 91
Phase lock loops (PLLs), 23
Ping-pong buffer operation, 825–826, 827f
Platform security architecture (PSA) certified
    analyze, 880–881
    architect, 881–882
    certify, 882–883
    design considerations, 895–896
    functional API certification, 887–888, 887–888f
    implementation, 882
    security evaluation levels
        IoT products, 883, 884t
        level 1, 884–885, 885f
        level 2, 885–886, 886f
        level 3, 887, 887f
        overview, 883–884
    security needs, thread models and security capabilities, 888
    security principles, 878–880, 879f
    stages, addressing security needs, 880, 881f
    technology ecosystem, 878
Platform security architecture-root of trust (PSA-RoT), 880, 880f
PMSA. *See* Protected memory system architecture (PMSA)
Polling method, 25
Pop preemption, 377
POP/PUSH instructions, 170–171
Postindex addressing modes, 163–165
Postindexed memory access instructions, 165t
Power management IC (PMIC), 8
Power on reset, 133
PPB. *See* Private peripheral bus (PPB)
PPCs. *See* Peripheral protection controllers (PPCs)
Preindexed addressing mode, 163–165
Preindexed memory access instructions, 164t
PRIMASK register, 364–365
Priority levels
    Cortex-M23 and Cortex-M33 processors, 311f
    exception, 310–312
    group priority field and subpriority field, 313t
    interrupt
        overview, 310–312
        priority grouping in Armv8-M Mainline, 313–314
    registers of Cortex-M23 and Cortex-M33 processors, 312f
    secure exceptions and interrupts, 314
    system exceptions, 313t
Private peripheral bus (PPB), 59, 61
Privileged thread mode, 101f

Privilege level transition
    non-secure API calls, 90f
    secure API calls, 89f
Procedure Call Standard for Arm Architecture (AAPCS), 679–681
Processors
    classification of, 3
    configuration options, 71
    internal components, 55–56t
    modes and states, 87–90
Process stack pointer (PSP), 104, 119–121, 308
Program counter (PC), 92–93, 308
Program flow control
    branch, 198–199
    compare and branch instructions, 201–203
    conditional branch, 200–201
    conditional execution, 203–206
    function call, 199–200
    overview, 198
    table branches, 206–208
Program generation flow, 42f
Program image
    application code, 36
    C library code, 36–37
    C startup code, 36
    data, 37
    reset handler/startup code, 35
    vector table, 35
Programmer's model
    application program status register (APSR)
        greater-equal (GE) bits, 109–110
        integer status flags, 107–109
        Q status flag, 109
    processor modes and states, 87–90
    registers (*see* Registers)
    TrustZone impact, 110–112
Programming
    accessing peripherals in C, 31–34
    data in static random access memory (SRAM), 37
    data types, C, 29–30
    microcontrollers, 14, 38–39
    program image (*see* Program image)
    vector table definition, 369–373
    wait for event (WFE) instruction, 397–399
    wait for interrupt (WFI) instruction, 396–397
    wake up conditions, 399–400
Program status register (PSR), 94–97, 308
Project options
    assembler, 658, 659f
    C/C++, 658, 658f
    debug, 660–661, 661f
    device, 654, 654f
    linker, 659–660, 660f

Project options *(Continued)*
    listing, 655–657, 656*f*
    output, 655, 656*f*
    tabs, 652, 653*f*
    target, 654–655
    trace, 661, 662*f*
    user, 657, 657*f*
    utilities, 661, 663*f*
Protected memory system architecture (PMSA), 466
PSA. *See* Platform security architecture (PSA)
PSA-RoT. *See* Platform security architecture-root of trust
    (PSA-RoT)
PSP. *See* Process stack pointer (PSP)
PSR. *See* Program status register (PSR)

Q
Q status flag, 109
QADD, 770
QADD8, 773–774
QADD16, 771

R
Radix point, 762, 763*t*
Real-time operating systems (RTOS), 3, 11, 29
    context switching in non-secure, 449–450, 449*f*
    Cortex-M processors, 450–462
    defined, 417
    TrustZone environment, 448–450
Real-time processors, 3
Receive event (RXEV) signal, 389
Recursive filter, 780
Reduced instruction set computing (RISC) architecture, 6
Re-entrant interrupt handler, 859–865, 861*f*
Region ID numbers, 289–292
Register-relative memory access instructions, 166*t*
Registers
    floating-point, 104–107
    interrupt and exception management, 306*t*
    read and write behaviors, 93*t*
    register bank, 91–94
    special registers, 94–104
    types, 90–91
Reset, 22–23
Reset and reset sequence, 133–136
Reset handler/startup code, 35
Resources, 22
Reverse instructions, 192*t*
RTOS. *See* Real-time operating systems (RTOS)

S
SADD8, 773
SADD16, 771
Saturation adjustment instructions, 195–197

SAU. *See* Security attribution unit (SAU)
SCB. *See* System control block (SCB)
SCS. *See* System control space (SCS)
Secure fault address register (SFAR), 694
Secure fault status register (SFSR), 503–504, 504*t*, 694
Secure gateway (SG), 78, 323, 695
Secure interrupt/exception prioritization, 314
Secure software design considerations
    entry points to prevent unintentional entry points, 748
    exception handler to unprivileged execution, 749
    input data and pointer validations
        CMSE pointer check functions, 742–743
        danger of "printf" in Secure API, 741–742
        non-secure memory, 735–739, 736*f*, 738*f*
        pointer checking, 739–740
    memory partitioning, 734–735
    non-secure callable (NSC), 733
    non-secure world, initial branching, 733
    parameter passing, 746
    peripheral driver code, 744–746
    peripheral interrupts, 746
    peripheral registers, 743–744
    platform security architecture (PSA) certification, 749
    reentrancy of secure functions, 748–749
    secure world not used, 749
    stack limit, 747
    stack underflow attack prevention, 747–748, 748*f*
    unprivileged execution level, 748
    XN (eXecute Never) attribute, 747
Secure software development
    address range and data object, 714–715*t*
    __ARM_FEATURE_CMSE macro, 702*t*
    calling non-secure function, 709–711
    Cortex-M Security Extension (CMSE), 686–687, 717
    creating simple secure API, 708
    design considerations (*see* Secure software design
        considerations)
    development platform considerations, 687
    fault handler, 719–720
    initial switching, non-secure world, 707–708
    Keil Microcontroller Development Kit (MDK),
        720–731
    overview, 701
    passing parameters across security domains, 718
    pointer checking, 711–716, 712*f*, 713–715*t*
    secure and non-secure, separation of, 685–686, 686*f*
    security setup, 702–707
    software environments, 718
    toolchains, 731–732
    trusted firmware-M (TF-M), 687
    TrustZone, 688–701
Security attribution unit (SAU), 60, 78, 115–116, 255,
    257–259, 283–285

address lookup summary, 692*f*
control register, 693, 693*t*
vs. implementation defined attribution units (IDAU), 689
region base address register, 694, 694*t*
region limit address register, 694, 694*t*
region number register, 693, 693*t*
registers and concepts, 691–693, 691*t*
secure fault address register (SFAR), 694
secure fault status register (SFSR), 694
type register, 693, 693*t*
Security aware peripherals, 296–297
Security requirements, 71–73
Security state transition, 79*f*
exception priority levels, 699–700, 700*f*
privileged level change, 698–699, 699*f*
Semaphores, 446, 447*f*, 851–854
Send event on pend (SEVONPEND), 388
Serial peripheral interface (SPI), 1
Serial wire debug (SWD), 575–576, 576*f*
Serial wire output (SWO), 131, 626–627, 627*f*
Serial wire viewer (SWV), 131, 580
SFAR. *See* Secure fault address register (SFAR)
SFSR. *See* Secure fault status register (SFSR)
SG. *See* Secure gateway (SG)
Sharable memory attribute, 253
Shareability grouping, 471, 471*f*
Shift and rotate instructions, 189–190*t*
Signed and unsigned extend instructions, 191–192*t*
Signed saturation (SSAT) operations, 195–197
SIMD. *See* Single-instruction, multiple-data (SIMD)
Single cycle I/O port feature, 271*f*
Single-instruction, multiple-data (SIMD), 4, 757–759, 757–759*t*, 758*f*, 765, 765*f*
data representations, 209*f*
data-types, 210
instructions, 209
operations, 211*t*
packing and unpacking instructions, 216–219
and saturating arithmetic instructions, 210
saturation instructions, 212–214*t*
syntax, 212–214*t*
Single memory access instructions, 159–161, 162*t*
Sleep extension/wakeup delay, 388–389
Sleep mode-related instructions, 227–228
Sleep modes, 53, 63, 383–384
Sleep-on-exit feature, 387–388
SMLABB, 772
SMLAD, 772
SMLAL, 769
SMLALBB, 772
SMLALD, 757, 758*f*, 772–773
SMMLA, 770

SMMUL, 769–770
SMULL, 769
SoCs. *See* System-on-chips (SoCs)
Software development
Armv8-M system, 682
caller saved and callee saved registers, 680, 681*t*
CMSIS-CORE software package, 637, 639*f*
Keil Microcontroller Development Kit (MDK), 639–679
non-secure software
secure world is not used, 682
secure world is used, 683
overview, 637
parameter passing and returning function call, 680, 681*t*
procedure call standard for Arm architecture, 679–681
scenarios, 637, 638*f*, 681
secure software where non-secure world is not used, 683
typical Cortex-M software project, 637–639
Software development flow, 41–44
Software optimization
assembly language level, 873–876
bit data handling in C/C++, 869–872
complex decision trees, 865–869
conditional branches, 865–867, 866*f*
performance considerations, 872–873
Software Trigger Interrupt Register (STIR), 305, 352–353
Solid-state disks (SSDs), 3
Special register access
CMSIS-CORE functions, 241–242*t*
instructions, 154–155
Special registers
CONTROL register, 99–102
exception/interrupt masking
BASEPRI, 367–369
FAULTMASK, 365–367
overview, 362–364
PRIMASK, 364–365
interrupt masking registers, 97–99
program status register (PSR), 94–97
stack limit registers, 103–104
SPI. *See* Serial peripheral interface (SPI)
SRPG. *See* State retention power gating (SRPG)
SSAT, 769
SSAT16, 771
SSDs. *See* Solid-state disks (SSDs)
Stack and heap sizes
assembly startup codes, 664–665, 664*f*
C startup codes, 665
required, 661–664

Stack frames
  exception handler in C, 326–327
  floating-point context, 331–332f
  formats, 327–334
  interface of C functions, 325–326
  stacking and unstacking overview, 325
  stack pointer, 334
Stacking and unstacking, 325
Stack limit checking
  main stack pointer(s) (MSP), 433–436, 435–436f
  overview, 432–433
  registers, 432–433, 432f
    access functions, 433, 434t
    symbols, 433, 434t
Stack limit registers, 103–104, 121–122
Stack memory, 117–121
Stack memory protection
  detecting stack overflow, 850–851
  usage, 849–850
Stack operations, 103–104, 117, 118–119f, 135
Stack overflow. See Stack limit checking
Stack overflow detection, 850–851
Stack pointer (SP), 121–122, 308
  selection, 102f, 334t
  stacking and unstacking, 334f
Stack pointer relative memory access instructions, 163t
Stack push and pop instructions, 170t
Stack size analysis, 849–850
Stack trace, 512–513, 514f
State retention, 384, 389
State retention power gating (SRPG), 390–391
Static random access memory (SRAM), 37
Store double-word (STRD) instructions, 374
Store-release instructions, 178–182, 851–854
Subpriority level, 314
Super loop, 25
Supervisor call (SVCall), 436–441, 437t, 437f, 439f
SWD. See Serial wire debug (SWD)
SWO. See Serial wire output (SWO)
SWV. See Serial wire viewer (SWV)
Synchronous and asynchronous exceptions, 340
System control block (SCB), 116–117
  application interrupt/reset control register (AIRCR)
    clearing all interrupt states, 410
    self-reset generation, 406–410
  configuration and control register (CCR), 410–413
  CPU ID base register, 406
  registers, 404–406, 415
  send event on pend (SEVONPEND), 388
  SLEEPDEEP, 385
  system exception management, registers
    application interrupt and reset control register,
      358–359

interrupt control and state register, 355
  summary, 354–355
  system handler control and state register, 360–362
  system handler priority registers, 355–358
System control register (SCR), 385
System control space (SCS), 116–117, 249, 286, 341, 346,
  466
SystemCoreClock, 421, 423
System exception management, 345
  access to functions, 341
  system control block (SCB) registers
    application interrupt and reset control register,
      358–359
    interrupt control and state register, 355
    summary, 354–355
    system handler control and state register, 360–362
    system handler priority registers, 355–358
System exceptions, 304t
System handler control and state register (SHCSR),
  360–362
System handler priority registers, 355–358
System-on-chips (SoCs), 8, 303
System reset, 133
System ticks, 418
SysTick, 54, 64, 70–71
SysTick calibration register, 421
SysTick calibration value register, 421, 423t
SysTick current value register, 421, 422t
SysTick_Handler(void), 422
SysTick timer
  address space, 425, 426f
  block diagram, 419, 420f
  CMSIS-CORE, 422–423
  considerations, 426–427
  control and status register, 421, 421t
  implementation options, 419, 419t
  operations, 419–422
  pending status behavior, 425, 426t
  purpose, 418–419
  registers, 419, 420f, 421t
  reload value register, 421, 422t
  real-time operating systems (RTOS), 422
  timing measurement, 425
  TrustZone, 425–426

T
Table branch, 206–208, 868–869
Tail-chaining optimization, 375–376
Task control block (TCB), 452–455
Technical reference manual (TRM), 86
Test target (TT) instructions, 287–292
TF-M. See Trusted firmware-M (TF-M)
Threat model, 879

Threat model and security analysis (TMSA), 880–881

Thumb instruction set, 140–141, 150–151, 163, 239

TLB. *See* Translation lookup buffer (TLB)

TMSA. *See* Threat model and security analysis (TMSA)

Toolchains
- GNU C compiler (GCC), 731–732, 732*f*
- IAR, 732

Trace connection, 132*f*

Trace point interface unit (TPIU)
- asynchronous clock prescaler register, 629, 629*t*
- block diagram, 627–628, 627*f*
- claim tag clear register, 630–632, 631*t*
- claim tag set register, 630–632, 631*t*
- current parallel port size register, 628, 629*t*
- formatter and flush control register, 630, 630*t*
- formatter and flush status register, 629–630, 630*t*
- output modes, 626
- periodic synchronization control register, 630, 631*t*
- registers, 628, 628*t*
- selected pin protocol register, 629, 629*t*
- serial wire output (SWO), 626–627, 627*f*
- supported parallel port size register, 628, 629*t*
- trace funnel, 584

Transient, 473–474

Translation lookup buffer (TLB), 464

Transmit event (TXEV), 392

TRM. *See* Technical reference manual (TRM)

Trusted firmware-M (TF-M)
- description, 889
- interprocess communication, 894–895, 895*f*
- microcontrollers, 895
- platform security architecture (PSA)functional APIs, 878, 882, 891–894, 891*f*, 893*t*, 893–894*f*
- secure and non-secure processing environments, 890, 890*f*
- secure software development, 687
- security requirements, 892*t*
- software execution environment, 889–891

TrustZone, 4
- address types, 115*t*
- Armv8-M, 76–79
- debug architecture, 590–594
- embedded systems, security, 73–76
- and exceptions, 126
- IoT microcontroller, 82
- life-cycle-states, 81*t*
- memory protection unit (MPU), 482–484, 482*f*
- memory system, 278
- operating systems (OS) features, 418
- operation states and modes, 88*f*
- partitioning of address spaces, 115–116
- programmer's model, 110–112
- real-time operating systems (RTOS), 448–450

secure software development
- BXNS and BLXNS instructions, 698, 698*t*
- instructions, 700–701, 700*t*
- memory separation, 689–690
- non-secure software calling, 695–696, 695*f*
- processor state, 688–689, 688*f*
- secure code calling, non-secure function, 696–697, 697*f*
- security attribution unit (SAU) programmer's model, 691–694
- security state transition, 698–700, 699–700*f*
- security requirements, 71–73
- on sleep mode support, 395
- stack pointer usage, 428–430, 429*f*
- support instructions, 231–232
- SysTick timer, 425–426
- target states of exceptions and interrupts, 322–325

Twiddle factors, 786

TXEV. *See* Transmit event (TXEV)

U

UFSR. *See* Usage fault status register (UFSR)

Unaligned data access support, 262–263

Unconditional branch instructions, 198*t*

Unified assembly language (UAL), 148, 150–151

Unprivileged access instructions, 171–172

Unprivileged execution level, 444–446

Unprivileged interrupt handler, 854–859, 860*f*

Unprivileged thread mode, 101*f*

Unsigned saturation (USAT) operations, 195–197

Unsupported coprocessor instructions, 235*t*

Unsupported hint instructions, 239*t*

Usage fault status register (UFSR), 503, 503*t*

V

Vectored floating-point (VFP), 525

Vector table, 35, 128–129, 315–318
- relocation, 371–373
- in startup code, 369–371

Vector table offset register (VTOR), 315–318, 373

Vector table relocation, 116

VFP. *See* Vectored floating-point (VFP)

Voltage level, 23

VTOR. *See* Vector table offset register (VTOR)

W

Wait for event (WFE) instruction, 397–399

Wait for interrupt (WFI), 396–397

Wake up conditions
- sleep-on-exit, 399*t*
- wait for event (WFE), 401*t*

Wakeup interrupt controller (WIC), 389–391

X

XOM. *See* eXecute-Only-Memory (XOM)

Printed in the United States
By Bookmasters